RISE OF THE AMERICAN NATION

Third Edition

LEWIS PAUL TODD
MERLE CURTI

"HISTORY AND THE SOCIAL SCIENCES"

MARK M. KRUG Professor of Education in History and the Social Sciences, University of Chicago
with the collaboration of:
GEORGE H. DANIELS Associate Professor of History, Northwestern University
MARGARET C. FALLERS Principal, University of Chicago Laboratory High School
JUDITH M. MEYER Chicago Public School System
PAUL E. PETERSON Assistant Professor of Education and Political Science, University of Chicago
WILLIAM D. RADER Associate Professor of Education, Northeastern Illinois State College

EDITORIAL CONSULTANTS:

JACK L. CASNER Supervisor, Secondary Curriculum, Kansas City, Missouri
EDWARD EISENHART Coordinator of Social Studies, Ridge High School, Basking Ridge, New Jersey
PAUL FLAUM Teacher, Social Studies, Smithtown Central High School, Smithtown, New York
MILDRED H. NORRIS Instructional Services, Education Service Center, Region II; Corpus Christi; formerly Consultant, Social Studies, Corpus Christi Public Schools, Texas
MARGUERITE MAY Curriculum Director, Jordan Education Complex, Los Angeles City Unified School District, California
ABRAHAM H. VENIT Chairman, Social Studies, Samuel J. Tilden High School, New York, New York

Maps: Harold K. Faye   **Drawings:** Samuel H. Bryant

ACCOMPANYING PROGRAM

Teacher's Manual and Resource Guide
Workbook
Tests
Living American Documents
Challenge and Change

Impressions of America

American History 400
(A full-color 35 mm. slide program)

United States History
(Overhead Projection Transparencies)

RISE OF THE

HARCOURT BRACE JOVANOVICH, INC.
NEW YORK   CHICAGO   SAN FRANCISCO   ATLANTA   DALLAS

THIRD EDITION

AMERICAN NATION

LEWIS PAUL TODD and MERLE CURTI

HISTORY AND THE SOCIAL SCIENCES
by MARK M. KRUG

LEWIS PAUL TODD has acquired national distinction as a teacher and writer on American history and related subjects. He taught American history for many years and was head of the Department of Social Studies in the Bound Brook High School, Bound Brook, New Jersey. He also has taught American history, historical geography of the United States, American government, and related courses at Queens College, New York, at Western Connecticut State College, Danbury, Connecticut, and at New York University.

Dr. Todd is widely known among social studies teachers for his textbook writing and for his many articles and editorials in social studies journals. He has contributed to the Yearbooks and other publications of the National Council for the Social Studies (NCSS). From 1947 to 1969 he was editor of *Social Education,* the official journal of the NCSS. Dr. Todd also is editorial writer for the *Civic Leader,* a publication of the Civic Education Service. In addition to his collaboration on *Rise of the American Nation,* he co-authored two series of social studies textbooks for elementary schools.

MERLE CURTI is Frederick Jackson Turner Professor of American History, Emeritus, at the University of Wisconsin and has been Visiting Professor of History at the University of Tokyo. He has also lectured at many American colleges and at Cambridge University in England. He is serving as honorary consultant in American cultural history, Library of Congress. Dr. Curti was formerly Professor of American History at Teachers College, Columbia University, where he and Dr. Todd began their collaboration on publications for use in high school American history classrooms.

Professor Curti has been president of the American Historical Association, the highest honor a historian in the United States can receive. He also received the award of the American Council of Learned Societies for particularly distinguished scholarship. His long list of distinguished historical writings includes *The Social Ideas of American Educators, The Making of an American Community, The American Paradox: The Conflict of Thought and Action,* and *The Growth of American Thought,* for which he won the Pulitzer prize for history.

MARK M. KRUG is Professor of Education in History and the Social Sciences at the Graduate School of Education, the University of Chicago, where he directs the training of history and social studies teachers in the M.A.T. program. Dr. Krug has been a social studies teacher and chairman of the social studies department of the Laboratory High School at the University of Chicago.

Dr. Krug is well known for his many contributions in the field of social studies. Dr. Krug's writings include many articles in *Social Education, Journal of Negro History,* and other periodicals, as well as biographies of Aneurin Bevan and Lyman Trumbull. He also is the author of two important recent books, *History and the Social Studies* and *The New Social Studies.*

ACKNOWLEDGMENTS: For permission to reprint copyrighted material, grateful acknowledgment is made to the following:
THE ANTIOCH REVIEW: From "The Limitations of History" by Martin Duberman from *The Antioch Review,* volume XXV, number 2.   DELL PUBLISHING COMPANY, INC.: Excerpt by Raymond Moley; excerpt by Arthur Schlesinger, Jr., and excerpt by Edgar Robinson from *Franklin Roosevelt and the Age of Action* edited by Alfred B. Rollins, copyright © 1961 by Dell Publishing Co., Inc.   ALFRED A. KNOPF, INC. and JONATHAN CAPE LTD.: From *The Age of Reform: From Bryan to F. D. R.* by Richard Hofstadter, copyright © 1955 by Richard Hofstadter.   ALFRED A. KNOPF, INC.: From *The Peculiar Institution: Slavery in the Ante-Bellum South* by Kenneth M. Stampp, copyright © 1956 by Kenneth M. Stampp.   THE MACMILLAN COMPANY: From *1787, The Grand Convention* by Clinton Rossiter. From "Anthropology" by Margaret Mead from *American History and the Social Sciences* edited by Edward Saveth.   W. W. NORTON & COMPANY, INC.: From *Thirteen Days: A Memoir of the Cuban Missile Crisis,* by Robert F. Kennedy, copyright © 1969 by W. W. Norton & Company, Inc.; copyright © 1968 by McCall Corporation.   THE UNIVERSITY OF CHICAGO PRESS: From "A New Frame for the Social Sciences" by C. Arnold Anderson from *The School Review,* Vol. 72, No. 4, Winter 1964.   WASHINGTON SQUARE PRESS, INC.: Excerpt by Bronislaw Malinowski from *Anthropology* edited by Samuel Rapport and Helen Wright.

ISBN 0-15-376070-2

PRINTED IN THE UNITED STATES OF AMERICA

Contents

Part 1
CREATING A NEW NATION 99

MAPS AND CHARTS

TEXT MAPS

TEXT CHARTS

HISTORICAL ATLAS OF THE UNITED STATES

xiv

SPECIAL FEATURES

LIVING AMERICAN DOCUMENTS

Introduction

The Colonial
Period

RISE OF THE AMERICAN NATION

INTRODUCTION: THE COLONIAL PERIOD	Unit One: Building the Colonies	1450–1763
PART 1: CREATING A NEW NATION	Unit Two: Winning Independence	1763–1789
	Unit Three: Building the Nation	1789–1845
PART 2: THE NATION DIVIDED	Unit Four: The Rise of Sectionalism	1820's–1860's
	Unit Five: The Nation Torn Apart	1845–1865
PART 3: THE NATION REUNITED	Unit Six: Rebuilding the Nation	1865–1900
	Unit Seven: The Rise of Industrialism	1860's–1890's
	Unit Eight: The Arrival of Reform	1897–1920
PART 4: THE NATION AS A WORLD LEADER	Unit Nine: Becoming a World Power	1898–1920
	Unit Ten: The "Golden Twenties"	1920–1932
	Unit Eleven: The New Deal and World War II	1932–1945
	Unit Twelve: The Challenges of a New Era	1945–1970's

UNIT ONE

Building the Colonies

1450–1763

■ *An early map of the New World published in 1532*

THE SPANISH ARMADA, a mighty and imposing fleet, set sail from Spain, while all Europe buzzed with rumors of war. The Spanish admiral hoped and prayed for victory as he gazed at the long lines of fighting ships under his command.

The vessels rose and fell upon the long swells, rolling slowly from port to starboard and back again as the seas swept under them. The admiral could see flags and pennants whipping in the wind, sailors clinging to the rigging, soldiers lining the rails, and the muzzles of cannon bristling from the gun ports.

The fleet was entering the English Channel. To the north, off the port quarter, was England, the land that the admiral intended to invade and conquer for his king. From the decks of their ships, the Spaniards could see smoke signals rising from the shore and tiny figures on horseback racing along the coastal roads. They knew that the alarm had been sounded. The English would be waiting for them.

The momentous day was Saturday, July 30, the year, 1588.

Attack at sea. On Sunday the English fleet sailed out to attack. The English ships were smaller than the lumbering Spanish men-of-war—smaller and swifter and manned by better-trained sailors and better gunners.

The Spanish ships sailed majestically up the Channel, keeping formation, their officers and crews confident of victory. But the English vessels swept in and out, picking off stragglers, firing broadsides, and then retreating outside the range of the Spanish guns.

The Spaniards were furious. They waved their swords and shouted at the Englishmen, daring them to come alongside and fight like men.

The English knew better. Outnumbered two to one and outgunned, they had no intention of making a frontal attack on the Spanish fleet. To be sure, Sir Francis Drake wanted to attack boldly. But

CHAPTER 1

European Settlements in the New World

1450 – 1624

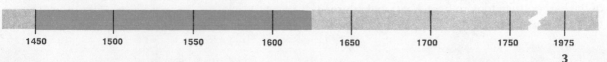

■ The defeat of the Spanish Armada marked the beginning of Spain's decline as a naval power and the turning point of Spain's fortunes in the New World.

Drake was only second in command. The admiral who commanded the English fleet, Lord Howard of Effingham, scorned Drake's tactics. "We'll pluck them feather by feather," said he.

The running battle continued for nearly a week. On Saturday evening, after a long, slow sail up the English Channel, the Spanish fleet anchored in the harbor of Calais (kal·AY) on the coast of France. The English ships stationed themselves just outside the entrance to the harbor and waited for the Spaniards to come out and continue the fight.

The Spanish admiral was in no hurry. England was only 20 miles away across the Channel. His fleet was still in fighting order, and he had reason to expect victory. Fate ruled otherwise.

Disaster for the Spaniards. On Sunday night the English set fire to several old vessels and headed them under full sail toward the Spanish fleet anchored in the harbor. English sailors stayed with the blazing ships until they reached the very mouth of the harbor, then took to open boats and returned to their own vessels.

The English trick worked. The Spaniards were terrified at the sight of the fire ships bearing down upon them. Word swept through the fleet that the burning vessels were loaded with explosives. The Spanish admiral gave the fatal order for his ships to cut their anchor cables and escape as best they could. Out of the harbor they fled, not in battle formation, but in wild disorder.

The Englishmen were waiting. Into the Spanish Armada the English gunners poured broadside after broadside. They kept firing until their guns were almost too hot to touch and their powder was gone.

What was left of the Spanish fleet fled to the north around Scotland, then turned south. But as the Spaniards tried to escape, a great storm came up and wrecked many of the remaining vessels. A shattered and broken fleet finally returned to Spain.

Turning point in history. The English defeat of the Spanish Armada was a decisive moment in world history—and in the history of the land that later became the United States. For nearly 100

4

years, Spain had been growing rich and powerful from trade and plunder in the New World. Unchecked, Spain might have gone on to build strong colonies along the Atlantic seaboard of North America from Florida to what is now Maine.

The sea battle in the English Channel in 1588 marked the turning point of Spain's fortunes in the New World. Though Spanish power continued strong for many years, Englishmen now could also begin to build permanent colonies in North America.

To understand why the famous sea battle of 1588 was so decisive a moment in the beginnings of our country, we must trace events that preceded and followed it. These explain the discovery, the exploration, and the settlement of the Americas.

THE CHAPTER IN OUTLINE

1. The search for an all-water route to Asia.

2. European exploration of the New World.

3. The rise and fall of Spanish power in the New World.

4. An English foothold in North America.

1 The search for an all-water route to Asia

Most men dream of discovering something new. Christopher Columbus was no exception. Almost 100 years before the defeat of the Spanish Armada, Columbus dreamed of discovering a new, all-water trade route between Europe and Asia. Like other men of his day, Columbus dreamed of the riches and honors that would be his if he succeeded.

In the latter half of the 1400's, many Europeans wanted to find new and better ways of trading with Asia. Many of Europe's keenest traders, indeed, were trying to solve this problem when Columbus was still a child in his father's small wool-combing shop in the Italian seaport of Genoa.

A time of energy and change. During the 1300's and 1400's Europe was stirring with new ideas. Many Europeans were filled with burning curiosity and intense energy. They were living in a period called the *Renaissance* (ren·eh·ZAHNS), meaning a time of "new birth."

■ This illustration, taken from a medieval manuscript, shows a group of Crusaders riding off to war. They wear protective mail armor and carry shields and weapons.

Through much of the preceding Middle Ages, Europeans had been primarily concerned with eking out a bare living and preparing through religion for life beyond the grave. Now their interest increasingly centered on the everyday world around them. Some men turned to the sea to search for new trade routes and to explore distant lands. Other men turned to art, architecture, and writing.

What started men thinking new thoughts and dreaming new dreams? No doubt the Crusades were partly responsible. Starting in 1096 and continuing for nearly 200 years until 1272, army after army of Crusaders set forth from Europe to battle the Moslems for control of the Holy Land in the Middle East. Many Crusaders died in battle. Others settled down to live in the Middle East. But those who returned brought back new ideas and new products. The ideas spread, creating new ways of living, and stimulating the Renaissance. The use of the new products also spread, creating new demands, and stimulating more trade between Europe and Asia.

Importance of trade. Since the days of the Crusades, Europeans had learned to want many Asian products that they could not produce for themselves. For several hundred years they had been

■ This African sculpture, intricately carved in ivory, depicts the Portuguese explorers who reached the African coast in the 1400's. Do you think the African artist regarded the Portuguese as peaceful traders or as warriors?

getting sugar and glass and steel from Damascus and Baghdad, rugs from Persia, and pepper or "black gold" from India. From the Spice Islands of the East Indies they got cloves and cinnamon and nutmeg, and from far-off China came fine porcelain and silks. To pay for these products, Europeans sent woolen goods and tin and gold and silver back along the trade routes.

Europeans needed the products they got from Asia. They needed the tough Damascus steel for their swords and armor. They needed rugs and porcelain and glass to make their cold, damp castles and manor houses more livable. More than anything else, perhaps, they needed spices, especially pepper. Spices gave variety and flavor to their coarse food, particularly to their meat.

Difficulty of trade. The old trade routes (see map, pages 8–9) had always been very difficult,

dangerous, and expensive. Months, sometimes years, passed before a box of spices or a bale of cloth reached Europe from Asia. Camel caravans carrying products overland from China and central Asia crossed vast wastelands and high mountain passes. Goods moving from the East Indies along the sea-land route made a long sea voyage westward across the Indian Ocean, then were carried over the burning Arabian Desert by plodding camel caravans. Next came another sea voyage, this time across the Mediterranean Sea on ships bound for the Italian cities of Genoa or Venice. The Italian merchants of Genoa and Venice had a *monopoly* ° on trade between the eastern Mediterranean and Europe. Finally, Asia's much-wanted products reached Europe's markets.

The search for new routes. The growing demand for products from Asia had a direct bearing on the discovery of America. Many European merchants wanted to get Asian goods more cheaply and end the virtual control of east-west trade enjoyed by the Venetians and Genoans. The Portuguese and Spaniards, and later the French, the English, and the Dutch, began to search for new ocean routes to Asia.

Thus, while Columbus was growing up in Genoa, a search for a new, all-water route between Europe and Asia was already under way. Before the search ended, European explorers had pushed back the frontiers of the known world. This expansion of trade out of the Mediterranean into world sea lanes is sometimes called the Commercial Revolution.

Portugal's sea route to Asia. Portuguese seamen led the search for an all-water route to Asia. They were financed by Prince Henry of Portugal, also known as Prince Henry the Navigator.

Prince Henry was interested in exploration. On the coast of Portugal he built a shipyard and a school for navigators. There he and his followers built new types of sailing ships seaworthy enough to brave the open waters of the Atlantic Ocean. He and his men experimented with newer methods of navigation, newer maps, and newer instruments for determining latitude, longitude, and direction—such instruments as the compass and astrolabe.

But Prince Henry did more than experiment. He sent expedition after expedition south along the unexplored coast of Africa (see map, page 9). And after his death in 1460, Portuguese seamen continued to explore the African coastline.

° *monopoly:* exclusive control over the supply of a product or service, free from competition.

At small harbor settlements where they anchored their ships, the Portuguese may have learned of African kingdoms inland. But they had little interest in exploring these kingdoms at that time. After trading such European goods as brass bowls, bracelets, beads, and textiles for fresh water and food, the Portuguese sailed on. Besides supplies, however, the Portuguese also took aboard African servants and slaves, carrying them back to Portugal and Spain on the return voyage. In later years, as you will see, some of these Africans or their descendants took part in the discoveries and explorations of the Americas.

With every expedition, Portuguese seamen pushed farther and farther south. Finally, in 1488, Bartholomeu Diaz (DEE-ahs) and his crew rounded the southern tip of Africa. Diaz wanted to continue toward Asia, but his men, weary from months at sea and fearful of the unknown, refused to go farther. Diaz turned back. But 10 years later, in 1498, Vasco da Gama, also from Portugal, followed Diaz's route around the Cape of Good Hope. He continued across the Indian Ocean, reaching Calicut in far-off India.

The voyages of Diaz and da Gama were enormously important to the little kingdom of Portugal and to the world. Within a few years Portuguese vessels were sailing back and forth along the new, all-water route to India and the Spice Islands.

In 1494 a treaty between Portugal and Spain established a Line of Demarcation about 1,100 miles west of the Cape Verde Islands. All new lands discovered west of this line were to belong to Spain; all new lands to the east were to belong to Portugal (see map, pages 8–9).

SECTION SURVEY

IDENTIFY: Crusades, Renaissance, Commercial Revolution; Christopher Columbus, Prince Henry the Navigator, Vasco da Gama; 1488.

1. Why was there a demand and a need in Europe for the goods from Asia?
2. What is meant by the statement that the old trade routes were difficult, dangerous, and expensive?
3. (a) Why were the voyages of the Portuguese important to the world? (b) What inventions enabled them to make these voyages?
4. The fact that there was an increased demand in Europe for Asian goods and the fact that the old trade routes were difficult, dangerous, and expensive are two unrelated facts of no major consequence. Do you agree or disagree? Why or why not?

2 European exploration of the New World

While Portuguese seamen were exploring the African coast, Columbus set out in 1492 under the flag of Spain on the first of four great voyages. Unlike the other explorers, who believed that the best all-water route to Asia was around Africa and eastward, Columbus headed westward. Knowing that the earth was round, a knowledge shared by informed people of his day, Columbus believed that if he sailed far enough to the west, he would reach Asia. In trying to prove his point, Columbus started what has been called the Geographic Revolution.

The expedition led by Columbus included three small ships, the *Niña,* the *Pinta,* and the *Santa María.* The able seamen who manned these ships were mainly Spaniards, but one of them has been described as a "man of color." He may have been one of the black Africans brought back to Europe from Africa by the Portuguese explorers.

(continued on page 10)

■ The explorations of Christopher Columbus in the New World constituted the opening chapter in Europe's colonization of the Americas.

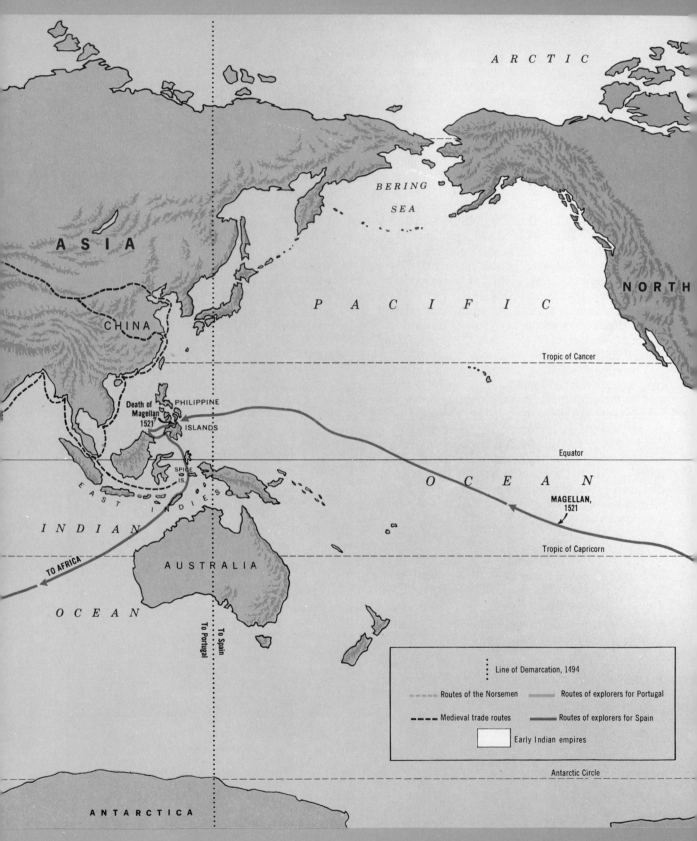

EXPLORING THE WORLD, EUROPEANS

A R C T I C

ASIA

BERING
SEA

CHINA

Tropic of Cancer

PACIFIC

NORTH

PHILIPPINE

Death of
Magellan
1521

ISLANDS

Equator

SPICE
IS.

O C E A N

E A S T   I N D I E S

MAGELLAN,
1521

INDIAN

Tropic of Capricorn

AUSTRALIA

TO AFRICA

O C E A N

To Portugal

To Spain

Line of Demarcation, 1494

Routes of the Norsemen   Routes of explorers for Portugal

Medieval trade routes   Routes of explorers for Spain

Early Indian empires

Antarctic Circle

ANTARCTICA

DISCOVER THE WESTERN HEMISPHERE

OCEAN

GREENLAND

Arctic Circle

ICELAND

NORSEMEN,
ABOUT 1000

NORWAY

SWEDEN

"WINELAND" ?

NEWFOUNDLAND

ENGLAND

NETH.

EUROPE

FRANCE

ASIA

AMERICA

Venice

Genoa
ITALY

PORTUGAL

SPAIN

Mediterranean

Sea

Damascus

PERSIA

A T L A N T I C

COLUMBUS,
1492

Baghdad

ARABIA

INDIA

BAHAMA

AZTEC

IS.

MAYA

BALBOA,
1513

PANAMA

CABRAL,
1500

AFRICA

DA GAMA,
1498

Calicut

SOUTH

O C E A N

INDIAN

INCA

BRAZIL

DIAZ,
1486-88

DA GAMA,
1497

AMERICA

VESPUCCI,
1501

To Portugal
To Spain

O C E A N

MAGELLAN,
1520

Cape of
Good Hope

MAGELLAN'S SHIP
"VICTORIA," 1522

Strait of
Magellan

TIERRA
DEL FUEGO

9

ANTARCTICA

■ The Norsemen were probably the first Europeans to reach the New World. They recorded their adventures in colorful tapestries like the one shown above.

Finding a new world. Instead of reaching Asia, Columbus landed at an island off the coast of an unknown world. Because his calculations showed the westward distance from Europe to Asia to be much shorter than it actually is, Columbus thought that he had reached Asia.

On the morning of October 12, 1492, Columbus and his crew went ashore on the island, which they called San Salvador. This island is now believed to be Watlings Island in the Bahamas (see map, page 9). Once on shore, they thanked God for leading them safely across the sea. Not a man among them realized that what they had discovered was a new world.

Columbus tried again and again and still again to discover an all-water route to the Spice Islands and the riches of Asia. But he failed, and he returned from his fourth voyage a poor, lonely, brokenhearted man. Columbus died in 1506 without knowing that his discovery would, in time, have more influence upon Europe than all the riches of Asia.

Before Columbus. The "first Americans" probably came from Asia many thousands of years ago across what is now the Bering Strait off Alaska. Through thousands of years, these people moved southward and eastward, settling in all parts of the Americas. The American Indians are descendants of these people.

In reality, Columbus "rediscovered" the New World. Other Europeans had explored there many years before.

The Norsemen were probably the first Europeans to reach the New World. In the late 900's, Eric the Red and his followers landed on Greenland and built a settlement there. In the year 1000, Eric's son, Leif the Lucky, and his crew were blown off course, finally landing safely on the northeast coast of North America. They called the country "Wineland the Good" after the wild grapes that grew there. Then they made their way back to Greenland. Other Norsemen also went to Wineland, or Vinland. Then their voyages stopped. Historians still do not know why the Norse voyages ended so abruptly.

Other Europeans may also have "discovered" the New World before Columbus. If so, no written records have remained. In any case, Columbus was not first. However, after Columbus' voyage the Americas stayed discovered.

Finding a new ocean. Soon after Columbus rediscovered the New World, a Spaniard named Vasco Nuñez de Balboa (NOO·nyez day bal·BOH·ah) discovered a new ocean.

In the year 1513 Balboa started on an expedition across the Isthmus of Panama (see map, page 9), searching for gold. Balboa's expedition, like many of the expeditions that pushed their way into the unexplored wilderness of the Americas, included Africans as well as Europeans. Thirty Negroes, in fact, traveled in Balboa's party.

Indian guides led Balboa and his men through a hot, steaming rain forest. After many hardships they reached the foot of a small mountain. Balboa climbed the mountain and caught his first glimpse of the mighty "South Sea," or what we now call the Pacific Ocean. Below him, a vast body of water stretched to the south and the west as far as his eyes could see. Was it another great ocean? Balboa could only guess that it was.

Circling the earth. Ferdinand Magellan proved Balboa's guess correct. Magellan's story began in 1519 when he set sail from Spain on one of the greatest voyages in human history. Magellan, a Portuguese, sailed under the flag of Spain. A year after his departure, he led his small fleet through a narrow waterway, now called the Strait of Magellan, at the southern tip of South America (see map, page 9).

For more than a month Magellan sailed westward through the strait. Snow-covered mountain peaks loomed on either side. At night the mountain slopes twinkled with Indian campfires, causing Magellan to call the land "Tierra del Fuego" (tih·EHR·a del foo·AY·goh), or Land of Fire. At last passing through the strait, Magellan sailed out upon an immense sea—a sea so vast and calm that he named it the Pacific Ocean.

Was this the great "South Sea" that Balboa had seen from the mountain in Panama? Magellan sailed on to find the answer.

Two years later, in September 1522, a small vessel named the *Victoria* sailed into a Spanish harbor. The 18 men aboard were the sole survivors of the 237 men who had sailed with Magellan from Spain three years earlier. These 18 men had done what no other men had done before—they had sailed around the world. Magellan, the original leader, was not among them. Killed in a battle, he lay buried in the Philippine Islands, half a world away.

Magellan's expedition proved to even the most stubborn European that the lands Columbus had discovered were indeed part of a new world. The expedition also gave Spain its claim to the Philippine Islands. In the years that followed, Spain sent soldiers to conquer the Filipinos, missionaries to convert them to Christianity, and merchants to open up trade. The Philippine Islands became a Spanish *colony.*°

Explorers and conquerors. After Columbus discovered the New World, other daring men began to explore its coastline and interior. Among the early explorers were Pedro Alvares Cabral (PAY·droh AHL·vah·rez cah·BRAHL), Amerigo Vespucci (ah·may·REE·go ves·POO·chi), and Ponce de León (PON·say day lay·OHN).

Cabral, sailing around Africa to India under the Portuguese flag, was blown off course. In the year 1500 he landed on the shores of what is now Brazil (see map, page 13). Cabral claimed this territory for Portugal.

In 1501 Amerigo Vespucci, a Florentine, sailed on a Spanish expedition along the coast of what is now South America. When he returned to Europe, he wrote a letter expressing the bold opinion that he had seen a new continent. News of Vespucci's conclusion reached a famous geographer, who proposed calling the newly discovered lands "America" in honor of Amerigo Vespucci. Columbus missed even the honor of having the new lands named after him.

A few years later, in 1513, Ponce de León, a Spanish nobleman, sailed along the coast of a peninsula which he named Florida (see map, page 13). On a later voyage, while leading his soldiers inland, he was killed by an Indian arrow.

Hernando Cortés (kor·TAYS), another Spaniard, was more fortunate. Cortés landed on the coast of Mexico in the year 1519 as leader of a small army that included several hundred Africans. Cortés was determined to conquer the Aztec Indians and their leader, Montezuma—or die in the attempt. He conquered the wealthy Aztec empire, winning glory and gold.

Several years later, in 1531–35, another Spaniard, Francisco Pizarro (pih·ZAHR·oh), led an expedition southward from the Isthmus of Panama. After sailing along the coasts of what are now Ecuador and Peru, Pizarro landed and marched into the interior. His march led him upward through the passes of the towering Andes Mountains and into the heart of the powerful Inca empire. There he and his men, Africans as well as Europeans, conquered the Incas and seized an immense treasure of gold and silver.

° *colony:* a settlement or territory created by a group of people who have left their native land, but who continue to live under the control of their mother country.

■ The meeting between Montezuma and Cortés, shown in the above picture, was a dramatic moment in history. It marked the beginning of Spain's conquest of the mighty Aztec empire.

The conquests of Cortés and Pizarro gave the Spaniards control of strategic parts of Mexico, Central America, and South America. For many years treasure from the Aztecs and the Incas and gold and silver from the mines of Mexico and Peru made Spain the wealthiest, most powerful nation in Europe.

Exploring northward. The treasure that Cortés and Pizarro had discovered fired men's imaginations. Spaniards called *conquistadores* (kohn·KEES·ta·DOH·res), or conquerors, set out in search of similar fame and fortune. Among them were Pánfilo de Narváez (day nahr·VAH·ez), Hernando de Soto, and Francisco Vásquez de Coronado (VAS·kehs day kor·o·NAH·doh).

In 1527–28 Narváez and a small army landed on the coast of Florida and pushed inland in search of gold. After wandering for three months through forests and swamps, and fighting off Indian attacks, they returned to the coast to find that their ships had sailed away.

In crude, homemade boats, the expedition searched the coast of the Gulf of Mexico hoping to find a Spanish settlement. All perished except four men, who reached the coast of what is now Texas. Among the four were a Spaniard named Alvar Cabeza de Vaca (day VAH·kuh) and an African named Estevanico (es·tay·vah·NEE·koh).

Striking inland and moving southwestward, the four men set out on an amazing journey that took them more than halfway across North America on foot. Several years later, after enduring many incredible hardships, they finally reached a Spanish settlement on the Gulf of California. De Vaca returned to Spain and wrote a book about the journey. Estevanico remained in Mexico.

In 1539 a Spanish expedition, led by de Soto, pushed into the southeastern part of what is now the United States. De Soto, clad in golden armor, wandered in search of riches, but found none. Finally, he discovered the Mississippi River, the "Father of Waters." There, in the heart of the New World, de Soto died in 1542. After weighting his body with stones and lowering it into the muddy water of the Mississippi, his followers abandoned the expedition.

Search for the cities of gold. Narváez, Estevanico, and other explorers learned from Indians about rich cities in the interior of North America, the "Seven Cities of Cibola." The Indians reported that the streets of these fabled cities were paved with gold and the walls of the buildings were studded with rubies and other gems.

In 1539 Estevanico led an expedition in search of these cities. Indians killed the African explorer, as well as his entire party. Like de Soto, Estevanico died in the land that he had explored.

In 1540 another Spanish conquistador, named Coronado, led a group northeastward from Mexico, also in search of the cities of gold. For months Coronado and his men explored what is now the southwestern United States. One of his lieutenants discovered the Grand Canyon of the Colorado River. Coronado himself marched eastward, reaching what is now eastern Kansas. Before returning to Mexico, he explored an immense territory, but discovered neither golden cities nor treasure.

English claims to new lands. Meanwhile the English were also establishing claims to large areas of the New World.

In 1497 John Cabot, an Italian sea captain commissioned by King Henry VII, sailed to North America out of the harbor of Bristol, England.

(*continued on page 14*)

EARLY EXPLORATIONS IN THE NEW WORLD

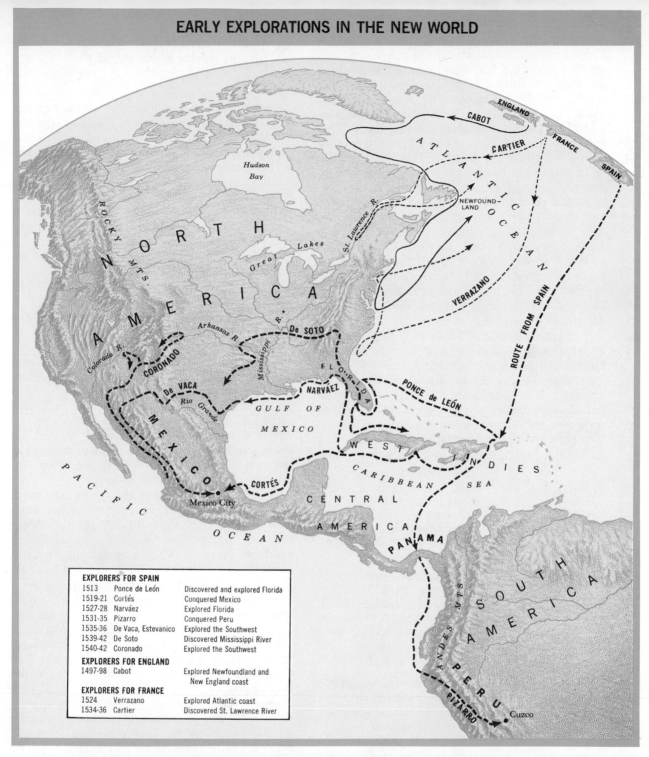

ENGLAND

CABOT

CARTIER

FRANCE

SPAIN

ATLANTIC OCEAN

Hudson Bay

NEWFOUND-LAND

ROCKY MTS.

NORTH

AMERICA

Great Lakes

St. Lawrence R.

VERRAZANO

ROUTE FROM SPAIN

Colorado R.

CORONADO

Arkansas R.

R.

Mississippi

De SOTO

FLORIDA

PONCE de LEÓN

De VACA

NARVÁEZ

Rio Grande

GULF OF MEXICO

MEXICO

WEST INDIES

PACIFIC

CORTÉS

Mexico City

CENTRAL

AMERICA

CARIBBEAN SEA

OCEAN

PANAMA

SOUTH AMERICA

ANDES MTS.

PERU

PIZARRO

Cuzco

EXPLORERS FOR SPAIN

1513	Ponce de León	Discovered and explored Florida
1519-21	Cortés	Conquered Mexico
1527-28	Narváez	Explored Florida
1531-35	Pizarro	Conquered Peru
1535-36	De Vaca, Estevanico	Explored the Southwest
1539-42	De Soto	Discovered Mississippi River
1540-42	Coronado	Explored the Southwest

EXPLORERS FOR ENGLAND

1497-98	Cabot	Explored Newfoundland and New England coast

EXPLORERS FOR FRANCE

1524	Verrazano	Explored Atlantic coast
1534-36	Cartier	Discovered St. Lawrence River

■ The explorers whose routes are shown above greatly expanded the limits of the known world.
The Spaniards, given a head start by Columbus, claimed vast areas in both North and South
America. Early English and French claims extended primarily along the North Atlantic coast.
These nations' claims played a vital role in the early history of the United States.

Little is known about Cabot, and even less about his famous voyage. It appears that on this voyage and another made the following year, he sailed along the coasts of what are now Newfoundland, Nova Scotia, and New England (see map, page 13), claiming these lands for England in the name of King Henry. It also appears that the thrifty king rewarded Cabot with a gift of 10 pounds and an annual pension of 20 pounds. This was small reward indeed for the explorer who gave England its first claim to a large part of North America.

French claims to new lands. French claims to a share of North America were based on the voyages of Giovanni da Verrazano (joh·VAHN·nee dah vayr·rah·TSAH·noh) and Jacques Cartier (kar·TYAY). Verrazano set out in 1524 to find a water route through America to Asia. He failed, but his explorations (see map, page 13) added to man's knowledge of the world and gave the French their first claim to new lands overseas.

Ten years later, in 1534, Cartier made the first of three voyages to the lands across the Atlantic. On the first voyage he explored the Gulf of St. Lawrence. On his second and third voyages he explored the St. Lawrence River as far as the present site of Montreal, and he tried to build a colony on a spot not far from where Quebec now stands. The colony was not a success, but Cartier helped to strengthen French claims to what is now Canada.

SECTION SURVEY

IDENTIFY: colony, "first Americans," Norsemen; Balboa, Ferdinand Magellan, Amerigo Vespucci, Estevanico, Hernando de Soto, Jacques Cartier, John Cabot; 1492–1542.

1. Why can it be said that Columbus "rediscovered" the New World?
2. Using the map on page 13, (a) indicate which areas were claimed by Spain, Portugal, France and England; (b) name the explorers making these claims.
3. Each new discovery aroused European interest in the lands across the seas. Why?
4. Black Africans were involved in New World discoveries. (a) Where were they involved? (b) What was their status in relation to the European explorers?
5. The Spanish conquistadores were amazed at the high level of civilization achieved by the Aztecs and the Incas. (a) Why do you suppose the Spaniards were amazed? (b) Do you think the Spanish point of view was a reasonable one? Why or why not?

3 The rise and fall of Spanish power in the New World

Settlers seeking new homes, as well as explorers and conquerors, traveled from Europe to the New World during the 1500's. Men and women from Portugal settled along the coast of what is now Brazil. Spaniards settled in other parts of South America, in Central America, in Mexico, and on islands in the Caribbean Sea.

The first Spanish settlement in what is now the United States was founded in 1565 at St. Augustine, Florida. Later, in 1609, Spaniards settled at Santa Fe, New Mexico. During this period Spaniards built ranches and missions in what is now northern Mexico and the southwestern United States.

Old ways in the New World. To their American colonies the Portuguese and Spaniards brought domestic animals, plants, and seeds never before seen in the New World. In pens and crates on the decks of their ships, they transported horses, donkeys, cattle, pigs, sheep, goats, and poultry. Using barrels cut in half and filled with earth, they carried fruit and nut trees—olive, lemon, orange, lime, apple, cherry, pear, fig, apricot, almond, and walnut. In bags they brought seeds of wheat, barley, rye, rice, peas, lentils, and flax. They also transplanted sugar cane and flowers.

By 1580 the Portuguese and the Spaniards had built prosperous farms, ranches, and cities in the New World. They were digging gold and silver from old Indian mines in Mexico and in Central and South America. They were carrying on a vigorous trade between the Old World and the New. They were printing books and building colleges in the New World. Churches and missions dotted the land. Toward the end of the 1500's, more than 150,000 Spaniards were living in the Americas.

Slavery in the New World. For the hard labor in their mines and on their plantations, the Portuguese and Spaniards used many slaves. At first they enslaved Indians, but the Indians rapidly died from European diseases or escaped by slipping silently into nearby jungles or mountains. To solve the labor shortage, the Portuguese and Spaniards, who were using some African slaves in Europe, began importing Africans to work as slaves in their New World colonies.

Some historians claim that slavery in Latin America was less harsh than it was in the English

■ The Portuguese and Spaniards brought African slaves to work in the mines and on the plantations of the New World. Above, Africans mine gold in Haiti.

colonies of North America. The claim rests on the fact that at home and in their Latin American colonies, the Portuguese and Spaniards followed a slave code based in part on ancient Roman law. This code tried to protect the slaves; for example, the code recognized marriages between slaves, forbade excessive punishment of slaves, and allowed severely beaten slaves to appeal to the courts.

Also, all Portuguese and Spanish slaveowners were members of the Roman Catholic Church. And the Church, interested in converting the Indians and Africans to Christianity, sometimes tried to defend the slaves and protect them from abuses.

Perhaps most important, the Portuguese and Spaniards had less color prejudice than northern Europeans. For centuries, dark-skinned Moors from North Africa had once dominated large parts of Spain and Portugal. As a result, the Portuguese and Spaniards accepted racial mixtures with some tolerance and without the severe legal and social disapproval that later prevailed among the English colonists.

Still, slavery in the Spanish and Portuguese colonies could be very harsh. Whenever Spaniards and Portuguese found it commercially profitable to exploit black slave labor, as on the sugar plantations of northeastern Brazil and the Spanish West Indies, they did so. Latin American slavery, like slavery at all times and places, was a cruel denial of human worth and dignity and often led to desperate resistance on the part of the slaves.

Colonies for the king. All Spanish colonies belonged to the king of Spain. He ruled with the help of advisers, but he could ignore the advisers if he wished. His was the final word. Because the Spanish rulers had complete, or absolute, power, they are sometimes called *absolute monarchs*. The people living in Spain and in the Spanish colonies had almost no voice in the government.

The Spanish rulers claimed that God had given them the right to rule. They claimed that they were God's representatives on earth, responsible only to God for their actions. This theory of government, common in Europe during this period, was called the *divine right of kings*.

15

■ In the above painting, a Spanish treasure ship is being attacked by pirates. Such ships carried precious cargoes of gold and silver from the New World.

In the New World itself, *viceroys,*° appointed by the king, ruled in his name with complete authority. For them, as for the humblest Spanish subject, His Majesty's orders were law. The Spanish king regarded the colonies as his personal possessions. The land was his, the people were his subjects, and the wealth of the New World was his to use as he pleased. And he used it in just this way. He rewarded his friends and advisers with rich gifts of gold and silver, large grants of land, trading privileges, and the right to operate the gold and silver mines.

Crest of Spanish power. The gold and silver of the New World were carried to Spain in great treasure fleets. These fleets included treasure-laden galleons—huge vessels for their day, slow and clumsy, but heavily armed—protected by a

° *viceroy:* a person appointed by the king to rule a country or colony as the representative of the king.

convoy of smaller, swifter warships. Year after year these fleets carried the wealth of the New World to the Old.

And then, in 1580, Spain had another stroke of good fortune. King Philip II of Spain became ruler of Portugal. The two kingdoms of Spain and Portugal were united. In the New World, Portugal's thriving colonies were joined to those of Spain. Portugal's rich trade with India and the Spice Islands of the East Indies brought still greater wealth to Spain. Spanish power seemed unbeatable. And yet, Spain's power gradually began to decline.

The Spaniards themselves were partly responsible for their failure to keep Spain the strongest nation in Europe. Their new wealth helped to ruin them. Instead of building industries to produce goods at home, the Spaniards used gold and silver from America to buy needed goods from other countries. As a result, when the flow of gold and silver diminished, Spaniards could neither pay for the goods that they needed, nor produce such goods for themselves.

Then, too, English and Dutch sailors called "sea dogs" hastened Spain's decline by attacking Spanish treasure ships at sea and seizing their precious cargoes.

Hawkins, first of the sea dogs. John Hawkins was the first famous English sea dog. Today we would call him a pirate—precisely what the Spaniards called him. But his fellow Englishmen and his queen, Elizabeth I, looked upon him as a daring hero.

In the 1560's Hawkins began to transport slaves from Africa to the Spanish West Indies. Although it was contrary to Spanish law for Spanish colonists to buy anything from Englishmen, Spanish landowners in the New World conveniently forgot the law and traded with Hawkins. The Spaniards were as eager to buy the slaves as Hawkins was to sell them. Before long, however, Hawkins discovered an easier—if riskier—way to make money. He began to raid Spanish seaports and attack Spanish treasure ships.

Drake, boldest of the sea dogs. Other daring English sea dogs followed Hawkins' example. Among the boldest was Francis Drake. In 1577 Drake left England with a fleet of swift, heavily armed vessels. He headed southward and sailed through the Strait of Magellan into the Pacific Ocean (see map, page 17). Then he turned northward, skirting the western coast of South America. In the coastal waters between Peru and Panama, he found exactly what he wanted—unprotected

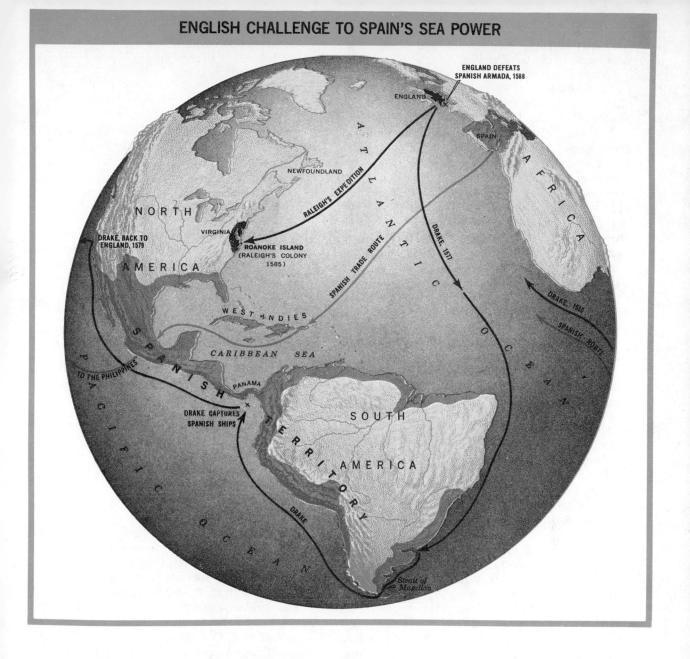

vessels loaded with treasure. The Spaniards, never expecting an enemy in these remote waters, had not provided convoys to protect their treasure ships.

Before long, Drake had seized all the plunder he could carry. He continued northward—not daring to return by the way he had come—and spent the winter on the coast of what is now California. When spring came, he sailed boldly across the Pacific in the *Pelican*, his only remaining ves-

sel. After crossing the Indian Ocean and going along the western coast of Africa, he arrived home in England in the autumn of 1580.

King Philip of Spain was furious. He knew that neither Drake nor the other English sea dogs could sail without Queen Elizabeth's permission. He also knew that much of Drake's plunder had enriched the English royal treasury. Philip therefore demanded that Queen Elizabeth punish Drake for piracy. Instead, Elizabeth welcomed Drake as a hero and knighted him on the deck of his ship, now renamed the *Golden Hind*.

Queen Elizabeth's action was a direct challenge to the Spanish king. Philip was quick to meet the challenge. He gave orders for a mighty fleet to invade and conquer England.

England, "Mistress of the Seas." As you have seen, Spain's attempt in 1588 to conquer England ended in disaster (page 4). The year 1588, therefore, was a turning point in history. Spain, with its powerful fleet destroyed, and weakened by troubles at home, began to decline in power. To be sure, for many years Spanish power remained strong in both the Old World and the New. But Spain was no longer the most feared nation in Europe.

While Spain became weaker, England and France and the Netherlands grew stronger. In time the English Royal Navy won for England the title of "Mistress of the Seas." By the end of the 1500's, no nation could prevent Englishmen from building colonies in the New World. And by this time many Englishmen were eager to do just that.

Failure of early colonies. Even before the defeat of the Spanish Armada, two Englishmen tried unsuccessfully to build colonies in America. Sir Humphrey Gilbert sailed across the Atlantic in 1583, intending to settle on the site of what is now St. John's, Newfoundland. But Gilbert and all his shipmates were lost in a storm.

The following year Queen Elizabeth gave permission to handsome, dashing Sir Walter Raleigh to build colonies in the New World, at his own expense. Raleigh spent a fortune in the attempt—and failed.

Raleigh's grant of land included all of eastern North America north of Spanish Florida. He named the land Virginia. With the backing of some wealthy Englishmen, he organized an expedition to explore the Atlantic coast. The expedition returned with good reports, and in 1585 Raleigh sent out his first group of colonists. They landed on Roanoke Island, off the coast of what is now North Carolina (see map, page 17).

The first Roanoke colony failed, however, and in 1587 Raleigh sent out a second group of colonists, who also settled on Roanoke Island. Unfortunately, the Spanish attempt to invade England in 1588 prevented Raleigh from sending fresh supplies for three years. When, in 1591, a relief expedition finally did reach Roanoke, the settlers were gone. To this day, the fate of this little band of colonists—the "Lost Colony"—remains a mystery.

Although Raleigh failed to build a colony, his efforts helped to strengthen England's interest in the New World.

SECTION SURVEY

IDENTIFY: slavery, absolute monarch, divine right of kings; John Hawkins, Sir Francis Drake, Sir Walter Raleigh; 1588.

1. Settlers seeking homes in the New World brought their "ways of living" with them. List these "ways" and the effects they had on the areas in which settlement took place.
2. (a) What accounted for the differences between slavery in the Spanish and Portuguese colonies and slavery in the English colonies? (b) Did these differences make slavery any "easier" for the slave? Explain.
3. (a) Upon what was Spain's power based? (b) Was this a stable economic base? Explain.
4. Explain why the defeat of the Spanish Armada was a decisive moment in the history of the land that later became the United States.
5. "Slavery is a cruel denial of human worth and dignity." Explain in your own words what this statement means.

4 An English foothold in North America

Sir Walter Raleigh had tried to start a colony on Roanoke Island but had lost his fortune in the attempt. A large business organization sponsored the next colonial venture. Hundreds of Englishmen invested money in the company, hoping to profit from colonial trade and development.

The famous charter of 1606. In 1606 King James I of England gave a single *charter* ° to two groups of men. One group, centered in Plymouth, England, was known as the Plymouth Company. The other, centered in London, was known as the London Company. The map on page 20 shows the land that King James granted to each of these companies in the large area then called Virginia.

The charter included a very important promise by King James: All people who served the company in the English colonies would retain their *rights and privileges* as Englishmen. In the words

° *charter:* an official document granting certain rights, powers, or privileges to a specific person or group; a written contract.

of the charter, they would "have and enjoy all liberties, franchises, and immunities . . . as if they had been abiding and born within this our realm of England, or any other of our said dominions."

Backgrounds of English liberty. The "rights" King James promised the settlers could be traced back nearly four centuries to the year 1215. In that year a group of English barons banded together against their monarch, King John, a harsh ruler who had been making excessive demands for money from the barons, and ignoring their traditional rights. The barons forced King John to sign the *Magna Carta,* or the Great Charter.

The Great Charter was important because it contained the idea that government should be *constitutional,* or conducted according to law and custom. Limits were set on what the king could demand from the barons. Some provision was made to protect the interests of clergymen, merchants, and townsmen, but the peasants were not affected. Nevertheless, when Englishmen of the 1600's and 1700's wanted to uphold what they called the "rights of Englishmen," they looked back to the Magna Carta as the foundation on which those rights rested.

Fifty years after the signing of the Magna Carta, in 1265, Englishmen asserted their right to *representative government* by establishing Parliament as the nation's lawmaking body. The English Parliament did not meet regularly for many, many years. In time, however, it did win the right to meet regularly and to help write law, or *legislation.* Long before the 1600's, England's Parliament had divided into two bodies—the House of Lords (or the "upper house") and the House of Commons (or the "lower house"). The House of Commons consisted of elected representatives.

The men who settled the American colonies carried these English ideas about government with them to the New World. In later years, as you will see, the English colonists again and again reminded the English government of its promise to respect their rights and privileges as Englishmen. Thus, the early colonists helped to strengthen the idea of self-government.

A poor start for Jamestown. It was Christmas time, 1606, when three small ships of the London Company moved down the Thames River, and sailed out upon the wintry sea. The London Company had wasted no time putting its share of the charter to use.

From the beginning the expedition was in trouble. The men did almost everything wrong.

■ The settlers of Jamestown worked together to clear the land for farming and to build cabins.

They took a roundabout way to America, following Columbus' route, and 16 of the 120 men died on the long voyage. When the colonists finally reached Virginia in the spring of 1607, they began to build a settlement named Jamestown in honor of the king (see map, page 20). They picked the poorest possible location—a low, wooded island in a river, which they called the James, near a marsh infested with malaria-carrying mosquitoes. The men did not take time to dig wells, but instead drank the dirty river water. Because they built only the flimsiest of shelters, they were drenched by rain in summer and half-frozen by cold when winter came.

Mistakes in England. Not all the fault for the colony's early failure lay with the settlers. The directors of the London Company, back in England, also made mistakes.

For one thing, the company, remembering Spain's rich discoveries, insisted that the settlers hunt for gold. The settlers did so willingly, but found none in the area. Thus, the men wasted valuable time that should have been spent in building houses and cultivating crops.

To make matters worse, the settlers were not allowed to own anything, and they received only as much food and clothing as they needed.

But the worst mistake of all, perhaps, was the failure of the directors to enlist enough real workmen to develop the resources of the settlement. The original group of 120 settlers that sailed for

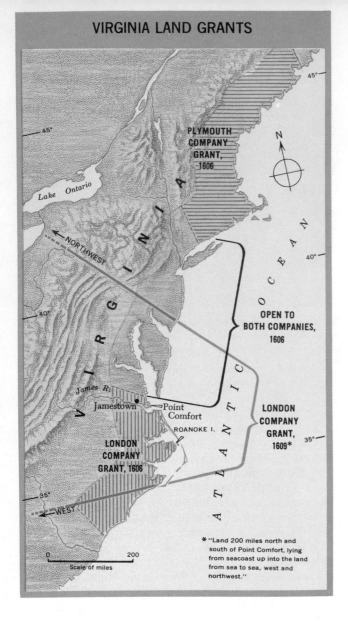

VIRGINIA LAND GRANTS

PLYMOUTH COMPANY GRANT, 1606

45°

45°

Lake Ontario

N

V I R G I N I A

NORTHWEST

40°

40°

OPEN TO BOTH COMPANIES, 1606

James R.

Jamestown

Point Comfort

ROANOKE I.

LONDON COMPANY GRANT, 1609*

35°

35°

LONDON COMPANY GRANT, 1606

A T L A N T I C

O C E A N

WEST

0   200
Scale of miles

* "Land 200 miles north and south of Point Comfort, lying from seacoast up into the land from sea to sea, west and northwest."

John Smith was a harsh ruler. Every morning he marched the men into the fields to cultivate the crops or into the forest to cut wood. They grumbled and complained, but the rule was "No work, no food." The men worked. And, thanks to John Smith, the colony survived.

When Smith returned to England, however, matters went from bad to worse. The winter of 1609–10 was terrible beyond belief. In later years the survivors called it "the starving time." When spring came, the sick, half-starved colonists were prepared to abandon Jamestown. Fortunately, just at this time ships arrived from England bringing more settlers and fresh supplies, giving the colonists new hope.

In 1609 the king granted a new charter, which gave more land to the Virginia colony (see map, this page).

Better times at Jamestown. Slowly, after 1610, conditions began to improve. Much to everyone's surprise, tobacco saved the colony.

Europeans first learned about smoking tobacco from the American Indians. By the early 1600's the habit of smoking was spreading throughout England and Europe.

Until Jamestown was settled, the Spanish West Indies supplied all the tobacco smoked by Englishmen and other Europeans. Then around 1612, John Rolfe (who later married the Indian princess Pocahontas) learned how to grow and cure tobacco in Virginia. Within a few years the colonists were shipping large quantities of this valuable product to England.

By 1619 most of the more than 1,000 men in the Virginia colony were making a living by raising tobacco. Tobacco farms dotted the banks of the James River for some 20 miles beyond the original settlement.

Jamestown grew for other reasons, too. Among the new settlers were many skilled workmen—carpenters, masons, blacksmiths, farmers, fishermen. Starting in 1618, each man who paid his way to Jamestown received 50 acres of land. The colonists now owned their fields and could sell their own products.

The start of self-government. In 1619 the London Company took another big step forward by giving the colonists the right to share in their own government.

July 30, 1619, is a memorable date in American history. On that date 22 *burgesses,* or representatives, two from each of the settled districts along the James River, met in Jamestown. Each of the

Jamestown included only 12 laborers and skilled workmen. The rest were "gentlemen"—in those days defined as men who had never done a day's work with their hands.

Difficult times at Jamestown. Not surprisingly, by the end of the first year only 53 settlers were still alive. They, too, might have perished had it not been for John Smith.

Smith set himself up as the leader of the colony. He ordered the men to dig wells, build better shelters, clear the land, and plant corn and other crops. Smith also made trips to Indian villages to get food.

burgesses had been elected by the voters of his own district. The House of Burgesses, as this lawmaking body came to be called, represented the men who owned land in the new colony. The first session, though short, was extremely important, for it marked the first step toward representative government in the New World.

The growth of Virginia. The date 1619 is memorable for other reasons. In that year 20 Africans arrived in the colony. These newcomers were the first of countless thousands of men and women from Africa who were brought to the New World. In the years that followed, Africans worked with people from many other lands in building the English colonies.

In the early years many, if not all, of the Africans were regarded as servants, bound for a period of years to the master who paid a ship captain for transporting them to America. At the end of a term of service, some of these black men acquired land and worked it for themselves. By the 1640's, however, Africans were being brought to the English colonies as slaves.

In 1619 also, the directors of the London Company sent 60 women to Virginia. The women were quickly married and, as the directors had foreseen, exercised a steadying influence upon the men.

The directors of the London Company, encouraged by Virginia's growing prosperity, began to send out hundreds of new settlers. Following orders from the company, some of the new settlers started an ironworks on the James River. Others planted olive trees and laid out vineyards. But most of the newcomers cleared a piece of land and began to grow tobacco.

Then disaster struck. Neighboring Indians had become alarmed by the rapid growth of the colony. In 1622, on a night that the survivors never forgot, the Indians attacked the outlying farmhouses, killing many of the settlers and burning most of the buildings. But Virginia quickly recovered from this blow. After striking back at the Indians, the colonists rebuilt their houses and started again. Between 1620 and 1624 about 4,000 men, women, and children arrived as settlers in the colony.

Virginia, a royal colony. In spite of the colony's growth, King James I decided that it had been badly managed. In 1624 he withdrew the charter from the London Company and took over the management of the colony. From that time on, Virginia was a *royal colony,* ruled by the king of England and his ministers. The king now appointed the

■ In 1619 the first Africans arrived in Jamestown. Brought there as captives, they became indentured servants.

governor and gave him power to veto, or reject, any laws. He also appointed a council, consisting of 12 members, to assist the governor.

But Virginia's government was not so restrictive as that of the Spanish colonies to the south and west, where the king of Spain and his viceroys still held absolute power. King James I did not attempt to end the House of Burgesses. The House of Burgesses continued to make the laws, subject to the approval of the governor and of the king. The settlers continued to elect the members of House of Burgesses.

SECTION SURVEY

IDENTIFY: charter, Magna Carta, constitutional government, representative government, House of Burgesses, royal colony; John Smith; 1619.

1. (a) What guarantee or promise was made by King James I in the charter of 1606? (b) Why was this promise important to the English colonists in the New World?
2. (a) What basic needs did the original colonists of Jamestown have to satisfy? (b) Were they successful? Explain.
3. Do you see any irony in the fact that the year 1619 marked the beginning of self-government, as well as the arrival of the first Africans in America? Explain.

TRACING THE MAIN IDEAS

Men have always lived in a changing world. There have been certain periods in history, however, when changes occurred with such speed and transformed so many different aspects of life that they were truly revolutionary. Such an age was the one that you have been reading about in this chapter.

The "revolutions" began in Europe. During the revolution now called the Renaissance, men became increasingly curious about the world around them. During the Commercial Revolution, traders from Spain, Portugal, England, and other nations facing the Atlantic discovered new, all-water routes to Asia and so destroyed the monopoly of the Italian traders of Genoa and Venice. During the Geographic Revolution, European explorers, led by Columbus, discovered a New World far across the Atlantic.

And, finally, in England a revolutionary spirit of independence began to grow. Englishmen had been insisting since the 1200's that they had a "right" to share in the government and to be "represented" in the lawmaking body called Parliament. This movement stretched over too long a period to be called a "revolution." But it was in full swing by the 1600's, and the changes it brought in the way men lived and governed themselves were nothing short of revolutionary.

In such an age—an exciting age in which new ideas and new ways of living were transforming the everyday affairs of life in Europe—Englishmen made their first permanent New World settlement and brought to it the principle of representative government.

As you will see in the next chapter, Englishmen soon carried the same principle of representative government to all the other settlements and colonies built along the Atlantic seaboard.

CHAPTER SURVEY

QUESTIONS FOR DISCUSSION

1. The years between 1450 and 1624 can be termed a revolutionary period. (a) What is meant by this statement? (b) Why did revolutionary changes take place in Europe at that time? (c) Why did these changes not take place in Europe during the years between 800 and 1000? (d) Did these changes benefit all the people in Europe? Explain.
2. In what ways are a colonist and an explorer (a) alike, (b) different?
3. Do you think that the "man on the street" in London or Madrid in 1600 was aware of the fact that he was living in a revolutionary age? Explain.
4. Explain each of the following terms in relation to the exploration and settlement of the New World: (a) freedom, (b) riches, (c) political rivalry between nations, (d) Christianity.
5. The seeds of troubled race relations in America were planted early in the history of European exploration and settlement of the New World. Comment.

RELATING PAST TO PRESENT

1. Do nations in the world today desire power for the same reasons that nations desired power in the 1500's?
2. Can we truly evaluate whether our period of history is as revolutionary as the period of history studied in this chapter? Why or why not?

USING MAPS AND CHARTS

1. Using the map on pages 8–9, answer the following questions: (a) If you had been a trader in the Middle Ages, which of the medieval trade routes would you have preferred? Why? (b) Which parts of the world were known to Europeans in 1500? Which parts were still unexplored?
2. Using the maps on pages 13 and 17, show why the routes from Peru and Mexico to Spain were so dangerous for the Spanish galleons.
3. Study the map on page 20. What future problems can you foresee as an outcome of the London Company grant?

ON SEPTEMBER 16, 1620, the *Mayflower* set sail from Plymouth harbor in England, bound for the New World. On November 11 the small, storm-battered ship finally dropped anchor off the tip of Cape Cod, a windswept arm of land jutting out from the mainland of North America. The passengers, the Pilgrims, were about to start the first permanent colony in New England.

Why had the Pilgrims come to this wild and lonely spot? Why did so many Europeans leave their homes in the Old World to face the dangers of an unknown New World?

If Europe had been a happier place, they might not have come. But, for many people, Europe in the 1600's was not a happy place. These people found the attractions of the lands across the sea very compelling indeed.

Men and women with little chance of improving their lives in Europe looked to America with new hope. Here was a rich but nearly empty land, almost unexplored, waiting for the ax and the plow of the pioneer. Here was opportunity, almost limitless, for men and women bold enough to seize it.

The settlers came first to Jamestown, then to New England, and then in ever-growing numbers to other wild and lonely places along the Atlantic seaboard. By 1733, when Georgia was started, European settlers had built thirteen colonies. And the boldest settlers, true pioneers, were pushing westward through the forest, clearing land and building homes in the wilderness.

Out of such simple beginnings a great new nation was to be born.

■ *Celebrating the first Thanksgiving, 1621*

CHAPTER **2**

The British Colonies in North America

1620 – 1750

THE CHAPTER IN OUTLINE

1. The search for a better life in North America.
2. Early settlements of the Pilgrims and Puritans in New England.
3. Expanding English settlements in New England.
4. The immigration of diverse peoples to the Middle Colonies.
5. The creation of a distinctive way of life in the Southern Colonies.

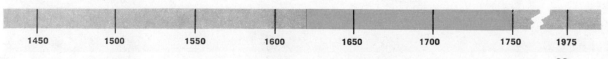

| 1450 | 1500 | 1550 | 1600 | 1650 | 1700 | 1750 | 1975 |

1 The search for a better life in North America

Opportunity! That was the great attraction. Like a magnet, opportunity drew men and women from Europe to the New World. But even so, people would not have come in such great numbers if conditions in Europe had been better.

Conflict over religion. During the 1500's and 1600's Europe was torn by religious strife. The conflict broke out shortly after Columbus discovered the New World. At that time virtually everyone in Western Europe belonged to the Roman Catholic Church. The conflict began when some men began to question Church practices and beliefs. One such man was Martin Luther in Germany. Another was John Calvin in Switzerland.

These men and others who shared their feelings broke away from the Roman Catholic Church and established Protestant, or "protesting," religious organizations. Roman Catholics called this movement the Protestant Revolt. Protestants called it the Reformation. By whatever name, this religious conflict was not just a battle of words and ideas. Armies marched, wars were fought, and thousands died in battle or were burned at the stake in the name of religion.

England broke with the Roman Catholic Church in 1534. At that time King Henry VIII established the Church of England, sometimes called the Anglican Church. The king of England became the head of the Church. According to English law, every English citizen, regardless of his own religious belief, had to belong to the Anglican Church and contribute to its support.

Search for religious freedom. In spite of the law, many Englishmen objected to the Anglican Church. Roman Catholics insisted upon their right to worship as they always had. Among those people who accepted the Protestant Reformation, some felt that the Anglican Church was too much like the Roman Catholic Church. They wanted to carry the Reformation further by simplifying, or "purifying," Anglican teaching, government, and worship. Broadly speaking, these people were known as Puritans or Dissenters.

One group of Puritans was willing to belong to the Anglican Church, but they wanted to reform, or "purify," it. Members of this group, as you will read, settled Massachusetts Bay Colony in the New World.

■ The great city of London, situated on the banks of the Thames River, looked like this in the late 1600's.

24

Other groups of Puritans refused to have anything to do with the Anglican Church. These people, who broke away and formed their own religious organizations, were called Separatists. The Pilgrims were one of these groups.

Life in England was often difficult for Puritans of all groups. They were persecuted by their neighbors, fined by the government, and sometimes sent to jail. At the height of such persecution, thousands left England, hoping to find greater religious freedom in the New World. As the years passed, other religious refugees—including Catholics, Protestants, and Jews—also fled to America from many European countries.

Search for political freedom. The desire to be free from political persecution also drove many Englishmen—as well as other Europeans—to the New World. For nearly 100 years, many Englishmen had hardly dared to express their political opinions.

Political problems in England came to a head during the reign of James I, who ruled from 1603 to 1625. King James I tried to make and enforce laws without the consent of Parliament, the law-making body of England. James believed in the "divine right of kings" (page 15), insisting that he was responsible to no earthly power for his actions. Most members of Parliament refused to accept this theory of government. As a result, an intense quarrel broke out between James I and Parliament.

The quarrel became even more intense when Charles I became king in 1625. For 11 years, from 1629 to 1640, Charles I ruled without Parliament. Then, in 1642, a civil war called the Puritan Revolution broke out in England. The war ended in 1649 when Charles I was beheaded. For the next 11 years, England was ruled by a group of Puritans, led by Oliver Cromwell until his death in 1658.

During this long period of political upheaval, many Englishmen moved to the New World to escape persecution by the government.

Widespread unemployment. Unemployment was another major reason why many Englishmen decided to leave England to settle in the colonies.

During the 1500's and 1600's many English landlords drove tenant farmers off their estates and turned the plowed fields into pastures on which they raised sheep. The landowners could make more money by selling wool than by collecting rents.

Many displaced tenant farmers moved to Eng-

■ Religious persecution in England took many forms—arrest, heavy fines, and sometimes even physical punishment, as shown here in an engraving from a book published in 1592.

lish towns and cities searching for jobs. But there were not enough jobs for all of them. Many had no place to go, no way to earn a living. Many of them became beggars. Some even became criminals—highwaymen, pickpockets, thieves.

But only a small proportion of the unemployed turned to crime or ended up in a debtor's prison. Most continued to look for work. Many were willing to risk anything to get a fresh start in life. America seemed to offer just such an opportunity. Many unemployed Englishmen signed contracts called *indentures*. In these contracts they promised that, in return for transportation to America, they would work without wages for periods ranging from two to seven years. The people who signed indentures were called *indentured servants*.

Economic ferment. The difficult times in England affected not only the unemployed, but thousands of working people. Prices were rising, and it was difficult to make ends meet.

When this happens today, we call it *inflation*. During a period of inflation, with prices soaring, a fixed amount of money buys fewer and fewer goods. People with a limited, or fixed, amount of income find it harder and harder to buy food and clothing.

One reason for rising prices in England—and throughout Europe—was the flow of gold and silver from the Spanish colonies of the New World. Gold and silver poured into the hands of Spaniards who used it to buy products from other countries. Because of the increased demand for their products, farmer and manufacturers in England and other countries could demand higher prices. The rising prices created hardships for thousands of Englishmen.

But higher prices also brought prosperity to some Englishmen, particularly businessmen—merchants, traders, and manufacturers. Thus, some of the New World treasure flowed through Spain into the hands of English businessmen. And as their fortunes grew, the businessmen began to look for profitable ways to invest their money. Many bought shares in the new overseas trading companies. The boldest began to think of financing colonies in the New World.

A dam about to burst. In the late 1500's and early 1600's, then, conditions in England favored colonization. Thousands of people longed for freedom to worship as they pleased. Thousands wanted to escape from political unrest and persecution. Poor people wanted jobs and the opportunity to earn a better living. Businessmen had money to invest in promising colonial ventures.

England in the opening years of the 1600's was like a dam behind which the water was rising higher and higher. When the dam finally burst, a flood of people poured out to populate the colonies overseas.

SECTION SURVEY

IDENTIFY: Protestant Reformation, religious freedom, indentured servants, inflation.

1. England in the early years of the 1600's was like a dam about to burst. What pressures or conditions finally caused the dam to break?
2. Explain why the New World can be termed a "safety valve."
3. Suppose you were an Englishman living in the early 1600's. Which of the following conditions would have upset you most: the fact that you could not (a) worship as you pleased, (b) express a political opinion, or (c) find a job? Explain.

2 Early settlements of the Pilgrims and Puritans in New England

When the Pilgrims arrived in 1620 aboard their ship the *Mayflower* to build the first permanent colony in New England, Jamestown in Virginia was the only established English settlement along the entire Atlantic seaboard. Twenty years later, however, thousands of Englishmen were living in flourishing settlements along the eastern coast of North America.

The "why" of the Pilgrim story. Why did the Pilgrims leave England to come to the New World? Not one of the 102 passengers on the *Mayflower* could have answered for all the others. Many were Separatists who refused to follow the practices of the Church of England. They wished to be free to worship in their own way.

Some of these Separatists had been living in the Netherlands, where the Dutch had allowed them to worship in their own way. But they did not want their children to grow up speaking Dutch instead of English, living like Dutchmen rather than Englishmen. Thus they came to the New World.

Others came for personal reasons. John Alden, a young cooper, or barrelmaker, had helped to ready the *Mayflower* for its voyage. He had decided to make the long journey largely out of a spirit of adventure.

Whatever their reasons for coming—and the religious motive was dominant—the passengers on board the *Mayflower* firmly agreed on one thing. They intended to establish new homes and a new way of life for themselves and their children in the New World.

The Mayflower Compact. Upon arriving in November 1620, the Pilgrims had to tackle the job of organizing a new government. The London Company (page 18) had given them a grant of land south of the Hudson River. But storms had blown the *Mayflower* off course, and the Pilgrims' ship had reached New England, where they had no legal right to land and settle. Nor did the Pilgrims have any plans for governing the colony once they landed.

While the crew furled the sails, the Pilgrim leaders gathered in the cabin. There, they wrote and signed what we now call the Mayflower Compact. In this compact, or agreement, they promised "all due submission and obedience" to the laws that they themselves would pass.

■ When the Pilgrims arrived at Plymouth, they saw a bleak and lonely landscape. A nineteenth-century artist imagined the scene of their landing in the painting shown above.

The Mayflower Compact was not a plan of government. It did not pledge the Pilgrims to a democratic way of life. Nevertheless, this short document marked an important step along the road to self-government in the New World.

Landing at Plymouth. By the time the Pilgrims signed the compact, it was too late in the day to lower a boat and row ashore. The next day was Sunday. Restraining their impatience to set foot on land, the Pilgrims remained on board the ship and devoted Sunday to prayer and worship. Early Monday they landed at what is now Provincetown, Massachusetts.

The Pilgrims spent more than a month looking for a place to settle. They finally selected a location on the other side of what is now Cape Cod Bay (see inset map, page 31). In earlier years English explorers had visited this place and named it Plymouth.

Plymouth had many advantages, including a small but good harbor, a brook of clear, fresh water, and a hill easily defended against attack. The Pilgrims were also attracted to it because, having once been the site of an Indian village, Plymouth was surrounded by cleared fields.

The Pilgrims sailed into Plymouth harbor late in December 1620 and, as William Bradford, one of the leaders, noted in his journal, "The twenty-fifth day began to erect the first house. . . ." Those who could work toiled through the cold, cheerless winter months. Many sickened and died. Before spring arrived, half the Pilgrims had perished. But not one settler left the colony to return to England when the *Mayflower* sailed back to England in April.

Those who were still alive might not have survived much longer had it not been for friendly Indians, and one man in particular called Squanto. Squanto taught the Pilgrims how to make effective use of the resources of forest, sea, and soil. Perhaps most important, he brought them seeds of native plants—pumpkin, squash, beans, and Indian corn—and showed them how to grow these crops in the cleared fields.

In the autumn of 1621, the Pilgrims celebrated their first year in the New World by setting aside

LIVING AMERICAN DOCUMENTS

Mayflower Compact (1620)

We whose names are underwritten, . . . having undertaken . . . a voyage to plant the first colony in the northern parts of Virginia, do . . . solemnly and mutually in the presence of God, and one of another, covenant and combine ourselves together into a civil body politic; . . . and by virtue hereof, to enact, constitute, and frame such just and equal laws, ordinances, acts, constitutions, and offices from time to time, as shall be thought most meet and convenient for the general good of the colony unto which we promise all due submission and obedience. . . .

27

Two Pilgrims speaking with an Indian

SQUANTO, FRIEND OF THE PILGRIMS

Before the Pilgrims landed at Plymouth, Captain Thomas Hunt, one of several Englishmen engaged in trade along the Massachusetts coast, kidnaped a Pawtucket Indian named Squanto and sold him into slavery in Spain. Squanto escaped to England, where he lived for two years. Then he returned to America on a trading vessel. But in 1618 he was back in England. A year later he crossed the Atlantic again (his fourth trip), sailing as guide and interpreter on a trading expedition that planned to operate in the Cape Cod area. When he reached New England, he discovered that all of his tribe had been wiped out by a terrible epidemic.

Squanto joined the Pilgrims shortly after they landed and helped them in many ways. William Bradford, the Pilgrim leader, tells the story: "Squanto continued with them [the Pilgrims], and was their interpreter, and was a special instrument sent of God for their good beyond their expectation. He directed them how to set their corn, where to take fish and to procure other commodities, and was also their pilot to bring them to unknown places for their profit, and never left them till he died."

28

several days for recreation and thanksgiving. Nearly 100 Indians and more than 30 settlers newly arrived from England joined them in the celebration.

Faith, courage, hard work, and an intense desire to be free enabled the Pilgrims to survive the first desperate period and build a permanent colony on the shores of New England. However, the colony never attracted many new settlers. Finally, under a charter granted in 1691, Plymouth became a part of its larger neighbor to the north, Massachusetts Bay Colony.

The roots of Massachusetts.   Like most of the Pilgrims of Plymouth, the Puritans of Massachusetts Bay Colony moved to the New World largely for religious reasons. Unlike the Pilgrims, many of the Massachusetts Bay settlers were willing to remain members of the Anglican Church, but wanted to change some of its practices. Charles I, who became king of England in 1625, refused to agree to such changes. He made life increasingly difficult for the Puritans. Finally, some prominent Puritan leaders, including John Winthrop and Sir Richard Saltonstall, decided to form a company and start a colony in America. In 1629 they secured a charter from the king and organized the Massachusetts Bay Company.

Fortunately for the Puritans, the charter neglected to name the place where the directors of the company would hold their annual meeting. The shrewd Puritan directors made the most of this oversight. They voted to take the charter and move to the New World, where they could run the company as they pleased. Thus, Massachusetts became a self-governing colony, almost independent of the English king and Parliament.

Arrival of the Puritans.   The Puritans began to arrive in Massachusetts during the summer of 1630 —nearly 1,000 men, women, and children aboard 17 ships. Unlike the Pilgrims, who arrived as nearly penniless refugees, the Puritan settlers had ample supplies of food, clothing, and tools. Among the colonists were skilled workmen—carpenters, masons, blacksmiths, shipbuilders, and men trained in other trades. Several colonists were graduates of Cambridge and Oxford, England's leading universities. The first governor, John Winthrop, was a well-educated man who kept a journal that was later published as a history of New England.

One by one the ships unloaded their cargoes, and the Puritans began to build villages along the coast north of Plymouth. Some settled at Shawmut, later called Boston (see map, page 31). Others settled in small villages near Boston. A few settled at Naumkeag (NOM·keg), later called Salem, which had been a fishing and trading village since the year 1626.

The Indians must have been astonished at this sudden burst of building activity. But these villages were only the beginning of English settlement in Massachusetts. During the next few years shipload after shipload of passengers from England arrived to join the early settlers. By the year 1640, there were more than 20,000 Englishmen living in Massachusetts Bay Colony.

Government in Massachusetts. Religion and government were closely intermingled in Massachusetts Bay Colony. The Puritan leaders wanted to establish a "Bible Commonwealth" in which the Scriptures served as the guide for every aspect of life. John Winthrop had warned the Puritans on the voyage to the New World that the Lord "will expect a strict performance from us." To make sure the settlers remained true to Puritan beliefs, the leaders established their Puritan version of the Church of England as the only recognized church. They also kept all government power in the General Court, the lawmaking body of the Massachusetts Bay Company. Only owners of stock or shares —a minority of the settlers—could belong to the General Court.

But from the start, some settlers rebelled against the rule of the leaders. They demanded the right to share in the government. Winthrop and the other leaders were soon forced to loosen their control. They granted the right to vote to all Puritan men who were good church members. They also granted each town the right to send representatives to the General Court. Thus, very early in its history Massachusetts, like Jamestown, had a representative form of government.

SECTION SURVEY

IDENTIFY: self-governing colony, Mayflower Compact; Squanto, John Winthrop; 1620.

1. What visions did the passengers on the *Mayflower* have of their life in the New World?
2. Compare the conditions confronting the Pilgrims who arrived in the New World in 1620 with the conditions confronting the settlers who arrived between 1630 and 1640.
3. (a) Of what importance was the fact that religion and government were closely intermingled in Massachusetts Bay Colony? (b) Are religion and government closely intermingled in the United States today? Why or why not?

3 Expanding English settlements in New England

The Puritan settlers of Massachusetts Bay Colony had left England mainly for religious reasons, hoping to find greater religious freedom in the New World. Yet, once settled in America, the Puritans were extremely harsh with people who did not believe in worshiping the same way that they did. Such people were forced to leave Massachusetts.

Besides those who fled from the strictness of Puritan rule, other colonists left Massachusetts to search for new and better farm land and greater opportunities. In this way, exiles and pioneers set up new colonies along the New England coastline.

The founding of Rhode Island. Of all the early settlers of Massachusetts Bay Colony, none created more of a stir than Roger Williams. A deeply religious young man, who was earnestly seeking spiritual truth, he arrived in the colony in 1631 and soon became pastor of a church in Salem.

Several ideas preached by the young pastor soon aroused the opposition of the leaders of Massachusetts Bay Colony. Williams taught that the colonists had no right to their land unless they first bought it from the Indians. He also preached that political leaders could have no authority over religious matters. He insisted that every individual had the right to worship God as his conscience directed him.

Williams was groping toward two important democratic ideas: first, that the church and the state ° should be separate, and second, that government should be based upon the will of the people. These two ideas eventually became widely accepted in the land that became the United States. However, Williams preached his ideas to Puritan colonists who believed that government's main purpose was to enforce God's law. Many Puritans rejected Williams and his teachings as wrong and dangerous.

Regarding Roger Williams as a menace to the peace and well-being of Massachusetts Bay Colony, the Puritan authorities decided to send him back to England. Williams escaped, fleeing for safety through the wilderness to his friends, the Narragansett Indians. He lived with them for several months.

° *state:* This term is often used in American history with two different meanings. It may refer to the government of any country or colony, as it does here. Or it may refer to one of the "states" of the United States.

■ The Narragansett Indians protected and cared for Roger Williams after his escape from Massachusetts Bay Colony.

Then, in 1636, with old friends from Massachusetts, he founded the village of Providence (see map, page 31) at the head of Narragansett Bay.

Other exiles from Massachusetts, among them Mrs. Anne Hutchinson, soon started other settlements along the shores of Narragansett Bay. In 1644 Roger Williams secured a charter for the colony of Rhode Island. Under this charter the government of Rhode Island rested upon the *consent of the governed*—in this instance upon the right of all adult males to vote and have a say in their government. The settlers were also guaranteed the right to worship as they wished.

A later charter, granted in 1663, deprived more than half of the adult males of their right to vote by requiring that a man must own a certain amount of property before he could vote. These so-called "property qualifications" caused much discontent. Even with this restriction on the right to vote, however, Rhode Island offered more freedom to more settlers than any other colony in New England. As you will see in Chapter 5, the charter of 1663 placed no restrictions on religious freedom. For this reason, Rhode Island attracted settlers of many religious faiths.

Westward to Connecticut. Connecticut, like Rhode Island, was an offshoot from the older colony of Massachusetts. But the men and women who settled Connecticut were not exiles. They were the first of many, many thousands of sturdy pioneers

who moved out to the *frontier,* or the unsettled wilderness land just beyond the settled areas, in search of greater opportunities.

In 1635 the Reverend Thomas Hooker and nearly all of the members of his church in Newtown (later Cambridge), Massachusetts, decided to move farther out. With the permission of the General Court, they moved southwest in the spring of 1636, traveling with all their property through the wilderness and settling finally at Hartford, Connecticut (see inset map, page 31).

Other pioneers started neighboring settlements. In 1639 the new settlements of Windsor and Wethersfield joined with Hartford and adopted a plan of government. This plan was called the Fundamental Orders of Connecticut.

More than 20 years later, in 1662, after 15 towns had been settled, Connecticut secured a charter from King Charles II. This charter extended the Connecticut boundaries to include settlements along Long Island Sound. The most important of these settlements was New Haven. The charter also gave the settlers the right to govern themselves, thus making legal a practice followed from the first days at Hartford. The charter of 1662 proved so satisfactory that the citizens of Connecticut kept it as their state constitution after winning their independence from Great Britain in the Revolutionary War.

Northward to New Hampshire and Maine. While Connecticut was growing into a self-governing colony, pioneers were pushing northward from Massachusetts into the area that later became the states of New Hampshire and Maine.

As early as 1622, John Mason and Sir Ferdinando Gorges (GOR·jez) had been granted the right to settle this territory. In 1629 the two men divided the land between them, Gorges taking the northern territory and Mason the southern. Both men tried to build colonies, but for a number of years their settlements remained little more than trading posts.

By the late 1630's settlers in substantial numbers were moving northward from Massachusetts, building settlements on the land claimed by Mason and Gorges. The Puritan authorities watched this development with keen interest and decided to claim the territory for Massachusetts. By the 1650's Massachusetts had gained control over both New Hampshire and Maine. It held control over Maine until 1820 when, more than 30 years after the Constitution of the United States had been adopted,

(*continued on page 32*)

SETTLEMENT OF THE THIRTEEN BRITISH COLONIES

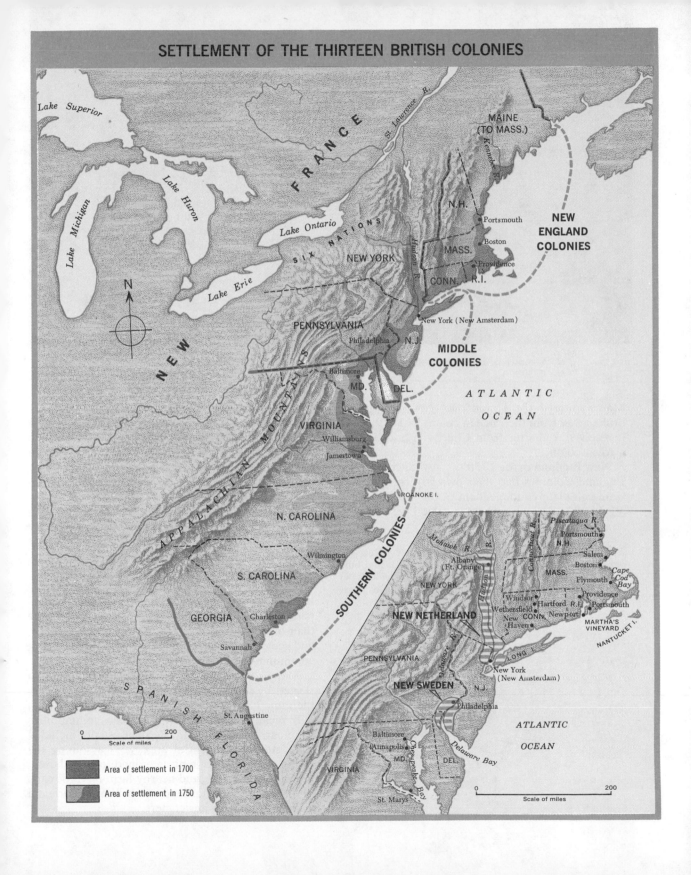

Lake Superior

Lake Michigan

Lake Huron

Lake Erie

Lake Ontario

St. Lawrence R.

F R A N C E

N E W

MAINE
(TO MASS.)

Kennebec R.

N.H.

NEW
ENGLAND
COLONIES

Portsmouth

SIX NATIONS

NEW YORK

Hudson R.

MASS.

Boston

Providence

CONN.   R.I.

PENNSYLVANIA

New York (New Amsterdam)

Philadelphia   N.J.

MIDDLE
COLONIES

A P P A L A C H I A N   M O U N T A I N S

Baltimore

MD.   DEL.

ATLANTIC

OCEAN

VIRGINIA

Williamsburg

Jamestown

ROANOKE I.

N. CAROLINA

Wilmington

SOUTHERN COLONIES

S. CAROLINA

GEORGIA   Charleston

Savannah

S P A N I S H   F L O R I D A

St. Augustine

N
↑

0   200
Scale of miles

| | Area of settlement in 1700 |
| | Area of settlement in 1750 |

Inset map:

Mohawk R.

Albany
(Ft. Orange)

NEW YORK

Hudson R.

Connecticut R.

Piscataqua R.

Portsmouth

N.H.

Salem

MASS.

Boston

Plymouth

*Cape
Cod
Bay*

NEW NETHERLAND

Windsor

Wethersfield

New
Haven

CONN.

Hartford   R.I.

Newport

Providence

Portsmouth

MARTHA'S
VINEYARD

NANTUCKET I.

LONG I.

New York
(New Amsterdam)

PENNSYLVANIA

Delaware R.

NEW SWEDEN

N.J.

Philadelphia

ATLANTIC

OCEAN

Baltimore

Annapolis

MD.

Chesapeake Bay

DEL.

Delaware Bay

VIRGINIA

St. Marys

0   200
Scale of miles

■ A center of important political activity as well as of trade, Boston was a flourishing city in the 1750's.

Maine entered the Union. But New Hampshire broke away from the Puritan colony in 1679, when it received a charter from Charles II and became a royal colony.

New England in the 1750's. Although the New England Colonies had their own governments and were completely independent of one another, they all developed along much the same lines.

■ Stone Fence. Before planting crops, many New England farmers collected stones from their fields and built fences, or walls. Early fences were low and wide; later ones as here were higher and narrower. Some of these later ones may still be seen in New England.

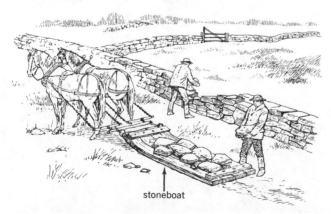

stoneboat

Most of the New England settlers shared similar origins, the vast majority coming from England and Scotland. However, Negro slaves could be found in all the New England Colonies. Unlike the European settlers who came to New England to gain freedom, the black slaves were brought from Africa against their will.

By the 1750's thriving towns and cities had been built around all the good harbors along the New England coast. Boston had a population of about 15,000. All of the seaport towns were busy, thriving places.

Inland, the colonies were dotted with small villages. From the beginning New England farmers had settled together in small communities rather than on remote farmsteads. Religion, the Indians, and geography influenced the development of small communities in New England.

Many New England communities had been started by friends and neighbors who belonged to the same local church. Hartford, Connecticut, you will recall, began this way. These communities were carefully planned. The plan usually included a "common," or central area; land adjoining the common for houses; a piece of land for the church, or "meetinghouse"; and nearby farm land for each of the settlers. Surplus land was held by the original settlers for sale to newcomers.

The need for defense, as well as the desire to be near the meetinghouse, also prompted the settlers to build compact communities. In frontier communities, where the danger from Indian attack was greatest, the first settlers also built a fort or blockhouse.

As one of their first tasks, the settlers usually organized a *militia*. The militia trained all adult male citizens for military service by drilling regularly on the common, or "the village green," as it was often called. The militia was called to active duty only during times of danger.

Geography also influenced the spread of small farming communities in New England. In many places the soil was shallow and filled with rocks and boulders, the land hilly and covered with forests. On such land, men could rarely clear a large area or build a big farm. Thus, New England communities remained small and compact.

SECTION SURVEY

IDENTIFY: frontier, will of the people, New England Colonies; Roger Williams.

1. Community living in New England was a result of religion, geography, and Indians. Explain.
2. What limitations did the physical environment impose upon settlers in Massachusetts?
3. Why was Roger Williams rejected by his society?
4. Relate or connect the reasons that caused settlers to come to the New World to the reasons that caused them to leave Massachusetts and establish new settlements elsewhere.

4 The immigration of diverse peoples to the Middle Colonies

People from the Netherlands and Sweden established the first settlements in the Middle Colonies (see map, page 31). In 1609, only two years after the founding of Jamestown, Henry Hudson, an Englishman sailing in the service of the Dutch East India Company of the Netherlands, explored the river that ever since has borne his name.

During the next few years Dutch traders made voyages to the Middle Atlantic coast. As a result of their favorable reports, Dutch investors secured a charter from the government of the Netherlands and organized the Dutch West India Company. The charter gave the company control over all trade and colonies in the New World. This charter conflicted with the charter granted by James I to the London Company, which founded Jamestown.

The rise of New Netherland. The Dutch West India Company acted promptly to secure the trade of the entire Middle Atlantic coast. The Dutch called the land they claimed New Netherland (see inset map, page 31). Around a fort that they built on the lower tip of Manhattan Island, they started the settlement of New Amsterdam, now New York City. They also established forts and trading posts on the Hudson River at the present site of Albany, on the Connecticut River near the present site of Hartford, and on the Delaware River below the present site of Philadelphia.

To attract settlers to New Netherland, the Dutch West India Company in 1629 offered huge land grants to any member who would settle at least 50 tenant farmers on his estate within four years. Some members who accepted the offer became large landowners, or *patroons*.

Most Dutch citizens, who were free men, would not move to the New World to live on a patroon's estate. As a result, the Dutch West India Company introduced slavery into the colony at an early date. Some of the patroons used African slaves to cultivate their estates. Still, New Netherland grew very slowly. Under the company's control, it never had more than 10,000 inhabitants. Most settlers lived in the trading center of New Amsterdam. They came from many European nations, as well as from Africa. In 1646 it was reported that 18 languages could be heard in New Amsterdam.

The Dutch threat to the English. From the beginning New Netherland posed a threat to the English colonies. From their strategic, fortified base at New Amsterdam, Dutch warships could strike at English ships bound to and from New England and the Southern Colonies. From New Amsterdam the Dutch also controlled the trade of three vital river valleys—the Hudson, the Connecticut, and the Delaware (see inset map, page 31). The Dutch strengthened their control even further when, in 1655, they seized Fort Christina and other Swedish settlements on the banks of the Delaware River, an area known as New Sweden.

Especially valuable to the Dutch was their control of the Hudson River. From a point north of Fort Orange (now Albany), the Mohawk Valley provided a route through the mountains into the Great Lakes region and the interior of the North American continent. The powerful league of Indians known as the Five Nations (later Six Nations) dominated this route. These Indians were

■ The Dutch town of New Amsterdam, located at the mouth of the Hudson River, is shown as it appeared in 1653. When the English gained control of the town, they renamed it New York.

friendly with the Dutch. They brought furs from the Great Lakes region to the Dutch posts on the Hudson River. But New England settlers also wanted to share in this rich fur trade. Dutch control of the Hudson River was a continual source of friction.

Conflict between English and Dutch. Dutch expansion eastward into Long Island and northward in the Connecticut Valley finally brought matters to a head. This expansion plunged the Dutch into conflict with traders and settlers from New England who were pushing southward into the same territory. In 1643, partly through fear of the Dutch, the colonies of Massachusetts, Plymouth, Connecticut, and New Haven united their military forces in the New England Confederation.°

Not only New England was threatened. Dutch expansion also threatened Maryland and Virginia to the south. The showdown between the English and the Dutch was not long in coming.

In 1664 an English fleet sailed into the Hudson River. Overwhelmed by superior English strength, Peter Stuyvesant, the Dutch governor, hauled down his nation's flag at New Amsterdam. Without firing a shot, the English thus ended the rival colonial power of the Dutch in North America.

The colony of New Jersey. Charles II, then king of England, presented all the territory that had once been New Netherland to his younger brother

° *confederation:* a political league in which members retain most of the power of government, while a central government body takes care of common problems, such as defense.

James, the Duke of York. The gift included not only the land between the Connecticut and the Delaware rivers, but also Long Island, the islands of Nantucket and Martha's Vineyard, and all of Maine east of the Kennebec River. This vast territory became the property of the 30-year-old Duke of York.

James gave the name New York to part of the former Dutch colony. Then he began to hand out generous gifts of land to his friends. The largest gift, New Jersey, which included the land between the Hudson and the Delaware rivers (see inset map, page 31), went to Lord John Berkeley and Sir George Carteret.

At the time, in 1664, New Jersey was almost all wilderness land, with only a few hundred settlers. Dutch and Swedish colonists had earlier built several small settlements along the Delaware River, and colonists from New England had settled a few villages in the north. Berkeley and Carteret tried to attract more settlers, but they had limited success. Finally, in 1702, after these lands had changed hands many times, the king of England claimed New Jersey as a royal colony.

New York under English rule. The newly created colony of New York had a much different history from that of New Jersey. The young Duke of York took a keen interest in the former Dutch colony. As one of his first and wisest acts, he ordered his colonial officials to treat the Dutch with "humanity and gentleness." He allowed the Dutch to speak their own language and worship in their own churches.

But in the long run the Duke was a harsh ruler.

He levied heavy taxes without the consent of the people, and, except for a brief two years (1683–85), he allowed them no voice in the government. Under his rule also, many more African slaves were brought into the colony. English interest in the slave trade continued to grow.

The end of absolute rule. In 1685 the Duke of York became King James II of England. A year later, in 1686, he combined New Jersey, New York, and the New England Colonies under a form of government called the Dominion of New England. He then abolished representative government in these former colonies and appointed Sir Edmund Andros as governor of the Dominion.

This period of absolute rule lasted about two years. Citizens in England resented the harsh rule of King James as much as the colonists resented his governor, Andros. In 1688 a revolt in England called the Glorious Revolution drove James II from the throne. In 1689 England adopted a Bill of Rights,° which included the right to representative government. The new king and queen, William and Mary of Orange, restored the colonial charters. The representative assemblies in the colonies regained their power.

Pennsylvania and Delaware. One of the most remarkable and successful of the Englishmen to found colonies in the New World was William Penn. Penn, the son of a prominent admiral in the Royal Navy, seemed destined for the fashionable life of the English court. But one day in 1667, at age 22, young Penn heard a Quaker sermon on the text, "There is a faith that overcometh the world." The sermon converted Penn. He became a member of the Society of Friends, often called Quakers.

Penn's father was shocked and angered by his son's conversion. The Quakers at this time were one of the most disliked religious groups in England. But Penn went his own way. His father finally forgave him and left him a large inheritance.

Part of Penn's inheritance was a debt that Charles II had owed his father. In place of the money, the king in 1681 gave Penn a charter making him full owner, or *proprietor*, of a huge grant of land in the New World. In this land Penn founded a colony which the king named Pennsylvania. As proprietor, Penn's power over this *proprietary colony* was almost as great as the king's power over a royal colony.

° *bill of rights:* a list, or bill, of certain rights and liberties guaranteed to every citizen by the government. (See "The Rights of Englishmen," page 106.)

Pennsylvania had no coastline. Penn solved this problem in 1682 by asking for, and receiving, another grant of land to the south on the west bank of Delaware Bay. This new grant, long called "the lower counties," was later named Delaware (see map, page 31). Until the Revolutionary War, the Penn family governed both land grants as separate colonies.

Pennsylvania, which Penn liked to call the "Holy Experiment," attracted many settlers. Penn wrote and published a pamphlet in English, French, Dutch, and German describing the colony he proposed to build. He invited honest, hardworking settlers to come, promising them religious toleration, representative government, and cheap land. Penn offered 500 acres of free land, with the right to buy additional land at one shilling an acre, to settlers who established their homes and families in the colony.

Settlers poured in—Quakers from England, Wales, and Ireland; Scotch-Irish Presbyterians; Swiss and German Protestants; Catholics and Jews from many countries of Europe. Africans were also brought to the Pennsylvania colony, but the black population grew slowly and was never large. However, in 1700, slavery in Pennsylvania was legally recognized.

Penn kept his promises to the settlers, and also treated the Indians fairly. Pennsylvania developed more rapidly than any of the other colonies.

The Middle Colonies in the 1750's. By the 1750's the Middle Colonies—Pennsylvania, Delaware, New Jersey, and New York—were extremely prosperous. Philadelphia, on the Delaware River, was the largest, busiest seaport in America. New York was almost as large.

From the beginning most people made their living by farming. But they did not settle in small farming villages, as in New England. Because the Indians presented no real danger except on the western frontier, the newcomers scattered freely over the countryside. Because the soil was fertile and the land gently rolling, settlers cultivated fairly large farms. On these farms they produced not only food for their families, but also a surplus for sale. Indeed, the Middle Colonies soon became known as the "breadbasket" of the New World. The harbors of Philadelphia and New York were always filled with ships loading flour, meat, and other foodstuffs for sale in England and the West Indies.

People in the Middle Colonies worked at a great variety of occupations. Although most were farmers, the colonists were also famous for their iron

Thomas Gilcrease Institute, Tulsa, Oklahoma

■ William Penn traveled through much of Pennsylvania in order to purchase land from the Indians who lived there and to establish friendly relations with them. Above, he meets with a group of Indians in 1682.

mines, their shipyards, and their manufacture of glass, paper, and textiles. And from the beginning these colonies were true "melting pots" of people from many different nations with many different backgrounds—much more so than any of the other colonies.

SECTION SURVEY

IDENTIFY: Middle Colonies, bill of rights, proprietary colony; Henry Hudson, Lord John Berkeley, William Penn; 1664.

1. (a) Why were the Dutch regarded as a threat by the English colonists? (b) Do you think the English were regarded as a threat by the Dutch colonists? Explain.
2. Why was the Pennsylvania colony a success?
3. Comment on how the Middle Colonies were different from the New England Colonies in terms of physical and social environments.

5 The creation of a distinctive way of life in the Southern Colonies

Virginia, the first Southern Colony, started with the struggling settlement at Jamestown. By 1632, when Maryland was chartered, Virginia was firmly established.

The founding of Maryland. As early as 1609, Sir George Calvert, the first Lord Baltimore, wanted to build English colonies in the New World. To this end, in 1620 he bought land in southern Newfoundland. The harsh climate and bleak landscape there discouraged settlers, however, and Lord Baltimore soon abandoned the attempt.

In 1628, after a visit to Virginia, Lord Baltimore decided to try again in a more favorable location. He died just before the king gave him a charter to Maryland. His son, the second Lord Baltimore, carried on the work and, as proprietor, succeeded in building the colony dreamed of by his father.

Lord Baltimore, a devout Roman Catholic, hoped to make his colony a refuge for persecuted Catholics, but with religious freedom for Protestants as well. The first 200 settlers included many Catholics. They sailed up Chesapeake Bay in the late winter of 1634 and settled at St. Marys (see inset map, page 31).

Because the settlers benefited from the earlier experience of the Virginia colonists, Maryland prospered from the start. Large plantations soon spread up and down the banks of the tidewater rivers.°

As the settlement grew, more and more Protestant settlers arrived. Fearing that the outnumbered Catholics would lose their freedom of worship, Lord Baltimore secured the passage of the Toleration Act of 1649. This act guaranteed religious toleration to everyone who believed in Jesus Christ. This was not complete religious freedom, since only Christians could settle in Maryland. Nevertheless, the Toleration Act marked another step forward in the continuing struggle for religious freedom.

Creation of the Carolinas. In 1663, Charles II gave a charter for Carolina to eight English noblemen, who were to be the proprietors of the new colony. The grant included all the territory

° tidewater river: a river with its mouth at an ocean and into which, at high tide, the ocean pushes salt water some distance upstream.

between Virginia and Spanish Florida and westward to the "south seas."

With the aid of John Locke, a young English philosopher, the proprietors drew up a constitution, or plan of government, for the new colony. This constitution provided an elaborate and rigid system of social classes, including a landed nobility. The ordinary colonists were at the bottom of the social ladder. Slaves were not even included on the ladder, for Locke had written: ". . . every freeman of Carolina shall have absolute power and authority over his Negro slaves, of whatever opinion or religion so-ever."

The proprietors' plan was doomed from the beginning. A project drawn on paper without reference to actual conditions in the New World could not determine Carolina history. From the first days, the colony began to divide into two parts (see map, page 31), as determined by geography and the desires of the settlers.

The northern section, North Carolina, was settled mostly by pioneers from Virginia. They built cabins, cleared the land, grew their own food, and raised tobacco to sell in England. Many also earned a livelihood from the pine forests, which supplied lumber and naval stores (tar, pitch, rosin, turpentine)—products needed by England's Royal Navy and merchant ships.

The southern section, South Carolina, proved more attractive to settlers from overseas. Through the seaport of Charles Town (later shortened to Charleston), settlers of many different religious faiths from many different nations passed to new homes in the New World. There were Anglicans and other religious groups from England; Scots in considerable numbers; French Huguenots (HYOO·guh·nahts), who were Protestants fleeing persecution in France; Germans; emigrants from the West Indies; and, as the years passed, growing numbers of African slaves. Many settlers built large, prosperous rice plantations on the rich coastal lowlands. Others gained a livelihood from the production of naval stores and, on the frontier itself, from the fur trade.

The early colonists of North and South Carolina waged a continuing struggle for a larger voice in the government. Finally, in 1729, the proprietors sold their rights to the king, and North Carolina and South Carolina became royal colonies with representative assemblies.

The founding of Georgia. In 1732, three years after North and South Carolina became royal colonies, the king granted a charter for Georgia (see

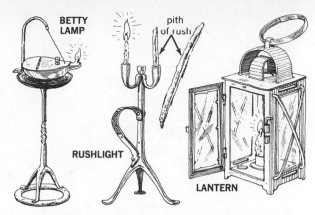

■ Colonial Lighting. The "Betty lamp" gave light from a burning wick floating in whale oil. Colonial housewives sometimes made a kind of candle by dipping a rush into tallow, producing a "rushlight." Another common source of light was the conventional wax candle, sometimes enclosed in a "lantern."

map, page 31). The British ° government hoped that Georgia could serve as a "buffer" against attacks from Spanish Florida.

But the compelling motive for starting Georgia had little to do with politics or business. Georgia was born out of man's love for his fellowman. A group of prominent Englishmen started the colony, and it was their desire to provide a place in which unfortunate English debtors could make a new start in life.

James Oglethorpe, the leader of the founders, arrived in Georgia in 1733 with the first debtors. They settled at Savannah, each man receiving 50 free acres of land. Slavery and the sale of rum were not to be allowed in the colony.

Oglethorpe and his fellow founders tried to recruit other settlers, offering liberal grants of land to all who came. But only a small number of immigrants arrived, among them New Englanders, Germans, and Scots. Some settlers demanded that slavery be allowed in the colony. After receiving three petitions asking for the introduction of slavery, the founders in 1750 reluctantly agreed to make slavery legal in Georgia. In 1752 the founders, as required by their charter, turned Georgia over to the king as a royal colony.

° **British:** In 1707 the separate countries of England and Scotland were united into a single country, properly called Great Britain. In common usage throughout the colonial period, however, the words "England" and "English" are often used to mean "Great Britain" and "British."

■ One of South Carolina's main crops was indigo, a plant which produced a blue dye. This old engraving shows indigo being processed by slaves on a plantation.

The effort to settle Georgia was not fruitless. Several thousand Englishmen were saved from debtor's prison and given a fresh start in life. And later Georgia became an active and prosperous state.

The Southern Colonies in the 1750's. By the 1750's the Southern Colonies—Maryland, Virginia, North and South Carolina, and Georgia—had all developed their own special ways of life. The great tobacco plantations in Maryland, Virginia, and North Carolina covered the rich lands near the tidewater rivers along the coast, and extended farther inland on the Atlantic coastal plains. Farther south the luxurious homes of wealthy rice planters were scattered over the coastal lowlands. The only large towns in the Southern Colonies at this time were Charleston, with a population of 10,000, and Baltimore, with 5,000.

A distinguishing characteristic of the Southern Colonies was slavery. The tobacco and rice plantations required large numbers of workmen. With plenty of land available on the frontier, free men would not work for wages on the plantations. As a result, the planters began to rely more and more upon black slave labor. By the 1750's the slavery system was firmly fixed in all the Southern Colonies.

If slaves could have been used profitably on the farms of the Middle Colonies or on the smaller farms of New England, no doubt slavery would have become more widespread in those colonies as well. In colonial times only a very small minority of people objected to slavery as such. Slavery was either profitable or unprofitable. In the Southern Colonies it was profitable, and slaves were used in ever-increasing numbers.

Although the planters set the pattern of southern life, most southern people lived in the back country —the inland areas that lay "back" from the seacoast. These people—pioneers and small farmers —lived much like pioneers in New England and the Middle Colonies.

SECTION SURVEY

IDENTIFY: Southern Colonies, Toleration Act of 1649; Lord Baltimore, James Oglethorpe.

1. What motives led to the settlement of the Southern Colonies?
2. How did the settlers adapt to the physical environment of the Southern Colonies?
3. In your own words, rephrase the Toleration Act of 1649 so that it establishes complete religious freedom.
4. (a) What two patterns of life were established in the Southern Colonies? (b) Was there potential here for conflict? Explain.
5. (a) Why is slavery wrong? (b) Why, then, did so many colonists accept the slave labor system?

38

TRACING THE MAIN IDEAS

English settlement began at Jamestown, and a few years later at Plymouth. As the years passed, settlers came in ever-growing numbers. Every good harbor along the Atlantic coast became a starting point in "the great adventure" of settling a new land.

The European settlers, men and women alike, came to the New World for many different reasons, bringing with them their own ways of life, their own religions, and their own languages. But all the colonists, regardless of their backgrounds or beliefs, shared one great purpose. They longed to win in the New World the opportunities they could not enjoy in the Old.

These were the colonial beginnings of the American nation—and of "the American way of life." You will learn more about the beginnings of the American way of life in Chapters 4 and 5.

But the colonies did not grow undisturbed. As you will see in the next chapter, both the Spaniards and the French—especially the French—threatened for a time to seize the English colonies and win control of the entire continent of North America.

CHAPTER SURVEY

QUESTIONS FOR DISCUSSION

1. Despite their different backgrounds and beliefs, the colonists shared common goals. How was this possible?
2. Differences in geographic conditions between the New England Colonies and the Southern Colonies were reflected in different patterns of land use and settlement. Explain.
3. How did geographic conditions influence the economic and social development of the Middle Colonies?
4. Why is agriculture considered an essential occupation for any new settlement of people?
5. Show how the European settlers in the New England Colonies, the Middle Colonies, and the Southern Colonies differed from one another (a) in how they made a living, (b) in their religious beliefs, (c) in their attitude toward slavery.
6. (a) If a person disagrees with his society's values, he should leave that society. Comment. (b) How should society regard a nonconformist? Why?
7. Some Americans today believe that the United States needs to return to the "Puritan ethic." (a) What do they mean by that statement? (b) Do you agree or disagree? Explain.

RELATING PAST TO PRESENT

1. Life in the colonies was characterized by undemocratic as well as democratic elements. Explain. Can we say the same of our society today? Explain.
2. Do immigrants arriving in the United States today come for the same reasons as those who came in the 1600's? Explain.

USING MAPS AND CHARTS

1. Using the map on page 31, answer the following: (a) What are the names of the Southern, Middle, and New England Colonies? (b) Which colonies —Southern, Middle, or New England—had the largest area of settlement in 1750? What natural geographic features formed protective barriers and eventually fostered a spirit of unity among the colonists?
2. Using maps in Chapters 1 and 2 to illustrate your points, show how inland waterways and oceans influenced the location of early settlements.
3. A broken coastline furnishes good harbors. On the map on page 31 name and locate the port cities that developed as a result of this geographic factor.

■ *British troops landing during the Battle of Quebec*

CHAPTER 3

The Growth of British Territory and Power

1750 – 1763

BY THE MIDDLE of the 1700's, a map of the land and sea areas of the world could be drawn with reasonable accuracy. Spread out on the map were vast colonial territories claimed by Portugal, Spain, the Netherlands, France, and Great Britain. These colonial areas were prizes for which each of the contending nations was ready to sacrifice blood and effort. Thus, during most of the 1600's and 1700's these European nations were engaged in almost constant warfare.

In the New World the British flag waved proudly over thirteen colonies along the Atlantic seaboard. Warships of His Majesty's Royal Navy stood guard over the 1,300-mile coastline and the nearly 1.5 million men, women, and children who lived in the colonies. The warships were needed, for Great Britain had powerful enemies.

To the south were the Spaniards. They had built a series of forts and missions that stretched from Florida to California along what is now the southern boundary of the United States. But during the 1600's and the 1700's Spain's power had been declining steadily. In 1754 the British did not think of Spain as a major threat.

To the north and west was New France. And this was a different story. The French were strong and growing stronger, not only in Europe, but in all their far-flung colonies—including New France. Between the British colonies and New France there was bitter rivalry and fear and an uneasy peace.

This is the story of the growth of New France, of British victory in the French and Indian War, and of troublesome policies adopted by Great Britain in controlling its American territory.

THE CHAPTER IN OUTLINE

1. The growing French threat to the British colonies.

2. Great Britain's victory over the French in North America.

3. Growing tensions between Great Britain and the colonies.

| 1450 | 1500 | 1550 | 1600 | 1650 | 1700 | 1750 | 1975 |

1 The growing French threat to the British colonies

French claims in North America were based, as you have read (page 14), on the early voyages of Verrazano (1524) and Cartier (1534–42). But the first Frenchman to establish settlements in the New World was Samuel de Champlain.

French claims in North America. Champlain made his first voyage to the New World in 1603. Before he died in 1635, he built a settlement at Quebec, won for France the friendship of the powerful Algonquin Indians, and explored most of the St. Lawrence Valley (see map, page 42).

Other Frenchmen pushed up the St. Lawrence River, explored the Great Lakes, and paddled their frail canoes into the heart of the vast North American wilderness. Among these daring explorers were Marquette, Joliet (joh·lee·ET), and La Salle.

In 1673 Father Marquette, a Jesuit missionary, and Joliet, a fur trader, crossed the Great Lakes and paddled down the Mississippi River as far as the mouth of the Arkansas River. Eight years later, in 1681–82, La Salle followed the same route to the Gulf of Mexico (see map, page 42). He claimed the entire Mississippi Valley for France, calling it Louisiana in honor of King Louis XIV. Later, in 1718, the French built New Orleans near the mouth of the Mississippi River.

By the early 1700's, then, the French controlled the two major gateways into the heart of North America. New Orleans gave them control of the southern entrance to the entire Mississippi Valley. Quebec and Montreal gave them control of the St. Lawrence River.

Combined with the Great Lakes, the St. Lawrence River provided a natural water route. By paddling and by carrying their canoes only a few miles overland, French explorers and traders could bring their canoes to the Mississippi or one of its tributaries, and have access to the entire region between the Appalachians and the Rockies.

French settlements. The rulers of France hoped to fill New France with large estates owned by nobles and worked by peasants. The peasants were to live in compact farming villages on the estates.

But compact French farming villages were never built. Each noble, or *seigneur* (seh·NYUR), wanted his estate to front on the St. Lawrence River, the only source of transportation—a smooth ribbon of ice in winter, a water route in summer. And when the seigneur brought tenants, called *habitants* (a·bee·TAHN), to work his estate, they also insisted upon water frontage. As a result, the settled area of New France consisted largely of farmhouses stretching along the banks of the St. Lawrence from Quebec to Montreal and up the Richelieu (RISH·eh·loo) River.

Most of the settlers of New France naturally came from the mother country, but some black slaves from Africa were brought to work on the

■ Most of the habitant farms in New France lay along the banks of the St. Lawrence River.

Detail from "The Habitant Farm" by Cornelius Krieghoff, The National Gallery of Canada, Ottawa.

NEW FRANCE THREATENS THE BRITISH COLONIES

Scale of miles
0   500

CHAMPLAIN, 1608-16

CANADA

C A N A D A

L. Superior

Quebec

Montreal

St. Lawrence R.

ACADIA

CHAMPLAIN, 1604-06

N
E
W

F
R
A
N
C
E

Mississippi R.

L. Huron

L. Michigan

L. Ontario

L. Erie

Lake Champlain

Portsmouth

Boston

Hartford

Providence

New York

Philadelphia

Wilmington

Baltimore

MARQUETTE AND JOLIET, 1673

LA SALLE, 1681-82

Ohio R.

MTS.

Williamsburg

APPALACHIAN

ATLANTIC

OCEAN

B
R
I
T
I
S
H

C
O
L
O
N
I
E
S

L
O
U
I
S
I
A
N
A

Arkansas R. River

Mississippi

LA SALLE, 1681-82

Wilmington

Charleston

Savannah

SPANISH

FLORIDA (SPANISH)

New Orleans (French)

GULF   OF   MEXICO

Area of British settlement in 1750

Chief area of French settlement in 1750

△ French wilderness posts

farms. Africans also came to New France as members of the French expeditions that explored the Great Lakes and the Mississippi Valley. The Negro population of New France, however, was never very large.

The fur trade.   Beyond the settled areas of New France lay an immense wilderness, partly charted by bold French explorers. The most easily exploited resource of this vast area was furs.

From its earliest days New France drew much of its wealth from the fur trade. Furs drew adventurous Frenchmen into the forested wilderness. Courageous *coureurs de bois* (KOO·RUR deh BWAH), or runners-of-the-woods, paddled their canoes into the interior, wintered with friendly Indian tribes, and returned in the spring with their Indian allies to the trading center at Montreal. They reached Montreal about the same time that cargo ships from France sailed into the harbor.

For several weeks active trading took place on the river below the city. Indians exchanged their furs for European goods—blankets, cloaks, cloth, beads, metal, ornaments, copper and iron kettles, spoons, knives, hatchets, guns, powder, and liquor. When the last cask of brandy had been emptied, the trading finally came to an end. Then the Indians and the coureurs de bois loaded their canoes and paddled back into the wilderness. The French ships weighed anchor and began their hazardous voyage back to Europe with their cargoes of furs.

The weakness of New France. On the map New France covered an immense area, including Canada and the entire Mississippi Valley (see map, page 42).

But the map was misleading. Except for Quebec and Montreal, the settled areas of Canada consisted largely of farmhouses strung along the St. Lawrence like beads on a string. And beyond the settled areas a chain of small forts and trading posts stretched in a long arc through the Great Lakes and the upper Mississippi Valley. Only the Indians and an occasional coureur de bois ever disturbed the age-old solitude of the forest in vast areas of New France.

The fur trade proved to be both a strength and a weakness for New France. The fur trade provided a livelihood for thousands—for manufacturers and workmen in the mother country, for shipowners and merchants, and for the coureurs de bois and their Indian allies. But the carefree life of the coureur de bois attracted the young and strong into the forests. As a result, the French never strengthened the settled areas along the St. Lawrence River.

French and British power. By 1750 the British had certain advantages over their French rivals to the north. The British colonies were well established, and British colonists outnumbered French colonists by 23 to 1. Also, most British settlements were confined to a fairly narrow belt of land along the Atlantic coast, whereas French settlements were scattered over half the continent (see map, page 42).

But the French also enjoyed advantages. New France, united under a single government, could act quickly when action was necessary. In contrast, the British colonies had separate governments. They seldom acted together, even when cooperation was needed.

The French also had the support of a great many more Indians than did the British. French fur traders did not destroy forests and drive away game as did British settlers who cleared the land for farming. However, the powerful Iroquois Indians, who lived in what is now New York State, refused to ally themselves with the French.

Iroquois Indians speaking in their council house

THE REMARKABLE IROQUOIS

No Indians in all North America were more greatly feared by their enemies or respected by their friends than the members of the Iroquois Confederation. Speaking of their qualities as warriors, a Frenchman declared that "they approach like foxes, fight like lions, and disappear like birds." In New York state the Mohawk River and lakes Seneca, Cayuga, Onondaga, and Oneida bear the proud names of the five original tribes. After 1700, when the Tuscaroras of North Carolina joined the Confederation, the Five Nations, as the Iroquois were called, became the Six Nations.

According to legend, the Iroquois Confederation was organized by two great leaders—Deganawidah and Hiawatha.

The legendary Deganawidah was a man of magnificent vision. He dreamed of a day when the Confederation would include *all* Indians, war would be abolished, and peace would reign across the face of the earth. We catch a glimpse of this noble ideal in the Iroquois "constitution," passed on by word of mouth from generation to generation: "I, Deganawidah, and the Confederated Chiefs now uproot the tallest pine tree, and into the cavity thereby made we cast all weapons of war. Into the depths of the earth, deep down into the underearth currents of water flowing to unknown regions, we cast all weapons of strife. We bury them from sight and plant again the tree. Thus shall the Great Peace be established."

Deganawidah's ideal was shattered when the Europeans began to settle the New World. Allied with the British, the organization that had been created as an instrument of peace became, for a time, a formidable instrument of war.

Conflicts in Europe and Elsewhere

War of the League of Augsburg	1689–1697
War of the Spanish Succession	1702–1713
War of the Austrian Succession	1740–1748
Seven Years' War	1756–1763

Conflicts in America

King William's War	1689–1697
Queen Anne's War	1702–1713
King George's War	1744–1748
French and Indian War	1754–1763

Finally, France in the early 1750's was the most powerful nation in Europe. French armies were second to none. French naval forces competed with the British for control of the seas.

Between 1689 and 1748 a fierce rivalry kept France and Great Britain at war with each other off and on for a total of nearly 25 years. The two nations fought for control of the seas and possession of distant colonies. In each war North America was only one of several prizes the British and French hoped to win. Armed forces of the two powers clashed on the seas and in Europe and Asia, as well as North America. But none of the wars proved decisive (see table).

In 1754 war clouds gathered once again. The two European nations began still another test of strength. This struggle determined the destiny of the North American continent.

SECTION SURVEY

IDENTIFY: gateway, *seigneur, coureurs de bois;* Samuel de Champlain.

1. Why did Frenchmen come to the New World?
2. Name the French explorers and the areas of the New World which they claimed for France.
3. Why are Montreal and New Orleans called "gateways"?
4. The French did not follow the British pattern of settlement. Why not?
5. Compare French and British power in 1754. Which was the stronger? Why?

2 Great Britain's victory over the French in North America

The decisive worldwide conflict between the British and the French started in the valley of the Ohio River. It started in 1754 when the expanding empires of France and Great Britain clashed in the land beyond the Appalachian Mountains. The contest was called the French and Indian War, or the Seven Years' War.

The first clash. Wealthy Virginians caused the first of a series of events that led to the French and Indian War. For business reasons, these men formed a company and secured from the British king a huge grant of land in the upper Ohio Valley. They intended to make a profit by dividing the land into small farms and selling the farms to settlers.

The French were alarmed by the Virginians' real estate activities on territory which the French claimed as their own. In 1753 the French started constructing a chain of forts connecting Lake Erie with the Ohio River (see map, page 45).

The governor of Virginia sent George Washington, a 21-year-old surveyor from Virginia, to warn the French that the land belonged to the British. (The land had been originally granted to Virginia by the charter of 1609. See map, page 45). The French ignored the warning of George Washington.

The following year Washington, now a major leading a force of militia, returned to the frontier and built Fort Necessity, a few miles south of the French Fort Duquesne (doo·KAYN). Fort Duquesne itself was situated at the strategic point where the Monongahela and Allegheny rivers join to form the Ohio River—the present site of Pittsburgh (see map, page 45). A small force of French and Indians defeated Washington in a battle fought at Fort Necessity on July 4, 1754.

Failure of the colonies to unite. The French were now entrenched along a line of scattered points from the Great Lakes south to the Ohio River, with outposts in the Allegheny Mountains. The entire northern frontier of the British colonies was exposed to attack from the Indian allies of the French. Moreover, the western country was closed to British traders and British settlers.

At this critical moment delegates from seven British colonies met at Albany, New York, to discuss united action against the French and their Indian allies. They were joined by Indian representatives from the Six Nations, earlier called the

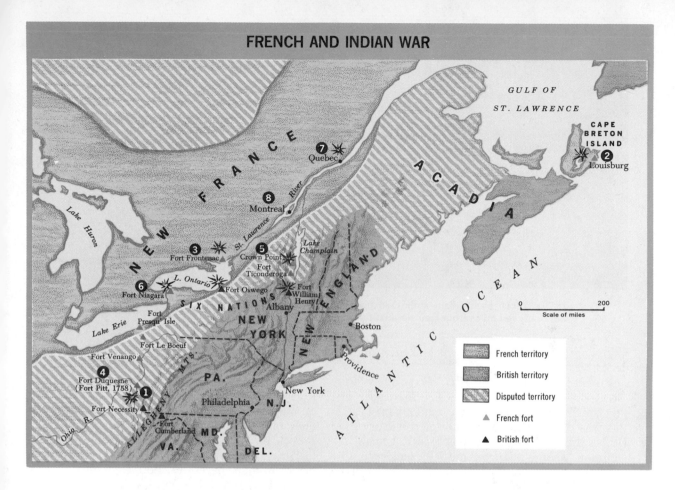

Five Nations (page 43). The Six Nations, also known as the Iroquois Confederation, occupied most of what is now central New York. Armed first by the Dutch and then by the English, they were the most powerful Indians in North America. And they were long-standing enemies of the French and of Indians friendly to the French. The British colonists welcomed the Iroquois representatives to the Albany congress.

At the congress, Benjamin Franklin proposed that the British colonies in America unite in a permanent union for defense. Both the British officials and the colonists rejected Franklin's proposal of 1754—known as the Albany Plan of Union. The colonists rejected it because they did not want each colony to give up its right to act independently. The colonists also rejected a somewhat similar proposal by officials of the British government. Although rejected, these proposals forced many colonists to think about the advantages of united action.

British disasters. Only a few months after the failure of the Albany congress, General Edward Braddock arrived from England with regiments of British regulars, or "redcoats." The British redcoats and a strong force of Virginia militiamen advanced through the wilderness toward the French forces at Fort Duquesne. They were ambushed when only 10 miles from their goal (see number 1 on map at top of this page).

Braddock and 63 of his 89 officers were killed. More than half his men were killed, wounded, or captured. The disaster would have been even greater if George Washington and the Virginia militia had not fought back, in Indian fashion, from the cover of trees and rocks.

Braddock's disaster left the 350-mile frontier of Pennsylvania, Maryland, and Virginia exposed to Indian attack. Matters got even worse when British expeditions against the French forts at Niagara and Crown Point also failed, and the French captured Fort Oswego and Fort William Henry (see

■ The French and Indians ambushed the British forces when General Braddock and his men were only ten miles from their destination, Fort Duquesne.

map, page 45). British prospects looked bleak indeed.

British success under Pitt. Fortunately for Great Britain, William Pitt became the leader of the British government in the autumn of 1756. Pitt was determined to win complete victory for British arms. He was a strong leader, a man of enormous energy and supreme self-confidence. "I know that I can save England and that nobody else can," he reportedly said.

Under Pitt's leadership the British Empire rallied. Pitt discharged incompetent officials and replaced them with able men. He gave colonial officers rank equal to those in the king's own troops. He strengthened the British navy and moved more troops to America. And everywhere throughout the British empire, Pitt took the offensive.

British victories. New France was like a tree. Its roots were the lines of communication for transporting soldiers, supplies, and messages across the Atlantic. Its trunk was the St. Lawrence River. Its spreading limbs and branches were the French-controlled waterways of the Great Lakes and the Mississippi Valley, with forts and trading posts scattered along them like leaves.

In 1758 the British destroyed the roots of the tree when a combined naval and land force under General Jeffrey Amherst captured Louisburg, a powerfully armed French fort on Cape Breton Island (see number 2 on map, page 45). The fall of Louisburg doomed New France. The victory gave the British navy an operating base for cutting off French reinforcements and supplies to America. During the same year the British also captured Fort Frontenac on Lake Ontario (see number 3 on map, page 45). This victory weakened French lines of communication to Fort Duquesne. The French promptly abandoned Fort Duquesne, and the British occupied it without a struggle (see number 4 on map, page 45). Fort Duquesne was renamed Fort Pitt.

During the year 1759 the British won even more sweeping victories. Amherst forced the French to retreat from their forts at Crown Point and Ticonderoga (see number 5 on map, page 45). Some of Amherst's forces seized Fort Niagara (see number 6 on map, page 45). This latter victory forced the French to abandon their forts in the upper Ohio Valley. And in September 1759 the British captured Quebec (see number 7 on map, page 45).

The fortress of Quebec had been considered impregnable because of its location on heights called the Plains of Abraham overlooking the St. Lawrence River. For more than two months a powerful British fleet under Admiral Charles Saunders and a landing party under General James Wolfe besieged the fort, which was commanded by the Marquis de Montcalm. Finally, in the gray dawn of a September morning, a daring landing party scaled the rocky cliffs, surprised the defenders on the Plains of Abraham, and then fought their way into the city.

The battle of Quebec was a magnificent victory for the British. Indeed, British historians refer to 1759 as "the wonderful year." In 1759 Great Britain won sweeping successes in America, in Europe, in the Mediterranean, and in India.

The following year, 1760, after only slight resistance, the French surrendered Montreal to General Amherst (see number 8 on map, page 45). In 1762 Spain, fearful of British victory, entered the worldwide conflict on the side of France. But Spanish aid was both too little and too late. The British kept winning all over the world. They completed their string of victories by seizing the Philippine Islands and Cuba from Spain, the West Indies sugar islands of Martinique (mahr·ti·NEEK) and Guadeloupe (gwah·duh·LOOP) from France, and French territory in India.

The spoils of war. Out of the worldwide struggle for trade, colonial empire, and naval supremacy, the British emerged victorious. Meeting in Paris, representatives of Great Britain, France, and Spain drew up the Treaty of Paris in 1763. Great Britain secured most of India and all of North America east of the Mississippi River, except New Orleans.

France, on the other hand, lost nearly all its possessions in India and in America. The British allowed France to keep only four relatively unimportant islands in the New World. Two of these were the sugar islands of Guadeloupe and Martinique.

As an ally of France, Spain was forced to give Florida to Great Britain. As compensation for this loss, however, the French gave the Spaniards New Orleans and the vast, almost unexplored territory of Louisiana west of the Mississippi River (see map, this page). The British returned Cuba and the Philippine Islands to Spain.

How war influenced the colonies. The American colonists, as well as Great Britain, profited from the long struggle. The colonial militias gained valuable new experience in methods of warfare. Their experience in fighting Indians was broadened by joint combat with the British against powerful French forces.

Although the colonial militias welcomed all able-bodied men, they were at first reluctant to accept black men. Most colonists did not like the idea of supplying Negroes with guns. But manpower shortages finally forced them to accept black men into the militia ranks.

The long struggle also taught the colonists that only by cooperating with one another could they

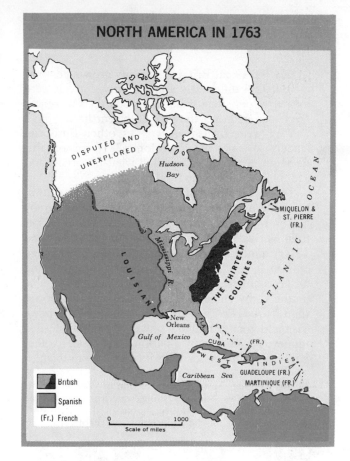

NORTH AMERICA IN 1763

hope to defend themselves. Yet colonial Americans in 1763 were still far from united. They did not fully grasp the absolute necessity for cooperation until faced with the American Revolution and the years of unrest following it.

SECTION SURVEY

IDENTIFY: French and Indian War, Treaty of Paris of 1763; Benjamin Franklin, William Pitt; 1754.

1. Was a clash between Great Britain and France inevitable? Why or why not?
2. (a) State the terms of the Treaty of Paris of 1763. (b) Of what significance were these terms to Great Britain, France, and the colonists in North America?
3. The New England Confederation (page 34), the Albany Plan of Union, and the French and Indian War were steps toward unifying the colonies. Is this statement true or false? Explain.
4. Before people can cooperate or unite, a "crisis situation" is necessary. Do you agree or disagree? Explain.

3 Growing tensions between Great Britain and the colonies

In 1763 Great Britain's steadily growing empire included 33 different colonies. Only thirteen were located along the Atlantic seaboard. The others were scattered over the face of the earth.

Why were British as well as other European leaders so eager to win colonies? To answer this question, we must understand what historians and economists have called "mercantilism."

The mercantile system of trade. *Mercantilism,* briefly, is an economic and political policy whereby a nation tries to gain greater wealth and power than its rivals. The mercantilism of the 1600's and 1700's aimed at building a powerful, self-sufficient empire in a world divided by religious wars and bitter commercial rivalry. Under mercantilism, a nation's government tried to gain greater power than its rivals by building a larger army and navy. To build greater military power, the nation needed money. To get money, a nation tried to sell to other countries more goods than it bought from them. It

■ This painting shows the intersection of Wall and Water streets near New York's bustling waterfront. At the left is the Tontine Coffee House, home of the city's stock exchange and a meeting place for merchants.

tried, in other words, to build a *favorable balance of trade.* A nation gains a favorable balance of trade when it *exports,* or sells abroad, more products than it *imports,* or buys from other nations.

If a nation secured a highly favorable balance of trade, it could (1) be self-sufficient, (2) become wealthy, and (3) build a powerful army and navy. Colonies were an essential part of the plan. The British, for example, thought that colonies would strengthen Great Britain in three ways. First, colonies would provide the raw materials essential to a small island kingdom with a growing population. Second, colonies would provide markets for goods produced in Great Britain, particularly manufactured goods. Third, the colonies would help to make Great Britain powerful. They would encourage the growth of a strong merchant fleet, which would serve as a training school for the Royal Navy. And colonies would also provide bases from which the Royal Navy could operate.

Restrictions on manufacturing. To apply the mercantile theory of trade, the British Parliament enacted many laws. One series of laws restricted nearly all the manufacturing of the British empire to England. A law passed in 1699, for example, forbade the colonists to export any wool or woolen cloth—even to a neighboring colony. Later laws forbade the colonists to manufacture beaver hats or iron products. The British government also tried to prevent skilled mechanics from leaving Great Britain, fearing that they would help the colonists start their own manufacturing plants.

The American colonists did not find these restrictions particularly burdensome. At this time the colonists had neither the money nor the skilled labor to establish industries.

Restrictions on shipping. Beginning in 1651, another series of laws, the Navigation Acts, restricted all trade within the empire to British ships. Only British ships could carry goods imported from Africa, Asia, and the non-British colonies of America into any port of the British empire.

Encouraged by the Navigation Acts, a powerful British merchant fleet was soon sailing the seas between the colonies and the mother country. The American colonists, being British citizens, could build, operate, and man their own vessels. Thus, they benefited greatly from the Navigation Acts. By the early 1770's, colonial shipyards were building one third of all merchant vessels sailing under the British flag, and many American colonial merchants were becoming wealthy men.

■ New York in 1757 was a growing center of merchant shipping. Ships flying the British flag carried manufactured goods into the colonies and raw materials bound for Great Britain.

Restrictions on selling. The Navigation Act of 1660 listed, or "enumerated," specific colonial products that could be shipped only to England. These *enumerated goods* included such important products as tobacco, cotton, and sugar. The colonists could not sell these products to other European countries, where they might have secured higher prices.

But by the 1700's the British government was paying *bounties* on some enumerated goods. Bounties are payments made to stimulate production of certain goods. The British paid bounties on tar, resin, turpentine, and hemp to stimulate colonial production of these so-called naval stores, needed urgently by the merchant fleet and the Royal Navy.

Restrictions on buying. In 1663 Parliament passed a new Navigation Act, requiring the colonists to buy most of their manufactured goods from England. Further, all European goods headed for the colonies had to be sent first to England, where the British unloaded the goods and collected an import *duty* ° on them. Then they reloaded the products on a British vessel and sent them across the Atlantic. These requirements enabled the Royal Navy to protect merchant shipping between England and America from enemy ships and pirates. They also protected British manufacturers from the competition of their European rivals.

Frictions under mercantilism. By passing

° *duty:* a sum of money collected on the import or export of goods; also called a *tariff.*

many laws, then, the British government applied its policy of mercantilism. Since other European nations with overseas colonies followed similar practices, mercantilism caused deepening rivalries between nations. As you have read, this competition was a basic cause of the long years of war between Great Britain and France.

■ Sawing Ship's Timber. Colonial shipbuilders' knowledge was advanced, but some of their tools were crude by our standards. In the illustration below, workmen use a "whipsaw" to cut timber for a ship.

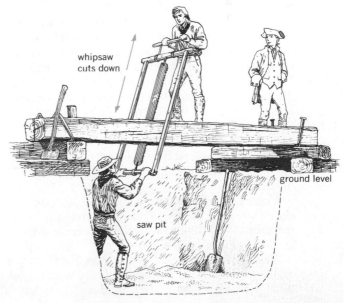

whipsaw cuts down

ground level

saw pit

49

■ **This diagram illustrates how slave ship captains crowded the maximum number of slaves aboard their vessels. Often only half the captives survived the horrors of the Middle Passage from Africa to the West Indies.**

The mercantile system of trade also created friction within the British empire itself, arousing jealousy even between colonial merchants. Colonial merchants with close family ties or other sources of influence in Great Britain received favors and privileges denied to less fortunate merchants. And mercantile policies created friction especially between Great Britain and some of its colonies in North America.

At first mercantilism seemed to threaten the prosperity of New England and the Middle Colonies. These colonies produced goods similar to those produced in Great Britain—grain, lumber, fish, cloth, iron, and other products. Great Britain did not want or need these colonial products, and actually passed laws barring them from Great Britain.

Fortunately, the New England and Middle Colonies soon established new markets for their goods. As a result, the mercantile laws did not seriously disturb them.

Colonial trade routes. The map on page 51 shows a major source of income for the colonial merchants—a *triangular trade* involving Africa, the West Indies, and the colonies.

Vessels from colonial ports set sail for Africa on the first leg of the triangle, their decks and holds piled high with kegs of rum produced in colonial

distilleries. On the west coast of Africa, they exchanged the rum for slaves or gold. From Africa the vessels set sail on the second leg of their voyage, with their human cargoes crowded in their holds. This took them to the West Indies, where they exchanged the slaves for molasses, sugar, or money. The final leg of the triangular trade route brought the ships home to the colonies loaded with sugar or molasses, for making more rum, and a balance of gold and silver.

Another busy trade route, also shown on the map on page 51, directly connected the colonies with the islands in the Caribbean Sea. Ships from New England and the Middle Colonies sailed southward with grain, fish, meat, cloth, soap, lumber, shingles, knocked-down shacks for the slaves, and casks for molasses and sugar. On the return voyage, the ships carried sugar, molasses, and money.

Evading the mercantile laws. Most of this trade was perfectly legal. But some of it directly violated British laws. One of the laws most violated was the Molasses Act of 1733.

Planters in the British West Indies had pushed the Molasses Act through Parliament, hoping to force the American colonists to buy all their sugar and molasses from the British West Indies. The Molasses Act thus provided that the colonists could buy similar supplies from the French, Dutch, or Spanish islands only by paying a very high duty. Since the British West Indies could supply only about one eighth of the molasses needed by the colonists, the colonial merchants felt compelled to evade the law.

If the British government had enforced the Molasses Act, many colonial merchants and businessmen would have been ruined, most rum distilleries would have been closed, and many workers would have lost their jobs.

A policy of salutary neglect. But for a long time Great Britain did not seriously attempt to enforce the Molasses Act. Indeed, the British government did not seriously attempt to enforce most of its mercantile laws. Instead, the British followed a policy of *salutary neglect,* which means that they deliberately failed to enforce the laws. The government was content, as one British statesman, Robert Walpole, expressed it, "to let sleeping dogs lie."

Trouble ahead. In 1763, however, the British government needed money to pay its war debt. It needed money to pay for the defense of its large and growing empire. It needed money to pay the officials required to govern the scattered colonies.

MAJOR COLONIAL TRADE ROUTES

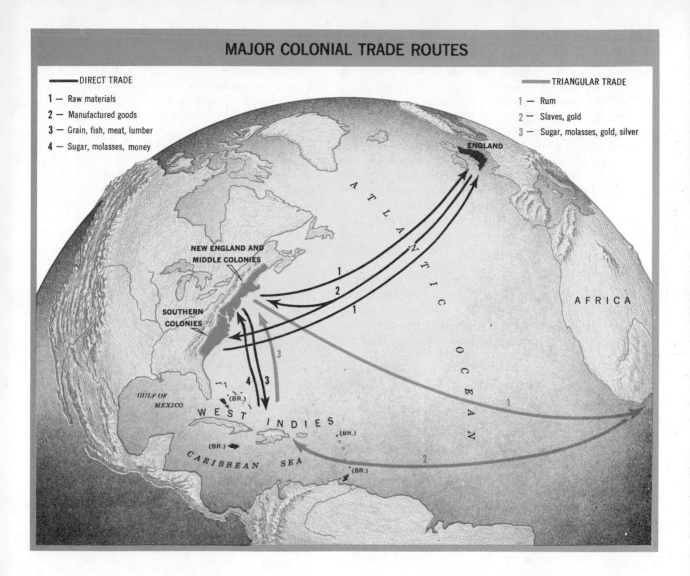

——— DIRECT TRADE
1 — Raw materials
2 — Manufactured goods
3 — Grain, fish, meat, lumber
4 — Sugar, molasses, money

——— TRIANGULAR TRADE
1 — Rum
2 — Slaves, gold
3 — Sugar, molasses, gold, silver

ENGLAND

ATLANTIC OCEAN

AFRICA

NEW ENGLAND AND
MIDDLE COLONIES

SOUTHERN
COLONIES

GULF OF
MEXICO

WEST   INDIES

(BR.)

(BR.)

(BR.)

CARIBBEAN   SEA

(BR.)

How could the British government obtain this money? One way was to adopt a new colonial policy. The earlier mercantile laws had regulated trade. The major purpose of the new laws would be to raise revenue.

When the British government began, after 1763, to develop this new policy, it ran into trouble. The conflict, as you will see in Unit Two, did not end until the thirteen colonies fought for and won their independence from Great Britain.

SECTION SURVEY

IDENTIFY: mercantilism, balance of trade, self-sufficient, exports, imports, triangular trade, salutary neglect.

1. Define the mercantile system of trade as an economic and political policy.
2. (a) What were the main purposes of mercantilism? (b) Why were colonies essential to the mercantile system of trade?
3. Explain the necessity under mercantilism for placing restrictions on the (a) manufacturing of goods, (b) shipping of goods, (c) buying and selling of goods.
4. What advantages and disadvantages did the mercantile system of trade have for the American colonies?
5. In the 1700's a nation that had a favorable balance of trade realized important national goals. (a) What does this statement mean? (b) Do you think the same statement would be true of a nation today? Explain.

TRACING THE MAIN IDEAS

During the 1600's and the 1700's a growing conflict among European nations disturbed much of the world. Powerful European nations were struggling for supremacy. They were driven by the rising spirit of nationalism, the desire for colonial empires, and the competition for trade.

By 1763 Great Britain had triumphed over its rivals. The Dutch and the French had been expelled from the mainland of North America. The Spaniards had been pushed west of the Mississippi River, holding only New Orleans on the east bank. British forces had also been victorious elsewhere in the world, notably in India. The British flag now flew over a large, growing empire.

Victory brought great prestige to the British people, but it also brought new problems. One major problem was that of governing the rapidly growing empire. Great Britain, like the other colonial powers of Europe, had tried to bind the colonies and the mother country together through a series of mercantile laws. As its empire grew, Great Britain found it increasingly necessary to adopt new laws and regulations governing its colonies.

As you will see in Chapter 6, Great Britain's efforts after 1763 to reorganize its empire antagonized people living in the colonies along the Atlantic seaboard and in 1775 plunged the colonists and the mother country into the Revolutionary War.

But the quarrel that led to armed conflict cannot be fully understood without some knowledge of everyday life in the colonies. In their efforts to adapt to the New World environment, the colonists developed ideas and ways of living different from those of people living in Great Britain. This steadily increasing spirit of "Americanism" is explained in Chapters 4 and 5.

CHAPTER SURVEY

QUESTIONS FOR DISCUSSION

1. Relate the conflicts among the powerful European nations for supremacy in Europe to their conflicts on the North American continent.
2. The statements in this exercise follow each other in cause and effect. Explain the cause and effect relationship in each statement, and then explain how the statement leads to the statement following it.
   (a) Nations desiring power [cause] needed to possess colonies [effect].
   (b) Nations possessing colonies [cause] needed large armies and navies [effect].
   (c) Large armies and navies [cause] meant large military budgets [effect].
   (d) Large military budgets [cause] meant . . . [What effects can you insert here?]
3. By 1750, there were fewer Negroes in New France and the New England Colonies than in the Southern Colonies. Why?

4. Do nations still consider a favorable *balance of trade* to be an important factor in their economic relations? Why or why not?

RELATING PAST TO PRESENT

1. Do nations today have the same reasons for possessing colonies that nations had during the period studied in this chapter? Explain.
2. Power struggles between nations today are different from those between nations in the 1600's and 1700's. How? Why?

USING MAPS AND CHARTS

1. Using the map on page 47, indicate the territory (a) won by Great Britain, (b) given to Spain, and (c) left to France by the Treaty of Paris of 1763.
2. Using the map on page 51, (a) explain Great Britain's mercantile policies and (b) describe and follow the triangular trade route and explain who profited from this trade.

IN 1751, a young man picked up a letter lying on a table in a colonial tavern. "Egad!" he cried, "I must know the contents of it." He rushed out of the room, taking with him someone else's mail.

As this incident reveals, the colonial postal system was in a sorry state. People often opened mail addressed to other people. The postriders, who carried the mail on horseback, were poorly paid and often dishonest.

Then Benjamin Franklin became Postmaster General of the colonies and quickly changed all this. Franklin required careful accounts from everyone handling the mails. He started new postal routes, some using horse-drawn stagecoaches instead of postriders. By providing this better means of communication, Franklin helped unite the colonies.

In 1763, Franklin made a trip of more than 1,600 miles, traveling over nearly every post road. On his travels, Franklin saw many colonists and learned how they lived and what they were thinking. He visited southern planters. He lived with townspeople. He stopped overnight with farmers. He talked with frontiersmen. And Franklin also saw two groups who lived in colonial America but were not really a part of it—Africans, most of whom were slaves, and the American Indians.

In this chapter you are going to look at each of these six groups of people. And you will see, as Franklin saw, that they were sharply divided on many matters. But you will also see, as Franklin saw, that by the 1760's, from one end of the British colonies to the other, many people were beginning to think of themselves as "Americans."

THE CHAPTER IN OUTLINE

1. Southern planters—holding on to an English life style.

2. Townspeople—the mixing of English and American ideas.

3. Pioneer farmers—the widening break with English ties.

4. Frontiersmen—emergence of the new Americans.

5. Africans in the colonies—emergence of a class apart.

6. The Indians—the clash of differing cultures.

CHANGING WAYS
OF AMERICAN LIFE

CHAPTER 4

The Start of an American Way of Life

1607 – 1763

1 Southern planters—holding on to an English life style

On Franklin's travels through the Southern Colonies in 1763 he saw few towns or cities. Baltimore, Maryland, founded in 1729, contained only a few thousand people. Charleston, South Carolina, the largest and wealthiest southern seaport, had only about 10,000 people.

Southern population. By the 1760's more than 2 million people lived in the British colonies of North America. Although most of these people came from Great Britain, thousands came from other lands, including Africa. About half of the total colonial population lived in the five Southern Colonies—Maryland, Virginia, North Carolina, South Carolina, and Georgia.

Throughout the colonies the majority of people lived in the country. In the South the proportion of country dwellers was especially high. Most southerners lived on small farms similar to those in New England and the Middle Colonies. Some lived on the frontier in small clearings cut from the forest. The wealthy planters lived on the fertile coastal plains, and a few owned plantations several

■ Southern Planter and Wife

thousand acres in size. These great planters lived much like English country gentlemen.

The planters. The southern planters earned their wealth from agriculture. Although they grew most of the food used on the plantation, their riches usually came from a single *cash crop,* that is, a crop raised to be sold at a profit. In Georgia and the Carolinas, especially South Carolina, rice was the important product. In Maryland, Virginia, and North Carolina the chief cash crop was tobacco.

The plantation. The large plantation was a complete economic unit. In the center stood a large house which was usually built in the Georgian style of architecture, then popular among the wealthy country gentlemen of England. Around the mansion were the simpler homes of the overseer, or supervisor, and the *artisans,* or skilled workers, many of whom were slaves. George Washington's estate at Mount Vernon, Virginia, for example, had cabins for carpenters, bricklayers, masons, blacksmiths, millers, and weavers.

Each plantation was almost self-sufficient—that is, it supplied almost all its own needs. Meat was butchered from herds of cattle and hogs. Other foods and clothing were secured from the land. The planter and his wife needed business ability to organize and administer the many details of running a plantation. Theirs was a luxurious way of life, but it carried heavy responsibilities.

English economic ties. Most of the planter's luxuries came from England. Even as late as the 1750's, American colonists produced few manufactured goods. Every year on the tobacco plantations slaves rolled the large hogsheads of tobacco to the wharves, and loaded them on vessels often owned by northern merchants. With his shipment, the planter often sent a list of goods that he wanted his agent in London to purchase for him. The agent sold the tobacco, rice, or indigo; bought the articles desired by the planter; and shipped them, together with a financial statement, to his client in America.

In this way the planters filled their homes with Old World luxuries—fine furniture, table silver, clothes, tapestries, wines, and books.

Social life. Since the plantations were more or less isolated, visits exchanged by the planters became great social events. Washington, during two months in 1768, entertained guests on 29 different days and dined out on 7 other occasions. The dinners were splendid affairs, followed by evenings of conversation or card playing. The gracious tradition of southern hospitality, which has continued

Detail from "Old Bruton Church" by Thompson. The Metropolitan Museum of Art. Gift of Mrs. A. Wordsworth Thompson.

■ In the country or in town, wealthy planters liked to meet at church, as did these Virginians at Bruton's Parish Church in Williamsburg.

to this day, developed out of the colonial custom of social visiting.

Most southern planters took pride in their horses and packs of hunting dogs. Dressed in scarlet hunting clothes from England, they enjoyed riding on fox hunts.

Many of the richer planters also owned town houses where they spent several months each year. During this period they enjoyed dancing, music, art, dramatics, and lectures. They also spent time playing cards, watching cockfights, and racing horses, as well as hunting foxes.

English influence. The plantations of the South reminded visitors of country estates in England. They were, in a sense, part of England carried to the New World. The wealthy planters dressed and talked and acted much like country gentlemen in the mother country. Indeed, in some ways they had more in common with Englishmen in the mother country than with the small farmers and frontiersmen who lived nearby.

And yet, as you will see, when the break with England finally came, some southern planters were among the first to fight for independence. A southern planter, Thomas Jefferson, wrote most of the Declaration of Independence. Another southern planter, George Washington, led the American armies to victory.

But it is also true that, when the Revolution began, some wealthy southern planters remained loyal to England, as did some wealthy people in the New England and Middle Colonies. Their ties with the mother country were too strong to break.

SECTION SURVEY

IDENTIFY: plantation, single cash crop, self-sufficient, artisans.

1. The large plantation was a complete economic unit eliminating the need for a local market town. Explain.
2. Describe the different social groups that lived in the South.
3. The plantation owner relied upon a single cash crop for his profit. (a) What is meant by this statement? (b) What disadvantages are faced by a community, region, or plantation that relies upon a single crop or industry for its economic life?
4. (a) What economic ties bound the southern planter to England? (b) Might these ties influence his feelings in a controversy between England and the other American colonies? Why or why not?

2 Townspeople—the mixing of English and American ideas

Like the southern planters, the wealthier townspeople in all the colonies dressed and acted like wealthier Englishmen in the Old Country. This is not surprising. Most colonial cities and towns were seaports with strong commercial ties to England. All travel and trade between the Old World and the British colonies flowed through these seaports.

By the 1750's Philadelphia, with 20,000 people, was the largest colonial city. In one year, 1754, a total of 471 trading vessels entered and left its busy harbor. New York and Boston were a close second and third in importance. Charleston, South Carolina, and Baltimore, Maryland, were the only towns of considerable size south of Pennsylvania.

Social divisions. By the 1760's merchants were the most influential citizens in all large northern towns. This was true even in New England, where clergymen had once been the leaders. The merchants, together with lawyers and the official families of the royal governors from England, set the fashions for the wealthier people. They drew their wealth from trade and from buying and selling land. Some owned country estates worked by tenant farmers.

Below the merchants on the social ladder were the majority of the townspeople—the free artisans and laborers. Below them were white indentured servants. And far below all these groups were Negro slaves.

These classes—the wealthy townspeople, the skilled workmen, and the servants and slaves—resembled similar classes in England. But class distinctions in the colonies were not so rigid as in England. Through hard work and ability, an artisan or even a white servant could make his fortune and join the society of the influential townsmen and southern planters. A black slave, however, could not.

Influence of the Old World. Old World influence could be seen in many features of town life. Some wealthy townsmen built houses similar to those seen on their visits to the Old World, sometimes even using bricks brought from England.

Like the wealthy southern planters, the wealthy townspeople imported furniture and household luxuries from England. The interiors of their houses, as well as the exteriors, reminded visitors of the Old World.

Like that of well-to-do people in England, the social life of the wealthy townsmen centered in the banquet hall and in elaborate dances. They rode to these festive occasions in gleaming coaches, drawn by white horses with silver trappings, driven by coachmen and outriders in blue coats and yellow capes.

Many well-to-do townspeople also enjoyed card playing, horse racing, cockfighting, and the theater. In Boston, however, strict Puritan ideas still prevailed, and such recreation was frowned upon or forbidden by law.

Only the wealthier townspeople enjoyed this brilliant social life. Household servants usually lived in simply furnished rooms over the family quarters. Artisans often lived behind their small shops that fronted on the streets.

A visit to Philadelphia. Imagine that we are in colonial America, strolling through the seaport of Philadelphia in, say, 1754. In other colonial towns the streets meander this way and that, following the early cowpaths and farm lanes. Philadelphia is different. Here William Penn's careful planning has proved worthwhile. The streets run neatly north and south, east and west. Some are paved with cobblestones; others are merely hard-pressed earth, and walking on these, our feet raise little clouds of

■ **Town Artisan and Wife**

■ Philadelphia was considered to be one of the handsomest colonial cities of the 1700's. Christ Church, which appears in the center of this picture, was a famous landmark of the day.

dust. We pass the homes of the wealthy—red brick and white stone houses surrounded by gardens and lawns. And we also pass the small shops of the artisans.

Hearing the sound of a bell, we pause to listen to the town crier. Introducing his news with "Hear ye, hear ye," he announces a sale of indentured servants just arrived from England.

On our way to the waterfront we pass the market house. Throngs of housewives and servants with baskets on their arms crowd around the stalls.

Farmers from the surrounding countryside are displaying their produce—butter, cheese, poultry, beef, mutton, and vegetables.

Along the waterfront. Reaching the water, we continue along Dock Street, which parallels the Delaware River. The noise of hammers and saws attracts our attention, and we see a shipyard where a small vessel is being built. Next to it, fishermen are heaving the day's catch onto the planks of the wharf. Beyond lies the English ship we have come

57

brick chimney with four
flues for four fireplaces

heavy wooden framing

wide wooden flooring

foundation stones

footing stone

■ Colonial Houses. Most houses in colonial times were simple one-story dwellings like these. They were designed to have a fireplace in any room requiring heat.

Approaching the ship, we find ourselves in the midst of bustle and confusion. Men carrying boxes and bales on their shoulders push their way toward the nearby warehouse. At one side a knot of colonists, eager for the latest news from the Old World, surrounds a sailor and asks him many questions. On the deck of the ship are the indentured servants, some looking extremely bewildered and unhappy.

The wealthy colonists, easily distinguished by their dress and self-assurance, pass among the servants, looking for a good bargain. Now and then a sale is made. The owner and his new servant leave the ship, the owner in front leading the way, the servant following with his belongings in a sack over his shoulder.

English ways of life. Walking back into town, it would be easy to think that we are walking through an English city. Passing the open door of a merchant's "counting house," we see clerks on tall stools patiently recording business transactions in their ledgers. Across the street is a tavern. A row of hitching posts stands in front of the tavern, and a hollow log serves as a watering trough for horses.

We have not seen the town hall or the jail with its pillory and stocks or the several churches that are important parts of the city. But we have seen enough to learn that life in the colonial towns is similar in many ways to life in English towns. The people dress and talk like Englishmen. The houses and public buildings are English in style. We see the same social divisions that exist in English towns.

The American "melting pot." But in some ways the colonial towns are different from the towns of England. Even though some people may want to do so, they cannot carry all the Old World ways to the New World.

For one thing, people from many different nations are learning to live together in colonial America. The colonial towns, as well as the frontier and the farming areas, are "melting pots." Many German settlers fill the section of Philadelphia known as Germantown. On the streets we pass men and women from Ireland and Scotland, many on their way to western frontier lands. And listening carefully, we hear the accents of people from France, Switzerland, Sweden, and many other European countries.

The "melting pot" of colonial America is producing a new American vocabulary. English visitors to the colonies hear many new, unfamiliar words. The colonists are speaking what Samuel Johnson, the famous English dictionary maker, in 1756 called the "American dialect." By the 1760's the new American vocabulary has borrowed many words from other languages. From the Indians it has borrowed *skunk, hickory, squash, raccoon, canoe, toboggan, moccasin, tomahawk,* and *wigwam.* From the Dutch it has borrowed *cruller, stoop, waffle, scow, boss,* and *cookie.* From the

French it has borrowed *bureau, gopher, chowder, bogus, portage,* and *prairie.* And the colonists have invented many new words—*bullfrog, eggplant, snowplow, cold snap, trail, popcorn, shingle,* and *backlog.*

Building the towns. The colonists are also trying to find new, workable solutions to the many problems faced by all townspeople. Working together, they are trying to solve problems of water supply, sewage, sanitation, health, and police and fire protection. In Philadelphia, Benjamin Franklin's newspaper, the *Pennsylvania Gazette,* publishes a steady stream of articles dealing with solutions to these problems. Largely because of Franklin's efforts, Philadelphia is one of the first cities in the world to have paved streets, street lights, police and fire departments, and a public library. Europeans are also working to introduce these same improvements in their cities. But the colonists take special pride in the cities they have built with their own hands.

A land of opportunity. The greatest difference between English and American towns can be summed up in the word "opportunity." There is plenty of work for everyone in Philadelphia, New York, Boston, and every other colonial town. Except for Negro slaves, who usually remain slaves for life, no one need remain a servant for very long. And if the town itself does not offer enough opportunity, the colonists can always move west. Many stay in town only long enough to save a little money. Then they are off over the roads that lead them to a new way of life.

SECTION SURVEY

IDENTIFY: social ladder, social classes, melting pot.

1. (a) Why would Philadelphia in 1754 remind you of England and English society? (b) Would you have the same thoughts after visiting a southern plantation? Explain.
2. How did the American variety of spoken English reflect the New World?
3. How does the word "opportunity" sum up a major difference between England and America?
4. (a) By the 1760's what factors determined a colonist's place on the social ladder? (b) Could all colonists move from one rung of the ladder to another? Explain.
5. The colonial immigrants could not bring all their Old World ways to the New World. (a) Why was this so? (b) Would this be true of immigrants today? Explain.

3 Pioneer farmers—the widening break with English ties

The area of America most different from the Old World lay back from the seacoast. Here, in the country, lived more than 90 percent of all the colonists.

Farming villages. Not far from the coast, particularly in New England, New Jersey, and Pennsylvania, were many small farming villages of 50 to 100 families, with a church or meetinghouse, a school, and several shops. Many villages had a cobbler to make shoes, a blacksmith to fix wagons, a doctor to give medical attention, and a general store to sell sugar, spices, and English cloth for dresses. Traveling barbers also came to the villages to cut hair and pull teeth.

To pay for these services, the farmers of the village and the surrounding territory hauled their surplus tobacco, grain, cattle, and hogs to the nearest seaboard or river-port town. There the farmers sold their products.

Before returning home, the farmers often stopped to make purchases in the shops displaying English luxury goods—tableware, silver and pewter vessels, and fine cloth. Thus, settlers living in areas where they could market their surplus products were able to live better than more isolated colonists.

Moving into new homes. People married young in colonial America. Some newly married couples settled on land near their parents. Many more became pioneers who moved farther inland where land was cheaper. It was a common sight to see a couple pass through a village on their way to a new home. The husband walked along, rifle in hand, knife in belt. Beside him was his wife. Behind them, an ox or a horse pulled a small cart containing a few boxes with all their belongings. Bringing up the rear, tied to the cart by a rope, was a scrawny cow.

Pioneer shelters. At first many pioneers lived in caves along the riverbanks, or in shallow pits roofed with branches and covered with sod to keep out the rain. Frequently newcomers put up three-sided log shelters with the open side facing away from the prevailing winds. Sooner or later those who stayed to farm the land built a full log cabin, a practical structure for forested country, introduced into the colonies by Swedish settlers.

The log cabins were usually crude, one-room affairs, with a dirt floor, no windows, and a door hung on leather hinges. The most important feature of most cabins was a huge fireplace where the settlers huddled for warmth, and where they cooked their food. Later, if the pioneers prospered, they improved the cabin. They laid a wooden floor, cut windows in the walls, and covered the openings with waxed paper or glass. They built a loft for the children to sleep in, added new rooms, and, if all went well, finally nailed clapboards on the outside walls over the rough logs.

The pioneers rose at dawn and went to bed at dusk. There were few books, even for those who could read, and the pioneers felt little need to light the cabins at night. Usually the glow from the fireplace furnished the cabin's only light. When more light was needed, people put large splinters of pine wood into cracks in the walls, where they burned with a bright, smoky flame. The pioneers used candles only on special occasions, for tallow was hard to get. Only wealthy townspeople used candles and oil lamps to any extent.

Household equipment. In the early log cabins, fireplaces furnished the only heat. The pioneers shivered as winter winds swept through cracks between the logs or down the drafty chimney. People often put warming pans in their beds, went to bed early, and bundled themselves in layers of blankets.

■ **Pioneer Farmer and Wife**

And every family that could afford to do so bought one of the stoves invented by Benjamin Franklin.

The pioneers also did all their cooking in the fireplace. They boiled vegetables, soups, and stews in large copper or iron kettles—prized possessions which hung from a pole in the chimney. The pioneers baked in Dutch ovens beside the fireplace, or in ovens built into the side wall of the fireplace itself.

Early pioneer furniture was homemade and crude. Beds were little more than wooden bunks placed along the wall. Logs, hewn smooth with an ax, became chairs and benches. Smooth boards placed on trestles served as tables. Since planks were hard to get, the colonists often broke up packing boxes from England and used the boards for table tops. Few settlers owned tablecloths.

Eating utensils were simple and few. Early pioneers often used wooden trenchers for dishes. These were slabs of wood 10 or 12 inches square and 2 or 3 inches thick with a hollow place in the center to hold food. The pioneers whittled spoons out of wood. They drank from gourds that they grew themselves, or from tankards that they made from wood, leather, or the horns of cattle. As the settlers grew more prosperous, they bought pewter and silver utensils.

Food for the pioneers. Once colonial Americans learned to use the abundant resources of the New World, they never lacked food and drink. The rivers and lakes were alive with fish, and the forests were filled with game. In the early days, settlers near the forts often saw herds of deer numbering several hundred animals. Turkeys weighing 30 pounds were seen in all the colonies, although the settlers rapidly wiped them out. Pigeons were so plentiful from Virginia northward that they sometimes darkened the sky and broke the limbs of trees in which they roosted. Wild rabbits and squirrels destroyed so many crops that bounty payments were offered for their pelts.

Pioneer clothing. The pioneer farmers also made their own clothing, using spinning and weaving skills learned in the Old World. They made thread from the wool of their own sheep and from the flax they grew in their own fields. The women and girls spun the thread, wove it into cloth, and cut and sewed their dresses. They also tanned deerskin to make moccasins, shoes, and jackets.

Social life and recreation. The hard life of a pioneer farm left little time or energy for recreation. Nevertheless, the settlers did occasionally combine work and play.

Detail from Flax Scutching Bee, Linton Park, National Gallery of Art, Washington, D.C. Gift of Edgar William and Bernice Chrysler Garbisch.

■ In this famous old painting, neighbors have gathered on a Pennsylvania farm for a "scutching bee." At such a party, flax was paddled or "scutched" before being made into linen thread. But some of the girls seem to be scutching their boyfriends instead of the flax.

When a newcomer was ready to build his log cabin, or when he had felled the trees and was ready to drag them from the land to clear a field, his neighbors came to help him. "House-raisings" sometimes lasted several days. In the morning the men lifted the logs into place to form the cabin walls. Meanwhile the women prepared dinner, baking great piles of cornbread and barbecuing an entire beef or deer over an open fire. After dinner there were sports, such as wrestling, foot racing, and shooting contests. In the early evening the settlers danced.

People who lived in areas that had been settled for some years had more opportunity to be neighborly. In these areas the farms were closer together and small villages had been built. On Sundays most settlers went to church. During the week, in appropriate seasons, they helped one another with the cornhusking, sheepshearing, sewing, and quilting. Weddings were always times of celebration. And most work also ceased on election days and on training days, when the local militia drilled in an open field in the morning and then spent the afternoon in sports and conversation.

Self-sufficiency. The pioneer farmer was a jack-of-all-trades. Give him a gun, an ax, a knife, a hoe, a sickle, and a kettle or two, and, helped by his wife and children, he could clear the land, build a house, and grow the crops. However, most pioneer farmers lived a harsh existence. They were self-sufficient not from choice, but because they had to be. The great majority had no doctors, no schools, and few churches. They usually had a roof over their heads, enough to eat, and freedom from oppressive laws and heavy taxes, but they paid for these advantages with lives of backbreaking labor.

New ideas among pioneers. Among these self-reliant pioneer farmers, certain ideas began to take root and grow. The pioneers were free men, who by their own efforts had created homes in the wilderness. They were individualists, for a man's success depended on his own strength and skill. They believed in cooperation, for only by helping one another could they clear the land and build their

61

houses. They felt themselves to be the equals of other men, for they saw most of their neighbors living similar lives. Finally, they were optimists, for they saw the forests yielding to their axes, homes and villages springing up in what had been wilderness land, and men who had started with nothing raising their families in security and growing comfort.

Those pioneer farmers who were of British descent still thought of themselves as British, but the ties with the mother country were weakening. More and more, they began to think of themselves as "Americans."

SECTION SURVEY

IDENTIFY: pioneer, adapt, self-reliant individualist.

1. To survive in a new environment, a person must adapt. Explain how the pioneer of colonial times adapted in terms of (a) shelter, (b) household equipment, (c) food, (d) clothing, (e) social life, (f) cooperation with his neighbors.
2. What is the relationship between self-reliance and feelings of freedom and equality?
3. Why were the pioneer farmers optimists?
4. "Learn by doing" could have been the motto of the pioneer farmer. (a) What does this statement mean? (b) Do you agree with it? Why or why not? (c) Could this motto be applied to our society today? Explain.

4 Frontiersmen—emergence of the new Americans

Most "American" of all the colonists were the frontiersmen. The frontier, or forest land to the west of the settled communities, was a man's world, and mainly a young man's world at that. Every year, in all the colonies, hundreds of adventurous youths left home to find excitement in the western forests.

Life on the frontier. Living in the wilderness, men shed many traces of European civilization. All that they owned they carried in their hands or on their backs—a hunting knife, a long rifle, powder, and shot. Yet with this meager equipment they managed to survive. They shed their European clothing for coonskin caps, buckskin shirts and trousers, and moccasins of deerskin. Game, fish, nuts, and berries furnished much of their food. They slept beneath the stars, in caves, or in crude log shelters.

Some frontiersmen built cabins, cleared patches

■ **Frontiersman and Wife**

of land, married, and raised families. But most frontiersmen were trappers and hunters who preferred the lonely life of the forest to the ties of a home. Now and then they appeared at a trading post to exchange a few furs for new supplies of powder, shot, and perhaps a little corn. But many frontiersmen never returned from their travels in the woods. Theirs was a wild and dangerous life, in which they constantly matched wits and skills against Indians and nature.

Recreation. Now and then frontiersmen for miles around gathered for companionship and sport. Their recreation reflected their hard, rough life. Hunting was both a necessity and a pleasure, and they were crack shots with a rifle. Shooting matches were common.

Games of physical strength also furnished fun— foot races, wrestling matches, jumping contests, and demonstrations of hurling the tomahawk and flinging a heavy wooden fence rail.

In the evenings, before a crackling log fire, they swapped colorful tales of forest adventure and told jokes about newcomers to the wilderness.

A new kind of talk. The "tall tales," full of highly exaggerated boasting, contained many new words and phrases borrowed from the Indians or coined to describe new objects and experiences.

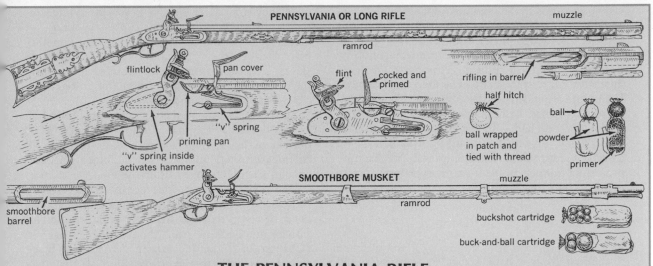

Labels in illustration:

PENNSYLVANIA OR LONG RIFLE — muzzle — ramrod — flintlock — pan cover — flint — cocked and primed — rifling in barrel — half hitch — ball — powder — "v" spring — priming pan — ball wrapped in patch and tied with thread — primer — "v" spring inside activates hammer

SMOOTHBORE MUSKET — muzzle — smoothbore barrel — ramrod — buckshot cartridge — buck-and-ball cartridge

THE PENNSYLVANIA RIFLE

The Pennsylvania rifle, sometimes called "the long rifle," was developed by German gunsmiths who settled in and around Lancaster, Pennsylvania, in the early 1700's. They had learned how to make rifles back in their homeland, but these were not good enough for the frontier. On the frontier a man needed a gun that would shoot straight and true. A hunter could carry only so much ammunition with him, and he had to make each shot count, even if the target was only a rabbit or squirrel for his next meal. And no man alone in the wilderness knew when a single shot might save his life.

By 1750 Pennsylvania gunsmiths were making rifles of amazing accuracy. Up to a range of 100 yards, they were about as accurate as an ordinary rifle is today. These rifles helped Americans to conquer the wilderness. With the rifle, the ax, and the Conestoga wagon—also invented in Pennsylvania—Americans pushed the frontier steadily westward.

Did the Pennsylvania rifle win the Revolutionary War that presently broke out between the American colonists and Great Britain? Maybe not. But it played a big part in the victory. In the reports they sent back to England, British generals referred to the "terrible guns of the rebels." Against the Pennsylvania rifle, the British—with a few exceptions—had only clumsy, smoothbore muskets with which a man could hardly expect to hit a target at more than 150 feet.

(*Explanation of Drawing.* The spiral rifling inside the barrel of the rifle, and its longer barrel, gave a rapid spin to the charge which carried it farther and truer than the charge from a smoothbore musket. Both weapons were loaded through the muzzle; the charge was pushed into position with a ramrod slung under the barrel. The charge might be a manufactured paper cartridge or a little loose powder that the soldier might pour down the barrel, ramming in after it a lead ball wrapped and tied in a linen patch. For firing, a pinch of powder in the priming pan was ignited by a piece of flint locked in the hammer.)

From the Indians the frontiersmen learned *pow-wow, peace pipe,* and *burying the tomahawk.* To describe strange features of the land, they coined such new words as *water gap, barrens, salt lick, underbrush,* and *bluffs.* Seaboard folk began to talk of the *back country,* of *backwoodsmen,* and of *taking to the woods.*

Frontier independence. The frontiersmen explored the "no man's land" between civilization and the wilderness. They discovered the fertile valleys and the passes through the mountains. They were individualists, brimming with independence, self-reliance, and initiative. But their individualism was cooperative as well as competitive, for an additional pair of strong arms and an extra rifle sometimes meant the difference between life and death.

In the forest the idea of equality—the core idea of democracy—took root and grew swiftly. A man

63

was judged not by fine clothes, eloquent language, or titles after his name, but by his skill in woodcraft and his knowledge of the wilderness.

Down the whole length of the frontier, from New France to Spanish Florida, frontiersmen lived much the same sort of life. The Germans, Scotch-Irish, and English on the Virginia frontier had more in common with the Massachusetts frontiersmen than they had with the rich planters of their own colony, or with the wealthy townsmen of the colonial seaports. Frontier life was an exciting process of mixing people from many different backgrounds into new, independent kinds of persons.

SECTION SURVEY

1. Explain how and why the life of a frontiersman differed from that of a planter, townsman, and pioneer farmer.
2. What new words or phrases used on the frontier demonstrated that the frontiersman had adapted to his new environment?
3. What typically American ideas developed on the frontier? Why?
4. How did frontier life act as a molder of people?
5. (a) How was a man judged on the frontier? (b) How was he judged in a colonial town? (c) Who did the judging? (d) Are the standards for judging a man dependent upon the environment in which he lives? Explain.

5 Africans in the colonies— emergence of a class apart

In the 1760's, of the 2 million people living in the British colonies, between 300,000 and 400,000 were Negroes of African birth or background.° These black colonists lived in, and helped build, all the colonies. Yet they were denied the opportunities that other colonial groups took for granted.

A class apart. For European settlers, America meant freedom and an opportunity to build a better life. For Negroes it meant nothing of the kind. Unlike the vast majority of European settlers, the Africans did not come to America freely. They were brought against their will, by force, literally in chains.

Nor did the position of the Africans improve

° Since no general census was taken until 1790, the estimates of the number of Negroes in the colonies in the 1760's often vary, but generally fall between 300,000 and 400,000 people.

once they arrived in the New World. White colonists regarded the black Africans as property—a valuable kind of property, but property nonetheless. Denied their humanity, Africans became slaves, and most remained slaves for life, as did their children. Every other group in colonial society regarded black men as inferior.

Slaveowners taught the Africans only as much as was necessary for them to do their work. Thus the slaves learned the simpler skills involved in colonial farming, building, and manufacturing, and enough English to obey orders.

The white colonists ignored the skills already possessed by the black arrivals. Few white colonists knew or cared that the Africans came from civilizations hundreds or even thousands of years old (Chapter 15). Coming ashore in America, black newcomers were forced to abandon all that they had held dear in the lands of their birth.

The Middle Passage. As colonial demands for slaves increased, the brutal African slave trade grew and flourished. From central and western Africa, long lines of Africans, captured by enemy tribesmen, were marched to west African seaports. To prevent their escape, the captives wore iron collars and were linked together by chains. The survivors of these long, cruel marches were sold to European or American sea captains, who bought only the strongest and healthiest young Africans.

Once the slaves were selected, they were branded and packed into the slave ships. Chained together two by two, they were packed together on ship decks that were often no more than three feet apart.

The weeks-long voyage to the New World, called the Middle Passage, was a nightmare. Some slaves managed to kill themselves by jumping overboard or choking themselves with their chains. Many died from spoiled food. And disease, fostered by overcrowding and filthy conditions, took many more lives. Sharks trailed the slave ships and fed on the bodies of the dead which were thrown overboard. Some slaves revolted against these inhuman conditions, but revolts were difficult to start, and they seldom succeeded.

Often only half of the slaves survived the horrors of the Middle Passage. But this heavy loss of life did little to discourage the slave traders, who made enormous profits from their trade.

British and American traders usually sold the surviving Africans to planters in the West Indies. Before being sent to the seaboard colonies, the African newcomers were "seasoned," or broken in, by white overseers and black slave foremen. Perhaps only about half the slaves survived the harsh seasoning period on the hot sugar plantations of the West Indies.

Slavery in the New England Colonies. By the 1770's, a relatively small number of Negro slaves, perhaps about 12,000, lived in New England. The small New England farms did not require the labor of large numbers of slaves. New England slaves worked as household servants for the wealthy, and as farm laborers, lumberjacks, carpenters, barrel-makers, blacksmiths, millers, fishermen, and ship-builders.

Slaves in New England had some legal rights. They could buy property and had the right to trial by jury in the courts. Slaves could attend church as long as they sat in "African pews," but they could not become church members. In Puritan New England church membership conferred political rights, such as the right to vote and to hold office. Such political rights were denied to slaves.

Most Puritan New Englanders looked upon their slaves as wards, or adopted children, of the family. Yet these "adopted children," even in rare instances when their owners taught them to read and write, were property to be bought and sold as their owners wished.

Although slaves in New England had some rights, New England slavery still was harsh. New England slaves, like slaves everywhere, rebelled against the central evil of slavery—the total and permanent ownership of human beings by other human beings. Many New England slaves fled from their masters, no matter how kind their masters might be.

Slavery in the Middle Colonies. Slaves in the Middle Colonies contributed their labor and skills to commerce and industry and farming. As in New England, however, the number of slaves was relatively small—perhaps about 35,000.

In New Netherland, Dutch patroons and merchants, like Puritan New Englanders, regarded their slaves as adopted children. When the British seized the area, this attitude changed. Under British rule, all black slaves in New York, except household servants, were strictly separated from white colonists. Severe rules of discipline governed the slaves. Violence between white colonists and black slaves became common in New York.

Attitudes toward slavery in Pennsylvania and much of New Jersey differed somewhat from those in New York. From the earliest days, at least some Quaker and German settlers in Pennsylvania and New Jersey doubted the morality of slave labor, as

■ **Black Colonist and Wife**

well as its usefulness. Some of them began to speak out against the evils of slavery.

Slavery in the Southern Colonies. Of the 300,-000 to 400,000 Negroes in colonial America in 1765, the vast majority, or nearly seven out of eight, lived in the Southern Colonies. Almost all of these black people were slaves.

Most southern slaves labored on tobacco, rice, and indigo plantations, but southern slaves also did many other kinds of work. Between 1732 and 1736, the *South Carolina Gazette* mentioned 28 trades using slave labor. Black slaves made an enormous contribution to the development of the Southern Colonies.

In the Carolinas, slavery grew rapidly, as it did in Georgia once it was allowed. The early colonists of Virginia and Maryland, however, came to depend upon slave labor only gradually. First they tried without success to enslave the Indians. Then they tried to rely on white indentured servants, but indentured servants were hard to get and harder to keep. Negro slaves provided a more dependable labor force—and a permanent one.

As you have read (page 21), the status of Africans in Virginia was for some time uncertain. The first African arrivals were regarded more or less as indentured servants, but their contracts did not always insure their freedom after their term of service was completed. After 1661 the institution

■ Slave labor was used on southern plantations to produce tobacco, rice, indigo, and other crops. Above, slaves work on a tobacco plantation in Virginia.

of slavery was clearly established in Virginia.

Throughout the late 1600's and the 1700's, slavery grew rapidly in the Southern Colonies. Southern planters developed new and larger plantations, requiring the labor of more and more slaves, and slave traders rushed to fill the demand.

The slave codes.   As the proportion of slaves to white people increased in the Southern Colonies, white southerners became alarmed. If plantation agriculture was to expand and be profitable, the southerners needed slaves. But white southern-

ers also feared that large numbers of black people would threaten white supremacy. Slaves, concentrated in large numbers, might successfully revolt against their masters. Occasional reports of slave revolts in the West Indies, where black slaves far outnumbered white settlers, stimulated these fears.

Beginning in the 1680's, southern slaveowners tried to solve this problem by passing slave codes. These laws had a twofold purpose. First, they safeguarded the slaveowner's investment in his slave property by setting up detailed regulations to prevent the theft or escape of his slaves. Second, they protected the slaveowner against slave violence by setting up strict rules for slave behavior.

To prevent slave revolts, the codes forbade slaves to meet together, leave the plantation, or own weapons. By law, slaves could not learn to read or write. Special guards circulated among the slaves to insure that these slave codes were not violated.

Black resistance to slavery.   In the 1600's and 1700's, punishments for all crimes were extremely cruel. Under the slave codes, however, punishments for black men were more severe than punishments for similar crimes committed by white colonists.

For minor crimes, slaves could be beaten severely or even have their noses split or their ears cut off. For major crimes, such as rape or murder, a slave could be hanged or burned to death.

Not all slaves submitted meekly to the slaveowners' attempts to own and control them. Slaves found many ways to harass their masters. Whenever possible, they purposely slowed down their work or did it poorly. Sometimes they struck back or even killed their white masters.

Slaves sometimes succeeded in running away from their owners, but because of their skin color, they did not automatically win their freedom. In all colonies, an unknown black man was immediately suspected of being a runaway slave.

Slaves could and did plot uprisings to secure their freedom. Slaveowners lived in terror of such revolts. The vaguest rumor of a slave uprising could cause panic in a white community. Whether the revolt was real or imagined, the punishment for the slaves was severe.

Vague rumors appear to have been the sole evidence used against more than 100 Negroes convicted of plotting a revolt in New York in 1741. Eighteen slaves were hanged, 13 burned to death, and 78 "transported," probably to the British West Indies, where the slave codes were extremely severe.

White opposition to slavery. A few white colonists condemned slavery. In 1700, Samuel Sewall of Boston, an influential judge, published a famous anti-slavery pamphlet called *The Selling of Joseph*. A devout Puritan, Judge Sewall gathered examples from the Bible to show that slavery was evil. Judge Sewall was promptly answered by another pamphlet that used Biblical examples to show that slavery was justified.

In 1688, twelve years before Judge Sewall's pamphlet appeared, the Quakers of Germantown, Pennsylvania, spoke out against slavery. These Quakers denounced the evils of selling men and of separating husbands from their wives and children.

Not until the mid-1700's, however, did Quakers generally begin to oppose the brutal slave trade and, gradually, slavery itself. John Woolman, a conscientious and thoughtful Quaker tailor, journeyed through the colonies persuading his fellow Quakers to free their slaves and educate them. His journal is still read and admired today.

Free black colonists. A few free Negroes lived in every colony. They had gained their freedom in several ways. Descendants of the early indentured Africans in Virginia inherited their freedom. Children of a white mother, regardless of the father's race, were regarded as free men. Occasionally a master freed a slave, sometimes to reward him for faithful service, sometimes to avoid supporting him in his old age. A few slaves bought their freedom, using savings their owners allowed them to earn and keep.

Most free black colonists earned their living as skilled workmen. A few owned their own small farms or businesses. Free black men could not serve in colonial militias in peace time, though both free black colonists and slaves were recruited into the militia in times of war. In the 1700's free Negroes were not allowed to vote in any of the Southern Colonies except, for a time, in North Carolina.

White colonists seldom associated with free black men except in casual, unimportant ways. An occasional free black man won a respected place in his community, but most had to endure some form of discrimination from the white colonists.

Separate and unequal. White colonists, especially the English, regarded Negroes, whether free or slave, as a class apart—and an inferior class at that. Most Negroes were forced to live apart from white colonists and under special laws enforced by white colonists. Black men contributed enormously to the growth of the colonies. White colonists not only expected hard labor from the Negroes, they

TO BE SOLD on board the Ship *Bance-Ifland*, on tuesday the 6th of *May* next, at *Afbley-Ferry*, a choice cargo of about 250 fine healthy NEGROES, juft arrived from the Windward & Rice Coaft. —The utmoft care has already been taken, and fhall be continued, to keep them free from the leaft danger of being infected with the SMALL-POX, no boat having been on board, and all other communication with people from *Charles-Town* prevented. *Auftin, Laurens, & Appleby.*

N. B. Full one Half of the above Negroes have had the SMALL-POX in their own Country.

■ During a smallpox epidemic, the owners of a slave ship anchored off Charleston were careful to stress in their advertisement that their cargo of slaves was free from infection.

demanded it. Yet in a new land abounding with opportunity, few Negroes were permitted to work, save, or build better ways of life for themselves or their families.

SECTION SURVEY

IDENTIFY: Middle Passage, slave codes, discrimination, racial prejudice, white supremacy, separate and unequal, "a class apart."

1. For each of the three colonial sections, answer the following: (a) How great was the need for slave labor? (b) What legal and social rights did slaves have? (c) What was the attitude of the white colonists toward the slaves? (d) What was the source, if any, of white opposition to slavery?
2. What purposes did the slave codes serve?
3. How did the slaves resist slavery?
4. (a) How did a slave gain freedom? (b) What was his status as a free man?
5. (a) How might slavery affect a slave's feelings toward white people? (b) How might slavery affect a slaveowner's feelings toward black people? (c) How might such feelings affect race relations today? (d) How might such feelings be overcome?

6 The Indians—the clash of differing cultures

When the Spaniards, French, and British came to the New World, they found the original inhabitants of the Americas—the Indians. The attitudes of the Spaniards, French, and British toward the Indians differed. Only the British, however, regarded the Indians as a constant threat to the way of life that they were trying to create in the New World. In the British colonies, the Indians were even less a part of colonial life than black colonists.

Spanish and French attitudes. The Spaniards, as you know, first overran and destroyed the Indian civilizations that they found, and then tried unsuccessfully to enslave the Indian survivors.

Finally, the Spaniards adopted one or the other of two attitudes toward the Indians. Sometimes they left the Indians alone to live as they chose in the vast forests, deserts, or mountains of Latin America. Or, in mission communities built throughout Latin America, Spanish priests taught Christianity to the Indians, as well as simple farming and industrial skills.

French colonists were more willing than the Spaniards or the British to accept the Indians as they were. Furs were the principal cash "crop" of New France. For this reason, the French did not want to interfere with the wilderness life of the Indians—a way of life that produced large quantities of furs. On the contrary, many French traders became a part of that way of life, taking Indian women for mates and living according to the customs of the Indian tribesmen with whom they traded.

From friendship to conflict. The first British settlers along the Atlantic seaboard owed much to the Indians, who received them with friendliness and curiosity. To survive in their strange new land, the British settlers had to learn many Indian secrets and skills. And learn they did. They learned how to grow and use Indian corn, or maize, and how to make canoes and paddle them on the waterways. They learned how to follow Indian trails and how to live off game, fish, and plants of the forest lands. The Indians, in turn, admired the marvelous tools and weapons of the British, and sometimes became too fond of European whisky and rum.

These early bonds of friendship were broken when the Indians realized that the advance of British settlement endangered their traditional ways of life. The Indians and the British came from utterly different cultural ° backgrounds. In the contacts and clashes between them, neither side could understand the other. That failure of understanding was to haunt relations between the settlers and the Indians throughout America's development.

British-Indian culture clash. To the British colonists, success and progress meant changing the natural environment. The British set out to chop down and burn the trees of eastern North America, to cultivate the land, to build homes and schools and churches, and to establish villages, towns, and cities.

To the Indians, nature was an essential part of life. They did not dream of changing it. As John Collier in his book *Indians of the Americas* put it, the Indians had a "reverence and passion for the earth and its web of life." The Indians had learned to gain a living from the land without destroying it. The Indians were deeply satisfied by their feeling of harmony with nature, a feeling which few British either understood or appreciated.

■ Huron Indian and Squaw

° *culture:* the whole way of life of a people, including their habits and customs, their religion and education, their government and their arts. In other words, the culture of a people includes everything the people do and all the ideas they share.

■ This scene of Eastern Woodland Indians illustrates many of their everyday activities. How many of these activities can you identify?

The British and the Indians also had different ideas about land and property. The British acquired the Indians' land by purchase or treaty or fraud. The British believed that property could be bought or sold by an individual. They did not understand that, for the Indians, property was held collectively by the tribe. An Indian chief was actually a trustee for the tribe. He had no right to sell or give away permanently any part of the ancestral lands. The Indians felt that they had no more right to sell the land than they had to sell the sky.

The British did not understand that treaties and agreements meant one thing to the Indians and something quite different to them. As for the Indians, they neither understood nor cared that British ways of farming, manufacturing, and commerce could provide good livings for many more people than could the Indian ways of life. Even if they had understood, the Indians could hardly have been expected to give up their traditional ways of living just because countless Europeans suddenly appeared on their lands, demanding that they do so. From these profound differences in the two

■ Fear and suspicion between British settlers and Indians repeatedly led to violence. Above, Indians and Frenchmen overrun the Massachusetts settlement at Deerfield during a war in 1704.

cultures, bitterness and suspicion—and eventually warfare—arose.

An atmosphere of violence. The British colonists had assumed that the Indians would eagerly abandon their traditional ways of life to adopt "superior" European ways. They were genuinely surprised when the Indians did not respond as expected. As a result, the British settlers soon decided that the Indians were a hopelessly inferior race of people.

Differing methods of warfare further deepened the fear, suspicion, and hatred between the British and the Indians. The Indians used what are now known as guerrilla tactics. They stole up silently in the night to burn villages and seize women and children as well as men, killing them on the spot or taking them into captivity.

If colonists pursued them, the Indians chose a good place of ambush, waited in utter silence, and then pounced upon the colonists and killed them.

This Indian use of the ambush and of guerrilla tactics directly contrasted with British tactics of open warfare and frontal assaults.

The colonists later adopted Indian methods of warfare, but in the early years the colonists thought that Indian tactics of war proved that the Indians were cruel savages, utterly untrustworthy, and utterly beyond the bounds of human civilization. Eventually, the colonists decided that they must exterminate the Indians or give up the whole purpose for which they had journeyed to America.

Efforts at conversion. Not all colonists regarded the Indians as cruel, inferior savages. Such Puritans as Roger Williams, John Eliot, and Jonathan Edwards tried to teach Christianity to the Indians and to deal fairly with them. Judge Samuel Sewall, while arguing against slavery for black people, also criticized his fellow New Englanders for regarding the Indians as little better than animals.

Other religious groups also tried to convert the Indians to Christianity. The Quakers especially tried to understand the Indians, to deal fairly with them, and to prove that love could overcome all barriers.

Efforts at education. A few attempts to educate the Indians in European ways of living met with scant success. In New England, Eleazar Wheelock raised funds for starting a college in New Hampshire where Indians could be educated and converted to Christianity. It had little success. In Virginia, at the College of William and Mary, a few Indian boys were taught in separate classes. When the boys returned to their tribes, the chiefs complained that they had been made unfit for Indian life.

Benjamin Franklin offered to supervise the education of some Indian boys. He was courteously told that Indian methods of education were better suited to the boys' development. The Indians offered instead to take some white boys and teach them Indian arts and skills. The colonists declined the offer.

Attempts at understanding. A few thoughtful British colonists took genuine interest in Indian life. Roger Williams in the 1600's learned one of the Indian languages and wrote an Indian dictionary. In the 1700's, Benjamin Franklin, Thomas Jefferson, and a few other scholarly colonists became interested in the customs as well as the languages of the Indians.

Thomas Jefferson admired the eloquence of Indian chiefs at treaty-making ceremonies. He also appreciated their dignity and nobility. Jefferson's views were related to an idea of "the noble savage" then common in European intellectual circles. People sharing this notion idealized "primitive" peoples and looked with disfavor upon what they called the shortcomings and artificial features of Europe's "over-civilization."

Locked in conflict. Genuine concern for the Indians was rare in colonial America. The vast majority of colonists did not include the Indians in their vision of an increasingly better and richer life in America. Most colonists made no effort to open the doors of opportunity to the Indians. Instead, they despised and feared them.

On their side, the Indians saw no reason to forsake their own customs. Nor were the Indians able to understand why the colonists feared and hated them so intensely.

With such profound misunderstanding on both sides, a long-lasting pattern of conflict between the Indians and the settlers was laid down in colonial America.

A legacy from the Indians. The value of the contributions that the American Indians have made to the world is beyond reckoning. Mankind will be forever in their debt.

Nearly 500 years have passed since men and women from the Old World began to settle the American continents. During all that time, none of the settlers nor their descendants have discovered and developed a single major agricultural product from the wild trees and plants of the New World. And yet, long before the first Europeans landed on the shores of the Americas, the Indians had developed more than 20 valuable products. In addition, they had learned to use many other products of the forests and grasslands. The amazing truth is that more than half of all the agricultural goods produced in the world today came from plants originally discovered and cultivated by American Indians.

The shelves of our stores are filled with these products, either in their natural form or processed into an almost endless variety of packaged and canned goods. How different our eating habits would be if we did not have corn, tomatoes, white and sweet potatoes, and the many varieties of beans! If we did not have peanuts, chestnuts, pumpkins, strawberries, blackberries, blueberries, cranberries, and crab apples! If we did not have chocolate and maple syrup! All these we owe to the American Indians.

SECTION SURVEY

IDENTIFY: culture, harmony with nature, exterminate.

1. (a) What were the Spanish and French attitudes toward the Indians? (b) Why did their attitudes differ?
2. Explain how the British-Indian culture clash was reflected in differing views of (a) nature, (b) land ownership, (c) treaties and agreements, (d) definition of success.
3. (a) What Indian ideas might have been useful to the British settlers? (b) What British ideas might have been useful to the Indians? (c) Why did such an exchange of ideas become impossible?
4. Comment on this statement: The Indians were doomed from the start because of European technological developments, such as guns and gunpowder.
5. The Indians had a "reverence and passion for the earth and its web of life." Could mankind today benefit by adopting this Indian attitude? Explain.

71

TRACING THE MAIN IDEAS

When immigrants from Europe first arrived in the New World, they were European in language, dress, customs, and ways of thinking and acting. They naturally tried to reproduce the familiar ways of life that they had known in the Old World. This proved to be impossible. They learned to change the material aspects of their life styles—houses, clothing, tools, weapons—to meet their needs. More slowly, they began to change the ideas and practices brought with them from the Old World.

The southern planters and the wealthy townsmen changed more slowly than the other colonial groups. Because of their close ties with England, they continued in some ways to be more English than American.

The pioneer farmers and the frontiersmen changed much more rapidly. Because they had so few ties with England, they became much more American than English.

There was another important fact about these groups of European colonists. They were growing apart. Many of the merchants and planters felt, as did many people in England, that family background or wealth made them "better" than the rank and file of people and entitled them to special privileges. The farmers and frontiersmen, on the other hand, were becoming more and more democratic in their ways of living and thinking.

At the same time, however, two important colonial groups—Negroes and Indians—were excluded from the mainstreams of colonial life. Black Africans were enslaved. The Indians were treated as enemy peoples. Thus, the seeds of prejudice were planted in the soil of the British colonies at the same time that democratic ideals began to take root. These seeds, in time, would grow and bear bitter fruit.

In the next chapter you will see how the ideas of the colonists influenced their schools, churches, and government. You will see how democratic ideas began to take root in colonial America.

CHAPTER SURVEY

QUESTIONS FOR DISCUSSION

1. The ways of life of the frontiersman and of the pioneer farmer made them more American than English. Explain.
2. The frontiersman's individualism was cooperative as well as competitive. Does this statement contradict itself? Explain.
3. (a) Many of the colonial planters and merchants were able to reproduce some of the familiar ways of life they had known in the Old World. Why? (b) Why were the pioneer farmer and the frontiersmen unable to reproduce as many Old World ways?
4. (a) What is meant by the phrase "a class apart"? (b) How did this condition apply to both Negroes and Indians in the colonial period? Why?
5. (a) In what ways is slavery contrary to American values? (b) In what ways is it contrary to human values?
6. In what ways is the white settlers' treatment of Negroes and American Indians during the colonial period a dramatic example of the fact that America's past shaped America's present?

RELATING PAST TO PRESENT

1. Do Americans today have the same outlook on life that the pioneer farmers had during the colonial period? Explain.
2. Are Americans today faced with the same problems that the colonists faced in learning to adapt to a new and changing environment? Explain.
3. Many people today are interested in restoring and preserving the ecology of the natural environment. In what ways would these people benefit from studying the attitudes toward nature held by the American Indians?

USING MAPS AND CHARTS

1. Geography influences people, and people influence geography. (a) Using the map on page 31, explain how the geography of the eastern seaboard influenced the lives of the early British settlers. (b) Explain how the British settlers affected the ecology (man's relationship to his environment in this question) and geography of the eastern seaboard by settling there.
2. Use the map on page 31 and the text of Chapter 4 to help you answer these questions: (a) What were the three largest cities (population) in the British colonies in the 1750's? (b) What is the approximate distance between Savannah and Boston? What means of travel did the colonists have to make the trip from Boston to Savannah? How did news travel from one colony to another? Would you say that communication was a problem during colonial times? Why? How did travel conditions affect trade between the colonies?

ROGER WILLIAMS, Puritan clergyman, fleeing for safety through snow-covered forests to live with his friends, the Narragansett Indians . . .

Lord Baltimore, wealthy Catholic proprietor of Maryland, arguing vigorously for the passage of his famous Toleration Act . . .

William Penn, Quaker, standing defiantly, hat placed firmly on his head, before the wigged and robed judges in an English courtroom . . .

John Peter Zenger, editor of the *New York Weekly Journal,* a lonely figure in a cold and cheerless prison cell writing articles for his paper . . .

They form a proud company, these and other colonial leaders who battled for man's right to be free. And there were others—many others. From the earliest days of settlement, and despite the blot of slavery, a substantial number of colonists struggled for freedom—for the right to worship as they pleased, for the right to secure an education, for the right to speak their minds freely, for the right to participate in government. When people possess these rights and freedoms, we say that they live in a "democratic society," or simply in a "democracy."

In Chapter 2 you saw how the colonists built their settlements along the Atlantic seaboard. In this chapter you will see how they began to carry the idea of freedom into their churches, schools, and government. This idea of freedom lies at the root of what we now call "the American way of life."

CHAPTER 5

Democratic Ideas in Colonial America

1607 – 1763

THE CHAPTER IN OUTLINE

1. The growth of religious tolerance in colonial America.

2. The planting of democratic freedoms in American soil.

3. The growing experience of the colonists in self-government.

4. The increasing power of colonial legislative assemblies.

1 The growth of religious tolerance in colonial America

When settlers first left Europe to build colonies in the New World, little or no religious freedom existed in the Old World. Each European nation had an official, or established, *state church*. In each nation, the government collected taxes to support the established church. Every citizen was required to join the state church and contribute to its support.

Old World religious beliefs. Naturally enough, the first settlers who came to the New World brought the idea of an established state church with them. In the French, Spanish, and Portuguese colonies of the Americas, the Roman Catholic Church was the established church. In part of New York and in all the Southern Colonies, including Maryland after 1692, the Anglican Church became the established church. The official church in the New England Colonies of Massachusetts, Connecticut, and New Hampshire was the Congregational Church. The Middle Colonies, on the other hand, had so many different religious groups that no single church was established, except the Anglican Church in part of New York.

The early settlers also brought to the New World the bitter religious conflicts and rivalries of the Old World. Border warfare often broke out between the Protestant British colonists of New England and the Roman Catholic French colonists of New France. Although these clashes were mainly caused by economic and political differences, they were aggravated by religious differences. Many border conflicts between British colonists in the Southern Colonies and Spanish colonists in Florida were also aggravated by religious differences.

Even within the colonies the various religious groups often persecuted one another. Many colonists came to the New World searching for religious freedom, but they were thinking of freedom only for themselves. Plymouth was for Separatists, Massachusetts Bay Colony for Puritans who had not as yet completely rejected the Anglican Church. Colonists who refused to accept the official religious beliefs were often thrown into jail or driven from the colony.

Roger Williams and a new idea. Roger Williams, as you have read (page 29), was one colonist who dared to fight against intolerance. The colony of Rhode Island of which he was the leading founder was small in size, but large in significance. It became a symbol of religious freedom for

■ The Pilgrims of Plymouth depended upon courage as well as spiritual strength to survive in the wilderness. This painting shows them on their way to church, carrying guns and Bibles.

America and the whole world. In Rhode Island there was no established church. No man could be taxed for the support of a church; no man could be forced to attend church; no man had to belong to a church in order to vote. All men could worship as they pleased, and all men could speak their minds freely.

Lord Baltimore and William Penn. In the struggle for greater religious tolerance, Lord Baltimore and William Penn also won notable victories. In both Maryland and Pennsylvania the principle of religious toleration became part of the basic law.

Maryland, as you have seen, was settled originally as a haven for persecuted Catholics, as well as for economic reasons. From the beginning the leaders welcomed both Catholics and Protestants. But friction developed, and Lord Baltimore secured passage of the Toleration Act of 1649.

The Toleration Act provided that anyone "professing to believe in Jesus Christ" was free to practice his religion and could not be persecuted because of his religious beliefs. The Maryland law, however, gave no protection to Jews and others who did not profess belief in Jesus Christ. Thus, it did not establish the complete religious freedom that existed in Rhode Island.

In Pennsylvania, religious toleration was broader than in Maryland, but not as broad as in Rhode Island. Any person could settle in Pennsylvania if he believed that "one Almighty and Eternal God" was the "Creator, Upholder, and Ruler of the World." Only Christians, however, could take part in the government.

The growth of toleration. With Rhode Island, Maryland, and Pennsylvania leading the way, all of the colonies eventually grew more tolerant in matters of religion. As time passed, individual religious groups found it increasingly difficult to regulate the lives of all the settlers.

For practical reasons, the leaders of each colony wanted as many people as possible to settle in their colony. Increased population was likely to bring wealth to the king, the proprietors, the businessmen, and the people in general. Thus, the colonial leaders found it almost impossible to keep out individuals simply because they held different religious beliefs. As people of many different religions began to settle side by side in the British colonies, the spirit of religious toleration began to grow.

Restrictions upon Negroes. White colonists did little to spread Christianity among black colonists, slave or free. The white colonists knew that

LIVING AMERICAN DOCUMENTS

Rhode Island Charter (1663)

No person within the said colony, at any time hereafter, shall be any wise molested, punished, disquieted, or called in question for any differences in opinion in matters of religion . . . but that all and every person and persons may, from time to time, and at all times hereafter, freely and fully have and enjoy his and their own judgments and consciences in matters of religious concernments. . . .

Maryland Toleration Act (1649)

Be it . . . enacted . . . that no person or persons . . . professing to believe in Jesus Christ shall . . . henceforth be any ways troubled, molested, or discountenanced . . . in respect of his or her religion nor in the free exercise thereof within this province. . . .

Pennsylvania Charter of Privileges (1701)

I [William Penn] do hereby grant and declare that no person or persons inhabiting . . . this province or territories who shall confess and acknowledge *One Almighty God* . . . shall be in any case molested or prejudiced in his or their person or estate because of his or their conscientious persuasion or practice. . . .

Christianity placed a great emphasis on the importance and dignity of every individual person. Slaveowners, especially in the 1600's, feared that if Negroes learned this Christian teaching they might rebel against slavery. Thus, during much of the colonial period, the majority of black people in the colonies were in effect excluded from Christianity.

There were exceptions. Some masters taught their slaves simple lessons about Christianity and included them in sessions of family worship. In the early 1700's, Anglican missionary societies urged slaveowners to give Christian instruction to their slaves. The Anglicans also set up schools in various colonial towns where black people could learn simple Christian teachings.

The Quakers did more than any other religious group to teach Christianity to black colonists. At Philadelphia in 1700 the Quakers established a yearly religious meeting for Negroes. An outstanding Quaker, Anthony Benezet, started a school in Philadelphia where black people could learn to read and write.

■ The Bethel African Methodist Episcopal Church in Philadelphia was built by black church-goers angered by the discrimination they had experienced in white churches.

In later colonial times, a few smaller religious groups made some efforts to include black members. In 1758, for example, a Baptist congregation in Virginia accepted black members.

Even black people who were allowed to join Christian churches, however, were almost always kept separate, or *segregated,* from white church members. Anglicans in the Southern Colonies sometimes built separate chapels on their plantations where slaves could worship. Puritans reserved an "African pew" for their few black members. As late as 1787 a Methodist congregation in Philadelphia forced black members to sit in the back row of the gallery. Angered by this discrimination, the black members withdrew and founded their own church—the African Methodist Episcopal Church.

Separation of church and state. Among the white colonists, a growing spirit of religious toleration weakened the foundations of the official state churches. The state found it harder to collect taxes for the support of a church to which many taxpayers did not belong.

As the years passed, the established state churches in the British colonies lost more and more power. State churches continued to exist in New England, except Rhode Island, and in the Southern Colonies until after the Revolutionary War. However, the movement that was to destroy their privileged position gathered strength in colonial America. By the 1760's, religious freedom, one of America's great democratic ideals, was slowly but steadily changing from a dream into a reality.

1. European settlers in the New World brought their Old World religious beliefs with them. What were these beliefs?
2. How did Roger Williams, Lord Baltimore, and William Penn contribute to the growth of religious tolerance in colonial America?
3. Would you consider Roger Williams a radical? Explain.
4. During most of the colonial period, most Negroes were in effect, excluded from Christianity. (a) Why was this so? (b) How were Negroes discriminated against? (c) Was this discrimination in accordance with Christian teaching? Explain.

2 The planting of democratic freedoms in American soil

In addition to religious freedom, freedom to learn, to think, to speak, and to publish are among the essentials of a democratic way of life. People who do not have these freedoms cannot vote intelligently or solve the problems, public and personal, which they face from day to day.

In the 1600's and 1700's freedom to learn, to think, to speak, and to publish was severely limited throughout most of Europe.

Old World ideas about education. Europeans in general believed that only wealthy men needed a formal education. Of course, every now and then an unusually able boy from a poor home secured an education and rose to prominence. On the whole, however, wealthy men made the laws and ran the governments of European nations. They usually had the best education money could provide. But most Europeans believed that this kind of education would be wasted on the ordinary people—the farmers, wage earners, and skilled workers.

The European settlers brought these Old World ideas about education to the New World. The wealthy colonial townsmen and planters hired tutors for their sons. They could also afford to buy books, pamphlets, and newspapers. Wealthy colonists could send their sons to private schools and universities in England. If an English education was beyond their means, they could send their sons to one of the colonial colleges.

Nine colonial colleges were started before the Revolutionary War. These colleges taught most of the same subjects as the English colleges on which they were modeled. Latin and Greek were required subjects.

Changing ideas in education. Before long, however, the well-to-do colonists began to feel that their children needed a different kind of education. In the first place, the planters, who made their money by exporting goods to England, were forced to take an active part in business. Many of the early planters' sons became prosperous and respected merchants, who wanted to know more about practical business affairs.

In the second place, the well-to-do colonists realized that they lived in a rural, isolated society. Their children could easily grow up in ignorance, no better educated than the mass of people whom the wealthy colonists considered their inferiors.

In the third place, as the merchants became more powerful, they began to ask the schools and colleges to provide more practical courses of study. Before the colonial period ended, some colonial schools offered courses in navigation, geography, modern languages, accounting, commercial law, and other subjects more immediately useful to businessmen than Greek and Latin.

Finally, the scarcity of books in the colonies led many merchants to organize private library societies. Libraries organized in this way were open only to society members. In some communities, however, civic-minded persons won enough support to establish a few small public libraries.

Thus, the environment of the New World modified the traditional ideas about education that the wealthy colonists brought with them from England.

Limitations on schooling. Most colonists—the small farmers living near the villages, the frontiersmen, and the tradesmen and artisans of the towns—did not have money to buy books, to travel, to hire tutors, or to attend private schools and colleges. Most of their energy went into the hard job of earning a living. Yet a great many colonists learned to read, write, and do simple arithmetic. Even on the frontier, where neither schools nor churches existed, some children were taught to read by their parents. In the towns some children, while learning a trade as apprentices, also learned to read and write and do simple arithmetic through the kindness of their master or his wife. And in all of the colonies there were a few elementary schools that children of poorer families could attend.

In the Middle and Southern Colonies, some

■ Harvard College, today Harvard University, was one of the first institutions of higher learning founded in the colonies. The picture above shows the college as it appeared in 1726.

schools were maintained by the various churches. But these schools were few and far between. South of Delaware the children of farmers and other workmen had only limited opportunities to go to school.

Few children of black parents, whether slave or free, could get an education in any of the colonies. Anglican missionary societies and the Quakers, as you have read, offered simple schooling to a few black people. Very rarely, a master or mistress taught a household slave to read and write. Phillis Wheatley was a slave child who learned in this way.

Phillis, brought to the New World from Africa when she was about nine years old, was sold to the Wheatley family in Boston. Mrs. Wheatley taught Phillis to read Latin as well as English. Phillis also studied geography, history, and astronomy. As a teenager, Phillis began to write lyric poems that were later published and highly praised. In 1773 Phillis Wheatley was granted her freedom and sent to England for her health.

The first public schools. New England colonists could get an education more easily than people in any of the other colonies. The Puritan leaders believed that people were more likely to become God-fearing and law-abiding citizens if they could read the Bible.

In 1647 the Massachusetts government passed a law requiring all towns except very small ones to provide schools for children. This was the first law of its kind passed in the colonies or in Europe.

For hundreds of years in Europe, the Bible had been copied mostly in Latin. During the Protestant Reformation, however, the Bible was translated and printed in German, French, English, and other European languages. The New England leaders were determined that the ability to read the English Bible should not die out in the New World.

To encourage reading and to prevent learning from "being buried in the grave of our fathers," the Massachusetts law ordered (1) that every town having 50 householders or more should at once appoint a teacher of reading and writing and pay him out of town funds and (2) that every town having 100 householders or more must provide a school good enough to prepare young men for college or pay a penalty. Families able to pay "rates" or tuition to the towns for the schooling of their children were required to do so. Tuition money for children from the poorest families, however, was paid directly out of town funds.

The Massachusetts law was not popular everywhere. Towns sometimes neglected to provide the education ordered by the law. Nevertheless, the law was a landmark in the history of education, for it expressed a new and daring idea about education —that education of all the people was a public responsibility.

The town schools of colonial New England, then, were one of America's greatest contributions to modern civilization. And free public education, paid for with government funds, has been—and is —one of the strongest roots of democracy.

The quality of schooling. Even where colonial schools existed, the quality of education provided was not always high. Many teachers were not much better educated than the children who sat before them. Often, especially in New England, the teacher of the very youngest children was a housewife, who heard the children's lessons while she did her washing and baking. Sometimes the village preacher conducted the classes.

In many schools indentured servants did the teaching. Although some indentured servants were able scholars of excellent character, others were inferior in every way.

Classes were often held in a church, a town hall, or a private home. Children of all ages generally sat in the same room and were taught by the same teacher. The terms were short. Attendance was irregular, for at any time a child might have to stay at home to help plant or harvest crops, or to cut wood.

Blackboards, slates, paper, and crayons were seldom available. Textbooks were rare. The one exception was the *New England Primer*. This little book first appeared about 1690, and more than 3 million copies were sold during the 1700's. The primer was more than a reader, for it taught school children to be obedient, to be law-abiding citizens, and to worship God.

Education on farms and frontier. The education of the ordinary people in the colonies was by no means limited to what they could learn from their parents' teaching, in the classroom, or as apprentices to a master craftsman. Much of the education of the frontiersmen and the pioneer farmers came from the practical school of experience. Face to face with problems for which they had nothing to guide them, men learned to think for themselves and to work out their own solutions. On the farm and frontier an individual had to be practical, inventive, self-sufficient, and flexible in his thinking.

This was a new kind of education and, as you will see, it was to have a profound influence upon the development of American democracy.

Few books reached the frontier, but many pioneer farmers owned copies of the Bible and much-thumbed almanacs. The almanacs contained a wide variety of information, from advice on medicine, recipes, planting, and harvesting to discussions of politics and religion. The almanacs also contained selections from the great European writers and many simple maxims urging the farmers to be content with their lot, obedient, respectful, thrifty, and industrious. The farmers also received some intellectual stimulation from public meetings and from Sunday sermons.

Education in the towns. The ordinary townspeople—owners of small shops, artisans, longshoremen, fishermen, and others—had more opportunities than the farmers or frontiersmen to secure an education. By the 1700's, in addition to the regular schools, an increasing number of private evening schools taught mathematics, accounting, modern languages, and other subjects useful to a man interested in business.

■ Phillis Wheatley was born in Africa and raised as a slave in Massachusetts. She received some education, unlike most slaves, and became one of the best-known poets of colonial New England.

i New England school children were often taught to read by means of a "hornbook." Pictured above, the hornbook contained a sheet of printed matter set in a frame and covered with transparent horn.

Townspeople could also obtain reading material more easily than farmers or frontiersmen. They had Bibles, almanacs, a few books, pamphlets, and, by the 1700's, a growing number of newspapers. People who could not afford to buy the newspapers could always read them or hear them read at a nearby tavern. The papers contained news, sermons, and articles contributed by readers. The townsmen also picked up news and ideas from public meetings, informal gatherings at the taverns, and debating societies that they sometimes organized. In these ways, many colonial townsmen learned to think for themselves and to express their opinions.

Victory for a free press. From the earliest days many colonial leaders disliked anything that threatened the respect that they felt the ordinary people owed them. These leaders believed that it was dangerous to educate men and women or allow them to read freely. This point of view was expressed by William Berkeley, governor of Virginia, who once boasted that while he was governor, Virginia had neither free schools nor printing presses.

Many colonists held a directly opposite point of view. They believed that people should be free to learn, to think, and to express their opinions. They also believed that printers should be free to print and distribute their own thoughts and the thoughts of others. Many colonists believed that a newspaper should be allowed to print the truth even if the truth offended the governing authorities.

One colonial printer, John Peter Zenger, was arrested in 1734 for publishing newspaper articles that criticized the royal governor of New York. Under British law, this made him guilty of criminal libel, even if his criticisms were true.

Fortunately for Zenger, he was defended by one of the ablest lawyers in America, Andrew Hamilton. Hamilton told the jury that, in deciding Zenger's case, they would be deciding the fate of every free man in the British colonies. Hamilton's plea won the day. The jury found John Peter Zenger innocent.

Zenger's victory in 1735 marked a long step forward toward freedom of the press. From this beginning in colonial times, freedom of speech and freedom of the press have developed into two of the strongest roots of the democratic way of life.

SECTION SURVEY

IDENTIFY: freedom of speech, public schools; Phillis Wheatley, John Peter Zenger.

1. (a) What Old World ideas about education did the colonists bring with them to the New World? (b) In what ways did conditions in the New World help to change these ideas?
2. Why was the Massachusetts education law of 1647 a landmark in the history of education?
3. Why was the trial of John Peter Zenger a step forward toward freedom of the press?
4. Why would you consider Phillis Wheatley's educational experience unique?
5. What is meant by the statement that free public education, paid for with government funds, is one of the strongest roots of democracy?

3 The growing experience of the colonists in self-government

In their colonial governments, as well as in religion and education, the colonists fought for more freedom. During their struggle, they gained experience in politics and firmly planted the roots of representative government.

Virginia led the way in 1619, as you have read, by creating the House of Burgesses. The House of Burgesses gave Virginia the first representative government in the New World. It also provided an example for the other colonies established by England along the Atlantic seaboard.

Types of colonial governments. England established three types of colonies in America: (1) royal colonies administered by the English government, (2) proprietary colonies belonging to proprietors, and (3) self-governing colonies largely independent of English control. Each colony had a governor, a council, and a representative assembly.

In a royal colony—and by the 1760's eight of the thirteen colonies were royal colonies—the governor and his councilors were appointed by the king. They administered the laws, sat as a high court of justice, and acted as the upper house of the legislature. The lower house, or assembly, was elected by the qualified voters. Although the lower house helped to make the laws, the king or his representative could veto its actions.

In proprietary colonies—including, by the 1760's, Maryland, Pennsylvania, and Delaware—the proprietor was granted a large amount of power by the king of England. The proprietor, who usually lived in England, appointed the governor and, in the case of Maryland, the councilors who formed the upper house of the legislature. The lower house was elected by the voters, just as in the eight royal colonies. Pennsylvania's legislature had only one house—the assembly.

The two remaining colonies, Rhode Island and Connecticut, were self-governing. Each was almost completely independent of England. The voters elected the governor and the representatives in both the upper and lower houses of the legislature.

Connecticut's written constitution. Connecticut was the first colony to adopt a *written constitution.*°

° *written constitution:* Some constitutions, like the Constitution of the United States, are in the form of a single written document. Other constitutions, like that of Great Britain, are referred to as unwritten because the principles of government are not listed in a single document.

This constitution, or plan of government, was known as the Fundamental Orders of Connecticut. As you have seen, it was adopted in 1639, only three years after Thomas Hooker and his fellow settlers arrived on the banks of the Connecticut River. Its eleven "orders" provided a detailed guide for organizing the government and electing government officials.

With the adoption of the Fundamental Orders, the Connecticut settlers established a government under written law. When disputes arose, the written law, not the opinions of the members of the legislature, provided the guide for deciding the issues. This principle of government under a written constitution became one of the cornerstones of American representative government.

It is important to remember, however, that none of the colonists, including the colonists of Connecticut, were thinking of what we call democracy. The idea of a representative assembly had already been established in England with the House of Commons, the lower house of Parliament. In organizing their representative assemblies, the colonists were simply following the British example. Thomas Hooker and his followers wrote the Fundamental Orders because they had to solve the immediate problem of how to govern themselves in a new community, and this seemed to be the best way to solve it.

Limitations on self-government. Regardless of the reason, the fact remains that many colonists had a voice in the government of the British colonies in North America. But in the colonies, as in England at that time, the voice was still a limited one.

The right to vote, or the *suffrage,* was limited in several ways. In the first place, only adult males

---

LIVING AMERICAN DOCUMENTS

Fundamental Orders of Connecticut (1639)

It is ordered . . . that there shall be yearly two general assemblies or courts: . . . The first shall be called the Court of Election. . . .

It is ordered . . . that no person be chosen governor above once in two years. . . .

It is ordered . . . that to the aforesaid Court of Election the several towns shall send their deputies. . . .

■ Above, Thomas Hooker and his followers are shown on their way to Connecticut. A few years after reaching their destination, they adopted the Fundamental Orders of Connecticut.

who owned a specified amount of property could vote. To vote, a man had to prove that he owned a farm or town lot of a certain size or that he had an income and paid taxes of a certain amount. These *property qualifications* existed even in the self-governing colonies of Connecticut and Rhode Island.

In the second place, *religious qualifications* kept many people from voting. In many colonies, particularly during the 1600's, men who did not belong to the established state church could not vote.

Negro slaves were not permitted to vote in any of the colonies.

In addition to the people who were not permitted to vote, many who might have voted never bothered to do so. Some of these people had never enjoyed political rights in the Old World. When they came to the colonies, they did not concern themselves with political problems, but were content to leave them to men of greater wealth and education. Finally, the isolation of frontier life kept many frontiersmen from voting and from otherwise participating in the government.

To be elected to the colonial assemblies, a man had to meet even higher qualifications than he did to vote. These qualifications varied from colony to colony. In South Carolina, for example, an assemblyman had to own 500 acres of land and 10 slaves, or own land, houses, and other property worth a substantial sum of money. Because of these qualifications, the representatives elected to the colonial assemblies generally were men of wealth and influence.

The struggle over the assemblies. Many ordinary people in the colonies quite naturally resented the concentration of political power in the hands of the well-to-do. Their resentment led to occasional outbreaks of violence.

This conflict between the well-to-do and the ordinary people, most of whom were farmers, is sometimes referred to as the conflict between the seaboard and the frontier. The wealthy people on the seaboard—great planters, rich town merchants, and influential lawyers—controlled the assemblies and tended to vote for laws that protected their own interests. The ordinary people—wage earners, farmers, and frontiersmen—had only a limited voice in the assemblies. They had few legal ways to pass laws that they wanted or to protect themselves from laws that harmed their interests.

Bacon's Rebellion. In Virginia in 1676 the conflict between the well-to-do and the ordinary people erupted into an outbreak of violence known as Bacon's Rebellion.

For many years the frontiersmen and small farmers of Virginia had been dissatisfied with the rule of Governor Berkeley. The farmers and frontiersmen claimed that they, the ordinary people, were not adequately represented in the colonial legislature. They complained that taxes were high and the price of tobacco was low. They further claimed that Governor Berkeley and the wealthy planters had deliberately refused to crush an Indian uprising, not wishing to anger the Indians, with whom many planters carried on a profitable fur trade.

When settlers in the outlying regions of Virginia were massacred by Indians, small farmers, led by an upper-class settler, Nathaniel Bacon, took matters into their own hands. Several hundred men marched to the frontier and killed more than 150 Indians. They then turned upon the rulers of the colony, seized Jamestown, gained control of the legislature, and passed laws favorable to the ordinary people.

Bacon's Rebellion was short-lived. When Nathaniel Bacon died a few months later, Berkeley and the great planters recovered power and crushed what was left of the resistance.

The need for local government. Out of their long struggle for control of the colonial legislatures, the colonists acquired practical experience in politics. It was in their local governments, however, especially in the communities of New England, that the colonists enjoyed the greatest opportunity to practice self-government.

From the very beginning every colonial community, large or small, had to establish rules, or laws, to carry on the everyday affairs of community life. In many early communities, defense against Indian attack was one of the most serious problems. All the communities also faced problems of fire and police protection, sanitation, schooling, the settlement of disputes between citizens, and many other practical matters.

No one questioned the need for local government. However, all the colonists had to answer one big question. Who would make and enforce the local laws?

Local government in New England. The Pilgrims anticipated this question even before they set foot in New England. As you have read (pages 26–27), in writing the Mayflower Compact, the Pilgrims took part in making an agreement under which they were to live.

After they settled at Plymouth, using the Mayflower Compact as their guide, the Pilgrims established a form of local government that was later adopted by other New England communities. This new form of local government came to be called the *town meeting.*

On town meeting days most citizens gathered in the town hall to discuss town problems, levy taxes on themselves, and elect town officers. The discussions sometimes became heated, for every citizen had the right to say what he thought.

The principal town officers were the "selectmen," usually three in number, who administered the laws that the voters adopted in the town meeting. Only the men voted, and in the early days the right to vote was limited by religious and property qualifications. Nevertheless, the New England town meetings provided larger opportunities to participate in government than citizens enjoyed in either the Middle or the Southern Colonies.

Local government in the other colonies. The town meeting type of government met the needs of people living in the compact farming villages and towns of New England. In the Southern Colonies, where most people lived on large plantations or on more or less isolated farms, local government

■ One hundred years before the American Revolution occurred, Nathanial Bacon and his followers rebelled against the colonial government in Virginia. But Bacon's Rebellion was short-lived.

had to cover a much larger area than a town. In the Southern Colonies, therefore, the people established the *county* as the unit of local government. Some southern counties covered several hundred square miles.

The chief officers of the county were the justices of the peace. These officers administered the laws, acted as judges in legal disputes, levied and collected taxes, provided for roads, and distributed county funds to widows, orphans, and other people who could not take care of themselves. A county lieutenant was responsible for defending the county against Indian uprisings and against serious disturbances by the colonists. These officers were usually appointed by the governor, but he chose them from people living in the county itself.

The Middle Colonies adopted a mixture of both the town and the county type of local government. In New York the town was generally the unit of local government. In Pennsylvania the county type of local government was more important.

Growing spirit of independence. The local governments, regardless of the type, dealt with everyday problems of immediate concern to the people. Therefore, most citizens received their first lessons in self-government at the local level. And, as you will see, the experience and confidence that they gained in local and colonial government strengthened their desire to exercise more control over the royal and proprietary governors.

SECTION SURVEY

IDENTIFY: Fundamental Orders, Bacon's Rebellion, suffrage, local government, town meeting, county; 1639.

1. Among the three types of colonial government, which would give the colonists more experience in self-government? Why?
2. Why is government under a written constitution considered a cornerstone of American representative government?
3. (a) What were the causes of Bacon's Rebellion? (b) Why did the frontiersmen and small farmers resort to violence? (c) Did they have an alternative? Explain.
4. There were many undemocratic practices in colonial America. Ilustrate this fact by referring to restrictions on voting and office holding.
5. Explain how the colonists, in organizing their representative assemblies, were simply following the British example.

4 The increasing power of colonial legislative assemblies

The struggle for a larger voice in the colonial governments was only one continuing conflict of the colonial period. In the royal colonies, as you have seen, the British king appointed the governors and the councilors; in the proprietary colonies the British proprietors appointed the governors and councilors. Except in the self-governing colonies of Rhode Island and Connecticut, then, the colonial governments were really split into two parts. In general, the governor and the councilors usually served the interests of the British empire as a whole. The assemblies, on the other hand, represented the interests of the colonists.

Attitude of British officials. Because of this divided control, political controversy in the colonies often centered on the royal governors. Most governors were selected from the ruling group in Great Britain—politicians, lawyers, and soldiers—although now and then the Crown ° appointed a favored or privileged colonist as governor.

In making appointments to the royal colonies, the Crown did not necessarily look for men with ability. Sometimes the king awarded the position to his friends and favorites. Some royal governors were excellent administrators who tried to balance British and colonial interests. A few were narrow-minded, shortsighted men who had few qualifications, by training or experience, for the offices they held.

But whether good, bad, or indifferent, most of the governors used their positions to increase their own fortunes. Many men were willing to pay handsomely to secure the jobs.

The military officers and clerks who served the royal governors were, as a rule, no better than their superiors. They were often appointed merely because they happened to be friends of the governor or his family. Such practices were common in Great Britain as well as in the colonies.

We should remember, however, that many able men held positions of authority in the colonies. We should also remember that the colonies, which enjoyed the advantage of being part of a growing British empire, owed a great deal to the mother country.

° *the Crown:* the king or the power of the king, in this case the king of Great Britain.

84

■ This old woodcut shows the Virginia House of Burgesses meeting in 1619. In what way were colonial assemblies such as this one an important step toward American independence?

Growing power of the assemblies. As representatives of the government of England, the royal officials naturally stressed the royal point of view. The majority of colonists, speaking through their representatives in the assemblies, held the opposite point of view. Why, they asked, should they pay taxes to furnish high salaries to countless outsiders from Great Britain, many of whom were lazy and incompetent? And what right had anybody to say that the interests of the colonists were less important than the interests of the British in the mother country?

Fortunately for the colonists, they had one extremely powerful weapon that helped curb the authority of the royal governors. The colonists controlled the purse strings. That is, the colonial assemblies had the power to vote all grants of money to be spent by the colonial governments.

Suppose the governor asked for money to pay the salaries of nine new clerks he wanted to appoint. The assembly could immediately say, "Yes, we'll grant you the money—provided you allow us to name the men you appoint." Or suppose the governor requested money to pay his official expenses. The assembly could say, "Yes, we'll grant the money—provided you *first* submit a statement explaining in detail how you will spend the money."

Sometimes the assemblies refused to grant funds to pay the governors' salaries until the end of each year. In this way, the colonists served notice upon the governors that they would do well to rule wisely. "Let us keep the dogs poor," one member of the New Jersey legislature remarked disrespectfully, "and we'll make them do what we please."

The governors hated these limitations upon their power, but they could not do much about them. They needed money to carry on the everyday business of the colonies and they wanted good salaries for themselves. This money could come only from the assemblies. Even before the Revolutionary War, the colonial assemblies were practically their own masters. They had, to a considerable extent, already won their freedom from British control.

SECTION SURVEY

1. Explain this statement: Due to a conflict of interests, colonial governments were split into two parts.
2. Why did political conflict in the colonies center on the authority of the royal governors?
3. How does control of the "purse strings" limit the power of political officials?

85

TRACING THE MAIN IDEAS

The first small roots of democracy found fertile soil in the British seaboard colonies. The colonists brought with them from Europe the idea of society built on a class system. They accepted, at first, the Old World restrictions on individual freedom in religion, education, and the right to vote and hold government office. But the colonists' discontent against these restrictions began to grow—slowly during the early years of colonization, then more rapidly.

Stimulated by the growth of freedom in England itself and even more by the environment of the New World, the settlers began to demand more freedom for themselves. During the course of their struggles, they gained practical experience in politics and self-government. In Europe, power tended to rest with monarchs or to be shared with a narrowly based parliament. By contrast, power in the colonies tended to be less concentrated and more fully shared by many more people. Far from the English throne, but sharing in the English heritage of freedom, the colonists developed their own principles of religious toleration, free public education, and representative government.

As you will see in Chapter 6, the colonists in the process of developing their own way of life had grown much further away from Great Britain than the British realized. This lack of understanding led to controversies, and finally, in 1775, to armed conflict.

CHAPTER SURVEY

QUESTIONS FOR DISCUSSION

1. The environment of the colonies gradually caused changes in the ideas and ways of life brought over from the Old World. Compare and discuss Old World ideas and New World ideas concerning religion, education, and representative government.
2. What connections can you see between the answer to question one and the spirit of independence that led to the American Revolution?
3. Compare education on the colonial frontier with education in colonial towns.
4. During the colonial period many Negroes were excluded from Christianity. Was this religious discrimination ultimately useful in maintaining slavery? Explain.
5. Are we in the United States still engaged in the process of furthering the democratic ideas and practices which were first developed during America's colonial period? Cite evidence to support your views.

RELATING PAST TO PRESENT

1. Which of America's current democratic practices can be traced to colonial ideas and institutions?
2. Does geography today affect the kind of local government found in various areas of the United States as much as it did during the colonial period? Explain.

USING MAPS AND CHARTS

1. Geographic differences between the Piedmont and seaboard areas in the Southern Colonies led to political differences. Explain this statement using the maps on pages 31 and 852–53 for reference.
2. What is the relationship between the geography of a colony and the colony's (a) settlement, (b) provisions for education, and (c) form of local self-government?

UNIT SURVEY

FOR FURTHER INQUIRY

1. If Columbus had not "rediscovered" America, it was inevitable that another explorer would have. Why?

2. From 1607 to 1760, certain forces were evolving in the colonies that (a) increased the colonists' spirit of independence and (b) weakened their ties with England. Discuss how (a) and (b) interacted; for example, how would an increase in the spirit of independence further weaken the ties with England, and how would a weakening of the ties with England further increase the spirit of independence? Then explain how each of the following contributed to the growing spirit of independence in the colonies: (a) reasons for coming to the New World, (b) geography—distance from England, (c) seeds of colonial democracy, (d) New World environment, (e) "salutary neglect," (f) colonial unity.

3. Do you think there is a contradiction between the existence of social classes in the colonies and the idea that the colonies were a "melting pot"? Explain.

4. How does protection of the rights of one religious group help to protect the rights of all religious groups?

5. By the end of the colonial period, the black colonist, slave or free, was virtually "closed out" from white society by discriminatory practices sanctioned by various established institutions in colonial America. (a) What were these institutions? (b) How did they prevent black Americans from being integrated into white colonial society?

PROJECTS AND ACTIVITIES

1. Prepare a talk or paper on the technological changes that enabled the period of exploration to take place when it did.

2. Describe a day in the life of a teenager in a colony of your choice.

3. Read Benjamin Franklin's *Autobiography*. Discuss why you think it has survived as a historical document.

4. Prepare a project on the art of colonial times. Discuss techniques or commentary on artists of the period (such as Charles Willson Peale, John Singleton Copley, and Benjamin West).

5. Prepare a photo history of your community using family photos, church records, and municipal collections.

6. Prepare a research project on the musical contributions made to American culture by the American Indians, Africans, or some other group.

7. Prepare a time line for classroom display covering the period 1450 to 1763. Above the line, using drawings or pictures for illustrations, insert important events in the American colonies; below the line, insert items of your own selection, such as biographical sketches, important events in Europe, or inventions.

8. Using maps of the United States, see how many cities, rivers, and mountains you can locate that have names that are French, Spanish, Dutch, or Indian. A translation of these names might also be of interest.

USING THE SOCIAL SCIENCES

(Read pages 89–98 before you answer the following questions.)

1. What is meant by social control?

2. What is the function of social control? In what areas of one's life is social control needed? Who decides this? Why?

3. What is the relationship between social control and the aims of a society?

4. On what *authority* did the Puritans base their ideas of social control? On what authority is social control in American society based today?

5. What challenges to social control arose in the Puritan community? What challenges to social control are present in American society today?

SUGGESTED FURTHER READING

General Reference Books

The following books may be useful throughout the study of American history.

ADAMS, JAMES T., *Album of American History*, Scribner, 6 vols. Pictorial.
——, *Atlas of American History*, Scribner, 11 vols.
——, *Dictionary of American History*, Scribner, 6 vols.

BAILEY, THOMAS A. *The American Spirit: United States History as Seen by Contemporaries,* Heath, 2 vols. A collection of readings about personalities and ideas chronologically presented. Maps, introductions, thought provokers, and bibliographies.

BUTTERFIELD, ROGER PLACE, *The American Past,* Simon and Schuster. Pictorial.

COCHRAN, THOMAS C., and WAYNE ANDREWS, *Concise Dictionary of American History,* Scribner.

COMMAGER, HENRY STEELE, ed. *Documents of American History,* Appleton-Century-Crofts, 2 vols. Comprehensive primary sources, with editorial annotations.

HACKER, LOUIS, *Major Documents in American Economic History,* Van Nostrand (Anvil Books), 2 vols. Each reading is placed in historical context by means of an introduction.

HOFSTADTER, RICHARD, *Great Issues in American History,* Random House (Vintage Books), 2 vols. Political issues debated in contemporary documents.

MORRIS, RICHARD, *The Encyclopedia of American History* (Revised Edition), Harper & Row. Valuable for ready reference.

———, *Great Presidential Decisions,* Lippincott. Primary sources with background material.

MUGRIDGE, DONALD H., and BLANCHE E. MC CRUM, *A Guide to the Study of the United States of America: Representative Books Reflecting the Development of American Life and Thought,* Government Printing Office.

STARR, ISIDORE, L. P. TODD, and M. CURTI, *Living American Documents,* Harcourt Brace Jovanovich. Selected primary sources.

Biography

GALT, THOMAS, *John Peter Zenger,* Thomas Y. Crowell.

LEIGHTON, MARGARET, *The Sword and the Compass,* Houghton Mifflin. About John Smith.

MILLER, PERRY, *Roger Williams and His Contribution to the American Tradition,* Atheneum (paper).

MORISON, SAMUEL ELIOT, *Admiral of the Ocean Sea,* Little, Brown. About Columbus.

ROBINSON, HENRY MORTON, *Stout Cortez,* Century House.

WOOD, WILLIAM C., *Elizabethan Sea Dogs,* Yale Univ. Press.

Other Nonfiction

ACHESON, PATRICIA, *America's Colonial Heritage.* Dodd, Mead. The conditions, problems, and developments that changed dependent settlements into independent colonies ready for revolution.

ADAMS, JAMES TRUSLOW, *The Founding of New England,* Little, Brown (paper).

ANGLE, PAUL M., ed. *A New Continent and a New Nation,* Fawcett (Premier Books, paper). Excerpts

from contemporary letters, diaries, and newspaper stories from 1492 to 1789.

BOLAND, CHARLES, *They All Discovered America,* Pocket Books (Permabooks, paper). Nineteen different explorations of America that predated Columbus' discovery.

COLLIER, JOHN, *Indians of the Americas,* New American Library (Mentor Books).

CRANE, VERNER W., *The Southern Frontier, 1670–1732,* University of Michigan Press (Ann Arbor Paperbacks).

DIAMOND, SIGMUND, ed. *The Creation of Society in the New World.* Rand McNally. Contemporary views of colonial Virginia and New England.

DRIVER, HAROLD E., ed. *The Americas on the Eve of Discovery,* Prentice-Hall (Spectrum Books, paper). Descriptions of American Indian cultures by early European explorers and modern scholars.

FISHER, SYDNEY, *Quaker Colonies,* Yale Univ. Press.

GOODWIN, MAUD, *Dutch and English on the Hudson,* Yale Univ. Press.

HORGAN, PAUL, *Conquistadores in North American History,* Farrar, Straus.

JOHNSTON, MARY, *Pioneers of the Old South,* Yale Univ. Press.

LANGDON, WILLIAM C., *Everyday Things in American Life,* Scribner.

LEVY, LEONARD W., *Freedom of Speech and Press in Early American History: Legacy of Suppression,* Harper & Row (paper).

MATTINGLY, GARRETT, *The Armada,* Houghton Mifflin.

NOTESTEIN, WALLACE, *The English People on the Eve of Colonization, 1603–1630,* Harper & Row (paper).

PARKMAN, FRANCIS, *The Parkman Reader.* Edited by Samuel Eliot Morison, Little, Brown. Selected from classic work on French-English conflict in North America.

QUARLES, BENJAMIN, *The Negro in the Making of America,* Macmillan (Collier Books). Up-to-date survey by an eminent black historian of the Negro's history in the United States.

Historical Fiction

CATHER, WILLA, *Shadows on the Rock,* Knopf. Colonial life in French Canada.

FORBES, ESTHER, *Mirror for Witches,* Houghton Mifflin.

HAWTHORNE, NATHANIEL, *The House of the Seven Gables,* Macmillan; and others.

———, *The Scarlet Letter,* Dodd, Mead; and others. Psychological novel of early Massachusetts.

IRVING, WASHINGTON, *Knickerbocker's History of New York,* Ungar.

ROBERTS, KENNETH, *Northwest Passage,* Doubleday.

SANDBURG, CARL, *Remembrance Rock,* Harcourt Brace Jovanovich. Book I is about the Pilgrims.

INTRODUCTION

HISTORY AND THE SOCIAL SCIENCES

The objective of history and of the social sciences—which include sociology, geography, economics, political science, and anthropology—is to learn about human societies and to throw light on the behavior of human beings as individuals and in groups.

The best way to try to understand how history and the social sciences go about this task is to imagine that each of them represents a different "lens" through which scholars look at human societies, both past and present. Each of these lenses throws light on a different aspect of human life and human behavior.

A sociologist, for example, is interested in investigating the social behavior of the various groups that make up society. An anthropologist studies the cultural behavior of various peoples all over the globe. A political scientist studies political behavior—how people set up institutions of government and how power is exercised in various societies throughout the world. An economist investigates the economic behavior of people in various societies and how they go about allocating and using their natural resources. A geographer, as social scientist, studies the world as the environment and home of man. A historian studies the record of man's past and tries to reconstruct past events and problems.

To put it yet another way, historians and social scientists ask different kinds of questions about the data, information, and evidence they assemble and about the phenomena they observe and study. When pieced together, the answers obtained from the questions posed and the information gathered through these various lenses enable us to better understand the behavior of nations, groups, and individuals. It is hoped that this knowledge can then be used for the betterment of human life.

Similarities and Differences

A historian is a social scientist because he uses scientific methods in his inquiry into the past. Historical investigations can usually be divided into three stages. In the first one, the research stage, the historian, like the social scientist, methodically collects his data, which may include artifacts, documents, letters, and diaries. In the second stage, the stage of analysis and interpretation, the historian also acts in a manner similar to that of the social scientist, subjecting his data to thorough testing and scrutiny, often comparing evidence from a variety of source materials. After this examining and testing of the evidence, the historian generally arrives at some tentative hypothesis about the historical problems or periods under study.

It is in the third stage of the historian's work, the stage of writing, that the paths of the historian and the social scientist take somewhat different turns. In the third stage the historian sets out to express his findings in a coherent and meaningful narrative. If his study concerns, for example, the Battle of Gettysburg, he does all he can to be as scientific and as objective as possible in describing the facts about what happened during this decisive battle in history. But in describing the complex natures of the two leaders, General Lee and General Meade, he also must use his psychological insights, and he must use his creative imagination in describing the battle itself. Thus, in this stage of his work, the historian, unlike the social scientist, becomes an artist as well as a scientist.

In addition, the historian writing about the Battle of Gettysburg, which marked a fateful turning point in the Civil War, must express value judgments

The Battle of Gettysburg

about the decisions taken by the commanders of the opposing forces. In other words, he assesses blame and gives praise where, in his subjective judgment, blame and praise are due. Social scientists, on the other hand, in pursuing their investigations, take great pains never to allow their own value judgments or subjective preferences to influence their inquiries in any way.

Another difference between history and the social sciences is that while social scientists attempt as a rule to make broad generalizations that throw light on some general, predictable aspects of human behavior, historians usually avoid generalizations. The historian writing about the Battle of Gettysburg, for example, a specific and concrete event in the story of man, would hesitate to generalize from this battle about other great battles in history. The reason for this is obvious. There are so many complex variables, or factors subject to change, in each historical event that broad historical generalizations would tend to be invalid and thus would be quite useless.

However, while the differences between history and the social sciences should be kept in mind, it must also be emphasized that collaboration between historians and social scientists has been growing steadily. Historians have recognized that insights, research findings, and modes of inquiry from the social sciences can be of invaluable help in illuminating many issues in history. Social scientists, on the other hand, find that historical knowledge and historical perspective are indispensable to many of their investigations.

Margaret Mead, the anthropologist, in speaking of the growing cooperation between history and anthropology, points out that, traditionally, "historians and anthropologists have been distinguished from one another by the materials which they have studied; the historian dealing with the past and the anthropologist with primitive peoples. This distinction is fast becoming obsolete, for both are turning their attention to contemporary problems of the great civilizations of the world—including our own."

Margaret Mead also suggests that another unique and unifying feature shared by history and anthropology is the loving preservation of detail. On the other hand, Martin Duberman, a distinguished young historian, argues that historians may be too interested in details and should become more interested in a broader analysis of issues. Historians must not, he states, allow their love of detail and the concrete to obscure the fact that lessons learned from the past can be applied to current social issues challenging mankind. He added: "No bit of information is too small to be worth having when used creatively as part of a larger mosaic, but all too frequently detail is elaborated in vacua, the dead specifics of past action tirelessly rehearsed for themselves alone, without reference to a broader framework which might rescue them from antiquarianism."

Case Studies in History and the Social Sciences

In the case studies presented in this textbook, we have endeavored to illuminate some important issues and periods in American history, using insights, concepts, and special modes of inquiry from both history and the social sciences.

The case studies in the social sciences concern a variety of human problems. In the case study on the Puritan community (page 96), a sociologist examines the social behavior of the Puritans living in Massachusetts Bay Colony. In the case study on the frontier (page 460), a geographer considers the evidence picturing the American frontier as a unique and definable region.

An economist, in his case study on scarcity, silver, and surplus (page 526), attempts to throw new light on the economic problems faced by Americans in the late 1800's during the period of the gold and silver controversy. A political scientist in his case study on big city political party "machines" (page 568) analyzes the city "bosses" and "machine" organizations that tended to dominate urban politics in the late 1800's and early 1900's.

In the case study dealing with immigration (page 678), an anthropologist attempts to describe and analyze the process of cultural change that accompanies the adjustment of immigrants to a dominant society. She chose a community of Greek-Americans in Chicago to illuminate her study.

Each of the case studies in history centers around a "case" or a special problem in American history which has been the subject of lively controversy among historians. For instance, historians have debated the questions of whether the Founding Fathers were motivated by private interests or by a sincere desire to act for the good of the nation (page 208), whether Jacksonian democracy was a myth or a reality (page 280), and whether the abolitionists were sincere fighters for human freedom or troublemaking fanatics (page 350). Historians have also recently re-examined the role of the black community in contributing to the cause of its own liberation during the Civil War (page 398), the debate between those favoring American expansion and those opposing it at the time of the Spanish-American War (page 622), the nature and legacy of the far-reaching changes wrought in American society by the New Deal (page 750), and the operation of the American decision-making process in times of crisis—in this case, the Cuban missile crisis of October 1962 (page 846).

Considered together, the case studies seem to confirm our premise that students of history can benefit a great deal from pooling the insights provided by the various social sciences. It should be added that the historian then tries to comprehend the total experience being studied and attempts to put it in some historical sequence and perspective.

One excellent example of a fruitful collaboration between history and the social sciences is a small but important book by Professor David Potter, entitled *The People of Plenty*. Potter set out to try to understand the concept of the American national character. What, he asked, are the basic components that make up the character of the American people?

Various social scientists gave different answers. Some questioned the validity of the idea of national character, but others found it a useful analytical concept. Margaret Mead, the anthropologist, isolated "mobility" and the "success drive" as the main components of the American character. David Riesman, the sociologist, said the answer lay in the great concern Americans have for the opinions and approval of their peer groups and neighbors—the "desire to keep up with the Joneses." Karen Horney, the distinguished psychologist and psychiatrist, stressed "competition" and "aggression" as the main characteristics of American culture.

Potter, the historian, then searched for one factor which would account for each of the separate components of the American character mentioned by these social scientists. Finally, he advanced the theory that "economic abundance," or affluence, was the single most important factor which has shaped the American national character. He argued that the fact that Americans have been and are the "people of plenty" explains the traits of "mobility" and "drive for success," the "desire to keep up with the Joneses," as well as the spirit of "competition" and "aggression."

Potter's book is a brilliant and largely successful example of how the insights and lenses—of both the historian and the social scientist—can be used to study problems of common concern to history and the social sciences.

Newly arrived immigrants in 1910

SOCIOLOGY

Nature of Sociology

Except perhaps for a few hermits, human beings everywhere live in groups. Sociologists want to find out about these groups—how they are set up and how they operate. Sociologists inquire not only into the structure of groups, but also into how members of any group behave. Sociology, then, is that branch of the social sciences devoted to the study of society in general and of groups in society in particular.

In their study of various groups in society, sociologists do not look for unique behavior or bizarre customs. Rather, they search for broad generalizations, for patterns of similarity, in a particular society or in particular groups in society. Suppose, for example, that in studying the American family group a sociologist finds a family in which the children are the breadwinners, earning the family's total income by performing as professional entertainers. Such a family would not be typical of the large majority of American families in which the father or mother or both are the breadwinners. The sociologist could not make a broad or accurate generalization about the American family by studying one such isolated case.

In studying the groups that make up human society, sociologists have found that some groups, such as the nation, the tribe, or the family, are permanent and seem to endure. Sociologists have found that in a modern industrial society like the United States relatively permanent groups include the family, the school, and the corporation. Sociologists are interested in studying these groups and the interaction among them, as well as their impact on American society as a whole. But sociologists also study groups that exist only briefly, then change or even disappear; for example, such groups as the Committee to Preserve the Redwoods or a group organized to work for the abolition of the death penalty in a particular state. Sociologists want to know how and why these groups are formed and how and why they change. Social change, then, is a subject of major interest to sociologists.

Sociologists also study the relationships between groups that are in conflict. For example, sociologists might investigate the relationship between railroad unions, representing labor, and the American Association of Railroads, representing management or the owners of the railroads. Sociologists also study relationships among members within a group. In the case of a labor union, for example, sociologists might study how union members are affected by changes in their environment or economic status. Do union members work harder under more pleasant working conditions—or does their work output remain the same? Why, as union members become more affluent, do they tend to become more conservative? Why do prosperous union members, for example, generally tend to disapprove of radical protest groups?

Sociologists also study the social behavior of minority groups, such as black Americans, Indians, and people of various ethnic backgrounds. Sociologists want to determine not only how these groups are set up, but also how the members of the groups behave. How do Indians of various tribes reconcile traditional tribal customs with the patterns of life in twentieth-century America? In studying black Americans, sociologists might investigate how life patterns among Negroes in northern cities differ from life patterns among black Americans living in rural areas of the South. How do these patterns affect the images that black Americans have of themselves? And how do these images affect the ways in which black Americans act—among themselves and in relation to white Americans?

How does socialization of Americans take place in the classroom?

In their search for a general theory of social behavior, some sociologists have examined entire societies in selected towns. In 1941, for instance, W. Lloyd Warner published a famous study called *Yankee City*. In this book, Warner described the class structure of an entire New England town which he and his associates had studied. Warner asserted that the inhabitants of "Yankee City" could be divided into six social classes—lower-lower, upper-lower, lower-middle, upper-middle, lower-upper, and upper-upper. Warner also contended that the inhabitants recognized themselves as belonging to one of these groups. Finally Warner made a broad generalization and concluded that the class structure of "Yankee City" applied to American society as a whole. Today, however, many sociologists no longer agree with Warner's analysis of class structure in America. They contend that his findings apply only to small towns, not to cities.

Sociologists also study deviant behavior—that is, the behavior of groups which are in conflict with the accepted standards and values of a society. Sociologists have made particularly important contributions in this area by investigating the behavior of criminals, juvenile delinquents, drug addicts, alcoholics, and compulsive gamblers.

Sociologists, then, are interested in describing and explaining the processes and the direction of social change in society. The complexity of life in modern industrial societies has made their task all the more challenging.

Concepts of Sociology

What is a concept? Webster's dictionary defines a concept as an "idea" or "a general notion." The basic concepts in the social sciences, then, are ideas—but ideas that have some general application. To expand the definition even more, we can say that in the social sciences a concept is a fundamental idea that helps to explain how people behave.

A concept in sociology is a fundamental idea that helps explain how people behave socially, or in groups. Many key concepts of sociology throw light on various phases of social behavior. This definition will become clearer as we look at some sociology concepts.

Consider, for instance, the concept of **socialization,** a key concept in sociology. Sociologists study the entire process of socialization; that is, the methods a society uses to transmit its values, its skills, and its accumulated knowledge to its children. Sociologists also examine the methods used to teach children how they are expected to act in various social situations—in school, in church, at home, and at play. How do children learn the behavior expected of them? And how does society evaluate whether or not a child is living up to its standards? These are questions investigated by sociologists.

Socialization is not a process affecting only the young. Adults also experience socialization every time they join a new group and try to adjust to what is expected of them. Adults can react to the pressures of socialization in several ways. Suppose, for example, a family joins a country club. The new members quickly learn that the older members expect them to dress a certain way and follow certain rules of behavior. When the family conforms willingly to these rules, they have chosen **assimilation** as their method of dealing with the expected standards of group behavior. Suppose, however, that members of a group adjust to a new situation unwillingly. Consider the example of young soldiers who dislike Army life, but adjust to it, rather than "buck the system." Sociologists would describe their adjustment as **accommodation.**

Three other methods of dealing with group pressures are **cooperation, competition,** and **conflict.** Consider the example of executives in a large cor-

In what ways does the army exemplify social control?

poration. These men are expected both to cooperate and to compete within their business society. They cooperate because they are working for identical goals imposed by the corporation—bigger sales and higher profits. At the same time, however, the executives compete to attain higher salaries and higher positions. When executives compete actively for the same job, conflict may arise. If the executives compete unfairly, the resulting conflict may be disruptive for the entire corporation.

Sociologists also study the concepts of **role** and **role conflict.** Members of a group are expected to follow certain modes of behavior, called roles. When a person is torn between two different sets of expectations in trying to fulfill what is expected of him, sociologists say that he is experiencing a role conflict. For example, consider a high school athletic coach who is also a classroom history teacher. The teacher-coach may experience a role conflict when the star of his football team fails his history examination. Similarly, a worker who has been promoted to foreman may undergo an acute role conflict because his loyalty to his fellow workers conflicts with his new responsibility to management.

Another important concept in sociology is **social control.** Social control is the power and authority that society exercises over its members; for example, a state's authority over its citizens or a principal's control over his students. In these examples, society exercises its control quite openly. Sociologists, however, have found that social control is sometimes exercised just as effectively by more subtle means, such as group pressures, gossip and ridicule, or veiled threats of ostracizing a member if he does not conform.

Two other important concepts in sociology are **status** and **social class.** Society not only assigns certain roles to individuals, it also evaluates these roles. The ranking of roles is called status. For example, the status of a Senator in Washington, D.C., society is invariably higher than that of a member of the House of Representatives. People who enjoy the same status are said to form a social class.

Sociologists also study the concept of **social mobility.** In American society, the distinction between classes is not static. Members of one class move up and down from one class into another. This is called social mobility. Southern slaveowners in the 1850's used social mobility as a powerful weapon for maintaining social control over their slaves. Members of the privileged class of house servants were kept under control by the constant threat that they could be moved down to the lowlier status of field hands. On the other hand, slaves in the fields often worked harder and endured harsh discipline in hopes of being promoted to the higher status of house servants. In uncovering these aspects of slave life, historians have used the concepts of sociology to throw light on particular events in history.

Methods of Sociology

Sociologists claim, with some justice, that they originated and refined the basic methods of inquiry and investigation now used in the social sciences. When a political scientist studies voting behavior, for example, he depends on sampling, polling, and interviewing. These are scientific methods of inquiry developed and refined by sociologists. On the other hand, sociologists often use mathematical and statistical methods developed by economists. The social sciences, then, although they differ greatly in the questions they ask of their data, do not differ greatly in their methods of investigation.

Sociologists depend mainly on empirical research; that is, their method of investigation is based on first-hand observation. A sociologist embarking on a research project begins by identifying the problem to be solved. Then he gathers pertinent data about the group or groups to be studied. After gathering this background information, the sociologist forms a hypothesis—a tentative conclusion or explanation of the problem. Then he selects appropriate groups to study and observes or interviews them to test his hypothesis. Finally, he analyzes his data to find out if his hypothesis has been validated.

In making his inquiries, the sociologist carefully tries to explain the actions of the group he is studying without judging them. He remembers the teaching of Max Weber, the founder of sociology, who warned that sociological research must be value-free. If the sociologist allowed his own personal preferences or biases to intrude upon his investigation, the results of his inquiry would be suspect and lacking in usefulness, as well as in objectivity.

Polling, sampling, and **interviewing** are methods of investigation very popular with sociologists. Sociologists have greatly refined the polling technique by developing methods to assure that the people being polled or questioned truly represent that part of the population whose views are sought. Suppose, for example, that a sociologist wants to determine the attitudes of older Americans toward college demonstrators. He might decide to question a representative sampling of people grouped according to social status, such as professional people, white collar workers, and blue collar workers. Or he might decide to question a cross section of people grouped according to their community residence, such as people living in cities, suburbs, and rural areas. Or he might decide to question people grouped according to age categories: 25 to 35, 36 to 45, 46 to 55, etc. Or he might decide to use a combination of these categories, depending on how he defined the problem to be solved.

In order to avoid sampling errors and errors due to the bias of the interviewers, sociologists developed and refined the technique of **random sampling.** Random sampling works on the principle that the final determination of who is to be polled is left to chance. Since the method is based on tested statistical laws, sociologists can determine the margin of error and discount it.

Sociologists have also greatly improved the use of **questionnaires** and **personal interviews** in collecting their data. Sometimes they develop and use **depth interviews.** Depth interviews are designed not only to determine the opinions of the people interviewed, but also to probe their attitudes, values, and prejudices. For example, a sociologist studying prejudice against certain minority groups might use a depth interview to determine if the people interviewed are telling the complete truth. Some people answering questions on prejudice might try to say what they think is expected of them. For example, if a person is asked if he likes members of a certain ethnic group, he might answer that he does, because he does not want to appear prejudiced. However, he might be harboring a deep dislike against members of that group. Or another person might honestly think that he is not prejudiced. But if faced with a specific situation, such as hiring a person of a certain minority group to work in his office, he might hesitate before acting. Or he might not act at all. A sociologist would use a depth interview to try to uncover all these hidden attitudes and get an accurate picture of prejudice and its effects.

Some sociologists, although not many, use the **historical analysis** technique to study the social behavior of people who lived in past societies, such as early Puritan settlers in New England or early Mormon settlers in Utah. Most sociologists, however, study contemporary social phenomena, which they can observe first hand, study empirically, and analyze statistically. In so doing, they try to contribute to a better understanding of contemporary social issues and problems.

CASE STUDY IN SOCIOLOGY

The Puritan Community

The Puritans who began to arrive in Massachusetts in the summer of 1630 came to practice their own version of the "Godly life." By coming to the New World, they had physically removed themselves from those Englishmen who did not worship God in the same way that they did. In a new, unsettled land, they planned to establish a community in which only the faithful would be allowed to settle; where the Puritans could enforce conformity to their own beliefs. The Puritans distinctly did *not* believe in freedom of religion.

The early settlers of Massachusetts Bay Colony were zealous Puritans who were certain that God's law, as given in the Bible, was an adequate guide to human affairs. They were determined to establish a community dedicated to the will of God. But in the long run, the Puritan experiment did not work. At the heart of the Puritan failure was the problem of **social control**—how to establish authority and maintain uniformity of behavior in their wilderness community. The methods the Puritans used to set up this social control over all members of the community—and why their methods failed—will be the objects of investigation in this case study.

Puritan Methods of Establishing Total Social Control

In America the Puritans intended to establish two great societies composed of the same people—a religious society and a political society. In principle these two societies—church and state—would be separate, but in practice they would be bonded together by rigid, precise rules established for the behavior of the two most important **social classes**—the ministers and the civil magistrates. Although the Puritans taught that their ministers had no special relationship with God denied to the ordinary worshiper, ministers were nevertheless recognized as men of special learning who were exceptionally skilled in explaining and interpreting difficult Biblical passages. Thus the Puritans believed that their ministers had the appropriate qualifications to supervise the daily activities of a people consecrated to God.

Since the Puritans regarded all occupations as holy callings, no occupation was outside the scope of the ministers' supervision. Thus, even though ministers were not eligible to hold civil office, they were expected to advise civil magistrates in state affairs. The civil magistrates, for their part, were expected to make and carry out good laws and to set good examples by leading good, moral lives in obedience to God's law. The magistrates were to have no final authority in religious matters but were to use their civil power if necessary to keep order in the church and to preserve the integrity of religious doctrine and practice. As long as the ministers and the magistrates carried out their roles properly and as long as the people generally respected these roles, an intimate association between church and society would be assured.

Within this overall structure of an intimate relationship between church and state, the Puritan leaders tried to establish total social control over their membership in a variety of ways—both formal and informal. The Puritans believed that men who had pledged themselves to observe the Word of God would by definition conform to the same standards and agree on all important matters of policy. Thus control over the faithful was to be exercised more through instruction and persuasion than through force.

In the Puritan community the family was the basic unit of social control and the most important vehicle for **socialization**—that is, for passing on Puritan values to each new generation. Puritan parents were obliged to make

A Puritan church service

sure that their children and all apprentices living with the family learned to read so that everyone would be able to see for himself what the Bible revealed of God's law. The mother and father disciplined not only their own children but also their servants and any boarders they might take in. To make certain that no one escaped this total control, Puritans were forbidden to live alone. Unmarried men and girls had to place themselves in some family if their own had been left behind. Thus the family was both a unit of early socialization and an important agency for the assimilation of later arrivals.

The role of the family in maintaining social control was supplemented by the role of the church, which had the primary function of instructing the Puritans in moral living. The sermon, which became enormously popular in Puritan Massachusetts, was designed to show how Biblical passages could be applied to everyday living. Although attendance at church was compulsory, the sermon had great drawing power on its own because of the scarcity of other amusements. Attending a sermon offered the Puritans a chance to meet distant neighbors and to exchange news and gossip.

For most Puritans the early socialization provided by the family and the continuing informal control exercised by the church were adequate to make them responsible, practicing members of the congregation. For a few Puritans, however, the discipline of the family and the church proved inadequate. In the cases of such "obstinate sinners," a group of elders would formally admonish the wrongdoers and try to convince them of the error of their ways. Excommunication, the severest punishment available to the church, was reserved for only the most extreme cases. A subtle method of social control, it was a much feared punishment. An excommunicated person was forced to live in virtual isolation. Other members could have nothing to do with him and except in matters essential for defense or safety could not even talk with him.

The Puritan leaders strengthened church control even further by limiting the right to vote in civil elections to those Puritan men who were church members in good standing. In so limiting the suffrage, the Puritan leaders were counting on the ministers to give the people sound advice and instruction concerning the kind of men fitted to rule. This was another important part of the social role of the clergy.

From the point of view of the established Puritan authorities, there was another advantage to this limitation. At a series of conferences, all candidates for church membership were questioned on their beliefs, their understanding of church doctrines, their personal conduct, and their willingness to accept all aspects of community life. Their one hope of gaining the right to vote was to convince the Puritan leaders that they were in hearty sympathy with the established order and could therefore fit into the group with no threat to the community consensus.

Puritan Attempts to Maintain Complete Social Control

For the Puritan community to maintain its identity, the leaders had to maintain total social control. They felt that it was their duty to establish a tight-knit, cohesive community, one that was totally insulated from differing religious points of view. At all times a majority of Puritans had to accept all Puritan ideals and goals. Without such wholehearted community support and consensus, the ideal working arrangement between church and state would collapse. This need explains the continuing efforts of the Puritan leaders as early as 1636 to restrict immigration into Massachusetts Bay Colony. It also

John Winthrop, strict Governor of Massachusetts Bay Colony

explains the well-known Puritan intolerance for dissent, an intolerance that extended to persecution and sometimes to the infliction of the death penalty. Persecution in New England, however, was generally used as a last resort. The heretic—a person who deviated from the accepted beliefs—was always offered the opportunity to leave in peace. Only when he refused to go did the authorities resort to sterner measures.

Particularly distasteful to the Puritans were dissenters like Anne Hutchinson and Roger Williams who, by imposing even more exalted standards of holiness than those imposed by the Puritan leaders themselves, threatened to divide and disrupt the community. Anne Hutchinson, for example, maintained that the Puritan test for church membership was far too lax. It was possible, she contended, to know exactly who was saved and thus to limit church membership only to those people. And, she went on to say, only two of the Puritan ministers of Massachusetts Bay were truly saved while most of the magistrates were not! The Puritan leaders concluded quite correctly that their community could not survive if such opinions were allowed. Accordingly, Mrs. Hutchinson was banished from the colony.

From the Puritan point of view, Roger Williams was likewise the bearer of dangerous doctrines which would have torn the community apart, for Williams insisted that there should be *no* connection between church and state. Any contact between the two, declared Williams, could serve only to corrupt the religious life. In other words, Williams was denouncing as sinful the role relationships worked out by the Puritans for their ministers and magistrates—relationships basic to the entire Puritan conception of their community. The Puritans could not tolerate such a teaching. Williams was expelled.

As the Puritan leaders knew only too well, their community could survive only so long as a large majority of the members shared group aims and willingly participated in community life. Their awareness of this fact explains the Puritans' vigorous persecution of the Quakers who began to arrive in the mid-1650's. Many Quakers were cast into prison, flogged, and banished from the colony. Several had their ears cut off and four were executed.

The Quakers' main offense was that they refused to take part in the ritual observances of Puritan community life. The Quakers, for example, often refused to attend the common religious services and when they did attend they disturbed the congregation by offering unsolicited remarks from the audience. Although these offenses hardly seem serious enough to warrant harsh punishments, it must be remembered that the Quakers' actions represented a special threat to Puritan control. The Quakers demanded a kind of freedom which the community could not confer and still maintain its identity.

The Quakers lacked a sense of commitment to Puritan ideals, a willingness to participate fully in Puritan rituals. They lacked the feeling of a common heritage and destiny which gives any society its underlying cohesion, and without which no community can exist as a special entity.

When Charles II came to the throne of England in 1660, he ordered that the persecutions against Quakers and other people of differing religious beliefs be halted. Because of this order, the Puritan community, for all practical purposes, could no longer survive as a separate, cohesive society.

■ "For the Puritan community to maintain its identity, the leaders had to maintain total social control." Explain. Cite evidence to support your answer.

■ What concepts from sociology are used in this case study? How do they contribute to an understanding of the Puritan community? Explain.

Anne Hutchinson was banished for her religious beliefs.

When Thomas Jefferson was born in 1743 on the frontier of Virginia, the thirteen American colonies were part of the British Empire. A thin line of settlement stretched along the Atlantic coast from New Hampshire south through Georgia. The colonists, nine out of ten of whom were farmers, looked eastward to Great Britain for political leadership.

During his lifetime, Jefferson took a leading part in a far-reaching political revolution. When he died in 1826, the United States was a proudly independent nation, a federal union of 24 states, and the advancing frontier had crossed the Mississippi River.

As late as the 1820's, however, nearly nine out of every ten Americans were still living on farms or in rural areas. When Jefferson was carried to his final resting place, the Industrial Revolution that was to transform America from an agricultural to an industrial nation was only beginning.

CREATING A NEW NATION

UNIT TWO

Winning Independence

1763 – 1789

IN THE YEAR 1763 the people of Great Britain felt a deep sense of pride. Victorious over all its rivals, Great Britain had established claims to an empire that circled the globe. British harbors were jammed with shipping. Battered ships of the British navy and weatherworn transports rode in on the incoming tides, bringing the fighting men of Great Britain back to their homes and families. Other British vessels weighed anchor and sailed out of the harbors carrying government and military officials to the far-flung outposts of the empire.

To the average Britisher the future appeared brighter than it had for many years. But thoughtful men of Great Britain and in other countries realized that the British empire faced many new and troublesome problems, particularly in the American colonies of the New World. One of these thoughtful observers was the French statesman Count Vergennes (vair·ZHEN).

Vergennes, mindful that France had been driven from the North American continent, predicted a similar, speedy end to Great Britain's moment of glory. "The American colonies stand no longer in need of England's protection," he said. England, he continued, "will call on them to help contribute toward supporting the burden they have helped to bring on her, and they will answer by striking off all dependence."

Vergennes proved to be an accurate prophet. Just 13 years after his prediction, the British colonies along the Atlantic seaboard declared their independence from Great Britain.

■ *British troops landing in Boston, 1768*

CHAPTER **6**

Moving Toward Independence

1763 – 1775

THE CHAPTER IN OUTLINE

1. Problems faced by the British in governing their empire.

2. Colonial opposition to taxation without representation.

3. Increasing tensions between Great Britain and the colonies.

4. The widening gap between Great Britain and the colonies.

| 1450 | 1750 | 1800 | 1850 | 1900 | 1950 | 1975 |

1 Problems faced by the British in governing their empire

In 1763 the British emerged victorious from the conflict known in Europe as the Seven Years' War and in America as the French and Indian War. But the peace that followed this victory brought no rest to governing officials in Great Britain. Candles and lamps in government offices burned late into the night as British leaders wrestled with the problems of reorganizing the rapidly growing empire.

Need for new taxes. One problem was the need for more money. Between 1689 and 1763 the British had fought four wars, which had left their nation heavily in debt. To make matters worse, the British government now needed even more money to maintain the military and naval defenses of its expanding worldwide empire.

British leaders quite naturally expected the American colonists to help pay the war debts. After all, the British reasoned, the colonists were subjects of the king. They ought to help pay for the cost of defense, especially their own defense. In short, the British government now intended to collect more taxes from the colonists.

Florida and Canada. Another troublesome problem was what to do with Florida and Canada —lands acquired by the British at the end of the French and Indian War. The governments of Florida and Canada had to be completely reorganized. Spaniards and Frenchmen in these areas, long-time enemies of Great Britain, were now British subjects, but British subjects in name only. How could they be made loyal subjects? What kind of government would work best in these new regions?

The western lands. No less troublesome was the problem of organizing a government for the wilderness land beyond the Appalachian Mountains. With the defeat of the French, law and order had vanished from this region. Fearful that colonial farmers would move across the mountains and destroy their hunting grounds, the Indians rebelled. The uprising known as Pontiac's Conspiracy started in 1763 under the able leadership of Pontiac, chief of the Ottawa Indians, a strong and mighty foe. Settlers fled eastward to escape the death and destruction that raged along the western frontier (see map, page 103) for nearly a year.

To add to the confusion, the British themselves did not agree on what policy to apply to the lands west of the Appalachians. One group, led by the Hudson's Bay Company, was interested solely in the fur trade. This group urged the government to keep settlers from crossing the mountains into the western lands. Another group, including most colonists, urged the government to encourage settlement and help turn the western lands into a farming region.

Even more complicated was the question of which colonies owned the lands beyond the Appalachian Mountains. As the map on page 103 shows, several colonies claimed land in this region. These claims were based on the original colonial charters. In several of these charters, the British government had granted territory "from sea to sea." In theory, then, some colonial claims reached to the Pacific Ocean! And, as the map on page 103 also shows, some of the colonies claimed the same land. Here was another troublesome problem that the British had to solve.

Weakness of British leaders. War debts and defense costs, the government of Florida and Canada, and the ownership of the western lands—these were only a few of the serious problems facing the British government in 1763.

To solve these problems, Great Britain needed wise statesmen—men with ideals, men broadly educated, men who could satisfy the needs of the colonies while also satisfying the needs of Great Britain. But men of this type were not in power at the time. George III, who was king from 1760 to 1820, was a stubborn, narrow-minded man who viewed the colonies as mere overseas territories owned by Great Britain. When he became king, he surrounded himself with "yes men"—ministers whose first thought was always to please their ruler.

The stage set for trouble. In 1763, then, serious differences of opinion separated British officials and American colonists. The British pointed out that they had saved the colonists from the French and Indian menace. They also pointed out that the colonists were still being protected by the British army and navy. The British believed, therefore, that the colonists should help pay the cost of protecting the empire and themselves.

To this argument, many colonists replied that the war was over and now they wanted to be left alone. Colonial farmers, frontiersmen, merchants, and manufacturers were anxious to pursue their own interests. They felt that the problems faced by the British in keeping an empire together were no concern of theirs. Settlers in all the colonies, although many were British, had begun to look upon their problems as being quite different from those of Great Britain.

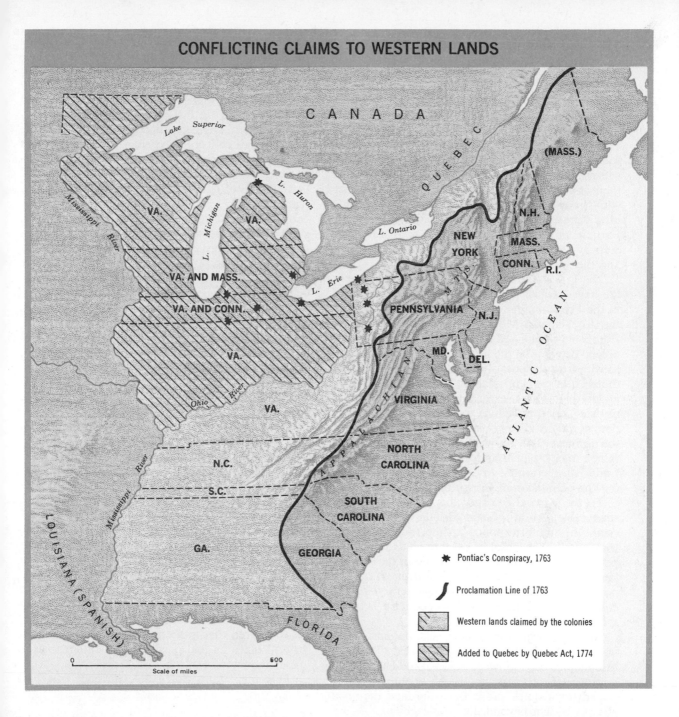

CONFLICTING CLAIMS TO WESTERN LANDS

CANADA

Lake Superior

L. Huron

L. Michigan

L. Ontario

L. Erie

Mississippi River

VA.

VA.

VA. AND MASS.

VA. AND CONN.

VA.

Ohio River

VA.

Mississippi River

N.C.

S.C.

GA.

LOUISIANA (SPANISH)

FLORIDA

QUEBEC

(MASS.)

N.H.

NEW YORK

MASS.

CONN.

R.I.

PENNSYLVANIA

N.J.

MD.

DEL.

VIRGINIA

NORTH CAROLINA

SOUTH CAROLINA

GEORGIA

ATLANTIC OCEAN

APPALACHIAN MTS.

0   500
Scale of miles

✹ Pontiac's Conspiracy, 1763

𝕁 Proclamation Line of 1763

▱ Western lands claimed by the colonies

▨ Added to Quebec by Quebec Act, 1774

SECTION SURVEY

IDENTIFY: Pontiac, George III; 1763.

1. (a) What problems did the British face in governing their empire after 1763? (b) Had the British faced these same problems before 1763? Explain.

2. (a) What arguments did the British use to persuade the colonists that they ought to help pay the cost of protecting the empire and themselves? (b) How did the colonists answer these arguments? Why?

3. (a) What led to Pontiac's uprising? (b) Do you think the Indians had valid reasons for resentment? Explain. (c) Do you think the colonists had valid reasons for wanting to move west? Explain.

103

2 Colonial opposition to taxation without representation

Starting in 1763, the British began to adopt measures to put the empire on a sound footing. The person responsible for these measures was George Grenville, who became prime minister, or leader of the British government, in 1763. To the surprise of Grenville and other British officials, their efforts to reform colonial administration met with strong opposition from the colonists. The colonists were especially angered by laws passed by a Parliament in which they were not represented. Step by step the gap between the mother country and the American colonies grew wider.

The Proclamation of 1763.   As a first move in the new colonial program, George III announced in the Proclamation of 1763 that all lands west of the Appalachian Mountains formerly claimed by France now belonged to the British Crown. In this official declaration the king also ordered all settlers to withdraw temporarily to the east of a line along the crest of the Appalachian Mountains (see map, page 103). This measure, prompted by Pontiac's uprising, tried to reduce conflict between the settlers and the Indians by reserving certain lands for the Indians. The fur trade of the entire western region was brought under royal control, and no trader was permitted to cross the mountains without the permission of British officials.

To the average Britisher the measure appeared reasonable. At last Great Britain was trying to establish a uniform policy for the Indians, the fur trade, and the disposal of western lands. This temporary stop to settlement and trade in the western lands would give the British government an opportunity to develop a long-range policy for the colonies without the distraction of conflicts between settlers and Indians.

But American fur traders and colonists who wanted to settle the western lands were filled with resentment. So, too, were colonial merchants who outfitted the traders and land speculators who hoped for a quick profit from the land they had already bought beyond the Appalachians.

The Sugar Act of 1764.   While the colonists were still angered by the Proclamation of 1763, Parliament landed another stinging blow by passing the Sugar Act of 1764. By this measure Parliament hoped to raise money to help pay the expenses of "protecting and securing" the colonies against attack. The Sugar Act raised the money by placing a duty on molasses, sugar, and other products imported from places outside the British empire. A similar law, the Molasses Act, had been enacted in 1733 (page 50). But the duty set by the act of 1733 was so high that the colonists had openly violated the law by smuggling.

Parliament was determined to enforce the new measure and collect the *revenue* ° the government needed. To make smuggling less profitable, Parliament set the new duty on molasses at only half —and in 1766 at only one sixth—of what it had been in 1733. Then British officials began to enforce the new law. British naval patrols inspected ships entering colonial harbors. Royal inspectors searched warehouses and even private homes, looking for smuggled goods. The revenue collectors also tried to enlist the aid of the colonists themselves by offering rewards to any citizen who reported that his friends or neighbors were smuggling.

Parliament hoped that the Sugar Act of 1764 would reduce taxes for citizens in Great Britain, who until now had borne almost all the defense costs of the entire empire, including the colonies in North America. The British felt that everyone who benefited from membership in the empire should share the cost of defending it. Parliament also hoped that the act would help the sugar planters of the British West Indies.

Despite the lower duty on molasses, the Sugar Act interfered severely with the business of colonial merchants, shipowners, and rum distillers. These colonists had been earning profits on duty-free molasses and other goods smuggled in from the French, Dutch, and Spanish islands in the Caribbean. Angry colonial merchants began to organize committees to discuss means of resistance.

The Currency Act of 1764.   Soon after the Sugar Act, Parliament passed another law forbidding the colonies to issue paper money. Parliament also required that in the future the colonists must pay all taxes in gold or silver coin rather than in paper money.

This regulation, called the Currency ° Act of

° *revenue:* the money collected by a government from taxes, duties, and the like.

° *currency:* This term refers to money that is "current" or used at a given time as the legal medium of exchange. Currency may be in the form of *coins,* that is, pieces of gold, silver, or other metals stamped and issued by the government. It may also take the form of printed or engraved paper, usually called *paper money.*

■ Colonial shipbuilders were kept occupied by the growing demand for merchant vessels. The painting above shows wharves along the Delaware River.

1764, antagonized many colonists, particularly colonial merchants. Money had been scarce in the colonies even before Parliament passed the new measure. Since 1750 the balance of trade between Great Britain and the colonies had shifted in favor of Great Britain. To equalize the balance, colonial merchants had to send large amounts of currency, in addition to trade goods, to Great Britain. These currency shipments were draining away the supply of currency in the colonies. Where, then, could the colonists find the money to carry on their business activities and pay their taxes?

The Quartering Act. While colonial tempers were still running high, Parliament passed still another unpopular law—the Quartering Act of 1765. This law required the colonial authorities to provide barracks and supplies for British troops stationed in America.

The Stamp Act of 1765. In the midst of growing colonial agitation, Parliament adopted the Stamp Act of 1765. The Stamp Act, like the Sugar Act, attempted to raise revenue to pay for the defense of the colonies. But the Stamp Act was far more sweeping. It levied taxes on licenses of all kinds, on college diplomas, playing cards, newspapers, advertisements, and legal documents such as deeds to land and mortgages on property. All such documents and materials had to bear a stamp showing that the tax had been paid.

George Grenville, the British prime minister, had announced in 1764 that he wanted Parliament to impose a stamp tax. Parliament, however, did not pass the act until 1765. Thus, the colonists had a full year to propose a more acceptable form of taxation. They failed to suggest an alternative. For this reason the British government was astonished when many colonists greeted the Stamp Act with angry protests. After all, the colonists had always paid taxes to support the empire.

The colonists, however, said that the earlier taxes had been *indirect taxes*—duties, for example, collected on goods entering colonial ports. These

The signing of the Magna Carta

RIGHTS OF ENGLISHMEN

In opposing British policies after 1763, the colonists were asserting what they believed to be their rights as Englishmen. Beginning with the *Magna Carta* in 1215, as you know, Englishmen had been recording these rights in formal documents. Following are excerpts from two of the most important of these documents—the Petition of Right and the Bill of Rights—written in England during the 1600's, while the colonists were struggling to build settlements in North America.

English Petition of Right (1628)

They [your subjects] do therefore humbly pray your most excellent majesty that no man hereafter be compelled to make or yield any gift, loan, benevolence, tax, or such like charge without common consent by act of Parliament; ... and that your majesty would be also graciously pleased, for the further comfort and safety of your people, to declare your royal will and pleasure that in the things aforesaid all your officers and ministers shall serve you according to the laws and statutes of this realm. ...

English Bill of Rights (1689)

Levying of money for or to the use of the crown ... without grant of Parliament ... is illegal.

It is the right of the subjects to petition the king. ...

The raising or keeping a standing army within the kingdom in time of peace, unless it be with the consent of Parliament, is against law. ...

Election of members of Parliament ought to be free.

The freedom of speech and debates or proceedings in Parliament ought not to be ... questioned in any court or place out of Parliament.

Excessive bail ought not to be required, nor excessive fines imposed, nor cruel and unusual punishments inflicted. ...

duties were finally paid only by those colonists who actually bought the products. Colonists often did not know that they were paying these duties because they were hidden in the price of the product. The earlier duties, the colonists insisted, had been levied to help regulate trade. The colonists argued that the stamp tax was different. It was a *direct tax*. Unlike an indirect tax, hidden in the price of the product, a direct tax had to be paid directly to the government.

Through the years, as you will recall, the colonial assemblies had won increasing control over the colonial purse strings (page 85). The colonists were used to paying direct taxes levied by their own colonial assemblies. The stamp tax, however, was a direct tax levied not by a colonial assembly, but by Parliament. The American colonists had no representatives in Parliament.

The Stamp Act, then, threatened to take money directly from the colonists without their consent. The settler buying a few acres of land on the frontier would have to pay a special tax on the deed to his property. Small farmers would have to pay taxes on warehouse receipts for tobacco or grain. Artisans in the towns would be required to pay taxes for playing cards and newspapers. And planters, merchants, lawyers, and editors would be paying taxes every time they turned around. This "vicious" tax, the colonists insisted, violated their right to tax themselves. It was levied without the consent of their own representatives. Here, indeed, was "taxation without representation."

Many colonists refused to listen to the British argument that Parliament represented all British subjects, including the colonists. True, British spokesmen admitted, colonial representatives did not sit in Parliament. But other large groups of Britishers also were not directly represented in Parliament. For example, many thousands of men living in the new, rapidly growing English cities of Manchester and Birmingham did not have the right to vote and were therefore not directly represented in Parliament. British spokesmen argued that representation of the American colonies in Parliament was similar to that of these British cities. It was, they said, "virtual representation." Parliament, they insisted, represented not only the citizens of Great Britain but all the people of the empire. What did the colonists mean by "no taxation without representation"? To these arguments the colonists turned deaf ears.

Opposition to the Stamp Act. With the passage of the Stamp Act of 1765, Parliament found that it had stumbled into a hornet's nest. Resolutions condemning the measure poured into England from the colonies. Colonial lawyers, merchants, and publishers met in protest. Colonial assemblies declared that all taxes were illegal except those levied by representatives of the people in their own legislatures.

In October 1765 delegates from nine colonies met in New York to hold a meeting known as the Stamp Act Congress. After asserting their loyalty to the king and promising "all due subordination" to Parliament, the delegates vowed to resist all taxes levied without the consent of their own colonial legislatures.

Many colonial merchants, joined by other leading citizens, went a step further. They signed *nonimportation agreements,* promising not to buy or import British goods. Within a few months products made in Great Britain almost vanished from colonial stores and warehouses.

Some colonial townsmen took even more direct action. Organized in societies called Sons of Liberty, they rioted in the large towns and destroyed the offices of stamp tax collectors. They burned stamps in the streets, destroyed the houses of royal officials, and applied tar and feathers to citizens sympathetic to Great Britain. They justified their violent actions by claiming that they were battling for their rights as Englishmen.

Repeal of the Stamp Act. The British accepted the news of colonial resistance to the Stamp Act with mixed feelings. George III exclaimed, "It is undoubtedly the most serious matter that ever came before Parliament."

British merchants were shocked. The colonial nonimportation agreements had brought British-American trade almost to a standstill. Many British merchants faced financial ruin. To prevent this, they demanded that Parliament repeal the Stamp Act. Powerful Britishers who sympathized with the colonists joined in the demand for repeal. Edmund Burke, a British statesman and writer, expressed his pride in men who fought such an "illegal" measure. William Pitt, a member of Parliament who later became prime minister of Great Britain, declared, "I rejoice that America has resisted."

Under such heavy pressure Parliament repealed the Stamp Act in March 1766. News of the repeal brought wild rejoicing in the colonies and sighs of relief from British businessmen and friends of the colonists. In New York City, Sons of Liberty erected a huge flagpole, called a liberty pole. Colo-

■ The Stamp Act of 1765 brought forth a violent reaction from the colonies. This old engraving shows a tax collector who has been strung up on a liberty pole by the crowd. A British sympathizer who protested the deed has been bound to the bottom of the pole.

nists gathered around the liberty pole to celebrate the repeal and to pledge their devotion to the cause of liberty.

The Declaratory Act of 1766. In the midst of the excitement, most colonists paid little attention to another law passed by Parliament—the Declaratory Act of 1766. In the Declaratory Act, Parliament asserted its "full power and authority to make laws to bind the colonies and people of America . . . in all cases whatsoever."

Thus, despite rejoicing in the colonies, the basic issue dividing the colonists from the mother country remained unsettled. Did the British Parliament have the right to make laws for the American colonists and to tax them when the colonists had no elected representatives in Parliament? This was the basic question.

1. Review the definition and purposes of mercantilism (Chapter 3).
2. Why did the Crown and Parliament approve the following measures and why did the colonists object to them: (a) the Proclamation of 1763, (b) the Sugar Act of 1764, (c) the Currency Act of 1764, (d) the Quartering Act of 1765?
3. The Stamp Act was adopted in 1765. (a) Why did the colonists oppose it? (b) How did they show their opposition? (c) Why was it repealed? (d) Why did many Britishers favor its repeal?
4. The Sons of Liberty justified their use of violence in opposing the Stamp Act. Do you? Explain.

3 Increasing tensions between Great Britain and the colonies

Money! This was Great Britain's crying need in 1766. Money to raise and maintain the armed forces needed to guard the far-flung outposts of the British Empire. Money to build and maintain the warships that guarded the sea lanes to and from the colonies. Money to pay the war debts left over from the Seven Years' War.

Lack of money, of course, was not a new problem. It was the same problem that the British government had faced in 1763. In 1766 the problem remained unsolved.

The Townshend Acts. In 1767, under the leadership of Charles Townshend, Parliament decided once again to try to raise revenue in America. But by now Parliament knew how deeply the colonists resented direct taxes. Parliament decided, therefore, to return to the long-accepted method of collecting duties on goods entering the seaports. Since the colonists had always paid indirect taxes of this kind, Parliament hoped the new duties would not cause any trouble.

The Townshend Acts levied import duties on articles of everyday use in America—tea, lead, glass, and colors for paint. If Parliament had stopped at this point, the colonists might not have objected. But Parliament, in an effort to insure that the new law would be enforced, legalized what were then called *writs of assistance*.

Writs of assistance. Writs of assistance were search warrants. "Writ" is an old word meaning "written." Writs of assistance, then, were written statements giving a government official the legal right to search a man's ship, his business establishment, or even his home.

The writs of assistance used in colonial times were quite different from present-day search warrants. Today, a search warrant must state the exact article sought and the specific premises to be searched. In colonial times, however, a British customs official, armed with a general search warrant, could enter any vessel or warehouse or home in America, at any time. And he could ransack the place in the bare hope that he might find smuggled goods.

For many years American colonial merchants had been arguing that the writs were illegal and an invasion of their "rights as Englishmen." As recently as 1761, when Boston customs officials had applied for a writ against colonial merchants, the merchants had taken their case to court. James Otis, their attorney, had often denounced the writs in fiery language. "What a scene does this open," he cried in one speech. "Every man, prompted by revenge, ill humor, or wantonness to inspect the inside of his neighbor's house, may get a writ of assistance."

Now, in 1767, Parliament had legalized the hated writs. The colonists could not change this fact. But they could and did protest, heaping their anger and contempt upon Parliament. How dare Parliament do such a thing to British citizens!

Arguments and resolutions. Many colonists openly expressed their resentment against the Townshend Acts, including the much-hated writs of assistance. New Yorkers refused to provide living quarters for British soldiers sent to enforce the law. Parliament promptly punished the colony by suspending its assembly, thus depriving New Yorkers of their right to representative government.

Other colonists picked up their pens and began to write. They poured out their resentment in a flood of angry pamphlets, resolutions, and petitions. Led by Samuel Adams, the legislature of Massachusetts drafted a letter to the other colonies, urging them to unite for resistance. The assemblies of Maryland, South Carolina, and Georgia promptly endorsed the letter. Parliament replied by forbidding the legislatures of these four colonies to meet.

The Virginia House of Burgesses adopted a set of resolutions summarizing the American case. The resolutions began with a statement by George

Washington referring to "our lordly masters in Great Britain." The resolutions then repeated the American claim that only colonial legislatures had the right to levy taxes on the colonists.

Direct action—and violence. While many colonial leaders protested in writing, other colonists decided to act. They signed new nonimportation agreements, promising not to import or buy British goods. The earlier agreements at the time of the Stamp Act of 1765 had almost ruined British merchants and had forced Parliament to repeal the measure. Many colonists reasoned that, since the agreements had worked then, they would work again now.

But some Americans were not content with these agreements. Once again mobs poured into the streets. They boarded and smashed British ships, attacked British customs officials, and freely applied tar and feathers to anyone who informed on smugglers. British soldiers sent to keep order were sometimes attacked.

In Boston crowds taunted the soldiers, calling them "lobsters," "redcoats," and "bloody backs." Now and then the more irresponsible members of a crowd hurled stones and snowballs at the soldiers. Every month friction between the citizens and the soldiers became more intense. Thoughtful colonial leaders and British commanders alike did everything possible to avoid more serious trouble. But an incident such as they dreaded finally occurred.

The Boston Massacre. On March 5, 1770, a large crowd gathered in Boston around a detachment of the 29th British Regiment. The crowd yelled insults and threw snowballs. Such outbursts had occurred many times before. But this time matters got out of hand. As the mob pressed closer against the soldiers, someone gave an order to fire. Three civilians were killed and two others were mortally wounded.

The first civilian killed was Crispus Attucks, a former slave, who had escaped 20 years earlier from his master. As a fugitive slave, he did not share the same degree of freedom as his fellow townsmen. Yet Crispus Attucks became the first person to die in the struggle between Great Britain and the colonies.

As news of the shooting spread, the citizens of Boston went wild with anger. A "massacre," they called the affair, and demanded that the British withdraw all troops from the city.

Later, when passions had cooled somewhat, the British soldiers were tried for murder. They were

■ Samuel Adams led the legislature of Massachusetts to draft a letter urging the other colonies to unite against the Townshend Acts. The assemblies of Maryland, South Carolina, and Georgia promptly endorsed the letter.

defended by Josiah Quincy, Jr., and John Adams, who later became the second President of the United States. Neither of these men had any sympathy for the British, but they insisted that every individual was entitled to a fair trial. All except two of the soldiers were acquitted. These two were convicted of manslaughter, but were soon released.

Repeal—and continued unrest. When Lord Frederick North became prime minister of Great Britain in 1770, the gap between Great Britain and the American colonies was wide indeed. The

■ **Crispus Attucks, a fugitive slave, was fatally wounded by a British soldier during the Boston Massacre. Attucks thus became the first to die in the struggle for American independence.**

new prime minister urged Parliament to repeal the Townshend Acts. As he pointed out, the non-importation agreements were once again ruining the business of many British merchants. Besides, the cost of enforcing the law was proving much too heavy.

In 1770 Parliament repealed the Townshend Acts. Parliament also allowed the Quartering Act to expire. But, in a new law, the British government was careful to retain a small import duty on tea as a symbol that Parliament had the power to tax the colonists. As George III put it, there must "always be one tax to keep up the right."

The repeal of the Townshend Acts brought a temporary end to much colonial unrest. But an occasional act of violence reminded the British that the basic issue remained unsettled.

One outbreak occurred in June 1772 when several boatloads of colonists attacked and burned the British revenue ship *Gaspee* a few miles south of Providence, Rhode Island. For the colonists, the most alarming thing about the *Gaspee* affair was

the British announcement that the suspected colonists would be sent to England for trial. This decision threatened to weaken the practice of self-government in Rhode Island.

Even more alarming was an announcement made at this same time by the royal governor of Massachusetts. From now on, Governor Thomas Hutchinson declared, the British Crown, not the colonial assemblies, would pay the salaries of the governor and the Massachusetts judges. This action freed the governor and the judges from all dependence upon the Massachusetts legislature.

Committees of Correspondence. These new threats to colonial freedom did not go unchallenged. Led by Samuel Adams, citizens of Boston met in a special town meeting and created a "Committee of Correspondence" consisting of 21 members, with James Otis as chairman. This committee had the job of keeping other colonies—and "the World"—informed about what was happening in Massachusetts. The idea worked so well that during the next few months other colonies organized similar committees. Many of the most prominent colonial leaders served on these committees. In Virginia, for example, the committee included Thomas Jefferson, Patrick Henry, and Richard Henry Lee.

Because the colonies had no central government where leaders of the various colonies could meet, the Committees of Correspondence performed an important service. They kept each colony informed of events and opinions in the other colonies. And, as it turned out, the colonists organized this new method of communication none too soon, for in 1773 Parliament adopted another measure that really started tempers boiling.

SECTION SURVEY

IDENTIFY: writs of assistance, "redcoat," Boston Massacre, *Gaspee;* Samuel Adams, John Adams, Crispus Attucks.

1. Why did the colonists object to (a) the Townshend Acts, (b) the writs of assistance?
2. How did the writs of assistance differ from present-day search warrants?
3. Of what importance were the Committees of Correspondence?
4. What is ironic about the fact that Crispus Attucks was the first man to die in the struggle between Great Britain and the colonies?
5. James Otis and Samuel Adams demonstrate how individual men can play important roles in history. Explain.

4 The widening gap between Great Britain and the colonies

The series of events that brought the American colonies to the verge of rebellion started in 1773 with the passage of the Tea Act. Parliament passed this measure to help promote the interests of the British East India Company, a well-established trading company with headquarters in England.

The Tea Act of 1773. The British East India Company was in trouble. It had 17 million pounds of unsold tea piled up in its warehouses—and no buyers. If the tea were not sold, and quickly, the company would be wiped out.

Part of the company's difficulties arose because many American colonists refused to buy English tea. When the Townshend Acts were repealed, the British government, you recall, had retained a small duty on tea as a symbol of its power to tax the colonies. The tax was a small one, but many colonists refused to pay it. In fact, they refused to buy tea imported from England.

Faced with this desperate situation, the British East India Company turned to Parliament for help. The members of Parliament, many of whom owned stock in the company, quickly worked out what they thought was a reasonable solution to the problem.

First, Parliament granted the company a large loan of public money. Parliament then passed a law enabling the company to lower its price on tea without losing any profits.

Before the new law was passed, the East India Company had been required to sell its tea only to British merchants. The merchants increased the price of the tea somewhat and then sold it to colonial retailers. The new law, known as the Tea Act, permitted the company to bypass the British merchants and sell the tea directly to the colonists. The Americans would still have to pay the Townshend duty, or tax, but the tea would cost less than ever before. Parliament figured that the colonists would be happy to buy the tea at the lowered price —and the British East India Company would be saved.

Why the colonists objected. Why, given the chance to buy tea at such a low price, did the colonists protest? For one thing, many colonists by now were opposed to all taxes imposed by Parliament.

In the second place, the new Tea Act allowed the British East India Company to undersell all of its competitors, even merchants who were smuggling tea into America without paying import duties. In effect, the company would have a monopoly on the sale of tea in America. Thus, many colonial middlemen, or merchants, who had been making profits in the tea trade would be driven out of business.

Nearly all colonial businessmen joined the tea merchants in their resistance. True enough, the act affected only the sale of tea. But if a monopoly were granted to one British company, what was to stop Parliament from granting monopolies to other British companies? The colonial merchants would have none of this.

Violence in the colonies. Faced with this threat to their businesses, the colonists reacted swiftly. Crowds rioted in the streets. The British East India Company could not sell a single pound of its tea. In Charleston colonists stored tea in damp cellars so it would rot. In Annapolis a ship

LIVING AMERICAN DOCUMENTS

Declaration and Resolves of the
First Continental Congress (1774)

**The good people of the several colonies . . . declare
. . . that the inhabitants of the English colonies in
North America, by the immutable laws of nature, the
principles of the English constitution, and the several
charters or compacts, have the following rights:**

Resolved,

**That they are entitled to life, liberty, and property,
and they have never ceded to any sovereign power
whatever a right to dispose of either without their
consent.**

**That our ancestors, who first settled these colonies,
were at the time of their emigration from the mother
country entitled to all the rights, liberties, and immunities of free and natural-born subjects within the
realm of England. . . .**

**That the foundation of English liberty and of all
free government is a right in the people to participate
in their legislative council. . . .**

and its cargo of tea were burned. Philadelphians
and New Yorkers refused to allow British ships
carrying tea to enter their harbors.

In Boston, late in 1773, colonists disguised as
Indians boarded ships and heaved the cargo into
the water. In one wild night they destroyed 342
chests of tea valued at thousands of dollars. The
Boston Tea Party, as it was called, attracted widespread attention. Many colonists approved, but
others were shocked at such violence.

The Intolerable Acts of 1774. British officials
and merchants were furious. It had been bad
enough for the colonists to refuse to pay taxes. It
was far worse for them to destroy property.

By overwhelming majorities Parliament passed
four measures to discourage further violence and
to strengthen British control over the colonists.
The colonists called these measures the Intolerable
Acts—that is, acts that they found unbearable and
not to be endured. One measure closed the port
of Boston to all shipping until the colonists paid
for the tea destroyed there. A second measure
revoked the Massachusetts charter of 1691 and
forbade Massachusetts colonists to hold town
meetings. A third measure, a new Quartering Act,
required the colonists to provide food and housing
for British soldiers sent to America to enforce the
laws. A fourth measure provided that British offi-

cials in Massachusetts charged with crimes committed while enforcing British laws could have
their cases tried not in that colony, but in England.

The Quebec Act of 1774. While passing what
the colonists called the Intolerable Acts, Parliament also passed a fifth measure, the Quebec Act.
The Quebec Act was intended to establish order
in Canada, which, as you recall, the British had
won by treaty from the French in 1763.

The Quebec Act, which greatly enlarged the
province of Quebec, established the southern
boundary of Canada at the Ohio River and the
western boundary at the Mississippi River (see
map, page 103). French laws were to continue in
Canada. French Canadians, most of them Roman
Catholics, were guaranteed religious freedom.

Parliament had no thought of passing the Quebec Act to punish the colonists. Indeed, the act
was a sound piece of legislation. But it came at the
same time as the Intolerable Acts. The colonists
regarded it as another attempt to punish them, by
destroying the claims of Massachusetts, Connecticut, and Virginia to the western lands, and by
strengthening the Catholicism which they disliked.

Reaction to the Intolerable Acts. Great Britain soon set out to enforce the Intolerable Acts.
General Thomas Gage, commander in chief of the
British armed forces in America, was named
governor of Massachusetts and was given more
troops to help him maintain order. The colonists
had defied British authority with physical force.
Very well, Great Britain would uphold the laws
with physical force.

"The New England governments are in a state
of rebellion," George III declared. "Blows must
decide whether they are to be subject to this country or independent."

Many colonists had no intention of submitting.
Great Britain, thinking only of punishing Massachusetts and warning the other colonies, had succeeded in arousing more antagonism throughout
America. Some colonists even talked about settling
the matter by force if necessary.

The First Continental Congress. Many colonists remained completely loyal to Great Britain.
They believed that the colonies should obey the
laws of Parliament without protesting. Other colonists tried to persuade the British to compromise.

On September 5, 1774, delegates from all of the
colonies except Georgia assembled in Philadelphia
at a meeting called the First Continental Congress.
The delegates quickly adopted a number of resolutions. Denying any thought of independence, the

■ In protest against the Tea Act of 1773, members of the Sons of Liberty dressed themselves as Indians and destroyed thousands of dollars worth of tea in Boston harbor.

delegates nevertheless demanded an immediate change in British policies. They solemnly asserted their rights to "life, liberty, and property"; to "all the rights, liberties, and immunities" of Englishmen; to the "free and exclusive power of legislation in their own several legislatures." They pledged each other mutual support. They revived the nonimportation agreements against British products. They agreed not to sell goods to Great Britain or the British West Indies if, by January 1775, the British had not made compromises. They resolved to create local "committees of safety and inspection" to provide firm and uniform action against the British government.

Finally, the First Continental Congress ended. The delegates agreed, however, to meet again in the spring of 1775 to take further steps if the Intolerable Acts had not been withdrawn by then.

SECTION SURVEY

IDENTIFY: Tea Act, Boston Tea Party, Intolerable Acts, First Continental Congress; General Thomas Gage.

1. (a) Why did so many colonists object to the Tea Act of 1773? (b) How did they express their opposition?
2. (a) What were the Intolerable Acts of 1774? (b) Why were the Intolerable Acts passed by Parliament?
3. Why did French Canadians favor the Quebec Act of 1774, while most American colonists opposed it?
4. (a) What actions were taken by the First Continental Congress? (b) Why do you suppose that the delegates at this first meeting did not talk of independence?

TRACING THE MAIN IDEAS

British victory in the Seven Years' War, called in America the French and Indian War, made Great Britain the leading colonial power in the world. British citizens had paid in blood and money to win their great empire. By 1763 the struggle was settled. France had been defeated. Peace had come at last.

But peace brought new problems. During the long years of colonial warfare, the American seaboard colonies had been growing away from the mother country. The people who settled these colonies had learned to think of them as *their* land, as a place different from England. They learned to love the new country that had brought most of them better lives than they or their fathers had known in the Old World. They began to think of themselves as Americans, although they did not ordinarily use the word "American" until after the Revolutionary War and although, until 1776, nearly all of them continued to think of themselves as loyal citizens of the British Empire.

A new way of life was developing in America. About 150 years had passed since the first English settlers had come to America, and the peoples of the Old World and the New were finding it increasingly difficult to understand each other.

The gap was already wide in 1763 when Great Britain decided to adopt a new policy and to make the colonies obey laws passed in London.

Step by step, between 1763 and 1775, the mother country and its colonies moved further apart. Yet by 1775 it was perhaps not too late to reconcile the differences. As you will see in Chapter 7, however, the reconciliation never came. Instead, the colonists declared their independence and won their freedom on the battlefield.

CHAPTER SURVEY

QUESTIONS FOR DISCUSSION

1. Explain how Great Britain applied the principles of mercantilism by means of (a) the Navigation Acts, (b) restrictions on colonial manufacturing, (c) the Currency Act of 1764.
2. Step by step, between 1763 and 1775, Great Britain and the American colonies moved further apart. Reread Count Vergennes' predictions in the introduction to this chapter. (a) What reasons did he give for the eventual independence of the American colonies? (b) Why do you think that British statesmen could not see what Vergennes saw?
3. By early 1775, leaders in Great Britain and in the colonies were lined up firmly against each other. Do you think it is unusual for two groups of people to see things so differently and reach such an impasse? Explain.
4. Wise men could have reconciled the gap between the mother country and the colonies in 1775. Do you agree or disagree? Explain.

RELATING PAST TO PRESENT

1. (a) Compare the reaction of the colonists to the destruction of property during the Boston Tea Party in 1773 and the reaction of Americans to the destruction of property today. (b) Is violence ever justified? Under what circumstances? What if the majority approves of it? What if the majority opposes it?
2. Does the use of violence breed more violence? Explain, using examples of violence in American society today.

USING MAPS AND CHARTS

1. Using the maps on pages 20 and 103, explain the reasons for the conflicting claims of certain colonies to western lands.
2. Using the map on page 103, describe the aim of the Proclamation of 1763.
3. Referring to the map on page 51, summarize the aims of British mercantilism and the importance of the triangular trade to the colonists.

J OHN HOWE, a private in the army of King George III, was a spy. Fortunately for him, he did not look like a spy. The people he met as he walked along the Massachusetts roads took him for an honest Yankee workingman. He even sounded like a Yankee. His regiment had been stationed in Boston long enough for him to learn how Yankees talked —and sometimes, what they were thinking about.

General Gage, British commander in Boston, had heard that the New Englanders were collecting arms and ammunition. He sent Private Howe and other spies out into the surrounding countryside to learn the truth. And John Howe was learning fast. He learned where the powder and shot were stored. He also learned that the Yankees were ready to fight. At a farmhouse near Lexington, he stopped to talk to an old man. The old man was cleaning a gun. Howe asked him what he intended to shoot. "A flock of redcoats at Boston," the man replied.

Howe heard the same story everywhere he went. He saw rebellious colonists—by now called Patriots—cleaning their guns and drilling openly on village greens. In taverns and public buildings he saw lists posted bearing the names of people who remained loyal to the king. He heard of Loyalists who had been tarred and feathered and of Loyalists whose homes had been burned because they dared to defend the British point of view.

This was the report John Howe carried back to General Gage in Boston. General Gage, who had heard the same story from other British spies, decided the time had come to act. By acting promptly he might, perhaps, nip the bud of rebellion. He decided to seize the ammunition that the colonists were storing at Concord and at several other towns.

THE CHAPTER IN OUTLINE

1. Open war between the British and the colonists.
2. The colonists' decision to declare their independence.
3. Waging the Revolutionary War in the early years.
4. Victory of the American Patriots over the British.
5. A favorable treaty of peace for the victorious Americans.

■ *Colonists toppling a statue of King George III*

CHAPTER 7

Winning a War for Independence

1775 – 1783

1 Open war between the British and the colonists

General Gage could no more hide his plans from the colonists than they could hide their activities from his spies and informers. In the spring of 1775 the Patriots in Boston were watching the British closely. They knew something was brewing. What is more, they made arrangements to warn the surrounding countryside if, and when, the British troops should march.

Lexington and Concord. Late at night on April 18 a group of Patriots in Charlestown saw two lights gleaming briefly from the window in the steeple of the Old North Church in Boston. The lights were a signal, arranged by a Patriot, to warn friends in Charlestown that British redcoats were crossing the Charles River on their way to Lexington and Concord, where the Patriots had secretly stored rifles and powder. The signal had been arranged in case the Patriot found it impossible to escape from the closely guarded city and give the message in person. After rowing under cover of darkness to Charlestown, the Patriot leaped into the saddle of a waiting horse and galloped off into the night—and into the pages of history.

The Patriot, of course, was Paul Revere. He and two fellow Patriots, William ("Billy") Dawes, Jr., and Dr. Samuel Prescott, rode through that fateful night, pounding on farmhouse doors, shouting their

cry of alarm. Behind them, as the hoofbeats of their horses faded into the distance, lamps winked on in kitchens. Wives, their eyes filled with worry, hastily prepared food while their menfolk hurriedly pulled on clothes and lifted their muskets and powder horns from the pegs on the wall. Then the men marched off across the fields to join their friends and neighbors at the appointed meeting place.

British troops, meanwhile, had rowed across the Charles River and were marching down the road toward Concord (see map, this page). They reached Lexington at dawn on April 19, 1775. The "minutemen"—militia members who had promised to be ready for action at a minute's notice—were there before them, gathered in ranks on the village green. Major Pitcairn, commander of the British patrol, ordered the colonists to drop their guns and leave the green. The colonists started to leave, but held on to their guns. Then someone fired a shot. Immediately, without waiting for orders, the British troops fired several volleys. When the smoke cleared, eight colonists lay dead. Ten others were wounded.

The British troops went on to Concord, where they cut down a liberty pole, set fire to the courthouse, and destroyed several gun carriages and a few tools. After encountering armed Patriot forces at Concord's North Bridge, the British started back toward Boston. But the countryside was swarming with angry colonists. From behind stone walls and the shelter of buildings, the colonists fired steadily upon the redcoats as they made their death march down the long road back to Boston. During that march British casualties amounted to 73 killed, 174 wounded, and 26 missing.

The redcoats reached Boston late in the day. Curious townspeople saw weary faces, bloody bandages, and men in tattered uniforms stumbling under the weight of wounded comrades. When night fell, campfire lights twinkled like fireflies around the rim of the city. These were the fires of rebellion, fed by many of the 16,000 minutemen from the surrounding countryside.

Ticonderoga and Crown Point. The days slipped by. Within a month, in May, came news that the "Green Mountain Boys," a small colonial force from what is now Vermont, under the command of Ethan Allen, had seized the British forts at Ticonderoga and Crown Point on Lake Champlain (see map, page 118). Most welcome of all was news that powder and shot and cannons from the captured forts were on their way to Boston.

WAR BREAKS OUT, APRIL 19, 1775

■ Above, the British start back from Concord to Boston. The British commander wrote, "There is not a stone-wall or house . . . from whence the Rebels did not fire upon us."

The Second Continental Congress.   As you recall, delegates to the First Continental Congress had agreed the previous year to assemble again if the British government did not meet their demands. On May 10, 1775, then, delegates to a Second Continental Congress met in Philadelphia.

Some of these delegates, among them Samuel Adams of Massachusetts and Patrick Henry of Virginia, were *radical* in their outlook. They were now ready to declare independence, seize British officials, and ask France and Spain for help. But most delegates were more *conservative*. They were reluctant to urge extreme changes in the relations between the colonies and the mother country.

The conservatives won. Led by John Dickinson of Pennsylvania, they assured the king that they had "not raised armies with ambitious designs of separating from Great Britain." To this plea for reconciliation, however, the delegates added a stern message. They made it clear that they would resist *tyranny* ° with force if necessary. And to show that they meant business, they appointed George Washington of Virginia as commander in chief of the Continental Army. In name at least, if not in might, the armed Patriots became an army.

The Battle of Breed's (Bunker) Hill.   Before Washington arrived to take command of the minutemen in the Boston area, blood had again been shed. General Gage, the British commander, ordered a frontal attack on the armed New Englanders who were encamped at Charlestown, overlooking Boston harbor. On June 17, 1775, in three

(*continued on page 119*)

° *tyranny:* the exercise of absolute power without regard for law and justice.

117

MAJOR CAMPAIGNS OF THE REVOLUTIONARY WAR

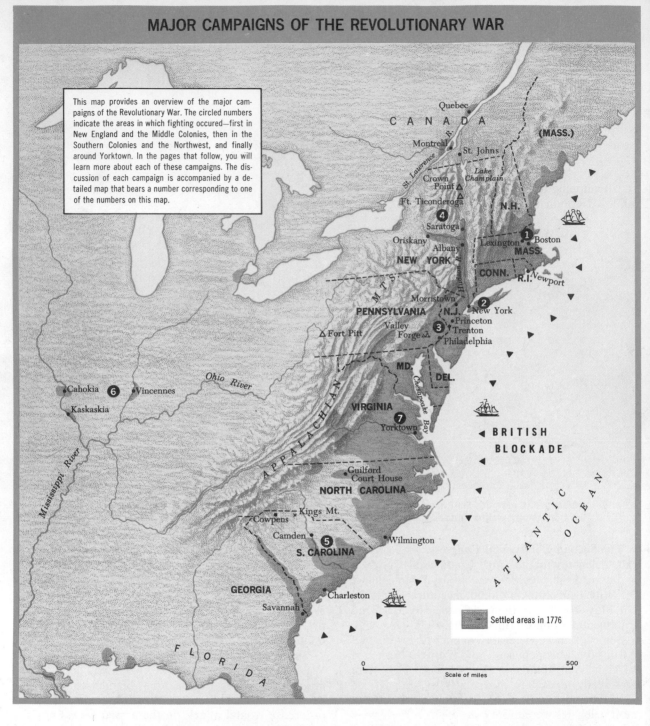

This map provides an overview of the major campaigns of the Revolutionary War. The circled numbers indicate the areas in which fighting occured—first in New England and the Middle Colonies, then in the Southern Colonies and the Northwest, and finally around Yorktown. In the pages that follow, you will learn more about each of these campaigns. The discussion of each campaign is accompanied by a detailed map that bears a number corresponding to one of the numbers on this map.

CANADA

Quebec

(MASS.)

Montreal

St. Johns

St. Lawrence R.

Lake Champlain

Crown Point △

Ft. Ticonderoga △

N.H.

④

Saratoga

Oriskany

Albany

Lexington

① Boston

MASS.

NEW YORK

CONN.

R.I. *Newport*

M T S.

Morristown

② New York

PENNSYLVANIA

N.J.

Princeton

③ Trenton

Valley Forge △

Philadelphia

△ Fort Pitt

Ohio River

Chesapeake Bay

MD.

DEL.

Cahokia ⑥ Vincennes

Kaskaskia

VIRGINIA

⑦

Yorktown

BRITISH
BLOCKADE

Mississippi River

A P P A L A C H I A N

Guilford Court House

NORTH CAROLINA

Kings Mt.

Cowpens

Camden

⑤

Wilmington

S. CAROLINA

A T L A N T I C   O C E A N

GEORGIA

Charleston

Savannah

Settled areas in 1776

F L O R I D A

0 ——————— 500
Scale of miles

■ As you read the text and examine each numbered map in the pages that follow, look frequently at the map above so that you will understand the progress of the war and the relationships among the various campaigns. On all the detailed maps, colored symbols stand for American forces, black symbols for British. These symbols are used on the detailed maps:

→ American advance   ----→ American retreat   ✳ American victory

→ British advance   ----→ British retreat   ✴ British victory

bold assaults, the British redcoats attacked the Americans on Breed's Hill, mistakenly called Bunker Hill (see map 1, this page). Both sides lost heavily. Finally, the Patriots, their ammunition exhausted, retreated with a loss of almost 450 men. But the British left more than 1,000 men killed or wounded upon the battlefield.

Shocked at news of this disaster, George III proclaimed the colonists rebels. He ordered the Royal Navy to begin a tight naval blockade to close off all shipping to the colonies. And he also hired 10,000 German soldiers, called Hessians (HESH-unz), to help fight and subdue the Americans.

British evacuation of Boston. The Second Continental Congress promptly took further steps to strengthen the colonial position. The Congress sent diplomatic agents to request aid from several European countries, including France, Spain, and the Netherlands. Late in 1775 the Congress also sent a military expedition to Canada, in the hope of encouraging the French Canadians to rise against the British. However, the French Canadians did not show much sympathy, and the expedition failed.

Early in 1776, however, the colonists were cheered by other news. In a surprise move at night, Washington occupied Dorchester Heights overlooking Boston, where the British fleet lay anchored in the harbor (see map 1, this page). The British, literally caught napping, awakened in the morning to find themselves looking across the bay into the mouths of cannon.

The British general, Sir William Howe, who had replaced General Gage as the commanding officer, decided that it was useless to try to hold Boston. The British fleet lifted anchor and sailed out of the harbor on March 17, 1776. With the fleet went the entire garrison of British soldiers and about 1,000 civilian Loyalists.

"The Lexington and Concord of the South." Meanwhile, another important military engagement had been fought in North Carolina—the Battle of Moore's Creek Bridge, sometimes called the "Lexington and Concord of the South." Fought at sunrise on the morning of February 27, 1776, the battle ended in a decisive victory for the Patriots.

During 1775 Governor Martin had recruited nearly 2,000 Loyalists, mostly Scottish Highlanders who had come to North Carolina since 1770. These Loyalist troops were to march on the seaports of Wilmington and Brunswick. There they were to be joined by regiments of British

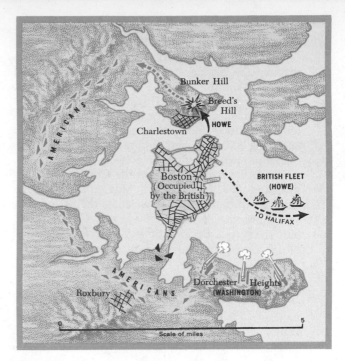

① Fighting Around Boston: June 1775–March 1776

troops under Lord Charles Cornwallis and Sir Henry Clinton, and by a powerful British fleet under Sir Peter Parker. Operating from these bases, this combined Loyalist and British force would then control the colony.

But the Patriots were fully aware of the plan. James Moore, a Patriot leader, stationed a force of about 1,100 men at Moore's Creek Bridge. This force ripped up the planking from the bridge and greased the log supports with soap and tallow.

LIVING AMERICAN DOCUMENTS

Patrick Henry's Speech
Before the Virginia Convention (1775)

Gentlemen may cry peace, peace. But there is no peace. The war is actually begun! The next gale that sweeps from the north will bring to our ears the clash of resounding arms! Our brethren are already in the field! Why stand we here idle? What is it that gentlemen wish? What would they have? Is life so dear, or peace so sweet, as to be purchased at the price of chains and slavery? Forbid it, Almighty God! I know not what course others may take; but as for me, give me liberty or give me death!

Then the men concealed themselves and waited.

The sun was just rising when the Loyalists reached the bridge, exhausted from marching all night. Attempting to cross on the slippery logs, they were met by a withering fire from the opposite bank. In a short but fierce fight, the Patriots, with only one killed and one wounded, won the battle and took 850 prisoners, many weapons and wagons, and a large supply of gold.

When the British forces under Cornwallis, Clinton, and Parker arrived in May, they found no Loyalist troops waiting to welcome them, and they sailed away. The Battle of Moore's Creek Bridge had shattered the ambitious British plan to hold North Carolina loyal to Great Britain.

SECTION SURVEY

IDENTIFY: Patriots, Loyalists, minutemen, radical, conservative, tyranny, Hessians; Paul Revere, Ethan Allen, Patrick Henry, Sir William Howe; April 19, 1775.

1. Show how General Gage's decision to "nip the bud of rebellion" led to open war between Great Britain and the colonies.
2. What was the military importance of (a) the Battle of Breed's Hill, (b) the seizure of Dorchester Heights, (c) Ticonderoga, (d) Moore's Creek Bridge?
3. (a) What is meant by the statement that most delegates to the Second Continental Congress took a conservative, rather than a radical, view of colonial relations with Great Britain? (b) Why would independence from Great Britain by a colony be considered a radical move in 1775?

2 The colonists' decision to declare their independence

Until the spring of 1776 most colonists refused to admit that they were fighting a war. In their opinion, they were merely resisting unjust acts of Parliament.

Reasons for caution. A few Patriots, as you know, had already urged the colonists to declare their independence. Most colonists, however, were reluctant to make the final break. For one thing, the British government maintained law, order, and stability in the colonies. Thoughtful colonists feared that, without British control, they would become victims of mob rule and anarchy. Local colonial leaders had seen mobs in action against tax collectors, British revenue officers, and Americans who were sympathetic toward king and Parliament. They did not want to exchange the tyranny of Great Britain for the greater tyranny of colonial mobs.

The colonists hesitated to declare their independence for other reasons, too. First, if they revolted and failed to win, they could be executed for treason. Second, as long as the colonists were merely resisting specific acts of Parliament, they could count upon powerful support from friends in Great Britain. Britishers like Edmund Burke, William Pitt, John Wilkes, and Isaac Barré (ba-REH) had joined British merchants in demanding that Parliament repeal objectionable laws. But the Americans knew that the moment they began to talk of separation from Great Britain, their British friends would turn against them and fight to preserve the British Empire. Indeed, many, perhaps most, men and women in the colonies were loyally devoted at this time to the British Empire.

Reasons for independence. Two bitter facts offset these arguments against a break with Great Britain. First, the British government had committed acts that many colonists believed violated their rights as Englishmen. Second, colonial blood had already been shed defending these rights.

In this explosive atmosphere Thomas Paine's pamphlet *Common Sense* was like a spark dropped in a keg of gunpowder. Paine was a former British political writer who had come to America in 1774. His widely read pamphlet appeared in January 1776.

"I offer nothing more than simple facts, plain arguments, and common sense," Paine wrote. In ringing words he pointed out that America had grown into a new and different nation with interests of its own. "... the period of debate is closed. Arms, as the last resource, must decide the contest. .... Everything that is right or reasonable pleads for separation. The blood of the slain, the weeping voice of nature cries, '*Tis Time to Part!*'" Paine's stirring words helped to kindle the spirit of independence.

In the debate over the declaration of independence, Americans took opposite sides on the basis of deep and sincere convictions. But, as Thomas Paine pointed out, by declaring their independence the colonists could gain immediate practical advantages.

First, as citizens of an independent nation, captured Patriot soldiers could demand to be treated as prisoners of war and avoid being shot as rebels. Second, the Patriot governments could seize the property of all Americans who remained loyal to the Crown. Third, the Patriots would have a better chance of winning foreign aid. The French and Spanish kings, for example, would probably favor a war that threatened to weaken the British empire.

Independence declared. Under the pressure of these arguments, colonial sentiment began to shift in favor of independence. On June 7, 1776, Richard Henry Lee of Virginia introduced a resolution in the Second Continental Congress declaring that "these United Colonies are, and of right ought to be, free and independent states." On June 11, before voting on Lee's resolution, the Congress appointed a committee of five men to write a formal Declaration of Independence. These five men were Thomas Jefferson, Benjamin Franklin, John Adams, Robert R. Livingston, and Roger Sherman. Jefferson was asked by the other four members of the committee to do the actual writing.

On June 28 the committee presented Jefferson's Declaration—with a few changes by Franklin and Adams—to Congress. Congress did not at once discuss the Declaration itself. Instead, it debated Lee's resolution and, by adopting it on July 2, officially declared the new United States of America to be independent of Great Britain. Then the delegates turned to Jefferson's statement, which they continued to discuss on July 3.

Before adopting Jefferson's document, the delegates made several changes. For example, Jefferson's original draft contained a passage condemning George III for the slave trade and blaming the king for failing to suppress it. However, delegates from the northern states, aware that people in their area had profited from the slave trade, did not feel that it was fair to blame only George III for this practice. And delegates from the southern states, where slavery and the slave trade were considered necessary, objected strongly to the passage. Thus, it was left out of the final document.

Finally, on July 4, Congress adopted the Declaration of Independence. In bold strokes John Hancock of Massachusetts, president of the Congress, signed the document. Then copies were rushed to the legislatures of the newly created states. Finally, on July 8, the Declaration was read and officially proclaimed in Philadelphia.

Reactions to the Declaration. Many Americans, especially the Patriots (also known as

A LIST of the Names of the PROVINCIALS who were Killed and Wounded in the late Engagement with His Majesty's Troops at *Concord*, &c.

KILLED.	
Of *Lexington*.	Of *Danvers*.
* Mr. Robert Munroe,	Mr. Henry Jacobs,
* Mr. Jonas Parker,	Mr. Samuel Cook,
* Mr. Samuel Hadley,	Mr. Ebenezer Goldthwait,
* Mr. Jona⁰ Harrington,	Mr. George Southwick,
* Mr. Caleb Harrington,	Mr. Benjamin Daland, jun.
* Mr. Isaac Muzzy,	Mr. Jotham Webb,
* Mr. John Brown,	Mr. Perley Putnam.
Mr. John Raymond,	
Mr. Nathaniel Wyman,	Of *Salem*.
Mr. Jedediah Munroe.	Mr. Benjamin Peirce.
Of *Menotomy*.	
Mr. Jason Ruffel,	
Mr. Jabez Wyman,	WOUNDED.
Mr. Jason Winship,	
	Of *Lexington*.
Of *Sudbury*.	Mr. John Robbins,
Deacon Haynes,	Mr. John Tidd,
Mr. —— Reed.	Mr. Solomon Peirce,
	Mr. Thomas Winship,
Of *Concord*.	Mr. Nathaniel Farmer,
Capt. James Miles.	Mr. Joseph Comee,
	Mr. Ebenezer Munroe,
Of *Bedford*.	Mr. Francis Brown,
Capt. Jonathan Willson.	Prince Easterbrooks,
	(A Negro Man.
Of *Acton*.	
Capt. Davis,	Of *Framingham*.
Mr. —— Hosmer,	Mr. —— Hemenway.
Mr. James Howard.	Of *Bedford*.
	Mr. John Lane.
Of *Woburn*.	
* Mr. Azael Porter,	Of *Woburn*.
Mr. Daniel Thompson.	Mr. George Reed,
	Mr. Jacob Bacon.
Of *Charlestown*.	
Mr. James Miller,	Of *Medford*.
Capt. William Barber's Son.	Mr. William Polly.
Of *Brookline*	Of *Lynn*.
Isaac Gardner, Esq;	Joshua Feit,
	Mr. Timothy Munroe.
Of *Cambridge*.	
Mr. John Hicks,	Of *Danvers*.
Mr. Moses Richardson,	Mr. Nathan Putnam,
Mr. William Maffey.	Mr. Dennis Wallis.
Of *Medford*.	Of *Beverly*.
Mr. Henry Putnam.	Mr. Nathaniel Cleaves.
Of *Lynn*.	
Mr. Abednego Ramsdell,	MISSING.
Mr. Daniel Townsend,	Of *Menotomy*.
Mr. William Flint,	Mr. Samuel Frost,
Mr. Thomas Hadley.	Mr. Seth Ruffell.

Those distinguished with this Mark [*] were killed by the first fire of the Regulars.

■ A list of American casualties constituted a powerful argument for declaring American independence.

■ The men who signed the Declaration of Independence must have done so with a deep sense of anxiety. They were risking everything in order to found the new nation.

Whigs °), greeted this news with wild rejoicing. Bells rang. Men sang and danced around bonfires and held banquets to celebrate. The long period of indecision had ended.

Other Americans greeted the news with indifference. These people—and there were many in every colony—were not much concerned one way or the other.

A third group, the Loyalists (also known as Tories °), refused to have anything to do with the celebrations. Some sat in silence behind closed doors and barricaded windows. They did not want to separate from Great Britain. Moreover, for them the bonfires were omens of terror. They had seen enough violence during the past 10 years to know what to expect—neighbor against neighbor, beatings, tar and feathers, burning houses, flights for safety to Canada or the British West Indies or

° Whig: a major political party in Great Britain which was opposed to taxing the colonies. For this reason, the Patriots of America were sometimes called Whigs.

° Tory: a major political party in Great Britain that opposed the Whigs. Since this party believed strongly in the power of the king, American colonists loyal to the king were sometimes called Tories.

122

England. And the Tories, now regarded as traitors in their own land, included many people with wealth and influence—merchants, lawyers, landowners, former officers of the king, members of the clergy.

The Declaration of Independence. The document in which Thomas Jefferson and his fellow Patriots declared American independence has become one of history's most cherished statements. For nearly 200 years freedom-seeking people all over the world have been inspired by its noble ideas and remarkable eloquence. Our admiration for the Declaration, however, should not obscure the fact that it was a practical document with three major purposes. As you read about these three purposes, turn also to the text of the Declaration of Independence (pages 124–26) and read the passages that correspond to the three following headings.

1. Preamble and reasons for separation. In the first place, the Declaration was an attempt to win public support for independence. This appeal to people in Europe and America was contained in the "preamble," or introduction, and in the 27 "reasons for separation" from Great Britain. The king was pictured as an evil ruler who intended to establish an absolute tyranny over the colonies. Each grievance pictured George III as a harsh tyrant. "He has forbidden . . . he has plundered . . . he has refused . . . he has constrained. . . ." In contrast, the colonists were pictured as patient, submissive, long-suffering citizens. "We have petitioned . . . we have warned . . . we have reminded . . . we have appealed. . . ."

2. A new theory of government. The second major purpose of the Declaration of Independence was to outline a new theory of government. This inspiring new theory explains why the Declaration remains today one of the most influential documents ever written.

In the opening lines of the second paragraph, Thomas Jefferson clearly and simply stated the basic principles of what today we call democracy: ". . . all men are created equal," he wrote. ". . . they are endowed by their Creator with certain unalienable rights; . . . among these are life, liberty, and the pursuit of happiness." "Unalienable rights" are rights which cannot be taken away from the people—not by any government, nor even by the people themselves.

What is the purpose of government? Jefferson replied that governments exist "to secure these rights." Where do governments obtain this authority? They derive "their just powers from the consent of the governed." What happens when a government begins to act like a tyrant? "It is the right of the people to alter or to abolish it, and to institute new government."

The Declaration of Independence, in this passage, clearly stated the right of the American colonists to revolt against their British rulers. It stated this idea in terms familiar to many people in both Europe and America.

Thomas Jefferson was not expressing merely his own ideas about government when he wrote the Declaration. His ideas came from two major sources. First, they came from scholars in Europe, among them John Locke, who during the 1600's and 1700's had been thinking about and developing new ideas about government. And second, Jefferson's ideas came from the practical experience of the American colonists in self-government.

The Declaration was an invitation to all men, in all times, to assume the right to rule themselves and to rid themselves forever from the tyranny of unwanted rulers.

3. A formal declaration of war. The third major purpose of the Declaration, contained in the final paragraph, was to announce formally that war

LIVING AMERICAN DOCUMENTS

Thomas Paine's "The Crisis" (1776)

These are the times that try men's souls. The summer soldier and the sunshine patriot will, in this crisis, shrink from the service of their country; but he that stands by it now deserves the love and thanks of man and woman. Tyranny, like hell, is not easily conquered; yet we have this consolation with us, that the harder the conflict, the more glorious the triumph. What we obtain too cheap, we esteem too lightly; it is dearness only that gives everything its value. Heaven knows how to put a proper price upon its goods; and it would be strange indeed if so celestial an article as FREEDOM should not be highly rated. . . .

existed. As Thomas Paine had predicted, this announcement had certain practical advantages for the Patriots. But it could also have grave consequences. If the Patriots failed to make good their claim to independence, the leaders of the revolution could be judged guilty of treason against the British Crown and executed as traitors.

The words in which the delegates pledged "our lives, our fortunes, and our sacred honor" to the successful outcome of the struggle were not idle words. The delegates who signed the document must have done so with a deep sense of anxiety. They were pledging everything to the cause. Failure would mean ruin. It might mean death.

SECTION SURVEY

IDENTIFY: mob rule, *Common Sense*, unalienable rights; Edmund Burke, Richard Henry Lee, Thomas Jefferson, John Hancock; July 4, 1776.

1. State the arguments for and against the final break with Great Britain in the spring of 1776.
2. (a) Which passages from *Common Sense*, quoted in your text, appeal to reason? (b) Which appeal to emotion?
3. The colonists were not unanimous in their reaction to the Declaration of Independence. Why not?
4. The Declaration was a practical document with three major purposes. Name and explain these purposes.
5. The slave issue was compromised in the Declaration. Why?
6. Show how the Declaration of Independence presented a theory for a new kind of government. Quote from the document.

THE DECLARATION OF INDEPENDENCE

In Congress, July 4, 1776

PREAMBLE

When, in the course of human events, it becomes necessary for one people to dissolve the political bands which have connected them with another, and to assume, among the powers of the earth, the separate and equal station to which the laws of nature and of nature's God entitle them, a decent respect to the opinions of mankind requires that they should declare the causes which impel them to the separation.

A NEW THEORY OF GOVERNMENT

We hold these truths to be self-evident: that all men are created equal, that they are endowed by their Creator with certain unalienable rights, that among these are life, liberty, and the pursuit of happiness.

That, to secure these rights, governments are instituted among men, deriving their just powers from the consent of the governed;

That whenever any form of government becomes destructive of these ends, it is the right of the people to alter or to abolish it, and to institute new government, laying its foundation on such principles, and organizing its powers in such form, as to them shall seem most likely to effect their safety and happiness. Prudence, indeed, will dictate that governments long established should not be changed for light and transient causes; and accordingly all experience hath shown that mankind are more disposed to suffer while evils are sufferable, than to right themselves by abolishing the forms to which they are accustomed. But when a long train of abuses and usurpations, pursuing invariably the same object, evinces a design to reduce them under absolute despotism, it is their right, it is their duty, to throw off such government, and to provide new guards for their future security.

REASONS FOR SEPARATION

Such has been the patient sufferance of these colonies; and such is now the necessity which constrains them to alter their former systems of government. The history of the present king of Great Britain is a history of repeated injuries and usurpations, all having in direct object the establishment of an absolute tyranny over these states. To prove this, let facts be submitted to a candid world.

He has refused his assent to laws the most wholesome and necessary for the public good.

He has forbidden his governors to pass laws of immediate and pressing importance, unless suspended in their operation till his assent should be obtained; and when so suspended, he has utterly neglected to attend to them.

He has refused to pass other laws for the accommodation of large districts of people, unless those people would relinquish the right of representation in the legislature, a right inestimable to them, and formidable to tyrants only.

He has called together legislative bodies at places unusual, uncomfortable, and distant from the depository of their public records, for the sole purpose of fatiguing them into compliance with his measures.

He has dissolved representative houses repeatedly, for opposing, with manly firmness, his invasions on the rights of the people.

He has refused, for a long time after such dissolutions, to cause others to be elected; whereby the legislative powers, incapable of annihilation, have returned to the people at large for their exercise; the state remaining, in the mean time, exposed to all the dangers of invasion from without and convulsions within.

He has endeavored to prevent the population of these states; for that purpose obstructing the laws of naturalization of foreigners, refusing to pass others to encourage their migration hither, and raising the conditions of new appropriations of lands.

He has obstructed the administration of justice, by refusing his assent to laws for establishing judiciary powers.

He has made judges dependent on his will alone for the tenure of their offices, and the amount and payment of their salaries.

He has erected a multitude of new offices, and sent hither swarms of officers to harass our people and eat out their substance.

He has kept among us, in times of peace, standing armies, without the consent of our legislature.

He has affected to render the military independent of, and superior to, the civil power.

He has combined with others to subject us to a jurisdiction foreign to our constitution and unacknowledged by our laws, giving his assent to their acts of pretended legislation:

For quartering large bodies of armed troops among us;

For protecting them, by a mock trial, from punishment for any murders which they should commit on the inhabitants of these states;

For cutting off our trade with all parts of the world;

For imposing taxes on us without our consent;

For depriving us, in many cases, of the benefits of trial by jury;

For transporting us beyond seas, to be tried for pretended offenses;

For abolishing the free system of English laws in a neighboring province, establishing therein an arbitrary government, and enlarging its boundaries, so as to render it at once an example and fit instrument for introducing the same absolute rule into these colonies;

For taking away our charters, abolishing our most valuable laws, and altering, fundamentally, the forms of our governments;

For suspending our own legislature, and declaring themselves invested with power to legislate for us in all cases whatsoever.

He has abdicated government here, by declaring us out of his protection and waging war against us.

He has plundered our seas, ravaged our coasts, burned our towns, and destroyed the lives of our people.

He is at this time transporting large armies of foreign mercenaries to complete the works of death, desolation, and tyranny already begun with circumstances of cruelty and perfidy scarcely paralleled in the most barbarous ages, and totally unworthy the head of a civilized nation.

He has constrained our fellow-citizens, taken captive on the high seas, to bear arms against their country, to become the executioners of their friends and brethren, or to fall themselves by their hands.

He has excited domestic insurrections among us, and has endeavored to bring on the inhabitants of our frontiers the merciless Indian savages, whose known rule of warfare is an undistinguished destruction of all ages, sexes, and conditions.

In every stage of these oppressions we have petitioned for redress in the most humble terms; our repeated petitions have been answered only by repeated injury. A prince whose character is thus marked by every act which may define a tyrant is unfit to be the ruler of a free people.

Nor have we been wanting in attention to our British brethren. We have warned them, from time to time, of attempts by their legislature to extend an unwarrantable jurisdiction over us. We have reminded them of the circumstances of our emigration and settlement here. We have appealed to their native justice and magnanimity; and we have conjured them, by the ties of our common kindred, to disavow these usurpations, which would inevitably interrupt our connections and correspondence. They, too, have been deaf to the voice of justice and of consanguinity. We must, therefore, acquiesce in the necessity which denounces our separation, and hold them, as we hold the rest of mankind, enemies in war, in peace, friends.

We, therefore, the representatives of the United States of America, in General Congress assembled, appealing to the Supreme Judge of the world for the rectitude of our intentions, do, in the name and by authority of the good people of these colonies, solemnly publish and declare, that these united colonies are, and of right ought to be, free and independent states; that they are absolved from all allegiance to the British crown, and that all political connection between them and the state of Great Britain is, and ought to be, totally dissolved; and that, as free and independent states, they have full power to levy war, conclude peace, contract alliances, establish commerce, and to do all other acts and things which independent states may of right do. And, for the support of this declaration, with a firm reliance on the protection of Divine Providence, we mutually pledge to each other our lives, our fortunes, and our sacred honor.

John Hancock
(MASSACHUSETTS)

NEW HAMPSHIRE
Josiah Bartlett
William Whipple
Matthew Thornton

NEW YORK
William Floyd
Philip Livingston
Francis Lewis
Lewis Morris

MARYLAND
Samuel Chase
William Paca
Thomas Stone
Charles Carroll
of Carrollton

CONNECTICUT
Roger Sherman
Samuel Huntington
William Williams
Oliver Wolcott

VIRGINIA
George Wythe
Richard Henry Lee
Thomas Jefferson
Benjamin Harrison
Thomas Nelson, Jr.
Francis Lightfoot Lee
Carter Braxton

MASSACHUSETTS
Samuel Adams
John Adams
Robert Treat Paine
Elbridge Gerry

NEW JERSEY
Richard Stockton
John Witherspoon
Francis Hopkinson
John Hart
Abraham Clark

SOUTH CAROLINA
Edward Rutledge
Thomas Heywood, Jr.
Thomas Lynch, Jr.
Arthur Middleton

PENNSYLVANIA
Robert Morris
Benjamin Rush
Benjamin Franklin
John Morton
George Clymer
James Smith
George Taylor
James Wilson
George Ross

GEORGIA
Button Gwinnett
Lyman Hall
George Walton

DELAWARE
Caesar Rodney
George Read
Thomas McKean

NORTH CAROLINA
William Hooper
Joseph Hewes
John Penn

RHODE ISLAND
Stephen Hopkins
William Ellery

3 Waging the Revolutionary War in the early years

In the spring of 1776, while the colonists were debating the question of independence, General Washington moved the Continental Army from Boston to New York. Washington was sure that the British would try to seize New York City and use it as a base of operations for their land and naval forces. By July Washington had nearly 30,000 men guarding the city.

Fighting around New York City. On July 2, the same day that the Second Continental Congress voted to declare the colonies independent, General Sir William Howe sailed into New York harbor and began to land British and Hessian troops on Staten Island (see map 2, this page). A few days later his brother, Admiral Lord Richard Howe, sailed into the harbor with powerful naval reinforcements. By the end of August British forces in the New York area numbered more than 30,000 men. More than 8,000 of them were Hessian soldiers hired by the British to fight in America.

Late in August General Howe landed about 20,000 men on Long Island, where General Washington had stationed the bulk of the Continental Army. Howe's troops forced the Americans back to Brooklyn Heights.

The Americans were now caught in a trap. The British army was in front of them. The British fleet was behind them, ready to sail into the East River to cut off their only avenue of escape.

Fortunately for Washington, General Howe did not attack immediately. Under cover of fog and darkness, the Americans crossed the East River in small boats and reached the temporary safety of Manhattan Island.

But the British fleet controlled the water around Manhattan Island, and Washington was unable to hold the city. After several sharp engagements he withdrew northward to White Plains, leaving the British in command of New York City and its splendid harbor.

Retreat across New Jersey. By late October 1776 Washington's position was becoming increasingly desperate. Winter was approaching. The Americans had lost heavily in men and supplies. The army was rapidly melting away as the men, faced with what seemed inevitable defeat, picked up their guns and returned to their homes.

In this difficult situation General Washington decided to retreat across New Jersey into Pennsylvania. Once in Pennsylvania, the Delaware River would separate him from the British, and he would gain time to regroup his battered forces.

During the retreat across New Jersey men continued to slip away from the army. By the time Washington reached the Delaware River, only about 3,000 troops remained under his command. Weary and discouraged, the soldiers combed the river for small boats, which they then rowed across to the Pennsylvania side (see map 2, this page). There Washington's troops went into a cold and cheerless winter encampment.

Victories at Trenton and Princeton. Confident that the war was almost won, General Howe prepared to celebrate Christmas in New York. To keep a watch upon the remnants of the American army, General Charles Cornwallis, commanding the British forces in the field, stationed 1,300 Hessians at Trenton and a second force a few miles farther south.

Howe's Christmas celebration was rudely interrupted. Opening a brilliant military campaign, Washington and his troops crossed the ice-choked

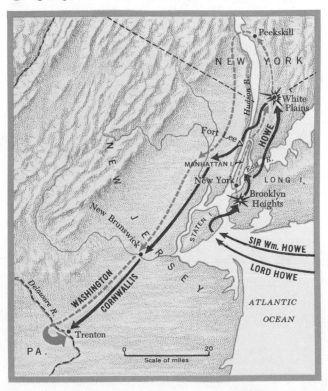

2 Fighting Around New York: July–December 1776

127

Delaware on Christmas night. Early the next morning they surprised the Hessians and took more than 1,000 prisoners.

British reinforcements under Cornwallis rushed to the Trenton area, arriving on January 2, 1777. Cornwallis, certain that he had Washington in a trap, prepared to attack in the morning. During the night the American troops slipped quietly away, leaving their campfires burning brightly to deceive the British into thinking that they were still there.

Instead of retiring to the safety of the west bank of the Delaware River, Washington struck inland, badly cut up three British regiments at Princeton, and withdrew swiftly to the hills around Morristown in northern New Jersey (see map 3, this page). From this position he could make raids upon the British lines of communication and supply between New York, New Brunswick, and Trenton. Since these cities were no longer of any particular value to the British, Howe pulled his troops out of New Jersey.

Washington's victories at Trenton and Prince-

3 New Jersey Campaigns: Winter 1776–77

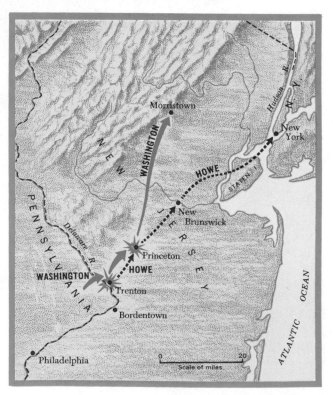

ton ruined British plans for ending the war in the winter of 1776–77. "All our hopes were blasted by that unhappy affair," declared Great Britain's colonial secretary. In contrast, American spirits began to revive. The Americans now had reason to believe they could actually win battles against British regulars. During the next few months volunteers began to swell the ranks of the Continental Army. Washington had taken great chances, but he had won the gamble.

British disaster at Saratoga. Aroused to more vigorous efforts by their defeats at Trenton and Princeton, the British now determined to end the war in 1777. They decided upon a plan that would separate New England from the rest of the states.

Lieutenant Colonel Barry St. Leger (SAYNT LEJ·er) was to lead an expedition, with some Indian allies, from Fort Oswego (os·WEE·goh) on Lake Ontario through the Mohawk Valley to the Hudson River (see map 4, page 130). General John Burgoyne was to lead a second expedition from Canada down the Richelieu River–Lake Champlain route. General Howe was to lead a third expedition from New York up the Hudson River. These three forces were to meet at Albany and crush the American forces.

The plan looked beautifully simple to the men drawing lines on a map in the warmth and comfort of the London War Office. What they did not know, or ignored, was that these lines crossed lakes, swamps, mountains, and trackless forests swarming with militiamen ready to defend their homes, villages, and farms.

St. Leger reached the Mohawk Valley on schedule and laid siege to Fort Stanwix, where American forces were stationed. If the fort fell, St. Leger would have a clear road open before him to Albany. General Nicholas Herkimer of New York and a force of German-American militiamen tried to reach Fort Stanwix and reinforce it, but a party of Tories and Indians ambushed them near the town of Oriskany (o·RIS·kah·ny).

General Herkimer, badly wounded and near death, had no choice but to retreat eastward, leaving the greatly outnumbered garrison in Fort Stanwix to make out as best it could. The situation for the Americans was desperate. Then suddenly, word spread through St. Leger's forces that Benedict Arnold was approaching with a large American army. St. Leger's Indians deserted, and the British had to retreat to Canada.

Meanwhile, a second British force was moving

■ This picture of the Battle of Princeton was painted by William Mercer about ten years after the battle occurred. Mercer's father, an American general, died in this conflict.

southward from Canada down the difficult Richelieu River–Lake Champlain route. General Burgoyne, its leader, knew as little about the American wilderness as his superiors in London. He reached and occupied Fort Ticonderoga without serious opposition. Then his troubles began. Trying to obtain additional supplies, he sent a small raiding party of some 500 Hessian troops into what is now Vermont. There they were destroyed at Bennington by General John Stark and a force of New England militiamen.

Burgoyne's position was now difficult, if not impossible. His provisions were almost gone. His lines of supply were stretched to a dangerous length from Canada through the forests. And the militia of New England and New York were swarming around him like angry bees. Moreover, Howe had failed to join him. Nevertheless, Burgoyne chose to advance.

At Bemis Heights near Saratoga, on the upper reaches of the Hudson River, Burgoyne met the main body of the American forces in the area. Outnumbered by more than two to one and outmaneuvered by the American leaders—Philip Schuyler of New York, Horatio Gates of Virginia, Benjamin Lincoln of Massachusetts, Daniel Morgan of Virginia, and Benedict Arnold of Connecticut—Burgoyne surrendered his entire force of nearly 6,000 men at Saratoga on October 17, 1777.

An unexplained blunder. Burgoyne might have been saved if the planned British expedition up the Hudson River had appeared in time. But it never did appear. Instead of marching northward from New York City, Howe embarked his troops and sailed southward. American scouts followed his progress down the coast. Much to their surprise, he passed the mouth of the Delaware

129

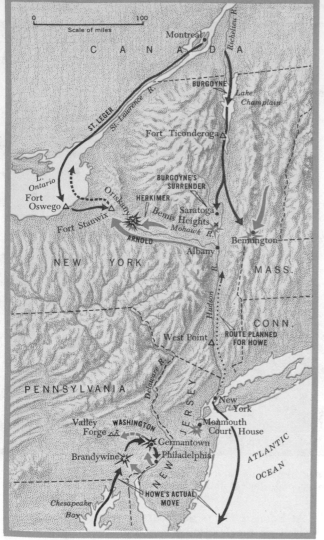

4 Saratoga and Philadelphia Campaigns: 1777–78

Burgoyne could handle the situation without help. For whatever reason, Howe's failure to proceed up the Hudson River contributed to the British disaster at Saratoga.

The British Parliament, sobered by the news of Burgoyne's defeat, sent commissioners to the Continental Congress with an offer to suspend the Intolerable Acts and pardon the Patriots. Unfortunately for the British, their concessions came nearly two years too late.

SECTION SURVEY

IDENTIFY: Battle of Saratoga; Charles Cornwallis, John Burgoyne, Benedict Arnold.

1. Why were Washington's victories at Trenton and Princeton so important?
2. Explain the British plan to separate New England from the rest of the colonies.
3. The Battle of Saratoga was one of the turning points of history. Explain.

4 Victory of the American Patriots over the British

Americans went wild with joy at the news of Burgoyne's defeat. Frenchmen, who were sympathetic to the American cause, celebrated as though they, too, had won a victory.

Aid from France. From the beginning, France had been secretly providing the Americans with desperately needed arms and supplies. Benjamin Franklin, one of the American commissioners in France, began some shrewd bargaining. His skillful negotiations were soon crowned with success. France, hoping to weaken its long-time rival, declared war on Great Britain. The French hoped to win revenge for their crushing defeat at the hands of the British in the Seven Years' War.

On February 6, 1778, France and the United States of America signed two treaties. In the first, a commercial treaty, the two nations agreed to give each other favored treatment in matters of trade. In the other, a treaty of alliance, France agreed to recognize the independence of the United States of America and to wage war upon Great Britain until America was free. America promised to defend the French West Indies. Both countries promised not to make a separate peace with Great Britain.

River, sailed to the head of Chesapeake Bay, and disembarked. Then he marched to Philadelphia, overcoming Patriot resistance in the battles of Brandywine Creek on September 11 and Germantown on October 4 (see map 4, this page). Once he was in Philadelphia, Howe settled down for the winter of 1777–78, while Washington went into encampment at Valley Forge, located about 18 miles west of the city.

Why Howe failed to carry through his part of the plan to split the colonies remains uncertain. Perhaps the British War Office blundered and neglected to send the orders in time. Perhaps Howe took matters into his own hands, deciding that

French cooperation was announced none too soon. Despite the victory at Saratoga, the Americans were in bad shape. Washington's army at Valley Forge was reduced to a handful of poorly equipped, sick, hungry men. But the glad news that they now had a powerful ally filled the Patriots with new hope. Recruits began again to fill the thinned ranks of the army.

Help from abroad. In addition to France, Spain and the Netherlands both supported the American cause, and volunteers from a number of European countries came to America. From Prussia came Baron von Steuben, who carried the main burden of organizing and drilling the Continental Army. From Poland came Casimir Pulaski (KAZ·ih·mihr poo·LAS·ky) and Thaddeus Kosciusko (koz·ih·US·koh), who planned the American defenses of West Point on the Hudson River and Bemis Heights near Saratoga. From France came the German-born officer Baron de Kalb, and the young Marquis de Lafayette (mar·KE deh la·fa·YET), who arrived in America with 12 other officers just before the Battle of Brandywine. After entering the war, France sent gold, powder, shot, equipment, a fleet, and a considerable number of troops to aid the American forces.

Changing British plans. French intervention forced the British to revise their plans for conquering their former colonies. As a first step, they replaced General Howe with Sir Henry Clinton.

Clinton had orders to strike the next blow at the southern states. Before doing this, however, he withdrew the British troops from Philadelphia and

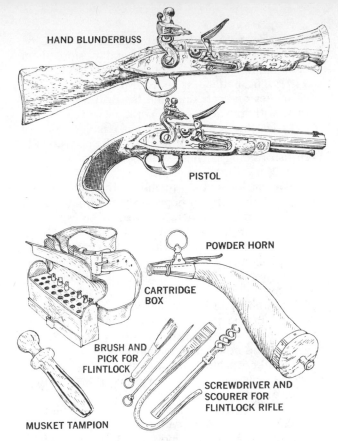

HAND BLUNDERBUSS

PISTOL

POWDER HORN

CARTRIDGE BOX

BRUSH AND PICK FOR FLINTLOCK

SCREWDRIVER AND SCOURER FOR FLINTLOCK RIFLE

MUSKET TAMPION

■ Firearms of the Revolution. Muskets and some rifles (page 63) were the chief weapons of the Revolution, but hand weapons, such as the blunderbuss and the pistol, were also used. In addition, the soldier often carried instruments for taking care of his weapons. The tampion, for example, kept water out of the gun barrel.

■ **Uniforms of the Revolutionary War**

AMERICAN REGULAR

AMERICAN ARTILLERY OFFICER

BRITISH REGULAR

BRITISH GRENADIER

set out across New Jersey toward New York City. Washington pursued the British and overtook them at Monmouth Court House (see map 4, page 130). The battle was indecisive, with about 350 casualties on each side, and the British continued their withdrawal to New York.

From then on, there were no major military activities in the North, although occasionally British raiding parties swept down on towns near New York City.

War in the South. In shifting the attack to the South, Great Britain hoped to profit from the aid of the Tories who were reported to be especially numerous in the southern states.

As in the North, the British had no great trouble occupying any seaports they wished. In December 1778 they seized Savannah, Georgia. In May 1780 they forced General Benjamin Lincoln to surrender Charleston, South Carolina, with 5,000 troops—practically the entire American army south of the Potomac River. From these bases General Cornwallis, who now commanded the British armies in the southern states, was able to move where and when he pleased. British forces raided the countryside, plundering and burning in an effort to terrorize the Patriots and force them into submission.

But for every Tory who rallied to the British, a Patriot sprang up to oppose the British war effort. In South Carolina guerrilla bands of farmers and hunters, under the command of such southern leaders as Francis Marion (called "the Swamp Fox"), Andrew Pickens, and Thomas Sumter, swarmed about the British forces. To aid these guerrilla bands, Congress sent a small army under the command of General Horatio Gates. Gates, however, was badly defeated at Camden, South Carolina, in August 1780 (see map 5, page 133).

The South seemed to be lost to the Patriot cause. But in October 1780 a band of frontiersmen led by Isaac Shelby, John Sevier, and others defeated a party of Tories at Kings Mountain, near the boundary between the Carolinas. At the same time Nathanael Greene of Rhode Island replaced Gates as commander of the American forces in the South.

Although General Greene won no major battles, he and General Daniel Morgan of Virginia, supported by the guerrillas, made the British occupation of inland regions extremely costly. In January 1781 Morgan defeated a British force at Cowpens in South Carolina. Two months later, in March, the Americans struck a serious blow against Cornwallis' forces at Guilford Court House, North Carolina (see map 5, page 133). Although Cornwallis won, his losses were so great that he finally abandoned the entire campaign and withdrew to the security of the coast, where the Royal Navy could support him.

Thus, by 1781, the British were back where they had been in 1778. They held only the city of New York and a few southern seaports. The cam-

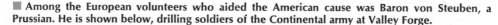

■ Among the European volunteers who aided the American cause was Baron von Steuben, a Prussian. He is shown below, drilling soldiers of the Continental army at Valley Forge.

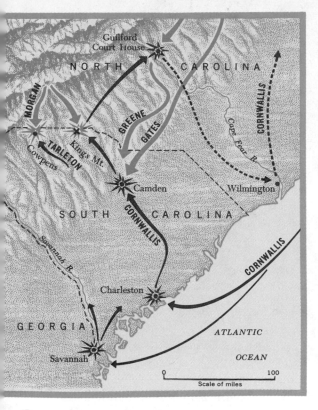

⑤ Fighting in the South: 1778–81

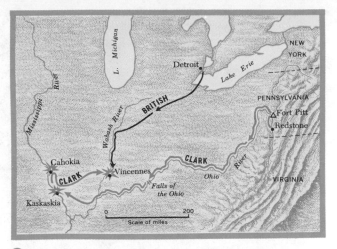

⑥ Fighting in the Northwest: 1778–79

paign in the South had been no more successful than the earlier northern campaigns.

Campaign in the Northwest.   Meanwhile, Lieutenant Colonel George Rogers Clark of Virginia had been clearing the western lands of British troops. From Virginia, whose claim to this territory went back to the charter of 1609, Clark secured money and supplies for the expedition. With a small band of hardened frontiersmen, he made his way down the Ohio River and up the Mississippi in the summer of 1778, won Indian aid, and surprised the British forts at Kaskaskia, Cahokia, and Vincennes (see map 6, this page). In December, however, Clark suffered a setback when the British recaptured Vincennes. But then in February 1779, in the dead of winter, Clark marched 170 miles eastward through the wilderness to surprise and overwhelm the British garrison at Fort Vincennes. This bold blow cleared the entire western lands of British forces.

The British surrender.   During the summer of 1781 the war proceeded swiftly to a conclusion.

Cornwallis moved northward into Virginia, basing his army at Yorktown on the peninsula between the York and James rivers (see map 7, page 134). He was supplied by the British fleet operating out of New York harbor. A small American army under generals Lafayette, Von Steuben, and Anthony Wayne of Pennsylvania watched the British closely, but the American forces were too weak to attack. Washington and a number of American and French soldiers remained at White Plains, New York. There they kept an eye on the British garrison that was under General Clinton in the city of New York.

This was the situation when a messenger from Admiral de Grasse, commander of the French fleet operating in the West Indies, arrived at Washington's headquarters. De Grasse reported that the fleet could be spared for a few months. Where, he asked, could General Washington use it most effectively?

With skill and speed, Washington quickly formulated a brilliant plan. Following Washington's instructions, de Grasse placed his fleet across the mouth of Chesapeake Bay, thereby cutting off Cornwallis from his supplies and reinforcements. The American army in White Plains then feinted at New York, leading General Clinton to believe that an attack upon the city was imminent. Instead of striking at New York, however, Washington made a forced march to Chesapeake Bay, where he and his army embarked on a fleet of transports and joined the French and American forces, including

Detail, John Trumbull, "Surrender of Lord Cornwallis at Yorktown," Yale University Art Gallery

■ The artist John Trumbull painted this scene of the surrender of the British at Yorktown. General Washington appears on horseback, in front of the American flag.

7 Fighting Around Yorktown: August–October 19, 1781

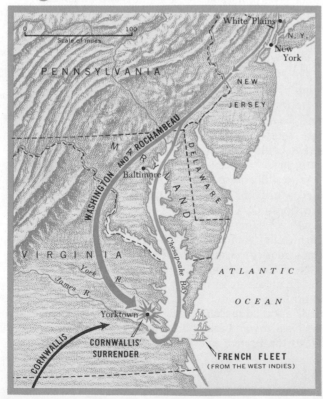

the southern militia, in front of Yorktown in Virginia (see map 7, this page).

Cornwallis was hopelessly trapped. Behind him was the French fleet. Before him was a greatly superior force of American troops, reinforced by 6,000 French troops. After a British squadron failed to break the French blockade, Cornwallis was ready to admit defeat. He surrendered his entire army of 7,000 men on October 19, 1781. Although the formal treaty of peace was not signed until 1783, all serious fighting on the American continent ceased with the American victory at Yorktown.

SECTION SURVEY

IDENTIFY: Baron von Steuben, Casimir Pulaski, Marquis de Lafayette; Valley Forge, Yorktown.

1. Why did the British campaign in the South fail?
2. In what ways did the geography of the colonies aid the Americans in their fight against the British?
3. (a) How did France hope to gain by helping the American cause? (b) Was self-gain the only reason that led France to help the Americans?
4. Have Americans ever gone abroad to aid in another country's fight for freedom? Comment.

5 A favorable treaty of peace for the victorious Americans

Both sides—the United States of America and Great Britain—faced serious problems during the eight long years of the war. In the end, however, the British problems proved to be much more difficult than those of the Americans.

Shortage of troops. One major American weakness was the relatively small number of men who were willing to fight in the war. Many Americans, indifferent to the outcome of the conflict, devoted their efforts to making the war as profitable for themselves as possible. Some merchants charged high prices for shoddy goods that they sold to the American armies. Some farmers sold their produce where it would bring the greatest profit, not caring whether it reached American or British hands. Because of this indifference and selfishness, Washington and his small band of faithful troops starved and froze at Morristown in the winter of 1776–77 and at Valley Forge in the winter of 1777–78, while in Philadelphia the British soldiers lived in comfort.

Early in his command, despite the shortage of troops, Washington ordered that no black men, slave or free, could be recruited. Some colonial leaders feared that slaves would revolt if given arms. Some of Washington's officers believed that Negroes did not make good soldiers, despite the fact that black men had fought—and fought well—in the French and Indian War and at Lexington, Concord, Ticonderoga, and Breed's Hill. At Breed's Hill, in fact, two black Americans, Peter Salem and Salem Poor, had been singled out for outstanding heroism. According to his superiors, Salem Poor "behaved like an experienced officer as well as an excellent soldier."

Washington and other leaders changed their thinking late in 1775 when Lord Dunmore, royal governor of Virginia, offered freedom to all slaves who joined the British forces. Washington now consented to the enlistment of free black men in the Continental armies. State militias, except in South Carolina and Georgia, enlisted slaves as well as free black men. Slaves were promised their freedom when the war ended; in most cases, however, the promise was not carried out.

Of some 300,000 Americans who fought in the war, about 5,000 were black. They served in the Continental navy and armies, and in the navies and militias of the states, with courage and skill. A French officer at Yorktown wrote: ". . . three quarters of the Rhode Island regiment consists of Negroes, and that regiment is the most neatly dressed, the best under arms, and the most precise in its maneuvers."

Other American weaknesses. Another major American weakness was the lack of any really effective central government. Until 1781, when, as you will see, the Articles of Confederation went into effect, the Americans fought under the weak leadership of the Second Continental Congress. The delegates to the Continental Congress, who were chosen by the legislatures of the states, had no real authority. They did make George Washington commander in chief of all the military forces, but they had no power to create any army for Washington to lead. They could only ask each state to furnish a certain number of men and supplies. If a state refused, the matter was ended.

Nor did the Continental Congress have the power to raise money by taxation. The Congress could—and did—borrow money from foreign countries and from American citizens. And it could ask the states for money—but if the states refused, Congress was helpless. In the end, Congress financed most of the war costs by issuing paper money known as "Continental currency."

Because of these problems the American military effort was weak and disorganized. Except for the first few weeks of the war, Washington never had more than 16,000 troops under his command at any one time, and he was never sure how many of these he could rely on. After each victory volunteers poured in; after each defeat the army melted away. "What we need is a good army, not a large one," Washington once remarked bitterly. He was destined to have neither. And yet his faith and courage never faltered. It was this faith combined with the unselfish devotion of many soldiers and citizens that finally carried the Patriots to victory.

British problems. Fortunately for the Americans, the British faced even more difficult problems. One of these was the problem created by geography.

When the war started, the Americans occupied the enormous territory from Canada to Florida. The only British foothold was the seaport of Boston. To win the war, the Americans needed only to hold on to what they had. The British, on the other hand, had to regain control of this enormous territory. And to regain control, they had to send troops and supplies 3,000 miles across the Atlantic in slow sailing ships. A number of British military experts were certain that the task was hopeless.

Handicapped by the problem of supply, the British were never able to conquer and hold any sizable inland area. Although the Royal Navy controlled the seas and could conquer any seaport it wished, the Americans could always move temporarily inland, where it was difficult for the British to suppy a regular army.

British blunders. The British were also guilty of many blunders and much mismanagement. They made no great effort to concentrate an overwhelming force against the Americans. To use an American expression, the British War Office "sent a boy to do a man's job."

Great Britain's major asset was its professional army. Well organized, well trained, well equipped, and well fed, the British regulars were more than a match for the Patriot troops in any engagement on open, unforested land. But the British regulars were often used badly. Their superiors in England often revealed a hopeless ignorance of the land and the people of America.

One of Great Britain's major mistakes was its reliance upon the Hessian soldiers hired by George III. Many of these unfortunate Germans had been seized forcibly by their rulers, who received payment for them from George III, and shipped them to America. Bewildered and homesick, they knew nothing about the war and cared less. As a result, they made poor soldiers.

The Loyalists or Tories who served under British colors, estimated at from 50,000 to 60,000, fought bitterly and even savagely against their former neighbors, as is common in civil war. But they, too, were untrained and unorganized, and their presence in the British ranks served to arouse the fighting spirit of the American Patriots.

Leaks in the blockade. The Royal Navy expected to sweep all enemy ships from the sea and by a tight blockade to cut off resources that the Americans needed to fight the war. But since America was a self-sufficient agricultural region, the blockade was an inconvenience rather than a disaster for the Americans.

Then, too, the Americans did have a navy. During the war more than 50 ships were built and commissioned by the Continental Congress and commanded by such men as John Paul Jones.

Jones' most memorable victory—and perhaps the greatest naval victory of the war—took place in 1779, when Jones' ship, the *Bon Homme Richard,* engaged the British ship *Serapis* in battle. With his own warship about to sink, Jones lashed the two ships together, and in desperate fighting won the victory. At the height of this battle, when asked to surrender, Jones made his famous defiant statement, "I have not yet begun to fight."

All the states except Delaware and New Jersey also built and manned their own naval vessels. Although these ships were small, the British had to spend much time in tracking them down and destroying them.

More difficult for the British to cope with were the American *privateers.* Privateers were privately owned ships whose owners were authorized by the Continental Congress or the state governments to attack enemy shipping. Slipping through the British blockade in fog or darkness, the privateers struck at defenseless British merchant vessels or small men-of-war. The money from the sale of captured ships and cargoes was divided among owners, captains, and crews. Since fortunes could quickly be made, this risky business attracted

■ Black soldiers fought—and fought well—in battles such as Breed's Hill, shown below. In all, some 5,000 black Americans served in the Continental navy and armies and in the navies and militias of the states.

thousands of adventurous colonists. The American privateers ranged far and wide searching for British ships. British losses were so heavy that marine insurance rates soared.

Opposition to British naval policy. The British fleet interfered with the shipping of neutral nations. Angered by the interference, several nations formed the League of Armed Neutrality. Before the war ended, this league included Russia, Sweden, Denmark, Prussia, Portugal, Naples, and several other European states. In addition, France, Spain, and the Netherlands were openly at war with Great Britain. Throughout the later years of conflict, the warships of these European nations, combined with the American navy and privateers, placed a heavy drain upon Great Britain's resources.

British opposition to the war. As a result, the war became increasingly unpopular in Great Britain. In fact, many leaders in Great Britain were opposed to the war effort. The situation was so bad that some British politicians and officers rejoiced at the news of an American victory, and some officers actually refused to serve overseas in America. British merchants, shipowners, and businessmen were losing heavily.

Great Britain could have continued to fight after Cornwallis' defeat at Yorktown in 1781. The British might have concentrated overwhelming forces against the Americans and, by a strict and long-continued blockade, might have finally worn them down to the point where they would have asked for peace. But the price of continuing the war was heavier than most British people were willing to pay.

The peace treaty of 1783. Negotiations to end the war began soon after the surrender of Cornwallis in October 1781. But the final treaty, called the Treaty of Paris, was not completed until September 3, 1783.

The four American commissioners—Benjamin Franklin, John Jay, John Adams, and Henry Laurens—could hardly have won better terms. By the terms of the treaty, the Americans gained (1) independence, (2) all the land between the Appalachian Mountains and the Mississippi River from the Great Lakes south to Florida,° and (3) the right to fish in the Gulf of St. Lawrence

---

° Florida, which Spain had turned over to Great Britain in 1763, was now returned to Spain. The northern boundary of Florida was not clearly defined and remained a source of friction between Spaniards and Americans until 1795 (see map above).

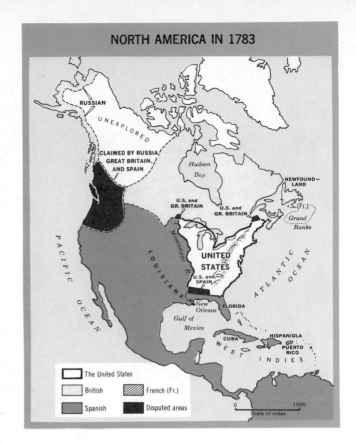

NORTH AMERICA IN 1783

The United States
British
Spanish
French (Fr.)
Disputed areas

and off the coast of Newfoundland (see map above).

A very difficult problem arose when Great Britain demanded that all property and land taken from the Tories be returned to them, and that all debts owed by Americans to Britishers be paid in full. Franklin and the other American commissioners insisted that this was impossible. The Tory property had been seized by the different states and had long since been sold. Large estates had been divided into many smaller pieces. The Continental Congress had no money to use for purchasing these properties and returning them to their former Tory owners.

Finally, after a long deadlock, the peace commissioners agreed to "recommend" that the new states allow persons with claims to use the American courts to recover their property.

The commissioners also agreed to "recommend" that private debts be handled in the same way. Actually, these recommendations were meaningless. Congress could not force the states to open their courts to Tory claims. But the British made

137

■ Benjamin Franklin traveled to France to negotiate the final Treaty of Paris in 1783. Above, dressed simply and not wearing a wig, he is presented at the French court.

the best of the situation and signed a preliminary treaty. Astonished at the liberal terms, the French foreign minister, Vergennes, declared, "The English do not make peace; they buy it."

The French, who were not represented in the peace talks until these decisions had been reached, were angry as well as surprised that the United States and Great Britain had agreed upon peace terms. Franklin had to use all his arts of persuasion to smooth the ruffled feelings of the French leaders. His success in negotiating the final Treaty of Paris in 1783 was a tribute to his skill as a diplomat.

The Americans were fortunate to be represented by such able men. They were even more fortunate that the peace commissioners decided to negotiate directly with Great Britain. Spain wanted to confine the United States of America to the land between the Atlantic and the Appalachians. If the American commissioners had been forced to sit around a peace table with representatives from Spain, France, and Great Britain, the thirteen colonies would have won only their independence—

nothing more. As it was, by making the most of Great Britain's desire for a quick end to the war, American peace commissioners won for their country a number of liberal concessions and a vast expanse of land west of the Appalachians.

SECTION SURVEY

IDENTIFY: privateers, Treaty of Paris; Salem Poor, Peter Salem, John Paul Jones; 1783.

1. List the advantages Great Britain had over the Americans at the start of the war.
2. Show how each of the following contributed to the American victory: (a) George Washington, (b) British problems in Europe, (c) British blunders.
3. (a) What role did black fighting men play in America's struggle for independence? (b) Why were white colonists at first reluctant to accept Negroes into the armed forces? (c) Were their reasons valid? Explain.
4. The Treaty of Paris of 1783 formally translated the Declaration of Independence from a wish to a reality. Explain by examining the terms of the treaty.

TRACING THE MAIN IDEAS

From the day the first English settlers in the New World began to adapt themselves to life in a strange environment, they began to grow away from their mother country. By 1763 the gap between the colonies and Great Britain was wide indeed. British efforts to draw the colonies into a firmer position in the British Empire, and to get them to help pay for the cost of running the empire, served only to antagonize the colonists. By the spring of 1775 the situation had become exceedingly tense.

Then the explosion went off. With the bloodshed at Lexington and Concord on April 19, 1775, and later at Breed's Hill, hope of compromise vanished.

In their Declaration of Independence, the American colonists broke their ties with Great Britain and proclaimed their message of freedom to the entire world. Aided by French troops on the battlefields of America and by French naval forces in the Atlantic, the Americans finally succeeded in wearing down the British and winning their independence.

With the Treaty of Paris in 1783, the world recognized that a new nation had been born. It was the first nation in the modern world to break the ties that bound it to the country that had colonized it and to launch out on its own.

As you will see in the next chapter, however, the people of the new nation faced many problems. The most difficult of these was how to organize an effective government around which Americans could rally with confidence and pride.

CHAPTER SURVEY

QUESTIONS FOR DISCUSSION

1. If, after 1763, Great Britain had maintained the same relationship it had had with the colonies before 1763, the Revolution might not have occurred. Comment.
2. British subjects in America fought, not to obtain freedom, but to confirm the freedoms they already had. Do you agree or disagree? Explain.
3. Why did the authors of the Declaration of Independence condemn George III instead of the idea of monarchy?
4. (a) What is the definition of the word "propaganda"? (b) Would you call Thomas Paine a propagandist? Explain.
5. Would you say that the American Revolution was caused more by (a) economic conflicts or (b) political differences between the colonists and the mother country? Find evidence in your textbook and library resources to support your position.
6. Some British textbooks attribute the American Revolution to a small group of radical agitators in America who were impatient with decision-making in Great Britain on matters affecting their immediate needs. (a) Do you agree or disagree with this interpretation? Explain. (b) Why do you think that British textbooks might present this interpretation of the Revolution?
7. What did Lincoln mean at Gettysburg when he said that our forefathers had "brought forth a new nation"? (Refer to the Declaration of Independence in preparing your answer.)
8. Even if the British had won a military victory over the colonists, in the long run they could not have prevented the colonies from achieving independence. Comment.

RELATING PAST TO PRESENT

1. The American Revolution provides an example of how an organized minority can bring about a revolution. Discuss with reference to current events.
2. Revolts against colonialism in Asia and Africa today can trace their beginnings to (a) the American Revolution and (b) the Declaration of Independence. Explain.
3. Despite the ideals of equality expressed in the Declaration of Independence, both slavery and racial hostility existed in the new nation; yet the ideas expressed in the Declaration are today forcing Americans to examine and try to resolve the contradiction between words and actions. Explain.
4. How does the Declaration give guidance to men who are trying to close the gap between what they are and what they might be?

USING MAPS AND CHARTS

1. (a) Using the map on page 118, point out the strategic importance of each of the campaigns in New England, the Middle Colonies, the Southern Colonies, and the Northwest. (b) Indicate the area included in the British naval blockade.
2. Locate each of the following places: Saratoga, Yorktown, Valley Forge, and Vincennes.
3. (a) Using the map on page 137, describe the boundaries of the United States after the Treaty of Paris of 1783. (b) Summarize the land claims of the European nations in North America at this time.

■ *Fort Detroit, in the Northwest Territory*

CHAPTER **8**

Creating a Confederation of States

1775 – 1787

"THE AMERICAN WAR is over," one of America's leaders declared in 1783, "but this is far from being the case with the American Revolution."

The speaker was Dr. Benjamin Rush, a prominent Philadelphia doctor and one of the signers of the Declaration of Independence. Dr. Rush knew—as did Thomas Jefferson and many other Americans—that it was easier to outline a new theory of government than it was to build a government that really worked.

Many problems faced the now independent American people. One of the most serious was whether the thirteen states, which for seven years had joined together in rebellion against British rule, would remain united now that the crisis was over. ". . . A long time, and much prudence, will be necessary to reproduce a spirit of union and . . . reverence for government," David Ramsay of South Carolina declared.

Actually, as it turned out, the American people developed a "spirit of union" and "reverence for government" in an amazingly short time. But even so, as you will see, there were moments between 1783 and 1787 when the future looked dark.

THE CHAPTER IN OUTLINE

1. Creating new state governments in the former colonies.

2. Union of the states under the Articles of Confederation.

3. The Confederation's lack of power to solve important problems.

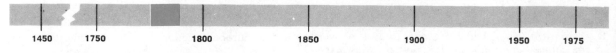

| 1450 | 1750 | 1800 | 1850 | 1900 | 1950 | 1975 |

1 Creating new state governments in the former colonies

In 1775, even before the start of actual fighting, the long-established governments of the colonies began to crumble. After the fighting at Lexington and at Breed's Hill, several royal governors returned to England. The more conservative members of the colonial legislatures also returned to their homes. By 1776 nearly all colonial government had disappeared. Only the local governments, most of them now in the hands of the Patriots, continued to meet and carry on business.

From old governments to new. The members of the Second Continental Congress were alarmed at this situation. They had no power to act as a government for the colonies. On the other hand, they knew that *someone* had to do something to prevent lawlessness and disorder from ripping the colonies apart. Thus, on May 10, 1775, the Second Continental Congress adopted a resolution urging the colonies to organize new governments to replace the colonial governments. John Adams, a delegate from Massachusetts, called this "the most important resolution that was ever taken in America."

The legislatures of New Hampshire and South Carolina, both controlled by Patriots, had already written new state constitutions. During the next few months all the other colonies except Connecticut, Rhode Island, and Massachusetts also adopted new state constitutions.

Connecticut and Rhode Island, as you recall, had always been self-governing colonies. Their colonial charters worked so well that Connecticut and Rhode Island continued to use them as state constitutions until well into the 1800's. Massachusetts, however, operated under a temporary government until near the end of the war.

Although the American people were fighting for the right to govern themselves, most of them had little or nothing to do with the writing of the new constitutions. In most states, the legislatures prepared the constitutions without consulting the people themselves.

This method of organizing the new governments did not suit Massachusetts and New Hampshire. Both these states held constitutional conventions at which specially elected delegates drafted the constitutions. When the delegates finished, the voters themselves had a chance to accept or reject the proposed constitutions.

Governments under law. The democratic ideas expressed in the Declaration of Independence helped to shape the new state constitutions. The men who wrote the constitutions wanted especially to provide ironclad guarantees of man's "natural rights"—his "unalienable rights" of "life, liberty, and the pursuit of happiness." As a result, each new state constitution began with a *bill of rights*. These bills of rights contained guarantees of religious freedom, the right to free speech and a free press, the right to assemble, the right to a fair trial by jury, and equality of all citizens before the law.

It was significant that the framers of the new state constitutions put the guarantees into *written constitutions*. In this way the guarantees became part of the fundamental law of each state. In the future, when an individual had a question about his rights under the law, he could turn to the written law itself. The law, not the opinion of a hereditary ruler or an appointed official, would provide the answer. And the law would give the same answer, the same rights, to everyone—at least to every white male citizen. Under these written state constitutions, the new American states were adopting *"government of laws, and not of men."*

■ John Adams declared that the resolution urging the colonies to replace their colonial governments with new governments was "the most important resolution that was ever taken in America."

To establish a government of laws, the new constitutions provided for a "separation of powers" among the three departments of government—the executive, legislative, and judicial departments. The constitution of Massachusetts provided that "In the government of this commonwealth, the legislative department shall never exercise the executive and judicial powers or either of them: the executive shall never exercise the legislative and judicial powers or either of them: the judicial shall never exercise the legislative and executive powers or either of them: to the end it may be a government of laws, and not of men." Although other state constitutions did not provide as clear a separation of powers as that of Massachusetts, all the states did limit the power of the executive department.

Separating church and state. Another important step taken by the states was to strengthen the principle of separation of church and government. When the Revolutionary War broke out, people in nine of the thirteen colonies were required by law to pay taxes to support an established state church. As you have read (page 74), the people had to pay these taxes even if they belonged to another church. By 1787, however, official churches existed in only three states—New Hampshire, Massachusetts, and Connecticut. In all the other states official churches had been abolished, or "disestablished." The people were free to contribute to the church of their own choice.

From that time on, the principle that the church and the state should be separate—that all individuals should be free to support the church of their

own choice and to worship as they pleased—has remained a cornerstone of American democracy.

Concern over slavery. The contradiction between the principles of the Declaration of Independence and the fact of slavery also troubled a growing number of Americans. Leading preachers, educators, lawyers, and public figures condemned slavery. In 1773 Patrick Henry said that slavery was "as repugnant to humanity as it is inconsistent with the Bible and destructive of liberty." This anti-slavery feeling led many slaveowners to free their slaves. Some did so because they were sincerely moved by the contradictions between slavery and the ideals of the Revolution. Other slaveowners freed their slaves because they thought that slavery was an expensive and inefficient way to get work done.

Thomas Jefferson was well aware that slavery contradicted the principles of freedom and equality set forth in the Declaration of Independence. In his writings he deplored the effects that slavery had of making slaveowners arrogant and of robbing slaves of human dignity.

Like many other Americans of the time, however, Jefferson was not certain about what the exact role of black people in American life should be. Jefferson did not want the full *abolition,* or ending of slavery, since he feared that white men and black men could not live peacefully side by side, especially in the southern states where slaves were so numerous. Jefferson also accepted the false, but common, thinking of his time that black men lacked the capacity for self-government. He suggested, but did not advocate, the idea that slaves might be freed and established in an area of their own on the western lands.

Some of the new state governments were moved to action by the clash between slavery and the ideals of the war they were fighting. The Continental Congress for a time prohibited the importation of slaves. Several states did the same. During the war many of the states enlisted slaves in their armed forces and granted them their freedom. Several states adopted laws providing for the gradual freeing of slaves and the eventual abolition of slavery. In Massachusetts, the Superior Court ruled that every slave within the state's borders had been freed by its constitution of 1780, which declared that "all men are born free and equal."

Anti-slavery sentiment stemming from the Revolutionary War also led to the formation of abolition societies, or groups working to end slavery. The first such society was founded by Philadelphia

LIVING AMERICAN DOCUMENTS

Virginia Statute for Religious Freedom (1786)

Well aware that Almighty God has created the mind free; *that* **all attempts to influence it by temporal punishments . . . tend only to . . . [produce] habits of hypocrisy and meanness; . . . to compel a man to furnish contributions of money for the propagation of opinions which he disbelieves is sinful and tyrannical; . . . truth is great and will prevail if left to herself. . . .**

. . . no man shall be compelled to frequent or support any religious worship . . . whatsoever; . . . all men shall be free to profess . . . their opinion in matters of religion; . . . the same shall in no wise diminish, enlarge, or affect their civil capacities. . . .

■ In spite of rising anti-slavery feeling after the Revolutionary War, slavery continued to exist in much of the country. Above, slaves work as coachmen on a southern plantation.

Quakers in 1775. By 1792 active abolition societies existed in all the states from Massachusetts southward to, and including, Virginia. These societies published pamphlets and sponsored speakers who condemned slavery as a contradiction of the Bible, of the principles of humanity, and of the principles set forth in the Declaration of Independence.

Moving toward democracy. During the Revolutionary War, then, Americans continued to strengthen the roots of democracy that had already been planted during the colonial period. But the democratic way of life did not emerge full blown from the Revolutionary War. In spite of rising anti-slavery feeling, slavery still existed in much of the country. The right to vote continued to be limited by religious and property qualifications. State governments continued to collect taxes to support the Congregational Church in New Hampshire, Massachusetts, and Connecticut. The right to hold government office in some states was denied to members of certain religious groups.

Because of these restrictions on the freedom of individuals, the ideals set forth in the Declaration of Independence were only partially realized in the 1780's. But the men and women who fought the Revolutionary War had taken a long step toward the democratic way of life, and it was evident in 1783 that they were about to take other steps. This is what Dr. Benjamin Rush had in mind when he wrote, "The American war is over, but this is far from being the case with the American Revolution."

SECTION SURVEY

IDENTIFY: bill of rights, "government of laws, and not of men," written constitution, abolition of slavery.

1. Why was it necessary for the colonists to organize new governments?
2. Why was it significant that each state put its bill of rights into writing?
3. Why did the new state constitutions provide for (a) separation of powers and (b) separation of church and state?
4. How was rising concern over slavery reflected in the revolutionary period?
5. In his writings Jefferson said that slavery was wrong. Yet Jefferson spared no effort to capture his runaway slaves and freed only five of his many slaves when he died. (a) How did Jefferson's actions contradict his words? (b) Why did so many Americans have contradictory views about the role of Negroes in American life?

2 Union of the states under the Articles of Confederation

By the summer of 1776, when independence was declared, the thirteen former British colonies had become thirteen states. Each of these states was separate and independent. The Second Continental Congress had no power to act for all the states. Nor did it have the power to compel the states to follow its wishes.

The problem of unity. The delegates to the Continental Congress agreed that the thirteen states must unite. But in what kind of union? And what kind of central government should they create?

Some delegates, including Benjamin Franklin, wanted a strong central government. They wanted the central government to be stronger than any of the state governments.

Most delegates, however, objected to a strong central government. They pointed out that the states were fighting a war to win their independence. Why, then, should the states deliberately create an American government that might turn out to be as tyrannical as British rule had been?

A plan for confederation. After long debate, the Continental Congress agreed that some kind of unity was needed to fight the war and appointed a committee to propose a workable plan of union.

LIVING AMERICAN DOCUMENTS

Articles of Confederation (1781)

Article 1. **The style of this confederacy shall be "The United States of America."**

Article 2. **Each state retains its sovereignty, freedom, and independence, and every power, jurisdiction, and right which is not by this confederation expressly delegated to the United States in Congress assembled.**

Article 3. **The said states hereby severally enter into a firm league of friendship with each other for their common defense, the security of their liberties, and their mutual and general welfare, binding themselves to assist each other against all force offered to or attacks made upon them or any of them on account of religion, sovereignty, trade, or any other pretense whatever....**

On July 12, 1776 the committee, headed by John Dickinson of Pennsylvania, presented a report to the Continental Congress, bearing the title "Articles of Confederation and Perpetual Union." After debating these "Articles" for more than a year, the delegates finally, on November 15, 1777, voted to adopt the Articles of Confederation.

The Articles of Confederation created a *confederation,* or league, of free and independent states known as "The United States of America." The central government of the league was to consist of a Congress having from two to seven delegates from each state. Each state delegation was to have only one vote in the Congress.

But this was only the first step in forming a union. Before the Articles of Confederation could become effective, each of the thirteen states had to *ratify,* or accept, the proposal.

Adoption of the Confederation. Not until 1781 did all the states agree to enter the Confederation. Maryland was the last.

During the discussion over the Confederation, the delegates from Maryland insisted that all the states with claims to land lying between the Appalachian Mountains and the Mississippi River (see map, page 149) must surrender their claims to the Confederation.

Maryland based its proposal on two arguments. First, the British were in actual possession of the western lands. To conquer this territory, the common effort of all the states was needed. Thus, the Maryland delegates argued, if all the states helped to free the western lands, then all the states should share the fruits of victory.

The men from Maryland advanced a second argument. Look into the future, they urged, to a time when the western lands would be filled with thriving towns and prosperous farms. At that time, the states owning these lands would overwhelm by sheer size and population the small states confined to the Atlantic seaboard. This being true, the Maryland delegates declared, they would not join the Confederation until the states owning western lands surrendered their claims.

Maryland's stand provoked heated debates. But finally the states with claims to western lands agreed to surrender their claims, and in 1781 Maryland ratified the Articles of Confederation. Thus the new league of states came into existence. The Articles of Confederation were an attempt to provide a kind of written constitution for the new nation. The attempt, as you will see, was successful in some ways but unsuccessful in others.

THE LAND ORDINANCE OF 1785: Township Land Survey

A WESTERN TOWNSHIP— 36 SQUARE MILES

6	5	4	3	2	1
7	8	9	10	11	12
Income reserved for school support → 16		15	14	13
19	20	21	22	23	24
30	29	28	27	26	25
31	32	33	34	35	36

6 miles (height)

6 miles

←1 mile→

One section (640 acres) one square mile

Half-section (320 acres)

Half quarter-section (80 acres)

Quarter-section (160 acres)

Quarter quarter-sections (40 acres each)

■ From an airplane, many parts of the United States show a neat pattern of farms and roads. This orderliness goes back to the township system of land survey first adopted in 1785. Income secured from the sale of Section 16 was for school support, but the school might be built in any of the sections.

Land—the first problem. Control of the land west of the Appalachian Mountains gave the Confederation its first real power and a great responsibility. Now, in 1781, the Confederation faced the same fundamental problems Great Britain and other colonial powers had faced when they first got colonies in the New World.

Settlers were already moving into the wilderness between the Appalachians and the Mississippi River. Nothing was more certain than that the tide of settlers would swell.

How was the land to be distributed among the men and women who "colonized" America's frontier? Who would profit from the sale of the land— a few land speculators or the settlers? Who would make laws for the towns and cities and states that would appear—the Confederation or the settlers?

These were real problems. To a large extent, the future of the new nation depended upon the answers.

Nature of the land problem. Great Britain had never developed a satisfactory land policy for the American colonies. As a result, the methods that new settlers used to secure land varied from colony to colony.

In colonial New England a fairly orderly system had been worked out. There, a person wishing to move west joined others of like mind and secured from the colonial assembly a grant of land which was carefully *surveyed,* or measured.

In other colonies, especially in Virginia, individuals generally went out into the new country, selected whatever land appealed to them, and settled on it. Naturally they took the best land, ignoring land that looked less desirable. Settlements were therefore thinly spread out, increasing the danger of Indian attacks. This method of settlement also led to frequent boundary disputes between settlers.

The government of the Confederation decided to work out a systematic method by which settlers could get clear *titles,* or guarantees of ownership, to land beyond the Appalachian Mountains. The government also decided to provide a system of granting land by which settlements could be made more compact and therefore easier to defend against Indian raids.

The Land Ordinance of 1785. The system of land settlement worked out by the Confederation was written down in the Land Ordinance of 1785.

145

Daniel Boone passing through Cumberland Gap

DANIEL BOONE, MAN AND MYTH

"Were you ever lost?" a friend asked Daniel Boone. "No," Boone replied, "but I was *bewildered* once for three days." One can multiply such stories by the hundreds. Which are true, which are fiction, it is hard to say, for Boone lives in history as part man, part myth.

Daniel Boone (1734–1820) was indeed a remarkable character, who spent most of his life in the wilderness. As a result of his skill and intelligence—as well as his luck—he lived to celebrate his 86th birthday.

Boone's age was remarkable. For most pioneers, life was exciting—but brief! In 1780, for example, 256 settlers in what is now Tennessee signed their names to a "constitution" for their new community. Ten years later all but a dozen were dead—and only one had died a natural death!

Boone is best known as the bold pioneer who, a few years before the Revolutionary War, blazed the Wilderness Trail through the Appalachians into the "dark and bloody ground" south of the Ohio River. There were others equally bold, who, about the same time, opened up the country that was to become Tennessee. But Boone had the good fortune to have a "publicity agent."

Boone was approaching 50 when he sat down with John Filson, a writer, to recall his life. Probably Boone colored the stories he told Filson, and Filson himself added much to the telling. Thus the man who finally emerged from the book bore only a limited resemblance to the rough-and-ready pioneer who lived, fought, and died on the frontier of the growing nation.

The method of westward expansion which it outlined was employed, with some changes, until 1862, when it was replaced by the Homestead Act (page 390).

The Land Ordinance of 1785 provided for government survey of squares of land six miles long and six miles wide to be known as *townships*. Each township was further surveyed and divided into 36 smaller squares of 640 acres, or one square mile, to be known as *sections*. One section in every township, section number 16, was to be set aside for the support of public schools. Four other sections were reserved for the United States. The remaining 31 sections were to be sold by the government at a price of not less than one dollar an acre (see chart, page 145).

This plan had several advantages. Since settlements would be close together, defense against the Indians would be less of a problem. Moreover, disputes over boundaries and titles would be largely eliminated, since government surveyors would determine the exact location of every section before settlers arrived. Finally, the sale of lands would provide the Confederation with desperately needed funds to meet current expenses and to pay off part of the Revolutionary War debt.

Government of new lands. After adopting a systematic plan for western settlement, the Confederation turned to another problem. How should the western lands be governed?

If the Americans had followed the British example, they would have regarded the whole western area as a colony. But Americans could hardly forget their recent war, waged in part against the mercantile theory of trade which put British interests and the interests of the empire as a whole above the interests of the colonies. With this in mind, the Continental Congress had already adopted, in 1780, a resolution promising that new western states could come into the Confederation equal in all respects to the older states.

This decision had been hastened by other developments. Before the Revolutionary War daring men like Daniel Boone had been penetrating the mountain passes and making settlements in what are now Kentucky and Tennessee (see map, page 149). This westward movement had, of course, been checked by the British in the Proclamation of 1763 and the Quebec Act of 1774, both of which closed the western lands to settlers. Once the Revolution began, however, more and more people crossed the mountains to enter the forbidden land. For these people the problem of government had to be solved as quickly as possible.

Land speculators also were eager for the Confederation to adopt a plan for governing the western country. These speculators stood a better chance of selling the land if they could assure settlers that a program for orderly land development and self-government had been adopted.

The Northwest Ordinance of 1787. In 1787 the Confederation partly fulfilled its earlier promise by passing the Northwest Ordinance. This ordinance provided for the governing of the Northwest Territory (see map, page 149).

In the beginning the Northwest Territory was to be ruled by a governor and three judges appointed by the Congress of the Confederation in Philadelphia. Later on, when the population included 5,000 free males of voting age, the settlers might elect a legislature to pass laws for themselves. They might also appoint a delegate to speak for them, but not to vote, in the Congress at Philadelphia. Still later, when the population of any part of the Northwest Territory reached 60,000 free inhabitants, the people could draft a constitution. Once this constitution had been approved by Congress, that part of the Northwest Territory would become a state, equal in every respect to the older states. Not less than three nor more than five states were to be carved out of the Northwest Territory.

Democratic achievements. Two other provisions in the Northwest Ordinance of 1787 encouraged the growth of democracy. One provision barred slavery from all the land composing the Northwest Territory. A second provision encouraged public education.

The fathers of the country believed that public

■ The land and territorial policies of the Confederation stimulated settlements that grew into today's large cities in the Middle West. By 1838, Cincinnati, Ohio, looked like this.

LIVING AMERICAN DOCUMENTS

Northwest Ordinance (1787)

Article 1. **No person . . . shall ever be molested on account of his mode of worship or religious sentiments. . . .**

Article 2. **The inhabitants of the said territory shall always be entitled to the benefits of the writ of habeas corpus and of the trial by jury. . . .**

Article 3. **Religion, morality, and knowledge being necessary to good government and the happiness of mankind, schools and the means of education shall forever be encouraged. The utmost good faith shall always be observed toward the Indians. . . .**

Article 6. **There shall be neither slavery nor involuntary servitude in the said territory, otherwise than in punishment of crimes. . . .**

SECTION SURVEY

IDENTIFY: central government, Confederation, Northwest Territory; Daniel Boone.

1. Were Americans satisfied with the government provided by the Articles of Confederation? Explain.
2. The period from 1783 to 1789 is sometimes called the "Critical Period." Do you think Americans living then would have agreed? Explain.
3. How did the Land Ordinance of 1785 resolve the problem that the British thought they had solved with the Proclamation of 1763?
4. Although the Northwest Ordinance of 1787 promised the "utmost good faith" toward the Indians, the Indians were in effect dispossessed of their lands. (a) Why did an undemocratic practice result from a most democratic policy? (b) Would you say that the British-Indian culture clash had become an American-Indian culture clash? Explain.

education was a necessary condition for the successful working of representative government. As a result, the Northwest Ordinance declared that "Religion, morality, and knowledge being necessary to good government and the happiness of mankind, schools and the means of education shall forever be encouraged." This provision stimulated public support of schools and colleges in the Territory.

The policy developed in the Northwest Ordinance was the most democratic colonial policy the modern world had known. It provided the machinery by which newer, less settled areas could eventually become equal members with parent communities. Under this general plan, almost all the new lands acquired by the United States in its march to the Pacific shores and beyond were admitted to the Union—first as *Territories,* later as *states.*

The inhabitants in the western Territories sometimes felt that they had many complaints against the national government. With one or two exceptions, however, no Territory ever seriously considered leaving the Union, for the people knew that, sooner or later, they would be admitted as equal members. And they also knew that, as their population grew, their influence on government policy would become more effective.

Years after the Northwest Ordinance was adopted, Daniel Webster gave his sober opinion of its importance: "I doubt whether one single law of any lawgiver, ancient or modern, has produced effects of more distinct, marked, and lasting character than the Ordinance of 1787."

3 The Confederation's lack of power to solve important problems

The government created by the Articles of Confederation was able, as you have seen, to solve some of the important problems facing the new nation. But there were other serious problems that the leaders of the new government could not solve.

The problem of weakness. Many Americans insisted that the central government was too weak. Actually, the men who wrote the Articles of Confederation had organized an effective "league of friendship." A mere league, or confederation, of independent states was not strong enough to solve all the critical problems confronting the newly independent states.

On paper the Confederation appeared to have certain powers. It could regulate weights and measures. It could create post offices. It could borrow money and coin money. It could direct foreign affairs and declare war and make peace. It could build and equip a navy. It could ask the states to provide men and money for an army.

These powers looked well enough on paper. But each state, jealous of its own rights, carefully guarded the use of these powers. The delegates who sat in Congress had no real authority. They were paid by the states and voted as their state legislatures directed them to vote. Each state delegation

(*continued on page 150*)

ORGANIZATION OF THE WESTERN LANDS

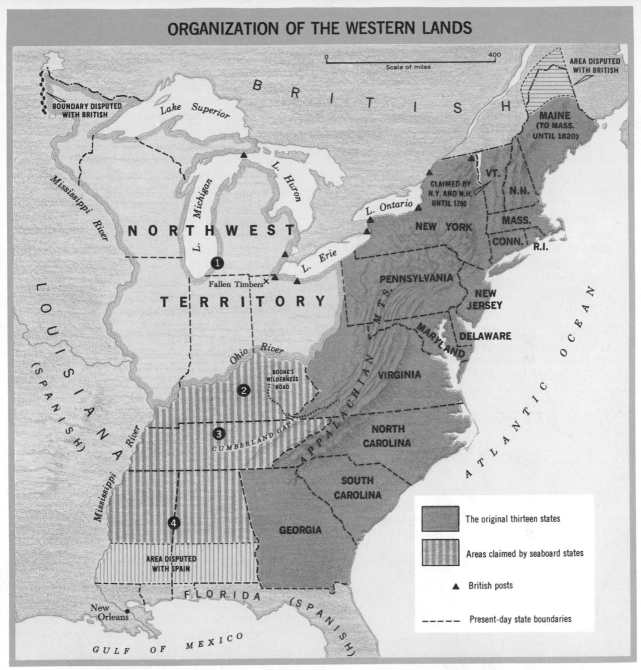

Notice the regions numbered 1 to 4 on the map above. As people moved into the unsettled lands in these numbered regions west of the Appalachian Mountains, new states were created and admitted to the Union. The following states were created out of the four regions north and south of the Ohio River:

1 These states were carved out of the Northwest Territory: Ohio (1803), Indiana (1816), Illinois (1818), Michigan (1837), Wisconsin (1848), and part of Minnesota (1858).

2 Originally claimed by Virginia; admitted as state of Kentucky in 1792.

3 North Carolina and South Carolina claims ceded to federal government in 1792; admitted as state of Tennessee in 1796.

4 Georgia claims relinquished by 1802; became part of Mississippi Territory; admitted as states of Mississippi (1817) and Alabama (1819).

was entitled to only one vote in Congress. Rhode Island, smallest of the states, had as much influence in deciding national issues as did the larger states of Virginia, New York, and Massachusetts.

No matter of importance could be settled without the consent of at least nine states, and changes in the Articles required the unanimous votes of the thirteen states. Finally, the Confederation lacked an executive, like our President now, with power to enforce measures adopted by Congress. And it had no central national court, like our Supreme Court, to protect the rights of citizens.

Lack of power to regulate finances. Money would have been a serious postwar problem even if the Articles of Confederation had created a stronger central government. As it was, the weakness of the Confederation made the money problem more difficult to solve.

This paper money, designed by Paul Revere, was issued in Massachusetts in defiance of British rule, even before independence was declared. But the money had little value under the Confederation.

TWENTY FOUR SHILLINGS

Issued in defence of American Liberty

Ense petit placidam, sub Libertate Quietem

MAGNA CHARTA

Aug.ᵗ 18. 1775.

To illustrate the problem, let us imagine a scene in a colonial store in 1783. The customer has just chosen some goods. He reaches into his pocket to pay his bill, and out tumbles a pile of coins and paper money. There are French, Spanish, English, Dutch, German, and Portuguese coins. There are pennies coined in Vermont, Massachusetts, Connecticut, New Jersey, and Pennsylvania. There is paper money issued by the Continental Congress during the opening years of the Revolutionary War and paper money issued by several of the states.

Some of the coins have been "clipped." That is, someone has stolen part of their value by scraping gold or silver from their edges. Some of the money may be counterfeit. The paper money is almost worthless, "not worth a Continental," many people grumble. Both the storekeeper and the customer would willingly exchange $1,000 of paper money issued by the Continental Congress for one dollar's worth of silver.

Obviously, only a government with authority to regulate finances in all of the thirteen states could bring order out of such chaos. But the states, each fearful of losing some of its newly won power, had not given this authority to the Confederation. The Confederation could coin its own money. But it had no way of obtaining gold and silver to be coined. The Confederation had no power to force the states to contribute money for the support of the general government. Less than one fourth of the money requested by Congress was ever raised.

No wonder the Confederation could not pay even the interest on the war debts. No wonder Europeans made bets as to how long the United States could survive.

Lack of power over interstate trade. Europeans had other reasons for regarding the new nation with scorn. The colonists had rebelled against Great Britain partly because they wanted to regulate their own trade. Now, with independence won, each state proceeded to make trade regulations to benefit its own citizens.

New York, for example, levied duties on products entering the state from New Jersey and Connecticut. New Jersey got even with New York by heavily taxing a lighthouse built on New Jersey soil by New York to guide ships into the Hudson River.

The resulting confusion led many Americans to think that perhaps the British had been right in insisting that only a central authority could regulate trade to the best advantage of all concerned.

Merchants who were opposed in theory to central control began to suggest that even the danger of tyranny was better than the confusion resulting from control of trade by the separate states. Here and there businessmen demanded that the Confederation be given power to regulate *interstate trade*.°

Lack of power over foreign trade. American merchants also found it difficult to carry on foreign trade in the years immediately following the peace treaty of 1783. This, too, was largely the result of the war. The British, now regarding the Americans as a foreign people, no longer gave them bounties and favored treatment in British ports.

Many people suffered from the government's lack of power to control foreign trade. Among them were the small but growing number of men engaged in manufacturing. During the Revolutionary War, when the British naval blockade made it difficult for Americans to import manufactured goods, Americans developed their own industries. But once the fighting stopped, British merchants flooded American markets with manufactured goods produced at low cost by well-established British industries.

American manufacturers began to talk about a

° *interstate trade:* trade between the people of different states. "Intrastate trade" is trade between people within a single state.

central government with power to levy import duties on manufactured goods from Great Britain and other countries. Such duties, added to the cost of imported goods, would make the prices of foreign goods and of American goods more nearly equal.

Lack of power to enforce treaties. To add to the confusion, the Confederation did not have the power to enforce its own treaties. When John Adams tried to negotiate a commercial treaty with Great Britain in 1785, the British only smiled. What value was a treaty, they politely asked Adams, when any one of the thirteen states could ignore it? No, the British said, under the system of government operating in America not one, but thirteen, treaties would be needed.

The British were right, of course. American leaders like John Jay were forced to admit that the peace treaty of 1783 was constantly being "violated . . . by one or other of the states." Britishers found it impossible to collect the debts owed them by Americans. Tories found it impossible to secure compensation for the property seized from them during the Revolution.

Quite naturally, Britishers grew increasingly angry at the failure of the Americans to pay the Tories. Using this failure as an excuse, the British refused to withdraw from the forts and trading posts in the Northwest Territory, as they had agreed to do in the Treaty of Paris in 1783.

Lack of military power. The refusal of the British to leave the western forts which protected their fur trade aroused the anger of the Americans living west of the Appalachians. The freedom-loving, independent westerners felt that the new government of the United States should drive the British away. The westerners wanted a display of military power, but the Confederation was powerless to meet their request.

Also because of its lack of military strength, the Confederation could not solve, or even partly solve, the problems between the settlers and the Indians. The Indians continued to resist the advance of the settlers, who continued to cut down forests and farm the land, ruining the game and furs on which the Indians depended. Conflict was inevitable.

To make matters worse, reckless Spanish and British officers in North America sometimes encouraged the Indians to attack western settlers. From their forts in the Northwest Territory, the British supplied the Indians with guns and ammunition. The Spaniards, who owned Florida and Louisiana, including all of the land west of the Mississippi River, also supplied the Indians with weapons.

John Adams tried but failed to get the British to give up their forts in the Northwest Territory. Nor were other Americans able to get the Spaniards to make any concessions.

Americans also failed to get the Spaniards to give them the right to use the port of New Orleans (see map, page 149). This port was important to settlers living in the Ohio Valley and in the land east of the Mississippi River. These settlers had no roads over which they could carry their products across the mountains to the eastern markets and seaports. The only possible way they could sell their produce was to float it down the Mississippi River to New Orleans. There they could load it on seagoing vessels and ship it to the Atlantic ports or to Europe. Unfortunately for the western settlers, the Spaniards who controlled New Orleans refused to guarantee Americans the right to use this seaport, and the American government was not strong enough to force Spain to grant this right.

The threat of civil war. Following the Revolution, the country experienced an economic slump —a sharp decline in business activity and jobs— what we now call a *depression*.

The farmers of Massachusetts were especially hard hit. Before the Revolutionary War much of their cash income had come from the sale of their farm and forest produce to the British West Indies. After the break with Great Britain this market was closed to them, and they found it increasingly difficult to get money to pay their taxes and the interest on their mortgages. To make matters worse, merchants and businessmen, mostly from Boston, controlled the Massachusetts state legislature. These men passed new laws that shifted the burden of taxation onto the farmers. Among these taxes was a heavy tax on land.

During the summer of 1786 farmers met in hastily assembled meetings to demand relief. But the Massachusetts legislature refused to act. As farm after farm was *foreclosed,* or seized for non-payment of taxes or interest on the mortgage, some Massachusetts farmers banded together and took matters into their own hands.

Shays' Rebellion. Led by Daniel Shays, the Massachusetts farmers demanded that the state legislature end the foreclosing of farms and give them a larger representation in the legislature. A group under Shays also tried to seize the arsenal at Springfield in an effort to secure guns, but they were too poorly armed to succeed.

Frightened by this defiance of the law, citizens of Boston raised funds to equip a militia to put down Shays' Rebellion. The troops hunted Shays and his men through the snowy woods, killing many and driving some across the state boundary into what is now Vermont. The rebellion was crushed.

Nevertheless, many Americans were thoroughly alarmed. Armed revolt threatened law and order and might even destroy the new nation. "There are combustibles in every state which a spark might set fire to," George Washington declared.

Signs of returning prosperity. Not all of the problems facing the country in the 1780's could be blamed, however, on the weaknesses of the Articles of Confederation. Hard times would have followed the war even if the government had been stronger. After all, property had been destroyed, long-established trade connections had been broken, and commerce and business in general had been seriously disturbed.

Even as early as 1785, only two years after the war ended, there were signs of better times ahead. By that date American ships were once again busily trading with countries outside the British empire. Sailors, shipowners, merchants, farmers, and manufacturers were sharing in the profits of this growing trade. Many of the interstate trade

☆UNDER ☆MY☆ ☆WINGS☆ ☆EVERY☆ ☆THING☆ ☆PROSPERS☆

■ New Orleans was a prosperous city in 1803, the year it became American. The strategic location of this port city was one of the most important reasons for the Louisiana Purchase.

barriers were not enforced. As a result, American products continued to cross state lines in considerable quantities.

By 1785 some Americans were satisfied with the government under the Articles of Confederation. They were pleased with the signs of returning prosperity. They were satisfied with the wise policy that the Confederation was developing for the western lands.

Despite these gains, the central government still was too weak to solve many of the problems facing the new country. It was not strong enough to establish a sound financial system, to regulate trade, to enforce treaties, or to use military force when force was needed. These government weaknesses disturbed groups of Americans—merchants and manufacturers, workmen of the cities, and westerners, who needed a strong central government to

protect them from the Indians and from the Spaniards and the British.

SECTION SURVEY

IDENTIFY: "not worth a Continental," interstate trade, duties, depression, foreclosure; John Jay.

1. What were the major weaknesses of the government under the Articles of Confederation?
2. What would have been your chief problem in the 1780's if you had been (a) a merchant, (b) a farmer?
3. Why did foreign countries show disrespect toward the government under the Articles of Confederation?
4. (a) What were the causes and results of Shays' Rebellion? (b) Why did this rebellion alarm many Americans?

153

TRACING THE MAIN IDEAS

Early in 1775, more than a year before the colonists declared their independence, the old colonial governments began to crumble. British officials began to leave the colonies. Tories, loyal to the British king and Parliament, began to flee to Canada, the British West Indies, and Great Britain. By 1776 the Americans faced the problem of creating new state governments and a new central government.

The new state constitutions written during the Revolutionary War reflected the deep-seated desire of Americans for a voice in their own government. All of the new governments were based upon written constitutions. The new constitutions contained bills of rights guaranteeing freedom to every citizen.

During the Revolutionary War Americans began to tackle the problem of building a central government. In their first efforts to govern themselves at the national level, the leaders of the thirteen free states wrote the Articles of Confederation. However, this experiment with a league of more or less independent states was only partially successful.

There were two basic problems. First, there was the problem of dividing powers between the states and the central government. To this problem the Confederation had given no answer. Second, the Confederation could not establish uniform laws binding upon the states and the people of the states.

Even before 1787 some American leaders had become convinced that only a stronger central government could provide order in the new nation. Once this conclusion had been reached, many American leaders began to take steps to change the existing form of government. As you will see in Chapter 9, these steps led to the drafting and adoption of the Constitution of the United States of America.

CHAPTER SURVEY

QUESTIONS FOR DISCUSSION

1. Despite their weaknesses, the Articles of Confederation were a great step toward building a strong and united nation. Do you think this is a valid statement? Explain.
2. Benjamin Rush of Pennsylvania, one of the signers of the Declaration of Independence, said at the end of the Revolutionary War: "The American war is over, but this is far from being the case with the American Revolution." Explain what he meant.
3. In 1790, there were approximately 700,000 slaves in the United States. (a) Why could emancipation have been successful at that time? (b) What were the consequences of allowing slavery to exist in the new nation?
4. Despite its treatment of the Indians, the Northwest Ordinance of 1787 produced lasting beneficial results essential to the establishment of the United States. Explain.

RELATING PAST TO PRESENT

1. Do the arguments presented in 1785 against a strong central government apply today? Why or why not?
2. Starting with the Articles of Confederation, American government has been faced with the continuous problem of finding (a) a balance between the power of the states and the power of the central government, and (b) a balance betwen liberty and authority. Explain.

USING MAPS AND CHARTS

1. Using the map on page 149, (a) describe the boundaries of the old Northwest Territory. (b) Point out the Cumberland Gap and indicate its importance. (c) Name and locate the new states formed out of the Northwest Territory. (d) Name and locate the new states formed out of the territory south of the Ohio River and east of the Mississippi River.
2. Referring to the chart on page 145, (a) explain the reasons for this township plan, and (b) show the relation between this plan and the rectangular pattern of several states. (For this pattern, see the map on pages 878–79.)

IN LATE April and the early weeks of May 1787, a number of the most distinguished men in America traveled toward Philadelphia. They came from all the states except Rhode Island, some on sailing vessels, some in carriages, some on horseback. These men were official delegates from the states to a meeting called the Constitutional Convention.

The decision by the Congress of the Confederation to hold this convention arose out of a meeting at Annapolis, Maryland, in 1786. The Annapolis meeting had been called to discuss a uniform system of trade regulations for all of the states.

Only five states, however, were represented at Annapolis. The delegates decided that it would be useless to try to accomplish anything with such a slim representation. Instead, they petitioned Congress to call another meeting of all the states, not only to discuss commercial problems, but also to study the weaknesses of the Confederation. Congress was slow to act on this proposal, but finally called the meeting for "the sole and express purpose of revising the Articles of Confederation. . . ."

The delegates to the Convention soon decided to go beyond their instructions and to write a wholly new Constitution, one that would do more than strengthen the Articles of Confederation. Between May and September of 1787, they drafted a Constitution which presently became, and still is, the foundation of all government in the United States. It has also become a model for representative government throughout the world.

■ *Washington addressing the Constitutional Convention*

CHAPTER 9

Creating a Federal Union

1787 – 1789

THE CHAPTER IN OUTLINE

1. A spirit of compromise at the Constitutional Convention.
2. Ratification of the Constitution after heated debate.
3. A workable form of government under the Constitution.
4. Separation of powers with checks and balances under the Constitution.
5. Safeguards for individual liberty under the Constitution.
6. The Constitution as a flexible, living document.

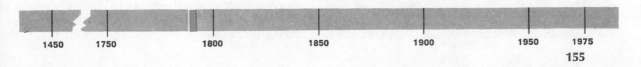

| 1450 | 1750 | 1800 | 1850 | 1900 | 1950 | 1975 |

1 A spirit of compromise at the Constitutional Convention

On the morning of May 14, 1787, the date set for the opening of the Constitutional Convention, Philadelphia's State House (later known as Independence Hall) was open and waiting for the delegates. Only two delegations appeared—one from Pennsylvania, the other from Virginia. By May 25, however, delegates from seven states—a majority—were present, and the most famous convention in American history began.

The delegates. The delegates to the Constitutional Convention were a remarkable cross section of American leadership. Most of them had played

■ Benjamin Franklin, 81 years old at the time of the Constitutional Convention, was its "elder statesman." Deeply respected by the other delegates, Franklin often helped to calm rising tempers.

active parts in their state governments. Many were learned in history and political philosophy. More than half had been members of the Second Continental Congress or the Congress of the Confederation. Eight had signed the Declaration of Independence, and nearly all had taken part in the American Revolution. Several had been diplomatic representatives from the United States to the governments of Europe. These men understood the problems their country faced.

Benjamin Franklin, now 81 years old, was the "elder statesman" of the Convention. Deeply respected by the other delegates, Franklin often helped to calm rising tempers. Most of the delegates, however, were relatively young. George Washington, unanimously chosen presiding officer of the Convention, was one of the older members at 55. Among the more active leaders, James Madison of Virginia was 36, James Wilson of Pennsylvania was 45, Alexander Hamilton of New York was only 32.

Several important men who had helped win the struggle for independence were not present at the Convention. Patrick Henry of Virginia refused to attend, saying that he "smelled a rat." He was afraid that the Convention would take away some of the power of the states, which he was convinced would be a setback for free government. Samuel Adams of Massachusetts had not been chosen as a delegate. Thomas Jefferson, John Adams, and Thomas Paine were in Europe.

Meeting in secrecy. The Convention was held in secret. Guards stood watch at every door. Each delegate agreed not to discuss Convention business with outsiders. Indeed, to prevent the aged and talkative Franklin from absentmindedly giving away important secrets at the dinner parties he liked to attend, a discreet Convention member was assigned to accompany him and restrain him if necessary.

Why all this secrecy? The delegates, being practical men, feared that news of what they were doing would plunge the country into argument. They also knew that it would be easier to iron out differences in a private conference room than in a public debate. They felt that they must first agree among themselves before presenting proposals to the public.

Official notes of the proceedings were kept, but they were not released until 1818. James Madison kept an unofficial record. He jotted down notes during the meetings and then labored far into the night writing them out with a quill pen. Madison's notes, which were far more complete than the official record, were kept secret until after his death in 1836.

Areas of agreement. The delegates to the Constitutional Convention represented different sections of the country with different interests. Yet from the beginning they agreed on a number of important matters. They agreed, first of all, that the nation's problems would not be solved by a mere revision of the Articles of Confederation. They believed that an entirely new Constitution was needed.

Most of the delegates also agreed that the country needed a strong central government. However, none of them favored a government with unlimited power.

The delegates agreed too that they must build a government in which no single section or group could dominate the rest. They agreed on a *republican* form of government—that is, a government in which the supreme power rested in the voters, who would elect men to run the government for them.

The delegates also agreed that they wanted a government in which the executive, legislative, and judicial powers would be separated. They recognized too that the new government would be respected only if it had the power to tax, to raise an army, and to regulate commerce. These lessons they had learned under the Articles of Confederation.

But there were many issues on which the delegates did not agree. Sectional issues and economic problems divided them. If the delegates had refused to compromise, the writing of the Constitution would have been impossible. Fortunately for later generations, most of the delegates at Philadelphia made generous concessions time and again.

The Great Compromise. One of the most serious conflicts of the Convention was a struggle between the large and small states over representation in Congress. Governor Edmund Randolph of Virginia, a large state, presented a plan of government now called the Virginia Plan. This plan provided that the population of each state would determine the number of representatives that it could send to Congress. William Paterson of New Jersey, speaking for the small states, presented what is now called the New Jersey Plan. Under this plan, each state would have equal representation in Congress. Paterson firmly opposed the Virginia Plan. "New Jersey will never confederate on

George Washington was chosen unanimously as presiding officer of the Constitutional Convention. He was described as "indeed, in every sense of the word, a wise, a good, and a great man."

the plan before the committee," he declared. "She would be swallowed up."

Speaking for the larger states, James Wilson of Pennsylvania threw back a challenging question: "Are not the citizens of Pennsylvania equal to those of New Jersey? Does it require 150 of the former to balance 50 of the latter? No," Wilson warned, "if the small states will not confederate on this plan, Pennsylvania . . . would not confederate on any other."

After a month of debate, the delegates finally adopted what is known as the Great Compromise. It is also sometimes called the Connecticut Compromise, since it was first proposed by Roger Sherman of Connecticut. By a narrow margin the

157

JOHN FITCH'S STEAMBOAT

On August 22, 1787, many delegates to the Constitutional Convention joined a crowd of Philadelphians on the banks of the Delaware River to witness a strange sight—the trial run of one of the first American steamboats. The trial was a success, and John Fitch, the inventor and builder, was encouraged to go on with his work.

In 1790 Fitch started regular passenger service between Philadelphia and Trenton and other towns along the river. During the summer and fall the boat, moving at about 8 miles an hour, traveled more than 1,500 miles.

"Fitch's steamboat really performs like a charm," wrote one of the passengers. "It is a pleasure, while one is on board of her in a contrary wind, to observe her superiority over the river shallops, sloops, ships, et cetera, who, to gain anything, must make a zigzag course, while this, our new invented vessel, proceeds in a direct line. . . . Fitch is certainly one of the most ingenious creatures alive, and will certainly make his fortune. . . ."

John Fitch never made his fortune. The steamboat would one day play an essential part in western settlement. It would carry settlers and their products over the water highways of the vast Mississippi Valley and thus help to bind the nation together. But Fitch was ahead of his time. People laughed at him and refused to lend him money for developing his invention. Poor and broken in spirit, he moved to Kentucky, where he died in 1798.

Convention voted for a Congress of two houses—a Senate and a House of Representatives. Each state, large or small, would be represented by two Senators, thereby giving each state equal power in the Senate. In the House, however, representation would be based upon population.

The three-fifths compromise. Some equally complicated differences arose between delegates from the northern and the southern states. These differences arose from a conflict between the economic interests of northern merchants and southern planters.

One dispute arose over the counting of slaves. Southerners wanted slaves to be counted when figuring the number of representatives to be elected to the House of Representatives. However, they did not want slaves to be counted when determining the amount of taxes to be paid. Northerners, on the other hand, thought that slaves should be counted when figuring taxes, but not when figuring representatives.

As a compromise, northerners and southerners agreed to count three fifths of the slaves for purposes of establishing both representatives and taxes. For example, if a state's population included 100,000 free men and 100,000 slaves, the state would be assigned a population figure of 160,000 for determining the amount of taxes to be paid and the number of representatives to be elected.

The commerce compromises. Another clash between the economic interests of the South and the North arose over the control of commerce and the regulation of the slave trade.

Northern merchants wanted the central government to regulate commerce with foreign nations, as well as among the states. Southern planters opposed this proposal. They feared that the government might pass tariff laws unfavorable to southern interests. For example, southern planters earned most of their income by exporting tobacco to Europe and the northern states. In turn, they imported either from Europe or the northern states many finished goods, such as household furnishings and farm equipment. If Congress imposed tariffs, or duties, on exports, overseas buyers would have to pay a higher price for southern tobacco. The planters feared that this rise in price would make them lose customers. Tariffs on imported goods, on the other hand, would raise the prices of products purchased by the planters. Under the circumstances, the southern delegates were opposed to all tariffs. They therefore opposed giving Congress unlimited power to regulate trade.

The delegates finally reached a compromise acceptable to both the North and the South. This compromise gave Congress the power "To regulate commerce with foreign nations, and among the several states," including the power to levy tariffs on imports. But Congress was denied the power to levy tariffs on exports of any kind.

The southern planters were troubled, however, by still another problem. Since Congress now had the power to regulate commerce and to tax imports, would it not be possible for Congress to outlaw the slave trade or to levy taxes on slaves imported into the country?

After a vigorous discussion, the Convention agreed that until 1808, or for 20 years, the states could continue to import slaves, and Congress could not interfere or forbid them to do so. During these years Congress could not levy an import tax in excess of 10 dollars per person. By this compromise the southerners won the right to import slaves for about a generation. But after 1808 Congress would have the right to decide whether to regulate or prohibit the further importation of slaves.

The slave trade compromise was probably necessary for the Constitution to gain needed support in the South. But it was a setback for the anti-slavery forces. At the time the Constitution was written, many Americans believed that slavery was gradually dying out in the United States and thus would no longer be a problem in 1808. However, by 1808, as you will read, circumstances had changed and the demand for slaves to work in the cotton fields of the southern states was growing rapidly. Years later a tragic war would finally bring an end to slavery in the United States.

Completing the Constitution. Finally, as the summer months of 1787 passed and as agreements were reached, the Constitution was completed. Time and again the Convention seemed near failure. Time and again angry men threatened to leave unless they got what they wanted. But in the end sober judgment prevailed. The delegates always found a way to compromise the differences that threatened to divide the country.

SECTION SURVEY

IDENTIFY: Great Compromise, three-fifths compromise, slave trade compromise; Benjamin Franklin, James Madison, Edmund Randolph, William Paterson; May–September 1787.

1. Why was the Constitutional Convention held in secret?
2. List and explain the areas of agreement the delegates reached at the very beginning of the Constitutional Convention.
3. How do you think the presence of Benjamin Franklin and George Washington added to the proceedings of the Convention?
4. The delegates reached compromises to settle their differences on three important issues. (a) Describe each issue. (b) Present the different points of view. (c) Explain the resulting compromise.
5. Do you think the slave trade compromise was a defeat for the anti-slavery forces? Why or why not?

159

2 Ratification of the Constitution after heated debate

On September 17, 1787, after 39 delegates had signed the document which they had prepared over the long, hot summer, the members of the Constitutional Convention met for a farewell dinner. The next day they began to leave Philadelphia. Each delegate was in a hurry to return to his own state, for the really big struggle was yet to be waged—the struggle over *ratification,* or approval, of the Constitution.

Differing opinions on the Constitution. The delegates had arranged that printed copies of the new Constitution be sent to each of the states. The Constitution would not become effective until nine of the thirteen states had ratified it.

Most of the men who left Philadelphia in September were prepared to lead the battle for ratification. These men believed that a strong *federal government* ° would be good for the country. They felt that it would establish law and order at home and command the respect of foreign governments. A few delegates who had refused to sign the Constitution hurried home to lead the fight against ratification.

In general, the American people divided into two groups in their thinking about the Constitution. One group, called the Federalists, favored the Constitution. The Federalists wanted a strong central government. The other group, the Anti-Federalists, opposed the Constitution. They did not favor a strong federal government, preferring instead to protect the rights of individual states. All over the country, people debated the issues heatedly, and began to bring pressure on the ratifying conventions.

Objections from opponents. During the debate over ratification by the state conventions, opponents of the Constitution raised some strong objections.

First, many opponents complained that the states were being asked to surrender too much power to the new federal government. These delegates preferred a constitution in which the states would retain most of their powers while the power of the federal government would be severely limited. In other words, they preferred a constitution like the Articles of Confederation.

° *federal government:* This term is used in the United States to refer to the national government as opposed to the separate governments of the individual states.

Second, still other opponents believed that the new Constitution did not give the voters enough control over the men who would run the new federal government. The Constitution allowed the states to decide who could vote and who could not. As you know, most states had property restrictions on voting, and several states had religious restrictions. To begin with, then, many Americans would be excluded from electing new federal officials.

To be sure, the Constitution did create a republican, or representative, form of government. But the Constitution limited the influence of even those men who were allowed to vote. The President and Vice-President were to be chosen by men called *electors.* The electors were to be selected, not by the voters, but "in such manner" as each state legislature should direct. Senators were to be chosen, not by the voters, but by the state legislatures. Only the members of the House of Representatives would be elected directly by the voters.

A third serious objection to the Constitution was the lack of a "bill of rights." Without a bill of rights, many Americans feared that the new federal government could take away their hard-won rights. Some states ratified the Constitution with the reservation that an adequate bill of rights be added. As you will see, this demand was later met with the first ten amendments.

Struggles for ratification. In December 1787 Delaware became the first state to ratify the Constitution. Before the year's end, New Jersey and Pennsylvania followed Delaware's example. Georgia and Connecticut ratified early in 1788.

In February 1788, Massachusetts, one of the larger, crucial states, ratified the Constitution by the narrow margin of 10 votes. Next came Maryland, South Carolina, and finally New Hampshire. Now the count stood at nine, the number needed.

Meantime, however, Americans directed their attention to the ratification struggles going on in Virginia and New York. The new government could hardly hope to succeed without these large and important states.

The battles in Virginia and New York were fought with much feeling on both sides. The final victory in favor of the Constitution was very close. A change of only six votes in Virginia and of two votes in New York would have defeated ratification in these states. The victory in Virginia was largely due to the enormous influence of George Washington. The victory in New York was to some extent a personal triumph for Alexander Hamilton, James Madison, and John Jay. These three

■ Philadelphia's State House (right) was the scene of many famous events in American history, including the signing of the Declaration of Independence and the Constitutional Convention.

men defended the Constitution in a series of brilliant essays that were printed in the newspapers and widely read. Later, the essays were collected and published in a famous volume known as *The Federalist.*

Time for celebration. When Virginia and New York ratified the Constitution, eleven states made up the Union. The new government could be started with some degree of confidence. Now only two states remained outside the Union. North Carolina did not enter until November 1789, and Rhode Island delayed ratifying the Constitution until the spring of 1790.

The fight over ratification had been a bitter one. The margin of victory was close. Nevertheless, it was a victory, and during the summer and fall of 1788 the country celebrated with bonfires and public demonstrations. The old government was ended. The new government was ready to start.

The first election. When all the states except North Carolina and Rhode Island had accepted the Constitution, elections were held. George Washington was unanimously elected President,

and John Adams Vice-President. Elections for the new Congress of the United States did not arouse much enthusiasm. In general, the men elected to Congress had favored the Constitution either in the Convention, or during the struggle for ratification, or both.

Traveling over the bad roads, the new Senators and Representatives slowly gathered in New York, the temporary capital of the nation. They awaited the coming of President-elect Washington and the inauguration of the new government.

SECTION SURVEY

IDENTIFY: federal government, electors, ratification, *The Federalist;* John Adams.

1. How was the new Constitution to be ratified?
2. (a) What were the differing opinions on the Constitution? (b) Which of these opinions are still held today?
3. How do you explain the fact that George Washington was unanimously elected President of the United States?

161

3 A workable form of government under the Constitution

The form of government created under the Constitution is based upon four fundamental principles. One is the principle of *federalism,* or the division of powers between the national government and the state governments.

Creating a federal union. Under the Articles of Confederation, the relations between the national government and the state governments had been a thorny problem. The Confederation left most power in the hands of thirteen free and equal states. The central government held no real authority over the states or over the people themselves. The delegates to the Constitutional Convention wanted to correct the weaknesses of this form of government.

From the outset, therefore, most delegates agreed that only a *federal union* would be strong enough to establish an orderly society. By creating a federal union, in which each state delegated some of its power to the national government, the framers of the Constitution corrected most of the weaknesses of the Articles of Confederation.

Individuals and the law. Having agreed to organize a federal union, the delegates were faced with another troublesome problem. How could the federal, or national, government enforce its laws? Suppose, for example, that a citizen of New Jersey refused to obey a federal law. Should the federal government ask New Jersey to punish the offender? And suppose New Jersey refused to comply. Would not the federal government have to have the power to maintain its authority?

The longer the delegates debated this question, the more convinced they became of the answer. To avoid trouble between the states and the federal government, all laws passed by the federal government *must apply equally to every individual* within the union. To insure obedience to these laws, the delegates decided that the federal government must have the power to reach into the states themselves to punish violators.

Because of this decision, Americans have always lived under two governments and two systems of law—federal and state. They have two citizenships, or "dual citizenship," since they are citizens both of the United States and of the state in which they live. The Tenth Amendment, adopted in 1791, specifies that there are three

■ The adoption of the Constitution was celebrated in New York City with a parade. The float in this picture honors Alexander Hamilton, the young New York delegate to the Convention.

groups of powers—(1) those delegated to the federal government, (2) those reserved for the states, and (3) those retained by the people.

Powers delegated to the federal government. The decision to give the federal government power to enforce its laws led the Convention to another difficult problem. What laws should the federal government be allowed to pass? Or, in different words, what powers should the states delegate, or surrender, to the federal government?

After long debate, the delegates decided to give certain specific powers to the Congress of the United States. All of these powers, known as *delegated* powers, are listed in the Constitution. They include the powers "To lay and collect taxes . . . To borrow money . . . To coin money . . . To regulate commerce with foreign nations, and among the several states . . . To raise and support armies . . . To provide and maintain a navy."

From this listing, it is clear that the delegates gave the federal government authority only over matters of common concern to the people of all the states. It is also evident that, in selecting the powers to be delegated to the federal government, the framers of the Constitution tried to correct major weaknesses of the Articles of Confederation —lack of financial power, lack of power to regulate commerce, and lack of military power.

Powers reserved for the states. Under a federalist form of government, the member states still retain freedom to act on matters not assigned to the federal government or expressly forbidden to the states. The states, in turn, commonly assign some of their powers to local governments. To guarantee this independence of action to the states, the delegates listed several powers that could not be exercised by the federal authorities. For example, the federal government is forbidden to levy any "tax or duty . . . on articles exported from any state."

By implication all powers not specifically granted to the federal government, nor denied to the states, were retained by the states. But to avoid any misunderstanding, the Ninth and Tenth Amendments were adopted in 1791. The Tenth Amendment leaves no room for doubt: "The powers not delegated to the United States by the Constitution, nor prohibited by it to the states, are reserved to the states respectively, or to the people." Those powers retained by the states are known as *reserved* powers. They include control over public education, transportation within the state, marriage, and divorce.

■ James Madison of Virginia jotted down notes during the course of each day's meetings and then labored far into the night writing them out with a quill pen. The notes were kept secret until after his death in 1836.

Shared powers. Every government must possess certain powers simply to exist and function effectively. All governments, for example, must have the power to raise money and to enforce law and order. Both the federal government and the states use the same methods to raise money— taxation and borrowing. Both governments also have police forces to maintain order. In addition, both governments have court systems for trying people who violate laws.

Powers shared by the federal government and the states are called *concurrent* powers. They exist concurrently with, or at the same time as, powers delegated to the federal government, on the one hand, and powers reserved for the states, on the other.

The supreme law of the land. The men who drafted the Constitution realized that conflicts might arise between federal and state laws. To settle such conflicts, the framers of the Constitution inserted this statement in the Constitution: "This Constitution, and the laws of the United States which shall be made in pursuance thereof, and all treaties made, or which shall be made, under the authority of the United States, shall be the supreme law of the land...." By including this statement, the Founding Fathers proclaimed that, in cases of conflict, the Constitution and the laws of the federal government should rank higher than state constitutions and state laws.

IDENTIFY: federalism, delegated powers, reserved powers, concurrent powers.

1. In what ways does a federal union differ from a confederation?
2. A citizen of the United States has a dual citizenship and must live under two governments and two systems of law. What does this mean?
3. How did the delegates resolve the problem of protecting the rights of the individual, while maintaining the power of the central government?
4. Why is the Constitution regarded as the "supreme law of the land"?

4 Separation of powers with checks and balances under the Constitution

The first basic principle of American government, as you know, is federalism, in which powers are divided between the federal, or national, government and the state governments. A second fundamental principle is the *separation of powers,* with "checks and balances," within the federal government.

Protection against tyranny. The men who wrote the Constitution believed in government under law. They wanted to protect the country from tyranny in any form. They believed that a misguided majority might be as dangerous to good government under law as a privileged minority or a power-mad dictator.

When they wrote the Constitution, therefore, the Founding Fathers tried to guard against what one of them called an "excess of democracy." At no time did they seriously consider including a guarantee of the right to vote in the Constitution. Instead, they left it to the states to decide who could vote and who could not.

The Founding Fathers were equally careful to guard against seizure of the government by a military dictator. They had not forgotten the troubled years before the Revolutionary War. Even closer to them were recent attempts to establish a military dictatorship over the thirteen states. In 1782, for example, army officers had offered the title of king to General Washington. If Washington had

wanted to be a dictator, the history of the United States might have been different.

Separation of powers. To help guard against tyranny in any form and to keep any one branch of the government from becoming too strong, the delegates agreed that the legislative, executive, and judicial powers of the government must be kept separate.

In developing this principle, the Founding Fathers were much influenced by the writings of a famous Frenchman, Montesquieu (mon·tes·KYOO). Montesquieu stressed that "men entrusted with power tend to abuse it." He believed that the best form of government was one in which the powers of government were divided among a number of governmental agencies.

With this idea in mind, the delegates set up three separate branches of the government, each having certain powers. To Congress they gave the legislative, or lawmaking, power (Article 1). To the Chief Executive, or President, they granted the power to execute, or carry out, the laws (Article 2). To the judiciary—that is, the federal courts—they gave the power to interpret the laws (Article 3).

In addition to separating the powers of the three branches of the federal government, the delegates wrote into the Constitution a system of *checks and balances.* Each branch was given certain powers that it could use to restrain, or balance, the powers of another branch if the other branch tried to abuse or exceed its powers.

Checks on the President. If a President is thought to be guilty of "treason, bribery, or high crimes and misdemeanors,"° he can be *impeached,* or accused of unlawful acts, by the House of Representatives and tried by the Senate. If he is found guilty, he can be removed from office. A President can make a treaty, but a two-thirds vote of the Senate is necessary to ratify it. A President can appoint important officers, but the Senate must confirm his appointments by a majority vote. Since Congress has control over taxes and money spending, it can interfere with any Presidential policy that requires expenditures of money. Finally, a two-thirds vote of Congress can overrule the President's *veto,* or rejection, of laws proposed by Congress.

Checks on Congress. The President, in turn, can check and balance the powers of Congress.

° *misdemeanor:* a minor violation of the law, such as disorderly conduct, in contrast to a more serious crime, such as murder, which is called a *felony.*

Perhaps his most important check is his power to veto Congressional legislation. He can also influence the thinking of many Congressmen through his annual "State of the Union" message and special messages to Congress. He can also bring pressure on Congress by calling a special session and asking for the passage of specific laws.

The President can also exert his influence by directing public attention to specific issues at press conferences or by speaking directly to the people. If a press conference or a public address results in a barrage of letters and telegrams to Congress, the President may win his points.

Checks by and on the judiciary. The federal judiciary—the Supreme Court and the lower federal courts—interprets the laws. As you will see later, the federal judiciary has the power to declare that a law passed by Congress and approved by the President is "unconstitutional."

However, this power of the Supreme Court and of other federal courts can be checked in several ways. Congress can impeach federal judges. Congress also determines by law the number of justices on the Supreme Court. At different times laws have set the number of justices at as few as five and at as many as ten.

The President, in turn, appoints all federal judges, with the consent of the Senate. The President's desire for a certain interpretation of the Constitution may sometimes conflict either with Congress or the Supreme Court. If the President appoints justices to the Supreme Court who are friendly to his point of view, and if he can get the Senate to approve his appointments, he is checking or balancing the power of Congress, of the judiciary, or of both. A further check on the judiciary is the President's power to pardon or reprieve persons convicted of crimes in the federal courts.

Pros and cons of checks and balances. The separation of powers with checks and balances in the federal government has sometimes been criticized for slowing down the workings of government. Important laws may be needed, but a President belonging to one party and a Congress dominated by another party may not be able to agree on a law. As a general rule, however, the system has worked well and has fulfilled the intentions of the men who wrote the Constitution.

In time of war or other crisis, Congress usually declares a national emergency and grants special powers to the President so that he can act quickly. When the emergency is over, the special powers are withdrawn.

■ Roger Sherman of Connecticut first proposed what is now known as the Great Compromise. The proposal was adopted after a month of debate, settling one of the most serious conflicts of the Convention.

The principle of the separation of powers with checks and balances was written into the Constitution as a safeguard for the future. It was meant to protect the liberties of the people.

SECTION SURVEY

IDENTIFY: legislative, executive, judicial, impeach, veto, unconstitutional; Montesquieu.

1. (a) What is meant by "separation of powers with checks and balances"? (b) Why did the framers of the Constitution adopt this principle?
2. (a) How can Congress check the President? (b) How can the President check Congress?
3. (a) How can the federal judiciary check Congress and the President? (b) How can Congress and the President check the federal judiciary?
4. The Founding Fathers feared "an excess of democracy." (a) What did they mean? (b) Do you agree with their thinking? Explain.
5. Montesquieu said that "men entrusted with power tend to abuse it." Do you agree? Why or why not?

5 Safeguards for individual liberty under the Constitution

A third fundamental principle of American government under the Constitution is *protection of the liberties of individuals.*

For a long time the American colonists had insisted upon protection of their rights as individuals against the powers of government—that is, protection of their *civil liberties.* The separation of powers with checks and balances is one way that the Constitution protects the rights of individuals. And there are many other safeguards. Some appear in the Constitution itself. Others were written into the first ten amendments—the Bill of Rights. Still others have been added in later amendments.

Guarantees in the Constitution. The Constitution itself provides important guarantees of civil liberty. For example, it prohibits *ex post facto laws* and *bills of attainder.*

An ex post facto law—that is, a law passed

■ Alexander Hamilton (shown below), together with James Madison and John Jay, defended the ratification of the Constitution in a series of essays. These essays were later published in one volume entitled The Federalist.

"after the deed"—sets a penalty for an act that was not illegal at the time it was committed.

A bill of attainder is a law that punishes a person by fine, imprisonment, or confiscation of property without first granting him a court trial. If Congress had the power to adopt bills of attainder, the lawmakers could punish any American, and he could do nothing to appeal the sentence. Instead, the Constitution provides that only the courts can impose punishment for unlawful acts, and then only by following the duly established law. To prevent arbitrary convictions by judges, the Constitution also provides that "The trial of all crimes . . . shall be by jury."

The Constitution also protects the citizen's right to the *writ of habeas corpus.* The writ of habeas corpus is a legal document that forces a jailer to release a person from prison unless he has been formally charged with, or convicted of, a crime. The Constitution states that "The privilege of the writ of habeas corpus shall not be suspended, unless when in cases of rebellion or invasion the public safety may require it."

The Constitution also gives special protection to people accused of *treason.* The men who drafted the Constitution knew that the charge of treason was an old device used by dictators to get rid of persons they did not like. Such rulers usually brought the charge of treason against persons who merely criticized the government, as well as against those who actually prepared an armed uprising against the government. To prevent the arbitrary use of this charge, the Constitution carefully defines treason: "Treason against the United States shall consist only in levying war against them, or in adhering to their enemies, giving them aid and comfort. No person shall be convicted of treason unless on the testimony of two witnesses to the same overt act, or on confession in open court."

The Constitution also protects the innocent relatives of a person accused of treason. Only the convicted person can be punished. No penalty can be imposed upon his family or relatives because of his wrongdoing.

These are only a few of the guarantees of personal rights that the Founding Fathers wrote into the Constitution. They are important examples of the way that the Constitution establishes a common standard of law for every American citizen, old and young, rich and poor alike.

The Bill of Rights. Despite the safeguards written into the Constitution itself, some states at first refused to ratify the Constitution because it did not offer greater protection to the rights of individuals. They finally agreed to ratification after they had been promised that a bill of rights would be added to the Constitution by amendment when Congress met.

Writing the Declaration of Independence in 1776, Jefferson had declared: "We hold these truths to be self-evident: that all men are created equal, that they are endowed by their Creator with certain unalienable rights, that among these are life, liberty, and the pursuit of happiness."

In 1789–90 the first Congress of the United States wrote these ideals into the Bill of Rights, the first ten amendments to the Constitution. The Bill of Rights protects individuals against any action by the federal government that may deprive them of life, liberty, or property without "due process of law."

Among the guarantees of liberty in the Bill of Rights, several are especially important. The First Amendment guarantees freedom of religion, speech, press, assembly, and petition. The Fourth Amendment upholds the principle that "a man's home is his castle" by forbidding unreasonable searches and seizures. The Fifth, Sixth, and Eighth Amendments protect individuals from arbitrary arrest and punishment by the federal government.

The Bill of Rights was ratified by the states in 1791. From that time it has remained one of the best-known features of the Constitution. The American people have turned to it for support whenever their rights as individuals have seemed to be in danger. No document in American history, except, perhaps, the Declaration of Independence, has been cherished more deeply.

In its attention to specific individual liberties, the Bill of Rights set an example for later amendments that extended the rights of the people even further. The Nineteenth Amendment, for example, ratified in 1920, extended voting rights to women. The Thirteenth, Fourteenth, and Fifteenth Amendments, ratified soon after the Civil War, became the Constitutional cornerstones for the long and continuing struggle of black citizens to secure equal rights in American society.

Interpreting individual rights. Although the Constitution, Bill of Rights, and later amendments guarantee certain rights equally to all Americans, individual rights are not absolute. The rights of an individual exist in relation to the rights of others. In guaranteeing freedom of speech and of the press, for example, the Bill of Rights does not grant an individual the right to say or print anything he likes at any time. For example, laws forbid the individual to say or print anything that may defame an innocent person's character. Freedom of speech and of the press, as well as all the other rights guaranteed by the first ten amendments, must be interpreted by the courts to have any real meaning.

SECTION SURVEY

IDENTIFY: civil liberties, ex post facto law, bill of attainder, writ of habeas corpus, Bill of Rights.

1. How does the Constitution guarantee civil liberties?
2. The protection of civil liberties is the essence of American democracy. Give your views on this statement.
3. What is the connection between the Declaration of Independence and the Bill of Rights?
4. (a) Why is it that individual rights are not absolute? (b) Why must your answer depend partly upon the interpretation of these rights by the courts?

6 The Constitution as a flexible, living document

The famous British statesman William E. Gladstone once referred to the Constitution of the United States as "the most wonderful work ever struck off at a given time by the brain and purpose of man." This was high praise indeed. But the most convincing proof of the Constitution's effectiveness is the fact that it has weathered the test of time. It stands today, as it has stood for nearly two centuries, as "the supreme law of the land."

The Constitution has successfully survived the years for two main reasons. First, it lays down rules of procedure that must be followed even when critical circumstances arise. Second, it is a "living" document, flexible enough to meet the changing needs of a growing nation. As you will see, Americans have been able to adapt the Constitution to changing ways and changing times. Thus the Constitution for the most part works as well today for an industrialized nation of fifty states and a population of more than 200 million people as it once worked for an agricultural nation of thirteen states and 4 million people.

The fourth fundamental principle of American government, then, is the Constitution's *adaptability* to changing times and changing circumstances.

Provision for amendments. The men who drafted the Constitution were as wise in what they did *not* write as in what they did write. They wrote down only the fundamental laws for the nation, leaving it to Congress to pass additional laws as they might be needed. Each time Congress meets, it passes such laws.

But even so the framers of the Constitution anticipated that changes in the fundamental law might have to be made from time to time. Accordingly, they wrote Article 5, which tells how the Constitution may be amended.

Because the amending process is slow and difficult, it is seldom used unless the need for change appears acute. Some people think the process is too slow and difficult. Others think it wise that no changes can be made in the "supreme law of the land" until the pros and cons have been thoroughly debated.

In any event, only 25 amendments have been adopted since 1789, including the first ten amendments—the Bill of Rights.

The "elastic clause." The delegates to the Constitutional Convention provided still greater flexibility to the Constitution by inserting what is known as the *elastic clause*. To the specific powers granted to Congress, this clause adds the power "To make all laws which shall be necessary and proper for carrying into execution the foregoing powers. . . ."

The elastic clause has become the subject of much debate in our country whenever Congress has stretched it to pass laws not specifically authorized in the Constitution. Congress, for example, has stretched its power to regulate commerce so that it includes the power to improve rivers and harbors and to require the payment of minimum wages to workers employed by industries engaged in interstate commerce.

Whenever Congress has stretched its powers in this way, a question has arisen over which branch of the government shall decide whether a law is "necessary and proper." The Constitution does not clearly state how this question should be answered. In 1803, however, Chief Justice Marshall established the tradition that this power rests in the Supreme Court (page 228).

The Supreme Court as referee. The power of the Supreme Court to decide whether or not a law or a treaty violates the Constitution is known as the power of *judicial review*. This means that the Supreme Court has the power to "review" or examine an act of Congress and to determine whether or not the act is in accord with the Constitution. When the Supreme Court exercises this power, it acts as a referee.

When the Supreme Court acts, its word is final. But the Supreme Court can—and sometimes does—reverse one of its earlier decisions. In 1954, for example, in *Brown v. Board of Education of Topeka*, the Supreme Court reversed the 1896 *Plessy v. Ferguson* decision in regard to civil rights (page 422). And the people of the United States can, by the process of amendment, alter the Constitution.

The "unwritten Constitution." The Constitution, then, has proved to be a flexible, enduring plan of government. Amendments have altered certain provisions of the Constitution and added others. Court decisions and acts of Congress, especially under the elastic clause, have given new meanings to certain provisions.

Other changes in American government have come about by custom. For example, the Constitution said nothing about political parties, which Washington and others distrusted as likely to cause quarrels. Neither did the Constitution provide for regular meetings of the heads of the executive departments concerned with defense, foreign affairs, the postal system, finances, and other matters. Such meetings, called cabinet meetings, nevertheless take place and have become an important part of the executive system.

Custom has established other important practices in the operation of the federal government. When the President, for example, needs to appoint a federal official to work in a state, he commonly seeks the advice of the Senators of that state, provided that they are from his own party. This custom is called "senatorial courtesy." Custom and the pressure of work have also led Congress to use an elaborate system of committees in its lawmaking procedures.

Practices such as these, growing out of custom and tradition, are sometimes called the *unwritten Constitution*. The Constitution does not refer to them, but they are so firmly established that they can be thought of as unwritten laws.

The admission of new states. The delegates, as you have seen, had drawn up a Constitution in which power was distributed between the states and the federal government. By making it possible for new states to enter the Union with minimum

■ This is a facsimile of the opening passages of the Constitution of the United States. The original copy of the Constitution and of the Declaration of Independence are on display under guard in the National Archives Building in Washington, D.C.

difficulty, they added still further flexibility and strength to the new government.

Since it was evident that the population of the western lands would grow rapidly, it was especially important to provide in advance for the easy admission of new states. So long as a western area remained a Territory, Congress was responsible for its government. But when the population of the Territory became large enough, the Territory could apply for admission to the Union as a state. In general, the laws passed to govern the admission of new states were the same as those established in the Northwest Ordinance (page 147).

SECTION SURVEY

IDENTIFY: "elastic clause," amending process, judicial review, "unwritten Constitution."

1. (a) Why can the Supreme Court be called a referee? (b) Why should every government have a referee?
2. Give three examples of the "unwritten Constitution" and explain why each arose.
3. How did the constitutional provision for the admission of new states add flexibility and strength to the American government?
4. Why has the Constitution successfully survived the years?

TRACING THE MAIN IDEAS

The delegates who met in the spring of 1787 to revise the Articles of Confederation included many of the ablest men in America. Convinced that the Confederation was not strong enough to bring order and prosperity to their country, they abandoned all thought of revision and proceeded to draw up a completely new constitution. Out of their long political experience, out of their keen intelligence, out of their great learning, the framers of the Constitution fashioned a plan of government for the United States of America. Revised, modified, and amended, the Constitution has served the American people for nearly 200 years. It stands as a lasting tribute to the wisdom and foresight of the Founding Fathers.

The Constitution created a republican form of government. It could not, however, create a strong, united nation overnight. In Chapter 10 you will see how men and women from many walks of life began to work at the task of unifying their country and of establishing it as a nation respected throughout the world.

CHAPTER SURVEY

QUESTIONS FOR DISCUSSION

1. The Declaration of Independence is the heart of the American nation, while the Constitution is the body. Comment.
2. How did the new Constitution reflect the political experiences of the colonies before 1775?
3. How did the new Constitution reflect the principles of the American Revolution?
4. What aims of the federal government are set forth in the Preamble to the Constitution?
5. In one column list ten rights guaranteed to every American in the Bill of Rights. In a second column, write the responsibility that goes with each right.

RELATING PAST TO PRESENT

1. Between 1945 and the present, colonies in various parts of the world have won their freedom from their mother countries. What problems have faced all of these nations in establishing governments that incorporate liberty under the law?
2. The Constitution says that Congress alone has the power to declare war. Many American Presidents, however, have sent troops abroad without Congressional authorization. (a) Do you think there is a need in today's fast-moving world for a President to have this power to send troops abroad? Explain. (b) Can you see any possible dangers in a President's use of this power? Explain.
3. (a) What authority determines an individual's rights in the United States? (b) Can one citizen determine for another the number or kind of rights he is entitled to? Explain.

USING MAPS AND CHARTS

1. Study the chart on page 177. (a) Why are there so many steps in the passage of a bill? (b) What steps can a citizen take to influence the introduction of a bill or the passage of a bill? (c) In your opinion, which step in the passage of a bill is the most critical? Why? (d) How does the Rules Committee play a most important role in the progress of a bill? (e) What is the purpose of the Conference Committee? (f) State the three courses of action that a President can follow when he receives a bill.
2. Turn to the chart on page 181. (a) Which, in your opinion, is the most important delegated power? the most important reserved power? the most important concurrent power? Why? (b) Explain why certain powers were denied to both the federal and state governments. (c) In your opinion, what is the most important advantage of the federal system of government? the most serious disadvantage?
3. Turn to the chart on page 172. (a) What is the basic function of each of the main branches of the federal government? Explain each function. (b) Choose five independent federal agencies and explain the importance of each today. (c) Name the present members of the President's cabinet and the department each heads. (d) Why are there two groups of courts in the judicial branch?
4. Turn to the chart on page 195. (a) How many Presidential electors did your state have in the last election? (b) Why are the November Presidential election results unofficial? (c) When is the President's election officially announced? (d) What minimum number of electoral votes was required to win the last Presidential election?

THE CONSTITUTION OF THE UNITED STATES

(The text of the Constitution is printed in BLACK; the commentary in BLUE. Portions of the text printed in brackets have gone out of date or have been changed by amendment.)

PREAMBLE

We, the people of the United States, in order to form a more perfect Union, establish justice, insure domestic tranquillity, provide for the common defense, promote the general welfare, and secure the blessings of liberty to ourselves and our posterity, do ordain and establish this CONSTITUTION for the United States of America.

¶ In addition to stating the purposes of the Constitution, the Preamble makes it clear that the government is established by consent of the governed. "We, the people, ... ordain and establish" the government. We, the people, have supreme power in establishing the government of the United States of America.

Article 1. LEGISLATIVE DEPARTMENT

SECTION 1. CONGRESS

All legislative powers herein granted shall be vested in a Congress of the United States, which shall consist of a Senate and House of Representatives.

¶ By separating the functions of government among branches concerned with lawmaking (Article 1), law executing (Article 2), and law interpreting (Article 3), the framers of the Constitution were applying the principle of separation of powers, and developing a system of checks and balances, as a defense against dictatorship. ¶ Practice has modified the provision that all lawmaking power granted in the Constitution shall be vested in Congress. For example, such administrative agencies as the Interstate Commerce Commission (p. 487) can issue regulations which in some ways have the force of laws.

SECTION 2. HOUSE OF REPRESENTATIVES

1. *Election and term of members.* The House of Representatives shall be composed of members chosen every second year by the people of the several states, and the electors in each state shall have the qualifications requisite for electors of the most numerous branch of the state legislature.

¶ The members of the House of Representatives are elected every two years by the "electors" (voters) of the states. Except for the provisions of Amendments 15, 19, and 24, the individual states decide who may or may not vote.

2. *Qualifications.* No person shall be a Representative who shall not have attained to the age of twenty-five years, and been seven years a citizen of the United States, and who shall not, when elected, be an inhabitant of that state in which he shall be chosen.

¶ *Qualifications for a Representative:* (1) At least 25 years of age. (2) A United States citizen for at least 7 years. (3) Residence in the state in which elected. (Custom has added the requirement of residence in the Congressional district from which a Representative is elected.) Each state is divided into Congressional districts for the purpose of electing Representatives; each district elects one. ¶ TERM OF OFFICE: 2 years.

THE THREE BRANCHES OF THE FEDERAL GOVERNMENT

Standing Committees of the House

Agriculture
Appropriations
Armed Services
Banking and Currency
District of Columbia
Education and Labor
Foreign Affairs
Government Operations
House Administration
Interior and Insular Affairs
Internal Security
Interstate and Foreign Commerce
Judiciary
Merchant Marine and Fisheries
Post Office and Civil Service
Public Works
Rules
Science and Astronautics
Standards of Official Conduct
Veterans Affairs
Ways and Means

Standing Committees of the Senate

Aeronautical and Space Sciences
Agriculture and Forestry
Appropriations
Armed Services
Banking and Currency
Commerce
District of Columbia
Finance
Foreign Relations
Government Operations
Interior and Insular Affairs
Judiciary
Labor and Public Welfare
Post Office and Civil Service
Public Works
Rules and Administration

LEGISLATIVE BRANCH

HOUSE OF REPRESENTATIVES — Membership based on state populations

SENATE — Two Senators from each state

Article 1 establishes the Legislative Branch.

Executive Departments

Heads of these departments form the President's cabinet.

Department of State
Department of the Treasury
Department of Defense
Department of Justice
Department of the Interior
Department of Agriculture
Department of Commerce
Department of Labor
Department of Health, Education, and Welfare
Department of Housing and Urban Development
Department of Transportation

EXECUTIVE BRANCH

Article 2 establishes the Executive Branch.

The Executive Office

The White House
Bureau of the Budget
Council for Urban Affairs
Council of Economic Advisers
National Security Council
National Aeronautics and Space Council
Office of Economic Opportunity
Office of Emergency Preparedness
Office of Intergovernmental Relations
Office of Science and Technology
Office of the Special Representative
 for Trade Negotiations

Independent Federal Agencies (Partial Listing)

Advisory Commission on Intergovernmental Relations
American National Red Cross
Applachian Regional Commission
Arms Control and Disarmament Agency
Atomic Energy Commission
Commission of Fine Arts
District of Columbia

Equal Employment Opportunity Commission
Farm Credit Administration
Federal Communications Commission
Federal Deposit Insurance Corporation
Federal Mediation and Conciliation Service

Indian Claims Commission
Interstate Commerce Commission
National Academy of Sciences
National Aeronautics and Space Administration
Ozarks Regional Commission
Panama Canal Company
President's Council on Physical Fitness and Sports

Securities and Exchange Commission
Selective Service System
Small Business Administration
Smithsonian Institution
Subversive Activities Control Board
Tennessee Valley Authority
U.S. Information Agency
Veterans Administration

THE SUPREME COURT
Courts of Appeals
District Courts
Courts of the District of Columbia

JUDICIAL BRANCH

Article 3 establishes the Judicial Branch.

Special Courts

Court of Claims
Court of Customs and Patent Appeals
Court of Military Appeals
Customs Court
Tax Court of the U.S.
Territorial Courts

3. *Apportionment of Representatives and direct taxes.* **Representatives [and direct taxes] shall be apportioned among the several states which may be included within this Union, according to their respective numbers [which shall be determined by adding to the whole number of free persons, including those bound to service for a term of years, and excluding Indians not taxed, three-fifths of all other persons]. The actual enumeration shall be made within three years after the first meeting of the Congress of the United States, and within every subsequent term of ten years, in such manner as they shall by law direct. The number of Representatives shall not exceed 1 for every 30,000, but each state shall have at least 1 Representative; [and until such enumeration shall be made, the state of New Hampshire shall be entitled to choose 3; Massachusetts, 8; Rhode Island and Providence Plantations, 1; Connecticut, 5; New York, 6; New Jersey, 4; Pennsylvania, 8; Delaware, 1, Maryland, 6; Virginia, 10; North Carolina, 5; South Carolina 5; and Georgia, 3.]**

¶ The bracketed portion of this clause beginning on line 3 forms what came to be called the three-fifths compromise (p. 158). Amendment 13 and Section 2 of Amendment 14 overruled this provision. ¶ Originally, each state was entitled to one Representative in Congress for every 30,000 people. Later, membership was limited by law to 435. A census of the population of the United States is taken every 10 years in order to determine the number of Representatives to which each state is entitled. Congress can change the number of members, as it did temporarily when Alaska and Hawaii were admitted to the Union before the 1960 census had determined the new number of Representatives for each state. A state, regardless of its population, is entitled to at least one Representative in Congress.

4. *Filling vacancies.* **When vacancies happen in the representation from any state, the executive authority thereof shall issue writs of election to fill such vacancies.**

5. *Officers; impeachment.* **The House of Representatives shall choose their Speaker and other officers; and shall have the sole power of impeachment.**

¶ *Clause 4.* The "executive authority" refers to the governor of the state; a "writ of election" is an order for a special election to fill the vacant seat. ¶ *Clause 5.* In actual practice, it is the majority party—the political party having the largest number of members in the House—which chooses the Speaker (chairman) of the House and other officials (clerk, doorkeeper, sergeant at arms, postmaster, and chaplain). The Speaker is the only official chosen from among the members of the House. ¶ The House, by a majority vote, can impeach (accuse) an Executive Department officer or a federal judge. The trial of the impeached official takes place in the Senate.

SECTION 3. SENATE

1. *Number of members and terms of office.* **The Senate of the United States shall be composed of two Senators from each state [chosen by the legislature thereof], for six years, and each Senator shall have one vote.**

¶ Under the provisions of Amendment 17, the 100 Senators are now elected directly by the voters of the states in the same manner as the Representatives. The method of electing Senators provided above, by which the state legislatures chose Senators, came to be considered undemocratic and was therefore changed.

2. *Classification; filling vacancies.* **[Immediately after they shall be assembled in consequence of the first election, they shall be divided as equally as may be into three classes. The seats of the Senators of the first class shall be vacated at the expiration of the second year, of the second class at the expiration of the fourth year, and of the third class at the expiration of the sixth year, so that one-third may be chosen every second year; and if vacancies happen by resignation, or otherwise, during the recess of the legislature of any state, the executive thereof may make temporary appointments until the next meeting of the legislature, which shall then fill such vacancies.]**

¶ One third of the Senate comes up for election every two years. This procedure was established in the first Senate, whose Senators were divided into three groups. One group was to serve for two years, the second for four years, and the third for six years. As a result, the terms of Senators today overlap, making the Senate a "continuing" body, in which two thirds of the members are "carried over" through every election. In contrast, the total membership of the House of Representatives is elected every two years. ¶ Under Amendment 17, if a Senator resigns or dies, the state governor can call a special election to fill the vacancy. The state legislature, however, may empower the governor to name a temporary Senator.

3. *Qualifications.* **No person shall be a Senator who shall not have attained to the age of thirty years, and been nine years a citizen of the United States, and who shall not, when elected, be an inhabitant of that state for which he shall be chosen.**

¶ *Qualifications for a Senator:* (1) He must be at least 30 years of age. (2) He must be a citizen for at least 9 years. (3) He must be a resident of the state in which he is elected. ¶ TERM OF OFFICE: 6 years.

4. *President of the Senate.* **The Vice-President of the United States shall be president of the Senate, but shall have no vote, unless they be equally divided.**

5. *Other Officers.* **The Senate shall choose their other officers, and also a president** *pro tempore,* **in the absence of the Vice-President, or when he shall exercise the office of the President of the United States.**

¶ *Clause 4.* To serve as President of the Senate is the only duty which the Constitution assigns to the Vice-President. He votes as a Senator only in case of a tie. After the illness of President Eisenhower in 1956 and 1957, the Vice-President undertook additional duties at the President's request. He attended cabinet meetings, traveled abroad on good will tours, and carried out ceremonial duties such as entertaining leading officials from abroad and representing the government at important events. ¶ *Clause 5.* "Other officers" include a secretary, chaplain, and sergeant at arms. These officers are not members of the Senate. *Pro tempore* is an expression in Latin meaning "for the time being," or "temporarily." Thus, whoever is the president pro tempore acts as a temporary president of the Senate.

6. *Trial of impeachments.* **The Senate shall have the sole power to try all impeachments. When sitting for that purpose, they shall be on oath or affirmation. When the President of the United States is tried, the Chief Justice shall preside; and no person shall be convicted without the concurrence of two-thirds of the members present.**

¶ Only the President, Vice-President, cabinet officials, and federal judges are subject to impeachment and removal from office. Members of the House and Senate cannot be impeached, but they can be censured and even removed from office by the members of their respective houses. ¶ Officials may be impeached only for committing "treason, bribery, or other high crimes and misdemeanors" (see Article 2, Section 4). The Chief Justice of the United States presides at the impeachment trial of a President. The Vice-President presides over all other impeachment trials. The Senate can find an impeached official guilty only if two thirds of the Senators present agree on the verdict. (A majority of the Senate must be present). ¶ The only President impeached was Andrew Johnson, in 1867 (p. 412); he was saved from conviction by one vote. In all the Senate has sat as a court of impeachment in 12 cases. A verdict of guilty was found in four of these.

7. *Penalty for conviction.* **Judgment in cases of impeachment shall not extend further than to removal from office, and disqualification to hold and enjoy any office of honor, trust, or profit under the United States; but the party convicted shall nevertheless be liable and subject to indictment, trial, judgment, and punishment, according to law.**

¶ The punishment for conviction in impeachment cases can consist only of removal from office and disqualification from holding any other federal office. However, the convicted person may also be tried in a regular court of law for the offense for which he was removed from office.

SECTION 4. ELECTIONS AND MEETINGS

1. *Holding elections.* **The times, places, and manner of holding elections for Senators and Representatives shall be prescribed in each state by the legislature thereof; but the Congress may at any time by law make or alter such regulations, except as to the places of choosing Senators.**

2. *Meetings.* **The Congress shall assemble at least once in every year, [and such meeting shall be on the first Monday in December,] unless they shall by law appoint a different day.**

¶ *Clause 1.* Under this provision, Congress has passed a law stating that, unless the constitution of a state provides otherwise, Congressional elections must be held on the Tuesday following the first Monday in November of even-numbered years. (Until 1960, Maine held elections in September.) Congress has also ruled that Representatives must be elected by districts, rather than by the state as a whole, and that secret ballots (or voting machines, where required by state law) must be used. ¶ *Clause 2.* Under Amendment 20, Congress now meets on January 3, unless it sets another day by law.

174

SECTION 5. RULES OF PROCEDURE

1. *Organization.* **Each house shall be the judge of the elections, returns, and qualifications of its own members, and a majority of each shall constitute a quorum to do business; but a smaller number may adjourn from day to day, and may be authorized to compel the attendance of absent members, in such manner, and under such penalties, as each house may provide.**

2. *Proceedings.* **Each house may determine the rules of its proceedings, punish its members for disorderly behavior, and with the concurrence of two-thirds, expel a member.**

¶ *Clause 1.* Each house of Congress may disqualify elected candidates and prevent them from taking office on the grounds of public policy. On one occasion the House refused to admit to membership an elected candidate who had violated the criminal laws. On another occasion the Senate refused to seat a victorious candidate whose election campaign had been characterized by "fraud and corruption." ¶ A *quorum* is the minimum number of persons required to be present to transact business; a majority of the House or Senate constitutes a quorum. In practice, business is often transacted with less than a quorum present, and may go on as long as no Congressman objects to the lack of a quorum. ¶ *Clause 2.* Each house has extensive rules of procedure. Each house can censure, punish, or expel a member. Expulsion requires a two-thirds vote.

3. *Journal.* **Each house shall keep a journal of its proceedings, and from time to time publish the same, excepting such parts as may in their judgment require secrecy; and the yeas and nays of the members of either house on any question shall, at the desire of one-fifth of those present, be entered on the journal.**

4. *Adjournment.* **Neither house, during the session of Congress, shall, without the consent of the other, adjourn for more than three days, nor to any other place than that in which the two houses shall be sitting.**

¶ *Clause 3.* Each house is required to keep a journal of its activities. These journals, called the *House Journal* and the *Senate Journal*, are published at the end of each session of Congress. A third journal, called the *Congressional Record*, is published every day that Congress is in session, and furnishes a daily account of what Representatives and Senators do and say. ¶ If one fifth of those present insist on a roll call of the members' votes, each member's vote must be recorded in the proper house journal. ¶ *Clause 4.* Both houses must remain in session for the same period of time and in the same place.

SECTION 6. PRIVILEGES AND RESTRICTIONS

1. *Pay and privileges.* **The Senators and Representatives shall receive a compensation for their services, to be ascertained by law and paid out of the Treasury of the United States. They shall in all cases, except treason, felony, and breach of the peace, be privileged from arrest during their attendance at the session of their respective houses, and in going to and returning from the same; and for any speech or debate in either house, they shall not be questioned in any other place.**

¶ In 1969 the salary of a Congressman was set by law at $42,500 a year. ¶ The provision concerning privilege from arrest establishes the principle of "Congressional immunity." According to this principle, Congressmen cannot be arrested or brought into court for what they say in speeches and debates in Congress. The aim of this provision is to enable members of Congress to speak freely. Congressmen are subject to arrest, however, if they commit a crime, and, under the laws governing slander and libel, they are liable for any false or defamatory statements that they may make outside Congress.

2. *Restrictions.* **No Senator or Representative shall, during the time for which he was elected, be appointed to any civil office under the authority of the United States, which shall have been created, or the emoluments whereof shall have been increased, during such time; and no person holding any office under the United States shall be a member of either house during his continuance in office.**

¶ This clause emphasizes the separation of powers in the federal government. Legislators cannot, while they are members of Congress, hold positions also in the Executive or Judicial Departments. Nor can a legislator resign his post and accept a position which was created during his term of office. Thus, Congressmen cannot set up jobs for themselves in the executive or judicial branches of the government. Furthermore, if a Congressman resigns and is appointed to an existing executive or judicial position, he cannot profit from any increase in pay in this position that was voted during his term in Congress.

SECTION 7. METHOD OF PASSING LAWS

1. *Revenue bills.* **All bills for raising revenue shall originate in the House of Representatives; but the Senate may propose or concur with amendments as on other bills.**

¶ All revenue, or money-raising, bills must be introduced in the House of Representatives. This provision grew out of a demand that the popularly elected branch of the legislature should have the "power of the purse." (Until Amendment 17 was ratified, the House of Representatives was the only popularly elected branch.) It was also felt that the voters had more control over Representatives, who are elected for two-year terms, than over Senators, who are elected for six-year terms; thus, Representatives would be more careful than the Senate in considering revenue bills. Since the Senate has the power to amend any bill, however, it can amend a revenue bill in such a way as actually to introduce a revenue bill of its own.

2. *How a bill becomes a law.* **Every bill which shall have passed the House of Representatives and the Senate shall, before it become a law, be presented to the President of the United States; if he approve, he shall sign it, but if not, he shall return it, with his objections, to that house in which it shall have originated, who shall enter the objections at large on their journal, and proceed to reconsider it. If after such reconsideration two-thirds of that house shall agree to pass the bill, it shall be sent, together with the objections, to the other house, by which it shall likewise be reconsidered, and, if approved by two-thirds of that house, it shall become a law. But in all such cases the votes of both houses shall be determined by yeas and nays, and the names of the persons voting for and against the bill shall be entered on the journal of each house respectively. If any bill shall not be returned by the President within ten days (Sundays excepted) after it shall have been presented to him, the same bill shall be a law, in like manner as if he had signed it, unless the Congress by their adjournment prevent its return, in which case it shall not be a law.**

¶ The process under which a bill becomes a law is shown on page 177. ¶ If the President does not approve of a bill, there are several things he may do. (1) He may veto, or refuse to sign, the bill. (2) He may permit the bill to become a law without his signature by holding it for 10 days (not counting Sundays) while Congress is in session. (3) Toward the end of a Congressional session, he may hold the bill in the hope that Congress will adjourn within 10 days or less. In that case, the bill fails to become a law, just as though the President had formally vetoed it. This type of veto is called a "pocket veto." ¶ A bill vetoed by the President can become a law despite his objections if two thirds or more of both houses vote for the bill a second time. When this happens, Congress is said to have "overridden the Presidential veto."

3. *Presidential approval or veto.* **Every order, resolution, or vote to which the concurrence of the Senate and House of Representatives may be necessary (except on a question of adjournment) shall be presented to the President of the United States; and before the same shall take effect, shall be approved by him, or being disapproved by him, shall be repassed by two-thirds of the Senate and House of Representatives, according to the rules and limitations prescribed in the case of a bill.**

¶ A *joint resolution* results from declarations passed by both houses of Congress on the same subject. It becomes a law in the same manner as a bill. A Congressional declaration of war takes the form of a joint resolution. ¶ A *concurrent resolution* represents only an expression of opinion on the part of either house of Congress. It does not have the force of law and, therefore, does not require Presidential approval. The process of amending the Constitution may start this way. A vote censuring a Representative or Senator, or an expression of sympathy, takes the form of a concurrent resolution.

HOW A BILL BECOMES A LAW

A typical successful bill follows this course on its way to becoming a federal law. A group of citizens or private organizations may have requested it; or the President may have recommended it; or a group in Congress, in either the House or Senate, may have believed it was needed and agreed to introduce it. The bill is drafted by one or more Congressmen and introduced in the appropriate house —in this case the House of Representatives. Bills pertaining to the raising of money must originate in the House of Representatives; other bills may originate in the House or Senate.

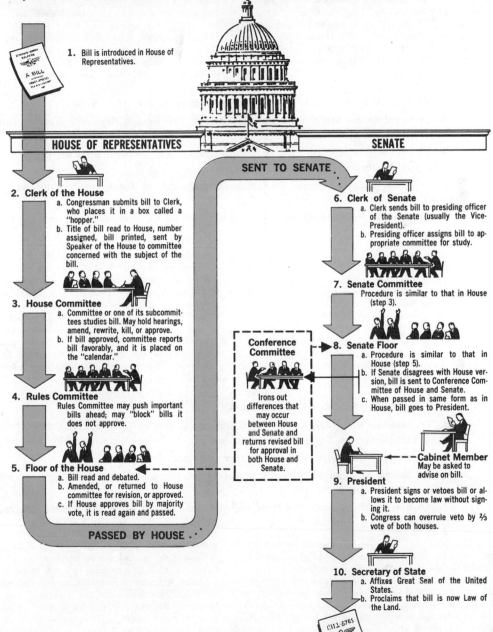

1. Bill is introduced in House of Representatives.

HOUSE OF REPRESENTATIVES

2. Clerk of the House
  a. Congressman submits bill to Clerk, who places it in a box called a "hopper."
  b. Title of bill read to House, number assigned, bill printed, sent by Speaker of the House to committee concerned with the subject of the bill.

3. House Committee
  a. Committee or one of its subcommittees studies bill. May hold hearings, amend, rewrite, kill, or approve.
  b. If bill approved, committee reports bill favorably, and it is placed on the "calendar."

4. Rules Committee
  Rules Committee may push important bills ahead; may "block" bills it does not approve.

5. Floor of the House
  a. Bill read and debated.
  b. Amended, or returned to House committee for revision, or approved.
  c. If House approves bill by majority vote, it is read again and passed.

PASSED BY HOUSE

SENT TO SENATE

SENATE

6. Clerk of Senate
  a. Clerk sends bill to presiding officer of the Senate (usually the Vice-President).
  b. Presiding officer assigns bill to appropriate committee for study.

7. Senate Committee
  Procedure is similar to that in House (step 3).

Conference Committee

Irons out differences that may occur between House and Senate and returns revised bill for approval in both House and Senate.

8. Senate Floor
  a. Procedure is similar to that in House (step 5).
  b. If Senate disagrees with House version, bill is sent to Conference Committee of House and Senate.
  c. When passed in same form as in House, bill goes to President.

Cabinet Member
May be asked to advise on bill.

9. President
  a. President signs or vetoes bill or allows it to become law without signing it.
  b. Congress can overrule veto by 2/3 vote of both houses.

10. Secretary of State
  a. Affixes Great Seal of the United States.
  b. Proclaims that bill is now Law of the Land.

The Congress shall have power

1. To lay and collect taxes, duties, imposts, and excises, to pay the debts and provide for the common defense and general welfare of the United States; but all duties, imposts, and excises shall be uniform throughout the United States;

¶ Section 8 places important powers in the hands of Congress, indicating that the framers of the Constitution were aware of the weaknesses of the Congress under the Articles of Confederation. This section lists 18 powers granted to Congress—the *delegated* or *enumerated powers*. The first 17 are "express" powers because they clearly designate specific areas in which Congress may exercise its authority. The eighteenth power is contained in the famous "elastic clause," from which has come the doctrine of "implied" powers. The elastic clause permits the "stretching" of the other 17 powers.

¶ *Clause 1.* This clause gives Congress the power to levy and collect taxes, duties or tariffs (taxes on imported goods collected at customhouses), and excises (taxes on goods produced, sold, or consumed within the country). The term "imposts" includes duties and excise taxes. Notice that these taxes must be uniform throughout the United States. According to this clause, the power to tax may be used for two purposes only: (1) to pay the government's debts, and (2) to provide for the common defense and general welfare. The Social Security tax on payrolls (p. 692) is a present-day use of the power to tax.

2. To borrow money on the credit of the United States;

3. To regulate commerce with foreign nations, and among the several states, [and with the Indian tribes];

4. To establish a uniform rule of naturalization, and uniform laws on the subject of bankruptcies throughout the United States;

5. To coin money, regulate the value thereof, and of foreign coin, and fix the standard of weights and measures;

6. To provide for the punishment of counterfeiting the securities and current coin of the United States;

¶ *Clause 2.* The power granted in Clause 2 enables the government to borrow money by issuing bonds for sale, on which the government pays interest. This clause, extended by Clause 18, has also given Congress the power to establish national banks and the Federal Reserve System (p. 179). ¶ *Clause 3.* Clause 3, included to remedy one of the major weaknesses of the Articles of Confederation, gives Congress direct control over interstate and foreign commerce. And this provision has been extended, by the use of Clause 18, to give Congress control over transportation, communication, and navigation. In order to exercise this broad power, Congress has set up various administrative agencies, such as the Interstate Commerce Commission and the Federal Communications Commission. ¶ *Clause 4.* Clause 4 provides the power to regulate the methods by which aliens become citizens of the United States and to form rules regarding bankruptcy. ¶ *Clause 5.* Clause 5 permits Congress to coin money, to determine the gold and silver content of money, and to order the printing of paper money. It also permits Congress to set up uniform standards for measuring weights and distances. ¶ *Clause 6.* Under Clause 6, Congress authorizes the Treasury Department to investigate counterfeiting of money or government bonds.

7. To establish post offices and post roads;

8. To promote the progress of science and useful arts by securing for limited times to authors and inventors the exclusive right to their respective writings and discoveries;

9. To constitute tribunals inferior to the Supreme Court;

10. To define and punish piracies and felonies committed on the high seas and offenses against the law of nations;

11. To declare war, [grant letters of marque and reprisal,] and make rules concerning captures on land and water;

¶ *Clause 7.* Clause 7 grants Congress the power to control post offices and the mail service. Through its power to appropriate money to run the various government departments, including the Post Office Department, Congress can also determine the postal rates. ¶ *Clause 8.* Clause 8 shows that the framers of the Constitution were eager to promote the progress of science and the arts. Under this power, Congress has passed laws providing that inventors be granted *patents* (exclusive rights to manufacture and sell their inventions for 17 years) and that authors and composers be granted *copyrights* (exclusive rights to control the publication or performance of their works for a 28-year period, renewable for an equal length of time). ¶ *Clause 9.* Clause 9 granted Congress the power to establish the federal district courts, the Courts of Appeals, and other special courts. ¶ *Clause 10.* Empowered by Clause 10, Congress protects and controls citizens and ships of the United States when they are out of the country. It may also punish counterfeiting in the United States of bonds and notes of a foreign government. ¶ *Clause 11.* Clause 11 gives Congress the power to declare war. Although Congress alone has this power, there have been instances when Presidents took military action without prior consent of Congress. In 1846 President Polk sent troops into an area which was claimed by both the United States and Mexico (p. 325). In 1950 President Truman ordered American troops into Korea to stop Communist aggression (p. 784). And in the mid-1960's, through executive order, increasing numbers of American troops became involved in the conflict in South Vietnam although there never was any formal declaration of war (pp. 800–04). ¶ "Letters of marque and reprisal" were licenses issued by the government to privateers (armed ships, privately owned), allowing them to attack enemy ships during wartime. In the War of 1812, the government of the United States issued many of these licenses, and American privateers took advantage of them to do extensive damage to British trade. Today, the issuing of such licenses is outlawed by international agreement.

12. To raise and support armies, but no appropriation of money to that use shall be for a longer term than two years;

13. To provide and maintain a navy;

14. To make rules for the government and regulation of the land and naval forces;

15. To provide for calling forth the militia to execute the laws of the Union, suppress insurrections, and repel invasions;

16. To provide for organizing, arming, and disciplining the militia, and for governing such part of them as may be employed in the service of the United States, reserving to the states, respectively, the appointment of the officers, and the authority of training the militia according to the discipline prescribed by Congress;

¶ *Clause 12.* The two-year limit in Clause 12 on money appropriations for the army was included to keep the major military power under strict civilian control. ¶ *Clause 13.* Notice that appropriations for the navy were not limited. An air force, of course, was not dreamed of when the Constitution was written. ¶ *Clause 14.* Under the power granted in Clause 14, Congress has established rules and regulations governing military discipline and the procedure of courts-martial. ¶ *Clauses 15, 16.* The term "militia" now refers to the National Guard units of the states. These units may now be called up by the President to keep law and order. They can become part of the United States Army in emergencies.

17. To exercise exclusive legislation in all cases whatsoever, over such district (not exceeding ten miles square) as may, by cession of particular states, and the acceptance of Congress, become the seat of government of the United States, and to exercise like authority over all places purchased by the consent of the legislature of the state in which the same shall be, for the erection of forts, magazines, arsenals, dock-yards, and other needful buildings;—and

¶ The power in Clause 17 enables Congress to exercise exclusive control over the District of Columbia, as well as over forts, arsenals, federal courthouses, post offices, dockyards, and other installations that are owned and operated by the federal government in the various states.

18. To make all laws which shall be necessary and proper for carrying into execution the foregoing powers, and all other powers vested by this Constitution in the government of the United States, or in any department or officer thereof.

¶ "Necessary and proper" are the key words in Clause 18, the so-called *elastic clause.* Only by combining the power granted in this clause with one of the other 17 powers can Congress use the implied powers granted to it in the Constitution. Laws based on this clause are, of course, subject to review by the judicial branch.

SECTION 9. POWERS DENIED TO THE FEDERAL GOVERNMENT

1. [The migration or importation of such persons as any of the states now existing shall think proper to admit shall not be prohibited by the Congress prior to the year 1808; but a tax or duty may be imposed on such importation, not exceeding $10 for each person.]

¶ Section 9 limits the powers of Congress. ¶ *Clause 1.* "Such persons" refers to slaves. This provision grew out of the commerce compromise at the Constitutional Convention held in Philadelphia in 1787 (p. 159). It was agreed that Congress would not prohibit the importation of slaves prior to 1808, and that it would not impose an import tax of more than $10 per slave. The importation of slaves into the United States became illegal in 1808.

179

2. The privilege of the writ of *habeas corpus* shall not be suspended, unless when in cases of rebellion or invasion the public safety may require it.

3. No bill of attainder or *ex post facto* law shall be passed.

¶ *Clause 2.* The guarantee of the *writ of habeas corpus* (meaning "you may have the body, or person") has been called the most important single safeguard of personal liberty known to Anglo-American law. It protects a person against being held in jail on insufficient evidence or no evidence at all. The lawyer of a person who is arrested can readily obtain a writ, or court order, which requires that the arrested person be brought before a judge who is to determine whether there are sufficient grounds to hold him in jail. If there are not enough grounds, the person must be free. ¶ *Clause 3.* A "bill of attainder" is a legislative measure which condemns a person and punishes him without a jury trial. Such measures were used in England where

Parliament could, by law, declare a person guilty of treason and punish him by death and confiscation of property. Under the Constitution, Congress cannot by law single out certain persons and inflict punishment on them. The power to punish belongs to the judiciary. ¶ An *ex post facto law* was a law which punished a person for doing something which was legal before the law was passed, or which increased the penalty for earlier actions. Because of this clause, the Lindbergh kidnaping law, for example, which was enacted by the federal government in the year 1932, cannot be applied to persons who committed the crime of kidnaping before the year 1932.

4. [No capitation or other direct tax shall be laid, unless in proportion to the census herein before directed to be taken.]

5. No tax or duty shall be laid on articles exported from any state.

6. No preference shall be given any regulation of commerce or revenue to the ports of one state over those of another: nor shall vessels bound to, or from, one state, be obliged to enter, clear, or pay duties in another.

¶ *Clause 4.* A "capitation tax" is a direct tax imposed on each person, such as the poll tax on persons voting. This provision was inserted to prevent Congress from taxing Negro slaves per poll, or per person, for the purpose of abolishing slavery. Amendment 16 overrules this clause as far as income taxes are concerned. ¶ *Clause 5.* Clause 5 also resulted from the

commerce compromises. The southern states wanted to make sure that Congress could not use its taxing power to impose taxes on southern exports, such as cotton and tobacco. ¶ *Clause 6.* This clause declares that the United States is an open market in which all states have equal trading and commercial opportunities.

7. No money shall be drawn from the Treasury, but in consequence of appropriations made by law; and a regular statement and account of the receipts and expenditures of all public money shall be published from time to time.

8. No title of nobility shall be granted by the United States; and no person holding any office of profit or trust under them, shall, without the consent of the Congress, accept of any present, emolument, office, or title, of any kind whatever, from any king, prince, or foreign state.

¶ *Clause 7.* This clause concerns the all-important "power of the purse." Since Congress controls expenditures, it can limit the powers of the President by limiting the amount of money he may spend to run the government. This clause has been described as the single most important curb on Presidential

power in the Constitution. Furthermore, the requirement to account for money spent and received helps to protect the public against misuse of funds. ¶ *Clause 8.* This clause prohibits the establishment of a nobility. It is also intended to discourage bribery of United States officials by foreign governments.

SECTION 10. POWERS DENIED TO THE STATES

1. No state shall enter into any treaty, alliance, or confederation; grant letters of marque and reprisal; coin money; emit bills of credit; make anything but gold and silver coin a tender in payment of debts; pass any bill of attainder, *ex post facto* law, or law impairing the obligation of contracts, or grant any title of nobility.

2. No state shall, without the consent of the Congress, lay any imposts or duties on imports or exports, except what may be absolutely necessary for executing its inspection laws; and the net produce of all duties and imposts, laid by any state on imports or exports, shall be for the use of the Treasury of the United States; and all such laws shall be subject to the revision and control of the Congress.

THE FEDERAL SYSTEM

DIVISION OF POWERS

FEDERAL GOVERNMENT

STATE GOVERNMENTS

FEDERAL AND STATE GOVERNMENTS

Important "enumerated" powers "delegated" to the Congress:

- To regulate interstate and foreign commerce
- To declare war
- To establish laws governing citizenship
- To coin money
- To control the postal system
- To regulate patents and copyrights
- To establish lower courts
- To establish and support the armed forces

Also there are "implied" powers provided by the so-called "elastic clause" (Art. 1, Sec. 8, clause 18) granting the power to pass all laws necessary and proper to carry out the enumerated powers.

Important "concurrent" powers shared by Federal and State Governments:

- To tax
- To borrow money
- To establish penal laws
- To charter banks
- To take property for public purposes (This power is called "eminent domain.")

Important "residual" or "reserved" powers retained by the State Governments:

- To regulate suffrage
- To maintain a system of public education
- To establish marriage and divorce laws
- To establish laws governing corporations
- To establish traffic laws
- To regulate intrastate commerce

Also, according to the 10th Amendment, all powers (1) not delegated to the federal government or (2) not prohibited by the Constitution are reserved to the states or to the people.

PROHIBITED POWERS

Powers denied the Federal Government:

- To suspend the writ of *habeas corpus* (except in cases of rebellion or invasion)
- To give preferential treatment in commerce or revenue to the ports of any state
- To draw money from the Treasury except by appropriation under a specific law
- To levy taxes on exports
- No person holding federal office can accept a gift from a foreign country without consent of Congress.

Powers denied the Federal and State Governments:

- To pass bills of attainder
- To pass *ex post facto* laws
- To grant titles of nobility

Powers denied the State Governments:

- To enter into treaties with other nations or with other states without the consent of Congress
- To coin money
- To impair obligations of contract
- To place a tax on imports or exports except to carry out its inspection laws
- To keep troops or ships in time of peace without consent of Congress

This chart describes the division of powers in the original Constitution. Additional limitations on the powers of the Federal Government are enumerated in the Bill of Rights.

3. No state shall, without the consent of Congress, lay any duty of tonnage, keep troops, or ships of war in time of peace, enter into any agreement or compact with another state, or with a foreign power, or engage in war, unless actually invaded, or in such imminent danger as will not admit of delay.

¶ According to Section 10, states cannot: (1) Make treaties. (2) Coin money. (3) Pass either bills of attainder or ex post facto laws. (4) Impair obligations of contract. (5) Grant titles of nobility. (6) Tax imports or exports without the consent of Congress. (7) Keep troops or warships in time of peace. (8) Deal with another state or foreign power without the consent of Congress. (9) Engage in war unless invaded. ¶ *Clause 1.* Because Shays' Rebellion (p. 152) was still fresh in the minds of the delegates to the Constitutional Convention, and since several of the states at that time were being urged to pass legislation relieving debtors from the payment of their debts, the delegates decided to protect creditors once and for all by denying states the right to pass laws that would impair obligations of contract. During the Great Depression which began in 1929, and the New Deal period (1933–45), the Supreme Court upheld state laws relieving debtors or mortgagees from paying their debts on the due dates, but payments were simply postponed, not canceled. ¶ *Clauses 2 and 3.* States may enter into agreements or compacts with each other, provided that they have the approval of Congress. There have been many such arrangements among states on problems concerning port development, conservation, minimum wages, crime prevention, flood control, the pollution of rivers, lakes, and harbors, and other matters.

Article 2. EXECUTIVE DEPARTMENT

SECTION 1. PRESIDENT AND VICE-PRESIDENT

1. *Term of office.* The executive power shall be vested in a President of the United States of America. He shall hold his office during the term of four years, and together with the Vice-President, chosen for the same term, be elected as follows:

¶ This provision gives the executive power to the President. He may use all of the means at his disposal to carry out the laws. He may also refrain from using some of these means. It should be understood, of course, that the power and prestige of the Presidency depend to some extent on the personality of the man who holds the office.

2. *Electoral system.* Each state shall appoint, in such manner as the legislature thereof may direct, a number of electors, equal to the whole number of Senators and Representatives to which the state may be entitled in the Congress; but no Senator or Representative, or person holding an office of trust or profit under the United States, shall be appointed an elector.

3. *Former method of using the electoral system.* [The electors shall meet in their respective states, and vote by ballot for two persons, of whom one at least shall not be an inhabitant of the same state with themselves. And they shall make a list of all the persons voted for, and of the number of votes for each; which list they shall sign and certify, and transmit sealed to the seat of the government of the United States, directed to the president of the Senate. The president of the Senate shall, in the presence of the Senate and House of Representatives, open all the certificates, and the votes shall then be counted. The person having the greatest number of votes shall be the President, if such number be a majority of the whole number of electors appointed; and if there be more than one who have such majority, and have an equal number of votes, then the House of Representatives shall immediately choose by ballot one of them for President; and if no person have a majority, then from the five highest on the list the said House shall in like manner choose the President. But in choosing the President the votes shall be taken by states, the representation from each state having one vote. A quorum for this purpose shall consist of a member or members from two-thirds of the states, and a majoriy of all the states shall be necessary to a choice. In every case, after the choice of the President, the person having the greatest number of votes of the electors shall be the Vice-President. But if there should remain two or more who have equal votes, the Senate shall choose from them by ballot the Vice-President.]

¶ *Clauses 2, 3.* These clauses established the electoral system, but very little that the Founding Fathers decided about electing a President has survived in the form they intended. The delegates to the Constitutional Convention, still fearful of popular rule, decided that the President and Vice-President ought to be elected by a small group of men called "electors," chosen according to a method determined by each state legislature. Until Andrew Jackson's Presidency, electors were chosen by state legislatures. Since then, the people have voted directly for the electors. Some changes in the method of electing a President have been made by formal amendment, as in Amendment 12; other changes have resulted from political practice. (The method of electing a President today is shown in the chart entitled "How a President Is Elected" on page 195. See also Amendment 23, page 200, for electors chosen by the District of Columbia and Amendment 24, page 200, for restrictions imposed on the states in fixing eligibility for voters in national elections.)

4. *Time of elections.* **The Congress may determine the time of choosing the electors, and the day on which they shall give their votes; which day shall be the same throughout the United States.**

5. *Qualifications for President.* **No person except a natural-born citizen [or a citizen of the United States, at the time of the adoption of this Constitution], shall be eligible to the office of President; neither shall any person be eligible to that office who shall not have attained to the age of thirty-five years, and been fourteen years a resident within the United States.**

¶ *Qualifications for President:* (1) A native-born citizen of the United States. (2) At least 35 years of age. (3) A resident of the United States for at least 14 years. ¶ TERM OF OFFICE: 4 years.

6. *Filling vacancies.* **In case of the removal of the President from office, or of his death, resignation, or inability to discharge the powers and duties of the said office, the same shall devolve on the Vice-President, and the Congress may by law provide for the case of removal, death, resignation, or inability, both of the President and Vice-President, declaring what officer shall then act as President, and such officer shall act accordingly, until the disability be removed, or a President shall be elected.**

¶ If a President dies or is removed from office, the Vice-President replaces him. John Tyler, in 1841, was the first Vice-President to succeed to the Presidency. By assuming the office of President and not simply serving as an acting President, he established a precedent that has since been followed. ¶ Under the Presidential Succession Act of 1947, if both the President and the Vice-President die or are removed from office, the order of succession is as follows: (1) Speaker of the House, (2) President pro tempore of the Senate, and (3) the cabinet members in the order in which their offices were created. ¶ Amendment 25, adopted in 1967 (p. 201), clarifies the procedure to be followed in cases of Presidential disability.

7. *Salary.* **The President shall, at stated times, receive for his services, a compensation, which shall neither be increased nor diminished during the period for which he shall have been elected, and he shall not receive within that period any other emolument from the United States, or any of them.**

8. *Oath of office.* **Before he enter on the execution of his office, he shall take the following oath or affirmation:—"I do solemnly swear (or affirm) that I will faithfully execute the office of President of the United States, and will to the best of my ability, preserve, protect, and defend the Constitution of the United States."**

¶ *Clause 7.* In 1969 the President's salary was set by law at $200,000 a year, plus a $50,000 expense account and a nontaxable fund for travel and official entertainment limited to $40,000. The Vice-President's salary was set, in 1969, at $62,500 a year, plus a $10,000 expense allowance. ¶ *Clause 8.* The President assumes his office officially only after taking the oath of office, which is administered by the Chief Justice of the United States.

SECTION 2. POWERS OF THE PRESIDENT

1. *Military powers.* **The President shall be Commander in Chief of the Army and Navy of the United States, and of the militia of the several states, when called into the actual service of the United States; he may require the option, in writing, of the principal officer in each of the executive departments, upon any subject relating to the duties of their respective offices, and he shall have power to grant reprieves and pardons for offenses against the United States, except in cases of impeachment.**

¶ The important point in this provision is that it places the armed forces under the control of a civilian. The President is a civilian, but he is superior in military power to any military officer. ¶ The words "principal officer in each of the executive departments" are the basis for the creation of the President's cabinet. Each cabinet member is the head of one of the executive departments. The President chooses his own cabinet, with the consent of the Senate. He can remove any cabinet official without asking Senate approval.

2. *Treaties and appointments.* **He shall have power, by and with the advice and consent of the Senate, to make treaties, provided two-thirds of the Senators present concur; and he shall nominate, and by and with the advice and consent of the Senate, shall appoint ambassadors, other public ministers and consuls, judges of the Supreme Court, and all other officers of the United States, whose appointments are not herein otherwise provided for, and which shall be established by law; but the Congress may by law vest the appointment of such inferior officers, as they think proper, in the President alone, in the courts of law, or in the heads of departments.**

¶ The President makes treaties with the advice and consent of two thirds of the Senate. A treaty ratified by the Senate becomes the supreme law of the land. The President can also enter into executive agreements with foreign governments. Although such agreements may have the same force as treaties, they do not require Senate approval. ¶ With the consent of the Senate, the President can appoint ambassadors, public ministers and consuls, and other diplomatic officials, federal judges, military officers, and members of administrative agencies. "Inferior officers" are those subordinate to the cabinet members or to federal judges. ¶ At the present time, a majority of federal government positions are filled by candidates who passed examinations given by the United States Civil Service Commission (p. 432).

3. *Filling vacancies.* **The President shall have power to fill up all vacancies that may happen during the recess of the Senate, by granting commissions which shall expire at the end of their next session.**

¶ If a vacancy in an important position occurs during a time when Congress is not in session, the President has the power to fill such a vacancy with an interim appointment. When Congress meets again, this appointment, or a new appointment, must be submitted to the Senate so that it may be approved.

SECTION 3. DUTIES OF THE PRESIDENT

He shall from time to time give to the Congress information of the state of the Union, and recommend to their consideration such measures as he shall judge necessary and expedient; he may, on extraordinary occasions, convene both houses, or either of them, and in case of disagreement between them, with respect to the time of adjournment, he may adjourn them to such time as he shall think proper; he shall receive ambassadors and other public ministers; he shall take care that the laws be faithfully executed, and shall commission all the officers of the United States.

¶ The President's duties include: (1) *Legislative duties:* delivering annual and special messages to Congress; calling special sessions of Congress; approving or vetoing bills (see Article 1, Section 7). (2) *Diplomatic duties:* receiving (or refusing to receive) ambassadors or ministers of foreign countries to indicate that the United States "recognizes" (or refuses to "recognize") the government of these countries. The President can also send home the ambassador of a foreign country as a sign that the United States is breaking off diplomatic relations with that country. (3) *Executive duties:* executing all the laws. In actual fact, the administration and enforcement of the laws are in the hands of the various government departments, commissions, and administrative agencies; but the President is responsible for seeing that they are carried out. (4) *Military duties:* commissioning all United States armed forces officers.

SECTION 4. IMPEACHMENT

The President, Vice-President, and all civil officers of the United States, shall be removed from office on impeachment for, and conviction of, treason, bribery, or other high crimes and misdemeanors.

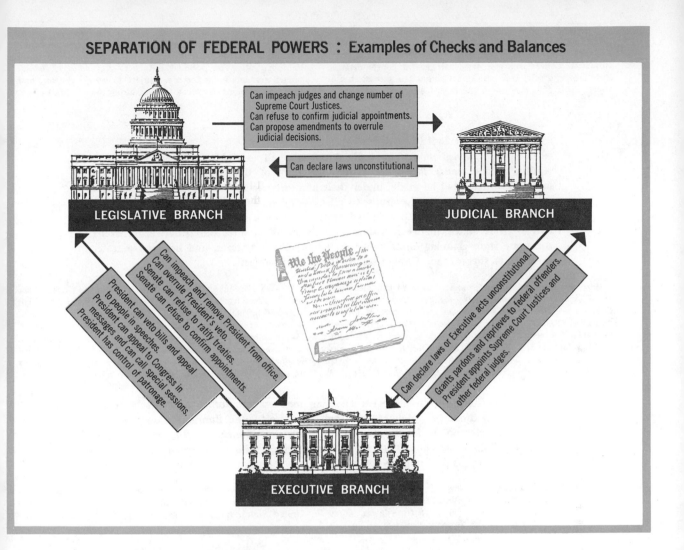

SEPARATION OF FEDERAL POWERS : Examples of Checks and Balances

LEGISLATIVE BRANCH

Can impeach judges and change number of Supreme Court Justices.
Can refuse to confirm judicial appointments.
Can propose amendments to overrule judicial decisions.

Can declare laws unconstitutional.

JUDICIAL BRANCH

Can impeach and remove President from office.
Can overrule President's veto.
Senate can refuse to ratify treaties.
Senate can refuse to confirm appointments.

President can veto bills and appeal to people in speeches.
President can appeal to Congress in messages and can call special sessions.
President has control of patronage.

Can declare laws or Executive acts unconstitutional.

Grants pardons and reprieves to federal offenders.
President appoints Supreme Court Justices and other federal judges.

EXECUTIVE BRANCH

Article 3. JUDICIAL DEPARTMENT

SECTION 1. FEDERAL COURTS

The judicial power of the United States shall be vested in one Supreme Court, and in such inferior courts as the Congress may from time to time ordain and establish. The judges, both of the Supreme and inferior courts, shall hold their offices during good behavior, and shall, at stated times, receive for their services a compensation, which shall not be diminished during their continuance in office.

¶ By authorizing the establishment of a system of federal courts, Article 3 creates the judicial power—the power to hear and decide cases. The lack of a federal court system was one of the weaknesses of the government under the Articles of Confederation. Under the judicial powers granted by the Constitution or developed through Supreme Court decisions, the courts have declared unconstitutional certain laws of Congress, acts of the President, laws of the state legislatures, and decisions of the state courts. ¶ Only the Supreme Court is established by the Constitution itself, but the Constitution gives Congress the authority to establish the lower courts which exist today. Since the Constitution does not state the number of justices to be appointed to the Supreme Court, Congress decides the number by law. At first, the Supreme Court had six justices. Congress has set the number at as many as ten and as few as five. ¶ Congress has created two types of lower courts. One type includes 90 federal district courts and 11 Courts of Appeals, which review cases sent up by the district courts. District courts and Courts of Appeals are called "constitutional courts" because they are general courts deriving their power directly from the Constitution. The second type of courts deals with cases of a specialized nature. The Court of Claims, the Tax Court, and the Court of Customs and Patent Appeals are included in this second group. ¶ The framers of the Constitution wanted to make sure that our federal judges would be independent of political influence. Accordingly, federal judges are appointed for life, subject to good behavior, and their pay cannot be reduced by law during their term of office.

SECTION 2. JURISDICTION OF FEDERAL COURTS

1. *General jurisdiction.* **The judicial power shall extend to all cases, in law and equity, arising under this Constitution, the laws of the United States, and treaties made or which shall be made, under their authority; to all cases affecting ambassadors, other public ministers and consuls; to all cases of admirality and maritime jurisdiction; to controversies to which the United States shall be a party; to controversies between two or more states; [between a state and citizens of another state;] between citizens of the same state claiming lands under grants of different states, and between a state, or the citizens thereof, and foreign states, citizens, or subjects.**

¶ Here the words "law" and "equity" have special meanings. "Law" means the common law—the laws that originated in England and that have been based on centuries of judicial decisions. "Equity" refers to principles of justice also developed in England to remedy wrongs in situations in which the common law was inadequate. Today, in the United States, law and equity are applied by the same judges in the same courts. ¶ The power of the federal courts extends to two types of cases: (1) those involving the interpretation of the Constitution, federal laws, treaties, and laws relating to ships on the high seas and navigable waters; and (2) those involving the United States government itself, foreign diplomatic officials (ambassadors, public ministers, and consuls), two or more state governments, and citizens of different states when the sum involved is more than $10,000; also cases involving a state or its citizens versus foreign countries or citizens of foreign countries.

2. *Supreme Court.* **In all cases affecting ambassadors, other public ministers and consuls, and those in which a state shall be a party, the Supreme Court shall have original jurisdiction. In all the other cases before mentioned, the Supreme Court shall have appellate jurisdiction, both as to law and fact, with such exceptions, and under such regulations as the Congress shall make.**

¶ "Original jurisdiction" means the right to try a case before any other court may hear it. "Appellate jurisdiction" means the right of a court to try cases appealed from lower courts. Most of the cases tried by the Supreme Court come up as a result of appeals from lower federal and state courts. Cases involving foreign diplomats and any of the 50 states of the United States, however, may be started directly in the Supreme Court.

3. *Conduct of trials.* **The trial of all crimes, except in cases of impeachment, shall be by jury; and such trial shall be held in the state where the said crimes shall have been committed; but when not committed within any state, the trial shall be at such place or places as the Congress may by law have directed.**

¶ Every person accused of a federal crime is guaranteed a jury trial near the scene of the crime. But the accused may give up this privilege, if he wishes. ¶ Amendments 5, 6, and 7 expand the provisions of this clause.

SECTION 3. TREASON

1. *Definition.* **Treason against the United States shall consist only in levying war against them, or in adhering to their enemies, giving them aid and comfort. No person shall be convicted of treason unless on the testimony of two witnesses to the same overt act, or on confession in open court.**

¶ Treason is the only crime specifically defined in the Constitution. To be found guilty of treason, a person must be shown to have helped wage war against the United States, or to have given aid and comfort to its enemies. A person cannot be convicted without the testimony of two witnesses to the same overt act, or his own confession in open court.

2. *Punishment.* **The Congress shall have power to declare the punishment of treason, but no attainder of treason shall work corruption of blood or forfeiture except during the life of the person attainted.**

¶ The punishment for treason, as determined by Congress, is death or a fine of $10,000 and imprisonment for not less than five years. This clause further states that the punishment for treason cannot be extended to the children of a traitor. They cannot be deprived of their rights and their property—as had been done in England.

Article 4. RELATIONS AMONG THE STATES

SECTION 1. OFFICIAL ACTS

Full faith and credit shall be given in each state to the public acts, records, and judicial proceedings of every other state. And the Congress may by general laws prescribe the manner in which such acts, records, and proceedings shall be proved, and the effect thereof.

¶ The purpose of this provision is to make sure that the official records of one state are respected in all the other states. Official records of this kind include birth certificates, marriage licenses, and death certificates; corporation charters, wills, and court decisions. This provision also protects a citizen's right to collect money that has been awarded him by a court decision in one state, even if the person who owes him the money moves to another state.

SECTION 2. PRIVILEGES OF CITIZENS

1. *Privileges.* **The citizens of each state shall be entitled to all privileges and immunities of citizens in the several states.**

2. *Extradition.* **A person charged in any state with treason, felony, or other crime, who shall flee from justice, and be found in another state, shall on demand of the executive authority of the state from which he fled, be delivered up, to be removed to the state having jurisdiction of the crime.**

3. *Fugitive slaves.* **[No person held in service or labor in one state, under the laws thereof, escaping into another, shall in consequence of any law or regulation therein, be discharged from such service or labor, but shall be delivered up on claim of the party to whom such service or labor may be due.]**

¶ *Clause 1.* The terms "privileges" and "immunities" simply mean the rights of citizens. Thus, a state cannot discriminate against citizens of other states in favor of its own citizens, except in certain very special areas—such as voting, for example. A state can impose residence requirements for voting, so that a citizen of another state will have to reside in the state for a specified period before he may exercise his right to vote as a citizen of his new state. ¶ *Clause 2.* This provision prevents a prisoner or a person charged with a crime from escaping justice by fleeing across a state line. It provides that a criminal be returned by the state in which he is captured to the state where the crime was committed—a process known as "extradition." A governor of a state cannot be forced to extradite, or return, a prisoner, however, if the governor feels that such action will result in injustice to the accused person. ¶ *Clause 3.* Since the ratification of Amendment 13 in 1865 brought an end to slavery in this country, the clause is now of historical interest only.

SECTION 3. NEW STATES AND TERRITORIES

1. *Admission of new states.* **New states may be admitted by the Congress into this Union; but no new state shall be formed or erected within the jurisdiction of any other state; nor any state be formed by the junction of two or more states, or parts of states, without the consent of the legislatures of the states concerned as well as of the Congress.**

¶ The Northwest Ordinance of 1787 (p. 147) provided that new states be admitted to the Union on completely equal footing with the original thirteen states. Although the Constitution declares here that new states may not be created within the territory of any other state without its consent, an exception did occur in 1863, when West Virginia was formed from the western part of the state of Virginia. This exception occurred during the Civil War, and West Virginia received permission from the loyal, rather than the secessionist, government of Virginia.

2. *Powers of Congress over territories and other property.* **The Congress shall have power to dispose of and make all needful rules and regulations respecting the territory or other property belonging to the United States; and nothing in this Constitution shall be so construed as to prejudice any claims of the United States, or of any particular state.**

¶ Under this provision, Congress has the power to control all property belonging to the federal government. It can set up governments for Territories and colonies of the United States. It can grant independence to a colony, as it did to the Philippines in 1946. It can set aside land for national parks and build dams for flood control.

SECTION 4. GUARANTEES TO THE STATES

The United States shall guarantee to every state in this Union a republican form of government, and shall protect each of them against invasion; and on application of the legislature, or of the executive (when the legislature cannot be convened) against domestic violence.

¶ If the President finds that public property is being destroyed and the public safety is endangered in a state, he may decide to send troops into that state without having been requested to do so by the local authorities. The President may even proclaim marital law in a state. This section also guarantees that states can govern only by consent of the governed.

Article 5.   METHODS OF AMENDMENT

The Congress, whenever two-thirds of both houses shall deem it necessary, shall propose amendments to this Constitution, or, on the application of the legislatures of two-thirds of the several states, shall call a convention for proposing amendments, which, in either case, shall be valid to all intents and purposes, as part of this Constitution, when ratified by the legislatures of three-fourths of the several states, or by conventions in three-fourths thereof, as the one or the other mode of ratification may be proposed by the Congress; provided that [no amendments which may be made prior to the year 1808 shall in any manner affect the first and fourth clauses in the Ninth Section of the First Article; and that] no state, without its consent, shall be deprived of its equal suffrage in the Senate.

¶ One of the most important features of the Constitution is that it can be amended, or changed. This adaptability is one of the four main principles of the Constitution. ¶ An amendment must first be *proposed*, and then *ratified*. There are four methods of amending the Constitution (see chart, page 189). So far, all amendments have been proposed by Congress and ratified by state legislatures, except Amendment 21, which was ratified by the convention method. ¶ The fact that only 25 amendments have been adopted since 1789—and only 15 since 1791—indicates that it is not easy to change the Constitution, and that changing it is a serious matter, requiring much thought and discussion in Congress, in the state legislatures, and among the people. ¶ Notice that there are two areas in which the Constitution cannot be amended under any circumstances. The first exception is obsolete because it is a reference to the period which preceded 1808. The second exception is still very important because it guarantees that every state shall have equal representation in the Senate.

Article 6.   GENERAL PROVISIONS

1. *Public debts.* **All debts contracted and engagements entered into, before the adoption of this Constitution, shall be as valid against the United States under this Constitution, as under the Confederation.**

¶ This provision was important because it announced to all that the new government would assume and pay back all debts incurred by the government under the Articles of Confederation. It was one of several actions advocated by Alexander Hamilton and undertaken by Congress in order to establish the credit of the new government.

188

HOW THE CONSTITUTION MAY BE AMENDED

Amendments may be proposed by ⅔ vote of Congress in both the House and Senate.

Or

⅔ of state legislatures may request Congress to call a Constitutional Convention.

Constitutional Convention proposes amendment.

Then

Amendment must be ratified by at least ¾ of the state legislatures,

Or

by a majority vote in ¾ of state conventions called to vote on amendment.

---

2. *The supreme law.* **This Constitution, and the laws of the United States which shall be made in pursuance thereof, and all treaties made, or which shall be made, under the authority of the United States, shall be the supreme law of the land; and the judges in every state shall be bound thereby, anything in the constitution or laws of any state to the contrary notwithstanding.**

¶ This is the famous "supremacy clause" of the Constitution. It declares that the "supreme law of the land" is: (1) the Constitution, (2) the laws of the United States passed under this Constitution, and (3) the treaties made under the authority of the United States. ¶ According to the supremacy clause, the power of the national government is superior to the power of the state governments, provided that its actions are in accordance with the Constitution. The Supreme Court determines whether the actions of the President and Congress are constitutional.

3. *Oaths of office.* **The Senators and Representatives before mentioned, and the members of the several state legislatures, and all executive and judicial officers, both of the United States and of the several states, shall be bound by oath or affirmation, to support this Constitution; but no religious test shall ever be required as a qualification to any office or public trust under the United States.**

¶ No religious qualification shall ever be required as a condition for holding public office. This provision results from the fact that in the United States there is separation of church and state, which means that a man's religion is supposed to remain a private matter, with no bearing on his consideration for public office.

Article 7. RATIFICATION

The ratification of the convention of nine states shall be sufficient for the establishment of this Constitution between the states so ratifying the same.

¶ The Constitutional Convention was summoned by the Congress under the Articles of Confederation for the purpose of amending the Articles. According to the Articles of Confederation, amendments had to be approved by all thirteen states. Instead of amending the Articles, however, the delegates to the Constitutional Convention drafted an entirely new plan of government. And realizing that it would be difficult to get the approval of all the states—Rhode Island, for example, had not even sent delegates to Philadelphia—the Founding Fathers provided that the Constitution would go into effect after ratification by only nine states, not thirteen. As a result, opponents of the Constitution said it had been adopted by revolutionary means.

DONE in Convention by the unanimous consent of the States present the seventeenth day of September in the year of our Lord one thousand seven hundred and eighty-seven and of the independence of the United States of America the twelfth. In witness whereof we have hereunto subscribed our names,

G Washington —*President and deputy from Virginia*

NEW HAMPSHIRE
John Langdon
Nicholas Gilman

NEW YORK
Alexander Hamilton

DELAWARE
George Read
Gunning Bedford
John Dickinson
Richard Bassett
Jacob Broom

NORTH CAROLINA
William Blount
Richard Dobbs
Spaight
Hugh Williamson

MASSACHUSETTS
Nathaniel Gorman
Rufus King

NEW JERSEY
William Livingston
David Brearley
William Paterson
Jonathan Dayton

MARYLAND
James McHenry
Daniel of St. Thomas
Jenifer
Daniel Carroll

SOUTH CAROLINA
John Rutledge
Charles Cotesworth
Pinckney
Charles Pinckney
Pierce Butler

CONNECTICUT
William Samuel
Johnson
Roger Sherman

PENNSYLVANIA
Benjamin Franklin
Thomas Mifflin
Robert Morris
George Clymer
Thomas FitzSimons
Jared Ingersoll
James Wilson
Gouverneur Morris

VIRGINIA
John Blair
James Madison

GEORGIA
William Few
Abraham Baldwin

AMENDMENTS TO THE CONSTITUTION

(The first ten amendments to the Constitution are called the Bill of Rights. The Bill of Rights limits the powers of the federal government but not the powers of the states. The Supreme Court has ruled, however, that the "due process" clause of Amendment 14 protects individuals against denial by the states of certain rights included in the Bill of Rights. For example, the Supreme Court has decided that neither the federal government nor the states can deprive any individual of his freedom of religion, speech, press, petition, assembly, or of several other rights that pertain to the fair treatment of an accused person.)

Amendment 1. FREEDOM OF RELIGION, SPEECH, PRESS, ASSEMBLY, AND PETITION (1791)

Congress shall make no law respecting an establishment of religion, or prohibiting the free exercise thereof; or abridging the freedom of speech, or of the press; or the right of the people peaceably to assemble, and to petition the government for a redress of grievances.

¶ Amendment 1 protects five great civil liberties: (1) Freedom of religion means that Congress cannot interfere with the right to worship as one sees fit. The Supreme Court, however, has ruled that Congress can require "conscientious objectors" to bear arms during wartime. Congress has, however, made special provisions to permit conscientious objectors to participate in war work without bearing arms. In interpreting the phrase "establishment of religion," the Supreme Court has decided that this phrase erects a wall of separation between church and state. In recent rulings the Supreme Court has prohibited state and local educational authorities from requiring prayers and devotional reading of the Bible in public schools. (2) Freedom of speech means the right to speak out privately and publicly. However, this right does not permit anyone to slander people (make false and malicious remarks about them), and under the Smith Act of 1940 (p. 720), no one can advocate the overthrow of the government by force and violence. Furthermore, the Supreme Court has declared that freedom of speech can be limited by the federal government if there is a "clear and present" danger that what is said may injure the general welfare. (3) Freedom of the press gives newspapers and magazines the right to print whatever they wish provided they do not libel people (publish false and malicious remarks about them) or advocate the violent overthrow of the government. Also, the use of the United States mails may be denied to those publications which spread indecent and fraudulent ideas. (4) Freedom to assemble is the right to attend meetings and join clubs. (5) The right to petition for redress of grievances means the opportunity to express complaints to any official of the federal government.

Amendment 2. RIGHT TO KEEP ARMS (1791)

A well-regulated militia, being necessary to the security of a free state, the right of the people to keep and bear arms shall not be infringed.

¶ The purpose of this amendment was to prevent Congress from depriving people of the right to bear arms in order to resist a tyrannical government. In the public interest, however, Congress and many of the states have regulated the ownership and use of weapons by private citizens through gun control legislation.

Amendment 3. QUARTERING OF TROOPS (1791)

No soldier shall, in time of peace, be quartered in any house, without the consent of the owner; nor in time of war, but in a manner to be prescribed by law.

¶ Amendments 3 and 4 are based on the important principle that "a man's home is his castle." ¶ Amendment 3 was designed to prevent the national government from requiring private citizens to house and feed military service personnel in their homes. The quartering of troops in private homes by the British government had been a source of friction between the American colonists and the British before the American Revolution.

Amendment 4.   SEARCH AND SEIZURE; WARRANTS (1791)

The right of the people to be secure in their persons, houses, papers, and effects, against unreasonable searches and seizures, shall not be violated; and no warrants shall issue but upon probable cause, supported by oath or affirmation, and particularly describing the place to be searched, and the persons or things to be seized.

¶ With the hated "writs of assistance" (p. 108) still fresh in their minds, the supporters of this amendment aimed to limit issuance of search warrants to the following conditions: (1) the warrant must be issued by a judge; (2) there must be a good reason for its use; (3) the officer who asks for a search warrant must take an oath in support of his reasons for demanding the warrant; and (4) the warrant must describe the place to be searched and the persons or things to be seized. ¶ The Supreme Court has decided that evidence illegally seized cannot be used in either federal or state courts. Under this amendment wiretapping cases have arisen. The federal government prohibits

wiretapping unless a court permit is obtained by showing a reasonable certainty that one of a certain list of crimes is being committed. ¶ In 1967 the Supreme Court held that eavesdropping and bugging by electronic means are also permissible within certain limits; police, for example, may use electronic eavesdropping devices provided a warrant is obtained in advance by showing probable cause. ¶ In 1968 the Supreme Court forbade the introduction of criminal evidence obtained by police by listening in on a party line, but evidence derived from wiretapping is permitted in federal courts in some crimes.

Amendment 5.   RIGHTS OF ACCUSED PERSONS (1791)

No person shall be held to answer for a capital, or otherwise infamous, crime, unless on a presentment or indictment of a grand jury, except in cases arising in the land or naval forces, or in the militia, when in actual service in time of war or public danger; nor shall any person be subject for the same offense to be twice put in jeopardy of life and limb; nor shall be compelled, in any criminal case, to be a witness against himself; nor be deprived of life, liberty, or property, without due process of law; nor shall private property be taken for public use, without just compensation.

¶ This amendment lists the rights of an accused person: (1) A person accused of a capital crime (one for which the death penalty may be imposed) or any other serious crime must first be accused by a grand jury (a jury of 12 to 23 persons) before he can be brought to trial. An "indictment" or "presentment" by a grand jury is merely a formal accusation. (2) A person cannot be tried twice for the same crime. (3) A person cannot be required to give testimony incriminating himself in a courtroom or before a grand jury or Congressional committee. However, under the Immunity Act of 1954, a witness can be required to testify in cases involving subversion (conspiracy

to overthrow the government), with the promise that he will not be tried on the basis of the evidence that he has furnished about himself. (4) A person cannot be deprived of life, liberty, or property without due process of law—or according to the law of the land. (5) Congress cannot take private property for public use without paying a fair price for it. This provision, an important protection of the property rights of individuals, establishes what is known as the principle of "eminent domain." ¶ Members of the armed forces are tried by military courts and commissions and are not subject to the provision calling for indictment by a grand jury.

Amendment 6.   RIGHT TO SPEEDY TRIAL (1791)

In all criminal prosecutions, the accused shall enjoy the right to a speedy and public trial, by an impartial jury of the state and district wherein the crime shall have been committed, which district shall have been previously ascertained by law, and to be informed of the nature and cause of the accusation; to be confronted with the witnesses against him; to have compulsory process for obtaining witnesses in his favor, and to have the assistance of counsel for his defense.

¶ This amendment continues the rights of an accused person. Notice that all witnesses against an accused person must appear on the witness stand, and that the government must help the accused to produce favorable witnesses. If an accused person cannot afford to hire a lawyer, the judge will assign one, and

the government will pay the lawyer's fee. These provisions under Amendment 6 apply to federal courts. However, under the "due process" clause of Amendment 14 (p. 196), the Supreme Court has decided that state courts must also assign a lawyer to defend an accused person who cannot afford one.

Amendment 7. JURY TRIAL IN CIVIL CASES (1791)

In suits at common law, where the value in controversy shall exceed twenty dollars, the right of trial by jury shall be preserved, and no fact tried by a jury shall be otherwise re-examined in any court of the United States than according to the rules of the common law.

¶ This amendment provides for a jury trial in those federal civil cases (trials where one person sues another) in which more than $20 is involved. By custom, however, people do not take their civil cases to be tried before federal courts unless these suits involve much more substantial sums of money than $20.

Amendment 8. BAILS, FINES, PUNISHMENTS (1791)

Excessive bail shall not be required, nor excessive fines imposed, nor cruel and unusual punishments inflicted.

¶ A person accused of a crime and awaiting trial may be permitted to leave jail if he or someone else posts "bail"—a sum of money serving as a guarantee that the accused will appear at his trial. The courts determine the amount of bail asked for. Cruel and unusual punishments, such as torture and beheading, are prohibited. ¶ In a series of rulings the Supreme Court declared invalid convictions of accused persons based on confessions secured by torture or other "third degree" methods.

Amendment 9. POWERS RESERVED TO THE PEOPLE (1791)

The enumeration in the Constitution, of certain rights, shall not be construed to deny or disparage others retained by the people.

¶ The Constitution does not describe specifically all the rights to be retained by the people. This amendment was added in order to guarantee that those fundamental rights that are not enumerated in the Constitution shall nevertheless be respected as inviolable rights by the national government at all times.

Amendment 10. POWERS RESERVED TO THE STATES (1791)

The powers not delegated to the United States by the Constitution, nor prohibited by it to the states, are reserved to the states respectively, or to the people.

¶ This is known as the "Reserved Power Amendment." Powers delegated to the national government are listed in Article 1, Section 8. Powers prohibited to the states are found in Article 1, Section 10. Amendment 10 makes it clear that all other powers—the so-called "reserved powers"—are left to the states or to the people.

Amendment 11. SUITS AGAINST STATES (1798)

The judicial power of the United States shall not be construed to extend to any suit in law or equity, commenced or prosecuted against one of the United States, by citizens of another state, or by citizens or subjects of any foreign state.

¶ This is the first amendment to the Constitution which was designed to overrule a Supreme Court decision. In the case of *Chisholm v. Georgia* (1793), the Supreme Court ruled that two citizens of South Carolina could sue Georgia in a federal court for property that Georgia had confiscated. The states objected, arguing that since the states were sovereign, it was undignified to permit a state to be sued by a citizen of another state in a federal court. As a result of this amendment, a citizen of the United States or of a foreign state who wishes to bring suit against any particular state of the United States is required to introduce his case in the courts of the state which is being sued.

Amendment 12. ELECTION OF PRESIDENT AND VICE-PRESIDENT (1804)

The electors shall meet in their respective states, and vote by ballot for President and Vice-President, one of whom, at least, shall not be an inhabitant of the same state with themselves; they shall name in their ballots the person voted for as President, and in distinct ballots the person voted for as Vice-President, and they shall make distinct lists of all persons voted for as President, and of all persons voted for as Vice-President, and of the number of votes for each, which lists they shall sign and certify, and transmit, sealed, to the seat of government of the United States, directed to the President of the Senate; the President of the Senate shall, in the presence of the Senate and House of Representatives, open all the certificates and the votes shall then be counted; the person having the greatest number of votes for President shall be the President, if such number be a majority of the whole number of electors appointed; and if no person have such majority, then from the persons having the highest numbers not exceeding three on the list of those voted for as President, the House of Representatives shall choose immediately, by ballot, the President. But in choosing the President, the votes shall be taken by states, the representation from each state having one vote; a quorum for this purpose shall consist of a member or members from two-thirds of the states, and a majority of all the states shall be necessary to a choice. [And if the House of Representatives shall not choose a President whenever the right of choice shall devolve upon them, before the fourth day of March next following, then the Vice-President shall act as President, as in the case of the death or other constitutional disability of the President.] The person having the greatest number of votes as Vice-President, shall be the Vice-President, if such number be a majority of the whole number of electors appointed, and if no person have a majority, then, from the two highest numbers on the list, the Senate shall choose the Vice-President; a quorum for the purpose shall consist of two-thirds of the whole number of Senators, and a majority of the whole number shall be necessary to a choice. But no person constitutionally ineligible to the office of President shall be eligible to that of Vice-President of the United States.

¶ This amendment alters Article 2, Section 1, Clause 3. Before the passage of this amendment, the electors each voted for two persons, without designating which was to be President and which Vice-President. As a result, in 1796 the people elected a Federalist President (John Adams) and a Republican Vice-President (Jefferson) (p. 223). In 1800 the electors of the victorious Republican Party each cast one vote for Jefferson, whom they wanted to be President, and one vote for Burr, whom they wanted to be Vice-President. The result, of course, was a tie (p. 227). Amendment 12, which instructs electors to cast separate ballots for President and Vice-President, prevents such situations. (See also Amendment 23, page 200, which makes provision for the choosing of electors of President and Vice-President by the District of Columbia.)

Amendment 13. SLAVERY ABOLISHED (1865)

SECTION 1. Neither slavery nor involuntary servitude, except as a punishment for crime whereof the party shall have been duly convicted, shall exist within the United States, or any place subject to their jurisdiction.

SECTION 2. Congress shall have power to enforce this article by appropriate legislation.

¶ Amendments 13, 14, and 15 resulted from the Civil War. Amendment 13 freed the slaves, Amendment 14 made Negroes citizens, and Amendment 15 forbade the states to deny black Americans the right to vote. ¶ Amendment 13 forbids slavery, and under Section 2, Congress has the power to enforce this order.

HOW A PRESIDENT IS ELECTED

TIME SEQUENCE		

SUMMER OF ELECTION YEAR

REPUBLICAN NATIONAL CONVENTION

A convention of party representatives from every state nominates candidates for President and Vice-President.

DEMOCRATIC NATIONAL CONVENTION

A convention of party representatives from every state nominates candidates for President and Vice-President.

BEFORE ELECTION

STATE REPUBLICAN HEADQUARTERS

The Republican Party in your state chooses electors* who promise to vote for the party's candidates for President and Vice-President.

STATE DEMOCRATIC HEADQUARTERS

The Democratic Party in your state chooses electors* who promise to vote for the party's candidates for President and Vice-President.

ELECTION DAY (NOVEMBER)

BALLOT BOX

In voting for a Presidential nominee, the voters actually vote for the electors of the nominee's party. This is the Popular Vote.

IF PARTY WINS...   **IF PARTY WINS...**

DECEMBER

The electors of the victorious party of each state assemble at their state capital and vote separately for their party's Presidential and Vice-Presidential candidates. This is the Electoral Vote.

Certified copies of these electoral votes are sent to the President of the United States Senate.

JANUARY

The President of the Senate counts the electoral votes in the presence of both houses of Congress.

Vice-President   President

To be elected, a candidate must receive at least a majority of the Electoral Vote.

*Each political party in each state is entitled to choose as many electors—delegates to the Electoral College—as it has Representatives and Senators in Congress.

Amendment 14. RIGHTS OF CITIZENS (1868)

SECTION 1. *Citizenship defined.* **All persons born or naturalized in the United States and subject to the jurisdiction thereof, are citizens of the United States and of the state wherein they reside. No state shall make or enforce any law which shall abridge the privileges or immunities of citizens of the United States; nor shall any state deprive any person of life, liberty, or property, wthout due process of law; nor deny to any person within its jurisdiction the equal protection of the laws.**

¶ This section contains a number of important provisions. By the definition of citizenship given here, black Americans were granted citizenship. The second sentence, forbidding states to abridge the privileges and immunities—the rights—of citizens, meant that the states could not interfere with the right of black Americans and other citizens to live a peaceful, useful life, or to travel. ¶ This amendment, like Amendment 5, contains a "due process of law" clause. Amendment 5 denies to Congress and Amendment 14 denies to the states the power to deprive any person of life, liberty, or property without "due process of law." This amendment, originally intended to protect Negro citizenship, has been broadly interpreted by the courts as a protection for corporations. Corporations, under this interpretation, are considered as "persons." Their property cannot be taken away except by fair, legal methods. Thus, for example, the Interstate Commerce Commission can fix railroad rates only after giving the railroad corporations an opportunity to present their side of the case. ¶ The "due process" clause also protects individuals from unfair actions by their state governments. It protects their rights of freedom of religion, speech, press, petition, and peaceful assembly, and the rights of persons accused of crimes against state abuses. It prevents a state, in the exercise of its police power (the power to do everything to protect the lives, health, morals, and safety of its people), from depriving anyone of civil liberties, except during a national emergency. ¶ The last provision of Section 1 prevents a state from denying to any person within its jurisdiction the equal protection of the laws. In 1954, in the case of *Brown v. Board of Education of Topeka*, the Supreme Court interpreted this provision to mean that segregation in public schools is unconstitutional. Also, in *Baker v. Carr* (1962) the Supreme Court ruled that unfair and unreasonable apportionment of representation in state legislatures violates the equal protection clause of this amendment..

SECTION 2. *Apportionment of Representatives.* **Representatives shall be apportioned among the several states according to their respective numbers, counting the whole number of persons in each state, excluding Indians not taxed. But when the right to vote at any election for the choice of electors for President and Vice-President of the United States, Representatives in Congress, the executive and judicial officers of a state, or the members of the legislature thereof, is denied to any of the male inhabitants of such state, being twenty-one years of age and citizens of the United States, or in any way abridged, except for participation in rebellion, or other crime, the basis of representation therein shall be reduced in the proportion which the number of such male citizens shall bear to the whole number of male citizens twenty-one years of age in such state.**

¶ This section was intended to guarantee that black Americans would be given the right to vote. If a state prevented any male citizen, 21 years of age or over, from voting, then the state's representation in Congress was to be reduced proportionately.

This section dealing with the apportionment of Representatives in a state is sometimes called the "dead letter clause" of Amendment 14 because its provisions have never been carried out.

SECTION 3. *Disability for engaging in insurrection.* **No person shall be a Senator or Representative in Congress, or elector of President and Vice-President, or hold any office, civil or military, under the United States, or under any state, who, having previously taken an oath, as a member of Congress, or as an officer of the United States, or as a member of any state legislature, or as an executive or judicial officer of any state, to support the Constitution of the United States, shall have engaged in insurrection or rebellion against the same, or given aid or comfort to the enemies thereof. But Congress may, by vote of two-thirds of each house, remove such disability.**

¶ This section aimed to punish the leaders of the Confederacy for having broken their oath to support the Constitution of the United States. All officials who had taken this oath and who later joined the Confederacy in the Civil War were disqualified from holding federal or state offices. Although many southern leaders were excluded under this section from holding office after the war, by 1872 most of them were permitted to return to political life. In 1898 all of the others were pardoned.

SECTION 4. *Public debt.* **The validity of the public debt of the United States, authorized by law, including debts incurred for payment of pensions and bounties for services in suppressing insurrection or rebellion, shall not be questioned. But neither the United States nor any state shall assume or pay any debt or obligation incurred in aid of insurrection or rebellion against the United States [or any claim for the loss or emancipation of any slave]; but all such debts, obligations, and claims shall be held illegal and void.**

¶ This section makes three important points: (1) The public debt of the United States incurred in fighting the Civil War was valid and could never be questioned by southerners. (2) The Confederate debt was void. It was illegal for the federal government or the states to pay any money on Confederate debts. This provision was meant to serve as a harsh lesson to all who had invested money in Confederate bonds. (3) No payment was to be made for the loss of former slaves.

SECTION 5. *Enforcement.* **The Congress shall have power to enforce, by appropriate legislation, the provisions of this article.**

Amendment 15.   RIGHT OF SUFFRAGE (1870)

SECTION 1. The right of citizens of the United States to vote shall not be denied or abridged by the United States or any state on account of race, color, or previous condition of servitude.

SECTION 2. The Congress shall have power to enforce this article by appropriate legislation.

¶ The purpose of this amendment was to extend the *franchise,* or the right to vote, to Negroes. Thus, according to the provisions of this amendment, any person who can meet all of the qualifications for suffrage in a particular state cannot be deprived of the right to vote simply because of his race or color.

Amendment 16.   INCOME TAX (1913)

The Congress shall have power to lay and collect taxes on incomes, from whatever source derived, without apportionment among the several states, and without regard to any census or enumeration.

¶ In 1894, as part of the Wilson-Gorman Tariff (p. 436), Congress passed an income tax law. The following year, in the case of *Pollock v. Farmers' Loan and Trust Company,* the Supreme Court declared this tax law unconstitutional. The Court stated that the income tax was a direct tax and, therefore, according to the Constitution (Article 1, Section 2, Clause 3; Article 1, Section 9, Clause 4) should have been apportioned among the states according to their population. This decision was unpopular because it prevented the government from taxing people on the basis of their incomes in order to pay for government expenses, which were already large, and growing larger. Amendment 16 overruled the Supreme Court decision and gave Congress the power to tax incomes from any source, and without apportionment among the states according to population. Today, income taxes are the federal government's major source of income.

Amendment 17.   ELECTION OF SENATORS (1913)

SECTION 1. *Method of election.* **The Senate of the United States shall be composed of two Senators from each state, elected by the people thereof, for six years; and each Senator shall have one vote. The electors in each state shall have the qualifications requisite for electors of the most numerous branch of the state legislatures.**

SECTION 2. *Filling vacancies.* **When vacancies happen in the representation of any state in the Senate, the executive authority of such state shall issue writs of election to fill such vacancies:** *Provided* **that the legislature of any state may empower the executive thereof to make temporary appointments until the people fill the vacancies by election as the legislature may direct.**

[SECTION 3. *Not retroactive.* **This amendment shall not be so construed as to affect the election or term of any Senator chosen before it becomes valid as part of the Constitution.]**

¶ Before the passage of this amendment, Senators were chosen by the state legislatures (see Article 1, Section 3, Clause 1). There was a great deal of dissatisfaction with this method because it gave the voters little control over the Senate. Amendment 17 provides for the direct election of Senators by the voters of each state, a method which helps to make Senators more responsive to the will of the voters who put them in office.

Amendment 18.   NATIONAL PROHIBITION (1919)

[SECTION 1. After one year from the ratification of this article the manufacture, sale, or transportation of intoxicating liquors within, the importation thereof into, or the exportation thereof from, the United States and all territory subject to the jurisdiction thereof for beverage purposes is hereby prohibited.

SECTION 2. The Congress and the several states shall have concurrent power to enforce this article by appropriate legislation.

SECTION 3. This article shall be inoperative unless it shall have been ratified as an amendment to the Constitution by the legislatures of the several states, as provided in the Constitution, within seven years from the date of the submission hereof to the states by the Congress.]

Amendment 19.   WOMAN SUFFRAGE (1920)

SECTION 1. The right of citizens of the United States to vote shall not be denied or abridged by the United States or by any state on account of sex.

SECTION 2. Congress shall have power to enforce this article by appropriate legislation.

¶ This amendment, extending the right to vote to all qualified women, marked the greatest single step the federal government has taken in extending the suffrage in the United States. The struggle to win this basic right for women began many years before the nineteenth amendment was finally ratified.

Amendment 20.   "LAME DUCK" AMENDMENT (1933)

SECTION 1. *Beginning of terms.* **The terms of the President and Vice-President shall end at noon on the 20th day of January, and the terms of Senators and Representatives at noon on the 3rd day of January, of the years in which such terms would have ended if this article had not been ratified; and the terms of their successors shall then begin.**

198

SECTION 2. *Beginning of Congressional sessions.* The Congress shall assemble at least once in every year, and such meeting shall begin at noon on the 3d day of January, unless they shall by law appoint a different day.

SECTION 3. *Presidential succession.* If at the time fixed for the beginning of the term of the President, the President-elect shall have died, the Vice-President-elect shall become President. If a President shall not have been chosen before the time fixed for the beginning of his term, or if the President-elect shall have failed to qualify, then the Vice-President-elect shall act as President until a President shall have qualified; and the Congress may by law provide for the case wherein neither a President-elect nor a Vice-President-elect shall have qualified, declaring who shall then act as President, or the manner in which one who is to act shall be selected, and such person shall act accordingly until a President or Vice-President shall have qualified.

SECTION 4. *Filling Presidential vacancy.* The Congress may by law provide for the case of the death of any of the persons from whom the House of Representatives may choose a President whenever the right of choice shall have devolved upon them, and for the case of the death of any of the persons from whom the Senate may choose a Vice-President whenever the right of choice shall have devolved upon them.

[SECTION 5. *Effective date.* Sections 1 and 2 shall take effect on the 15th day of October following the ratification of this article.

SECTION 6. *Time limit for ratification.* This article shall be inoperative unless it shall have been ratified as an amendment to the Constitution by the legislatures of three-fourths of the several states within seven years from the date of its submission.]

¶ When the Constitution was written, the means of transportation and communication were so slow that it was decided that a new President and new Congressmen elected in November could not reach the capital to take office until March 4. However, since sessions of Congress began in December, a session including newly elected Congressmen could not be held until 13 months after their election. Thus, even if a Congressman running for re-election were defeated in November, he would serve in the session of Congress which began the month after his defeat, and continue to serve for several months. Since defeated candidates had been politically rejected by the voters, they were called "lame ducks," suggesting that their "political wings" had been clipped. One purpose of Amendment 20 was to limit the term and power of "lame duck" Congressmen.

Amendment 21. REPEAL OF PROHIBITION (1933)

SECTION 1. The eighteenth article of amendment to the Constitution of the United States is hereby repealed.

SECTION 2. The transportation or importation into any state, territory, or possession of the United States for delivery or use therein of intoxicating liquors, in violation of the laws thereof, is hereby prohibited.

[SECTION 3. This article shall be inoperative unless it shall have been ratified as an amendment to the Constitution by conventions in the several states, as provided in the Constitution, within seven years from the date of the submission hereof to the states by the Congress.]

¶ This amendment, which repealed Amendment 18, was the only amendment ratified by special state conventions instead of state legislatures. Congress felt that a popular referendum (vote) would give the people a better chance to voice their opinions on prohibition. As in Amendments 18 and 20, Congress included a provision that the amendment, to become law, have a seven-year limit for ratification by the state legislatures.

Amendment 22. TWO-TERM LIMIT FOR PRESIDENTS (1951)

SECTION 1. No person shall be elected to the office of the President more than twice, and no person who has held the office of President, or acted as President, for more than two years of a term to which some other person was elected President shall be elected to the office of the President more than once. [But this Article shall not apply to any person holding the office of President when this Article was proposed by the Congress, and shall not prevent any person who may be holding the office of President, or acting as President, during the term within which this Article becomes operative from holding the office of President or acting as President during the remainder of such term.]

[**SECTION 2.** This article shall be inoperative unless it shall have been ratified as an amendment to the Constitution by the legislatures of three-fourths of the several states within seven years from the date of its submission to the states by the Congress.]

¶ The original Constitution placed no limit on the number of terms a President could be elected to office. Washington and Jefferson, however, set a two-term precedent. In 1940 this tradition was broken when Franklin D. Roosevelt was elected for a third term, and in 1944, when he won a fourth term. The purpose of this amendment was to write the two-term precedent into law. The bracketed portion was included so that the amendment would not apply to President Truman, who was holding office at the time the amendment was ratified. Note, too, that anyone who succeeds to the Presidency and completes less than two years of another person's term may be elected for two more terms.

Amendment 23. PRESIDENTIAL ELECTORS FOR DISTRICT OF COLUMBIA (1961)

SECTION 1. The District constituting the seat of Government of the United States shall appoint in such manner as the Congress may direct:

A number of electors of President and Vice-President equal to the whole number of Senators and Representatives in Congress to which the District would be entitled if it were a State, but in no event more than the least populous State; they shall be in addition to those appointed by the States, but they shall be considered, for the purposes of the election of President and Vice-President, to be electors appointed by a State; and they shall meet in the District and perform such duties as provided by the twelfth article of amendment.

SECTION 2. The Congress shall have power to enforce this article by appropriate legislation.

¶ Amendment 23 enables residents of the District of Columbia to vote for President and Vice-President. In effect, the amendment gives the capital city three members in the Electoral College, the number elected by each of the six least populous states: Alaska, Delaware, Hawaii, Nevada, Vermont, and Wyoming.

Amendment 24. POLL TAX BANNED IN NATIONAL ELECTIONS (1964)

SECTION 1. The right of citizens of the United States to vote in any primary or other election for President or Vice-President, for electors for President or Vice-President, or for Senator or Representative in Congress, shall not be denied or abridged by the United States or any state by reason of failure to pay any poll tax or other tax.

SECTION 2. The Congress shall have the power to enforce this article by appropriate legislation.

¶ Ratified by 38 states, three fourths of the state legislatures in the United States, this amendment forbids the collection of any taxes as a requirement for voting in federal elections. Notice that the amendment does not apply to state or local elections. At the time of ratification, five southern states (Alabama, Arkansas, Mississippi, Virginia, and Texas) still had poll taxes—taxes persons had to pay before they had the right to vote.

Amendment 25. PRESIDENTIAL DISABILITY AND SUCCESSION (1967)

1. In case of the removal of the President from office or his death or resignation, the Vice-President shall become President.

2. Whenever there is a vacancy in the office of the Vice-President, the President shall nominate a Vice-President who shall take the office upon confirmation by a majority vote of both houses of Congress.

3. Whenever the President transmits to the President pro tempore of the Senate and the Speaker of the House of Representatives his written declaration that he is unable to discharge the powers and duties of his office, and until he transmits to them a written declaration to the contrary, such powers and duties shall be discharged by the Vice-President as Acting President.

4. Whenever the Vice-President and a majority of either the principal officers of the executive departments or of such other body as Congress may by law provide, transmit to the President pro tempore of the Senate and the Speaker of the House of Representatives their written declaration that the President is unable to discharge the powers and duties of his office, the Vice-President shall immediately assume the powers and duties of the office as Acting President.

Thereafter, when the President transmits to the President pro tempore of the Senate and the Speaker of the House of Representatives his written declaration that no inability exists, he shall resume the powers and duties of his office unless the Vice-President and a majority of either the principal officers of the executive department or of such other body as Congress may by law provide, transmit within four days to the President pro tempore of the Senate and the Speaker of the House of Representatives their written declaration that the President is unable to discharge the powers and duties of his office. Thereupon Congress shall decide the issue, assembling within 48 hours for that purpose if not in session. If the Congress, within 21 days after receipt of the latter written declaration, or, if Congress is not in session, within 21 days after Congress is required to assemble, determines by two-thirds vote of both houses that the President is unable to discharge the powers and duties of his office, the Vice-President shall continue to discharge the same as Acting President; otherwise, the President shall assume the powers and duties of his office.

¶ This amendment, ratified in 1967, alters Article 2, Section 1, Clause 6, by making it more clear, particularly in the case of a temporary disability of the President. No such law covered the situation in which President Wilson was an invalid for 17 months but refused to give up his Presidential powers. In more recent times the question of temporary disability was again raised when President Eisenhower suffered a heart attack. ¶ (1) If a President is removed from office, dies, or resigns, the Vice-President replaces him. (2) The new President will then nominate a new Vice-President, who will take office when both houses of Congress approve by a majority vote. (3) If a President should state in writing to both heads of Congress that he is unable to carry out his duties, the Vice-President will perform these duties as Acting President until the President states in writing that he is once again able to carry out his duties as President. (4) If the Vice-President and a majority of the President's cabinet or a group selected by Congress states in writing to the heads of both houses of Congress that the President is unable to perform his duties, the Vice-President will perform these duties as Acting President until the President states in writing that he is once again able to carry out his duties. ¶ If, however, when the President states in writing that he is able to resume his duties, the Vice-President and a majority of the cabinet or a group selected by Congress disagrees with him, then Congress must decide by a two-thirds vote whether the President shall take up his duties or whether the Vice-President shall continue in his place as Acting President.

Amendment 26. VOTING AGE LOWERED TO 18 (1971)

SECTION 1. The right of citizens of the United States, who are 18 years of age or older, to vote shall not be denied or abridged by the United States or any state on account of age.

SECTION 2. The Congress shall have the power to enforce this article by appropriate legislation.

¶ Amendment 26 lowers the minimum voting age to 18 in all federal, state, and local elections.

UNIT SURVEY

FOR FURTHER INQUIRY

1. The colonists resented being treated as the "tail" to the British "kite." Explain the meaning of this statement.
2. What part did each of the following persons play in the history of the Declaration of Independence: (a) John Locke, (b) Thomas Paine, (c) Richard Henry Lee, (d) John Hancock, and (e) Thomas Jefferson?
3. What attitude was held by each of the following groups toward the Articles of Confederation: (a) merchants, (b) bankers, (c) artisans, (d) farmers, and (e) property holders?
4. If you had been a delegate to one of the state conventions which were called to ratify the Constitution, would you have been in favor of the ratification, or opposed to it? Give your reasons.

PROJECTS AND ACTIVITIES

1. The Department of State regularly sends broadcasts to Europe over the "Voice of America," the radio station of the United States Information Agency. Assume that you have been asked to address European teenagers on the topic, "An American Student's View of American Democracy." Prepare a ten-minute talk on the topic based on the material in Units One and Two.
2. Draw a time line for the years 1763–83, indicating on it all the events leading to the Revolutionary War, as well as the important battles of the war.
3. Imagine that you are the editor of a newspaper in colonial America, and compose a newspaper editorial (a) opposing the separation from Great Britain, (b) supporting the ratification of the Constitution.
4. On an outline map of the United States, indicate (a) the original thirteen states, (b) Philadelphia, (c) New York City, (d) Boston, (e) Williamsburg.

5. Construct a bulletin board display on the Bill of Rights. Use illustrations from newspapers and magazines to show the Bill of Rights in action today.

USING THE SOCIAL SCIENCES

(Read pages 204–210 before you answer the following questions.)

1. Clinton Rossiter said that all evidence concerning the motives of the Founding Fathers must be examined thoughtfully "in the context of 1787." What did he mean?
2. How does the context of time influence the gathering of historical evidence and the interpretation that will be given to that evidence?
3. Reread the first sentence of the case study. Do you think that Rossiter should have said "I must conclude" rather than "one must conclude"? Explain.
4. Was there a problem of social control under the Articles of Confederation? Explain.
5. Alexander Hamilton told the convention, "Take mankind in general, they are vicious." How did Hamilton's view of the average man's basic nature influence his political beliefs?
6. Judging from the Constitution that the Founding Fathers framed, do you think they held a high or low opinion of the nature of the average man? Explain.
7. What problems in research and interpretation are faced by the historian who tries to resolve the Rossiter-Beard controversy?
8. Can one be completely objective in trying to understand and explain a historical event? Explain.

SUGGESTED FURTHER READING

Biography

BAKELESS, JOHN, *The Life of George Rogers Clark,* Lippincott.

BOWERS, CLAUDE G., *The Young Jefferson,* Houghton Mifflin.

BRANT, I., *James Madison: Father of the Constitution,* Yale Univ. Press.

CALLAHAN, NORTH, *Daniel Morgan: Ranger of the American Revolution,* Holt, Rinehart & Winston.

CRANE, VERNER WINSLOW, *Benjamin Franklin and a Rising People,* Little, Brown.

CUNLIFFE, MARCUS, *George Washington: Man and Monument,* Little, Brown.

EATON, JEANETTE, *Young Lafayette,* Houghton Mifflin.

FORBES, ESTHER, *Paul Revere and the World He Lived in,* Houghton Mifflin.

FRANKLIN, BENJAMIN, *Autobiography,* Dutton; and others.

MAUROIS, ANDRÉ, *Washington: The Life of a Patriot*, Oxford Univ. Press (Toronto).

MEADE, ROBERT D., *Patrick Henry: Patriot in the Making*, Lippincott.

MORISON, SAMUEL ELIOT, *John Paul Jones: A Sailor's Biography*, Little, Brown (paper).

PADOVER, SAUL K., *Jefferson*, New American Library (Mentor Books).

SCHACHNER, NATHAN, *Alexander Hamilton: Nation Builder*, McGraw-Hill.

——, *Thomas Jefferson: A Biography*, A. S. Barnes, 2 vols.

THAYER, THEODORE, *Nathanael Greene: Strategist of the American Revolution*, Twayne Publishers.

VAN DOREN, CARL, *Benjamin Franklin*, Viking.

WOODWARD, W. E., *Tom Paine: America's Godfather*, Dutton.

Other Nonfiction

ALDEN, JOHN RICHARD, *The American Revolution: 1775–1783*, Harper & Row (paper).

RECKER, CARL, *The Declaration of Independence: A Study in the History of Political Ideas*, Random House (Vintage Books). Discusses how the ideas expressed in the Declaration originated, and how they have been accepted and modified by succeeding generations.

——, *The Eve of the Revolution*, Yale Univ. Press.

CATER, DOUGLASS, *The Fourth Branch of Government*, Random House (Vintage Books). The role of the newspaper, the press conference, and public opinion in today's politics.

CATTON, BRUCE, ed., *American Heritage Book of the Revolution*, Simon and Schuster. Pictorial.

COYLE, DAVID CUSHMAN, *The United States Political System and How It Works*, New American Library (Mentor Books).

GIPSON, LAWRENCE H., *The Coming of the Revolution: 1763–1775*, Harper & Row (paper).

JAMESON, JOHN F., *The American Revolution Considered as a Social Movement*, Harper & Row (Beacon, paper).

JENSEN, MERRILL, *The Making of the American Constitution*, Van Nostrand (Anvil Books).

KNOLLENBERG, BERNHARD, *Origin of the American Revolution, 1759–1766*, Macmillan.

LANCASTER, BRUCE, and J. H. PLUMB, *The American Heritage Book of the Revolution*, Dell (paper).

LASSWELL, HAROLD D., *Politics: Who Gets What, When, How*, World Publishing (Meridian Books, paper). The competition for political influence and power among small groups within our society.

MC CLOSKEY, ROBERT G., *The American Supreme Court*, Univ. of Chicago Press (paper). Covers the periods 1789–1865, 1865–1937, and 1937–1959; includes law cases that illustrate the main trends of each period.

MILLER, JOHN C., *Origins of the American Revolu-tion*, Little, Brown.

——, *Triumph of Freedom*, Little, Brown. About the Revolution itself.

MONTROSS, LYNN, *Rag, Tag, and Bobtail*, Harper & Row. About the Continental Army.

MORGAN, EDMUND SEARS, *The Birth of the Republic: Seventeen Sixty Three–Eighty Nine*, Univ. of Chicago Press (paper).

MORRIS, RICHARD B., *The American Revolution: A Short History*, Van Nostrand (Anvil Books). Part I is a narrative of the American Revolution, and Part II contains original documents related to the period.

NEUSTADT, RICHARD E., *Presidential Power*, New American Library (Signet Books, paper). The role of the Chief Executive.

PADOVER, SAUL K., *The Living Constitution*, New American Library (Mentor Books).

——, *The Meaning of Democracy*, Praeger (paper). Analyzes both the shortcomings and advantages of the democratic process.

PECKHAM, HOWARD, *The War for Independence: A Military History*, Univ. of Chicago Press (paper).

ROSSITER, CLINTON, *The American Presidency*, New American Library (Mentor Books, paper). The author considers the American Presidency "one of the few truly successful institutions created by men in their endless quest for the blessings of free government."

——, *Political Thought of the American Revolution*, Harcourt Brace Jovanovich (paper).

SCHRAG, PETER, ed., *The Ratification of the Constitution and the Bill of Rights*, Heath (paper). A collection of original source material reflecting the controversies regarding the ratification.

VAN DOREN, CARL, *The Great Rehearsal*, Viking. The Constitutional Convention.

Historical Fiction

ALLEN, HERVEY, *Bedford Village*, Holt, Rinehart & Winston. Frontier life in Pittsburgh.

BOYD, JAMES, *Drums*, Scribner. Realistic story set during American Revolution.

EDMONDS, WALTER D., *Drums Along the Mohawk*, Little, Brown. Story of Indian raids.

LANCASTER, BRUCE, *Guns of Burgoyne*, Lippincott.

——, *From Lexington to Liberty*, Doubleday.

MASON, F. VAN WYCK, *Three Harbors*, Lippincott; Grosset & Dunlap. Seacoast merchants.

ROBERTS, ELIZABETH MADOX, *The Great Meadow*, Grosset & Dunlap. A woman's life on the frontier.

ROBERTS, KENNETH, *Arundel*, Doubleday. About a soldier on Benedict Arnold's expedition against Quebec.

——, *Oliver Wiswell*, Doubleday. Sympathetic picture of the Tories.

——, *Rabble in Arms*, Doubleday. About Burgoyne's surrender.

HISTORY AND THE SOCIAL SCIENCES

HISTORY

Nature of History

"History" and "the past" are not, as is sometimes assumed, synonymous terms. In fact, they are quite different.

The past is the entire story of the human race—of all human beings everywhere in the world. History, on the other hand, is what historians have written and are writing *about* the past. This does not include the entire past because some aspects of the past are not of great interest to historians and, more important, some events in the past have left few traces, artifacts, or documents on which historians can base an accurate reconstruction. Historians, therefore, reconstruct only a small part of some fragments of the past which are of particular interest to them.

In spite of these limitations, however, history is a vast enterprise. It records not only the story of civilizations, of nations, of kings, rulers, wars, and conquests, but also tells us how men grew corn and wheat, how they sold their wares, how they organized their governments, how they worshiped their gods, how they built their houses, how they made their clothes, how they lived, and how they died.

Historians in every generation write histories dealing with the same subject. There always seems to be room for new or newer interpretations. In that sense all history is contemporary history because every historian digs out new facts, discovers new data, or interprets old data from his own particular point of view. This is what makes the reading of history so fascinating.

It is obvious from what we have said that history is an inquiry into the past. In fact the word "history" comes from the Greek word meaning "to inquire." If history is inquiry, then the historian is an inquirer and the study of history is an enterprise in inquiry. Indeed, the historian has much in common with a detective. The historian can reconstruct the event and the detective the crime only if clues are available and only if they have trained imaginations. Both painstakingly gather data and clues, evaluate the testimony of witnesses (unfortunately for the historian, he cannot cross-examine his witnesses), and then formulate their conclusions. Neither the historian nor the detective can ever be sure that the event they are investigating really happened exactly as they have reconstructed it. They can only hope that it did. Often the discovery of new clues or new testimony makes it clear that the original judgment was wrong. Then, in the case of the detective, there is need for a new trial; in the case of the historian, there is need for a new study.

History provides a collective memory for people in every generation. Individuals usually cherish their memories, even the bad ones. The same is true of the human race as a whole. All people all over the world were and are curious about their past. People want to know what those who preceded them have done and thought. Even more intent in knowing about the past are political and religious leaders, who also want to make sure that future generations will know of their deeds, their thoughts, their beliefs. Kings, emperors, generals, popes, and presidents have exhibited great curiosity about what history will say about them. Often, in fact, they have spared no efforts to "help" future historians reach a favorable verdict on their lives and accomplishments.

In making their inquiries into the past, historians are wary of making broad generalizations. Social scientists, on the other hand, want to discover broad generalizations—patterns of similarity that lead to "laws" which may

Crusaders

be used to predict some aspect of human behavior. Historians, however, are often inhibited from making broad generalizations because of lack of adequate evidence. Even more important, historians are impressed by the uniqueness of each historical event and by the variability of human nature, including the often inexplicable behavior of political leaders. Very often an irrational explanation of a particular event or action taken by a historical figure is more correct than a rational explanation.

After allowing for these variables, however, historians do formulate generalizations within a limited scope. In using the word "Crusades," for example, the historian is in fact generalizing because the word "Crusades" includes a whole series of events and images—the call of the pope to Christians to free the Holy Land, the several European armies sent to the Holy Land, the campaign of Richard the Lionhearted, and so on. Historians also predict, but their predictions usually point to several possible alternatives based on their analysis and interpretation of past events.

History differs from the social sciences in another important aspect. Social scientists refrain as much as possible from passing value judgments on the subjects or groups they are dealing with. Historians, on the other hand, after analyzing the available objective data, do not hesitate to pass judgments if they believe such judgments are warranted. Historians thus might condemn Hitler for the crimes he committed during World War II, censure President Buchanan for his indecisiveness on the eve of the Civil War, praise Lincoln's fortitude in the face of great adversities, or commend Franklin D. Roosevelt for acting boldly to combat the Great Depression.

In spite of these differences, however, historians in recent years have increasingly used the insights and methods of the social scientists to aid them in their own investigations.

Uses of History

Our everyday language reflects our preoccupation with history. We often use such expressions as "History is on our side," "History teaches us . . . ," "The lesson of history is . . . ," "The verdict of history will be. . . ." All these expressions indicate a widespread acceptance of the idea that history is a teacher and a judge of the past. It has also often been said that nations that do not learn from their past mistakes are condemned to repeat them.

Basically these assumptions are correct, but they need to be amplified, clarified, and qualified. History, the difficult and ever-changing reconstruction of the past, does teach us a great deal about ourselves and our life today, but its lessons are often neither simple nor direct. Leaders of nations who read about a particular crisis in the past in hopes of finding guidance for dealing with a present crisis may be disappointed. The reason is simple. A conflict that happened 50 years ago may look similar to a present one, but in fact many new variables make comparisons extremely difficult. The people involved have changed, as has the world's technology. International relations and alliances present a different picture, and, often most important, the values, beliefs, and aspirations of the people involved have probably undergone a great deal of transformation.

But while the study of past events may not supply us with direct answers to present troubles, the study of history is most helpful in that it teaches us the variety of ways in which people in the past have dealt with their problems. Knowledge of history is indispensable for obtaining a sense of historical perspective. And a sense of historical perspective is essential for making a sound evaluation of the present. Because human societies are so complex and

Adolf Hitler at a Nazi rally

because the variables of human life are so numerous, the direct application of past solutions to present problems is not possible—or even desirable. What the study of history can do is to help us see the wide range of available alternatives which have led to the resolution of human conflicts and may do so again.

History has been a powerful force in the creation and the continued existence of national pride, or nationalism. Nationalism, however, can be and often is a double-edged sword. On the one hand, excessive nationalism and uncritical acceptance of a nation and its policies can become a destructive force, especially when manipulated by unscrupulous or incompetent leaders. Hitler, for example, led the German people to catastrophe with his slogan "Deutschland über alles" (Germany over all else).

But love of country, nurtured by the thoughtful and sound teaching of a nation's history, can be a constructive force which may inspire people, especially a nation's youth, to creative endeavors. National history taught in a spirit of inquiry which allows students to become aware of their nation's basic strengths and its occasional blunders, of its accomplishments and failures, and of its future tasks, is likely to result in a deep and abiding loyalty toward one's country, as well as a personal commitment to legitimate national interests and aspirations.

In some areas, the knowledge of the past does help directly in understanding the present. The story of the long rivalry between China and Russia over the control of Mongolia and Sinkiang, for example, is indispensable to an understanding of the present conflict in that area. The same is true of the history of the Middle East and the conflict between the Israelis and the Arabs.

But more often the lesson of history is neither so direct nor so obvious as these examples would indicate. It is wiser to speak of *lessons* of history rather than a lesson of history and of the *uses* of history rather than the use of history. History as the story of man's struggle to conquer the forces of nature and of his faltering attempts to attain the goal of a better and happier life makes men better equipped to deal with the problems of their own existence. The knowledge of how men acted in the past and of how they have striven to order the lives of their respective societies may not always provide ready-made answers to present crises, but it undoubtedly makes the task easier by providing examples of various modes and styles of life.

Methods of History

Like the social scientist, the historian uses the scientific mode of inquiry in making his investigations. The historian traditionally begins his inquiry into the past by posing three questions: What happened? How did it happen? Why did it happen? With these questions in mind, he begins his investigation.

First of all, the historian must select the subject for his investigation. To avoid duplication of effort, he must determine who else has written on the subject and what they have written. Even more important, he must make sure that there are enough data and evidence on his chosen subject to make an investigation possible and worthwhile. Without such evidence and data, of course, the historian cannot ask the basic questions to begin his inquiry.

Having chosen the subject for his inquiry, the historian then sets out to collect as much evidence as possible, carefully taking pains to verify the genuineness, reliability, and validity of the sources he uncovers. When he has collected and verified the authenticity of his evidence, he is ready to formulate a hypothesis—a tentative conclusion to be tested. The historian then reads and analyzes all the evidence to test his hypothesis. After making a thorough inquiry, he finally organizes his data into a readable narrative into which he incorporates his conclusions.

In the course of his investigation, the historian is careful to check and recheck his sources, always approaching every available historical source with an attitude of doubt. Thucydides, the great Greek historian, wrote: "And with reference to the narrative of events, far from permitting myself to derive it from the first sources that come to hand, I did not even trust my own impressions, but it rests partly on what I saw myself, partly on what others saw for me, the accuracy of the report being always tried by the most severe and detailed tests possible."

In subjecting their sources of evidence to "the most severe and detailed tests possible," historians use scientific modes of inquiry and thus act as social scientists. However, when a historian reaches the last stage of his work, the stage in which he has completed the testing and analysis of his data and is ready to begin the narrative in which he will write down his conclusions, opinions, and judgments, he becomes an artist. The reason for this is that in his final reconstruction of some portion of the past, the historian, while basing his narrative on the objective evidence he has analyzed, must also use his creative imagination. No matter how diligent the historian has been in amassing all the available information on the assassination of Lincoln, for example, his narrative on how the murder scene actually looked and what the assassin did before, during, and after the assassination will have to be substantially augmented by his imaginative intelligence. And this imaginative reconstruction will, of course, be based on the author's accumulated knowledge of events and circumstances.

In recent years some historians have begun to use concepts and modes of inquiry from the social sciences in their investigations. For example, some have found concepts from sociology, such as **status** and **social class,** and concepts from political science, such as **leadership** and **power structure,** very useful in their work. Still other historians have found great advantage in the quantitative approaches used by many political scientists. For example, the use of computers has helped historians in their analyses of such factors as the voting behavior of certain groups in the American population or the identification of voting blocs in the Senate and House of Representatives.

However, for most historians, history remains a thoughtful and rational "contemplation based upon sources." In the historical case studies in this book, we will endeavor to inquire into some important aspects of American history aided by the studies and findings of American historians as well as the evidence of primary sources; that is, original historical sources such as documents, letters, and speeches. The conclusions to be drawn from these case studies, like conclusions from all historical investigations, are subject to evaluation, that is, intelligent interpretation. They are also, in accordance with the usual practice of historians in all generations, subject to revisions and reinterpretations in the light of new evidence and new data.

In a sense, written history is a "dialogue" between the historian and the student of history. In the same way, in the classroom, history can become a dialogue between the teacher and the students. The historical case studies in this book are intended to encourage students to think about important problems in American history, to analyze these problems using historical evidence, and finally, to evaluate the evidence and to form their own conclusions using intelligent and imaginative interpretation to guide them in their inquiries into the past.

The assassination of Abraham Lincoln

George Washington (upper right) presiding at the Convention

CASE STUDY IN HISTORY

The Motives of the Founding Fathers

"When all the evidence has been examined thoughtfully in the context of 1787, one must conclude that both the revealed and the concealed purposes of most framers [of the Constitution] . . . were largely public in character, and that to explain their actions exclusively in terms of private ambitions and interests is an affront to historical truth."

This is a conclusion of a modern American historian, Clinton Rossiter, who has made an authoritative study of the Constitutional Convention of 1787. However, Rossiter's appraisal of "the miracle in Philadelphia," a phrase used by George Washington, stands in sharp contrast to the conclusion of another great American historian, Charles A. Beard. In his book *An Economic Interpretation of the Constitution* (1913), Beard maintained that the text of the Constitution reflected basically the private interests of the Convention members. He believed that the Founding Fathers voted as they did primarily to protect their own property—their own businesses, land, and slaves—which they identified with the public interest. Which interpretation is the more accurate? This is the question we shall investigate as we read about the Constitutional Convention—the proceedings which Jefferson labeled "an assembly of demigods."

Profiles of Some Leading Delegates

The 55 delegates from 12 states (Rhode Island was not represented) who assembled in the red brick State House in Philadelphia in May 1787 included many talented men. Of the 55 delegates, 34 were lawyers; most of the others were merchants or planters. Many of the delegates were rich men.

George Washington was President of the Convention, and there had never been any doubt that he would hold this post. The delegates agreed that Washington was the most able to preserve the dignity and the secrecy of the deliberations and that he alone was aloof enough and respected enough to mediate the many differences of views which might disrupt the proceedings.

Benjamin Franklin, the 81-year-old delegate from Pennsylvania, was known and respected both in the states and in Europe. Franklin used his great reputation and prestige to promote a spirit of compromise at the Convention.

James Madison from Virginia, a small, slender man of 36, had a profound knowledge of government and political theory. Because he trusted the judgment of the people, Madison's instincts were usually on the side of popular democracy. Madison kept a daily journal of the Convention—the only eyewitness account of the secret proceedings. To make his report as accurate as possible, Madison sat facing the delegates, with his back to Washington who presided. "In this favorable position," Madison wrote later, "for hearing all that passed, I noted in terms legible and in abbreviations and marks intelligible to myself what was read from the Chair or spoken by the members and losing not a moment . . . was enabled to write out my daily notes during the session or within a few finishing days after its close." Madison's notes were published by order of Congress after his death.

Alexander Hamilton, a handsome 32-year-old delegate from New York, was brilliant but erratic, famous but widely hated. At the Convention "the Little Lion," as Hamilton was called, represented the aristocratic point of view. The new government, he argued, must be put in the hands of the wealthy and well-educated because the mass of the people could not be trusted. Arrogantly he told the Convention: "Take mankind in general, they are vicious." Hamilton was a nationalist and a supporter of a strong central government. He fought hard for his views but when defeated, as he often was at the Convention, he loyally supported the decisions taken.

Besides these giants, or "demigods," there were at the Convention other men of great ability and influence. We can mention only a few: Roger Sherman of Connecticut, whom John Adams called "the old Puritan, honest as an angel"; Elbridge Gerry of Massachusetts, a Harvard man, who contributed a great deal to the formulation of important compromises, but who in the end did not sign the document; and Gouverneur Morris of Pennsylvania, whose well-timed speeches, diligent committee work, and disdain for slavery marked his as one of the most influential delegates at the Convention.

These, then, were the leading delegates, uniquely independent men representing many different points of view. Many historians have argued that the delegates' genius lay in their ability to resolve their differences for the good of the Union. Was this true? Or were the Founding Fathers motivated mainly by private interests, which they, in turn, identified with public interests? These are the questions we should keep in mind as we examine the major areas of disagreement at the Convention and how they were resolved.

Four Areas of Major Disagreement Resolved by Compromise

1. The conflict over whether or not slaves should be counted for purposes of representation.

In the debate over the Great Compromise, Roger Sherman of Connecticut proposed that representation in the House be determined on the basis of the census of the free population. The southerners were in a quandary. They demanded that slaves be included in counting population; yet at the same time they maintained that slaves were property. Northerners were quick to point out the obvious contradiction in the southern position. But the southerners would not back down. Finally the Convention voted for representation in the House in proportion to the whole number of free persons and "three fifths of all other persons [Negro slaves] except Indians not paying taxes." Thus the Constitution, in fact, accepted the idea that slaves were not full persons.

2. The conflict between the southern slave states and the northern free states over the slave trade and slavery.

The debate over the slave trade lasted all summer. Charles Pinckney of South Carolina warned that his state would never accept the Constitution if the slave trade were prohibited. On the other hand, Gouverneur Morris of Pennsylvania declared that slavery was "a nefarious institution, the curse of heaven on the states where it prevailed." John Rutledge of South Carolina answered that slavery had nothing to do with humanity or religion—that it was simply a matter of economic interest, and he repeated the warning that the issue would determine whether the South would be part of the Union.

Faced with this ultimatum, the North accepted a compromise allowing the slave trade to continue for 20 years until 1808 when it would cease. In addition, in Article 4, Section 2, the North accepted a provision which not only accepted the existence of slavery, but also made the return of fugitive slaves obligatory on all law officers in the country. Historians agree that this was a high price to pay for the participation of the southern states in the Union, but they argue that northerners had no choice if the United States was to become a reality.

Alexander Hamilton

3. The dispute over the powers of Congress to tax imports and exports.
The agricultural states opposed giving Congress the right to tax imports and exports while the manufacturing states wanted Congress to have the power to levy taxes (tariffs) on imports to protect domestic industry.

4. The controversy between the "aristocrats" and the "democrats" over the extent of the direct participation of the people in electing their leaders and representatives.

Compared to the other compromises, the differences between the agricultural and manufacturing states and between the "aristocrats" and the "democrats" were resolved with relatively little difficulty. The Commerce Compromise provided that Congress could tax imports but not exports. The compromise on the direct election of the President and the Vice President provided that there would be a popular vote for Presidential electors in each state, but then the Electoral College would elect the President. Members of the House were to be elected by popular vote, while Senators were to be elected by state legislatures.

"The Genius for Compromise"

The Constitution represented the fruits of the American genius for compromise. There is no doubt that the delegates, individually and as representatives of the states, were zealous in defending their interests. There also is no doubt that many delegates were aware that the establishment of a strong central government would increase the value of their holdings in land, slaves, and securities. Yet there is overwhelming evidence from their own testimony that their purpose went far beyond such limited considerations.

George Mason of Virginia wrote to a friend, "The eyes of the United States are turned upon this assembly. . . . May God grant we may be able to gratify them by establishing a wise and just government. For my own part, I declare I would not, upon pecuniary motives, serve in this convention for a thousand pounds per day." John Rutledge of South Carolina, a wealthy planter, declared that the delegates "ought to take a permanent view of the subject and not look at the present moment only."

These were noble words. Yet the delegates never claimed that they wrote the best Constitution in the world. They did claim, however, that they wrote the best Constitution that was possible for them to write. Benjamin Franklin expressed this opinion when he said in a speech to the Convention:

"I agree to this Constitution, with all its faults, if they are such; because I think a general government necessary for us. . . . I doubt, too, whether any other convention we can obtain may be able to make a better constitution. For, when you assemble a number of men to have the advantage of their joint wisdom, you inevitably assemble with these men all their prejudices, their passions, their errors of opinion, their local interests, and their selfish views. From such an assembly can perfect production be expected? It therefore astonishes me, sir, to find this system approaching so near to perfection as it does. . . . Thus I consent, sir, to this Constitution, because I expect no better, and because I am not sure that it is not the best."

John Rutledge

■ Do you agree with the conclusions of historians like Rossiter or do you agree with those of Beard in his 1913 study? What evidence can you cite to support your opinion?

■ Rossiter said that all the evidence must be examined thoughtfully "in the context of 1787." What did he mean?

UNIT THREE

Building the Nation

1789 – 1845

Detail from "Lady Washington's Reception," by Daniel Huntington.
In the Brooklyn Museum Collection.

■ *President Washington entertaining at his home*

CHAPTER **10**

A Strong Start for the Nation

1789 – 1801

IT IS April 30, 1789. At New York City, the temporary capital of the nation, a crowd has gathered in Wall Street to watch the inauguration of the first President of the United States. Above the crowd, on the balcony of Federal Hall, stands George Washington. Robert R. Livingston, Chancellor of the State of New York, administers the oath of office. For a moment there is silence. Then a roar of applause breaks from the crowd.

What thoughts may have passed through Washington's mind as he gazed down on the sea of faces and as the waves of sound rose around him?

Perhaps Washington weighed in his mind the chances for the new government's success. He knew that most people still thought of themselves as citizens of New York, Delaware, or Virginia, and not yet as citizens of the United States. The people might hail him as President of the United States, but Washington was fully aware that the United States was not yet a nation.

Indeed, many of Washington's close associates were somewhat pessimistic about the future of the new nation. John Adams, newly elected Vice-President, feared that the Republic would not last beyond his own lifetime. Alexander Hamilton considered that the Constitution was "frail and worthless." Washington himself thought of the United States as an "experiment entrusted to the hands of the American people."

For better or worse, however, this great American experiment was now under way.

THE CHAPTER IN OUTLINE

1. The task of organizing the new federal government.
2. Successful solutions to the nation's money problems.
3. The new nation's policy toward foreign nations.
4. The role of political parties in American government.
5. President Adams' struggles with a divided party.
6. Federalist ideas and methods under the Republicans.

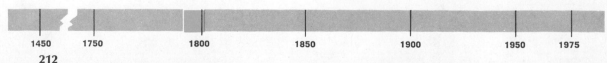

1450   1750   1800   1850   1900   1950   1975

1 The task of organizing the new federal government

Washington's trip from Mount Vernon, his home in Virginia, to New York City had been a triumphant journey. All along his route crowds turned out to watch him pass, to cheer him, and to scatter flowers in his path.

But now the celebrations were over. President Washington and the other elected officials—Vice-President John Adams; the 26 Senators, two from each state; and the 59 Representatives—had taken the oath to uphold the Constitution. Now they had to face the task of organizing the new government and making it work.

Basic problems. To guide them, the newly elected federal officials had only the general principles written into the Constitution and the experience gained from their work in the various colonial governments and in the Confederation. They had to build everything from the ground up.

They had, as yet, no federal laws, no courts, no law-enforcement officers. Serious financial problems had to be met, but there was no federal treasury and no method for collecting taxes. Worse still, the American people had little money to use to pay the taxes that the new government would certainly have to levy. And on top of all the other problems, the new government owed a large debt inherited from the Revolutionary War and from the government under the Confederation.

Difficult problems also lay ahead for the new nation in its relations with other nations. The President had to work out a foreign policy acceptable to Congress. He had to appoint ambassadors and instruct them in their duties. If trouble should arise, the President had little military strength to call upon. The navy built by the Continental Congress had been decommissioned and the army now included only some 600 officers and enlisted men.

The Constitution gave the new government the power to deal with these and other problems. But dealing with them successfully called for hard work and statesmanship on the part of the President and Congress.

■ George Washington was rowed across the Hudson River to New York City's Wall Street for his inauguration. His little boat had a crew of thirteen men, one for each state in the Union.

■ This picture shows the members of the first Presidential cabinet. They are, from left to right, Henry Knox, Thomas Jefferson, Edmund Randolph, and Alexander Hamilton. Washington stands at the far right.

Congress at work. As one of its first and most important measures, Congress adopted the Judiciary Act of 1789. This act provided for a Chief Justice and five Associate Justices of the Supreme Court. The first Chief Justice appointed by the President and approved by the Senate was John Jay.

The Judiciary Act also established thirteen district courts and three circuit courts. Congress thus carried out its power under Article 1 of the Constitution "To constitute tribunals inferior to the Supreme Court."

The Judiciary Act further stated that all disputes over the meaning of the Constitution, federal laws, and treaties must, in the last resort, be settled by the Supreme Court. If this power—the power of judicial review—had not been granted to the Supreme Court, each state would have been free to interpret federal laws in its own way. The United States would have been a league of *sovereign,* or independent, states, not a federal union. For this reason, the Judiciary Act was essential to building the federal system.

The first Congress also took other important steps. It sent the Bill of Rights to the states to be ratified. It re-enacted, or passed for a second time, the Northwest Ordinance providing a government

for the Northwest Territory. Mainly to raise revenue, it levied a small tariff on imports.

Creating a "cabinet." Congress also created three executive departments to help the President with his work. The Department of State was created to help the President handle foreign and other affairs, the Department of the Treasury to deal with financial problems, and the Department of War to manage military matters.

The heads of these departments came to be known as the President's *cabinet.*° However, the cabinet as we know it today was not officially recognized in law until 1907. The heads of these departments, called Secretaries, met with the President for informal conferences. The Secretaries, however, could only advise the President. Then, as now, the responsibility for making final decisions in the Executive Department rested with the President alone.

President Washington filled his first "cabinet" by appointing Thomas Jefferson as Secretary of State, Alexander Hamilton as Secretary of the Treasury, and Henry Knox as Secretary of War.

Finally, Washington chose Edmund Randolph to fill the position of Attorney General. Randolph, the fourth member of Washington's cabinet, advised the President on matters of law. The Attorney Generalship was at first a part-time job; the Department of Justice was not created until 1870.

Washington also appointed Samuel Osgood as Postmaster General. Postal affairs were then administered by the Treasury Department; the Post Office Department was not created until 1829.

° *cabinet:* This term, which now means a group of advisers, originally referred to a "cabinet," or private office, in which advisers gathered for conferences.

SECTION SURVEY

IDENTIFY: Judiciary Act, tariff, cabinet; Henry Knox, Samuel Osgood.

1. List the basic problems faced by the young republic in 1789 in the area of (a) domestic, or internal, affairs and (b) foreign affairs.
2. What guidelines did the newly elected officials have for organizing the new government?
3. Describe the measures adopted by the first Congress in its effort to solve some of the basic problems faced by the new republic.
4. The President makes all final decisions in the Executive Department. (a) What are some advantages of this procedure? (b) What are some disadvantages?

2 Successful solutions to the nation's money problems

Among the many problems faced by the new federal government, the most urgent was that of raising money. The government needed money to pay salaries, to build and maintain the army and navy, to operate the post offices, and to carry on other activities. It also needed money to repay the debt owed to foreign countries and to American citizens.

The problem of finances. During the first year or two, the government's problem of raising money was exceptionally difficult. To be sure, the Constitution gave Congress the power "To lay and collect taxes. . . ." And as you have seen, the first Congress used this power when it levied a small tariff on articles imported into the United States. But the revenue from this tariff did not even begin to pay the expenses of running the new government. More money had to come from other taxes. But what kinds of taxes?

There was another big question: Where would Americans get the gold and silver coin or the paper money to pay their taxes? In 1789 there was very little currency in the United States. The Constitution gave Congress the power to coin money. But where would the gold and silver come from?

Looking for solutions to its many financial problems, Congress turned to the new Secretary of the Treasury, Alexander Hamilton, for help. In turning to the Secretary of the Treasury, the first Congress set an important precedent. While Congress is responsible for passing laws, it has always relied heavily on the Executive Department for advice and guidance.

Repaying the war debt. Hamilton devised a program that would put the nation's finances on a sound basis. In the first of a series of reports, he asked Congress to establish the nation's credit by paying its debts. Hamilton knew that a nation, like an individual, must pay its debts or lose the respect and trust of its neighbors and find it impossible to borrow in the future.

The United States and the separate states owed a combined war debt of more than $80 million—a staggering sum for those days. Hamilton proposed to repay all of this debt.

Everybody agreed that the United States should pay $12 million owed to France, the Netherlands, and Spain. The United States "funded" these international debts. That is, the United States arranged to repay with interest, over a fixed period, the money that these countries had lent.

The domestic debt was another matter. Many Congressmen objected to Hamilton's proposal to repay $44 million borrowed from American citizens during the Revolutionary War. The Continental Congress had borrowed this money by issuing paper money and selling *government bonds*. Government bonds are certificates issued by a government in exchange for a loan of money. The certificate is a promise that the loan, plus interest, will eventually be repaid. But, as you know, the government's credit during and after the war was so low that its paper money was "not worth a Continental." The government's bonds were equally low in value.

By now many people who had originally held the bonds and paper money had sold them to speculators for a fraction of their original, or "face," value. Hamilton now proposed that the bonds and paper money be redeemed, or paid off, at their face value. Hamilton's opponents objected. Why should the entire country pay out its hard-earned money to benefit a few speculators? However, Hamilton convinced Congress that, if the nation's credit was to be established, all debts must be paid.

The remainder of the total debt, about $25 million, was owed by several states to American citizens. Hamilton wanted the federal government to take over, or assume, this debt and pay back every penny the states owed. This proposal started a violent argument. States with small debts and states whose war debts were already paid argued that it was unfair for them to assume their neighbors' burdens. Southerners protested that most state bonds, like the bonds of the Continental Congress, were in the hands of speculators, who would again profit at the expense of the people.

Defeat seemed certain, but at the last moment a compromise was arranged. In the so-called Assumption Bill, southerners, led by Thomas Jefferson, agreed that the national government should assume the state debts. In return, northerners, led by Hamilton, agreed to vote for a bill to locate the new national capital along the banks of the Potomac River on land donated by Virginia and Maryland. The government was moved to the new capital, Washington, D.C., in 1800.

Hamilton's bank proposal. Equally brilliant was Hamilton's proposal that Congress pass a bill creating a *national bank* to be called the Bank of the United States. By a national bank Hamilton did not mean just one bank, but a banking system.

The system would consist of a large central bank, with branch banks located in major American cities.

This proposal was almost revolutionary for its time. In the early 1790's the United States had no centralized banking system. There were only small local banks, chartered by the different states.

Hamilton carefully pointed out the advantages of a national banking system. The branch banks would provide safe places for tax officials to deposit money collected from the people. When the government wanted to transfer money from one place to another, the branch banks could do this by sending checks rather than by taking the risk of actually shipping gold and silver. Moreover, a national banking system would be large enough to lend money to the government as well as to private individuals. When the central bank did not have as much money to lend as the government wanted to borrow, it could always turn to its branch banks for help.

Finally, the Bank of the United States would provide what Hamilton called "a sound, uniform currency," that is, currency having the same value all over the country. People would have faith in paper money, or *bank notes,* bearing the name of the Bank of the United States. People would prefer these bank notes to the paper money printed by small local or state banks. As a result, Hamilton predicted, small shaky banks would close down, while others would work hard to win the public's confidence. All this would be good for business— and for the country as a whole.

Adoption of the bank proposal. Hamilton's arguments in favor of a Bank of the United States were sound. But his opponents, led by Jefferson, also had sound arguments.

First, according to Hamilton's proposal, the Bank of the United States would sell 25,000 shares of stock at $400 each, amounting to a total *capital stock,* or money value, of $10 million. The government would buy one fifth of all the shares. The other four fifths would be bought by private investors, who would, of course, be wealthy Americans. Jefferson argued that this would give wealthy people a monopoly control over the country's money power.

Jefferson also argued that a national bank would have an unfair advantage over local or state banks. Again he was right. All government funds would be deposited in the Bank of the United States and its branches. These funds could be lent to individuals at a profit to the national bank. Private banks would have no opportunity to earn profits on the deposit and loan of government funds.

Finally, Jefferson claimed that the bank would be unconstitutional. The Constitution did not give the federal government power to create a bank. In reply Hamilton pointed to the "elastic clause" of the Constitution, which gave Congress the right "To make all laws which shall be necessary and proper for carrying into execution the foregoing powers . . ." including the power "To lay and collect taxes . . ." and "To borrow money on the credit of the United States." Hamilton said that it was "necessary and proper" for Congress to create a bank that would help carry out its responsibility for collecting taxes and borrowing money.

Thus the arguments ran for and against Hamilton's proposal. But, in spite of violent debate in the cabinet, Washington leaned toward Hamilton's side. In 1791 Congress passed a bill granting a charter to the Bank of the United States over strenuous opposition.

Hamilton's tariff proposal. Hamilton also urged Congress to pass another tariff law. As one of its first acts, Congress had levied a small tariff on imported goods. Congress had passed this measure mainly to raise revenue. But now Hamilton proposed a new kind of tariff—what we call a "protective" tariff.

The difference between a "revenue" tariff and a "protective" tariff is one of purpose and therefore of rates. If, for example, Congress placed a low tariff, or duty, on a blanket manufactured in England, English manufacturers could pay the duty and still compete with American manufacturers for American trade. This would be a *revenue tariff.* But if Congress placed a very high tariff on each English blanket, say as high as 100 percent of its value, then the English blanket would have to be sold in the United States for twice what it cost the English manufacturer to make it. As a result, the English manufacturer could not sell blankets in America in competition with American manufacturers. A tariff of this kind would not raise revenue for the government, since the English manufacturer would abandon his American markets. But it would "protect" the American manufacturers from competition and thus would be a *protective tariff.*

Congress did not even consider Hamilton's proposal for a protective tariff. Nevertheless, the proposal shows how completely Hamilton wanted

Detail from "View of the Capitol" by Burton. The Metropolitan Museum of Art, Joseph Pulitzer bequest, 1942.

■ Washington, D.C., the new national capital, was located along the banks of the Potomac River. The Capitol Building, only partially completed, is shown above as it appeared in 1824.

to bind the wealthy people, in this case the manufacturers, to the government by ties of self-interest. This proposal also reveals how well Hamilton understood the young nation's needs. He saw that the United States could not become truly independent until it could produce most of the goods that it needed.

The Whisky Rebellion. In a fourth proposal Hamilton urged Congress to levy an *excise tax* ° on distilled liquors. The distiller himself would have to pay this tax on every gallon of liquor that he produced and sold.

Hamilton knew that the excise tax would not raise much revenue. That was not his goal. Rather,

° *excise tax:* a tax levied upon goods produced within the country where they are consumed, or used.

he wanted to impress the frontiersmen with the power of the federal government. What better way than to pluck money from the pockets of the freedom-loving frontiersmen by taxing them for every gallon of whisky that they distilled?

In the 1790's the frontiersmen were almost isolated from the settled areas along the Atlantic coast. Only the roughest of trails cut through the forests. As a result, the frontiersmen could not transport their corn to markets in the settled areas. And corn was their most important crop. But they could and did distill the corn into whisky. Then they loaded the jugs or kegs of whisky onto the backs of mules and drove the mules castward to market. Whisky, in short, was the most important source of cash for many frontier farmers. The excise tax would hit them hard.

Hamilton knew that the tax would cause resentment. Indeed, this was exactly what he wanted, for the new government would then have a chance to demonstrate its power. As Hamilton expected, the frontiersmen rebelled. They refused to pay the tax, and the "Whisky Rebellion" broke out on the frontiers of western Pennsylvania in 1794. But the rebellion melted away when the federal government sent 15,000 militiamen to the scene. Hamilton himself accompanied the militiamen, who were commanded by "Light-Horse Harry" Lee of Virginia, a cavalry officer in the Revolutionary War. No lives were lost, but the federal government had demonstrated its strength.

The success of Hamilton's program. Hamilton's financial program proved a great success. By paying off its debts, the new government showed that it meant to meet its obligations. The national banking system provided a sound, uniform currency. The excise tax brought in a small amount of much-needed revenue. More important, it extended the influence of the government to the frontier.

To be sure, Hamilton's financial program put money into the pockets of the well-to-do. Americans who owned government bonds, who invested in the Bank of the United States, and who needed a sound, uniform currency were delighted—and became staunch supporters of the new government.

But Hamilton's financial program benefited not only the wealthy. It aided all Americans, for it gave the United States a workable money system and a credit reputation that few of the older nations of Europe enjoyed.

SECTION SURVEY

IDENTIFY: precedent, revenue tariff, protective tariff, excise tax, Whisky Rebellion; Alexander Hamilton.

1. What important precedent did the first Congress set when it turned to the Secretary of the Treasury for help?
2. What policies did Hamilton propose to establish the nation's credit?
3. Compromise is vital to the democratic process. How does the Assumption Bill prove this statement?
4. (a) What were Hamilton's arguments for a national bank? (b) What were Jefferson's arguments against it?
5. Of what significance was the role of the federal government in the Whisky Rebellion?
6. Why did Hamilton's financial program prove a great success?

3 The new nation's policy toward foreign nations

The United States was born in a world torn by revolution and warfare. The world situation enormously complicated the problems of the new government.

The French Revolution. Even while the first American Congressmen were gathering to organize the government in the spring of 1789, a revolution of the common people and a few nobles and churchmen broke out in France. Fighting under the slogan "liberty, equality, fraternity," the French revolutionists shared some of the ideas expressed in the American Declaration of Independence. But they were divided in their viewpoints and more violent than the American revolutionists in insisting upon their ideas.

The revolutionists soon gained complete power in France. They mobbed and beheaded thousands of people in the French upper classes, including King Louis XVI and Queen Marie Antoinette. Thousands of other upper-class Frenchmen escaped to neighboring countries. There, safe from the sharp blade of the guillotine, they laid plans to regain control of France.

Europeans looked at the French Revolution with mixed feelings. Many people, particularly the ruling classes, were filled with horror. They feared that the example set by the French revolutionists might spread to their countries. As a result, they wanted to see the revolution crushed. By 1793 the new government of France, called the Republic, was at war with Great Britain and other European countries.

American reactions. It was impossible for American citizens to remain untouched by the turmoil in Europe. The French seized American ships carrying goods to Great Britain or its possessions. The British seized American ships carrying goods to France or its colonies and *impressed,* or kidnaped, American sailors to serve in the British navy. Most of these sailors were citizens of the United States, but some were, in fact, deserters from the British navy.

American citizens took sides. Hamilton and his followers favored Great Britain. Jefferson and his followers favored France and the French Revolution. Social gatherings often broke up in vigorous arguments.

American neutrality. What would the policy of the United States be? According to a treaty made with France in 1778 (page 130), the United States was obliged to defend the French West Indies. But if the United States aided France, it would soon find itself at war with Great Britain. War would be suicidal. The new nation was not prepared for armed conflict on either land or sea. The situation confronting President Washington was grave indeed.

In April 1793, Edmond Genêt (zheh·NEH), minister from the French Republic, arrived in the United States. "Citizen" Genêt, as he was called in France, did not insist that the United States come to the defense of the French West Indies, but he did demand that American seaports be opened to French naval vessels and privateers.

Many Americans welcomed Genêt and urged the President to honor the American obligation to France. Others, friendly to Great Britain, urged Washington to break off all relations with France.

Backed unanimously by his cabinet, the President ignored the popular outcry and on April 22, 1793, issued a Proclamation of Neutrality. The proclamation forbade American citizens to take part in any hostilities on land or sea with any of the warring nations. Congress endorsed the President's action by passing a neutrality act.

War with Great Britain avoided. In spite of the neutrality act, conflict with Great Britain seemed certain in 1793.

To save its West Indian colonies from starvation, France for the first time permitted Americans to trade with the French West Indies. The British promptly seized American ships, claiming that trade not permitted in time of peace was not permitted in time of war.

As American ships were confiscated and American sailors were impressed into the British navy, many Americans became increasingly angry. Men began to drill on village greens, to fortify harbor entrances, and to build warships. Congress closed all American ports and began to talk of forbidding Americans to buy British products.

Trying to prevent war, President Washington sent Chief Justice John Jay of the Supreme Court to London to try to settle the differences between Great Britain and the United States. Jay was only partly successful. The British won the best of the bargain. They won the right to trade freely in all American ports. In return, they did promise to withdraw their troops by 1796 from certain forts still occupied on the northwestern frontier. But they insisted upon the right of British fur traders to carry on their business in American territory.

Jay's Treaty, as it was called, greatly disappointed many Americans. Some of Jefferson's more hotheaded followers said that Hamilton and the government had "sold out" to Great Britain. Mobs burned Jay in effigy and threw stones at Hamilton.

Finally, however, when the name calling and arguments died away, most Americans agreed that Jay's Treaty had accomplished its major purpose: It had prevented war with Great Britain. It had also prodded the Spaniards into actions that proved extremely helpful to the United States.

The end of differences with Spain. News of Jay's Treaty came as a blow to Spain. The Spaniards had just signed an agreement with the French Republic. Because of this agreement, the Spaniards faced a possible war with Great Britain. When the United States and Great Britain settled their differences, Spain acted to insure American neutrality in the war that Spain and France were waging against Great Britain.

In 1795, in a treaty negotiated by Thomas Pinckney, United States minister to Great Britain, the Spaniards granted everything that Americans had been demanding since 1783. The treaty settled the long-standing dispute between the United States and Spain over boundaries between Florida and Georgia (see map, page 857). Spain also agreed to curb Indian attacks upon settlements in Georgia and in the western lands. Even more important, Spain gave Americans the right to navigate the Mississippi River freely. This right included the privilege of transferring goods at the port city of New Orleans from river boats to ocean-going vessels without paying duties to Spain.

This right—the *right of deposit*—was especially important to western farmers. The westerners sent bundles of furs and jugs of whisky eastward over the mountain trails on the backs of mules and donkeys. But they could not use pack trains to send heavy or bulky products eastward. Instead, they floated heavy products down the Ohio and the Mississippi to New Orleans. There they sold their products to shipmasters bound for Europe or the Atlantic coast ports. After completing the sale, the men broke up their rafts and sold the lumber.

Although this was a clumsy method of carrying on trade, it was cheaper than sending goods by pack train directly to eastern markets. Pinckney's Treaty seemed to assure westerners that Spain would no longer threaten to close their vital trade route, the Mississippi River.

■ Western farmers floated their produce to New Orleans on flatboats. Early flatboats were cruder than the one shown in this picture painted by George Caleb Bingham. Crews of early flatboats broke them up at New Orleans, sold the lumber, and returned on foot or horseback.

LIVING AMERICAN DOCUMENTS

George Washington's
Farewell Address (1796)

The great rule of conduct for us in regard to foreign nations is in extending our commercial relations to have with them as little political connection as possible. So far as we have already formed engagements, let them be fulfilled with perfect good faith. . . .

Europe has a set of primary interests which to us have none or a very remote relation. Hence she must be engaged in frequent controversies, the causes of which are essentially foreign to our concerns. . . .

It is our true policy to steer clear of permanent alliances with any portion of the foreign world, so far, I mean, as we are now at liberty to do it. . . .

Washington against foreign alliances.   In 1796 President Washington, refusing to serve a third term, prepared to return to Mount Vernon. During his two terms he had helped to establish the new nation on a solid foundation. His administration had organized the machinery of government. It had avoided war with Great Britain and France. It had settled the long-standing argument with Spain. These were solid accomplishments.

Nevertheless, Washington was troubled. Disliking political factions, he was troubled by the sharp, often bitter arguments between Hamilton and his followers and Jefferson and his followers. He was also troubled about United States relations with other countries.

As one of his last public acts, President Washington prepared his Farewell Address to Congress and his fellow citizens. In this address Washington urged the American people to remain devoted to the Union and to avoid the formation of political parties. He also warned them to avoid "permanent alliances" with "any portion of the foreign world." At that time, the United States was still a struggling young nation. Washington feared that foreign alliances might prevent the United States government from acting in its own best interests.

SECTION SURVEY

IDENTIFY: impressment of seamen, neutrality, Jay's Treaty, Pinckney's Treaty, right of deposit, Farewell Address.

1. (a) Why did the ruling classes in Europe look with horror upon the French Revolution? (b) Did they look upon the American Revolution with the same horror? Explain.
2. What effects did events in Europe during the period just studied have on Americans?
3. (a) What conditions led Washington to issue his Proclamation of Neutrality in 1793? (b) Was the Proclamation successful? Why or why not?
4. What hopes, fears, and warnings did Washington express in his Farewell Address? Quote directly from the Address to support your answers.

4 The role of political parties in American government

The development of political parties deeply troubled President Washington. But by September 1796, when Washington in his Farewell Address warned against "the danger of parties," a two-party system already existed. The names Federalist and Republican were being applied to the two opposing parties.

Rise of the two-party system. The Constitution said nothing about political parties. Many Americans besides George Washington hoped that party divisions could be avoided. It soon became apparent that this was impossible.

As early as the Presidential election of 1792, something resembling two major parties appeared in American politics. Washington was re-elected by unanimous vote. Vice-President John Adams was also re-elected, but against considerable opposition. He was opposed by George Clinton of New York, a candidate sponsored by Thomas Jefferson and his followers.

Hamilton's followers came to be called Federalists. The Federalist Party was strongest in New England and along the Atlantic seaboard. It included many wealthy merchants, manufacturers, lawyers, and clergymen. John Adams, himself a Federalist, said that Federalists represented "the rich, the well-born, and the able." The Federalists had little faith in the ability of the average person to play an intelligent part in government.

The opposition party was led by Thomas Jefferson. The members of this party took the name Democratic-Republicans. Before long, they simply called themselves Republicans. Although some wealthy people were Republicans, most of Jefferson's supporters were the owners of small farms or wage earners in the growing towns.

Party differences. Jefferson's beliefs were quite different from Hamilton's. Hamilton had little faith in the ability of the average people to govern themselves. Jefferson, on the other hand, had great faith in the average man's ability to play an effective part in government. Jefferson expressed this faith in the Declaration of Independence, in his statement that all governments should secure their power from "the consent of the governed."

Hamilton, distrusting average people, wanted to give power to wealthy people by creating a strong federal government under their control. A *strict,* or literal, interpretation of the Constitution would not permit a sufficiently strong federal government. Thus Hamilton chose to read his own meaning into the Constitution by a *loose,* or elastic, interpretation.

Jefferson, on the other hand, wanted the people, particularly the small farmers who made up 90 percent of the total population, to have controlling power in the country. Therefore he favored the weakest possible federal government, strong state governments, and ironclad guarantees of individual liberties. He believed that the Constitution *as written* gave sufficient power to the government. When a question arose as to the meaning of the Constitution, Jefferson chose a *strict* interpretation.

Because of their differing interpretations of the Constitution, Hamilton and Jefferson often had clashes of opinion. For example, in 1791, as you recall, disagreement arose when Hamilton proposed the creation of a national bank. Jefferson, insisting on a "strict" interpretation of the Constitution, argued that Congress could not create the bank because there was no mention of banks or banking in the Constitution. Hamilton, interpreting the Constitution "loosely," had a ready answer. The Constitution did give Congress power to regulate money, he argued, and since a national bank was needed to carry out this regulation, Congress could create such a bank.

By 1794 most voters had chosen the political

■ Political party feelings ran high in the late 1790's. The cartoon shown above satirizes a fight that broke out in the House of Representatives when a Federalist and a Republican exchanged insults.

party they preferred. From that day to this, American political life has revolved around the *two-party system.*° "Third parties" have also developed from time to time to press for policies they felt the major parties were neglecting.

Nominating candidates. On March 4, 1797, President John Adams, a Federalist, took the oath of office. A few minutes later Thomas Jefferson, a Republican, was sworn in as Vice-President.

A Federalist President, a Republican Vice-President! How did such a curious situation develop? The answer lies in the election of 1796. This election also provides an example of how custom helped to shape American political institutions.

° The political parties of 1794, however, were not political parties in the modern sense. Rather, they were loosely grouped alliances centering around leaders of different political persuasions. The American two-party system, with its committees, conventions, and voting discipline, developed only gradually.

Both the Federalists and the Republicans entered the election year determined to win. President Washington had announced his intention of retiring, and the Presidency and the Vice-Presidency were wide open.

The Constitution, as you know, gave no directions for nominating candidates for the Presidency and Vice-Presidency. The political leaders of the two parties were thus ~free to choose their own methods. They decided to keep political power in their own hands by holding Congressional conferences, later called *caucuses,* in which they chose the candidates. The voters at large could say nothing about who was nominated as they now can by voting in primary elections or by taking an active part in the affairs of political parties.

Months before election day the Federalists in Congress met in a private conference, or caucus. They chose John Adams and Thomas Pinckney as the Federalist candidates for President and Vice-President. Republican Congressmen, meeting in a similar party conference, chose as their candidates Thomas Jefferson and Aaron Burr. Thus, the leaders of the political parties selected the men that they, the leaders, wanted to run. But in the 1790's the final decision rested, not with the political parties nor with the voters, but with a group of men called "electors."

Role of the electors. On election day, voters all over the country traveled to polling places and voted for officials to serve them in local, state, and federal government. According to the Constitution the voters did *not,* however, vote directly for the President and Vice-President. Instead, they voted for electors who had been chosen by the state legislatures. These chosen electors in each state then voted, as the Constitution provided, "by ballot for two persons." That is, they cast electoral votes for President and Vice-President. The voting results were then forwarded to the President of the Senate who, in the presence of the Senate and the House of Representatives, opened the returns and had them counted. The candidate receiving the largest vote, provided it was a majority, was declared President. The candidate with the second largest vote was declared Vice-President.

The Constitution did not say that the electors had to vote for the two candidates previously nominated by each political party. According to the Constitution, the electors could vote for anyone they wished. This small, select group was supposed to be better informed, and therefore able to choose more wisely, than the American voters at large.

But the framers of the Constitution had not known that the country would divide into two political parties. They had not foreseen that the electors might choose a President from one political party and a Vice-President from another. In 1796, however, this happened.

The election of 1796. When the electors gathered to vote for the President and the Vice-President, they had before them four names—the Federalist candidates, John Adams and Thomas Pinckney, and the Republican candidates, Thomas Jefferson and Aaron Burr.

It was expected that the electors would choose either *both* Federalist candidates or *both* Republican candidates. But some leading Federalists did not like John Adams. These Federalists worked out a plan to make Pinckney President and Adams Vice-President. The plan backfired. When the electoral votes were counted, John Adams had the largest number of votes, Thomas Jefferson the next largest. As a result, the United States had a Federalist President and a Republican Vice-President.

Custom and the Constitution. Custom, rather than law, prevented a similar situation from happening again. Gradually, after 1796, electors came to understand that they were expected to vote only for the previously nominated candidates. The Federalist electors, for example, understood that they should vote for the Federalist candidates. Likewise, the Republican electors understood that they were to vote for the Republican candidates.

■ George Caleb Bingham painted this scene of a county election in the middle 1800's. On the steps, candidates tip their hats to voters, who wait in line to cast their spoken ballots.

■ This 1799 cartoon concerns the XYZ Affair. It depicts the French Directory as a five-headed monster, demanding money from the American representatives at daggerpoint.

This custom became part of our "unwritten Constitution." °

° The group of Presidential electors in each state has come to be known as an Electoral College. Sometimes the entire body of electors in the United States is referred to as the Electoral College.

SECTION SURVEY

IDENTIFY: two-party system, caucus, electoral votes, Electoral College.

1. (a) What caused the appearance of the Federalist Party and the Republican Party? (b) Who belonged to each?
2. In the election of 1796, the elected President and Vice-President belonged to different political parties. (a) How did this happen? (b) Why is it unlikely to happen again?
3. (a) What did Jefferson and Hamilton believe about the "common man"? (b) What is the connection between the kind of government men build and the beliefs they hold about the nature of the "common man"—whether he is basically good or evil?
4. (a) Compare the two parties with regard to their views on the strength of the federal government and their interpretation of the Constitution. (b) How do the differences reflect Hamilton's and Jefferson's views of man and his nature?

5 President Adams' struggles with a divided party

President John Adams was not pleased at having a Republican Vice-President in his administration. But he had little time to worry about it, for when he took office, the United States was threatened by war with France.

On the verge of war. American relations with France had grown steadily worse since 1793. The French resented America's refusal to aid France by honoring the Treaty of 1778, and the American Proclamation of Neutrality of 1793. The French also resented Jay's Treaty, which France regarded as pro-British.

As a result, France had become increasingly hostile during Washington's second administration. The French navy had seized American ships and had kept them from reaching British ports. The French Directory, a committee of five men who governed France after 1795, had refused to receive the minister sent by President Washington to Paris. Speaking of this insult, President Adams said that France "treated us neither as allies nor as friends nor as a sovereign state." Nevertheless, President Adams decided to make one more effort toward peace.

The XYZ Affair. Early in 1797 President Adams sent three prominent Americans to Paris to try to reach an agreement with France. The French government refused to receive the Americans officially. While waiting for an official reception, the Americans were visited by three Frenchmen.

The Frenchmen, later identified by President Adams as merely "X, Y, and Z," made three insulting demands. First, the American government must apologize publicly to France for remarks made by President Adams in a speech to Congress. Second, the United States must grant a loan to France. Third, the American envoys must pay a bribe of $250,000 to the five members of the French Directory.

When news of this insult reached America, many Americans demanded war. Rallying around the slogan "Millions for defense, but not one cent for tribute," Americans began war preparations. In 1798 the government created the Navy Department. Warships were built and harbors were fortified. The government also strengthened the army and recalled former President Washington from

Mount Vernon to assume chief command. Although war was not officially declared, a state of war actually existed. Within a few months American warships captured more than 80 vessels flying the French flag.

War avoided. President Adams then performed one of the most courageous acts of his career. Although many members of his own party were clamoring for war, Adams tried once again to secure peace. In 1799 he sent another group of commissioners to Paris.

By the time the Americans arrived, Napoleon had overthrown the corrupt Directory and made himself dictator of France. Napoleon wanted to begin his rule free from conflicts with foreign nations. Thus, he was eager to reach a settlement with the United States.

The Americans and the French quickly reached an agreement. Both countries agreed to abandon the old treaty of 1778. The United States agreed to drop its claims against France for illegally seizing American ships. Nevertheless, a major source of friction remained, for the French continued to seize American ships that attempted to trade with the British.

In spite of the agreement's shortcomings, President Adams had avoided full-scale war with France. Like Washington before him, Adams believed that the infant nation could survive only if it avoided European conflicts.

By safeguarding America's interests in this crucial period, President Adams deliberately sacrificed any popularity that he might have enjoyed with his own party.

The Alien and Sedition Acts. In 1798, while anti-French feeling was running high, the Federalist majority in Congress passed a series of laws designed, they said, to unite the country. It was generally understood, however, that the laws would also weaken the Republican Party.

These measures, often called the Alien and Sedition Acts, included four different laws: (1) the Naturalization Act, (2) the Alien Act, (3) the Alien Enemies Act, and (4) the Sedition Act. Congress passed these laws against the advice of President Adams and other leaders of the Federalist Party.

The Naturalization Act stated that an alien, or foreigner, must reside in the United States for 14 years before he could become a naturalized citizen. Up to that time, only 5 years of United States residence had been required. Congress said that this act would help protect the country from enemy

"John Adams," after John Singleton Copley, painted after 1783. 28. 180. Courtesy Museum of Fine Arts, Boston, Seth Kettell Sweetser Residuary Fund.

■ President John Adams, like Washington before him, believed that war would be disastrous for the new nation. But by safeguarding America's interests and keeping the country out of war during this crucial period, Adams sacrificed his own popularity.

aliens in wartime. But since most newcomers joined the Republican Party as soon as they became citizens, the partisan implications of the measure were clear. The Federalist Party wanted to remain in office.

The Alien Act authorized the President to expel from the country "all such aliens as he shall judge dangerous to the peace and safety of the United States . . ." or those involved in plots against the government. The Alien Enemies Act authorized the President, in time of war or invasion, to imprison or banish any foreigners he considered a menace to public security. The Federalists said that these two acts were necessary war precautions, but it was evident that they could also be used to silence anti-Federalist opinion. After all, a Federalist President would be able to decide exactly which aliens were "dangerous" to American security.

The Sedition Act was intended to silence American citizens themselves. Sedition means, among other things, the use of language to stir up discontent or rebellion against a government. Under the Sedition Act fines and imprisonment could be used to silence anybody who wrote, said, or printed anything "false, scandalous, and malicious" against the government, the Congress, or the President, "with intent to defame."

If these laws had been enforced, they would have ended all opposition to the Federalist Party. The Naturalization Act went into effect at once. The Alien Act and the Alien Enemies Act were not enforced, but the mere threat of being imprisoned or deported drove many Frenchmen from the country. Likewise, fear of punishment under the Sedition Act undoubtedly kept many Americans from criticizing the government. To this extent, then, the Sedition Act interfered with freedom of the press and freedom of speech, two principles deeply cherished by Americans then and now. Many Americans believed that the Alien and Sedition Acts were unjust attempts by the government to interfere with the rights of individuals—aliens and citizens alike. The acts pointed in the direction of what we today call "a police state."

Virginia and Kentucky Resolutions. The Republicans were furious. They claimed that these measures destroyed free speech and greatly increased the power of the federal government, particularly the power of the President. They voiced their protest in the Kentucky and Virginia Resolutions.

The Kentucky Resolutions, prepared by Thomas Jefferson, were adopted by the legislature of the new state of Kentucky in 1798 and 1799. The Virginia Resolutions, prepared by James Madison, were adopted by the legislature of Virginia in 1798. Together, these resolutions outlined the *states' rights,* or *compact,* theory of the Constitution. This theory included these ideas: (1) the federal government had been created by the states; (2) the federal government was merely an agent for the states, operating under a "compact," or agreement, which had delegated to the federal government certain specific powers and no more; (3) the federal government, or its agent, could be criticized by its

creators, the states, if it committed unauthorized acts. And who would determine when an act was unauthorized, or unconstitutional? Why, the states, of course.

Carried to an extreme, the states' rights, or compact, theory of the Constitution would give the states the power to declare *null and void* ° any act of Congress that the states considered unconstitutional. The theory could lead to *secession,* or withdrawal, of one or more states from the Union. Of course, this interpretation of the Constitution was a complete contradiction of the views expressed by Hamilton and the Federalists. The Federalists claimed that the government had been created by the people, not by the states, and that the Supreme Court was the sole judge of whether or not an act of Congress was unconstitutional.

The Kentucky and Virginia Resolutions were sent to the other state legislatures. But to the disappointment of Jefferson and Madison, the Resolutions did not receive favorable action. Federalist majorities controlled most of the state governments, and the Resolutions were "tabled"; that is, action on them was indefinitely postponed. Nevertheless, the Resolutions proved to be effective political weapons. They offered the voters a choice between a strong federal government and a weaker union in which the power of the states would be greater than the power of the federal union.

° *null and void:* not legal and therefore not binding on anyone.

SECTION SURVEY

IDENTIFY: "Millions for defense, but not one cent for tribute," alien, naturalized citizen, sedition, compact theory of the Constitution, null and void, police state.

1. What were the causes and results of French-American friction between 1793 and 1799?
2. John Adams and Napoleon both wanted peace. Why?
3. (a) In what ways did the Alien and Sedition Acts violate the Bill of Rights? (b) How did they reflect the emotional feelings of the times? (c) What was their relationship to the Kentucky and Virginia Resolutions?
4. (a) Show how the idea of "Union" in Washington's Farewell Address would be threatened by the states' rights, or compact, theory of government. (b) How did the Federalists respond to the compact theory?

6 Federalist ideas and methods under the Republicans

By the time President Adams' administration was drawing to a close, the Federalists had lost much of their earlier influence. Many Americans, including many Federalists, were dissatisfied with the high taxes made necessary by preparations for war. Most damaging to the Federalists, however, was the public's angry reaction to the Alien and Sedition Acts.

The election of 1800. When election year 1800 rolled around, Congressmen of both parties met in caucuses, as they had done in 1796, to select candidates. The Federalists chose President John Adams to run for a second term, with Charles C. Pinckney as his running mate for Vice-President. The Republicans again chose Thomas Jefferson for President and Aaron Burr for Vice-President. Burr was a brilliant New York lawyer and a top-ranking leader of the Republican Party.

The Republicans won the election, gaining control of the Presidency and of both houses of Congress. Despite their victory, however, the Republicans and the country faced an extremely serious situation. There were even rumors of civil war.

The problem was that Jefferson and Burr had both received the same number of electoral votes. The candidate with the largest number of electoral votes was to be President; the candidate with the second largest number, Vice-President. Now there was a tie.

At first glance, this problem seemed easy to solve. The Constitution clearly stated that in case of a tie the House of Representatives would make the final decision, with the total representation from each state having a single vote. Ordinarily, the House would have given the Presidency to Jefferson, for the Republican caucus had nominated him for this position. But some Federalists in the House preferred Aaron Burr. Burr was a Republican, but was not as strong a supporter of Republican principles as Jefferson.

The Federalists did not have enough voting strength to win the office for Burr, but they prevented Jefferson from winning a majority of the votes on 35 successive ballots. Finally, on February 17, 1801, with Inaugural Day little more than two weeks away, the deadlock broke and Jefferson won on the thirty-sixth ballot. Burr then became Vice-President.

Because of this confusion, Congress drew up

■ John Marshall remains to the present day one of the most highly regarded of America's Chief Justices. He helped the Supreme Court to mold the political and economic structure of the nation.

the Twelfth Amendment, and sent it to the states for ratification. Finally ratified in 1804, the amendment stated that electors must vote on separate ballots for President and Vice-President.

The midnight appointments. Having lost control of the executive and legislative branches of the government, the Federalists began, as soon as the elections were over, to strengthen their hold on the judicial branch. During the four months between Election Day and Jefferson's inauguration on March 4, 1801, the Federalist majority in the old Congress passed a new Judiciary Act. This act of 1801 increased the number of judges in the federal courts by 16.

President Adams promptly appointed Federalists to these positions. The President labored until late in the evening of his last day in office signing the commissions of the new judges. His appointees were given the scornful name of "midnight judges."

227

LIVING AMERICAN DOCUMENTS

Marbury v. Madison (1803)

The powers of the legislature are defined and limited; and that those limits may not be mistaken, or forgotten, the Constitution is written. To what purpose are powers limited, and to what purpose is that limitation committed to writing, if these limits may, at any time, be passed by those intended to be restrained? . . . It is a proposition too plain to be contested that the Constitution controls any legislative act repugnant to it . . . A legislative act contrary to the Constitution is not law. . . . It is emphatically the province and duty of the judicial department to say what the law is. . . .

—United States Supreme Court

Chief Justice John Marshall. The most significant appointment made by Adams—though not one of his midnight appointments—was that of John Marshall of Virginia as Chief Justice of the Supreme Court. Probably no single act of President Adams' administration had more far-reaching results.

John Marshall remains to the present day one of the most highly regarded of America's Chief Justices. A staunch Federalist, he largely dominated the other justices on the Supreme Court during the 34 years he served, from 1801 to 1835. In more than 500 opinions from his mind and pen, Chief Justice Marshall helped to mold the political and economic structure of the new nation.

Basic principles under Marshall. During his long term as Chief Justice, John Marshall established three basic principles of American law. These principles became foundation stones of the federal union.

Marshall stated (1) that the Supreme Court had the power to determine when a law of Congress was unconstitutional. Although this principle—the power of judicial review—had been included in the Judiciary Act of 1789, it was not made clear until John Marshall handed down in 1803 a famous decision in the case of *Marbury v. Madison*. In this decision Marshall declared that part of the Judiciary Act passed by Congress in 1789 was unconstitutional. "It is emphatically the province and duty of the judicial department to say what the law is," Marshall stated. Jefferson and others were shocked

at this interpretation of the Constitution. As Jefferson expressed it, Marshall made the Constitution "a mere thing of wax in the hands of the judiciary, which . . . [they] may twist and shape into any form they please."

In later decisions Marshall established two other basic principles. He declared (2) that the Supreme Court had the power to set aside laws of state legislatures when these laws were contrary to the federal Constitution, and (3) that the Supreme Court had the power to reverse the decision of a state court.

Significance of Marshall's work. In these decisions Marshall strengthened the federal government at the expense of the states by weakening the legal basis for the states' rights, or compact, theory of government. He thus helped to shape the loose collection of states into a *national* union of the people.

As the years passed, and as the Supreme Court handed down its decisions, Jefferson's alarm increased. From his home at Monticello, Virginia, the former President wrote: "The great object of my fear is the federal judiciary. That body . . . ever acting, with noiseless foot . . . gaining ground step by step, and holding what it gains, is engulfing insidiously the special [state] governments. . . ."

Despite his fears Jefferson could not alter the course of events. In decision after decision, the Supreme Court broadened the meaning of the Constitution. Owing largely to John Marshall's efforts, the federal government became increasingly powerful. Owing to the force of events, moreover, Jefferson himself helped to strengthen the federal government, even though this was contrary to his beliefs.

SECTION SURVEY

IDENTIFY: "midnight judges," judicial review, *Marbury v. Madison;* Aaron Burr, John Marshall.

1. How did the Twelfth Amendment correct the conditions that made the elections of 1796 and 1800 most unusual?
2. Explain how each of three decisions by Chief Justice John Marshall established basic principles that strengthened the federal government.
3. (a) Why did Jefferson fear the power of the federal judiciary? (b) Were his fears justified? Explain.
4. Of what importance is the "control" of the judiciary to a political party? What does "control" mean in this case?

TRACING THE MAIN IDEAS

Between 1789 and 1800 the Founding Fathers breathed life into the Constitution. During these years they organized a new government and welded the more or less independent states into a union.

Under President Washington and President Adams the Federalists made important advances. They set the machinery of government in motion and successfully launched the United States into the current of world affairs.

These early years of life under the Constitution had been difficult years for the young nation. Yet when President Adams and most of the Federalist Congressmen left office on March 4, 1801, they could look with pride upon a growing nation which was slowly becoming more unified.

Americans were still a divided people, not yet sure of themselves and of their future, but the division was more and more between national political parties. State boundaries were gradually becoming less and less important, while the national government was steadily growing in strength. The American nation was taking form.

In the next chapter you will see how the new nation acquired a vast new territory beyond the Mississippi River, survived the strain of war, and grew in strength and unity of purpose.

CHAPTER SURVEY

QUESTIONS FOR DISCUSSION

1. Compare the actions of the federal government during Shays' Rebellion with the actions of the federal government during the Whisky Rebellion.
2. (a) Discuss the reasons for the rise and fall of the Federalist Party. (b) What were the lasting contributions of this party to domestic and foreign policy?
3. Why is George Washington a good example of (a) the importance of individuals in history? (b) the kind of leader needed to serve as President?
4. What foreign policy did Washington formulate in 1793? Why?
5. Could you have predicted the differing views of Hamilton and Jefferson concerning the French Revolution? Why?
6. What purpose did political parties serve in the 1790's? What do you think might have happened without them?

RELATING PAST TO PRESENT

1. Can the advice given in Washington's Farewell Address be applied to America today? Why or why not?
2. Does the United States maintain a policy of neutrality in its foreign affairs today? Why or why not?
3. Compare and contrast some of the domestic problems faced by the United States in 1789 with those of today.
4. Why do you think the Electoral College has been criticized in recent years? Do you think its abolition is a good idea? Why or why not?
5. Are state governments more or less powerful today than they were in 1800? Explain.

6. Can we judge a President's ideas about government on the basis of the persons he recommends to serve on the Supreme Court? Explain.
7. Compare the views of Hamilton and Jefferson on (a) government, (b) industrial society versus agricultural society. Then consider our society today, and decide which man would be more pleased by modern America. Explain the reasons for your decision.

USING MAPS AND CHARTS

1. Using the charts on page 854, give the area of the United States in 1783. Compare the relative size of that area with the area of the United States today.
2. Using the charts on pages 858–59, indicate the approximate population of the United States in 1790 and the percentages of this population living in urban and rural areas. Compare these statistics with those of 1970.
3. Using the map for 1790 on page 860, locate the areas which had the largest population per square mile in 1790.
4. Using the map on page 149, explain the importance of the Mississippi River to the settlers living west of the Appalachian Mountains. Indicate the connection between the settlers' dependence on the Mississippi River and the Pinckney Treaty of 1795.
5. Referring to the same map, explain why the farmers of western Pennsylvania preferred to transport whisky rather than grain to the eastern markets.

■ *The frigate* United States *on its launching day*

CHAPTER **11**

The Nation's Growing Size and Power

1801 – 1817

ON MARCH 4, 1801, John Adams, the outgoing President, left the "President's House" too troubled in mind to pay Thomas Jefferson, the newly elected President, the courtesy of remaining for his inaugural ceremony. A staunch Federalist, Adams feared that the victory of Jefferson and the Republican Party meant the end of the new nation.

While Adams' carriage was jolting over the rough road leading out of Washington, D.C., Jefferson was reading his Inaugural Address. In his address, Jefferson tried to quiet the fears of Federalists who believed with John Adams that a revolution was about to sweep across the country.

Jefferson pledged himself to "the honest payment of our debts" and promised to preserve "the general government in its whole constitutional vigor." The best government, he said, is "a wise and frugal government, which shall restrain men from injuring one another, shall leave them otherwise free to regulate their own pursuits of industry and improvement, and shall not take from the mouth of labor the bread it has earned." This, he said, "is the sum of good government."

Jefferson's moderate statement pleased the Federalists. Alexander Hamilton accepted it as "a pledge . . . that the new President will not lend himself to dangerous innovations, but in essential points will tread in the steps of his predecessors."

The inauguration of Thomas Jefferson marked the beginning of a long period of Republican control in the United States. During these years the United States more than doubled in territorial size, fought a war to protect its rights, and emerged from the war stronger than it had ever been.

THE CHAPTER IN OUTLINE

1. Doubling of the nation's territorial size under Thomas Jefferson.

2. National growth at home and abroad under Jefferson.

3. Complex issues and forces leading to the War of 1812.

4. The Americans against the British in the War of 1812.

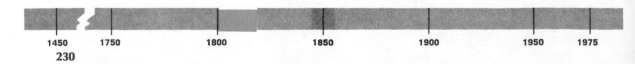

| 1450 | 1750 | 1800 | 1850 | 1900 | 1950 | 1975 |

1 Doubling of the nation's territorial size under Thomas Jefferson

Thomas Jefferson's pledge that the Republicans would act with moderation did not prevent him from exercising vigorous leadership as President. When the opportunity came to double the territorial size of the United States, he acted quickly and efficiently, even though he was not at all sure that the Constitution gave him the power to act as he did.

A rising threat. In 1800 Napoleon, then the ruler of France, secured from Spain the territory of Louisiana, which Spain had held since 1762.

In the early 1800's Louisiana covered an enormous area stretching westward from the Mississippi River to the Rocky Mountains and northward to Canada (see map, page 232). Some people believed that it included Texas. Whatever its boundaries, both Spain and France tried to keep the transfer of this vast area secret from the rest of the world. But rumors of the deal reached the United States Department of State.

Reasons for concern. Jefferson was alarmed. When the weak Spanish nation had held the mouth of the Mississippi River, the United States had not been especially concerned. But France, unlike Spain, was a mighty nation, with a steadily growing empire. French control of the Gulf of Mexico and the mouth of the Mississippi would deprive westerners of the "right of deposit" at New Orleans and severely limit their trade. French possession of Louisiana would check American expansion into the interior of the continent. It would also place France, a powerful and aggressive nation, upon the western border of the United States.

President Jefferson had a strong interest in the western country. Unlike many Federalists, who were concerned with eastern shipping and finance, the Republican Jefferson believed that the strengthening of western lands was desirable and necessary. He believed that the westerners would be loyal and contented citizens only if the federal government insured a free outlet for their goods into the Gulf of Mexico.

Warning to France. Accordingly, the President wrote to Rufus King, the United States minister in England. If the rumors about Louisiana were true, Jefferson wrote, it would be necessary to "marry ourselves to the British fleet and nation." These were strong words for a man who had recently promised in his Inaugural Address to avoid all "entangling alliances." Nevertheless, to keep France from controlling the Mississippi River and the great American West, Jefferson was prepared to form an alliance with Great Britain.

But Jefferson did not assume that war with France was inevitable. He urged the American minister to Paris, Robert R. Livingston, to offer Napoleon as much as $10 million for New Orleans and for West Florida—an area immediately east of New Orleans. This would guarantee American control of the Mississippi River and provide the western farmers with an outlet for their products. To aid Livingston, Jefferson sent James Monroe to Paris.

The sale of Louisiana. When the American commissioners made their offer to Napoleon's representative, there was a moment of silence. Then the Frenchman smiled. How much would they pay for *all* of Louisiana, he asked. The Americans tried to conceal their astonishment. After some discussion they agreed that the United States would pay the equivalent of about $15 million for the entire area. This land transaction, probably the largest in history, was negotiated early in 1803.

Why did Napoleon sell this valuable French territory? The answer can be seen on the map on page 233. Notice particularly the West Indian island of Santo Domingo. Before France could take possession of Louisiana, French forces had to establish a strong naval base in the West Indies. From such a base French warships could dominate the South Atlantic and the Caribbean Sea. With this in mind, Napoleon had decided to reconquer

LIVING AMERICAN DOCUMENTS

Thomas Jefferson's First
Inaugural Address (1801)

It is proper you should understand what I deem the essential principles of our government: ... Equal and exact justice to all men, of whatever state or persuasion, religious or political; peace, commerce, and honest friendship with all nations, entangling alliances with none; the support of the state governments in all their rights, as the most competent administrations for our domestic concerns and the surest bulwarks against anti-republican tendencies; the preservation of the general government in its whole constitutional vigor, as the sheet anchor of our peace at home and safety abroad; a jealous care of the right of election by the people. ...

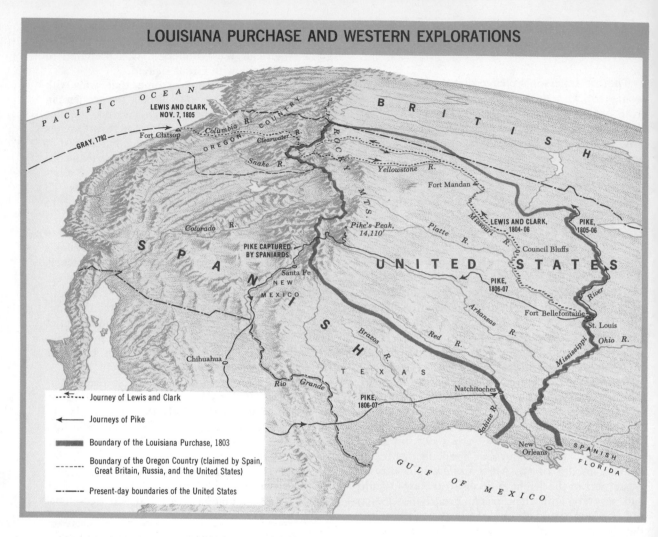

Haiti, a former French colony on the western half of the island of Santo Domingo.

In 1791, during the French Revolution, the black people of Haiti, most of them slaves, had risen in revolt against their French masters. Under the leadership of a remarkable black man, Toussaint L'Ouverture (too·SAN loo·vair·TYUR), they had won their independence. In 1800 Napoleon had tried to reconquer the entire island of Santo Domingo, but had failed. For one thing, the Haitians had fought fiercely. For another, yellow fever had wiped out many of Napoleon's troops.

Without control of Santo Domingo, France had little use for Louisiana. Moreover, by 1802 Napoleon was planning to conquer all of Europe, which would mean a renewal of war between Great Britain and France. Napoleon knew that the British

navy could easily seize his overseas possessions, including those in the New World. Therefore, he decided to save what he could, and $15 million was better than nothing.

Purchase despite complications. Napoleon's offer to sell Louisiana pleased Jefferson. But the offer also troubled him.

Jefferson, as you know, had always opposed giving the federal government any powers not specifically granted by the Constitution. The Constitution said nothing about the government's right to buy territory from a foreign nation. Jefferson felt that an amendment to the Constitution would be necessary before the purchase could be made. But his advisers warned him that Napoleon might change his mind while the amendment was being adopted. Jefferson therefore sent the treaty of pur-

■ An expedition led by Meriwether Lewis and William Clark spent more than two years exploring the territory of Louisiana. Above, the expedition is shown at the Columbia River.

chase to the Senate for approval. He later admitted that he had been inconsistent and had "done an act beyond the Constitution."

In the Senate, Jefferson's political enemies, the Federalists, strongly objected to the treaty. They declared that $15 million was too high a price for an empty wilderness. They frankly expressed their fear that when farmers filled this vast western territory, the eastern commercial interests in Congress would be outvoted. If this occurred, how could the Federalists get Congress to pass any measures that would help eastern commerce and finance?

To strengthen their arguments, most Federalists insisted that the Constitution did not give the federal government power to buy territory. The Federalists' arguments were as inconsistent as those of Jefferson, for the Federalists had claimed that the Constitution should be broadly interpreted and that it gave the federal government all powers not specifically denied to it.

The stands taken by Jefferson and the Federalists on the Louisiana issue illustrate how ideas change as interests and situations change. Despite Federalist objections, the treaty of purchase was approved. In 1803 Louisiana, or the Louisiana Purchase, became part of the United States.

The Lewis and Clark expedition. Nobody knew what the boundaries of Louisiana were or what lay within the territory. Jefferson decided to find out just what the nation had bought. He assigned the task to a United States army expedition led by Meriwether Lewis and William Clark (see map, page 232).

The expedition of about 30 men left the Mississippi at St. Louis on May 14, 1804, and traveled up the Missouri River to its headwaters. There they

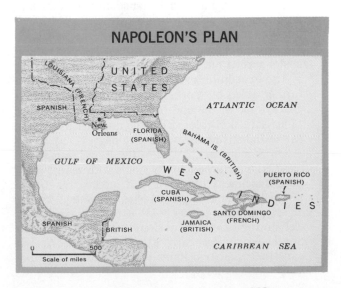

NAPOLEON'S PLAN

■ President Thomas Jefferson seized the opportunity of buying the territory of Louisiana, even though he was not at all sure that the Constitution gave him the power to act as he did.

Importance of the purchase. The purchase of Louisiana, with its immense area and rich resources, was an outstanding event in American history. It was a guarantee that the new nation would one day become a leading world power. As Robert R. Livingston observed when the treaty of purchase was signed, "From this day the United States take their place among the powers of the first rank."

SECTION SURVEY

IDENTIFY: Louisiana Purchase; Toussaint L'Ouverture, Lewis and Clark, York, Zebulon Pike, Sacajawea; 1803.

1. In his Inaugural Address, Jefferson expressed his ideas about government. (a) What were these ideas? (b) How did they follow the ideals of the Declaration of Independence?
2. (a) Why did Napoleon decide to sell Louisiana? (b) Why did Jefferson decide to purchase it? (c) What objections were made to the purchase? (d) How was the Constitution involved in these objections?
3. What does the uprising of the black people of Haiti in 1791 reveal about man's desire to be free?

hired Indian guides and horses, and journeyed 300 miles over perilous mountain trails to the headwaters of the Clearwater River. Then they built canoes and made their way down the Clearwater and the Columbia to the Pacific.

The expedition was marked by good luck as well as good management. During the first winter Lewis and Clark hired a French-Canadian fur trader and his Indian wife, Sacajawea, to serve as guides and interpreters. At the headwaters of the Missouri, the expedition encountered its first Indians, whose leader turned out to be Sacajawea's brother!

The expedition's relations with the Indians were further aided by York, Clark's black slave, whom Clark freed at the end of the expedition. Because of his dark skin color, York did not seem as strange to the Indians as the white men did.

On September 23, 1806, the Lewis and Clark expedition returned to St. Louis with maps, journals, specimens of plants and insects, the bones and pelts of animals, and boxes of soil and stones.

Meanwhile, other bold explorers, including Zebulon Pike, were pushing into the American Southwest. These early expeditions gave Americans their first real knowledge of the country beyond the Mississippi.

2 National growth at home and abroad under Jefferson

Thomas Jefferson's prompt action in the purchase of Louisiana was only one of several vigorous steps he took as President. Immediately upon taking office, he urged Congress to repeal a number of Federalist laws that he felt were harmful to the country's best interests. He also did not hesitate to use military force to protect American rights.

Federalist laws repealed. The Alien and Sedition Acts of 1798, which Jefferson strongly opposed, had expired before he became President. But the Naturalization Act, also passed in 1798, was still in effect. Congress, at Jefferson's urging, promptly repealed it. Congress also repealed the excise tax on whisky, which Jefferson regarded as unconstitutional. Congress likewise repealed the Judiciary Act of 1801 so that the "midnight judges" appointed by President Adams on the eve of Jefferson's inauguration could not assume office.

Jefferson then turned his attention to the army and the navy. He persuaded Congress to cut their appropriations and reduce them in size. Jefferson was opposed to a strong military establishment because it would greatly strengthen the federal gov-

234

ernment. Moreover, by reducing the armed forces, Jefferson could operate the government more economically.

Federalist programs continued. The Republicans, however, did not wipe out all the work of the Federalists. Jefferson acted with moderation. During his administration he continued many Federalist programs and kept many Federalists in office.

Hoping to end the bitterness between the Federalists and the Republicans, Jefferson said in his Inaugural Address: "We are all Republicans, we are all Federalists." Then he proceeded to show through actions that he meant what he said about bringing unity to the nation.

Although Jefferson had argued that the Bank of the United States was unconstitutional, he could do nothing to disturb it, for its charter ran until 1811. And even though Jefferson had opposed Hamilton's plan to have the federal government assume the state debts, his Secretary of the Treasury, Albert Gallatin, paid off installments on the public debt as rapidly as possible.

Defending American rights. In a war with the pirates of North Africa, Jefferson actually pushed forward the Federalist ideal of a strong federal government.

The Moslem rulers of the Barbary States of North Africa—Morocco, Algiers, Tunis, and Tripoli—had long been seizing the ships of Christian nations and holding their crews for ransom. Instead of declaring war on the pirates, the European governments had decided that it was cheaper to make the yearly payments of tribute, or bribes. Since 1783 the United States, whose merchants traded with the Mediterranean countries, had also been paying tribute to the pirates of North Africa. But when the rulers of Tripoli made exorbitant demands upon the United States, and had the flagpole of the American consulate chopped down, Jefferson decided to meet the challenge. He sent a squadron of naval ships to the harbor of Tripoli in the Mediterranean (see map, this page).

On a night in February 1804, Lieutenant Stephen Decatur rowed into the harbor of Tripoli with a handful of men. They boarded the *Philadelphia,* an American warship that had been seized by the pirates. Decatur and his men surprised the pirate crew, set fire to the ship, and rowed back to their own vessel through a hail of gunfire from the shore.

Despite Decatur's daring exploits, however, tension continued until 1805, when the ruler of Tripoli threatened to kill American captives. The Americans then accepted a peace that ended the payment

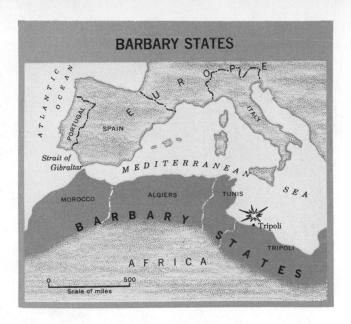

BARBARY STATES

of tribute to Tripoli. However, the Americans agreed to make ransom payments for Americans captured by the pirates. The piracy of other Barbary States continued until 1815. Then an American fleet under Decatur, reinforced by European warships, won honor and victory for the American navy, finally bringing to an end the payment of tributes to the pirates along the Barbary coast.

American ships could now sail the Mediterranean freely. Europeans regarded the United States with new respect and admiration. Moreover, American naval forces gained valuable experience during the war. And Americans took great pride in the heroic exploits of Stephen Decatur and other naval commanders. These new heroes, shared in common by people in every section of the United States, stimulated pride in the growing nation.

The election of 1804. The Republicans entered the Presidential election of 1804 confident of victory. For their Presidential candidate they turned again to Thomas Jefferson. But they dropped Aaron Burr, who had served as Vice-President during Jefferson's first term, and chose George Clinton of New York as Jefferson's running mate. Jefferson and Clinton won a sweeping victory, carrying all the states except Delaware and Connecticut.

Hamilton's tragic death. In the meantime Burr had switched to the Federalist Party, and in the spring of 1804 ran for the governorship of New York on the Federalist ticket. Alexander Hamilton,

235

■ This picture shows the destruction of the ship Philadelphia in the harbor of Tripoli in 1804. Daring naval exploits such as this inspired Americans with pride in their growing nation.

who did not trust Burr, urged the Federalists to vote against him. Burr lost the election. Blaming Hamilton for his defeat, Burr sent his enemy a note, demanding an immediate apology for an uncomplimentary remark concerning Burr which Hamilton supposedly made during the election campaign. When Hamilton refused to apologize, Burr challenged him to a duel.

The two men met in the early morning of July 11. At the signal to fire, Burr raised his pistol and took careful aim. Hamilton, who had not tried to fire, fell mortally wounded and died shortly afterward. Such was the tragic end of Alexander Hamilton, a man who had contributed much to building the new nation.

Burr's inglorious end. Aaron Burr's next adventure puzzled Americans at the time and has puzzled historians ever since. In 1805 and 1806 he involved several prominent Americans in vague schemes—perhaps to persuade westerners to leave the Union and set up a separate republic, perhaps to conquer Mexico and establish an independent empire. While fleeing in disguise, Burr was arrested

236

by officers of the federal government and charged with treason.

Chief Justice John Marshall, who presided at the trial, followed the strict definition of treason given in the Constitution (page 186). Burr was acquitted, and chose to live in Europe in exile. Later he returned to New York, where he lived and died under the shadow of disapproval by his fellow Americans.

SECTION SURVEY

IDENTIFY: tribute, Barbary States; Stephen Decatur.

1. (a) What important changes did the Jefferson administration make in the Federalist program? (b) Which Federalist policies did the Republicans continue? Why?
2. How did the war with the Barbary pirates strengthen the federal government and stimulate national pride?
3. The Presidential election of 1800 brought a change in faces rather than a change in measures. Do you agree or disagree? Explain.

3 Complex issues and forces leading to the War of 1812

In 1803 Napoleon began his conquest of Europe. By 1807, after a series of brilliant victories, Napoleon had almost attained his goal. But he still faced major obstacles. To the east stood Russia. To the west, across the English Channel, stood Great Britain. British troops had been driven from the European mainland, but the British navy was powerful at sea, and Napoleon knew that Great Britain might soon put its troops back on European soil.

Wartime profits. One of Napoleon's desperate problems was that of supply. The British navy controlled the seas across which France had to bring products.

America was an important source of supply for both France and Great Britain, but especially France. Great Britain could send its merchant fleet to any part of the world to obtain imports, but France had few ships and therefore relied upon American merchant vessels. American merchants made handsome profits from the European war. From 1789 to 1805 the tonnage, or carrying capacity, of the American merchant marine increased enormously, from about 100,000 tons to nearly 1 million tons. During this same period America's total imports and exports increased four times. Much of this trade was with France and its colonies.

Interference with America's trade. Great Britain was determined to destroy America's trade with France for two major reasons. First, American goods strengthened Napoleon in his life-or-death struggle with Great Britain. Second, the expansion of the American merchant fleet threatened to make the United States a major competitor with British merchants and shipowners.

In 1807 the British adopted a series of measures called Orders in Council. These Orders forbade American vessels to enter any ports under Napoleon's control, either in Europe, the West Indies, or India.

While Great Britain was trying to shut off all trade with France, Napoleon attempted to blockade, or seal off, the British Isles. In a series of Orders, he forbade all nations, the United States included, to trade with the British. He further warned that he would confiscate every vessel that entered French ports after stopping at Great Britain or any British colony. Moreover, he threatened to seize every ship that submitted to inspection by British cruisers or that paid duties to the British government.

The British Orders in Council and Napoleon's Orders did not arise out of hostility toward the United States. They arose out of the war raging between Great Britain and France in Europe. But whatever their reason, the Orders violated a principle that was then becoming, and has since remained, an important pillar of American foreign policy—the principle of *freedom of the seas.*

For many months American merchants matched wits with the French and British naval commanders by engaging in the dangerous but highly profitable practice of blockade running. The profits attracted so many merchants and seamen that in 1807 United States foreign trade soared to the highest level in the nation's history. This risky trade involved the United States in constant conflict with both the British and the French.

Another source of conflict between the United States and Great Britain was continuing British seizure, or impressment, of American seamen (page 218).

In the summer of 1807 the commander of the British ship *Leopard* demanded the right to search the American frigate *Chesapeake* for deserters from the British navy. The commander of the *Chesapeake* refused, whereupon the *Leopard* opened fire. Three Americans were killed and 18 wounded. Four *Chesapeake* sailors were seized and taken aboard the *Leopard*. Many outraged Americans demanded war.

The Embargo Act of 1807. Jefferson did not want war, but he did want to end the continuing American conflict with Great Britain and France. He decided that the only answer short of war was to remove American ships from the high seas.

With this in mind and with his cabinet's approval, Jefferson urged Congress to pass an *embargo,* that is, a law forbidding Americans to trade with any foreign nation, including, of course, Great Britain and France. Congress late in December 1807 passed the Embargo Act, which forbade American vessels to leave for foreign ports. With this act, the United States temporarily abandoned the principle of freedom of the seas in hopes of avoiding war.

From the outset the Embargo Act could not be fully enforced. Americans smuggled goods across the border to Canada. Some merchants kept their vessels abroad, where, sailing under British or French licenses, they continued to earn large prof-

■ Above, Napoleon, Emperor of France, is about to crown his wife Empress. Why did France have to rely upon American merchant vessels as a source of supply for imported goods?

its. Nevertheless, American trade suffered badly.

New England merchants were the first to feel the pinch. They angrily demanded repeal of the Embargo Act, claiming that Jefferson was deliberately trying to ruin them. Farmers, unable to sell their crops to foreign buyers, and unemployed sailors joined the merchants in demanding repeal. Even western farmers were hard hit.

Reluctantly, Jefferson gave in to the growing pressure. On March 1, 1809, three days before he left office, Congress, with his support, ended the embargo by repealing the Embargo Act.

Drifting toward war. Following the precedent started by George Washington, Jefferson refused to run for a third term. In the Presidential election of 1808, James Madison of Virginia, a Republican, won by a substantial vote, and George Clinton was re-elected Vice-President.

Madison was a quiet, scholarly man. For eight years before becoming President, he had served as Jefferson's Secretary of State. Madison shared Jefferson's views. He was determined to gain respect for American rights on the high seas by peaceful means. However, during his first administration the country moved toward war.

Madison's attempts at diplomacy. In place of the Embargo Act, Congress in 1809 passed the Non-Intercourse Act. This act forbade American merchants to do business with Great Britain or France, although trade with other nations was allowed. But trade with Britain and France was precisely what Americans were demanding. Because of continued pressure from merchants, Congress in 1810 allowed the Non-Intercourse Act to expire. As far as Congress was concerned, American ships could now sail where and when they pleased. American shipowners and captains returned to the dangerous business of blockade running.

Still searching for a way to avoid war, President Madison on May 1, 1810, signed a new law urging Great Britain and France, the warring nations, to remove their restrictions on American shipping, and promising that when either power did this, the United States would promptly refuse to trade with the other power.

Failure of Madison's policy.   President Madison was playing a dangerous game, one that could easily lead to war. If the United States refused to trade with one of the warring nations, that nation would accuse Americans of taking sides against it.

The keen-witted Napoleon recognized this fact and in August 1810 announced that France was removing all restrictions against American shipping. Madison was warned by the British and several of his own advisers that Napoleon could not be trusted. Madison ignored these warnings and issued orders forbidding trade with Great Britain.

Madison's policy failed, for Napoleon continued to interfere with American shipping. The policy had won the United States little, if anything, from France. On the other hand, it had antagonized Great Britain.

Madison's demands met by Britain.   The British, however, were facing a serious economic depression. During the winter of 1811–12 grain crops failed, food prices rose, trade slumped, factories closed, and many workers lost their jobs.

Under pressure from British merchants, businessmen, and workers, Parliament decided to withdraw the Orders in Council that had interfered with American trade and freedom of the seas. Parliament suspended these Orders on June 16, 1812. Great Britain's need for American trade persuaded the British to meet President Madison's demands.

Declaration of war.   The British Parliament had met President Madison's demands. But there was no Atlantic cable or telephone in those days, and the Americans had not heard of the British action. Thus, on June 18, 1812, two days after Parliament had withdrawn the Orders in Council, Congress declared war on Great Britain. Why?

Most historians agree that the War of 1812 was fought mainly over freedom of the seas and the impressment of American seamen. But these were not the only reasons for the American decision to fight Great Britain. Congressmen from the eastern states with their strong interests in trade were divided, while the great majority of Congressmen from the agricultural southern and western states favored the war. How can this be explained? What other forces led to the outbreak of war?

Land hunger.   Western land hunger was an old story. Pioneer farmers quickly exhausted the fertility of their soil and then moved westward in search of new lands, which they cleared, planted— and eventually wore out. By 1812 they had almost reached the end of the forested areas.

The northwestern farmers did not want to move into the treeless prairies of the United States, where there was no timber to build houses and fences. Some farmers mistakenly believed that the prairie soil was poor. All of them knew correctly that the tough prairie sod would be difficult to plow. Northwestern farmers preferred to move northward into the rich, wooded sections of southern Canada. A war with Great Britain might make this Canadian land part of the United States.

The farmers living in Tennessee, western Georgia, and what is now northern Alabama longed for the lands of Spanish Florida bordering the Gulf of Mexico (see map, page 244). They wanted this land not only for farming, but also because it was being used as a safe hiding place for runaway slaves and by Indians who kept attacking American frontier settlements. People from this section of the country clamored for the conquest of Florida. A war with Great Britain would provide an excuse for this conquest, because Spain had been virtually an ally of the British ever since Napoleon had invaded Spain.

National pride.   The rising spirit of pride in the new nation also led to the War of 1812. Americans resented impressment of American sailors and insults to the flag. Many Americans now believed that the United States was destined to expand until the American flag flew over the entire Western Hemisphere from the North Pole to the Strait of Magellan. At the very least, they said, Canada and Mexico and the land as far as the Pacific Ocean should belong to the United States.

Indian relations.   Troubled relations with the Indians also led westerners to demand war against Great Britain. The Indians of the northwestern areas had been persuaded or forced to give up more and more of their land to the advancing Americans. Time after time, they had been promised that this was the last land they would be forced to give up. And every time the promise had been broken.

Encouraged by Canadian fur traders, a great Indian leader named Tecumseh decided to make a final stand against American expansion. He began to form a confederation of Indian tribes.

Tecumseh and the Prophet.   In the early 1800's Tecumseh and his brother, the Prophet, kindled a religious revival among the Indians of the Northwest. Indian warrior and Indian priest, they traveled far and wide among the scattered tribes, urging them to preserve their traditions and beliefs.

Tecumseh had no wish to start a war. He asked only that the white men leave the Indians alone and stop taking their lands. Although Tecumseh was opposed to warfare, he finally took up arms against the United States. But no organization of Indians could hope to stop the westward movement.

Demands of the "War Hawks."   As the influence of Tecumseh and his brother began to spread along the frontier, westerners became alarmed. Most of them believed that British fur traders in Canada were supplying the Indians with arms. Why not seize Canada, they asked, and thus end once and for all the dangers of an alliance between the British and the Indians?

In the Congressional elections of 1810, the citizens of the frontier regions elected several young men to Congress. Among these men were Henry Clay of Kentucky, John C. Calhoun of South Carolina, Felix Grundy of Tennessee, and Peter B. Porter of western New York. Known as "War Hawks," these young Congressmen helped to whip up war spirit in Congress. "We shall drive the British from our continent," declared Felix Grundy. "They will no longer have an opportunity of intriguing with our Indian neighbors. . . . That nation [Britain] will lose her Canadian trade, and by having no resting place in this country, her means of annoying us will be diminished."

Because of western demands, in the late autumn of 1811 General William Henry Harrison, the Governor of Indiana Territory, led American troops against a force of Indians led by Tecumseh. The Indians were encamped where the Tippecanoe River flows into the Wabash River (see map, page 244) in what was soon to become the state of Indiana. The Indians fought bravely, and Harrison lost many men. When he left the battlefield, he was not sure of the outcome. But the Indians, who had also suffered badly, quickly fled northward. Harrison was somewhat surprised to discover that he had won the battle. Although the Battle of Tippecanoe was not a decisive victory, it helped to establish Harrison's reputation as a frontier military hero and, as you will see, paved the way for his election to the Presidency in 1840.

Tecumseh was killed in battle in 1813. The confederation that he and his brother had organized fell apart.

SECTION SURVEY

IDENTIFY: freedom of the seas, blockade running, Embargo Act of 1807, "War Hawks"; Tecumseh, James Madison; 1812.

1. How did American merchants profit from the Napoleonic Wars in Europe?
2. (a) Why did Great Britain want to destroy American trade with France? (b) How did Great Britain carry out this aim?
3. In the Embargo Act, the United States abandoned a cherished principle to avoid war. (a) What was the principle? (b) Was the embargo a practical measure? Explain. (c) Why was it hard to enforce?
4. Explain how each of the following led to the War of 1812: (a) land hunger, (b) national pride, (c) American-Indian conflict, (d) fur trade, (e) desire for freedom of the seas, (f) impressment of American seamen.

4 The Americans against the British in the War of 1812

Many circumstances led to the War of 1812—among them land hunger, national pride, Indian troubles, and the fur trade. But in his war message to Congress, President Madison emphasized two major reasons—the continued seizure of American ships and the impressment of American seamen.

Thus, as you know, Congress declared war on June 18, 1812, two days after the British Parliament had suspended the Orders in Council—President Madison's major reason for advocating the war. Many Americans, among them Henry Clay, believed that the Kentucky militia could conquer Canada in three weeks. However, the war dragged on for more than two years.

The election of 1812. In May, only a few weeks before war was declared, Republican leaders nominated Madison for a second term. The Federalists, most of whom opposed the war, nominated De Witt Clinton of New York, a Republican who had broken with the dominant leadership of the Republican Party. Although Madison won the election by a comfortable margin, Clinton carried all the New England and Middle Atlantic states except Vermont and Pennsylvania. Moreover, the Federalists made heavy gains in Congress.

The election of 1812 clearly revealed that many Americans opposed the war. This feeling was especially strong in New England.

A divided country. Even after the conflict started, many Federalists continued to feel that it was unnecessary. Merchants realized that war would ruin what was left of their shipping. Furthermore, they objected to proposals to annex Canada and Florida to the United States, for they saw clearly that additional land would greatly increase the power of the farmers. Why, the Federalist merchants asked, should we fight a war that will weaken our influence in the federal government?

Even some Republicans had misgivings about the war. John Randolph of Virginia raised an issue that would haunt the halls of Congress for many years. He declared that the annexation of Canada would increase the strength of that part of the United States that did not have slavery and weaken the power of the southern states. Randolph also feared that a war would so increase the powers of the federal government that the traditional rights of the states would be endangered.

Handicaps to the war effort. The opposition of most Federalists and some Republicans weakened the war effort in other ways as well. Governors of New England states would not permit their state militias to invade Canada. When Congress debated the question of a compulsory draft law to raise men for the army, the New England Federalists denounced the measure.

Daniel Webster, a gifted young orator from Massachusetts, declared that compulsory military service was unconstitutional. "Where is it written in the Constitution?" Webster cried. "In what article is it contained that you may take children from their parents and parents from their children and compel them to fight the battles of any war in which the folly or the wickedness of the government may engage it?" New Englanders in general, and Federalists in particular, contemptuously referred

■ President James Madison, sometimes called the "Father of the Constitution," was a quiet, scholarly man. He tried unsuccessfully to use peaceful means to gain respect for American rights on the high seas.

to the War of 1812 as "Mr. Madison's War."

When the war dragged on without success and American ships were swept from the seas, New England Federalists became increasingly bitter. Finally, on December 15, 1814, a group met in secret session at Hartford, Connecticut, in what was known as the Hartford Convention. The delegates proposed several amendments to the Constitution increasing the influence and power of the commercial sections of the country.

Perhaps most important, the delegates to the Hartford Convention proclaimed that when any minority within the country considered laws of the federal government unconstitutional, the minority had the right to declare such laws null and void.

■ Above, black and white sailors cheer as the Americans win a victory in the Battle of Lake Champlain. This was one of the most important American victories in the War of 1812.

This was a restatement of the Virginia and Kentucky Resolutions (page 226). But this time the statement came from the Federalists, not from the Republicans. However, the Hartford Convention met too late to have any effect upon the war.

Although most southerners and westerners favored the war, they too were divided. Southerners wanted to conquer Florida. Westerners were just as eager to conquer Canada. As a result, the American military leaders found it difficult to plan a strategy that would please even those who supported the war.

Lack of preparation. The country was not prepared for war. The navy's fleet of a dozen ships was helpless before the more than 800 warships of the British Royal Navy.

The army and the militia were also unprepared. The army had fewer than 7,000 men at the outbreak of the war. Its commanders frequently were well-meaning but elderly Revolutionary War veterans who proved no match for superior British commanders. Another weakness was the American failure to appoint a single commander to direct the entire war effort. Moreover, the militia on which the Americans chiefly depended was poorly equipped and trained.

Many Americans fought gallantly in the War of 1812. Nevertheless, courage on the part of individuals could not make up for lack of readiness.

Black soldiers and sailors. Little effort was made during the War of 1812 to recruit Negroes, except in New York, where the legislature passed a special act for raising two regiments of black troops. Yet many black men, slave and free, took part in the war. Fugitive slaves, hoping to win their freedom, fought both on the American side and on the British side.

The black fighting men on the American side made many contributions. After British forces seized Washington, D.C., American leaders in Philadelphia, also fearing seizure, appealed to local Negroes to help secure the city's defenses. About

2,500 responded and won the praise of the authorities.

In Louisiana, General Andrew Jackson, ignoring the fear of many white officers that it would be dangerous to arm black troops, called on "the free men of color" to fight the British. He promised them the same pay as white soldiers and the same bonuses in cash and land that white soldiers would receive after the war.

When the war was over, Jackson addressed his black troops: "I expected much from you," he said, "but you have surpassed my hopes." The President, Jackson declared, would be informed of their conduct and "the voice of the representatives of the American nation shall applaud your valor, as your General now praises your ardor."

Naval officers also testified to the bravery of black sailors under fire. Captain Oliver H. Perry had at first been disgruntled when he was sent "blacks, soldiers, and boys" as naval reinforcements. He later wrote that the Negroes in his crew "seemed absolutely insensible to danger."

Despite their contributions and bravery, however, not many of the slaves who fought in the War of 1812 were granted their freedom.

Ending in stalemate. The primary American objective in the War of 1812 was the conquest of Canada. Despite several attempts, the Americans failed to achieve this goal.

On the other hand, by securing control of Lake Erie, the Americans did succeed in preventing a Canadian force from occupying American territory for any length of time. Lake Erie was secured in 1813 through the victory of Captain Oliver H. Perry and his small naval force. His report of the victory, "We have met the enemy and they are ours," is still an honored part of American naval tradition. Equally important was the victory of Captain Thomas Macdonough on Lake Champlain, near Plattsburg, New York, in 1814. Macdonough's victory prevented a British invasion of the United States from Canada by way of the Champlain Valley.

The one outstanding American military victory of the War of 1812 was that of General Andrew Jackson at New Orleans. Jackson, born near the border between North and South Carolina, had already won fame as a vigorous Indian fighter in the Tennessee country. When he heard of British operations near New Orleans, he rushed there. In a large-scale encounter with British forces under General Pakenham, Jackson won. This victory helped promote the future political fortunes of General Jackson. It also gave the people of the United States the impression that they had won the War of 1812.

Actually the victory at New Orleans had no effect upon the war's outcome. Negotiations for a peace treaty between the Americans and the British at Ghent in Belgium had been under way for some time. The Americans and the British had reached an agreement before the battle of New Orleans was fought. Lack of modern means of communication prevented this news from reaching New Orleans in time to stop the battle.

The Treaty of Ghent. The Treaty of Ghent, signed on Christmas Eve, 1814, was somewhat limited in its direct results. It said nothing about the impressment of American seamen or about neutral rights on the high seas. But it did arrange for the release of all prisoners of war and for the restoration of all occupied territory. It also provided for a commission to settle disputes over the boundaries between the United States and Canada. Most important, it restored peace, and led eventually to greatly improved relations between the United States and Great Britain.

Settling disputes peaceably. Shortly after the war ended, the United States and Great Britain created a number of other commissions to tackle the long-standing problems of trade, furs, and fishing rights along the North Atlantic coast.

These commissions produced worthwhile results. One commission, which finished its work in 1815, did away with trade discriminations and allowed American ships to sail to all British ports except those in the West Indies. Another commission gave Americans the right to fish along the Canadian coast and to dry their fish on Canadian shores.

The Rush-Bagot Agreement. While the commissions were at work, the United States and Great Britain signed another treaty of even greater importance.

Immediately after the war, both the United States and Canada had begun to build warships on the Great Lakes to defend their frontiers. American, Canadian, and British statesmen agreed that this was a needless expense and an invitation to future trouble. The Rush-Bagot Agreement, signed in Washington in 1817, provided that the United States and Canada would maintain only a few small vessels for police purposes on Lake Champlain and the Great Lakes. Years later the agreement was

(*continued on page 245*)

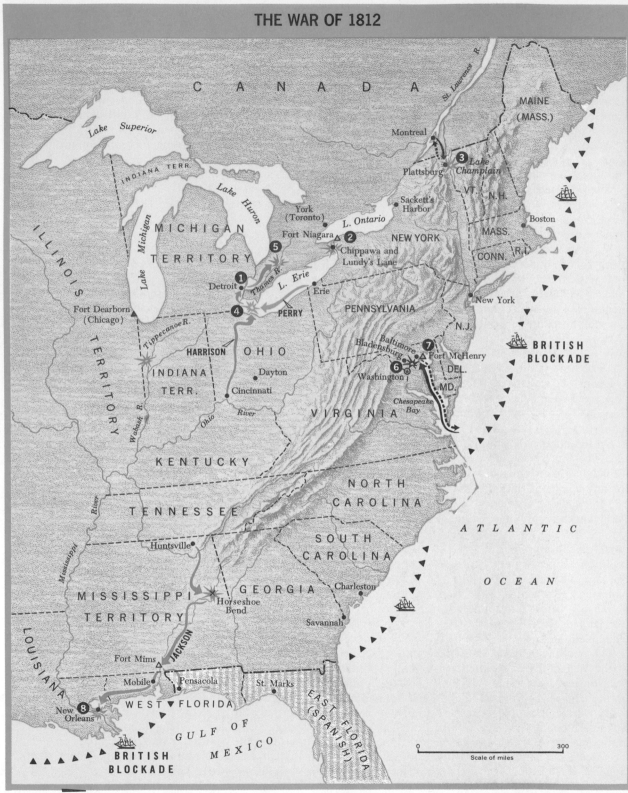

THE WAR OF 1812

CANADA

St. Lawrence R.

MAINE
(MASS.)

Lake Superior

Montreal

Lake Huron

INDIANA TERR.

Plattsburg ③ Lake Champlain

VT. N.H.

York (Toronto)

Sackett's Harbor

Boston

MICHIGAN

L. Ontario

NEW YORK

MASS.

Fort Niagara ⚔ ② ⑤

Chippawa and Lundy's Lane

CONN. R.I.

TERRITORY

Lake Michigan

① Detroit ④ L. Erie

Erie

New York

Thames R.

PERRY

PENNSYLVANIA

ILLINOIS

Fort Dearborn (Chicago)

Tippecanoe R.

N.J.

HARRISON

OHIO

Baltimore ⑦

Bladensburg

Fort McHenry

TERRITORY

INDIANA TERR.

Dayton

⑥ Washington

DEL.

Wabash R.

Cincinnati

MD.

BRITISH BLOCKADE

Ohio River

River

VIRGINIA

Chesapeake Bay

KENTUCKY

ATLANTIC

NORTH CAROLINA

TENNESSEE

Huntsville

OCEAN

SOUTH CAROLINA

MISSISSIPPI

Charleston

Horseshoe Bend

GEORGIA

TERRITORY

Savannah

JACKSON

Fort Mims

⑧

New Orleans

Mobile

Pensacola

St. Marks

LOUISIANA

WEST FLORIDA

EAST FLORIDA (SPANISH)

GULF OF MEXICO

BRITISH BLOCKADE

Mississippi River

0   300

Scale of miles

The United States entered the War of 1812 with a plan for a three-pronged drive into Canada. The three attacking forces, composed mainly of poorly trained militia, were to start their drives from Detroit ❶ the Niagara area ❷ and Plattsburg ❸.

1812—The year 1812 brought a series of disasters for the American side. In July, General William Hull crossed the Detroit River into Canada ❶. Then, fearing his lines of communication would be cut by a strong force of British and Indians, Hull withdrew from Canada and surrendered Detroit without firing a shot. Farther west, the American garrison at Fort Dearborn, where Chicago now stands, was wiped out. Later in the year, the British repulsed two feeble attacks across the Niagara River ❷. And in November, a drive launched from Plattsburg ❸ against Montreal ended on the Canadian border when the American militia refused to leave United States territory.

1813—The situation improved somewhat in 1813. In April, a combined naval and military expedition sailed from Sackett's Harbor, raided York (now Toronto), and, contrary to orders, burned the public buildings of that city before withdrawing. Some months later, Captain Perry's naval victory on Lake Erie ❹ forced the British to abandon Detroit. General William Henry Harrison pursued the retreating troops and their Indian allies, overtook them at Moravian Town on the north bank of the Thames River ❺, and on October 5 won a decisive victory. With the death of their leader Tecumseh, who was killed in this battle, the Indians who had been helping the British deserted the British cause.

1814–1815—In 1814, with the defeat of Napoleon in Europe, the British were able to send strong forces to America. Before the reinforcements arrived, however, an American army under General Jacob Brown had crossed the Niagara River and on July 5 had defeated the British troops in the Battle of Chippawa ❷. A second battle, fought on July 25, near the Canadian village of Lundy's Lane, ended in a draw.

The British, in 1814, launched three campaigns. A powerful British invading force of more than 10,000 regular troops was stopped by Captain Macdonough's victory on Lake Champlain ❸. A second invading force landed on the Potomac below Washington, marched into the city against only token resistance, and burned the public buildings before retiring ❻. This same force was prevented from landing at Baltimore by the fierce resistance put up by the troops manning Fort McHenry —when Francis Scott Key wrote "The Star-Spangled Banner" ❼. The third invading force, which landed near New Orleans ❽ was decisively defeated by American troops commanded by Major General Andrew Jackson, in a battle fought two weeks after a peace treaty had been signed.

extended to include land fortifications as well. Thus the agreement was one of the enduring outcomes of the War of 1812.

In 1818 another commission established the boundary between the United States and Canada extending from the Lake of the Woods, west of Lake Superior, to the Rocky Mountains. The northeastern boundary from the Atlantic Ocean to the Lake of the Woods was later settled by the Webster-Ashburton Treaty of 1842. The boundary from the Rocky Mountains to the Pacific Ocean was fixed by treaty in 1846 (see map, pages 856–57).

The war as a turning point. The War of 1812 also marked a turning point in American history. From 1789 to 1815, events in Europe had helped to shape United States policies, especially foreign policies. After the Treaty of Ghent, the United States became much more independent of Europe. Equally important, the nations of Europe treated with growing respect the young country that had not hesitated to go to war with the greatest naval power in the world.

For the next 100 years, as you will see, the United States was not directly involved in European wars. Americans concentrated upon the job of developing their own country. After 1815 the American people as a whole turned their backs on Europe and began to tackle with renewed vigor the exciting task of opening up the western lands.

SECTION SURVEY

IDENTIFY: Hartford Convention, "Mr. Madison's War," compulsory military service; Daniel Webster, Oliver H. Perry, Andrew Jackson.

1. The War of 1812 can be attributed to a communications gap between the United States and Great Britain. Comment.
2. Why did most Federalists oppose the war?
3. (a) What changes in white attitudes toward Negroes took place during the war? Why? (b) Do you suppose these changes were widespread or permanent? Explain.
4. Explain how the results of the War of 1812 can be found in part in each of the following: (a) Treaty of Ghent, (b) Rush-Bagot Agreement, (c) Canadian-American relations, (d) European-American relations.
5. The War of 1812 revealed the existence of "sectionalism"—the belief that one's own section is the most important and that the nation's policies should satisfy that section's needs. Explain.

TRACING THE MAIN IDEAS

Between 1801 and 1815 the young, struggling United States doubled in size, adding the vast territory of Louisiana to its domain. The Louisiana Purchase was one of Thomas Jefferson's outstanding accomplishments as President. By 1815 the Indians had been driven from the new state of Ohio and the Territory of Michigan, both of which had been carved out of the Northwest Territory. The way was open for the advance of pioneers into the unsettled lands of the Mississippi Valley.

During this period the United States became involved in the Napoleonic Wars, which plunged Europe into turmoil between 1796 and 1815. Although the United States failed to maintain for itself the freedom of the seas, and although it failed to stay out of war, it emerged from the conflict without loss of territory or national strength. The War of 1812 marked a turning point in the relations between Canada and the United States. Despite bitterness generated by armed conflict, the way was paved for the peaceable settlement of future disputes.

Finally, the troubles that Americans faced in this period of turmoil helped to draw them together into a united nation. The American people emerged from the War of 1812 with a strong feeling of unity. American victories on land and sea were proudly remembered. Military defeats and failures were largely forgotten.

In the next chapter you will see how the growing nation undertook to become economically as well as politically independent of Europe and to stand on its own feet as an equal member of the family of nations.

CHAPTER SURVEY

QUESTIONS FOR DISCUSSION

1. The epitaph on Jefferson's tombstone reads: "Here lies Thomas Jefferson, author of the American Declaration of Independence, of the Statute of Virginia for Religious Freedom, and father of the University of Virginia." (a) Why do you think Jefferson wanted to be remembered in this manner rather than as President of the United States? (b) Which qualities of Jefferson do you think are most admired by the American people? Why?
2. In his first Inaugural Address, Jefferson called for "peace, commerce, and honest friendship with all nations, entangling alliances with none." Compare Jefferson's attitude with the ideas expressed by George Washington in his Farewell Address (see Starr, Todd, and Curti's *Living American Documents* [Harcourt Brace Jovanovich, Inc.], pages 101 and 108.
3. It is argued that the War of 1812 was really the Second War of Independence. Do you agree or disagree with this statement? Explain.
4. Americans feared an alliance between the Indians and the British. How would such an alliance have profited the Indians? the British?
5. Alexander Hamilton labored to give the country a strong central government; Jefferson championed the rights of the individual. What specific contributions did each man make to American government?

RELATING PAST TO PRESENT

1. Does Jefferson's Inaugural Address apply to the United States today? Why or why not?
2. Thomas Jefferson made the following statement: "Were it left to me to decide whether we should have a government without newspapers or newspapers without a government, I should not hesitate a moment to prefer the latter." Explain. Would you have the same preference? Why or why not? Would you include television news reports as a modern addition to newspapers? Explain.
3. During the War of 1812, the country was divided over the issue of compulsory military service in a democracy. What arguments were made then concerning this issue? What arguments are made now?

USING MAPS AND CHARTS

1. Turn to the map on page 232. What was the geographic importance of the explorations of (a) Lewis and Clark and (b) Pike for the future history of the United States?
2. Referring to the charts on page 854, compare the area of the original United States with that of the Louisiana Purchase. Was your state one of those carved out of the Louisiana Purchase?

THE WAR of 1812 marked a turning point in American affairs. Freed at last from involvement in the affairs of Europe, Americans in 1815 could now turn their full attention to developing America.

The war itself had greatly stimulated a feeling of national pride. So strong was this feeling during the years from about 1817 to 1825, and so united were Americans in their determination to strengthen the growing nation, that this period came to be known as the "Era of Good Feelings."

However, the term "Era of Good Feelings" was not entirely accurate. The spirit of "sectionalism" was also gaining strength as different sections of the country continued to develop in different ways.

The Northeast, particularly New England, was being reshaped by the Industrial Revolution. The South, primarily an agricultural region, was devoting more and more of its effort to the cultivation of cotton. The "West," which most Americans still thought of as the land between the Appalachian Mountains and the Mississippi River, was attracting growing numbers of pioneer settlers.

Members of Congress naturally looked out for the special interests of their states and their own sections of the country. But Congress and the President also had to deal with the problem of welding the three sections of the rapidly growing country —the Northeast, the South, and the West—into a unified whole. They solved this problem, at least temporarily, by means of a program called the "American System."

THE CHAPTER IN OUTLINE

1. The spread of the Industrial Revolution from Great Britain to America.

2. The development of the "American System" under new national leaders.

3. The growing nation's struggles with new and complex problems.

4. The nation's role as guardian of the Western Hemisphere.

5. The expression of national pride in American education and arts.

■ *A New England textile mill*

CHAPTER **12**

Prosperity and Respect for the Unified Nation

1817 – 1825

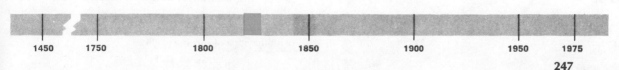

| 1450 | 1750 | 1800 | 1850 | 1900 | 1950 | 1975 |

1 The spread of the Industrial Revolution from Great Britain to America

The *Industrial Revolution* was a revolution in manufacturing and industry that began in the 1700's with the invention and development of power-driven machines. As the revolution gained momentum, more and more manufacturing was done in factories and less and less in the homes and small shops of workers.

The arrival of Samuel Slater. Samuel Slater, who landed in New York in 1789, was one of many inventors and skilled workmen of his time who became pioneers of the Industrial Revolution.

The Industrial Revolution began in England, but even in colonial America skilled mechanics built water-powered mills for grinding grain, sawing wood, treating cloth, and making iron. Nevertheless, Samuel Slater's arrival in New York proved to be an important event, for Slater became known as the "Father of the American Factory System."

Although only 21 when he left England, Slater was already a highly skilled mechanic. Having worked in a cotton textile mill, he knew a great deal about the new spinning and weaving machines built by British inventors. What is more, he knew that British businessmen wanted to keep the secrets of these new machines from other countries. For this reason, the British government had forbidden the machines to be sold and had forbidden textile workers to leave the country.

Slater nevertheless slipped away and arrived in New York with empty hands and almost empty pockets. But he knew how to build power-driven machines for spinning and weaving cloth.

Factories in place of home industries. Samuel Slater went to Rhode Island. There, with the financial aid of Moses Brown, a Quaker merchant, Slater reproduced from memory the machines he had used in England. Indeed, he even improved them.

Before long, Slater was operating a successful cotton factory, or mill, using water power to turn the spindles. Other men soon began to operate mills at water-power sites in New England and the Middle Atlantic states. At first the new mills did nothing more than spin thread with power-driven machines. The mill owners then distributed the thread to homes scattered over the surrounding countryside. Working at hand looms in their own homes, women wove the thread into cloth, which they then returned to the mill owners. Within a few years, however, mills began to weave the cloth as well as spin the yarn. During the early 1800's less and less work was done in the home; more and more work was done in the new textile mills.

But the power-driven machines and the buildings to house them were very expensive to build and maintain. Individual craftsmen could not afford them. Thus, *capitalists* ° like Moses Brown built the factories, installed the machinery, purchased raw materials, hired workers, and distributed the finished products. After starting in the textile industry, the Industrial Revolution spread rapidly to the manufacturing of many other products, among them firearms, clocks, and watches.

The Industrial Revolution would have come to America even if Samuel Slater had never been born. As it turned out, however, Slater was a pioneer in developing the American *factory system*.

The search for laborsaving machines. From the earliest days of settlement, the colonial towns and villages never had enough manpower to develop the seemingly limitless natural resources of the New World. Slowly but steadily, pioneer men

° *capitalist*: a person who invests money in a business with the hope of earning profits.

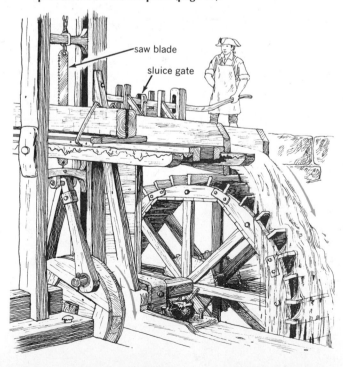

■ **Water-powered Saw.** Water power had been used for many years for various purposes before Samuel Slater adapted it to bring power to his textile machinery. In this water-powered saw, a shaft from the water wheel turned the reciprocating wheel, which produced the saw's up-and-down motion. This "up-and-down saw" was an improvement on the whipsaw (page 49).

saw blade

sluice gate

■ This old print shows cotton thread being spun in a New England textile mill. Notice the child at work behind the spun thread, at the lower lefthand corner of the picture.

and women pushed westward. With so much un-occupied land available, they preferred to own their own farms rather than work as hired hands. Faced with this labor shortage, American farmers put their numerous sons and daughters to work at an early age.

The growing towns also had more work to be done than they had people to do it. This shortage of labor stimulated men to invent laborsaving machines, to install them in factories and on farms, and to provide better working conditions and higher wages than prevailed in Europe.

Encouraging inventors. Because of these conditions, the American government took steps to encourage inventors. In 1790 Congress enacted a law granting inventors, as well as authors, exclusive rights for 14 years to all profits made from their ideas. This law meant that the new tool or the new book belonged to the inventor or author, and could be produced and sold only with his permission for a period of 14 years.°

New sources of power. Another important development in the Industrial Revolution was the discovery and use of new sources of power to run machinery. The textile machinery first used in Great Britain was driven by water power. In 1769, however, James Watt, a Scotsman, took out an English patent for a steam engine. By the 1790's steam power was rapidly replacing water power in British mills.

Although Americans in the 1790's knew about steam engines and were even building some of their own, steam power did not come quickly to the United States. By 1812 there were only 10 steam-powered mills in the new nation. The reason was

° Inventions can now be "patented" for 17 years. Publications can be "copyrighted" for 28 years, and the copyright may be renewed for an additional 28 years.

249

not that Americans were uninterested in steam as a power source, but simply that their rivers and streams, especially those in New England, provided ample water power to operate the first factories.

Interchangeable parts. Eli Whitney, a Connecticut resident, hit upon the idea of building machines with *interchangeable parts*. It was this development, in which French inventors also pioneered, that made *mass production* possible.

Whitney's idea grew out of his work with guns. Before the early 1800's all guns were manufactured by gunsmiths who hammered out each part separately and assembled the parts by hand. When any gun part was damaged, a new part had to be made by hand to replace it.

In 1789 Eli Whitney decided that he could manufacture guns using a new principle of production. He wrote to the Secretary of the Treasury, requesting a contract. "I should like," he wrote, "to undertake the manufacture of 10,000 or 15,000 stand of arms. I am persuaded that machinery moved by water, adapted to this business, would greatly diminish the labor and facilitate the manufacture of this article. Machines for forging, rolling, floating, boring, grinding, polishing, etc., may all be made use of to advantage."

Although Whitney's request was unusual, he got his contract from the government. But when more than two years had passed, people began to think Whitney's project had failed.

Then the young inventor made a trip to Washington. Before a group of skeptical officials, he unpacked a box containing the parts of 10 identical guns. At Whitney's request an official selected one part from each of the piles scattered about the table. The first gun was then assembled. This process was repeated until all 10 guns had been assembled and fired. Those present witnessed what was actually the beginning of mass production.

A look ahead. Not even the most far-sighted American ever dreamed that the developments taking place around him were the first steps in a revolution destined to change life everywhere.

In years to come the Industrial Revolution would help to unite the American people. It would help solve problems of transportation by binding the nation together with a web of steel rails. It would help solve the labor shortage, providing Americans with laborsaving devices beyond the wildest imaginations of the early colonists. It would help Americans conquer the wilderness, make use of the rich resources of forest and sea and soil, and transform the United States into the wealthiest country on earth. The Industrial Revolution would, through the work of the scientists and the engineers, help people conquer disease, solve many of the problems of community life, and build a very different, and in many respects a better, way of life.

SECTION SURVEY

IDENTIFY: Industrial Revolution, home industries, capitalist, interchangeable parts; Samuel Slater.

1. Why is Samuel Slater known as the "Father of the American Factory System"?
2. Relate the following terms to the Industrial Revolution: (a) water-power sites, (b) factories, (c) capitalism, (d) growth of cities.
3. How did a labor shortage and government protection encourage inventions?
4. (a) How did Eli Whitney and James Watt contribute to the revolution of industry? (b) Why were their contributions significant?
5. (a) In what ways has the Industrial Revolution helped the American people and transformed the United States? (b) Has the Industrial Revolution created any new problems? Explain.

■ **Iron Furnace.** To produce "molten iron" which could be poured into molds, "iron ore, charcoal, and limestone" were poured in the top of the furnace. In the bottom of the furnace, in white-hot heat, the iron drained out and impurities called "slag" were collected and removed. The white-hot heat was produced by a water-powered "bellows," which forced a blast of air through the burning charcoal.

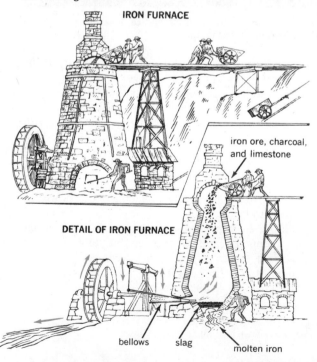

IRON FURNACE

iron ore, charcoal, and limestone

DETAIL OF IRON FURNACE

bellows   slag   molten iron

2 The development of the "American System" under new national leaders

Most of the men who tackled the job of running the new nation in the years following the War of 1812 were new on the national scene. The older men who had led the American people through the Revolutionary War and the opening years of the nation's history were passing from the scene.

The famous three. Three of the new leaders were particularly outstanding. They were destined to play prominent roles in the nation's history for the next 35 years. Each came from a different section of the country.

Henry Clay, a Republican from Kentucky, entered Congress in 1811. Clay, as you know, was one of the "War Hawks" who had clamored for war with Great Britain in 1812. Trained in the law and striking in appearance, Henry Clay became an impressive orator and the acknowledged spokesman for the western parts of the country.

John C. Calhoun of South Carolina also entered Congress in 1811. He, too, was a lawyer, a persuasive speaker, and a Republican. Like Clay, he had also favored the War of 1812. With his keen mind and his devotion to politics, Calhoun began his career as a spokesman for the nation at large, but soon became the major spokesman for the southern states and for the doctrine of states' rights.

Daniel Webster, a Federalist from Massachusetts, entered Congress in 1813. He was born on a farm in New Hampshire. Like Clay and Calhoun, Webster became a lawyer, practicing first in New Hampshire and later in Boston, Massachusetts. Like Clay and Calhoun, Webster was a powerful speaker. In Congress, he quickly became the outstanding spokesman for the northeastern part of the country. At first Webster worked for low tariffs. But as industrial interests in the Northeast replaced shipping interests, he became a defender of high protective tariffs.

The elections of 1816 and 1820. It was an older statesman, however, who won the Presidential election of 1816. James Monroe, Republican, who had served as Secretary of State under President Madison, easily defeated the Federalist candidate, Rufus King. King, a brilliant and able Senator from New York, represented a dying party. By 1816 the Federalists were so weakened that they won only three states.

When President Monroe toured New England after his inauguration in 1817, even a Boston pub-

■ Henry Clay was a Republican from Kentucky who became the acknowledged spokesman for the western parts of the country. Like John C. Calhoun from the South and Daniel Webster from the Northeast, Clay was to play a prominent role in the nation's history for the next 35 years.

lication, the *Columbian Centinel,* which had opposed him in the election, said that the times would prove to be an "Era of Good Feelings." This phrase pleased the new President, and, as the years passed, it did seem to describe national life. The different groups in the country began to work together on common problems. The Federalist Party as such disappeared, and for more than 10 years the Republican Party, originally founded by Thomas Jefferson, was the only political party in the United States.

By 1820 political harmony was so widespread, at least on the surface, that President Monroe actually ran for re-election without opposition. He won all of the electoral votes but one, and was re-elected President.

The American System. In 1816, even before President Monroe was elected for the first time, the Republicans took steps to strengthen the growing nation. In so doing they increased the powers of the federal government at the expense of states' rights. To justify their actions, they used a "loose" interpretation of the Constitution, like the one favored earlier by Alexander Hamilton and the Federalists. This was one reason that the Federalist

■ The Monroe Doctrine became a cornerstone of United States foreign policy. Above, President Monroe, with one hand touching a globe of the world, discusses the policy with members of his cabinet.

Party disappeared. By 1816 the Republicans were doing many things the Federalists had been advocating for years.

Nationally minded statesmen like Henry Clay of Kentucky insisted that the nation could be strengthened only by developing a sound economic program that would enable the United States to become independent of the rest of the world. The economic program that the Republicans adopted in 1816 came to be called the *American System,* a term later used by Henry Clay in a speech in Congress.

The American System developed by the Republicans rested on three major foundations: (1) a national bank to provide a sound, uniform financial system; (2) a protective tariff to provide a wall behind which American factories could grow and prosper; and (3) a transportation system to facilitate trade between the northeastern manufacturers and the western and southern farmers.

The second Bank of the United States.   To promote the nation's economic well-being, the Republicans borrowed from the Federalists the idea of a national bank. In 1816 Congress granted a charter to the second Bank of the United States.

To understand why the Republicans took this action, we must go back to 1811. In that year the charter of the first Bank of the United States expired. State legislatures, especially in the West, immediately granted new charters to private individuals allowing them to organize and operate banks.

Between 1811 and 1816 the number of banks chartered by the states nearly tripled. Many of these state banks were subject to only a limited amount of regulation. Some of them issued far more paper money than they could back up with gold or silver. Inevitably the value of this paper money declined. As a result, the Treasury of the United States found itself accepting for taxes a growing amount of almost worthless bank notes.

This unhealthy financial situation caused the Republicans to remember Alexander Hamilton's Federalist belief that a national bank was essential to the nation's well-being.

The protective tariff of 1816.   In 1816 the Republicans enacted a protective tariff, thus adopting another of Hamilton's basic ideas and making it part of the American System. During the early 1800's, and especially during the war years from

252

1812 to 1815, Americans had found it difficult to get manufactured goods from Europe. As a result, new factories had sprung up on American soil. But when the War of 1812 ended, British manufacturers naturally wanted to drive their American competitors out of business.

The ink was hardly dry on the Treaty of Ghent in 1815 before British vessels began to deliver cargoes of factory-made goods to American ports. The British manufacturers were resorting to a practice known as "dumping"—that is, selling large quantities of their goods below cost to drive rival manufacturers out of business. Once American factories closed, the British manufacturers would raise the price of their products and recover their earlier losses, knowing that they would have little competition from the ruined Americans.

American factory owners had no intention of being driven out of business. They demanded government protection against their British rivals. Thus, Congress adopted the Tariff Act of 1816, which levied high duties on manufactured goods shipped into the United States. The new tariff was designed to protect America's so-called infant industries.

In 1816 most Americans favored the protective tariff. Even Thomas Jefferson, who had earlier opposed the protective tariff recommended by Hamilton, now believed the Tariff Act of 1816 was desirable. John C. Calhoun of South Carolina, who later became an arch foe of tariffs, supported the Tariff Act of 1816, assuming that the South would develop industries of its own. In protecting its infant industries, the young nation was looking forward to becoming self-sufficient and economically independent of England.

SECTION SURVEY

IDENTIFY: American System, "dumping"; Henry Clay, John C. Calhoun, Daniel Webster, James Monroe.

1. Why was the period from about 1817 to 1825 known as the "Era of Good Feelings"?
2. (a) What were the three major foundations of the American System? (b) How did each of these promote national unity?
3. By 1816 what conditions forced the Republicans to use the "loose interpretation" of the Constitution earlier favored by Hamilton and the Federalists?
4. (a) What is the function of a protective tariff? (b) Did all the sections or regions of the United States favor one in 1816? Why or why not?

3 The growing nation's struggles with new and complex problems

The new nation was growing by leaps and bounds. Soon after the Constitution went into effect, four new states were added to the original thirteen—Vermont (1791), Kentucky (1792), Tennessee (1796), and Ohio (1803). Between 1810 and 1820 the population west of the mountains more than doubled, from about 1 million to more than 2 million, and five new states entered the Union—Louisiana (1812), Indiana (1816), Mississippi (1817), Illinois (1818), and Alabama (1819).

Demand for better transportation. Until shortly after the War of 1812, the western settlers depended almost entirely upon the rivers or upon very poor roads for transportation. Using flatboats or rafts, they shipped their surplus products down the Ohio and other rivers into the Mississippi, then down the Mississippi to New Orleans.

But the westerners could not use flatboats or rafts to transport manufactured goods upriver. Keelboats, invented for this purpose, were laborious and slow. As a result, most manufactured products from the eastern areas reached the western lands by means of rough roads across the mountains. Transporting goods by wagon over these roads was costly and time-consuming.

The building of a good transportation system was as essential to the new nation as a good Constitution and a strong federal government. Westerners needed roads and canals to carry their products to eastern markets. Northeastern manufacturers needed roads and canals to move their manufactured goods into the sparsely settled areas of the country. And southerners were also interested in improving transportation. As John C. Calhoun of South Carolina put it, "We are greatly and rapidly —I was about to say fearfully—growing. This is our pride and our danger, our weakness and our strength. . . . Let us, then, bind the republic together with a perfect system of roads and canals."

First steps by private enterprise. The need for better transportation had long been apparent. During the 1790's and early 1800's businessmen throughout the country organized private companies to build roads and canals. The first important road project, begun in 1791, was the building of the Lancaster Turnpike between Philadelphia and Lancaster, Pennsylvania (see map, page 287). Soon roads were being built in other states. By

1811 New York, for example, had granted 137 charters to private companies, and businessmen had built more than 1,400 miles of improved *toll roads* in New York state alone. These toll roads were private roads charging a fee, or toll, to those who used them.

Nearly all of the new roads and canals built by the early 1800's started in the coastal cities—Boston, New York, Philadelphia, Baltimore, Charleston—and ran into the surrounding country. These new roads and canals, financed by private companies, helped to meet the demand for improved transportation in the coastal areas. But the improved roads and canals did not run into sparsely settled regions. None ran through the Appalachian Mountains. Businessmen did not want to spend their money to build a transportation system in thinly populated areas. They feared that the risks were too great and the profits too small.

Improvements at public expense. This situation prompted a growing number of citizens to demand that the federal government finance and build the needed highways and canals. During President Jefferson's administration Albert Gallatin, Secretary of the Treasury, proposed that the federal government construct a network of highways covering the entire United States. Congress did not adopt Gallatin's ambitious proposal. It did, however, appropriate money in 1806 for building a road from

LIVING AMERICAN DOCUMENTS

McCulloch v. Maryland (1819)

The power to tax involves the power to destroy.... If the states may tax one instrument, employed by the [federal] government in the execution of its powers, they may tax any and every other instrument. They may tax the mail; they may tax the mint; they may tax patent rights; they may tax the papers of the customhouse; they may tax judicial process; they may tax all the means employed by the government, to an excess which would defeat all the ends of government. This was not intended by the American people. They did not design to make their government dependent on the states....

The question is, in truth, a question of supremacy; and if the right of the states to tax the means employed by the general government be conceded, the declaration that the Constitution, and the laws made in pursuance thereof, shall be the supreme law of the land, is empty and unmeaning declamation....

Cumberland, Maryland, across the mountains into what is now West Virginia.

Construction began in 1811. Within a few years this road, called the Cumberland Road or the National Road, was pushed westward from Cumberland as far as Ohio. Later, between 1822 and 1838, because of additional grants of money from Congress, the National Road was extended across Ohio and Indiana to Vandalia, Illinois—(see map, page 287). As each section was finished, the federal government turned it over to the states through which it ran. Thousands of settlers poured into the western country over the National Road, particularly after the War of 1812.

In 1816, with the National Road progressing westward, John C. Calhoun introduced in Congress the so-called Bonus Bill. This bill asked that additional "internal improvements" be made at government expense. Calhoun's plan was approved by Congress early in 1817. But President Madison objected. He vetoed the Bonus Bill, not because he disapproved of internal improvements, but because he felt that the Constitution did not give Congress the power to spend money in this way. President Monroe shared Madison's convictions, and Congress abandoned plans for further internal improvements at public expense.

Even so, the economic program adopted by Congress during Madison's administration had accomplished a great deal. It had set up a national bank that provided Americans with a reasonably sound currency. It had given the manufacturers a protective tariff. It had helped to open up the western areas by pushing the National Road farther westward. In general, it had strengthened the different sections and had drawn them closer together.

The Panic of 1819. By 1818 all sections of the country were enjoying prosperity. Conditions were so prosperous, in fact, that various groups began to indulge in *overspeculation,* or excessive, risky investment in land, stock, or commodities, in the hope of making large profits. Southerners, tempted by rising prices for cotton, bought land at exorbitant prices. Western settlers, tempted by rising prices for grain and meat, also scrambled to buy land. Manufacturers in the northeastern states, eager to take advantage of the general prosperity, bought land and built new plants and factories.

All of these groups were borrowing money to finance their enterprises. And many banks encouraged the frenzy of speculation by lending money too freely on the flimsiest security.

Then came the crash. Late in 1818 the directors

■ The nation's need for good roads increased steadily as settlers traveled farther and farther westward. The painting above shows Mormon pioneers making their way to Utah in the 1850's.

of the Bank of the United States ordered all their branch banks not to renew any personal mortgages. The directors also ordered the branch banks to present all state bank notes to the state banks for immediate payment in gold or silver or in national bank notes. State banks could not meet their obligations. They closed their doors. Farmers and manufacturers could not renew their mortgages. They lost their property.

By mid-1819, because of numerous foreclosures, the Bank of the United States had acquired huge areas of land in the South and West and many businesses in the East. People ruined by foreclosure blamed the bank for their troubles and called it "The Monster."

Increased federal power. In the midst of the financial panic, Chief Justice Marshall of the Supreme Court handed down one of his most important decisions in the case of *McCulloch v. Maryland*. The Maryland state legislature had attempted to tax the Baltimore branch of the Bank of the United States. When the bank refused to pay the tax to Maryland, the case went first to the state

Court of Appeals and finally to the Supreme Court.

Three major issues were involved: (1) Who has sovereign power—the federal government or the state governments? (2) Does the Constitution give Congress power to create a national bank? (3) If Congress does have this power, does the state have the right to tax the bank?

In 1819 Marshall decided all these issues in favor of the federal government. Referring to the first point, he declared that "The government of the Union, then . . . is emphatically and truly a government of the people." Thus, concluded Marshall, since the federal government was created by the people, not by the states, the power of the federal government was supreme.

Referring to the second point, Marshall admitted that the Constitution did not specifically give Congress the power to create a bank. But, he went on to say, the Constitution did give Congress the right to do whatever was "necessary and proper" to carry out any of its specific powers. Thus, reasoned Marshall, since Congress had the power to levy and collect taxes and to borrow money, it also had the

255

Fairview Inn on the National Road

WESTWARD ON THE NATIONAL ROAD

In the spring of 1817 Morris Birkbeck, an Englishman, started westward on the National Road. During his travels Birkbeck recorded the following observations of American transportation in the 1800's.

"So here we are," he wrote in his journal, "nine in number, one hundred and thirty miles of mountain country between us and Pittsburgh. We learn that the stages which pass daily from Philadelphia and Baltimore are generally full and that there are now many persons at Baltimore waiting for places. No vehicles of any kind are to be hired, and here we must either stay or *walk* off. The latter we prefer, and separating each our bundle from the little that we have of traveling stores, we are about to

undertake our mountain pilgrimage—accepting the alternative most cheerfully after the dreadful shaking of the last hundred miles by stage....

"Old America seems to be breaking up and moving westward. We are seldom out of sight, as we travel on this grand track toward the Ohio, of family groups, behind and before us....

"To give an idea of the internal movements of this vast hive, about twelve thousand wagons passed between Baltimore and Philadelphia and this place [near Pittsburgh] in the last year.... Add to these the numerous stages, loaded to the utmost, and the innumerable travelers on horseback, on foot, and in light wagons, and you have before you a scene of bustle and business...which is truly wonderful."

right to create a national bank to carry out these financial powers.

Referring to the third point, Marshall declared that "the power to tax involves the power to destroy." If a state had the power to tax a national institution such as the Bank of the United States, it could severely weaken or destroy federal power. Therefore, Marshall stated, neither Maryland nor any other state had the right to tax the Bank of the United States.

Marshall's continuing influence. In 1819, the same year of his famous ruling in the case of *McCulloch v. Maryland,* Marshall wrote another decision of far-reaching consequences. In the case of

Trustees of Dartmouth College v. Woodward, Marshall set aside an act of the state legislature of New Hampshire. The original charter of Dartmouth College had been granted by George III in 1769. In 1816 the New Hampshire legislature passed a law altering this charter. The Dartmouth College trustees claimed that the new law was unconstitutional. When the case came before the Supreme Court, John Marshall supported the trustees. Marshall pointed out that a charter was a valid contract guaranteed by the Constitution. Thus, no state had the power to interfere with such a contract.

This decision was important for two reasons. First, it asserted the right of the Supreme Court to set aside state laws when such laws were unconstitutional. Second, it guaranteed that corporations operating under state charters would not be subject to the whims of state legislators. For this reason, the Dartmouth College case is sometimes called the "Magna Carta" of the corporation.

Five years later, in 1824, in the case of *Gibbons v. Ogden,* Marshall declared another state law unconstitutional. The case involved an attempt by the New York legislature to give Robert Fulton and his business associates a monopoly over all steamboat traffic on the Hudson River. Marshall argued that the Constitution had given the federal government the power to regulate interstate commerce. Since navigation on the Hudson River involved interstate commerce, the state had no right to grant a monopoly. The monopoly granted by the state legislature was therefore unconstitutional.

Marshall's argument greatly broadened the definition of interstate commerce. His decision thus paved the way for later federal control of such "interstate commerce" as telegraph, telephone, radio, and television, as well as kidnaping and car theft if the criminals crossed state lines.

John Marshall's decisions did much to strengthen the powers of the federal government. While Congress through the American System was seeking to build a stronger, more unified nation, Marshall on the Supreme Court bench was moving toward the same goal.

Rifts in the spirit of unity. Much bitterness grew out of the Panic of 1819 and was directed especially against "The Monster," the Bank of the United States. As you will see later, this bitterness helped to bring about upheavals that by 1829 put Andrew Jackson, representative of the newer areas of the country, into the White House. And, as you will also see later, differences over the question of slavery and the admission of Missouri into the Union hung like a dark cloud over the nation.

The Jacksonian upheavals and the issue concerning Missouri are discussed in later chapters. It is necessary now to see how the United States, through the Monroe Doctrine, asserted its growing power in foreign affairs.

SECTION SURVEY

IDENTIFY: toll road (turnpike), overspeculation, interstate commerce, Bonus Bill, National Road.

1. Because of geography, Americans had need for better transportation. Explain this statement as it applies to (a) westerners, (b) northeastern manufacturers, (c) southerners.

2. (a) What caused the Panic of 1819? (b) Why did many people blame the Bank of the United States for their troubles?
3. State specifically the constitutional arguments of Chief Justice Marshall that helped to strengthen the federal government.
4. What does the picture of the Fairview Inn on page 256 tell you about American life at this time and place?

4 The nation's role as guardian of the Western Hemisphere

After the War of 1812, as you have seen, the growing spirit of national pride and the growing fact of national power began to have a strong influence on developments within the United States. These new feelings of pride and strength also influenced American foreign policy.

At this time, the people of Latin America were struggling to win their independence from Spain and Portugal. Americans were deeply interested in the revolutions taking place in the lands to the south of the United States.

Revolutions in Latin America. In the early 1800's, as you know, Napoleon was trying to secure mastery over all of Europe. In 1808 he conquered Spain. This was the signal for Latin Americans to rise in revolt.

The enormous South American continent is broken into fragments by mighty mountain barriers, such as the Andes, and by dense rain forests, such as those of the Amazon River Valley. As a result, the Latin-American struggle for independence took place in a number of separate revolutions (see map, page 259).

The Latin-American armies, separated though they were, all fought for essentially the same objectives: freedom and independence.

By 1822 the American continents were almost free of foreign control. Russia still claimed the vast unexplored territory of Alaska. Great Britain still ruled Canada, British Honduras, British Guiana (gee·AHN·ah), and a number of West Indian islands. Spain still ruled Cuba and Puerto Rico. France and the Netherlands still ruled French and Dutch Guiana and several of the islands in the Caribbean. But Europeans were on their way out. The growing forces of democracy and the drive toward national independence were remaking the map. These independence movements also struck a massive blow at slavery in Latin America. The institution persisted only in Cuba and Brazil.

American control of Florida. The revolutions in Mexico and other Latin-American countries greatly affected the United States. Many Americans viewed the struggle of their Latin-American neighbors as a continuation of their own earlier struggle for independence. Some of them supplied the revolutionists with arms in spite of repeated Spanish and Portuguese protests. Other Americans saw in the conflicts an opportunity to settle long-standing border disputes with Spain and to win additional territory for the United States.

The American government officially took a position of neutrality in the conflicts between Spain and Portugal, on the one hand, and their colonies, on the other. However, between 1810 and 1813 the United States annexed the territory known as West Florida (see map, page 856). Spain protested, but was powerless to act.

A few years later, in 1818, Andrew Jackson and an American military force, hotly pursuing a group of marauding Seminole Indians, invaded East Florida. Acting on his own and without orders from the United States government, Jackson seized two Spanish forts, and hanged two men accused of giving arms to the Indians. Once again the Spaniards, deeply involved in their troubles in Latin America,

■ Osceola, a leader of the Seminole Indians, led his people in a long war against the United States government. The war began in 1835 when the Seminoles refused to sign a treaty giving up their land in Florida.

were powerless to act. But Jackson's invasion convinced Spain that the United States would not rest until all of Florida was under the Stars and Stripes. Spain decided to sell while it still held the territory.

In 1819 the two countries signed the Adams-Onís Treaty, giving the United States all the land east of the Mississippi River, together with any claims that Spain might have to the Oregon country (see map, page 857). In return the United States agreed to assume claims totaling $5 million that American citizens held against Spain for damages to American shipping during the Napoleonic Wars. More important in the long run was the agreement by the United States to abandon its claim to Texas as part of the Louisiana Purchase.°

British support of the revolutions. Great Britain favored the revolutionists of Latin America. The British, like many United States citizens, were looking forward to an increasingly profitable trade with a Latin America no longer tied economically to Spain and Portugal. They were determined to retain the trade of Latin America, which, since the start of the revolutions, had been carried largely in British ships. If the Spanish colonies were restored to Spain, British merchants would lose the profitable Spanish-American trade.

European interference. Other nations did not join the British and the Americans in supporting the Latin American revolutions. Until 1815, when Napoleon was finally defeated at the Battle of Waterloo, the European nations were too occupied with their own problems to take an active part in Latin American affairs. With the fall of Napoleon and the breakup of his once mighty empire, however, Russia, Prussia, Austria, and Great Britain organized an alliance to preserve the peace of Europe, calling it the Quadruple Alliance. Later, when the continental members pledged to crush democratic revolutions in Europe, Great Britain withdrew.

As long as the Quadruple Alliance (often mistakenly called the "Holy Alliance") confined its activities to the Old World, it aroused no concern in the United States. But when it began to talk of restoring the former Spanish colonies to Spain, Americans became concerned.

To make matters worse, in 1821 the tsar of Russia warned the vessels of other nations to avoid the Pacific coast from Alaska southward to the 51st

---

° The southwestern boundary of the United States at this time was placed along the Sabine River, from its headwaters north and west to the 42nd parallel, and along the 42nd parallel to the Pacific (see map, pages 856–57).

GREAT BRITAIN

FRANCE

PORTUGAL

SPAIN

AFRICA

CANADA (BR.)

ATLANTIC OCEAN

UNITED STATES, 1776

PROTECTED UNDER THE MONROE DOCTRINE, 1823

PACIFIC

MEXICO, 1821

CUBA

SANTO DOMINGO, 1821

HAITI, 1804

PUERTO RICO

(BR. AND FR.)

(BR.)

CENTRAL AMERICA, 1821

VENEZUELA, 1811

GUIANAS

COLOMBIA, 1819

ECUADOR, 1822

BRAZIL, 1822

PERU, 1824

BOLIVIA, 1825

PARAGUAY, 1811

OCEAN

CHILE, 1818

URUGUAY, 1825

ARGENTINA, 1816

Liberated countries

Present-day boundaries

Countries under foreign control

1776 Dates of declarations of independence

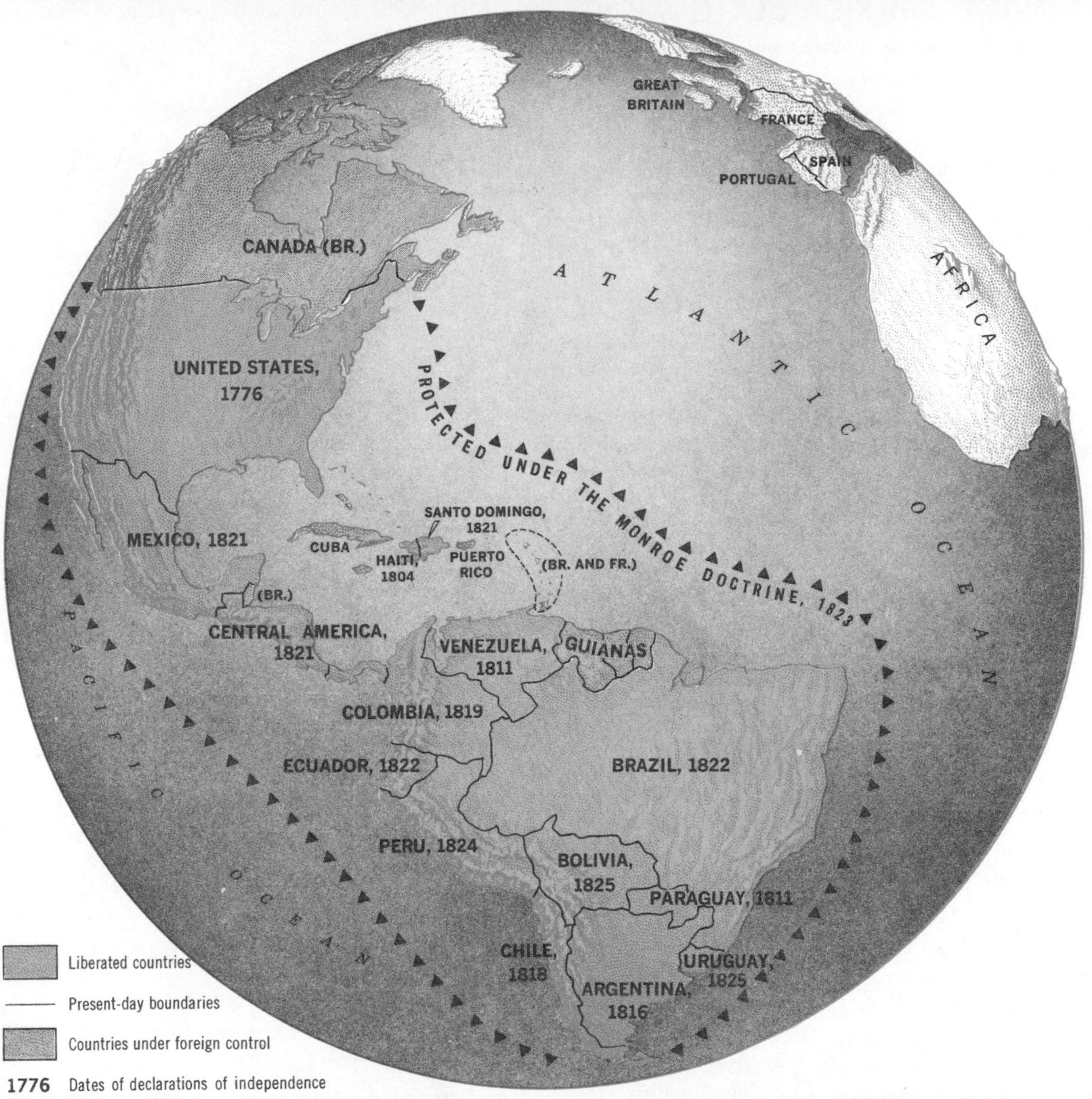

parallel. This order barred American vessels from the Oregon coast, which the United States claimed jointly with Great Britain. The Oregon country was already a useful port of call for Yankee traders, who traded trinkets to the Indians in exchange for valuable furs. Russia was also establishing trading posts along the coast of northern California.

For these reasons the American government did not permit the tsar's order to go unchallenged.

America's reply: the Monroe Doctrine. The United States met the challenge of the Quadruple Alliance and of the Russian threat by three specific actions. First, Secretary of State John Quincy Adams addressed a strong note of protest to Rus-

LIVING AMERICAN DOCUMENTS

Monroe Doctrine (1823)

The American continents ... are henceforth not to be considered as subjects for future colonization by any European powers.... We owe it, therefore, to candor and to the amicable relations existing between the United States and those powers [Quadruple Alliance] to declare that we should consider any attempt on their part to extend their system to any portion of this hemisphere as dangerous to our peace and safety. With the existing colonies or dependencies of any European power, we have not interfered and shall not interfere. But with the governments who have declared their independence and maintained it, and whose independence we have ... acknowledged, we could not view any interposition for the purpose of oppressing them, or controlling in any other manner their destiny, by any European power in any other light than as the manifestation of an unfriendly disposition toward the United States....

Our policy in regard to Europe, which was adopted at an early stage of the wars which have so long agitated that quarter of the globe, nevertheless remains the same, which is, not to interfere in the internal concerns of any of its powers....

---

sia, bluntly asserting American rights to sail the Pacific waters. Second, the United States recognized the independence of the revolutionary governments of Latin America. Third, President Monroe, in his annual message to Congress delivered on December 2, 1823, announced an American foreign policy that came to be known as the Monroe Doctrine. The Monroe Doctrine was actually an extension of the policy started by Washington in his Farewell Address and by Jefferson in his statements on foreign policy.

In this famous message President Monroe made four clear declarations: (1) The Western Hemisphere was no longer open to colonization by European powers. (2) Any attempt by any European country to establish colonies in the New World or to gain political control of any American country would be viewed as an unfriendly act toward the United States. (3) The United States would not interfere in European affairs or in the affairs of American colonies already established. (4) In return, Europe must not in any way disturb the political status of any free country in the Western Hemisphere.

Enforcing the Doctrine. With the Monroe Doctrine the United States proclaimed a policy of "America for Americans." The important question, of course, was whether the United States could enforce the Monroe Doctrine.

Fortunately, the United States was supported by Latin Americans to the south, as well as by Great Britain. Although Latin Americans knew that the United States was acting in its own self-interest, they realized that the Monroe Doctrine practically guaranteed their independence from Europe.

Great Britain gave the Doctrine its real strength. In 1823 and, in fact, until well into the 1900's, the British navy controlled the Atlantic sea lanes. Only with British consent could ships of any nation, including United States vessels, move between Europe and the Americas. Americans were fortunate that British merchants were keenly interested in preserving the independence of the countries of Central and South America. At the first hint of interference from the continental powers, Great Britain sided with the Americas.

Significance of the Doctrine. The Monroe Doctrine was a direct warning to the European powers that the United States was vitally concerned in the affairs of all the nations in North, Central, and South America. The Doctrine became a cornerstone of United States foreign policy.

The Monroe Doctrine also revealed the growing spirit of American strength and unity. President Monroe spoke for a united people of more than 10 million citizens. He spoke for a nation that was becoming increasingly conscious of its own strength. He spoke for a nation that was determined to retain its hard-won independence from Europe and to decide its own policies.

SECTION SURVEY

IDENTIFY: Monroe Doctrine, Adams-Onís Treaty, tsar; 1823.

1. Describe how the United States acquired all of Florida.
2. How did the following lead to the Monroe Doctrine: (a) revolutions in Latin America, (b) American foreign policy, (c) business reasons, (d) the Quadruple Alliance?
3. (a) What were the provisions of the Monroe Doctrine? (b) How did this policy reflect growing feelings of American pride and strength? (c) Upon what would enforcement of the Doctrine depend? Why?
4. Does the United States follow a policy of "America for Americans" today? Explain.

5 The expression of national pride in American education and arts

In developing the American System, Americans revealed their intention of becoming *economically* independent of Europe. With the Monroe Doctrine Americans declared their complete *political* independence from Europe. Both these developments were long steps forward in the new nation's growth. So, too, was another development which is apt to go unnoticed because of its less dramatic form.

This third step in the nation's growth was the development of truly American religion, education, art, and literature. With this new development, the United States began to become less *culturally* dependent on Europe.

After the American Revolution, American Protestant churches severed their close ties with church authorities in Europe. And many, though not all, educators, artists, and writers of this period revealed in their work the growing spirit of *nationalism,* or national pride. These men helped to unite the nation fully as much as the businessmen and the political leaders who were working for economic and political independence.

A national university proposed. Pride in their new nation prompted some Americans to speak out in favor of a national university. Many Americans shared the view of George Washington that a national university would help to train people for public service, as well as provide the nation with a growing body of educated citizens. During the early years of the country's history, this proposal received considerable support. John Quincy Adams, who became President in 1825, was only one of many men who tried, although unsuccessfully, to establish such an institution.

Noah Webster—author and educator. Another illustration of the growing spirit of independence was Noah Webster's project for molding a national "American" language, distinct from English. "America," Webster had declared in 1783, "must be as independent in *literature* as she is in *politics,* as famous for *arts as for arms."* With this in mind, Webster labored at the tremendous task of publishing a dictionary—*An American Dictionary of the English Language*—in which the British spelling of many words was simplified. When his dictionary was finally published in 1828, Webster hoped that it would help Americans to achieve a uniform language.

Webster also prepared a spelling book. Published as early as 1783, it was used in nearly every elementary school in America. By the time Webster died in 1843, more than 15 million copies had been sold, and nearly 100 million copies were sold before the book went out of general use. Like the dictionary, the spelling book helped Americans develop a uniform national language.

American history and geography. In addition to his work on the dictionary and the spelling book, Webster edited a famous school reader, *An American Selection of Lessons in Reading and Speaking.* Hoping to arouse a spirit of national pride as well as a reverence for American heroes, Webster devoted more than half of his school reader to material from American history. Webster later wrote other books entirely concerned with American history.

Meanwhile another scholar, Jedidiah Morse, was introducing American youth to the geography of their country. Morse, like Webster, wanted to teach American history, and his geographies were largely devoted to the story of American life.

Books for the study of the nation's history were prepared by a number of other writers. Before the "Era of Good Feelings" ended, the study of American history had become an accepted part of the curriculum of many American elementary schools.

■ America's political independence from Europe was a long step forward in the new nation's growth. Below, citizens gather to vote in Philadelphia's Independence Hall on election day in 1815.

■ Benjamin Banneker, a free Negro from Maryland, was a self-taught mathematician, astronomer, and almanac-maker. He played an important role in the surveying and planning of Washington, D.C., the nation's capital.

One indication of growing national pride was legislation passed in 1827 by Massachusetts and Vermont requiring all the larger schools in these states to teach American history.

The arts. During the early years of the nation's growth, a number of artists were also influenced by the spirit of nationalism. This influence showed in their work.

There were, for instance, the architects who designed the nation's capital. Although a French engineer, Major Pierre L'Enfant (lahn·FAHN), planned the city of Washington, L'Enfant was dismissed before work actually began because he was impossible to work with. L'Enfant left, taking his maps and drawings with him. Fortunately, however, one of L'Enfant's associates—Benjamin Banneker—was able to reproduce the plans from memory. Banneker, a free Negro from Maryland, was a self-taught mathematician, astronomer, and almanac-maker.

Other Americans also played a large part in the design and construction of the city of Washington. The versatile Thomas Jefferson, for example, proposed the locations of the Capitol and the White House. As the city of Washington grew, it helped give American citizens a feeling of permanence, a growing conviction that the new nation was solidly planted and destined to endure.

During this same period, such painters as Charles Willson Peale, Gilbert Stuart, and John Trumbull painted many portraits of the nation's leaders. Although these painters lacked sufficient originality and skill to be great artists, their portraits helped to make the nation's founders known to many Americans.

Writers. During the early 1800's some writers began to draw upon the American environment for the material in their stories. Some, like Mason Locke Weems, better known as Parson Weems, who published a biography of the first President of the United States, wrote in glowing terms about the fathers of the nation.

Other writers, among them Washington Irving and James Fenimore Cooper, began to write about America itself. Irving turned chiefly to the Dutch society of the Hudson Valley, producing such works as "The Legend of Sleepy Hollow," "Rip Van Winkle," and the *Knickerbocker History of New York*. In his early novels Cooper turned to the Indians and the frontier. The *Leatherstocking Tales*, a series of novels, are only a few of the books that he produced.

A new feeling of unity. National unity, or nationalism, was one of the forces that helped to shape American life during the first 30 or more years of the nation's history. This national pride stimulated rich and poor alike in all sections of the country. It stimulated the frontiersmen cutting their way through the forests, the businessmen in the growing cities, and the statesmen in Washington. It stimulated educators, artists, and writers as well as the men, women, and children who listened to their ideas and read their books and looked at their paintings. Thus, the new nation became stronger and more unified as the years went by.

SECTION SURVEY

IDENTIFY: nationalism; Benjamin Banneker, Gilbert Stuart, Parson Weems.

1. What contributions were made to American education and American nationalism by (a) Noah Webster, (b) Jedidiah Morse?
2. How did American architects, painters, and writers in the early 1800's contribute to rising American nationalism?
3. How did the writers of this period reflect faith in the free individual and in democracy?

TRACING THE MAIN IDEAS

The desire for independence and for national unity reached a peak in the United States during the decade following the War of 1812. Because Americans were so united in their efforts to strengthen the new nation, the period from about 1817 to 1825 was called the "Era of Good Feelings."

During the "Era of Good Feelings," Americans from all walks of life worked to make their nation strong and independent. Congress, supported by many businessmen and farmers, adopted the so-called American System. This system was designed to make the United States self-sufficient and *economically* independent of Europe. It consisted of a national bank to provide a sound financial system, a high tariff to protect American industry, and a national transportation system to connect the East and the West.

Meanwhile, through the Monroe Doctrine, President Monroe and his advisers took steps to make the United States politically independent of Europe. Through the Monroe Doctrine, the United States asserted its growing power in foreign affairs.

During these same years, educators, artists, and writers were devoting their efforts to American themes and heroes, thus helping to make the United States less dependent *culturally* on Europe.

But the "Era of Good Feelings" was soon to end. Beneath the surface forces of division were at work. The new nation shortly was to be split by sectional controversy that would finally plunge it into four terrible years of warfare.

Before turning to the story of sectional controversy, however, it is necessary to look at another important development—the growing democratic spirit in the United States. During the years that the American people were building a new nation, they were also strengthening the spirit and practices of democracy. This is the story told in the next chapter.

CHAPTER SURVEY

QUESTIONS FOR DISCUSSION

1. Explain how each of the following contributed to the growth of industry: (a) trade restrictions and the War of 1812, (b) the shortage of labor, (c) the government.
2. Explain how each of the following revealed the growing spirit of nationalism: (a) the American System, (b) Supreme Court decisions, (c) Webster's dictionary, (d) use of the bald eagle emblem on American coins.
3. Because of America's location, the nation could remain isolated enough from European affairs to concentrate on its own internal development during the period just studied. Explain.
4. Why was the development of the nation largely dependent on the growth of its transportation system?
5. As political situations change, ideas and attitudes held by political parties also change. In what instances during the period just studied did the Republicans adopt positions previously held by the Federalists?

RELATING PAST TO PRESENT

1. Study the excerpt from *Living American Documents* on page 260. Which of the ideas put forth in the Monroe Doctrine are still important today? Name some recent world incidents that have caused the United States to apply ideas expressed in the Monroe Doctrine.
2. Study the pictures on pages 247 and 250 and compare the sources of power with those of today.
3. Can isolationism achieve peace in today's world? Why or why not?
4. How is today's interstate highway system the fulfillment of the proposal put forth by Albert Gallatin during the Jefferson administration? Does Gallatin's reasoning still apply?

USING MAPS AND CHARTS

1. Referring to chart 1 on pages 866–67, summarize the factors that contributed to the start of the Industrial Revolution in the United States.
2. Using chart 4 on page 873, compare the tariffs of 1789 and 1816. Explain the difference in rates.
3. Refer to the map on page 259. (a) Describe the events that led President Monroe to formulate the Monroe Doctrine. (b) According to the Monroe Doctrine, which areas in the Western Hemisphere could remain under foreign control?

■ A rural court in the 1840's

CHAPTER 13

The Nation's Growing Democratic Strength

1825 – 1845

W HAT IS *democracy?* Abraham Lincoln partly defined it when he referred to "government of the people, by the people, for the people." The right of every qualified person to vote and hold office—that is, to participate in his own government—is sometimes called *political* democracy.

But we know that there is more than this to democracy. We sometimes speak of *economic* and *social* democracy, that is, a society in which all people have an equal opportunity to gain an education, to choose the careers they want, and to live from day to day as free men, equal in the eyes of the law to all their neighbors.

This larger conception of democracy had begun to develop roots in the early years of America's history. For most Americans, however, democracy remained a sharply limited concept. The noble words of the Declaration of Independence—"all men are created equal"—did not yet apply to black Americans, to American Indians, or to other minority groups.

Even political democracy was limited in the early years. When the Constitution was adopted, the right to vote and to hold public office was restricted in varying degrees in different states.

During the early years of the nation's history, however, political democracy made increasing gains. By the late 1820's many of the earlier voting restrictions on white, male adults had been removed, and in 1828 political democracy scored a major victory with the election of Andrew Jackson as President.

THE CHAPTER IN OUTLINE

1. Emergence of Andrew Jackson as "the people's choice."

2. The increasing role of Americans in government.

3. Jackson's active role in dealing with national problems.

4. Economic depression at the end of the Jacksonian era.

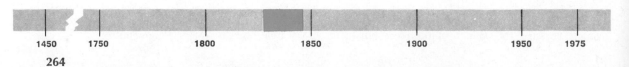

| 1450 | 1750 | 1800 | 1850 | 1900 | 1950 | 1975 |

1 Emergence of Andrew Jackson as "the people's choice"

By 1824 the "Era of Good Feelings" was drawing to a close. The Republican Party and the American public were increasingly divided. The growing power of the ordinary people, as well as the rivalry among the major sections of the country, was clearly revealed in the political struggles from 1824 to 1828. During these years the Democratic Party —the same party that bears that name today— began to take shape.

The election of 1824. In 1824 four men ran for the Presidency, and all four called themselves Republicans. At least three were *favorite son°* candidates, nominated to represent different sections of the country. John Quincy Adams of Massachusetts—the son of John Adams, the second President—represented the northeastern states. William H. Crawford of Georgia represented the southern states. Andrew Jackson of Tennessee represented the western states. Henry Clay thought of himself as a national leader, although he came from Kentucky, then a "western" state.

Of the four candidates Henry Clay had the most definite program. Clay urged support for the American System that he had done so much to develop. In the American System, as you have seen, Clay and other leaders in Congress tried to serve, and at the same time to balance, the interests of the different sections of the country. Even in these early years of his career, Clay was beginning to establish himself as "the Great Compromiser"—a role he was to play many times in the years ahead. Crawford and Jackson hedged on most specific issues, including the tariff and the development of roads.

When the electoral votes were counted, Jackson had 99, Adams had 84, Crawford had 41, and Clay had only 37. No one candidate had the 131-vote majority needed for election. In such a situation, according to the Twelfth Amendment to the Constitution, the House of Representatives had to choose the President from the top three candidates. Clay, who was automatically eliminated, being the fourth candidate, persuaded his followers in the House to vote for Adams. With Clay's support, Adams won. John C. Calhoun of South Carolina became Vice-President.

° *favorite son:* In current usage, the term usually refers to a candidate placed in nomination on the first ballot by his state's delegation—as an honor, but with little chance of being nominated.

Jackson against Adams. The new President, John Quincy Adams, appointed Henry Clay as his Secretary of State. Jackson and his followers claimed that this was part of a "corrupt bargain." They maintained that Clay had supported Adams in exchange for the top post in the cabinet.

The charge of a "corrupt bargain" was false. Both Clay and Adams had done what they thought was best for the country. But Jackson believed that the charges were true. He was especially bitter because he had won the largest number of electoral votes.

Jackson was so angry that he resigned from the Senate in 1825 and launched a vigorous campaign to become President in 1828. During this three-year battle, both Adams and Jackson called themselves Republicans. Adams, however, referred to himself as a National-Republican, while Jackson called himself a Democratic-Republican.

As the months passed, some of Jackson's supporters, including Vice-President Calhoun, began to call themselves Democrats. In those days the word "Democrat" was a radical term. Jackson avoided it publicly, although he used it often in private. By the 1830's, however, Jackson's party was officially calling itself the Democratic Party. Jackson's opponents organized the Whig Party in 1834, taking their name from the old Whig Party in England which had opposed the tyranny of George III. For the next 20 years the Democrats and Whigs were the two major political parties in the country.

The election of 1828. By 1828 most white adult male citizens had won the right to vote. Many of these new voters considered Jackson to be their leader. They made much of the fact that he had been born in a log cabin and had risen by his own efforts.

In the election of 1828 Jackson won a sweeping victory over Adams. Jackson won every state west of the Appalachian Mountains and south of the Potomac River. He also won in Pennsylvania and New York. John C. Calhoun was re-elected as Vice-President.

Americans differed violently in their reactions to the election. Because the votes of average people had figured decisively in an election for the first time, many wealthy and powerful Americans, including President Adams, felt that "King Mob" had triumphed.

Other Americans were jubilant. They believed that democracy had finally triumphed, and that the ordinary people were entering a new era.

■ Crowds of people overran the White House during Jackson's inaugural celebration. The wild scene led some observers to believe that "King Mob" had replaced law and order in America.

Jackson's first inauguration. On March 4, 1829, political democracy celebrated its greatest victory up to that time. Everywhere many rank and file Americans rejoiced at Jackson's victory. As one writer said, "It was the people's day, and the people's President, and the people would rule." The nation's tiny capital on the banks of the Potomac was jammed with 10,000 visitors. "A monstrous crowd of people is in the city," Daniel Webster wrote. "I never saw anything like it before. Persons have come five hundred miles to see General Jackson, and they really seem to think that the country is rescued from some dreadful danger."

The inaugural celebration was itself a symbol of a new era. After his Inaugural Address the new President held open house in the Executive Mansion—the White House. Jackson's followers jammed in to greet him. Men with muddy boots climbed on chairs and tables to get a better view, furniture was broken, trays of food were knocked over, fights broke out, and women fainted.

The President himself narrowly escaped injury from the excited crowd, and had to flee from the mansion. The crowd was finally dispersed by placing tubs of punch and other refreshments on the lawns of the White House. Dignified citizens watching the scene with horror feared that "King Mob" had replaced law and order in America.

Jackson the man.   What was he like, this man who aroused such conflicting emotions?

Born on the Carolina frontier in 1767, Jackson was the son of immigrant parents from northern Ireland. He grew up without formal schooling. Like many other Americans, he moved westward with the advancing line of settlement. Like most of them, he was honest and hard-working.

Jackson's opponents made fun of him, claiming that he could not spell, that he told rough stories, chewed tobacco, and wore strange-looking "backwoods" clothes. Whether or not these claims were ever true, they certainly did not apply to Jackson's later life. When he became a wealthy planter and a famous American hero, Jackson cultivated the manners of a gentleman. Tall and slender, with thick white hair, he was a distinguished-looking man. His followers often called him "Old Hickory."

Jackson's outlook and attitudes seem to have been the same as those of many ordinary white Americans. This was especially true of his attitude toward Negroes. Although his attitude was often contradictory, Jackson apparently was not aware of the contradictions. During the War of 1812, as you recall, he addressed "free men of color," praising them for their courage, patriotism, and valor. Yet later, as a slaveowner and national leader, he wrote letters to his son expressing different, very unfavorable, opinions about slaves. However, on at least one occasion he instructed that "My Negroes shall be treated humanely."

Jackson's attitude toward the Indians was also contradictory. Before becoming President, he had won a reputation as an Indian fighter. In ruthless, hard fighting, Jackson had defeated the Creek Indians in Mississippi and Alabama and the Seminoles in Florida.

Jackson respected the Indian military leaders and honored them in defeat. But at other times, like most white Americans, he regarded the Indians as childish, inefficient, incapable of "improvement," and altogether inferior.

Significance of the 1828 election.   Jackson's triumph in the election of 1828 was largely the result of advancing democratic forces in America. Fundamental changes had clearly taken place since the days of President Washington and the Federalists. For one thing, political power was now more evenly divided between well-to-do people and people in average circumstances. Average people no longer stood in awe of leaders who, it had been

supposed, were especially qualified by birth and education to lead the nation. Before the inaguration of 1829, all the Presidents were men from wealthy backgrounds. Andrew Jackson, in contrast, had been born into poverty and had risen through his own efforts. He was identified with the hopes and ambitions of a majority of white Americans, who claimed him for their own.

In the second place, Jackson's election indicated that the western section of the country was a new force to be reckoned with in national politics. Andrew Jackson was from Tennessee. He was the first President from a state that did not border on the Atlantic. Now for the first time a frontiersman, a westerner, sat in the White House.

But Jackson's followers were not all westerners. Of course, many western frontiersmen had voted for him because he had been a frontiersman and had won fame as a vigorous Indian fighter. Frontiersmen felt that he would understand their problems. But some small farmers everywhere voted for him for the same reason. Many southern planters voted for him because, as a planter and slaveowner himself, he would understand their point of view. Some city workers as well as small businessmen voted for him because they believed he would help them to get the laws they wanted. Many small businessmen, fearful of the growth of big business organizations, wanted the opportunity to expand their own enterprises. They believed that Andrew Jackson, a self-made man, would help them to keep the doors of opportunity open.

Thus, with the support of a majority of ordinary white Americans, Andrew Jackson became President.

SECTION SURVEY

IDENTIFY: "favorite son" candidate, political democracy, "King Mob"; John Quincy Adams.

1. Explain the violently different reactions to Jackson's election in 1828.
2. Jackson was representative of "the people." (a) Who were "the people"? (b) In what ways did Jackson represent them?
3. (a) What was the significance of the election of 1828? (b) Why can it be called the "Revolution of 1828"?
4. In this period, if a man had been born in a log cabin, had risen by his own efforts, and had seen military service, he was regarded as an attractive political candidate. (a) Why? (b) Is this still true today? Explain.

2 The increasing role of Americans in government

Andrew Jackson, the new President, had no carefully developed political program. Yet despite his lack of a clear-cut program, Jackson, as President, held three firm convictions.

First, he believed in political democracy. He believed that the government belonged to all of the people who could vote, and he was determined that the majority must rule. Second, although Jackson believed that the powers of the federal government should be limited, he also believed in the Union—the United States as a whole. Thus, he believed that the new nation must be preserved at any cost. Third, Jackson believed in the power of the Presidency.

Extending the "spoils system." As one of his first steps, the President removed many of his political opponents from public (government) office and replaced them with his supporters. "No . . . rascal who made use of an office or its profits for the purpose of keeping Mr. Jackson out of power is entitled to the least leniency save that of hanging," cried one ardent Jacksonian.

Under the *spoils system,* as it came to be called, a victorious political party could dispose of public offices, giving them to party supporters, often without regard for their abilities or qualifications. The name "spoils system" came from the popular expression "to the victor belong the spoils." The spoils system had already become common in some northern and western states. It had also been used to some extent in the federal government, but Jackson applied it more vigorously than ever.

In general, Jackson removed those officeholders he suspected of having supported his political opponents. Older men, some but not all of them experienced and competent, were replaced by younger and often poorly qualified men. Although Jackson actually replaced only about one fifth of all federal officeholders, he established a precedent that later Presidents followed with drastic results.

Defending the spoils system. Jackson maintained that the spoils system actually improved the government. He claimed that one man was as good as another. "The duties of all public officers are, or at least admit of being made, so plain and simple that men of intelligence may readily qualify themselves for their performance," Jackson stated.

Jackson also believed that it was sound policy to keep changing officeholders. He felt that a man who remained too long in office became indifferent to the public welfare and forgot that he was a servant of the people.

Above all, Jackson believed that as many men as possible should have the opportunity to learn by experience how the government functioned. He felt that it was good democratic procedure to "rotate" the offices among as many men as possible. He maintained that the more people who held office, the more the government would be responsive to the changing needs of the people.

Jackson's policies brought politics into the range of the ordinary white citizen. Even a poor man could risk devoting his time to political activities if he could hope for a job as a reward for faithful service.

Defects of the spoils system. Because of Jackson's policies, however, political parties came to be led and supported by officeholders who were paid by the government. These officeholders also contributed a certain percentage of their salaries to maintain their political organizations.

The spoils system also encouraged many individuals to use the public payroll for their own gain, enriching themselves at the taxpayers' expense. As you will see later, the professional politician and the "city boss" were born during this period. Many professional politicians have labored unselfishly for the nation, but some have used their positions largely for self-interest, bringing discredit upon the American political system.

Andrew Jackson was not entirely responsible for these political abuses, but, by extending the spoils system, he helped to open the door through which such abuses entered national politics.

The start of nominating conventions. During Jackson's administration, political democracy gained an important victory with the increasing use of nominating conventions to choose candidates for federal office. Until this time, as you know, candidates for federal office had been selected by legislators gathered in closed meetings, or caucuses. The voters at large had enjoyed little if any voice in the nominating process. In the meantime, however, a different practice had been developing at the local level. Groups of voters, meeting in their own communities, chose delegates for county conventions, which in turn nominated men for county offices.

This practice gradually spread upward into state politics and eventually into national politics. By 1832 the present practice of nominating the President and Vice-President in nominating conventions had been established.

■ Jackson's Indian policy forced many eastern tribes to give up their land and move out West. The Cherokees, shown above, called their long, bitter journey "The Trail of Tears."

Jackson's "kitchen cabinet." Hoping to bring the government and the people closer together, Andrew Jackson surrounded himself with a group of unofficial advisers. Jackson's political enemies dubbed these advisers the "kitchen cabinet." The term was meant to imply that these advisers entered the White House by a back door and met with the President in secret.

Some members of the "kitchen cabinet" were newspaper editors. Recognizing the importance of friendly relations with the press, Jackson placed a number of prominent editors in public office. In return, they helped him to mold public opinion, to gain good publicity, and to win support for his policies.

Speaking for "the people." On most great issues of his time, Jackson tried to speak for the nation as a whole. Most other leaders spoke for their own section of the country. Of course, not all the people in each section of the country shared the same interests or agreed on all issues. Still, by 1830 the viewpoints of the three sections of the nation were becoming more sharply defined. Each section had its outstanding champion. Daniel Webster of Massachusetts represented the interests of the Northeast—the merchants, manufacturers, bankers, and men of property in general. John C. Calhoun of South Carolina was the spokesman for the planters of the South. Thomas Hart Benton of Missouri became the advocate of the West, especially of western farmers and land speculators, who wanted to secure cheap, or even free, public land. Henry Clay of Kentucky, the Great Compromiser, tried to find a formula for balancing the interests

269

of the three sections and, in the process, to become President.

Andrew Jackson seemed to speak for most ordinary white Americans everywhere. He placed himself, as he said, at the head of "the humbler members of society—the farmers, mechanics, and laborers" who had "neither the time nor the means" to secure for themselves the things that they wanted from the government.

Jackson's Indian policy. Like many other white Americans of his time, as you know, Jackson's attitudes toward people of other races were filled with contradictions. And his attitudes often affected his policies.

As an old Indian fighter and frontiersman, Jackson shared with other westerners the belief that the Indians were a threat. All along the frontier, people believed that the very existence of the Indians interfered with the "right" of white Americans to occupy the Indian homelands and put them to more productive use.

The process of uprooting the Indians had been going on for a long time. Many tribes had been persuaded, often by trickery, to give up their claims to ancestral lands and move across the Mississippi River into lands set aside for them by Congress. But sometimes the Indian resettlement took place at bayonet-point. Often it was marked by dishonesty and brutality on the part of government officials.

During Andrew Jackson's two terms as President, many Indians were driven from Georgia, Florida, Alabama, and Mississippi. Little or no preparation was made for their resettlement. Deeply tragic stories are told of how the Indians— thinly clad, without moccasins, sometimes in chains, often without food—were driven during the bitter cold of winter into a strange and barren wilderness beyond the Mississippi River.

Even though Jackson, as President, was responsible for the removal of these Indians, he did show some concern for their plight. But his official position remained one of uncompromising support for Indian resettlement. He turned a deaf ear to white missionary groups who wanted to help the Indians achieve orderly, settled lives. He also ignored political critics who opposed his Indian policy, including Henry Clay.

Nor did Jackson pay heed to the Supreme Court which was still presided over by Chief Justice John Marshall. In two decisions the Court sided with a group of Cherokee Indians, declaring that forcibly removing the Indians from their lands violated their treaty rights. Jackson is reported to have said, "John Marshall has made his decision; now let him enforce it."

More important than Jackson's political opinion was his personal conviction that Indians were a primitive people who were blocking the western movement of white Americans. Thus, it was easy for Jackson to conclude that the Indians would be happier and better off across the Mississippi River, remote from white neighbors. In these areas, they might preserve their own way of life or gradually accept the ways of life of the white majority. When Jackson left the White House, the first major Indian removals had largely been carried out. He regarded this achievement as one of his major accomplishments.

A product of his times. In the 1820's and 1830's, most white Americans shared Andrew Jackson's attitudes toward Negroes and Indians. Although American ideas of equality and justice had been stated, they were not yet widely practiced. Criminals and insane people, for example, were still badly mistreated, and few Americans saw anything wrong with such treatment. Employers often treated their employees harshly and unjustly.

Andrew Jackson, in the light of his times, took long strides toward fuller political democracy for average white Americans. But important though these steps were, the democratic ideal of equal opportunity for every individual still remained a distant goal.

SECTION SURVEY

IDENTIFY: "spoils system," nominating conventions, Indian resettlement.

1. What three convictions determined Jackson's actions as President?
2. Why did Jackson claim that democracy was furthered (a) by changing officeholders often, (b) by the spoils system?
3. How do nominating conventions bring the government and the people closer together?
4. By 1830 sectionalism, or regionalism, was sharply defined. How do the following men illustrate this statement: (a) Daniel Webster, (b) John C. Calhoun, (c) Thomas Hart Benton?
5. (a) What was Jackson's attitude toward American Indians? (b) Why was the Indian resettlement policy particularly harsh?
6. During Jackson's administration the American ideals of equality and justice were not applied to black Americans or to American Indians. Why not?

3 Jackson's active role in dealing with national problems

One of Jackson's bitterest fights was against the Bank of the United States. Many small businessmen, farmers, and workmen had fought this battle since the original Bank was created by Alexander Hamilton in 1791. President Jackson, in his first message to Congress early in 1829, opened his attack against the second Bank of the United States. As the months passed, he became more and more vigorous in his opposition.

Opposing the Bank. Jackson's attack came partly because he disliked banks and failed to understand banking. He saw the Bank of the United States as a "money power"—a monopoly which "the rich and powerful" used to their own advantage. He pointed out that a majority of the shares of Bank stock were owned by wealthy investors living mainly in seaboard states. The handful of investors living west of the Appalachians owned only a small fraction of the stock.

Why, the President asked, should the government continue to grant control of the Bank to a few wealthy people, most of them easterners? "Many of our rich men," he declared, ". . . have besought us to make them richer by acts of Congress. By attempting to gratify their desires, we have in the results of our legislation arrayed section against section, interest against interest, and man against man, in a fearful commotion which threatens to shake the foundations of our Union."

The President's followers were delighted by these words. But Nicholas Biddle, president of the second Bank of the United States, called Jackson's statement "a manifesto of anarchy."

To his charge that the Bank was a tool of rich easterners, Jackson added the serious charge that it engaged in questionable political activities. He charged, for example, that by granting loans to Congressmen, the Bank was able to influence legislation. There is little doubt that it did, at least after Jackson made his accusation—an accusation which many people considered unfair. Once the Bank directors were convinced that the President intended to destroy their institution, they fought back with every weapon at their command. "This worthy President," Biddle angrily stated, "thinks that because he has scalped Indians . . . he is to have his way with the Bank. He is mistaken."

Jackson also claimed that the mere existence of the Bank was unconstitutional. In so doing he was expressing his belief in the limited powers of the federal government. He was also ignoring the Supreme Court decision of 1819 in *McCulloch v. Maryland* that had ruled that the Bank was acceptable under the Constitution (page 255). Jackson indicated that he did not intend to be bound by verdicts of the Supreme Court. "Each public officer who takes an oath to support the Constitution swears that he will support it as he understands it, and not as it is understood by others . . ." Jackson bluntly asserted. "The opinion of the judges has no more authority over Congress than the opinion of Congress over the judges, and, on that point, the President is independent of both."

Many Americans joined Jackson in opposing the Bank. Farmers and wage earners who wanted easy credit opposed the Bank's lending policies. These people were angry because the Bank refused

■ Jackson's military reputation was one of his political assets. Years after the event, Alonzo Chappel painted this portrait of the hero of the battle of New Orleans.

Chicago Historical Society

271

to lend them money unless they could give adequate security in money or goods as a pledge of repayment. From a banker's point of view, this was sound business. Bankers pointed out that they had no right to lend money without adequate guarantees that the borrowers could repay.

Men with rising business interests also resented the sound banking policies of the second Bank of the United States. Being refused easy credit by the national Bank, they turned to private and state banks. Powerful banking interests centering in New York City also resented the special privileges enjoyed by the Bank of the United States. Popular slogans of the day denounced the Bank as a monstrous monopoly.

The Bank as an election issue.   Angered at the opposition, the supporters of the Bank, including Henry Clay, decided to force a showdown. They persuaded Nicholas Biddle to apply for a renewal of the Bank's charter. The bill passed both houses of Congress in the summer of 1832, four years before the charter was due to expire.

Henry Clay and the National-Republicans deliberately raised the issue at this time. They hoped that Jackson would veto the bill. If he did, the National-Republicans could make the Bank a major issue in the election of 1832. President Jackson did as they wished. He vetoed the bill to re-charter the bank in forceful terms.

The National-Republicans nominated Henry Clay for the Presidency late in 1832. Clay and his followers campaigned in favor of rechartering the Bank. Andrew Jackson, running for re-election as the Democratic candidate, continued his vigorous opposition. The Bank question became the major campaign issue.

Jackson won the election, with Martin Van Buren of New York as his Vice-President. Clay and the National-Republicans suffered a crushing defeat. Under these circumstances, everyone understood that the Bank charter would not be renewed in 1836.

Destroying the Bank.   Not content to wait for the Bank to die a natural death in 1836, Jackson set out to destroy it by gradually withdrawing all federal deposits. Federal funds were now deposited in certain state banks. These so-called "pet banks" were selected, Jackson's enemies claimed, on the basis of their loyalty to President Jackson and to his party.

The Bank of the United States, now deprived of federal deposits, was badly crippled, but it managed to survive until 1836. In that year, the charter of the Bank of the United States expired.

Andrew Jackson and his supporters felt that they had won a great victory over a government-approved monopoly of the money power by wealthy easterners. In their opinion, this was another triumph for democracy.

Jackson's support of the Union.   In his fight with the Bank of the United States, Andrew Jackson flatly stated that he, as President, did not intend to be restricted by the Supreme Court. But this statement did not indicate any lack of respect for the federal Union established by the Constitution. Indeed, beginning in 1830 Jackson took such a fighting stand in support of the Union that southern champions of states' rights, who had supported Jackson, were completely confused. The issue that forced Jackson into his firm position was a revolt of South Carolina planters against a high protective tariff.

Rising tariffs.   When America's source of manufactured goods was cut off by the Embargo Act of 1807 and the War of 1812, Americans, as you know, were forced to build their own factories. When the war ended in 1815, British manufacturers tried to destroy their new rivals by "dumping" British goods in America. The United States then tried to encourage its own manufacturers by the protective tariff of 1816. The tariff rates of 1816 were raised in 1824 and again in 1828.

Southern reaction.   Because of its high rates the Tariff Act of 1828 was called the "Tariff of Abominations" by its enemies. The tariff was passed by such a large majority in Congress that southern planters became alarmed. Reflecting their alarm, John C. Calhoun, the Vice-President, wrote—but did not sign—a pointed statement expressing his views about the tariff and the larger issue of states' rights. Calhoun argued that each state had the right to *nullify,* or refuse to obey, any act of Congress that it considered unconstitutional. This was a restatement of the compact theory of government earlier set forth in the Kentucky and Virginia Resolutions (page 226).

The legislature of South Carolina adopted Calhoun's statement, which came to be known as the "South Carolina Exposition and Protest," together with a set of resolutions calling the tariff unconstitutional and unjust. Georgia, Mississippi, and Virginia adopted similar resolutions.

Webster's defense of the Union.   Calhoun's doctrine of states' rights provoked bitter debate in Congress. A widely held southern view was clearly expressed by Senator Robert Y. Hayne of South

Carolina. Hayne argued that, in opposing the tariff, southerners were simply resisting "unauthorized taxation." Hayne also restated Calhoun's views that the states could nullify unconstitutional acts of Congress.

Another viewpoint, widely held in the North, was eloquently expressed by Daniel Webster of Massachusetts in one of the most famous speeches ever given in the Senate. Webster declared that the United States was not a mere league, or compact, of states. He argued that it was "the people's government, made for the people, made by the people, and answerable to the people." No state had the power to declare an act of Congress unconstitutional, Webster insisted. If each state could obey only those laws it chose to accept, Webster declared, the Union would become "a mere rope of sand."

Webster maintained that only one agency had the power to decide whether acts of Congress were unconstitutional. The agency, he said, was the Supreme Court. In thunderous words he flung out his challenge to Calhoun and Hayne and all who accepted the doctrine of states' rights and nullification: "Liberty *and* Union, now and forever, one and inseparable!"

Jackson's defense of the Union. Which side would the President support? The answer was not long in coming.

At a dinner in April 1830 President Jackson rose from his chair, fixed his eyes upon Vice-President Calhoun, held his glass in the air, and proposed a toast: "Our Federal Union—It must and shall be preserved."

A long moment of silence followed. Then the fiery Calhoun, spokesman for the southern planters, rose to his feet and threw back a defiant challenge: "The Union—next to our liberty, the most dear! May we always remember that it can only be preserved by respecting the rights of the states. . . ."

The battle was on. The leaders of both sides were able fighters who were reluctant to compromise when principles were at stake.

The conflict smoldered for two years. Then, in 1832, Congress adopted a new tariff measure. The Tariff Act of 1832 provided somewhat lower rates than the "Tariff of Abominations." But the new act was still a protective tariff and southerners therefore felt that it was no better than the old tariff. Convinced that the supporters of a protective tariff controlled Congress, South Carolina decided to act.

■ This moving portrait was made late in Andrew Jackson's life. His face, though aged and marked by grief, retains the strength that made him a symbol of a strong, united nation.

South Carolina's threat to secede. In November 1832 South Carolina adopted the Ordinance of Nullification, which declared the tariff acts of 1828 and 1832 "null, void, and no law," and not "binding upon this state, its officers, or citizens." The ordinance was a clear defiance of the United States government. It closed with a solemn warning: If the federal authorities tried to enforce the tariff law after February 1, 1833, South Carolina would secede from the Union.

The President's reaction. The President now moved into the spotlight. As Chief Executive of the United States, he was charged with enforcing the laws. He acted promptly. In "off-the-record" statements he lived up to his reputation as a fighting man, warning that he was prepared to "hang every leader . . . irrespective of his name or political or social position. . . . Tell them," he said to a Congressman, "that they can talk and write resolutions and print threats to their hearts' content. But if one drop of blood be shed there in defiance of the laws of the United States, I will hang the first man of them I can get my hands on to the first tree I can find."

For the public record Jackson was more moderate. In a long, carefully worded statement he repeated his belief in the Union and his determination to uphold it at whatever cost, but he left the way open for a peaceable solution.

Calhoun was out on a limb. The other southern states had refused to follow South Carolina along the road to secession. Calhoun and his followers stood alone against the full might of the United States. With possible violence facing the country, political leaders proposed to end the crisis by compromise.

A compromise tariff. Under the leadership of Henry Clay, the Great Compromiser, Congress adopted a compromise measure, the Tariff Act of 1833. Under this act, tariff rates were to be reduced gradually to the level of 1816, which Calhoun had once supported. This reduction was part of what many southern leaders demanded. But the reductions in the rates were to take place over 10 years so that manufacturers would be better able to adjust to the lack of high tariff protection.

Along with the compromise tariff act, Congress in 1833 also adopted the Force Act. This act gave the President the power to enforce federal tariff laws by military force if necessary.

Secession had been avoided. "Old Hickory" became a symbol of a strong, united nation.

SECTION SURVEY

IDENTIFY: "pet banks," "Tariff of Abominations," nullify, doctrine of states' rights, Force Act; Nicholas Biddle, "Old Hickory."

1. (a) Explain how Jackson expanded the power of the Presidency over the issue of the Bank. (b) Did he weaken the power of any other branch of the government? Explain.
2. (a) Summarize Calhoun's defense of states' rights. (b) Summarize Webster's defense of the Union.
3. How did the debate over the tariff reflect the different economic interests of the major sections of the country?
4. How did Clay's compromise tariff of 1833 satisfy (a) the South, (b) the North, (c) Jackson?

4 Economic depression at the end of the Jacksonian era

In March 1835 Andrew Jackson passed the midpoint of his second term as President and paused to consider his accomplishments. From Jackson's point of view, his administration had been a great success. He had won every major battle with his political opponents. His supporters were devoted to him. One of them expressed a widely held opinion when he wrote that "General Jackson may be President for life if he wishes." But Jackson made it clear that he was ready to retire.

The election of 1836. In 1835, after Jackson announced that he would not run for a third term, the Democratic Party held a nominating convention in Baltimore. The convention chose Martin Van Buren of New York as its Presidential candidate.

Martin Van Buren had served in Jackson's first administration as Secretary of State, and in his second as Vice-President. Van Buren was a shrewd politician, sometimes called the "little magician" or even the "sly fox." He entered the race with Jackson's strong support.

The Whig Party, organized in 1834, was made up of assorted groups, united chiefly by their dislike of "King Andrew" Jackson and the policies of the Democratic Party.

The Whigs did not unite behind a single candidate. They chose instead to use a "favorite son" strategy. In each section of the country, the Whigs selected a "favorite son" to run for President. They thus hoped to divide the total vote and prevent Van Buren from getting a majority. This would throw the election into the House of Representatives, where the Whigs hoped to have enough strength to choose one of their own candidates.

The Whig strategy failed. Van Buren won a majority of the electoral votes.

In his Inaugural Address on March 4, 1837, Van Buren announced that he would follow in Jackson's footsteps. He soon discovered that this was impossible. He was hardly in office before the nation plunged into an economic depression.

The roots of the depression. The depression of 1837 had its roots in events that occurred largely during Jackson's administration. After his election in 1832, as you know, Andrew Jackson gradually withdrew federal funds from the Bank of the United States and then deposited this money in "pet banks," many in the West. With the federal money as security, the "pet banks" printed large amounts of their own bank notes. Many "pet banks" were also "wildcat banks" which issued bank notes far in excess of the federal funds on deposit. Because they were so plentiful and had so little real value, these bank notes were easy to borrow. People borrowed this "easy money," often with a minimum of security, to buy land and to invest in the nation's growing transportation system. For a time it seemed as though almost everyone in the country was speculating with borrowed money.

Land speculators were especially active. Between 1830 and 1836 yearly federal income from the sale of public land rose from about $2 million to about $24 million. Much of this money was in the form of "wildcat" bank notes. The United States Treasury was flooded with this unsound currency.

In July 1836 President Jackson acted to check the wave of speculation sweeping across the country by issuing the "Specie Circular." This Executive Order forbade the Treasury to accept as pay- ment for public land anything except gold and silver, known as *specie,* or bank notes backed by specie.

The panic of 1837. Shortly after Jackson issued his order, the trouble began. The sale of public land dropped off sharply because few people had gold or silver coins to pay for the land. Persons holding bank notes began to ask the banks to exchange the bank notes for the gold or silver itself. Many banks could not redeem their own bank notes. As a result, banks began to fail. By the end of May 1837, soon after President Van Buren took office, every bank in the United States had suspended specie payment. Before the panic ended, hundreds of banks had gone out of business.

As the banks failed and sound money disappeared from circulation, business began to suffer. Factories closed. Construction work ended on buildings and roads. Thousands of wage earners lost their jobs. Hungry people rioted in the streets of New York and Philadelphia.

President Van Buren and other leaders of his day did not think that the government could or

■ The panic of 1837 created situations like those shown in this contemporary cartoon. Workmen stand idle. Women and children are reduced to begging. The signs on the custom house and the bank illustrate the dilemma—the government demanded that payments be made to it in specie, but people could not obtain specie because banks were not redeeming bank notes with it.

"HURRAH FOR OLD TIPPECANOE."

HARD CIDER
AND
LOG CABIN
ALMANAC
18 FOR 41
HARRISON AND TYLER.

■ The campaign of 1840 was one of the most boisterous in American history. The illustration above shows Harrison entertaining his supporters with hard cider, while Van Buren tries to put a stop to these tactics.

of Ohio, with John Tyler of Virginia as his running mate.

The campaign of 1840 was one of the most boisterous in American history. General Harrison, who owned a prosperous 2,000-acre farm, was nevertheless pictured as a poor but honest man who lived in a log cabin and earned his daily bread in the hardest way. The Whigs built log cabins for headquarters and entertained the crowds at political rallies with barrels of hard cider. Recalling General Harrison's battle with the Indians on the banks of the Tippecanoe River in 1811, the Whigs aroused enthusiasm for their candidates by shouting, "Tippecanoe and Tyler too." To ridicule their opposition, the Whigs shouted, "Van, Van is a used-up man."

The Whigs won an overwhelming victory. But General Harrison did not live to enjoy his triumph. He died shortly after he took office. Vice-President John Tyler, a states' rights Democrat who intensely opposed Jackson, succeeded to the Presidency.

A look ahead. During President Tyler's administration and that of his Democratic successor, James K. Polk, who was inaugurated in 1845, the boundaries of the nation were extended to the Pacific Ocean. During these same years the differences between the North and South became increasingly serious.

What was happening in the North, the South, and the West to create these conflicts? As you will see in Unit Four, two strikingly different ways of living and working had been developing in the northern states and the southern states. Out of these different ways of life arose tensions that became increasingly severe from the 1820's to the 1860's and finally led to the outbreak of a tragic war.

should do anything to try to stop the depression. Van Buren believed and had stated that "The less government interfered with private pursuits, the better for the general prosperity." Under the circumstances, he could only sit back and watch the depression run its course.

The depression was only one problem faced by President Van Buren. But the depression more than anything else cost him re-election.

The election of 1840. In December 1839 the Whig Party held a nominating convention at Harrisburg, Pennsylvania. The delegates sniffed victory in the air. They did not attempt to publish a *platform,* or statement of the party's political policies. Instead, they chose to fight the campaign entirely on the issue of the depression, which they of course blamed on Van Buren and the Democrats. To lead the fight, they nominated a hero of the War of 1812, General William Henry Harrison

TRACING THE MAIN IDEAS

During most of the years between 1824 and 1841, Andrew Jackson occupied the center of the national stage. During these years Jackson stood as a symbol of democracy and national unity.

But Jackson was far more than a symbol. He firmly believed that the President should assume an active role as the nation's leader, and that "the people" should share in the task of government. In general, he favored limiting the powers of the federal government through a strict interpretation of the Constitution. But he firmly believed that the Union established by the Constitution was a *national* Union. In the eight years of his administration, he did much to promote the forces which had been making the government more democratic. He brought ordinary white Americans into closer touch with the government. During the tariff controversy he struggled to maintain national unity.

The depression that started in 1837 and continued through the administration of Democrat Martin Van Buren gave the Whigs a chance to win control of the government. They made the most of their opportunity in the campaign of 1840, sending General Harrison to the White House. With the Whig victory, the colorful Jacksonian era came to an end.

But the democratic impulse continued strong. Democracy is more than the right to vote and to hold public office. It is, in a larger sense, a way of life that offers every person an equal opportunity to live and work as a free individual. This democratic impulse helped to put Andrew Jackson in the Presidency in 1829. It also set in motion a wave of reforms, including a rising protest against the evils of slavery, that affected many phases of American life.

As you will see in Unit Four, these reforms were taking place side by side with the division of the nation into three distinct sections—the North, the South, and the West.

CHAPTER SURVEY

QUESTIONS FOR DISCUSSION

1. Compare the relationship of the Democratic and Whig parties with that of the Federalist and Democratic–Republican parties.
2. (a) Describe four steps in the growth of democracy during the Jacksonian period. (b) How was the treatment of black Americans and American Indians undemocratic during this period?
3. Show the connection between the Kentucky and Virginia Resolutions, the Hartford Convention, and the "South Carolina Exposition and Protest." What precedents did they create?
4. How did the election of Jackson to the Presidency in 1828 illustrate the development of democracy in America?
5. Describe the circumstances under which the following statements were made: (a) "Liberty *and* Union, now and forever, one and inseparable." (Webster) (b) "Our Federal Union: it must and shall be preserved." (Jackson) (c) "The Union: next to our liberty, the most dear." (Calhoun)
6. Jackson's enemies called him "King Andrew," while his friends called him "a man of the people." Explain.
7. Why were Clay and Calhoun considered great statesmen in their day?

RELATING PAST TO PRESENT

1. Many people today have attitudes toward black Americans and American Indians similar to those that were common during the period just studied. Explain.
2. Some observers, both here and abroad, view Presidential nominating conventions as circuses. Do you agree or disagree? Explain.
3. Would today's federal government respond to a depression or recession in the same way that the federal government responded to the business panics of 1819 and 1837? Explain.
4. Why has the number of positions in the Presidential cabinet grown since the days of Andrew Jackson?
5. The issue of states' rights versus federal power is as important today as it was in Jackson's era. Comment.

USING MAPS AND CHARTS

1. Using the map on pages 856–57, locate the boundaries of the United States when Jackson was President.
2. (a) Using chart 4 on page 873, compare the tariffs of 1789, 1816, and 1828. (b) Explain these rises in tariff rates and their political effect.

UNIT SURVEY

FOR FURTHER INQUIRY

1. Why will there always be conflicts between the powers of the nation and the powers of the states in a federal system of government?
2. The character of George Washington strengthened the new government, and the brilliance of Hamilton enabled it to function successfully. Comment.
3. The goal of George Washington's foreign policy may be summed up in one word—peace. Why?
4. How do you explain the difference between what was said and what was done concerning minority groups in America between 1789 and 1845?
5. By 1830, what principles of American foreign policy had been established by (a) Presidential proclamations, (b) the War of 1812, (c) the Monroe Doctrine?
6. What is your opinion of Andrew Jackson as President? Why?

PROJECTS AND ACTIVITIES

1. Prepare newspaper clippings for a file or bulletin board display on recent Supreme Court decisions. Comment on whether these decisions broaden or limit federal power.
2. Make a graph showing the growth of the American population from 1790 to 1840. (Consult an almanac for this information.) Check your graph against the graph of population growth on page 858.
3. Draw a map to illustrate the territorial expansion of the United States between 1790 and 1842.
4. Write a newspaper editorial protesting or defending Jackson's treatment of the Indians.

5. For a deeper insight into Jacksonian democracy, read Chapter 13 of Joseph E. Gould's *Challenge and Change: Guided Readings in American History* (Harcourt Brace Jovanovich). Report to the class.

USING THE SOCIAL SCIENCES

(Read pages 280–82 before you answer the following questions.)

1. What was Jackson's concept of the Presidency? of the function of the federal government?
2. What is meant by reality in our everyday use of the word? What is meant by reality as used in this case study?
3. In Chapter 13 what position do the authors take regarding the reality of Jacksonian democracy? Explain.
4. What kinds of data do you think you would need in order to evaluate for yourself what Jacksonian democracy really was like?
5. Do you think that reading a biography of Jackson would be helpful in evaluating Jacksonian democracy? Why or why not?

SUGGESTED FURTHER READING

Biography

BAKELESS, JOHN, *Lewis and Clark: Partners in Discovery*, Morrow.

BOWERS, CLAUDE G., *Jefferson and Hamilton*, Houghton Mifflin.

——, *Jefferson in Power*, Houghton Mifflin.

BRANT, IRVING, *James Madison*, Bobbs-Merrill, 6 vols.

CUNLIFFE, MARCUS, *George Washington: Man and Monument*, New American Library (Mentor Books, paper). A brief, lively account of the legendary figure as well as the human being who was our first national hero.

CURRENT, RICHARD N., *Daniel Webster and the Rise of National Conservatism*, Little, Brown (paper). Traces the change in Webster from champion of states' rights and exponent of free trade to national conservative and protectionist.

FRANK, WALDO, *Birth of a World: Bolivar in Terms of His People*, Houghton Mifflin.

FRIED, ALBERT, ed. *The Essential Jefferson*, Macmillan (Collier Books, paper). Jefferson's writings arranged chronologically, each group preceded by the editor's comments.

JAMES, MARQUIS, *Andrew Jackson: Border Captain*, Grosset & Dunlap (Universal Library, paper). The story of a national hero.

LOTH, DAVID, *Chief Justice Marshall and the Growth of the Republic*, Norton.

MILLER, JOHN C., *Alexander Hamilton: Portrait in Paradox,* Harper & Row.

MIRSKY, JEANETTE, and ALLAN NEVINS, *The World of Eli Whitney,* Macmillan.

MITCHELL, BROADUS, *Alexander Hamilton: Youth to Maturity,* Macmillan.

MORRIS, RICHARD B., ed. *Basic Ideas of Alexander Hamilton,* Pocket Books.

PADOVER, SAUL K., *Jefferson,* New American Library (Mentor Books).

RICHARD, L. E., *Abigail Adams and Her Times,* Appleton-Century-Crofts.

SAEGER, ROBERT, *And Tyler Too: A Biography of John and Julia Gardiner Tyler,* McGraw-Hill.

SCHLESINGER, ARTHUR M., JR., *Age of Jackson,* Little, Brown; New American Library (Mentor Books).

THORP, LOUISE HALL, *Until Victory: Horace Mann and Mary Peabody,* Little, Brown.

WALTERS, RAYMOND, JR., *Albert Gallatin,* Macmillan.

WILMERDING, LUCIUS, *James Monroe: Public Claimant,* Rutgers Univ. Press.

Other Nonfiction

BASSETT, JOHN SPENCER, *The Federalist System,* Harper & Row.

BEIRNE, FRANCIS F., *The War of 1812,* Dutton.

BOWERS, CLAUDE G., *Party Battles of the Jackson Period,* Houghton Mifflin.

CARR, ALBERT Z., *The Coming of War: An Account of the Remarkable Events Leading to the War of 1812,* Doubleday.

CHASE, RICHARD, *American Folk Tales and Songs,* New American Library (Signet Books, paper).

CUNLIFFE, MARCUS, *The Nation Takes Shape: 1789–1837,* Univ. of Chicago Press (paper). A topical approach to government, politics, international relations, territorial expansion and industry.

DANGERFIELD, GEORGE, *The Era of Good Feelings,* Harcourt Brace Jovanovich.

DE VOTO, BERNARD, *The Course of Empire,* Houghton Mifflin.

——, *Across the Wide Missouri,* Houghton Mifflin. Describes the West in the 1830's; illustrated.

FLEXNER, JAMES T., *The Pocket History of American Painting,* Simon and Schuster (Washington Square Press, paper). The lives and works of American artists, Copley through Benton.

FORD, H. J., *Washington and His Colleagues,* Yale Univ. Press.

FORESTER, C. S., *The Age of the Fighting Sail,* Doubleday. Naval war of 1812.

HAMILTON, ALEXANDER, and others, *The Federalist Papers,* Dutton (Everyman's Library); and others. Essays on government and politics. Best known are numbers 10, 78, 84.

HORSMAN, REGINALD, *Causes of the War of 1812,* A. S. Barnes (Perpetua Books, paper). Basic causes of the war traced to Europe.

KROUT, JOHN ALLEN, and DIXON RYAN FOX, *The Completion of Independence,* Macmillan. Social and cultural history, 1790–1830.

LORANT, STEFAN, *The Presidency: A Pictorial History of Presidential Elections from Washington to Truman,* Macmillan.

MILLER, JOHN C., *The Federalist Era: 1789–1801,* Harper & Row (paper).

PADOVER, SAUL K., *Thomas Jefferson on Democracy,* New American Library (Mentor Books).

PERKINS, BRADFORD, *Prologue to War: England and the United States, 1805–1812,* Univ. of California Press.

PERKINS, DEXTER, *A History of the Monroe Doctrine,* Little, Brown (paper). Includes the Cuban Missile Crisis of 1962.

PRATT, FLETCHER, *The Heroic Years,* Random House. The years 1801–1815.

ROZWENC, EDWIN C., *Ideology and Power in the Age of Jackson,* Doubleday (Anchor Books, paper).

SANFORD, CHARLES L., ed. *Quest for America, 1810–1824,* Doubleday (Anchor Books, paper). Decline of agrarian society and the beginning of the Jacksonian Era; includes 73 documents, photographs.

SCHACHNER, NATHAN, *Founding Fathers,* Putnam (Capricorn Books, paper). The first twelve years of the United States as a nation.

TURNER, F. J., *The Rise of the New West,* Peter Smith.

VAN DEUSEN, GLYNDON G., *The Jacksonian Era, 1828–1848,* Harper & Row.

WILTSE, CHARLES M., *The New Nation: 1800–1845,* Hill & Wang.

Historical Fiction

ADAMS, SAMUEL HOPKINS, *Canal Town,* Random House; and others. Building of the Erie Canal.

——, *The Gorgeous Hussy,* Houghton Mifflin; Grosset & Dunlap. Politics in Jacksonian Washington.

ATHERTON, GERTRUDE, *The Conqueror,* Lippincott. About Hamilton.

CARMER, CARL, *Genesee Fever,* Doubleday. About land speculation.

CHURCHILL, WINSTON, *Richard Carvel.* Macmillan. Eighteenth-century Britain and America.

DOBIE, FRANK J., *The Mustangs,* Bantam. Tales of old Texas.

FORESTER, C. S., *Captain from Connecticut,* Little, Brown.

HALE, EDWARD EVERETT, *The Man Without a Country,* Houghton Mifflin; Revell. An American classic.

ROBERTS, KENNETH, *Captain Caution,* Doubleday. Novel about War of 1812.

SHEPARD, ODELL, *Holdfast Gaines,* Macmillan. An Indian is the hero.

TUFTS, ANNE, *As the Wheel Turns,* Holt, Rinehart & Winston. New England mill town in 1814.

HISTORY AND THE SOCIAL SCIENCES

Jacksonian Democracy—Myth or Reality?

One issue that has long divided historians is the question of whether or not President Andrew Jackson was really the "people's choice"—whether or not his two terms as President can rightly be called the era of "Jacksonian democracy."

Some historians maintain that Jackson was a man of the people who was elected in a democratic upsurge of new voters from the middle and lower classes. President Jackson, they say, encouraged a broad program of demo-cratic reforms including extension of the suffrage and a greater rotation of offices in the federal bureaucracy. In attacking the Bank of the United States, they contend, Jackson helped to free American business from special privileges enjoyed by the high-born and the very rich. These reforms, the pro-Jackson historians maintain, justify the use of the term "Jacksonian democracy."

Other historians point out that Andrew Jackson was a slaveowner, a land speculator, and a vigorous Indian fighter, who, as President, was unrelenting in his insistence on taking over all Indian lands—peacefully if possible but by force when necessary. These historians argue that Jackson did not institute voting reforms, but benefited instead from the extension of the suffrage which preceded his election. They maintain further that the greater rotation in the ranks of federal officials led to the introduction of a "spoils system" which amounted to the wholesale replacement of experienced officeholders with Jackson's followers and supporters. The anti-Jackson historians argue, also, that Jackson's defeat of the Bank of the United States had extremely harmful effects on the nation's economy.

What is the real truth in this controversy? Was Jacksonian democracy a myth or a reality? This is the question we shall investigate in this case study.

Extension of the Suffrage

Jackson's election to the Presidency in 1828 was indeed the first election marked by a growing determination to make the popular vote the crucial factor in electing a President and thereby reduce the vote of the Electoral College to a mere formality. Four years earlier, in the election of 1824, Jackson had received 155,872 popular votes to John Quincy Adams' 105,321, Henry Clay's 46,587, and William Crawford's 44,282. Despite his clear victory in the popular count, however, Jackson was denied the Presidency because he did not have the required majority of electoral votes. John Quincy Adams was subsequently elected President by the House of Representatives.

In the election of 1828 Jackson's suppoters were determined to see to it that the will of the people as reflected in the popular vote would prevail. The Congressional caucus system which had been used to elect state representatives to the Electoral College was abolished. Under the old caucus system, the electors had been free to disregard the popular voting results in their own states. Under the new system, the electors were selected by the state legislatures and were instructed, in most states, to heed the mandate of the popular vote.

In 1828 Jackson, who ran as the Democratic candidate, received 647,231 votes, while Adams, his National-Republican opponent, got 509,097 votes. The increase in the total popular vote from about 352,000 in 1824 to over 1.1 million in 1828 attested to the fact that ever-growing numbers of white male citizens were beginning to participate in the American democratic process. While the extension of the suffrage was not Jackson's accomplishment,

Voters gathered to hear election returns

his emphasis on the importance of the popular vote helped in the building and strengthening of American democracy.

In contrast to the aristocratic and aloof Adams, the good-natured, straight-talking Jackson was accepted by most ordinary Americans as their representative. It is true that this image of Jackson contrasted sharply with the fact that he was also a wealthy planter and slaveowner, but in the eyes of his contemporaries his frontier background and his lack of a college education stamped him as a man of the people. Jackson's career had truly taken him from the log cabin to the White House, and most ordinary Americans found in this fabulous rise the fulfillment of their own personal dreams.

The Spoils System

Once in office, Jackson began his reform of the civil service, emphasizing that he was improving the government by ridding the federal bureaucracy of incompetent officials. Many historians, however, have maintained that Jackson's spoils system was a device intended to put Jackson's supporters into government offices. Regardless of his motives, however, President Jackson was able to justify his actions to his contemporaries.

In his message to Congress dealing with the subject, the President promised to discharge all "unfaithful and incompetent" officials who had acquired a "habit of looking with indifference upon the public interests." "In a country where offices are created solely for the benefit of the people," the President went on to say, "no one man has any more intrinsic right to official station than another. Offices were not established to give support to particular men at the public expense. No individual wrong is, therefore, done by removal, since neither appointment to nor continuance in office is a matter of right. . . . It is the people, and they alone, who have a right to complain when a bad officer is substituted for a good one."

His reforms, Jackson maintained, were intended to broaden democratic principles by making officials more responsive to the needs of their constituents and to the popular will. Jackson's emphasis on the fact that federal officials must first and foremost be servants of the people was a new idea—and one which quickly became very popular.

Jackson's Fight Against the Bank

One serious struggle faced by Jackson as President was his attempt to abolish the Bank of the United States. The Bank was regarded by Jackson as a monster which served the privileged few by exploiting the people. Jackson disliked banks in general, and, in particular, he disliked the president of the Bank of the United States, the rich and aristocratic Philadelphia banker Nicholas Biddle. The President was convinced that Biddle and the Bank possessed too much power—and that this power must be destroyed.

Some historians are convinced that the destruction of the Bank was a very costly economic blunder. However, Jackson's attack on the Bank drew the support of many of his contemporaries—small businessmen across the nation, eastern wage earners who did not trust the value of the paper money issued by the Bank which they received in wages, and western farmers who did not trust the eastern bankers and who wanted to use gold and silver as currency rather than paper money.

In 1832 Nicholas Biddle, hoping to force a showdown with the President, applied for a renewal of the Bank's charter even though it was not due to expire until 1836. Jackson sent two messages to Congress urging that the Bank not be rechartered. But the bill was passed by both houses of Congress.

KING ANDREW THE FIRST.

Some of Jackson's critics saw him as a demagogue and an absolute ruler.

When Jackson was informed of the vote, he exclaimed, "The Bank is trying to kill me, but I will kill it." Jackson decided to veto the bill.

Much of Jackson's reputation as a President of the people and the molder of a more democratic nation can be traced to his veto message, one of the most powerful in American history. In his message Jackson appealed for the support of the people over the heads of Congress. This expression of confidence in the judgment of the mass of the American people over the judgment of their chosen representatives introduced a new element into American politics. Many later Presidents adopted Jackson's approach and openly urged Americans to influence their Congressmen to reverse their votes on a particular issue. Woodrow Wilson, for example, appealed to the American people to support the Treaty of Versailles after Congress rejected it, and Harry Truman also appealed directly to the people when he made the "do-nothing Congress" a major issue in his campaign for re-election.

Most important in helping us to appraise Jackson and his era were the arguments Jackson used to justify his veto. The President charged that the Bank was a monopoly serving the privileged few. "The many millions," he wrote, "which this act proposes to bestow on the stockholders of the existing Bank must come directly or indirectly out of the earnings of the American people."

After making it clear that as President he considered himself the defender of the rights of *all* the people, Jackson went on to spell out in eloquent language the principles on which he believed a just government must rest: "It is to be regretted that the rich and powerful too often bend the acts of government to their selfish purposes. Distinctions in society will always exist under every just government. Equality of talents, of education, or of wealth cannot be produced by human institutions. In the full enjoyment of the gifts of Heaven and the fruits of superior industry, economy, and virtue, every man is equally entitled to protection by law; but when the laws undertake to add to these natural and just advantages artificial distinctions, to grant titles, gratuities, and exclusive privileges to make the rich richer and the potent more powerful, the humble members of society—the farmers, mechanics, and laborers—who have neither the time nor the means of securing like favors to themselves have a right to complain of the injustice of their government.

"There are no necessary evils in government. Its evils exist only in its abuses. If it would confine itself to equal protection, and, as Heaven sends its rains, shower its favors alike on the high and the low, the rich and the poor, it would be an unqualified blessing. In the act before me there seems to be a wide and unnecessary departure from these just principles. . . ."

It has been argued that in affirming these advanced populist ideas, Jackson was merely acting as a clever politician and a dangerous demagogue. There is undoubtedly some truth in these accusations, but what is more important is the fact that Jackson gave expression to an important conception of the role of the federal government—one which was later broadened and refined by many American Presidents from Theodore Roosevelt in his "New Nationalism" through Franklin Roosevelt in his "New Deal" and John Kennedy in his "New Frontier" to Richard Nixon in his attempt to bring America together.

■ On balance do you think that Jacksonian democracy was a reality or a myth? Cite evidence to support your conclusion.

■ Would Jackson's contemporaries have been more or less inclined than modern historians to accept Jackson as the "people's choice"? Why?

PART **2**

The major themes in Part 1 of this book were the political developments that transformed the British colonies along the Atlantic seaboard into an independent nation and strengthened democracy by extending the right to vote. Thomas Jefferson (1743–1826) was one of many Americans who lived through these creative years.

Abraham Lincoln was 17 years old when Jefferson died. Jefferson, the elderly statesman, had lived to see the nation born. Lincoln, the youth, lived to see the Union tested by fire and sword in one of the most tragic conflicts in history.

Lincoln also lived to see revolutionary changes in the economic life of the nation. When he was born in a log cabin in 1809, nine out of ten Americans were living on farms, and the frontier had not yet reached the Mississippi River. When he died in 1865, the Industrial Revolution was in full swing, and the smoking factory chimney was replacing the farmhouse as the symbol of the nation's economy.

THE NATION DIVIDED

UNIT FOUR

The Rise of Sectionalism

1820's – 1860's

By the 1840's the Industrial Revolution was moving steadily ahead in the United States. "I visited the . . . factory establishment at Waltham, within a few miles of Boston," Harriet Martineau, an English traveler, wrote of a trip she made in 1834–35. "Five hundred persons were employed at the time of my visit."

The Waltham textile plant was one of the largest in the country, but there were many others, most of them only a few years old. The mills and factories, simple structures of wood or stone or brick, stood on the banks of swift-flowing rivers and streams, which provided their power source. Nearby were the small houses of the workers and the larger houses of the owners.

Factories, and the towns springing up around them, were becoming an increasingly important part of American life by the 1840's, particularly in the northeastern states. They were the visible evidence of the changes that were slowly beginning to alter life in the Northeast and that would, in time, affect the entire nation.

In her travels the English visitor also saw other signs of change. She saw new roads, new canals, and new railroads connecting the growing towns with one another and with the surrounding countryside, and reaching across the Appalachians to the farms and towns in the growing western regions. The rapidly developing transportation system and the new mills and factories were part of the Industrial Revolution that was beginning to transform the United States from an agricultural to an industrial nation.

CHANGING WAYS
OF AMERICAN LIFE

CHAPTER 14

Building New Industries in the Northern States

1820's – 1860's

THE CHAPTER IN OUTLINE

1. The effects of improved transportation on the growing nation.

2. The role of wage earners in creating the early industrial system.

3. The effects of immigration on American life.

1 The effects of improved transportation on the growing nation

Without a good system of transportation, the United States could never have expanded westward to the Pacific coast. Just as the Constitution gave the American people a strong federal union of states, so roads, canals, railways, and steamboats made it possible for Americans to exchange material products and ideas and to work together for the common good.

Roads and highways. The development of better roads and highways was well under way by the 1820's. Especially in the East, as you have seen, private companies had built hundreds of miles of good roads and turnpikes (page 287). To open up the western region, state legislatures had financed the building of state-owned roads leading into the interior. Pennsylvania, for example, had completed the Philadelphia-Pittsburgh Turnpike in 1818 (see map, page 287).

But the most important road project was the National Road, started in 1811. Financed by the federal government, the National Road cut across state boundaries and progressed slowly westward. By 1833 it was open to traffic as far as Columbus, Ohio. By 1852 it reached Vandalia, Illinois, not far from the Mississippi River (see map, page 287). In 1853 the 834 miles of the National Road were turned over to the states.

By 1860 Americans could look with pride at the roads and highways that crisscrossed the eastern half of the nation. In 1790, according to estimates of the Bureau of the Census, there had not been a single important stretch of hard-surfaced road in the entire United States. By 1820 more than 9,000 miles of surfaced roads had been completed; by 1860, more than 88,000 miles.

Effects of the roads. The roads built with private, state, and federal money began to change the lives of many thousands of Americans. Farmers in the outlying parts of the eastern states and in the lands west of the Appalachian Mountains could at last buy and sell products in the city markets of the East. The roads were crowded with freight wagons and other traffic.

Although moving produce by wagon cost less than carrying it on the backs of horses or mules, wagon transportation still was quite expensive. In 1817, for instance, it cost $13 to transport a barrel of flour some 250 miles from Pittsburgh to Philadelphia—and this was over one of the nation's best highways. Farmers, businessmen, and others began to demand less expensive means of transportation.

The Erie Canal. Canals were one answer to the demand for cheaper transportation. As early as the 1780's leaders of New York state had urged that a canal be built between Albany and Buffalo. Such a canal would provide inexpensive water transportation from New York City to the Great Lakes.

Agitation for the canal grew stronger when the National Road was started. New Yorkers saw that Baltimore would be connected to the western areas by the only highway through the mountains. Baltimore might thus become the leading Atlantic port. Thoroughly alarmed, the New York legislature, acting under the leadership of Governor De Witt Clinton, authorized the construction of the Erie Canal.

In 1817 the dirt began to fly in one of the major engineering feats in American history. Immigrants, many from Ireland, did most of the hard work. When the canal was finished in 1825, a man-made waterway, 42 feet wide and at least 4 feet deep, stretched westward for 363 miles from the Hudson River at Troy to Lake Erie at Buffalo (see map, page 287).

The Erie Canal was an immediate success. Heavy barges were drawn through the water by ropes tied to horses and mules who walked on a towpath bordering the canal, urged along by a driver. At the stern of each barge stood a helmsman. Passengers rode in luxury barges with gaily colored curtains at the windows.

Cities began to grow along the canal route, among them Utica, Syracuse, and Rochester. New York City became the "gateway to the West" and the nation's leading commercial port, doubling its population within 10 years after the canal's opening. Cheap water transportation had done all this. Because a horse could pull 50 times as much weight in still water as it could pull over a road, freight rates dropped to a new low. Before the canal was completed, transporting a ton of goods by road from Buffalo to New York had cost more than $100. After the canal was finished, the same ton of goods could be carried through the canal for $5 to $10.

The canal-building era. As New York City businessmen began to make huge profits, businessmen in other commercial cities, such as Philadelphia and Baltimore, also began to build canals. Pennsylvania, eager to share in the western trade, built a canal through the Allegheny Mountains, connect-

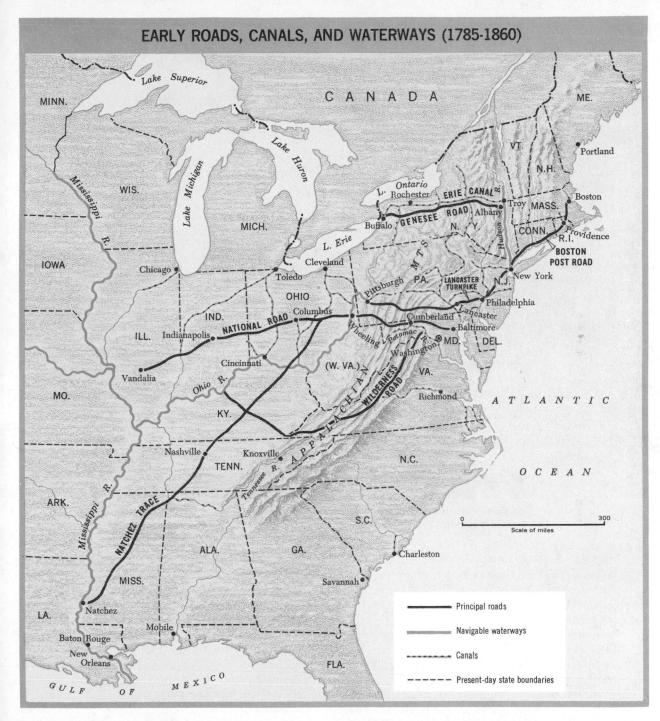

EARLY ROADS, CANALS, AND WATERWAYS (1785-1860)

Principal roads

Navigable waterways

Canals

Present-day state boundaries

ing Philadelphia with the headwaters of the Ohio River (see map, this page).

By the 1830's canals were being dug throughout the country. When the depression of 1837 hit, more than 3,000 miles of canals had been built,

most of them in the northern part of the country. With the depression, however, the enthusiasm for canal building ended abruptly, partly because railroads were becoming important, partly because the states now were unable or unwilling to invest in

287

■ This Currier and Ives print, made in 1863, is entitled " 'Wooding Up' on the Mississippi."
Wood from a riverside woodyard is being loaded onto the steamboat to be used for fuel.

canals. Several states defaulted on their canal bonds. That is, they failed to repay money that people had invested in them. Some states sold the state-owned canals to private companies. Others continued to operate the canals they had built. But for some time, state development of transportation facilities ended.

River steamboats. Another essential link in the new transportation system was the steamboat, or steamer. Before 1800 inventors in both Europe and America had built steam-driven boats. In 1787, for example, a steamboat invented and built by John Fitch had made a successful trial run on the Delaware River. But it was Robert Fulton's demonstration of the *Clermont,* on the Hudson River in 1807, that first attracted widespread American attention.

Fulton and his business associates realized that

huge profits could be earned in the western areas. Up to this time, as you know, river boats could not navigate economically upstream. In 1811 Fulton and his associates built a steamboat at Pittsburgh and took it down the Ohio River to the Mississippi. Called the *New Orleans,* it ran successfully up and down the Mississippi for several years. Other steamboats were soon built, and by the 1820's steam-driven vessels were fairly common sights on the Mississippi and Ohio rivers.

From the 1820's to the 1860's, river steamers transported most of the cargo of the Mississippi Valley. They chugged up and down the Mississippi and threaded their way east and west to villages and towns along the numerous tributaries of the river. By 1840 four fifths of all traffic in the Mississippi Valley was carried by steamboats, and steamers were appearing on the Great Lakes.

Building railroads. Like the early roads and canals, the railroads grew out of commercial rivalry among the eastern cities. Baltimore led the way. Construction of the first section of the Baltimore and Ohio Railroad began on July 4, 1828, the fifty-second anniversary of the Declaration of Independence.

Present at the start of the construction in Baltimore was Charles Carroll, at 91 the only surviving signer of the Declaration of Independence. The famous patriot said that this was the greatest event of his life. Even Carroll, however, could not have foreseen how railroads would reshape the United States. As time passed, the railroad, more than any other part of the American transportation system, made possible the development of the United States into the greatest industrial nation in the world.

But in 1828 there were few signs of the railroad's future success. The first locomotive on the Baltimore and Ohio—the *Tom Thumb,* built by Peter Cooper of New York—was a crude, undependable contraption. The rails on which the engine ran were wooden timbers with thin strips of metal along the top. With much clanging of metal, fearsome showers of sparks, and loud hissing of steam, the *Tom Thumb* could reach a maximum speed of about 10 miles an hour.

This was a feeble beginning, but railroads soon made rapid progress despite violent opposition from the stagecoach lines. Rival seaports began to build rail lines into the interior. By 1833 merchants of Charleston, South Carolina, had financed a 136-mile railroad into the interior of the state (see map, page 290). At the time it was the longest railway line in the world under a single management. Boston, New York, and Philadelphia followed suit. Better locomotives were developed. Rails made entirely of iron replaced the early wooden ones, and the cars were improved.

By 1840 nearly 3,000 miles of track had been laid; by 1850 the total had grown to more than 9,000 miles. By 1860, 30,000 miles of rails linked the East and the western regions as far as the Mississippi River (see map, page 290). Most of the new lines were in the northern part of the country.

Effects of improved transportation. It was a difficult and costly job for the young nation to build its transportation system. But the job was done—by roads, canals, steamboats, and railroads.

As each new stage of the transportation system was completed, new western areas were linked with

■ **By the middle of the 1800's, railroads were swift and safe. Below, a train stops in Stratford, Connecticut, to pick up and unload passengers and freight.**

The Metropolitan Museum of Art, bequest of Moses M. Tannenbaum, 1937.

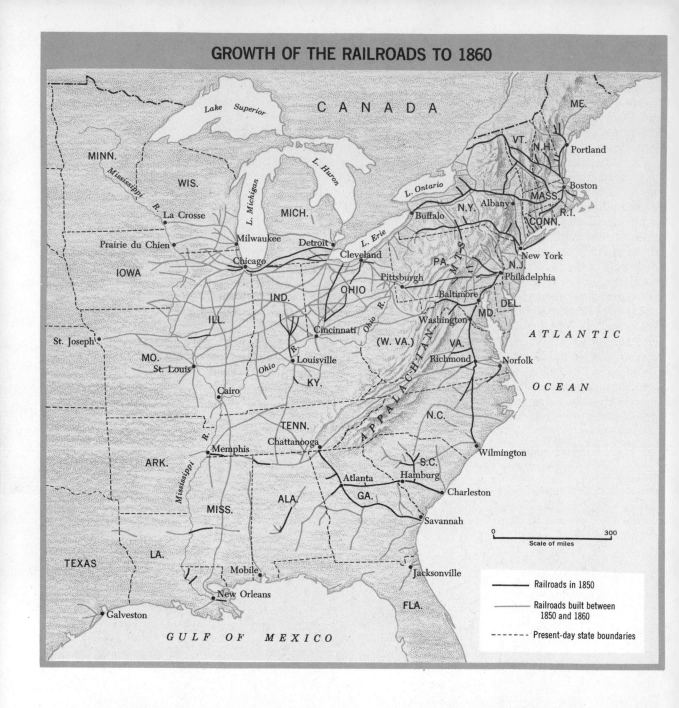

GROWTH OF THE RAILROADS TO 1860

CANADA

Lake Superior

ME.

MINN.

WIS.

MICH.

L. Michigan

L. Huron

VT.

N.H.

Portland

Boston

MASS.

R.I.

CONN.

L. Ontario

Albany

N.Y.

Buffalo

New York

La Crosse

Mississippi R.

Prairie du Chien

Milwaukee

Detroit

Cleveland

Chicago

IOWA

ILL.

IND.

OHIO

Pittsburgh

PA.

Philadelphia

N.J.

Baltimore

DEL.

MD.

Washington

ATLANTIC

St. Joseph

MO.

St. Louis

Cincinnati

Ohio R.

Ohio R.

Louisville

KY.

(W. VA.)

VA.

Richmond

Norfolk

OCEAN

Cairo

TENN.

Chattanooga

APPALACHIAN MTS.

N.C.

Memphis

Mississippi R.

ARK.

S.C.

Hamburg

Wilmington

Atlanta

GA.

Charleston

ALA.

MISS.

Savannah

TEXAS

LA.

Mobile

New Orleans

Jacksonville

FLA.

Galveston

GULF OF MEXICO

Scale of miles

0   300

Railroads in 1850

Railroads built between
1850 and 1860

Present-day state boundaries

the eastern seaboard. Eastern products began moving west in ever-growing volume, stimulating the development of eastern factories.

The new means of transportation also stimulated the development of the western regions. Pioneer settlers could now travel to these promised lands more easily than ever. Once settled, the pioneers

could send their surplus crops to the eastern cities. The improved system of transportation brought the western farms and eastern factories closer together.

At the same time western villages began growing into large towns and even cities. At first these communities served mainly as centers of trade between western farms and eastern factories. But by 1860 the towns and cities in what is now called the Middle West were developing thriving industries of their own.

As the Industrial Revolution continued to gain momentum in the United States, many new factories were built. Some were built in the South, and an increasing number were built in the Middle West. But most were built in New England and the Middle Atlantic states.

Because of the developing transportation system, manufacturers could sell their goods over a larger and larger area of the country. At the same time their new industries were protected from European competition by a tariff wall (page 272). Although the upward trend of the tariff was checked after 1832, the manufacturers continued to receive some tariff protection.

The growing nation.   Manufacturers also benefited from a rapidly growing nation. In 1790 there had been only 13 states in the new nation. By 1840 there were 26 states. By 1860 the total reached 33 states.

The population was also increasing. From about 4 million in 1790, it grew to more than 17 million in 1840. By 1860 it had swelled to more than 31 million.

The overwhelming majority of these people were farmers, as were their fathers and grandfathers before them. In 1840 nearly nine out of every ten Americans still lived in rural areas.

But the towns were growing in number and in size. In 1790 there had been only 24 towns with populations larger than 2,500. In 1840 the census takers reported 131 towns and cities having more than 2,500 inhabitants, some of them west of the Appalachian Mountains. By 1860 there were 392.

Investment of capital.   By 1840 the United States was a big nation, growing bigger every year. Its growing population needed the products of the new industries. Where did the manufacturers get the money, or the capital, to invest in the new mills and factories?

Some of the necessary capital came from European investors, but much came from well-to-do Americans—especially merchants. During the years of the Embargo Act (1807–09) and the War of 1812, American businessmen had money to invest. By 1820, $50 million had been invested in manufacturing in the United States. By 1850 the amount had risen to $500 million. By 1860 it totaled more than $1 billion.

This money was used mainly to build small, *individually owned* factories or mills. The owner

■ No other sailing ships ever built could match the Yankee clippers in speed or beauty. Even their names— Zephyr, Flying Cloud, Lightning—suggest swift and graceful motion. The clipper Lightning is shown above.

was often the manager, who hired and directed the workers and worked side by side with them. Sometimes larger businesses were organized as *partnerships,* in which two or more men shared ownership and operation of the business. Widespread use of the *corporation* as a form of business organization was still to come (Chapter 23).

The merchant marine.   While industry was growing, American seamen were carrying American goods to all parts of the world. Even before 1800 Yankee sailing vessels had been familiar sights in the ports of China, Java, Sumatra, Siam (now Thailand), India, and the Philippines. The vessels left their home ports with cargoes of beads, knives, gunpowder, cotton goods, pottery, and rum. Stopping at harbors in the Pacific Northwest, the captains traded these goods with the Indians in

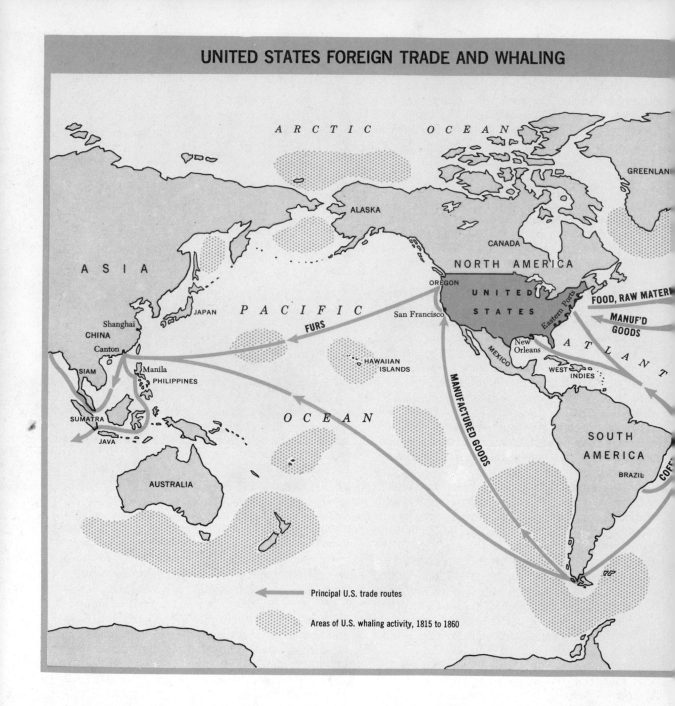

Principal U.S. trade routes

Areas of U.S. whaling activity, 1815 to 1860

exchange for furs. The furs were then carried to China and sold. The returning vessels brought tea and other luxuries to the United States.

This long voyage was dangerous, but enormously profitable if successful. In a few hours of trading, one captain secured 560 otter skins from the Indians of the Pacific Northwest in exchange for goods that had cost him only $2. He sold the otter skins in Canton, China, for $22,400. In 1797, 30 boys and young men, the oldest only 28, sailed around the world, returning with a net profit of more than $50,000 on an initial investment of less than $8,000.

From the 1820's to the 1860's American mer-

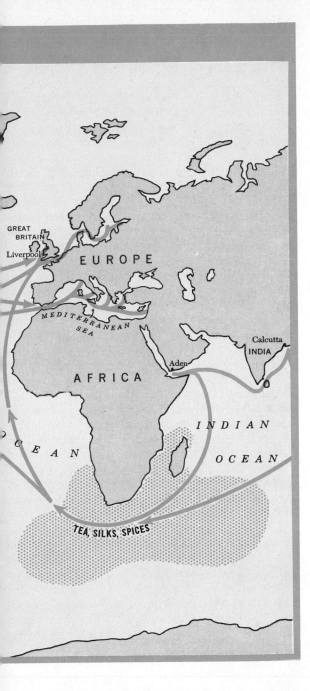

GREAT
BRITAIN
Liverpool
EUROPE
MEDITERRANEAN
SEA
AFRICA
Aden
Calcutta
INDIA
INDIAN
OCEAN
OCEAN
TEA, SILKS, SPICES

trading along the Yangtze (YANG-tsee) River in China; and American whalers were likely to appear for water and provisions in almost any port of the world (see map at left).

Yankee seamen were equally successful on the Atlantic. As early as 1824 they carried most of the traffic in passengers and freight between Liverpool, England, and the ports of Boston and New York. An Englishman explained how the Yankees achieved this success. "The reason will be evident to anyone who will walk through the docks at Liverpool," he said. "He will see the American ships, long, sharp built, beautifully painted and rigged, and remarkable for their fine appearance and white canvas. He will see the English vessels, short, round, and dirty, resembling great black tubs."

Clipper ships. During the 1840's and 1850's the sailing ships of American merchants became world-famous. The celebrated "clipper ships" were the pride and glory of the seas, outdistancing every other ship afloat. The clippers made the run from China to New York in as little as 75 days, thereby capturing the rich trade of the Orient from slower vessels that required nearly a year to make the same journey. The activities of the merchant fleet kept American shipyards busy, and the fortunes made from commerce helped to finance America's growing factories and railroads.

But at this time the British, who had been outdistanced by the Yankee sailors and shipbuilders for 50 years, were busily constructing ocean-going steamships. By 1860 steamships had demonstrated their superiority over sailing vessels. During the Civil War American shipowners lost much of their already dwindling business. Thereafter, the decline in the United States merchant marine went on until the 1900's.

SECTION SURVEY

IDENTIFY: Erie Canal, *Clermont, Tom Thumb,* partnership, clipper ship.

1. In your opinion, which of the following was most important in the development of the United States: (a) roads, (b) canals, (c) steamboats, or (d) railroads? Give reasons for your choice.
2. (a) How did improved transportation affect the various regions of the nation? (b) Which section benefited most? Why? (c) Which section benefited least? Why?
3. (a) What accounted for the success of the American merchant marine between 1820 and 1860? (b) Why did it decline after 1860?

chants kept building larger and faster sailing ships to add to the American merchant marine. In these faster vessels American seamen continued to carry on a flourishing trade with China and other Asian countries. By 1860 Americans had secured more than half of all the commerce to and from the great Chinese port of Shanghai; American seamen were

2 The role of wage earners in creating the early industrial system

As more and more factories were built, mainly in the northern part of the country, manufacturers had to find workers to run the machines and do other work in the new industrial plants. Where did they find these workers?

Early labor supply. Until about 1830 most wage earners were native-born American women and children. In 1831, for instance, children under 12 years of age made up about 40 percent of all the wage earners in the cotton textile mills of Rhode Island. In other industries and other areas the percentage of child labor was not so high, but everywhere children performed many factory tasks.

Women were quite willing to work in the textile factories. Since they were used to spinning and weaving in their homes, they saw little difference in transferring their work to a factory. As for the children, they did whatever their parents told them, at a time when it was commonly believed that hard work was good for children.

During the early 1800's factory owners often contracted for the labor of an entire family. Advertisements like the following, which appeared in Providence, Rhode Island, in 1828, were frequently printed in the newspapers of the industrial towns: "Families Wanted—Ten or twelve good respectable families, consisting of four or five children each, from nine to sixteen years of age, are wanted to work in a cotton mill in the vicinity of Providence." Of course, employers also hired individual men and women.

Conditions of labor. The family system of labor had certain advantages for the workers. The family was kept together, instead of being split up to work in different towns. The work was not always difficult. Machinery ran much more slowly than it does today, and the children did the lighter tasks. In a textile mill, for example, children might mend broken threads or carry boxes containing bobbins, or spools. Although the hours were long—12 to 14 hours a day six days a week—the workday was no longer than that on the farm, which lasted from sunrise to sunset.

British labor compared. During the first 30 or 40 years of the 1800's, conditions in British factories were grim and degrading compared to those in the United States. During the early 1800's young children in Great Britain were taken from orphanages and poorhouses to do hard work in factories,

mills, and mines. As late as 1830, a Parliamentary investigating committee reported that children only eight and nine years old were working from dawn to dusk or even longer, under the harshest and most unsanitary conditions.

This report led Parliament in 1833 to pass a "factory act," placing limits on the working hours of children. Later acts helped to eliminate the worst, but not all, evils of the British factory system.

Most American workers were better off, partly because they had a means of escape. If conditions became too bad, American workers could return to their farms or perhaps take up new land on the frontier. Moreover, labor was scarce in the United States. A harsh employer would soon find himself with an empty building and idle machines. And some employers, honestly wanting to treat their workers decently, tried to provide good working conditions.

The Waltham system. A notable but short-lived experiment was the one worked out at Waltham, Massachusetts, beginning in 1813. Only persons of good character were employed in the Waltham textile plant. The women and girls lived in company-owned boarding houses, run much like college dormitories of today, with matrons in charge to see that certain rules were observed. Employees were discharged for lying, profanity, and laziness. All employees were required to attend church. Educational programs, lectures, debates, and social gatherings were organized. The factories were clean and cheerful, with flower boxes at the windows and pictures above the looms.

The Waltham system spread to several other factories. For a while it worked well. Women and girls, as well as men, welcomed a chance to leave home and get at least a little "book learning," often unavailable on the farm. By 1840, however, the system began to break down as factories grew in size, and as employers began to hire immigrants who had begun to stream into the country during the 1830's.

Rising discontent. Although working conditions in American factories were generally better than those in Great Britain, by the 1830's and 1840's many American workers were laboring under extremely harsh conditions. Some workers were forced to toil as many as 16 hours a day in the dirty, crowded tenement areas of cities like Boston, New York, and Philadelphia. This situation existed particularly in the clothing industries, where workers, mostly women and children, la-

■ Winslow Homer painted this scene of a young woman on her way to work in an early New England mill. Until about 1830 most wage earners in America were native-born women and children.

bored in the dark, dirty, upper stories of buildings, called lofts. Equally depressing was the plight of women and children who picked up unfinished garments from a central plant and took them to their slum lodgings to complete the sewing, receiving a small payment for each garment that they completed.

As time passed, the argument that hard work was good for children began to break down. More people, including the workers themselves, began to demand educational opportunities for children. They agreed that democracy could not work among illiterate people and that opportunity to improve oneself required schooling. To meet these demands, some manufacturers opened Sunday schools and evening schools for the boys and girls. But these efforts were unsuccessful, for children who had worked long hours six days a week were in no condition to attend classes in their few hours of free time.

Early labor organizations. The wage earners' discontent with many features of the new industrial economy led some skilled workers, especially bootmakers and printers, to form workingmen's organizations. These organizations—the earliest American labor unions—tried to get higher wages and better working conditions for their members. Thus, the growth of the nation's labor movement paralleled the growth of its industry.

The labor movement was especially active during the late 1820's and the early 1830's. During these years, the newly organized local unions even thought of a great national union of all workers.

By 1834, when representatives of labor met in their first national convention, there may have been as many as 300,000 organized workers in the United States. In 1834, also, a group of workmen organized the National Trades Union. The National Trades Union never became powerful, but it did represent a significant beginning for labor organizations and for labor thinking.

The workers' demands. The workers' organizations made a number of demands, with higher wages heading the list. Hand in hand with this demand went agitation for a 10-hour working day. The workers won partial success in 1840 when President Martin Van Buren established the 10-hour day for all government workers.

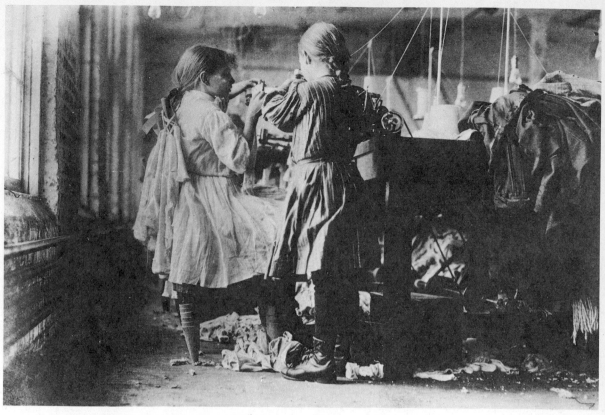

■ Although the argument that hard work was good for children began to break down in the 1800's, it was not until the early 1900's, the time of this photograph, that child labor was abolished.

But the wage earners looked upon shorter hours not merely as desirable ends in themselves, but also as a means to even more important ends. Many workers wanted equality of educational opportunity. This meant that working children must be released from manual toil and given the chance to attend school. And this, in turn, meant that schools must be built with public funds in all parts of the country. By demanding the education of their children, the wage earners helped to speed the development of tax-supported public schools.

Wage earners also demanded an end to the practice of throwing a man into prison when he could not pay his debts. By the early 1840's nearly all of the states had ended this practice.

By the 1830's and 1840's organized labor had become a new force in American life. Workers had begun to develop the idea of unions and of *collective bargaining*—bargaining, that is, between union representatives and employers over wages, hours, and working conditions. Unions had begun to develop the *strike,* or the union members' refusal to

work until their employer met their demands, and the *picket line,* or the parading of union members outside a plant during a strike, trying to persuade other workers not to take their jobs.

Problems of black workers.   The aims of the early labor unions did not include better working conditions for Negro workers. Since competition for jobs was often fierce, white workmen resented the fact that black workers, to get jobs at all, often accepted lower wages. That meant that the wages of white workers were also forced down.

White workers refused to work in the same shops and factories with Negroes. Black workers were barred from membership in the trade unions. Excluded from the unions, black workers often served as strike-breakers. That is, they took the jobs of white workmen during the strikes, weakening the effect of the strikes. On rare occasions when white workers and black workers did agree to organize to improve wages, the white workers insisted on separate unions.

Things were no better for Negroes in the unskilled trades. During hard times, Negroes working at unskilled jobs in canal construction and railroad building were often fired and replaced by white workers.

Because of these conditions, resentment and bitterness on both sides led to workingmen's riots in Philadelphia, New York, and other cities. In 1855, for example, violence erupted when black workmen took the jobs of white longshoremen on the New York City waterfront.

Weakness of organized labor. In these early years, the American labor movement was not yet strong enough to win many of the workers' demands. There were several reasons for this weakness.

In the first place, many wage earners did not realize that they formed a new and important group in the nation's economic life and that they had interests in common. This feeling was partly the result of tradition. From the earliest days, most Americans had been farmers, and the early factories and mills drew most of their labor supply from the farms. The Americans' strong spirit of independence and individualism made it difficult for labor organizations to draw workers into unions. Wage earners continued to think of themselves as individuals who could look after their own interests. They were reluctant to follow the rules laid down by a union.

In the second place, cheap land was always available. This cheap land did not actually attract many dissatisfied workers. They could not afford the simple equipment needed to move west, and many preferred town to country life. But cheap land did draw westward thousands of farmers who might otherwise have turned to the cities for employment.

In the third place, until 1842 labor unions were not recognized by law. In that year the Supreme Court of Massachusetts, in the case of *Commonwealth v. Hunt,* decided that labor unions had a legal right to exist in Massachusetts. This decision set a precedent, though not a strong one. Wage earners had to struggle in one state after another for the right to organize. The struggle was a long one, for businessmen in general were opposed to the formation of unions.

In the fourth place, the depression of 1837 threw thousands of men out of work. These unemployed workers could not afford to pay union dues and had to accept any job they could get, regardless of what it paid. This situation slowed the growth of the labor movement.

Finally, during the 1830's immigrants began to come to the United States in large numbers. Many of them were willing to work for low wages. Immigration, therefore, forced down the wages of many native-born American workers and almost brought the labor movement to a halt.

IDENTIFY: Waltham system, collective bargaining, strike, picket line, strike-breakers.

1. Who supplied the labor in the factories during the early 1800's?
2. (a) Compare working conditions in Great Britain with those in the United States at that time. (b) Why did conditions in the two countries differ?
3. (a) What led to the formation of early labor unions? (b) What did these unions want?
4. Why were early attempts at unionization only partially successful?
5. (a) How were black workers discriminated against in regard to jobs and unions? (b) How were Negroes "used" by employers to weaken the labor movement?

3 The effects of immigration on American life

Between 1790 and 1830 the population of the United States more than tripled, increasing from about 4 million to nearly 13 million. Nearly all of this growth resulted from births in the United States itself. During these years fewer than 400,000 immigrants entered the country.

Growing immigration. In the 1830's, however, the small stream of immigration swelled to a great flood. From 1830 to 1840 more than half a million immigrants poured into the United States (see chart, page 858). Forty-four percent came from Ireland, 30 percent from Germany, 15 percent from Great Britain, and the remainder from other European countries. Between 1840 and 1850 a million and a half immigrants arrived in the United States, 49 percent of them from Ireland.

Irish immigrants. The Irish came to escape terrible conditions in their homeland. In Ireland during those years, many people worked as tenant farmers on the estates of landlords who lived in England. The landlords did little or nothing to improve the conditions of their tenants, who barely managed to make a living. And then, in 1846, a terrible famine struck Ireland. Thousands died during the "Potato Famine," as it was called. Other thousands fled to America.

The people who left Ireland were attracted to the United States for several reasons. They liked what they had heard about American democracy. They were thrilled at the reports of plenty in the United States. Moreover, American contractors encouraged them to come and work on the roads, canals, and railroads, and manufacturers attracted them into the new mills and factories.

Hardships of immigration. The immigrants endured incredible hardships in their efforts to reach the United States. The following news item from the *Edinburgh Review* of July 1854 gives a glimpse of their sufferings: "Liverpool was crowded with emigrants, and ships could not be found to do the work. The poor creatures were packed in dense masses in ill-ventilated and unseaworthy vessels, under charge of improper masters, and the natural result followed. Pestilence [disease] chased the fugitive to complete the work of famine. Fifteen thousand out of ninety thousand emigrants . . . in British bottoms [ships] in 1847 died on the passage or soon after arrival. The American vessels, owing to a stringent passenger law, were better managed; but the hospitals of New York and Boston were nevertheless crowded with patients from Irish estates. . . ."

Poor, unable to move to the western lands, many of the Irish immigrants found homes in the slums of such growing cities as New York, Boston, Albany, Baltimore, St. Louis, Cincinnati, and New Orleans. Many Irish men went to work as unskilled laborers on roads, canals, and railroads. Many Irish women took jobs in factories, where they displaced native-born American wage earners.

German immigrants. Although people from many countries came to America during these years, the Germans formed the second largest group after the Irish. Between 1845 and 1860 more than 1.3 million Germans landed in the United States.

Many Germans came because, after 1815, Europe (and the German states in particular) was controlled by harsh rulers. Thousands of Germans who rebelled against political oppression fled when their revolutions failed. Other Germans came to earn a better living.

Most German immigrants settled in the Middle Western states—Ohio, Indiana, Illinois, Wisconsin, Iowa, and Missouri. Able, thrifty farmers, they built prosperous farms. Many also settled in the cities, and by the 1860's formed a substantial pro-

portion of such communities as Buffalo, Detroit, Cleveland, Cincinnati, Chicago, and St. Louis.

Immigrants resented. Most immigrants quickly became American citizens. Because many had come to the United States in search of political freedom, they helped to strengthen political democracy. Because they were eager to work, they contributed to the wealth of the growing nation. But despite these contributions, the immigrants were resented by many native-born Americans, who were afraid that large numbers of "foreigners" would change the older ways of living in America.

Some Germans, for instance, aroused suspicion because they organized their own clubs, gathered in social halls to talk and sing, established their own churches and schools, published their own newspapers, and continued to speak German. Many native-born Americans viewed these activities with misgivings.

But the Irish became the chief targets of American resentment. Like many newcomers to a strange land, they tried to settle near their friends from the Old Country. As a result, clusters of Irish people kept growing in the cities. Many dressed as they had in Ireland. Their accent sounded strange to other Americans. Many native-born Protestants disliked the Irish immigrants simply because most of them were Roman Catholics. Because the Irish were "different" in these and other ways, some Americans at first looked upon them with suspicion. Suspicion of this kind has unfortunately been the fate of every large immigrant group.

Resentment against the immigrants often led to friction and violence. Riots broke out in several cities. As more immigrants arrived, resentment against them increased. In 1845 a national organization of native-born Americans was started. A year later, this society was reorganized as a secret order called the Supreme Order of the Star-Spangled Banner or the Sons of the Sires of '76. Members solemnly promised to oppose foreigners and to support only American-born Protestants for public office. When asked about the society, members would answer, "I know nothing." Because of such answers the organization came to be known as the Know-Nothing Party.

During the early 1850's the Know-Nothing Party, officially called by now the American Party, was very strong in American political life. In the election of 1854 it polled one fourth of the total vote of New York and two fifths of Pennsylvania's vote. In Massachusetts it elected every state officer and nearly the entire legislature. In Baltimore the

■ This remarkable picture, painted in 1855, shows crowds of immigrants debarking at New York City. They were fleeing famine in Ireland and seeking a new life in America.

Know-Nothings organized the "Plug-Uglies," so-called because they went to the polls carrying carpenters' awls to "plug," or stab, voters who did not give a secret password. However, the election of 1854 was the high tide of the movement. In the national convention of the Know-Nothing Party in 1855, southern members and northern members split over the question of slavery. As a result of this split, the Know-Nothing Party gradually lost its strength.

Changing ways of life. From the 1830's to the 1860's, older Americans were bewildered and upset as they saw familiar, traditional ways of life replaced by new and unfamiliar ways. Most older Americans did not realize that machines, factories, and an *urban,* or city, way of life were causing the revolution taking place around them. Foreigners were only one of many new elements in the changing pattern of American society. But many native-born Americans blamed all their troubles, real and imaginary, on the new arrivals.

SECTION SURVEY

IDENTIFY: Potato Famine, Know-Nothing Party, urban.

1. (a) What conditions led the Irish to emigrate to the United States? (b) Where did they settle? Why?
2. (a) Why did the Germans come to the United States? (b) Where did they settle? Why?
3. (a) What was the aim of the Know-Nothing Party? (b) Give your opinion of this party.
4. (a) Why would immigrants tend at first to hold on to their old ways? (b) Why would this lead to resentment against them? (c) Would the children and grandchildren of immigrants be as likely to follow the "old ways"? Explain.
5. What were the contributions of the immigrants to the United States at this time?

TRACING THE MAIN IDEAS

Between the 1820's and the 1860's the Industrial Revolution continued to gain momentum in the United States. Every part of the country was affected by the influences of expanding industry. Even in the South, textile mills and ironmaking plants began to appear. But for the most part industrial development was concentrated in New England, New York, Pennsylvania, and in the growing cities of the Middle West. Immigrants settled mainly in the Northeast and the Middle West, where they took advantage of the opportunities provided by railroad building and other industrial enterprises, and by farming.

The industrial towns and cities, with their factories, their whirring machines, and their manufacturers, financiers, and wage earners, were becoming a major influence in America. Industrialism strengthened democracy by making it possible for the people to buy goods never before available to them and by raising their standards of living. It strengthened national unity by binding the nation together with roads, canals, and railroads.

But industrialism also created new problems. Wage earners, more and more dependent for their daily bread upon forces beyond their individual control, began to join together in labor unions; conflict between workers and owners became increasingly common. And widespread resentment of older white American workers toward black workers and toward immigrants helped to weaken the early labor movement. Finally, industrialism transformed the North into a new and distinct section of the country, creating serious differences between the North and the South.

CHAPTER SURVEY

QUESTIONS FOR DISCUSSION

1. The development of better methods of transportation was as important in uniting the country as the Constitution itself. Comment.
2. During the period just studied, two thirds of the immigrants to America were between the ages of fifteen and forty, and about two thirds were males. What do these figures indicate to you?
3. Describe four conditions which encouraged the development of manufacturing in the period before 1860.
4. (a) The growth of the labor movement paralleled the growth of industry. Explain this statement. (b) Summarize the obstacles confronting the labor movement during the period just studied. (c) What were the achievements of the labor movement during that period?
5. (a) Compare the reasons for immigration during colonial times with the reasons for immigration during the period 1830–50. (b) Why did native-born Americans heap the blame for many of their troubles on immigrants?
6. (a) In what ways did industrialization strengthen democracy and unite the nation? (b) In what ways did it promote sectionalism? (c) In what ways did it create new problems?

RELATING PAST TO PRESENT

1. Do groups similar to the Know-Nothing Party of the 1840's have the right to exist in our society today? Explain.
2. Is there a need in our society today for a "Know-Nothing Party"? Explain.

3. "Workers are dependent for their livelihood upon forces beyond their individual control." What does this statement mean? What "forces" are referred to?
4. Are minority groups still discriminated against in regard to (a) jobs, (b) unions? Explain.
5. For each of the following, compare current conditions in America with conditions during the period just studied: (a) strength of labor unions, (b) rights of women, (c) child labor, (d) working conditions.

USING MAPS AND CHARTS

1. Using the map on page 287, answer the following: (a) What determined the routes of the Erie Canal and the National Road? (b) Who benefited from these routes?
2. Using the map on page 290, answer the following: (a) What is the period covered by the map? (b) Where were most of the railroads located? Why? (c) Explain the reason for the smaller number of railroads built in the South.
3. Using the map on pages 292–93, (a) indicate the shortcuts available to world shipping during the period covered by the map. (b) What were the chief exports and imports of the United States at that time? (c) Explain America's great interest in whaling.
4. Refer to charts 1 and 2 on page 858 in answering the following: (a) Compare United States population in 1820 and 1860. (b) Compare immigration in 1820 with that in 1860. (c) What conclusions can you draw from these facts?

"COTTON is king" was an expression heard often in the South during the 1840's and 1850's. Travelers journeying in the autumn along the dusty southern roads saw the major wealth of the South in every field—ripe cotton, ready to be picked, cleaned of seed, packed in bales, and shipped to mills in New England and Great Britain.

Cotton was indeed important to a great majority of the people living in the southern states. By the 1850's the cotton grown, shipped, and sold by southerners was worth more than all the rest of America's exports put together.

But in talking about the importance of "King Cotton," southerners were not thinking of themselves alone. They knew that countless other people —in the northern states, in Europe, and around the world—depended upon southern cotton for their living. They were thinking of merchants who traded and shipped cotton and of the sailors who manned the ships; of owners of cotton textile factories and of the workers in them; of storekeepers and traders who sold cotton shirts and trousers and dresses in the United States, in Europe, in Africa, in India— wherever, in fact, they could find buyers.

Southerners could ask in the 1840's and 1850's: "What other product grown by man and fashioned into finished articles affects so many people in so many different parts of the world?" The answer was, "None."

Great changes had taken place in the southern states since the 1790's. When the Constitution was adopted, tobacco, not cotton, had been the most important southern crop. At that time also, many people in the South as well as in the North had thought that slavery would soon disappear in the United States. But now, in the 1850's, "cotton was king," and nearly 4 million slaves lived and worked in the South. The "Cotton Kingdom," with its system of slave labor, was becoming increasingly different from the North with its growing cities, its expanding population, and its free labor.

CHANGING WAYS
OF AMERICAN LIFE

CHAPTER 15

Creating a Cotton Economy in the Southern States

1820's – 1860's

THE CHAPTER IN OUTLINE

1. The development of the "Cotton Kingdom" in the South.
2. The role of the planters as leaders of the South.
3. The role of the slaves in building the "Cotton Kingdom."

301

1 The development of the "Cotton Kingdom" in the South

The southern states, by the 1840's and 1850's, covered a vast area stretching southward from Maryland and the Ohio River to the Gulf of Mexico. The states of Louisiana, Arkansas, and Texas were also included in this great cotton-growing region.

The farm lands. Travelers in the South at this time were most impressed by the endless acres of cotton fields. But they also saw many acres planted in other staple crops, such as tobacco, rice, and sugar cane. In Virginia, North Carolina, Kentucky, Tennessee, and Missouri, where the climate and soil were most favorable for tobacco growing, the fields were green with broad, flat tobacco leaves. Rice fields flourished in the swampy coastal areas of South Carolina and Georgia. To the west, in the delta of the Mississippi River, huge stands of sugar cane swayed and ripened in the warm winds that swept in from the Gulf of Mexico. Travelers in Virginia might see large fields of wheat and corn. In Texas they could see herds of long-horned cattle.

Southerners received much of their cash income from their staple crops—mainly cotton, tobacco, rice, and sugar cane. Most, though not all, of these staple crops were grown on large plantations.

But travelers in the South in the 1850's also saw many small *subsistence farms,* much like those that existed in the Northeast and Middle West, where families raised food crops and livestock for their own use.

Towns and industries. Since the southern economy depended mainly on agriculture, industries and towns naturally grew more slowly in the South than in the North. But the southern states had many towns and a few important cities, among them Richmond, Virginia; Charleston, South Carolina; and New Orleans, Louisiana.

The southern towns and cities had their tradesmen, skilled workers, and professional people—doctors, lawyers, clergymen, and teachers. Along the wharves and on the streets, visitors could see sawmills, paper mills, brickyards, leather tanneries, blacksmith shops, turpentine and whisky distilleries, and a few cotton mills.

By 1860 about 10,000 miles of railroad tracks had been laid throughout the southern states. Along the rivers and coastlines hundreds of steamboats were busy exporting the South's staple crops

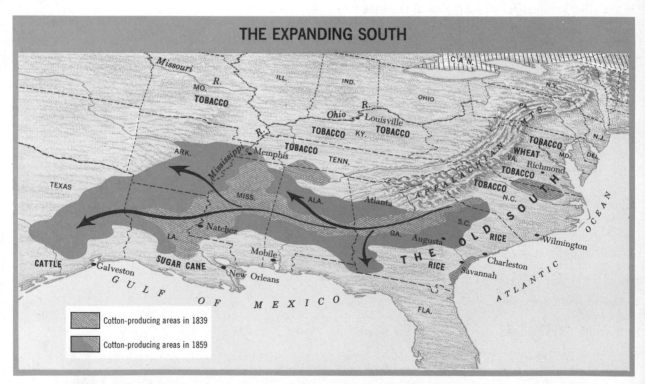

THE EXPANDING SOUTH

Cotton-producing areas in 1839
Cotton-producing areas in 1859

■ The famous French painter Edgar Degas painted this picture of a New Orleans cotton buyer's office in the 1870's. The scene would have looked much the same in the 1840's or 1850's.

to northern and European markets and importing manufactured goods.

By the 1850's some leading southerners were urging further development of southern industry and commerce. The southern economy, in short, was varied and complex. But southerners never lost sight of the all-important reality that "cotton was king."

The growing cotton economy. In the late 1700's, as you know, British inventors developed power-driven machinery for spinning thread and weaving cloth. Before long, textile mills were operating in the New England and Middle Atlantic states. As the textile mills produced more and more cloth, mill owners on both sides of the Atlantic began clamoring for more raw cotton fiber.

The heart of the cotton plant, called the boll, is

a tangle of fibers and seeds. Eli Whitney, inventor of interchangeable gun parts (page 250), in 1793 invented a machine that could separate the cotton seeds from the fibers much faster than could be done by hand. Whitney's machine, called the cotton gin, broke a bottleneck in the production of raw cotton fiber.

Before the invention of the cotton gin, cotton could be grown profitably only along the South Atlantic coast. Along this coast grew a limited amount of "sea-island cotton," whose long fibers could be separated from the seed fairly rapidly by hand. However, much larger amounts of "upland cotton" were grown in the interior of the southern states. The shorter fibers of upland cotton clung so tightly to the seed that a man could separate by hand only about a pound of cotton fiber a day.

303

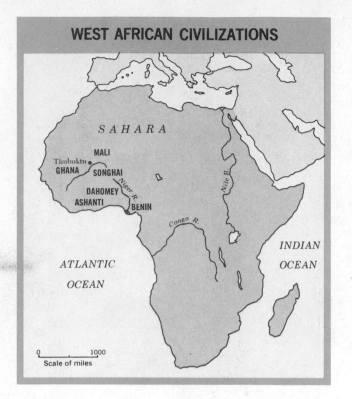

WEST AFRICAN CIVILIZATIONS

SAHARA

MALI
Timbuktu
GHANA
SONGHAI
DAHOMEY
ASHANTI
BENIN

Niger R.

Nile R.

Congo R.

ATLANTIC
OCEAN

INDIAN
OCEAN

0   1000
Scale of miles

In 1791 total American production of cotton fiber had been only 4,000 bales. By 1830 it had jumped to 732,000 bales. In 1860 the figure stood at more than 4 million bales, two thirds of the world's total production of cotton. Cotton alone represented about two thirds of the value of the entire nation's exports in the year 1860.

Cotton and slavery. From 1800 to 1860 southern prosperity became increasingly dependent on cotton. Textile manufacturers, needing more and more cotton, paid higher and higher prices for the supply that was often too small to meet their needs. Rising prices tempted southern planters to clear more land and grow more cotton.

As the demand for cotton increased, the rich soils of the Gulf states and the Mississippi Valley attracted cotton growers. Many southerners saw a chance to get ahead by moving west, clearing the soil, and starting cotton plantations. Thus, by 1845 the states of Louisiana, Mississippi, Alabama, Arkansas, Florida, and Texas were added to the original southern states.

By the late 1850's the cotton economy had reached the height of its power. The cotton lands, or cotton belt, stretched in a long crescent from North Carolina in the east to Texas in the west (see map, page 302).

To clear the land and grow cotton, a large supply of inexpensive labor was needed. The northern Europeans who were migrating to the United States preferred to find work in the North. Cotton planters therefore depended more and more on black slave labor.

Southern social groups. By 1860 the population of the South had risen to approximately 12 million. About 4 million were black slaves. The rest were mainly white southerners of English and Scotch-Irish ancestry. However, some southerners of French ancestry lived in the coastal plains of the Carolinas and around New Orleans, and some of German ancestry lived in Texas. But on the whole, European immigrants were not attracted to the South. More than 4 million immigrants were living in the United States by 1860, but only 13.5 percent of them lived in the southern states.

In the South as in other parts of the country, the population was divided into a number of social and economic groups. Except for slaves, who had almost no opportunity to better their lot, and for the free black people, whose opportunities were severely restricted, energetic and ambitious men were continually moving from lower to higher economic

Whitney's cotton gin, when operated by hand, enabled one man to separate 50 pounds of upland cotton a day. And when power was used to operate the cotton gin, a man operating the machine could separate more than 1,000 pounds a day.

More and more southern farmers now began to raise and sell cotton, first in Georgia and South Carolina, and later in the rich soils of the Gulf coast states and the Mississippi Valley (see map, page 302). Big 500-pound bales of raw cotton fiber were shipped in ever greater quantities to the textile mills of New England, the Middle Atlantic states, and Great Britain.

The expanding cotton market. By 1850, also, new methods of long-distance transportation had been developed—notably the steamship and the railroad. Mill owners in the United States and Europe could sell their finished products to more people in ever more distant markets. As cotton cloth became cheaper, the whirring looms of Great Britain and the northeastern United States began supplying bolts of cotton cloth to be made into clothing to peoples all over the world. Before long, clothing manufacturers began selling ready-made dresses, shirts, and trousers in worldwide markets.

groups. In the words of one southern historian, a man could mount "from log cabin to plantation mansion on a stairway of cotton bales. . . ."

What were the major economic and social groups in the South in 1860?

The slaves and their background. At the bottom of the social and economic pyramid in the South were the slaves from Africa. Numbering fewer than 1 million in 1800 and about 1.6 million in 1820, the slave population had increased to roughly 4 million by 1860. No other newcomers to America were so completely separated from their past as were the Africans. Theirs was a supremely tragic story.

When traders began transporting black slaves to the New World, Africa was then the homeland—as it is today—of many different social groups. Each group had developed its own way of life, its own culture. African social organization ranged from tribal groups and city-states to kingdoms and empires.

Long before the New World was discovered, a number of African societies had attained a high degree of civilization. In western Africa, for example, the ancient empire of Ghana (see map, page 304), from which the modern nation of Ghana has taken its name, reached the peak of its power 500 years before Columbus sailed for America. Ghana's empire was held together by an efficient political system and a well-trained army. The empire drew its main strength and wealth from trade across the Sahara. Because of this trade, flourishing commercial cities grew up in Ghana.

When Ghana finally declined, the kingdom of Mali rose in its place. Mali reached the peak of its power in the 1300's. The government of Mali was well organized and stable, its international trade prosperous. Most of the people were farmers, but many also worked as weavers, builders, miners, and metal craftsmen.

One of the most important cities of ancient Mali was Timbuktu, which became a famous center of learning. Moslem scholars and statesmen from many cities of the Middle East traveled regularly to Timbuktu. African scholars from the university at Timbuktu won fame for their intellectual activities. Many of them served as professors at various universities of the Middle East.

By the late 1400's the kingdom of Mali and much other west African territory became part of the powerful empire of Songhai. With a strong government and flourishing trade, Songhai was

■ Many beautiful works of art have come down to us from the West African kingdom of Benin. This mask, carved from ivory in the 1550's, probably was worn on the belt of a Benin king as a symbol of office. Notice the design on the collar and headdress; the faces represent Portuguese explorers who first visited Benin in the late 1400's.

prosperous. Much of its wealth was spent on education. Moslem students from abroad, as well as native Africans, learned literature, grammar, geography, law, and surgery in Songhai's schools and universities.

Another outstanding African culture developed in the Ashanti (ah·SHAN·ti) kingdom on the Gold Coast. When the first British visitors arrived in the Ashanti capital in 1817, they were astonished at what they found. The British saw a well-organized society with trained soldiers and an elaborate social

■ Here are two more works of art made by Benin artists. Below is a bronze plaque cast in the late 1500's or early 1600's. It depicts a Benin king with his attendants and gives us some idea of the pomp and ceremony of Benin court life. Above is a bronze statue of a leopard made about 1750.

life. They saw the high craftsmanship of the Africans revealed in beautifully woven silk robes and skillfully fashioned jewelry.

The first European visitors found similar conditions in the West African kingdom of Dahomey (dah·HOH·mi). The roads were broad and well laid out. Buildings were clean and neat. Law and order prevailed. Trade prospered. Taxes and custom duties were collected. Wood carving had reached an advanced state of development.

Still another advanced kingdom in West Africa that impressed European visitors was Benin. Benin developed during the 1200's and was a flourishing center of activity when the Portuguese arrived there in 1483. Artists of Benin created ivory carvings, iron work, and bronze sculpture of great beauty.

When the slave trade began, Africans from kingdoms and empires such as these, as well as men and women from the most primitive tribes, were torn from their homes and families. Arab and African slave traders drove them to the coast. There they sold these unfortunate African captives to European traders.

Between 1500 and the mid-1800's, at least 15 million Africans were taken from their homeland and transported to the New World. The effects on African society were devastating. Africa was drained of its most valuable resource—its people.

Slavery in the cotton lands. By 1860, as you know, about 4 million slaves lived in the South. About 500,000 of them lived and worked in southern towns and cities. The rest, about 3.5 million, worked on farms and plantations.

As white planters moved from the older southern states into the rich new cotton areas of the Gulf states, some of them took their slaves with them. Others sold their slaves before leaving and bought new ones on arrival. The increasing demand for slaves in the Gulf states led to a flourishing interstate slave trade. Professional slave traders bought slaves in the border states and transported them to slave auction centers at Natchez and New Orleans. There the slaves mounted auction blocks, to be sold to the highest bidder.

The interstate slave trade was often criticized for causing the breakup of many slave families. A few efforts were made to outlaw it, but after 1820 these efforts were abandoned.

By the 1840's and 1850, then, slavery was spreading across the South, and the number of southern slaveowners was increasing. By 1840 more than half the people in Mississippi were slaves, as were almost half of the people in Alabama and

Louisiana. Yet by 1860 less than 385,000 southern families owned slaves. This means that only about one fourth of all southern white families were slave-owners. Three fourths were not. In addition, most of the southern slave-owning families had only a few slaves. By 1860, in fact, less than 10,000 southerners owned 50 slaves or more.

Free black southerners. By 1860 about 250,000 free Negroes lived in the South, most of them in towns and cities. Some of them, as you know, had been freed by their owners. However, as slavery became more of an established institution, it became more and more difficult for masters to free their slaves. At the same time, "free" Negroes in the South enjoyed less and less freedom.

After 1830 the legislatures of all the southern states passed laws severely restricting the movements of free black people. Free Negroes had to register with the town authorities and carry a pass. Often they had to post *bonds*—money or a pledge of property—to guarantee their good behavior. Their property was taxed, but they could not vote. Nor could they testify in court against white citizens or slaves, although slaves as well as white citizens could testify against them.

There were many other discriminations. Free black southerners could not assemble freely for any purpose. In many places they were forbidden to attend churches, even all-Negro churches, unless a white person was present. Laws in some areas forbade them to learn how to read and write.

Although these severe laws and regulations were not always enforced, free black southerners lived under the constant threat that they might be. In addition, free Negroes never knew when some new law or discrimination might be imposed upon them or when they might be punished or even sold into slavery for some minor violation.

The poor whites. "Poor whites," who made up about 10 or 12 percent of the southern white population, formed another distinct group in the social and economic pyramid of the South. Other white southerners looked down on the poor whites, calling them "hillbillies," "crackers," or "piney woods folks."

Most of the poor whites were frontier families, many of whom lived in log cabins. Their standard of living was low, partly because they lived on the poorer soils, called "pine barrens," or along the rugged Appalachian mountainsides and other hilly areas that were hard to cultivate. These people often suffered from poor health, but they had pride and a fierce independence.

■ Slaves worked on farms and plantations, in cities and towns, in a variety of skilled and unskilled jobs. The poster above includes mention of a cook and nurse, a painter-carpenter, a bilingual maid, and a coachman.

Laborers and tenants. White farm laborers and tenant farmers formed another large southern group. The farm laborers were hired to work for wages during the harvest season or to do some work regarded as too dangerous for the expensive slaves. The tenant farmers rented and tilled fields that were usually worn out from overuse. These tenant farmers generally lived in debt.

The small farmers. Many small independent farmers in the South owned several acres of productive land and lived much like small farmers in other parts of the country. These people, often called "yeomen," lived in rudely constructed but reasonably comfortable frame houses, considerably better than the one-room log cabins of the poor whites. Each year the small farmers sold a bale or two of cotton as a cash crop. Their food came largely from the corn, potato, and vegetable patches around their houses. They were almost self-sufficient and had in addition a small cash income of about $100 a year. Some owned more land and were fairly prosperous.

The small slaveowners. Some small southern farmers who prospered bought a slave or two, or perhaps a slave family. A really prosperous small farmer might have 8 or 10 slaves.

When a small farmer acquired a few slaves, his scale of living did not usually change. He often continued to work in the fields himself, alongside his newly purchased slaves. Although his cash income might increase to perhaps several hundred dollars a year, he remained a member of a distinct social group, separated from the rich planters on the one hand and the poor whites on the other. Some small farmers lived in the cotton belt, with only a fence separating them from the plantations. However, most of them lived to the north of the cotton belt and in the fertile valleys of the Appalachian Mountains.

The planters. The most influential people in the South—the planters—were also the fewest in number. According to the Bureau of the Census, a southern "planter" was a person engaged in agriculture who owned 20 slaves or more. In 1860 the Bureau of the Census reported that there were only about 50,000 southern planters.

SECTION SURVEY

IDENTIFY: "King Cotton," staple crop, cotton gin, subsistence farm, Timbuktu, Songhai, interstate slave trade.

1. What factors enabled the South to become the world's greatest cotton-producing area between 1800 and 1860?
2. Explain the relation (a) between cotton production and westward expansion and (b) between cotton production and slavery.
3. "No other newcomers to America were so completely separated from their past as were the Africans." Explain.
4. Compare the life of (a) poor whites, (b) farm laborers, (c) tenant farmers, (d) small independent farmers, and (e) free Negroes.
5. Due to slavery, African society was drained of its most valuable resource—its people. (a) Comment on this statement. (b) Why are people the most valuable resource that a society has?

2 The role of the planters as leaders of the South

As a general rule, the planters held the leading political positions in the South. They usually represented the southern states as Senators and Representatives in the Congress of the United States.

Who were the planters? Many southern planters were descendants of the wealthy colonial planters of the eastern seaboard states. Others were self-made men who had worked their way up the economic and social ladder. For example, Joseph Emory Davis, a brother of Jefferson Davis, produced 3,000 bales of cotton each year on Mississippi land that he had carved out of frontier wilderness. Southerners who started life as small farmers and rose to positions of influence included such prominent leaders as John C. Calhoun of South Carolina and Andrew Jackson of Tennessee.

The plantation home. Travelers who journeyed through the South in the 1850's occasionally passed an imposing mansion set well back from the road with close-clipped lawns sweeping down to a river. The house itself, shaded by tall trees and surrounded by formal gardens, looked cool and inviting with its wide verandas and its white Grecian pillars supporting the roof.

Many of these mansions, often having 12 or 15 luxuriously furnished rooms, were places of distinction and beauty. These were the homes of the wealthy planters who owned 100 to 500 slaves or more. However, even as late as 1860 fewer than 2,500 planters could afford such luxury.

The planter who owned from 20 to 100 slaves lived well, but more modestly. His home might have as many as 8 or 10 rooms, with wide halls and deep verandas surrounded by spacious, shaded grounds. The furnishings inside the house were usually comfortable but not luxurious, for most of the planter's wealth was tied up in land and slaves. He could not afford expensive household goods or lavish entertainment. In fact, such planters and their families often lived lonely, isolated lives.

Educational leadership. For the most part, the wealthy planters and their families received excellent educations. This in itself helps to explain their strong influence. Believing firmly in the importance of education, they hired private tutors for their children or sent the boys to private schools. A high proportion of the older boys went to college. Most attended William and Mary College, the University of Virginia, or some other southern institution, but many went north to Yale, Harvard, Princeton, West Point, and Annapolis. Hundreds of these young graduates of southern and northern colleges rose to positions of leadership in the South.

Political leadership. The form of local government that prevailed throughout the South had been introduced into Virginia by the first English settlers and had later spread throughout the southern states. This form of local government enabled the planters to control the machinery of southern government and to hold all the leading political offices in the South.

The county was the most important southern political unit, and the most important county officers were the justices of the peace. These men—in varying numbers up to 35 for each county—were appointed by the governor of the state, who usually was a wealthy planter himself. The justices had broad powers. They levied taxes. They provided for the building of roads, bridges, and schoolhouses. They appointed sheriffs to enforce the law.

Once a month the justices met as a judicial body to try law cases. The justices also met informally and unofficially to choose candidates for election to the state legislature and to the Congress of the United States. Without their approval it was difficult if not impossible for any southerner to win an election for county, state, or national office.

The planter's duties. When the planter was not away from home on public business, his life was comfortable but not easy. He had to attend to an endless number of details.

In addition to supervising the work on the plantation itself, the planter had to keep records of his business transactions. And he had to write numerous letters to shipowners and bankers and to the agents who sold his cotton to the textile mills.

In terms of money in the bank, the planter was not usually a rich man. He shipped his cotton in care of an agent in the North Atlantic states or in Great Britain. The agent sold the cotton and shipped back whatever agricultural tools, clothing, books, and household furnishings the planter wanted. Frequently, after his cotton was sold and his purchases made, the planter found himself in debt to the agent, who handled his business on commission.

Even more time-consuming was the day-by-day routine of managing the plantation. Each morning the planter or his overseer assigned jobs to the slaves, such as tending the cotton, hoeing corn, cultivating other food crops, cutting wood, hauling water, feeding livestock, and doing household

■ Many southerners came to feel that slavery was not only necessary for the South, but also profitable. The "Oakland House and Racecourse," painted in 1839 and shown above, illustrates the elegance of wealthy southern life at this time.

chores. There was always much work to be done, for a cotton grower also raised most of the food eaten by his family and slaves.

Was slave labor profitable? It is impossible to say whether or not slave labor was really profitable for the southern planters. Many planters and most small farmers did not keep accurate accounts and did not know from one year to the next just how much they had earned or lost.

Before 1840 some southerners believed that slave labor was becoming less profitable than hired labor. In 1837 George Tucker, a professor at the University of Virginia, argued in a book entitled *The Laws of Wages, Profits, and Rents* that slavery was an inefficient system of labor. To support this argument, Tucker and others pointed to the high cost of buying slaves; to the fact that unwilling workers were usually poor workers; to the expensive supervision that was required to keep slaves at work; to the cost of food, clothing, and shelter,

309

■ The rare photograph above was taken in 1862. It shows a group of slaves—men, women, and children—on a South Carolina plantation.

which continued even when slaves could not work; and to the economic losses caused by a slave's illness or death.

But after 1840 such arguments were heard less frequently. Many southerners had come to feel that slavery was not only necessary for the South, but that it was also profitable. Thus southerners were angered when, in 1857, a small farmer from Carolina published a book that tried to prove that the South was economically inferior to the North because of the inefficiency of slavery. The author, Hinton Rowan Helper, called his book *The Impending Crisis*. Feeling in the South ran so high against Helper that he found it wise to move to the North.

Actually, there is evidence that the large rice, sugar, and cotton plantations were often profitable to their owners, depending partly upon weather conditions and market prices and depending especially on managerial skill. On the other hand, some planters were regularly in debt, and many were just barely breaking even.

The pro-slavery argument. Whether or not slavery was a profitable labor system, by 1860 it had become a firmly established institution on all southern plantations and many small southern farms. And as slavery grew and spread, it became the subject of increasingly bitter controversy between southerners and northerners. In defending their way of life, southerners developed what has come to be called "the pro-slavery argument."

The pro-slavery argument declared, in part, that slavery was necessary because, without it, southern planters would not have an adequate labor supply. The argument held further that the institution of slavery was not only necessary, but was of positive value to the slaves themselves. It provided them with shelter, clothing, and food; it took care of them in sickness and old age; it provided them with a secure and stable existence.

The champions of slavery often contrasted the secure life of the Negro slave with the uncertain lot of white wage earners in the mills, factories, and mines of the North and of Europe. These white workers, it was argued, were exploited mercilessly by their employers, who had no concern for their well-being, who paid them barely enough to live on, who fired them when there was no work to do, and who discarded them when they were too ill or too old to work.

The pro-slavery arguments were popularized throughout the South by leaders at political rallies, by newspaper editors, by novelists and short-story writers, and by preachers. The arguments were mainly advanced by, or on behalf of, the large plantation owners. But small planters, who often wanted to become large planters, also accepted the pro-slavery argument, as did small farmers who owned no slaves, but who hoped in time to acquire some. Even the poor whites accepted the pro-slavery argument because it added to their sense of solidarity and pride in being members of the white society of the South.

Most average white southerners, then, as well as wealthy southerners, accepted the arguments in defense of slavery and spurned the arguments of men who opposed slavery. White southerners largely accepted the leadership of the great plantation owners and the institution of slavery itself. They identified slavery with the distinctive southern way of life. They regarded any criticism of slavery, or any efforts to restrict it, as hostile to their homes, their land, and their way of life.

SECTION SURVEY

1. Explain the conditions that enabled the large planters to hold many of the leading political positions in the South.
2. The life of the planter was "comfortable but not easy." Explain.
3. State the arguments that were presented to show that slavery was not profitable.
4. Summarize the main points of the pro-slavery argument.
5. Slavery was identified with the distinctive southern way of life. Comment.
6. Why did the average white southerner accept the institution of slavery?

3 The role of the slaves in building the "Cotton Kingdom"

Probably no modern American, black or white, can fully imagine what it was like to be a slave. But based on the records available to them, historians have tried to reconstruct an accurate picture of slave life in the southern states in the years before 1860.

The study of slavery. On the basis of documents and records alone, no historian can accurately reconstruct what it was like to be a slave. There are many records, but most of them were written by white southerners or by white travelers from the North or from Europe.

A few slaves who could write left short accounts of their lives. A larger number who escaped to the North or to Canada wrote more detailed autobiographies. Long after slavery ended, scholars interviewed former slaves and recorded their memories.

In addition to written records, historians have also examined the surviving work songs and religious spirituals in which the slaves expressed some of their feelings. And in trying to reconstruct an imaginative but accurate picture of slave life, historians have also used some of the scholarly methods of sociology, anthropology, and psychology. What, then, are some things that can be said about slavery as the slaves actually lived it?

The work the slaves did. By 1860 the nearly 4 million slaves in the South performed a wide variety of jobs. Many worked in the homes of the planters, cooking the meals, doing the housekeeping, and tending the children.

Some of the slaves became skilled workers. Women learned to spin, weave, and sew. Some became cooks, maids, laundresses, dairymaids, and nurses. Men became blacksmiths, painters, shoemakers, jewelers, and silversmiths. Others learned to do the carpentry, bricklaying, and other tasks required to build a house. Some could not only build the house, but could also make necessary plans, draw up contracts, and complete the entire structure.

Some slaves were hired out by their owners to work in tobacco factories, in sugar and flour mills, and in iron works. A great many did hard, unskilled work in building canals, roads, and railroads, and in draining swamps. Large numbers worked as stevedores at seaports, lifting and carrying heavy loads on and off ships.

The great majority of the slaves on the cotton,

rice, and sugar cane plantations did the hard work of the fields. Men and women planted the crops in the spring and cultivated them through the summer. In the fall the slaves picked cotton, cut sugar cane, harvested rice and grain, and slaughtered livestock. In the winter they mended fences and cleared new land.

How slave labor was organized. On farms and small plantations, the slaves were usually supervised by their owners. On small farms, owners sometimes worked alongside their slaves.

On large plantations, work was organized either by the task system or by the gang system. Under the *task system,* each slave was assigned a particular job to do each day and was free when the job was finished. At such times, some slaves earned wages by working for someone else. Under the more widely used *gang system,* an overseer, or foreman, assigned groups of slaves to work under "drivers," who were also slaves. The gang worked as long and as hard as the overseer or driver saw fit. The purpose of the gang system was to get as much work as possible out of the slave labor force.

How slaves were treated. Although records are scanty, there is some evidence that slaves were more humanely treated on small farms and small plantations than on large ones. On large plantations, where overseers were frequently in command, slaves were often treated harshly if not brutally. But the records are mixed. There is evidence that slaves on some large plantations of the lower South received better food, living quarters, and medical care than slaves on poorer farms and small plantations.

Many planters treated their slaves reasonably well because the slaves were valuable property. For example, imagine a planter who owned 50 slaves. Allowing from $1,000 to $1,500 for each slave, an average price in the 1850's, the planter's investment in slaves was from $50,000 to $75,000.° The death of a single slave meant a serious financial loss; even the illness of a slave was a setback. Any illness or injury resulting from ill-treatment was against the planter's interests. To protect his investment, therefore, the planter was apt to keep his slaves adequately fed, clothed, and housed.

Much of the pro-slavery argument was based on these grounds. Advocates of slavery argued that the living standards of the slaves—their working day, their food, clothing, and shelter—were better

and more secure than those of free white workers in the mills and factories of the North.

But that argument left much out of account. The industrial worker of the North could quit his job and look for another. If he had some cash, he could move to the relatively cheap farm lands of the western regions. He was a free person. The slave, by contrast, was property. He had no voice in deciding the conditions of his work or even of his life. The free worker, to be sure, had to submit to the discipline and rules of the mill or factory where he worked, but that discipline differed sharply from slave discipline.

Slave discipline. Slaveowners had to teach their slaves to be slaves—that is, to be obedient and accept their lot. Slaveowners did this partly by persuasion. They taught their slaves that it was their religious duty to obey their master, mistress, or overseer. Slaves were taught to believe that any white person was superior by nature to any black person.

These efforts were conscious and deliberate. Plantation owners bought handbooks on how to manage slaves. Some handbooks contained question-and-answer lessons, which the slaves had to memorize. These lessons were meant to teach them always to obey and respect white people, never to argue with them, and to accept their own condition as slaves.

Under these psychological pressures, and dependent as they were upon their masters for food, clothing, and shelter, many slaves came to regard themselves as children. Some masters encouraged this attitude by giving small gifts or special privileges to obedient slaves, as is often done with children.

When persuasion failed, masters and overseers could and did resort to brutality. If a slave showed signs of disobedience, stubbornness, or independence, he might be flogged or whipped. If this did not work, the slave might suffer even more painful and degrading punishments, such as being branded or having his nose slit. The worst threat facing many a slave was that he might be sold and thus deprived of the few cherished family ties he had developed.

This discipline encouraged many slaves to be outwardly childlike and obedient toward white people, but it also encouraged deceitfulness. Many slaves wore masks of outward respect and subordination to escape penalties or win rewards. But these masks sometimes concealed resentment and hatred toward white people.

° In terms of today's dollar value, of course, this amount would be many times greater.

■ This Currier and Ives print shows a rather idealized scene of a southern plantation. The planter is talking to his wife (foreground) as slaves harvest cotton.

How slaves resisted. Despite the many efforts to control them, many slaves, as you know, found ways of resisting slavery (page 66).

No one knows how many slaves ran away from the plantations, some to join relatives from whom they had been separated, others to seek freedom in the North or in Canada. The number of fugitives probably ran into thousands each year. Many, however, were captured by professional slave catchers who used bloodhounds to pursue the runaways.

Slaves even in colonial times had plotted uprisings to secure their freedom (page 66). These rebellions continued into the 1800's.

In 1791 the slaves of Haiti carried out a successful revolt against their French masters (page 232). In Henrico County, Virginia, a slave named Gabriel Prosser heard of this revolt and was inspired by it. He secretly organized a group of slaves, forged weapons, and set a date for an uprising in 1800. Gabriel Prosser's plot was betrayed by two fellow slaves. Pursued by Virginia militiamen, the con-

spirators disbanded but were caught and punished.

An uprising was said to have been organized in Charleston, South Carolina, in 1822 by Denmark Vesey, a former slave. But reports of this plot may have rested largely on unfounded fears among white southerners, since no actual act of rebellion took place. Whatever the facts may have been, 37 Negroes were put to death and others were severely punished.

In 1831 a slave named Nat Turner led a slave uprising in Southampton County, Virginia. Outwardly obedient, Nat Turner had learned to read the Bible and was deeply religious. Believing that God had chosen him to slaughter white people and free the slaves, Nat Turner began his rebellion. Before troops suppressed it, 60 white people and more than 100 slaves were killed. Turner was captured, brought to trial, and hanged. After this rebellion, all southern states severely tightened their control over black people, free as well as slave.

Most slaves, of course, took no part in rebellions.

313

■ Nat Turner, believing that God had chosen him to slaughter white people and free the slaves, led a slave uprising in Virginia. Looking at the above picture, what kind of a man does Turner (shown with outstretched arm) seem to be? Would you have pictured Turner differently?

Most never tried to run away. But they did express their unhappiness and misery under bondage in haunting religious songs called spirituals. These hymns, rich in Biblical lore, were modeled in part on the "gospel hymns" sung by white Christians, but they were also influenced by traditional African musical forms. Nearly all Negro spirituals poignantly expressed the slaves' deep longing for freedom.

The heritage of slavery. The slaves made enormously valuable contributions to the wealth of their owners and to the wealth of the entire southern economy. However, these contributions were made at enormous costs to the slaves. While the institution of slavery existed in the United States, black people were deprived of the opportunities and freedoms enjoyed by all other Americans.

314

SECTION SURVEY

IDENTIFY: task system, gang system; Gabriel Prosser, Denmark Vesey, Nat Turner.

1. (a) What resources have historians employed in reconstructing a picture of southern slave life in the years before 1860? (b) Can the picture ever be complete? Why or why not?
2. (a) What work did slaves do? (b) How was their labor organized? (c) How were they treated? (d) What was the basic difference between southern slaves and northern white workers?
3. (a) Why was it necessary to teach slaves how to be slaves? (b) Why did the methods of disciplining the slaves lead to role playing on the part of many Negroes?
4. Enumerate the ways in which slaves resisted slavery.

TRACING THE MAIN IDEAS

The South, as well as the Northeast, was greatly influenced by the Industrial Revolution that began in England in the late 1700's and soon spread to many other countries in the Western world. The invention of power-driven machines for spinning and weaving yarn created a growing demand for cotton fiber. The invention of the cotton gin gave planters an effective machine for cleaning the seeds from cotton. The invention and development of better methods of transportation made it possible for planters to ship their cotton to the new factories in England and the Northeast.

Except for the cotton gin, however, few machines were used on southern farm lands. Slaves cleared the land, plowed the fields, planted the seeds, and harvested the white and fluffy crop of cotton. As the years passed and larger areas of the South were planted in cotton, slaves became increasingly numerous and increasingly valuable.

By 1860, nearly 4 million slaves in the South were farming cotton and other major crops, or working as skilled laborers. Although treatment of slaves varied, slave owners in general used a variety of methods to train and control their slaves. Despite these efforts, some slaves revolted and many others ran away. Other evidence, such as that found in the Negro spirituals, also expressed the slaves' deep longing for freedom. Slaves contributed enormously to the southern economy, but were deprived of the opportunities and freedoms enjoyed by other Americans.

Only a small percentage of southerners owned slaves. But, in general, the slaveowners were the wealthiest, the best educated, and the most influential men in the South. They were the political leaders who ran the governments in the southern states and who represented the South in the Congress of the United States. These men—and their wives and families—created a way of living different from that in any other section of the country.

You have now seen how distinctive ways of living and working developed in the North and the South. We turn now to the third section of the United States—that vast and rapidly expanding region known as the West. As you will see, it, too, was transformed during the first half of the 1800's.

CHAPTER SURVEY

QUESTIONS FOR DISCUSSION

1. (a) The southern economy before 1860 was varied and complex. Explain. (b) If you had lived in a southern town, what jobs would have been available to you?
2. When the Civil War broke out, why were poor whites and small farmers who owned no slaves willing to fight on the Confederate side?
3. Study the various illustrations that appear throughout the chapter you have just studied. (a) What conclusions can you draw concerning life in the South before the Civil War? (b) Do you think that these illustrations present a realistic picture of life at that time? Explain.
4. Describe he aspects of slavery that made it a dehumanizing institution.

RELATING PAST TO PRESENT

1. What effects of slavery can you find in today's society?
2. Does today's South still have its own distinctive way of life? Explain.
3. Did the poor people of the North and the South prior to 1860 have goals that were different from the goals of poor people today? Explain.

USING MAPS AND CHARTS

1. Using the map on page 302, (a) explain the shift of cotton-producing areas between the 1830's and the 1850's, (b) locate the Old South, and (c) justify the statement that economic life in the South was varied in spite of the dominance of "King Cotton."
2. Name the two least populated southern states in 1860 (see map, page 861).
3. (a) If you had been a cotton planter living in the 1830's who planned to buy a new plantation, and you had before you the map on pages 852–53, in which area would you have decided to buy land? Why? (b) Turn to the map on pages 864–65, examine it, and then decide whether your choice would have been a practical one.
4. Using the map on page 304, list the West African kingdoms shown and give dates for each.
5. Explain the nature of American exports in 1850. Consult chart 2 on page 873.

CHAPTER 16

Expanding the Nation's Boundaries to the Pacific

1820's – 1860's

Bᴇɢɪɴɴɪɴɢ in earliest colonial times, hardy pioneers had been attracted to the untamed frontier lands of the New World. Generation after generation of American settlers had been drawn ever farther westward. By the 1840's it was clear that the United States was about to fulfill its "manifest destiny"—the occupation of the vast area between the Mississippi River and the Pacific Ocean. A majority of Americans believed that their nation's historic mission, or manifest destiny, was to possess all the lands stretching from sea to sea.

From the 1820's to the 1860's, Americans continued to move into the lands between the Appalachian Mountains and the Mississippi River. But many restless pioneers were casting eager eyes on lands farther west. In 1821 Missouri, west of the Mississippi, was admitted to the Union. In the 1820's and 1830's pioneers also crossed the Mississippi into what in 1838 became the Iowa Territory.

Immediately ahead lay the Great Plains, known to the pioneers as the Great American Desert. This vast, almost treeless expanse, covered with grass and sagebrush, did not appeal to the pioneers until a later time.

But beyond the Rockies, far to the northwest, beckoned Oregon—a fertile and forested land, well watered. To the south lay the magnet of Texas, a rich land thinly settled by Spaniards and Mexicans. Far to the west of Texas and even more thinly settled by Spaniards and Mexicans was California.

From the 1820's to the 1860's, as you have seen, the Industrial Revolution was creating a distinctive way of life in the North, while cotton cultivation was creating a different way of life in the South. In this chapter you will learn how the third great section of the United States—the "West" as we know it today—was added to the nation.

THE CHAPTER IN OUTLINE

1. Expansion of fur traders and settlers into the Oregon country.
2. Creation of the Lone Star Republic of Texas by American settlers.
3. Adding the entire Southwest to the nation after war with Mexico.
4. California's entry into the Union after a surge of migration.

1 Expansion of fur traders and settlers into the Oregon country

Far to the northwest of Missouri, beyond the Rocky Mountains, lay an enormous area of towering mountains, magnificent forests, and fertile valleys drained by rivers teeming with fish—the area now called the Pacific Northwest. This rich area, then known as the Oregon country or simply as Oregon, stretched northward from the 42nd parallel, the northern border of California, to the parallel of 54° 40', the southern boundary of Alaska (see map, page 319). Until the early 1820's the Oregon country was claimed simultaneously by four nations—Spain, Russia, Great Britain, and the United States.

Conflicting claims. The Spanish claim to the Oregon country dated back to an agreement made between Spain and Portugal in 1494 (page 7). Spain, however, gave up its claim in 1819, under the same treaty in which Spain ceded Florida to the United States (page 319).

Russia based its claims to the Oregon country on the explorations of Vitus Bering, a Dane who had explored the area for Russia in 1741. Following Bering's explorations, the Russians had established missions and trading posts in Alaska and then northward along the coast as far as northern California.

Increasing Russian pressure along the Pacific coast after 1815, you will recall, had partly led the United States to issue in 1823 what became known as the Monroe Doctrine. President Monroe had warned Russia and other European nations that the United States would not tolerate any further colonization in the Western Hemisphere. The Russian tsar decided not to force the issue, and, in 1824 the Russians withdrew their remaining claims to all land south of the 54th parallel.

Great Britain based its claim to the Oregon country on voyages made to the Pacific by Francis Drake in 1577–80 and by Captain James Cook in 1776–78. The government of Great Britain encouraged British fur traders to develop a profitable fur trade with the Indians of the Pacific Northwest.

The United States had established its first claim to the Oregon country in 1792, when Captain Robert Gray, a merchant sea captain from Boston, discovered the Columbia River and began trading for furs. The American claim was strengthened when American fur traders began traveling overland to the Oregon country in the early 1800's.

In 1818 Great Britain and the United States

Charles Degs, "The Trapper," Yale University Art Gallery, The Mable Brady Garven Collection

■ The Mountain Men were a hardy breed, as rough and ready a group of men as one could find in America in the early 1800's. They discovered trails and passes through the Rockies that were later used by settlers moving west.

agreed to occupy the Oregon country jointly for 10 years. Ten years later, after Spain and Russia had given up their claims, Great Britain and the United States renewed their agreement.

American fur traders. The American interest in the far western fur trade began in earnest after the Lewis and Clark expedition of 1804–06 (pages 233–34). Centering in St. Louis, the western trade was gradually organized by enterprising business concerns like the Rocky Mountain Fur Company. This company outfitted rugged "Mountain Men" who roamed the West searching for animal pelts. During the trapping season the Mountain Men lived like the Indians and traded with them. In the spring they returned to St. Louis, where their employers paid them for their loads of pelts. The pelts were then marketed in the East and in Europe.

The Mountain Men were a hardy breed, as rough and ready a group of men as one could find in America in the early 1800's. Jedediah Smith and

James P. Beckwourth were typical of these adventurous fur traders.

Jedediah Smith, in a few brief years in the 1820's, explored more of the Far West than any white man before him. He was the first white American to cross the desert into California. As a trapper, hunter, and leader, Smith was outstanding. At age 33, however, his fur-trading days came to an abrupt end when he was killed by a band of Comanche Indians.

James P. Beckwourth, another outstanding Mountain Man, joined his first fur trading expedition at St. Louis in 1823. Beckwourth, who was part Negro, was probably hired as a groom to care for the expedition's horses. As time passed, he became a full-fledged Mountain Man, marrying a succession of Indian maidens from the Blackfoot, Snake, and Crow tribes, as other Mountain Men did also. He lived among the Crows for six years and, according to his own claim, became their chief. After leaving the Crows, Beckwourth roamed throughout the West, discovering in 1850 a mountain pass that is still named for him.

In their explorations of the Far West the Mountain Men discovered trails and passes through the Rockies that were later used by settlers moving west. The most important of these passes, the South Pass in what is now Wyoming, led to a trail that crossed the Continental Divide and cut through the Snake and Columbia river valleys to the Pacific Ocean. In the 1830's it was found that covered wagons could be driven over this route. Later, the route came to be known as the Oregon Trail (see map, page 319).

Rivalry for furs. The Rocky Mountain Fur Company, which employed many Mountain Men, was a very successful business venture. Even more successful was the American Fur Company formed in 1808 in New York by John Jacob Astor, a German immigrant. Astor engaged in bitter contests with his American and British rivals for control of the North American fur trade.

By the 1820's the American Fur Company controlled most of the American trade in the Upper Mississippi Valley, in the Rockies, and in the Oregon country. Astor soon had sales offices in St. Louis, New York, England, France, Austria, and China. In 1832 the company sold 25,000 beaver skins, nearly 50,000 buffalo hides, about 30,000 deerskins, and many other pelts.

Rivalry between the fur trade companies, and their greed for profits, often led to unfair dealings and trouble with the Indians. The federal government tried for a while to solve these problems by setting fixed prices for animal pelts. But the government gave up its effort in 1823, largely because of pressure from the private traders.

Missionaries in Oregon. The fur trade led to the exploration of the river routes over the Great Plains, the mountain passes, and the Oregon country itself. It also led in the 1830's and 1840's to the settlement of that part of the Oregon country south of the Columbia River. The surge of settlement was stimulated mainly by missionaries and by New England businessmen interested in trade and fishing.

The first missionaries traveled to the Oregon country with fur traders. Jason Lee, a Methodist, built a mission and a school for Indian children in the fertile Willamette Valley in 1834. Samuel Parker, a Presbyterian minister, followed him a year later. In 1836 Marcus Whitman and H. H. Spalding, both Presbyterians, made the long overland journey with their young brides. In 1840 Father Pierre De Smet, a Jesuit priest, arrived in the Oregon country.

The early settlers. The missionaries sent back east for more settlers. By the 1840's pioneers were entering the Oregon country at the rate of a thousand a year. They usually traveled in groups, partly to protect themselves when crossing the Indian country. The pioneer groups followed the Oregon Trail through the South Pass and along the Snake River and Columbia River into the Oregon country.

The pioneers came in ever-growing numbers, some bringing with them their Negro slaves. A few free black men came also. Although some southerners wanted to establish slavery in the Oregon country, most of the settlers were opposed to it. Thus, as early as 1845 slavery in the Oregon country was forbidden by law. However, the same law set up severe discriminations against free Negroes, ordering them, under the threat of flogging, to leave the country within two years.

From the beginning the settlers in the Oregon country felt a need for government. In 1843 nine men drew up a resolution which said in part: "We the people of Oregon territory, for the purposes of mutual protection and to secure peace and prosperity among ourselves, agree to adopt . . . laws and regulations, until such time as the United States of America extend their jurisdiction over us. . . ."

Settling British-American claims. According to the agreement reached in 1818 and later re-

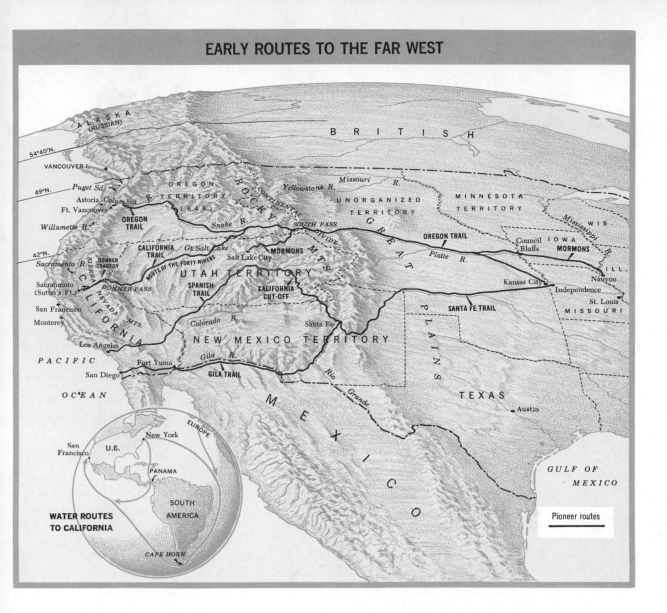

Pioneer routes

WATER ROUTES
TO CALIFORNIA

newed, Great Britain and the United States were to occupy the Oregon country jointly. But by 1840 it was clear that a new solution was needed to settle rival British-American claims.

Many Americans were demanding that the British withdraw all claims to the land south of the line 54° 40'. This demand became a major issue in the Presidential election of 1844. The Democrats, under the leadership of James K. Polk of Tennessee, made western expansion the keynote of their campaign.

Although some Americans spoke with bitter and even warlike words, calmer minds prevailed. Through compromise Great Britain agreed in the Treaty of 1846 to give up its claims to the Oregon country south of the 49th parallel (see map, this page).° Thus, by 1846 a boundary existed between the United States and Canada from the Atlantic to the Pacific Ocean. At first this boundary was

° Earlier, in 1818, a treaty between the United States and Great Britain had established the boundary between the United States and Canada as far west as what is now Montana (page 245).

319

■ Going west on the Oregon Trail was a long, rugged trip through dry lands, mountains, and Indian country, but at the end lay rich and inexpensive land. Albert Bierstadt, the artist of the picture shown above, has painted a scene of the trip.

marked by a few minor fortifications. Since then it has been completely unfortified.

In 1848 that part of the Oregon country which now clearly belonged to the United States was organized as Oregon Territory.

SECTION SURVEY

IDENTIFY: Oregon Trail, Mountain Men, Treaty of 1846 (with Great Britain); John Jacob Astor, Jedediah Smith, James P. Beckwourth.

1. (a) Why was there a dispute over the Oregon country? (b) Why did the United States and Great Britain at first agree to occupy the Oregon country jointly?
2. Show how each of the following helped to lay the basis for American claims to the Oregon country: (a) Captain Gray, (b) Lewis and Clark, (c) Mountain Men, (d) Astor, (e) missionaries, (f) settlers.
3. How did the United States finally acquire the Oregon country?

2 Creation of the Lone Star Republic of Texas by American settlers

In the early 1820's, when Americans first began showing interest in the Oregon country, other traders and settlers were already moving southwestward into Spanish lands. As the traders and settlers moved in, they began a chain of events that eventually led the United States to acquire the vast area now occupied by Texas, New Mexico, Arizona, California, Nevada, and Utah, as well as parts of Colorado and Wyoming.

Spanish settlements. Spanish claims to this vast country were based upon explorations made by De Soto, Estevanico, and Coronado in the 1540's (page 12).

In the 1600's and 1700's the Spaniards began to spread thinly northward from Mexico City—the heart of their New World empire. In 1609 they established Santa Fe, in what is now New Mexico. For a long time Santa Fe remained their chief northern outpost. In the 1700's, fearful of possible threats from the French and the British, the Spaniards renewed their colonizing efforts. Throughout the present states of Texas, New Mexico, Arizona, and California, they established forts, missions, villages, towns, and scattered ranches of enormous size.

The missions. The missions were an important part of the Spanish colonizing system. Some missions were founded by Jesuit and Dominican priests, but most were established by Franciscans. The missions tried to convert the Indians to Christianity, to teach them Spanish ways of life, and to make them loyal subjects of the Spanish Crown.

The center of each mission was the church, often a beautiful structure built of stone or *adobe* (ah·DOH·bih), bricks of baked clay. The mission also included living quarters for the priests and workshops in which the Indians learned weaving, silverworking, blacksmithing, and other crafts. Generally the main buildings were enclosed within an adobe or a stone wall. Around the mission were farming areas, where the priests and Indians grew grain, grapes, and other crops and sometimes raised cattle. After the Indians had become Christians and had learned Spanish ways of living, they were sometimes given farm lands of their own near the mission.

The Spaniards hoped that vigorous communities would develop around the missions, with each mission as the center of community life. Although this goal was only partly realized, the missions exercised a strong influence along what is now the southern border of the United States from Texas northward to San Francisco Bay. To this day this area is dotted with remains of the old Spanish missions—some still used as churches, some preserved for visitors, and some in ruins.

Attitude toward outsiders. Thus, for almost two centuries after the founding of Santa Fe in 1609, the Spaniards occupied or claimed much of what has become, roughly, the southwestern quarter of the United States.

Then, after the Louisiana Purchase of 1803, Americans began to move westward toward the Spanish frontiers. The Spanish authorities tried to protect themselves by forbidding all trade with the Americans and by seizing American explorers and traders who entered their lands. But the Spanish policy of excluding Americans began to weaken late in 1820. At that time Moses Austin, a Connecticut-born pioneer, received permission to establish a colony of a few hundred American families in what is now Texas, with the understanding that they would become loyal subjects of Spain.

A more liberal attitude. Moses Austin died in 1821 before he could establish his colony. Also in 1821 the Mexicans, after a successful revolt against Spanish rule, established the Republic of Mexico (see map, page 259). The new government of Mexico adopted a more liberal attitude toward American traders and settlers.

Soon a flourishing overland trade developed between Independence, Missouri, and Santa Fe. Long trains of American wagons—loaded with all sorts of manufactured goods, from pins and needles to rifles—set out from Independence on the long and dangerous Santa Fe Trail (see map, page 319). In Santa Fe they traded their goods for silver, gold, or hides, and then began the long journey home. Hostile Indians—especially the Comanches—often attacked the traders along the way.

Settlers in Texas. In addition to letting down barriers against trade, the new Mexican government also opened its doors to settlers. It gave Stephen F. Austin, the son of Moses Austin, a renewal of the grant of land that his father had received from the former Spanish authorities. Stephen Austin, a well-educated man noted for fairness, good judgment, and organizing ability, began in 1821 to build a vigorous American colony in Texas. Austin's "Old Three Hundred" settlers were hand-picked pioneers.

Other settlers soon followed. By 1830 more than

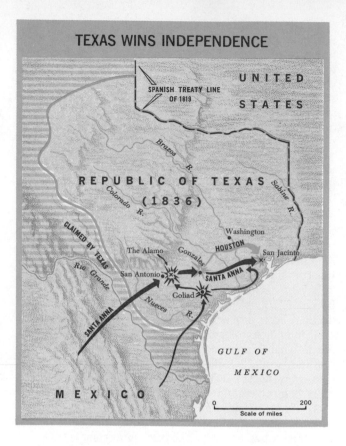

TEXAS WINS INDEPENDENCE

SPANISH TREATY LINE OF 1819

UNITED STATES

Brazos R.

REPUBLIC OF TEXAS
(1836)

Colorado R.

Sabine R.

CLAIMED BY TEXAS

Rio Grande

Washington

The Alamo   Gonzales   HOUSTON

San Antonio   SANTA ANNA   San Jacinto

Goliad

Nueces R.

SANTA ANNA

MEXICO

GULF OF MEXICO

0   200
Scale of miles

Mexican authorities would not reconsider. After several clashes with Mexican officials, fighting broke out.

An event sometimes called "the Lexington of Texas" took place on October 2, 1835. The commander of the Mexican troops stationed at San Antonio tried to seize a cannon that had been given to the settlers at Gonzales (gon·ZAH·lehs) for defense against the Indians (see map, this page). A group of Texans blocked his efforts. He returned to San Antonio without the cannon.

Later, a band of Texas volunteers led by Ben Milam defeated a large Mexican force in desperate house-to-house fighting in San Antonio. Prisoners taken in the battle were permitted to return to Mexico.

Infuriated by this defeat, General Santa Anna, the dictator president of Mexico, promptly led a large army back into Texas. The Mexican army besieged a force of almost 200 Texans in the Alamo, a fortified former mission at San Antonio (see map, this page). Among the defenders were a number of famous Texans, including James Bowie and William B. Travis, the joint commanders, aided by newcomer Davy Crockett. They refused to surrender despite overwhelming odds. When Santa Anna stormed the fort on March 6, 1836, they were killed to the last man. On March 27 another force of Texans was massacred at Goliad (goh·lih·AD) after it had surrendered and laid down its arms.

The desperate Texans rallied under the cry, "Remember the Alamo! Remember Goliad!" Led by Sam Houston, the Texans destroyed Santa Anna's advance guard at San Jacinto (SAN jah·SIN·toh) on April 21, 1836, and Santa Anna was captured. After a secret treaty was signed, Santa Anna was released with the understanding that he would use his influence to make Mexico recognize the independence of Texas, with its southern boundary at the Rio Grande.

Independence for Texas. Back in March, while the defenders of the Alamo were still holding off the Mexicans, a group of delegates assembled at Washington-on-the-Brazos (BRAZ·us), then a small village of 10 or 12 rude dwellings. There, in a cold, drafty gun shop, the Texans on March 2, 1836, declared their independence. They also drafted a constitution for a new Republic of Texas, often called the Lone Star Republic. Sam Houston, a former governor of Tennessee, became the first elected president of the Republic of Texas.

Annexation delayed. During the revolution American sympathy was, of course, with the Tex-

---

20,000 Americans, many of them southerners, had entered Texas. By that time, slavery had been outlawed in Mexico; thus, it was technically illegal for southerners to bring slaves into Texas. However, since the Mexican authorities were lax in enforcing this law, many southerners brought their slaves along anyway.

The Mexican authorities soon saw that their liberal policies were encouraging the growth of an American community, or even an American state, within Mexico itself. Convinced that too many independent-minded Americans were entering, the Mexican government began to close its doors to further settlement. In 1830 it passed a law which tried to restrict further settlement in the Mexican states bordering the United States. Land grants not already taken up were canceled. The Mexicans also restated that slavery on Mexican lands was forbidden. To enforce their laws, the Mexicans strengthened their army posts throughout Texas.

The fight for independence. The Americans in Texas protested vigorously against what they said were restrictions on their individual rights. But the

■ Davy Crockett, one of the heroes of the Alamo, is shown using his rifle as a club as he tries to defend himself against advancing Mexican soldiers.

ans. Volunteers, recruited in the United States, crossed into Texas and fought against Santa Anna. But when the new republic petitioned to join the United States, strong opposition developed. Since Texas wanted to permit slavery, northerners in Congress feared that its admission would unduly increase southern influence in Congress. Others feared that to admit Texas would be to invite war with Mexico, which had not recognized Texas' independence. Thus, the admission of Texas was delayed.

Free black settlers in Texas. Although Texas wanted to allow slavery, it did not want free Negroes to live within its borders. In 1840 the new Lone Star Republic ordered all free black settlers to leave Texas or be sold into slavery. The free black men, many of whom had fought in the struggle for Texan independence, protested. The Texans then decided that free Negroes could remain—but only if they made a special appeal to the Congress of the Lone Star Republic.

In some southeastern counties of Texas, free Negroes formed a sizable minority. The Ashworth family, for example, had come to Texas in the early 1830's to take up land granted to them by the Mexican government. The Ashworths, as well as other free black settlers in Texas, owned land, cattle, and even slaves. For a time they got along fairly well with their white neighbors, but as the war between North and South approached, tensions and even feuds arose.

SECTION SURVEY

IDENTIFY: Lone Star Republic; Moses Austin, Stephen F. Austin, Sam Houston, Santa Anna, Ashworth family.

1. What were the aims of the Spaniards in establishing missions?
2. Why did the Texans revolt against Mexican rule?
3. (a) Explain the historical importance of the slogan "Remember the Alamo! Remember Goliad!" (b) What is the function of slogans?
4. Describe the role played by Sam Houston in the history of Texas.
5. Why was the annexation of Texas to the United States delayed?
6. (a) In what ways were free black settlers in Texas similar to white settlers? (b) What was the position of free Negroes when Texas became a republic? Why?

3 Adding the entire Southwest to the nation after war with Mexico

The annexation of Texas in 1845 moved the United States one step closer to war with Mexico. But other factors also led to the Mexican War which finally broke out in 1846.

Sources of friction. At the root of the conflict was the fact that two different ways of life met and clashed in the vast region west of Texas, including the Mexican area known as Upper California (the California we know today). Mexico's claim to all this territory, a claim inherited from the Spaniards, dated back to 1494, more than a century before the first English settlement appeared on the Atlantic coast. Spanish law, Spanish architecture, Spanish customs, and the Spanish language prevailed throughout the area.

Against this frontier of Spanish culture with its leisurely tempo of life pressed an irresistible tide of energetic, land-hungry Americans. These Americans believed firmly that it was the "manifest destiny" of their nation to expand to the Pacific Ocean.

In the 1830's and early 1840's ill feeling between Mexico and the United States steadily mounted. During most of these years, the Republic of Mexico was torn by revolutions; its government was often corrupt and irresponsible. As a result, Americans —whom the Mexican authorities were now trying to keep from settling on Mexican soil—were often thrown into Mexican jails and mistreated. Indeed, 22 Americans suspected of plotting a revolution were executed by the Mexicans in 1835 without a trial.

Debts owed by the Mexican government to United States citizens also contributed to the ill feeling. During Mexico's struggles to win its independence from Spain, the property of many Americans living in Mexico had been damaged or destroyed. In 1839 an international commission examined American claims and awarded United States citizens about $2 million. By 1845 Mexico had paid only three installments.

The Mexicans also had many grievances against the United States. They were bitter about American expansion into Texas and the Texas revolution of 1836, which they blamed on the United States. They feared that Texas was only the beginning of an American attempt to win control of the entire Southwest.

Rising war fever. American naval and military commanders in the Pacific area had standing orders to seize Upper California if war broke out between the United States and Mexico. In 1842 Commodore Thomas A. C. Jones, hearing a false rumor that war had been declared, sailed swiftly to Upper California, seized the capital at Monterey, hauled down the Mexican flag, and raised the Stars and Stripes. The next day, learning that he had made a mistake, Commodore Jones apologized profusely and withdrew in haste.

In the Presidential election of 1844, the Democrats demanded that Texas, as well as Oregon, be annexed to the nation. When the Democrats won the election, the government took steps to admit Texas to the Union without delay. To the Mexicans, who had never recognized the Republic of Texas, this was the final blow. The Mexican government broke off diplomatic relations with the United States.

Texas was finally admitted to the Union in December 1845. Meantime, the new President, James K. Polk, had even greater plans. He wanted the United States to acquire the whole vast area stretching from Texas to the Pacific Ocean. But he hoped to do so by peaceful means. In November 1845 he sent Ambassador John Slidell to the Mexican government with an offer to buy Upper California and New Mexico. The Mexican government refused to receive Slidell, and he returned empty-handed.

Outbreak of war. President Polk was now sure that Mexico would never willingly give up New Mexico and Upper California, or its claim to Texas. However, he still wanted this vast area to belong to the United States, and he was ready to declare war to get it. Several members of his cabinet urged him to delay, saying that if he waited long enough, Mexico would probably commit some act that would justify war.

In January 1846, however, Polk ordered troops under General Zachary Taylor to move southward from the Nueces (noo·AY·ses) River to the north bank of the Rio Grande (see map, page 326). Ever since Texas had declared its independence from Mexico, Texans had claimed that their territory reached southward to the Rio Grande, but the Mexicans had insisted that it ended farther north at the Nueces River. By sending troops into this disputed area, Polk could claim that he was acting defensively. But the Mexicans could claim that the United States was acting aggressively.

Months passed, and President Polk's impatience mounted daily. Finally, on May 9, the President notified his cabinet that he intended to recommend

■ Spanish law, architecture, customs, and language prevailed in the territory of Upper California. A Spanish mission, founded there in 1770, is shown above.

war with Mexico within a few days. But that very night he received the news he had long been wanting. Mexican troops had crossed the Rio Grande and had fought with American forces.

Convinced that the American people would approve his action, Polk sent his war message to Congress on May 11. "But now after reiterated menaces," he declared, "Mexico has passed the boundary of the United States, has invaded our territory and shed American blood upon American soil. . . . War exists, and notwithstanding all our efforts to avoid it, exists by the act of Mexico herself. . . ." On May 13, Congress declared war.

Who started the war? Many people at the time and many people since have believed that the United States started the Mexican War by a deliberate act of aggression. One person who questioned American actions was Abraham Lincoln, a young Illinois lawyer, then serving his only term in Congress. In 1847 he introduced in Congress his famous Spot Resolutions, questioning whether the "spot" on the north bank of the Rio Grande where American blood had been shed was really United States soil.

On the other hand, some historians have maintained that Mexico deliberately sent troops across the Rio Grande, hoping to start a war that it thought it could win.

Despite the great difference in size between the United States and Mexico, many Mexican military leaders believed that they could defeat the Americans. The Mexicans had expelled the Spaniards in 1821 and had overthrown revolutionists in their own country since that time. Thus they were confident of their military abilities. They also hoped that Great Britain would come to their aid, because the British, wanting to develop their own trade with the Republic of Texas, had opposed its annexation to the United States. The Mexicans believed, too, that the people of the United States would never support a war.

Mexican hopes were misplaced. The Mexicans did not have the necessary military power. Great Britain did not support them. And, although some northerners feared that slavery might expand into the vast area that might be acquired as a result of the conflict, the American people in general supported the war once it had begun.

Military operations. Armed forces of the United States operated in three different areas (see map, page 326). One area included Upper California and New Mexico. Upper California fell al-

MAJOR CAMPAIGNS OF THE MEXICAN WAR

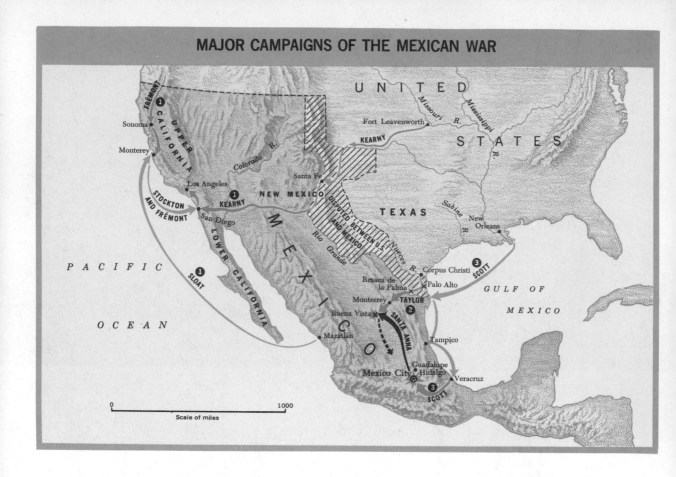

most without a struggle. Even before news reached Upper California that war had been declared, a few dozen Americans led by William B. Ide had begun to plot against Mexican rule. They carried on their discussions in the camp of Captain John C. Frémont, a famous explorer who had arrived in California the previous autumn with 62 men picked for their marksmanship. At Sonoma on June 14, 1846, Ide and a band of American settlers proclaimed the Republic of California, or the Bear Flag Republic, and hoisted a flag with a bear and a star painted on it as a symbol of independence.

On July 7 Commodore J. D. Sloat of the United States Navy, hearing of the outbreak of war, landed naval forces at Monterey on the California coast, raised the American flag, and proclaimed California a part of the United States. Frémont then organized most of the Americans, including the Bear Flaggers, into a "California battalion," and, with Commodore Robert F. Stockton, moved south and captured Los Angeles. At the same time

an overland expedition led by Brigadier-General S. W. Kearny left Fort Leavenworth on the Missouri River, occupied Santa Fe, and thereby won control of New Mexico. Kearny then continued into California.

Meanwhile, in a second area south of the Rio Grande, an expedition under General Zachary Taylor won victories at Palo Alto and Resaca de la Palma (reh·SAH·kah day lah PAHL·mah) on May 8 and 9, 1846, before war was actually declared. Taylor then went on to capture Monterrey, Mexico, in September 1846 and to check the Mexican forces under Santa Anna at Buena Vista (BWAY·nah VEES·tah) in February 1847.

Despite these defeats the Mexicans continued to fight. Polk ordered a third expedition to advance against Mexico City, the capital of Mexico, over the route once traveled by Cortés. Under the leadership of General Winfield Scott, an expeditionary force including marines was landed from naval ships near Veracruz on the Gulf of Mexico. Nearly

326

every step of the long, mountainous road to the "Halls of Montezuma" was bitterly contested. Hard battles were fought at several places, but on September 14, 1847, American troops entered Mexico City as conquerors.

End of the war. By 1848 Upper California, New Mexico, and the entire Southwest were in American hands. General Taylor's troops held northern Mexico, and General Scott's forces walked the streets of the Mexican capital. Hopelessly defeated, the Mexicans had to end the war on American terms as written down in the Treaty of Guadalupe Hidalgo (gwah·dah·LOO·pay e·DAHL· goh) in 1848.

From the Mexican point of view, these terms were severe indeed. Mexico was forced to give up Texas, New Mexico, and Upper California—two fifths of Mexico's land. In return for this huge area, called the Mexican Cession (see map, pages 856–57), the United States gave Mexico $15 million and agreed to assume debts totaling over $3 million that Mexico owed to Americans.

The dreams of all Americans who had believed in their nation's "manifest destiny" had come true. The southwestern boundary of the United States reached to the Pacific.

Finally, in 1853, Congress approved a payment to Mexico of $10 million for the Gadsden Purchase (see map, page 856), an area of land south of the Gila River needed to construct a southern transcontinental railroad. The purchase was named for James Gadsden of South Carolina who, as minister to Mexico, negotiated the purchase. Except for Alaska, the Gadsden Purchase rounded out the present continental boundaries of the United States.

(see map, pages 856–57)

SECTION SURVEY

IDENTIFY: "manifest destiny," Spot Resolutions, Bear Flag Republic, "Halls of Montezuma"; James Polk, Zachary Taylor, Winfield Scott.

1. What were the reasons for the Mexican War from (a) the American point of view, (b) the Mexican point of view?
2. Do you think the war was justified or not? Give reasons.
3. (a) What were the terms of the Treaty of Guadalupe Hidalgo of 1848? (b) What was the significance of this treaty in American history? (c) Why did the Mexicans think the treaty terms were harsh?
4. What was the importance of the Gadsden Purchase?
5. Two cultures were in conflict in Texas and the region west of Texas. Explain.

4 California's entry into the Union after a surge of migration

While government officials in the United States, Canada, Great Britain, Mexico, and Texas were wrestling with the problems created by American expansion into the Oregon country and the Southwest, settlers continued to cross the Great Plains and thread their way through the passes to the Rocky Mountains and beyond.

The Mormons and Utah. One of the largest groups was the Mormons. The Mormon Church, or the Church of Jesus Christ of Latter-Day Saints, had been founded in western New York in the 1820's by young Joseph Smith. Smith announced that he had found golden plates on which sacred scriptures were engraved. When translated, these became the "Book of Mormon." Thousands of converts joined the new religious faith.

In three different places—Kirtland, Ohio; Independence, Missouri; and Nauvoo, Illinois— Mormons attempted to build an ideal society where they could live and worship in their own way. Each time, they were driven away by hostile neighbors who did not understand them and who disliked their idea that they were a chosen people with a special revelation of truth. In Illinois, many people further disapproved of the Mormons because of their open acceptance of polygamy. In Missouri, people who favored slavery disliked the Mormons because they feared that the Mormons would oppose slavery—simply because most Mormons came from the Northeast. It apparently made little difference to the pro-slavery Missourians that Joseph Smith opposed the abolition of slavery.

The Nauvoo community in Illinois prospered more than the other two. By 1844 it had become a thriving town of 15,000 persons. In that year, however, nearby communities organized against the Mormon leadership. Joseph Smith and his brother Hiram were shot by a brutal mob which invaded the prison in which the leader and his brother were lodged for their own protection. Once again the Mormons were forced to move.

Under the able leadership of Brigham Young, the Mormons moved out of Nauvoo. Their long caravan of loaded wagons moved westward across the plains, through the towering Rockies, and finally stopped in 1847 on the eastern shore of Great Salt Lake (see map, page 319). There the Mormons plowed and irrigated the fields, learning many lessons about desert farming which they passed on to later western settlers. They laid out Salt Lake City on the Jordan River, and erected a temple which became world-famous. The Mormons also sent missionaries to the ends of the earth and organized ways of transporting converts to their new communities in Utah.

Utah was not admitted to the Union until 1896. By that time it was a settled and prosperous region, born out of a desire similar to that which had driven the Pilgrims, Roger Williams, and others to worship God in their own way.

Spanish rule in California. Beyond the shore of Great Salt Lake, hidden by the towering Sierra Nevadas, lay Upper California. Neither Spain nor Mexico had ever been strong enough to exploit this rich land.

From the beginning the ruling authorities in Mexico City had looked upon Upper California as an outpost of their empire, a defense against invaders, but for a long time there was little threat of invasion. The Spaniards became concerned in the 1700's, however, when Russians began to establish fur trading posts in the Oregon country and when Russian vessels began to appear off the coast of northern California. To strengthen their claims to the area, the Spaniards in 1769 sent soldiers and missionaries to build forts and missions in Upper California.

Led by Gaspar de Portolá and Father Junípero Serra, Spaniards moved northward along the Pacific coast until they reached San Francisco Bay. For the next 15 years Father Serra, a Franciscan priest, worked to strengthen the authority of the Spanish Crown and the Roman Catholic Church in California. Before his death in 1784, Father Serra, aided by other Franciscans, had built a chain of missions in the fertile valleys along the coast from San Diego to San Francisco Bay.

After Father Serra's death other devoted friars continued his work. Indians gathered around the missions to till the fields, to learn handicrafts, and to be instructed in the ways of God. Besides the missions there were a few forts and a few small towns, among them San Diego, Los Angeles, Monterey, and Yerba Buena (YAIR·bah BWAY·nah), where San Francisco now stands. Scattered sparsely over this immense territory were the estates of powerful Spanish landowners.

In this rich land of rare beauty, of vast distances, of unbelievable contrasts of climate and topography, life moved at a slow and leisurely tempo. There was little trade with the outside world or even with Mexico itself. The Californians sold some hides, mostly to American trading vessels that stopped now and then at the ports, but on the whole each ranch and each mission was self-sufficient.

Mexican rule in California. Neither Spain before 1821 nor Mexico after 1821 exercised firm control over California. In fact, Mexico weakened its strongest hold over the area in 1834 when it forced the Church to sell its mission lands to private owners. After this happened, the Indians began to leave the missions, drifting back into the interior. One by one the missions closed.

In 1846, when a handful of Americans staged the Bear Flag Revolt, there were no more than 4,000 Mexicans in all of California, and only 500 of them were soldiers, scattered among half a dozen forts. The forts themselves and their armament were completely out of date.

Even though Spanish and Mexican control was weak, to this day the influence of Spanish culture can be seen everywhere in California. Many towns, rivers, and mountains have Spanish names. Spanish laws, customs, and architecture still continue to enrich California life.

Settlers in California. A region as rich and beautiful as Upper California could not long be hidden from the eyes of restless Americans pressing steadily westward. In 1841 a party of men, women, and children, led by John Bidwell, "the prince of California pioneers," set out from Missouri. Their trip across the plains and mountains, as revealed in the journal of their leader, is a tribute to human courage. "We knew only," Bidwell wrote, "that California lay to the west."

The Bidwell pioneers were followed by many others, including the ill-fated Donner party. Caught in 1846 in the Sierra Nevada mountains by the icy grip of an early winter, the Donner party built crude shelters and struggled to survive. Soup made of boiled leather and powdered bones became a luxury. Of the 79 persons who started, 34 died before an expedition out of California rescued the survivors.

The Gold Rush. By 1848 several hundred Americans had settled in California. Among the early settlers was John A. Sutter from Switzerland, whose sawmill and fort at Sacramento were the center of bustling activity. On the morning of January 24, 1848, one of his employees, James W. Marshall, detected flakes of yellow metal at the bottom of a stream where a new mill was being

328

■ "California News" was painted by William S. Mount in 1850. It shows an eastern post office, where people gathered to talk of California, and of the Gold Rush.

built. The shining substance was gold. Despite Sutter's desire to keep the discovery secret until a new mill was built, the news spread like wildfire. The small flow of California settlers swelled into a powerful flood. In 1849, a year after the discovery of gold, the entire male population of the eastern half of the United States seemed to be moving west.

Stories of huge fortunes made overnight circulated through the nation. Some stories were true; most were false. True or false, the stories stirred men's imaginations. By the thousands they sold all they owned and joined the mad rush of the "Forty-Niners" to the gold fields of California.

Adventurers from Europe and the eastern United States converged upon California by three routes

■ This photograph shows a prospector panning for gold. He is squatting by a creek bed, swirling sand and water together in his pan. As he does so, flakes of gold sink to the bottom of the pan, while the lighter sand spills over the edge.

(see map, page 319). The longest route was the safest and most comfortable, as comfort went in those days. This route was by ship around Cape Horn.

The quickest, most crowded, and most expensive route was by ship to Central America, by land across the Isthmus of Panama, and by another ship from there to San Francisco. Every old ship that could float was pressed into service. Crowds of men in bright shirts and slouch hats, armed with bowie knives and pistols, raced to get across the bottleneck of the Isthmus and on to one of the few ships sailing between Panama and California.

A third route, fit only for the rugged and the brave, led across the Great Plains and through the mountain passes—the route of the Bidwell and Donner parties. Many of the wagon trains of the "Forty-Niners" took as long as five months to make the trip from the eastern seaboard. Many trails along the route were lined with household goods thrown away to lighten the load and with dead bodies of animals and men struck down by Indians, disease, hunger, thirst, cold, or heat.

The first wave of "Forty-Niners" jammed into lawless mining camps. Some found riches beyond their wildest dreams. Most found only disappointment. As the months passed, two streams of travelers passed on the trails and roads leading from San Francisco to the mining regions. Going west were newcomers eager for fortunes; returning east were disappointed gold seekers who had given up the search.

Included in the wave of "Forty-Niners" were black men, slave and free. Some worked as servants. Others searched for gold in crews under the direction of a slaveowner. A few became independent miners. Moses Rodgers, for example, born a slave in Missouri, became a mining authority whose advice was often sought by other gold seekers.

Statehood for California. Gradually the uproar subsided, and some men began to build houses, hotels, stores, and shops in the rapidly growing towns and cities. Some settled on the land and began to farm. Settlers built schools and churches. A government that was partly military and partly civilian was formed.

Late in 1849 a convention met and drafted a state constitution, which was accepted by the people. The constitution outlawed slavery in California. In 1850 Congress approved the constitution, and California promptly entered the Union as a free state, adding another star to the American flag.

SECTION SURVEY

IDENTIFY: Donner expedition, "Forty-Niners"; Joseph Smith, Brigham Young, Father Serra, John Bidwell, John Sutter; 1849.

1. (a) Why were the Mormons persecuted? (b) How did they respond to persecution?
2. The influence of Spanish culture in California is still apparent. Explain.
3. (a) Who were the "Forty-Niners"? (b) Why did they go to California? (c) How did they get there?
4. Did California make its entry into the Union as a slave state or as a free state?

TRACING THE MAIN IDEAS

The "Westward Movement" began with the first settlers along the eastern seaboard of North America. Driven by the excitement of exploring the unknown and by the desire for land, generation after generation of pioneers followed the setting sun across the vast, untamed continent.

By the early 1800's the frontier had advanced to the Mississippi River. By 1850 bold pioneers had crossed the 2,000-mile stretch of plains and mountains and were building new homes in Oregon and California on the Pacific coast. Other pioneers had moved into Texas and the Southwest. Only the plains and mountains remained to be settled. "Manifest destiny" had been fulfilled. The United States extended from ocean to ocean.

This immense area reaching from the Mississippi Valley to the Pacific coast was populated by people whose means of livelihood and ideas about government were in many respects different from those of people who lived in the North and in the South. The differences were less important, however, than the fact that the West was growing rapidly in population and in political strength.

As you will see in the next unit, both the North and the South struggled for control of the West. They struggled in the halls of Congress as well as on the plains themselves. This struggle is one of the keys to understanding American history during the generation before the outbreak of armed conflict between North and South. Before turning to this story, however, you will read in the next chapter about some of the developments that were transforming American life during the years between the 1820's and the 1860's.

CHAPTER SURVEY

QUESTIONS FOR DISCUSSION

1. Illustrate the importance in American history of (a) the frontier, and (b) the idea of "manifest destiny."
2. What was the basis for claims to the Oregon country by (a) Spain, (b) Russia, (c) Great Britain, and (d) the United States?
3. The northwest boundary of the United States is 49° north latitude. What is the story behind this boundary line?
4. Compare the motives of the Americans who pioneered in the Pacific Northwest and Texas.
5. Americans viewed the acquisition of Florida, of Texas, and of Oregon each in a different way. Explain.
6. Critics have attacked the United States' annexation of Texas and the war with Mexico as being imperialistic. Others have defended both as necessary to our "manifest destiny." What evidence can you find to support each of these views?
7. Compare the motives that led Americans to settle Utah and California.

RELATING PAST TO PRESENT

1. A westward movement is still going on in our country. In an almanac, find population figures for the state of California in 1950, 1960, and 1970. Why do you think this population movement is continuing? What other states have had a substantial growth in population since 1950? What states have declined in population since 1950? Why?
2. Using a modern road map of the western United States, together with the map on page 287, (a) determine whether the modern highways follow the old western trails; (b) determine which modern cities were in existence during the period 1820–60.
3. In what ways are our lives easier than the lives of the frontiersmen? In what ways are they more difficult?
4. In the period just studied, America's foreign policy was based on the idea of a "manifest destiny" to expand to the Pacific Ocean. What do you believe is the main goal of American foreign policy today?

USING MAPS AND CHARTS

1. Using the map on page 319, answer the following: (a) If you had been living in St. Louis in the 1840's and wanted to go west, which area would you have chosen for settlement? Why? (b) Describe the route that you would have followed. (c) Which route to the West would you have preferred to take if you had been living on the east coast? Why?
2. (a) Referring to the map on page 326, indicate the major objectives of the military moves by Frémont, Sloat, and Kearny. (b) What were the major objectives of the expeditions of General Taylor and General Scott?
3. Referring to chart 2 on page 854, answer the following: (a) Compare the area, in square miles, of Texas with that of the Mexican Cession. (b) What percentage of the present United States area did these two constitute? (c) What states were formed out of the acquisition of Texas and the Mexican Cession?

CHAPTER 17

Stirring the American People with Ideas of Reform

1820's – 1860's

THE TERM "to ferment" means "to be inwardly active, agitated, or excited; to seethe mentally or emotionally. . . ."

It would be difficult to find a more accurate term than "ferment" to describe the activities of the American people in the years from the 1820's to the 1860's. The United States was indeed in ferment during these years. Changes were taking place with bewildering speed.

The very appearance of America was changing. Industrialism was transforming the North. Cotton growing was bringing prosperity to large areas of the South. Land-hungry pioneers were pushing the frontiers across the Great Plains, through the Rocky Mountains, and into the fertile valleys of the Pacific Northwest and sunny California. In outward appearance the United States by the 1830's and 1840's was a much different country from the United States of the 1790's.

The ideas of the people were also changing. By the time Andrew Jackson became President in 1829, all white male adults had won the right to vote. Political democracy brought new hope to the people. Those who had won the right to vote, and those who hoped to win it, expected to use their newly won power to make the ideals of democracy work more effectively in everyday affairs.

During the period from the 1820's to the 1860's, reformers were seeking to improve almost every aspect of society. Millions of Americans were "inwardly active, agitated, or excited."

"We are all a little wild here with numberless projects of social reform," Ralph Waldo Emerson, the New England writer and philosopher, wrote to a friend in England.

The story of this period of reform, this age of "ferment," is told in this chapter.

THE CHAPTER IN OUTLINE

1. The struggle of reformers to improve American life.
2. A promising start for free publicly supported education.
3. Development of a vigorous movement to abolish slavery.
4. Rising tensions and their effects on the abolition movement.
5. Expression of a deep faith in individual liberty.

1 The struggle of reformers to improve American life

One of the many reforms Americans were working for in the period from the 1820's to the 1860's was a more important place for women in American life.

The status of women. From the earliest days women worked together with men in the development of America. They shared the loneliness, the dangers, the desperately hard work involved in transforming the wilderness into a land of prosperous farms and thriving towns and cities.

But even as late as the 1830's women had legal rights far inferior to those of men. In some states a married woman had almost no right to own property. When a woman married, all her property went to her husband. If she earned money or inherited property after marriage, it too belonged to her husband.

Moreover, a married woman had almost no legal claim to her children. The husband controlled his sons and daughters while he lived. He, not both parents, decided what the children should do. Indeed, if a man wished, he could leave a will placing his children under a guardian after his death, even though their mother was still alive. However, men rarely used their full legal rights over their wives and children.

As for politics, that was entirely a man's job. Women often exercised a strong influence over husbands and friends, but the rights to vote and to hold office were a man's rights.

Declaring women's rights. By the 1820's and 1830's women were protesting loudly and defiantly against their lowly place in society. Women frequently tried to force their way into men's meetings, even into political conventions. The men, astonished at this "unladylike" conduct, usually turned them away.

A few leaders of the women's rights movement came from Europe, where a similar struggle was under way. For example, Ernestine L. Rose of Poland, Frances Anne Kemble of England, and Frances Wright of Scotland crossed the Atlantic to help American women in their struggle for equal rights.

But American women bore the brunt of the struggle. Among the American leaders were Lucretia Mott and Elizabeth Cady Stanton. These two women were largely responsible for organizing the first women's rights convention, held at Seneca Falls, New York, in July 1848. The women delegates adopted a Declaration of Sentiments, which said, "All men and women are created equal . . ." and went on to list demands for political, social, and economic equality with men. But decisive gains in these fields did not come until after 1850. Early victories came mainly in the field of education.

Education for women. By the 1820's education for girls and women was getting under way. Emma Hart Willard opened the Troy Female Seminary at Troy, New York, in 1821, and began to teach mathematics, science, history, and other subjects. During the next few years Catharine Esther Beecher, Mary Lyon, and other dedicated women opened schools for girls.

The coeducation movement made some headway in the Middle West. The first male college to open its doors to women was Oberlin Collegiate Institute in Ohio, which admitted women four years after it was founded in 1833. Other colleges in the Middle West followed Oberlin's example. In 1856 the University of Iowa became the first state university to admit women.

Early achievements. Slowly, and against strong opposition, women began to win places in what had been considered a "man's world." Dr. Elizabeth Blackwell, the first woman to win a medical diploma in the United States, began to practice medicine in New York City in 1850. She founded the first school of nursing in the United States and in 1875 became a professor in the London School of Medicine for Women. Her sister-in-law, Antoinette Louisa Blackwell, became the first fully ordained female minister in the United States.

Other women won distinction as writers and editors. Louisa May Alcott wrote a number of

LIVING AMERICAN DOCUMENTS

The Seneca Falls Declaration of
Sentiments and Resolutions (1848)

We hold these truths to be self-evident; that all men and women are created equal. . . . Now, in view of this entire disfranchisement of one half of the people of this country, their social and religious degradation —in view of the unjust laws above mentioned, and because women do feel themselves aggrieved, oppressed, and fraudulently deprived of their most sacred rights, we insist that they have immediate admission to all the rights and privileges which belong to them as citizens of the United States. . . .

■ Although women made up much of the industrial labor force, they often received very low wages. This 1860 picture shows women factory workers on strike in Massachusetts.

children's books, among them *Little Women,* which was translated into several languages. Harriet Beecher Stowe wrote *Uncle Tom's Cabin* (page 343). Margaret Fuller became editor of *The Dial,* a philosophical and literary magazine. She also served as literary critic for the New York *Tribune.*

Dorothea Lynde Dix. Another woman who exerted enormous influence was Dorothea Lynde Dix. Miss Dix ran a boarding school in Boston until ill health forced her to close it. But in 1841, after inspecting the East Cambridge jail near Boston, she began a new career as a reformer.

Miss Dix was horrified by the cold, bare, and filthy conditions of the jail where mentally ill persons were kept next to other prisoners. She laid the facts before the Massachusetts legislature, but the male lawmakers were indifferent to her remarks.

Goaded to further action, Dorothea Dix decided to visit every jail and poorhouse in Massachusetts and to present overwhelming evidence to the legislature. She packed notebook after notebook with horrors almost beyond belief. In all of the jails and poorhouses, she found old men, young girls, the

poor, and the mentally ill thrown together in cold, dirty prisons. Some were chained to walls, beds, or floors. Some wore iron collars or strait jackets. Some had been confined in cages for years.

Finally, Miss Dix went again to the Massachusetts legislature with her evidence. This time the legislators listened. They began to pass laws to improve conditions in jails and poorhouses. During the next few years Miss Dix repeated her reform work in Connecticut, New York, Pennsylvania, and Kentucky. Moreover, her efforts attracted the attention of European reformers and helped to improve conditions in European jails and institutions for the poor and insane.

By the 1850's, largely because of Miss Dix and others who shared her views, important reforms had been made in the United States. The death penalty for some crimes had been abolished, and a growing number of people were demanding the "complete abolition of capital punishment." Most states had outlawed the whipping of prisoners. Imprisonment for debt had been ended. Men and women were confined in separate sections of prisons, and the mentally ill were separated from other prisoners. More attention was given to the individual criminal, and more effort was made to reform rather than to punish.

When Dorothea Dix died in 1887, at the age of 85, a famous English doctor said, "Thus has died and been laid to rest . . . the most useful and distinguished woman that America has ever produced."

Crusade against alcohol. Another reform movement in which women as well as men took part was the battle against excessive drinking. This battle, known as the "temperance movement," got under way on a national scale in 1833 when advocates of temperance held a convention in Philadelphia. The delegates included businessmen who believed that drinking was physically harmful and caused many accidents. Most of the reformers, however, believed that drinking was a sin.

The temperance movement grew rapidly. In 1836 several groups joined to form the American Temperance Union. Politicians, hoping to attract votes, took up the cause. The reformers flooded the country with literature, some for adults, much of it for children.

Some reformers were not satisfied to fight for moderation, or temperance, in drinking. Insisting that any drinking was harmful and sinful, they demanded state laws prohibiting the manufacture and sale of all alcoholic drinks.

Because of this widespread agitation, the reformers began to produce results. In 1834, the year after the temperance movement got under way, Congress forbade the sale of alcoholic beverages to Indians. Quakers, missionaries, and some Indian leaders had long been trying to stop the sale of rum and whisky to Indians. They believed that unscrupulous white men sold liquor to the Indians and then defrauded them of their treaty rights while the Indians were under the influence of liquor. But the law of 1834 was hard to enforce and was generally ignored. White men continued to sell liquor to the Indians.

The temperance movement won a notable victory in Maine in 1846. In that year the Maine legislature passed a law prohibiting the use of intoxicants. Other states followed suit.

Many people, especially brewers and distillers, opposed these laws. Other citizens protested that the states had no power to decide what a man should or should not drink.

Vigorous though the temperance and prohibition movements were, they did not bring an end to drinking. An unexpected by-product of the prohibi-

tion laws was a sharp rise in sales of patent medicines with a high alcoholic content. But the reformers did produce some results. Drinking among women almost ceased. In many communities a drunken man became an object of curiosity or even of contempt.

Efforts to end war. From about 1820 to 1860 many Americans, as well as Europeans, began to devote their efforts to the peace movement. Quakers in the United States had always opposed the use of force, except when necessary for police purposes. However, an organized anti-war movement did not develop in America until after the War of 1812. In 1828 numerous local peace societies joined together to form the American Peace Society. The members insisted that war was anti-Christian, inhumane, and uneconomical.

One leader of the peace movement was Elihu Burritt, a self-educated Connecticut blacksmith. He developed a pledge card against war which was signed by more than 40,000 persons in America and England. With the cooperation of William Ladd, a Maine sea captain and farmer known as "the apostle of peace," Burritt urged the nations of the world to form an international organization and a world court for settling international disputes.

■ Dorothea Lynde Dix was once called "the most useful and distinguished woman that America has ever produced." Her efforts led to improved conditions in prisons and institutions for the mentally ill.

Efforts to build ideal communities. Not all the people who longed for a better world tried to change existing institutions in the world of everyday affairs. Some men and women, following the example of religiously inspired groups, withdrew from the world around them to build *utopian* (yoo·TOH·pi·an), or ideal, communities.

Robert Owen, a wealthy British manufacturer, started a utopian community in 1825 at New Harmony in Indiana. It failed, but its failure did not discourage other experiments. Two well-known but short-lived experiments were Brook Farm, near Boston, and the Oneida (o·NI·dah) Community in New York.

SECTION SURVEY

IDENTIFY: reformer, capital punishment, temperance movement, prohibition, American Peace Society, utopian; Dorothea Dix.

1. Even as late as the 1830's, women had legal rights far inferior to those of men. Discuss.
2. Describe three notable accomplishments by women during this period.
3. (a) Describe the growth of the temperance movement at this time. (b) What were its results? (c) Why did Congress forbid the sale of liquor to Indians?
4. Why were so many utopian communities started during this period?
5. (a) In your opinion, which of the reform movements discussed in this section had the most lasting effects on American society? (b) Which had the least? Explain.

2 A promising start for free publicly supported education

Of all the reform programs of the period from the 1820's to the 1860's, none was more closely related to the democratic upsurge than the movement for free public schools. This movement was also related to the desire of many conservative-minded Americans to strengthen the social order by training young people to be economically useful as well as patriotic.

The problem of education. In colonial times New England towns were required by law to provide elementary schools. These New England schools were not entirely free. Parents who could afford to do so paid tuition fees for their children; the town paid only for the children of poor parents.

By the early 1800's, however, these so-called "common" schools of New England had reached a very low level. Buildings were inadequate; the quality of teaching was generally poor. Conditions were even worse in the Middle Atlantic and southern states, where people lived farther apart. Indeed, in many areas schools run by churches provided almost the only chance children had to get an elementary education.

By the 1820's and the 1830's this situation was changing. Many people were demanding public, tax-supported schools.

Leaders in the movement. Among the outstanding leaders of the struggle for free and improved public education were Horace Mann and Henry Barnard. Horace Mann turned from a brilliant legal and political career to become a crusader for public schools in Massachusetts. When the Massachusetts legislature created a state Board of Education in 1837, Mann became its first secretary. He used his growing power to establish "normal schools" for training teachers. He also began to organize the local school districts into a statewide system of education.

Henry Barnard did for Connecticut and Rhode Island what Horace Mann was doing for Massachusetts. For his efforts, Henry Barnard won national recognition. In 1867 he became the first United States Commissioner of Education.

The work of these and other leaders, among them Calvin E. Stowe of Ohio, Caleb Mills of Indiana, and John Swett of California, helped to set the pattern of free public education throughout the United States.

Objections to public education. The struggle for free, tax-supported elementary schools was not easily won. Churches that had already established religious schools, or that hoped to do so, objected strongly. Private schools, both religious and secular, were vigorous in their opposition. Many taxpayers objected to using tax money to pay for schools.

Many Americans also had strong prejudices against "book larnin'." A pioneer in Illinois said that he "didn't think folks was any better off for reading, an' books cost a heap and took a power of time. 'Twant so bad for men to read," he admitted, "for there was a heap of time when they couldn't work out and could jest set by the fire; and if a man had books and keered to read he mought; but women had no business to hurtle away their time. . . ."

Detail E. L. Henry, "Country School," Yale University Art Gallery, The Mable Brady Garven Collection

■ By the 1860's, most children in the United States could expect to receive an elementary school education. The painting above shows a scene in a country school in the late 1800's.

Early victories. In spite of prejudice against "book learning," and in spite of organized opposition, the movement for tax-supported elementary schools began to gain strength. In 1832 New York City established a system of free public elementary schools. Four years later, in 1836, Philadelphia followed suit. By the 1850's nearly all children, at least in northern cities, could secure a free elementary education.

Meanwhile, New England led the way in efforts to provide free high school education. The first public high school in America, the English High School of Boston, opened in 1821. Six years later, in 1827, Massachusetts adopted the first state law requiring towns with 500 or more families to provide a high school education for town youths at public expense.

In response to this law and growing voter demand, some Massachusetts towns established high schools, as did some other towns in other states. But the movement grew slowly. By 1850 the nation had only 55 public high schools, although there were more than 6,000 private high schools, or *academies,* as they were called. A high school edu-

cation was still beyond the reach of most American youths.

The educational ladder. The democratic system of free public education in the United States has been called "a great educational ladder." By the 1860's the "ladder" was beginning to be erected. Most children could expect to receive an elementary school education. In many larger towns they could attend free public high schools unless

LIVING AMERICAN DOCUMENTS

Horace Mann on Education (1848)

Education, then, beyond all other devices of human origin, is a great equalizer of the conditions of men— the balance-wheel of the social machinery . . . it gives each man the independence and the means by which he can resist the selfishness of other men. It does better than to disarm the poor of their hostility toward the rich: it prevents being poor. . . .

■ In 1862 Mary Jane Patterson became the first black American woman to receive a college degree. Later she served as the principal of a high school for black students in Washington, D.C.

the fact that there were so many of them shows how deeply Americans valued education.

Equally significant was the fact that the principle of the separation of church and state (page 191) was being written into all of the state constitutions. By the 1830's no person could be compelled to pay taxes to support any church or any school that taught particular religious doctrines.

Black students in college. In the period from the 1820's to the 1860's, the doors of higher education began to be opened to qualified black students, but only barely opened. In 1826 the first Negroes to be graduated from American colleges, Edward A. Jones and John B. Russworm, received degrees from Amherst and Bowdoin.

Three special colleges for black students were established in this period: Avery College and Lincoln College in Pennsylvania and Wilberforce College in Ohio. But the only truly coracial as well as coeducational college was Oberlin in Ohio. Oberlin was founded in 1833 by people who believed in abolition. Out of 8,800 young men and women who attended Oberlin between 1833 and 1861, 245 were black. Some were fugitive slaves or the sons and daughters of fugitives.

Most of the Negro coeds at Oberlin were enrolled in a Preparatory Department or in a special Ladies' Course. Mary Jane Patterson became, in 1862, the first black American woman to receive a college degree. After graduation, Miss Patterson taught school in Philadelphia for several years. Then, in 1871, she became the first black principal of a newly established high school for Negroes in Washington, D.C.

SECTION SURVEY

IDENTIFY: free public school, academy, Oberlin; Calvin E. Stowe, Mary Jane Patterson.

1. Describe the contributions made to American education by (a) Horace Mann and (b) Henry Barnard.
2. Why was there opposition to free public schools?
3. List four achievements accomplished by the supporters of free public schools.
4. Show why political democracy depends on free public schools.
5. Why was it an accomplishment for students, black or white, to receive a college education at this time?
6. Horace Mann spoke of education as the "great equalizer of the conditions of man." Relate this statement to the effects of education on Americans of different social, economic, and racial backgrounds.

they were held back by poverty or by parents who preferred to have them work.

A growing number of states established public universities. North Carolina pioneered by providing in 1776 in its constitution for the establishment of a state university. The University of North Carolina graduated its first class in 1798. Other states followed North Carolina's example. By the late 1850's, 16 states had established universities supported in part by public funds.

Alongside this system of free public schools and universities was the older system of private educational institutions—private elementary schools, academies, and more than 100 church-supported colleges. Most of these colleges were small, with 100 to 300 students and 6 to 12 professors. But

3 Development of a vigorous movement to abolish slavery

The most vigorous of all the reform movements between the 1820's and the 1860's was the anti-slavery, or *abolition,* crusade. No other single development did as much to arouse controversy and to drive a wedge between the North and the South.

Background of abolition. A few Americans in colonial days objected to slavery, as you have read (page 67). After the Revolutionary War this anti-slavery sentiment grew. Thus, in the 1780's and 1790's, several anti-slavery societies were organized in the North. For example, the American Convention for Promoting the Abolition of Slavery and Improving the Condition of the African Race was formed during this period. This society tried to convince people that slavery was immoral and a contradiction of the American ideal of freedom and equality before the law.

In the nation's early years, thoughtful southerners, as well as northerners, believed that slavery was morally wrong. These southerners found support among planters who believed that slavery was no longer profitable. Tobacco growing exhausted the fertility of the soil and decreased the value of land and crops. At the same time, the cost of feeding, clothing, and housing slaves remained the same or increased.

Problems of freeing slaves. A few planters, as you know, freed their slaves (page 67). But the problem was a complex one. Some southern slave-owners, even though they believed that slavery was wrong or unprofitable, felt that it was unfair to set slaves free to take care of themselves in a difficult and even hostile society. This view was strengthened by the common belief that black people were inferior and not able to become equal citizens.

Slavery and cotton. The conflict in southerners' minds over whether or not to free their slaves was largely erased after Eli Whitney's invention of the cotton gin in 1793. Because of the cotton gin, the demand for slaves grew by leaps and bounds. Moral and political questions about slavery were raised less and less as the "Cotton Kingdom" became prosperous.

But the renewed value of slaves did not wholly stop the anti-slavery movement, even in the South. As late as 1830 several Virginians publicly opposed slavery and proposed measures for doing away with it gradually.

In the early 1820's Benjamin Lundy, a mild-mannered but persistent Quaker, published a weekly anti-slavery newspaper in Baltimore called *The Genius of Universal Emancipation.* Like most spokesmen against slavery in the 1820's, Lundy was moderate in his approach. He hoped to bring about the gradual emancipation of the slaves through appeals to the good and moral instincts in all men.

Attempts at colonization. Lundy, like many anti-slavery men, supported the American Colonization Society. This society was founded in 1817 to colonize free blacks and to buy slaves to be settled as free men in Liberia, which the society created in West Africa on the model of Sierra Leone, a nearby British refuge for free blacks.

Lundy sincerely hoped to encourage emancipation by giving financial help to owners who wanted to free their slaves. But the most influential members of the society—planters in Kentucky, Virginia, and Maryland—were not opposed to slavery. These planters wanted to rid the nation of free Negroes because they believed that such people encouraged slaves in their desire to be free. The planters thought that colonization offered the best solution to "the race problem."

Faults in colonization. The colonization experiment was impractical and not very successful. The American Colonization Society could never have raised enough money to make a dent in American slavery. Each year the number and value of slaves was increasing. Each year the institution of slavery was becoming more deeply rooted in the cotton-planting areas of the South. By 1831 only 1,420 black Americans had been settled in Liberia.

The colonization movement also was unsuccessful because most American Negroes opposed it. There were exceptions, of course. Even before the American Colonization Society was formed, Paul Cuffee, a successful Negro merchant, had sent 38 black Americans to West Africa at his own expense. But most free black people later opposed colonization.

Conventions of free black Americans, which met to promote freedom and oppose discrimination in the North as well as the South, regularly denounced colonization. Reports of hardships in Liberia were discouraging. To most black Americans, Africa was a strange, far-off place. Despite their grim lot, most black Americans had come to think of America as home.

Early efforts by black people. In addition to condemning colonization, free Negroes began taking steps early in the nation's history to improve their own lot, and, if possible, that of the slaves. They formed their own Afro-American churches. They organized societies for mutual aid and for improving opportunities in education and social life for black people.

Free Negroes also began early to take legal action to improve their circumstances. In 1794 free Negroes asked Congress in a formal petition to take steps for "the relief of our people." In 1800 free black Americans of Philadelphia petitioned Congress to correct injustices in a law requiring fugitive slaves to be returned to their owners, or to men who falsely claimed to be their owners. The same petition also asked Congress to provide for gradual emancipation of all slaves.

The first of a new, more vigorous series of conventions held by black Americans met in Philadelphia in 1830. The delegates suggested that some black Americans might like to move to Canada. Those who did not choose to emigrate were urged to use every legal means to improve their lives in the United States.

David Walker's *Appeal.* These moderate activities were overshadowed in 1829 by the publication of an essay called *Appeal* by David Walker. Walker, a black American, began his *Appeal* by describing Negro slaves as "the most degraded, wretched, and abject set of beings that ever lived since the world began."

But Walker's essay was not only a powerful attack on slavery, it was also a call for bold and vigorous action by black Americans. Negroes were men, said Walker, and the time had come for them to act like men. Southern Negroes, slave and free, must strike for their freedom—violently if necessary. If white Americans wanted to prevent racial war, insisted Walker, they must at once recognize the rights and humanity of black Americans.

Northerners, including white anti-slavery forces, condemned Walker's book as inflammatory and dangerous. Southerners put a price on Walker's head and tried to halt circulation of his *Appeal*.

A new militant mood. Up to this time anti-slavery voices, white and black, had tried to convince the public that slavery was immoral and must be ended gradually. Now in the 1830's, the abolition movement began to be more militant, or aggressive. David Walker's *Appeal* was one example of growing opposition to moderate efforts. William Lloyd Garrison's newspaper, the *Liberator,* was another.

In his very first issue of the *Liberator,* published in Boston in 1831, Garrison, a white abolitionist, wrote: "I shall strenuously contend for the immediate enfranchisement of our slave population. . . . I am in earnest—I will not equivocate—I will not excuse—AND I WILL BE HEARD. . . ."

Slavery, Garrison insisted, contradicted the Bible and the Declaration of Independence. It was both a sin and a crime. It must be abolished, and abolished at once.

Garrison condemned southern slaveowners, but he also condemned northerners who apologized for slavery or kept silent about it. Equal rights for black Americans in the North was a leading object of Garrison's crusade.

Garrison's outspoken language offended many moderate white Americans who were against slavery. For that reason, most of the *Liberator's* subscribers were black.

The religious and moral fervor of Garrison and his New England followers was shared by rising abolitionist leaders elsewhere. In New York Arthur and Lewis Tappan, deeply religious men and wealthy merchants, fought for abolition, as did Isaac Hooper, a Quaker who aided runaway slaves.

The most important abolitionist leader outside the East was Theodore Weld. He trained 70 young men who followed his example in carrying militant abolitionism into hundreds of communities in Ohio, western Pennsylvania, and upstate New York. Weld's students were very successful in winning thousands of supporters to the anti-slavery movement.

The new anti-slavery militancy found a few followers in the South, who freed their own slaves and moved to the North, where they worked for immediate emancipation. Among these southern abolitionists were Sarah and Angelina Grimké, daughters of a prominent South Carolina slaveowner, and James G. Birney of Alabama. Few southerners, however, followed their example. The abolition movement was mainly confined to the Northeast and the West, where people had no investment in slaves.

SECTION SURVEY

IDENTIFY: abolition movement, militant, *Appeal*, the *Liberator*; Benjamin Lundy, David Walker, William Lloyd Garrison, Theodore Weld.

1. By 1800 many southerners and northerners believed that slavery was wrong. Why?
2. How did the belief that Negroes were inferior justify not setting them free?

3. (a) Why did attempts at colonization fail? (b) What democratic principles would have been overthrown if separatism had succeeded?
4. (a) How did free Negroes try to improve their own lot and that of the slaves? (b) What was Walker's position on how to achieve equality? Why? (c) How would Walker's views hold up today?
5. (a) What caused the abolition movement to become militant? (b) How did the *Liberator* contribute to this militancy?
6. Why was the abolition movement confined mainly to the Northeast and the West?

4 Rising tensions and their effects on the abolition movement

In 1833 the movement to abolish slavery gained new momentum when the British Anti-slavery Society forced Parliament to abolish slavery in the British Empire. In 1833, also, American abolitionists formed the American Anti-slavery Society, modeled on the British Society. The American Anti-slavery Society, a national organization, had many affiliated groups on the local and regional level. These affiliated groups quickly multiplied. By the mid-1830's there were more than 1,000 of them in the United States, with about 150,000 members.

The American Anti-slavery Society tried to influence public opinion by appealing to the conscience of white America. It circulated pamphlets and tracts and poured petitions into Congress and into state legislatures. The society also supported many lecturers, including Theodore Weld and the young men he had trained.

Frederick Douglass. Probably the most effective lecturer of the American Anti-slavery Society was Frederick Douglass, a former slave.

In moving words, Douglass told his northern and western audiences of his cruel treatment as a young slave in Maryland and how his master had tried to keep his mistress from teaching him how to read. He told how a professional slave-breaker had overworked, beaten, and nearly starved him, and of how, finally, he had attacked and beaten the slave-breaker. Of this experience Douglass said, "I was a changed being from that night. I was nothing before, I was a man now... with a renewed determination to be a free man."

Douglass condemned slavery and demanded its immediate abolition. He also insisted that it was time for the American people to listen to his message. "The lesson which they must learn, or neglect to do so at their own peril," he warned, "is that Equal Manhood means Equal Rights, and further, that the American people must stand each for all and all for each without respect to color or race...."

Split in the movement. The American Anti-slavery Society was soon split by differences among its members. In particular, the militant positions of William Lloyd Garrison alienated more moderate members.

Garrison insisted that women speak at anti-slavery meetings on terms equal with men. He also demanded that women hold high offices in anti-slavery societies. Garrison's opponents resisted this policy, insisting that the struggle for women's rights should be kept separate from the anti-slavery movement.

Garrison antagonized many other members of the Society in other ways. He denounced the churches and the federal government for compromising with slavery. Claiming that the Constitution itself protected slavery, Garrison maintained that anti-slavery men should refuse to vote or hold office.

Other leaders of the American Anti-slavery Society deplored Garrison's militant views and actions. Thus, in 1840 the society split apart. Garrison continued to control the original organization,

■ Probably the most effective lecturer of the American Anti-slavery Society was Frederick Douglass, a former slave. In addition to lecturing, Douglass also published an abolitionist newspaper called The North Star and was active in aiding escaped slaves.

■ Frederick Douglass escaped from slavery when he was 21. He later married, and he and his wife settled in the North. The picture above shows the young couple on the way to their new home.

while a new society promoted the more moderate program of his opponents.

Moderate programs. In their first major attempt at political action, moderates formed the Liberty Party and in 1840 nominated James G. Birney, a former Alabama slaveowner, as its Presidential candidate. In the election of that year, Birney polled only 7,000 votes. Four years later, in the election of 1844, the Liberty Party won more votes, but only 62,000 out of 2.5 million votes cast.

But the political abolitionists were not discouraged. They kept working to influence policies of the major political parties even though they might not win national elections on their own.

Militant activities. Some abolitionists kept demanding more vigorous action. In their eyes, the laws protecting slavery were immoral and should be defied. The most outspoken of these abolitionists was Henry Highland Garnet, a former slave from Maryland.

In a fiery speech before the National Convention of Colored Citizens in Buffalo in 1843, Garnet proclaimed, "Brethren, Arise, Arise! Let every slave throughout the land do this, and the days of slavery are numbered. You cannot be more oppressed than you have been; you cannot suffer greater cruelties than you have already. Rather die like free men than live as slaves." By a majority of one, the Buffalo convention voted to suppress Garnet's speech. Several years later, however, it was published.

The underground railroad. Some anti-slavery Americans took more direct action in the abolition movement by helping runaway slaves escape. These activities, kept secret out of necessity, came to be known as the "underground railroad." Slaves who learned about the "railroad" might slip away into the woods until pursuit died down, and then flee north across the Ohio River or the Mason-Dixon line.°

Crossing the Mason-Dixon line or the Ohio River, however, did not bring the slaves their freedom. According to a Fugitive Slave Law passed by Congress in 1793, the owner of a runaway slave could recover his slave merely by appearing before a magistrate and declaring that a captured slave belonged to him. Thus, fugitive slaves were not safe until they reached Canada.

Once across the Mason-Dixon line or the Ohio River, however, runaway slaves hoped to contact an "agent" on the underground railroad, who would arrange for their escape. Hiding in attics and haylofts by day and taken to the next "station" by night, the slaves slowly made the long trip northward. In time, with good luck, the hazardous journey was completed and the slaves found freedom in Canada.

Negroes as well as white Americans were active in the underground movement. Some of these black men were well-to-do, like James Forten, a Philadelphia sailmaker, and Robert Purvis, a free Negro born in Charleston, South Carolina, and educated at Amherst College. Purvis' zeal in assisting slaves

° The Mason-Dixon line was originally drawn as the boundary between Pennsylvania and Maryland, but it, along with the Ohio River, came to be considered as the dividing line between the free states of the North and the slave states of the South.

to freedom won him the title of "president" of the underground railroad.

Other black Americans active in the underground movement were themselves escaped slaves. Frederick Douglass was one. Another was William Wells Brown, the first black American novelist. Harriet Tubman, a fugitive slave, returned to the South time and time again at great personal risk to lead hundreds of slaves to freedom by way of the underground railroad. She was often called "the Moses of her people."

Uncle Tom's Cabin. The perils of trying to escape from slavery were vividly portrayed by Harriet Beecher Stowe, a northern white woman, in her famous novel *Uncle Tom's Cabin,* published in 1852.

In *Uncle Tom's Cabin,* Mrs. Stowe described the inhumanity of the slave system and efforts to escape from slavery, as she had heard about them from fugitives. Although the book was often moralistic in tone, as was common in the writing style of the times, the characters "came alive" in a way that readers never forgot. *Uncle Tom's Cabin* also was made into a play, which became one of the most popular melodramas in the history of the American theater.

In the South, *Uncle Tom's Cabin* was bitterly denounced as presenting a false and distorted picture of slavery. Southerners were angered in spite of the fact that the book gave examples of kindness on the part of masters toward slaves and of loyalty and affection on the part of slaves toward masters. Southerners were especially furious because the book encouraged support for the underground railroad.

Northern resistance. The abolitionists aroused widespread opposition in the North, as well as in the South. William Lloyd Garrison once remarked that he found "contempt more bitter, opposition more stubborn, and apathy more frozen" in New England than in the South.

Garrison's remark was, of course, an overstatement, but not by much. Abolitionist preachers in the North were sometimes forced to quit by their congregations. Influential citizens like Wendell Phillips of Boston, a gifted writer and orator, were barred from clubs and social gatherings because of their anti-slavery activities. William Lloyd Garrison was once forced to flee for safety to a Boston jail. More than once Theodore Weld and his students were manhandled by angry audiences. Elijah P. Lovejoy, an abolitionist editor who lived in Alton, Illinois, was murdered as he tried to prevent a hostile mob from destroying his printing press.

Many wage earners and businessmen opposed the abolition movement. Northern wage earners, fearing the job competition of free black workers, often broke up anti-slavery meetings. Most northern trade union leaders were either indifferent to the anti-slavery movement or actively opposed to it. They feared that abolition of slavery would flood northern cities with low-paid, competitive black workers. Most northern businessmen frowned upon the abolitionists, believing that anti-slavery activities would hamper trade between the North and the South.

Some northerners feared that abolitionist activities, especially the underground railroad and encouragement of slave revolts, might lead the South to leave the Union—which was exactly what Garrison and his militant followers hoped would happen. Most northerners dreaded the thought of emancipation, which might flood the North with a large immigration of free black people.

Southern reactions. Southerners, understandably, were most embittered by the anti-slavery movement. The Nat Turner rebellion of 1831 (page 313) occurred at the very time that the new, militant abolition movement was beginning. Many southerners, dreading the thought of widespread slave revolts, angrily blamed abolitionists in general, and William Lloyd Garrison in particular, for the Nat Turner rebellion.

As losses from runaway slaves mounted, slave-

■ This house in Fountain City, Indiana, belonged to an abolitionist named Levi Coffin and was an important station on the underground railroad.

owners became furious. Trying to prevent further rebellion and to protect slave property, southern legislatures tightened the "slave codes" (page 66). Free Negroes, as well as slaves, fell under strict supervision.

Even federal officials put up resistance. When southern postmasters refused to deliver abolitionist literature, the United States Post Office Department supported them. In 1836, southerners in the House of Representatives pushed through the so-called "gag rule," which forbade any member to read an anti-slavery petition in the House.

Such actions by federal officials violated freedom of speech and of the press—basic civil liberties guaranteed by the Constitution. The "gag rule" was finally repealed, mainly through the efforts of former President John Quincy Adams, who had become a Congressman from Massachusetts. But the struggle for civil liberties was just beginning.

Influence of the abolitionists. Between the early 1830's and 1860, as you will read, the North and the South drew further and further apart in their interests and opinions. Finally, unable to compromise their differences, they fought a bloody war. One of the issues, perhaps the greatest issue, was the institution of slavery. There is no question that the abolitionists helped force this issue by causing more and more northerners to see the evils of slavery, and by causing southerners to be even more determined in defending their way of life.

SECTION SURVEY

IDENTIFY: Liberty Party, "slave codes," "gag rule," Mason-Dixon line; Frederick Douglass, William Wells Brown.

1. How was the anti-slavery movement in step with the times (a) outside the United States, (b) inside the United States as a result of the general ferment for reform?
2. How did each of the following aid the abolition movement while increasing sectional bitterness: (a) Garrison, (b) Douglass, (c) Garnet, (d) "underground railroad," (e) *Uncle Tom's Cabin,* (f) Harriet Tubman, (g) "gag rule"?
3. (a) What were the reasons for northern and southern opposition to the abolition movement? (b) Which of these reasons might apply to the black experience today?
4. (a) What was the influence of the abolitionists? (b) Do you think that war could have been avoided if the abolitionists had not forced the issue? Explain.

5 Expression of a deep faith in individual liberty

Michel Chevalier, a French visitor to the United States in the year 1834, was impressed by the young nation's vigor. "All is here . . . boiling agitation," he commented. "Experiment follows experiment. . . . Men change their houses, their climate, their trade, their condition, their sect; states change their laws, their officers, their constitutions."

All of this activity—mental as well as physical—was reflected in the work of writers and scholars.

Henry David Thoreau (1817–62). Henry David Thoreau hated the industrial society that he saw rising in the United States. To Thoreau, machines were unnecessary gadgets that complicated life. "Nature is sufficient," Thoreau declared. To prove his point, he lived alone for more than two years in a cabin that he built with his own hands on the banks of Walden Pond near Concord, Massachusetts. There, free from the burden of machines and from institutions that he believed imprisoned the human spirit, he wrote the classic book *Walden*.

Thoreau distrusted the power of the national government as much as he feared the new industrial society. Objecting strongly to a government that allowed slavery to exist, Thoreau wrote, "I cannot for an instant recognize that political organization as *my* government which is the *slave's* government also."

But Thoreau did not limit his distrust to verbal or written criticism. In 1846, believing that war with Mexico was an unjust attack and an attempt to extend slavery, he refused to pay his poll tax to the government. Thoreau was jailed but released the next day when a member of his family paid the tax without his knowledge.

Thoreau argued that it was a man's duty to disobey unjust laws, even at the cost of imprisonment, if his conscience told him that the laws were unjust. He explained these ideas in an essay published in 1849, which has become famous as "Civil Disobedience." Its ideas later influenced Leo Tolstoy in Russia, Mohandas Gandhi in India, and Martin Luther King, Jr., in the United States.

Looking ahead, Thoreau foresaw two grave dangers to human liberty: one, industrialism, with its concern for the material things of life and its disregard for the individual; the other, the national state, with its indifference to the individual and its glorification of power.

A whale hunt

HIGHLIGHTS OF AMERICAN WRITING

Herman Melville (1819–1891) drew upon his years as a seaman on a whaling ship in writing his epic whaling novel *Moby Dick,* a powerful allegory of the struggle between good and evil.

Richard Henry Dana, Jr. (1815–1882) recorded in *Two Years Before the Mast* his adventures as an ordinary seaman on a voyage from Boston to California and back again.

Nathaniel Hawthorne (1804–1864) was a descendant of one of the "witch-judges" of early Salem and of a man who was active in persecuting Quakers. Perhaps this background gave Hawthorne the preoccupation with themes of sin and guilt evident in his novels *The Scarlet Letter* and *The House of the Seven Gables* and in his famous short story "The Minister's Black Veil."

Henry Wadsworth Longfellow (1807–1882) won fame for his long narrative poems *The Song of Hiawatha, Evangeline, The Courtship of Miles Standish,* and also for his shorter poems "Paul Revere's Ride" and "The Ship of State."

John Greenleaf Whittier (1807–1892) described scenes and events of his boyhood in rural New England in his long poem *Snow-Bound.*

Edgar Allan Poe (1809–1849), critic, short-story writer, and poet, wrote such horror tales as "The Pit and the Pendulum" and "The Cask of Amontillado"; the classic detective story "The Gold Bug"; and such melodic poems as "To Helen," "The Bells," "The Raven," and "Annabel Lee."

Oliver Wendell Holmes (1809–1894) had already established a fine reputation as a physician when he became editor of the *Atlantic Monthly* Magazine, in which he published *The Autocrat of the Breakfast Table,* a series of light essays on varied subjects. He also wrote the poem "Old Ironsides" after he read that the *Constitution,* a heroic frigate of the War of 1812, was about to be destroyed.

Ralph Waldo Emerson (1803–1882). Thoreau and Ralph Waldo Emerson were close friends. They both lived in Concord, Massachusetts. They both believed in the supreme importance of individual freedom.

Emerson started his career as a Unitarian minister. But he left his pulpit in 1832, at age 29, to become a "preacher to the world." For most of the next 50 years, Emerson wrote and lectured. He traveled widely, and wherever he went he urged men to stand on their own feet, to free themselves from ignorance and prejudice, to think for them-

■ Ralph Waldo Emerson urged men to stand on their own feet, to free themselves from ignorance and prejudice, to think for themselves, and to respect their fellow men.

selves, and to respect their fellow men. Democracy with its free institutions would not work, he said, if the individuals in a democratic society were not free.

Emerson had a deep faith in America, in democracy, and in the ability of men and women to solve their problems and build a better world. Although Emerson was critical of the growing emphasis on material things and the growing power of the national government, he did not share Thoreau's fear of industrialism.

Nor was Emerson troubled, as many Americans were, by the swelling tide of immigration. Welcome the immigrants, he urged, for "The energy of Irish, Germans, Swedes, Poles, and Cossacks, and all the European tribes—and of the Africans, and of the Polynesians—will construct a new race, a new religion, a new state, a new literature, which will be as vigorous as the new Europe which came out of the smelting-pot of the Dark Ages. . . ."

Walt Whitman (1819–1892). One day in 1855 Emerson received a copy of a newly published volume of poems entitled *Leaves of Grass.* Much impressed, he wrote the author, Walt Whitman: "I greet you at the beginning of a great career."

In *Leaves of Grass,* Whitman "sang" the praises of the growing nation. Even more than Emerson, he believed deeply in democracy and in the ability of the people to build an ever-better way of life for themselves and for their children. "The old and moth-eaten systems of Europe have had their day,"

he wrote. "Here [in America], we have planted the standard of freedom, and here we will test the capacities of men for self-government."

Whitman did not share Thoreau's fear of industrialism. On the contrary, he hailed science and industry as liberating forces which would lift from men's backs the age-old burdens of superstition and toil. In his "Carol of Occupations," he glorified the working people and the machines they operated. In "Pioneers! O Pioneers!" he challenged his fellow Americans to share his faith in the future. "We must march . . ." he wrote,

"We the youthful sinewy races, all the rest on us
  depend,
          Pioneers! O Pioneers! . . ."

The larger meaning. Emerson, Thoreau, and Whitman raised powerful voices in praise of freedom and democracy. But theirs were by no means the only voices. Americans who had no gift for words, and many immigrants who did not yet speak the English language, or spoke it only haltingly, also shared this faith.

This faith in the individual and in democracy lay at the roots of the reform movements you have read about in this chapter.

Years earlier, in 1776, Thomas Jefferson had expressed the same faith in the words: "We hold these truths to be self-evident: that all men are created equal, that they are endowed by their Creator with certain unalienable rights, that among these are life, liberty, and the pursuit of happiness. . . ."

Emerson, Thoreau, Whitman, the reformers you have been reading about, and many others were trying to apply the principles of the Declaration of Independence to the everyday affairs of life.

SECTION SURVEY

IDENTIFY: *Walden,* "Civil Disobedience," *Leaves of Grass.*

1. (a) What two major developments did Thoreau fear as threats to human liberty? (b) Why is it significant that Thoreau went to jail for his beliefs? (c) If it is a man's duty to disobey unjust laws, is it also his duty to accept the penalty society metes out for disobeying those laws? Discuss.

2. (a) Why did Emerson think of himself as a "preacher to the world"? (b) Summarize the main ideas of his "message."

3. Explain Whitman's idea that Americans are "pioneers" who must march forward.

4. Have science and industry been the liberating forces envisioned by Whitman? Explain.

TRACING THE MAIN IDEAS

From the 1820's to the 1860's new developments began to transform the United States with bewildering speed. Factories and factory towns sprang up in the northern states. Slavery became increasingly important in the cotton-growing areas of the South. New means of transportation stimulated trade and sped the westward movement of land-hungry pioneers. Immigrants in steadily mounting numbers poured into the growing cities and out upon the farm lands.

During the 1830's a Frenchman, Michel Chevalier, visited America and described it as a place of "boiling agitation." Chevalier was referring to the intense physical activity of the American people as they plunged headlong into the job of building the nation. He was also referring to their enthusiasm for new ideas and their desire to make democracy work.

This faith in democracy stimulated wave after wave of reform movements—among them the struggle for women's rights, for more humane treatment of criminals and the mentally ill, for equality of educational opportunity, for the abolition of slavery. These reform movements continued through the 1830's, 1840's, and 1850's.

As you have seen, democracy made large advances during these years. But, as you will see in the next unit, the problem of slavery became increasingly acute, reaching a bitter climax in armed conflict between North and South.

CHAPTER SURVEY

QUESTIONS FOR DISCUSSION

1. Reread the Preamble to the Constitution of the United States (page 171). What steps toward fulfilling the ideals stated in the Preamble were taken during the period just studied?
2. Humanitarian striving was a characteristic of the new democratic spirit. Give evidence of this characteristic in the fields of education, temperance, abolition, and the treatment of the criminal and the insane.
3. Thoreau, Emerson, and Whitman were spokesmen for the American spirit at this time. Give reasons to support this statement.
4. The years 1828–50 have been described as the era of "The Rise of the Common Man." Why?
5. How did the views of the militant abolitionists differ from the views of the moderate abolitionists?
6. What American ideals were reflected in the literature of this period?
7. Which of the women reformers of this period do you think made the most significant contribution to American life? Explain.

RELATING PAST TO PRESENT

1. Do women and men have an equal choice of careers in our society today? Explain.

2. Has the dream of Burritt and Ladd of an international organization and a world court been realized? Explain.
3. Compare the ideas of Thoreau and Whitman concerning the effects of science and industry. Considering our society today, which of the two foresaw the future more accurately? Explain.
4. How do the statements by Frederick Douglass and Henry Garnet about their fellow black Americans apply to the position of black Americans today? Explain.
5. Which of the reform movements just studied are still going on today? Why does reform often take a great deal of time?

USING MAPS AND CHARTS

1. Referring to chart 8 on page 859, discuss the trend of movement of people from the country to the city between 1790 and 1850.
2. Using chart 6 on page 858, discuss the increase in life expectancy for people living in America between 1790 and 1850.
3. In the Chronology of Events, refer to the events of the Jacksonian era (page 882), and discuss which event had the most constructive effect on United States history, and which had the most injurious effect.

UNIT SURVEY

FOR FURTHER INQUIRY

1. If the Industrial Revolution had not occurred, do you think slavery could have taken root in the North? Why or why not?
2. Except for the cotton gin, machines were not as important in the South as they were in the North. Explain.
3. Was it inevitable that westward-moving Americans would clash with Mexicans in California? Why or why not?
4. How did the various reform movements reflect faith in democracy?

PROJECTS AND ACTIVITIES

1. Read Thoreau's "Civil Disobedience" and then explain why you think it influenced men like Martin Luther King, Jr., and Mohandas Gandhi.
2. For the views of foreigners in America during the early 1800's, see *Impressions of America*, edited by Brown and Brown (Harcourt Brace Jovanovich). Compare some of these views with each other as well as with the views of Americans living at the same time.
3. If you are interested in poetry, read some of the poems of Bryant, Emerson, Longfellow, Poe, Thoreau, and Whitman, and comment on how these poets viewed America and the American character.
4. Find songs of the early 1800's about immigration, labor, and slavery. Discuss how music reflects the times in which it is written.

USING THE SOCIAL SCIENCES

(Read pages 350–52 before you answer the following questions.)

1. Now that you have read this case study, what questions do you have regarding the abolitionists?
2. Why do you think people joined the crusade for abolition? Why do you think people usually join a crusade?
3. Did the anti-slavery movement in the United States reflect what was going on outside the United States (for example, in Russia, Europe, Latin America)?
4. Did the Founding Fathers make any moral judgments regarding slavery? Explain.
5. Do you think that a democracy can endure if slavery exists within it? Why or why not?

SUGGESTED FURTHER READING

Biography

BARTLETT, IRVING H., *Wendell Phillips: Brahmin Radical*, Harper & Row (Beacon).

COIT, MARGARET, *John C. Calhoun: An American Portrait*, Houghton Mifflin.

CURRENT, RICHARD N., *Daniel Webster and the Rise of National Conservatism*, Little, Brown.

DANA, R. H., *Two Years Before the Mast*, Macmillan; and others. Seaborne adventures.

EATON, CLEMENT, *Henry Clay and the Art of American Politics*, Little, Brown.

GREEN, CONSTANCE, *Eli Whitney and the Birth of American Technology*, Little, Brown.

HAYS, ELINOR RICE, *Morning Star: A Biography of Lucy Stone, 1818–1893*, Harcourt Brace Jovanovich.

JAMES, MARQUIS, *Andrew Jackson: Portrait of a President*, Bobbs-Merrill.

——, *The Raven*, Coronet (Paperback Library). Pulitzer prize-winning biography of Sam Houston.

JONES, NARD, *The Great Command: The Story of Marcus and Narcissa Whitman and the Oregon Country Pioneers*, Little, Brown.

LUTZ, ALMA, *Emma Willard: Daughter of Democracy*, Houghton Mifflin.

NEVINS, ALLAN, *Frémont, Pathmaker of the West*, McKay.

——, ed. *Polk: The Diary of a President, 1845–1849*, McKay.

NYE, RUSSELL B., *William Lloyd Garrison and the Humanitarian Reformers*, Little, Brown.

SMITH, ELBERT B., *Magnificent Missourian: The Life of Thomas Hart Benton*, Lippincott.

SYRETT, HAROLD C., *Andrew Jackson*, Bobbs-Merrill.

THOMAS, JOHN L., *The Liberator: William L. Garrison*, Little, Brown.

THOREAU, HENRY DAVID, *Walden*, Dutton; and others. Autobiographical.

VAN DEUSEN, GLYNDON G., *The Life of Henry Clay*, Little, Brown (paper).

WADE, MACON, *Margaret Fuller*, Viking.

Other Nonfiction

BILL, A. H., *Rehearsal for Conflict*, Knopf. About Mexican War.

BILLINGTON, RAY ALLEN, *The Far Western Frontier: 1830–1860*, Harper & Row (text ed.).
——, with JAMES BLAINE HEDGES, *Westward Expansion*, Macmillan.
BINGHAM, EDWIN R., ed. *California Gold*, Heath (paper). A clergyman, a journalist, a merchant, a doctor's wife, and two miners describe life during the gold rush.
BOATRIGHT, MODY C., *Folk Laughter on the American Frontier*, Collier (paper).
BRANDON, WILLIAM, *American Heritage Book of Indians*, Dell (paper). Traces the history of the American Indian from prehistoric times to the present.
BUGG, JAMES L., *Jacksonian Democracy, Myth or Reality*, Holt, Rinehart & Winston (paper).
COMMAGER, HENRY STEELE, *Era of Reform, 1830–1860*, Van Nostrand (Anvil Books, paper). Original documents, including writings on Utopianism, women's rights, and land reform.
DE VOTO, BERNARD, *Across the Wide Missouri*, Houghton Mifflin (Sentry Editions, paper). The West in the 1830's; illustrated.
——, *The Year of Decision*, Houghton Mifflin. The West in 1846.
DICK, EVERETT, *The Dixie Frontier*, Putnam (Capricorn Books, paper). Covers many aspects of southern frontier life before the Civil War.
DODD, WILLIAM E., *The Cotton Kingdom*, Yale Univ. Press. The plantation system.
EDITORS OF AMERICAN HERITAGE, *Westward on the Oregon Trail*, Harper & Row.
FILLER, LOUIS, *The Crusade Against Slavery*, Harper & Row (paper).
FISH, CARL R., *Rise of the Common Man*, Macmillan. Democratic innovations of Jacksonian period.
FORBES, JACK D., *The Indian in America's Past*, Prentice-Hall (Spectrum Books, paper). Descriptions by European explorers and settlers, speeches of Indian chiefs, etc.
FRANKLIN, JOHN HOPE, *From Slavery to Freedom: A History of American Negroes*, Knopf.
FULLER, EDMUND, *Tinkers and Genius: The Story of the Yankee Inventors*, Hastings House.
HANSEN, MARCUS LEE, *The Atlantic Migration, 1607–1860*, Harvard Univ. Press; Oxford Univ. Press.
HULBERT, A. B., *The Paths of Inland Commerce*, Pocket Books.
LANGDON, W. C., *Everyday Things in America, 1776–1876*, Scribner.
MACY, JESSE, *The Anti-Slavery Crusade*, Yale Univ. Press.
NYE, RUSSELL B., *The Cultural Life of the New Nation*, Harper & Row (paper).
OWSLEY, FRANK L., *Plain Folk of the Old South*, New York Times Co. (Quadrangle Books, paper). Describes an often neglected middle class of "yeoman farmer" in the Old South.

PAINE, R. D., *The Old Merchant Marine*, Yale Univ. Press.
PHILLIP, U. B., *Life and Labor in the Old South*, Little, Brown.
RAPPAPORT, ARMIN, ed. *The War with Mexico: Why Did It Happen?*, Rand McNally (paper). Introductory essay, original source documents, and current essays present various points of view on this question.
SAMS, HENRY W., *Autobiography of Brook Farm*, Prentice-Hall (paper). An experiment in Utopian living described in selected readings.
SCHLESINGER, ARTHUR, JR., *The Age of Jackson*, Little, Brown (paper).
SINGLETARY, OTIS A., *The Mexican War*, Univ. of Chicago Press (paper).
STEPHENSON, NATHANIEL W., *Texas and the Mexican War*, Yale Univ. Press.
THOMPSON, HOLLAND, *The Age of Invention*, Yale Univ. Press. Inventions before the War Between the States.
TURNER, FREDERICK JACKSON, *The Frontier in American History*, Holt, Rinehart & Winston.
TYLER, ALICE, *Freedom's Ferment: Phases of American Social History to 1860*, Harper & Row (paper).
VAN DEUSEN, GLYNDON G., *The Jacksonian Era, 1828–48*, Harper & Row (paper).
WEBB, WALTER P., *The Great Plains*, Ginn. The story of adaptations to a new region.
WHITE, STEWART EDWARD, *The Forty-Niners*, Yale Univ. Press.
WILSON, MITCHELL, *American Science and Invention*, Simon and Schuster.
WITTKE, CARL, *We Who Built America*, Prentice-Hall. Immigration.

Historical Fiction

BRESLIN, HOWARD, *The Tamarack Tree*, McGraw-Hill. Political rally in New England.
DESMOND, ALICE D., *Glamorous Dolly Madison*, Dodd, Mead.
EDMONDS, WALTER D., *Rome Haul*, Random House (Modern Library). Life on the Erie Canal in the 1820's.
GUTHRIE, ALFRED B., *The Big Sky*, Morrow; Pocket Books. Novel about mountain men.
——, *The Way West*, Pocket Books. Novel of pioneers going to Oregon.
HOUGH, EMERSON, *The Covered Wagon*, Dutton; Pocket Books. About pioneers.
RICHTER, CONRAD, *The Trees*, Knopf. Struggles of a pioneer family.
STONE, IRVING, *Immortal Wife*, Doubleday. Jessie and John Frémont.
——, *The President's Lady*, Doubleday. Rachel and Andrew Jackson.
WHITMAN, WALT, *Leaves of Grass*, Doubleday; and others. Poetry praising American democracy.

HISTORY AND THE SOCIAL SCIENCES

CASE STUDY IN HISTORY
The Abolitionists

Abolitionists have for a long time fared poorly at the hands of American historians. They were and still are often branded as fanatics who caused as much trouble as their opponents, the pro-slavery forces. In fact, some distinguished historians have maintained that the abolitionists were as guilty as pro-slavery agitators in creating the conditions that led to the Civil War. James G. Randall stated that William Lloyd Garrison, a leading abolitionist, "was a detriment to the cause he so devotedly served [abolition of slavery], for the extremism of his editorials and the vitriol of his attacks doubtless alienated many moderates in the North and certainly antagonized the slaveholders of the South." David M. Potter wrote that "without the abolitionists there might have been no Civil War." Avery Craven was convinced that if Garrison were alive today he "could profitably consult a psychiatrist."

On the other hand, Professor Kenneth Stampp contended that historians have condemned abolitionists "for their distortions and exaggerations. But are historians really being 'objective' when they combine warm sympathy for the slaveholders' point of view with cold contempt for those who looked upon the enslavement of 4 million American Negroes as the most shocking social evil of their day?"

What is the truth in this controversy? Were most abolitionists agitators and fanatics? Or did they genuinely hate slavery and champion human freedom? How much did the abolitionists contribute to the emancipation of the slaves? How much did they contribute to the conditions that led to the Civil War? These are the questions that will direct our inquiry.

The Abolitionists—Extremist Agitators or Fighters for Freedom?

There is no question that some abolitionists were extremists who advocated any methods, including violence, to achieve their goal—freeing the slaves. John Brown was such an abolitionist. Brown, a passionate opponent of slavery, was determined to keep Kansas free of slavery—no matter what the cost. In 1854 he attacked some settlers near the Pottawamie River in Kansas, killing a number of innocent people. In October 1859, in hopes of inciting widespread slave revolts, Brown attacked the federal arsenal at Harpers Ferry, Virginia. The attack failed. Brown was tried for treason, convicted, and executed. During his trial Brown made an eloquent speech condemning slavery as a violation of the Christian faith. Although most northerners condemned Brown's actions, many praised his speech, thus helping to widen the rift between North and South.

Unlike Brown, William Lloyd Garrison, the leading white abolitionist, rejected and abhorred violence and carried on his crusade against slavery through the written and spoken word. But when he wrote or spoke, Garrison was indeed fiery and outspoken. Garrison knew that critics would label him an extremist, but he accepted that risk. "I am aware," wrote Garrison in the first issue of his abolitionist newspaper, the *Liberator*, "that many object to the severity of my language; but is there not cause for severity? I *will be* as harsh as truth, and as uncompromising as justice. On this subject I do not wish to think, or speak, or write, with moderation. No! No! Tell a man whose house is on fire to give a moderate alarm ... but urge me not to use moderation in a cause like the present. . . . I swear, while life-blood warms my throbbing veins, still to oppose and thwart with heart and hand . . . till Africa's chains are burst and Freedom rules the rescued land, trampling Oppression

Detail from The Last Moments of John Brown, The Metropolitan Museum of Art, Gift of Mr. and Mrs. Carl Stoeckel, 1897.

John Brown on the way to his execution

and his iron rod; such is the vow I take—So Help Me God!"

In Garrison's time as now, most Americans regarded the Constitution as a sacred document. Thus, Garrison and his followers were denounced with particular vehemence for their attacks on the Constitution. On one occasion Garrison burned a copy of the Constitution on a public square. Another time he outraged many Americans by calling the Constitution "a covenant with death and an agreement with hell." What led Garrison to make such outspoken attacks against the supreme law of the land? Garrison opposed the Constitution because he could not accept the "slavery clauses" included in the document—clauses which have since been repealed.

Garrison argued that slavery was sanctioned in the Constitution not in one, but in two, places. For different reasons, white southerners never tired of reminding the North of this fact, too. The Constitution stated in Article 1, Section 2, that for the purpose of apportioning Representatives from the states, each slave would count as three fifths of a person—not as a whole person. In addition, in Article 4, Section 2, the Constitution included a strong law, providing that fugitive slaves must be returned to their owners.

Southerners, basing their claims on these clear and specific provisions in the Constitution, proclaimed that abolitionist propaganda, as well as northern opposition to the return of the fugitive slaves, was unconstitutional. They demanded that northern authorities comply with the law and outlaw abolitionist attempts to end slavery as blatant violations of the Constitution.

William Garrison and his followers felt that, in view of the South's great strength in Congress, there was little chance that a constitutional amendment abolishing slavery could be adopted. Confronted with this situation and faced with the pressure not to act in violation of the Constitution, Garrison decided instead to advocate the abrogation of the Constitution and the division of the United States into two separate parts—the free states and the slave states. It should be noted, however, that many abolitionists opposed Garrison's stand on these issues and preferred to work for the abolition of slavery within the existing political system.

Turning the Struggle Against Slavery into a Moral Crusade

Theodore Weld, another important abolitionist, greatly aided the antislavery movement by lecturing against slavery as a moral evil which violated basic Christian beliefs. Weld's conviction that slavery was a moral evil was shared and preached throughout the land with increasing effectiveness by the evangelist Charles G. Finney and the famous preacher Henry W. Beecher. In a relatively short time these men and others succeeded in making slavery not only a political and economic issue, but predominantly a moral one. As Finney put it, "Christians can no more take the neutral ground on this subject. . . . It is a great national sin. . . . It is in vain for the churches to pretend it is merely a political sin. I repeat, it is the sin of the Church, to which all denominations have consented."

Frederick Douglass

Black abolitionists were also active in the crusade for their own freedom. The most outstanding black abolitionist leader was Frederick Douglass, about whom Garrison once exclaimed, "White men and black men had talked against slavery, but none had ever spoken like Frederick Douglass." Douglass spoke of the horrors of slavery on the basis of his own experiences, having escaped from a slave plantation when he was 21. He told his audiences that "he who has endured the cruel pangs of slavery is the man to advocate liberty." The recital of Douglass' own experiences as a slave greatly aided the abolitionists' drive to show slavery as being contrary to the values of religion and humanity.

Black abolitionists were chiefly responsible for organizing the underground railroad which helped many hundreds of slaves escape to the North or to Canada. One of the most effective operators of the railroad was Harriet Tubman, a black woman. Herself a runaway slave, she returned to the slave states 19 times and personally escorted more than 300 slaves to freedom.

Not all slaves fleeing from the South, however, won their freedom. Some were seized by local police authorities, who, acting in accordance with Article 4, Section 2, of the Constitution and local laws, were ready to return the fugitive slaves to their owners. In most such cases, the abolitionists by mobilizing public opinion were able to pressure the authorities into granting the prisoners jury trials. During these trials the abolitionist lawyers invoked the supremacy of the moral law over what they claimed were unjust and immoral political laws. Invariably, northern juries refused to return the slaves.

Faced with the onslaught against their "sacred institution," southerners formulated a vigorous campaign in defense of slavery. Southern pro-slavery spokesmen argued that Negro slaves were "inferior" beings who needed the protection and guidance of their owners. Southern preachers and theologians argued that the Bible supported slavery—that the Old Testament accepted the existence of slavery and that Paul, in the New Testament, advised a servant to return to his master. The Lord, they argued, had intended Negroes to be slaves and the freeing of the slaves would thus violate the will of God.

But the sharpest counterattack against abolitionist propaganda came not from southern preachers, but from southern political leaders. Southern politicians charged that the abolitionists were violating the Constitution, were instigating slave insurrections, and if not silenced would force the southern states to secede from the Union. Senator John Calhoun of South Carolina, the leading spokesman of the South, put the issue with characteristic bluntness: "If the agitation [abolitionist activity] goes on, the same force, acting with increased intensity, as has been shown, will finally snap every cord, when nothing will be left to hold the states together except force."

In December 1861, when South Carolina issued an official explanation of its secession from the Union, abolitionism was cited as the main cause. The South Carolina declaration blamed the northern states for "the open establishment among them of societies, whose avowed objective is to disturb the peace of and claim the property of citizens of other states. They have encouraged and assisted thousands of our slaves to leave their homes; and those who remain have been incited by emissaries, books, and pictures to servile insurrection."

As Calhoun's testimony and South Carolina's declaration indicate, abolitionist propaganda became greatly feared in the South. By branding slavery a moral evil, the abolitionists had succeeded in making slavery obnoxious to millions of northerners and had also incited many slaves to rebel against their servitude. But at the same time, by their very success in turning their anti-slavery struggle into a moral crusade, the abolitionists had helped to make attainment of any meaningful compromise on slavery between the North and the South impossible.

Harriet Tubman

■ Were most abolitionists fanatics or sincere champions of human freedom? Cite evidence to support your conclusion.

■ Without the abolitionists slavery might not have been eradicated from American society. Comment.

■ Without the abolitionists there might have been no Civil War. Comment.

UNIT FIVE

The Nation Torn Apart

1845–1865

Chapter 18   A Time of Crisis and Compromise (1845–1861)

19   A Nation Divided by War (1861–1865)

■ *John Brown*

CHAPTER **18**

A Time
of Crisis
and
Compromise

1845 – 1861

THE GROWING conflict among the three sections of the country—North, South, West—this is the large and tragic theme of American history during the years preceding the Civil War, or the War Between the States, as this conflict is also sometimes called. The story that unfolds as we review this unhappy period is one of compromise, of brief intervals of uneasy balancing of interests, of breakdowns of compromise, of growing conflict, and of ever more desperate attempts to restore harmony among the sections of the country.

The basic problem was that the North and South and West had developed along very different lines. To be sure, many people in all sections shared common institutions and beliefs. It is also true that there were many differences within each section. Yet each section had developed its own characteristic way of life.

The industrial North had its growing factories and towns. The agricultural South was increasingly dependent upon the single crop of cotton. And the West was filled with restless pioneers pressing against ever new frontiers.

Given these differences, it is not surprising that men from each of the three sections held radically different views about such issues as internal improvements at federal expense, tariffs, banking and currency, public lands, and the question of slavery.

To understand the tensions rising among the three sections of the country in this period, it is necessary to review events that had been taking place between the administrations of President Monroe and President Polk.

THE CHAPTER IN OUTLINE

1. An uneasy political balance between North and South.

2. Easing of mounting tensions through the Compromise of 1850.

3. The end of the long period of political compromise.

4. The steady movement of North and South toward war.

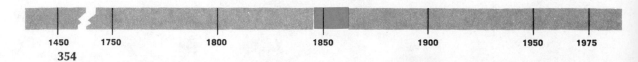

1450   1750   1800   1850   1900   1950   1975

354

1 An uneasy political balance between North and South

The first serious clash between the sections—in this case the North and the South—had arisen in 1819–20, when President Monroe was in office, over the question of admitting Missouri to the Union. At times the controversy had become so heated that men talked boldly of "disunion" and "civil war." Former President Thomas Jefferson, following the debates from his hilltop home, wrote that "This momentous question, like a fire bell in the night, awakened and filled me with terror. I considered it at once as the knell ° of the Union."

Dispute over Missouri. To understand Jefferson's grave concern, we must turn back to 1819, when the United States was composed of 11 free states and 10 slave states. Alabama was about to be admitted to the Union as the eleventh slave state. With Alabama in the Union, the North and the South would each have 22 Senators.

Then the Territory of Missouri, in which slavery already existed, asked to be admitted to the Union. If Missouri were allowed to enter as a slave state, the balance of power in the Senate would be upset. The South would have 24 votes and the North would have only 22.

Tallmadge's explosive proposal. On February 13, 1819, before Alabama was admitted, Representative James Tallmadge of New York rose on the floor of the House to present an amendment to Missouri's application. Tallmadge proposed to outlaw the further introduction of slaves into Missouri. He also proposed to free, on their twenty-fifth birthday, all children born into slavery in Missouri after it became a state.

Tallmadge and his supporters argued that Congress had the power to prohibit slavery in any Territory of the United States. They pointed out that Congress had earlier prohibited slavery in the Northwest Territory (page 147). They argued that, in dealing with the Territory of Missouri, Congress should follow the precedent established when it outlawed slavery in the Northwest Territory.

The Missouri Compromise. The House of Representatives, where the North held a majority of the seats, adopted the Tallmadge Amendment by a close vote. But the Senate rejected it.

° *knell:* the tolling of a bell, especially one announcing a death.

Why, with 11 free states and only 10 slave states represented in the Senate at this time, was the South able to win this victory? The answer is that certain northern Senators voted with the southern *bloc,* or solid group of Senators, to defeat the amendment. In other words, although in 1819 the issue of slavery had been raised, the differences between North and South had not yet hardened.

But Congress was now deadlocked. The House favored the amendment, while the Senate opposed it. The deadlock was broken, however, through mutual concessions known as the Missouri Compromise.

At this time Maine was also petitioning Congress to enter the Union—as a free state. To keep an even balance of free and slave states, the Senate approved a proposal combining the admission of Maine with that of Missouri. Senator Jesse Thomas of Illinois introduced an amendment that received strong support from Henry Clay of Kentucky. This amendment proposed that Missouri be admitted as a slave state, but that slavery be prohibited in the rest of the Louisiana Purchase, north of latitude 36° 30′ (see map, page 356). Southern Congressmen accepted this restriction because cotton could not be grown profitably on the land north of the 36° 30′ line.

The crisis seemed to have passed. But the next year, 1820, the anti-slavery forces in Congress threatened to exclude Missouri from the Union because Missouri's constitution contained discriminations against free Negroes. Henry Clay then proposed the so-called second Missouri Compromise. Clay argued that the proposed constitution of Missouri could not deny any citizen of Missouri the privileges and protections he was entitled to under the Constitution of the United States. When this proposal was accepted, Missouri was admitted to the Union as a slave state.

Thus, the crisis of 1819–20 passed. But thoughtful men realized that danger lay ahead for the young nation. "This is a reprieve only, not a final sentence," Jefferson declared. And John Quincy Adams wrote in his diary that the conflict over Missouri was a "mere preamble—a title page to a great, tragic volume."

The tariff issue. During the years from 1828 to 1832, as you have seen, conflicting views on the tariff question brought the United States uncomfortably close to disunion (page 273). In condemning the "Tariff of Abominations" of 1828, South Carolina had threatened to secede from the Union. This crisis also passed, however, when the

North and the South agreed to another compromise proposed by Henry Clay, the Tariff Act of 1833. This compromise tariff provided for a gradual reduction of tariff rates.

Growing anti-slavery forces. Meanwhile the shadow of the slavery issue continued to darken the land. In spite of opposition in the North as well as the South, the abolition movement grew. By 1836 more than 500 abolitionist societies were active in the North. In 1840 the abolitonists organized the Liberty Party and, as you know, nominated James G. Birney for the Presidency.

The deadlock over Texas. As the shadow of the slavery issue grew larger and more ominous, the struggle for control of the western areas became more intense. Every time a Territory applied for admission to the Union as a state, northern and southern Congressmen marshaled their forces for a struggle.

In 1836 and 1837 Congress admitted Arkansas and Michigan into the Union without any controversy, for one was slave and the other free. But trouble arose when the newly organized Republic of Texas (pages 322–23) applied for admission. Since slavery already existed in Texas, Congress would have to admit Texas as a slave state, thereby upsetting the balance between the North and the South.

As it happened, President Van Buren and many Congressional leaders were eager at this time to keep the slavery issue out of politics. But Texans could not afford to let the matter rest. Only 50,000 free people lived in the Lone Star Republic. If Mexico, with its population of 6 to 7 million, decided to reconquer its former territory, Texas would be in serious difficulty. Texans needed a powerful ally to protect them against Mexico. Faced with this situation, Texas negotiated treaties of friendship and trade with France, Belgium, the Netherlands, and Great Britain.

For several years the issue of Texas hung in the balance. Mexico refused to recognize Texas' independence. Great Britain and France, on the other hand, continued to support an independent Texas. And American opinion remained divided.

The election of 1844. Such was the situation in the United States in the election year of 1844. Henry Clay, the Whig candidate, tried to avoid the issue. James G. Birney, again the candidate of the anti-slavery Liberty Party, firmly opposed the admission of Texas. But James K. Polk of Tennessee, the Democratic candidate, came out for "The re-

MISSOURI COMPROMISE OF 1820

■ Abolitionist activities often aroused violent opposition, even in free states. This picture shows a mob in Alton, Illinois, burning down the printing plant of the Reverend Elijah P. Lovejoy, editor of an abolitionist newspaper. Lovejoy was killed during the attack.

annexation of Texas and re-occupation of Oregon!"

The Democratic Party's 1844 slogan was clever politics. It implied that the United States had always owned Texas and Oregon. This was not true, but the slogan shifted the focus from the troublesome issue of slavery to the popular issue of expansion. Northerners and southerners alike wanted their country to expand westward.

Polk won the election. In February 1845, shortly before he took office, Congress by a joint resolution voted to admit Texas into the Union. The resolution included the following provisions: (1) With the consent of Texas, a total of five states could be carved out of the territory. (2) If Texas did divide, any land north of the 36° 30′ line would be closed to slavery. (3) The United States would take over the boundary dispute with Mexico. (4) Texas would retain its lands and pay its own debts.

Texas accepted these terms and entered the Union in December 1845. Thus the balance between North and South swung by two states in favor of the South. (It had already swung in favor of the South when Florida entered the Union in March 1845.) But the balance was restored by the admission of Iowa in 1846 and Wisconsin in 1848, both free states.

Thus, for more than 25 years, from the Missouri

Compromise of 1820 to the year 1846, Congress had walked a tightrope. By a series of compromises, the North and the South had managed to resolve the troublesome problems that had threatened to split them apart. This was the situation in 1846 when the United States went to war with Mexico.

SECTION SURVEY

IDENTIFY: Tallmadge Amendment, "The re-annexation of Texas and re-occupation of Oregon!"; Henry Clay, James G. Birney.

1. (a) Why did Missouri's application for admission to the Union create a crisis? (b) How was the crisis settled?
2. (a) What did the North and South each gain by the Missouri Compromise? (b) Why did Jefferson call the Compromise "a reprieve only, not a final sentence"?
3. What were the reasons behind the long delay in admitting Texas to the Union?
4. How did the election of 1844 reflect the issues of the time?
5. (a) Why would southern planters oppose a high protective tariff? (b) What type of tariff would westerners want?
6. What does the phrase "balance of power" mean in reference to the Senate?

357

2 Easing of mounting tensions through the Compromise of 1850

On February 2, 1848, the United States brought the Mexican War to a victorious conclusion. As you recall, Mexico ceded to the United States a huge area of land in the Southwest—the Mexican Cession. Would slavery be permitted or prohibited in the states that were to be carved out of this new area?

Division over the Southwest. In general, Americans divided along four different lines in their views as to what should be done with the land acquired from Mexico.

First, President Polk and many citizens felt that the problem could best be solved by building upon the Missouri Compromise of 1820. The Missouri Compromise, you recall, outlawed slavery in all remaining areas of the Louisiana Purchase north of latitude 36° 30' (see map, page 356). President Polk now proposed to extend this line to the Pacific, prohibiting slavery north of the line and allowing slavery south of the line.

Second, citizens strongly opposed to slavery accepted the Wilmot Proviso. In August 1846, shortly after the Mexican War started, David Wilmot, a Democratic representative from Pennsylvania, presented a resolution to Congress. The Wilmot Proviso flatly declared that "neither slavery nor involuntary servitude shall ever exist" in the lands acquired from Mexico. All but one of the northern states adopted resolutions approving the Wilmot Proviso.

Southerners took a third point of view. John C. Calhoun, probably the most influential southern spokesman, insisted that Congress had no right to prohibit slavery in the Southwest. Indeed, he insisted, Congress had a duty to protect the rights of slaveowners to their "property," the slaves, in *all* the Territories. Calhoun based his argument on the Fifth Amendment to the Constitution, which guarantees that no person shall "be deprived of life, liberty, or property, without due process of law."

A fourth group, led by Senator Lewis Cass of Michigan and Senator Stephen A. Douglas of Illinois, argued that the people of each Territory should decide whether or not to permit slavery in their Territory. This proposed solution came to be known as "popular sovereignty" or "squatter sovereignty."

Straddling the issue. The problem of slavery in the Territories was the burning issue in the Presidential election of 1848. But both major parties refused to take a stand on this issue. Both parties included southerners as well as northerners, and any strong stand would have split either party in two.

President Polk, exhausted by his four years in office, refused in 1848 to run for re-election on the Democratic ticket. With Polk out of the running, the Democrats turned to Lewis Cass of Michigan, one of the authors of "popular sovereignty."

The Whigs nominated General Zachary Taylor, who had earned the title "Old Rough and Ready" as a fighter in the Mexican War. General Taylor was a southerner, but he had never been seriously involved in politics, and his political views were virtually unknown.

Effects of a third party. The efforts of the Whigs and Democrats to straddle the slavery question drove many northerners to a newly formed third party—the Free-Soil Party. The Free-Soilers opposed any further extension of slavery into the Territories. Adopting the slogan "Free Soil, Free Speech, Free Labor, and Free Men," they nominated former President Martin Van Buren of New York.

Van Buren and the Free-Soilers had great influence on the election, even though they failed to carry a single state for the Presidency. By capturing Democratic votes, especially in New York state, Van Buren unintentionally helped to throw the election to the Whig candidate, General Zachary Taylor. More important, the Free-Soilers won 12 seats in the House of Representatives. Otherwise, the House was almost evenly divided between Whigs and Democrats. The Free-Soil Party therefore held the balance of power in the lower house.

Another crisis. The Congress that assembled in December 1849 was torn by dissension. In fact, tempers were so on edge that the members of the House of Representatives had to vote 63 times before electing a Speaker of the House and getting down to business.

One issue facing Congress was California's application to enter the Union as a free state. Southerners refused to consider the application. If California entered the Union as a free state, the existing balance of 15 slave and 15 free states would be upset in favor of the North.

Another issue before Congress was the controversy between the state of Texas and the newly acquired but as yet unorganized territory of New Mexico. Texas, where slavery was permitted, claimed that its boundary extended westward into country that the federal government had recog-

■ Above, southwesterners of Spanish, Mexican, and Indian ancestry watch over a herd of cattle. After the Mexican War ended, many southwesterners stayed on as American citizens.

nized as belonging to New Mexico. Anti-slavery men in Congress naturally tried to confine Texas to the smallest possible limits. Southerners just as naturally resented northern attempts to limit the area of Texas.

Arguments over other issues echoed through the halls of Congress. Southerners strongly resisted a proposal to abolish slavery in the District of Columbia. They also resisted a proposal to organize New Mexico and Utah into Territories since the proposal made no reference to slavery. Southerners wanted the proposal to state clearly their right to own slaves in New Mexico and Utah during the Territorial period.

Many northerners, on the other hand, were just as strongly opposed to a southern proposal for a new and more effective fugitive slave law. According to the original Fugitive Slave Law of 1793, state and local officials were responsible for capturing runaway slaves and returning them to their owners. In 1842, however, the Supreme Court had ruled that state officials did not have to help federal officials in the capture and return of runaway slaves. Southerners now wanted a new law that once again required state officials to assist in capturing runaway slaves.

All of these issues were loaded with political dynamite. Any one could lead to a break between the North and the South. In the opening months of 1850 many people felt that the United States stood on the brink of disunion, if not indeed on the brink of war.

Clay's compromise. Henry Clay of Kentucky, whose compromises had saved the Union from previous disasters, was known and respected as "the Great Compromiser." Now, in 1850, ill and weary from years of devoted effort to the Union, he stood before the Senate to plead once more for reason and moderation.

Clay's proposals included: (1) the admission of California as a free state. (2) The organization of the land acquired from Mexico (except California) into Territories on the basis of "popular sovereignty," so that the settlers might decide for themselves whether or not they wanted slavery in their Territory. (3) A payment of $10 million to Texas by the United States, if Texas abandoned all claims to New Mexico east of the Rio Grande. (4) The abolition of the slave trade—that is, of the buying and selling of slaves—but not of slavery itself in the District of Columbia. (5) A more effective fugitive slave law, one that would compel state and

359

■ Above, Henry Clay proposes the Compromise of 1850 to the Senate. Seeking to preserve the Union, he said, "I know no South, no North, no East, no West to which I owe allegiance."

local law enforcement officials to cooperate with federal officials in the capture and return of runaway slaves.

The Great Debate. For more than six months Clay's proposals provoked one of the most critical debates in American history. Daniel Webster—like Clay a veteran Whig leader—supported Clay's compromise by arguing that slavery was not likely to prosper in the newly acquired lands. For this reason, Webster declared, it would be unnecessary and unwise for the North to insist on excluding slavery from this area. But many northerners opposed Webster and accused him of betraying the cause of freedom. Stephen A. Douglas of Illinois, who had argued for "popular sovereignty," supported Webster and Clay.

John C. Calhoun of South Carolina spoke for the South. He opposed "popular sovereignty" and all other compromises on the question of slavery. Calhoun was an old man. Like Webster and Clay, he had served his country in Congress for almost 40 years. He was so weak that he had to be carried into the Senate, where a colleague read his speech condemning the compromise. Calhoun insisted, as he had always done, that a slaveowner had the right to take his property anywhere in any of the Territories and that Congress had the duty to protect him in this right. Most southern Senators supported Calhoun.

But others, Whigs and Democrats alike, strongly opposed Calhoun. Among this group were Thomas Hart Benton of Missouri, Salmon P. Chase of Ohio, and William H. Seward of New York. These men sternly denied that the Constitution protected slavery. They opposed the proposed fugitive slave law and urged Congress to exclude slavery from the Territories. Many of them agreed with Seward that there is a "higher law than the Constitution" and that "all legislative compromises are radically wrong and essentially vicious."

Victory for compromise. As it turned out, most Americans in both the North and the South favored compromise. In September 1850 Congress adopted all of Clay's compromise measures by substantial majorities.

John C. Calhoun did not live to see the outcome of the Great Debate. He died in March, leaving a great gap in the ranks of southern leaders. Nor did President Taylor live to see the outcome. After he died in July, his successor, President Millard Fillmore of New York, signed the compromise bills and made them law.

Thus compromise, sometimes called "the essence of politics," once again saved the day. Throughout the nation Americans hailed the work of Clay and his colleagues as a great triumph for national unity. Businessmen spoke enthusiastically for it, expressing their fear that continued controversy between the North and the South would ruin business everywhere.

Would the compromise endure? This was the major question on the lips of many Americans in the fall of 1850.

SECTION SURVEY

IDENTIFY: Wilmot Proviso, "popular sovereignty," Free-Soil Party; Zachary Taylor, Stephen A. Douglas, Millard Fillmore; 1850.

1. Why did American victory over Mexico in 1848 aggravate the slavery issue?
2. Read on page 358 the four proposals for handling the slavery issue in the Mexican Cession. Evaluate each one.
3. "In the opening months of 1850 . . . the United States stood on the brink of disunion, if not indeed on the brink of war." What issues led to this situation?
4. (a) State and evaluate the terms of Clay's Compromise of 1850. (b) Which section of the country profited most from this compromise?
5. Why is compromise sometimes called "the essence of politics"?
6. What did Seward mean by saying that there is a "higher law than the Constitution"?

3 The end of the long period of political compromise

The Compromise of 1850 lasted about four years. As you will see, these four years were the lull before the storm.

Prosperity and growth. Prosperity and growth —these were two of the striking characteristics of the United States during the early 1850's. The South prospered as the price of cotton rose and the annual production of cotton more than doubled. The Northeast prospered as new factories and a growing demand for manufactured products provided plenty of jobs at good wages for great numbers of people, including thousands of immigrants. The Middle West prospered and expanded as railroads opened up the fertile prairie lands, enabling farmers to transport and sell their products. The population of California was growing rapidly.

The railroads were becoming a vital part of the nation's growing economy. Between 1847 and 1861 railroad mileage in the United States increased from about 9,000 to more than 30,000 miles. Most of the new railway lines reached from the Northeast into the Middle West, helping to bind these two areas together (see map, page 290). As a result, when war did come in 1861, the South faced a much more powerful combination than it would have faced had war broken out in 1850 or earlier.

Because the attention of Americans in both the North and the South had for the moment shifted from the problem of slavery to prosperity and growth, the election of 1852 was uneventful. Both major parties condemned further argument over slavery; both accepted the Compromise of 1850 as final. When the votes were counted, the Democratic candidate, Franklin Pierce of New Hampshire, had won 27 states. His rival, the Whig candidate, General Winfield Scott, a hero in the Mexican War, had won only 4 states.

Ominous undercurrents. In his Inaugural Address, President Pierce urged the people to work for national harmony. But harmony was being undermined by dissension.

The publication of Harriet Beecher Stowe's *Uncle Tom's Cabin* in 1852 (page 343) infuriated southerners, who insisted that her picture of slavery was a vicious falsehood. Many northerners, on the other hand, accepted the picture as absolute truth.

The Fugitive Slave Law of 1850, which was

FREE STATES	SLAVE STATES
Thirteen Original States	
Pennsylvania	Delaware
New Jersey	Georgia
Connecticut	Maryland
Massachusetts	South Carolina
New Hampshire	Virginia
New York	North Carolina
Rhode Island	
States Admitted 1791–1819	
(before Missouri Compromise)	
Vermont (1791)	Kentucky (1792)
Ohio (1803)	Tennessee (1796)
Indiana (1816)	Louisiana (1812)
Illinois (1818)	Mississippi (1817)
	Alabama (1819)
States Admitted 1820–48	
(before Compromise of 1850)	
Maine (1820)	Missouri (1821)
Michigan (1837)	Arkansas (1836)
Iowa (1846)	Florida (1845)
Wisconsin (1848)	Texas (1845)

part of the Compromise of 1850, also helped to keep the issue of slavery before the people. Ralph Waldo Emerson, highly regarded as a philosopher and writer, expressed the feelings of most militant abolitionists about the Fugitive Slave Law when he wrote, "This filthy enactment was made in the nineteenth century by people who could read and write. I will not obey it. . . ."

Several northern states responded to the pressure of abolitionists and openly defied the Fugitive Slave Law by passing "personal liberty laws." These laws forbade local officials to help in the capture and return of fugitive slaves.

While northerners defied the Fugitive Slave Law, southerners also helped to fan the flames of misunderstanding. Some southerners began to talk of increasing their power in Congress by acquiring new slave territory. The Spanish colony of Cuba seemed especially attractive.

The Ostend Manifesto. In 1848 President Polk had tried to buy Cuba for $100 million. Spain had refused to consider the offer. But some southerners continued to cast longing eyes at Cuba. Finally, in 1854, the American ministers to Great Britain, France, and Spain met in Ostend, Belgium, and issued a statement that has come to be known as the "Ostend Manifesto."

The ministers declared that, if Spain refused to sell Cuba to the United States, the United States would have every right to seize Cuba by force. President Pierce promptly disavowed this statement. But northern abolitionists were furious. They pointed out that southerners were obviously prepared to plunge the whole nation into war in order to add new slave territory to the Union.

The Kansas-Nebraska Act. In 1854, while undercurrents like these were undermining national unity, Senator Stephen A. Douglas of Illinois increased the tensions, without meaning to do so. Douglas wanted support for building a transcontinental railroad westward from Chicago. He felt that if the country west of the Missouri River were organized as a Territory, it would be settled faster, and its need for a railroad would be increased. To achieve these ends, Douglas sponsored and carried through Congress the Kansas-Nebraska Act. This act had the effect of repealing the Missouri Compromise.

The Missouri Compromise of 1820, as you know, had established the 36° 30′ parallel of latitude from the Mississippi River to the Rocky Mountains as the boundary between slave and free territory, Missouri being the only exception. The Kansas-Nebraska Act created two new organized Territories in the West—Kansas and Nebraska (see map, page 363). Both these Territories were north of the old 36° 30′ line and, therefore, closed to slavery. But the Kansas-Nebraska Act of 1854 abolished the Missouri Compromise dividing line, declaring it "inoperative and void" and stating that the Territories were now "perfectly free to form and regulate their domestic institutions in their own way. . . ."

Northern reaction. Both major political parties were split by the Kansas-Nebraska Act. Most southern Democrats and southern Whigs voted for the bill. Many northern Democrats joined northern Whigs in opposing it. From 1854 until 1861, when war broke out, neither party was able to reunite its northern and southern wings.

Indeed, the Kansas-Nebraska Act plunged the entire nation into violent controversy over the slavery question. Out in Illinois an obscure lawyer, Abraham Lincoln, protested against opening the new Territories to slavery. And up in Boston, the day after the Kansas-Nebraska Act was passed, armed forces were needed to enforce the Fugitive

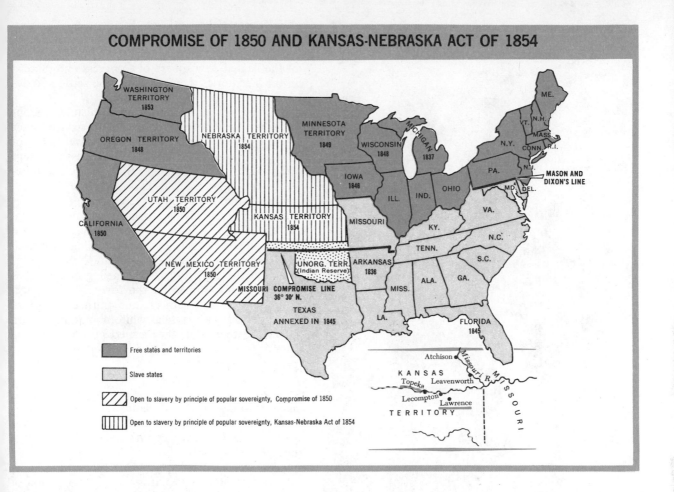

COMPROMISE OF 1850 AND KANSAS-NEBRASKA ACT OF 1854

Free states and territories

Slave states

Open to slavery by principle of popular sovereignty, Compromise of 1850

Open to slavery by principle of popular sovereignty, Kansas-Nebraska Act of 1854

Slave Law. A battalion of United States artillery, four platoons of marines, and a sheriff's posse were called out to escort a runaway slave from the courthouse to the ship waiting to carry him back to the South.

Everywhere throughout the North people once again talked about slavery. The Fugitive Slave Law became increasingly difficult to enforce. And in "anti-Nebraska" meetings men denounced Douglas for reopening the slavery dispute.

The race for Kansas. Senator Charles Sumner of Massachusetts was one of many militant abolitionists who believed that the Kansas-Nebraska Act would plunge the country into serious trouble. "It puts freedom and slavery face to face and bids them grapple." And "grapple" they did, on the plains of the new Territory of Kansas.

Settlers had already begun to drift into Kansas; most of them had no strong feelings about slavery one way or the other. But the ink was hardly dry on

the Kansas-Nebraska Act before northerners and southerners began a race to move into and to control the new Territory. Conflict was the more likely since many newcomers were squatters on land to which they had not obtained legal title.

Northerners formed an "Emigrant Aid Company" and sent anti-slavery settlers into Kansas. These men and women founded Lawrence, Topeka, and other settlements. Meanwhile, pro-slavery settlers from Missouri began to move over the border into Kansas. The pro-slavery settlers started the towns of Atchison, Leavenworth, and Lecompton (see map, this page).

Then the time came for the settlers in Kansas to draw up a constitution and organize a Territorial government. Was slavery to be allowed in Kansas or not? The pro-slavery forces rushed voters from Missouri over the border and elected a pro-slavery legislature which promptly passed laws favoring slaveowners. The anti-slavery forces then drafted

■ In "bleeding Kansas," violence raged between pro-slavery forces bent on making Kansas a slave state and abolitionists determined to make Kansas a free state. Above, "border ruffians" cross into the Territory.

a constitution forbidding slavery and elected an anti-slavery legislature. Thus, by the end of 1855, the Territory of Kansas had two different governments—one pro-slavery, one anti-slavery.'

Dilemma in Washington. Back in Washington, Congressmen watched the struggle with dismay—and no one with greater dismay than the author of

the Kansas-Nebraska Act, Stephen A. Douglas. When Douglas had argued for "popular sovereignty," he had hoped to take the slavery issue out of the heated atmosphere of Congress and place it in the Territories themselves for the settlers to decide.

Obviously, Douglas had been mistaken. Congress now had to take sides and recognize either the pro-slavery or the anti-slavery government of Kansas. President Pierce urged Congress to accept the pro-slavery government. But Douglas, who believed that most Kansans favored a free Territory, opposed the President's recommendation. Congress, hopelessly divided, could reach no decision.

"Bleeding Kansas." Meanwhile, violence raged in what men called "bleeding Kansas." Northerners and southerners began to pour weapons into the Territory. An armed group of pro-slavery men marched on the town of Lawrence, center of the free settlers, and burned a part of it. In revenge, a fanatical white abolitionist, John Brown, gathered another armed group, including his own sons, and one night murdered five unarmed pro-slavery men.

The violence over the slavery issue was heightened by conflicts between the pro-slavery and anti-slavery forces over land claims. At least 200 citizens lost their lives in the bitter strife. Neither side was guiltless. In the end federal troops were brought in to restore order.

The Republican Party. One immediate result of the struggle over Kansas was the formation of a new political party. Neither of the two major parties, the Whigs and the Democrats, dared take a stand on Kansas or any other issue involving slavery. Each party needed the support of its members in the Middle West, where the Kansas-Nebraska Act was popular. For this reason, anti-slavery men in both parties decided that the time was ripe to organize a new party pledging to prevent the further expansion of slavery in the Territories.

Many towns and cities in the Middle West claim to be the birthplace of the Republican Party. It was at a convention in Jackson, Michigan, on July 6, 1854, however, that the delegates voted to adopt the old label of Thomas Jefferson's party for their new organization, and to call themselves "Republicans."

The election of 1856. By 1856 the Republicans were strong enough to enter the Presidential contest. They chose John C. Frémont of California, a famous explorer, to head their ticket. The

FIRST REPUBLICAN CONVENTION HELD AT LAFAYETTE HALL, PITTSBURG, PA, FEB, 22ᴰ 1856.

■ This picture commemorates the first Presidential nominating convention held by the Republican Party. In the Roll of Honor are listed Republicans elected to the Presidency up to 1901.

Democrats nominated James Buchanan of Pennsylvania. The Whigs and the American, or "Know-Nothing," Party nominated Millard Fillmore of New York.

The election returns showed that sectional lines were rapidly stiffening in the nation. The Whigs, who had tried to dodge the slavery issue, came in a poor third, with only 8 electoral votes. The Democrats, who in the end supported the Compromise of 1850 and the Kansas-Nebraska Act "as the only sound and safe solution of the slavery question," came in first with 174 electoral votes (14 slave and 5 free states). The Republicans, who had come out just as squarely against any further expansion of slavery, gave their opponents a good race. Running under the slogan "Free Soil, Free Speech, Free Men, and Frémont," the new Republican Party collected 114 electoral votes (11 free states). The new Republican Party was obviously a purely sectional political organization drawing all its support from the North.

The electoral votes failed to reveal the fact that many people in both the North and the South did not share the views of the majority of voters. Yet the election of 1856 appeared to point to new alignments of political strength in the North and in the South. It seemed likely that the long period of compromise had come to an end.

SECTION SURVEY

IDENTIFY: Ostend Manifesto, Fugitive Slave Law, "bleeding Kansas"; Franklin Pierce, John C. Frémont, James Buchanan.

1. Although the period of 1850–54 was a prosperous one, the issue of slavery continued to cause trouble. Comment.
2. (a) Describe the undercurrents that were undermining national unity before the passage of the Kansas-Nebraska Act in 1854. (b) What were the provisions of the Kansas-Nebraska Act? (c) Describe the consequences of the act's passage.
3. Explain the conditions that led to the formation of the present-day Republican Party.

365

4 The steady movement of North and South toward war

By 1857 the prospect of compromising the struggle between the North and the South seemed remote. From 1857 to 1861 the nation drifted toward disunion.

The Dred Scott decision. On March 6, 1857, two days after President Buchanan took the oath of office, the Supreme Court handed down an explosive decision. The decision involved a slave named Dred Scott.

Dred Scott's owner had taken him from Missouri, a slave state, into Illinois, a free state, and into Minnesota Territory, which was free under the terms of the Missouri Compromise. His owner then took him back into Missouri. A group of abolitionists brought the Dred Scott case into court, claiming that since Scott had lived in a free state and in free Territory he was a free man. The case went through two lower courts, one of which decided for Scott, the other against. Eventually, the case reached the Supreme Court.

The Supreme Court ruled that residence in a free Territory and free state had not given Dred Scott his right to freedom. It declared that Scott (and therefore all slaves) was not a citizen of the United States or of the state of Missouri. Therefore, he had no right to sue in either a state or a federal court.

LIVING AMERICAN DOCUMENTS

Dred Scott v. Sandford (1857)

The right of property in a slave is distinctly and expressly affirmed in the Constitution. The right to traffic in it, like an ordinary article of merchandise and property, was guaranteed to the citizens of the United States, in every state that might desire it, for twenty years. And the government in express terms is pledged to protect it in all future time, if the slave escapes from his owner.... And no word can be found in the Constitution which gives Congress a greater power over slave property, or which entitles property of that kind to less protection than property of any other description. The only power conferred is the power coupled with the duty of guarding and protecting the owner in his rights....
                                 —*United States Supreme Court*

Had the Supreme Court stopped at this point, the Dred Scott case might have gone almost unnoticed by the general public. But the Supreme Court went on to rule that the Missouri Compromise was unconstitutional because Congress had no power to exclude slavery from the Territories. The Court based this decision on the Fifth Amendment, which prohibited Congress from depriving any person of ". . . property, without due process of law." The only other time that the Court had declared an act of Congress unconstitutional was in the case of *Marbury v. Madison* in 1803.

The abolitionist forces in the North were severely jolted by the Dred Scott decision. According to this decision the basic principle of the new Republican Party—the exclusion of slavery from the Territories—was unconstitutional. Now, because of the Supreme Court decision, only an amendment to the Constitution could keep slavery out of the Territories. But an amendment had to be ratified by three fourths of all the states. In view of southern opposition, such a majority was out of the question. Anti-slavery men determined to gain strength and win the election of 1860.

A new leader. The contest for the office of United States Senator from Illinois in 1858 turned out to be a prelude to the general election of 1860.

Stephen A. Douglas was running for re-election as a Democrat. He knew that if he won the Senate race in 1858 he had a good chance of winning the Democratic nomination for the Presidency in 1860.

To oppose Douglas, the Illinois Republicans put up Abraham Lincoln. Born in a log cabin in Kentucky, Lincoln was a self-made man. Gifted with a down-to-earth sense of humor and with much political shrewdness, Lincoln was a match for Douglas in wit, in logical argument, and in general ability.

Lincoln was not an abolitionist. However, he believed that slavery was morally wrong, and he steadfastly accepted the basic principle of the new Republican Party that slavery must not be extended any further. In accepting his nomination for the senatorship, he declared: "A house divided against itself cannot stand. I believe this government cannot endure permanently half slave and half free. I do not expect the Union to be dissolved—I do not expect the house to fall—but I do expect it will cease to be divided. Either the opponents of slavery will arrest the further spread of it, and place it where the public mind shall rest in the belief that it is in the course of ultimate extinction, or its advocates will push it forward till it shall become alike

lawful in all the states, old as well as new, North as well as South."

The Lincoln-Douglas debates. Confident of his position and of his ability to defend it, Lincoln challenged Douglas to a series of debates. Throngs of people came to seven Illinois towns to hear Lincoln and Douglas vigorously debate the issues of the day. Newspapers in every section of the land reported the debates. Lincoln greatly impressed those who heard him and many who read what he said.

In the debates Lincoln asked Douglas how he could reconcile his principle of "popular sovereignty" with the Dred Scott decision. This put Douglas in a tight spot. In the Dred Scott decision the Supreme Court had ruled that no one had the right to outlaw slavery in any Territory. Douglas, on the other hand, had argued for "popular sovereignty," allowing the people in each Territory to make their own decision about slavery. If Douglas answered Lincoln by stating that he believed in the Dred Scott decision, he would win the support of southerners, but lose much northern support. If he continued to argue in favor of "popular sovereignty," he would lose southern support, but win many northern votes. With his eye on the Presi-

dency in 1860, what could Douglas say to please both northerners and southerners?

Douglas was a brilliant politician. He answered Lincoln with a clever reply that became known as the Freeport Doctrine, after the Illinois town of Freeport, where the debate took place. Douglas replied that the legislature of a Territory could refuse to pass a law supporting slavery and thus in effect could exclude slavery from the Territory. Douglas' statement met with enough approval in Illinois to win him the senatorship. Nevertheless, the Freeport Doctrine weakened Douglas in the South and, in so doing, cost him the nomination for the Presidency in 1860 by a united Democratic Party.

Southerners began to realize that Douglas' devotion to "popular sovereignty" did not mean that he favored the expansion of slavery.

John Brown's raid. In the fall of 1859 John Brown tried to start a slave rebellion in Virginia. With money obtained from abolitionists in New England and New York, Brown armed a party of about 18 men. On October 16 he seized the federal arsenal at the town of Harpers Ferry, in what is now West Virginia. He planned to seize the guns stored in the arsenal, give them to nearby slaves, and lead the slaves in what he hoped would be a widespread rebellion.

It was a bold idea, almost certain to fail. Brown and his followers were captured by Colonel Robert E. Lee of the United States Army in command of a unit of marines. After a trial that Brown admitted was more fair than he had reason to expect, he was found guilty and hanged for "murder, criminal conspiracy, and treason against the Commonwealth of Virginia."

Many southerners believed that most northerners approved of Brown's action. In reality most northerners were shocked at the news of John Brown's raid and quickly condemned it as the act of an irresponsible fanatic. But some northern abolitionists did regard Brown as a hero and a martyr. Emerson declared that Brown was a "new saint." Frederick Douglass, who had refused to join Brown's scheme because he felt that it was doomed to fail, now applauded Brown's courage. Southern newspapers quoted the opinions of this small minority of abolitionists as typical of what the whole North was thinking. To southerners, John Brown's raid was convincing evidence that the North was determined to abolish slavery.

Widening split. By 1860 the ties binding the North and the South had almost disappeared. The break between the two sections was reflected in the tensions dividing the political parties. The widening split became clear in 1860 when the national political parties met to draw up platforms and to nominate candidates for the Presidency.

End of the Whig Party. The Whig Party had virtually disappeared by 1856, when most southern Whigs went over to the Democrats and most northern Whigs joined the Republicans. In 1860 what was left of the old Whig Party nominated John Bell of Tennessee for the Presidency. Changing their name to the Constitutional Union Party, they adopted a platform which called upon all who loved the nation to recognize "no political principles other than the Constitution of the country, the Union of the states, and the enforcement of the law."

Division in the Democratic Party. The Democratic Party split wide open in 1860. One group, consisting mostly of southerners, took a strong proslavery position. This group nominated John C. Breckinridge of Kentucky for the Presidency and demanded federal protection for slavery in the Territories. The other group, mostly northern Democrats, nominated Stephen A. Douglas for the Presidency and took the position that "popular

sovereignty" should decide the slavery question in the Territories.

Growing Republican strength. The Republicans, meeting in Chicago, determined to make the most of the split in the Democratic Party. They abandoned one candidate, Governor William H. Seward of New York, partly because he seemed to be identified with eastern "money interests" and partly because a candidate from the Middle West was more likely to win the election. The convention then named Abraham Lincoln as its candidate.

The Republican platform was a purely sectional platform, designed to win the support of northern industrialists and wage earners and of farmers, particularly in the Middle West. The platform opposed the extension of slavery into the new Territories.

Four parties—four views. Thus, four political parties entered the Presidential race in 1860. The Republicans, with Lincoln at their head, were supported by many northern industrialists and midwestern farmers who opposed any further extension of slavery. Aligned against the Republicans in the North were Democrats led by Douglas. The Douglas Democrats wanted to keep things much as they were. Douglas urged the people to vote for him on the ground that, if Lincoln were elected, the South would leave the Union.

In the South the contest was between the moderate Constitutional Unionists, led by Bell, and the southern Democrats, led by Breckinridge. The southern Democrats made it clear that they would regard the election of Lincoln as proof that the North was using its superior strength to encroach upon the rights and interests of the South.

Results of the election. Lincoln won the election, receiving 180 electoral votes, all from the northern free states. Breckinridge mustered 72 electoral votes, all from the southern slave states. Douglas drew 12 electoral votes, while Bell received 39.

The count of the popular vote showed that Lincoln had polled 40 percent, Douglas 29 percent, Breckinridge 18 percent, and Bell nearly 13 percent. Lincoln was elected President, but by a minority of the popular vote.

Thoughtful observers noted with alarm that in both the North and the South Lincoln and Breckinridge, who opposed any compromise on the issue of slavery in the Territories, won more votes than the moderates, Douglas and Bell. Did this mean that the southern states would carry out their threat to secede?

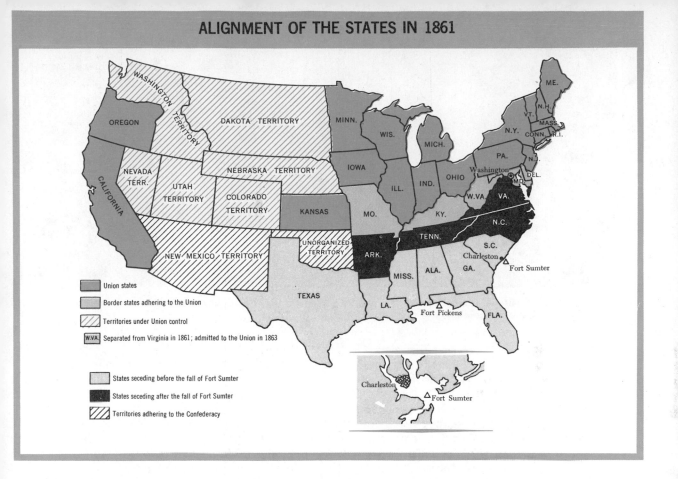

ALIGNMENT OF THE STATES IN 1861

Union states

Border states adhering to the Union

Territories under Union control

W.VA. Separated from Virginia in 1861; admitted to the Union in 1863

States seceding before the fall of Fort Sumter

States seceding after the fall of Fort Sumter

Territories adhering to the Confederacy

Secession from the Union. The fateful answer came quickly. Shortly after the November election the legislature of South Carolina called a special convention to consider secession. The delegates unanimously voted that South Carolina was no longer a state of the Union. Other southern states, not without some opposition, followed South Carolina's example and passed acts of secession (see map, this page).

Early in 1861 delegates from six of the seven seceding states met at Montgomery, Alabama, and drafted a constitution for the Confederate States of America. The Confederate Constitution resembled the Constitution of the United States. It created a federal government. But there were some important differences. The Confederate Constitution stressed "the sovereign and independent character" of each state. It also guaranteed the right to own slaves.

The Montgomery convention elected as President of the Confederacy Jefferson Davis, a Mississippi planter who had formerly served as United States Senator and Secretary of War. The delegates also elected Alexander H. Stephens of Georgia as Vice-President.

Buchanan's inaction. While southern states were seceding from the Union, what did President Buchanan do? Unfortunately, he did almost nothing. He did announce that no state in the Union had the right to secede. But he also stated that the federal government had no power to hold any state in the Union against its will. Thus, for four months, from Lincoln's election until his inauguration, the only efforts to meet the crisis were several half-hearted proposals for compromise. All these proposals were quickly rejected by leaders in both the North and the South.

In fairness to Buchanan, it should be said that his policy did prevent war for several months and gave compromise proposals a chance to be heard. Since he had only four months more in the White House, Buchanan may have concluded that the incoming President should be allowed to settle the problem in his own way.

369

■ A tattered Confederate flag flew over Fort Sumter after Union forces surrendered the fort to Confederate soldiers. The Civil War had begun.

Outbreak of war. During this time Confederate troops occupied—without resistance—all but two of the forts and navy yards in the states that had seceded from the Union. By the time Lincoln was inaugurated on March 4, 1861, only Fort Pickens at Pensacola, Florida, and Fort Sumter at Charleston, South Carolina (see map, page 369), remained in the hands of the federal government. Southerners—or at least those southerners who held the most extreme point of view—claimed that these forts belonged to the Confederate States of America, not to the United States of America. Confederate troops moved into strong positions against these two forts, but did not attack.

In March, Major Robert Anderson, commanding Fort Sumter, notified the War Department in Washington that his supplies were almost gone. This situation presented President Lincoln with a major problem. If he sent new supplies to Fort Sumter, the Confederacy would consider this to be an act of war. If he failed to send supplies, the fort would pass into Confederate hands. Were this to happen, many people would conclude that the United States government had recognized the right of the southern states to secede.

Finally, toward the end of March, and against the advice of the majority of his cabinet, Lincoln sent a relief expedition to Fort Sumter. When the Confederate government heard this news, it notified General Pierre Beauregard (BOH·reh·gahrd), commander of the Charleston district, to fire upon Fort Sumter if such action were necessary to prevent United States reinforcements from reaching it.

On April 12 at 4:30 in the morning, the Confederate guns around the harbor opened fire on Fort Sumter. Major Anderson, in command of the fort, promptly returned the fire while the relief expedition, unable to pass the Confederate batteries, lay helpless outside the harbor. Two days later, on April 14, Major Anderson led his men out of the fort, which then passed into Confederate hands.

News of the fall of Fort Sumter ended all hope of compromise. Men in the North and the South rushed to join the armed forces. War had begun.

SECTION SURVEY

IDENTIFY: secede, Confederacy; Abraham Lincoln, Jefferson Davis, John Brown; April 12, 1861.

1. (a) What was the decision of the Supreme Court in the Dred Scott case? (b) Why did this decision arouse widespread opposition in the North?
2. Describe the Lincoln-Douglas debates.
3. Describe the reactions of northerners and southerners to John Brown's raid.
4. In the form of a chart, compare the parties, candidates, issues, and results in the election of 1860.
5. Lincoln was elected President by a minority of the popular vote, and a sectional minority at that. Explain.
6. In the election of 1860, "those who opposed any compromise on the issue of slavery won more votes than the moderates." Comment.
7. Why did the southern states secede in 1860–61?

TRACING THE MAIN IDEAS

Historians have come up with a variety of names for the war that broke out in 1861, the two most common being the Civil War and the War Between the States. Northern historians have preferred the label "Civil War," describing a conflict between two groups seeking power within the *same nation*. Some southern historians, however, have preferred "War Between the States," using the word "states" to mean "nations," and thus describing a conflict between *two different nations*. From a southern point of view, the Confederacy formed an independent nation with an organized, responsible government and a legitimate constitution.

Northern and southern historians have also differed in their explanations as to why the war broke out. In the decades immediately following the war, northern historians saw the conflict as one to preserve the Union against southern "rebels" who sought to disrupt it. Southern historians viewed the war as a struggle to preserve southern liberty and constitutional guarantees of states' rights, which southerners insisted northerners had repudiated.

In the 1900's an increasing number of historians emphasized basic differences in the economic and social systems of the North and the South. These differences were revealed, they said, in conflicts over the tariff, over internal improvements at public expense, over money and banking, over the disposal of public lands, and over the struggle to control the West. Other historians held that war came because of mistakes committed by blundering leaders who failed to work out possible compromises. Some historians have always emphasized that the conflict over slavery was an important cause of the war. And in recent years a growing number have insisted that slavery was the basic issue over which the war was waged.

These and other explanations do not mean that all or some of the historians are wrong. Each has put his finger on one or more of many forces that contributed to the armed conflict between the North and the South.

The thoughtful historian does not now try to give a simple explanation of the Civil War. He can point out that some southerners believed that a new nation based on slavery and states' rights had come into existence and had to be defended. He can also point out that many southerners who loved the Union, and would have preferred to stay in it, supported the Confederacy out of loyalty to states' rights, out of a determination to protect their homes and institutions, or out of consideration for the position taken by relatives and friends.

The historian can also point out that the great majority of northerners held that the benefits of the Union were too important to be destroyed. Most northerners, as you will read, at first believed that the preservation of the Union was the only real issue at stake. But as time passed, many more northerners came to feel that the war had *two* major purposes: preserving the Union and freeing the slaves.

CHAPTER SURVEY

QUESTIONS FOR DISCUSSION

1. (a) Is compromise the best way of solving an issue as important as slavery? Why or why not? (b) List possible courses of action that could have been followed regarding the issue of slavery. (c) How do strong emotions hinder problem solving?
2. Show how each of the following increased sectional bitterness: (a) the Mexican War, (b) the Wilmot Proviso, (c) William Lloyd Garrison, (d) Harriet Beecher Stowe, (e) the Compromise of 1850, (f) the Dred Scott decision, (g) John Brown's raid, and (h) the Ostend Manifesto.
3. (a) Do you believe that white southerners were the only Americans prejudiced against Negroes during the period just studied? Explain the reasons for your opinion. (b) What inaccuracies and misunderstandings may result from the generalization that all southerners were pro-slavery and all northerners were anti-slavery?

RELATING PAST TO PRESENT

1. The North, as well as the South, has a history of anti-black attitudes. Gather evidence from the period just studied and from current news stories to support this statement.
2. Who would you say are today's counterparts to the abolitionists of the 1840's and 1850's? Explain.

USING MAPS AND CHARTS

1. (a) Using the map on page 363, point out the lines that divided free states from slave states, beginning on the east coast and ending at the Pacific. (b) Explain how each of these was agreed upon.
2. Consult the map on page 369, and identify (a) the border states, (b) the southern states seceding before the fall of Fort Sumter and those seceding afterward, (c) the Union states, and (d) the Territories under Union control.

■ *A young Union soldier*

CHAPTER **19**

A Nation Divided by War

1861 – 1865

On MONDAY, April 15, 1861, the day after Fort Sumter was evacuated by Union troops, President Abraham Lincoln declared that the government of the United States was confronted with an armed revolt against its authority and called for 75,000 men to volunteer for three months' service in the army.

In the northern states, men enthusiastically answered Lincoln's call to arms. From all walks of life they rushed to join the colors—Republicans and Democrats, native-born Americans and newly arrived immigrants who had not yet learned to speak the language of their adopted country. For the time being, the North was united as it had never been united before in its history.

The poet Walt Whitman remembered the opening weeks of the war and managed to recapture in verse the feeling of unity that gripped northerners in those trying days:

Beat! beat! drums!—blow! bugles! blow!
Through the windows—through the doors—burst like a ruthless force,
Into the solemn church, and scatter the congregation;
Into the school where the scholar is studying;
Leave not the bridegroom quiet—no happiness must he have now with his bride;
Nor the peaceful farmer any peace, ploughing his field or gathering his grain;
So fierce you whirr and pound, you drums—so shrill you bugles blow.

In the South as well as in the North, the beat of drums and the shrill voice of the bugle summoned men to war.

THE CHAPTER IN OUTLINE

1. Development of war strategies in the North and the South.

2. Victory for the Union after four years of war.

3. The struggle to free the slaves and preserve the Union.

4. Severe hardships for the South during the war years.

5. Important changes in life behind Union lines.

6. Political problems for the Union at home and abroad.

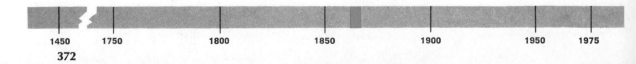

| 1450 | 1750 | 1800 | 1850 | 1900 | 1950 | 1975 |

1 Development of war strategies in the North and the South

On April 15, 1861, when President Lincoln called for Union volunteers, there were only seven states in the Confederate States of America, or the Confederacy—South Carolina, Georgia, Florida, Alabama, Mississippi, Louisiana, and Texas. But with Lincoln's call to arms, every state in the Union had to make its fateful choice.

Choosing sides. Virginia, on April 17, became the eighth state to join the Confederacy. When Virginia left the Union, the United States Army lost several of its ablest officers. The most famous Virginia officer to take up arms for the South was Robert E. Lee, to whom President Lincoln had offered command of the Union forces. Arkansas, Tennessee, and North Carolina soon followed Virginia into the Confederacy. By May 20, five weeks after Fort Sumter fell, 11 states had joined the Confederacy (see map, page 369).

The mountainous counties in northwestern Virginia did not follow the rest of the state into the Confederacy. In 1863 these counties were admitted to the Union as the state of West Virginia. Control of this area, part of which lay on the Ohio River, was important to the North because it helped to keep open the lines of communication between the Northeast and the Mississippi River.

The "border states"—Delaware, Maryland, Kentucky, and Missouri—were also important to the Union, but for a time it was uncertain on which side some of them would fight.

Maryland was especially important, for if it joined the Confederacy, the Union capital at Washington, D.C., would have been isolated from the northern states. For a time Maryland hung in the balance. Many Marylanders were sympathetic to the Confederacy, and on April 19 a mob of angry citizens attacked the Sixth Massachusetts Regiment as it passed through Baltimore. To prevent the passage of Union troops and to avoid further bloodshed, Maryland authorities burned the railroad bridges connecting Baltimore with Philadelphia and Harrisburg. But Lincoln, determined to keep Maryland in the Union, sent federal troops into the state and arrested the leading Confederate sympathizers. Pro-Union leaders then won power, and Maryland remained in the Union.

The other border states—Delaware, Kentucky, and Missouri—also decided in favor of the Union. Delaware never hesitated. Kentucky at first ignored Lincoln's call for volunteers and tried to remain neutral. But when the Confederate army invaded Kentucky in September, the state declared for the Union. Missouri's government was controlled by southern sympathizers. After several battles had been fought, however, Missouri officially lined up with the North.

"The North" also included the Pacific coast states of California and Oregon. In 1863, after

■ **Uniforms of the Civil War**

CONFEDERATE CAVALRY OFFICER

CONFEDERATE RIFLEMAN

UNION RIFLEMAN

UNION CAVALRY OFFICER

West Virginia joined the Union, a total of 24 states were fighting on the northern side.

In many states, especially in the border states, families were torn apart as some members enlisted with the Confederacy, others with the Union. Three of Mrs. Lincoln's brothers fought and died for the South. Robert E. Lee's nephew commanded Union naval forces on the James River in Virginia while his famous uncle was fighting Union army forces not many miles away. The division within families and the breakup of lifelong friendships were some of the tragic results of the war.

Northern advantages. The North had tremendous material advantages over the South. It was greatly superior in population, in manufacturing, in agricultural and natural resources, in finances, and in transportation facilities. Northern strength had recently been increased by the admission of three new states to the Union—Minnesota (1858), Oregon (1859), and Kansas (1861).

The population of the 24 northern, western, and border states totaled 22 million, plus about 800,000 immigrants who entered the United States during the war years. About 400,000 foreign-born men served in the Union armies.

Varied economic resources gave the North an enormous advantage over the predominantly agricultural South. When the war began, the North had 92 percent of the nation's industries and almost all the known supplies of coal, iron, copper, and other metals. The North also owned most of the nation's gold. Confederate wealth was largely in land and slaves.

Northern transportation facilities were also far superior to those of the South. Most of the nation's railroad lines were located in the North and the Middle West. Thus, the North could move men and supplies almost at will, and could transport food from the midwestern farm lands to workers in the eastern cities and to soldiers in the field. Moreover, with control of the navy and a large part of the merchant marine, the North could carry on trade with nations overseas.

Southern advantages. The 11 states of the Confederacy had a combined population of only about 9 million, including more than 3.5 million slaves. Northerners therefore outnumbered white southerners by more than four to one. But southerners took comfort from the fact that other outnumbered people had managed to win wars.

Southerners also felt confident because, to win, they had only to fight a defensive war. The South needed only to protect its territory until the North tired of the struggle. The North, on the other hand, had to penetrate and conquer an area almost as large as Western Europe.

The Confederacy also had the advantage that many of its ablest officers were West Point graduates with long years of army experience. Also, southerners were used to outdoor living, and were generally more familiar with firearms and horses than many men from the Northeast who had been raised in cities.

Another reason for southern optimism was the conviction that "cotton was king." Southerners believed that the textile mills of Great Britain and France were so dependent on raw cotton that these countries would have to come to the aid of the Confederacy.

War aims. Another advantage that southerners had over northerners was the fact that, from the start, southerners were fighting for more clearly defined goals and more personal and concrete aims.

The major aim of the Confederacy never varied. Southerners fought to win their independence—the right to govern themselves as they saw fit. Also, once northern armies invaded the Confederacy, southerners fought to defend the things that men cherish most—their homes and families. In addition, many southerners—slaveholders and nonslaveholders alike—were fighting to preserve slavery. By this time, as you know, slavery had become a firmly established southern institution—widely identified with the distinctive southern way of life.

In contrast, northerners who supported the war were fighting for less tangible goals, no matter how

■ Improvements in Weapons. By 1860, muzzle-loading weapons (page 63) were replaced by various kinds of breechloaders using metal-jacketed cartridges. The "single-shot rifle" could be fired quite rapidly, the "7-shot carbine" even faster.

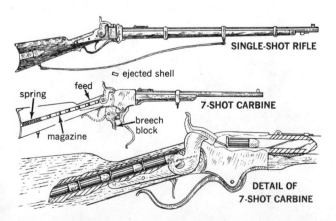

SINGLE-SHOT RIFLE

ejected shell

spring

feed

magazine

breech block

7-SHOT CARBINE

DETAIL OF
7-SHOT CARBINE

■ The North's industrial strength gave it an important advantage over the South. Above, a painting by John Ferguson Weir shows a cannon being cast for use by the Union army.

deeply felt. At the start of the war, most northerners believed with President Lincoln that they were fighting for one major aim—the preservation of the Union. Only a few extreme abolitionists saw the war as a means to end slavery. But as the war dragged on, more and more northerners came slowly to believe that freeing the slaves was as important as restoring the Union—that the two aims, indeed, were inseparable.

War strategies. The overall strategy of the South was as clear and simple as its war aims. Southerners proposed to fight a defensive war, holding the North at arm's length until northerners grew war-weary and agreed to peace on southern terms. The only exception to this defensive strategy was a plan to seize Washington, D.C., and strike northward through the Shenandoah Valley into Maryland and Pennsylvania. By this plan the South hoped to drive a wedge between the Northeast and the Middle West, disrupt Union lines of communication, and bring the war to a speedy end.

Overall northern strategy included three different plans of attack: (1) to cripple the South by blockading the Confederate coastline; (2) to split the Confederacy in two by seizing control of the Mississippi River and interior railroad lines; (3) to seize Richmond, Virginia, which had become the

Confederate capital in May 1861, and then to drive southward and finally link up with Union forces driving eastward from the Mississippi Valley.

Such were the war aims and plans of the two opposing sides. In the spring of 1861, as the northern "Boys in Blue" and the southern "Boys in Gray" trudged to their first battlefield, no one knew that four long, cruel years of fighting lay ahead.

SECTION SURVEY

IDENTIFY: "Boys in Blue," "Boys in Gray"; Robert E. Lee.

1. (a) Name the states that joined the Confederacy. (b) Name the four "border states."
2. Make a chart comparing the North and the South with respect to (a) number of states, (b) population, (c) industrial development, (d) transportation facilities, (e) financial resources, (f) naval power. Evaluate each as a factor for strength in fighting the war.
3. If you had been a southern sympathizer in 1861, why would you have thought that the Confederacy might win the war?
4. (a) Compare the war aims and military strategy of the North and the South. (b) Why were southern goals more clearly defined than those of the North?

375

2 Victory for the Union after four years of war

The first important battle of the Civil War was fought on July 21, 1861, near a stream called Bull Run in northern Virginia (see map 1, page 378). In this engagement, the First Battle of Bull Run, the Confederates defeated the northern recruits, who fled in confusion to Washington, D.C.

Results of Bull Run. Northerners were stunned. If the Confederate commanders had taken advantage of their victory, they could easily have captured Washington, D.C. But the Confederate troops, elated by victory, scattered to celebrate.

The outcome of the First Battle of Bull Run surprised both the North and the South. Northerners, shocked by defeat, prepared for a long war. Southerners, misled by what seemed an easy victory, became overconfident.

The Union blockade. Meanwhile, Union warships and other vessels hastily converted into naval service had begun to blockade the 3,550 miles of Confederate coastline stretching from Virginia around Florida and the Gulf of Mexico to southern Texas (see map, page 377).

As time passed, the blockade became increasingly effective. For example, in 1860, the year before war broke out, 6,000 ships entered and left southern ports, whereas during the first year of the war only about 800 ships slipped through the blockade. Daring Confederate sea captains kept trying to "run the blockade," but as the years wore on fewer and fewer ships slipped through.

The blockade was a severe handicap to Confederate plans. The South had counted on exporting cotton, tobacco, sugar, and other products to obtain money to buy European military equipment and manufactured goods. As the blockade tightened, European products vanished from southern stores. Southern manufacturers could not make up the deficiencies.

As products became increasingly scarce, the prices of southern goods shot skyward, and patriotic southern women began to make substitutes. Using looms and spinning wheels brought down from dusty attics, they began to spin and weave fabrics for clothing and uniforms. Before the war ended, southerners were melting church bells to make cannons.

War at sea. Although the Confederacy failed to break the Union blockade, daring Confederate seamen made the sea lanes dangerous for northern shipping. Between Lincoln's election and the fall of Fort Sumter, the South seized a number of United States vessels then in southern harbors. During the war southerners also purchased in England the *Alabama,* the *Florida,* and 17 other warships. Although these few vessels posed no serious threat to the United States Navy, they did sink more than 250 merchant ships before the war ended.

More important to the war's outcome was the ever-present possibility of a Union naval attack on a southern harbor and the landing of a Union army behind Confederate lines. Fortunately for the South, all of its important harbors had been heavily fortified long before the war. Early in 1861 the Confederacy seized these fortifications and continued to man them throughout the war. But this meant that many thousands of Confederate troops, badly needed on the fighting front, had to remain in the coastal fortresses to guard against Union attack. Despite southern precautions, Union forces captured New Orleans and several forts along the Atlantic coast.

The Union on the offensive. The Appalachian Mountains divided land operations into two major theaters of war—the eastern theater and the western theater.

Shortly after the Union disaster at the First Battle of Bull Run, President Lincoln gave 34-year-old General George B. McClellan, a West Point graduate, command of the eastern theater of war. A superb organizer, and popular with his men, McClellan quickly turned a mob of untrained volunteers into the highly effective Army of the Potomac. In November 1861 Lincoln elevated McClellan to General-in-Chief of all the Union armies. But McClellan was overly cautious, refusing to attack until he was thoroughly prepared. The saying "All quiet along the Potomac" became a public joke. Lincoln finally commented, "If General McClellan does not want to use the army, I would like to *borrow* it."

While the Army of the Potomac marked time in the East, Union forces in the western theater fought small skirmishes in Missouri, hoping to prevent that state from joining the Confederacy. By 1862, however, Missouri was secure, and General Henry W. Halleck, in command of the western theater, opened a drive into Tennessee.

War in the West. Beginning in western Kentucky where the Tennessee River empties into the Ohio River, an infantry unit commanded by General Ulysses S. Grant—one of General Halleck's

(*continued on page 378*)

MAJOR CAMPAIGNS OF THE CIVIL WAR

Battle between Merrimac and Monitor, March 9, 1862

Mason and Dixon's Line

Legend:

Union states

Union plans to split the Confederacy and seize Richmond

Union blockade of Confederate shipping

Confederate states

▲ Forts seized by Confederate forces

■ This map shows the main points of Union strategy and provides an overview of the major campaigns of the Civil War. The circled numbers indicate the areas in which fighting occurred. In the pages that follow, you will learn more about each of these campaigns. The discussion of each campaign is accompanied by a detailed map that bears a number corresponding to one of the numbers on this map. As you read the text that follows and examine each numbered map, look frequently at the map above so that you will understand the sequence of the war. On the map above and on the detailed maps, Union states appear in yellow, Confederate states in green. On all of the detailed maps, colored symbols stand for Union forces, black symbols for Confederate forces. The following symbols are used:

→ Union advance   ⇢ Union retreat   ✸ Union victory

→ Confederate advance   ⇢ Confederate retreat   ✷ Confederate victory

377

1 First Battle of Bull Run: July 21, 1861

subordinate officers—moved southward. On February 6, 1862, Grant captured Fort Henry on the upper Tennessee River, and on February 16 he captured Fort Donelson on the Cumberland River (see map 2, page 379). These victories opened the way for an invasion of the deep South by way of the Tennessee and Cumberland rivers. But General Nathan Bedford Forrest, one of the South's best generals, escaped and proved so dangerous that Union General William T. Sherman later ordered his men to hunt Forrest down "if it costs ten thousand lives and bankrupts the federal treasury."

In the operations along the Tennessee, the Union infantry was assisted by gunboats, small warships capable of steaming along the shallow river waters. Indeed, in both this campaign and the Mississippi River campaign, gunboats proved extremely useful to both sides.

With Fort Donelson in Union hands, Grant continued southward along the Tennessee River to Pittsburg Landing, sometimes called Shiloh (SHY·loh), in Tennessee. Here General Albert S. Johnston of Texas, Confederate commander in the West, surprised and completely defeated him. But with Johnston's death and the arrival of reinforcements, Grant again took the offensive and after desperate fighting finally drove the Confederate army from the field. At the end of May, Union forces occupied Corinth, in northern Mississippi.

At the same time, other Union forces were fighting to the south and north to gain control of the Mississippi River. On the night of April 23 Union

Flag Officer (later Admiral) David G. Farragut of Tennessee ran his gunboats past the forts guarding New Orleans and captured the city. Meanwhile a combined Union naval and land expedition under Commodore A. H. Foote and General John Pope was moving southward down the Mississippi. In June this expedition seized Memphis, Tennessee, and then continued as far south as Vicksburg, Mississippi (see map 2, page 379).

Thus, by the summer of 1862, Union forces in the western theater had almost succeeded in splitting the Confederacy in two along the Mississippi. Casualties had been enormous on both sides, for the Confederate armies made the Union troops pay dearly for every foot of ground. But Union armies had driven the Confederate troops out of Kentucky and western Tennessee. Only a short length of the Mississippi, and Port Hudson, Louisiana, remained in Confederate hands.

War in the East. Union victories in the western theater during 1862 were more than balanced by Confederate victories in the eastern theater.

In April 1862 General McClellan finally started the long-awaited offensive against the Confederate capital at Richmond, Virginia. Leaving General Irvin McDowell with 40,000 men to guard Washington, D.C., McClellan transported more than 100,000 troops down the Potomac River, seized Yorktown, Virginia, and began a slow, cautious advance up the peninsula between the York and the James rivers (see map 3, page 379). By mid-May, McClellan's troops were within a few miles of Richmond. Here McClellan paused to wait for reinforcements.

Because of the actions of the brilliant Confederate officer General Thomas J. ("Stonewall") Jackson, McClellan's reinforcements never arrived. In May and June, with only 18,000 men, Jackson fought engagements in the Shenandoah Valley, defeating Union forces three times his size and holding a constant threat over Washington, D.C.

Meanwhile, in June, Confederate troops defending Richmond launched furious counterattacks, known as the Seven Days' Battles, against McClellan's army. Led by General Robert E. Lee, General "Stonewall" Jackson, and the dashing cavalry officer General James E. B. ("Jeb") Stuart, the Confederate troops forced McClellan to drop back to the James River.

On August 29–30, two months after the successful defense of their capital, the Confederates won another victory at the Second Battle of Bull Run (see map 3, page 379). Union General John Pope,

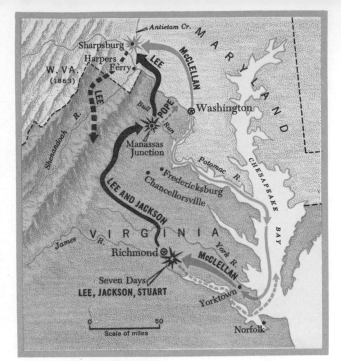

War in the East: 1862

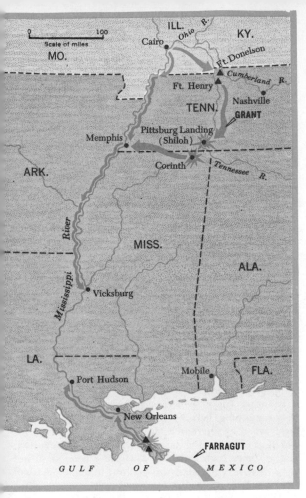

2 War in the West: 1862

overconfident because of his victories in the western theater, launched a new drive toward Richmond. But Lee and Jackson caught him at Bull Run and defeated him. The light from Pope's burning wagons could be seen in Washington, D.C., and the city was in panic.

Encouraged by these successes, the Confederacy decided to stage three powerful offensives designed (1) to regain control of the Mississippi, (2) to recover the ground lost in Tennessee and Kentucky, and (3) to invade Maryland and draw that state into the Confederacy. All three offensives failed.

On September 4 General Lee crossed the Potomac into Maryland with 40,000 picked troops, confident of victory. On September 17, at Sharpsburg near Antietam Creek (see map 3, this page), he engaged General McClellan and a force of 70,000 men. The Battle of Antietam was the bloodiest of the war. Both sides were so exhausted

that McClellan did not try to pursue the Confederate troops and win a decisive victory.

The Battle of Gettysburg. The year 1863 opened with both sides discouraged. The southern offensive in the fall of 1862 had failed, and the South had begun to despair of winning support from Great Britain and France. The North, although victorious in the western theater, had suffered defeats in the East, and the Union capture of Richmond seemed extremely remote.

Such was the situation when, in June 1863, General Lee again struck into the North hoping to drive a wedge into the Union and deal a fatal blow to the northern war effort. By the end of the month his army of 75,000 men was moving northward across Maryland into Pennsylvania. On June 30 advance patrols of the Confederate and Union armies met at Gettysburg, Pennsylvania (see map 4, page 380). For two days the main armies fought desperately as they maneuvered for position on the hills around the town.

On July 3 Lee staked the fate of his army and, as it turned out, of the Confederacy itself on a bid for victory. Led by General George E. Pickett, 15,000 of Lee's finest troops charged up Cemetery Ridge through the devastating fire of Union troops under the command of George G. Meade. For a brief moment the Confederate battle flag floated on

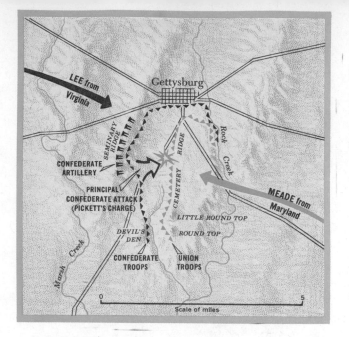

④ Battle of Gettysburg: July 1–3, 1863

LIVING AMERICAN DOCUMENTS

Abraham Lincoln's Gettysburg Address (1863)

Four score and seven years ago our fathers brought forth on this continent a new nation, conceived in liberty, and dedicated to the proposition that all men are created equal.

Now we are engaged in a great civil war, testing whether that nation, or any nation so conceived and so dedicated, can long endure. We are met on a great battlefield of that war. We have come to dedicate a portion of that field as a final resting place for those who here gave their lives that that nation might live. It is altogether fitting and proper that we should do this.

But, in a larger sense, we cannot dedicate—we cannot consecrate—we cannot hallow—this ground. The brave men, living and dead, who struggled here, have consecrated it far above our poor power to add or detract. The world will little note nor long remember what we say here, but it can never forget what they did here. It is for us, the living, rather, to be dedicated here to the unfinished work which they who fought here have thus far so nobly advanced. It is rather for us to be here dedicated to the great task remaining before us—that from these honored dead we take increased devotion to that cause for which they gave the last full measure of devotion; that we here highly resolve that these dead shall not have died in vain; that this nation, under God, shall have a new birth of freedom; and that government of the people, by the people, for the people, shall not perish from the earth.

the crest of the ridge. But the Union forces were too strong, and the broken remnants of Pickett's force fell back.

The next day, July 4, Lee started his sorrowful but skillful retreat back to Virginia. To Lincoln's disappointment, the overcautious Meade did not pursue the Confederate forces. "Our army held the war in the hollow of their hand," Lincoln said, "and they would not close it. Still," he added, "I am very grateful to Meade for the great service he did at Gettysburg."

The battle for Vicksburg. On July 4, 1863, the Union won another victory with the fall of Vicksburg, Mississippi. Starting in March 1863, General Ulysses S. Grant marched his army southward from Memphis, rapidly overcame Confederate opposition in five battles, and on May 22 laid siege to Vicksburg, the stronghold of Confederate forces on the Mississippi (see map 5, page 381).

For six weeks Vicksburg held out, suffering terrible punishment from Grant's cannons and from Union gunboats in the river. Finally, on July 4, reduced to starvation, the Confederate defenders surrendered. Five days later Port Hudson, Louisiana, fell into Union hands. Within a week a Union steamboat from St. Louis arrived in New Orleans, which had been held by Union forces for more than a year.

With Union control of the Mississippi River, the Confederacy was finally split in two along the Mis-

sissippi. Another of the North's major objectives had been accomplished. The time was approaching for the final drive to end the war.

A Union breakthrough. On September 9, 1863, two months after the fall of Vicksburg, a Union army under General William S. Rosecrans occupied Chattanooga, Tennessee, a key railway center and gateway to the deep South (see map 6, page 381). Rosecrans then set out after the Confederates, commanded by General Braxton Bragg, who turned on him at Chickamauga Creek and defeated him, driving him back into Chattanooga. Indeed, if troops under General George H. Thomas had not held back the Confederates long enough to allow Rosecrans to withdraw his main forces, the battle would have ended in utter disaster for the North. For his part in the battle, General Thomas won the title "Rock of Chickamauga," and replaced Rosecrans as commander of the Union army at Chattanooga.

The Union army stayed in Chattanooga until late November. Then, reinforced with fresh troops, the army, under the command of General Grant himself, and with generals Thomas, Hooker, and Sherman as his subordinates, opened an offensive. In two bitterly contested engagements—Lookout Mountain and Missionary Ridge—the Union troops broke through Confederate defenses and opened the way into the deep South.

Beginning of the end. On March 9, 1864, General Grant became supreme commander of all Union armies. Two months later, acting on Grant's orders, General William T. Sherman set out from Chattanooga with 100,000 men to invade Georgia. The greatly outnumbered Confederate army under General Joseph E. Johnston fell back, fighting heroically and destroying railroads and bridges as it retreated. Sherman pushed on relentlessly, and on September 2 he entered Atlanta. Two months later, with some 60,000 men, he left Atlanta and started toward Savannah, Georgia (see map 7, page 382). On December 22 Sherman wired President Lincoln, "I beg to present you as a Christmas gift the city of Savannah."

Behind him on his "March to the Sea" Sherman left a swath of destruction 300 miles long and 60 miles wide. Railroad tracks, heated red-hot in giant bonfires, were twisted around trees and telegraph poles. Bridges lay in tumbled ruins. Crops were uprooted, livestock slaughtered, and farmhouses reduced to ashes. Sherman intended to weaken southern resistance, but he also left a legacy of southern bitterness.

By the spring of 1865 Sherman's army was moving northward through the Carolinas with General Joseph E. Johnston's weary army trying to slow him down.

Meanwhile, General Grant in May 1864 had been hammering away at Richmond, Virginia, pushing through difficult terrain against fierce Confederate resistance (see map 8, page 382). Despite enormous losses in this Wilderness Campaign, Grant fought on. "I propose to fight it out along this line if it takes all summer," he wrote.

Grant did fight all summer and into the fall and the winter. The superior resources and manpower of the Union were beginning to have a decisive effect.

Lee's surrender. In the spring of 1865 Sherman's army continued to move northward, and

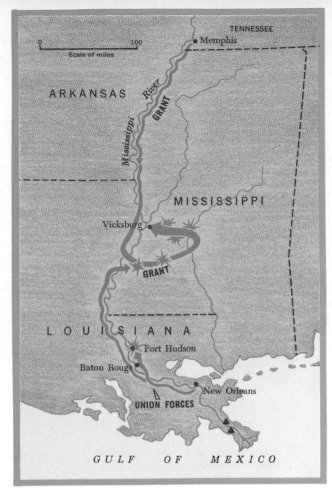

5　War in the West: March–July 1863

6　Fighting Around Chattanooga: Fall 1863

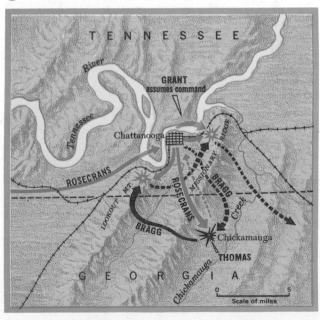

⑦ Sherman's Drive to the East and North: May 1864–April 1865

⑧ Grant's Campaign Around Richmond: May 1864–April 9, 1865

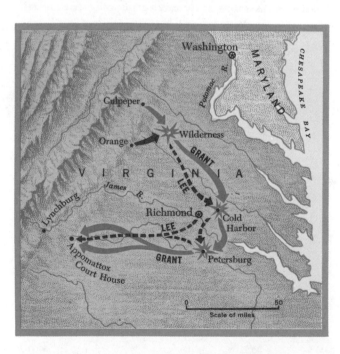

Grant's troops were hammering at the doors of Richmond. On April 2 General Lee withdrew from the city, and the Stars and Stripes at last flew over the former Confederate capital.

From Richmond, Lee moved swiftly westward toward Lynchburg, Virginia, with Grant close on his heels (see map 8, this page). Lee thought for a time that he might escape with his army into North Carolina and there join forces with General Johnston, who was as yet undefeated. But Lee's position was hopeless. Finally, on April 9, General Lee surrendered.

Appomattox Court House. The two men, Lee and Grant, met in a house in the small village of Appomattox Court House in Virginia. Lee was in full dress uniform with a jewel-studded sword at his side. Grant wore a private's blouse, unbuttoned at the neck.

Grant offered Lee generous terms. He allowed the officers and men to return to their homes after their promise that they would not again take up arms against the Union. The troops had to surrender their weapons, but Grant permitted Lee's officers to keep their pistols and swords. When Lee mentioned the distressing condition of southern agriculture, Grant said, "Let all the men who claim to own a horse or mule, take the animals home with them to work their little farms. This," he said, "will do much toward conciliating our people."

The meeting ended, Lee mounted his horse and ⌐ode off. Union troops started to cheer. Grant ordered them to be silent. "The war is over; the rebels are our countrymen again," he said.

Thus the long, bitter conflict ended.

SECTION SURVEY

IDENTIFY: Battles of Bull Run, Army of the Potomac, Sherman's "March to the Sea"; George McClellan, Henry Halleck, Nathan Forrest, Albert S. Johnston, David Farragut, John Pope, "Stonewall" Jackson, "Jeb" Stuart, Joseph E. Johnston; April 9, 1865.

1. It has been said that the Union blockade was as effective in overpowering the South as were the armies of Grant and Sherman. Explain.
2. Compare the significance of the Union victories in the West with that of the Confederate victories in the East in 1862.
3. Discuss the significance of the battles of Gettysburg and Vicksburg.
4. What were the terms of surrender that Grant offered Lee?

3 The struggle to free the slaves and preserve the Union

Southerners dying for the Confederacy and northerners dying for the Union were not the only Americans willing to sacrifice everything for their beliefs. As the war dragged on, a small but growing number of northern abolitionists began to speak out more loudly. They were determined at all costs to link the freeing of the slaves to the saving of the Union.

Growing abolitionist activity. Far from suspending the long struggle to end slavery, the war quickened abolitionist activities. Frederick Douglass, a well-known black spokesman, expressed the view of all abolitionists when he declared that the Union could not be preserved unless the slaves were *emancipated,* or given their freedom.

The abolitionists added practical reasons to their moral and humane arguments for freeing the slaves. Emancipating the slaves, they said, would encourage slaves to flee the South, thus striking a heavy blow at the southern wartime economy, which depended heavily on slave labor. Moreover, freeing the slaves would rally strong anti-slavery sentiment elsewhere in the world to the Union side. Soon after the war started, the abolitionists pressured the national government to issue an immediate declaration of emancipation.

Lincoln's early opposition. President Lincoln had long believed slavery to be wrong, but he now insisted that, in the national crisis, the issue of slavery must be subordinated to the main issue of saving the Union. Lincoln feared the emancipation of the slaves would force the border states—Missouri, Kentucky, and Maryland—to leave the Union.

Like Thomas Jefferson before him, moreover, Abraham Lincoln was convinced that white Americans and black Americans could never live together in peace. He therefore tried to persuade slaveowners in the border states to accept his policy of gradual emancipation, including payment for the loss of their slaves. At the same time, he tried to persuade free Negro leaders to start a new colonization movement of black Americans into Central America or the West Indies.

As late as August 1862, Lincoln expressed his reluctance to turn the war into a crusade to free the slaves. "My paramount object in the struggle," he declared, "is to save the Union, and it is not either to save or to destroy slavery. If I could save the Union without freeing any slave, I would do it, and if I could save it by freeing all the slaves, I would do it. And if I could save it by freeing some and leaving others alone, I would do that. What I do about slavery and the colored race I do because I believe it helps to save this Union. And what I forbear, I forbear because I do not believe it would help to save this Union."

Abolitionist gains. Deeply disappointed, the abolitionists were quite outspoken in condemning Lincoln. Anti-slavery forces in Congress were strong enough to challenge the President's position.

In April 1862 Congress abolished slavery in the District of Columbia, paying owners for the loss of their slaves. A short time later Congress abolished slavery in United States Territories. Congress also supported a plan for giving financial aid to states that would adopt a program for freeing slaves over a period of years. But to committed abolitionists, these moves were far from enough.

The Emancipation Proclamation. By September 1862 Lincoln had reluctantly decided that a war fought, at least partly, to free the slaves would win welcome European support, lessening the danger of foreign intervention on the side of the Confederacy. It would also strike a blow at the Confederacy and win some needed, wholehearted support for the Union from growing numbers of American abolitionists.

Lincoln prepared an Emancipation Proclamation but kept it secret, waiting for news of a northern victory to add to its impact. On September 22, 1862, five days after Union forces stopped Lee's troops at the bloody Battle of Antietam, Lincoln issued a preliminary Proclamation of Emancipation. In this proclamation President Lincoln declared that all slaves in states or parts of states still fighting against the United States on January 1, 1863, would from that time on be forever emancipated—free, that is, wherever Union armies could liberate them or they could escape to the North.

On January 1, 1863, Lincoln issued his final Emancipation Proclamation. Abolitionists, although pleased, were still skeptical of Lincoln's intentions. For one thing, the Emancipation Proclamation did not free any slaves in states then in the Union—the border states, that is—nor in certain parts of Virginia and Louisiana that were under Union control. Lincoln made these exceptions because he was still worried about antagonizing the border states and driving them out of the Union. He was also uncertain that the Constitution gave him the authority to free any slaves anywhere.

■ These men, members of the 4th United States Infantry, were among the 186,000 black soldiers and sailors who fought in the Union army and navy during the Civil War.

Despite criticism of the Emancipation Proclamation, however, most people in the United States and overseas now concluded that Lincoln had at last clearly stated a second, vital issue of the war.

The Thirteenth Amendment.   When President Lincoln issued his Emancipation Proclamation, he based it upon his constitutional authority as commander in chief of United States military forces. Whether this authority gave him the right to free the slaves—whether, that is, his Proclamation had the force of law—was an unanswered question.

To settle the slavery question once and for all, Congress early in 1865 approved an amendment to the Constitution, freeing slaves everywhere in the United States and its Territories. This, the Thirteenth Amendment, was finally ratified by the necessary three fourths of the states eight months after the war ended.

Negro contributions to the war effort.   While abolitionists kept up their pressure upon the government, black Americans made important contributions to northern victory.

Early in the war, some runaway slaves who reached the Union lines in search of freedom were sent back to Confederate lines. In 1862 Congress finally forbade these practices. In so doing, Congress supported such Union officers as Benjamin Butler and John C. Frémont, who had welcomed the fugitives and put them to work at important noncombatant tasks. At that time, northern commanders were forbidden to use black men, slave or free, as fighters.

Before the war ended, about 200,000 Negroes served the northern fighting forces as noncombatants. Among them were cooks, teamsters, nurses, scouts, spies, and steamboat pilots.

Early exclusion from military service.   There were several reasons why black Americans, slave and free, were forbidden to fight in the war.

First, official northern policy stated that the war was being fought to suppress rebellion and restore the Union. Thus, the issues of slavery and of Negro participation in the war were officially downgraded, although they could not be ignored. Second, as you know, President Lincoln and other northern officials feared that the use of black soldiers would antagonize the loyal border states. Third, many white northern recruits made it clear that they did not want to fight with black men as fellow-soldiers. Some northern officers even ques-

384

tioned whether Negroes had the ability or the courage required to make good soldiers.

Abolitionists, white and black, denounced the policy of excluding black men from the Union forces. They declared that it was unfair to keep willing Negroes from fighting for the emancipation of their enslaved brethren.

Practical necessities presently reinforced the arguments of abolitionists. When it proved harder and harder to recruit white northern soldiers, as it did, the rejection of black volunteers could no longer be justified. Several Union generals in the conquered areas of the South asked permission to use black troops and test their fighting ability. In Louisiana, Union commanders wanted to use free Negroes who had organized their own regiment and were eager to fight.

Changing policy. These increasing pressures led at last to a change in northern military policy. In the summer of 1862 the War Department authorized General Rufus Saxton to raise five regiments of black troops in the sea islands off the coast of South Carolina, which had been occupied by Union forces. In Massachusetts and other northern states free Negroes were organized into regiments. Before the war ended, about 186,000 black Americans served in northern armed forces, including 29,000 in the navy.

Discrimination against Negro troops. The reluctant admission of black Americans into the fighting forces did not mean that they lived and fought on equal terms with white men. Black soldiers were less well trained than white soldiers and received less adequate medical services. They often were assigned fatigue duty—the menial, nonmilitary chores around camp. Although Negroes served as noncommissioned officers, only a handful received commissions.

Black soldiers were often badly treated, not only by white fellow soldiers but also by white northerners. Through most of the war, black soldiers received less pay than white soldiers; some Negro troops, in fact, refused to accept any pay at all until the injustice was ended. Finally, after great pressure, Congress in 1864 provided that black fighting men were to receive the same pay as white soldiers.

Black troops under fire. Despite the discriminations against them, after 1862 black soldiers and sailors fought bravely in almost all battles of the war. Their courage and ability often astounded their officers and foes. For unusual valor in the Civil War, 21 black fighting men received the Con-

■ Members of the 54th Massachusetts Regiment stormed Fort Wagner, South Carolina, on July 18, 1863. Charles and Lewis Douglass, sons of Frederick Douglass, were members of this regiment.

gressional medal of honor from the government.

One outstanding example of what black troops could do took place at Fort Wagner in South Carolina.

The 54th Massachusetts Regiment. On the evening of July 18, 1863, the men of the 54th Massachusetts Regiment were trying to relax on the sands of Morris Island on the southern side of the Charleston harbor. The day-long bombardment had ended, but the evening was uneasily quiet.

In front of the troops, across a narrow neck of windswept land, loomed the sloping walls of Fort Wagner. The Union bombardment had done no visible damage to the fort. It would have to be taken, if at all, by a desperate frontal assault. The 54th, commanded by Colonel Robert Gould Shaw and backed by other regiments, had been selected to spearhead the attack.

The 54th Massachusetts was composed of the first black soldiers recruited for the Union armies. This was the first time black troops had been assigned a key role in a major battle. They would carry the heaviest responsibility and surely suffer the greatest losses. Also, the Confederacy had declared that Negro soldiers in the Union forces were outlaws. If captured, they could be shot, hanged, or sold into slavery without trial.

At the command "Forward!" the men of the 54th started across the open ground toward the fort. The fort turned into a solid mass of gunfire aimed at the ranks of the advancing troops. Other Confederate forts in the harbor opened fire. It seemed impossible that any man could remain alive in this inferno. But somehow Colonel Shaw and more than 90 of his men courageously clawed their way up the sloping sides of the fort to the parapet at the top. For a moment they stood outlined against flame and smoke. And then Colonel Shaw was hit and fell inside the fort. About 80 of his men leaped in after him. They surrounded his lifeless body and fought hand-to-hand until every one of them was killed.

On the fierce battleground before Fort Wagner, Union troops were repulsed with terrible losses, some 1,500 being killed or wounded. Black troops would fight with equal gallantry in other battles of this and later wars. But the men of the 54th had won a special place in American history.

SECTION SURVEY

IDENTIFY: Emancipation Proclamation, Thirteenth Amendment, 54th Massachusetts Regiment.

1. (a) How did the Civil War affect abolitionist activities? (b) How did abolitionist activities affect the war?
2. (a) Why did Lincoln at first oppose emancipating the slaves? (b) Why did he change his mind?
3. Read the Thirteenth Amendment on page 194. Why was it passed?
4. (a) Cite Negro contributions to the war effort. (b) Why were Negroes at first excluded from military service? (c) Of what significance is it that 21 black Americans received the Congressional medal of honor?
5. How were black troops discriminated against?
6. Why is Fort Wagner, South Carolina, significant in (a) black military history, (b) American history?

4 Severe hardships for the South during the war years

The appearance of former slaves in the ranks of invading northern armies was dramatic proof that the War Between the States was completely transforming the lives of people in the Confederacy.

During the first few weeks of the war, there was excitement—and sadness—as southern men and boys left for the battlefields, confident and in high spirits. After a few months, as casualty lists grew longer and as food and supplies became scarce, the war became a grim reality, relieved on occasion by news of a Confederate victory. From 1861 to 1865 the South was a nation in arms.

Manpower and the draft. During the war, by volunteer enlistments and the draft, the Confederacy maintained an army of about 400,000 men. All together, from 1861 to 1865, the Confederacy enlisted or drafted 1.3 million men.

In the first year of the war the Confederacy relied entirely on volunteer enlistments. On April 16, 1862, however, it turned to *conscription,* or the draft, making every white man between the ages 18 and 35 liable for military service unless lawfully exempt.

The draft was unpopular, and many southerners claimed that it was unfair. The original conscription law exempted workers in many occupations. It also permitted a drafted man to hire a substitute. Since the "substitute" provision favored wealthy people who could afford to hire substitutes, poorer people grumbled that the conflict was "a rich man's war and a poor man's fight." Late in 1863 the Confederate government stopped the privilege of hiring substitutes, and in 1864 it reduced exemptions and increased draft limits to include all white men between 17 and 50. In the last months of the war the Confederacy became so desperate for manpower that it reluctantly decided to recruit slaves, promising to set them free if they remained loyal to the end of the war.

States' rights. Many southerners insisted that conscription was contrary to their constitution. Believing strongly in states' rights, they therefore denied that the Confederate government had the authority to reach into a state and force a man into military service. The state authorities in North Carolina refused to enforce the conscription law.

Southerners also objected to other policies of the central government at Richmond on the ground that states' rights were violated. When President

■ General Lee surrendered to the Union forces on April 9, 1865, and the Civil War ended. Above, Lee's soldiers furl the Confederate flag for the last time.

Davis suspended the writ of habeas corpus (page 180), the state courts promptly denied his right to do so. Many southerners applauded the decision of the courts and South Carolinians even talked about seceding from the Confederacy. Thus, the strong belief of southerners in states' rights weakened the efficiency of the Confederate war effort.

Southern finances. Raising money was a far more difficult problem for the Confederacy than raising manpower, for most southern wealth was in land and slaves. The Union blockade, which cut off most southern trade, also prevented the Confederacy from raising money from customs duties.

Early in the war, patriotic southerners lent $100 million to the Confederacy in return for war bonds, but this source of income was soon exhausted. The government borrowed another $15 million from abroad, and raised about $100 million from taxation. But all this income was far from adequate, and the Confederacy had to rely mainly on "paper money."

Before the war ended the government had printed more than $1 billion in Confederate bank notes. The value of these notes depended on the promise of the Confederate government to redeem them—that is, exchange them for gold or silver—"after the ratification of a treaty of peace between the Confederate States and the United States of America." As southern victory became increasingly remote, the Confederate currency steadily declined in value. By 1865 each dollar bill was worth only 1.6 cents in gold. With northern victory the Confederate war bonds and bank notes became worthless.

Meanwhile prices soared. People with goods to sell demanded more and more Confederate bank notes in return for their commodities. It was said that a woman could take money to market in a basket and bring her purchases home in a pocketbook.

Southern industry. But paper money was only one reason for skyrocketing prices. Another was the shortage of goods. The Union blockade deprived southerners of practically all luxuries, such as tea and coffee, as well as many essentials— clothing, hardware, medicines, and soap. As one historian put it, "The blockade was the real destroyer of the South."

Despite heroic efforts, manufacturing establishments in the Confederacy could not supply the needs of either the army or the civilian population. Confederate soldiers often marched without shoes, slept without blankets, and lived in ragged clothing. Fortunately for the Confederate troops, they won many battles and captured large supplies of food, clothing, and munitions.

Agriculture and transportation. Civilians felt the pinch of hard times even more than the soldiers. City people especially suffered from the shortage of goods and the soaring prices. By 1863 many southerners faced near-starvation.

This tragic situation was not caused by lack of food, for the South was an agricultural region. Despite the flight of slaves to the Union lines there was still enough labor, slave and free, to work the farms and plantations. The serious problem was lack of transportation.

When the war started, the Confederacy had only about 9,000 miles of railroads out of a total of more than 30,000 miles for the entire country. Southern planters had depended largely on the rivers to send their cotton to the seaports. As the war continued, the Confederacy had difficulty keeping even its limited railroad mileage in operation. With no way to replace worn-out equipment, southerners tore up branch lines and used branch line engines, cars, and rails to keep main lines in operation. The southern transportation problem was so severe that, before the war ended, people in Richmond rioted for food while barns in the Shenandoah Valley were filled with wheat.

During the last few months of the war the food shortage became so desperate that many Confederate soldiers deserted to get back home and help feed their families. The war brought sorrow and suffering to rich and poor alike in the South.

SECTION SURVEY

IDENTIFY: conscription, writ of habeas corpus.

1. On what grounds did many southerners object to military conscription?
2. What methods did the Confederate government use to raise money for the war?
3. Why was issuance of huge amounts of paper money harmful to the southern people?
4. How did lack of industry and lack of transportation help to defeat the South?

388

5 Important changes in life behind Union lines

The North, with its superiority in material resources, never experienced the hardship and suffering endured by southerners. Nevertheless, the war created problems and brought many changes in northern life.

Manpower and the draft. During the war more than 2 million men, including 186,000 Negroes, served in the Union armies. The North, like the South, at first recruited its troops by volunteer enlistments. On March 3, 1863, however, Congress passed a conscription law making all ablebodied male citizens between 20 and 45 liable for military service. As in the South the law allowed a drafted man to hire a substitute. The federal law also permitted a drafted man to buy exemption by paying $300 to the government.

The Conscription Act aroused violent opposition, especially among recent immigrants from Ireland. The Irish newcomers did not want to be forced to fight a war which was likely to increase the number of free black workers, with whom they competed for unskilled jobs. Moreover, when black workmen, unable to get jobs, broke strikes organized by Irish longshoremen and other workers, racial tension reached the boiling point.

Riots, combining opposition to the draft with opposition to black Americans, broke out in a number of cities. The most serious riot, beginning on July 13, 1863, in New York City, lasted for four terror-filled days. Mobs of white Americans burned to the ground an orphan asylum for Negro children. They demolished shops and houses of black Americans as well as those of white abolitionists. Seventy-six people were killed before federal troops could restore order.

The bounty system. The draft provided only a small fraction of the Union troops. Much more effective as a means of raising troops was the "bounty system." To attract volunteers, federal, state, and local governments each paid a bounty to all who volunteered for service. When the bounties were totaled, a man might receive as much as $1,000 for enlisting.

While the bounty system was an effective recruitment device, it did give rise to the dishonest practice of "bounty jumping." A man would enlist in one locality and collect his bounties, then desert and re-enlist under another name in another locality and collect additional bounties. Some "bounty

■ The famous photographer Mathew Brady took this picture of Union artillery ready for action at Fort Sumter, Virginia. The date of the photograph is June 1862.

jumpers" enlisted and deserted 20 or 30 times before they were caught.

Northern finances. To raise money for the war, the North relied on four sources of revenue: the tariff, war bonds, an income tax, and issuance of paper money.

From 1832 to 1861 southern planters and many western farmers had opposed high tariffs. In 1861, however, with several southern states out of the Union, the Republicans in Congress promptly passed the Morrill Tariff Act, raising import duties to an average of 25 percent of the value of the imported goods. The Morrill Tariff Act protected American manufacturers from the competition of European rivals. After war broke out, Congress raised the rates until by 1864 they reached an

average of 47 percent, the highest up to that time.

Southern planters and midwestern farmers had also favored a decentralized banking system. In such a system, state and local banks could issue their own bank notes and make loans with little if any federal control. After 1861, however, the Republican Congress adopted a law that did away with state bank notes and established a system of national banks.

In 1863 Congress passed the National Banking Act. The new law permitted five or more individuals with a capital of $50,000 to organize a national bank. The bank directors were required to invest at least one third of the bank's capital in United States bonds. When the bank had deposited these bonds with the Secretary of the Treasury, it was

■ This photograph shows Richmond militiamen of the 1st Virginia Regiment. It is an early picture, taken before the First Battle of Bull Run.

allowed to issue national bank notes up to 90 percent of the value of the bonds. This provision had two important effects. First, it encouraged banks to buy government bonds (that is, to lend the government money). Second, it provided a sound and uniform currency for the entire country.

Neither the tariff nor the sale of government bonds, however, provided enough money to pay northern war costs. Therefore, Congress passed an income tax. By the war's end, incomes between $600 and $5,000 were being taxed 5 percent, incomes of $5,000 or more were being taxed 10 percent.

Congress also issued paper money, known as *greenbacks* because the back of the money was usually printed in green. The value of the "green-backs," like the value of the Confederate paper money, depended upon the government's ability to redeem them in gold or silver at some future date. Thus, their value rose with every northern victory and fell with every northern defeat. At one point the "greenbacks" were worth only 35 cents of a dollar's worth of gold, but by the war's end they were worth 78 cents. Paper money helped to drive prices upward, but inflation never got out of hand as it did in the South.

Booming northern industry. Inflation did not get out of hand in the North partly because northern industry could produce all the materials needed by the armed services and the civilian population. With the tariff to protect them from foreign competition and huge war orders to meet, manufacturers built new factories during the war years. In Philadelphia alone 180 new factories opened between 1862 and 1864.

The war also stimulated the development and use of laborsaving machines. Elias Howe's sewing machine, first patented in 1846, enabled clothing manufacturers to produce uniforms more rapidly for the Union armies. An improved version of a machine for sewing uppers to the soles of shoes, which was patented by Gordon McKay in 1862, put shoe manufacturing on a mass production basis.

There was a great deal of "profiteering" during the war as greedy businessmen took unfair profits at a time of national necessity. Even worse, there were cases of outright business deceit. Some manufacturers sold the government blankets and uniforms of such poor quality that they fell apart in the first heavy rains.

But "profiteers" were a by-product of a development far more enduring—the expansion of American industry during the war years.

Agricultural expansion. Northeastern and midwestern agriculture, as well as industry, was greatly stimulated during the war by government aid, war orders, and the development of laborsaving machines.

The Republican Party, as you have seen, represented a combination of midwestern farmers and northeastern businessmen. It is not surprising, therefore, that the Republican Congress passed laws favorable to farmers.

The Homestead Act of 1862 gave 160 acres of land to anyone who paid a small registration fee and lived on it as his *homestead*° for five years.

° *homestead*: a tract of land, with its house and other buildings, occupied as a home.

Under this act, between 1862 and 1865 the United States government gave about 2.5 million acres of land to some 15,000 settlers. Most of the new homesteads were in the Middle West.

In 1862 the government also adopted two other measures to aid agriculture as well as industry: (1) It created the United States Department of Agriculture, and (2) with the Morrill Act of 1862 it launched the United States upon a huge program of agricultural and industrial education. The Morrill Act gave each state 30,000 acres of land for each Senator and Representative it had in Congress under the 1860 census. The income from the sale or rental of this land was to be used to support a special kind of education. Each state was to support at least one college in which agriculture and the "mechanic arts," such as engineering, were to be emphasized. These colleges came to be called "land grant colleges."

Farmers of the northeastern and midwestern states prospered with rising prices and a ready market for all they could produce. With money in their pockets, thousands of farmers were able to buy such laborsaving machinery as mechanical reapers, which had been invented by Obed Hussey and Cyrus H. McCormick in the early 1830's. The reaper, improved plows, and other farm machinery helped to speed the revolution in agriculture that was gaining momentum during the war years.

Growth of the railroads. Railroads also prospered during the war. For example, the value of Erie Railroad stock increased sevenfold in three years. New lines were built, many with the help of government *subsidies,* or financial aids, and land grants. These lines helped to unite the Northeast and the Middle West.

During the war the Republican Congress decided to build a transcontinental railroad, which people had been talking about for a long time. In 1862 Congress granted a charter to the Union Pacific and the Central Pacific railroads, authorizing them to build a railway between Omaha, in Nebraska Territory, and California. Congress also promised the railroads liberal cash subsidies and generous gifts of land along the right of way. Although actual construction did not begin until after the war (page 440), the subsidies and land grants showed how far the new Republican government was prepared to go in providing federal aid for business and industry.

The changes that took place behind the Union lines during the years from 1861 to 1865 were of great importance to the nation's future. As you will see, the growth of industry, stimulated by the war, gained momentum in the years following the war.

SECTION SURVEY

IDENTIFY: New York draft riot, "bounty jumpers," "greenbacks," "profiteering," Homestead Act of 1862, "land grant colleges"; Elias Howe, Cyrus McCormick.

1. (a) What methods did the North use to raise an army? (b) What abuses developed? (c) Why did some recent Irish immigrants object to the draft? (d) Why did some men rush to enlist?
2. Describe the methods used by the North to finance the war.
3. Give the reasons for the boom in northern industry during the war.
4. What conditions stimulated agricultural prosperity in the North?
5. What steps were taken by Congress during the war to encourage railroad building?

6 Political problems for the Union at home and abroad

The war thrust an almost unbearable burden on President Lincoln. Even while he was occupied with the fighting itself, he had to deal with a host of other problems, including foreign affairs.

Great Britain and France. During the first two years of war, the governments of Great Britain and France were friendly to the Confederate States of America. This friendship deeply concerned President Lincoln and the federal government.

There were reasons why many Europeans wanted the South to win. European manufacturers, particularly the British, looked forward to the creation of a new nation that would provide them with cotton and other raw materials and, at the same time, placed no tariffs on the importation of their manufactured goods. European shipowners looked forward to the weakening of their business competitors in New England and the Middle Atlantic states if the North lost.

To be sure, millions of Europeans hoped for the end of slavery in the South. But Lincoln at first discouraged these people when he made it clear that he was not fighting the war to free the slaves, but to preserve the Union.

Strained relations. Only a few months after the war started, an incident occurred that nearly led to a disastrous break between the United States and Great Britain. The trouble started when a Union warship commanded by Captain Charles Wilkes stopped a British steamer, the *Trent,* and seized two Confederate commissioners to Great Britain and France—James M. Mason and John Slidell. The British, furious at this violation of their rights as a neutral, talked of war with the United States and actually sent troops to Canada. But President Lincoln avoided trouble by releasing the two Confederate agents and admitting that Captain Wilkes had been wrong.

Even more serious was the problem of Confederate warships built in British shipyards. Some of these warships, among them the *Florida* and the *Alabama,* left Great Britain in the summer of 1862 and began to destroy Union merchant vessels. But Great Britain stopped the construction of other Confederate warships when the American minister to Great Britain pointedly warned the British for-eign minister, "It would be superfluous in me to point out to your lordship that this is war."

Fortunately for the Union, during the closing months of 1862 northern victories on the battle-field and the Emancipation Proclamation issued by President Lincoln ended the threat of foreign na-tions intervening in the war in order to give aid to the Confederacy.

The Copperheads. The danger of foreign in-tervention was not the only danger that the Union faced. In the North—as well as in the South—there was from the beginning active opposition to the war. Leaders of the opposition in the North were called "Copperheads" by Union sympathizers, after the poisonous snake of that name. The Copper-heads argued that the war's costs in lives, money, and loss of personal liberty were too great to be justified. They also argued that the South could not be defeated and that the war was therefore use-less. Finally, they insisted that even if the North

■ The Confederate warship **Alabama** destroyed no less than 58 Union vessels before it finally was sunk (see below) by the U.S.S. Kearsage in 1864.

should win, a Union based on compulsion was a denial of the Constitution and of democracy.

The strength of the Copperheads, most of whom were members of the Democratic Party, varied from place to place and from month to month. The more extreme Copperheads organized secret societies called the Knights of the Golden Circle and the Sons of Liberty. They discouraged enlistment and encouraged men to desert. They also helped Confederate prisoners to escape and smuggled war materials into the Confederacy.

The most influential Copperhead leader was Clement L. Vallandigham, a member of Congress from Ohio. He was finally arrested in 1863 and convicted of opposing the war effort. Lincoln banished him to the Confederacy, but Vallandigham promptly moved to Canada. While he was in exile, he was nominated by the Democrats for the governorship of Ohio, but lost.

The election of 1864. Dissatisfaction over the war split the Democratic Party. In the election of 1864, many Democrats joined the Republicans to form the Union Party. This party chose Lincoln for the Presidency and Andrew Johnson, a former Democratic Congressman from Tennessee but an opponent of the Confederacy, for the Vice-Presidency. The Democratic Party named General George B. McClellan as its candidate for the Presidency.

Anti-war feeling was running so high in 1864 that President Lincoln fully expected to be defeated. "We are now on the brink of destruction," he wrote to a friend. "It appears to me that the Almighty is against me, and I can hardly see a ray of hope."

But the tide of the war turned in favor of the North shortly before the election. Sherman's capture of Atlanta convinced many voters that the end of the war was near. Moreover, Lincoln's opponent, General McClellan, refused to support the platform of his own Democratic Party, which declared that the war was a failure and ought to be stopped immediately. As a result, Lincoln won an overwhelming victory, receiving 212 electoral votes to 21 for the Democratic candidate. The mere fact that a Presidential election was successfully held in wartime was in itself a victory for representative government.

The fight against discrimination. The continuing strength of representative government during the war years did not include, however, the broadening of the suffrage for black Americans, even for those who were free when the war started. In addi-

■ Sojourner Truth spoke dramatically and sincerely for causes such as abolition, temperance, prison reform, and women's suffrage. Her speeches had the power to move black and white audiences alike.

tion to fighting for their voting rights, Negroes in the North had to fight many other kinds of discrimination.

During the war, black and white abolitionists in the North continued their campaign against racial discrimination on federal, state, and local levels of government. As a result of these pressures, Congress repealed a law forbidding black Americans to be employed as mail carriers. Congress in 1865 also passed a law that required horse-drawn street-

■ This sewing school was established in Richmond, Virginia, by the Freedmen's Bureau. The Bureau was a government agency created in 1865 to aid refugees, freedmen, and those people left poverty-stricken by the war.

cars in Washington, D.C., to carry black passengers without discrimination. A black woman, Sojourner Truth, boldly defied conductors and passengers to test this law, and was successful.

The Department of State and the Department of Justice, again under pressure from abolitionists, ruled in individual cases that black men were citizens. The Supreme Court of the United States for the first time permitted a Negro lawyer to argue a case before the Court. Because of these actions by branches of the federal government, the Dred Scott

decision of 1857 was in effect repudiated. That decision, you recall, had denied that a Negro could be a citizen (page 366).

With the help of white abolitionists, black opponents of discrimination campaigned in several states for the right to vote and to receive legal equality in courts. In California, Illinois, and Indiana, laws forbidding black Americans to enter these states were challenged. Negroes vigorously attacked segregated public schools. Where they were not able to bring about school desegregation, they demanded improvements in the inferior all-black schools their children attended—when they were able to attend any school at all.

Not all of these campaigns for civil rights succeeded during the war, nor for a long time thereafter, but they did start to break down barriers that had set black Americans apart as less than equal citizens.

Aid to fugitives. Northern Negroes also took part in efforts to bring relief to fugitive slaves, or *contrabands* as they were called. During the war years, these people were held in federal camps, often under conditions of gross neglect.

Church groups and black and white abolitionists organized volunteer aid societies that sent clothing and medical supplies to the contrabands. Through petitions and delegations to Congress and the War Department, these societies also prodded the federal government into organizing work and relief opportunities, as well as schools, for the contrabands. Teachers in these schools were dedicated young abolitionists from the North, black and white. Nevertheless, the efforts made on behalf of the contrabands were small compared with the need.

SECTION SURVEY

IDENTIFY: *Trent* affair, *Alabama* settlement, suffrage, contrabands; Clement L. Vallandigham, Sojourner Truth.

1. Why did some European governments sympathize with the Confederacy?
2. (a) Who were the Copperheads? (b) What were their opinions on the war?
3. (a) What were the issues in the election of 1864? (b) Why was this election a victory for representative government?
4. During the war, abolitionists continued to fight against discrimination. (a) At what levels did they make their fight? Why? (b) What specific issues did they attack?

TRACING THE MAIN IDEAS

In 1865 the terrible trial by fire and sword came to an end and the nation could estimate what it had lost and what it had gained. The conflict had been frightfully expensive in men and money. It cost the southern states more than a billion dollars, the northern states several times that amount. After all pensions and other costs were paid, the war probably cost the American people a total of 10 billion dollars. It was also frightfully costly in life. Not counting those permanently injured, the North lost about 359,000 men; the South lost about 258,000 men.

The war had many far-reaching results. It ended the doctrine of secession. It strengthened the Union by increasing the power of the federal government at the expense of the states. Not least important, the four-year war helped to speed the development of American industry.

The war also strengthened the forces of democracy. It showed that a representative form of government could operate successfully in wartime. The war opened the door to freedom for all black Americans, and proved the ability and willingness of black Americans, despite discrimination, to fight for the national interest and to make heroic sacrifices for their freedom and recognition as human beings.

In the spring of 1865 Americans stood on the threshold of a new era. New opportunities were opening before them. Of course they could not know this at the time. They could look only into the immediate future. And northerners and southerners alike faced huge problems. They had to define the place of the newly freed slaves in the nation's life, "to bind the nation's wounds," and to join hands as a reunited people.

CHAPTER SURVEY

QUESTIONS FOR DISCUSSION

1. Contrast economic conditions in the North and South during the war.
2. Compare the economic measures adopted by the Republican administration of 1861–65 with the measures advocated earlier by Henry Clay in his famous "American System."
3. Explain the differences between the Emancipation Proclamation and the Thirteenth Amendment.
4. Lincoln's leadership was one of the major reasons for the North's victory. Do you agree or disagree? Explain.
5. It has been said that the Gettysburg Address contains one of the great definitions of democracy. (a) What important democratic ideals are explained in the speech? (b) Which ideas are held in common by the Declaration of Independence, the Preamble to the Constitution, and the Gettysburg Address?
6. Citing evidence from your textbook, discuss Lincoln's attitude toward black Americans. Do you think that some of his beliefs contradicted each other? Explain.
7. General Sherman's attitude toward the South was harsh, and he believed that old and young, rich and poor, should feel the hard hand of war. His goal was to destroy the enemy's will to fight—whether they were soldiers or civilians. This is called "total war." Do you accept this attitude? Why or why not?
8. Without the issue of slavery, there would have been no conflict between the North and the South. Do you agree or disagree? Explain.
9. Despite discrimination, black Americans demonstrated their faith in America during the Civil War. Explain.
10. Lincoln suspended the writ of habeas corpus and suppressed freedom of speech and freedom of the press during the war. Does a national crisis justify suspension of civil liberties? Should the President have this power? Should Congress have this power? Explain your answers.

RELATING PAST TO PRESENT

1. Sojourner Truth, a black woman, challenged the law concerning discrimination on streetcars in Washington, D.C. In 1955, approximately one hundred years later, Mrs. Rosa Parks, a black woman, challenged the law concerning discrimination on buses in Montgomery, Alabama. Comment on the relationship between the two events.
2. Discuss the following statement in reference to events during the Civil War: The nation admired the willingness of black Americans to take up arms in order to obtain their rights. Discuss this statement in reference to today's militant black leaders. Does the statement have bearing in this case or not? Explain.

USING MAPS AND CHARTS

1. (a) Using the map on page 377, identify the major land and sea campaigns undertaken by the North and South. (b) Check your identifications by referring to the individual maps on pages 378–82.
2. Referring to the map on page 861, compare the population of the North and South in 1860. What does this information tell you?

UNIT SURVEY

FOR FURTHER INQUIRY

1. The Civil War demonstrated once and for all that a state may not lawfully secede from the Union, even if it does so in order to protect its rights from the power of the federal government. Comment.
2. The creation of the Republican Party assured the break between the North and South. Explain.
3. The strength of democracy was demonstrated by the fact that the election of 1864 was held on schedule. Do you agree or disagree? Explain.
4. The abolitionists were not the first Americans to justify lawbreaking in the name of a higher moral law (consider the events leading to the American Revolution). How is a government threatened by the principle that laws may be broken if they go against a higher moral law? What positive and negative results have occurred through the breaking of laws in the United States?

PROJECTS AND ACTIVITIES

1. On an outline map of the United States, indicate the following boundary lines and compromise provisions: Ohio River, Mason and Dixon's line; Northwest Ordinance of 1787; Missouri Compromise of 1820; Compromise of 1850; Kansas-Nebraska Act.
2. Read Lincoln's First Inaugural Address in Starr, Todd, and Curti's *Living American Documents* (Harcourt Brace Jovanovich), and comment on it in the light of subsequent events.
3. The causes of the Civil War are among the most challenging problems in the study of American history. This subject can be explored by studying Chapter 18 of Joseph E. Gould's *Challenge and Change* (Harcourt Brace Jovanovich). Present a class report on what you have read.
4. The Civil War still fascinates Americans today. What evidence can you find to support this statement?

USING THE SOCIAL SCIENCES

(Read pages 398–400 before you answer the following questions.)

1. Black Americans proved their capabilities and loyalty with blood in the Civil War; yet in subsequent wars, they continued to face discrimination in the armed forces of the United States. Explain.
2. Do you think it is important to know whether the black community contributed to the cause of its own liberation? Why or why not?
3. Was slavery the problem of the black man or the white man? Explain.
4. Do you think the author has injected his own values into this case study? Explain. How does this case study reveal the problem a historian has in being objective?

SUGGESTED FURTHER READING

Biography

BASLER, ROY P., ed. *Abraham Lincoln: His Speeches and Writings,* Grosset & Dunlap (Universal Library, paper). Extensive collection of speeches, official papers, and letters, with the editor's commentary and a preface by Carl Sandburg; covers the years 1832–1865.

CAPERS, GERALD N., *Stephen A. Douglas, Defender of the Union,* Little, Brown.

CATTON, BRUCE, *Grant Moves South,* Little, Brown.

——, *U.S. Grant and American Military Tradition,* Little, Brown.

COMMAGER, HENRY STEELE, *America's Robert E. Lee,* Houghton Mifflin.

CURRENT, RICHARD N., *The Lincoln Nobody Knows,* McGraw-Hill.

DOUGLASS, FREDERICK, *Life and Times of Frederick Douglass,* Macmillan (Collier Books, paper). Autobiographical account of the first twenty-seven years in the life of one of the great black American leaders.

EHRLICH, LEONARD, *God's Angry Man,* Pocket Books. About John Brown.

FORTEN, CHARLOTTE L., *The Journal of Charlotte L. Forten,* Macmillan (Collier Books, paper). A young teacher's experiences in instructing former slaves; a description of Negro self-help during the Civil War.

FREEMAN, DOUGLAS, *Robert E. Lee: A Biography,* Scribner, 4 vols.

FREMANTLE, ARTHUR J. L., *The Fremantle Diary: The*

South at War. Edited with commentary by Walter Lord, Putnam (Capricorn Books, paper). Diary of a young English army officer visiting in the South during the war.

HENDRICK, BURTON J., *Statesmen of the Lost Cause: Jefferson Davis and His Cabinet,* Little, Brown.

HORAN, J. D., *Mathew Brady: Historian with a Camera,* Crown.

LORANT, STEFAN, *The Life of Abraham Lincoln: A Short Illustrated Biography,* New American Library (Signet Books).

PETRY, ANN, *Harriet Tubman: Conductor on the Underground Railroad,* Thomas Y. Crowell.

RANSOM, JOHN, *John Ransom's Diary,* Dell (paper). A young soldier's account of life in Confederate military prisons during the war.

ROSS, ISABEL, *Angel of the Battlefield: The Life of Clara Barton,* Harper & Row.

SANDBURG, CARL, *Abraham Lincoln: The Prairie Years* and *The War Years,* one-volume edition, Harcourt Brace Jovanovich.

——, *Storm over the Land,* Harcourt Brace Jovanovich. Lincoln during the war.

STERN, PHILIP VAN DOREN, *The Man Who Killed Lincoln,* Random House.

WATKINS, SAM R., "Co. Aytch," Macmillan (Collier Books, paper). A personal, often humorous, narrative of a Confederate soldier's life.

WILSON, FORREST, *Crusader in Crinoline,* Lippincott; and others. About Harriet Beecher Stowe.

WOODWARD, W. E., *Meet General Grant,* Liveright; Tudor.

Other Nonfiction

ANGLE, PAUL M., *The Lincoln Reader,* Rutgers Univ. Press; Pocket Books. Selections about Lincoln by sixty-five authors.

——, and EARL SCHENCK MIERS, *The Living Lincoln,* Rutgers Univ. Press.

BISHOP, JIM, *The Day Lincoln Was Shot,* Harper & Row; Bantam.

CATTON, BRUCE, *Glory Road,* Doubleday. Nonfiction by a leading authority on the Civil War.

——, *Mr. Lincoln's Army,* Doubleday.

——, *A Stillness at Appomattox,* Doubleday; Pocket Books.

——, *Terrible Swift Sword,* Doubleday.

——, *The Coming Fury,* Doubleday.

——, *This Hallowed Ground: The Story of the Union Side of the Civil War,* Doubleday.

EATON, CLEMENT, *The Growth of Southern Civilization, 1790–1860,* Harper & Row.

FILLER, LOUIS, *The Crusade Against Slavery, 1830–1860,* Harper & Row (Torchbooks, paper). Relates the abolition movement to other reform movements such as women's rights and public education.

FRANKLIN, JOHN HOPE, *The Emancipation Proclamation,* Doubleday.

FURNAS, J. C., *Goodbye to Uncle Tom,* Apollo Editions (paper). An analysis of stereotypes of black Americans, the origins of these stereotypes, and the forms they take in our society today.

HIGGINSON, THOMAS WENTWORTH, *Army Life in a Black Regiment,* Harper & Row (Beacon, paper). The story of the first official Negro regiment of the Civil War, told by its commander, an abolitionist.

KETCHUM, RICHARD M., *The American Heritage Picture History of the Civil War,* Harper & Row. Narrative written by Bruce Catton; contains over 800 pictures, maps.

MC PHERSON, JAMES M., *The Negro's Civil War,* Random House (Pantheon Books, paper). Contains eyewitness accounts and editorial commentary.

MILTON, GEORGE F., *The Eve of Conflict,* Houghton Mifflin. Controversy over Slavery.

NEVINS, ALLAN, *Ordeal of the Union,* Scribner, 2 vols. The decade 1847–1857.

——, *The Emergence of Lincoln,* Scribner, 2 vols.

PIERCE, FREDERICKS, ed. *The Civil War as They Knew It,* Bantam (paper). Chronological study of the war utilizing the photographs of Mathew Brady and the writings of Lincoln.

PRESSLY, THOMAS J., *Americans Interpret Their Civil War,* Macmillan (Collier Books, paper). Various interpretations of the causes and significance of the Civil War.

QUARLES, BENJAMIN, *The Negro in the Civil War,* Little, Brown. Contributions of Negro soldiers and labor battalions.

STAUDENRAUS, P. J., *The Secession Crisis, 1860–1861,* Rand McNally (paper).

STERN, PHILIP VAN DOREN, *Prologue to Sumter,* Fawcett (Premier Books, paper). Speeches and articles by John Brown, Mark Twain, Lincoln, Sam Houston, and others present both southern and northern views.

WILEY, B. I., *The Life of Billy Yank,* Bobbs-Merrill. Union soldiers.

——, *The Life of Johnny Reb,* Bobbs-Merrill. Confederate soldiers.

Historical Fiction

CHURCHILL, WINSTON, *The Crisis,* Macmillan. Famous novel about the war.

CRANE, STEPHEN, *The Red Badge of Courage,* Appleton-Century-Crofts; and others.

DOWDEY, CLIFFORD, *Bugles Blow No More,* Holt, Rinehart & Winston. Picture of southern defeat.

KANTOR, MAC KINLAY, *Andersonville,* World Publishing; New American Library (paper). Southern prison camp.

LONGSTREET, STEPHEN, *Gettysburg,* Farrar, Straus.

STREET, JAMES, *Tap Roots,* Dell (Dial Press); McKay. Southern abolitionists.

HISTORY AND THE SOCIAL SCIENCES

CASE STUDY IN HISTORY
Black Soldiers in the Civil War

The Civil War not only preserved the Union but also brought about the end of slavery—though at a staggering cost in human life. More than 1 million northerners lost their lives. The extent of the enlistment of Negro soldiers in the Union army and their contribution to the Union victory needs and deserves a thorough examination. It is important to know whether or not black Americans contributed to the cause of their own liberation.

Did Negro troops contribute to the Union victory over the Confederacy? Did the black community contribute to the cause of its own liberation? These are the questions we shall try to answer in this case study as we investigate the role of black fighting men in the Civil War.

Overcoming Early Opposition to Black Participation

At first Negroes who wanted to enlist in the Union forces encountered many obstacles and much opposition. For some time after the outbreak of the war, most northerners contended that the war was being fought mainly to preserve the Union—not to free the slaves. Further, many northerners doubted that Negroes, after years of slavery, could make good soldiers.

At the start of the war, President Lincoln, fearing the hostile reaction of the border states, opposed Negro recruitment. On August 4, 1861, Lincoln told a group of delegates from Indiana, who proposed the formation of black regiments, that "to arm the Negroes would turn 50,000 bayonets from the loyal border states against us that were for us." On another occasion Lincoln, expressing his lack of confidence in black fighting ability, said, "If we were to arm the Negroes, I fear that in a few weeks the arms would be in the hands of the rebels." Nonetheless, in spite of Lincoln's apprehensions, several Union generals attempted to form black regiments, but encountered strong opposition from the War Department.

As the war intensified, three basic factors caused the government to change its policy toward Negro recruitment. First, after the Union forces suffered a series of sharp defeats, many northerners became convinced that the North must use all available manpower to prevent an imminent southern victory. Second, it became apparent that the Confederate war effort was greatly aided by the use of black slave labor. Third, once the border states were securely on the side of the North, Lincoln, pressured by the Radical Republicans, dropped his opposition to black troops.

In March 1862 the Secretary of the Army ordered the recruitment of black troops in the Mississippi Valley. In July of the same year Congress passed the Confiscation Act giving the President power "to employ as many persons of African descent as he may deem necessary and proper for the suppression of the rebellion." And in response to the Militia Act of 1862, which authorized Negro enlistment, the first Negro regiments were formed.

In March 1863 President Lincoln wrote to Andrew Johnson, the war governor of Tennessee, encouraging him to recruit black troops. The President wrote that the black population "is the greatest available and yet unavailed of force for restoring the Union. The bare sight of 50,000 armed and drilled black soldiers upon the banks of the Mississippi would end the rebellion at once." Apparently, early in 1863 Lincoln wanted black troops—but mainly for the psychological effect they would have on the southern forces.

Faced with the opportunity of joining in the war for their own freedom, black leaders urgently appealed to their people to enlist. In the most elo-

Storming Fort Wagner

quent appeal, entitled "Men of Color, To Arms," Frederick Douglass, the famous abolitionist, wrote in part: "Liberty won by white men would lose half its luster. Who would be free themselves must strike the blow. . . . I now, for the first time during this war, feel at liberty to call and counsel you to arms. I urge you to fly to arms, and smite with death that power that would bury the government and your liberty in the same hopeless grave."

Many thousands of Negroes responded to the appeal of Douglass and other black leaders. By the end of the war, more than 186,000 Negroes had served in the Union armed forces.

Even after Negroes were allowed to wear the Union uniforms, however, they were forced to endure many discriminations (page 385). Black leaders and soldiers and many white political leaders protested against these discriminatory policies and demanded full equality for black soldiers. The most dramatic appeal was made personally to President Lincoln by Frederick Douglass. In his *Autobiography* Douglass describes vividly his meeting with the President. At this meeting Douglass told Lincoln that black soldiers should receive the same pay as white soldiers. He also urged Lincoln to retaliate against the southern policy of executing captured black soldiers by informing the Confederacy that, for any black prisoner executed by the South, a Confederate prisoner would be executed by the North.

Lincoln, Douglass relates, listened attentively and then told Douglass that black soldiers must receive less pay "to smooth the way to their employment at all as soldiers," but he assured Douglass that ultimately their pay would be equalized. As to the retaliatory policy, Lincoln said that the mere thought of hanging an innocent man for a crime committed by somebody else was repugnant to him. Douglass concludes: "In all this I saw the tender heart of the man rather than the stern warrior and commander in chief of the American army and navy, and, while I could not agree with him, I could not but respect his humane spirit."

As the war went on, discriminating practices against black troops were gradually removed. On June 14, 1864, the War Department issued an order which said in part: "The practice which has hitherto prevailed . . . of requiring these troops [black troops] to perform most of the labor of fortifications, and the labor and fatigue duties . . . will cease, and they will be required to take their fair share of fatigue duty with white soldiers." In 1864, also, the pay for all soldiers, black as well as white, was equalized. These measures greatly raised the morale of the black troops fighting for the Union cause.

The all-Negro 54th Regiment of Massachusetts, which brought honor to its colors in the assault on Fort Wagner (page 386), had a favorite song which revealed some of the feelings and hopes of the black soldiers:

McClellan went to Richmond with two hundred thousand brave;
He said, "Keep back Negroes," and the Union he would save.
Little Mac he had his way—still the Union is in tears—
Now they call for help of the colored volunteers.

Chorus: O, give us a flag all free without a slave,
            We'll fight to defend it, as our fathers did so brave,
            The gallant Company "A" will make the rebels dance,
            And we'll stand by the Union if we only have a chance.

So rally, boys, rally, let us never mind the past;
We had a hard road to travel, but our day is coming fast,
For God is for the right, and we have no need to fear—
The Union must be saved by the colored volunteer.

Members of the 4th U.S. Infantry, at Fort Lincoln

The number of black fighting men serving in the Union army grew steadily as military commanders became convinced of the valor of Negro troops.

Negro troops played a vital role in the battle around Petersburg, Virginia, in June 1864. In a comment to a newspaper reporter on the battle, the Secretary of War said that "the hardest fighting was done by the black troops." After the battle was over, the commanding officer of the operation, General William F. Smith, went personally to thank and commend the black soldiers for their courage under fire.

Black troops fought valiantly and courageously on many other battlefields, including Milliken's Bend in Louisiana, Vicksburg in Mississippi, and in the seige of Atlanta, Georgia. At Fort Pillow in Tennessee, the cold-blooded massacre of some 350 black soldiers by Confederate troops so outraged the North that President Lincoln ordered that: ". . . for every soldier of the United States killed in violation of the laws of war, a rebel soldier will be executed; and for every one enslaved by the enemy or sold to slavery, a rebel soldier shall be placed at hard labor. . . ."

The official records of the Civil War show that 178,985 black soldiers and 7,122 black officers served in the Union army. They fought in many engagements and in 39 major battles. About 37,300 Negro soldiers died in the war, and 17 black soldiers and 4 sailors won the Congressional medal of honor.

These achievements did not go unrecognized. President Lincoln was particularly impressed. On August 26, 1863, Lincoln wrote to James G. Congling, a long-time supporter in Illinois, who objected to the Emancipation Proclamation: "You say that you will not fight for the Negroes. Some of them seem willing to fight for you; but no matter. . . . Peace does not appear so distant as it did. . . . And there will be some black men who can remember that with silent tongue, and clenched teeth, and steady eye, and well-poised bayonet, they have helped mankind on to this great consummation, while I fear there will be some white ones unable to forget that with malignant heart and deceitful speech they have striven to hinder it."

In January 1864 Lincoln went even further in expressing his deep gratitude and admiration for black contributions to the Union cause. In a letter to General James Wadsworth, a Union general commanding the District of Columbia, Lincoln stated: "You desire to know, in the event of our complete success in the field . . . if universal amnesty should not be accompanied with universal suffrage [for Negroes]. . . .

"How to better the conditions of the colored race has long been a study which has attracted my serious and careful attention; hence I think I am clear and decided as to what course I shall pursue . . . regarding it a religious duty, as the nation's guardian of these people, who have so heroically vindicated their manhood on the battlefield, where, in assisting to save the life of the Republic, they have demonstrated in blood their right to ballot, which is but the humane protection of the flag they have fearlessly defended.

"The restoration of the Rebel States to the Union must rest upon the principle of civil and political equality of both races; and it must be sealed by a general amnesty."

Portrait of a Union soldier

■ How did Lincoln's attitudes toward black troops change between 1861 and 1864? How do you account for this change?
■ Did black troops contribute to the Union victory and to the cause of their own liberation? Cite evidence to support your answer.

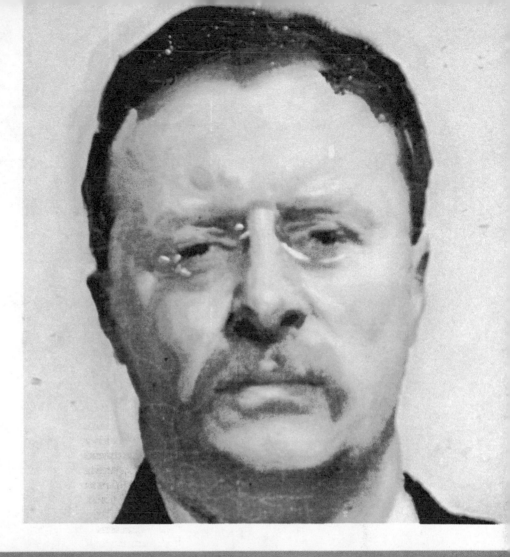

PART **3**

The major themes in Part 2 of this book were the growth of the nation from 17 to 36 states and the swift advance of the frontier from east of the Mississippi to the Pacific Ocean; the rise of sectionalism and the crisis of armed conflict between the North and the South; and the changes that were taking place in everyday life as the Industrial Revolution gathered momentum. All these developments took place during the lifetime of Abraham Lincoln (1809–65).

Theodore Roosevelt was six years old when Lincoln was shot down by an assassin. During his rich and full life Roosevelt saw the reunited nation grow from 36 to 48 states, expand overseas, and fight a war "to make the world safe for democracy." During Roosevelt's boyhood the United States was still a predominantly agricultural country. Before he died in 1919, the United States had become one of the leading industrial powers of the world.

THE NATION REUNITED

UNIT SIX

Rebuilding the Nation

1865–1900

A<small>FTER THE</small> Civil War came to an end, bitterness between the North and the South continued for many years. In part this was the inevitable result of a terrible conflict in which most people on each side believed that their cause was right and just.

But equally important as a cause of resentment was the decade of *reconstruction,* or rebuilding the Union, that followed the war. During this period, bitter feelings arose over the stubborn political and constitutional problems involved in bringing the southern states back into the Union. There were also the grave economic problems of rebuilding devastated southern industries and reopening normal trade relations among the states. Finally there was the continuing social problem of bringing the black American into the mainstream of national life.

As you will see in this chapter and in Chapter 21, the problems of Reconstruction had to be dealt with at a time when both the North and the South faced a breakdown of public morality, with graft and corruption reaching into every level of government—local, state, and national. This breakdown was due not only to the war, which had dislocated long-established ways of life in every section of the country. As you will read, it was brought about also by the changes that were taking place in the United States during the latter half of the 1800's—the rapid development of industry, a flood of immigration, and the phenomenal growth of cities.

THE CHAPTER IN OUTLINE

1. A lenient plan of reconstruction under President Lincoln.

2. Attempts to establish order in the war-ravaged South.

3. A severe program of reconstruction under the Radical Republicans.

4. The short-lived era of Radical control in the South.

5. Advances in agriculture, industry, and education in the New South.

6. The struggle of black southerners to find their place in the New South.

Chicago Historical Society

■ *A civil rights speech in the House of Representatives*

CHAPTER **20**

Restoring the South to the Union

1865 – 1900

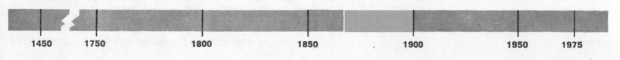

1450   1750   1800   1850   1900   1950   1975

1 A lenient plan of reconstruction under President Lincoln

On March 4, 1865, near the end of the war, President Lincoln stated his policy of reconstruction for the South. The roar of cannon fire at Richmond would soon be stilled but Lincoln's Second Inaugural Address was destined to live on.

"With malice toward none," he said; "with charity for all; with firmness in the right, as God gives us to see the right; let us strive on to finish the work we are in; to bind up the nation's wounds; to care for him who shall have borne the battle, and for his widow, and his orphan—to do all which may achieve and cherish a just and lasting peace among ourselves and with all nations."

Lincoln's program. Lincoln's were not idle words. He had already begun to develop a program of reconstruction based upon "charity for all," and he fully intended to carry out that program.

As early as December 8, 1863, Lincoln outlined his program for restoring the South to the Union in his Proclamation of Amnesty ° and Reconstruction. It was a practical, flexible program rather than one based on rigid and theoretical ideas about the Constitution. The program did rest, to be sure, on Lincoln's theory that the Confederate states had never succeeded in leaving the Union. They had for a time left the "family circle," but they were still part of the family, and the immediate problem was to get them back into the circle quickly.

Lincoln's plan for restoring what he called the "proper political relation" consisted of two major steps.

First, he offered full pardon to all southerners who would take an oath of allegiance to the Union and promise to accept the federal laws and proclamations dealing with slavery. The only southerners excluded from this offer were men who had resigned civil and military positions under the federal government to serve in the Confederacy, members of the Confederate government, Confederate army officers above the rank of colonel, Confederate navy officers above the rank of lieutenant, and Confederates who had mistreated Negro as well as white prisoners of war.

Second, Lincoln declared that a state could draw up a new constitution, elect new officials, and return to the Union on a basis of full equality with all

° *amnesty:* a broad pardon for offenses against a government.

404

other states when it met certain conditions. A minimum number of persons (at least 10 percent of those who had voted in the election of 1860) must take the oath of allegiance. Each person taking the oath must have been a qualified voter in his state before its secession from the Union.

In 1863 this program applied only to areas conquered by Union armies. Lincoln intended to apply it to all other Confederate areas as soon as they were in Union hands. But he did not insist that this proposal was the only acceptable one. He understood, and stated, that Congress must give final approval to admitting Congressmen from the reconstructed states. Moreover, as time passed Lincoln revealed flexibility in his own thinking. For example, in a letter written in 1864 he stated that the restoration of the southern states to the Union "must rest upon the principle of civil and political equality of both races; and it must be sealed by a general amnesty." And in his last public address, delivered on April 11, 1865, only four days before his death, he declared that he favored giving the vote to those Negroes who had fought for the Union and to those with some educational qualifications.

Opposition to Lincoln's policy. Not all Republican leaders agreed with Lincoln's ideas on reconstruction. A good many opposed the idea of pardoning former Confederates and allowing them to vote and hold office. These Republican leaders doubted the loyalty of former Confederates. They also doubted whether, if given political power, the former Confederates would permit black Americans to enjoy legal and political rights.

The Republicans who were most opposed to Lincoln's speedy and lenient reconstruction policy were called Radicals. The Radical Republicans were by no means a well-defined group. Different Radicals took different positions on political and economic issues and on methods of readmitting the former Confederate states to the Union. The public at the time, and some historians since, often overlooked these differences. They incorrectly assumed that the two most outspoken Congressional Radicals—Senator Charles Sumner of Massachusetts and Representative Thaddeus Stevens of Pennsylvania—expressed the views of all Radical Republicans.

Senator Sumner insisted on measures to guarantee the political and legal equality of black Americans and to educate them so that they could carry out the responsibilities of freedom. Congressman Stevens wanted to punish the South for all the injustices and discriminations that black southerners had suffered under white rule. Stevens also wanted to do everything possible to ensure that, in the future, southern freedmen would be treated justly. Believing that political and legal rights for Negroes would be meaningless if Negroes did not have economic independence, Stevens urged that the estates of "rebel traitors" be confiscated and divided up among the freedmen. Few Radical Republicans accepted so extreme a policy.

While the war was being fought and in the months following Confederate surrender, a majority of Republican leaders, more moderate in their views, lined up with Lincoln's reconstruction policies. But many moderates agreed with the Radicals on one point. They believed that President Lincoln, in exercising his war powers, had encroached upon the constitutional powers of the legislative branch. They all felt that Congress, not the President, was responsible for laying down the rules for restoring the southern states to the Union.

Some Republicans frankly admitted that their thinking about reconstruction was influenced by practical political considerations. They had every reason to believe that, when the war ended, white southerners would reject the wartime Republican Party and flock to the Democratic Party. Southern Democrats returning to Congress would probably support northern Democrats, thus making the Republicans a minority party. Such a combination might endanger measures that had the support of many, though not all, Republicans—a high tariff, national banks, free land, and federal aid to railroads (pages 389–91).

The Republicans could keep the Democrats from gaining majority power in state as well as federal governments in two ways. First, they could give voting rights to former slaves, now freedmen, who would support the Republicans at the polls in gratitude for emancipation. Second, they could keep former Confederate leaders from voting and holding public office.

Political considerations of this kind played some part in shaping attitudes of many Republicans toward reconstruction—historians disagree as to how large a part. However, it should also be emphasized that many Republican Congressmen approached the complicated problems of reconstruction with a genuine desire to help the freedmen and guarantee them fair opportunities in American life.

The Wade-Davis Bill. Opposition to President Lincoln's plan for reconstruction found expression in the Wade-Davis Bill. Although some Radical Republican Congressmen thought the bill was too

■ The fateful and lonely decisions that American Presidents sometimes have to make are reflected in this brooding photograph of President Lincoln. It was taken at the White House by Mathew Brady in 1862.

mild, enough moderate Republicans supported it so that the bill was passed by a slender majority in early July 1864.

The Wade-Davis Bill provided for readmitting the southern states into the Union under more stringent conditions than those favored by President Lincoln. The bill was intended to give political power to southerners who had been loyal to the Union. It was also intended to insure that the new constitutions of the southern states would recognize the freedom of black southerners. Finally, the bill was intended to insure that southern war debts were *repudiated,* or not paid.

President Lincoln refused to sign the Wade-Davis Bill. He felt that its rigid provisions would restrict him when the time came to rebuild the

THE NATION MOURNS.

Lincoln's funeral cortege, Washington, D.C.

THE DEATH OF ABRAHAM LINCOLN

On the evening of Friday, April 14, 1865, the President and Mrs. Lincoln left the White House and went with friends to Ford's Theater. They were going to see an English play called *Our American Cousin.* Lincoln watched the play from an armchair in a box overlooking the stage. Shortly after ten o'clock John Wilkes Booth, a former actor, entered the box and fastened the door behind him. Armed with a Derringer pistol and a dagger, he rested the pistol on the back of the chair and shot President Lincoln through the head. An officer named Major Rathbone rushed to the President's aid, but Booth slashed at Rathbone with the dagger and leaped to the stage, tripping and injuring himself as he fled.

Witnesses disagreed as to what Booth shouted as he escaped. Some thought he cried "Sic semper tyrannus!" ("Thus be it ever to tyrants!" spoken in Latin). Others thought he said "The South is avenged!"

A young army doctor came to the aid of the President, but Lincoln never regained consciousness. He was carried to a house across the street, where he died the next morning.

Booth was eventually found hiding in a barn in Virginia. He refused to give himself up, and shots were fired, but whether he died by his own hand or was killed by a Union soldier is not known.

The entire nation mourned the President's death. Carl Sandburg, poet and Lincoln biographer, has described the slowly moving funeral train that carried Lincoln's body to its final resting place at Springfield, Illinois: "There was a funeral," he wrote. "It took long to pass its many given points. Many millions of people saw it and personally moved in it and were part of its procession. The line of march ran seventeen hundred miles. As a dead march nothing like it had ever been attempted before."

Union. He also believed that Congress did not have the constitutional authority to compel a state to abolish slavery. Abolition of slavery, he believed, would require an amendment to the Constitution.

Lincoln's assassination. Whether or not Lincoln's tact and moderation could have won acceptance of his policy must remain an unanswered question, for on April 14, 1865, he was assassinated by John Wilkes Booth, a former actor.

Sorrow and anger gripped the country—South

as well as North, black as well as white. White southerners had despised Lincoln during the war, but many had now come to feel that he was a wise, compassionate leader who offered their best hope for a workable program of reconstruction.

But Lincoln was gone. Flags flew at half-mast, bells tolled, and weeping crowds filed through the funeral train as it stopped in cities between Washington, D.C., and Lincoln's burial place in Springfield, Illinois. Meanwhile, Vice-President Andrew Johnson became President.

President Johnson. Andrew Johnson was a self-educated man. Deprived of the opportunity to have any formal schooling, he had spent his boyhood as a tailor's apprentice. Later his devoted wife had helped him to improve his meager writing ability. While still a young man, he was elected mayor of his community, a small mountain village in eastern Tennessee. This was the beginning of a political career in the Democratic Party that took him in 1857 to the Senate of the United States. Although he owned a few slaves, Johnson disliked the large planters who were so influential in the South, and he had resisted the secession of Tennessee in 1861.

Johnson's service for the Union during the war won him an appointment as military governor of Tennessee, responsible for controlling those areas of his state occupied by Union troops. When the Republicans, including Lincoln himself, despaired of winning the Presidential election in 1864 (page 393), Johnson, a Democrat, was placed on the "Union" ticket in the hope that he would draw votes for Lincoln.

Andrew Johnson had many good qualities, among them a stubborn fighting spirit and the moral courage to act according to his convictions. Unfortunately, he was not a flexible man. Whereas Lincoln always tried to understand the positions of his political opponents, Johnson tended to insist upon the rightness of his own point of view. Johnson lacked sufficient patience, tact, and political skill to be an effective leader at this critical time.

Johnson and reconstruction. One of Johnson's first decisions as President was to offer rewards for the arrest of Jefferson Davis and other former Confederate leaders. Most Radical Republicans were pleased with Johnson's action, for they thought he would help them carry out their program.

President Johnson soon disappointed the Radicals, however, by adopting a more conciliatory attitude toward the South and by claiming that he intended to follow Lincoln's program. For a time

he seemed to be doing so. He officially recognized the reconstructed governments of Tennessee, Arkansas, Louisiana, and Virginia. He retained all of Lincoln's cabinet.

In several ways, however, Johnson did not follow Lincoln's program—neither in details nor in general approach. Lincoln had kept an open mind about the best method of reconstructing the Union. Johnson refused to consider any plan but his own. His stubbornness antagonized the Radical Republicans, as did his policy of pardoning former Confederates. When the Radicals objected to his policies, Johnson further antagonized them by answering their arguments with name-calling and personal abuse.

Johnson managed even to antagonize the moderate Republicans. Most moderates shared with the Radicals the conviction that any program of reconstruction must provide civil and political equality for both races. Johnson opposed this viewpoint.

End of the first stage of reconstruction. In spite of strong differences of opinion, the reconstruction program proceeded for a time along the lines laid down by Lincoln and modified by Johnson. Within a few months all the former Confederate states except Texas had adopted new constitutions and organized new governments.

When Congress assembled on December 4, 1865, Senators and Representatives from the southern states, most of whom had been leaders in the Confederacy, were waiting outside the doors to take their seats in the national legislature. To many observers it looked as though the long and dreadful war was finally ended and the restored nation was about to start anew.

SECTION SURVEY

IDENTIFY: amnesty, freedman, Wade-Davis Bill; John Wilkes Booth, Charles Sumner, Thaddeus Stevens, Andrew Johnson; April 14, 1865.

1. (a) What did Lincoln mean when he said, "With malice toward none; with charity for all"? (b) By referring to the terms of Lincoln's reconstruction plan, show that he practiced what he preached in his Second Inaugural Address.
2. Outline the opposition to Lincoln's reconstruction plan. Be sure to include the reasoning of those who opposed him.
3. (a) State the provisions of the Wade-Davis Bill. (b) What were Lincoln's objections to this bill?
4. Compare the ideas of Lincoln, Johnson, and the Radical Republicans on reconstruction.

2 Attempts to establish order in the war-ravaged South

A new chapter in American history opened when Congress assembled on December 4, 1865, but it was not the chapter outlined by either Lincoln or Johnson. It was, instead, one of the most troubled chapters in the nation's history.

Economic chaos in the South. The scene in the South at the end of the war was one of utter poverty. Crumbling chimneys rose from the ashes of once lovely mansions, grass grew in the roads, broken bridges lay in ruins, and two thirds of the railroads were destroyed.

The devastation in the cities was especially grim. A visitor reported that Columbia, South Carolina, was "a wilderness of crumbling walls, naked chimneys, and trees killed by flames." The business section of Richmond, Virginia, one of the great southern manufacturing centers, lay in ruins. An observer said it consisted of "beds of cinders, cellars half filled with bricks and rubbish, broken and blackened walls, impassable streets deluged with debris." The scene in Atlanta, Georgia, was one of blackened devastation. In city and country alike, wherever armies had fought, the land lay largely desolate.

Social chaos. The southern economy, as well as southern property, had been torn apart by the war. A citizen of Mississippi wrote in April 1865 that "our fields everywhere lie untilled. Naked chimneys and charred ruins all over the land mark the spots where happy homes . . . once stood. Their former inhabitants wander in poverty and exile, wherever chance or charity affords them shelter or food. Childless old age, widows, and helpless orphans beggared and hopeless, are everywhere." Conditions were not everywhere so bad as this writer supposed, but they were bad enough.

The plight of some 4 million freedmen was far worse. The former slaves were at last free, at least in name, but free to do what? Most of them had never been given an opportunity to learn how to read and write. None had owned land. Few knew what it was like to work for their own wages. Nor could most of their former owners pay them wages, for Confederate money was worthless and United States currency was almost nonexistent in the South. The land itself remained, but seeds and agricultural tools had almost disappeared.

Disease, always the companion of hunger and lack of sanitation, swept across the South. It was especially serious in the cities and their outskirts, where uprooted people struggled to survive in makeshift shelters. Thousands died during the summer and winter of 1865–66. In some crowded urban areas, disease swept away as many as one quarter to one third of the black population, and the death rate among the white population was almost as grim.

The Freedmen's Bureau. The United States Army provided some relief in the form of food and clothing for white and black southerners alike. But the major responsibility for helping the South through the difficult period of readjustment fell upon the Freedmen's Bureau, the first important example of federal support for needy and underprivileged people. The Freedmen's Bureau was headed by General Oliver Otis Howard of Maine, who also, in 1867, founded Howard University in Washington, D.C., for the primary purpose of offering higher education to freedmen.

Congress passed the bill creating the Freedmen's Bureau on March 3, 1865, the month before Lincoln's death, and made it responsible for looking after "refugees, freedmen, and abandoned lands." The bureau agents, who were everywhere in the South, were expected to help poverty-stricken white people also, but their major responsibility was to the freedmen. The agents were expected to guide the freedmen in their first steps toward self-support and, if necessary, to protect them against people who might try to take advantage of them.

Northerners and southerners differed in their attitude toward the Freedmen's Bureau. Most northerners regarded it as an honest effort to help the South bring order out of chaos. Most white southerners, on the other hand, resented the bureau. They charged that many bureau agents deliberately encouraged the freedmen to look upon their former owners as enemies, and were therefore responsible for creating racial friction.

White southerners also charged the bureau with raising false hopes among the freedmen, thereby making the process of readjustment increasingly difficult. One of these "false hopes" was the freedmen's belief that they would all receive farms. During the summer and fall of 1865 the rumor circulated that every former slave would get "forty acres and a mule" as a Christmas gift from the federal government. This rumor was based on the vague promise in the Freedmen's Bureau bill that land which had been abandoned, or for which taxes had not been paid, would eventually be distributed among the freedmen. But the freedmen accepted

■ After the war, southerners faced the enormous task of rebuilding countless cities, towns, and farms. This photograph shows an area of Richmond, Virginia, destroyed during the war.

the rumor as truth. Overjoyed at the prospect of soon owning farms, and understandably associating freedom with the right to choose where and how they worked, some freedmen decided not to work for white southerners.

Restrictions on freedmen. Faced with such a new situation, southern leaders began to take steps to restore life as they had known it. One step was the adoption of laws to regulate the conduct of freedmen.

Laws of this kind, known as "slave codes," had existed before the war (page 66). The new black codes, which varied from state to state, contained many of the same provisions as the old slave codes. As white southerners pointed out, however, they also included certain improvements in civil rights for the former slaves. Under the new codes, freedmen were permitted to own personal property, to sue and be sued in court, to act in court cases involving one or more Negroes, and legally to marry members of their own race.

But in general, the black codes denied Negroes their basic civil rights. Mississippi, for example, using its old code, merely substituted the word "Negro" for "slave." Black southerners were forbidden to possess firearms unless licensed to do so. They were forbidden to assemble unless white southerners were present. Nor could Negroes ap-

pear on the streets after sunset or travel without permits. Above all, the codes established white control over black labor. They prohibited black southerners from starting businesses, and provided for tight labor contracts, including severe apprenticeship regulations and stern punishments if contracts were broken. Some codes also restricted black southerners from renting or leasing farm land. The black codes indicated the widespread determination of white southerners to confine the freedmen to a clearly defined, subordinate way of life.

Such was the situation in December 1865 when the newly elected Senators and Representatives from all the former Confederate states except Texas appeared in Washington to take their seats in Congress. The former Confederate states had taken some, but not all, of the steps required by both President Lincoln and President Johnson for readmission to the Union. The new Senators and Representatives fully expected to take their seats in Congress and to share with northern Congressmen the task of rebuilding the Union.

Congress, however, refused to admit the southern Senators and Representatives. What motives prompted Congress to reject the South's newly elected Congressmen? Why did Congress refuse to accept Lincoln's and Johnson's programs for restoring the South to the Union?

409

Reasons behind rejection. From the time Lincoln's program began to take shape, as you know, Radical Republicans had argued that southern leaders could not be trusted. Now, in December 1865, they pointed to the legal restrictions placed on freedmen as evidence that white southerners were unwilling to recognize the complete freedom of black Americans.

The Radical Republicans also disagreed with the Lincoln and Johnson theory about the nature of the war. Both Lincoln and Johnson had argued that the conflict was *a rebellion of individuals.* This being so, the President could use his pardoning power, granted him by the Constitution, to restore the South to the Union.

Charles Sumner, leader of the Radical Republicans in the Senate, opposed Lincoln's theory with the "state suicide" argument. According to Sumner, the southern states, as complete political organizations, had committed "state suicide" when they seceded from the Union. Now, with the war over, they were in the same position as any other unorganized Territory of the United States. This being the case, Congress alone had the constitutional right to establish the terms for admitting them to the Union.

Thaddeus Stevens, majority leader of the House, held an even more drastic point of view. According to Stevens, the former Confederate states did not exist even as Territories. In Stevens' opinion they were "conquered provinces," and should be treated as such.

The historian cannot be sure of the motives that led Radical Republicans to take the positions they did. Some Radicals, as you have read, were influenced by economic and political considerations (page 405). But a good many Republicans, both Radicals and moderates, were strongly influenced by a sincere feeling of obligation to the freedmen. They genuinely wanted to make sure that white southerners did not deprive black southerners of their freedom and reduce them to a permanently inferior way of life.

Many moderate Republicans shared Lincoln's attitude toward the South. If Johnson had been less insistent upon having his own way, if he had been willing to work with the moderate Republicans, they and their Democratic colleagues in the House and Senate might have carried through a reconstruction program acceptable to white southern leaders. But President Johnson would not change his views. As a result, control of Congress passed into the hands of the Radicals.

410

IDENTIFY: "forty acres and a mule," "state suicide" theory, "conquered provinces" theory, black codes.

1. If you had been living in the South in 1865, what would have been the most pressing problems you and your family would have had to face?
2. (a) Describe the work of the Freedmen's Bureau. (b) Contrast northern and southern opinion of this bureau.
3. (a) List the restrictions placed on black southerners by white southern leaders. (b) What argument did white southerners use to defend these restrictions?
4. What reasons led Congress to reject (a) southern Congressmen, (b) Lincoln's and Johnson's reconstruction programs?
5. How did Andrew Johnson contribute to the problems of reconstruction?

3 A severe program of reconstruction under the Radical Republicans

By refusing in December 1865 to seat the southern Congressmen, the Radical Republicans practically guaranteed their own control of both houses of Congress. Within a few months they restored military rule in the South, thereby sowing seeds of bitterness that were to live for many years.

The first steps. Congress immediately appointed a joint committee of six Senators and nine Representatives to study the entire question of reconstruction. While Congress waited for the committee's report, it proceeded to safeguard the rights of the freedmen.

As one step in this direction, Congress passed a bill enlarging the powers of the Freedmen's Bureau. The new law gave the bureau power to prosecute in military courts, rather than in civil courts, any person accused of depriving a freedman of his civil rights. President Johnson promptly vetoed the bill, arguing (1) that trial by military courts violated the Fifth Amendment of the Constitution, and (2) that Congress had no power to pass *any* laws with 11 states unrepresented. Johnson's veto infuriated the Radical Republicans. After long debate they finally gathered enough votes to pass the bill over the President's veto.

In the meantime, Congress passed a civil rights bill, the first in a series of federal acts designed to give black Americans full citizenship and guarantee them complete equality of treatment with all other citizens. Johnson also vetoed this bill on the ground that it was an unconstitutional invasion of states' rights. Enough moderate Republicans joined the Radicals in Congress to pass this measure, the Civil Rights Act, over Johnson's veto.

Johnson's vetoes of the Freedmen's Bureau bill and the Civil Rights Act had two immediate results. First, the vetoes cost him the support of moderate Republicans who, without any desire to "punish" white southerners, believed that Congress should protect the rights of freedmen, which the black codes endangered. Second, the vetoes strengthened the influence of Thaddeus Stevens and other Radical Republicans. The Radicals argued that Johnson, the Democrats, and the old ruling white class in the South were making victory by arms hollow and meaningless.

The Fourteenth Amendment. Congress, fearing that the Supreme Court might declare the Civil Rights Act unconstitutional, decided to write the provisions of the act into the Constitution by amendment. This amendment, the Fourteenth, was the outcome of compromise between moderate and Radical Republicans. Some Radicals had hoped to outlaw all forms of racial segregation and discrimination. That objective does not seem to have been shared by the moderates, nor even by all Radicals who shaped the Amendment.

The Fourteenth Amendment (page 196) made black Americans citizens of the United States and of the states in which they lived. It forbade states to deprive citizens of the rights of life, liberty, and property without due process of law, or to deny any citizen "the equal protection of the laws." It went further and excluded former Confederate leaders from holding public office, state or federal. It provided for reduction of Congressional representation of states that deprived Negroes of their rights as citizens. It also forbade southern states to repay Confederate war debts or to compensate former slaveowners for their loss of slaves.

Radical Republicans in control. Tennessee ratified the Fourteenth Amendment in July 1866 and was immediately readmitted to the Union. But, on the advice of President Johnson, all of the other southern states rejected the amendment by overwhelming votes.

What would Congress do next? The answer depended in part on the Congressional elections in the fall of 1866. If the Democrats won control of Congress, they might return to Lincoln's and Johnson's programs, or some modification of them. If the Radical Republicans won, the nation might expect further restrictions on the political role of the former Confederates and stronger guarantees of the rights and opportunities of the freedmen.

At this point several events helped to swing voters toward the Radical Republicans. Violent race riots were especially influential in shaping public opinion. In Memphis, Tennessee, 46 black Americans were killed, and 12 Negro schools and 4 Negro churches were burned. In a riot at New Orleans about 200 people, mostly black, were killed or wounded. Many northerners, shocked by such violence, began to feel that perhaps the Radical Republicans were right in demanding further federal protection for the freedmen.

In the late summer of 1866 President Johnson made a trip to Chicago, stopping along the way to make election speeches. When opponents heckled him, Johnson's answers often seemed to reflect a lack of understanding of the election issues, as well as bitter hatred of Radical Republicans. His language, often blunt and uncouth, antagonized many voters.

More important, however, as a reason for Radical Republican strength was the memory of the war itself. During the terrible conflict, both sides had suffered immense casualties. Voters who did not want to risk losing the fruits of hard-won military victory voted for Radical Republican candidates.

In the election the Radical Republicans increased their hold on both houses of Congress. With more than a two-thirds majority in both the Senate and the House, the Republicans, if they held together, could override Presidential vetoes.

Reconstructing the South. In March 1867 a combination of Radical and moderate Republicans passed, over Johnson's vetoes, a number of measures that provided a complete program for reconstruction. The new program, which the majority in Congress was determined to force upon the South, contained five major provisions.

First, Congress divided the 10 southern states that had rejected the Fourteenth Amendment into five military districts, each under a military governor, with federal troops to maintain law and order while the states drafted new constitutions and organized new governments.

Second, Congress deprived most former Confederate leaders of the right to vote and hold office. The restrictions were the same as those Congress had earlier written into the Fourteenth Amendment.

Third, Congress gave the freedmen the right to vote and hold office.

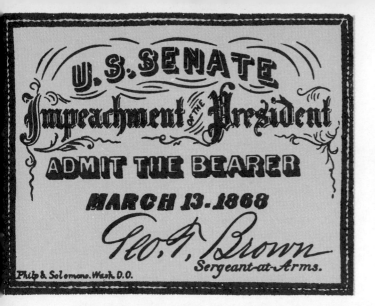

U.S. SENATE
Impeachment of the President
ADMIT THE BEARER
MARCH 13. 1868
Geo. T. Brown,
Sergeant-at-Arms.

Philp & Solomons. Wash. D.C.

■ The Radical Republicans did not succeed in removing President Andrew Johnson from office. However, the charges that they brought against Johnson, and his subsequent impeachment trial, did put an end to his influence as President. Pictured above is a ticket to the trial.

Fourth, Congress authorized the states to write new constitutions which guaranteed Negroes the right to vote.

Fifth, Congress required the states to ratify the Fourteenth Amendment.

The white southern governments that had been formed under the Presidential plan of reconstruction now had no choice but to bow to the new Congressional program. One by one, the states held conventions, drafted new constitutions, organized new governments, and entered the Union under the terms laid down by Congress.

Johnson's impeachment and trial. By the summer of 1868 all but three southern states had returned to the Union on the terms laid down by Congress. (Mississippi, Texas, and Virginia finally accepted the terms and were readmitted in 1870.) Meanwhile, the Radical Republicans determined to remove their hated "enemy," President Johnson, from office.

Several things led the Radical Republicans to this decision. They certainly were affected by the emotional hatreds and tensions of the times. But, more important, the Radicals knew that the success of their reconstruction program depended heavily on its enforcement. They were convinced that President Johnson would not enforce Congressional policy. And Johnson confirmed their suspicions when, by executive order, he restricted the power

of commanding military officers in the South and removed commanders known to be sympathetic to Radical programs.

To find grounds for impeachment and to reduce the President's power, Congress in 1867 adopted the Tenure of Office ° Act over Johnson's veto. Under this law the President could not dismiss important civil officers without the Senate's consent. Believing the law unconstitutional, Johnson decided to put it to a test. In February 1868 he demanded the resignation of Secretary of War Edwin M. Stanton, who had consistently cooperated with Johnson's enemies, the Radical Republicans.

The House immediately adopted a resolution that "Andrew Johnson, President of the United States, be impeached of high crimes and misdemeanors in office." Having passed the resolution, the Radicals then hunted for other charges to bolster their case against the President.

The Radicals charged that Johnson, ". . . unmindful of the . . . harmony and courtesies which ought to exist and be maintained between the executive and legislative branches of the government . . . did attempt to bring into disgrace, ridicule, contempt, and reproach the Congress of the United States. . . ." The Radicals cited various occasions when the President publicly made "with a loud voice certain intemperate, inflammatory, and scandalous harangues" against Congress, "and did therein utter loud threats and bitter menaces."

Under the Constitution, a President may be impeached on grounds of "treason, bribery, or high crimes and misdemeanors" (pages 174 and 184). On these grounds, the controversial charges brought by the House against President Johnson were quite dubious. Nevertheless, he was impeached.

Johnson's trial before the Senate, presided over by Chief Justice Salmon P. Chase, lasted about two months. After prolonged debate it became clear that Johnson was not guilty of any offense for which he could legally be removed from office. Nevertheless, when the Senate vote was counted, it stood 35 to 19 against Johnson, just one vote short of the necessary two-thirds majority required for removal from office. Johnson continued to serve as President until his term expired on March 4, 1869, almost a year after his trial. But his influence as President was at an end.

Decline of Radical power. It soon became apparent, however, that the Radical Republicans had

° *tenure of office:* the period during which an individual has the right to continue in office.

overreached themselves by attacking the President, even though much of his behavior had been provocative. For two years, with some support from other Republicans, the Radicals had been able to ignore the moderate program of reconstruction and to override Johnson's repeated vetoes of their own program. But when they tried to remove the President from office, they lost the support of many moderate Republicans. Moreover, public opinion finally began to turn against them.

The election of 1868. As the election of 1868 approached, the Republicans realized they were in trouble. In hopes of winning the election, they unanimously nominated Ulysses S. Grant for the Presidency. Grant had no political experience. He did not share the moral conviction of many Radical Republicans of the need to protect the freedmen. Nevertheless, he was popular with the public as a war hero.

The Democrats chose as their Presidential candidate Horatio Seymour, a wealthy New Yorker and former governor of his state. The Democratic platform denounced the Radical Republican program of reconstruction, declaring it unconstitutional. It condemned the Radicals for their attempt to remove President Johnson from office.

Economic issues were also important in the election of 1868. The platform of the Democratic Party, for example, contained a plank advocating a "cheap money" policy. During the war the government had issued $450 million in paper money known as "greenbacks" (page 390). After the war, in 1866, the Republican Congress had provided for the gradual withdrawal of the greenbacks from circulation. By 1868 nearly $100 million had been withdrawn. In their 1868 platform the Democrats promised, if elected, to reverse this policy and reissue the paper money. They proposed to use the greenbacks to redeem those war bonds not specifically redeemable in gold.

The Democrats knew that this "cheap money" plank would antagonize wealthy bondholders, who fully expected that the money they had lent the government would be repaid in gold. But they also knew that the proposal would appeal to many less well-to-do voters, particularly those who owed money, for with more currency in circulation they could more easily pay off their debts.

Republican candidate Ulysses S. Grant barely squeaked through to victory. Although he won by an overwhelming electoral vote of 214 to 80, capturing 24 of the 36 states, his popular majority was only 309,000 out of almost 6 million votes. A shift

General Ulysses S. Grant, head of all the Union armies, emerged from the Civil War as a military hero. But as President of the United States, he seemed unable to come to grips with graft and corruption in the government.

of only a few thousand votes in a handful of states would have swung the election to Horatio Seymour, the Democratic candidate.

The Radical Republicans studied the election returns with growing concern. They realized that many voters had turned against the Republicans because of their "hard money" policy. They also realized that only the Negro vote had given them a majority, though small, of the popular vote.

The Fifteenth Amendment. With this disturbing conclusion in mind, the Radicals drew up the Fifteenth Amendment and submitted it to the states for ratification. The Fifteenth Amendment was short and to the point: "The right of citizens of the United States to vote shall not be denied or abridged by the United States or any state on account of race, color, or previous condition of servitude."

The Fifteenth Amendment was ratified by the necessary three fourths of the states and became part of the Constitution in 1870. Mississippi, Texas, and Virginia—the last three southern states to return to the Union—were required to ratify the amendment as a condition for readmission.

SECTION SURVEY

IDENTIFY: due process of law, equal protection of the laws; Ulysses S. Grant.

1. (a) Explain how the new Freedman's Bureau law and the Civil Rights Act aimed to protect the freedmen. (b) Why did Johnson veto both? (c) What were the results of Johnson's vetoes?
2. (a) Why did Congress propose the Fourteenth Amendment? (b) Read the Fourteenth Amendment on pages 196–97 and summarize the main ideas in each of its sections.
3. Describe the five major provisions of the Congressional plan for reconstruction.
4. What were the reasons for Johnson's impeachment?
5. Read the Fifteenth Amendment on page 197. (a) What does it provide? (b) Why was it passed?

4 The short-lived era of Radical control in the South

The Radical Republican program of reconstruction brought far-reaching changes to the South, but only for a relatively short time. For varying periods —as long as 10 years in only three states—Radical Republicans and their allies controlled the former Confederate states.

Help from the North. In the 10 years after the surrender of the Confederacy, the main concern of the federal government was the restoration of the Union. Providing aid to the war-ravaged South and to needy southerners took second place. The Freedmen's Bureau, during its brief existence, did provide the healing benefits of food, clothing, and medical supplies, as well as opportunities, however inadequate, for freedmen to obtain an education. But the Freedmen's Bureau was severely limited by lack of funds and by opposition from most white southerners and many northerners.

The work of the Freedmen's Bureau was supplemented, however, by teachers and missionaries who were supported by northern churches and relief societies, black as well as white. Most of the northerners who tried to help the freedmen were motivated by humanitarian and democratic ideals. Many were successful in winning the confidence of the men, women, and children whom they had come to help. Others, equally well-meaning but unfamiliar with southern ways of life and perhaps less tactful, antagonized the people with whom they tried to work.

Carpetbaggers and scalawags. White southerners especially resented the arrival in the South of northerners whom they jeeringly called "carpetbaggers." This nickname implied, wrongly, that the newcomers were all fly-by-night adventurers who carried everything they owned in suitcases made of carpeting material, which were common at the time.

The carpetbaggers came for many different reasons. Some sincerely wanted to help the freedmen exercise their newly acquired rights. Some hoped to get themselves elected to political office. Some came to make their fortunes, as Americans had long been doing, by acquiring farm land or by starting new businesses.

But some carpetbaggers came for reasons of outright greed or fraud. Horace Greeley, editor of the New York *Tribune,* wrote of these carpetbaggers that they were "stealing and plundering, many of them with both arms around the Negroes, and their hands in their rear pockets, seeing if they cannot pick a paltry dollar out of them."

Most white southerners and some northerners scorned the northern carpetbaggers who moved into the South. Special scorn, however, was heaped upon native-born southerners who cooperated with northern authorities. Some of these native-born southerners were prompted by the best of motives. Having opposed slavery and secession, they had sympathized with the Union during the war; now they believed that the best way to restore peace and prosperity to the South and to the nation was to forgive and forget. But others were selfish and ambitious men who seized any opportunity to advance their own fortunes at the expense of their neighbors.

Whatever the motives of these native-born southerners, most were held in contempt by other white southerners, who referred to them as "renegades," "mangy dogs," and "scalawags," a word familiarly used for scoundrels.

Reconstruction governments. Such were the men—scalawags and carpetbaggers, good and bad alike—who largely controlled southern state governments during part of the Radical reconstruction period. Northerners held most of the important political offices, at least during the early years. They

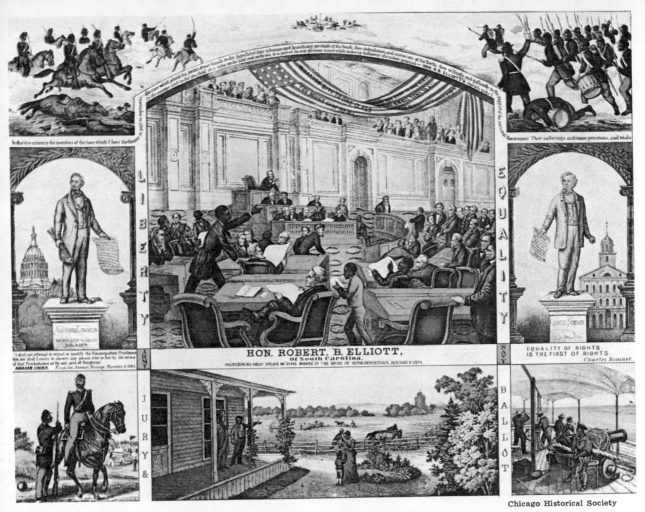

■ Robert Brown Elliott was a brilliant lawyer, scholar, and Congressman. He is shown in the center illustration speaking on civil rights before the House of Representatives in 1874.

were able to get themselves elected partly because they persuaded the freedmen to vote for them, and partly because many white southerners were deprived of the right to vote while others refused to take part in political activities.

The enormous influence of northerners in southern politics can be seen by examining the election results in the seven southern states readmitted to the Union by 1868. As a result of the first postwar elections held in these states, 4 of the 7 governors, 10 of the 14 United States Senators, and 20 of the 35 United States Representatives were carpetbaggers. In general, southern scalawags and freedmen had to be content with the less important state and federal offices.

Black southerners in public life. Negroes were elected to the southern "carpetbag" governments, and they played an important role in some of them. In recent years, however, some historians have pointed out that the Negro's role in these governments has often been exaggerated. Only one Negro served briefly as a southern governor. In only one southern state—South Carolina—did the Negroes for a time hold a majority in the state legislature. Only Mississippi sent black Senators, two of them, to Washington. One was Hiram Revels, a native of South Carolina who, after studying at Knox College in Illinois, had been a teacher and minister. The other was Blanche K. Bruce, who had escaped from slavery in Virginia and who had also been a teacher.

415

The record of black citizens in reconstruction politics also has often been misrepresented, according to recent historians. Many Negroes, to be sure, who had been denied an education and experience in public life through no fault of their own, were victimized by clever carpetbaggers and scalawags, whose leadership they followed. Others showed independence and political skill, among them Robert Brown Elliott of South Carolina, a brilliant lawyer and scholar, and P. B. S. Pinchback of Louisiana, son of a Mississippi planter and a black mother.

The Negroes in public life during reconstruction did not demand revenge upon white southerners. In fact, most black leaders favored returning the right to vote to their former white masters. The records of those elected to the United States Congress compared well with the records of many of their white colleagues.

The record of reconstruction governments. White southerners who had once dominated public life rightly deplored extravagant expenditures for needless luxuries authorized by legislators, white and black, in some reconstruction governments. They also rightly denounced some reconstruction legislators for outright corruption and graft.

Some of the new legislators were all too willing to enrich themselves while granting favorable railroad and corporation charters to businessmen, often northerners, who wanted to develop southern enterprises. But southern Democrats who briefly controlled southern legislatures in the first years after the war had followed some of the same corrupt practices. And, as you will read later, public morality in all sections of the United States sank to an extremely low level during the years following the Civil War.

The southern reconstruction legislatures, controlled by carpetbaggers, scalawags, and freedmen, did increase the debts of their states. But this was often the result of borrowing for much needed and long overdue public improvements. The new legislatures, for example, strengthened public education and, for the first time, made it available to large numbers of black children.

The reconstruction governments also pushed forward other constructive programs. They spread the tax burden more equitably. They introduced overdue reforms in local government and the judicial system. Imprisonment for debt was abolished. The legal rights of women were extended. Laws were passed to protect homes and farms against illegal foreclosures—that is, against unjustified seizure by dishonest officials. And most of the southern state constitutions drafted during the period of reconstruction continued in effect for many years.

Secret societies. Whatever the merits and demerits of the reconstruction governments may have been, most white southerners resented them. Since many former Confederate leaders were denied the vote and since others chose to boycott politics, some white southerners expressed their opposition by defying the law through intimidation and violence. By 1867 some white southerners were striking telling blows at carpetbaggers, scalawags, and politically active freedmen through a number of secret societies. The best known were the Knights of the White Camelia and the Ku Klux Klan.

These secret organizations tried to frighten black southerners and their white leaders and thus keep them out of politics. Bands of hooded men clad in ghostly white costumes rode through the countryside at night, stopping now and then at a house to issue warnings. When warnings failed, cabins and churches were burned, and some freedmen were beaten or killed. White sympathizers and friends of Negroes sometimes received the same treatment. Moderate white southerners, disgusted with the brutality and fearful of northern reaction, disapproved of these actions. But for a time they failed to make their disapproval effective.

Congress tried to end the lawlessness by passing a series of Military Enforcement Acts, sometimes called the Force Acts (1870–71). These acts gave the President power to use federal military forces to control the secret societies, to call upon the state militias when necessary, to suspend the writ of habeas corpus, and to provide for federal supervision of southern elections.

To many white southerners, the Force Acts seemed unduly harsh. Yet compared with the treatment of the losers in civil wars elsewhere, the former Confederates were not severely punished. There were never more than 25,000 federal troops in the occupied states after the war. No political or military leader was executed. Few were imprisoned. President Johnson made liberal use of his pardoning power. Jefferson Davis was released from prison within two years. Except for the loss of slaves, property was seldom seized as punishment for what many northerners regarded as treason.

Further leniency prevailed in 1872, when Congress passed the Amnesty Act. This act restored political rights, including of course the right to vote, to about 160,000 former Confederates. After 1872 only about 500 white southerners were still barred from political activity.

The Force Acts, the withdrawal of many southerners from the secret societies, and finally the Amnesty Act virtually ended the power of the Ku Klux Klan and other such groups at that time. As most white southerners began to vote again, and as white southern leadership re-emerged, the reconstruction governments in several states were replaced by governments representing traditional white southern rule.

The end of Radical reconstruction. During the early 1870's northerners began to lose interest in the problems of southern reconstruction. Radical Republican power was reduced, and its leadership diminished, by the death of Thaddeus Stevens in 1868 and of Charles Sumner in 1874. More northerners began to believe that political chaos in the South would continue as long as former southern leaders were kept out of power.

At first many northerners had championed the cause of the freedman. Now they became disillusioned at reports, often exaggerated, of the political ineptness of black southerners. Many northerners seemed to ignore the fact that because most freedmen had been slaves, they had little, if any, education and no political experience. Many northerners grew weary of the problems of the freedmen and less willing to press for an effective program to help the freedmen learn their new political roles as citizens.

Weary of tensions in the South, many northerners began to say that perhaps the freedmen *did* need the supervision of white southern leaders. Perhaps it would be better, they now said, to let southerners work out their own problems of government and race relations. Northerners justified their retreat by referring to the federal system embodied in the Constitution, which left many powers in the hands of the states. No doubt many northerners, sincere enough earlier in demanding equal rights for the freedmen, now became increasingly and uncomfortably aware that black Americans were not treated as equal citizens in most northern states. Thus, many northerners now found it easier to concentrate on strengthening national unity and to give less attention to the place of black Americans in national life.

This decision was stimulated by a growing number of northern businessmen who wanted to stop the Radical program of reconstruction. A disor-

■ Members of secret societies such as the Ku Klux Klan dressed in ghostly costumes and rode through the countryside at night. By the use of intimidation and violence, they tried to frighten black southerners and their white sympathizers from engaging in political activities.

ganized, poverty-stricken South was not good for business on either side of the Mason-Dixon line.

In 1877, shortly after the inauguration of President Rutherford B. Hayes, the last of the federal troops of occupation were withdrawn from the southern states.

The era of reconstruction left many major problems unsolved and created a number of new and equally urgent problems. This was true even though many forces in the North and the South were working for the reconciliation of the two sections of the Union.

1. (a) Define carpetbagger and scalawag. (b) Why did the carpetbaggers go south?
2. Why is the period of reconstruction sometimes called the "tragic era"?
3. (a) What was the record of the reconstruction governments? (b) How did white southerners express their opposition to these governments? (c) Was their opposition justified? Explain. (d) What was the attitude of black southern leaders toward white southerners?
4. How did the federal government react to the secret societies and the violence that developed in the South during this period?
5. Many northerners who favored the withdrawal of federal troops from the South were exhibiting racial prejudice. Discuss.

5 Advances in agriculture, industry, and education in the New South

During the 1880's many southerners began to speak of the "New South." Those who used this term, including editor Henry W. Grady of the Atlanta *Constitution,* urged their fellow citizens to abandon the one-crop system of agriculture and develop all the resources of a rich land—the minerals and the forests as well as the soil. Above all, Grady and others who shared his beliefs urged southerners to convert the region's raw materials into manufactured goods in southern mills and factories.

Breakup of plantations. One characteristic of the postwar South was the breakup of many, though by no means all, of the large plantations. This process started in 1865, immediately after the war ended. Planters, who had little if any cash to hire farm laborers, began to sell portions of their plantations to the more prosperous independent farmers. Because of the breakup of the large plantations and the opening of new lands, between 1865 and 1880 the number of small farms more than doubled, while the size of the average southern farm decreased.

Some black southerners, who had emerged from slavery without education, without land, and almost without clothes, also benefited from the breakup of the large plantations. As the years passed, a small but growing number of freedmen acquired small farms.

Tenant farming and sharecropping. While some poor white southerners and a few black southerners became owners of small farms, many others entered into a *tenant* relationship with the large landowners. Under the tenant relationship, which had existed even before the war, a planter usually rented portions of his land to several tenants, who supplied their own seed, mules, and provisions. The owner managed the scattered tenant holdings much as if these made up the old-time plantation, thus retaining some advantages of large-scale production. Many tenants remained tenants all their lives. Others saved enough money to buy a plot of land and become small landowners.

Less fortunate was the *sharecropper.* He furnished nothing but his labor, getting his cabin, seed, tools, mule, and a plot of land from the owner. In return for his labor, the sharecropper received a percentage of the crop that he produced. Since the sharecropper did not get paid until harvest time, he had to buy provisions for himself and his family on credit. To obtain credit, he had to give a "lien," or mortgage, on the crops that he expected to plant and harvest. The debts he could not pay at harvest time were added to his bill to be paid a year later.

When the crops were harvested, almost all of the sharecropper's share of the money usually went to pay his bills. Because he also had to pay interest on his debt, the sharecropper found it very difficult to get out of debt. And as long as he was in debt, he was practically bound to the soil, since the law forbade him to leave the state until his bills were paid. Frequently the landlord also owned the store where the sharecropper bought his provisions and where he could buy on credit. Since the sharecropper was seldom free from debt and almost never had any cash, he had to buy at the landlord's store.

Many sharecroppers raised only cotton or tobacco since the landlord insisted on cultivating these crops exclusively. The landlord argued that the sharecroppers did not know anything about other crops and that cotton and tobacco were the only dependable cash crops.

Although tenant farming and sharecropping existed in other parts of the country, these practices were especially widespread in the South. Indeed, tenant farming and sharecropping provided a workable solution to the frequently desperate economic situation confronting southerners in the postwar years. But tenant farming and sharecropping also made it difficult for the South to abandon its traditional one-crop system and develop diversified farming.

Agricultural progress. Despite the problems facing southern farmers, the South made considerable progress during the postwar years. Southerners, like farmers elsewhere in the nation, benefited from new developments in science and technology. During the 1870's and 1880's improved machines for sowing, cultivating, fertilizing, and reaping were introduced. In 1872 Alabama and Virginia established agricultural colleges; by 1900 the other southern states had followed their example. Because of these institutions and the development of scientific agriculture in other parts of the country, the cultivation of traditional crops was improved and some new plants were introduced.

Cotton continued to be the most important single crop. Indeed, by 1871 the South was growing more cotton than it had in 1860. The older states increased their yield per acre by using commercial fertilizers and improved farming methods. Much of the total increase, however, came from the opening of new cotton lands in the Southwest. By 1900 Texas alone produced one third of all the nation's cotton.

Improved farming methods led to greatly increased production of tobacco, rice, sugar, corn, and other traditional crops. But the most important change in southern agricultural life was the development of truck farming and fruit growing. Because of railroad expansion and the invention of the refrigerator car, fresh vegetables and fruit could be shipped to northern urban centers. The long growing season in the South and an abundance of cheap labor also stimulated truck farming. As early as 1900 thousands of refrigerator cars were rolling northward, hauling welcome supplies of green vegetables, watermelons, strawberries, oranges, apples, and peaches to northern cities.

Industrial development. An even more remarkable development in the New South was the growth of industry. In industry, as in agriculture, the South responded to forces that were transforming economic life in other regions of the United States and, for that matter, in most of Europe.

Southern industrial development actually started before the outbreak of the Civil War. By 1860 about 10 percent of the manufactured wealth of the United States came from southern textile mills, iron works, lumber projects, and sugar refineries. But the war and reconstruction ruined many southern industries, and for nearly 20 years the South made little if any industrial progress.

By the late 1870's, however, more and more southerners were concluding that southern prog-

■ Industrial development in the New South led to the growth of cities. This engraving of a busy section of Atlanta, Georgia, was made in 1887.

ress depended upon industrialization. The development of industry would enable the South to take fuller advantage of its rich natural resources.

Money to build factories, mines, steel mills, railroads, and other industries came in part from northern investors, in still larger part from the South itself. Profits from expanding agriculture were poured into new industrial ventures. In community after community the people themselves gathered in mass assemblies to plan a factory, often a textile mill, and to raise the necessary capital. By 1900 more than 400 cotton textile mills had been built. Throughout the South farming villages were transformed into mill towns within a few short years. The labor force for the new factories was supplied in large part by poorer white people. Black laborers were almost entirely excluded from the new industrial development.

Many early mills were controlled by a single family or a small group of persons, who owned the houses in which the workers lived, the stores where they bought their goods, and the other town buildings. The workers depended on the owners for their jobs and had to spend their wages to rent company-owned dwellings and to buy provisions from company-owned stores. As a result, the labor organizations that were developing rapidly in the North during these years made little headway in the South.

The growth of southern industry depended not only on local and northern capital, natural resources, and a cheap labor supply, but also on improvements and extensions of southern railroads. The war left southern railroads in terrible condition. But old railroads were quickly rebuilt, and new lines constructed. By 1890 the southern railroad system was twice as large as it had been in 1860.

Industrial development in the New South led to the growth of cities. Between 1870 and 1890 Durham, North Carolina, developed from a small village to a flourishing tobacco center. Richmond, Virginia, and Nashville, Tennessee, became leading urban centers. The population of Atlanta, Georgia, increased from 37,000 to 65,000 between 1880 and 1890. Birmingham, Alabama, founded in 1871 on the site of a former cotton field, was transformed within a few years into a bustling iron and steel center, often called "the Pittsburgh of the South."

By 1900 southern manufactured products were worth four times as much as in 1860. With its growing industrial cities, its factories and mills and mines, and its developing transportation system, the South was beginning to be more and more like other regions of the United States. But with all its industrial progress, the New South had a long way to go to catch up industrially with other sections of the country.

Educational developments. During the closing years of the 1800's, able and far-seeing southern leaders urged their fellow citizens to improve their educational system and thus make better use of their human resources. Southern education did improve, but every forward step was taken in the face of tremendous handicaps. Southern leaders had to deal with widespread poverty despite improving economic conditions, traditional reluctance to support public education by adequate taxation, and the high cost of maintaining separate schools for white and black children.

Among the outstanding contributions to southern education were the gifts of northern philanthropists. Especially noteworthy were the gifts of George Peabody and John F. Slater, both northern millionaires. The Peabody Fund was created in 1867, the Slater Fund in 1882. Income from these funds helped to provide educational opportunities for white and black southerners alike in the postwar years.

The money provided by private sources, however, was only a fraction of what was needed. Most of the burden of rebuilding schools and opening up educational opportunities for white as well as black southerners had to be shouldered by the southern states. Slowly, as the economic situation improved, the South was able to provide more opportunities.

The "Solid South." Most southerners belonged to the Democratic Party. There were southern Republicans, to be sure, but they were completely outnumbered in local, state, and national elections. For example, when the Presidential elections rolled around, the former Confederate states cast all their electoral votes for the Democratic candidates. Thus, people began to refer to the southern states as the "Solid South."

The "Solid South" was born during reconstruction days when Radical Republican governments composed largely of carpetbaggers, scalawags, and freedmen controlled the southern states. In their determination to rid themselves of Radical Republican rule, white southerners poured into the Democratic Party. After 1877, when the last federal troops were withdrawn from the South, most white southerners continued to support the Democratic Party.

SECTION SURVEY

IDENTIFY: New South, one-crop agriculture, "the Pittsburgh of the South," philanthropist, "Solid South."

1. (a) Define tenant farming and sharecropping. (b) Explain why these agricultural relationships were especially widespread in the postwar South.
2. Show how science and technology contributed to agricultural progress in the postwar South.
3. (a) Give three reasons for southern industrial development. (b) What were some results of industrial growth?
4. Summarize the factors which influenced the development of education in the South. (b) What handicaps hindered this development?

6 The struggle of black southerners to find their place in the New South

Black southerners had hoped to share in the agricultural, industrial, and educational progress of the New South, and in the nation's ideals of freedom and equality. Their hopes did not materialize for several reasons. First, the federal government suspended its program for helping the freedmen make the transition from slavery to freedom. Second and equally important, white Americans in both the North and the South continued to think of black Americans not as equals but as inferiors. And third, since so many Negroes lived in the South, white southerners feared that the white southern way of life would be threatened if black southerners were not firmly "kept in their place."

Disenfranchisement of the Negro. For more than a decade after white southern Democrats regained control of their governments in 1877, many Negroes continued to vote, and a few even held public office.

Early in the 1890's, however, the Populist Party, a radical third-party movement, began to threaten the power of both the Democratic and Republican parties (Chapter 21). In the South, Populist organizers had their greatest success among poor and disadvantaged white people, but they also worked hard to win the support of black voters. Southern Democrats, alarmed by this development, tried to prevent Negroes from voting.

Beginning with Mississippi in 1890, the southern states began to adopt laws and to frame new constitutions that excluded most black southerners from the polls, or voting places, on grounds other than "race, color, or previous condition of servitude." By the early 1900's the guarantees of civil rights in the Fourteenth and Fifteenth Amendments had become largely ineffective in the South. In many southern areas few Negroes voted and fewer still held public office, even in minor positions.

A number of states adopted a *poll tax*—a flat tax imposed on every person as a requirement for voting, and a *literacy test*—an examination to determine whether a person can read or write or has a certain amount of education. Since many black southerners had little money and little if any education, these laws kept large numbers from voting.

But the poll tax and the literacy test also deprived many "poor whites" of the vote. To remedy this situation, several states, starting with Louisiana in 1898, added a "grandfather clause" to their constitutions. This clause declared that, even if a man could not pay the poll tax or pass the educational test, he could still vote if he had been eligible to do so on January 1, 1867, or if he were the son or the grandson of a man who had been eligible to vote on January 1, 1867. Under this clause many "poor whites" were allowed to vote, but Negroes, whose fathers or grandfathers had not had the suffrage at that time, could not.

The "grandfather clause" was declared unconstitutional by the Supreme Court in 1915. So long as it remained in force, however, many black southerners were effectively deprived of their right to vote.

■ Black Americans took part in municipal elections held in Washington, D.C., in 1867. This sketch of the scene appeared in a contemporary magazine and was accompanied by an account of the long lines of black citizens who began to assemble early on the morning of Election Day.

Segregation of the races. Meanwhile, a pattern of segregation, or separation, of white and black southerners was taking shape.

Except in a few instances, the Radical Republicans had not tried to bring white and black children together in southern public schools. But black and white southerners used the same transportation facilities and other public services. The Civil Rights Bill of 1875 had declared that "all persons within the jurisdiction of the United States shall be entitled to the full and equal enjoyment of the accommodations, advantages, facilities, and privileges of inns, public conveyances on land or water, theaters and other places of public amusement; subject only to the conditions and limitations established by law and applicable alike to citizens of every race and color, regardless of any previous condition of servitude."

Even after white southern rule was restored in 1877, southerners of both races often used the same transportation facilities and other public services. But in 1883 the Supreme Court ruled against the Civil Rights Act of 1875 on the ground that the Fourteenth Amendment forbade states, not individuals or corporations (such as railroads), from discriminating against black citizens. However, black and white southerners in many places continued to use the same public accommodations.

In 1881 Tennessee passed the first of the so-called "Jim Crow" laws. Under this law, white southerners and black southerners were required to ride in separate railway cars. Other states followed Tennessee's example. By the 1890's all southern states required such separation, not only in schools but in streetcars, railroads, and railroad stations. Within a few years this pattern of separation, or segregation, spread to parks, playgrounds, and other public facilities.

Then, in 1896, the Supreme Court added legal support to segregation. In the case of *Plessy v. Ferguson,* the Court ruled that it was not a violation of the Fourteenth Amendment to provide "separate but equal" facilities for black Americans. This 1896 ruling by the Supreme Court was a serious blow to the efforts of black Americans to improve their lives.

Negro reactions. Confronted by segregation and denied their political and civil rights, some black Americans became disheartened and migrated to other nearby states, such as Oklahoma and Kansas, or moved to the growing northern cities. Most, however, stayed in the South, and worked to develop their own black communities.

Black southerners strengthened their own churches, lodges, and mutual aid societies, developed their own business enterprises, and, against handicaps, tried to secure an education. Their efforts began to produce results. In 1865 only about 5 percent of all Negro adults could read and write; by 1900 more than 50 percent had achieved these basic skills.

Southern Negro leaders also protested the growing pattern of segregation and discrimination, and the denial of civil rights guaranteed by the Fourteenth Amendment. On the lecture platform, in churches, in the press, and in conventions, they demanded recognition of their constitutional rights. In 1889 the former black abolitionist Frederick Douglass, now an old man, asked whether "American justice, American liberty, American civilization, American law, and American Christianity could be made to include and protect alike and forever all American citizens in the rights which have been guaranteed to them by the organic and fundamental laws of the land." In Baltimore E. J. Waring, a black lawyer, urged Negroes to fight discrimination by law suits against officials and citizens guilty of violating their rights.

Booker T. Washington. Alongside such protests, the leading Negro spokesman from 1890 to 1915, Booker T. Washington, followed a different course. Washington, the son of a slave mother and a white father, received a vocational education at Hampton Institute in Virginia. He then founded and built Tuskegee Institute in Alabama. Convinced that Negroes needed a vocational education, not a classical or liberal one, Washington insisted that black Americans must improve their lives by acquiring job skills and training. They must prepare themselves for the skilled trades, small business enterprises, farming, and domestic service. He urged black southerners to make themselves, by self-help, so indispensable to the southern economy that white southerners would gradually respect their ability and recognize them as useful and respectable members of the community.

Such a policy was acceptable to leading white southerners as well as to northerners. Washington's influence also became very great among black Americans. He sponsored many programs to support Negro educational institutions, and he encouraged the development of black businesses. Washington also spoke out against lynching and illegal discrimination, especially in the years just before his death in 1915. Nevertheless, he remained convinced that black southerners should avoid protests and emphasize vocational training, farm and home ownership, and the development of small business enterprises.

W. E. B. Du Bois. Booker T. Washington's views met a strong challenge from a much younger Negro, W. E. B. Du Bois. Born and reared in western Massachusetts, Du Bois studied in German universities and earned his Ph.D. at Harvard. At first he believed that if white southerners and northerners came to understand past Negro achievements and present Negro conditions and problems, their attitudes toward black Americans would change for the better. His pioneer sociological studies of Negroes in Philadelphia and in the South, which he pursued at Atlanta University, were directed toward this end.

Gradually, however, Du Bois came to believe that only vigorous and continuous protests against inequalities and injustices, and effective appeals to black pride, could change existing conditions. *The Souls of Black Folk,* a book of eloquently written essays, criticized Booker T. Washington's exclusive emphasis on vocational training, urged broader education for at least the more talented young Negroes, and called on all black Americans to assert their rights vigorously. With a few like-minded black leaders, Du Bois organized a meeting in 1905 at Niagara Falls which demanded an end to all unequal treatment based on race and color.

The appeals and demands of the Niagara Movement, which included criticisms of Booker T. Washington's program, aroused many Americans, white as well as black. One outcome was the formation of the National Association for the Advancement of Colored People (NAACP). The NAACP worked through the courts to end disenfranchisement and other civil injustices. In time it succeeded in winning Supreme Court decisions which declared unconstitutional the "grandfather clause" in southern state constitutions, jury trials conducted under mob pressure, and segregation by local law of housing for black people. The Urban League, likewise organized by both black and white Americans, concentrated on securing equal job opportunities for black workers and fought discrimination in urban housing.

The work of the NAACP and the Urban League brought some progress for black citizens in the North and West. These national organizations were also represented in the South, but they made less progress there. Most black southerners continued to experience discrimination, segregation, and denial of equal rights.

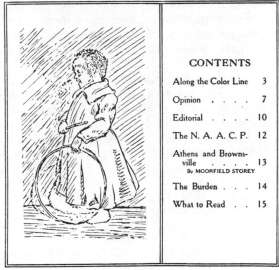

THE CRISIS
A RECORD OF THE DARKER RACES

Volume One   NOVEMBER, 1910   Number One

Edited by W. E. BURGHARDT DU BOIS, with the co-operation of Oswald Garrison Villard, J. Max Barber, Charles Edward Russell, Kelly Miller, W. S. Braithwaite and M. D. Maclean.

CONTENTS

Along the Color Line   3
Opinion   7
Editorial   10
The N. A. A. C. P.   12
Athens and Brownsville   13
   By MOORFIELD STOREY
The Burden   14
What to Read   15

PUBLISHED MONTHLY BY THE
National Association for the Advancement of Colored People
AT TWENTY VESEY STREET   NEW YORK CITY

ONE DOLLAR A YEAR   TEN CENTS A COPY

■ The Crisis, the official publication of the NAACP, was first edited by W. E. B. Du Bois. Its object was "to set forth those facts and arguments which show the danger of race prejudice."

SECTION SURVEY

IDENTIFY: "Jim Crow" laws, *Plessy v. Ferguson*, "separate but equal," NAACP, Urban League; Booker T. Washington, W. E. B. Du Bois.

1. Why did black southerners not share in the progress of the New South?
2. Show how each of the following affected the right of black southerners to vote: (a) poll tax, (b) literacy test, (c) "grandfather clause."
3. (a) Why did southern states pass laws barring Negroes from voting? (b) How did this affect black southerners?
4. (a) How was a new pattern of segregation established in the South? (b) How did the Supreme Court contribute to the separation of the races?
5. How did black Americans react to discrimination?

TRACING THE MAIN IDEAS

In 1865, just before his tragic death, President Lincoln urged the victorious North to act "With malice toward none; with charity for all"; and in this way to build "a just and lasting peace. . . ."

President Johnson's efforts to apply Lincoln's policy by quickly restoring the Union were effectively blocked by the Radical Republicans who controlled Congress. For various reasons, the Radical Republicans wished to decide how the former Confederate states should be reconstructed. The more extreme members of the Radical group wanted to revolutionize the South by transferring political power from the white leaders to the Negroes.

White southerners were disturbed at the prospect of living in a position of political, economic, and social equality with former slaves. Without power to resist by armed force, they used every means at their command to defeat the northern program of reconstruction. Unable to enforce their will upon the South, northerners gradually lost interest, and in 1877 the last federal troops were withdrawn from the former Confederate states.

During the 1880's and 1890's the outline of a New South began to appear. Southern agriculture grew steadily more diversified. Southern mines began to supply increasing amounts of ore to southern furnaces. Textile mills and other factories began to transform southern villages into growing cities.

In 1900 the South was still basically an agricultural region. Southerners were still struggling to recover from the economic disaster of the war. But, like people in the North and the West, they were being swept into the future by the growing forces of industry. Most black southerners, however, did not share in the progress of the New South.

CHAPTER SURVEY

QUESTIONS FOR DISCUSSION

1. To what extent do you think revenge was the motivating factor in the behavior of the Radical Republicans in Congress?
2. (a) Compare the Presidential plan of reconstruction with the Congressional plan, as to purpose and provisions. (b) Why do you think the Presidential plan was more lenient than the Congressional plan?
3. The experience of losing the war and of Congressional reconstruction was so bitter and humiliating that southerners found it hard to forgive and even harder to forget. Discuss.
4. What, in your opinion, is the historical significance of the impeachment of President Andrew Johnson?
5. Compare the attitudes of Booker T. Washington and W. E. B. Du Bois. In your opinion which of these two men had greater faith in the democratic system? Explain the reasons for your opinion.
6. If Lincoln had lived to carry out his plan of reconstruction, do you think he would have encountered the same difficulties that President Andrew Johnson did? Explain.
7. How did the Supreme Court decision in the case of *Plessy v. Ferguson* reflect the spirit of the times?
8. (a) How did northern attitudes serve to encourage the South's segregation practices? (b) How did the attitudes of the federal government serve to encourage segregation and discrimination in the country at that time?
9. How were the conflicts of the reconstruction period rooted in the issue of slavery?
10. If you had been a northerner in Congress during the period 1850–70, what would have been your position on the South and reconstruction?
11. Did the black codes and "Jim Crow" laws reestablish slavery in the South? Explain.

RELATING PAST TO PRESENT

1. Black Americans have striven to achieve equality, not dominance. Comment.
2. Both the North and the South missed the opportunity after 1865 to bring the ex-slave into the mainstream of American life. In the 1970's, there is new hope that black Americans, as well as other minority groups, will for the first time participate fully in the life of the nation. Do you think this hope is well founded? If the opportunity of the 1970's is missed, do you think there will be another opportunity in the future? Explain your answers.
3. Compare the federal government's attitude toward minorities during reconstruction and today.
4. During reconstruction only the South was prejudiced against black Americans; today, there is little difference in the various sections of the nation regarding racial prejudice. Do you agree or disagree with this statement? Explain.

USING MAPS AND CHARTS

1. (a) Using the map on pages 864–65, list the agricultural products produced in the South today. (b) Explain the change in southern farming.
2. (a) Using the map on pages 870–71, make a list of the mineral and power resources of the New South. (b) What historic forces brought about this development of industrial production?

CHANGE is often disturbing, and in no period of American history was change more disturbing than in the generation following the Civil War. You have seen how drastic changes came to the South during reconstruction and how white and black southerners struggled to adjust to these changes. Equally striking changes were occurring in the Northeast, the Middle West, and the West during these years.

The major cause of these changes was the rapid growth of industry after the war. New power-driven machinery was invented and installed in large factories, giant corporations were organized, and new methods of mass production were adopted. These exciting developments made many new products and services available to more and more Americans and helped to raise their standard of living.

But there were dark shadows in this bright picture. As industries grew, cities grew and became overcrowded, creating new problems—problems of sanitation, disease, fire, and transportation.

In order to see this dramatic and disturbing period of American history clearly, it is necessary to take several looks at it. In later chapters you will see how the growth of "big business" created complex problems, not only for many businessmen, large and small, but also for farmers, miners, and wage earners. In this chapter you will see how graft and corruption plagued American political life during the postwar years, and how repeated efforts were made to root out this dishonesty in government.

THE CHAPTER IN OUTLINE

1. Similarities and differences between the two major political parties.

2. The spread of graft and corruption in the postwar years.

3. Initial moves toward restoring honesty to government.

4. Increasing political reforms in government despite setbacks.

■ *Americans celebrating Independence Day*

CHAPTER **21**

Severe
Trials
for
Democracy

1865 – 1897

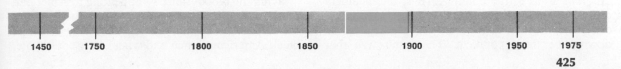

| 1450 | 1750 | 1800 | 1850 | 1900 | 1950 | 1975 |

1 Similarities and differences between the two major political parties

Political behavior is an important and complicated aspect of every modern society. In the United States, for example, the political behavior of American voters often stems from habit and tradition. Americans sometimes cross party lines to cast their vote, but more often they vote for candidates of one party—the party they have "always" supported.

The political behavior of American leaders is also complex—as complex, in fact, as human nature itself. Why do people seek political office? Some run out of a genuine desire to make a contribution to American life. Some are motivated by the competitive spirit, the satisfaction of winning out over the other fellow. Some run to win prestige and power, which can be used either to enrich the lives of all Americans or to enrich only the lives of the officeholders.

In the years from 1865 to 1897, the character and structure of the Democratic and Republican parties reflected these and other characteristics of American political behavior. The makeup of the political parties, in turn, explains a good deal about political leadership and election contests during these years. The problems and functions of the political parties at this time were also related to the political corruption that shocked many Americans and led to a demand for reform.

Similarities between the parties. The Republican and Democratic parties in the years between 1865 and 1897 shared many common features. Each party counted on the votes of thousands of men whose fathers and even grandfathers had preferred that party, and who voted for it more or less from habit.

In terms of votes cast in national elections, the parties were fairly evenly matched. This meant that in spite of—or perhaps because of—a good deal of public indifference to politics, competition between the two parties was sharp. Eagerness to win when the race was close led spokesmen of each party to criticize their rivals with slogans and name-calling. Sometimes these slogans and names appealed to the American sense of humor, but often they also were unfair and emotionally charged.

Each party was made up of members from many different areas of the country. Thus, the members often had conflicting regional and economic interests. In order to win elections, each party had to downgrade these conflicts. The result was that neither party was able or wanted to face squarely some of the most serious issues of the time.

In each party, factional rivalries centered around the rival ambitions of the leaders, or "bosses," of the several organizations, or "machines," making up the party. These personal rivalries often led to the selection of undistinguished "compromise" candidates.

The Republican Party. The Republican Party after the Civil War continued to enjoy the support of a great many northern and western farmers, who had been important pillars of Republican strength in the party's early years. These farmers voted, almost out of habit, for the Republican Party because they believed that the Republicans, by supporting the free homestead policy, had opened the frontier areas of the West to settlement.

But the Republicans also increasingly attracted industrialists. The influence of manufacturers and other businessmen became more and more important as the Republicans encouraged the growth of business and industry and refrained from trying to control business enterprises. In an age of industrial growth and the rise of huge new fortunes in business, many Americans seemed to approve such success no matter how it had been achieved. Operators of railroads, mines, and other enterprises often did not hesitate to ask politicians for favors or to return such favors with cash payments or other rewards. Many of these operators sought favors from both political parties. As it happened, the Republicans dominated the federal government for much of the period between 1865 and 1897.

Since victory at the polls depended on the support of both businessmen and farmers, and since farmers and businessmen often differed on such economic issues as currency, banking, and tariffs, Republican leaders tried to keep the support of both groups by not taking a firm stand on important issues when party platforms were written.

In addition to support from farmers and businessmen, the Republicans could count upon other voters. Most of 1 million northern Civil War veterans, appreciative of the Republican Party's role in the war and of its liberal pension policy for "old soldiers," voted Republican. By identifying the Democratic Party as the party of secession and defeatism in the war, the Republicans successfully used the political tactic that came to be known as "waving the bloody shirt"—appealing to American patriotism. Finally, as the party of emancipation, the Republicans could count on the votes of most black Americans when and where they could vote.

The Democratic Party. The Democratic Party was also made up of various groups with conflicting interests. After 1877 the party could count on the support of the "Solid South," which was still primarily agricultural. Democratic leadership, however, passed to men engaged in banking and importing interests in northern cities, and to the lawyers who served them.

While bankers and importers favored low tariffs and "sound money," southern and western farmers generally wanted "easy credit," a plentiful money supply, and decentralized banking. Thus, the Democrats tried to avoid taking clear-cut positions on these important issues. Moreover, while a great many Democrats favored low tariffs, some did not. For example, Pennsylvania Democrats who developed the steel industry, and Louisiana sugar planters and processors, both wanted tariffs to protect their special interests against competing foreign producers. In general, however, the Democratic Party did not favor government measures to promote industrial growth. It clung to the traditional doctrine of *laissez faire,* meaning that the federal government should not interfere with business and industry.

A chief source of Democratic strength was the immigrant vote in the northern cities. The newcomers were helped in various ways by the well-organized party "machines," such as Tammany Hall in New York City. At a time when city governments provided little or no help to needy people, the "machines" performed a necessary function. They did so, of course, for political reasons—they wanted the immigrants' votes at election time.

The Democratic city "machines," like those in the Republican Party, made profitable deals with contractors eager to get bids for public buildings and concessions for street lighting, streetcars, sewers, and other public services. Thus, when Democrats pointed to the Republican corruption in the nation's government during these years, they ignored their own record in the northern cities.

Third parties. Many honest men in both parties opposed political corruption. However, these reformers often were unable to make much progress inside their own parties. Moreover, many Americans were dissatisfied because the two major parties refused to take clear-cut stands on many serious issues. Thus the way was opened to third-party movements.

Third-party movements also were confronted by many problems. They faced the opposition of well-financed, powerful "machines" in the two major

The Boss

In the Republican Party and in the Democratic Party, factional rivalries centered around the ambitions of the "bosses" of the several "machines' making up each party. These bosses used their influence to deliver large blocs of votes to the political candidates they favored.

parties. Third parties also had to contend with the reluctance of many Americans to risk "throwing away" their votes on a new party which had only slight chances of winning elections. As you will read, however, third parties sometimes caused the two older parties to take a stand on important election issues or sometimes even to change their policies.

SECTION SURVEY

IDENTIFY: "waving the bloody shirt," *laissez faire,* party "machines."

1. Make a chart listing the similarities between the two major political parties in the period from 1865 to 1897.
2. (a) Who supported the Republican Party? Why? (b) Who supported the Democratic Party? Why?
3. What is meant by the statement that government should not interfere with business and industry?
4. Describe how the character and structure of the Democratic and Republican parties from 1865 to 1897 reflected certain characteristics of American political behavior.

427

2 The spread of graft and corruption in the postwar years

It was Ulysses S. Grant's unhappy destiny to occupy the White House during the period in which graft and corruption infected every level of American government—federal, state, and local.

President Grant. In 1868, when he won the election for the Presidency on the Republican ticket (page 413), Grant enjoyed the respect of millions of Americans. His well-earned reputation rested upon his success as commander of the Union armies during the latter years of the Civil War. Had he never served as President, Grant would have lived and died a popular hero. Unfortunately, his lack of political experience was a great handicap, and his eight-year administration proved to be a dark page in the history of the Presidency.

Grant himself was honest and upright. His great weakness—which could have been a virtue if tempered by reason—was a blind loyalty to friends. Being honest himself, he could not believe that his associates were any less honest, and he stubbornly refused to admit that some of his "friends" used him to advance their own fortunes.

The Crédit Mobilier scandal. Even before Grant took office, the federal government was involved in an unsavory scandal.

In 1862 Congress had granted a charter to the Union Pacific Railroad and to the Central Pacific Railroad to build a transcontinental railroad. The Union Pacific was to build westward from the Missouri River at Omaha, in Nebraska Territory. Meanwhile, the Central Pacific was to build eastward from Sacramento, California.

Building such a railroad was extremely expensive and risky. But since the completed railroad would be important to national development, the federal government gave various subsidies to the railroad companies, as you will read later.

The small group of men who owned the controlling shares of stock in the Union Pacific Railroad saw a chance to make enormous profits. They organized a construction company called the Crédit Mobilier (kray·DEE moh·bee·LYAY), to which they awarded construction contracts. These contracts were paid for by other stockholders of the Union Pacific Railroad at several times what the job actually cost. As a result, much of the money invested by stockholders in the Union Pacific, as well as a large share of the government subsidies, enriched a small group of greedy men.

When Congressional committees finally investigated, they discovered that some Congressmen had owned stock in the Crédit Mobilier company. The company owners had given the Congressmen the stock, or had sold it to them at half price, in an effort to bribe them and to block investigations.

The "salary grab." The Crédit Mobilier scandal was occupying the attention of Congress when the Senators and Representatives voted themselves a 50 percent increase in salaries—from $5,000 to $7,500 per year. Congressmen pushed the salary bill through on the last day of the session, March 3, 1872. To make matters worse, they made the measure retroactive for two years, meaning that each Congressman would receive two years' back pay, or $5,000, besides his future salary increase. The public was so outraged at this "salary grab" that Congress hastily repealed the act at the opening of its next session. Although the "salary grab" was perfectly legal, it does indicate the "something for nothing" philosophy which motivated many public figures—Democrats and Republicans alike—during these unsettled years.

The Treasury Department scandal. Public resentment had hardly died when another scandal made newspaper headlines. Secretary of the Treasury William A. Richardson signed a contract with a private citizen, John D. Sanborn, giving Sanborn authority to collect some overdue federal taxes, with the right to pocket half of all he could collect. By various devious methods, Sanborn collected $427,000, retaining about $213,000 for himself.

When called to explain the affair, Sanborn swore that he had kept only a small part of the "commission," having been forced to give $156,000 to his "assistants"! These "assistants" were politicians who had used their influence to swing the tax-collection contract to Sanborn. But the contract was legal, and the "commission" was paid in full. A new law prevented the situation from recurring, however, and Richardson resigned.

The "Whisky Ring." The new Secretary of the Treasury, Benjamin H. Bristow, was an honest official who promptly discovered other corrupt practices in his department. Investigation disclosed that taxes were not being collected on about seven eighths of the liquor distilled in the United States. Further investigation revealed that high public officials were guilty of blackmail and fraud.

According to the tax law, a distiller who failed to pay revenue taxes on distilled liquor would be compelled, if caught, to pay a double tax. Any informer who revealed to the government that a company had failed to pay its taxes received 10 percent of the tax penalty as a reward. Informers soon saw, however, that they could collect more by blackmailing the tax-evading company than by reporting the evasion.

The Secretary of the Treasury discovered that a ring of whisky distillers and blackmailers had been defrauding the United States government of a million dollars annually. The Supervisor of Internal Revenue in St. Louis, John McDonald, who was involved in the conspiracy, went to prison for a year, but not before the trail of corruption was traced even to President Grant's private secretary.

Other scandals. Meanwhile, it was discovered that Secretary of War William W. Belknap had accepted $24,500 in bribes from a trader at Fort Sill in what is now Oklahoma. Belknap had decided to give the profitable and exclusive trading concession to a New York friend. The trader, who was making a huge profit from the Indians around Fort Sill, agreed to pay Belknap and his friend each $6,000 a year if allowed to retain his concession.

When evidence of this bribery was presented, the House of Representatives voted unanimously to impeach Secretary Belknap, who then hastily resigned. Despite all the evidence, the Senate's impeachment trial failed to convict the ex-Secretary of War. The Senators who voted "not guilty" claimed that because Belknap had resigned he was no longer subject to trial by the Senate.

There were still other evidences of graft in the federal government. The Secretary of the Navy "sold" business to builders and suppliers of ships. The Secretary of the Interior worked hand in glove with land speculators. President Grant himself had no part in these unsavory activities, but many people felt that he was at fault for allowing his "friends" to hide behind his good name.

Corruption in state governments. Corruption was as bad, if not worse, in the state governments. In 1868 when the Erie Railroad, which was controlled by Daniel Drew, James ("Jim") Fisk, Jr., and Jay Gould, wanted to sell $10 million worth of additional stock, Gould went to the New York state capital at Albany with a trunk full of money to bribe the legislators to legalize the sale of the stock. A steady stream of greedy legislators passed through Gould's hotel room. Evidence suggested that the governor of New York sold his influence for $20,000 and that state senators got $15,000.

The Tweed Ring. Perhaps worst of all was the corruption in municipal, or city, government. William M. Tweed, an uneducated chairmaker, rose

THOMAS NAST, MASTER CARTOONIST

Thomas Nast (1840–1902), one of the greatest political caricaturists of all time, came to the United States from Germany when he was only 6 years old. By the time he was 20, Nast had demonstrated his amazing skill. In the early 1870's, while attacking the Tammany Hall political machine, he was offered $500,000 to drop his work and move abroad.

It was during his anti-Tammany campaign that Nast drew one of his most famous cartoons, "The Tammany Tiger Loose." In this cartoon he showed a ravenous beast in an arena with the bodies of his victims lying around him. The beast was about to devour the "Republic" pictured as a helpless young woman. The corrupt political boss, "Emperor Tweed," was seated in the stands, surrounded by his henchmen. Under the cartoon Nast asked readers, "What are you going to do about it?" Aroused New York citizens took such vigorous action that Tweed and his associates fled the country. But they could not escape Nast. Several years later, in Spain, Boss Tweed was identified by a person who recognized him from one of Nast's drawings, and Tweed was returned to New York and sent to prison.

The "Tammany Tiger" is only one of many famous symbols created by Thomas Nast. He invented the Republican elephant and the Democratic donkey. But his most popular creation was the lovable image of Santa Claus. It was Thomas Nast who first portrayed Santa Claus as the merry old gentleman with the long white beard.

in 15 years to be a multimillionaire "dictator" of New York City in the 1860's and 1870's. Working with Tammany Hall—the Democratic political organization and the so-called political "machine" of the city—"Boss" Tweed completely controlled the government of the city.

Tweed gained control very simply. He or his men met immigrants when they landed, fed them, found them jobs, gave them coal, left them baskets of food at Thanksgiving and Christmas. After they secured the right to vote, the newcomers returned Tweed's "friendship" by voting for the men he favored. Moreover, when election outcomes seemed doubtful, men stuffed the ballot boxes with votes in favor of Tweed's candidates. Some men voted several times, using different names and addresses each time.

How did Tweed use his power? He overloaded city payrolls with friends. He demanded "kickbacks" from people who wanted city jobs. He demanded bribes from companies that wanted to provide city services. A courthouse, started in 1868, was to cost $250,000; three years later, still uncompleted, it had cost $8 million. In three years Tweed and his crooked "ring" stole from New York City an estimated $20 million. It is further estimated that between 1868 and 1871 Boss Tweed's "ring" and his business friends cost the city close to $100 million.

Reasons for corruption. Why was public morality at such a low level in the years following the Civil War?

The war itself was partly responsible. In the crisis of wartime the all-important consideration is to get things done quickly. Cost is secondary to national survival, and money flows freely into war industries. During the war years, with business booming, unscrupulous businessmen and legislators had a rare opportunity to engage in dishonest practices. These practices were carried into the postwar years.

A related and equally significant explanation of the postwar graft was the rapid growth of large-scale industry, about which you will read in Chapter 23. In earlier times, when factories and businesses were small, a businessman was well known. If his practices were dishonest, he was apt to lose his neighbors' good will. But the new large corporations were impersonal. The men who controlled them were hardly known even by many of their own stockholders. Within the corporations, it was easier for unscrupulous men to get away with questionable practices.

IDENTIFY: Crédit Mobilier, "salary grab," Whisky Ring, Tammany Hall, Tweed Ring; William Belknap, Jay Gould, "Boss" Tweed.

1. Ulysses S. Grant's administration was a dark page in the history of the American Presidency. Describe four scandals that support this conclusion.
2. Although Grant was not personally involved in these scandals, people blamed him for them. Why?
3. Show that graft and corruption also existed on the state and local levels.
4. Why was public morality at such a low level in the postwar years?

3 Initial moves toward restoring honesty to government

Newspapers in the late 1860's and the early 1870's were filled with stories and cartoons attacking government graft among federal, state, and local officials. The most famous American cartoonist was Thomas Nast of New York, whose powerful cartoons in *Harper's Weekly* helped to reveal to the public the abuses of "Boss" Tweed and his friends.

These revelations of corruption stimulated a widespread demand for reform. No reform movement aroused greater interest than the proposal to appoint men to government jobs on the basis of merit. Under the "spoils system," which Andrew Jackson had helped to extend (page 268), government jobs were given to political favorites. Under the proposed "merit system," those who received the highest grades in competitive examinations would get the jobs, whether they were Republicans or Democrats. All these public jobs in the federal, state, and local governments would be called *civil service* jobs.

Growth of the reform movement. A halfhearted attempt by Congress and President Grant to reform the civil service failed. In 1875 the chairman of the recently appointed civil service commission resigned in disgust, and the commission was discontinued.

Meanwhile, in 1872, a varied group of reform-minded Republicans, who called themselves the Liberal Republican Party, nominated Horace Greeley, the editor of the New York *Tribune*, as their Presidential candidate to run against the regular Republican candidate, President Grant. The Democrats, meeting two months later, also nominated Greeley, hoping by this means to benefit from the split in the Republican Party.

The Liberal Republican platform included a pledge to fight corruption in public life and a specific plank, or section, urging civil service reform. But Grant was elected President by an overwhelming electoral vote—286 to 66.

The defeat at the polls in 1872 was a disheartening blow to the reformers. Within a year, however, they began to gather strength. For one thing, new public scandals drove more Americans into the reform movement. Although the two major parties were quite evenly matched at the national level, growing dissatisfaction with Grant's Republican administration enabled the Democrats to win control of the House of Representatives in the Congressional elections of 1874.

The election of 1876. The Democrats, heartened by the growing demand for reform, approached the 1876 elections confident of victory. They chose as their Presidential candidate Governor Samuel J. Tilden of New York. Governor Tilden had won national attention by helping to break up the Tweed Ring in New York. The Democratic platform demanded civil service reform and an end to graft in public life.

The Republicans, who were "running scared," nominated a man well known as a reformer, Governor Rutherford B. Hayes of Ohio. Hayes promised to work for civil service reform in the federal government. He also promised to end the troubled and troublesome period of reconstruction.

Both Tilden and Hayes were wealthy men. Both were closely associated with industrialists and businessmen. Tilden's one big asset was the fact that he was running against a party that for eight years had been identified with scandal after scandal.

Disputed election returns. The election gave Tilden 250,000 more popular votes than Hayes received. The first count of the electoral votes, based on early returns, also gave Tilden an advantage over Hayes—184 to 165. As a result, most newspapers at first said Tilden had won.

But the papers had jumped to the wrong conclusion. Tilden with his 184 electoral votes was one short of the necessary majority. Ordinarily, when no Presidential candidate has a clear majority of the electoral vote, the House of Representatives chooses the President. But this was no ordinary election. Four states—South Carolina, Florida, Louisiana, and Oregon—had each sent in *two* different sets of returns. In all, 20 electoral votes from these four states were claimed by both the Repub-

licans and the Democrats. Tilden needed only one of these disputed votes to win. Hayes, however, needed all 20.

The single disputed vote from Oregon was quickly settled in favor of Hayes. But the remaining 19 votes from the three southern states aroused a storm of controversy. The Republicans claimed all three states for Hayes, but the Democrats insisted that, since these states were still under carpetbag rule, the will of the majority had not been expressed. For a time the controversy threatened to plunge the nation into violence.

Settling the dispute. Unfortunately, the Constitution provided no explicit procedures for solving this complicated situation. According to the Constitution, the votes had to be counted, but by whom? If the Republican-controlled Senate counted the votes, the Senators would throw out the Democratic returns and give the election to Hayes. If the Democratic-controlled House counted the votes, the Representatives would throw out the Republican returns and give the election to Tilden.

In order to break the apparently hopeless deadlock, Congress created an Electoral Commission of 15 members—five Senators, five Representatives, and five Supreme Court Justices. By previous arrangement the Senate chose three Republicans and two Democrats; the House, two Republicans and three Democrats. Four Justices—two Republicans and two Democrats—were to name a fifth member of the commission—an independent voter without ties to either party.

It was generally understood that the one "independent" member of the Electoral Commission would be Justice David Davis. At the last minute, however, Davis resigned from the Supreme Court because of his election to the Senate, and his place on the Electoral Commission went to a Republican. It was not surprising therefore, that when the disputed votes were counted, the returns from South Carolina, Florida, and Louisiana went to the Republicans by a "straight" party vote of eight Republicans as opposed to the seven Democrats on the commission.

Thus it was that Hayes, who had received a minority of the popular votes, entered the White House as President on March 5, 1877. The controversial election of 1876–77, however, had a larger significance. It represented a victory for compromise and for the process of orderly government. It showed that violence and bloodshed could be avoided even in an extremely close and hotly contested election.

Difficulties for Hayes. President Hayes had four difficult years in the White House. Throughout his administration the Democrats controlled the House, and for two years, from 1879 to 1881, the Senate as well. Although the Democrats did not try to upset the decision of the Electoral Commission, they called Hayes "His Fraudulency" and "Old Eight to Seven" to remind him that they questioned his right to the Presidency.

Hayes also faced opposition from his own party. The election of 1876 split the Republicans into two groups—the "Stalwarts" and the "Half-Breeds." The Stalwarts, led by Senator ("Boss") Roscoe Conkling of New York, included most of the Radical Republicans who had created and for a time enforced the program of southern reconstruction. The Stalwarts, sometimes called "Old Guard" Republicans, were against reform and reformers, including the President himself, whom they called "Granny Hayes." The "Half-Breeds," led by James G. Blaine of Maine and John Sherman of Ohio, agreed with Hayes that at least some reform was needed.

To fulfill his promise of ending reconstruction, President Hayes named a former Confederate leader to his cabinet and withdrew what were left of federal occupation troops from the South (page 416). As the remaining reconstruction, or "carpetbag," governments lost power, southern Democrats were free to manage state affairs in their own way. Southern Democrats elected to Congress from the "Solid South," in alliance with northern Democrats, now broke the power of the Radical Republicans who had controlled Congress during the years of reconstruction.

Hayes' battle for reform. The opposition he faced did not prevent President Hayes from fighting for reform legislation. He was the first President to take serious steps to reform the civil service. He refused to follow the practice of many earlier Presidents of discharging thousands of officeholders and replacing them with political favorites. He also insisted that all persons recommended by Congressmen for jobs should be carefully investigated.

One of Hayes' cabinet members, Carl Schurz, a German-born Republican, introduced the merit system into the Department of the Interior. And the President himself courageously removed a prominent Republican leader, Chester A. Arthur, from his job as Collector of Customs in New York because of his undue political activity. Many "Old Guard," or Stalwart, Republicans were furious, but Hayes stood his ground.

The election of 1880. Well before the nominating conventions for the 1880 elections, President Hayes announced that he would not run for re-election. The Stalwart wing of the Republican Party, fed up with talk of reform and eager to return to the "good old days," tried to win the nomination for former President Ulysses S. Grant. But the Half-Breed wing of the party managed to block this attempt. Finally, the Republican convention nominated a war veteran, General James A. Garfield of Ohio. To win the support of the disappointed Stalwarts, the convention nominated for Vice-President Chester A. Arthur, a leading Stalwart.

The Democrats also pinned their hopes for the Presidency on a war veteran, General Winfield S. Hancock of Pennsylvania.

Divided into groups with conflicting interests and eager to win elections, neither the Democrats nor the Republicans faced up to basic problems of the new industrial age—labor legislation, regulation of railroads and other "big business," the money issue, and an income tax. Thus, it was a third party, the Greenback-Labor Party, as you will see, that squarely faced the new and controversial issues of the time.

The election of 1880 was a close one. Garfield won with an electoral vote of 214 to Hancock's 155. But the popular vote totaled 4,449,053 for the Republicans, 4,442,035 for the Democrats.

Civil service reform. On July 2, 1881, President Garfield was shot by Charles J. Guiteau, a disappointed—and mentally unbalanced—government job seeker. Garfield died in September.

The President's tragic death shocked the country into seeing the evils of the old spoils system. Chester A. Arthur, the new President, responded to the widespread demand for reform and supported the Pendleton Civil Service Act.

The Pendleton Act, which became law in 1883, provided for a three-man *bipartisan* commission—one on which both parties were represented—to give competitive examinations to candidates for government jobs. The first examinations were to be for only about 12 percent of federal jobs, but the President was given authority to broaden the list. The Pendleton Act also forbade the party in power to ask for campaign contributions from federal officeholders. President Arthur appointed as head of the commission a well-known champion of civil service reform and extended the list of "classified" federal positions—positions for which civil service examinations had to be taken.

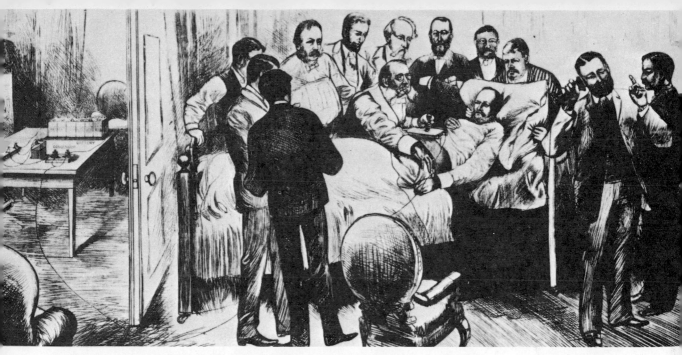

■ After President Garfield was shot, a device invented by Alexander Graham Bell was used to find the exact location of the assassin's bullet. But Garfield's life could not be saved.

Thus, after years of agitation, reformers at last managed to write into law the principle that federal jobs below the policy-making level should be filled by "merit," using competitive examinations. A long step had been taken toward making government more honest and efficient.

Presidential candidates in 1884. When the election year of 1884 rolled around, Chester A. Arthur made it clear that he wanted to run for the Presidency again. But his fellow Republican Stalwarts had lost faith in him because of his reform activities. Instead, the leader of the Half-Breed wing of the Republican Party, James G. Blaine, won the nomination.

Blaine was a handsome, colorful, and persuasive candidate. But during his long political career he had made many enemies, including the reformers in his own party. These enemies now accused Blaine of having used his political influence to secure favors for big business—at a generous profit for himself. Disgruntled at his nomination, a large group of Republicans, nicknamed "Mugwumps," bolted the party and voted for the Democratic candidate.

The Democrats made the most of Blaine's reputation as "a tool of the special interests" by choosing a reformer for their Presidential nominee. Grover Cleveland, who had been governor of New York, was known to be thoroughly honest, courageous, independent—and stubborn when fighting for a principle. His reform activities also had provoked strong opposition within his own party.

Democratic victory. In the campaign the big issues of the day were almost forgotten as the politicians heaped abuse upon the rival candidates. Each party diligently raked over the personal life of the opposition candidate, searching for misconduct that could be held against him.

Throughout the election campaign the two candidates, Blaine and Cleveland, ran neck and neck. And then, on the very eve of the election, at a reception given for Blaine by a group of Protestant clergymen, a speaker called the Democrats the party of "Rum, Romanism, and Rebellion."

The speaker's use of the word "rum" was a deliberate attempt to "smear" the Democrats. His use of the word "rebellion" referred to the alliance between northern Democrats and the "Solid South" Democrats. Both these references were indiscreet, but the speaker's reference to "Romanism"—the Roman Catholic religion—was fatal. It was generally agreed that Blaine's failure to rebuke the speaker for this insult to Roman Catholic voters cost him the election. Cleveland won the Presidency, squeaking through with 219 electoral votes to Blaine's 182.

The election of 1884 was the first Presidential victory for the Democrats in 28 years. It was one sign that memories of the Civil War were beginning to recede.

SECTION SURVEY

IDENTIFY: civil service, "Old Guard" Republicans, "Mugwumps"; Samuel Tilden, Rutherford Hayes, "Boss" Conkling, James Blaine, James Garfield, Chester Arthur, Thomas Nast.

1. Contrast the "spoils system" with the "merit system" of appointment to government jobs.
2. In what ways was the election of 1876 one of the most unusual in American history?
3. What position did each of the following take concerning reform: (a) Liberal Republicans, (b) Stalwarts, (c) Half-Breeds?
4. Explain the provisions and the significance of the Pendleton Act of 1883.
5. Discuss the factors that led to Cleveland's election in 1884.

4 Increasing political reforms in government despite setbacks

When President Cleveland entered the White House in 1885, the movement for political reform entered a new phase.

Cleveland's firm stand. President Cleveland, who strongly believed that "a public office is a public trust," took a firm stand on important issues even though he knew that his action would antagonize influential members of his own party.

He supported civil service reform by doubling the number of federal offices on the classified list. He took a step toward conserving the nation's natural resources by recovering more than 80 million acres of public land illegally held by railroads, lumber companies, and cattle interests. He also signed a bill in 1887 creating a federal Division of Forestry.

One of his most courageous acts was his attempt to block pension "grabs" by veterans of the Union army. For many years the Pension Bureau had been very generous in handing out pensions. Now and then, however, requests for pensions were based on such flimsy grounds that even the bureau rejected them. Often, when this happened, the dis-

appointed pension seeker asked his Congressman to get the pension for him by pushing a special bill through Congress. President Cleveland vetoed more than 200 of these bills. He thus antagonized many ex-soldiers, who were united in the politically powerful veterans' organization the Grand Army of the Republic, known as the G.A.R.

Important laws. In addition to Cleveland's personal accomplishments, Congress adopted several important laws during the years from 1885 to 1889.

The Presidential Succession Act of 1886 provided that, if both the President and the Vice-President died or were disabled, the cabinet officers would succeed to the Presidency in the order in which their offices had been created.

The Electoral Count Act of 1887 was designed to prevent another disputed election similar to the election of 1876. The act provided that, if a state sent in more than one set of electoral returns, Congress had to accept the returns approved by the governor of the state.

In 1887 Congress, in an effort to quiet the clamor of small businessmen and farmers against unfair business practices by the railroads, passed the Interstate Commerce Act. For some time the act did not achieve its stated objectives, but it did initiate what was to become a far-reaching policy change in relations between government and business (Chapter 24).

Congress refused, however, to accept President Cleveland's vigorous recommendation that tariff rates be lowered. Despite the President's urging, high-tariff men in the Senate blocked the administration bill providing lower tariff rates.

The election of 1888. President Cleveland's reform activities, and especially his campaign for lower tariffs, antagonized political leaders in his own party. Nevertheless, in 1888 the Democrats nominated him for a second term.

Although Cleveland won nearly 100,000 more popular votes than his opponent, Benjamin Harrison, he lost the election by an electoral count of 233 to 168. The Republicans won the Presidency and control of both houses of Congress.

Cleveland's policies reversed. Benjamin Harrison was a successful lawyer, a veteran of the Union army, and the grandson of former President William Henry Harrison. He was not, however, a "strong" President. In his opinion, his duty as Chief Executive was to follow the wishes of the Senators and Representatives, who in turn had the responsibility of carrying out the wishes of the people.

During President Harrison's administration the Republicans reversed many of President Cleveland's policies. They did little to change the spoils system, and replaced Democratic officeholders (except those on the classified list) with Republicans. Congress passed the Dependent Pension Act that granted a pension to nearly every disabled Union veteran. Congress also adopted the highest protective tariff the country had seen up to that time. The McKinley Tariff of 1890, introduced by Congressman William McKinley of Ohio, raised rates from an average of about 38 percent to an average of close to 50 percent.

But "Old Guard" Republicans did not have everything their way. In an effort to appeal to farmers, laborers, miners, small businessmen, and the American public in general, Congress passed two important laws in 1890. The Sherman Silver Purchase Act was intended to appeal to western mining interests and to increase the amount of money in circulation as a benefit to farmers, wage earners, and small businessmen. The Sherman Antitrust Act was intended to protect the public at large from monopoly practices and other abuses of free enterprise that had arisen with the growth of industry. You will read about these two important laws in Unit Seven.

Growing dissatisfaction. Neither the Sherman Silver Purchase Act nor the Sherman Antitrust Act served to overcome the growing dissatisfaction with President Harrison's Republican administration. Wage earners, united in the newly organized American Federation of Labor (Chapter 25), had no reason to hope their demands would be met by Republicans. Many farmers, abandoning hope of help from either party, began to take steps with the support of organized labor to secure control of the government and bring about long-sought reforms. And Americans in general, struggling to make ends meet in the face of rising prices, blamed their troubles on the Republican-sponsored McKinley Tariff.

Of course, the problems Americans faced in the 1890's could not be explained simply in terms of a tariff act or the policies of a political party. Basic to everything else was the fact that a new industrial civilization was being born. Enterprising business leaders were creating new industries; technology was creating new jobs and opportunities—and, in the process, displacing men from older lines of work; and the entire economy was growing ever more rapidly. American wage earners on the whole were better off than workers in industrial Europe;

some wage earners were doing very well indeed; and the large middle class was growing. But there was poverty, too, and insecurity for millions of American workers. And many large problems were clamoring for attention.

Need for reform. Two widely read books expressed growing dissatisfaction with the concentration of wealth in the hands of a few men. Henry George's *Progress and Poverty,* first published in 1879, contrasted the wealth of the few with the poverty of many people. George thought that this inequality was due to the fact that a few men had monopoly control over the nation's choicest land sites and other natural resources. George proposed a new system of land taxation which, he thought, would abolish great fortunes and provide good livings for everyone.

In 1894 a book by Henry Demarest Lloyd was published entitled *Wealth Against Commonwealth.* The author concluded that the giant new corporations and business enterprises were running the new industrial economy for their own gain.

Lloyd's book expressed the deep-seated discontent of millions of Americans. It was not industrialism that the people feared and hated. They agreed with Lloyd that the new industrial age held the promise of a brighter future for people everywhere. What concerned many Americans was that the new industrialism had created extremes of poverty and wealth. Expanding industries brought vast wealth to a few owners, while the majority of workers lived in poverty. For a solution to this problem, many Americans turned to government—whether controlled by Republicans or Democrats.

By 1892 the demand for government action had reached clamorous proportions. Owners of small businesses, wage earners in every section of the country, and especially the western farmers, were calling for reform.

The election of 1892. Rising discontent turned the election of 1892 into a spirited three-way contest. Both the Republicans and the Democrats realized that they had to do something about reform. They were prodded into action by the strength of a new party, the Populist Party, which had been created in 1891. The Populist Party was organized, as you will see later, by farmers. But it also attracted wage earners and many other voters who were discontented with the two major parties.

The Republicans were on the defensive. President Harrison and the Republican Party received widespread criticism. The President himself had almost completely abandoned civil service reform.

Congress had opened the door to a flood of pensions for disabled veterans. Congress had also adopted the McKinley Tariff, the highest protective tariff in history. Despite criticism, the Republicans decided to stand on their record, and nominated President Harrison for a second term.

The Democrats, eager to take advantage of the demands for reform from both wage earners and farmers, nominated Grover Cleveland, who was already known as a champion of honest politics.

The Democrats won, with Cleveland gathering 277 electoral votes to Harrison's 145. The Democrats also won control of Congress. But the new Populist Party—an out-and-out reform party—made a remarkable showing. Although the Populist candidate, James B. Weaver, collected only 22 electoral votes, his popular vote totaled more than 1 million, and the party itself managed to elect three governors and send numerous representatives to state legislatures and to Congress.

Cleveland in trouble. From the beginning President Cleveland was in trouble. He antagonized wage earners with his labor policy, and farmers with his money policy, as you will see later. People in general blamed him for a depression that hit the country shortly after he took office. In the Congressional elections of 1894, the voters expressed their dissatisfaction by electing enough Republican Senators and Representatives to give the Republicans control of Congress.

The Wilson-Gorman Tariff Act. Cleveland's election had stemmed in part from his promise to lower the McKinley Tariff. Acting on the President's recommendations, in December 1893 Representative William L. Wilson of West Virginia introduced a bill that provided substantial reductions in existing tariff rates. The bill passed the House without great difficulty. In the Senate, however, high-tariff men, led by Senator Gorman of Maryland, added more than 600 amendments to the original bill.

The Wilson-Gorman bill, as it was called, provided lower average tariff rates than the act it was designed to replace—39.9 percent to the McKinley Tariff's 48.4 percent. But it was still a high protective tariff, and President Cleveland was furious. He did not veto the bill, for he thought it was better than the McKinley Tariff. But he refused to endorse it by signing it, preferring instead to leave it on his desk for 10 days, after which it automatically became law without his signature.

Dissatisfaction with the tariff. During the tariff debates in the Senate, powerful *lobbies,* or pressure

groups, tried in every way possible to influence the votes of doubtful Senators. Producers of iron, steel, wool, glass, and hundreds of other commodities demanded tariff protection.

One of the most active lobbies was the American Sugar Refining Company, usually called "the sugar trust." ° The original House bill had completely removed the tariff on raw and refined sugar. The sugar trust, determined to get the tariff restored, immediately went to work on the Senate. After a long and heated debate, the trust won, and the tariff on sugar was restored.

The Wilson-Gorman Tariff cost the Democrats the support of millions of Americans who were convinced that the Democrats had broken their campaign promise to do away with a high protective tariff.

Decision against an income tax. The original tariff bill introduced by Representative Wilson would have drastically lowered the tariff rates. Expecting a loss in government revenue because of the lower rates, the House Ways and Means Committee added a clause to the tariff bill providing for a 2 percent tax on all incomes of more than $4,000.

The income tax clause provoked violent debate, but it finally became law. Opponents of the income tax immediately tested the new measure in the courts, and in 1895 the Supreme Court declared it unconstitutional. The Supreme Court ruled against the income tax because it was a direct tax not apportioned among the states according to population, as required by the Constitution (page 180).

The Democratic administration could by no stretch of the imagination be held responsible for the Supreme Court's negative decision on the income tax. Nevertheless, millions of rank and file Americans considered this decision as merely one more example of how the government favored "big business." Thus, the Supreme Court's rejection of the income tax helped to fan the flame of protest sweeping the country.

Financial panic and depression. On May 5, 1893, only two months after Cleveland took office, a financial panic began as the value of stocks on the New York Stock Exchange suddenly plunged downward. As the weeks passed, the situation rapidly became worse. Thousands of businesses failed. Factories closed their doors. Perhaps as many as 4 million workers were unemployed. The prices of farm produce dropped so low that farmers could

° *trust:* a group of companies centrally controlled to regulate production, reduce expenses, and eliminate competition.

■ On May 5, 1893, only two months after Cleveland took office, a financial panic began. The value of stocks on the New York Stock Exchange, shown above, suddenly plunged downward.

not afford to pay the freight to market. By the end of the year, the American nation was in the grip of one of the worst depressions in its history.

There were a number of reasons for the depression that hit the country in 1893, but, as the depression deepened, money became the central issue. In the Republican convention of 1896 the Republicans, favoring a money policy demanded by businessmen and industrialists, nominated William McKinley of Ohio as their candidate. The Democrats, adopting the money policy of the Populist Party, nominated William Jennings Bryan of Nebraska. You will read a full account of this dramatic Presidential election in Chapter 24. McKinley won the election, as you will see, and the Populist Party died out. But the forces of reform soon rallied, in the early 1900's, to a new and more powerful banner—the banner of the Progressive movement.

SECTION SURVEY

IDENTIFY: pension "grabs," McKinley Tariff of 1890, Populist Party, lobbies, trust, panic of 1893; Benjamin Harrison.

1. What did Grover Cleveland mean by saying that "a public office is a public trust"?
2. Explain how each of the following laws helped to solve an important national problem: (a) Presidential Succession Act of 1886, (b) Electoral Count Act of 1887, (c) Interstate Commerce Act of 1887.
3. Between 1890 and 1896 workers and farmers felt that the government favored "big business" and the well-to-do. What events made them feel this way?
4. What was the significance of the writings of Henry Demarest Lloyd and Henry George?
5. Why was the income tax declared unconstitutional in 1895?

TRACING THE MAIN IDEAS

Change, unrest, new ways of living, and new problems—these were characteristics of every section of the United States during the years from 1865 to 1900. Many of the new problems that Americans faced were the inevitable result of the war that for four long years had convulsed the nation and disrupted long-established ways of living. To an even greater extent, however, the new problems were the result of the Industrial Revolution that was transforming the United States from an agricultural nation into a great industrial power.

The war itself had hastened the process of industrialization. Keyed to feverish pitch during the war years, northern industry continued to expand after 1865—and with ever-increasing speed. Nor was the process of industrialization confined to the North. It was transforming life in the South, and, as you will see in the next chapter, it helped men to conquer the last frontiers of the West.

But the new ways of living brought serious problems as well as excitement and drama. Morality in public life rapidly declined as a "get-rich-quick" spirit and greed for power infected millions of Americans. Wealth and power became dangerously concentrated in the hands of a relatively few businessmen and bankers—the creators of the new industrial age. Through their control of the giant corporations that were springing up in the nation, of the railroads, and of the mines, factories, and banks, this relatively small group of men was able to exert powerful influence over government at every level.

There is, however, another side of the story. As Americans became increasingly aware of these serious problems, they began to take steps to correct the situation. In later chapters of this book you will see how the American people undertook to solve the numerous problems that faced them.

CHAPTER SURVEY

QUESTIONS FOR DISCUSSION

1. (a) What, in your opinion, are the causes of political corruption? (b) Why were graft and corruption so widespread after the Civil War?
2. (a) Explain the Pendleton Act's significance regarding democratic government. (b) Why has the act been called the "Magna Carta of civil service reform"?
3. Compare and explain the positions of the Republican and Democratic parties concerning the tariff issue during the period 1865–96. Refer to specific tariff laws.
4. According to some historians, the Hayes-Tilden election of 1876 is an example of a secret political bargain. Search historical sources to find out what various historians say about this issue. What evidence do these historians use to support their positions?

RELATING PAST TO PRESENT

1. What in your opinion is the function of the news media regarding government policies and practices?
2. Has civil service reform fulfilled the expectations of the men who proposed it? Do you think the civil service has contributed to bureaucracy and red tape in our government today? Explain your answers.
3. Does the word reform have a different meaning today from the one it had during the period just studied? Explain.
4. Compare the present Presidential Succession Law of 1967 (Amendment 25) with the one enacted in 1886.
5. What part of the population made up the majority of Republican and Democratic party members during the period 1865–97? What part of the population constitutes the majority of political party members today? Compare and comment.
6. Would any military man elected to the Presidency in 1868 have encountered the same difficulties that Grant did? Explain.

USING MAPS AND CHARTS

1. Consulting the Chronology of Events on pages 884–85, point out and explain the most important political, economic, and social developments during the administrations of each of the following Presidents: Grant, Hayes, Arthur, Cleveland (two terms), and Harrison.
2. Which of these Presidents, in your opinion, had the most impressive achievements to his credit? Defend your position.
3. Analyze the cartoons on pages 427 and 429 by identifying the characters and explaining the aim of each cartoonist. Is this form of commentary still practiced today?

CHIEF JOSEPH, leader of the Nez Percé (NAY per·SAY) Indians, stood before his conquerors. "I am tired of fighting," he said. "Our chiefs are killed. . . . It is cold and we have no blankets. The little children are freezing to death. . . . My heart is sick and sad. From where the sun now stands I will fight no more, forever."

The year was 1877. The time, sunset. The place, the plains of Montana, near the Canadian border.

The Nez Percé Indians had dwelt in peace for half a century in the Oregon country. But after 1865 pioneers, looking with greedy eyes at the Nez Percé hunting grounds, had begun to pour into the Pacific Northwest. And soon a federal order arrived: The Indians were to be moved to a reservation—a tract of land set aside by the federal government as a dwelling place for the tribe.

But the Nez Percé refused to submit. Chief Joseph tried to lead his people to safety in Canada. With 200 warriors and 600 women and children he traveled more than 1,300 miles in two months, closely pursued by United States troops. Chief Joseph and his people were within sight of the Canadian border when they were surrounded and forced to surrender.

In 1877 Chief Joseph and his conquerors stood on the last frontier of the West—the Great Plains, a vast area stretching from what are now Montana and North Dakota southward to Texas. From time immemorial this land had belonged to the Indians. Now it was being claimed by people from the North and South and from distant Europe.

This is the story of the conquest of the Indians. It is also the story of the West itself and of new ways of life on the "last frontier."

THE CHAPTER IN OUTLINE

1. Troubled relations with the American Indians.
2. The short-lived kingdom of cattlemen on the plains.
3. The rapid settlement of the "last frontier" by pioneering farmers.
4. The discovery of mineral treasures in the western mountains.

Thomas Gilcrease Institute, Tulsa, Oklahoma

■ *Chief Joseph surrendering*

CHAPTER 22

Conquering the "Last Frontier"

1865 – 1900

1 Troubled relations with the American Indians

On their western edge the prairies of the Middle West merge into the Great Plains. Although no sharp line separates the prairies from the plains, the 100th meridian is usually accepted as the dividing line. Usually, as one travels westward from the 100th meridian to the Rocky Mountains, the rainfall decreases and the grass gets shorter.

Obstacles to settlement. It was along the 100th meridian that the westward advance halted for at least a generation during the early 1800's. The reluctance of the pioneers to settle on the Great Plains arose in part from misinformation. Earlier explorers, accustomed to wooded country with abundant rainfall, had established the idea that the Great Plains were mainly uninhabitable desert. Maps of the time called the plains the "Great American Desert." By the 1850's, however, this notion was being dispelled. Traders and pioneers who crossed the plains on their way to California and the Pacific Northwest reported that much of the plains country was good for settlement.

But a tremendous obstacle to settlement remained—the Plains Indians.

Bows and arrows against long rifles. The Plains Indians had learned what the white settlers would have to learn—how to adapt to the plains environment. The buffalo, or bison, provided the Indians with food, clothing, and shelter.

The Indians were powerful enemies. They rode horses with superb ease. Before they secured rifles, they fought with spears and with short bows, from which they could drive their arrows with amazing rapidity and penetrating force. They were protected by shields of buffalo hide, which they coated with glue made from horses' hooves and hardened over the fire to an almost iron-like consistency. A favorite Indian tactic was to gallop around the enemy, hiding behind horses and shields, deliberately drawing enemy fire. When the enemy's ammunition was exhausted, the Indians darted in to strike him down with arrows and long spears.

Faced with these weapons and tactics, white settlers at first were at a great disadvantage. Their long rifles could be reloaded and fired only with great difficulty from the back of a galloping horse.

A new weapon. The invention of the revolver in the late 1830's soon ended the Indians' temporary superiority in weapons. The revolver could be reloaded easily at full gallop, and several bullets could be fired in rapid succession without reloading. Armed with this new weapon, frontiersmen in the 1850's began to move out onto the plains with new confidence.

New transportation. The early pioneers who crossed the plains on their way west depended upon horses and oxen for transportation. A man on horseback, however, could not transport goods in bulk. To fill his need, caravans of covered wagons lumbered out upon the plains, forming circles around campfires at night for protection against Indian attack. As time passed, stagecoach lines provided speedier transportation.

But it was the railroad that finally provided adequate transportation. Construction of the first transcontinental railroad to the Pacific coast began in 1866. Chinese workers were imported to do most of the physical labor on the Central Pacific. Most of the workers on the Union Pacific, building from Omaha, in Nebraska Territory, were recent Irish immigrants. All work was done under the eyes of scouts, who protected the railroad builders from bands of hostile Indians. The meeting of the rails of the Central Pacific and the Union Pacific at Promontory in what is now Utah (see map, page 445) in 1869 was an occasion of jubilation. Silk-hatted gentlemen, surrounded by workmen, drove a golden spike to hold the last rails in place while the news was telegraphed to Americans everywhere.

The first transcontinental railroad contributed enormously to the nation's economic growth. It brought the Atlantic and the Pacific seaboards within a week's journey of each other, and opened a route to the rich resources of the West.

The railroad carried northerners and southerners alike into the untamed West. It also split the buffalo herds in two. The herds were split again and again as new railroad lines crept across the grasslands. The completion of the Northern Pacific Railway in 1883 sealed the fate of the final, northernmost buffalo herd (see map, page 445).

Destruction of the buffalo. For a few brief years there was wholesale slaughter of the buffalo. Parties of hunters debarked from trains with horses and equipment, killed the buffalo at will, and loaded the hides on trains bound for eastern markets. It has been estimated that between 1871 and 1874 hunters killed nearly 3 million buffalo each year. By 1875 buffalo hides were selling from 65¢ to $1.15 apiece. The waste was frightful. Buffalo carcasses were abandoned, and for every hide taken, four were left on the plains.

■ The telegraph, like the railroad, marked the advance of United States settlement. Perhaps a Plains Indian listening to the "talking wires" also was aware that the telegraph symbolized an end to his own way of life.

The disappearance of the buffalo doomed the Plains Indians, who had built their hunting culture upon the buffalo herds. In destroying the buffalo, white hunters destroyed the Indians' only source of food, clothing, and shelter. Almost the last of the free Indians in the United States were driven on to remote reservations, where they lived as wards —that is, under the protection and control—of the federal government.

Thus the revolver and the railroad, both products of the Industrial Revolution, helped to sweep the Indians from the Great Plains and to open the way for white settlement.

The last Indian wars. Despite their advantages over the Indians, white settlers had to fight long, hard, and ruthlessly to drive the Plains Indians from their hunting grounds. Between 1865 and 1886 the United States conducted a costly and brutal campaign against the Plains Indians. In all the engagements of this campaign, men who had fought on the southern and northern sides in the Civil War now fought together against the Indians.

In 1866 Congress decided to recruit four all-black regiments—the 24th and 25th Infantries, and the 9th and 10th Cavalries—to fight in the Indian wars. One fifth of the army's soldiers on horseback in the western campaigns were enrolled in the 9th and 10th Cavalries.

During the 30-odd years of the Indian wars, the Indians fought back against white and black military forces in an effort to hold on to their lands and to keep their distinctive ways of life. The smaller the area into which they were driven, the more savagely the Indians fought back. But the savagery was by no means all on one side. White leaders fought with broken promises as well as with guns. In 1877, the same year in which Chief Joseph made his heroic attempt to lead his people to freedom in Canada, President Hayes himself told Congress, "Many, if not most, of our Indian wars have their origin in broken promises and acts of injustice on our part."

By the mid-1880's, however, the bloody warfare was over. The Indians were forced onto reservations, often located far from their homelands and with different terrain and climate. Sometimes, to make matters worse, when the Indians had adjusted to life on one reservation, they were uprooted and moved to another. Indians who tried to escape from the reservations were captured and punished. A few Indians continued to resist, but by the mid-1880's their power as a people had been destroyed.

"Americanizing" the Indians. From the point of view of the white settlers, a serious Indian "problem" still remained. About 200,000 to 300,000 of the "original Americans" had to be assimilated into American life. According to the prevailing thought of the time, it was necessary for the Indians to give up their way of life and accept the culture of the white majority. To the Indians, this meant abandoning many Indian customs, such as collective, or tribal, ownership and use of land; marriage traditions; religious beliefs; even their clothing and adornments. Indian braves resented, for example, the efforts of reservation agents to make them cut their long, braided hair.

The vast majority of white Americans neither understood nor appreciated the Indian cultures, and did not recognize their importance to the Indian peoples. The Indians, of course, had no desire to abandon their culture and traditional ways. Thus, the task of "Americanizing" the Indians was to be anything but easy.

Reform activites. Some Americans, however, were deeply troubled by the long history of the white settlers' injustice to the Indians. Helen Hunt Jackson in her book *A Century of Dishonor* (1881) provided documentary evidence of the white man's broken promises. The reformers were also profoundly disturbed by the corruption, inefficiency, and lack of leadership in the Bureau of Indian Affairs.

One reform group, the National Indian Defense Organization, argued that the deep-rooted cultures of the Indians could not be rapidly changed without grave consequences. Members of this group argued that the Indians should be allowed to retain their own traditions and customs. Most other reform organizations, however, believed that the Indians could and should be speedily "Americanized" by persuading them to adopt Christianity, the white man's forms of education, and individual land ownership.

Reformers who urged Americanization of the Indians through individual land ownership, without intending to, actually strengthened the more selfish interests of land speculators, miners, ranchers, and farmers who were already occupying the unsettled areas of the West. These men, coveting the more valuable parts of Indian reservations, supported the reformers' policy of individual Indian ownership, since this would open remaining reservation lands to white occupation.

Writing the policy into law. Responding to such pressures, the federal government in the Dawes Act of 1887 made a general policy of what it had been trying to do in a piecemeal fashion. With the Dawes Act, Congress hoped to hasten the time when the Indians living on reservations would be "Americanized."

The Dawes Act provided that each head of an Indian family could, if he wished, claim 160 acres of reservation land as his own. Bachelors, women, and children were to be entitled to lesser amounts. Legal ownership of the property was to be held in trust by the federal government for 25 years. During this period the Indians could neither sell their land nor use it as security for a mortgage. This restriction was intended to protect the Indians from unscrupulous land speculators. The Burke Act of 1906 modified this provision. It gave the Secretary of the Interior authority to reduce the 25-year period in any case in which he was convinced that the Indian himself was capable of handling his own affairs.

The Dawes Act and the Burke Act also provided that Indians who accepted the land and abandoned their tribal way of life were to be given citizenship, including the right to vote. Meanwhile, Congress appropriated larger but still inadequate funds for the education of Indian children in regular day schools or in boarding schools far from their homes.

Failure of the "Americanization" policy. This federal legislation persuaded and enabled some Indians to adopt the way of life of the white majority and to become American citizens. Even so, Indians who left the reservations to live in American towns and cities often met with discrimination in jobs and unfair treatment. Most Indians remained on the reservations, clinging as best they could to their tribal customs, and living as wards of the federal government. The government policy of encouraging individual land ownership and individual farming among the Indians largely failed when land speculators found loopholes in the Dawes Act. Between 1887 and the 1920's much of the reservation land was, in one way or another, taken from the Indians, and their lot became more desperate.

By the 1920's it was becoming increasingly clear that federal policy was a failure. Nothing in the Indians' tradition had prepared them to be individual farmers. Those who did try to change their way of life were often forced to struggle with the poorest land possible. Moreover, government-sponsored education failed to equip Indian children for the new lives they were expected to live. It also led the children to dislike their elders for stubbornly resisting the tide of "white progress." All too often Indian young people tried to live in two different worlds, neither of which really suited their needs.

In 1924 the Indian population as a whole was given citizenship, partly as a reward for the services of Indian young men who fought in World War I. But citizenship did not lessen the harsh fact that Indian poverty was perhaps greater than that of any other group in the United States. To be sure, the discovery of oil on some Indian lands, among them the Osage reservation in Oklahoma, brought unexpected riches to a few Indians. But for Indians as a whole, conditions remained harsh. The Indian death rate, because of infant mortality and disease among adults, was so high that the Indian population was decreasing. Nor did citizenship diminish the discrimination against and unfair treatment of the Indians by most white Americans.

A new Indian policy. During the 1920's and 1930's the federal government began to move toward a new Indian policy. In 1934 Congress made a notable shift when it adopted the Wheeler-Howard Act.

The new law, sometimes called the Indian Reorganization Act, put a stop to the practice of breaking up the reservations. Indeed, going a step further, it tried to restore to the tribes portions of their land that had not yet been converted into farms. Instead of forcing the Indians to accept changes, as earlier laws had done, the new act permitted tribes to choose whether or not they wanted to practice self-government and whether or not they wanted to strengthen their own community life by emphasizing traditional customs, beliefs, and crafts. The act emphasized local control rather than administrative control from Washington.

The Indian Reorganization Act of 1934 also tried to provide a more effective type of education —an education designed to teach Indians to use their land more effectively through soil conservation and improved methods of raising and marketing their farm products and their livestock. The new educational program, which included adults as well as children, made the schools a center of community life. Encouraged by the new policy, many Indian tribes began to rebuild their tribal way of life and to face the future with new hope.

But problems still remained. Some tribes had succeeded fairly well in becoming Americanized. They rejected the new policy, claiming that it would keep them in an inferior status in relation to the white majority. Tradition-minded chiefs discovered that many of the 25,000 young men who had served in the armed forces during World War II resisted a return to traditional tribal customs. These Indian veterans felt that the full recognition of their rights as citizens was more important than the perpetuation of tribal customs.

Government reversals. During the early 1950's the federal government, preoccupied with other concerns, showed little interest in preserving Indian cultures. Instead of encouraging the development of tribal life, the government tried to persuade Indians to leave the reservations and find work in the cities. At the same time many functions of the Bureau of Indian Affairs were handed over to other federal departments—for example, the Public Health Service. Further, some functions of the federal government concerning the Indians were delegated to the states in which large numbers of Indians lived.

This shift in policy, however, did not last. By the early 1960's the federal government was once again encouraging the development of tribal life on Indian lands. More and more Americans, including Indians themselves, were demanding a better life for the "first Americans." New Indian leaders established national organizations to emphasize their cultural identity while also working for an end to discrimination and unfair treatment.

By the early 1970's the Indians were working to solve their greatest problems—poverty, prejudice, and lack of opportunity—and some progress was being made. The Indian population of the United States, which had been reduced to about 240,000 in the 1920's, had grown to more than 500,000 by the early 1970's. Indians lived in almost every state in the Union, although the great majority lived west of the Mississippi River.

A forward step. Despite limited gains, however, the Indian population continued to face the threat of "forced termination." Forced termination was a long-standing federal policy designed to end all ties between the federal government and the Indians. It involved the eventual ending of government responsibility for Indian welfare, including the tax-exempt status of Indian lands.

In the summer of 1970, President Nixon declared that the federal government was renouncing its policy of forced termination. "Termination," the President said, "implies that the federal government has taken on a trusteeship responsibility . . . as an act of generosity toward a disadvantaged people, and that it can therefore discontinue this responsibility on a unilateral basis whenever it sees fit." But, Nixon continued, this was not the case: "The special relationship between Indians and the federal government is the result . . . of solemn obligations which have been entered into by the United States government. . . ." These obligations "carry immense moral and legal force. . . ." They "cannot be abridged without the consent of the Indians."

At the same time, President Nixon urged Congress to act on a number of proposals aimed at giving the Indians greater control over their own affairs. These proposals included Indian responsibility for the management of federal funds for Indian housing, education, medical services, public works, and economic development.

The Nixon program offered the American Indians a larger measure of control over their own destiny than they had had since the first Europeans landed on the shores of the New World. It remained for Congress to adopt the legislation necessary to put the new program into effect.

SECTION SURVEY

IDENTIFY: Indian reservation, Great Plains, prairies, buffalo, Dawes Act of 1887, Wheeler-Howard Act of 1934; Chief Joseph, Helen Hunt Jackson.

1. (a) In combat, what advantages did the Indians at first have over the frontiersmen? (b) How did the following contribute to the defeat of the Indians—the revolver, the railroads, the destruction of the buffalo?
2. President Hayes said, "Many, if not most, of our Indian wars have had their origin in broken promises and acts of injustice on our part." Explain.
3. What part did each of the following play in the Americanization of the Indians: (a) government policies, (b) reformers?
4. Give arguments for and against the policy of Americanization.
5. (a) What did government Indian policies after 1920 attempt to accomplish? (b) Were these policies successful? Why or why not?

2 The short-lived kingdom of cattlemen on the plains

Cattlemen began to move out onto the Great Plains in the 1860's, long before the Indians were conquered. By the 1890's the cattle industry had become "big business," its products passing from the western ranges through the stockyards, slaughterhouses, and packing plants to become a major item of domestic and world trade.

Rise of the "Cattle Kingdom." Many of the animals for the cattle industry came from ranches in southeastern Texas formerly operated by Spaniards and Mexicans. These ranches were occupied by the Texans, who also took over the huge herds of wild cattle, called longhorns, estimated in 1865 to number about 5 million head. The wild herds sprang from cattle lost by the Spaniards and by the American wagon trains crossing the plains in earlier days.

It was no easy task for the first Texans to learn how to handle the cattle, wild or tame. A writer in the 1870's warned that "the wild cattle of Texas . . . animals miscalled tame, are fifty times more dangerous to a footman than the fiercest buffalo."

In learning how to handle cattle, the Texans owed a good deal to Mexican *vaqueros*° (vah-KAIR·ohs), and to Indians. These men helped to train many slaves in the dangerous business of handling cattle. After emancipation, freedmen provided perhaps one third of the manpower for cattle raising. With the aid of the horse, the saddle, the rope, and the revolver, white and Negro cowboys learned how to handle the longhorns on the open grasslands. Cattle ranching became a profitable occupation and a distinctive way of life.

The "long drive." People in the nation's growing cities needed enormous quantities of beef. The problem was to find a means of transporting the steers to urban markets. Transportation was provided by the railroads, which in the 1860's began to push out upon the Great Plains.

As the steel rails moved westward, enormous herds of steers were driven from Texas north on "long drives" to towns that grew up along the railroads. By 1870 Kansas cattle towns like Abilene, Ellsworth, and Ellis (all on the Kansas Pacific Railroad) and Dodge City and Wichita (on the Atchison, Topeka, and Santa Fe Railway) had become roaring, riotous, lawless communities (see map, page 445).

° *vaquero:* the Spanish word for cowboy.

During the early years of the long drives, nearly all the steers driven from Texas were sold in the cattle towns at good prices. In time, however, the number of cattle began to exceed the demand, and Texans who arrived in late fall were either unable to sell their steers or had to sell them at a loss.

The open range. At this point, enterprising cattlemen began to winter their surplus steers on the open range, or unfenced grazing lands, near the cattle towns. After fattening them during the winter, they sold them at high prices in the towns before the new cattle drives from Texas arrived to glut the market.

This was not the first time that cattle had been pastured on the short grass of the Great Plains. Pioneers crossing the plains to the Southwest and to the Pacific Northwest in the 1830's had watched buffalo grazing. In addition, many wagon trains had wintered on the plains, and the pioneers had discovered that their horses and cattle grew fat on the short and thin, but nutritious, grass. The great freight carriers and stagecoach companies regularly pastured their stock on the open range. The open-range cattle industry did not develop, however, until the railroads provided access to markets, and the Texans provided the cattle.

445

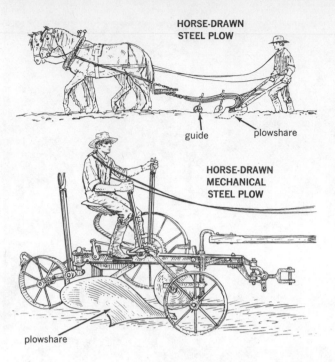

HORSE-DRAWN
STEEL PLOW

guide   plowshare

HORSE-DRAWN
MECHANICAL
STEEL PLOW

plowshare

■ **Improved Farm Implements. Steel "plowshares" (above) were developed to turn in furrows the tough sod of the prairie. Better implements (below) were also developed for breaking the furrows and pulverizing the soil.**

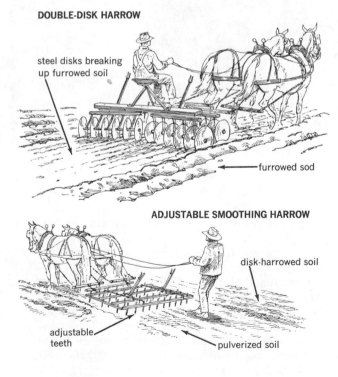

DOUBLE-DISK HARROW

steel disks breaking
up furrowed soil

furrowed sod

ADJUSTABLE SMOOTHING HARROW

adjustable
teeth

disk-harrowed soil

pulverized soil

The cattle rush. News that quick money could be made in the open-range cattle business soon reached the eastern seaboard and spread to Europe. The cattle rush that followed was quite similar to the gold rush that had populated California in 1849–50. Prices for land and steers soared as men on the Great Plains staked out their claims.

Men rushed to the cattle country to make their fortunes. They built dugouts, sod huts, or simple ranch houses, and pastured their herds on the open grasslands. Some, though by no means all, became wealthy.

Until the 1880's the cattlemen ruled the Great Plains. This was the period of the long drive, the open range, the roundup, and the picturesque roving cowboy.

End of the open range. The open-range cattle industry passed, however, almost as quickly as it had started. As the supply of steers rapidly increased, beef prices fell disastrously low. In 1885 a severe drought burned up the grasses on the overstocked range, and cattle starved by the thousands.

Even more disastrous for the cattlemen was the arrival of sheepherders and farmers in the 1880's. Sheep cropped the grass so close that little was left for the cattle. Farmers broke up the open range with their farms and barbed-wire fences (page 449). The cattlemen fought desperately to keep the range open. But they fought a hopeless battle. By the late 1880's the open, unfenced range was fast becoming a thing of the past.

Ranches and fences. By the 1890's the western cattle industry centered in the high plains running through eastern Montana, Wyoming, Colorado, the New Mexico Territory, and western Texas. Most ranchers by now owned and fenced their property with barbed wire.

Ranches varied in size from 2,000 to 100,000 acres. To an easterner, accustomed to small farms of a few hundred acres at most, western ranches seemed enormous. But the ranches had to be large since each steer required a grazing area of 15 to 75 acres, depending upon the amount of rainfall and the resulting growth of grass.

With the invention of better instruments for drilling into the ground and the improvement of windmills for pumping water, many cattlemen watered their stock from wells scattered over their ranches. In years of abundant rainfall, cattlemen might prosper, since their herds could fatten on the natural grasses, but in years of drought cattlemen were forced to feed their cattle hay or cottonseed cake, a costly practice which often wiped out their profits.

■ The cowboys in this 1898 photograph have stopped their hard and dusty work for a quick meal served off the tailgate of a chuck wagon.

Growth and specialization. The development of the railroads revolutionized the cattle industry, which tended to become more and more specialized. Many ranchers on the plains began to concentrate on breeding and raising cattle. The steers were then sold to farmers in the rich corn and pasture lands of the prairies. After being fattened for market, the cattle were shipped to nearby stockyards in Omaha, Kansas City, St. Joseph, Sioux City, St. Paul–Minneapolis, and Chicago (see map, page 445). There they were slaughtered and transported in refrigerator cars to eastern cities and sometimes from there to Europe.

Ranchers used the prairies, the semiarid plains, the high plateaus, and the mountain valleys of the West for cattle grazing lands. On these lands they produced a substantial portion of the nation's meat and wool. By the 1890's the western livestock industry had become an organized, specialized business, closely tied to the nation's economic life.

SECTION SURVEY

IDENTIFY: Cattle Kingdom, longhorns, roundup, ranch, vaqueros.

1. What is the relationship between the railroads and the "long drive"?

2. Explain how cattlemen used the open range of the Great Plains.
3. Give the reason for the cattle rush of the 1870's.
4. Why did the open range disappear?
5. Show how the development of the railroads helped to bring about specialization in the cattle industry.

3 The rapid settlement of the "last frontier" by pioneering farmers

Farmers followed the cattlemen out on the prairies and plains. In about one generation, from 1870 to 1900, pioneers settled more land than had all their American forefathers combined.

In the 263 years from the first tiny settlement at Jamestown in 1607 until 1870, Americans transformed 407,734,041 acres of wilderness into farm land. Mighty though this achievement was, its pace was leisurely compared to the speed with which men conquered the prairies and the plains. In the 30 years between 1870 and 1900 pioneers settled an additional 430 million acres—an area roughly equal to the combined areas of Norway, Sweden, Denmark, the Netherlands, Belgium, Germany, and France.

What was happening in America to make possible this rapid settlement of the last frontier?

Free land for settlers. One attraction of the West was free land. In 1862, as you have read (page 390), Congress enacted the Homestead Act granting 160 acres to any individual who wished to settle a farm, or, as it was called, a "homestead."

Farmers, as well as land speculators, rushed to accept the offer. Thousands were ex-soldiers who sought new homes in the West. Thousands of others came from worn-out farms in the East, particularly from New England, in the hope of finding more fertile land. Still other thousands came from Europe. In many areas of the Middle West, more than half of the pioneers were immigrants—Germans, Norwegians, Swedes, Danes, Czechs, Finns, and Russians.

The railroads and settlement. Without the railroad, however, the free land in the West, no matter how attractive, would have remained unpopulated. During the 1870's and the 1880's four great transcontinental railroads crossed the prairies and the plains. These railroads along with their branch lines opened up the western country for settlement.

The rail lines into and through the wild western country were built only at enormous cost. Moreover, the investment was extremely risky. Investors did not know when, if ever, the new railroads would begin to make a profit and reward them for their risks. Thus the government, which was eager to have the railroads built, encouraged the pioneer railroad companies with cash subsidies and grants of land (see diagram, page 466). The companies used the cash subsidies and money raised from the

sale of some of the land to lay the rails, build the bridges and stations, and buy the engines and cars.

At the time the grants were made to the railroads, the land itself was almost worthless. Before the railroad companies could profit from their grants, they had to persuade people to move into the unsettled areas. Because the land was close to the railroads and therefore would be valuable, the railroad companies could hope to sell it, even though free land was available in more remote areas. But even more important was the fact that once the land was settled, the railroads would gain revenue from passengers and freight. In addition, any land that the railroads could not sell would rise in value as settlers built farms, villages, and towns along the right of way.

With these considerations in mind, the railroads launched extensive advertising campaigns, sending literature and agents even into Europe. Life on the plains was pictured in glowing colors, and as an added inducement the prospective purchaser was frequently offered free railroad transportation to any land that he might buy. The transatlantic steamship lines, always eager to obtain passengers and freight, also launched advertising campaigns in Europe.

The problem of houses and fences. Despite these inducements, settlers did not at first pour into the plains. For one thing, many still believed the old myth of the "Great American Desert." An even more important factor was the scarcity of wood.

The pioneers solved the problem of housing, as men have always done, by making use of the best available building material. On the plains this was sod. Cut out of the soil, bricklike chunks of sod formed the walls of shelters. With a few precious pieces of wood the settlers framed the roof, finishing it with a layer of sod to keep out wind and rain and snow.

Fencing presented an even more difficult problem. The pioneers could not farm without fences to protect their crops, and on the plains there was no material for fences.

During the 1870's nearly every newspaper on the edge of the plains carried long articles on the problem of fencing. The first pioneers tried everything, even mud walls, but without success. Ordinary wire strung between a few precious wooden posts was not effective, for cattle could get their heads through the smooth strands of wire and gradually work an opening in the fence.

The problem of fencing was finally solved by a New Hampshire-born Yankee, Joseph Glidden,

■ **Barbed-wire Fence.** On the Great Plains, which were largely treeless, farmers could not build fences from tree-stumps or boards. "Barbed wire," which cattle learned to avoid, was finally the answer. Fence posts were made from scrap lumber or from limbs of the few trees that grew on the plains.

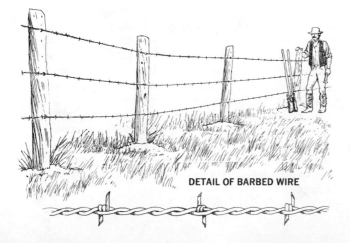

DETAIL OF BARBED WIRE

■ This farm family had their picture taken outside their sod home in Custer County, Nebraska, in 1888. Why was their house not made of wood?

who had moved to De Kalb, Illinois. His solution was barbed wire—that is, wire with sharp, projecting points. Glidden took out his patent in 1874. Barbed-wire fences proved effective as a barrier to cattle, and within 10 years the open range was criss-crossed by a network of barbed-wire fences.

The problem of water. Scarcity of water, like scarcity of wood, was a problem that the pioneer farmers had never had to face in the eastern part of the United States or in the European countries from which they had migrated. Eastern farmers secured their water from springs bubbling to the surface or from shallow wells dug 20 to 30 feet to the *water table* ° underground. They hauled it to the surface in buckets or pumped it up easily by hand; later, in the 1900's, they pumped it by gasoline-driven or electric pumps. But on the Great Plains, where the water table was much deeper, machinery was needed to drill deeper wells. And once the well shafts had reached the water table, the farmers needed mechanical pumps to draw the water to the surface.

° *water table:* the depth below which the ground is saturated with water.

In a search for oil during the 1860's, petroleum companies developed new drilling machinery capable of penetrating farther beneath the surface than ever before. This machinery speedily found its way to the Great Plains, where it was used to tap underground water supplies.

Meanwhile, other inventors were developing windmills capable of operating pumps to draw water to the surface. Another New Englander, Daniel Halladay of Connecticut, developed the self-governing windmill that automatically adjusted itself to wind pressure, and thus operated at a uniform speed.

Windmills were first used, as you know, by cattlemen to provide water for their stock and for steam locomotives crossing the plains. But the windmill really came into its own when farmers began to settle on the semiarid lands. Factories producing windmills were soon doing a thriving business.

Other problems of the settlers. Railroads, barbed wire, factory-made windmills—all products of the new industrial age—helped the farmer conquer the Great Plains. So, too, did the development of "dry farming," a better method for farming areas with limited amounts of rainfall. "Dry farming"

449

■ In the latter half of the 1800's, states, railroads, and private land companies advertised the western lands in glowing colors to attract settlers.

involved deep plowing and careful cultivation to keep the surface of the soil pulverized and thus conserve as much precious moisture as possible. The development of improved farm machinery also helped to lighten the farmer's work.

But the pioneers had other problems to solve, problems for which inventors, manufacturers, and agricultural experts had no ready answers. For one thing, the cattlemen resented the settlers who broke up the open range with their fences. Bitter fights raged in the early days between cattlemen and farmers, and many unmarked graves soon dotted the plains. But it was an unequal struggle, for by sheer force of numbers the farmers eventually won.

Nature also contributed to the settlers' difficulties. Until men learned how to deal with the plains environment, life was sometimes harsh beyond endurance. The unrelieved round of daily labor impressed writers who tried to describe the life of the farmers on the Great Plains. The novels of O. E. Rölvaag (ROHL·vahg), *Giants in the Earth* and *Peder Victorious,* give a picture of empty plains and lives spent beneath a burning sun, of grasshopper plagues, of drought, of ruined crops, of bitter cold and blinding blizzards. Many pioneers gave up the struggle and moved back east. But others remained and forced the plains to yield their treasures.

In addition to the same problems faced by the early settlers, farmers in the 1880's and 1890's encountered many new problems created by industrialism. In the new industrial age, as you will see, the farmer became increasingly concerned with freight and shipping charges, prices established in distant markets, the cost of farm machinery, interest rates on mortgages, and many other factors he could not control.

The Oklahoma "Sooners." In spite of all obstacles, however, land-hungry farmers continued to push out upon the plains, fencing the land as they advanced, building homes and villages—and new states.

One dramatic example of the land hunger of American pioneers occurred in 1889. On March 23 of that year, President Benjamin Harrison issued a proclamation that set in motion a wild rush toward the "District of Oklahoma." The President announced that free homesteads of 160 acres would be available "at and after the hour of twelve o'clock noon, on the twenty-second day of April." The army immediately established patrols along the district boundaries to guard against premature entry, and waited for the rush to begin.

It was a short wait. By April 22 almost 100,000 land-hungry pioneers—some in wagons, some on horseback—were packed solidly along the boundary line. Exactly at noon the officer in charge fired a shot, and the wild stampede began.

But even the swiftest riders discovered that they were not there "soon" enough. Despite army precautions, many "Sooners" had evaded the patrols, slipped across the boundary, and staked out claims before the area was officially opened.

Within a few hours of the deadline, every inch of "Oklahoma District" was occupied. Thousands of disappointed landseekers started back along the roads they had eagerly traveled earlier.

The last frontier. The roll call of states entering the Union in the half-century after 1865 is an impressive one—Nebraska in 1867; Colorado in 1876; North Dakota, South Dakota, Montana, and Washington in 1889; Idaho and Wyoming in 1890; Utah in 1896; Oklahoma in 1907; and New Mexico and Arizona in 1912.

In 1890 the Superintendent of the United States Census made a significant statement: "Up to and including 1880," he declared, "the country had a frontier of settlement, but at present the unsettled area has been so broken into by isolated bodies of settlement that there can hardly be said to be a frontier line."

SECTION SURVEY

IDENTIFY: sod houses, "dry farming," Oklahoma "Sooners," the last frontier; Joseph Glidden, Daniel Halladay.

1. How was western settlement speeded by (a) the Homestead Act, (b) the railroads?
2. How did the farmers on the plains solve the problems of housing and fencing?
3. Discuss the importance of the windmill to the Great Plains farmers.
4. If you had been living on the Great Plains in the late 1800's, what problems and pleasures might you have experienced?

4 The discovery of mineral treasures in the western mountains

Developments of the new industrial age made it possible for the farmer to conquer the last western frontiers. But the West in turn helped to speed the Industrial Revolution. From western farms came unending food supplies for the growing city populations. From western mines came an apparently limitless supply of gold and silver to provide capital to build industries. From other western mines came a steadily swelling volume of iron, copper, and other metals.

From "Forty-Niners" to "Fifty-Niners." The discovery of gold in California drew men by the tens of thousands to the Pacific coast in 1849–50. Some of the "Forty-Niners" made fortunes, but most were disappointed. Refusing to admit defeat, prospectors began to explore the valleys and slopes of the mountainous regions between the Pacific Ocean and the Great Plains.

In 1859 prospectors discovered gold near Pikes Peak in the unorganized territory of Colorado. More than 100,000 "Fifty-Niners" rushed to the scene to stake their claims. Caravans of covered wagons lumbered across the plains with the slogan "Pikes Peak or bust" lettered on the white canvas. Some men shouldered packs and crossed the plains on foot. Others pulled handcarts behind them. Perhaps half of the fortune hunters returned the way they had come, with their slogan changed to "Busted, by gosh!" Nevertheless, enough remained to organize the Territory of Colorado in 1861; in 1876, as you know, the state of Colorado was admitted to the Union.

Even more valuable than the Colorado deposits were the discoveries of silver in 1859 in the western part of the Territory of Utah. Within a decade nearly $150 million worth of silver and gold had been extracted from the famous Comstock Lode in what is now Nevada (see map, page 445), and by 1890 the total had reached $340 million. Enough of the original prospectors stayed after the stampede of 1859 to organize the Territory of Nevada, which became a state in 1864.

Gold in the Black Hills. In 1874 other prospectors discovered gold in the Black Hills of South Dakota (see map, page 445), and another gold rush followed. This area was Indian territory, the Sioux Reservation, and the federal government tried to keep the prospectors out of the region. The lure of gold was too strong, however, and the government soon abandoned its efforts to protect the Indians. In 1877 the government opened the entire area to white settlers.

Early mining communities. During and after the Civil War, mining communities sprang up literally overnight in many areas of the West. Life in these mining camps has been described vividly in *The Luck of Roaring Camp* by Bret Harte and in *Roughing It* by Mark Twain. These and other contemporary accounts present a picture of wild, lawless communities of tents, rough board shacks, and smoke-filled saloons strung along a muddy street.

Each mining camp passed through several stages of development. At first, every man was a law unto himself, relying for safety upon his fists or his guns. Then some citizens began to organize their own private police force, often called "vigilantes" (vij·i·LAN·tees), in an effort to maintain order. Soon they built schools and churches—crude shacks, perhaps, but important steps toward civilized liv-

■ As this painting shows, the lack of women in western mining camps did not prevent the miners from holding dances. "Ladies" at the dance were designated by a patch on their clothing or a handkerchief worn on their sleeves.

ing. With the schools and churches came organized local government. Then came the appeal to Congress for recognition as a United States Territory, and eventually the adoption of a constitution and admission to the Union as a state.

Today the mountain regions, the valleys, and the high plateaus of the West are dotted with abandoned mining communities—ghost towns, as they are called. The abandoned mine shafts and the sagging, windowless cabins stand as mute testimony to the fact that prospectors and miners once pioneered on this vast frontier.

Systematic exploration.   The early discoveries of gold and silver acted like magnets, drawing adventuresome prospectors into the unexplored mountainous regions of the West. Before long, however, exploration was conducted on a more system-

atic basis, partly through federal efforts. Between 1865 and 1879 the federal government sent many expeditions into the mountains, and in 1879 the United States Geological Survey was organized. Private industry also sent out carefully organized expeditions. The picturesque prospector with his pack horse and hand tools continued to roam the mountains, but long before the end of the 1800's an increasing number of the mineral deposits were being discovered by expeditions equipped with the latest technological devices and knowledge of geology.

Minerals for industry.   The development of the nation's industries brought a growing demand for metals of all kinds. The list of minerals discovered in the western mountains is impressive. Copper, needed when the electrical industry developed, was found in enormous quantities around Butte, Montana; Bingham, Utah; and in Nevada and Arizona. Lead and zinc were discovered in the same area. These and other metals have helped the United States to become the leading industrial nation in the world.

Mining as big business.   The systematic exploration for mineral wealth was paralleled by other developments that brought about great changes in mining. New methods of extracting the metal from the ore were discovered, colleges of mining engineering were opened, powerful machinery was invented, great corporations were organized, and armies of skilled technicians and engineers moved into the mining regions. New equipment and the growing knowledge of chemistry and metallurgy enabled companies to work low-grade ores with profit.

By the 1890's mining had become "big business." Engineers, equipped with the latest tools of science and technology, were converting the West into a region of enormous value to the industrial development of the nation.

SECTION SURVEY

IDENTIFY: "Pikes Peak or bust," Comstock Lode, vigilantes, ghost towns; Bret Harte, Mark Twain.

1. Who were the "Fifty-Niners"?
2. Describe life in the early mining communities and the stages of development they went through.
3. How and why was the picturesque prospector replaced by systematic exploration?
4. Why did mining become "big business" by 1890?
5. What is the connection between the West and the Industrial Revolution?

TRACING THE MAIN IDEAS

The conquest of the Plains Indians and the settlement of the lands west of the Mississippi River took place, for the most part, in the years following 1865. Although by the 1890's the process was not complete, settlers had poured into the prairies and plains in such numbers that the Superintendent of the Census could announce that the frontier no longer existed.

The development of the resources of this vast region, almost one half the total area of the present United States, called forth all the courage and intelligence that men could command. The West was not one region, but many regions, each basically different from the others. Each group of settlers—cattlemen, farmers, and miners—learned to adapt themselves to their environment and to make use of the most easily developed natural resources—the grasslands, the fertile soil, and the metals. As the years passed, they learned how to modify the environment and to seek out and develop other resources.

The conquest of the West was, in one sense, merely a prelude to an even larger chapter in American history—the transformation of the nation from a predominantly agricultural country to one of the great industrial giants of the modern world. That transformation is the subject of Unit Seven and of later chapters in this book.

CHAPTER SURVEY

QUESTIONS FOR DISCUSSION

1. (a) Which of the reform groups concerned with the Indians best understood their problems? Explain the reasons for your choice. (b) Should the question of how to "Americanize" the Indian ever have arisen? Why or why not?
2. Technological developments such as railroads, barbed wire, and factory-made windmills helped the farmer to conquer the Great Plains. Explain.
3. The last frontier disappeared in 1890. (a) Explain how this occurred. (b) What in your opinion is the significance of the frontier in American history?
4. (a) How well do you think western stories and movies show life as it really was in the West between 1870 and 1890? (b) Which aspects of western life are overstressed? (c) Which are neglected?
5. Why does the life of the open range and the mining camps still appeal to the imaginations of millions of Americans?
6. In what ways did the federal government encourage the settlement and development of the West?

RELATING PAST TO PRESENT

1. What part has racial prejudice played in the history of the American Indian?

2. Compare early government policies regarding the Indian with the policies of today. Are they different? Explain.
3. Is scarcity of water still a problem in the West today? Cite evidence to support your answer.
4. President John F. Kennedy named the reform program of his administration the "New Frontier." What historical appeal was he making to Americans?

USING MAPS AND CHARTS

1. Using the map on pages 852–53, locate the Great Plains. Describe the characteristics and climate of this region.
2. Consulting the maps on pages 864–65 and 870–71, describe the agricultural and industrial development that has taken place in the Great Plains region.
3. Using the map on page 445, answer the following: (a) How many railroads connected the Middle West with the Far West? (b) What was the significance of Promontory? of the Comstock Lode? (c) Where did the western cattle business begin? (d) How many railroads were available to cattlemen using the Chisholm Trail? the Western Trail?

UNIT SURVEY

OUTSTANDING EVENTS

1868 Fourteenth Amendment is ratified.
1868 House of Representatives impeaches Johnson.
1868 Ulysses S. Grant is elected President.
1869 First transcontinental railroad is completed.
1870 Fifteenth Amendment is ratified.
1872 Grant is re-elected President.
1876 Rutherford B. Hayes is elected President.
1880 James A. Garfield is elected President.
1881 Garfield is assassinated, Chester A. Arthur becomes President.
1884 Grover Cleveland is elected President.
1888 Benjamin Harrison is elected President.
1892 Grover Cleveland is elected President.

FOR FURTHER INQUIRY

1. Describe the views held by W. E. B. Du Bois with regard to the status of the Negro in American life.
2. Beginning in the 1880's and continuing until the 1930's the United States tried to solve the Indian problem by getting rid of the Indian. Do you agree or disagree? Explain.
3. In 1954, the Supreme Court ruled in *Brown v. Board of Education of Topeka* that "separate but equal" facilities for Negroes were unconstitutional. Compare this case with the *Plessy v. Ferguson* decision in 1896. How did each decision affect the status of the black American?

PROJECTS AND ACTIVITIES

1. Imagine that you are a journalist in the South immediately after the Civil War, and write a feature story describing the political, economic, and social conditions you see around you.
2. Research a report on the individual experiences of ex-slaves after the Civil War.
3. Two students can present opposing views of the reconstruction governments in the South: one student can defend the accomplishments of these governments and the other student can attack their failings.
4. A group of students can prepare and present a dramatization of the impeachment of Andrew Johnson.
5. For an account of the removal from their lands of the Indians, see pages 201–13 of Joseph E. Gould's *Challenge and Change* (Harcourt Brace Jovanovich, Inc.).
6. Research and present a report on the history of Indian reservations in the United States. The report should include an account of actions currently being taken by American Indians to secure their full civil rights.

USING THE SOCIAL SCIENCES

(Read pages 456–62 before you answer the following questions.)

1. Explain how the same region of the United States might comprise several different frontiers.
2. Do you think the frontier region in the Soviet Union influenced that nation's history in the same way that the frontier region of the United States influenced American history? Explain. What kind of research must you do in order to arrive at an understanding of this question?
3. Are Americans of today less influenced than earlier Americans by the region in which they live? Why or why not?
4. Among the geographical concepts discussed in this case study are the conflicts due to differing ideas on the use of resources, and how resources affect settlement patterns. How do these concepts apply to the North and South before the Civil War? Can these concepts help to explain some of the causes of the Civil War? If so, how?

SUGGESTED FURTHER READING

Biography

BROWN, DEE, *The Gentle Tamers: Women of the Old Wild West*, Putnam.

BURGER, NASH K., and JOHN K. BETTERSWORTH, *South of Appomattox*, Harcourt Brace Jovanovich. Ten biographies of southerners.

CLEMENS, SAMUEL L., *Life on the Mississippi*, Harper & Row; and others. Mark Twain's life as a river pilot.

——, *Roughing It*, Harper & Row; Holt, Rinehart & Winston (paper). Silver rush to Nevada.

DUBERMAN, MARTIN B., *Charles Francis Adams*, Houghton Mifflin.

FUESS, CLAUDE M., *Carl Schurz, Reformer*, Dodd, Mead.

GRAHAM, SHIRLEY, and GEORGE LIPSCOMB, *George Washington Carver, Scientist*, Messner.

HOWE, MARK DE WOLFE, *Oliver Wendell Holmes: The Proving Years, 1870–1882*, Harvard Univ. Press.

KORNGOLD, RALPH, *Thaddeus Stevens*, Harcourt Brace Jovanovich.

MC KITRICK, ERIC L., *Andrew Johnson and Reconstruction*, Univ. of Chicago Press.

NEVINS, ALLAN, *Grover Cleveland: A Study in Courage*, Dodd, Mead.

SEITZ, DON CARLOS, *Horace Greeley*, Bobbs-Merrill.

STRYKER, LLOYD PAUL, *Andrew Johnson, A Study in Courage*, Macmillan.

VAN DEUSEN, GLYNDON, *Horace Greeley: Nineteenth-Century Crusader*, Hill & Wang (paper).

WASHINGTON, BOOKER T., *Up from Slavery*, Houghton Mifflin; and others. Autobiographical.

WINSTON, R. W., *Andrew Johnson, Plebeian and Patriot,* Holt, Rinehart & Winston.

Other Nonfiction

ATHERTON, LEWIS, *The Cattle King,* Indiana Univ. Press.

BILLINGTON, RAY ALLEN, with JAMES BLAINE HEDGES, *Westward Expansion,* Macmillan.

BOWERS, CLAUDE G., *The Tragic Era,* Houghton Mifflin. Reconstruction.

BUCK, PAUL, *The Road to Reunion, 1865–1900,* Random House (Vintage Books); Peter Smith.

CASH, W. J., *The Mind of the South,* Random House (Vintage Books, paper). Analysis of southern philosophy, temperament, and mores by a small-town newspaper editor.

CLARK, IRA G., *Then Came the Railroads,* Univ. of Oklahoma Press.

COULTER, E. MERTON, *The South During the Reconstruction, 1865–1877,* Louisiana State Univ. Press.

CURRENT, RICHARD, ed. *Reconstruction, 1865–1877,* Prentice-Hall (Spectrum Books, paper). Primary sources.

DICK, EVERETT NEWTON, *Sod House Frontier, 1854–1890,* Johnson. Social history.

DRISKO, CAROL F., and EDGAR A. TOPPIN, *The Unfinished March,* Doubleday (paper). The civil rights movement.

DURHAM, PHILIP, and EVERETT L. JONES, *The Negro Cowboys,* Dodd, Mead. Negro cowboys who rode the western trails after the Civil War; contains photographs.

FRANKLIN, JOHN HOPE, *From Slavery to Freedom: A History of American Negroes,* Knopf.

——, *Reconstruction After the Civil War,* Univ. of Chicago Press.

HOLBROOK, STEWART, *American Lumberjack,* Macmillan (Collier Books, paper). A history of lumberjacks, their camp lore, and the age they lived in.

——, *The Story of American Railroads,* Crown.

HOOGENBOOM, ARI, *Outlawing the Spoils: A History of the Civil Service Reform Movement, 1865–1883,* Univ. of Illinois Press.

JACKSON, HELEN HUNT, *A Century of Dishonor,* Torch.

JOSEPHSON, MATTHEW, *The Politicos,* Harcourt Brace Jovanovich. The political parties and the professional politicians who emerged after the Civil War.

LA FARGE, OLIVER, *A Pictorial History of the American Indian,* Crown.

MELTZER, MILTON, *In Their Own Words,* Thomas Y. Crowell (paper). Includes text and documents written by black Americans during reconstruction; illustrated.

MILTON, GEORGE FORT, *The Age of Hate,* Coward-McCann. Andrew Johnson and the radicals.

MOODY, JOHN, *The Railroad Builders,* Yale Univ. Press.

NELSON, BRUCE, *Land of the Dacotahs,* Bison.

ORTH, S. P., *The Boss and the Machine,* Yale Univ. Press.

PARKHILL, FORBES, *The Last of the Indian Wars,* Crowell Collier and Macmillan.

PAUL, RODMAN WILSON, *Mining Frontiers of the Far West, 1848–1880,* Holt, Rinehart & Winston.

RANDALL, JAMES G., *The Civil War and Reconstruction,* Heath.

SIMKINS, F. B., *History of the South,* Knopf.

SPENCER, SAMUEL REID, *Booker T. Washington and the Negro's Place in American Life,* Little, Brown.

STILL, BAYRD, ed. *The West: Contemporary Records of America's Expansion Across the Continent, 1697–1890.* Putnam (Capricorn Books, paper). Primary sources and eyewitness accounts pertaining to America's expansion.

STONE, IRVING, *The Men to Match My Mountains,* Doubleday. About the West.

WEBB, WALTER PRESCOTT, *The Great Plains,* Ginn; Grosset & Dunlap (paper).

WOODWARD, C. VANN, *Origins of the New South, 1877–1913,* Louisiana State Univ. Press.

——, *The Strange Career of Jim Crow: A Brief Account of Segregation,* Oxford Univ. Press (Galaxy Books, paper). Segregation in the South from 1877 to the present.

Historical Fiction

BUSCH, NIVEN, *Duel in the Sun,* Morrow; and others. Excellent western.

CATHER, WILLA, *Death Comes to the Archbishop,* Knopf. Novel about the West.

——, *My Antonia,* Houghton Mifflin. Novel about the West.

——, *O Pioneers!,* Houghton Mifflin. Novel about settlement of West.

CLARK, WALTER VAN TILBURG, *The Ox-Bow Incident,* New American Library (Signet Books). Western novel.

FERBER, EDNA, *Cimarron,* Doubleday; and others. The rush of settlers into Oklahoma.

FORD, PAUL LEICESTER, *The Honorable Peter Sterling,* Hillary House. Rise of a political boss.

GREY, ZANE, *The U. P. Trail,* Grosset & Dunlap; Pocket Books. Railroad building.

JACKSON, HELEN HUNT, *Ramona,* Little, Brown; Grosset & Dunlap. Plight of the Indians.

LA FARGE, OLIVER, *Laughing Boy,* Houghton Mifflin; Pocket Books. Navajo culture.

MITCHELL, MARGARET, *Gone with the Wind,* Macmillan; Pocket Books. Famous novel about the Civil War and the reconstruction period.

RÖLVAAG, OLE EDVART, *Giants in the Earth,* Harper & Row. Pioneers in North Dakota.

WISTER, OWEN, *The Virginian,* Macmillan; and others. Novel with cowboy hero.

HISTORY AND THE SOCIAL SCIENCES

GEOGRAPHY

Nature of Geography

Of all the social sciences, geography is probably the most misunderstood. Most people think that geography is concerned primarily with the reading of maps or with the listing of mountains, rivers, cities, crops, and resources in order to describe a particular country. Geographers maintain that this is, in fact, a misrepresentation of their discipline.

Geography, or the New Geography, is interested primarily in studying regions—or particular places on the face of the earth. The geographer wants to find the common characteristics that identify various places and regions of the world. The modern geographer, however, does not want to make a mere listing of these characteristics. Rather, he wants to find out how these characteristics are related. He is interested in understanding how the physical, human, and cultural characteristics of a particular place have blended to make that place a region.

A region can be large or small. It can be the Mekong Valley in Vietnam or the city of Chicago in Illinois. To identify the common characteristics that identify a place as a distinct region, a geographer must study land formations, water supply, and climate. He must also study patterns of population density, occupations of people living in the area, income per capita, diet, and, very often, values and beliefs. And finally, and most important, the geographer must determine the relationships that exist among these characteristics. How do they affect one another? How do they all combine to form a unique region—one that is distinct from all other regions of the world?

Some geographers look upon themselves as natural scientists rather than social scientists. These geographers deal with earth science—an important branch of geography. Earth science focuses on the study of the earth, mountains, oceans, and atmosphere, as well as the relationship between the earth, man, the sun, and the planets.

But many other geographers regard themselves as social scientists. Geography as a social science is man-centered. It studies the earth as the home of man. The cultural geographer, as he is sometimes called, studies the physical environment—but only insofar as it is the theater of human operations. It is the way in which man uses, shapes, and lives in the physical environment that is of major interest to cultural geographers.

Cultural geographers reject the simplistic notion that man is shaped by his physical environment. Instead they suggest that man, more often than not, reshapes and remakes his physical environment. Different cultures have in the past, and do now, use the same physical environment in different ways. The physical environment in the United States was basically the same for the Indians and for later settlers, but the Indians used it differently than the later settlers did. How do men use their available resources? How do they adapt to their physical environment? How do they change their physical environment by using their special skills and accumulated knowledge? These are questions investigated by geographers.

To understand the interrelationships and interaction between man and his physical environment, the geographer, as social scientist, studies cultural and social factors. He studies the distribution of languages, technological skills, religious beliefs, types of housing, and the use of domestic animals. This is not to say that the cultural geographer ignores physical characteristics. He does not. But he maintains that, in order to obtain an accurate picture of

The Mekong Valley region in Vietnam

a region, it is absolutely essential to study cultural as well as physical characteristics, for customs, traditions, and cultural and religious beliefs have often shaped the landscape and changed the physical environment. The cultural geographer would contend, for example, that the religious beliefs of the ancient Egyptians had a decisive influence on the use they made of their physical environment and on the type of buildings they constructed and left behind. He would also maintain that cultural mores, educational values, and idealistic aspirations have shaped and transformed the physical landscape of present-day Israel.

Whereas historians are interested in examining the totality of human experience within the framework of *time* relationships, geographers concentrate on examining the totality of human experience within the framework of *space* relationships. A geographer tries to know and to understand all that he can about a human environment on the face of the earth in the same way that a historian attempts to learn all that he can about a human event in the past.

Geographers try to find patterns of similarity that distinguish various regions of the world—characteristics that endow the regions with some degree of unity and some degree of uniqueness. In so doing, geographers help to throw light on the world in which we live—from small units like our local community or our city to larger units like our nation and our world—thus helping us to observe our environment more intelligently and perceptively.

Concepts of Geography

Geographers believe that the face of the earth can be divided into many different regions. **Region** is undoubtedly the most important concept in geography.

Geographers define a region as an area of any size that has a considerable number of common physical and cultural characteristics. The physical characteristics examined by geographers in their attempt to define a region would include climate, rivers, mountains, and resources. The cultural characteristics would include population density, religious beliefs, technical skills, food habits, and availability of health services.

Modern geographers study an area from every possible aspect, trying to comprehend the arrangement of things and forces that make a particular region or area different from all other regions or areas. They want to study the character of various regions on the surface of the earth to attempt to learn about their unifying features. In looking at the region of Soviet Siberia, for example, geographers would study the climate, the landscape, the rainfall, the density of population, the cities, the industrial centers, and the beliefs and customs of the people living in the area. Under the new geography, too, such a study, to be complete, would include the political aspects of the Soviet government's drive to colonize Siberia, as well as a study of the region's military and strategic importance.

However, modern geographers want to do much more than make a listing of a region's physical and cultural characteristics. They are interested primarily in understanding the relationships among these characteristics. In other words, they want to examine **spatial relationships,** or relationships in space—another important geographic concept.

Geographers assume that a region's characteristics do not exist in a haphazard, unrelated fashion, but rather that they are related and interact to affect one another. In studying the physical and cultural characteristics of a region, then, a geographer would try to determine how these characteristics affect one another. How, for example, is landscape related to the location of industrial centers? How are climate and rainfall related to population density? How do religious beliefs and cultural traditions affect the way the people use their physical environment? And how do all these characteristics combine to give a region its distinctive pattern—the individuality which distinguishes it from any other place? His study of an area's spatial relationships, then, helps a geographer capture the uniqueness of a specific region of the world.

Another important concept studied by geographers is **spatial interaction.** This means that geographers study one place as it relates to another. Geographers might, for example, study the spatial interaction that exists between Chicago and the nearby suburb of Evanston. Chicago and Evanston interact because they have a connecting relationship. They share certain common interests and problems, such as air and water pollution, police and fire protection, and maintenance of roads. It is to the mutual benefit of both communities to work together in tackling these problems.

Chicago and Evanston are interdependent in other ways also. For example, most people in Evanston work in Chicago and use Chicago as their chief center for shopping and for entertainment. Conversely, many people working in Chicago live in suburbs such as Evanston. Geographers are interested in determining the spatial relations and the spatial interaction that exist between such interdependent localities.

Geographers have found that spatial relations and spatial interaction are not static. They are always changing. They are always being redefined. For example, the building of the Hoover Dam led to a new system of spatial relations and spatial interaction among communities in the area. This interaction included the use of water, effects on new and old industries, changes in modes of living, new amusement areas, new communcation systems, a new distribution of churches and schools, and, of course, new ways of thinking and behaving by the people involved.

Geographers stress also that neither regions nor places are static. A place designated by a geographer as a central location—meaning that it is a place to which people, goods, and ideas gravitate—may in time lose its importance. The Suez Canal, as recent events in the Middle East have shown, has lost much of its previous importance. On the other hand, the new Aswan Dam, built in the same area, has become a new place of centrality.

Methods of Geography

Many geographers study and identify regions on the surface of the earth. What methods do they use to pursue this task?

In pursuing their inquiries, geographers use many of the methods used by other social scientists. The geographer is committed to a scientific method of investigation. He studies his subject as objectively as possible, collecting all available information. Then he carefully classifies and measures the data and information he collects.

The geographer begins by postulating a hypothesis. For example, he might state that a given area under study *is* a region, meaning that it has a sufficient number of unifying physical and cultural characteristics to make it a distinct area on the face of the earth. When a geographer proceeds in this way, he is using a **regional approach.**

Sometimes a geographer approaches his inquiry by posing a more general

How is climate related to population density in this Alaskan community?

question, such as: What are the major electric power stations in India and why are they where they are? If the geographer proceeds in this manner, he is using a **topical approach.**

Whether he is using a regional or a topical approach, the geographer next begins to collect data to test his hypothesis or to answer the question that he has posed. One way of collecting the necessary data is to make and study **maps.**

Some maps will aid the geographer in his analysis of the physical features of the area he is studying. Others will give him a graphic picture of the yearly rainfall. And still other maps will provide him with information on population density, crops grown, and the area's communication and transportation network. A thorough knowledge of cartography—or the ability to make and interpret maps—is an essential skill required of the geographer in collecting his data.

Another method a geographer uses to collect his data is **field observation.** Geographers feel that it is not enough for them to read about an area or to study it on maps. They believe that it is necessary for them to go out into the field to observe the area they are studying first hand. Geographers know that men have always influenced and continue to influence and change their physical environment. And geographers know that, to make a thorough investigation of a region, they must study these humanized landscapes for themselves.

In the course of his field observation a geographer might study, for example, an area's farm land to see how it has been changed by human hands, by machines, and by human ingenuity. A geographer would also make the same kind of first-hand observation of the humanized landscape of the area's lakes, mountains, cities, and suburbs.

After gathering his data, a geographer must analyze it. Modern geographers, like many of their colleagues in the other social sciences, have begun to rely more and more on **statistical analysis** of their data; often using computers. Instead of just describing or listing the spatial relationships which he has observed, such as the relationship of rainfall to population density, a geographer attempts to measure these relationships with mathematical precision. Although geographers differ on the exact significance of the use of statistical methods in their studies, they all agree that use of mathematical models can be important.

Finally, after gathering and analyzing his data statistically, the geographer must form his conclusions by testing his original hypothesis in the light of his research and observations. Suppose, for example, that he has been using the regional approach and now wants to decide whether the area he has studied is indeed a unique region with unifying characteristics. Out of hundreds or even thousands of features of the area he has examined, he must now select only those features which give the area an identity—an overall character. Like a historian, he must study and then carefully discard hundreds of unimportant details that do not focus on the area's dominant features. Finally, after examining his data, the geographer concludes his study by confirming, rejecting, or revising his original hypothesis. He may find, for example, that the area under study is indeed a region, but that the boundaries of that region, as he originally conceived them, were incorrect.

To reach a valid conclusion, the geographer must be able to comprehend how the various areas on the earth differ from one another—and how they are interrelated. As you can see, the knowledge, judgment, and skills required of the modern geographer are impressive indeed.

Why must a geographer have a thorough knowledge of cartography?

CASE STUDY IN GEOGRAPHY

The Concept of the Frontier

The word "frontier" undoubtedly evokes immediate pictures in your mind. Cowboys driving cattle along dusty trails. A ramshackle mining community perched on the side of a hill. A lonely farm dwelling sitting in the middle of a vast treeless plain. All of these scenes are typical of a frontier in the United States. But what, if anything, do they have in common that might help us understand the frontier as a single phenomenon?

One similarity common to all the frontier scenes described above appears to be the exploitation of physical resources—the grasslands for cattle raising, the valuable minerals for mining, the land for farming. However, exploitation of physical resources alone is not sufficient for defining a frontier. After all, the Indians had been exploiting the grasslands of the Great Plains long before the United States called the area a frontier.

Another essential factor common to all frontiers is that they must, by definition, be associated in some way—by settlement or by control—with a particular society. The frontiers of the United States advanced into territory that was, for the most part, owned by the United States but not occupied at first by white Americans.

Also essential in defining the frontier is the characteristic of newness. All the frontiers of the United States were new areas of exploitation for settlers from the settled portions of the United States or Europe. Either the resource itself was new—the minerals or the grasslands—or the type of exploitation was new—farming on the Great Plains.

When we talk about a frontier, we are talking about a specific area on the face of the earth. But this area can and does change—in both time and space. For example, in the United States, the farming frontier tended to be a zone which gradually moved westward from its starting point on the east coast. The movement of the mining frontier, on the other hand, tended to be more sporadic, moving from California where gold was discovered in 1849 to various other points in the western mountains at different times.

In the remainder of this case study, we will look at **spatial relationships** and **spatial interactions** on the frontier, to determine if there is enough evidence for us to picture the American frontier as a definable **region,** or whether the data lead us to think of various "frontiers."

How People's Ideas Affect Their Use of Physical Resources

Different people assign different values to a region's physical characteristics. Thus, a region's resources become valuable or worthless according to the value assigned to them by the people using them. For example, gold had been in the western mountains while the Indians lived there, but was not as highly regarded by the Indians as it was by the white Americans who flocked to the areas during the various gold rushes.

Frequently, a resource is labeled valuable or worthless by a small group of people within a society, and this evaluation persists. Until after the Civil War, the unfavorable description the "Great American Desert" was readily accepted by most Americans, who came to regard the plains as suitable only for Indians and buffalo hunters. Railroad entrepreneurs were influential in changing the prevalent negative attitude of settlers toward the plains. In order to get more passengers and freight for their transcontinental lines, as well as to sell some of the land granted free to them by the government, the railroads engaged in extensive positive advertising. After buffalo hunting,

Thomas Gilcrease Institute, Tulsa, Okla.
A cowboy of the Great Plains

the major resource of the plains utilized by white Americans was the grass—for cattle raising. Shortly thereafter, settlers began venturing onto the plains to utilize still another of the area's resources—the land for farming.

This illustrates another factor about a nation's frontiers. The same area may be a frontier several different times. The Great Plains underwent a series of frontier periods: first, the frontier of the traders and buffalo hunters; then, the cattlemen's frontier; and, finally, the homesteaders' or farmers' frontier.

Changing technology also has an impact on how an area's resources are used. Some resources simply do not become valuable until technological invention or improvements are available to help man utilize them to his full advantage. Before farmers could really hope to profit from a move to the Great Plains, for example, practical fencing materials (barbed wire), equipment for obtaining water (a specially designed windmill), and special farming equipment had to be developed.

On the other hand, improved technology sometimes heralded the end of a frontier period. This was especially true of many mining frontiers. As long as individual men or small groups of men could continue to mine the mineral, an area was likely to maintain its rough, rugged frontier atmosphere. However, when elaborate machinery available only to large-scale investors became necessary for further mining, the area took on a more settled character, and the adventuresome miners moved on to new mining frontiers.

Conflicts Due to Differing Ideas on the Use of Resources

Conflict—and violence—often developed on the American frontier because different groups of people regarded a particular resource from different points of view. From the beginning, the Indians and most white Americans disagreed in their evaluation of how the resources of the land should be used. For example, the Plains Indians' dependence on the buffalo as a long-term source of support brought them into conflict with white hunters who viewed the buffalo as a short-term source of immediate wealth.

The continual encroachment of white settlers into Indian territory resulted in numerous wars. Any geographer mapping the changing agricultural frontiers in the United States would undoubtedly find maps of Indian battles helpful in delimiting the frontier as a region. In some areas, in fact, the westward movement of the farming frontier was effectively halted, at least temporarily, by the presence of Indians. However, when the resources in a particular area were considered sufficiently valuable, no treaty was sacred enough to protect Indian property.

Conflicts on the frontier, of course, were not confined to those between Indians and white Americans. Anyone who has watched "western" movies is familiar with the conflicts between cattlemen and sheep herders, between ranchers and homesteaders, or among miners. Thse conflicts also resulted from different interpretations of, or conflicting claims on, the same resource.

How Resources Affect Settlement Patterns and Spatial Interaction

The type of resource utilized on a frontier will undoubtedly have an effect on how people distribute themselves in an area. Settlement patterns are an obvious reflection of spatial relationships, showing how men react to the demands of their physical and cultural environment.

Settlement on the mining frontiers was clustered; all the prospectors tried to get as close as possible to the known source of a valuable mineral.

Harvey T. Dunn (1884–1952), American. *Something For Supper* (detail). South Dakota Memorial Art Center, Brookings. Gift of the artist.

How did conflicts arise over the use of the Great Plains?

461

This density contrasted sharply with the low density of settlement of cattlemen on the Great Plains, who spread out in order to have sufficient grazing land for their cattle. The settlement patterns which developed on the westward-moving farming frontier were somewhat haphazard. If the first settlements were successful, new immigrants continued to arrive, settling at some distance from the early settlers, until the frontier area was gradually filled up and the frontier period came to an end.

Towns developed on the farming frontiers as they did on the mining frontiers, and were an important link in the essential spatial interaction between the frontier and the settled areas. However, the type of spatial interaction depended on circumstances. For example, gold and silver mined in frontier areas did not decrease in value if they had to undergo a long, slow journey to reach the markets of the settled areas. The same, however, was not true of cattle and wheat. For the wheat and cattle frontiers to be profitable, railroad transportation was essential.

The Frontier as a Region

Can the American frontier be defined as a region? Until 1890, the United States Census Bureau did in fact attempt to establish a "frontier line," using population density as its defining characteristic. The evidence presented in this case study, however, seems to indicate that an attempt to define the American frontier as a region can be both a hindrance and an aid.

Obviously there are characteristics shared by all American frontier areas: exploitation of "new" physical resources by people with psychological and economic ties to the settled areas of the United States, accompanied by conflict with previous "tenants." If the geographer were to map areas which manifested such conditions, making different maps for different time periods, he would probably be able to delimit "the frontier region" of the United States. The early maps for such a study would either show the entire trans-Mississippi West as frontier or would have a western boundary somewhere near the "Great American Desert." Later maps would include the mountain and plateau areas of the western mining states as well as the westward-advancing farming frontier on the plains.

However, the accuracy and value of such a portrayal of the American frontier leaves something to be desired. For one thing, the mining frontier is quite different from the farming frontier in terms of people involved, settlement patterns, and interaction with settled areas. Also, to portray the mining frontier spatially in the same manner as the farming frontier would be quite misleading since mining activity tended to cluster rather than disperse. The farming frontier might be regionalized fairly adequately as a westward-moving zone, but the cattlemen who advanced from the southwest into the Great Plains would complicate even that definition.

If a geographer were to use regionalization as a tool in his study of the frontier, he would probably decide to use several categories of frontiers based on the varying types of resources utilized. In this way his study would reveal the important contrasts as well as the similarities concerning the American frontiers.

■ What concepts are used to study the American frontier in this case study?
■ "An attempt to define the American frontier as a region can be both a hindrance and an aid." Cite evidence to support or refute this statement.

California gold miners

UNIT SEVEN

The Rise of Industrialism

1860's – 1890's

Chapter 23 Business Pioneers and the Growth of American Industry

24 The Revolt of American Farmers Against Big Business Practices

25 The Struggle of American Workers to Organize

26 Changing Ways of Life in the New Industrial Age

CHAPTER 23

Business Pioneers and the Growth of American Industry

1860's – 1890's

IN THE 1870's a large majority of Americans lived in the country or in small rural villages and towns. This was the age of dirt roads; of carriages and wagons; and of covered bridges, their wooden sides plastered with circus posters and notices of county fairs. It was the age of oil lamps; woodstoves; the handpump or the open well; and the Saturday-evening bath in a washtub in the center of the kitchen floor.

This was the age of sewing circles and spelling bees; the one-room schoolhouse; and the country store with its tubs of butter and pickles, its cracker barrel, and its clutter of groceries and clothing and household articles hanging from the ceiling and spilling over the shelves. Symbols of the age were the small family-owned factory and the blacksmith shop at the crossroads with its charcoal fire, its huge bellows, and its burly smith in grimy leather apron exchanging quips with loungers while he shaped and fitted new shoes to a neighbor's horse.

But a new age was coming into being. Symbols of the new age were rapidly growing cities, large factories with smoke pouring from their towering stacks, long lines of railroad cars rumbling across the countryside, and a growing number of farm machines standing outside barns or operating in the fields. In brief, life in the new industrial age was being transformed in many ways.

This, then, is the story of how America began to change from a rural, agricultural economy to an urban, industrial way of life.

THE CHAPTER IN OUTLINE

1. Binding the nation with systems of transportation and communication.

2. Creating more products for more people through expanding business.

3. Developing new forms of business organization as industry expands.

4. The rise of business pioneers in the new industrial society.

1 Binding the nation with systems of transportation and communication

The heart of an industrial society is the city. It is here that most factories and workers are concentrated and that most raw materials are fashioned into finished products. It is also here that most goods and services are bought and sold.

If the city is the heart of an industrial society, the routes of transportation are the veins and arteries. Into the city flow the vital resources gathered from farm and mine and forest and sea. Out of the city flow the unending supplies of manufactured articles, moving day and night over a vast transportation network to every corner of the land and overseas to other lands.

Just as the human body cannot function without heart and veins and arteries, so an industrial economy cannot function without its urban manufacturing centers and an efficient system of transportation and communication.

The growth of cities. One of the most striking developments during the years between 1865 and 1900 was the rise of the modern city with its busy railroad yards, its smoking factories, its factory workers, and its office workers. During these years, scores of American cities grew from sprawling towns to huge urban centers. In 1870, for example, about 75 percent of the people lived in the country or in communities of fewer than 2,500 inhabitants. By 1900 only about 60 percent of all Americans lived on farms or in small rural communities. The urban population had skyrocketed. While in 1870 only about 10 million of the nation's total population of 40 million were urban dwellers, by 1900 more than 30 million of America's 76 million people were living in urban areas.

The growth of cities was the result of many revolutionary developments, including the discovery of new sources of power, the application of hundreds of new inventions and new processes, and the enormous expansion of the nation's transportation and communication network.

The growth of railroads. Between 1870 and 1900 railway mileage in the United States increased from 53,000 miles to more than 190,000. During these same years the railroads improved in speed, comfort, and safety. Double sets of tracks replaced single sets, allowing streams of traffic to flow in two

■ The years 1865 to 1900 saw the rise of the modern city in America. Chicago, the biggest city in the Middle West, is shown here as it appeared in the 1890's.

Pattern of sections in a typical land grant

Section 1-mile square granted to railroad

Section 1-mile square sold to other holders

Right of way: 100 yards wide

The depth of the grants varied from 5 to 40 miles on both sides of the right of way.

(Map labels: NORTHERN PACIFIC, SOUTHERN PACIFIC, CENTRAL PACIFIC, UNION PACIFIC, SOUTHERN PACIFIC, KANSAS PACIFIC, ATLANTIC AND PACIFIC)

directions at once. Iron rails, which had shattered beneath heavy loads, were replaced by steel rails. Bridges of iron and later of steel replaced wooden bridges. Coal, a more efficient fuel, replaced wood in the tenders of locomotives. In 1869 George Westinghouse patented the air brake, a system of power braking more efficient than the old hand brake.

Railroad passenger comfort increased. In the 1850's railroad cars had been overcrowded wooden boxes, but during the next 20 years George M. Pullman and others invented and placed in operation sleeping cars, dining cars, and parlor cars.

A nationwide network of steel. The success of the first transcontinental line (page 440) quickly led to the construction of several others. By 1893 a half-dozen major, or trunk, lines crossed the plains and mountains to the Far West, while north of the Canadian border the Canadian Pacific furnished an additional route to the Pacific coast. All over the United States, feeder, or branch, lines were also built to link the trunk lines with surrounding areas. Presently a network of steel rails served every part of the country, however remote from the major centers of industry and transportation.

Financing the construction of railroads. The construction of railroads, especially lines reaching into the still unsettled West, was enormously expensive. To encourage the building of new lines, the government provided grants of land and loans of money.

The original land grants set aside large areas of land within which the railroad could claim a specified amount. Until the railroads exercised their claim, none of the land could be sold to the public.

Some railroads ran into construction or other difficulties and did not exercise their choice for 10 years or more. Others never exercised the right, and the land reverted to the government. In round figures, the national government turned over 131 million acres of land to the railroads. At the time, this land was worth a total of approximately $123 million.

But that is only one side of the story. In return, the land-grant railroads and their competitors carried government troops and military freight for one half the standard rates until October 1, 1946. In addition, the railroads carried United States mail for four fifths of the standard rates. In March 1945 a Congressional committee reported that the railroads had already "contributed over $900 million in payment of the lands which were transferred to them under the Land Grant Act."

The government also provided subsidies in the form of bonds loaned to the railroads. These bonds bore interest at 6 percent. The railroads eventually repaid the original loans of close to $65 million with payments of interest and principal totaling about $168 million.

Importance of steamships. While land transportation was being improved, traffic on the sea lanes and inland waterways was also being developed. After 1850, sailing ships on the oceans and on the Great Lakes were replaced by steam-driven, steel-hulled freighters and sleek passenger liners. These ocean-going vessels carried millions of emigrants from Europe to the rest of the world, mostly to the United States. They also carried raw materials and manufactured goods to and from the expanding world markets.

466

Urban transportation. Meanwhile, in the growing urban areas new methods of transportation enabled people to move quickly within the crowded cities. By the late 1800's electric trolleys were rapidly replacing horse-drawn cars. Steam-driven and, later, electric-powered elevated trains rumbled along above crowded city streets. By the early 1900's subway trains carried passengers below the streets of New York and Boston.

As steel-framed skyscrapers climbed higher into the air, elevators, powered first by steam and then by electricity, began to carry passengers and freight from story to story. Indeed, without the elevator, skyscrapers could not have been used.

From telegraph to telephone. Equally important developments came in the field of communications. Until the 1870's the telegraph had been the most significant advance in communication since the invention of printing from movable type. From the 1870's on, however, new inventions appeared one after another.

The telegraph had been first successfully developed in the United States by Samuel F. B. Morse and in England by Charles Wheatstone during the late 1830's and the early 1840's—just as the new steam railroads began to appear. The telegraph moved across the country with the railroads—indeed, without the telegraph the railroads could not have operated safely.

In 1866, about 25 years after Morse's invention, Cyrus W. Field succeeded in laying a transatlantic telegraph cable. During the next few years additional underwater cables connected North America with other continents, giving Americans almost instantaneous communication with the rest of the world.

In 1876 Alexander Graham Bell, a teacher of the deaf in Boston, applied for a patent on a telephone he had invented. Bell's telephone quickly captured the public's imagination, and in 1885 the American Telephone and Telegraph Company was organized to put the new invention into widespread use. The first crude instrument was rapidly improved, benefiting from Thomas Alva Edison's work in the field of electricity. Soon there were webs of telephone wires throughout the nation's cities, and telephone lines began to reach out into rural areas.

Other influential inventions. The telegraph, the underwater cable, and the telephone were landmarks in the history of communications. But in the late 1800's other important inventions and developments also began to reshape American life.

In the 1860's Christopher Sholes of Wisconsin developed the typewriter, which was improved by other men until it became an essential part of all business operations. An improved postal system, without which modern business could not function, was also developed.

The improvement of machines for making cheap paper from wood pulp and for printing newspapers, books, and magazines also played a vital part in developing more effective means of communication. And then, of course, there was the camera, which later provided new forms of recreation as well as new techniques for industry and research.

By 1900 improvements in transportation and communications were binding all parts of the United States into a single complex economic unit. Specialized business enterprises, both agricultural and industrial, were springing up in all parts of the land, each playing its part in the ever-expanding, interlocking economic system.

SECTION SURVEY

IDENTIFY: urban center; George M. Pullman, Samuel F. B. Morse, Cyrus W. Field, Alexander Graham Bell, Thomas Alva Edison, Christopher Sholes.

1. "If the city is the heart of an industrial society, the routes of transportation are the veins and arteries." Explain.
2. (a) Why did the federal government help finance the building of the railroads? (b) What methods did it use?
3. The communications revolution at this time bridged space and time. Explain.

2 Creating more products for more people through expanding business

"Which came first, the chicken or the egg?" is a good question to keep in mind when thinking about the Industrial Revolution. For example, did improvements in transportation and communications come first, and then the big factories and mass production? Or was it the other way around?

The answer, of course, is that the Industrial Revolution was the product of many different developments in many different fields, all going on at the same time, and all combining to transform, or "revolutionize," the older ways of life. These developments included new sources of power, new machines, new and bigger industries, and new ways of selling.

■ This early oil well was one of the many drilled in the United States after 1859. First used to make a fuel for lamps, oil became a source of power that virtually revolutionized American life.

In the late 1800's man learned to use two new sources of power—oil and electricity.

Power from petroleum.   From the earliest times people had known about the dark, thick substance that oozed from the earth in certain places and that we now call "petroleum," or "oil." In the early 1850's it was discovered that kerosene, an efficient and inexpensive fuel for lamps, could be refined from petroleum. The growing demand for kerosene

prompted Edwin L. Drake, a retired railroad conductor, to try to drill an "oil well" near Titusville, Pennsylvania. This was in 1859. While he was drilling, people thought he was crazy. When the oil began to flow, however, people quickly began sinking wells of their own.

Kerosene rapidly replaced whale oil as an efficient fuel for lamps. In every American city, peddlers carted kerosene through the streets, selling their product from door to door. And as the years passed, oil was used more and more as a lubricant for the nation's many new machines.

It was the development of the internal combustion engine, which burned gasoline or, later, diesel fuel, that finally turned oil into one of the nation's major sources of power. In Chapter 29 you will see how oil as a source of power virtually revolutionized American life.

Power from electricity.   Electricity, like oil, was known to man long before he put it to practical use. The work of two Italians, Galvani and Volta, led in the late 1700's and early 1800's to the invention of the storage battery. The storage battery, which supplied small amounts of electric current at low "voltages," greatly aided Americans and Europeans who were experimenting with the uses of electricity. Even more far-reaching in their consequences were the discoveries of the principles governing the electric motor and the dynamo. Although many men contributed to these discoveries, a major share of the credit belongs to England's Michael Faraday and America's Joseph Henry.

Thousands of Americans first learned about the dynamo at the Centennial Exhibition at Philadelphia in 1876, where they saw one in operation converting mechanical energy into electrical energy. In 1882, six years after the Philadelphia Centennial Exhibition, Thomas Edison built in New York City the first large central power plant in the United States for generating electricity. Edison drove his dynamos with steam engines. Other steam-powered electric generating plants soon appeared in other cities. Another giant stride forward was made in 1895 with the opening at Niagara Falls of the first large hydroelectric plant for producing electricity from water power. In spite of these developments, by 1900 only about 2 percent of America's manufacturing industries were powered by electricity. The revolutionary impact of this new source of power was to come after 1900.

Steel for the new industries.   Behind the story of new sources of power lies still another story— the discovery of new ways of producing steel.

468

The United States had an abundance of the raw materials vital to the new industrial age—iron ore and coal. Immense deposits of iron ore lay near the western shores of Lake Superior. Perhaps 500,000 square miles of coal fields, or about one half of the world's known deposits, were waiting to be tapped, the largest of them in Pennsylvania.

Steel, a hard, tough metal containing iron, carbon, and other elements, was not a new material. Men had made it for centuries and fashioned it into weapons, tools, and utensils. But until the mid-1800's no one knew how to produce steel cheaply and in large quantities.

In the 1850's an Englishman, Henry Bessemer, and an American, William Kelly, independently discovered a new process for making large quantities of steel cheaply by burning out impurities in molten iron with a blast of air. During the next few years the "Bessemer process," as it was called, was steadily improved and other even more effective processes were developed.

The annual production of steel in the United States soared steadily upward. In 1870, for example, the United States produced only about 68,000 tons of steel. By 1900, however, Americans produced more than 10 million tons of steel annually, and by 1918 production had increased to 44 million tons.

Without steel—as well as copper and other metals—the Industrial Revolution as we know it would not have occurred in the United States. Steel, power, rapidly growing factories, efficient transportation and communications—these were the keys to the new industrial age.

The growth of mass production. Much of the growing steel production at this time was going into the construction of railroads, bridges, heavy machinery, factories, mills, and other industrial enterprises. American businessmen were laying the foundations of an industrial system that eventually would make the United States the most productive country in the world and would provide Americans with the highest national standard of living in history.

As businesses expanded and factories grew larger, their owners and managers continually developed more efficient methods of production. During the first half of the 1800's, Eli Whitney had developed interchangeable parts (page 250). This development in turn called for a *division of labor*. For instance, a shoemaker no longer made an entire shoe. Instead, in great shoe factories—mostly in New England—parts of the shoes were cut and

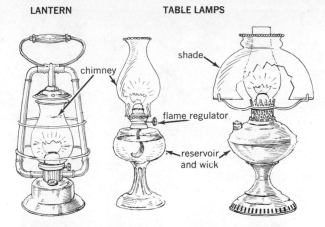

LANTERN   TABLE LAMPS

chimney

shade

flame regulator

reservoir and wick

■ **Kerosene Lighting.** A "wick" soaked in kerosene extended upward from the "reservoir" through the "flame regulator" to the point where it could be lighted. The glass "chimneys" had to be cleaned frequently because soot from the flame accumulated inside.

■ **Bessemer Converter.** Steel is made by removing impurities from "pig iron" which has previously been made in an iron furnace (page 250). In this Bessemer converter of 1863, a very strong blast of hot air was forced through the molten pig iron, blowing away the impurities and leaving molten steel. The steel could then be poured out and shaped into various forms.

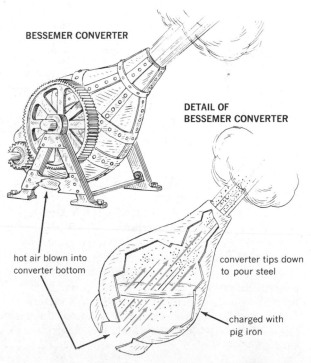

BESSEMER CONVERTER

DETAIL OF BESSEMER CONVERTER

hot air blown into converter bottom

converter tips down to pour steel

charged with pig iron

The *department store* combined many specialty stores under one roof. John C. Wanamaker opened one of the first department stores in the United States in Philadelphia in 1876. Marshall Field opened another in Chicago in 1881. Other merchants soon opened department stores in other cities.

Chain stores—stores with branches in many cities—also began to appear. Pioneers in this field of selling were the Great Atlantic and Pacific Tea Company (A&P), founded in 1859, and the chain of stores started by Frank Woolworth in 1879. Chain stores, like department stores, sold goods at lower prices because they bought the goods they sold in large quantities at low prices.

Manufacturers in the 1880's also began to develop large-scale, professional advertising. Such advertising introduced new products, promoted mass purchasing, and helped create a large national market for an ever-increasing stream of manufactured products.

Mail-order houses. Specialty stores, department stores, and chain stores were all part of the urban scene. In 1872, however, Aaron Montgomery Ward started in Chicago a mail-order business aimed at the rural market. A few years later, the Sears, Roebuck mail-order business was started. Montgomery Ward and Sears, Roebuck used the same business methods. Customers placed orders and paid for them by mail; their goods were shipped to them by mail or railway express. Catalogs from these two mail-order houses became prized possessions in every rural household and in many a cattleman's or sheepherder's bunkhouse or camp. They helped to bring the outside world to isolated farms and speeded the transformation of farm life.

■ In 1879, F. W. Woolworth opened a "5 & 10¢ store" in Lancaster, Pennsylvania. It was the first in a chain of stores that sold only goods priced at a low figure. By 1899, Woolworth owned 54 such stores.

shaped by men working at machines that performed only a single operation at a time. The different parts—heel, sole, lining—were then brought together at a central location in the factory and assembled into a shoe. In this way, vast quantities of shoes could be made quickly and cheaply.

This division of labor was soon adopted by most American factories in every industry, making possible the *mass production* of products of every kind.

New ways of selling products. The small general store, as well as the small family-owned factory, became less important in America during the late 1800's. Completely new types of stores appeared to handle the ever-growing quantity of products pouring forth from the nation's factories.

The *specialty store* concentrated upon a single line of goods—hardware, clothing, groceries, shoes, and so forth.

SECTION SURVEY

IDENTIFY: "Bessemer process," division of labor (specialization), mass production; Edwin L. Drake, Michael Faraday, Joseph Henry, Marshall Field.

1. Of what significance was the revolution in power to (a) workers, (b) manufacturers?
2. Relate an abundance of natural resources and advanced technological techniques to the growth of a nation as an industrial power.
3. What basic premise or idea did the following men have regarding the merchandising of goods? (a) Frank Woolworth, (b) John Wanamaker, (c) Montgomery Ward.
4. Why did changes in the selling of merchandise, or goods, take place at this time?

3 Developing new forms of business organization as industry expands

Most of America's factories and stores in the 1860's and 1870's were *individual proprietorships* —small enterprises owned by individuals or families. The individual or the family members who owned a small factory knew all the workmen— often by their first names. Most wage earners in the 1860's lived in small towns, worked in small factories, and took part in community activities with their employers.

During the next 30 years much of this small-town, personal relationship began to disappear. It was crowded out by the huge industrial plant located in or on the outskirts of a large city and employing hundreds, even thousands, of wage earners, who were often strangers to one another and even more remote from the men who owned the business.

Partnerships. As businesses grew in size, businessmen had to find ways of sharing expanding costs and responsibilities. The *partnership* as a form of business organization became more common. The partnership, even then, was an old form of business organization.

When two or more men go into partnership, they have the advantage of greater capital and greater skill than one man, for generally each partner invests both money and time in the enterprise. But partnerships have one major weakness for the partners. Each partner is completely liable, or responsible, for anything that happens to the business.

Corporations. As industries grew larger in the 1800's, another form of business organization, the *corporation,* became more common. It gradually became the leading form of business organization in the United States.

To start a corporation, three or more persons must apply to a state legislature for a *charter,* or license, to start a specific business enterprise. Once granted, this charter allows the interested persons to organize a corporation and sell shares of *stock,* or certificates of ownership, to raise the capital needed to carry on the enterprise. The *stockholders* or *shareholders*—those who invest their money in the enterprise—may periodically receive *dividends,* that is, a share of the corporation's profits. Legally, a corporation is regarded as an individual—an "artificial person" entirely separate from its owners—possessing certain rights, such as the right to make contracts, to buy and sell property, and to sue and be sued in court.

The corporation has important advantages over the individual proprietorship and the partnership. Two advantages are especially important to the corporation itself. First, the corporation can draw upon very large reservoirs of capital because it can sell shares of stock to many people. Second, the charter gives the corporation "perpetual life"; that is to say, the corporation is not ended by the death or resignation of one or several of its owners.

For the owners, or investors, the corporation also offers two important advantages. First, a stockholder can sell all or part of his stock whenever he chooses. Second, an investor has only "limited liability." That is, if the corporation fails, he loses only the money he has invested in its stocks; he cannot be made to pay any debts owed by the bankrupt corporation. This makes the corporation a far safer investment than, say, a partnership, in which each partner has "unlimited liability" and may lose his home and everything else he owns if the business fails.

Corporations after 1860. During the first half of the 1800's, only a few large American industries were organized as corporations, and these were usually owned by only a handful of persons. By the 1860's, however, businessmen needed increasing amounts of capital to build, equip, and operate the new manufacturing enterprises that utilized the vast resources of America's forests, soils, mines, and waters. Because the corporation proved ideal for gathering large amounts of capital, it became very common after 1860.

Business consolidation. During the latter half of the 1800's, there was also a growing trend toward business combination, or consolidation. Corporations that were engaged in the same type of business joined together to create large combinations.

Economists have pointed out that these combinations were, in many ways, a stronger form of business organization. Several corporations, when banded together, could save some of the costs of production and distribution. They could eliminate competing salesmen and advertising. They could purchase larger quantities of raw materials at lower prices and make better use of by-products. They could arrange better bargains with banks, transportation companies, and workers. It was thought, too, that they could put an end to "cutthroat competition," in which rival companies kept undercutting prices until none was earning any profits. In short, through consolidation, business-

■ The Shadwell Rope Works is an example of the large factories employing hundreds of workers that began to appear in the United States after the 1870's.

men could substitute cooperation for competition and thus reduce waste, costs, and risky losses.

But these large enterprises sometimes presented dangers to important principles of freedom in the American economic system. Through consolidation, a group of corporations might gain monopoly control over a particular line of business. Monopoly control could lead to great economic evils by operating "in restraint of trade." That is, it could reduce competition, which lies at the heart of a free enterprise economy.

For example, a business combination might have so much power that it could "freeze out" competitors by undercutting prices until the competitor failed. Then the combination could raise prices to make up its losses. Or if a consolidated enterprise gained monopoly control in a given line of business, it could charge any price it chose, denying purchasers their right to shop around for the best bargains. These and other economic evils stemming from monopoly control presently became problems, as you will see, for American government, for American businessmen, and for the American people as a whole.

Corporation pools.   One of the earliest ways in which corporations combined was by organizing *pools*. To form a pool, several corporations simply agreed to divide all their business opportunities among themselves. For example, several railroads serving the same city might agree on what percentage of local business each would handle. Or they might agree to charge uniform freight rates so that none would gain a price advantage. Or a group of manufacturing corporations might agree to divide the country into several market areas, each reserved for the salesmen of one of the corporations in the pool and "off limits" to all the others.

Pools were merely "gentlemen's agreements." Unlike the corporation, which operated under a legal charter, a pooling agreement had no legal standing. For that reason, courts refused to judge cases in which a member of a pool violated his agreement with the other members. In 1887 pools were declared illegal in interstate commerce (page 434), and practically disappeared.

Powerful trusts.   Meanwhile, other businessmen developed a second form of business consolidation, called the *trust*.

Businessmen who wanted to organize a trust first had to reach an agreement with the principal stockholders in the several corporations involved. The promise of greater profits from a larger organization was often all that was needed to persuade stockholders to enter a trust.

Under the trust agreement, the promoters of the trust, called the "trustees," gained control of the stock in all the corporations and thus of the corporations themselves. In exchange, the trustees gave the stockholders of the corporations "trust certificates" on which dividends were paid out of the profits of the trust.

With control of the stock in their hands, the trustees could run several corporations as a single giant business enterprise. If the trustees could get control of enough corporations they could secure monopoly control of an entire business field and charge whatever prices or rates they desired. They could, for example, lower prices temporarily in one area to drive a competitor out of business, while raising prices everywhere else.

During the 1870's and the 1880's, giant trusts swallowed up corporations in many of the nation's largest industries, including oil, steel, sugar refining, and whisky distilling. When a trust did get control of enough corporations to secure a monopoly and eliminate competition, it often raised prices on the products it controlled. The consumers who purchased and used these products complained bitterly about the high prices. The smaller competing businesses complained even more bitterly as the trusts closed in on them.

Magazines and newspapers of the time were filled with articles, letters, and editorials pointing out the evils of the "all-powerful monopolies," and pleading with the government to step in and restore freedom of enterprise. But local, state, and federal governments were powerless. There were no laws that said that trusts and monopolies were illegal, although under the *common law*,° which courts might or might not enforce, "conspiracies in restraint of trade" were forbidden.

The Sherman Antitrust Act.   Finally, in 1890, during the administration of President Benjamin Harrison, Congress passed the Sherman Antitrust Act. The public assumed that the act was intended to restore a larger measure of free competition by breaking up giant "trusts"—a term that had come to mean any monopoly or near-monopoly of an industry. This also seemed to be what Congress intended, for Section 1 of the act declared: "Every contract, combination in the form of trust or otherwise, or conspiracy, in restraint of trade or commerce among the several states or with foreign nations is hereby declared to be illegal. . . ." The act further stated that individuals and corporations found guilty of violating the law would be liable to legal penalties.

° *common law:* a system of law based upon custom, tradition, and precedents established by courts of law.

Weakness of the Sherman Antitrust Act.   Actually, few Americans, including even corporation lawyers and Congressmen, were able to explain precisely what the new law did and did not prohibit. The act failed to define such words as "trust," "combination," "conspiracy," and "monopoly."

Because of its loose wording, the Sherman Antitrust Act was extremely difficult to enforce. The government lost seven out of the first eight cases that it brought against giant business combinations, or trusts.

In 1895 the Supreme Court handed down a decision in the case of *U.S. v. E. C. Knight Company* that made the antitrust law almost meaningless. The Court ruled that the company, which had secured control of 98 percent of the sugar refining business, was not guilty of violating the antitrust law because its control of the refining process alone did not involve restraint of interstate trade. A monopoly itself was not illegal, the Court stated. It became illegal only when it served to restrain interstate trade.

This and other decisions by the Supreme Court convinced businessmen that they were free to consolidate. Thus, the movement to form business consolidations actually gained momentum in the years following the passage of the Sherman Antitrust Act.

And yet, despite its glaring weakness, the Sherman Antitrust Act marked the first attempt by the federal government to make rules for the conduct of big business. It established an important precedent for later and more effective laws.

Holding companies.   After 1890 some of the nation's business leaders abandoned the trust for another form of business consolidation—the *holding company*. To form such a consolidation, it was necessary to get a charter from one of the states. The directors of the holding company then issued stock in the holding company itself. With the money raised by selling this stock, the directors bought controlling shares of stock in two or more corporations that were actually engaged in producing goods or services, such as manufacturing companies, mining companies, or transportation companies. The holding company did not itself produce either goods or services. But the company did control all the corporations whose stock it held.

After the 1890's the holding company became very popular. It was legal. It was responsible for its actions because, unlike the trust, it operated under a charter that could be revoked if the terms were violated. And when a holding company threatened to monopolize an industry, it was liable, like a

■ This cartoon of 1889 pictures giant trusts looming over the Senate floor. Notice that there is an open entrance for monopolists, but that the "people's entrance" is closed.

trust, to prosecution under the Sherman Antitrust Act, although conviction was unlikely.

Other forms of consolidation. Another form of consolidation that often defied prosecution was the *interlocking directorate*. In an interlocking directorate some or all of the directors of one company served as directors of several other companies. By this means they could develop a uniform policy for the entire industry.

There were, of course, other ways to establish a uniform policy. Directors of different companies could simply meet and make secret "gentlemen's agreements" on prices they would charge and other matters.

Men who tried to establish uniform policies for an entire industry—either through interlocking directorates or through "gentlemen's agreements"—were subject to prosecution under the Sherman Antitrust Act. But, as you have seen, it was difficult to prove that a monopoly existed. And its existence was especially difficult to prove when the

monopoly had been created by means of interlocking directorates and secret agreements.

SECTION SURVEY

IDENTIFY: business consolidation, stock, dividends, cutthroat competition, monopoly.

1. What advantages does the corporate form of business organization have over the partnership?
2. On a four-column chart entitled "Forms of Business Consolidation," define (a) pools, (b) trusts, (c) holding companies, and (d) interlocking directorates. Give reasons for their creation, objections to them, and methods used to control their abuses.
3. How did Supreme Court decisions in the late 1800's aid businessmen?
4. (a) Summarize the provisions of the Sherman Antitrust Act of 1890. (b) Why was this law difficult to enforce? (c) Would it be as difficult to enforce today? Explain.

4 The rise of business pioneers in the new industrial society

The men who presided over the new world of throbbing machines, noisy factories, and crowded cities were the business leaders and the financiers. The influence of the businessman was reflected in local, state, and national politics.

Growing influence of the businessman. Between 1789 and 1860 thirteen Presidents had been elected—seven from the South, six from the North. Between 1860 and 1900 each of the seven Presidents elected was from the industrial regions of the Northeast or from the Middle West. On nearly all essential issues, moreover, the major differences between the Republicans and the Democrats largely disappeared during these years (page 426).

The business leaders of this period do not fit into a single type. They varied greatly in personalities, abilities, and methods of doing business. They were pioneers, possessing the virtues as well as the shortcomings of pioneers. Some were rough. Some were urbane, polished men. All were energetic men, eager to seize upon the unlimited opportunities of the new industrial world emerging around them. Some were fabulously successful. Others, the "small businessmen," never amassed fortunes or won great power. But all—"big" business leaders and "small" businessmen alike—shared the ideal of self-reliant individualism.

Cornelius Vanderbilt. "Commodore" Cornelius Vanderbilt was born in 1794 when George Washington was President of the United States. By 1865 Vanderbilt, who had started life as a poor boy, had accumulated great wealth and owned a fleet of steamships worth $10 million. Twelve years later, when he died at 82, he was worth $105 million.

Even in his seventies Commodore Vanderbilt was a tall, erect, energetic man, with a defiant bearing. He could hardly write, his spelling was impossible, and his temper won him many enemies. He seemed to act on impulse, following his intuitions, or even consulting astrologers or fortunetellers, in his business affairs. An extremely vain man, he printed his own picture on all the stock certificates of his Lake Shore and Michigan Southern Railroad.

What did Vanderbilt contribute to American life? For one thing, he consolidated the railroad companies that provided service between New York and Chicago. Before he secured control of the different lines, passengers and freight had to be transferred 17 times between the two cities during a 50-hour trip. When he had completed the consolidation, one train made the entire trip in about 24 hours. He replaced iron rails and wooden bridges with steel rails and steel bridges. He built double tracks to make two-way traffic safe and speedy. He constructed new locomotives and terminals. Achievements such as these made possible the rapid development of America's industrial economy.

Andrew Carnegie. Andrew Carnegie was another fabulous business leader who arose during the early decades of industrialism. Born in 1835 in

■ Some of the business pioneers in the new industrial society amassed enormous fortunes. "Commodore" Cornelius Vanderbilt, for example, was worth $105 million when he died. His grandson later built a summer "cottage" for $4 million. The mansion's dining hall, with its two crystal chandeliers, is shown below. © Arnold Newman

Scotland, Carnegie came to America at age 12 and settled with his parents in Allegheny, now a part of Pittsburgh. At 14 he was working 12 hours a day as a bobbin boy in a cotton mill for $1.20 a week. He studied hard, and at 16 was a telegraph clerk earning about $4.00 a week—a fair salary in those days. A likable lad, at 17 Carnegie became private secretary to the president of the Pennsylvania Railroad.

In 1850 Carnegie bought an oil well, and he made money in the new oil industry. But he soon turned to the steel industry, and it was here that he spent the rest of his business life.

Carnegie frankly admitted that he knew nothing about steel manufacturing. His success lay in his ability as a salesman and promoter. He knew how to gather around him men who were specialists. He was a relentless driver, never satisfied with himself or with others. One day he received a telegram from one of his plant superintendents: "We broke all records for making steel last week," the telegram read. "Congratulations," Carnegie wired back. "Why not do it every week?"

Carnegie, however, also recognized the achievements of others. People he liked rose rapidly up the ladder to financial success. Charles M. Schwab, for instance, who entered one of Carnegie's plants as a stake driver at a dollar a day, became president of the Carnegie Steel Company at age 34, and his share of profits in 1896 was $1.3 million. Similar stories are told of Carnegie's friendship for Henry Phipps, Henry C. Frick, and others.

By 1900 Andrew Carnegie, who began as a poor immigrant boy, was said to be the second richest man in the world. He owned all the types of property and equipment necessary for the mass production of steel, including deposits of iron ore, limestone, and coal; ships and railways to carry the raw material to his smelters and mills; and huge steel plants from which the finished products poured forth. Carnegie sold his steel property in 1901 for $225 million. This tremendous financial deal was negotiated by J. P. Morgan, the most famous investment banker of the time, and his banking associates. Out of the negotiations, in which 11 steel companies were merged, was born the mighty United States Steel Corporation, then the largest corporation in the world. Many economic historians have regarded this huge transaction as a critical point in the development of American capitalism. It marked a shift from "industrial capitalism," in which corporations were controlled by their industrial owners, to "finance capitalism," in which whole industries were dominated by bankers.

Carnegie retired in 1901. He spent much of the rest of his life giving away his money for education and other causes. "I started life as a poor man," he once said, "and I wish to end it that way." Before his death he had disposed of more than $350 million. Many public libraries stand today as monuments to Carnegie's generosity, while foundations created by his money still support causes such as education, world peace, and medical research.

John D. Rockefeller. Even richer than Carnegie was John D. Rockefeller, born in 1839, who started life as a poor boy and accumulated the world's greatest fortune. One of five children, Rockefeller left high school after one year to work as a clerk for about $3 a week. In 1858, at age 19, he went into the wholesale food business with an Englishman named M. B. Clark. The Civil War brought large profits to the new company. Rockefeller promptly invested his money in oil refineries, and from this point on oil became his major interest. He pioneered in developing the trust as a form of big business organization. Although ruthless in forcing competitors to choose between joining him or going down to ruin, Rockefeller is credited with bringing order and efficiency to the highly chaotic and wasteful oil industry.

By 1900, however, Rockefeller's interests had broadened. He owned controlling stock in the gigantic Standard Oil Company, in railway lines, in steamship lines, in iron ore deposits in Colorado and in the Lake Superior region, in steel mills, and in many other enterprises. When the United States Steel Corporation was being organized by J. P. Morgan, Rockefeller sold to the newly formed corporation his iron ore deposits and Great Lakes steamers, receiving $80 million for the iron ore deposits alone.

Like Carnegie, Rockefeller in his later life gave away many millions, and the foundations created with his money today foster research and promote the public welfare.

Pioneers of industrialism. These were only a few of the many pioneers of the new industrial society. Like other pioneers—cattlemen, prospectors, frontier farmers, and workingmen—they helped to develop the resources of a new land. They were endowed with great energy and rare ability. They were gamblers, willing to take chances in the hope of gain. They were highly competitive men in a highly competitive society, at a time when few laws

■ **The dangerous, back-breaking labor in early steel mills is vividly shown in this painting done in 1877 by John Ferguson Weir. The workmen are guiding a shaft of steel out of a heating furnace.**

had been enacted to bring order into the mad rush of business enterprise. They were absorbed in the wild excitement of building a new industrial world, of creating huge fortunes, of securing power.

These men have often been condemned for their selfishness and for the ruthless business methods they used to destroy their competitors and climb to power. At the same time, their critics have acknowledged that these men built new industries, introduced efficient organization, and provided opportunities that enabled many people to invest their savings profitably in the new industries springing up all over the nation.

Leaders of this type were the products of their time. It is unlikely that they will ever again appear in American life. But while onstage, they played an important part in an important period of the nation's development, and they helped to give new directions to American life.

SECTION SURVEY

IDENTIFY: industrial capitalism, finance capitalism, Standard Oil Company; J. P. Morgan.

1. Draw up a list of characteristics which entitle Vanderbilt, Carnegie, and Rockefeller to be called (a) "pioneers of industrial society," (b) "robber barons."
2. What important contributions did the business pioneers of the late 1800's make to American economic life?
3. The leading businessmen of the late 1800's had different personalities but made use of the same methods to achieve success. Comment.

477

TRACING THE MAIN IDEAS

During the years between 1865 and 1900, the United States grew by leaps and bounds. By the opening years of the 1900's, the United States had become the leading industrial nation in the world. Smoking factory chimneys, the rumble of steam-driven and electric machinery, and long trains of freight cars pulling into and out of congested urban centers were symbols of the Industrial Revolution.

Particularly in the Northeast and Middle West, and to a lesser extent elsewhere in the nation, industrialism was transforming people's lives. Raw materials from America's vast reservoir of natural resources poured into the mills and factories. Finished products in ever-growing quantities poured out of the mills and factories.

Mass production led to specialization. Financiers raised the capital to build the railroads and the factories. Manufacturers developed more efficient methods of producing goods. Merchants developed new methods of advertising and selling. Many workers—clerks, stenographers, managers, factory workers, and others—manned the new industrial plants. New methods of business organization were developed, and great corporations and combinations of corporations increasingly replaced the earlier family-owned businesses.

Throughout America a new spirit of fierce competition drove men at a faster and faster pace. It was an exciting and a productive period in the nation's history. But some of the changes created problems for many people. Much of the nation's history since 1865 has been concerned with the efforts of Americans to adjust their ways of life to the new forces of growing industrialism.

CHAPTER SURVEY

QUESTIONS FOR DISCUSSION

1. What is meant by the statement that America has changed from a rural, agricultural economy to an urban, industrial economy?
2. The Civil War provided momentum for industrial expansion. Comment.
3. Technological changes often meet with resistance. Why do you think this is so?
4. Would you rather live and work in a rural, agricultural society or in an urban, industrial society? Why?
5. Did the Industrial Revolution change the relationship between man and his environment? Explain.

RELATING PAST TO PRESENT

1. Should industries in the United States bear responsibility for what happens to our environment as a result of their activities? Why or why not?
2. What methods are used by business today to consolidate and control vast economic enterprises?
3. Are today's objections to new technology comparable to the objections raised during the period just studied? Explain.

USING MAPS AND CHARTS

1. Using chart 1 on page 868, compare railroad mileage in 1830 with that in 1880 and explain the increase and its significance for economic expansion.
2. (a) Referring to the chart on page 466, explain the federal plan for land grants to railroads. (b) What monetary grants were made?
3. (a) Using chart 8 on page 859, compare the ratio of rural to urban population in the United States in 1790 with the ratio in 1900. (b) What were the causes of the change? (c) Of what significance was the change?
4. Using the charts on pages 866–67, answer the following: (a) What advances in American industry between 1850 and 1900 were most significant in helping to create big business? (b) Which of these major advances help explain large-scale development of railroad transport? (c) What connections can you see among increasing output per worker, the shifts in power sources, and major advances in American industry? (d) How are increasing output per worker and the shifts in power sources related to the change in the average number of hours worked per week? (See also chart 4 on page 877.)

After 1865 American farmers stood on the threshold of the new industrial age. To be sure, neither the farmers nor the great majority of their fellow Americans were aware of the sweeping developments that were about to transform life in America, in Western Europe, and eventually throughout the world.

Even by 1870, however, the symbols of the new industrial age were beginning to appear everywhere. Steel rails were creeping out onto the prairies, across the plains, and through remote mountain valleys, opening up new farm lands and bringing older farm lands in closer touch with the cities. Farm machines had begun to appear on some of the nation's more prosperous farms, enabling the farmer to produce more with less labor. The rapidly growing industrial cities were opening up ever-larger markets for farm products. As a result of these and other related developments, the farmer was becoming an increasingly important part of the new industrial economy.

In the 1870's farmers had every reason to assume that better times lay ahead for the nation's rural population. Better times did come, but not in the 1880's and 1890's. Instead, as industrialism swung into full stride, American farmers in general were confronted with a host of new problems.

CHAPTER 24

The Revolt of American Farmers Against Big Business Practices

1860's – 1890's

THE CHAPTER IN OUTLINE

1. A simple but laborious life for farmers up to the 1870's.

2. Complex new problems for farmers in the industrial age.

3. The farmers' increasing influence on government.

4. The farmers' failure to win control of the national government.

1 A simple but laborious life for farmers up to the 1870's

Every 10 years, in accordance with the requirement laid down in the Constitution, a federal census has been taken across the highways and byways of America. Every household and every person has been contacted. Occupations, income, and other information have been recorded and sent to the nation's capital, where they have been compiled and published.

The farm population in 1870. The returns from the 1870 census showed that the nation's urban population was growing more rapidly than the rural population. Whereas in 1860 80 percent of all Americans had lived in rural areas, by 1870 only about 75 percent lived on farms or in small towns and villages. Even so, the United States was still predominantly a farm country.

The 2.7 million farms that the census takers visited in 1870 varied greatly. Some were large, others small. Some farmers were prosperous; others just managed to earn a living. But regardless of size or degree of prosperity, the farms of 1870 shared certain characteristics.

The day of hand tools. Manual labor and a few simple hand tools characterized work on most farms in 1870. It is easier, perhaps, to visualize the typical farm of 1870 by starting with things the farmer did not have.

No farmers, for instance, had gasoline-driven machines or machines powered by electricity. The farmers pumped water by hand, hoisted it in buckets from open wells, or, if they were fortunate, connected a pipe to a hilltop spring and allowed the water to flow into the barn and the farmhouse. There were no electric or gas ranges; farm wives cooked on iron, wood-burning stoves or, rarely, on the newly developed kerosene stoves. There were no gas or electric lights; for illumination farmers used smoky kerosene lamps and lanterns. There was no central heating; there were only stoves and, in the milder climate of the South, open fireplaces. There were no mail-order catalogs from which a farmer could order ready-made clothing, tools, or equipment. In 1870 these "modern" conveniences had not yet been developed.

On some of the nation's large and more prosperous farms, improved machines were becoming increasingly important. Steel plows were in general use. More horse-drawn corn planters, mowers, hay-rakes, reapers, and threshers were being manufactured and bought. But in 1870 relatively few farmers could afford this equipment.

In 1870 farmers depended almost entirely upon hand tools—axes, saws, spades, pitchforks, sickles, scythes, and rakes. For power they relied on their muscles and on horses, mules, or oxen.

There was nothing new in this situation. For many farmers, American farm life in 1870 was not essentially different from American farm life in, say, 1770 or 1820.

The self-reliant workman. The farmer's lot was never easy. He and his sons rose at daybreak—and even earlier in winter—to milk the cows, bring in firewood, feed the hens and pigs, and fill the water trough for the livestock. When night fell—and even after dark in winter—the farmer was still busy with his unending chores.

But this hard life had its compensations. A farmer was his own boss. His land and his labor furnished most, if not all, of life's essentials—food, clothing, and shelter. The farmer who had to rely mainly on his own efforts developed a spirit of independence that no wage earner could hope to enjoy.

■ **Heating and Cooking.** The parlor stove for heating and the kitchen range for cooking and heating were commonly used in cities and towns, as well as in the country, until the development of central heating, the gas range, and the electric range. Coal or wood was burned and ashes had to be removed frequently.

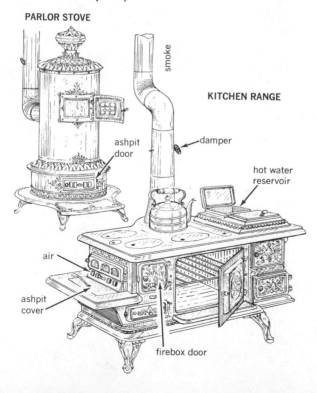

PARLOR STOVE

smoke

KITCHEN RANGE

ashpit door

damper

hot water reservoir

air

ashpit cover

firebox door

■ **Winslow Homer painted this picture of a group of boys playing "Snap the Whip." Their one-room country school is shown in the background.**

But not all American farmers in 1870 shared this feeling of independence. Nearly one fourth of the families living on farms at this time did not own the land they worked. They either rented farms as tenants or operated them as sharecroppers. Share-cropping, as you have read, was especially common among black farmers in the South.

Social life. Except for farmers who lived close to a growing city or a large town, opportunities for social activities in 1870 were limited. Most farm families had only three centers of social activity—the nearest town, the church, and the school.

The Saturday drive to town in a wagon or buggy behind "Old Dobbin" was a big weekly event. Even a 10-mile trip meant about 4 hours on the road. As for the "town," it might be nothing more than a country store at the crossroads, with a blacksmith shop on the opposite corner. Or it might be a sizable village, or even a county seat with a courthouse, a railroad station, several stores, a bank, a doctor's office, a lawyer's office, and a cluster of houses, including the homes of a handful of retired farmers.

These Saturday trips combined business with pleasure. While the mother shopped, and while the farmer arranged for the sale of his cash crops or settled his account at the bank or the store, the children played with their friends. But the shopping and the business brought the opportunity to chat with neighbors, to watch some horse trading in front of the blacksmith shop, and to get the latest news.

The Sunday trip to church was another bright spot in the week. Once again "Old Dobbin" was hitched to the wagon or buggy, and the entire family, freshly scrubbed and dressed in their best clothes, drove to church. There they sang, listened to the sermon, and afterward gathered in front of the church for leisurely talk before driving home.

The local school. On weekdays the children attended a one-room elementary school, some of the boys and girls walking two or three miles each way along the country roads. School terms were short, for the children had to help with spring planting and fall harvesting. The teacher, usually a young woman, taught all grades. The emphasis in

481

1870, as in earlier times, was on "readin', 'ritin', and 'rithmetic." During the school term the teacher often lived in the homes of the pupils, staying a month in one home, then a month in another, and so on throughout her stay.

The school was also a community center. Graduation day was a big occasion, and now and then there were spelling bees and other events for parents as well as for their children.

Loneliness of farm life. For most farm families, however, farming in 1870 was a hard, lonely way of life. It was especially hard and lonely for the pioneers living on the prairies and plains.

Hamlin Garland, who spent his boyhood on farms in Wisconsin, Iowa, and the Dakotas, pictured in his books and short stories the dreary loneliness in isolated farming communities. In his famous collection of tales, *Main-Traveled Roads,* Garland wrote:

"The main-traveled road in the West (as everywhere) is hot and dusty in summer, and desolate and drear with mud in fall and spring, and in winter the winds sweep the snow across it; but it does sometimes cross a rich meadow where the songs of the larks and bobolinks and blackbirds are tangled. Follow it far enough, it may lead past a bend in the river where the water laughs eternally over its shallows.

"Mainly it is long and wearyful, and has a dull little town at one end and a home of toil at the other. Like the main-traveled road of life, it is traversed by many classes of people, but the poor and the weary predominate."

Especially difficult was the lot of immigrant farmers from Europe who, by 1870, were moving out onto the prairies and plains (page 448). These immigrant pioneers had to adjust not only to a strange physical environment but also to a strange and bewildering social environment. Churches were different, schools were different, life in nearly every way was different from what they had known in the Old World. At first they did not understand the language and customs of their neighbors. Nor did their neighbors understand the language and customs of the newcomers.

Hardest of all, perhaps, was the lot of black settlers who ventured into the new areas of the prairies and plains. One "great exodus" of about 15,000 Negroes from the southern states arrived in Kansas in 1879, where they hoped to start new lives free from discrimination. These black newcomers —penniless, wearing patched and tattered clothing, weary and often ill from their long journey—

took up homesteads in the new and unfamiliar lands. To buy a calf, a pig, a few chickens, or a plow, the men worked for wages on nearby farms, on railroads, or in mines. Despite these hardships, many of the black settlers managed to carve out homes for their families in Kansas. Smaller groups of Negroes settled in other parts of the West. Most of them endured some form of discrimination from their white neighbors.

New problems. Most American farmers of the 1870's were not unhappy with their lot. They expected to work hard, and they expected to live more or less apart from their neighbors.

The most troublesome problems confronting America's farmers in the late 1800's were not the age-old problems of hard manual labor and the loneliness of farm life. The problems that troubled them most were new problems growing out of the new industrial economy that was bringing changes to every part of American life.

SECTION SURVEY

1. Explain why farm life in 1870 was not very different from farm life in 1770 or 1820.
2. Although farm life in 1870 was not easy, it had compensations. Explain.
3. (a) Describe the social life of a farm family of the 1870's. (b) How different was this social life from that back east?
4. Compare the adjustments of immigrants in the 1870's settling on the plains and prairies with the adjustments of immigrants in the 1700's who settled along the eastern seaboard.
5. Do you think the reasons for the exodus of Negroes to Kansas in 1879 parallel the reasons for the exodus of Europeans to the New World? Explain.

2 Complex new problems for farmers in the industrial age

For American farmers in general, the last 25 or 30 years of the 1800's brought new problems. Not all farmers were equally affected by these problems. Farmers who remained self-sufficient continued to live much as their parents had lived before them. And many farmers living near city markets, especially farmers concentrating on truck gardening and dairying, were fairly well off. In fact, many wheat growers and other single-crop farmers turned to dairying in the 1870's and 1880's.

The majority of the nation's farmers, however,

were in serious trouble during the last quarter of the 1800's. What were the new problems the farmers faced?

Overproduction and falling prices. The most fundamental causes of agricultural discontent—overproduction and falling prices—were rarely understood by the farmers themselves.

From 1865 to about 1900, farmers produced more food than people could afford to buy. This increase of food in the American markets was the result of (1) the rapid opening of new farm lands on the prairies and plains, and (2) the development of new farm machinery and improved methods of farming.

Why did American farmers not sell their surplus products to other countries? They did. But competing agricultural countries such as Russia, Canada, Argentina, and Australia were also seeking customers abroad and often with the same products that American farmers wanted to export. Thus there was an increased amount of certain kinds of food on the world market as well as in the United States.

Whenever the supply of any commodity is greater than the demand for that commodity, prices fall. Since the 1930's, as you will see later (Chapter 37), the federal government has tried to "support" farm prices in the United States, but in the late 1800's nobody even suggested such a possibility. Thus, farm prices kept falling.

Wheat, which had brought $2.50 a bushel in 1868, dropped to about 78 cents a bushel in the late 1880's. Because of high transportation costs and for other reasons, however, the farmers actually often got only 30 cents a bushel. Corn fell to 15 cents a bushel and, being cheaper than coal, was often used for fuel. Cotton, which in the late 1860's had sold for 65 cents a pound, dropped to 5 cents a pound in 1895. Thus, growers of these important staple crops were farming at a loss.

High farm costs. The situation was even more desperate than these figures indicate. To add to their difficulties, the farmers paid high prices for their shoes, clothing, kerosene, furniture, farm machinery, household equipment, and other goods. In many instances prices were high because cheaply made European goods had been excluded from American markets by the high tariffs put on imports to protect American manufacturers. And in some instances prices were high because they had been artificially raised by monopolies.

Mortgages and increased debts. To make matters worse, the farmers almost always owed money. Many had borrowed money in the form of mortgages to pay for their land, homes, and barns. They had added to this burden of debt by borrowing money to pay for fences, livestock, seed, and machinery. As prices for farm products fell with overproduction, the farmers could not pay their debts. To ward off disaster, they increased their mortgages by borrowing more money, thus adding to their burden of debt.

The 1880's were often called "the decade of mortgages." Of the total number of farms in the country, 43 percent were mortgaged. In Kansas the number reached 60 percent.

Of course, these mortgages often were necessary. By means of mortgages, men with little or no money could borrow the capital they needed to buy a farm, purchase farm machinery, or make improvements on existing farms. It was not mortgages themselves, but hard times and high interest rates that troubled the farmers.

High interest rates. During the late 1800's interest rates on western farm loans ran from 8 to 20 percent. These rates were higher than interest rates charged to industrial and commercial enterprises. Bankers and other money lenders justified the higher rates on farm loans on the ground that farming was a riskier business than industry or commerce. In addition to these high interest rates, money brokers charged a commission for arranging farm loans. In Kansas, 200 loan brokers, starting with nothing, were said to have become millionaires within a few years.

The problem of money. The farmer blamed his troubles on the shortage of money, which was only part of the problem, but an important part. To understand the farmer's point of view, it is necessary to see how money affected his everyday life.

The first thing to remember is that money is a *medium of exchange*—that is, something of value given in exchange for goods or services. Its value is determined by the goods or services it will buy. A flour miller might say, "One dollar will buy one bushel of wheat." A farmer might say, "One bushel of wheat will buy one dollar." The miller and the farmer are saying the same thing; both are stating the value of a dollar *and* the value of a bushel of wheat.

The second thing to remember is that there are two ways to change the value of a dollar *and* the value of a bushel of wheat. All other things being equal, if we *increase the amount of wheat,* let us say double it, then "one dollar will buy two bushels of wheat" or "two bushels of wheat will buy one dollar." If we *decrease the number of dollars in circulation,* say by one half, we can accomplish the same result, for one half as many dollars will now buy just as much wheat. That is, "50 cents will buy one bushel of wheat" and "one dollar will buy two bushels of wheat"; or again "two bushels of wheat will buy one dollar."

In actual practice, the problem of money value is not this simple. But the illustration may help to clarify the problem of the western farmer in the late 1800's.

Falling farm prices. Between 1865 and 1900 the price, or value, of farm products fell lower and lower. Or, to state it differently, the value of money rose higher and higher. Let us take a specific example. In 1868 Olaf Erickson sold 1,000 bushels of wheat at $2.50 a bushel. In 1868, then, his wheat brought him $2,500. Since his interest payments that year amounted to $250, Olaf could pay this interest with the income from 100 bushels of wheat, or one tenth of his income. Each year from 1868 on, Olaf continued to grow and sell 1,000 bushels of wheat. But by 1890 wheat was bringing only 75 cents a bushel. Olaf's income in 1890, therefore, was only $750. Since his interest payments were still $250, he now had to pay his debt with the income from 334 bushels of wheat, or one third of his total income.

As far as Olaf could tell, he had done nothing to cause this state of affairs. He owned the same farm. He worked just as hard every day from sunup to sundown. Yet his income had dropped from $2,500 to $750 a year. Something was wrong. Olaf was working as hard and raising as much wheat as ever. Clearly, Olaf reasoned, the *value of money* had changed. Money was harder to get. Money was scarce. Money was "tight" or "expensive." It had gone up in value. That was why, Olaf thought, the same amount of wheat brought him fewer dollars each year.

Olaf, of course, forgot that there were many more farmers in 1890, both in the United States and in other countries, than there had been in 1868, and that most of his fellow farmers were producing far more wheat than they had produced in 1868.

Although Olaf did not understand the whole complex problem, he did have his finger upon one key to his difficulties. The supply of money in the United States was not expanding rapidly enough during the late 1800's to meet the needs of the new industrial economy. The answer, as Olaf saw it, was simple enough: Let the government increase

the amount of money in circulation. This would "cheapen" the dollar and raise the price of farm products. Olaf could pay his debts, buy what he needed, and enjoy a decent standard of living.

The middlemen. Farmers also blamed many of their difficulties on the so-called *middlemen* who bought from the farmer and sold to wholesalers and retailers. The services performed by these middlemen—the brokers, produce buyers, grain-elevator operators, and stockyard owners—were important in the distribution of farm products. But farmers believed that the middlemen were taking too large a share of the wealth produced on farms and ranches.

Many middlemen no doubt did take advantage of the farmers. Farmers, having little cash and credit, and needing money to pay their debts, had to sell their goods at harvest time even if prices were disastrously low. The middleman, backed by considerable capital, could afford to store what he bought from the farmer until prices went up. Of course, prices did not always go up, and middlemen were sometimes ruined when prices fell.

The railroads. Farmers, especially on the prairies and plains, reserved their chief hatred, however, for the railroads. Like other Americans, including small businessmen, farmers had at first welcomed the railroad with enthusiasm. They believed that it would open distant markets to them and increase the value of their farm lands by bringing more farmers into the community. Farmers who could afford to do so often bought a few shares of railroad stock. And the governments of small farming communities often invested money in railroad stocks and bonds in return for the railroad's promise to build a branch line to the community.

Unfortunately, events did not always develop as the farmers expected. In the first place, the railroad stock that farmers owned was so small a part of all the stock sold that the farmers had little voice in determining railroad policies.

In the second place, the farmers expected that competition among the railroads would keep freight rates low. In this hope they were also disappointed because the railroads charged "differential freight rates." The different railroads were competitors only at terminal points in the major cities, not in the towns and villages along any given stretch of track. To state it differently, railroad officials bid against each other for "long-haul" shipments between two distant cities served by two or more lines, sometimes cutting their rates so low that they operated at actual losses. They made up these losses,

For the farmer in the late 1800's, the country store was an important institution. Here farmers gathered to buy and sell, to get mail, to exchange gossip, and to discuss politics.

however, by charging much higher rates for "short-haul" shipments to communities served by only one railroad.

Farmers and other small shippers protested, of course, against this so-called "long-haul, short-haul abuse" on the part of the railroads. But it was very difficult for them to do anything about the situation.

Many of the problems that farmers faced in the late 1800's were new, strange, and complicated. Most farmers did not at first understand the new problems of overproduction, falling prices, "tight" money, high interest rates, middlemen, and high shipping costs. Like all other Americans, the farmers had to grope their way into the industrial age.

IDENTIFY: medium of exchange, "tight" money, differential freight rates, long-haul shipments.

1. Explain the connection between overproduction and declining farm prices in the period following the Civil War.
2. The 1880's were often called the decade of mortgages. Why?
3. Describe the reasoning of farmer Olaf Erickson when he blamed the shortage of money for the decline in farm prices.
4. What were the farmers' grievances against (a) middlemen, (b) railroads?
5. The new problems faced by the farmer were related to the industrial age. Explain.

485

3 The farmers' increasing influence on government

One of the first lessons that farmers learned as they began to tackle the problems facing them in the late 1800's was the need for cooperative action.

The Grange. The first national farm organization, started in 1867, was called the Grange, or the Patrons of Husbandry. Its founder, Oliver Hudson Kelley, was familiar with the hardships and loneliness of farm life. He proposed, therefore, to establish a national organization with a local chapter in every farm community, where farm families could meet for recreation and to listen to discussions on better ways of farming.

At first Kelley fought an uphill battle in organizing the Grange. By 1872, however, farm prices were falling rapidly, and the farmers, bewildered and disturbed, joined the Grange in growing numbers. By 1875 some 1.5 million farmers, most of them in the Middle West, were Grange members.

Farmers' cooperatives. Kelley had started the Grange primarily to combat social isolation and lack of educational opportunity. The farmers who joined in the 1870's, however, were more interested in economic problems and in the slogans "Cooperation" and "Down with monopoly."

Working together in the Grange and in many local farm organizations, farmers organized cooperative associations, usually called *cooperatives*. A farm cooperative owned and managed by the farmers themselves could bypass middlemen by (1) selling the produce of a group of farmers directly to big city markets and (2) buying farm machines, clothing, and household goods in large quantities at wholesale prices. Before long, farmers began to set up not only cooperative stores but also cooperative grain storage elevators, creameries, and even factories to manufacture their own farm machines and equipment.

Some of these early cooperative ventures were successful, but most failed, partly because of the farmers' lack of business experience, partly because the farmers did not have enough capital to compete successfully with established businesses. But the farmers did not give up, for they still had the possibility of political action.

Influence in state politics. As early as 1870 farmers in Illinois forced the state legislature to investigate unfair practices by the railroads. As a result, in 1871 the Illinois legislature created a commission to fix maximum freight rates, and made it illegal for a railroad to charge "differential freight rates." Encouraged by the passage of these so-called "Granger laws" in Illinois, farmers in Minnesota, Iowa, and Wisconsin persuaded their legislatures to adopt similar laws.

The railroads opposed these laws, of course, and sometimes refused to obey them. But in 1876 and 1877 the Supreme Court, in a series of decisions known as the "Granger cases," of which the most far-reaching case was *Munn v. Illinois,* ruled that state legislatures had the right to regulate businesses that affected the public, including grain elevators and railroads.

Unfortunately for the farmers, the railroads either evaded the laws or exerted enough pressure on the legislators to get the laws repealed. The most serious blow for the farmers, however, came in 1886, when the Supreme Court qualified its decision in the "Granger cases" by ruling that state legislatures had no power to regulate traffic that moved across state boundaries. Or, stating it differently, only the federal government had the power to regulate interstate activities of railroads.

The Interstate Commerce Act. The 1886 Supreme Court decision led Congress to pass the Interstate Commerce Act of 1887. This act was needed to correct a number of unfair practices.

"Pooling" arrangements by the railroads were one of the practices opposed by farmers and by the public at large. Several railroads operating in the same area and across state borders would get together to form a pool (page 472). All members of the pool then agreed not to compete, but instead to charge certain agreed-upon rates. As a result, farmers and others using the railroads often had to pay exorbitant rates.

LIVING AMERICAN DOCUMENTS

Munn v. Illinois (1877)

Property does become clothed with a public interest when used in a manner to make it of public consequence, and affect the community at large. When, therefore, one devotes his property to a use in which the public has an interest, he, in effect, grants to the public an interest in that use, and must submit to be controlled by the public for the common good, to the extent of the interest he has thus created. He may withdraw his grant by discontinuing the use; but, so long as he maintains the use, he must submit to the control. . . .

—United States Supreme Court

486

Another practice the public wanted corrected was the granting of special favors. In order to get business, competing railroads often gave large corporations especially low rates. Or instead of actually lowering the rates, the railroads sometimes agreed to grant *rebates,* that is, to refund, or return, part of the shipping charges.

Farmers, small businessmen, and the public also complained, as you know, that railroads sometimes charged more for a short haul than for a long haul. It sometimes cost more to send goods a few miles than to send the same goods from, say, Chicago to New York.

Provisions of the act. The Interstate Commerce Act, adopted in 1887 and applying to all railroads passing through more than one state, made it illegal for railroads to (1) make "pooling" arrangements, (2) give special favors in the form of lower rates or rebates, (3) charge more for a short haul than for a long haul over the same line, or (4) charge unjust or unreasonable rates. The act also required railroads to print and display their rates, and give a minimum of 10 days' public notice before changing rates.

Finally, the Interstate Commerce Act created an Interstate Commerce Commission (ICC) of five members appointed by the President and confirmed by the Senate. The commission had authority to (1) investigate complaints against railroads, (2) summon witnesses, (3) examine a railroad's accounts and correspondence, and (4) require railroads to file annual reports of operations and finances and to adopt a uniform system of accounting.

The commission, however, had no real authority to fix rates and to enforce its orders. If a railroad refused to accept the commission's proposals, the commission had to appeal to the courts for an order compelling the railroads to obey. In some instances the courts refused to grant such orders. In other instances the courts reversed the commission's decision. Some big businessmen regarded the Interstate Commerce Act as a sop to disgruntled farmers and small businessmen, who, however, soon demanded more effective legislation.

And yet, despite its limitations, the Interstate Commerce Act was highly significant. It was the first important attempt by the federal government to regulate transportation and to create a federal "regulatory commission." Because the act set a precedent for more sweeping measures later adopted by Congress, it marked a turning point in the history of the relations between government and business.

Detail from A. Logan's, "The Circus," 1874. Oil on Canvas. Gift of Edgar William and Bernice Chrysler Garbisch. Collection Whitney Museum of American Art, New York.

THE GREATEST SHOW ON EARTH

The circus, the Fourth of July, and the county fair—these were the big events of the year for farm children and their parents. Most exciting of all was the circus, and the most famous circus was that operated by Phineas T. Barnum.

Barnum started his circus in 1871, billing it as "The Greatest Show on Earth." Ten years later he joined with his major rival, J. A. Bailey, to form the famous Barnum and Bailey Circus.

Every spring the circus started its tour, traveling from town to town in wagon trains over dusty country roads. Agents traveled ahead of the show, plastering colorful posters on the sides of barns, on fence posts, and in the windows of general stores. For weeks in advance farm boys from miles around saved every penny they could get their hands on in anticipation of the big event.

Under the big tent farm youths saw a strange and exciting world. They saw "Jumbo, the King of Elephants," trained bears, snarling tigers and roaring lions, giants and dwarfs, fat men and bearded ladies, sword swallowers and clowns, acrobats and jugglers and other entertainers who performed feats the like of which they had never seen.

When the show was over, many a farm lad dreamed of leaving home and following the circus. A few did run away, but most were content to live with their memories and to begin counting off the months until the circus appeared again.

Politics and paper money. While struggling with railroad legislation, farmers also turned to a more serious problem—the problem of falling prices for farm produce. Ignoring the facts of (1) overproduction and (2) competition from farmers overseas, they blamed low farm prices solely on the scarcity of money.

The farmers' analysis of their problem was partly right, for during the late 1860's and the 1870's money was becoming increasingly scarce. In 1865, for example, the amount of "currency," or money of all kinds, in circulation in the United States averaged $31.18 per person. By 1878 the average had dropped to $17.08.

Faced with growing hardship, farmers demanded that the government increase the supply of currency in circulation. When neither the Republicans nor the Democrats promised to help them, farmers began to join the Greenback-Labor Party, commonly called the Greenback Party.

The Greenback Party took its name from the paper money known as "greenbacks" which had been issued by the government during the Civil War (page 390). After the war the government began to withdraw the greenbacks from circulation. Farmers and other "cheap money" advocates protested. They wanted *more,* not fewer, greenbacks in circulation.

Greenbacks redeemed in gold. But the "cheap money" people did not get what they wanted. Instead, in 1875 Congress adopted the Resumption Act. This act ordered the Secretary of the Treasury to redeem *in gold* all greenbacks presented to the Treasury on or after January 1, 1879. As a result of this action, by January 1, 1879, greenbacks were worth their full, or face, value in gold. Under these circumstances, owners of greenbacks did not bother to redeem them, and Congress decided to allow 346 million of them to remain in circulation as a permanent part of United States currency.

Meanwhile, in 1875, dismayed by Congress' decision to redeem the greenbacks in gold, the "cheap money" advocates decided to take their case to the people at the polls. That was when they organized their own political party. Although the newly organized Greenback Party did not win a significant number of votes in the 1876 election, the Greenbackers continued their battle for "cheap money."

The silver issue. President Rutherford B. Hayes, who entered the White House in 1877, successfully opposed the pressure of the Greenbackers to get more paper money into circulation. But he was unable to block another move by the "cheap money" people to increase the volume of currency in circulation.

Back in 1834 the government had adopted a law providing for the coinage of both gold and silver, at a ratio of about 16 to 1. That is, the government offered to buy 16 ounces of silver for the same price it paid for one ounce of gold. At the time silver was relatively scarce, and silver producers could sell 16 ounces of silver to private buyers for *more than* one ounce of gold. As a result, they did not take silver to the United States Mint to be coined into silver dollars.

In the 1870's however, this situation changed. With the discovery of huge silver deposits in Colorado and Nevada (page 451), the supply of silver increased tremendously and the value of silver *bullion,* or uncoined metal, began to fall. In 1874, for the first time in more than 30 years, 16 ounces of silver bullion were sold on the open market for *less than* one ounce of gold.

Faced with falling prices, silver producers remembered the government's offer to buy silver at the ratio of 16 to 1. But in trying to sell their silver bullion to the Treasury Department, they discovered that in 1873 Congress had passed a law removing silver dollars from the list of standard coins.

Furious at the loss of a profitable market for their bullion, silver producers denounced Congress for what they called the "Crime of '73." Actually Congress had passed the law because for more than 30 years the silver producers had not wanted to sell their bullion to the government.

But the "Crime of '73" became a rallying cry for those who demanded that the government buy silver. This demand came mostly from the West. But the silver people were also supported by other Americans, including farmers, who wanted more currency in circulation.

The Bland-Allison Act. In 1877 Representative Richard P. Bland of Missouri introduced a bill calling for free and unlimited coinage of silver dollars at a ratio of 16 silver dollars to 1 gold dollar. When this bill reached the Senate, it was modified by Senator William B. Allison of Iowa to become the Bland-Allison bill.

The Bland-Allison bill authorized the Treasury Department to buy and to mint not less than $2 million and not more than $4 million worth of silver each month. President Hayes vetoed the bill, but Congress passed it over his veto in 1878. The new law was a partial victory for the silver interests, the Greenbackers, and other "cheap money" people.

Failure of the Greenback movement. The Greenback Party reached its high-water mark in 1878, when it polled 1 million votes and elected members to Congress. This was a shock to the two major parties. But the triumph was short-lived. Two years later the Greenback Presidential candidate, General J. B. Weaver, received only 300,000 votes.

Although it failed to achieve its goal, the Greenback movement, like the Grange movement, taught the farmers several valuable lessons. The farmers learned from their experience with the Grange that they could, if united, gain influence in state legislatures. They learned from the Greenback movement that their influence might be felt even in the national legislature. And, above all, they learned that the secret of power lay in organization.

Farmers' Alliances. Even before the Greenback Party began to break up, farmers began to form organizations called "alliances." During the early 1880's the different state alliances in the North and Northwest organized a loose federation called the Northern, or Northwestern, Farmers' Alliance. The southern groups joined in a much more tightly knit organization known as the Southern Alliance.

Like the Grange, the alliances experimented with cooperative buying and selling organizations. They were prepared to take action to protect the farmers from the exploitation of manufacturers, railroads, and middlemen.

Hard times in the late 1880's transformed the alliances into influential political organizations. By 1890, for example, the Southern Alliance had 3 million white members, while 1 million southern black farmers were enrolled in an affiliated Colored Alliance. A proposal to merge the Southern Alliance and the Northwestern Farmers' Alliance failed, however, because southerners insisted upon separate white and black lodges in the merged alliance. Northern leaders refused to accept this arrangement.

Desperate conditions for farmers. Starting in 1886, a 10-year series of droughts on the Great Plains turned farm lands into arid desert. Driven to desperation, thousands of farmers finally gave up and moved back east. But others remained and continued to fight the land and the men that they held responsible for much of their trouble—the owners of railroads and factories, the directors of banks and insurance companies that held farm mortgages, and the middlemen who bought and sold farm produce. The farmers also continued

Harvey T. Dunn (1884–1952), American. *The Homesteader's Wife* (detail). South Dakota Memorial Art Center, Brookings. Gift of the artist.

■ Starting in 1886, a 10-year series of droughts on the Great Plains turned farm lands into arid desert. The picture shown above reflects the hard life of farm people on the Great Plains.

their pressure, along with other "cheap money" interests, to get the government to put more money into circulation.

The Sherman Silver Purchase Act. During the administration of President Benjamin Harrison, the Republicans in Congress were eager, as you have seen, to increase tariff rates. They succeeded when the McKinley Tariff Act became law in 1890 (page

436). But to get enough votes to pass this tariff act, the Republicans had to make a deal with the "cheap money" people.

In 1889 and 1890 six new states entered the Union—North Dakota, South Dakota, Montana, Washington, Idaho, and Wyoming. These states, all in the West, greatly increased the political strength of the farmers and the silver mining interests in Congress. Congressmen representing farming and silver mining areas agreed to vote for the McKinley Tariff Act if the high-tariff Congressmen voted for a "cheap money" bill.

As a result of this "deal," the Sherman Silver Purchase Act became law in 1890. This act required the United States Treasury to purchase 4.5 million ounces of silver each month at the prevailing market price and to pay for this silver with paper money that could be redeemed in gold or silver.

Silver miners hoped that the law would raise the price of silver, and farmers hoped that, by increasing the supply of money, it would raise the prices of farm produce. These expectations were not realized. The purchased silver was not coined, and the money in circulation did not greatly increase.

New farm leaders. Leaders of the Farmers' Alliances were active in securing passage of the Sherman Silver Purchase Act and other legislation favorable to farmers. Some of the leaders became national figures by reason of their powerful oratory, their vigor, and the depth of their convictions. Among the nationally famous leaders was Ignatius Donnelly of Minnesota, a spellbinder on the platform and a pamphleteer with a biting literary style. In Kansas there was "Sockless Jerry" Simpson, who denounced the rich eastern monopolists. Kansas also produced Mrs. Mary Elizabeth Lease, a colorful and able lawyer whose fervent speeches fanned the flame of political unrest.

In the South a new group of political leaders representing the poorer farmers arose to challenge the traditional leaders of the Democratic Party. Among the most picturesque and eloquent of the new leaders were Governor James Hogg of Texas, Tom Watson of Georgia, and "Pitchfork Ben" Tillman of South Carolina.

The big question. By 1890 American farmers were facing a major question: Should they form a third party? Many northern farmers favored a third party; most southern farmers opposed it. The opposition of southern farmers arose from a split within the southern Democratic ranks.

Since reconstruction days, prosperous, white, conservative southerners, called "Bourbon" ° Democrats, had regained major political strength in the South. They were opposed by agrarian reformers within the Democratic Party who were demanding greater economic opportunity and justice for poor white farmers. The voices of these southern Democratic reformers and their followers were strong within the Southern Alliance of farmers.

In 1890 many southern Negroes were still permitted to vote. As a rule, the Bourbon Democrats were less determined than poorer white farmers in discriminating against black southerners. Thus, many black tenant farmers voted for Bourbon candidates.

Leaders of the southern Democratic reformers had differing opinions on the issue of Negro suffrage. A few, recognizing the common economic interests of the poorer farmers, white and black, favored an effort to enlist black voters on their side. But the majority feared that competition with the Bourbons for black votes would endanger white supremacy in the South. They especially feared that a third political party would divide the southern white vote and thereby enable Negroes to become a political power again in the South, as they had been during reconstruction. Thus most leaders of the Southern Alliance were opposed to a new farmers' political party. These leaders preferred to continue their efforts to capture control of the southern Democratic Party from the Bourbon Democrats.

° **Bourbon:** in politics, an extremely conservative or reactionary person, named after France's Bourbon family of rulers.

SECTION SURVEY

IDENTIFY: the Grange, rebates, pooling, "cheap money," ratio of 16 to 1, bullion, "Crime of '73," Sherman Silver Purchase Act of 1890; Oliver H. Kelley.

1. (a) What was the original purpose of the Grange? (b) Why were farmers' cooperatives formed?
2. Discuss the strengths, limitations, and significance of the Interstate Commerce Act of 1887.
3. Explain the reasons for the formation of (a) the Greenback Party, (b) Farmers' Alliances.
4. Farmers learned that one way to power was through organization. Discuss.
5. In the political struggle in the South, black southerners were caught in the middle. Comment.

4 The farmers' failure to win control of the national government

Should the farmers form their own national political party? This was the question that farmers discussed in schoolhouses and Grange halls during the summer of 1890.

Birth of the Populist Party. The Congressional elections in the fall of 1890 drew farmers and their wives into what seemed to be a fiery crusade. Led by spokesmen like Mary Elizabeth Lease, the farmers bluntly stated their grievances.

In a powerful speech Mrs. Lease proclaimed: "Wall Street ° owns the country. It is no longer a government of the people, by the people, and for the people, but a government of Wall Street, by Wall Street, and for Wall Street. The great common people of this country are slaves, and monopoly is the master. The West and South are bound and prostrate before the manufacturing East.... There are thirty men in the United States whose aggregate wealth is over one and one-half billion dollars. There are half a million looking for work. ... We want money, land, and transportation.... We will stand by our homes and stay by our firesides by force if necessary, and we will not pay our debts to the loanshark companies until the government pays its debts to us. The people are at bay, let the bloodhounds of money who have dogged us thus far beware."

Fired by this new militant spirit, Republican and Democratic farmers decided in 1891 to forget their political differences and form a third party. A meeting made up chiefly of Farmers' Alliance leaders from the West and Middle West launched the People's Party, or the Populist Party, at Cincinnati, Ohio, in 1891. In Omaha, Nebraska, the following year, the Populists drew up a platform and nominated James B. Weaver of Iowa for President of the United States.

The farmers' "Declaration of Independence." On July 4, 1892, the Populists adopted their platform, demanding far-reaching reforms.

"We meet in the midst of a nation brought to the verge of moral, political, and material ruin," stated the platform. "The people are demoralized.... The newspapers are largely subsidized or muzzled; public opinion silenced; business prostrated; our homes covered with mortgages; labor impover-

ished; and the land concentrating in the hands of the capitalists. ... We have witnessed for more than a quarter of a century the struggles of the two great political parties for power and plunder, while grievous wrongs have been inflicted upon the suffering people. We charge that the controlling influences dominating both these parties have permitted the existing dreadful conditions to develop without serious effort to prevent or restrain them. Neither do they now promise us any substantial reform.... They propose to sacrifice our homes, lives, and children on the altar of Mammon.° ..."

Specific Populist demands. The Populist platform then listed the specific demands of the farmers: (1) an increase in the currency, to be secured by the "free and unlimited coinage of silver at a ratio of 16 to 1"; (2) government ownership of railroads, telegraphs, and telephones; (3) the return to the government of all land held by railroads and other corporations in excess of their needs; (4) a graduated income tax, requiring people with higher incomes to pay a proportionally higher tax; (5) a system of national warehouses where farm produce could be stored until market conditions improved, with the government providing loans on each deposit by a farmer; (6) political reforms, including the direct election of United States Senators, and the adoption of the secret ballot, the initiative, and the referendum (Chapter 27).

The Populist Party had strong support from many industrial wage earners, as well as from farmers. Thus, the Populist platform also demanded shorter working hours and restrictions on immigration, which many workers held responsible for unemployment and low wages.

The election of 1892. In the campaign of 1892, great crowds of farmers in the Middle West gathered at outdoor meetings and picnics to listen to eloquent Populist speakers. James B. Weaver, the Populist Presidential candidate, traveled widely and spoke to enthusiastic audiences in the Middle West.

In the South, however, the story was different because of the racial situation. Conservative Democrats and Populists alike were willing to let black southerners vote—but only if it seemed certain that they could control the black vote. Populist leaders, however, urged poor farmers, white and black, to vote together against their "exploiters," the well-to-do planters and businessmen of the Demo-

---

° **Wall Street:** a street in New York City's financial district, the nation's principal financial center; often used as a symbol of large banking and business interests.

° **Mammon:** an ancient god, used to symbolize wealth, greed, and materialism, to whom human sacrifices were made.

cratic Party. This angered many white southerners, rich and poor alike, who feared that the Populist bid for black support might endanger white supremacy. Populist speakers in the South were greeted with howls and jeers.

The southern Populist bid for Negro votes was not very successful. The Populists did not attempt to build a strong or lasting alliance between poor white and black southerners. They did not support a move toward federal supervision of elections, which would have guaranteed the right of black southerners to vote. Nor did the Populists support other efforts of southern Negroes to overcome their grievances. Thus, Populist candidates in the election of 1892 were generally defeated in the South.

President Benjamin Harrison, running for reelection on the Republican ticket, was defeated, as you know, by the Democratic candidate, Grover Cleveland. The Democratic victory was a sweeping one. But the Populists made an impressive showing in the nation as a whole, despite their failure in the South. They polled more than 1 million popular votes, won 22 electoral votes for their Presidential candidate, and gained seats in state legislatures and in Congress. No third party had ever shown such strength within a year after its birth. Democrats and Republicans alike realized that the Populist movement was much more than the protest of a few discontented Americans.

Depression and growing resentment. For the two older political parties, however, the Populist movement was only the beginning of their problems. In 1893 the country sank into a serious economic depression (pages 436–37). Farm prices plunged downward. Factories closed their doors, and thousands of unemployed workers walked the streets, desperately looking for jobs.

Farmers and wage earners blamed the depression on "tight money." They demanded that the government increase the amount of currency in circulation by the "free and unlimited coinage of silver at a ratio of 16 to 1."

President Cleveland blamed the crisis on the Sherman Silver Purchase Act of 1890. He believed that it was not "tight money" that had led to the depression, but rather uncertainty over the "value

■ In the election of 1892, a Republican and a Democrat in Chicago each promised to pull the other through the streets in a wagon if his candidate lost. The Democrat, a Cleveland banker, won the bet. The painter, Joseph Klir, included in his picture a number of his fellow immigrants who had come to the United States from what is now Czechoslovakia.

Chicago Historical Society

of money." Cleveland insisted that the only way to end the depression was to accept gold as the single standard of value for the nation's currency. This was an oversimplified explanation, for the depression was worldwide. But there was some truth in the President's analysis.

Reviewing the money problem. As you have seen, during the 1870's and 1880's farmers blamed their difficulties, in part at least, on the government's refusal to increase the supply of money, or currency, in circulation. Farmers and other *debtors* wanted "cheap money" with which to pay their overwhelming debts. On the other hand, *creditors* and businessmen in general wanted to be paid back in dollars worth at least as much as the dollars they had lent or invested. Creditors and businessmen wanted, therefore, to restrict the amount of money in circulation. They wanted what they called "sound money."

Acting under the authority of the Sherman Silver Purchase Act, the Treasury had begun in 1890 to buy silver in large quantities. Mine owners now had a sure market for almost the entire output of their mines, but the price of silver continued to drop. Farmers and other "cheap money" people considered the new law merely a halfway measure. What they demanded in the Populist platform of 1892 was the "free and unlimited coinage of silver at a ratio of 16 to 1."

The shrinking gold reserves. By 1893, however, the Treasury Department was becoming deeply concerned about the policy of *bimetallism*—meaning that two metals, gold and silver, furnished the security for all the nation's currency. The value of silver had fallen until the actual silver in a silver dollar was worth only 60 cents. Since silver as well as gold provided the "backing," or security, for the nation's currency, more Americans began to grow uneasy about this situation. As a result, more people began to exchange their silver bank notes for gold coins, rather than for silver coins. By the time Cleveland entered the White House in March 1893, the gold reserves had shrunk to only a little more than $100 million.

The shrinkage in gold reserves created a serious government crisis. If the gold reserves completely disappeared, the government would no longer be able to keep its promise with gold coins. It would, instead, have to pay with silver. And, since by mid-summer of 1893 the value of the silver in a silver dollar had fallen to 49 cents, prices would soar in a runaway inflation, and the nation would head toward economic disaster.

Repeal of the Sherman Silver Purchase Act. President Cleveland acted promptly. He called a special session of Congress to repeal the Sherman Silver Purchase Act. The President's recommendation provoked violent debate. Representatives of silver mines, farmers, and "cheap money" people in general refused to consider repeal. But in the late fall the administration finally secured enough votes to push the repeal bill through Congress.

Repeal of the Sherman Silver Purchase Act stopped the flow of silver into the Treasury. But the gold reserves continued to shrink, for there were still many millions of silver bank notes in circulation and the Treasury kept on redeeming them in gold. By 1895 the gold reserves had dropped to only $41 million. It seemed to be only a question of time before the United States would go off the gold standard—that is, would stop redeeming its paper currency with gold—and runaway inflation would start.

Cleveland aided by bankers. At this critical point President Cleveland accepted the recommendation of a group of bankers headed by J. P. Morgan. The bankers offered to lend gold to the government, receiving government bonds as security.

The arrangement worked. When people heard that J. P. Morgan and other leading bankers were behind the government, confidence returned and the run on the gold reserves ended. Many Americans, those with "sound money" views, felt that President Cleveland and the bankers had acted wisely and had saved the nation from disaster. But "cheap money" Americans were furious. Pointing out that the bankers had charged a generous commission for their services, they insisted that the President had made a "deal with Wall Street."

Battle lines drawn. By the time of the Presidential election of 1896, both major parties were split between the "sound money," gold-standard people and the "cheap money," silver people.

The Republicans chose as their Presidential candidate William McKinley of Ohio. Although McKinley tried to straddle the money issue, he came to be regarded as the leader of those people who favored the gold standard.

The Democratic convention opened with a bitter struggle between the "sound money" wing of the party and the "silver" wing. The "sound money" delegates were soon howled down, and "cheap money" delegates adopted a platform demanding "free and unlimited coinage of both gold and silver. . . ."

The battle lines were drawn, with the Republicans on the "sound money" side and the majority of Democrats on the "cheap money" side. But the Democrats had not yet selected a Presidential candidate. Rejecting President Cleveland, the "silver" Democrats began to look for a man who could lead them to victory.

William Jennings Bryan. The field was wide open when a handsome young lawyer stepped forward to address the convention. Only 36 years old, William Jennings Bryan of Nebraska had served in the House of Representatives for four years. This was his only political experience in the national capital. But when he began to speak at the convention, people listened.

"We do not come as aggressors," Bryan cried. "Our war is not a war of conquest; we are fighting in the defense of our homes, our families, and prosperity. We have petitioned, and our petitions have been scorned; we have entreated, and our entreaties have been disregarded; we have begged, and they have mocked when our calamity came. We beg no longer; we petition no more. We defy them! . . .

"You come to us and tell us that the great cities are in favor of the gold standard; we reply that the great cities rest upon our broad and fertile prairies. Burn down your cities and leave our farms, and your cities will spring up again as if by magic; but destroy our farms and the grass will grow in the streets of every city in the country. . . .

"Having behind us the producing masses of this nation and the world, supported by the commercial interests, the laboring interests, and the toilers everywhere, we will answer their demand for a gold standard by saying to them: You shall not press down upon the brow of labor this crown of thorns, you shall not crucify mankind upon a cross of gold!"

With the closing words of Bryan's "Cross of Gold" speech, wild tumult broke out at the convention. Here was the Democratic standard-bearer. Here was a fitting leader for a crusade to wrest power from the big business, "sound money" groups.

The Democratic nomination of Bryan and the adoption of a platform demanding free and unlimited coinage of silver left the Populists in an awkward position. The Democrats had stolen their thunder. When they met in convention, the Populists decided to support Bryan as their Presidential candidate, but they tried to preserve their party identity by nominating Tom Watson of Georgia for the Vice-Presidency rather than Arthur Sewall of Maine, the Democratic nominee.

Bryan's crusade. Bryan turned the election campaign into a crusade. In 14 exhausting weeks Bryan, traveling thousands of miles by railroad, accomplished the almost superhuman feat of making 600 speeches to 5 million people in 27 states. Bryan's speeches roused his supporters into frenzies of enthusiasm.

The "sound money" people threw all their energy and resources into defeating Bryan. Under the leadership of Mark Hanna of Ohio, McKinley's campaign manager and a wealthy businessman, the Republicans raised at least $3.5 million to offset Bryan's $300,000 campaign fund. Nearly every influential newspaper in the country backed the Republicans. Many factories paid their workers on the Saturday before election with the warning that they would have no jobs if William Jennings Bryan won the election.

McKinley's victory. Bryan lost with 176 electoral votes to McKinley's 271. But the popular vote was much closer—7 million for the Republicans, 6.5 million for the Democrats. Although the country had decided in favor of the gold standard, the farmers and other "cheap money" advocates had come close to winning the Presidency and control of Congress.

Defeat in the 1896 election and the arrival of better times for the farmers ended the power of the Populist Party. As you will see, however, during the early 1900's a new third party, the Progressive Party, as well as progressive Democrats and Republicans, won many of the reforms that the Populists had demanded.

SECTION SURVEY

IDENTIFY: Populists, free and unlimited coinage of silver, "sound money," bimetallism, "Cross of Gold" speech; James B. Weaver, William McKinley, William Jennings Bryan, Mark Hanna.

1. In your opinion, which four planks in the Populist Party platform of 1892 would have aided the farmers most at that time?
2. Which ideas in Bryan's "Cross of Gold" speech were most effective in winning him the nomination?
3. If all the underprivileged people in the nation in the 1890's had been able to form an alliance or had been able to organize, what do you think might have been the result?

TRACING THE MAIN IDEAS

Machines, science, and industry transformed American life with increasing speed after 1870 and created many new problems for farmers as well as for all other Americans. Most farmers lost the individual freedom they had possessed when they had produced a good part of what they needed on their own land. Overproduction brought falling prices and growing distress. Increasingly, farmers became dependent upon forces that they could not control—the railroads that carried their goods to market, prices fixed in distant markets, tariffs that sometimes raised the cost of manufactured goods, the supply of currency made available by the federal government.

Faced with these new problems, farmers began to organize new political parties and to increase their influence in the old parties in an effort to gain influence in state and federal governments. They hoped by these methods to secure laws that would regulate the railroads, the industries, and the other parts of the economic system and thus make life easier for farm people.

But industrialism brought benefits as well as problems. Power-driven machines made life immeasurably easier. Increased production enabled the farmer to feed himself and his fellow citizens far better than men had ever been fed before. Developments in transportation and communications broke down the isolation of farm life and brought the farmer and his family into touch with the life of the world beyond the farm.

It was difficult for farmers, as it was for all other Americans, to adjust to the new industrial age. The problems were all too real. By the 1900's, however, farmers began to understand that Americans were becoming increasingly interdependent and that their best hope of realizing the bright promise of the new age was to learn to work together.

CHAPTER SURVEY

QUESTIONS FOR DISCUSSION

1. Third parties in national politics have never won a Presidential election. What then has been their function in our political system?
2. (a) Discuss the reasons why the farmer wanted cheap money (greenbacks) and free and unlimited coinage of silver. (b) To what extent were farmers successful in achieving this goal?
3. Explain why you would have felt as you did about cheap money vs. sound money, if you had been a (a) debtor farmer, (b) creditor businessman, (c) retired person living on a fixed income, (d) banker, (e) worker.
4. How did each of the following complicate the farm problem: (a) railroads, (b) interest on mortgages, (c) protective tariff?
5. Why was the Populist Party so fiercely opposed to the financiers, railroads, and corporate businessmen of the United States?
6. By referring to the "Cross of Gold" speech, explain why William Jennings Bryan came to be known as "the voice of populism."

RELATING PAST TO PRESENT

1. Search current newspapers and magazines for articles on migrant farm workers in the United States. Compare the difficulties these migrant workers have with the problems faced by early Grange members.
2. Do dissident groups need a crisis in order to mobilize behind one leader and one platform? Does a society have to be confronted with a crisis or an emergency before it listens to those who are in need? Explain your answers.
3. Does mechanization continue to bring about change in our society today? Explain.

USING MAPS AND CHARTS

1. Consult chart 1 on pages 866–67 in answering these questions: (a) What major advances in American agriculture were made between colonial times and 1900? (b) How does the progress in agriculture compare with the advances made in the fields of transportation, communication, and manufacturing?
2. Refer to charts 5 and 6 on page 863 in answering the following: (a) Compare the average size of farms in 1850, 1900, and today. What does this information tell you? (b) Compare the number of farms in 1850, 1900, and today. What does this information tell you?

CHAPTER 25

The Struggle of American Workers to Organize

1860's – 1890's

On APRIL 14, 1865, when President Lincoln was shot in Ford's Theater in the nation's capital, the United States was still a predominantly agricultural country. By 1900 it had become the leading industrial and manufacturing nation in the world.

America's amazing industrial growth was possible only because of immense improvements in transportation, notably the railroad and the steamship; the development of power-driven machines; the organization of business into large corporations; the construction of giant factories and other industrial plants; the development of more efficient production techniques; and the rapid growth in the number of workers.

The workers—women and children as well as men—came from farms and rural areas. They also came from Europe, in a mighty flood of immigration numbering hundreds of thousands every year.

Both the older Americans and the newcomers entered a new world when they moved into America's growing industrial communities. In the early days of power-driven machines and mass production, they were as much pioneers as the men and women who had earlier pushed America's frontiers westward to the Pacific. And, like pioneers in every age, wage earners in the late 1800's faced complex problems.

THE CHAPTER IN OUTLINE

1. Complex new problems for wage earners in the industrial age.

2. The influence of immigrant workers in American society.

3. The role of labor organizations in dealing with workers' grievances.

4. Opposition to organized labor's early efforts to win reforms.

496

1 Complex new problems for wage earners in the industrial age

The industrial developments that were transforming the United States from 1865 to 1900 created new problems as well as new opportunities for wage earners. Like all other Americans, wage earners had to adapt themselves to a rapidly changing industrial society.

New owner-worker relations. For one thing, large corporations hiring thousands of workers changed the old-time relations between owners and employees. In earlier days when factories were small, the owner knew his workers and often took a personal interest in their welfare. But in the huge factories workers seldom saw the owners, most of whom were stockholders living in widely separated parts of the country.

Nor did many owners know at first hand what working conditions were like in their factories and mines. They bought shares of stock as an investment. They employed managers to run the plants.

Moreover, the workers themselves often were less interested in the new, large impersonal corporation. As the factory grew larger, the worker, as an individual, became less important. If he objected to the way the factory was run, he could easily be replaced. Single-handed, he could not hope to change or improve his working conditions. Nor could he reasonably hope to become an owner beyond, perhaps, buying a few shares of stock. To be sure, some workers did become foremen and managers, and a few rose to positions of wealth and power.

But in general, as factories grew larger and more impersonal, it became harder for individual workers or small groups of workers to "bargain" with their employers over wages and working conditions.

Company towns. Workers in so-called "company towns" labored under the greatest disadvantages. There were mining districts in Pennsylvania and West Virginia and textile-mill regions in the South where companies owned entire towns—all the houses, stores, and other buildings. The companies employed the teachers and the doctors. The local magistrates and the policemen owed their jobs to the company. In these towns no worker dared to protest the rent he paid for his company-owned house or the prices he paid in the company-owned store. Frequently, the worker received part of his wages, not in cash, but in credit at the company store.

Effects of mechanization. The use of power-driven machines in factories also created new problems for wage earners. For one thing, work became increasingly specialized and increasingly monotonous. Moreover, the new machinery often did the work of several wage earners. Indeed, the new machines might produce much more than the displaced wage earners. Thus, the installation of new machines often caused *technological unemployment* by throwing workers out of jobs. Of course, the new machines often created new and different jobs because workers were needed to build and repair the machines. Further, the higher output of the machines increased the nationwide production of goods, and thereby created new jobs of many kinds. But displaced workers often found it difficult to learn new skills and get new jobs.

Machines were also physically dangerous. Until about 1910 little was done to safeguard workers from accidents. When an accident occurred, the worker himself was usually blamed. If he was disabled, he received no compensation to pay for doctors and hospitalization. When a worker was

■ One effect of the growth of industry was the crowding of workers and their families in big-city slums. This photograph was taken in the early 1900's.

killed, his family was usually left without an income, for employers did not insure the lives of wage earners. Yet industrial hazards were a problem of primary importance. Between 1900 and 1910, for example, 3 percent of all employed workers in the United States were killed or injured annually in industrial accidents.

Effect of the railroads.   Before the nationwide network of railroads was built, American manufacturers usually sold their products only in nearby market areas, without competition from other areas. With the railroad network, however, a manufacturer could sell his products anywhere in the country, provided that his prices were as low as those elsewhere.

This creation of a competitive national market for goods also created a competitive national market for labor. For example, if cotton goods were being made cheaper in southern mills because of lower wage rates, then New England manufacturers of cotton goods were inclined to lower their wage rates to compete with the lower-priced output of the southern mills.

The business cycle and unemployment.   Like other citizens, workers were greatly influenced by what economists call the *business cycle*—the expansion of business and industry during periods of prosperity and their contraction during periods of depression. Businessmen and government officials had not yet learned how to cushion the effects of depression. Workers lived in constant dread of being laid off or having their wages sharply reduced whenever business conditions took a downturn. Even when business was good, unemployment brought hunger and misery to many industrial workers.

Between 1870 and 1900 hundreds of thousands of jobless men searched for work. In 1889, a fairly typical year, about 19 percent of the workers in manufacturing and transportation were jobless.

The closed frontier.   As long as the frontier remained open, farmers on worn-out eastern land could choose between migration to the frontier or migration to the city. Many chose to continue farming and moved west. After about 1900, however, as eastern farmers had less and less opportunity to find good cheap western land, they turned increasingly to the cities for work. Thus they helped to swell the population of the cities and to drive down the wages of the industrial worker. In this respect the labor market was like any other market. An oversupply of workers tended to push wages down.

Low wages and long hours.   During the last quarter of the 1800's, many wage earners complained with increasing bitterness about their low wages. Unskilled workers might earn no more than $10 a week. Skilled workers—those whose jobs required a certain amount of training and education —might earn no more than $20 a week. Actually, industrial expansion brought higher *real wages°* to workers as a whole. Nevertheless, large numbers of workers believed that they were not receiving a fair share of the profits from the country's great industrial growth.

Wages tended to be low for several reasons: the increasing power of employers over employees; the creation of a competitive national labor market; depressions; and the flooding of the labor market by new workers.

Wage earners also complained about their long working hours. After 1865 an 11-hour day was common in American industry. Yet even in the 1880's textile workers in many places toiled from 12 to 14 hours daily.

From 1900 to 1920 working hours began to be shortened. The average working hours in factories decreased from 57 per week in 1909 to 50 per week in 1919. But even as late as this, the 12-hour day prevailed in the steel industry, for example.

It was indeed a new and rapidly changing world with which the American wage earner wrestled in the late 1800's. The problems of wage earners were complex ones, and neither the workers, the owners of the industries, nor Americans in general had any ready answers. And, as you will see, immigrants entering the country during this period encountered these same problems and others.

° *real wages:* wages reckoned in terms of actual purchasing power, or what the money will buy.

SECTION SURVEY

IDENTIFY: "company town," technological unemployment, business cycle, real wages.

1. Compare relations between owners and workers in the small, privately owned mills and the huge, corporation-owned factories.
2. Discuss the problems faced by workers as a result of increasing mechanization.
3. How did each of the following affect workers: (a) railroads, (b) business cycle, (c) end of the frontier?
4. What were two of the most common complaints of workers in the 1880's and 1890's?

2 The influence of immigrant workers in American society

Immigrants played an essential part in the amazing industrial development of the United States from 1865 to 1900. Immigrants came in the first place as workers seeking new opportunities. In trying to find places for themselves in their new homeland and in the industrial age, the immigrants were often greeted with distrust and suspicion.

The problem of numbers. Part of the difficulty was the overwhelming number of immigrants who poured into the country. During the 29 years from 1870 to 1899, more than 11 million men, women, and children entered the United States.

The changing character of immigration. The changing character of immigration, as well as the swelling tide, alarmed many Americans. Until the early 1880's most immigrants came from northwestern Europe—from Great Britain, Ireland, Scandinavia, Germany, and the Netherlands. But after 1890 an increasingly large number came from southern and eastern Europe. The languages, customs, and ways of living of these immigrants were quite different from those of immigrants from northwestern Europe.

Effect of immigration on labor. The immigrants had an enormous influence on American life. Although some settled on farms, the great majority moved to the densely crowded slum areas of the cities. Here they competed with native Americans for housing, thereby driving up housing costs.

Most immediate of all, however, was their effect upon established workers. Immigrants competed with established American wage earners for jobs, thereby lowering wages. To be sure, immigrants helped to stimulate the economy by creating new demands for factory and farm products. But the average wage earner was more disturbed by the job competition of the immigrants than he was impressed with the stimulating effects of large-scale immigration.

Tension on the Pacific coast. Chinese workers on the Pacific coast, particularly in California, were the first victims of the rising distrust against all

■ Many Chinese laborers, after helping build the western railroad, stayed on as track workers, or "gandy dancers." In this painting, Chinese workers are waving as a Central Pacific train puffs along between snowsheds built as a protection against avalanches. The painting was made by the artist Joseph Becker in 1869.

immigrants. By the terms of the Burlingame Treaty of 1868, the Chinese had the right to immigrate to the United States. For some years, Chinese laborers had been welcome additions to the labor supply. They had been willing to do the hardest and least desirable jobs for very low wages. They were the backbone of the construction gangs that built the western section of the first transcontinental railroad (page 440). By the 1870's, nearly 75,000 Chinese workmen had entered the country. Most of them had settled in California, where they made up about 20 percent of all workers.

Such was the situation in 1873 when a depression hit the country. As unemployment mounted, California workmen feared that the Chinese would take their jobs at low wages. Fear and insecurity were intensified because the Chinese, for reasons not always of their own choosing, lived entirely to themselves, and did not learn American ways of living.

Restrictions on Chinese immigrants. Ill feeling, already running high, was fanned into violence by crowds of unemployed California workmen who gathered on street corners and sand lots. The "sand lotters" presently fell upon the unfortunate Chinese, killing some and burning the property of others.

In cooperation with distressed farmers, California workingmen were able to influence the writing of a new state constitution in 1879. California's new constitution discriminated against Chinese by prohibiting them from owning property or working at certain jobs.

The opponents of Chinese immigration also succeeded in getting Congress to pass an "exclusion bill" in 1879. The 1879 bill prohibited all but a few Chinese from settling in the United States in any year. Because this bill violated the Burlingame Treaty of 1868, President Hayes vetoed it. But under pressure the Chinese government agreed not to object if the United States regulated immigration, and in 1882 Congress enacted a new Chinese Exclusion Act which, with several extensions, continued in effect until World War II. The Chinese Exclusion Act forbade the immigration of Chinese laborers and denied American citizenship to Chinese born in China. Only students and a few other groups of Chinese could enter the United States.

Other immigration restrictions. The Chinese Exclusion Act of 1882 was the first of a long series of restrictions on immigration, enacted mainly because of pressure from worker groups. The second was the repeal in 1885 of the Contract Labor Law.

The Contract Labor Law had been adopted by Congress in 1864, when booming wartime industries were in desperate need of workers. This law permitted American employers to recruit laborers in Europe. Under the law it was legal for employers to have workmen abroad sign contracts agreeing to come to the United States to work for a specified employer for specified wages for a specified time. It was illegal for the workers to leave the job while the contract was in force. American workers objected to the law because (1) it came dangerously close to setting up a slave-labor system and (2) it subjected American workers to the unfair competition of cheap foreign labor.

After the repeal of the Contract Labor Law, American wage earners pressured Congress to pass other restrictive measures. One bill that kept coming up for 30 years would have forbidden entry to any immigrant who could not read and write. Congress actually did pass this law on several occasions, but each time the President then in office vetoed the bill. In 1917, however, Congress passed a "literacy test" bill over President Woodrow Wilson's veto, and the door to immigration was shut a little further.

The role of immigrants. From 1865 to 1900 the restrictions placed on immigration were relatively minor. And without the more than 11 million immigrants who poured into the United States between 1870 and 1900, America's industrial progress would have been much slower. Immigrant muscles and brains helped to transform the United States from a predominantly agricultural country into a giant industrial power.

SECTION SURVEY

IDENTIFY: immigrants, slums, "sand lotters," "literacy test" bill.

1. Describe the changing character of immigration after 1880.
2. Discuss three ways in which immigration affected American workers.
3. (a) Give the reasons for the passage of the Chinese Exclusion Act of 1882. (b) How would you feel about this if you were Chinese?
4. Why was the Contract Labor Law of 1864 repealed?
5. "Immigrant muscles and brains helped to transform the United States." Explain.
6. Is there any irony in the fact that the United States, a nation of immigrants, restricted immigration? Comment.

3 The role of labor organizations in dealing with workers' grievances

Faced with numerous problems in the new industrial age, wage earners, like farmers, began increasingly to seek solutions for their problems through organization.

The National Labor Union. Labor organizations were not new. During the war years 1861–65, however, as industry boomed and the cost of living soared, the labor movement gained new momentum.

In 1866 the National Labor Union was launched under the leadership of William Sylvis, an experienced and able organizer of iron molders. In 1868 the National Labor Union helped push through Congress a law establishing an 8-hour working day for laborers and mechanics employed by or in behalf of the federal government. But after unsuccessfully supporting a third-party movement in the election of 1872, this union faded away.

The Knights of Labor. Far more important than the National Labor Union was the Knights of Labor, founded in 1869 in Philadelphia by Uriah S. Stephens, a tailor. The Knights of Labor tried to unite all American workers into one great union—skilled and unskilled workers; men and women; white and black workers; foreign-born and "natives." The Knights aimed "to secure to the toilers a proper share of the wealth that they create; more of the leisure that rightfully belongs to them." Among other things, they favored an 8-hour day and abolition of child labor.

The Knights of Labor also tried to organize and operate their own cooperative stores and manufacturing plants, as some farmers had done (page 486). They hoped by this means to save for themselves the profits that normally went to manufacturers and middlemen and at the same time to produce lower-priced goods. However, most of their cooperative enterprises failed, largely because they did not have enough money to buy good machinery and to hire qualified managers.

■ In the new industrial age, wage earners, like farmers, were faced with numerous problems. The picture below, showing steelworkers on their lunchbreak, was painted about 1890.

Reasons for the Knights' success. In some of their efforts the Knights of Labor were more successful. They were influential, for example, in causing Congress to pass the Chinese Exclusion Act in 1882 and to repeal the Contract Labor Law in 1885 (page 500).

The Knights of Labor officially frowned on strikes, preferring to settle disputes between managers and laborers through industrial *arbitration*.° However, a successful railroad strike in 1885 did much to boost the group's membership. For the first time in American labor history, railroad operators met strike leaders on equal terms and agreed to labor's chief demands. When the railroad strike occurred, the Knights numbered about 500,000 members, but by 1886 their membership had reached 700,000. This remarkable growth also owed much to the idealism and enthusiasm of Terence V. Powderly, who succeeded Uriah S. Stephens as leader of the Knights of Labor.

Reasons for decline. The decline of the Knights was almost as rapid as their rise. In 1888 only 260,000 members were enrolled and by 1890 this figure had dropped to about 100,000.

There were several reasons for this decline in membership. For one thing, the Knights lost an important railroad strike in 1886 against the southwestern railroad system controlled by financier Jay Gould. This strike antagonized the public because of violence accompanying it and because of shortages of food and coal resulting from it. In the second place, the Knights included too many opposing groups to develop real strength. The skilled craftsmen especially disliked the Knights' policy of taking in unskilled workers, with whom they felt they had little or nothing in common.

Finally, Terence V. Powderly's aims came to be too general to satisfy numerous workers. Many wage earners were now convinced that a strong labor movement must avoid political crusades and concentrate instead on improving working conditions for specific groups of workers. This conviction accounted for the rise of a rival organization of workers, the American Federation of Labor (A. F. of L.).

Rise of the A. F. of L. Started in 1881 under another name and reorganized in 1886, the A. F. of L. quickly replaced the Knights of Labor as the leading American labor organization.

Unlike the Knights of Labor, the A. F. of L. was a federation of separate national *craft unions,* each representing a group of skilled workers in a separate trade, or craft, such as carpentry, welding, or typography. It sought to organize all skilled workers by their craft rather than by the industry in which they worked. However, the A. F. of L. did include a few *industrial unions* which tried to organize all workers in a single industry, unskilled as well as skilled.

Each A. F. of L. union was free to bargain collectively for all its members, to call strikes, and to manage its own affairs.

The A. F. of L. also differed from the Knights of Labor in keeping itself aloof from general reform movements and from independent or third-party political activities. The A. F. of L. was an economic organization of workers emphasizing craft unionism —"pure and simple unionism."

Program of the A. F. of L. The A. F. of L. program called for an 8-hour working day and a 6-day working week; for legislation protecting workers on dangerous jobs and compensating them and their families in case of injury or death; for higher wages and for generally better working conditions. The A. F. of L. threw its weight in political contests to whichever party or candidate came closest to representing its aims.

The A. F. of L. accepted the capitalistic free-enterprise system. It did insist, however, on controlling the skilled labor market, on getting a larger share of the output of industry through higher wages and shorter hours, and on improving labor conditions.

With the exception of a single year, the president of the A. F. of L. from 1886 to 1924 was its principal founder, Samuel Gompers. Under Gompers' leadership the A. F. of L. grew rapidly. In 1890 it had only 100,000 members, but by 1900 membership had climbed to 500,000.

SECTION SURVEY

IDENTIFY: National Labor Union, skilled worker, unskilled worker, arbitration, craft union, industrial union; Uriah Stephens, Terence Powderly, Samuel Gompers.

1. Why did American workers decide to organize unions?
2. Describe the (a) purpose, (b) successes, and (c) reasons for the decline of the Knights of Labor.
3. How did the A. F. of L. differ from the Knights of Labor?
4. What is meant by the statement that the A. F. of L. was "job-conscious rather than class-conscious?"

° *arbitration:* the judging of a dispute by an impartial person accepted by both sides to act as referee.

4 Opposition to organized labor's early efforts to win reforms

When American workers began to organize during the late 1880's, they encountered numerous obstacles in their efforts to improve labor conditions. Their attempts to form unions and to seek recognition of their unions' right to bargain for them met widespread opposition.

Public opposition to unions. During the late 1880's Americans in general, as well as government, usually supported employers in any conflicts between employers and unions or between employers and workers striking for union recognition.

This opposition to unions is not hard to understand. Most Americans had grown up in the older, rural America where the individual worker had more control over his fate than he now had in the giant corporations. They believed that every employer had the right to hire and fire as he pleased.

Many Americans resented union demands for the *closed shop.* Businesses that had closed-shop agreements with a union could hire only union members. Employers resented this restriction on what they considered their right to hire anyone they pleased. Many workmen also resented closed-shop agreements, which forced them to join a union whether they wanted to or not.

Moreover, many Americans believed that most workers were quite content with their lot. And the fact that as late as 1914 only about one worker out of ten belonged to a labor organization seemed to support this belief. Many Americans held that the best workers could still rise to become managers and even owners. Most Americans blamed the entire labor problem, as well as industrial conflict itself, on "power-eager" labor leaders interested in their own personal advancement.

The Haymarket affair. On May 4, 1886, a large group of workingmen gathered in Haymarket Square in Chicago. They were there to protest an attack on strikers in which, on May 3, one striker had been killed and a number of others wounded.

The meeting was orderly and the crowd was just beginning to leave when nearly 200 policemen appeared. Suddenly, without warning, a bomb burst in the midst of the policemen, killing one and wounding many others.

No one ever identified the bomb thrower. Nevertheless, eight "radicals," who on earlier occasions had advocated violence, were arrested. Seven of the men were sentenced to death, the eighth to 15 years in prison.

Attention Workingmen!

GREAT

MASS-MEETING

TO-NIGHT, at 7.30 o'clock,

AT THE

HAYMARKET, Randolph St., Bet. Desplaines and Halsted.

Good Speakers will be present to denounce the latest atrocious act of the police, the shooting of our fellow-workmen yesterday afternoon.

Workingmen Arm Yourselves and Appear in Full Force!
THE EXECUTIVE COMMITTEE

■ Nothing during the 1880's did more to turn public opinion against organized labor than the Haymarket affair. For many years large numbers of Americans continued to identify organized labor with anarchy and radicalism.

No evidence was ever produced to indicate that organized labor was responsible for the violence in Haymarket Square. Yet nothing during the 1880's did more to turn public opinion against organized labor than the tragic Haymarket affair.

Immigrants and labor unions. Many union leaders were of foreign birth. In several labor organizations, especially in the textile and coal mining industries, immigrant workers were a source of strength. On the other hand, however, a great many immigrants opposed labor unions. Coming from rural backgrounds in the Old World, most immigrants had no previous experience with labor organizations. Bewildered by their new and strange environment, they often did not feel a need to join with native American workers in presenting a united front to promote common interests.

Many immigrants had left Europe partly to be as free as possible from all sorts of restrictions. Thus, they did not like labor unions, with their dues, their rules, and their insistence that no one work for less than a certain wage. Many immigrants felt that, however bad working conditions in the United States might be, they were better than conditions in the Old World.

Most immigrants, also, were unskilled workers. Thus, the A. F. of L. made little or no effort to admit them to the craft unions. Finally, there was widespread prejudice among native American workers toward immigrant workers. This prejudice

■ The virtual exclusion of Negroes from the American labor movement weakened the movement's effectiveness. Above, black workers who had been denied union membership take temporary jobs by strikebreaking during a 1905 dispute between teamsters and Chicago employers.

was deepened when foreign-born workers were recruited by business managers to break strikes.

Black workers and the unions. Because of the racial prejudice of many white workmen, Negroes were excluded from most labor organizations. A notable exception was the Knights of Labor, which, proclaiming the solidarity of all workingmen, enrolled black workers without discrimination, at least until the organization's waning years.

At first the leaders of the A. F. of L. favored including skilled black workers in their craft unions. They believed that, if this was not done, black workingmen might undermine the purposes of the federation by accepting lower wages. But when the machinists' union and others refused to admit Negroes, Samuel Gompers, by now the dominant power in the A. F. of L., backed down. He insisted that union constitutions should not specifically exclude black members, but he admitted that in practice the unions might do so. The United Mine Workers and a few other A. F. of L. unions admitted black members on equal terms with white members. Most other unions insisted, however, that any black workers admitted to A. F. of L.

membership be organized in separate unions.

Most northern Negroes were unskilled workers. Thus, after the decline of the Knights of Labor, the A. F. of L. policy of organizing only skilled workers meant, in effect, that black workmen were excluded from northern labor organizations. In the South, where there were many skilled black workingmen, the labor market in the skilled trades was controlled by all-white A. F. of L. unions. As a result, many skilled black workers were forced into the ranks of unskilled labor.

By 1902, in both the North and the South, 43 national labor unions had not a single black member, and 27 others had only a handful. Gompers tried to argue that Negroes had only themselves to blame for their exclusion because few were skilled workers and fewer still were willing to accept the self-discipline and cooperation necessary in trade unionism. Booker T. Washington, however, declared in 1897 that the union movement was holding back the economic progress of black workmen by refusing to admit them as apprentices and by making no effort to organize them.

The virtual exclusion of Negroes from the American labor movement closed off to the great mass of black Americans an important opportunity to be included in the mainstream of American life. It also weakened the effectiveness of the labor movement itself.

Division in the ranks of labor. The mechanization of industrial plants also weakened the power of wage earners to unite. When factories were small, skilled workers could see that the work of unskilled workers, however minor, was an essential part of the production process. But when factories grew large and workers became strangers, skilled workers came to look down on unskilled workers.

Thus the wage earners themselves divided into two groups: (1) a small number of skilled workers who gained more and more bargaining power with employers, and (2) a larger number of unskilled, unorganized laborers whose voices and interests counted very little.

Industry against the unions. With a majority of Americans generally distrustful of unions, huge industrial enterprises did not find it difficult to influence public opinion and government in their own favor. They hired lawyers to fight their battles in the courts. They spent money on advertising and publicity to win public sympathy. They paid skillful lobbyists to get favorable laws passed or to defeat bills that employers did not like. Some corporations contributed handsomely to the political party most likely to win an election, thus hoping to secure government favors.

To discourage workers from joining unions, employers also developed more direct methods. For example, employers' associations, made up of several manufacturers, compiled *black lists,* or lists of certain workers considered as undesirable— sometimes because the workers were incompetent, sometimes because they were labor organizers, sometimes merely because they belonged to a union. The black list was circulated throughout an entire industry, all over the country. No man whose name appeared on such a black list could get a job in that industry, at least under his own name.

Many employers also required workers applying for a job to sign a written agreement not to join a union. The workers called these agreements *yellow-dog contracts.* A worker who violated such a contract promptly lost his job.

Employers used still other methods to prevent workers from organizing. Sometimes private detectives, posing as workers, joined unions and reported strike plans to employers, as well as names of union leaders. Sometimes when strikes broke out, unscrupulous employers actually paid agents to commit acts of violence, which were then blamed on labor. At other times, of course, the workers themselves resorted to violence. Such violence provided employers with a good excuse for calling in the local police, the state militia, or even federal troops to restore order and break the strike.

Sometimes employers fought strikes with another weapon—the *lockout.* They closed their plants, thus "locking out" the workers. Then they brought in "strikebreakers"—nonunion workers hired to do the work of those on strike—and the plant was reopened despite the angry strikers outside its gates. On other occasions owners simply locked their plants and waited until the hungry, impoverished strikers were willing to work on any terms.

State support of industry. With public opinion on their side, employers counted on government aid in conflicts with workers. There were, it is true, some exceptions to this general rule.

In most serious labor disputes, however, governors sent the state militia to the scene, where their presence worked to the employers' advantage. Whenever they sent the militia, the governors argued that the troops were needed to protect property, prevent violence, and maintain order. Since the governors were sworn to uphold law and order, this seemed reasonable. On the other hand, the arrival of the state militia often made it impossible for the workers to continue to strike.

Federal support of industry. In the last quarter of the 1800's, the Presidents of the United States in general followed the example of the state governors in ordering troops to a scene of trouble. Thus, during a series of railroad strikes in Pennsylvania and Maryland in 1877, when state troops could not restore order, President Hayes sent federal soldiers to keep the trains running. The strikes collapsed.

A famous case of federal intervention occurred near Chicago in 1894 when a strike was called against the Pullman Palace Car Company by the American Railway Union under the leadership of Eugene V. Debs. The strike was supported by railway workers around Chicago and elsewhere, who refused to handle trains which included Pullman cars. When Governor Altgeld of Illinois refused to call out the state militia or ask for federal help, President Cleveland sent federal troops anyway. Cleveland declared that such action was justified in order to guarantee mail delivery, although mail trains were in fact running and the mails were being delivered. Whatever the merits of the arguments for and against the use of troops in the Pullman strike, organized labor was bitter about their use.

Court support of industry. In the late 1800's the courts, no less than governors and Presidents, generally used their powers in behalf of management. For example, during the Pullman strike mentioned above, the railroad owners asked a federal court in Chicago to issue an *injunction,* or court order, forbidding Debs and other labor leaders to continue the strike. The court issued the injunction. It justified this action on the ground that the strikers had entered into "a conspiracy in restraint of trade" and were therefore violating the Sherman Antitrust Act of 1890, which declared such conspiracies illegal (page 473).

Debs defied the court order. He was promptly arrested, and sentenced to six months in jail for refusing to obey the injunction. Labor denounced this conviction as "government by injunction." But the Supreme Court in 1895 upheld the ruling, Debs was placed behind bars, and the strike was broken.

President Cleveland's role in strikes consistently aroused the opposition of organized labor. Thus, organized workers vigorously supported the Populist Party during the early 1890's. And they rallied to the support of William Jennings Bryan in the election of 1896.

After 1895 the injunction became a powerful weapon against organized labor since employers often secured injunctions to prevent or break up strikes. Labor leaders complained bitterly, but their only possible relief was (1) that the Supreme Court would reverse its decision of 1895 or (2) that Congress would modify the Sherman Antitrust Act so that it could not be used against labor unions.

Radical movements. After the Haymarket affair of 1886, many Americans, believing that organized labor was filled with anarchists, began to identify the labor movement with radicalism. But most Americans in the 1880's and 1890's did not distinguish among the three major radical movements—anarchism, Communism, and socialism.

The anarchists believed that men could work and live happily together in voluntary associations if they could be freed from the restraints of government. They believed that the idealistic society they advocated could be achieved only by the violent overthrow of the government and of capitalism—the economic system under which industry is owned and controlled by private individuals. Although the anarchists were few in number, their reputation for violence deeply alarmed the nation.

The followers of Karl Marx believed that, under capitalism, wage earners would always be exploited. They argued that capitalism must be replaced by an economic system in which the workers themselves would own and control the means of production.

In time, the followers of Marx developed into two separate groups. One group, known as Communists, insisted that the only way to build the new society of workers was by means of revolution and the violent seizure of power.

The other group, known as socialists, did not advocate revolution. The socialists believed that the workers, organized in a political party, could vote themselves into power and by democratic means could reconstruct the economic and social foundations of society.

The influence of the radical movements upon American labor organizations was never as strong as it became in some parts of Europe. Union members, by and large, continued to support Republicans, Democrats, or third party candidates and policies according to the union members' personal judgment of current issues and their own best interests.

Influence of organized labor. As you have seen, the labor movement of the late 1800's faced much opposition. But despite setbacks, organized labor continued to fight for its aims and for public recognition and support. By the early 1900's, as you will see, the lot of American workers was beginning to improve.

SECTION SURVEY

IDENTIFY: closed shop, Haymarket affair, Pullman strike, "government by injunction," capitalism, anarchism, socialism, Communism; Eugene Debs.

1. (a) Explain why public opinion in the late 1800's usually supported employers over workers. (b) What role did prejudice play in this attitude?
2. Why did immigrants oppose the labor movement?
3. (a) Why were Negroes excluded from the labor movement? (b) What have been the long-term effects of this discrimination?
4. Show how employers used each of the following against organized labor: (a) publicity, (b) lobbyists, (c) political contributions, (d) black lists, (e) yellow-dog contracts, (f) lockouts.
5. What evidence is there to support the belief that in the late 1800's government, federal and state, was on the side of industry?

TRACING THE MAIN IDEAS

The rapid development of large-scale industry between 1865 and 1900 created new problems for American wage earners. They attempted to solve these problems by organizing labor unions. Through the labor movement Samuel Gompers and other labor leaders outlined a program of democracy that differed in many respects from the traditional ideas of democracy.

Democracy in the earlier days was largely based on the ability of the individual to help himself. But the growth of great corporations made it increasingly difficult for the individual worker to solve his problems. As a result, the workers organized unions through which they could act as a united group. They began to demand government protection in the form of laws providing maximum hours of work, minimum wages, and accident compensation.

By 1900 labor organizations were beginning to exert considerable influence upon government at both the state and the federal levels. They were beginning to support those candidates in the major political parties who were most friendly to the progress of the workers. They also insisted that it was their democratic right to organize, to bargain as an entire group, and to strike if necessary to protect their rights.

In their demands and in their actions, wage earners were reacting to the new industrial society that was transforming the United States. Like farmers and all other Americans, they were seeking to adjust themselves to the industrial age.

CHAPTER SURVEY

QUESTIONS FOR DISCUSSION

1. How did the Haymarket affair help turn public opinion against the labor unions?
2. In human terms, what price did the United States pay for becoming an industrialized nation? What advantages did it gain?
3. During the period just studied, there was a shortage of skilled labor. How did this encourage manufacturers to mechanize as much as possible?
4. The majority of immigrants coming to the United States during the period just studied were between the ages of 14 and 45. What significance for the nation's economy can you derive from this fact?
5. In the period 1870–1900, what were the major grievances of workingmen against (a) employers, (b) state governments, and (c) the federal government?
6. Machines widened the gap between skilled and unskilled wage earners. Comment.
7. What democratic "safety valves" prevented a political revolution in the United States during the economic conflicts of the Industrial Revolution?

RELATING PAST TO PRESENT

1. Compare the power of labor unions during the period 1865–1900 with their power today.
2. Compare the demands labor unions make today with the demands made during the period 1865–1900.
3. In recent years, have American labor unions changed their policies regarding the admission of minority groups? Support your answer with evidence found in news stories or encyclopedia articles dealing with present-day labor unions.
4. Do you think most Americans today can differentiate between radical political movements and lawful dissent? Explain.
5. Radical political movements were not able to gain control of the labor movement during the period just studied. Do you think that they could today? Explain.

USING MAPS AND CHARTS

1. Using charts 1, 2, and 5 on page 858, answer the following: (a) Explain the connection among charts 1, 2, and 5. (b) What were the conditions in Europe that explain the rise in immigration between 1820 and 1914?
2. Refer to charts 1 and 4 on pages 876–77 for the following questions: (a) Compare the increase in total population with that in the labor force between 1850 and 1910. (b) What connection, if any, is there between these figures and the rise of organized labor? (c) Compare the average number of hours worked per week in 1850 with the number in 1900. Discuss the economic developments that contributed to this change. (Consult also chart 1 on pages 866–67.)
3. (a) Using chart 3 on page 866, compare the number of workers in manufacturing in 1870 with the number in 1900. (b) What connection, if any, is there between these figures and the rise of organized labor?

CHANGING WAYS
OF AMERICAN LIFE

CHAPTER **26**

Changing Ways of Life in the New Industrial Age

1860's – 1890's

"WE CANNOT all live in cities," Horace Greeley once remarked, "yet nearly all seem determined to do so." Greeley, the famous newspaper editor, was speaking of a new phenomenon in American life—the movement of many people away from the rural areas and into the great urban centers—the trend toward "urbanization" in America. From 1865 to 1900, growing numbers of young men and women and a considerable number of older people left the farms and country villages and headed cityward. The majority of these people moved to the larger cities, those having populations of 25,000 to 50,000 or more.

What was the compelling attraction of the growing cities? The answer was "opportunity"—opportunity for adventure, opportunity to win fame and fortune. The city offered jobs in offices and factories, work in the building trades, employment for skilled and unskilled alike, the chance to carve out a successful career in any of hundreds of lines of enterprise. Many people, especially young people, were eager to share in the excitement of the new age, and they found the attractions of urban life irresistible.

For a number of years ways of life in the city and the countryside drew far apart, and terms like "city slicker" and "country hick" were often heard. As the years passed, however, the differences between life in rural and urban areas became less marked.

THE CHAPTER IN OUTLINE

1. Changing life patterns in American cities in the industrial age.

2. Changes in American education in response to changing life patterns.

3. Reflections of the industrial age in new styles of American writing.

4. New trends in architecture and other fine arts in a changing society.

5. The enrichment of American life through new forms of recreation.

1 Changing life patterns in American cities in the industrial age

The city had many faces. It was stores and banks and offices, museums and libraries and theaters, churches and schools. It was freight yards—and, in seaports, waterfronts—ringed by factories, warehouses, stockyards, and wholesale markets. It was slum areas with drab tenement buildings crowded along narrow, dirty streets and alleys littered with rubbish. It was row after row of houses arranged, in newer cities, in a neat pattern of "blocks" or "squares." It was pretentious mansions, the costly show places of the self-appointed leaders of "society."

But mainly the city was people—rich people, people with modest incomes, poor people—all affected, more or less, by the new power-driven machines and new methods of mass production steadily transforming the world around them.

Concentration of wealth. One of the most obvious characteristics of this new industrial age was the concentration of wealth in relatively few hands. To be sure, some Americans had always been rich while others had been poor, but the gap between the richest and the poorest had never been as great as it was in the late 1800's.

Many of the new, self-educated millionaires built huge mansions, filled with expensive and gaudy furnishings. They bought race horses, yachts, and summer estates. They traveled abroad. Sometime they gave parties costing tens of thousands of dollars.

The rich as public benefactors. As time went on, however, the newly rich, and especially their college-educated children, smoothed off the rougher edges. Many successful businessmen began to accept the responsibility for using their money to improve their communities. They increasingly gave money to build and support churches, colleges, art galleries, opera houses, and libraries.

For example, during his lifetime Andrew Carnegie, a self-made man, gave $60 million to help towns and cities establish free public libraries. Men of enormous wealth, such as Ezra Cornell, Leland Stanford, John D. Rockefeller, Sr., Jonas Clark, Matthew Vassar, and Cornelius Vanderbilt, founded or gave endowments to colleges and universities. J. P. Morgan, Henry C. Frick, Andrew W. Mellon, and dozens of others built up costly and valuable art collections, many of which were in time opened to the public. Other men gave financial support to American symphony orchestras.

Thus, American arts and education began to benefit from fortunes made in railroads, the stock market, and industry. Some of the new business "magnates" became patrons of art and culture, much as the kings and princes of the Renaissance had helped the artists of their day.

The middle-income group. Lower down on the economic ladder were the professional people, the smaller businessmen, the clerks, the managers, and the more successful skilled workers. These people raised their standard of living and enjoyed the new "modern conveniences," such as gas and electric lighting, modern plumbing, and new household appliances. They went to the theater, used libraries, bought magazines and books, and increasingly sent their children, not only through high school, but also to college.

Opportunities for women. The continuing development of coeducational universities in the Middle West and the West, and the establishment in the East of such women's colleges as Mount Holyoke, Wellesley, Vassar, and Smith, meant that more young women could obtain an education equal to that once enjoyed only by young men. The battle for the higher education of women was a real one, for many people doubted that girls had the physical and mental ability to do college work. But the experiment proved successful. Women college graduates became increasingly active in civic affairs. Some became business executives, and others entered the professions. By 1900 there were 1,000 women lawyers, 3,000 women ministers, and 7,500 women doctors in the United States.

Girls who did not go to college but who wanted careers found new opportunities in business, especially as stenographers in offices, banks, and industrial plants. The development of the typewriter was a tremendous benefit to business as well as to women eager to work outside the home.

In addition to these new activities, a great many women of the urban middle class joined the women's clubs which rapidly multiplied after the Civil War. These clubs at first concentrated mainly on discussions of literary and cultural topics, but before 1900 they were also fighting political corruption, working for better health and recreational conditions, and in some instances battling for woman suffrage.

Women's organizations generally excluded black members. Mrs. Joseph St. Pierre Ruffin and Mrs. Mary Church Terrell, both of mixed parentage, unsuccessfully challenged these organizations to

admit Negro women. They also led in establishing the National Federation of Afro-American Women and the National Association of Colored Women.

Although by 1900 only a few western states had given women the right to vote, in the next 15 years the number grew. Meanwhile, in states which gave them limited suffrage, women took part increasingly in local elections of school board members. Gradually, opposition to women's participation in public affairs began to yield to the steady and vigorous pressure of such champions of women's rights as Elizabeth Cady Stanton, Lucy Stone, Susan B. Anthony, Anna Howard Shaw, and Carrie Chapman Catt.

Jane Addams. Jane Addams (1860–1935) was one of America's most influential women—a social reformer, humanitarian, and crusader for peace. Horrified by the suffering she saw in sprawling city slums, Miss Addams decided to dedicate her life to helping the poor. She purchased a building called Hull House in the slums of Chicago and opened it to the public in 1889.

At Hull House, Miss Addams provided kindergartens for the children of working mothers, classes in child care, and recreational facilities for youth and adults. For a time many business and political leaders opposed her as a dangerous meddler. Eventually, however, even her most bitter critics admitted that she was performing a great service. Social workers from all parts of the United States and from foreign countries visited Hull House, and then returned to their own communities to apply what they had learned.

Jane Addams was also influential in securing child-labor laws and appropriations for public parks. In 1931 she received the Nobel peace prize for her active work in the cause of world peace. But her most enduring memorial was the growing recognition by people in all walks of life that they shared a responsibility for helping to alleviate poverty and suffering.

The lower income groups.   On the lower rungs of the economic ladder in American life were the very poor people, including large numbers of immigrants, and almost all black Americans. The people in these lower income groups enjoyed only a few of the advantages of the new urban culture. They could not afford to send their children to school beyond the elementary grades. Frequently, in fact, children from poor families had to take jobs in factories even before they finished elementary school. Nor could most of the poorer people afford adequate medical care or go to hospitals when they were sick.

Yet improvements in urban living affected at least a few of the poor. In the late 1880's a group of high-minded men and women founded social "settlement houses" in some of the worst slum areas of the major cities. Jane Addams' Hull House in Chicago was one of the most famous of these. These centers for recreation, education, and decent living affected only a small part of the slum population, but they were nevertheless important. In addition, the Salvation Army, a religious group founded in England, provided food, shelter, and some hope to many of the most poverty-stricken urban citizens. And by 1900 some cities were building a few playgrounds in the poorest areas.

Moreover, opportunities to climb the economic ladder existed, even for the poor, and the opportunities far surpassed those in the Old World. These opportunities drew immigrants to the American cities in an ever-swelling volume. And a determination to increase the opportunities and to provide a better way of life for all Americans motivated the numerous reform programs and the development of more and better schools in the late 1800's and early 1900's. Finally, these opportunities caused many poorer people to exert strenuous efforts to acquire an education and to rise above the environment into which they had been born.

One group remained a notable exception. Negroes found their opportunities limited because of racial prejudice, which set the great mass of black Americans apart from even the most disadvantaged white Americans. Their struggle was yet to come.

SECTION SURVEY

IDENTIFY: suffrage, settlement house, Salvation Army; Jane Addams, Susan B. Anthony, Mary Church Terrell.

1. Explain what is meant by the statement, "The city had many faces."
2. "American arts and education began to benefit from fortunes made in railroads, the stock market, and industry." Why was this so?
3. What "class" divisions existed in the United States by 1890?
4. What is the relationship between the nation's industrialization and the emancipation of American women?
5. (a) Whose responsibility is it to try to improve the condition of the poor in the United States? Explain. (b) Who took the responsibility in 1890?

2 Changes in American education in response to changing life patterns

Like almost every other aspect of American life, education was transformed by the rising force of industrialism. Most obvious were (1) increased school enrollments, (2) new methods of teaching, and (3) new courses of study.

Expansion of the schools. In 1870 about 7 million children were enrolled in American schools, most of them in the lower grades. Only 30 years later, in 1900, the number had more than doubled. During this same period the number of high schools multiplied 10 times. And still the demand for education grew.

Between 1900 and 1920 the growth of enrollment and increase in construction of school buildings was even more striking. In 1900 about 16 million children attended American schools; by 1920 the number had risen to about 23 million. This growth reflected the increasing throngs of children in America's cities, but it also testified to the rapid accumulation of wealth that could be taxed to support education.

From old ways to new. The character of the schools—including courses of study and methods of teaching—was also changing.

Pupils in the earlier rural classrooms were all too familiar with the sharp sting of the hickory stick, wielded by teachers on the theory "spare the rod and spoil the child." This earlier education emphasized the memorization of facts that were often unrelated to meaningful ideas. Children learned reading, writing, and arithmetic and memorized a few more or less related facts about geography and history. The few students who went to high school or to a private "academy" spent much time learning Latin, Greek, and mathematics. Most educators believed that these subjects provided mental training and therefore fully equipped students for later life.

As science and industry began to transform American life and as the urban population grew, some reformers demanded a new program of education better suited to the industrial age. A few educational pioneers, such as Colonel Francis W. Parker of Chicago, began to stress the idea that education is not just the memorization of facts, but also the broadening of a child's experience. Education, Parker insisted, must prepare children to live in an expanding and complex world of science and industry. John Dewey was another educational

■ The growth of American technical knowledge was dramatized in 1883 when the great Brooklyn Bridge was opened with a showy display of fireworks. The advanced engineering knowledge that went into its design, and especially into its powerful supporting cables, was provided by John Roebling, an immigrant from Germany, and his son.

pioneer who stressed the idea that education is not something apart from the rest of life but an essential part of life itself. By the 1890's Dewey's experimental school in Chicago was attracting attention for its program of "learning by doing" and for its emphasis upon making children physically sound, intellectually competent, socially well adjusted, and able to work with other people.

Most schools, it is true, continued along more traditional lines, but the influence of Colonel Parker, John Dewey, and other pioneers began to cause changes in American education.

Direct influence of industrialism. The needs of the new industrial society were also reflected in new courses of study in elementary and secondary schools. By 1900 educational programs were being broadened to include the natural sciences and such "practical" and "useful" subjects as industrial designing, business arithmetic, bookkeeping, typing, stenography, shopwork, home economics, and manual arts.

Many school administrators also reflected the growing influence of business and industry. Superintendents and principals became more and more like businessmen in their emphasis upon efficiency and organization.

New trends in higher education. The colleges and universities no less than the elementary and the secondary schools responded to the needs of the new age. New technical schools, such as the Columbia University School of Mines, the Massachusetts Institute of Technology, and the Case School of Applied Science, turned out growing numbers of men prepared to take important jobs in railroad building, in mining, and in other engineering projects. The state universities and land-grant colleges (page 391) especially reflected the newer emphasis on practical training for a wide variety of fields.

Even the older colleges which emphasized the classics often felt obliged to add more scientific and "practical" subjects to their traditional courses of

512

study. Under the influence of President Charles W. Eliot of Harvard, President Andrew D. White of Cornell, and other educational leaders, the colleges modified the old, rigid curriculum in which students studied mainly Latin, Greek, and mathematics.

Colleges and universities also enriched their educational programs by adding courses in the social sciences and modern languages, as well as in the natural sciences. It was no longer possible for every student to take all the subjects in the curriculum. To meet individual differences, the "elective" system was introduced.

At the same time marked progress was made in the professional studies of medicine and law. This was especially important, for people living in the congested and complex urban centers increasingly needed the services of good lawyers and doctors.

In these and many other ways, education responded to the changing patterns of everyday life after 1865.

SECTION SURVEY

IDENTIFY: "learning by doing," elective system; Colonel Francis W. Parker, John Dewey.

1. How did the rise of industrialism influence American education in the late 1800's?
2. (a) What changes were made in the courses of study in public schools to meet the needs of the new industrial society? (b) Do you agree with these changes? Why or why not?
3. Describe the ways in which colleges and universities responded to the needs of the new age.
4. Do you think education should provide you with the means of making a living or should it enable you to understand yourself and your society? Explain.

3 Reflections of the industrial age in new styles of American writing

Newspapers, magazines, and novels also revealed the influence of the new urban industrial way of life. Most obvious was an enormous increase in circulation of printed material. Only slightly less obvious were changes in appearance and content.

Growth of newspapers and magazines. Between 1870 and 1900 the number of daily newspapers in the country increased from 600 to nearly 2,500. Their circulation multiplied six times—a jump far greater than the growth in population.

This huge expansion reflected gains in the reading ability of many Americans and a growing interest in the world beyond the local community. It also reflected a new trend in journalism.

Several important mechanical inventions enabled men to print more newspapers, magazines, and books at lower costs. Most important of these inventions were the typewriter, improved printing presses, and the Linotype, a fast and efficient typesetting machine invented by Ottmar Mergenthaler in 1885.

Mass circulation was also stimulated by the rapidly developing art of advertising. Businessmen were ready to advertise, but only in newspapers and magazines that had mass circulation. The desire to secure advertising stimulated publishers to capture an ever-wider reading public. Thus the publishers used more and more "popular" articles written in a "catchy" style to attract the largest possible number of readers.

New "titans of the press." Three of the outstanding leaders of the new trend in journalism were Charles A. Dana, Joseph Pulitzer, and William Randolph Hearst.

Dana, publisher of the New York *Sun*, dug up sensational news and gave it prominent space on the front pages of his paper. Pulitzer, publisher of the New York *World*, followed much the same technique. His paper appealed to the general reader because it contained human-interest stories and many articles on the scandalous activities of the rich and the tragedies of the poor. Pulitzer also developed the comic strip, the sports page, and the section with columnists, puzzles, and advice to the lovelorn.

Hearst, who was Pulitzer's chief rival, outdid Pulitzer at his own game. Hearst bought the New York *Journal* in 1895 and ran up its circulation beyond that of any other paper. By denouncing the irresponsibility and selfishness of some of the well-to-do, Hearst appealed to the masses of people. But his special success rested on his ability to hire gifted feature writers, able sports reporters, and popular comic artists. He also was able to get the most sensational news before anyone else and to play it up for all it was worth—frequently for far more than it was worth.

Journalism as big business. Well before 1900 journalism began to adopt the methods of other big business enterprises. Leading publishers began to buy up small papers and to consolidate great newspaper chains. Large chains could use the same feature articles, the same comic strips, and even

ALGER SERIES No. 49

FACING THE WORLD

BY HORATIO ALGER. JR.

■ Horatio Alger, Jr., turned out dozens of success stories for boys. In a sense these stories glorified an urban society in which a hard-working boy, no matter how humble his beginnings, could succeed by pluck—and luck.

the same editorials. This was especially true as the different parts of the nation and the world became increasingly interdependent, with public interest reaching out beyond the local community to national and world affairs. Moreover, the newspaper chains subscribed to great news-reporting services, or "syndicates," such as the Associated Press (AP) and the United Press (UP), which collected news items from every corner of the earth.

Even the newspapers that remained independent were influenced by the trend toward standardized practices in journalism. Many of them also subscribed to the big news-reporting services and bought columns, comic strips, and other features from syndicates.

By 1900 there also were numerous foreign lan-

guage newspapers for immigrants and about 150 newspapers for black Americans. Although these publications had limited resources, they served important functions. They gave their readers a "sense of identity" with other people of the same national origin or racial background. Most of them, also, were uncompromising in opposing discrimination and in supporting the rights and interests of their readers.

Mass circulation magazines. Magazines, like newspapers, adapted themselves to the changing times. To be sure, some of the older magazines, such as the *Atlantic Monthly, Harper's, Scribner's,* and others, continued to appeal to the better educated. Even before the Civil War, however, a new type of low-priced, popular magazine began to appear, which contained material aimed at mass circulation among "average" readers. The *Ladies' Home Journal,* established in 1883, was one of the most successful. It provided reading material that interested millions of women, and it further built up its circulation by setting its price at 10 cents. Under the editorship of a Dutch immigrant, Edward Bok, the *Ladies' Home Journal* sponsored many crusades to raise standards of living and improve community life.

Literature about urban life. American literature—no less than schools, newspapers, and magazines—reflected the growing influence of urban industrialism. Extremely popular were the success stories for boys which Horatio Alger, Jr., and W. T. Adams (under the name of Oliver Optic) turned out by the dozens. These stories in a sense glorified an urban society in which a hard-working boy, no matter how humble his beginnings, could climb to the top by sheer pluck—and luck.

William Sydney Porter (O. Henry) struck a very different note with short stories that presented realistic pictures of American life, both urban and rural. Different again were the novels of Edith Wharton, which pictured the conflicts between the newly rich and older well-to-do families of New York in the 1880's. Henry James suggested the tensions of members of America's leisure class who chose to live in the sophisticated urban centers of Europe.

One of the best-known novels of the period was *The Gilded Age,* written by Samuel L. Clemens (Mark Twain) and Charles Dudley Warner. In a humorous but biting manner, the writers described the corrupt activities of many politicians and land speculators operating in the nation's capital. Edward Bellamy's *Looking Backward: 2000–1887,* another widely read book, described an imaginary society in which poverty and corruption had been eliminated and men lived in freedom and dignity.

One of the ablest writers was William Dean Howells, whose realistic stories furnished a faithful picture of middle-class life in America. Howells, in *The Rise of Silas Lapham,* was especially successful in telling of the triumphs and tragedies of a self-made man.

Notable exceptions. There were, of course, many authors whose work was in no way influenced by the changing times. Emily Dickinson, for example, was one of a number of authors interested in literature for its own sake. Miss Dickinson, a sheltered New England writer, created many thought-provoking short poems that have since been recognized as poetry of great distinction and originality.

Even many of the books written for the general public had no apparent relation to the new issues of industrialism. For instance, General Lew Wallace's *Ben-Hur,* a widely read novel, dealt with the conflict between paganism and Christianity in the early days of the Roman Empire. The growing reading public also enjoyed highly romantic and sentimental novels, as well as colorful Wild West adventure stories which enterprising publishers put out in paper covers for only 10 cents—the famous "dime novels."

"Local-color" writers. Partly in reaction against the more or less standardized ways of city life, another group of writers concentrated upon describing those regions of the United States that were still largely under the influence of the older, rural ways of living. One of these writers, Edward Eggleston, touched a "folksy" note in describing life in rural Indiana in his book *The Hoosier Schoolmaster.*

The greatest of these "local-color" writers was Samuel L. Clemens (Mark Twain), the first important writer from west of the Atlantic seaboard states. His *Life on the Mississippi* dramatized the crude, vigorous, racy aspects of the American steamboat era. *The Adventures of Tom Sawyer* and *The Adventures of Huckleberry Finn* were landmarks in the literary and psychological representation of the adolescent American boy. At the same time, these books satirized the middle-class values and racial prejudices of a rural community in Missouri. Twain's *Roughing It* vividly portrayed the raw life of western mining camps.

The colorful and heroic verses of Joaquin (hwah·KEEN) Miller and the realistic stories of mining camps written by Bret Harte brought the

Far West into the nation's literature. Helen Hunt Jackson (page 442) also increased the awareness of the Far West with her stories of Spanish missions and of Indian life in old California. Hamlin Garland, in *Main-Traveled Roads* (page 482) and other books, wrote of the harsh conditions endured by pioneers on the northern prairies.

The South, too, had its share of local-color writers. George Washington Cable and Grace King presented to readers a picture of life among the French-speaking Creoles of Louisiana. Thomas Nelson Page popularized a romantic image of master-slave relations on Virginia plantations before the Civil War. Joel Chandler Harris of Georgia won fame for his "Uncle Remus" tales, folk stories brought from Africa by slaves.

The writings of black authors also partly reflected the influence of the local-color school of writing. Local color distinguished *My Southern Home,* the last book of the pioneer black novelist William Wells Brown. Another important Negro writer, Paul L. Dunbar, was hailed by a leading white critic as the first black American writer "to feel the Negro life esthetically and express it lyrically." Some of the novels and tales of Charles W. Chestnutt, a black writer of North Carolina, also reflected the local-color school of writing.

New England, like other regions, excited the imaginations of local-color authors. A number of writers, among them Mary E. Wilkins Freeman and Sarah Orne Jewett, pictured the changes in rural life in New England as young people abandoned the rocky, unproductive family farms to seek their fortunes in the growing cities.

SECTION SURVEY

IDENTIFY: journalism, dime novels, local color; Horatio Alger, O. Henry, Mark Twain, William Wells Brown, Paul L. Dunbar, Bret Harte, Emily Dickinson.

1. New developments made possible the mass circulation of newspapers and magazines. Of what significance is this fact?
2. Indicate the contributions of each of the following to the field of journalism: (a) Dana, (b) Pulitzer, (c) Hearst.
3. (a) What is meant by the statement that newspaper publishing became big business? (b) How would this affect the reading public?
4. (a) How did magazines adapt to the changing times? (b) What influence do you think magazines had upon the people reading them?
5. Show how the novels of this period reflected the "growing influence of urban industrialism."

4 New trends in architecture and other fine arts in a changing society

Architecture and art, no less than journalism and literature, revealed the influence of urban life and the growth of industry after 1865.

Decline and revival of architecture. For a number of years after the Civil War, American architecture reached what many have regarded as a low level. During the 1870's and the 1880's many successful businessmen and financiers poured fortunes into huge, gaudy mansions. These overdone show places, as well as many equally tasteless public buildings and smaller houses, were a far cry from the dignified and beautiful structures Americans had designed and built along simple classical lines in the late 1700's and early 1800's.

■ The 21-story Flatiron Building, New York City's first skyscraper, towered above its neighbors when it was completed in 1903.

Toward the end of the 1800's, however, a number of architects, notably Henry Hobson Richardson and Richard Morris Hunt, began to design more pleasing and practical houses and public buildings in a more dignified and restrained style.

The World's Columbian Exposition, or World's Fair, held in Chicago in 1893, helped to quicken public interest in good architecture. Many of the buildings that housed the exhibits were designed in the simple classical style. Thousands of visitors carried back to their home communities memories of beautiful structures with noble pillars and clean, direct lines.

New trends in architecture. One structure at the Chicago World's Fair, the Transportation Building, heralded a really new day in architecture. Its architect, Louis H. Sullivan, taught that "form follows function," meaning that the best-designed building is one that has a style and uses materials perfectly suited to the purposes of the building. Gradually this idea was adopted by more and more architects, among them Frank Lloyd Wright, who started to practice his profession in Chicago in 1893 and became one of the world's foremost architects.

The availability of such new building materials as steel, concrete, and plate glass, plus the necessities of urban life, did much to stimulate a new type of business structure.

The "invention" of skyscrapers. As city business districts became more crowded and as real-estate values soared, architects tried to solve the problem by building upward. How could men erect taller buildings? Ingenious architects provided the answer by constructing huge steel frames and filling the spaces with stone, brick, concrete, and glass. The Home Insurance Building, built in Chicago in 1884, set the example for these towering structures. During the next few years, in both Chicago and New York, builders erected taller and taller skyscrapers.

But the new towering buildings turned the narrow streets below into dark, gloomy canyons. To solve this problem, the governing authorities of New York City finally adopted an ordinance requiring architects to "set back" the higher stories of all tall buildings so that more light would reach the streets. This ordinance accomplished its purpose. It also relieved the rectangular lines of the boxlike skyscraper and accounted for the magically beautiful and unique character of the New York sky line. Like many other activities of American life, architecture began to reveal more and more the influence of new times and new ways of living.

Painting and sculpture. The new industrial age had less influence on painters and sculptors than it did on architects. Between 1865 and 1900 the most important development in the fine arts was the increasing skill of American artists who had studied in European art centers. The improving standards in American art also rested in part on the ability and the willingness of wealthy Americans to collect masterpieces, to establish art schools, and to buy the works of American artists.

The themes that painters and sculptors chose often seemed to have little to do with the growing urban industrial society. Gifted sculptors created great statues of Lincoln and other national heroes. One outstanding creation was the "Adams Monument" in Rock Creek Cemetery in Washington, D.C., made by Augustus Saint-Gaudens (saynt-GAW·d'nz). This monument, sometimes referred to as "The Peace of God," represents a brooding, hooded figure and suggests the mystery of life and death.

A number of painters did equally outstanding work. George Inness captured on canvas the beauties of woodland scenes. Winslow Homer's brilliantly colored seascapes suggested the strength and primitive force of the sea. Albert Ryder's mystical, legendary paintings showed a world remote from the market place and factory.

The influence of industrialism on art. The work of a number of artists, however, did reveal the influence of industrial and urban America. Thomas Eakins, for example, painted famous and wealthy Americans with such frank realism that they would not buy his works. But Eakins refused to change his style for the sake of immediate popularity and profit, and continued to paint life as he saw it. In a painting designed to reveal the surgeon's scientific skill, the "Clinic of Dr. Gross," Eakins suggested very concretely the new scientific trend of his age.

SECTION SURVEY

IDENTIFY: architecture, fine arts; Frank Lloyd Wright, Augustus Saint-Gaudens, Winslow Homer, Albert Ryder, Thomas Eakins.

1. What did Louis Sullivan mean by the statement that in architecture "form follows function"?
2. Describe the themes that inspired the noted American sculptors and painters of this period.
3. How do skyscrapers reflect the American spirit?

5 The enrichment of American life through new forms of recreation

Recreation, like all other aspects of everyday living, was transformed by the new urban industrial age. The well-to-do, having time and money, enjoyed such new and, at first, exclusive sports as tennis and golf. Gradually, however, the middle-income groups also began to enjoy such forms of recreation.

New types of rural recreation. For many thousands of American children and their parents in the early 1900's, one of the most memorable events of the year was the arrival of the circus. P. T. Barnum's tent circus, started in Brooklyn in 1871, was called "the greatest show on earth."

Equally awaited was the arrival of the Chautauqua. The Chautauqua movement was an educational enterprise started in 1874 on the shores of Chautauqua Lake in upper New York state. Each year thousands of Americans from all over the United States traveled to Chautauqua Lake to enjoy a summer vacation and to benefit intellectually and spiritually from the lectures and sermons provided for them. Study groups using Chautauqua publications were organized in many towns and villages. As the years passed, the program at Chautauqua Lake became increasingly varied, adding illustrated travel talks, stage presentations, and humorous acts to the more serious lectures and the religious services. Other enterprising leaders also organized traveling tent programs similar to those earlier developed on the shores of Chautauqua Lake. By the early 1900's the traveling Chautauquas were bringing a glimpse of the outside world into many rural communities.

New types of urban recreation. During the 1880's the bicycle changed from a clumsy, high-wheeled, dangerous contraption into something like the machine we know today. As a result, bicycling became a popular fad, as well as a means of getting to and from work for many people.

The theater also gained popularity, particularly for middle-income groups. At its best the theater in this period offered admirable plays performed by great actors, American and foreign-born. Some of the most appealing programs, however, were the melodramas that reminded city dwellers of their own rural background. Such plays as *Way Down East* and *The Old Homestead* attracted large audiences. There was also an equally popular series

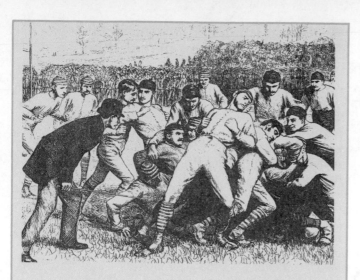

FOOTBALL IN THE 1880'S

The following report of the Yale-Princeton game of 1884 appeared in the New York *Evening Post*. Although the reporter probably exaggerated, the account does remind us that football in the 1880's was still a rough-and-tumble game with only the most rudimentary rules.

"The spectators could see the elevens hurl themselves together and build themselves in kicking, writhing heaps. They had a general vision of threatening attitudes, fists shaken before noses, dartings hither and thither, throttling, wrestling, and the pitching of individuals headlong to earth; and all this was an exceedingly animated picture which drew from them volley after volley of applause. Those inside the lines, the judges, reporters, and so on, were nearer and saw something more. They saw real fighting, savage blows that drew blood, and falls that seemed as if they must crack all the bones and drive the life from those who sustained them."

of melodramas on significant urban themes, such as *Bertha, the Sewing-Machine Girl*. Vaudeville shows, providing a variety of singing, dancing, and gymnastic arts, also attracted large audiences.

By 1900 amusement parks were attracting crowds of city people and making fortunes for their owners. In many cases trolley car companies built amusement parks just outside the city, thereby reaping profits from the parks as well as from trolley fares.

Physical exercise and American sports. During the last quarter of the 1800's an increasing number of middle-class city dwellers became aware of the need for physical exercise, especially for youth. One answer was gymnasiums, which appeared in growing numbers in cities and towns as well as in schools and colleges.

These same years also saw the rapid development of three major spectator sports—baseball, football, and basketball.

Baseball in various forms had been played long before the first professional team, the Cincinnati Red Stockings, was formed in 1869. Seven years later, in 1876, the National League was organized. In 1900 the American League was formed. Well before 1900 urban dwellers in growing numbers were packing ball parks to watch what was becoming one of America's favorite spectator sports.

Football, which evolved from the English game of Rugby, also became increasingly popular. The first intercollegiate football contest, played between Rutgers and Princeton in 1869, had 25 men on each side. Within a few years intercollegiate contests were being held in the West as well as in the East. Played mostly by college men, football in the early days was a rough-and-tumble game, so rough, in fact, that some people protested against its "brutality" and demanded its abolition. As the years passed, however, new rules were developed, and the game became better organized.

Basketball, which also became a typically American sport, was first played in 1892 by students at the Y.M.C.A. college in Springfield, Massachusetts. Its inventor, Dr. James Naismith, then an instructor in physical education, created the game to provide the same opportunities for recreation in the winter that baseball provided in the spring and football in the autumn. Within a few years the game was being played all over the country.

The older rural forms of recreation—picnics, amateur baseball, horseshoe pitching—continued to be popular. Increasingly, however, the ways in which people relaxed and amused themselves were being transformed in the new industrial age.

SECTION SURVEY

1. Show how the circus and the Chautauqua movement affected rural and urban recreation.
2. What three major spectator sports were developed in the late 1800's?
3. How do recreational activities reflect people and their values?

TRACING THE MAIN IDEAS

Between 1865 and 1900 the United States was transformed from an essentially agricultural nation to a predominantly industrial nation. Growing numbers of people poured into the great urban centers which each year exerted a more and more powerful influence upon all aspects of American life, including education, journalism, literature, architecture, art, and recreation.

What had made the cities such a powerful influence?

In trying to answer this question we must remember that the cities were the centers of industry. Thus we find ourselves going back to the factories and mass production. And when we look at the factories, with their mass production, we find that they depended upon power-driven machines. And when we look at the power-driven machines—and the almost countless number of inventions and discoveries that made the new machines possible —we find ourselves face to face with science and technology—that is, with the application of science to industry. Or to put it in other terms, we come face to face with scientists, engineers, manufacturers, businessmen, and financiers. Without science and technology there would have been no thriving factories and no large industrial cities.

The world of the late 1800's was changing with bewildering speed. New leaders were appearing, and new ways of living and working, too. The American people—rich and poor, city dweller and country farmer—had to adjust to the new conditions.

The new age was full of promise for a richer and fuller life for all men everywhere. But before the promise could be realized many problems had to be solved. You will read about some of these problems and the ways in which the American people tried to solve them in the following chapters.

CHAPTER SURVEY

QUESTIONS FOR DISCUSSION

1. Show how architecture and art were affected by urban life and the growth of industry.
2. Explain how each of the following terms reflects the changing ways of American life during the period just studied: (a) concentration of wealth, (b) settlement house, (c) elective system, (d) mass circulation of magazines, (e) skyscrapers, (f) spectator sports.
3. Examine the pictures on pages 510 and 516 and indicate how they help to show the changes taking place during the period just studied.
4. What is the relationship between education and an effective democracy?
5. To what extent should the press be "free"? Why?
6. What is the relationship between functionalism in architecture and an industrialized society?
7. What accounts for the emphasis on reform during the period just studied?

RELATING PAST TO PRESENT

1. Does education today reflect the needs of our society? What changes, if any, would you recommend be made in the high schools and colleges today?
2. What in your opinion is the role of newspapers today?
3. Do you think the federal government should be involved in the support of the arts? Explain.

USING MAPS AND CHARTS

1. How were the major advances in American industry during the period 1850–1900 interrelated? (Consult chart 1 on pages 866–67.)
2. Using charts 6 and 8 on pages 858–59, answer the following: (a) How did average life expectancy change between 1790 and 1900? (b) Explain the reasons for this change and its significance. (c) Summarize the shift from rural to urban population during 1790–1900 and explain its causes.

UNIT SURVEY

FOR FURTHER INQUIRY

1. What is the relationship between the United States having an abundance of resources and its becoming an industrial power?
2. After 1865 how did the attitude of government in the United States encourage the expansion of business and industry?
3. In your opinion, why did radical political movements fail to gain a foothold in America during the Industrial Revolution?
4. "America was built on the back of the immigrant." Comment.
5. Which view of America—Jefferson's or Hamilton's—was confirmed by the end of the nineteenth century? Refer to text page 221 in answering this question and explain the reasons for your answer in detail.

PROJECTS AND ACTIVITIES

1. Contrast the lives of two famous immigrants: for example, Andrew Carnegie and Samuel Gompers. What do you think caused them to become leaders in their respective fields?
2. America has been described as a nation of immigrants. Look into your own family background to discover where your relatives or ancestors were born and why they came to the United States. If possible, interview a member of your family, or of a friend's family, who immigrated to the United States from another country—such an interview would be considered a primary source in historical investigation.
3. Research the story of John Peter Altgeld, former Governor of Illinois, who pardoned some of the participants in the Haymarket Riot because he believed they had not had a fair trial.
4. Present a report on the problems and contributions of one of the immigrant groups in the United States.

USING THE SOCIAL SCIENCES

(Read pages 522–28 before you answer the following questions.)

1. Define the following terms: scarcity of resources, price, supply and demand, Gross National Product (G.N.P.), economizing, market, fiscal policy.
2. By using the example of a bushel of wheat, explain how supply and demand affects price.
3. How does scarcity of resources make the process of compromise a necessary part of our national economy? Compare compromise as an economic process with compromise as a political process.
4. Do you agree or disagree with the economic ideas of Karl Marx? Why? of Adam Smith? Why?
5. Can history be explained solely in economic terms? Explain.

SUGGESTED FURTHER READING

Biography

ALLEN, FREDERICK LEWIS, *The Great Pierpont Morgan,* Harper & Row; Bantam.

BEARD, ANNIE S., *Our Foreign-born Citizens,* Thomas Y. Crowell. Famous immigrants.

CARNEGIE, ANDREW, *Autobiography of Andrew Carnegie,* Houghton Mifflin.

FANNING, LEONARD M., *Fathers of Industry,* Macfadden-Bartell Books (paper). A biographical history of the leaders of the Industrial Revolution.

FLYNN, JOHN T., *God's Gold: The Story of Rockefeller and His Times,* Harcourt Brace Jovanovich.

GARST, SHANNON, *Buffalo Bill,* Messner. About a famous scout.

GINGER, RAY, *Eugene V. Debs: A Biography,* Macmillan (Collier Books, paper). The life of a leader of American Socialism; describes his activities in the railroad unions and the founding of the I.W.W.

GLAD, PAUL M., *The Trumpet Soundeth: William Jennings Bryan and His Democracy, 1896–1912,* Univ. of Nebraska Press.

GOMPERS, SAMUEL, *Seventy Years of Life and Labor: An Autobiography,* Dutton, 2 vols.

HUGHES, RUPERT, *The Giant Wakes,* Borden. About Samuel Gompers.

NEVINS, ALLAN, *John D. Rockefeller: The Heroic Age of American Enterprise,* Scribner, 2 vols.

WERNER, M. R., *Bryan,* Harcourt Brace Jovanovich. About William Jennings Bryan.

WINKLER, JOHN K., *Incredible Carnegie,* Doubleday. About Andrew Carnegie.

WOODWARD, C. VANN, *Tom Watson: Agrarian Rebel,* Oxford Univ. Press. A biography of the southern Populist leader.

Other Nonfiction

BUCK, S. J., *The Agrarian Crusade,* Yale Univ. Press. Farm problem.

——, *The Granger Movement,* Univ. of Nebraska Press (paper).

GINGER, RAY, *Altgeld's America: The Lincoln Ideal Versus Changing Realities,* New York Times Co. (Quadrangle Books, paper). The transformation of America from a rural society to an urban industrial society during the years 1892–1905.

GLAAB, CHARLES N., *The American City: A Documentary History,* Irwin (Dorsey Press, paper). Relates political events and social developments to urban history; selected essays by well-known authors.

HACKER, LOUIS, *The Triumph of American Capitalism,* Columbia Univ. Press. Economic history before 1900.

HANSEN, MARCUS L., *The Immigrant in America,* Harper & Row (paper).

HAY, SAMUEL P., *The Response to Industrialism, 1885–1914,* Univ. of Chicago Press (paper). Economic development and human adjustment during the industrial period in American history.

HENDRICK, B. J., *Age of Big Business,* Yale Univ. Press.

HICKS, JOHN D., *The Populist Revolt,* Univ. of Minnesota Press.

HIGHAM, JOHN, *Strangers in the Land, Patterns of Nativism, 1860–1925,* Rutgers Univ. Press.

HOLBROOK, STEWART H., *The Age of the Moguls,* Doubleday. Anecdotal account, often humorous, of the creators of immense wealth, such as Vanderbilt and Carnegie.

JONES, ALLEN M., *American Immigration,* Univ. of Chicago Press (paper).

JOSEPHSON, MATTHEW, *The Robber Barons,* Harcourt Brace Jovanovich (Harvest Books, paper). A critical study of the great industrialists.

KIRKLAND, EDWARD C., *Industry Comes of Age: Business, Labor, and Public Policy, 1860–1897,* Holt, Rinehart & Winston.

KRAMER, DALE, *The Wild Jackasses: The American Farmer in Revolt,* Hastings House. Political action by farmers.

MAXIM, HIRAM P., *Horseless Carriage Days,* Dover (paper). The author was a pioneer in the development of the gas engine and the auto; covers the years 1893–1901.

MOODY, J., *The Railroad Builders,* Yale Univ. Press.

MORRIS, RICHARD B., and JAMES WOODRESS, *The Shaping of Modern America, 1865–1914,* McGraw-Hill (paper). Selected excerpts from diaries, documents, newspapers, etc.

MUMFORD, LEWIS, *The Brown Decades: A Study of the Arts in America, 1865–1895,* Dover.

NEVINS, ALLAN, *The Emergence of Modern America, 1865–1878,* Macmillan.

ORTH, S. P., *The Armies of Labor,* Yale Univ. Press.

PELLING, HENRY, *American Labor,* Univ. of Chicago Press (paper).

RIIS, JACOB A., *How the Other Half Lives,* Scribner. Slums of New York.

SALOUTOS, THEODORE, *Farmer Movements in the South, 1865–1933,* Univ. of California Press.

SCHLESINGER, ARTHUR M., *Rise of the City,* Macmillan. Development of urban life.

SHANNON, FRED A., *The Farmer's Last Frontier: Agriculture, 1860–1897,* Holt, Rinehart & Winston.

STOVER, JOHN F., *American Railroads,* Univ. of Chicago Press.

WARE, NORMAN J., *The Labor Movement in the United States, 1860–1895: A Study in Democracy,* Random House (Vintage Books, paper). Covers the Knights of Labor and the emergence of the A.F. of L.

WILSON, MITCHELL A., *American Science and Invention, A Pictorial History,* Simon and Schuster. The important persons and developments in American science and technology.

Historical Fiction

BELLAMY, EDWARD, *Looking Backward,* Random House (Modern Library). The United States in the year 2000.

CLEMENS, SAMUEL L., and C. D. WARNER, *The Gilded Age,* Grosset & Dunlap. Materialism after the Civil War.

DAVENPORT, MARCIA, *The Valley of Decision,* Scribner; Grosset & Dunlap. Rise of steel industry and unions.

DREISER, THEODORE, *The Financier,* Harper & Row. Novel about materialism and greed.

——, *The Titan,* World Publishing. Novel about a millionaire.

GARLAND, HAMLIN, *Main-Traveled Roads,* Harper & Row; Holt, Rinehart & Winston. Short stories of life on the Great Plains.

——, *A Son of the Middle Border,* Macmillan. Great Plains in late 1800's.

HOWELLS, WILLIAM DEAN, *The Rise of Silas Lapham,* Houghton Mifflin; Random House (Modern Library). About a businessman.

NORRIS, FRANK, *The Octopus,* Doubleday. Novel about railway abuses.

——, *The Pit: A Story of Chicago,* Grove. Novel about wheat exchange.

HISTORY AND THE SOCIAL SCIENCES

ECONOMICS
Nature of Economics

All societies are faced with a central economic problem: their natural and human resources are scarce or limited while the wants and needs of their people are virtually limitless. Economics is the social science concerned with the ways in which societies all over the world deal with this problem of unlimited wants and limited resources.

Economists study the ways in which societies use their human and natural resources to produce the many goods and services required to satisfy their people's wants and needs. In other words, they study the ways in which various societies allocate and use their resources. Since no society, including the affluent American nation, has ever had enough productive resources to satisfy all the wants of its people, all societies must devise ways of economizing—or choosing how to use the limited resources that are available.

Obviously, the choices available in economizing resources are much more limited in some nations than in others. The United States has long been considered the richest country in the world because it has allocated its abundant resources to satisfy the wants of such a large proportion of the American people. Yet even America's "affluent society" faces the constant problem of economizing. The problem, however, is much more severe and the choices much more limited in underdeveloped nations. In an underdeveloped nation of Africa or Asia, for example, the government may need to limit strictly the people's use of resources in order to build up the nation's productive capacity as a whole.

In order to understand how a particular country or society allocates and uses its scarce resources, economists study that country's economy. This is a complex task. Among other things, it involves studying the natural and human resources available; the market system—the ways in which goods and services are exchanged; the available supply of land, labor, and capital. In each nation, organizations and institutions have been developed to operate and function in these and many other areas. You are familiar with many of the most important groups and structures in the American economy—corporations, labor unions, banks, small businesses, stock exchanges, etc. This formal structure is known as the nation's **economy,** or **economic system.**

All parts of a nation's economic system are closely interrelated. Thus, changes in one part usually have direct and indirect consequences on many other aspects of the economy. In the United States, for example, suppose Congress, with the consent of the President, decided to increase the rates of personal income taxes. This action would have immediate consequences on the ability of millions of citizens to meet their financial needs—on their ability to make a living. The government's tax policy also influences the rate of industrial production, affects the rate of personal and corporate savings, and helps to determine the rate of home building and business construction.

Obviously, no study of a nation's economy can overlook the very important matter of **economic policies.** Each society decides, by its economic policies, the all-important question of how resources in that society are distributed: namely, *what* goods and services are produced, *how* they are produced, and *for whom* they are produced. Suppose, for example, that the government of an American city or state decides to increase its sales tax on purchased goods. The increased sales tax might adversely affect the distribution of these goods to those with limited incomes—poor people might not be able to buy the taxed goods, or, at least, not as many of these goods.

An industrial complex in Tacoma, Washington

One of the most important aims of economics is to study man's economic behavior and to formulate principles, or theories, that help us to understand this behavior. These theories are useful in studying the behavior of individuals in their daily task of making a living. They are equally useful to decision-makers in business and government in helping them analyze the complex process of interaction that makes up the economic system of an entire nation.

Economists study and analyze economic behavior objectively. When they study the economic problems facing a society, they make a careful analysis of the alternative solutions that a given society may choose. Economists stress that their discipline is not a set of fixed doctrines—it is rather, they say, a way of thinking rationally about any economic system or economic problem.

Concepts of Economics

Like the other social sciences, economics has developed certain concepts, or fundamental ideas, that help to explain economic behavior, or how any economy functions. You have already studied one of the basic concepts of economics, the **scarcity of resources.** As you have seen, the problem of allocating resources in any society is an important and difficult one because there are never enough available resources to fulfill the wants and needs of all people and all groups in society. As economists study any complex economic system, they attempt to find general explanations of how the scarce resources of land, labor, and capital are allocated in that society. This allocation, of course, differs in underdeveloped societies and in advanced technological societies as well as in capitalist nations and in Communist nations.

Another important concept studied by economists is the concept of **factors of production.** The factors of production are the natural and human resources which form the basis of any nation's economy. These natural resources include land (property, mineral resources, buildings), labor (manpower and brainpower), and capital (money and machinery). The ways in which these factors are used help to determine what goods and services are produced in any society.

To measure the amount of goods and services produced, economists use the concept of the **Gross National Product,** or the **G.N.P.** The G.N.P. is the total value of all goods and services produced in a country in any one year. In using the G.N.P., economists must adjust the total figures in relation to price changes in the goods and services listed. An analysis of the G.N.P. helps economists to understand a nation's economic behavior.

The concept of **price** is another important tool economists use to study the behavior of a nation's economy. In the simplest terms, price refers to the amount of money paid for specific goods and services. Prices are determined, in large part, by **supply and demand**—another key concept in economics. Supply is the amount of any product offered for sale. Demand is the quantity of any product people are willing to buy. Supply and demand thus determine the price of a product.

Another important concept in economic analysis is the **market.** Every product or service has a market; that is, it is exchanged by buyers and sellers. We are all familiar with the market for automobiles, houses, clothing, and medical care. But a market exists for labor, capital, and land, as well. Economists often study the labor market to understand employment patterns, job trends, and workers' productivity. Economists studying the labor market often examine the activities of labor unions. For example, representatives of each major union negotiate new labor contracts with the large business corporations in their industry to agree on wages and working conditions for the next two

What is meant by the "Gross National Product"?

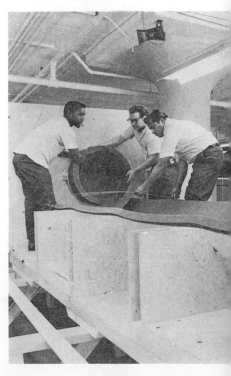

or three years. These union contracts play a major role in shaping the labor market.

Economic growth and development is another key concept in modern economics. The continuing growth of a nation's economy can be measured by a rise in the G.N.P., as well as many other indexes of the economy's behavior, such as national income, cost of living, housing starts, and labor productivity. A country is enjoying real economic growth if its G.N.P. is rising steadily, if nearly all of its available work force and most of its industrial capacity is being used, and if it maintains a balance between its increasing capacity to produce goods and services and its people's ability to pay for these goods and services.

In the United States and many other nations, economic growth is a shared objective of business, labor, and government. Obviously, a rising G.N.P. accompanied by runaway inflation—a rapid decrease in the consumer's purchasing power and an inordinate rise in prices of food, goods, and essential services—would not signify economic growth. In the same way, industry's decision to reduce its efforts in developing new technology and products, or industry's failure to expand into new markets, might lead to a declining rate of economic growth.

Economists also make considerable use of the concept of **fiscal policy.** This concept refers to the policies, implemented through laws and regulations, which determine the income and expenditures of the government. The United States government, and most other governments, use fiscal policy to help promote or slow down the growth of the economy. A government's fiscal policies, especially its tax and spending programs, have a great influence on the production of goods and on the purchasing power available to consumers. When the government cuts income taxes, for example, people have more money, they can then buy more goods, and this increased demand stimulates greater production of goods and services.

Until recently the traditional goal of most government fiscal policies was to balance the budget, or to make expenditures equal income. More recently, governments have been willing to experience budget deficits and to borrow money if necessary to stimulate economic development in their nation.

Methods of Economics

The National Task Force on Economic Education defined economics as "a rational way of thinking about economic problems, not a party line or a set of answers."

This definition of economics applies only to capitalist countries. It does not apply to Communist countries such as the Soviet Union where economics is indeed a party line. Communist countries follow the theories of Karl Marx, who believed that private property was the source of most evil in society and the root of much of the selfishness in men. Marx taught that there was a constant struggle between the large classes of workers and farmers and the smaller class of landowners and industrialists for control of the means of production—land, factories, businesses. Once private property was abolished, Marx argued, all members of society would share the wealth produced by the nation's economy.

Capitalist nations like the United States reject Marx's theories. Instead they accept the economic theories of Adam Smith, who taught that private property and individual self-interest were the best bases for a nation's economy. In the United States, free enterprise and free competition long have been the foundations of our nation's economic system.

Obviously, because of their differing beliefs in the nature of their discipline, economists in Communist and in capitalistic countries go about their work in markedly different ways. Here, we shall limit our discussion to the methods used by economists in capitalist countries.

To provide information on economic trends, economists rely heavily on statistical and quantitative data. They use these data in **economic models** and in **measurements** they have designed to study the economy. In gathering these data, economists have found large-scale electronic computers to be extremely useful. Computers can collect and tabulate tens of thousands of figures and, what is more important, can quickly analyze this enormous amount of raw economic data and indicate correlations, or relationships, that help to predict economic trends and outlooks.

However, even the use of the most accurate statistical tools does not solve all the economist's problems. Suppose, for example, that, after a thorough statistical and quantitative study, economists find that in order to stop inflation in the United States the rate of unemployment must reach 5.6 percent of the potential labor force. The question then arises as to whether or not it is feasible—or politically possible—to stop inflation by forcing so many people out of work and into the ranks of the unemployed. In this example, the answer to an economic problem requires a value judgment which has far-reaching social and political implications. All that economists do in such a case is to provide the specific figures to indicate how a rise in unemployment would affect the rate of inflation.

In making their investigations, economists sometimes need to interpret and make **forecasts,** or predictions, from their data. This need to forecast is often seen in the work of economists called stock analysts who are employed by large corporations and by stock brokers. Stock analysts study the factors which have influenced stock market prices in the past, such as trends in international events, the level of personal incomes, interest rates, and the rate of federal spending. They then examine these same data in the present stock market, as well as the mood of institutional investors and potential investors. On the basis of this careful analysis, they try to predict the performance of various kinds of stock in the short term or on a long-term basis.

Different stock market analysts may come up with different predictions—not so much because the data they gather may differ significantly but because they assign different importance to different economic factors. This does not mean that economics is an imprecise science. The different conclusions result from the reality that economic factors are greatly affected by the international scene, by shifts in government policy, and by the changing mood of investors in the economy.

In making their studies, economists, like other social scientists, try to analyze economic behavior objectively. Yet most economists emphasize that there are limitations in understanding, and especially in predicting, economic behavior. Economists are well aware that the economic behavior of individuals, of groups, and of nations is very complex and erratic. No one can predict with absolute certainty whether a majority of American families will live within their budgets or whether most Americans will save money regularly in any given year. Neither can anyone predict whether there will be peace or war, whether a mood of confidence or uncertainty will dominate the national and international scenes. Thus, in making their predictions, economists must proceed with great caution, relying on an objective statistical analysis of their data as well as an analysis of the many factors that often have a decisive influence on economic life.

How do stock market prices reflect the state of the national economy?

CASE STUDY IN ECONOMICS

Scarcity, Silver, and Surplus: A Paradox

A Look at Scarcity

Many of the main problems facing Americans during the last decades of the 1800's were economic ones. Most serious, especially for American farmers, were the related problems of rising crop production and falling crop prices. Farmers were growing more wheat and corn, but receiving less money for their products. Silver producers faced similar problems when tremendous increases in the amount of silver available led to decreases in silver prices.

Earlier you learned that **scarcity of resources** is a constant problem faced by people in every society. Scarcity was a problem for Americans living in the 1800's as much as it is a problem for Americans today. But how can we speak of scarcity of resources in the late 1800's when the main economic problem faced by farmers and by silver producers was one of surplus? Rather than a scarcity of corn, wheat, and silver, there was an overabundance of these products. How can apparent contradiction be explained?

First of all, let us make sure that our economic data are correct. Is it true that, in general, the production of silver, corn, and wheat was increasing in the years between 1875 and 1900? You can find the answer in Table 1.

Everson Museum, Syracuse, New York

"Corn Husking"

TABLE 1
Production of Silver, Corn, and Wheat: 1875–1900

Year	Silver (Millions of Fine Troy Ounces)	Corn (Thousands of Bushels)	Wheat (Thousands of Bushels)
1875	24.5	1,450	314
1880	30.0	1,706	502
1885	39.9	2,058	400
1890	54.5	1,650	449
1895	55.7	2,535	542
1900	57.6	2,662	599

It is evident from an analysis of Table 1 that, in general, the production of silver, corn, and wheat *was* increasing in the years between 1875 and 1900. What was happening to the price of these products during the same time period? For the answer, examine Table 2.

TABLE 2
Prices of Silver, Corn, and Wheat: 1875–1900

Year	Price of Silver (Cents per Fine Troy Ounce)	Price of Corn (Cents per Bushel)	Price of Wheat (Cents per Bushel)
1875	124.0	41.9	101.0
1880	115.0	39.0	95.2
1885	106.5	32.2	77.2
1890	104.6	49.6	83.7
1895	65.3	25.2	50.5
1900	61.3	35.0	62.1

As you can see, prices for silver, corn, and wheat were considerably lower in 1900 than in 1875. Notice, however, that while the prices of corn and wheat did not decline during each 5-year period, the price of silver did.

In the last quarter of the 1800's, then, the supply of silver, corn, and wheat was increasing while the prices for them were decreasing. The **price** of each of these products—or of any product—is a reflection of the balance between **supply and demand.** If the price of a product is falling, the explanation may be that the demand for that product is less than the supply, or stated another way, that the supply of the product is greater than the demand for it. Usually, when suppliers have a surplus supply of any product, some of them, in order to sell their product, will be willing to accept a lower price, thus forcing other suppliers to do the same or find no market for their product.

Combining this information with what we have learned from Tables 1 and 2, we can make a general statement about the supply of and demand for silver, corn, and wheat during the last 25 years of the 1800's: Between 1875 and 1900 the supplies of silver, corn, and wheat increased faster than did the demand for them, causing prices to fall. This means that there actually was a surplus of these products during those years.

Now that we have verified our economic data, we can go back to our original question. How can a surplus be explained when economists insist that the basic economic condition in all nations is that of scarcity?

The scarcity concept, as economists use it, refers to the total of all the resources of a nation which can be used to satisfy all of the wants and needs of that nation. A society's wants are nearly unlimited; its resources are not. Silver, wheat, and corn represent only a small part of a nation's total resources. Thus, it is not inconsistent for an economist to assert, on the one hand, that we live in a world of scarcity while asserting, on the other hand, that certain parts of the economy may produce surpluses.

The Supply of Money

Much of the concern of the late 1800's involved America's supply of money. In a growing economy it is important for a nation to maintain some measure of economic stability; depressions or panics as well as inflationary periods are to be avoided. In the last quarter of the 1800's American agricultural production was growing rapidly. American industrial production, according to one estimate, increased by 250 percent during the same period.

In order for a growing economy to maintain stability, economists generally agree that the total supply of money in circulation must also increase. As specialization increases and more people are employed, more money is also needed to keep goods and services flowing.

For decades prior to 1896 the United States had maintained a gold standard. Increases in the supply of currency in circulation were tied to increases in the United States Treasury's gold supply. By the late 1800's some Americans, identified by William Jennings Bryan as "those who live upon the Atlantic coast," wanted gold to remain the only backing for United States currency. Many other Americans, however, especially farmers suffering from falling prices, wanted a bimetallic standard. That means that they wanted the Treasury to maintain reserves in both gold and silver as backing for American currency. They hoped in this way to increase the amount of money in circulation, halt the falling price levels, and thus ease the farmers' plight.

But the actual amount of currency in circulation was not decreasing in the last quarter of the 1800's. Between 1873 and 1896 the total amount of

William Jennings Bryan

currency in circulation rose by almost $700 million. However, because of the population growth during the same period, the amount of currency available to each American increased only slightly. And between 1890 and 1896, the amount of currency per capita actually decreased. Thus, the farmers' cry that not enough money was in circulation had some basis in fact.

The term **Gross National Product (G.N.P.),** as you recall, refers to the total dollar value of all goods and services produced in an economy during a year. Although the concept of G.N.P. is a product of twentieth-century economic theory, economists have made estimates of G.N.P. for the latter quarter of the 1800's.

Economist Simon Kuznets has estimated that the per capita G.N.P. rose from $165 a year, on the average, in 1869–1873 to $210 in 1889–1893. An estimate of G.N.P. for the period 1892–1896 placed the G.N.P. per capita at $199. This decline provides additional evidence that the 1890's were an economically troubled period. In fact, three business contractions occurred between 1891 and 1897. Between 1879 and 1897 prices fell more than 1 percent a year.

The prices of the goods and services that people, businesses, and governments buy change over time. In order to compare G.N.P. levels for different years, it is necessary for economists to estimate the amount of price change from one year to another and compare years in terms of dollars of equal purchasing power. If this adjustment were not made, it would be impossible to tell how much of a G.N.P. increase or decrease was real and how much was due to price increases or decreases.

Economists are not yet able to provide us with completely refined G.N.P. data for the period between 1875 and 1900. They do know, however, that prices during this period were falling rather than rising. Thus, in calculating *real* G.N.P. for the last 25 years of the 1800's, they must allow for the price decreases. Their calculations lead them to believe that between 1875 and 1900, in spite of the panics or depressions that occurred, *real* G.N.P. was increasing at the rate of 2 percent a year. This economic growth was perhaps less noticeable to Americans living in those years than to later economists; nonetheless, it was characteristic of the period. It may be that the conflict over gold and silver and the plight of the farmer, in fact, tended to obscure this economic growth.

The efforts made in the last 25 years of the 1800's to create a bimetallic standard were aimed at increasing the supply of money in circulation. An increase in the supply of money, it was theorized, would lead to a halt in the falling price levels. Price levels would be maintained at a steady level and might even be increased. If one regards unchanging prices as preferable to falling prices, then silver would have been preferable to gold in the late 1800's. With the election of McKinley in 1896 and a rapidly increasing world gold supply, however, the United States remained committed to the gold standard.

A farming family on the Great Plains

■ How is the concept of scarcity useful in analyzing the gold and silver controversy of the late 1800's? Explain.
■ What is the paradox regarding surplus and scarcity that an economist finds in this case study? What data are used to analyze this paradox?

UNIT EIGHT

The Arrival of Reform

1897–1920

■ *Electioneering in an American town*

27

The Start of Reforms Under the "Square Deal"

1897 – 1909

THE FORTUNES of nations as well as of individuals sometimes change with bewildering speed. But men have no certain ways of foreseeing when change will come or of predicting its directions.

The administration of President McKinley, from 1897 to 1901, is a case in point.

Who on McKinley's inauguration day could have foreseen that within little more than a year the nation would be at war with Spain in a conflict called the Spanish-American War, and that before McKinley's four years in office were over the United States would become a great colonial power with possessions in the Pacific and the Caribbean? (You will read about these striking international developments in Unit Nine.)

And who, looking at the solid triumph of big business in the election of 1896, would have dared to predict that within six years a new reform movement, the Progressive movement, would begin to sweep the country, and that a progressive President and Congress would draw up new rules for the conduct of business?

The reform movements of the early 1900's were really a continuation, on a broader front, of earlier efforts to preserve and strengthen democracy in the new industrial age. As you will see, however, the progressives also tackled other problems, including the increasingly serious issue of the conservation of the nation's natural resources.

THE CHAPTER IN OUTLINE

1. Reforms in government as a result of the Progressive movement.

2. A "square deal" under President Theodore Roosevelt's leadership.

3. Conservation of natural resources under Theodore Roosevelt.

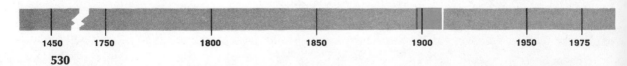

| 1450 | 1750 | 1800 | 1850 | 1900 | 1950 | 1975 |

1 Reforms in government as a result of the Progressive movement

To many Americans, the victory of William McKinley and the Republicans in the election of 1896 (page 494) spelled the doom of the reform movement. In 1897 the conservative Republicans seemed to have a clear road before them. Having just defeated William Jennings Bryan in his bid for the White House, their leaders in Congress now passed the Dingley Tariff of 1897, which raised average tariff rates to a new high of 57 percent.

In the meantime the depression of 1893–96 gave way to prosperity. New corporations sprang up, and older corporations merged to form giant trusts and industrial concerns. Even the short-lived Spanish-American War of 1898 (Chapter 30) did not interrupt the nation's economic growth.

Surrounded by prosperity and caught up in the fervor of war and overseas expansion, many Americans in the late 1890's began to forget the demands of the Populists and other reform groups. Yet by 1900 a new reform impulse, an offspring of and successor to the Populist movement, was under way. Historians have called this the Progressive movement.

Aims of the Progressives. The Progressive movement cut across party lines. It included men from the Bryan wing of the Democratic Party, as well as discontented Republicans.

Leaders of the Progressive movement had specific aims. (1) They wanted to restore control of the government to the rank and file of people. (2) They wanted to correct the abuses and injustices that had crept into American life in the age of urban industrialism. (3) They wanted to restore greater equality of economic opportunity by drawing up new rules for the conduct of business.

The progressives were optimists. They believed that these reforms would create a more prosperous and a more democratic country. They hoped to set new standards of honesty for both business and government.

Robert M. La Follette. Robert M. "Fighting Bob" La Follette of Wisconsin was one of the outstanding leaders of the Progressive movement. After graduating from the University of Wisconsin in 1879, La Follette fought his way upward in local and state politics. He won victories over the opposition of the Republican political machine that dominated Wisconsin, and in doing so won a reputation for fearless honesty. An excellent speaker,

he sought support from the farmers and working people, and won the governorship of Wisconsin in 1900.

As governor, La Follette helped to break the power of the political "machine" that had been running the state, and restored control of the government to the majority of the people. He persuaded hesitant legislators to levy heavier taxes on the railroads and on the newer public utilities—the gas, electric, and streetcar companies. He also persuaded the legislators to create commissions to regulate the public-utility companies. In cooperation with Charles Van Hise, president of the University of Wisconsin, La Follette inaugurated a movement for the conservation of Wisconsin's forests and water-power sites, which had largely come under the control of large industrial corporations.

The La Follette administration also promoted good government in Wisconsin by using university men to help legislators find needed facts and draft laws that the courts could not easily set aside. He also appointed university men to serve on the new state regulatory commissions. The "Wisconsin Idea," as the La Follette movement was called, attracted nationwide attention.

Other progressive leaders. Encouraged by La Follette's example, other governors and public officials began to attack corrupt government and powerful corporations. Joseph W. Folk became governor of Missouri in 1906 largely as a result of his success in prosecuting a ring of corrupt politicians in St. Louis. Charles Evans Hughes became governor of New York in 1907 chiefly because of his success in uncovering the highly questionable business practices of certain insurance companies. Hiram Johnson became governor of California in 1910 after fighting the political "bosses" and great railroads that had so powerful an influence in the state.

By no means were all of the progressives public officials. Jane Addams, the social worker, for example, attacked the problem of newly arrived immigrants living in the slums of Chicago. Miss Addams, as you know, organized a community center known as Hull House, which became a model for numerous other social-service centers in urban areas throughout the country.

The "muckrakers." The Progressive movement also included many scholars, journalists, preachers, and novelists. Theodore Roosevelt applied the name "muckrakers" to the writers who exposed the evils and corruption they found in politics and the business world. Although Roosevelt used the term

APROL, 1904

Enemies of the Republic
By LINCOLN STEFFENS

The Breaking Up of the
Standard Oil Trust
By IDA M. TARBELL

The Negro—Part Two
By THOMAS NELSON PAGE

SEVEN SHORT STORIES

Illustrations in Color

S. S. McCLURE CO. NEW YORK AND LONDON

■ The Progressive movement included many scholars, journalists, preachers, and novelists. Their written attacks on abuses in American life often were published in periodicals such as McClure's Magazine. Can you identify any of the articles featured in the issue shown above?

in a disparaging manner, the writers accepted it with pride, and it came into popular use.

The "muckraking" movement as such, however, is usually dated from an article, "Tweed Days in St. Louis," written by Lincoln Steffens and Claude H. Wetmore for the October 1902 issue of *McClure's Magazine.* The following month *McClure's* began the serial publication of Ida M. Tarbell's critical *The History of the Standard Oil Company.* Soon many other magazines began publishing attacks on abuses in American life.

Muckraking novelists as well as journalists attacked many of the evils of their day. Upton Sinclair, in his sensational novel *The Jungle,* exposed unsanitary practices in the meat-packing industry

—and, incidentally, turned many of his readers into vegetarians. Frank Norris's novel *The Octopus* exposed the railroads' control over rural political and economic life. And Jack London in *The War of the Classes, The Iron Heel,* and *Revolution* warned of a revolution that could wipe out private capitalism.

A few, though not many, of the muckrakers called attention to the plight of American Negroes. The most impressive work was *Following the Color Line* by Ray Stannard Baker, a series of magazine articles published as a book in 1908.

Following the Color Line was a competent and honest report of segregation in the South and of racial discrimination in the North. As such, it put the problem of white-black relations in a nation-wide context. In general, Baker favored Booker T. Washington's gradual approach to the difficult problems facing black Americans. In so doing, he reflected the optimistic faith that men of good will, once aware of the facts, could be counted upon to support policies to help Negroes improve their lives and enjoy greater opportunities.

The root of the problem. The muckrakers brought to light many abuses in American life. Lincoln Steffens, however, pinpointed the basic problem in a series of articles later published as a book entitled *The Shame of the Cities.* Years later, in his *Autobiography,* Steffens summarized his conclusions. The basic problem facing Americans was not the development of industrialism or of business, large or small. The source of the evil was "privilege"—the understandably human demand for special privileges from government. This had to be controlled, according to Steffens, or abuses and corruption would follow.

Millions of Americans in the late 1800's and the early 1900's shared Steffens' views. They also agreed that one way to combat the evils of special privilege was to restore control of government to the people.

The Australian ballot. One of the first steps in the direction of more democratic government was the adoption of the *Australian ballot,* or secret vote. Until about 1890 voting had not been done in secret. Each political party printed its own ballots in a distinctive color. Thus, when a voter cast his ballot—as he did in open view of anybody who cared to watch—it was easy to determine how he had voted. The secret ballot, developed in Australia and adopted in the United States, made this open voting impossible by placing the names of all candidates on a single sheet of paper, printing all ballots at public expense, and requiring voters to mark and cast their ballots in secrecy.

The initiative, referendum, and recall. In trying to secure a more democratic government the progressives supported the use of the initiative, referendum, and recall. All of these reform measures had been advocated by the Populists in the 1890's.

The *initiative* enabled voters in a state to initiate, or introduce, legislation at any time. Suppose, for instance, that a group of citizens wanted to increase the amount of state money spent for public schools. They would draw up a bill and attach to it a petition containing the signatures of a certain percentage of the voters in the state (usually from 5 to 15 percent, depending upon state law). When the petition was presented to the state legislature, the representatives were required by law to debate it openly.

The *referendum* was a logical companion to the initiative. Suppose that a bill was pending before a state legislature to give excessive privileges to a public utility company. By securing a specified number of signatures to a petition, voters could compel the legislature to place the bill before *all* the voters of the state for their approval or disapproval. In effect, the referendum enabled every qualified voter to act as a legislator.

The *recall* enabled voters to remove an elected government official before his term expired. When a specified number of voters, usually 25 percent, presented a petition, a special election had to be held. In this election all of the voters had an opportunity to cast their ballots for or against allowing the official to continue in office.

South Dakota, in 1898, was the first state to adopt the initiative and the referendum. Eventually 20 states adopted initiative and referendum procedures, and 12 states adopted the recall.

The direct primary. In trying to make government more responsive to the people's wishes, the progressives also advocated the *direct primary*.

Under long-established custom, all candidates for government office were nominated in political conventions. Since the conventions were easily controlled by professional politicians, rank and file voters had little opportunity to express a preference for any candidate.

The direct primary remedied this situation by providing "a nominating election" well in advance of the regular election. A man who wanted to run for office could, by securing a specified number of signatures to a petition, have his name printed on the primary ballot of any one of the political parties. On the day of the primary election, the registered voters of each party then marked their ballots for their candidate.

First adopted by Wisconsin in 1903, the direct primary soon spread to almost every state.

Women's suffrage. The vote for women also became part of the progressive program. By 1900 four states—Wyoming, Utah, Colorado, and Idaho—had granted full voting privileges to women. As a result of progressive efforts, between 1910 and 1914 seven other states, all west of the Mississippi, gave women the right to vote. In 1920, with the adoption of the Nineteenth Amendment, women's right to vote was written into the Constitution of the United States.

Direct election of Senators. Another reform advocated by the progressives was the direct election of United States Senators. According to the Constitution, Senators were chosen by state legislatures. During the early 1900's, however, progressive members of the House of Representatives urged the adoption of an amendment that would allow the people to vote directly for Senators. But the Senate, which was often criticized as a "rich man's club" and which included many politicians who owed their jobs to political bosses and political "machines," blocked every attempt to get this amendment before the states.

In the end, however, the rising power of the progressives proved too much for the "machine" politicians. In 1913, in the Seventeenth Amendment, the right to choose Senators was taken from the state legislatures and given to the voters at large.

Reform of city government. While winning victories at the state and federal level, the progressives were also trying to reform corrupt city governments. Most municipal governments consisted of a mayor and a large city council, elected by the voters and given complete responsibility for running city affairs. This system made it relatively easy for a well-organized political "machine," using corrupt election procedures, to win control of city government and use its power as it saw fit.

Galveston, Texas, led the way to a new type of government in 1900 after a disastrous hurricane and tidal wave killed one sixth of the city's people and destroyed a third of its property. To meet the emergency, Galveston gave a commission of five men extraordinary power to run the city. The experiment proved so successful that the *commission* form of government soon spread to other cities.

■ Thirty thousand demonstrators marched in this suffragette parade of 1912. But American women could not vote until 1920, when the Nineteenth Amendment was adopted.

By 1912 more than 200 American communities had adopted the commission form of government. Supporters argued that it was simpler, more efficient, and less expensive than older types of city government. Also, since each elected commissioner was directly responsible for a separate function of the city government, such as the police, the fire department, sanitation, and public works, it was easier to fix responsibility for the proper conduct of city affairs.

In 1908 Staunton, Virginia, led the way in developing another effective innovation in city government—the *city manager* plan. The plan received national attention in 1914 when it was adopted by Dayton, Ohio, after the mayor and council were unable to cope effectively with a flood emergency. The city manager, an expert in municipal administration, without political connections, is appointed by an elected city council or board of commissioners to run the city as efficiently and economically as possible. After 1914 city manager government spread to numerous cities.

The progressives were, indeed, a powerful force in American life in the early 1900's. In the remaining pages of this chapter you will see how a progressive President, Theodore Roosevelt, and a progressive-minded Congress used their power to bring about long-demanded changes in the relations between government and business.

SECTION SURVEY

IDENTIFY: Progressive movement, "muckrakers," "Wisconsin Idea," Australian ballot, initiative, referendum, recall, direct primary, the Seventeenth and Nineteenth Amendments, city manager plan; Lincoln Steffens, Upton Sinclair.

1. In what ways did La Follette reform the government of Wisconsin?
2. (a) Muckrakers exposed many abuses in American life. Explain. (b) How did the mass circulation of newspapers and magazines relate to the muckrakers' influence?
3. (a) Was reform of the Negroes' plight a major progressive concern? Why or why not? (b) Why were Booker T. Washington's views accepted by many white Americans?
4. (a) In the early 1900's there was extensive need for reform in many areas of American society. Why was this so? (b) To what did critics attribute the abuses that existed at this time?

2 A "square deal" under President Theodore Roosevelt's leadership

President McKinley and the Republicans entered the elections of 1900 confident of victory. The Democrats, who had again nominated William Jennings Bryan, tried to make free silver a major campaign issue. But Americans in general, including most farmers, were enjoying prosperity, and they returned President McKinley to the White House with an electoral vote of 292 to 155.

Six months after his second inauguration, on September 6, 1901, McKinley was shot by a half-crazed assassin. He died a few days later and, to the dismay of conservative Republicans, Vice-President Theodore Roosevelt became the nation's Chief Executive.

Theodore Roosevelt's background. Theodore Roosevelt was born in 1858 into a well-to-do New York family. He studied at Harvard, where he acquired a taste for history and politics. After graduation he served a two-year term, from 1882 to 1884, as a member of the New York state legislature. Part of the next two years he lived on a cattle ranch in the Dakota Territory. Returning home in 1886, he unsuccessfully ran for mayor of New York City. He devoted the following three years to the study and writing of history, a task that had occupied much of his spare time since his college days.

In 1889 President Harrison appointed Roosevelt to the Civil Service Commission, where he served effectively for six years. In 1895 he became president of the New York City Police Commission, leaving this job in 1897 to become Assistant Secretary of the Navy. When war with Spain broke out in 1898, he resigned his Navy post to organize, with Leonard Wood, a volunteer cavalry regiment known as the "Rough Riders." After the war he became the Republican governor of New York, but his vigorous, independent actions so alarmed the Republican political bosses that in 1900 they decided to get him out of active politics by "kicking him upstairs" into the Vice-Presidency.

Such was the man who at age 42 became the youngest President the United States had ever had —and, as the conservative Republicans had rightly feared, one of the most independent.

Roosevelt as a progressive. Roosevelt had a great gift for sensing public opinion and expressing it in telling phrases. A man of immense energy, he fought zealously for things he believed to be right.

Theodore Roosevelt was also a good politician. That is to say, he was ready to compromise, taking half a loaf when the whole loaf could not be had. He did not start the Progressive movement. Nor did he go as far as many progressives felt he could and should go. But he gave the Progressive movement dramatic national leadership. His general popularity, his enthusiasm, his ability as a speaker, and his position enabled him to promote reforms.

The election of 1904. Roosevelt's progressive ideas antagonized many Republicans leaders. When election year 1904 rolled around, the Republican political leaders would have abandoned him in favor of a more conservative candidate had they dared. But by this time "Teddy" Roosevelt enjoyed widespread popularity. No other Republican candidate had a chance of winning the nomination.

Roosevelt went on to win a resounding victory at the polls—336 electoral votes to 140 for his Democratic opponent, Judge Alton B. Parker of New York.

What was the secret of Roosevelt's popularity with the rank and file of voters? During the campaign, he had announced that he was "unhampered by any pledge, promise, or understanding of any kind, save my promise, made openly to the American people, that so far as my power lies I shall see to it that every man has a square deal, no less and no more." This promise carried weight, as you will see, because Roosevelt's record during his first term in office convinced millions of voters that he meant what he said.

LIVING AMERICAN DOCUMENTS

Theodore Roosevelt's
"New Nationalism" Speech (1910)

Our country—this great republic—means nothing unless it means the triumph of a real democracy, the triumph of popular government, and, in the long run, of an economic system under which each man shall be guaranteed the opportunity to show the best that there is in him. . . .

I stand for the square deal. But when I say that I am for the square deal, I mean not merely that I stand for fair play under the present rules of the game, but that I stand for having those rules changed so as to work for a more substantial equality of opportunity and of reward for equally good service. . . .

535

In Theodore Roosevelt's era, working conditions in American coal mines were grim. Young boys as well as men mined long hours for low wages. This photograph of child miners was made in the early 1900's.

Settling a coal strike. Less than a year after succeeding McKinley as President, Roosevelt showed where he stood on the question of organized labor. In the spring of 1902 a strike broke out in Pennsylvania in the coal mines owned largely by railroad companies serving the region. The miners worked long hours, lived in company towns, bought from company stores, and because of low wages found it hard to make ends meet. Organized as part of the United Mine Workers Union, they had asked for a 9-hour day, a 20 percent wage increase, improved working conditions, and recognition of their right

to bargain as a union. The mineowners refused to negotiate with the union, whereupon the miners went out on strike.

By autumn the country faced a coal-less winter with factories closed and homes without heat. The mine owners demanded that the President send federal troops into the area to break the strike. Roosevelt refused. Instead, he summoned representatives of the owners and of the union to a White House conference.

At this conference the mineowners refused to listen to a proposal for impartial arbitration. Furious at this lack of cooperation, Roosevelt let it be known that he might send the army to take over the mines in the name of the government. Faced with this prospect, the mineowners agreed to accept the decision of a board of arbitration.

After four months of study, the board gave its decision. The miners won a 9-hour day and a 10 percent wage increase. But the board did not grant the miners the right to negotiate as a union.

Although the miners won only part of their demands, the case was a landmark in the history of organized labor. For the first time the federal government had stepped into a labor controversy with the idea of protecting the interests of all concerned —wage earners, owners, and, by no means least important, the public.

The Danbury Hatters' case. Organized labor was not pleased, however, with the outcome of another labor dispute that began in 1902. In that year the hatters' union started a nationwide effort to boycott, or to halt the purchase of, the hats produced by a hat manufacturer of Danbury, Connecticut. The hat company claimed that the boycott restrained trade and was therefore illegal under the Sherman Antitrust Act. After a long delay, in 1908 the Supreme Court decided in favor of the hat manufacturer. As a result, the members of the hatters' union were held liable for three times the damages suffered by the hat manufacturer.

Theodore Roosevelt was in no way responsible for the Supreme Court ruling. But organized labor, thoroughly alarmed at the outcome of the Danbury Hatters' case, held the government responsible for failing to draft laws that gave reasonable protection to labor unions.

Roosevelt and black Americans. Some progressives fought the exploitation of black workers, established settlement houses for Negroes, and organized national societies to protect the legal rights of black citizens. But the progressives, on the whole, did not focus attention on the plight of black Americans. Many progressive leaders, to be sure, spoke out against racial injustice, but most of them believed that this problem could, at that time, be dealt with realistically only at state and local levels.

Theodore Roosevelt, too, did little to try to improve the conditions of black Americans. But Roosevelt did become involved in southern politics, where questions of segregation and black leadership were important issues. Especially during his first term, he wanted to strengthen his influence in southern Republican organizations. Thus, against the opposition of segregated southern Republican organizations, Roosevelt sometimes supported the claims of black politicians to federal office and to participation as delegates at Republican national conventions.

In such matters Roosevelt often used Booker T. Washington as a middleman. Once, after a conference with Washington, Roosevelt invited the black leader to lunch with him at the White House. When the episode became known, a storm of criticism swept the South. Roosevelt did not repeat the invitation.

Roosevelt's failure to include Negroes in his "square deal," except when politically expedient to do so, reflected the attitudes and prejudices of most white Americans during these years, including most of the progressives.

Roosevelt as "trust buster." During Roosevelt's administration, the federal government took a number of steps toward regulating business practices in the interests of the public welfare. Before this time, as you recall, the federal government, with few exceptions, had not become much involved in business affairs.

Early in his first term Roosevelt directed his Attorney General to bring suit under the Sherman Antitrust Act against the Northern Securities Company. This was a holding company that controlled the three leading railroads serving the country between Lake Michigan and the Pacific Northwest. "We do not wish to destroy corporations," Roosevelt announced, "but we do wish to make them subserve the public good." In 1904 the Supreme Court held that the Northern Securities Company did restrain trade and was illegal under the Sherman Antitrust Act.

Early in 1903, while the Northern Securities Company case was still pending in the courts, Congress passed two important laws. The first measure,

■ A portrait of Edward A. Johnson appears below with a page from his School History of the Negro Race in America. Studies such as his contributed to a growing literature on Negroes.

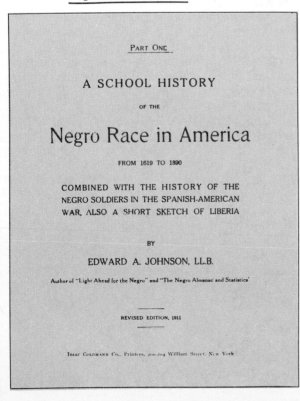

PART ONE

A SCHOOL HISTORY

OF THE

Negro Race in America

FROM 1619 TO 1890

COMBINED WITH THE HISTORY OF THE
NEGRO SOLDIERS IN THE SPANISH-AMERICAN
WAR, ALSO A SHORT SKETCH OF LIBERIA

BY

EDWARD A. JOHNSON, LL.B.

Author of "Light Ahead for the Negro" and "The Negro Almanac and Statistics"

REVISED EDITION, 1911

Isaac Goldmann Co., Printers, 200-204 William Street, New York

the Expedition Act, speeded up antitrust cases by giving them a priority over other cases in federal courts. The second measure created the Department of Commerce and Labor, with a Secretary in the President's cabinet. The new department included a Bureau of Corporations, authorized to investigate and report on corporation activities.

After 1904, encouraged by the Supreme Court decision in the Northern Securities Company case and by his own victory at the polls, Roosevelt started action against a number of other trusts. Altogether, 44 suits against trusts were started during Roosevelt's administration.

But even when the Supreme Court ordered a trust to dissolve, the men who had controlled the various corporations in the trust often continued to run them as a unit by meeting informally and sharing in the decisions of the separate corporations. By arrangements of this kind—often called "communities of interest" or "gentlemen's agreements" —the corporations continued to do informally

■ President Theodore Roosevelt liked to hunt big game. Here, in a political cartoon by Clifford Berryman, hunter Roosevelt has shot down harmful trusts and tamed other trusts by means of "restraint."

what they had previously done as a trust. The possible advantages of large-scale operations, both for the consumer and for the corporations, were obviously very great. Moreover, big business was so tied together that any attempt to break up a monopoly was like trying to unscramble the eggs in an omelet. The trend of the times was toward larger and larger business combinations, and neither Roosevelt nor anyone else could reverse this trend.

"Good" and "bad" combinations. Before leaving office in 1909, Roosevelt concluded that the problem of trusts was not simply one of size. What really mattered was whether a business combination, regardless of size, was "good" or "bad" for the public as a whole. He asked Congress to pass laws defining "good" and "bad" practices, but Congress refused.

Finally, in 1911, two years after Roosevelt left office, the Supreme Court adopted his point of view. In two cases involving business combinations, the Court ruled that the Sherman Antitrust Act's prohibition of "all combinations in restraint of trade" should mean "all *unreasonable* combinations in restraint of trade." In applying the "rule of reason," as it was called, the Supreme Court from then on decided whether a large business combination was "reasonable" or "unreasonable" by looking not merely at its size, but also at its effect upon the public.

Important railroad legislation. The Roosevelt administration had much better success in regulating railroads than in breaking up trusts. Following the President's recommendations, Congress adopted two laws which put teeth into the Interstate Commerce Act of 1887 and strengthened the Interstate Commerce Commission (page 487).

The Elkins Act of 1903 made it illegal for a shipper to accept a rebate, just as the Interstate Commerce Act had made it illegal for a railroad company to give one. Many railroads approved of this act, for it freed them from the necessity of giving special privileges to large shippers.

The Hepburn Act of 1906 provided for more thorough regulation over railroads by giving the Interstate Commerce Commission authority (1) to regulate express and sleeping-car companies, oil pipelines, bridges, railroad terminals, and ferries doing business across state lines; (2) to fix "just and reasonable" rates, subject to approval by the federal courts; (3) to restrict the granting of free passes; and (4) to require that railroads use uniform methods of accounting.

In 1910, after President Roosevelt had left office, Congress also passed the Mann-Elkins Act, which placed telephone, telegraph, cable, and wireless companies under the control of the Interstate Commerce Commission.

Laws protecting public health. President Roosevelt also gave leadership to a movement to protect public health.

Government chemists had long known that the products of some distilleries, drug companies, and meat-packing plants were endangering public health. Many canned foods were spoiled or were treated with poisonous preservatives. Patent medicines often contained harmful habit-forming drugs or ingredients that could not possibly relieve any ailments. And, as Upton Sinclair had pointed out in his book *The Jungle,* meats in the packing houses were often from diseased animals.

Against the powerful opposition of the meat-packing interests, Roosevelt and the progressives in Congress in 1906 succeeded in getting the Meat Inspection Act passed. This act gave the federal government power to inspect all meat shipped from one state to another.

Congress also adopted the Pure Food and Drug Act of 1906. This act forbade the manufacture, sale, or transportation of adulterated or poisonous patent medicines and foods. It also required the makers of patent medicines to put labels on containers indicating their exact contents. Five years later, in 1911, Congress supplemented this law by making it illegal to use false or misleading labels.

These acts helped to strengthen the developing theory that the federal government had a responsibility for protecting the public welfare.

SECTION SURVEY

IDENTIFY: "square deal," Danbury Hatters' case, Northern Securities Company case, "communities of interest," "rule of reason."

1. Explain why organized labor was pleased with Roosevelt's handling of the 1902 coal strike.
2. How did Roosevelt's attitude toward black Americans reflect the attitudes and prejudices of most white Americans of the time?
3. Do the facts support Roosevelt's claim to the title of "trust buster"? Why or why not?
4. The Elkins Act, the Hepburn Act, the Meat Inspection Act, and the Pure Food and Drug Act were important steps toward a new interpretation of government responsibility and of the general welfare clause in the preamble to the Constitution. Do you agree or disagree with this interpretation? Explain.

3 Conservation of natural resources under Theodore Roosevelt

"The first work I took up when I became President," Roosevelt wrote in his *Autobiography* "was the work of reclamation." This, the job of reclaiming and conserving the nation's natural resources, proved to be one of his greatest contributions.

Wasted natural resources. When Theodore Roosevelt became President, almost nothing had been done to safeguard the nation's resources. Indeed, Americans had always used their natural resources without regard for the future. Pioneer farmers had cut and burned their way westward, with ax and fire transforming forest lands into farm lands. With careless generosity the federal and state governments had encouraged waste, especially during the latter half of the 1800's, handing over to private individuals and to corporations priceless natural resources—agricultural and grazing lands, forest regions, mineral deposits, oil fields, and water-power sites.

By 1900 only 200 million of the nation's original 800 million acres of virgin forest were still standing, and four fifths of the timber was privately owned. The men who controlled the nation's corporations were, in general, no more concerned about waste than the pioneer settlers had been. Lumber companies destroyed forests without regard for wildlife, flood control, fire protection, replanting, or the preservation of young trees. Cattlemen and sheepmen overgrazed semiarid lands, stripping them of their protective covering of grass and often converting them into dust bowls.

Coal companies worked only the richest and most accessible veins, leaving the bulk of the coal buried in abandoned mines. Oil companies allowed natural gas to escape unused into the air. The growing cities polluted rivers and streams with sewage and industrial wastes, destroying fish and creating a menace to public health. The only excuse for these wasteful practices was that Americans had been accustomed to thinking that their natural resources were inexhaustible.

Early conservation efforts. By the late 1800's the situation was becoming increasingly serious. A rapidly growing population was making heavier and heavier demands upon the nation's resources. The growing industries were devouring raw materials in ever larger quantities. A few thoughtful Americans realized that the nation's resources could not last forever.

As early as 1873 the American Association for the Advancement of Science demanded some action to prevent the waste of natural resources. Because of these efforts and the efforts of other farsighted people, Congress in 1887 established the Forest Bureau in the Department of Agriculture. And in 1891 Congress authorized the President to withdraw timberlands from public sale. Acting under this law, President Harrison set aside a national forest reserve of 17 million acres, and Presidents Cleveland and McKinley more than doubled this area.

A small beginning toward the conservation of natural resources had been made. But the public as a whole had not yet learned to think of the need for conservation as a serious national problem.

Roosevelt's leadership. During his administration, President Roosevelt awakened public interest to the need for conservation, aroused Congress to action, and managed to get the federal and the state governments to adopt new policies.

In 1901, the year he became President, Roosevelt warned his fellow Americans that "The forest and water problems are perhaps the most vital internal problems of the United States." In a special message to Congress he reminded the legislators that "The mineral wealth of this country, the coal, iron, oil, gas, and the like, does not reproduce itself. . . . If we waste our resources today," he warned, "our descendants will feel that exhaustion a generation or two before they otherwise would. . . ."

But Theodore Roosevelt was never content with mere talk. During his administration he withdrew from public sale 150 million acres of forest land— an area substantially larger than France. He also withdrew millions of acres of coal and phosphate lands and potential water-power sites. In response to his urging, Congress created wildlife sanctuaries and national parks. Needless to say, in all of these activities Roosevelt met strong opposition from private interests.

■ In 1903, Roosevelt and John Muir (at Roosevelt's right), a famous naturalist, camped for four days at Yosemite Park in California, where they discussed conservation.

The Newlands Reclamation Act. For one of the most important acts of his administration, however, President Roosevelt received considerable support, especially from western Congressmen. Early in his Presidency he supported the Newlands Reclamation Act, which provided that money from the sale of public lands in 16 western states and Territories was to be used to build irrigation projects that would reclaim wasteland—that is, make it suitable for farming. Money from the sale of water to farmers who settled on the reclaimed land was to go into a revolving fund that would finance additional irrigation projects.

Reclamation work started at once. Within four years 28 different irrigation projects were under way. By 1911 the Shoshone (shoh·SHOH·nee) Dam in Wyoming and the Roosevelt Dam in Arizona were in operation. Water from the enormous reservoir created by the Roosevelt Dam flowed through irrigation canals and ditches to transform 200,000 acres of desert into rich farm land. As other projects were completed, additional thousands of acres of wasteland were brought under cultivation.

The White House Conference. In 1907 Roosevelt took another important step when he created the Inland Waterways Commission. After studying nearly every aspect of the conservation program the commission urged the President to organize a national conference to publicize the need for conservation.

Roosevelt immediately issued invitations for a White House meeting in May 1908. Those invited included state governors, Congressmen, Supreme Court justices, leading scientists, and scores of prominent citizens.

The White House Conservation Conference was a great success. One result was the appointment of a 50-man National Conservation Commission made up of roughly equal numbers of scientists, businessmen, and political leaders. This commission went to work at once on a systematic study of the country's mineral, water, forest, and soil resources.

Another important outgrowth of the White House Conference was the appointment of state conservation agencies in 41 of the states by governors convinced of the need for them.

Thus, Theodore Roosevelt had succeeded in arousing public opinion to the need for conservation. Equally important, he had established the foundations of a solid conservation program for the future.

■ Arizona's Roosevelt Dam, which was in operation by 1911, created an enormous reservoir. Water from this reservoir flowed through irrigation canals and ditches to transform 200,000 acres of desert into rich farm land.

SECTION SURVEY

IDENTIFY: conservation, reclamation, natural resources.

1. Show how Theodore Roosevelt tried to arouse the nation to the need for conservation.
2. What was the significance of the Newlands Reclamation Act of 1902?
3. Why was there opposition to the concept of conservation proposed by Roosevelt?
4. In what ways did "Teddy" Roosevelt establish "the foundations of a solid conservation program for the future"?
5. Pioneers, corporations, state and federal governments, and Americans in general were and are responsible for the waste of America's natural resources and the pollution of the natural environment. Comment on why this was true in the early 1900's and why it is still true today.

TRACING THE MAIN IDEAS

The victory of the Republicans in the election of 1896 broke the strength of the Populist movement. With the triumph of the Republicans and with the return of prosperity, many people concluded that the reform movement had lost its force.

But the reform movement was not dead. On the contrary, during the opening years of the 1900's it gained new life in the Progressive movement. Guided by the progressives, including President Theodore Roosevelt, the relationship of government and business began to change. In earlier times—until, say, the 1880's—the government's role had been, in general, that of a referee who stood on the sidelines and was called in only when one of the players disobeyed the rules. Now, in the twentieth century, the government began to take a more active part, to accept more responsibility for regulating the activities of business in the interest of the public welfare. Both Republicans and Democrats were responsible for this changing conception of the role of government in the new industrial age.

As you will see in the next chapter, the reforms started under President Roosevelt were continued under the Republican administration of President Taft and, to an even greater degree, under the Democratic administration of President Wilson.

CHAPTER SURVEY

QUESTIONS FOR DISCUSSION

1. How did the role of government change during the period just studied?
2. To what extent did Roosevelt's domestic policies follow the goals of his "square deal" program?
3. Theodore Roosevelt's main goal was not to "bust the trusts" but rather to assert the power of the federal government over big business. Do you agree or disagree with this statement? Explain.
4. Was reform necessary for the preservation of American business and the free enterprise system in the United States? Why or why not?
5. Did the ideals of Progressivism agree with the ideals expressed in the Declaration of Independence? Explain.

RELATING PAST TO PRESENT

1. In what ways did Theodore Roosevelt extend the powers of the Presidency?
2. In *Following the Color Line* (1908), Ray Stannard Baker stated that the plight of the Negro in America was more of a white man's problem than a black man's problem. Comment.
3. How does today's federal government protect the American public from unfair business practices?
4. Which critics in our society today might qualify for the title "muckraker"? What are they criticizing?

USING MAPS AND CHARTS

1. Consult the Chronology of Events for Theodore Roosevelt's administration (page 886) in answering the following: (a) Indicate and explain the events relating to conservation. (b) Indicate and explain the laws relating to railroads. (c) Which of the laws were designed specifically to help the consumer? (d) Which events were favorable to labor?
2. Referring to the Business Activity chart (pages 884–86), compare the depression of 1907 with those of 1873 and 1893 in length and severity. What were the consequences of these depressions?

A Woodrow Wilson campaign poster, 1912

F<small>ROM</small> 1901 to 1921 the White House opened its doors to three different Presidents. From 1901 to 1909 "Teddy" Roosevelt—colorful, dynamic, forceful—promised to give Americans a "square deal" and, on the whole, did much to fulfill his promise. From 1909 to 1913 William Howard Taft —a huge man, genial, highly intelligent, thoroughly competent, but without "Teddy's" ability to capture the public's imagination—made important contributions to the reform program. From 1913 to 1921 Woodrow Wilson—scholar, idealist, in his own quieter way sharing Theodore Roosevelt's conviction that the President's job was to lead Congress and the country—promised a "New Freedom" to his countrymen and took important steps toward fulfilling that promise before World War I interrupted his program.

Each of the three Presidents had to grapple with one basic issue—the role of government in the new industrial age. Should government try to guarantee vigorous competition by breaking up the giant industries? This was what the reformers of the 1880's and 1890's had demanded, and this was what they thought they had secured with the passage of the Sherman Antitrust Act of 1890.

Or should government accept the trend toward larger and larger industrial combinations and be content to make rules under which "good" combinations could prosper and "bad" combinations could be broken up? This was the view that Theodore Roosevelt came to accept.

CHAPTER **28**

The Extension of Reforms Under the "New Freedom"

1909 – 1920

THE CHAPTER IN OUTLINE

1. Gains and losses of the Progressive movement under President Taft.

2. Expanded opportunities under Woodrow Wilson's "New Freedom."

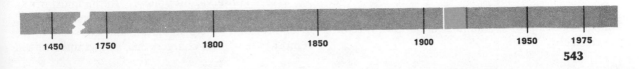

| 1450 | 1750 | 1800 | 1850 | 1900 | 1950 | 1975 |

1 Gains and losses of the Progressive movement under President Taft

Despite a financial panic and depression in 1907, President Roosevelt's popularity with the public was at its peak. It was clear that the Republican nomination for another term was his for the asking. But Roosevelt stood by an earlier announcement that he would not run again.

The election of 1908. At the Republican convention in Chicago, Roosevelt threw his support to his close friend and associate William Howard Taft of Ohio, who won the nomination on the first ballot. Roosevelt also played a leading role in drafting the Republican platform. The platform called for strengthening the Interstate Commerce Act of 1887 and the Sherman Antitrust Act of 1890, for conserving the nation's resources, developing an improved highway system, and revising the tariff.

The Democrats again chose William Jennings Bryan as their Presidential candidate. The Democratic platform condemned the Republican Party as the party of "privileges and private monopolies." It called for a lower tariff, new antitrust laws, and a federal income tax.

One unusual feature of the election campaign was the action taken by the American Federation of Labor. Until 1908 the A. F. of L. had consistently refused to throw its support behind any political party, choosing instead to support friends of organized labor in both parties. In 1908, however, the A. F. of L. abandoned this traditional policy and came out for Bryan and the entire Democratic ticket.

Despite the support of organized labor, the Democrats lost by a considerable margin, with Taft receiving 321 electoral votes to Bryan's 162. The Republicans also retained control of both houses of Congress.

Reforms under Taft. William Howard Taft, a Cincinnati lawyer and judge, had served the Roosevelt administration in the Philippines and in the War Department. Taft was a cautious man. Both his legal training and his temperament led him to stress the legalistic restrictions on his Presidential power. As one commentator put it, the transfer of the Presidency from Roosevelt to Taft was like changing from an automobile to a horse-drawn carriage. Despite his conservative nature, however, Taft recognized the force of the Progressive movement and supported a number of important reform measures.

Taft's administration chalked up an impressive list of accomplishments which progressives had favored. Taft's Attorney General started 90 antitrust suits against big corporations compared with 44 suits started under President Roosevelt. Following Taft's recommendation, Congress strengthened the Interstate Commerce Act by passing the Mann-Elkins Act of 1910. This act (page 538) placed telephone, telegraph, cable, and wireless companies under the jurisdiction of the Interstate Commerce Commission. Congress also established a Bureau of Mines in the Department of the Interior, and created a new department with cabinet rank—the Department of Labor. In response to the growing attack upon the evils of child labor, Congress established a Children's Bureau in the Department of Labor. It also established an 8-hour day for all workers on projects contracted for by the federal government.

In addition to its antitrust measures and efforts to improve the lot of wage earners, the Taft administration also took steps to create a healthier political climate. President Taft himself added a considerable number of federal jobs to the civil service list, and Congress adopted the Publicity Act requiring political parties to make public the sources and amounts of money spent in political campaigns.

Taft's administration was also partly responsible for the adoption of a constitutional amendment to make possible a federal income tax. The Sixteenth Amendment, which had been recommended by Taft and proposed in July 1909, was ratified by the required number of states by February 1913.

Progressive opposition to the tariff. In spite of these impressive reform measures, President Taft early began to lose the support of the progressives in the Republican Party. As a result, he relied more and more on conservative members of the party.

The split between President Taft and the progressives appeared as early as April 1909, when Congress adopted the Payne-Aldrich Tariff. The progressives had worked for lower tariff rates, and at first Taft had supported their position. Then he switched to the high tariff point of view, and swung his influence behind the Payne-Aldrich measure. In the new act some reductions were in fact made, but rates on many thousands of items were actually increased.

Taft's conservation policy. In the midst of the tariff controversy, Taft was also violently attacked for his stand on conservation. Indeed, some of his most bitter critics charged that he had undermined

Theodore Roosevelt's conservation program. Although this was an unfair charge, it is true that the conservation movement suffered a setback during the opening months of Taft's administration.

Taft's Secretary of the Interior, Richard A. Ballinger, was a cautious lawyer. After examining the timber law of 1891, he concluded that the President's authority to withdraw land from sale extended only to timber lands. He therefore restored to public sale valuable water-power sites that President Roosevelt had previously withdrawn. Gifford Pinchot, head of the Forest Service under both Roosevelt and Taft, promptly protested. Taft sided with Pinchot, and the lands in question were returned to the forest reserve. But Pinchot, an ardent conservationist, was convinced that Ballinger was on the side of private interests and opposed to the conservation program.

Pinchot's fears were strengthened when Ballinger allowed extensive coal lands and timber lands in Alaska to pass into private hands. This action aroused a storm of controversy throughout the country. In the midst of the storm, Taft removed Pinchot from office.

Although Ballinger resigned in 1911 and the new Secretary of the Interior restored the Alaskan lands to the federal forest reserve, the damage had been done. Taft's stand on the Ballinger controversy cost the Republicans large numbers of votes in the Congressional elections of 1910. For the first time in 16 years the Republicans lost control of the House of Representatives.

Actually, Taft did a great deal to advance the conservation program. After receiving authorization from Congress, he withdrew almost 59 million acres of coal lands from public sale. He also signed the Appalachian Forest Reserve Act, which enabled the government to add about 1.3 million acres of land in the White Mountains of New Hampshire and the Southern Appalachians to the federal reserves.

A political victory for progressives. Early in 1910 the progressive wing of the Republican Party launched an attack upon the Speaker of the House. Since 1903 Speaker Joseph G. Cannon of Illinois, nicknamed "Uncle Joe," had been one of the most powerful officers in the government. As Speaker, he appointed all House committees and selected the chairmen. He appointed himself chairman of the powerful Committee on Rules, which determined the order of business in the House. Acting in this capacity, he could prevent any bill to which he objected from coming out of committee for debate on

■ President William Howard Taft was conservative by nature. Yet he recognized the force of the Progressive movement and supported a number of important reform measures.

the floor of the House. Moreover, as presiding officer of the House he could determine who should speak during debate by recognizing or refusing to recognize anyone he pleased. As a result of these powers, "Uncle Joe" was able to rule the House with an iron hand.

The progressives charged that Cannon, a conservative, had used his great power to block progressive legislation. Determined to put an end to Cannon's control, in March 1910 Representative George W. Norris of Nebraska proposed an amendment to the House rules. He moved that in the future the Committee on Rules be elected by the members of the House instead of being chosen by the Speaker, and that the Speaker himself be excluded from membership on the Rules Committee.

Speaker Cannon, solidly supported by the conservatives, fought desperately to maintain his power. After a heated debate, about 40 progressive Republicans voted with the Democrats in favor of

Norris' motion and stripped the Speaker of his traditional powers over the Committee on Rules. A year later the House deprived the Speaker of his power to appoint members of the remaining committees. The Speaker remained an extremely influential figure, but his power to rule had been taken from him.

Split in the Republican Party. By 1912 the Republican Party was split wide open, with the "old guard" on one side and the progressives on the other. Theodore Roosevelt, by now dissatisfied with Taft's leadership, decided to run again for the Presidency. To do so, Roosevelt had to brush aside the obvious candidate of the progressive forces, Robert M. La Follette of Wisconsin. Roosevelt also had to line up enough delegates to the nominating convention to insure his own nomination.

But President Taft had the advantage that a President always has at a political convention. When the Republican convention began to organize, the Roosevelt supporters claimed that many of their delegates were refused seats by the steamroller methods of the Taft forces. The convention named Taft as its candidate. Disgruntled at this turn of affairs, Roosevelt's supporters called another convention, which nominated him for the Presidency and launched a new third party—the Progressive Party, sometimes called the "Bull Moose" Party.°

The "Bull Moose" Republicans with "Teddy" Roosevelt at their head adopted a platform calling for numerous reforms. The platform favored legislation in the interest of labor; it advocated tariff reform; it endorsed the initiative, referendum, and recall; and it declared that it stood for government control over unfair business practices. In a spirited campaign, full of an almost frenzied zeal, Roosevelt popularized his "New Nationalism" program. By the phrase "New Nationalism" he meant the extension of the powers of the federal government so that it might become an effective instrument in the battle for progressive measures and social reform.

Wilson as the Democratic candidate. The Democrats had every reason to believe that the split in the Republican Party would insure their own victory. As their standard bearer, they chose Governor Woodrow Wilson of New Jersey. The Democratic platform called for tariff reduction, banking reform, laws on behalf of workers and farmers, and the enforcement of stronger antitrust laws. Both the platform and the nomination of Wilson indicated that the Democratic Party was under the influence of its progressive wing.

Wilson, the son of a southern Presbyterian minister, had been educated at Princeton, the University of Virginia, and Johns Hopkins University. In 1902 he became president of Princeton University. His writings emphasized the idea that the President of the United States ought to be the real leader of the government, taking the initiative and interpreting the will of the people.

Not until Wilson became governor of New Jersey in 1910 did he favor the newer progressive ideas. As governor he fought the political "machine" bosses of his party, showing a remarkably astute independence. He also took the lead in pushing through the legislature laws designed to reform the lax corporation laws of the state. And he showed more and more interest in other progressive measures. Thus he became the logical choice of the progressives in the Democratic Party.

An idealist and a man of convictions, Wilson was determined, courageous, and independent. He sensed the popular discontent in the country, and his neatly turned phrases about establishing a "New Freedom" for the common man greatly appealed to those who were convinced that special privilege menaced the nation.

Democratic victory. The election proved to be a clear-cut victory for the progressives, a defeat for the conservatives. Wilson received 435 electoral votes to 88 for Roosevelt and 8 for Taft.

Despite his overwhelming electoral vote, Wilson was a "minority" President. He received only 6 million popular votes out of a total of more than 15 million. Nevertheless, he could count upon widespread public support for his progressive "New Freedom" program.

SECTION SURVEY

IDENTIFY: Department of Labor, Publicity Act, Sixteenth Amendment, "Bull Moose" Party, "New Nationalism."

1. Make a chart comparing the parties, candidates, issues, and results of the 1908 and 1912 elections.
2. (a) What were the reasons for the revolt against "Uncle Joe" Cannon? (b) What were the results?
3. "Taft's administration chalked up an impressive list of accomplishments which progressives had favored." Explain.

° The party adopted as its emblem the powerful bull moose as a tribute to Roosevelt, who often used the term to describe a person's strength and vigor.

2 Expanded opportunities under Woodrow Wilson's "New Freedom"

With his "New Freedom" program President Wilson hoped to restore the equality of opportunity that many Americans had enjoyed when the frontier was still open to settlers. Wilson believed that this equality of opportunity had for the most part been destroyed by the closing of the frontier, by great corporations, and by the often corrupt alliance between government and business.

Wilson's plea for the "New Freedom." President Wilson at once recommended to Congress a positive program to promote the public welfare. Opposed by pressure groups and lobbies representing special business interests, Wilson used all his oratorical skills to win popular support.

The legislation enacted during Wilson's first administration did not fully realize the President's ideal of economic freedom and equality for the common man. But it went far in that direction.

Tariff reform. Like most Democrats, Wilson believed that high protective tariffs benefited the trusts by excluding from the country products which foreign manufacturers could make and market more cheaply. It was also true, of course, that tariffs protected jobs and helped workers maintain higher wages than European workers received.

To check the trend toward monopoly and reduce the cost of living, the Wilson administration pushed through Congress the Underwood Tariff Act of 1913. This act did not establish *free trade*,° but it went further toward reducing tariffs than had any act adopted in the past 50 years. It lowered duties on almost a thousand items, including cotton and woolen goods, iron, steel, coal, wood, agricultural tools, and many agricultural products. The average of all duties was reduced from 41 to 29 percent.

To make up for the revenue thus lost, the Underwood Tariff Act took advantage of the recently ratified Sixteenth Amendment to the Constitution by including a section providing for an income tax. The new law provided for a "graduated" tax ranging from 1 to 6 percent on incomes over $3,000 per year.

The Underwood Tariff was passed against strong opposition. Its opponents claimed it would seriously harm American business. Whether these claims were justified, however, remained unanswered, for

° *free trade:* the exchange of goods between countries unhampered by regulations or high protective tariffs aimed to keep out foreign goods.

in 1914 war broke out in Europe and many normal trade relations were shattered. During World War I American business boomed, and American manufacturers did not need a tariff to protect them from foreign competition.

But the Underwood Tariff did answer the widespread cry for tariff reform. Moreover, in its income tax provision, it laid down the principle that those with more income must bear a heavier share of the expenses of government. This rule is sometimes called the "ability-to-pay" principle of taxation.

Demand for a new banking system. The second important achievement of Wilson's "New Freedom" administration was in the field of money and banking. Almost everyone was dissatisfied with the existing banking system. But people disagreed on how to reform it. Some favored a strongly centralized banking system under *private* control, and others wanted the *government* to exercise greater control over money and banking.

In general, the more conservative business groups wanted greater private control over the existing banking system. They argued that this control would enable the stronger banks to help the less favored banks in times of financial crisis.

On the other side were the Bryan Democrats and the progressive Republicans. They believed that the existing banking system was already too much under the control of the great bankers and financiers—the "money trust." They wanted the government, not private bankers, to control the banking system. This control, they argued, would enable the government to regulate the amount of currency in circulation and thus help to stabilize prices.

LIVING AMERICAN DOCUMENTS

Woodrow Wilson's
"New Freedom" Speech (1912)

I take my stand absolutely, where every progressive ought to take his stand, on the proposition that private monopoly is indefensible and intolerable. And there I will fight my battle.... I am for big business, and I am against trusts. Any man who can survive by his brains, any man who can put the others out of the business by making the thing cheaper to the consumer at the same time that he is increasing its intrinsic value and quality, I take off my hat to, and I say: "You are the man who can build up the United States, and I wish there were more of you."...

■ The artist George Bellows painted an overcrowded, urban America, teeming with life, in his "Cliff Dwellers." The painting was done in 1913.

The Federal Reserve System. The Federal Reserve Act of 1913 was a compromise between these two proposals. It provided for the establishment of 12 Federal Reserve districts, each with a Federal Reserve Bank. The operations of these district banks were to be supervised and coordinated by a Federal Reserve Board in Washington, D.C. All national banks were to be members of a Federal Reserve Bank, and all of the state banks which met certain requirements were invited to join.

The Federal Reserve Banks were strictly "bankers' banks," established to provide services only for member banks, not for business concerns or private citizens. In times of crisis, when weak banks were on the point of failing, the Federal Reserve Banks could transfer money reserves and thus help to prevent failure and the loss of people's savings.

The Federal Reserve System also provided a more "elastic" currency by making it possible to put more money into circulation or to withdraw some from circulation according to the needs of the time. It provided this elastic currency by controlling the amount of lending that member banks could do.

Antitrust laws strengthened. The third great achievement of Wilson's "New Freedom" program was its effort to strengthen the antitrust laws. The Clayton Antitrust Act of 1914 helped to put teeth in the older Sherman Antitrust Act.

The Clayton Act was aimed at business practices that until then had not been illegal. (1) It prohibited business organizations from selling at lower prices to certain favored purchasers *if* such price discrimination helped to create a monopoly. (2) It prohibited "tying contracts"—that is, contracts requiring a purchaser to agree that he would not buy or sell the products of a competitor. (3) It declared interlocking directorates illegal in companies with capital investments of $1 million or more. (4) It prohibited corporations from acquiring the stock of another company *if* the purchase tended to create a monopoly.

The Clayton Act also attempted to protect the farmer and the wage earner. As you have seen (page 506), the Sherman Antitrust Act of 1890 had been used on a number of occasions against labor unions. The Clayton Act, on the other hand, declared that labor unions and farm organizations had a legal right to exist and could not "be held or construed to be illegal combinations or conspiracies in restraint of trade, under the antitrust laws."

The Clayton Act also prohibited the granting of an injunction in a labor dispute *unless* the court decided that an injunction was necessary "to prevent irreparable injury to property." This act also declared that strikes, peaceful picketing, and boycotts were legal under federal jurisdiction.

Organized labor hailed the Clayton Act as a great victory. But as you will see, the courts tended to interpret the act in such a way that the injunction continued to be used as a weapon against strikes.

The Federal Trade Commission. The Federal Trade Commission, created by Congress in 1914 as part of President Wilson's "New Freedom" program, was authorized to advise and regulate industries engaged in interstate and foreign trade. The commission was to be a bipartisan body of five members.

The commission was authorized to (1) require annual and special reports from corporations; (2) investigate the business activities of persons and most corporations; (3) publish reports on its findings; and (4) order corporations to stop unfair methods of competition. Among the unfair practices investigated by the commission were mislabeling, adulteration of products, and false claims to patents. If a corporation refused to obey an order to "cease and desist" such practices, the commission could appeal to the courts to enforce its ruling. But the law protected the corporation by providing that it also could appeal to the courts if it considered the "cease and desist" order to be unfair.

The Federal Trade Commission was intended to prevent the growth of monopolies and to help bring about a better understanding between big business and the government.

Other "New Freedom" measures. The tariff, money and banking, regulation of trusts—these were the major problems tackled by Congress during Wilson's first administration. Much more reform legislation might have been adopted if the outbreak of World War I in Europe in the summer of 1914 had not interfered. Even so, Congress found time to pass several other important measures.

In 1914 Congress adopted the Smith-Lever Act. Among other things, this act provided federal funds for rural education. The educational programs were to be carried on by the Department of Agriculture in cooperation with the land-grant colleges. Federal grants of money were to be matched by similar grants from the states receiving this aid. Three years later, in 1917, just before the United States entered World War I, Congress adopted the Smith-Hughes Act. This additional measure provided federal funds for vocational education in both rural and urban areas of the country. You will learn more about these acts in Chapter 29.

The Federal Farm Loan Act of 1916 made it easier for farmers to borrow money. This act divided the country into 12 agricultural districts. It established a Farm Loan Bank for each district where farmers could get mortgages at rates lower than those available at regular banks.

Negroes and the "New Freedom." During the election campaign of 1912 Woodrow Wilson promised an officer of the National Association for the Advancement of Colored People (NAACP) that, if elected, he would promote the interests of black Americans in every way possible. Such was not the case, however. As President, Wilson seemed to agree with most white Americans that segregation

---

LIVING AMERICAN DOCUMENTS

Woodrow Wilson on
American Ideals (1914)

My dream is that, as the years go on and the world knows more and more of America, it will also drink at these fountains of youth and renewal; that it also will turn to America for those moral inspirations which lie at the basis of all freedom; that the world will never fear America, unless it feels that it is engaged in some enterprise which is inconsistent with the rights of humanity; and that America will come into the full light of the day when all shall know that she puts human rights above all other rights and that her flag is the flag not only of America, but of humanity.

■ Black Americans were not allowed to take part in Wilson's "New Freedom" and continued to live in a segregated environment. Above is a photograph of a black teacher with his class, taken in the early 1900's.

was in the best interests of black Americans and white Americans alike.

During Wilson's administration, which was largely dominated by white southerners, white employees and black employees in government offices in Washington, D.C., were segregated. And many black office workers were dismissed in southern cities. A Negro journalist expressed the bitterness of his people when he remarked that Wilson had given black Americans no part in the "New Freedom."

Presidential candidates in 1916. By 1916 President Wilson had established himself as a vigorous leader. The delegates to the Democratic convention pointed with pride to his solid list of achievements and enthusiastically renominated him for a second term.

The Republicans chose Supreme Court Justice Charles Evans Hughes, former governor of New York, as their standard bearer. The Progressive

Party nominated Theodore Roosevelt. But Roosevelt, unwilling to split the Republican vote again, refused the nomination and supported Hughes. The Progressive Party, deprived of Roosevelt, decided not to nominate another candidate. As a result the Republicans, once more united, entered the campaign hopeful of victory.

Wilson's victory. Debate during the campaign of 1916 centered not only upon Wilson's record on domestic issues, but also upon America's relation to the war which had broken out in Europe in 1914 (Chapter 32). During the campaign Hughes toured the country, criticizing the Democrats for the Underwood Tariff and for their handling of foreign affairs. Wilson, on the other hand, contented himself with delivering a number of speeches from the front porch of his summer home in New Jersey. Speakers for the Democratic Party adopted the slogan "He kept us out of war."

The election itself turned out to be one of the closest in American history. The final electoral vote was 277 for Wilson, 254 for Hughes. California proved to be the decisive state—the Democrats won in California by a margin of only 3,773 popular votes! And yet, despite the closeness of the vote, Wilson had won against a united Republican Party, as had not been true in the election of 1912. Even more reassuring, he had collected nearly 600,000 more popular votes than Hughes.

Wilson seemed to feel that his first term in office had accomplished his goals, though many progressives held that much remained to be done. In any event, it was not the "New Freedom" that occupied the President during his second administration. As you will read later, within a month of his second inauguration on March 4, 1917, the United States entered World War I.

SECTION SURVEY

IDENTIFY: "New Freedom," Underwood Tariff, Federal Farm Loan Act, free trade, elastic currency, "ability-to-pay" principle of taxation.

1. (a) Why did Wilson institute the "New Freedom" program? (b) What did this program reveal about his view of the role and purpose of government?
2. How did the Clayton Antitrust Act of 1914 "put teeth in the older Sherman Antitrust Act?"
3. What was the function of the Federal Trade Commission?
4. Why can the Federal Reserve Act of 1913 be considered a victory for the progressives?
5. Were black Americans included in Wilson's "New Freedom" program? Why or why not?

TRACING THE MAIN IDEAS

In 1909, when William Howard Taft entered the White House, the Progressive movement was in full swing. His predecessor, Theodore Roosevelt, had captured the imagination of the American people and won wide support for his "square deal." Taft was less forceful, less imaginative, much more conservative than "Teddy" Roosevelt. Nevertheless, during his administration Congress adopted an impressive number of significant reform measures. But Taft did not move rapidly enough or far enough to please the progressive wing of his party, and in the election of 1912 the Republicans split, with the progressives voting for Roosevelt and the conservatives voting for Taft. The Republicans lost, and Woodrow Wilson, a Democrat, became President.

President Wilson breathed new life into the movement for progressive reforms. He shared the belief of many leaders in both parties that the rise of giant industries threatened to destroy the equality of opportunity that had for so long been an important part of the American way of life. He agreed with millions of Americans that the government had to assume the responsibility for safeguarding free enterprise and democracy.

In his "New Freedom" program President Wilson undertook to restore a larger measure of competition to the economic life of the country. He undertook to provide rules that would insure greater equality of opportunity for most of his fellow Americans.

Both the "New Freedom" and the earlier "square deal" were attempts by America's leaders, Democratic and Republican, to come to grips with the problems created by the transformation of the United States from an agricultural country to one of the leading industrial powers of the world.

CHAPTER SURVEY

QUESTIONS FOR DISCUSSION

1. The basic issue with which Theodore Roosevelt, Taft, and Wilson had to grapple was the role of government in the new industrial age. Explain.
2. Compare Theodore Roosevelt's "Square Deal" and Woodrow Wilson's "New Freedom" in regard to (a) aims, (b) legislative accomplishments, and (c) influence upon later history.
3. Do you agree or disagree with the basic principle of the income tax—the "ability to pay" principle? Why?
4. Black Americans were not included in Wilson's "New Freedom" program. Why? From what other reform programs had black Americans been excluded previously? Why?
5. Woodrow Wilson made the following statement: "Democratic institutions are never done—they are, like the living tissue, always a-making." Comment on this statement with regard to the events dealt with in this chapter.

RELATING PAST TO PRESENT

1. Has the attitude of the American public toward the graduated income tax changed from what it was during the period just studied? Explain.
2. What reforms are currently being proposed by the national government to help remedy the ills of our society? How do the problems of today compare with those of the period just studied?
3. Will black Americans and other minorities benefit from reform measures being proposed or enacted by the national government today? Explain.

USING MAPS AND CHARTS

1. Basing your answer on chart 1 on page 868, compare railroad mileage in 1880 with that in 1920 and explain the reason for the increase. Why is this information significant?
2. What conclusions for the period 1890–1920 can you draw from charts 2 and 3 on page 868?

CHANGING WAYS
OF AMERICAN LIFE

CHAPTER 29

"The Big Change"
in American
Ways of Life

1900 – 1920

As the United States approached the middle of the twentieth century, Frederick Lewis Allen wrote a book reviewing and interpreting 50 years of American history. He called his book *The Big Change,* and added the subtitle *America Transforms Itself, 1900–1950*. Note that Allen did not say "America *was* transformed," but chose instead to emphasize that Americans were themselves responsible in large part for "the big change."

The transformation, as Allen saw it, was "in the character and quality of American life by reason of what might be called the democratization of our economic system, or the adjustment of capitalism to democratic ends." It was, he went on to say, "the way in which an incredible expansion of industrial and business activity, combined with a varied series of political, social, and economic forces, has altered the American standard of living and with it the average American's way of thinking and his status as a citizen."

In 1900 the United States was in full process of passing from a predominantly rural economy to a predominantly industrial economy. Americans as a whole were struggling to adjust their daily lives and institutions to the new world created by the Industrial Revolution. It was a world of crowded cities, of new sources of power, of machines, of mass production, and of an economy that each year was providing more and more people with more of the necessities and the luxuries of life.

During the years from 1900 to 1920 a growing number of Americans, including businessmen, became increasingly aware of the need to modify some of the attitudes and practices carried over from the early days of the Industrial Revolution. In 1920 there were still many large and difficult problems that remained unsolved. But "the big change" was already beginning to have an important influence on the direction of American life.

THE CHAPTER IN OUTLINE

1. A revolution in American industry through new inventions and ideas.

2. Improvements in the life of the American farmer in the early 1900's.

3. Improving conditions for American industrial workers.

1 A revolution in American industry through new inventions and ideas

In 1900 America was still in the horse-and-buggy age. But that age would not last much longer. Great changes were transforming the country, and even greater changes lay ahead.

Older ways of living. In 1900 Americans still rode in horsedrawn streetcars; hitching posts for horses were common sights; livery stables and blacksmith shops were centers of activity in every town; at nightfall the lamplighter made his rounds, lighting gas lamps that still furnished illumination for most American streets.

It is easier, perhaps, to picture the America of 1900 by listing the things that people did not have and did not know. There were no rock groups, no beauty parlors, no income taxes. No one had heard of vitamins, Salk vaccine, or penicillin. Women could vote in only four states—Wyoming, Colorado, Utah, and Idaho. Boy Scouts and 4-H Clubs did not exist. Neither did motion pictures, radios,

television, or airplanes. Automobiles were still curiosities; people often called them "horseless carriages."

Signs of change. And yet, in 1900, Americans stood on the threshold of a new way of life. Indeed, much of the new was already apparent. By 1900 railroad builders had constructed 192,566 miles of track. All the great trunk lines had been built across the continent. Day and night, long lines of freight cars rumbled across the country loaded with products of America's farm lands, mines, mills, and factories. New railroad lines were being built—by 1920 the nation's railroad mileage reached its high mark of 260,000 miles of track.

Automobiles and highways. While railroad builders were feverishly building their network of steel rails, inventors in Europe and America were experimenting with a new source of power—the "internal combustion" engine, in which fuel, usually gasoline, was converted into a vapor and exploded within the engine walls. Among the American experimenters were Charles E. Duryea, George B. Selden, Elwood Haynes, Alexander Winton, and

■ In 1900 America was still in the horse-and-buggy age, but changes were beginning to come with ever-increasing rapidity. Below is a painting of an elevated railway in New York City.

DEVIL WAGONS OF THE EARLY 1900's

Until about 1905 automobiles were luxuries that only wealthy people could afford, and expensive toys for mechanically minded men. To the average person they were public nuisances, noisy contraptions that frightened horses and sometimes caused accidents. Some people called them "devil wagons." Others joked about their undependability. Typical of the jokes was this one that appeared in *Life* Magazine in 1904:

"Do you enjoy your automobile?"
"Yes, I enjoy my automobile immensely."
"But I never see you out."
"Oh, I haven't got that far yet. I am just learning to make my own repairs."

Henry Ford. These men and others developed the gasoline engine.

By 1900 "horseless carriages" were appearing on the road. At first the automobile was an expensive toy for wealthy people. Mass production soon lowered costs, however, bringing the automobile within reach of people with modest incomes. Whereas in 1900 there were only 8,000 automobiles in the United States, by 1920 there were 1 million trucks and 8 million passenger cars.

The development of the automobile depended,

of course, upon other inventions and developments. One was the discovery by Charles Goodyear of the process for vulcanizing, or hardening, rubber, for which he obtained his first patent in 1844. Other inventions led to improvements in refining petroleum into gasoline, and in developing batteries, generators, and other electrical devices.

The development of the automobile also depended upon—and helped to stimulate—the construction of paved roads. In 1904, for example, nearly all rural roads were little better than dirt lanes, although some were "surfaced" with gravel, clay, or crushed oyster shells. By 1924, however, 472,000 miles of rural highways had paved surfaces. By 1924 older roads were being widened, graded, and paved at the rate of about 40,000 miles a year, and at an annual cost of approximately $1 billion.

The airplane. By 1900 Europeans and Americans were experimenting with powered flight. Samuel P. Langley of Washington invented the first power-driven airplane. But it was the Wright brothers, Orville and Wilbur, who on December 17, 1903, first put such a machine in the air. Their first flight went only about 120 feet, and did not attract much attention. Within a few years, however, the first crude flying machines were being replaced by more effective planes, and men were making longer and longer flights. In 1919 a Navy seaplane crossed the Atlantic by way of the Azores, and two English fliers, John Alcock and A. W. Brown, flew nonstop from Newfoundland to Ireland.

Wired and wireless communications. Equally revolutionary were developments in communications. Europeans and Americans were barely getting used to the idea of the telephone when, in 1895, a 21-year-old Italian inventor, Guglielmo (goo-LYEL-moh) Marconi, gave the first demonstration of wireless telegraphy. Eight years later, from a station at Cape Cod, Massachusetts, he transmitted an entire message across the ocean to England and received a reply.

Within a few years wireless equipment had been installed on all large vessels, and wireless messages were being sent over land and sea by powerful transmitters. Meanwhile, scientists and engineers were experimenting with the transmission of the spoken word through the air, as distinguished from mere signals. But commercial radio broadcasting did not become a reality until the 1920's.

One of the most significant inventions in the field of communications was the three-element vacuum tube, invented by Lee De Forest in 1906. The telegraph and the telephone, as well as wireless communication, benefited from this invention, which could be used to relay telegraph and telephone impulses over long distances. By 1915 New York and San Francisco were linked by telephone.

The motion picture. Thomas Armat's invention of the motion picture projector in 1895 made possible the development of a new method of communication and a new form of recreation.

In the early days, films ran only a few minutes.

Then, in 1903, a pioneer "picture story" called *The Great Train Robbery* demonstrated the possibilities of the motion picture. Soon directors and producers, among them D. W. Griffith, who won fame in 1914 for his film *The Birth of a Nation,* were proving to ever larger audiences that the motion picture could do a great deal that was impossible on the stage. Night after night people crowded into the "nickelodeons," as the early movie theaters were called, and for the usual admission of five cents watched such popular stars as Mary Pickford, Douglas Fairbanks, and Charlie Chaplin.

New methods of production. The new world that was coming into being in the early 1900's depended upon the development of an old source of power—steam—and the even faster development of new power sources—oil and electricity. Between 1900 and 1920 oil production in the United States jumped from 63 million to about 443 million barrels annually. By 1914 nearly one third of the nation's factory machines were driven by electricity, and the use of electric power was rapidly increasing. High-voltage transmission lines carried the pulsing energy of dynamos—steam-driven or water-driven—to widely scattered cities. Smaller transmission lines, or "feeders," carried electricity to small towns and villages and even to some isolated farms.

Productivity of America's factories was greatly increased not only by the use of new sources of power, but also by the development of the *assembly line*. On an assembly line, individual parts were moved from station to station along a slowly mov-

■ **Gas Lighting. Inflammable gas was led through walls to fixtures. Some fixtures used an "open fishtail flame" (left). Others used "mantles" made of a heat-resisting material which glowed when a flame burned inside of them (right).**

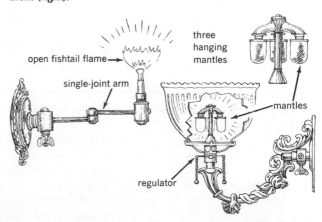

open fishtail flame →

single-joint arm

three hanging mantles

mantles

regulator

ing track, or "conveyor belt." At each station, workers added a new part to the product on the track. Finally, a steady succession of finished products came off the end of the assembly line. Developed in the early 1900's by Henry Ford in the manufacture of automobiles, the assembly line soon became an essential part of America's developing industrial economy.

Increasing efficiency. *Efficiency engineering* also increased the productivity of America's factories. Credit for originating this development is usually given to Frederick W. Taylor.

Taylor wanted to secure greater efficiency from machines and from the men operating the machines. In an effort to do this, he developed "time-and-motion" studies of plant operation. Using a stop watch, Taylor carefully watched a worker operating a machine and counted the number of motions the worker made to complete a particular operation. Then he worked out ways to reduce the number of movements of the worker's hands and feet. Sometimes the worker was trained to use his hands and feet more effectively. Sometimes the machine was redesigned, and its controls placed in more convenient locations.

The development of Taylor's methods made great economies possible in every stage of mass production. Each process in the mechanized industrial plant was simplified and speeded up along the assembly line. Each worker performed a highly specialized task, working with the least possible effort to produce the maximum output.

The "Ford idea." Henry Ford had made a major contribution to American industry in developing the assembly line. But he made perhaps an even more fundamental contribution by introducing a revolutionary new theory of wages.

On January 5, 1914, Ford announced that he was nearly doubling the wages of the workers in his plants. Beginning immediately, he said, his 13,000 employees would receive a minimum wage of $5 for an 8-hour day. This announcement swept almost all other news off the front pages of America's newspapers. The New York *Herald* called it "an epoch in the world's industrial history."

Ford was both warmly applauded and sharply criticized for his action. But the criticism did not prevent the "Ford idea" from spreading to other industries. Rising wages gave American workers greater purchasing power. They could buy more and more of the products of America's expanding industry. As the years passed, more people came to understand that mass production and mass pur-

chasing power are mutually interdependent. This understanding was an essential part of what Frederick Lewis Allen called "the big change" transforming America in the opening years of the twentieth century.

SECTION SURVEY

IDENTIFY: nickelodeons, assembly line, efficiency engineering; Charles Goodyear, Samuel Langley, Wright brothers, Guglielmo Marconi, Frederick Taylor.

1. Why was transportation vital to the creation of a modern America?
2. Henry Ford made an important contribution to the American economic system. Comment.
3. In 1900 the United States was in full process of passing from a rural to an industrial economy. (a) What changes were taking place in the "new world" created by the Industrial Revolution? (b) What conflicts did these changes create? (c) Why was it difficult for people to adjust to these changes?

2 Improvements in the life of the American farmer in the early 1900's

The life of the farmer, like the lives of other Americans, was being transformed during the years between 1900 and 1920.

Growing demand for farm produce. One of the most significant developments in the early 1900's was the startling growth of America's city population. Between 1900 and 1920 the urban population increased by about 24 million, the rural population by only about 6 million. Between 1900 and 1920 urban dwellers increased from about 40 percent of the total population to more than 50 percent.

The swelling urban population came in part from the nation's farms as many farm youths left home to seek their fortunes in the cities. But it came in much larger part from the more than 14 million immigrants who poured into the United States between 1900 and 1920. Regardless of the source, however, the growing urban population meant more mouths to feed and a growing demand for farm products.

Rising prices and prosperity. The rapidly growing demand for farm products enabled farmers to receive higher prices. Indeed, between 1900 and 1920 farm prices increased threefold.

"Cheaper" money, as well as the increased de-

Have you placed a Sentimental Value on your Horses out of proportion to the work they are able to perform?

BAILOR MOTOR CULTIVATORS

■ This advertisement reflects the changes that were transforming the life of the American farmer during the years between 1900 and 1920.

mand for farm products, helped to raise prices. Just as the Republicans had firmly planted the nation on the gold standard, new discoveries of gold in the Klondike region of Canada and in Alaska in 1897, and the invention of more efficient methods of extracting gold from ore, greatly increased the gold supply. As the supply of gold increased, the value of gold fell. And as the value of gold fell—making money "cheaper"—the prices of all other products rose.

Moreover, the value of farm lands increased, rising on the average fourfold between 1900 and 1920. As a result, many farmers were able to sell their surplus acres for a handsome profit and either retire or buy new farm machines.

Laborsaving machines. Farmers had been using laborsaving machines long before the turn of the century. Not until after 1900, however, did the shift from hand tools to power-driven machines begin to transform the farming industry. According to census records, in 1870 the total value of all farm implements and machinery in the United States amounted to $271 million. By 1900 the figure had risen to $750 million; by 1920 to $3.6 billion.

Whereas in 1900 farmers still carted their produce to market in wagons, by 1920 many were using trucks. Census figures show that in 1910 farmers spent $32 million for motor vehicles; in 1920, $392 million.

Even more revealing as a measure of the machine age was the use of tractors. In 1910 there were only 1,000 tractors on American farms; by 1920 there were 246,000.

Gasoline and electricity—these new sources of power were revolutionizing rural as well as urban life in the early 1900's. Power-driven machinery—pumps, plows, seeders, harvesters, milking machines, trucks, and tractors—began to lift the burden of labor from the farmer, enabling him to

557

produce far more products with much less toil.

The growth of scientific agriculture. Scientific knowledge, as well as power-driven machinery, helped to revolutionize farming. Chemists discovered secrets of the soil, enabling farmers to use new fertilizers and better methods of cultivation to stop soil exhaustion and replenish worn-out land. Biologists improved the life span and the productivity of livestock, plants, grains, and fruits. Bacteriologists discovered ways to check blights and diseases in both plants and animals.

Scientists also began to develop new grains and fruits resistant to disease and better adapted to varying climatic conditions. One of their most important discoveries was that of vitamins.

Federal aid to farmers. Much of the new research and experimentation was carried on by the federal government or in state institutions created with the aid of federal grants. As you have read (pages 390–91), in 1862 a Republican Congress adopted three measures of great importance for farmers: (1) it enacted the Homestead Act, granting farmers free land; (2) it passed the Morrill Act, granting land to the states for the establishment of "land grant" colleges of agriculture and mechanical arts; and (3) it created the Department of Agriculture.

In later years the federal government greatly expanded this program of aid to farmers. The Hatch Act of 1887, for example, provided money for agricultural experiment stations and farms in each state. The Smith-Lever Act of 1914 provided additional money for the employment of "county extension agents" who were to carry "useful and practical information on subjects relating to agriculture and home economics" to the farmers of each county. The Smith-Hughes Act of 1917 provided money for the support of vocational education in the public schools, including education in agriculture, industries, trade, home economics, and the training of teachers.

Farmers as businessmen. By the early 1900's the farmer had become an important part of the nation's industrial economy. To be sure, on thousands of small farms tucked away in mountain valleys and in other remote areas, farm families lived much as their forefathers had lived 100 years earlier. But these more or less self-sufficient farms were exceptions. Most of the nation's farm produce was raised by farmers who, whether they liked it or not, had in many respects become businessmen.

The commercial farmer specialized in one or two crops, or in dairy farming, or in raising livestock. He needed money, or capital, to buy his machinery and to hire labor. He had to keep careful accounts and to pay careful attention to market conditions. He was, in brief, one part of an abstract thing known as the "nation's economy." When the economy prospered, the farmer could hope to prosper; when the economy went into a depression, the farmer was certain to suffer.

Changing ways of living. Equally revolutionary was the impact of the new industrial age on the everyday lives of farm families. By 1920 loneliness and social isolation were becoming memories to many of the nation's farmers. The slender threads of telephone wires were spinning a net of communications across the countryside. The automobile—notably Henry Ford's "Tin Lizzie"—was bringing the farm closer to the town and the city. Whereas a five-mile drive to town had once meant a one- or two-hour trip behind "Old Dobbin," by 1920 the same trip could be made in the family car in half an hour or less. This meant more trips to town, often for an evening at the movies.

With better communication and transportation and with more money in their pockets, farmers could provide better education for their children and better living conditions for their families. The one-room school continued to dominate the rural educational scene, but more and more farm children began to come from miles around to enjoy the advantages of "consolidated schools," and many were able to continue their education at the state university. For farm children, no less than for their parents, life "down on the farm" in the early 1900's was far more comfortable and interesting than it had ever been before.

SECTION SURVEY

IDENTIFY: subsistence farming, commercial farming, "consolidated schools."

1. Explain how each of the following affected and changed the life of the farmer in the years from 1900 to 1920: (a) urbanization, (b) mechanization, (c) scientific agriculture, (d) federal aid.
2. How did the social life of farm families change as a result of mechanization?
3. By having a national, rather than a local, transportation system, farmers had wider markets as well as more competition. Comment on how this would affect their economic freedom.
4. By 1920 farmers had become businessmen who wanted to make money rather than to subsist, or merely make a living, from the land. Comment.

3 Improving conditions for American industrial workers

Conditions for the industrial worker as well as for the farmer improved considerably during the early 1900's. First, as you have seen, wage earners benefited from the fast-increasing productivity of America's economic system. Second, through organization, wage earners were beginning to gain enough strength to exert real influence on state legislatures and on Congress. Third, many Americans, including many industrialists, were beginning to realize that the industrial age had raised serious problems—problems that had to be solved if democracy itself was to survive. Fourth, through articles in popular magazines and in the daily newspapers, the general public was becoming increasingly aware of the need for eliminating many of the wage earners' grievances.

Early social legislation. In an effort to improve the conditions of wage earners, European and American legislators began to pass laws commonly referred to as "social legislation." In the United States these laws mainly were passed by the northern and western states; the South, with its newer industrial development and its special problems, did little during this period to promote the welfare of workers through state laws.

In general, the first state laws limited hours of work and improved working conditions. As early as 1879 a Massachusetts law prohibited women and children from working more than 60 hours a week. Oregon enacted a similar law in 1903, and other states followed suit. Meanwhile, New York state initiated a series of laws protecting workers as well as consumers.

The recognition that certain types of work involved special risk led Utah in 1896 to pass a law limiting the working day of miners to 8 hours. New York in 1910 passed the first important state law to compensate workers for accidents that took place on the job.

In 1912 Massachusetts set a precedent by passing the first "minimum-wage law." The Massachusetts act established a minimum-wage rate—employers could not ask a wage earner to work below this rate. These early laws represented a new approach to the problems of wage earners in the emerging industrial society.

Early Supreme Court objections. Much of the early social legislation was declared unconstitutional by the Supreme Court. The Court argued that such laws deprived owners of the property rights guaranteed them by the Constitution. The Court said that a law limiting a man's control over his business, including his employment policies, actually deprived him of part of his property without the "due process of law" guaranteed in the Fifth and Fourteenth Amendments.

The Supreme Court also objected to social legislation on the ground that it violated an individual's right to enter into any contract he wished. According to the Court, when a worker accepted employment and an employer agreed to pay him, a "contract" had been made even though the terms were not written down. Following this "freedom-of-contract" line of reasoning, the Supreme Court declared unconstitutional in 1905 a New York law which had fixed a maximum working day of 10 hours for New York bakers.

Changing Court attitudes. Many people objected that such an interpretation of the Constitution was unjust to labor. They argued that it was unrealistic to assume that the individual worker could actually bargain with a corporation that employed thousands of men. They insisted that, in reality, the Supreme Court was depriving every worker of any freedom to bargain with his employers.

Supreme Court justices, like many other Americans, gradually changed their attitude toward social legislation. Like other citizens, they were influenced by the progressive temper of the times. The justices found other clauses in the Constitution that enabled states to limit the individual's right to do as he pleased with his property. The Court increasingly held that the Constitution had reserved to each state the power to enact laws necessary to protect the health and well-being of all its citizens. On these grounds the Supreme Court, in the case of *Muller v. Oregon* (1908), upheld an Oregon law that provided a 10-hour day for women, thereby setting a precedent for the Court's approval of other social legislation.

Federal laws in favor of labor. The states rather than the federal government enacted most of the early social legislation. But workers found this situation unsatisfactory since certain states, especially in the South, lagged behind others. This situation prompted organized labor and its champions to seek relief through federal laws.

Except for its constitutional power "to promote the general welfare" and "to regulate interstate commerce," the federal government had little power to control labor relations. To be sure, the

■ During the early 1900's, social legislation was needed to improve the working conditions of wage earners by regulating hours, minimum-wage rates, and the abuses of child labor.

federal government did have the power—and used it—to control working conditions for its own employees. In 1868, as you have seen, Congress established an 8-hour day for laborers and mechanics employed by or in behalf of the United States government. In 1892 all federal government employees were given an 8-hour day.

Later, in 1908, acting under its power "to regulate interstate commerce," Congress enacted an Employers' Liability Act protecting railroad workers from bearing all the costs of accidents that occurred on the job. And in 1916, when the railroad workers' unions, known as the railroad brotherhoods, threatened to strike for an 8-hour day, Congress passed the Adamson Act. This act gave railroad workers the same pay for an 8-hour day that they had been getting for a 10-hour day.

During President Wilson's administration Congress also granted labor's request that it be exempt from the charge of conspiring "to restrain trade." As you have seen, the Clayton Antitrust Act of 1914 helped to modify some of the clauses in the Sherman Antitrust Act of 1890 to which labor had objected.

By the time World War I broke out in Europe in

1914, labor still had many grievances, and it was still far from its goals. But it could look back upon a number of reforms gained through 50 years of struggle. And, perhaps most important, organized labor enjoyed a small but steadily growing measure of support from public opinion.

SECTION SURVEY

IDENTIFY: social legislation, minimum wage, freedom of contract, *Muller v. Oregon,* Employers' Liability Act.

1. Why did the conditions of wage earners begin to improve in the early 1900's?
2. Describe the various kinds of social legislation passed by the states to aid workers.
3. (a) On what grounds did the Supreme Court declare this early social legislation unconstitutional? (b) How do Supreme Court decisions sometimes reflect the times in which they are made?
4. (a) Why was it that for many years the federal government did not enact social legislation? (b) Why did it become necessary for the federal government to become involved in social legislation?

TRACING THE MAIN IDEAS

During the years between 1900 and 1920 the United States completed the process of passing from a predominantly agricultural economy to a predominantly industrial economy. By 1920 the United States had become the most productive industrial nation on earth.

In 1900 Americans were still living in the horse-and-buggy age. It was, however, a dying age. Old ways were rapidly giving way to new. People living during the years between 1900 and 1920 saw the advent of automobiles, airplanes, radio, motion pictures, the assembly line, and many other developments destined to transform older ways of living.

But the rapidly increasing productivity of the nation's economy and the steadily rising standard of living were only the most obvious signs of the new America that was coming into being. Less obvious, but equally significant, were the changes beginning to take place in the thinking of many Americans. More and more people were beginning to modify some of the attitudes and practices that they had carried over from the early days of the Industrial Revolution. More and more people were beginning to realize that organized labor had an important role to play in the new industrial economy. Slowly but surely, Americans were beginning to take the first halting steps toward what Frederick Lewis Allen called "the adjustment of capitalism to democratic ends."

In 1920 the American people still had a long, hard road to travel. But although they had no way of knowing it, the road along which they were beginning to move would bring them by mid-century to the highest standard of living in history.

CHAPTER SURVEY

QUESTIONS FOR DISCUSSION

1. Industrialization strengthened the existing belief that America was the land of opportunity. Comment.
2. In general, whom do you respect more, the person who inherits his money or the person who "makes it" on his own? Explain how your answer relates to your belief about America and opportunity.
3. (a) What is meant by "the American dream"? (b) Do you think this concept originated during the period just studied? Why or why not?
4. Comment on how the automobile affected the American way of life with regard to (a) where people worked, (b) where people lived, (c) individual freedom.
5. (a) Compare American transportation in 1900 and 1920. (Make use of the charts on pages 868–69.) (b) What do these figures tell you about change in the United States during the period 1900–20?
6. In what ways did the revolution in communication help initiate reform movements and the growth of political democracy?
7. Why was it necessary for farmers to receive federal aid during the period just studied?

RELATING PAST TO PRESENT

1. Explain why you agree or disagree with the following statement: In America, if an individual tries hard enough, he is bound to succeed.
2. Are we still making what Frederick Lewis Allen called "the adjustment of capitalism to democratic ends"? Explain.
3. American citizens increasingly look toward the federal government to meet the needs of our modern society. Do you think that the state and local governments could deal more effectively with some of our modern problems? Explain.

USING MAPS AND CHARTS

1. Using the charts on pages 866–67, explain the increase in output per worker in the period 1900–20. What does this figure mean in relationship to a higher standard of living?
2. Consulting chart 1 on page 862, answer the following: (a) How did our farm population change between 1900 and 1920? (b) What accounted for the change?

UNIT SURVEY

FOR FURTHER INQUIRY

1. Thomas Jefferson and Andrew Jackson both believed with Thoreau that "that government is best which governs least." Do you think this viewpoint became less practical by the twentieth century? Explain your answer, referring to events described in this unit.
2. Labor unions came as a direct response to the problems created by industrialization. Comment.
3. During the period in which the United States was transformed by industrialization and urbanization, new situations arose in which black Americans were discriminated against. Name some of these new situations.

PROJECTS AND ACTIVITIES

1. Study paintings and music of the period 1897–1920. How well do the art and music of the period reflect the times?
2. If possible, obtain a Sears Roebuck catalog that dates from the period just studied. What do the ads tell you about American life at that time? What seems particularly old-fashioned? What seems to have remained more or less the same?
3. Examine old newspapers or magazines printed in your town or state during the year 1900. Compare the prices of the food and clothing in the advertisements with current prices. Then consult an almanac to find out what the average family income in the United States was in 1900 and what it is now. Was it easier or more difficult to support a family in 1900?

USING THE SOCIAL SCIENCES

(Read pages 564–70 before you answer the following questions.)

1. Some sociologists say that political participation may be associated with social and economic status. How would you relate this statement to the case study you have just read?
2. How does the author of the case study explain why the "machine" dominated the urban power structure?
3. Political systems and processes are related to the values and goals of the society in which they operate. What were the values and goals of the urban centers that enabled the political "machine" to operate?
4. What is the viewpoint of the author of this case study toward reformers and reform movements?
5. Today, minority groups in American cities are becoming increasingly active politically. How might the author of the case study account for this phenomenon? What other explanations could you offer?

SUGGESTED FURTHER READING

Biography

ADDAMS, JANE, *Twenty Years at Hull House,* New American Library (Signet Books, paper). Autobiography of a leading reformer; history of the first settlement house in the United States.

BARUCH, BERNARD, *Baruch: My Own Story,* Pocket Books (paper). Autobiography of an adviser to Presidents from Wilson to Eisenhower.

BLUM, JOHN MORTON, *The Republican Roosevelt,* Harvard Univ. Press.

BOWEN, CATHERINE DRINKER, *Yankee from Olympus: Justice Holmes and His Family,* Little, Brown; Bantam. Semifictional biography of Oliver Wendell Holmes, Jr.

BUSCH, NOEL F., *TR: The Story of Theodore Roosevelt and His Influence on Our Times,* Reynal.

FAUSOLD, MARTIN L., *Gifford Pinchot: Bull Moose Progressive,* Syracuse Univ. Press.

FRANKLIN, JOHN HOPE, ed. *Three Negro Classics,* Hearst (Avon Books, paper). Includes *Up from Slavery* by Booker T. Washington; *The Souls of Black Folks* by W. E. B. Du Bois, and the *Autobiography of an Ex-Colored Man* by J. W. Johnson.

GARRATY, JOHN A., *Henry Cabot Lodge: A Biography,* Knopf.

GINGER, RAY, *The Bending Cross: A Biography of Eugene V. Debs,* Rutgers Univ. Press.

GRAYSON, CARY, *Woodrow Wilson: An Intimate Memoir,* Holt, Rinehart & Winston.

HARBAUGH, WILLIAM H., *Power and Responsibility: The Life and Times of Theodore Roosevelt,* Farrar, Straus.

HIDY, RALPH, FRANK ERNEST HILL, and ALLAN NEVINS, *Timber and Men: The Weyerhauser Story,* Macmillan.

HOOVER, HERBERT, *The Ordeal of Woodrow Wilson,* McGraw-Hill.

LINK, ARTHUR, *Wilson: Road to the White House,* Princeton Univ. Press.

——, *Wilson: The New Freedom,* Princeton Univ. Press.

——, *Woodrow Wilson and the Progressive Era,* Harper & Row.

LORANT, STEFAN, *The Life and Times of Theodore Roosevelt,* Doubleday.

LOWITT, RICHARD, *George W. Norris: The Making of a Progressive, 1861–1912,* Syracuse Univ. Press.

MC GEARY, M. NELSON, *Gifford Pinchot: Forester-Politician,* Princeton Univ. Press.

MAXWELL, ROBERT S., *La Follette and the Rise of the Progressives in Wisconsin,* Wisconsin State Hist. Soc.

MORGAN, WAYNE, *William McKinley and His America,* Syracuse Univ. Press (paper).

MOWRY, GEORGE E., *Theodore Roosevelt and the Progressive Movement,* Univ. of Wisconsin Press.

PRINGLE, HENRY F., *Theodore Roosevelt: A Biography,* Harcourt Brace Jovanovich (Harvest Books).

STEFFENS, LINCOLN, *Autobiography of Lincoln Steffens,* Grosset & Dunlap; Harcourt Brace Jovanovich (text ed.).

WHITE, WILLIAM A., *The Autobiography of William Allen White,* Macmillan.

Other Nonfiction

BAKER, RAY STANNARD, *Following the Color Line: An Account of Negro Citizenship in the American Democracy,* Torch.

BOWERS, CLAUDE, *Beveridge and the Progressive Era,* Houghton Mifflin.

DUNNE, F. P., *Mr. Dooley at His Best,* Scribner. Satirical humor.

——, *The World of Mr. Dooley,* Crowell Collier and Macmillan (paper).

FAULKNER, HAROLD U., *The Decline of Laissez Faire: 1897–1917,* Holt, Rinehart & Winston.

——, *The Quest for Social Justice: 1898–1914,* Macmillan.

FILLER, LOUIS, *Crusaders for American Liberalism,* Antioch Press.

FRANKLIN, JOHN HOPE, *From Slavery to Freedom,* Random House (Vintage Books, paper). A survey of black Americans' efforts to advance during the period just studied; discusses the ideological debate between Booker T. Washington and W. E. B. Du Bois.

GOLDMAN, ERIC, *Rendezvous with Destiny: A History of Modern American Reform,* Random House (Vintage Books).

HOFSTADTER, RICHARD, *The Age of Reform: From Bryan to F. D. R.,* Knopf (text ed.).

JOSEPHSON, MATTHEW, *The President Makers,* Harcourt Brace Jovanovich.

LORD, WALTER, *The Good Years,* Bantam (paper). Various events reflecting the spirit of the times in 1900–1914.

MANN, ARTHUR, *Yankee Reformers in the Urban Age,* Harvard Univ. Press.

REGIER, C. C., *The Era of Muckrakers,* Peter Smith.

RIIS, JACOB A., *How the Other Half Lives,* Hill & Wang (American Century Series, paper). Written in 1890, this indictment of slum life has become a classic document of social reform.

STEFFENS, LINCOLN, *Shame of the Cities,* Hill & Wang (American Century Series, paper). Originally published in 1904, this book by a leading muckraker tells how American cities were being corrupted during this period.

WEINBERG, ARTHUR, and LILA WEINBERG, eds. *The Muckrakers,* Putnam (Capricorn Books, paper). A collection of articles by writers who shocked the nation into an era of reform.

YOUNG, JAMES H., *The Toadstool Millionaires: A Social History of Patent Medicines in America Before Federal Regulation,* Princeton Univ. Press.

Historical Fiction

DAVIS, CLYDE B., *The Great American Novel,* Farrar, Straus. Covers events of the Progressive Era.

DOS PASSOS, JOHN, *42nd Parallel.* Houghton Mifflin. America around 1900.

FAIRBANK, JANET A., *The Lion's Den,* Bobbs-Merrill. A Progressive Wisconsin farmer in Congress.

——, *Rich Man, Poor Man,* Houghton Mifflin. About the Progressive era.

NORRIS, FRANK, *The Octopus,* Bantam (paper). One of the earliest novels of social protest (1901), it dramatizes struggles of California farmers against the abuses of the railroads.

SINCLAIR, UPTON, *The Jungle,* Harper & Row. Novel about Chicago's meat-packing industry and the life of factory workers.

STONE, IRVING, *Adversary in the House,* Doubleday. Fictionalized life of Eugene V. Debs.

TRAIN, ARTHUR, *Yankee Lawyer,* Scribner.

HISTORY AND THE SOCIAL SCIENCES

POLITICAL SCIENCE

Nature of Political Science

Political scientists have traditionally studied government. In recent years, however, they have enlarged their area of interest to study also the exercise of power. Political science today, then, is the study of government and of the exercise of power in society.

Political scientists study government and the institutions of government. They try to understand how various systems of government work. In studying the government of the United States, for example, political scientists analyze how the American government is organized. They examine the role of American institutions of government, such as the Senate and the House of Representatives. They study, for example, the ways in which the Senate carries out its responsibilities. In the area of international politics, political scientists study and compare various systems of government in different countries of the world. They might compare, for example, the role of elections in a democratic country such as the United States to the role of elections in a totalitarian country such as the Soviet Union.

But political scientists are interested not only in the structure of government; they also are interested in the process of government. That is, they study the question of who exercises political power and how it is exercised in various governmental systems. In other words, political scientists are trying to analyze the nature of the entire political process, or the nature of *politics*

Harold Lasswell, a very influential political scientist, wrote a book entitled *Politics: Who Gets What, When and How?* Lasswell's title provides a good working definition of politics. The study of politics, as well as the study of government, is at the heart of political science. To understand American politics, for example, political scientists have found it necessary to look for answers to many questions: What are the roles of the Democratic and Republican parties in American politics? What are the differences between the two parties? Do certain groups of Americans tend to vote in certain ways? What affects group voting patterns? What are the effects of special interest groups—such as the labor unions, veterans' groups, business lobbys—on American political life? In seeking the answers to these questions, political scientists are trying to analyze the crucial issue of how political decisions are made.

Political scientists want their studies of American politics to be useful to both students and leaders of government. Thus, they try to find sound, working generalizations, or patterns, that accurately describe how our political system works. In studying voting patterns, they try to form generalizations that describe and predict the voting behavior of various groups. They try, for example, to find a pattern that describes how people living in wealthy suburbs tend to vote in Presidential elections. How does this compare with the voting habits of white collar workers living in the cities?

In searching for generalizations, political scientists are trying to find a general theory of political behavior. That is, they are trying to act scientifically, and in this sense, political science is a *science*. The new political *science* explores questions about politics and tries to find regular patterns or "laws" that describe or explain the political process.

However, not all political scientists look at the nature of their work in the same way. Some emphasize the scientific aspect more, some less. In general, political scientists go about their tasks in one of two ways.

President Nixon addressing Congress

Some political scientists look on political science as a behavioral science. This means that they place greater emphasis on studying the behavior of individuals than on studying political institutions. To carry out their studies, they use empirical, or observable, data and then analyze their data statistically. In general, they study politics to gain a deeper insight into why men behave the way they do.

Other political scientists study political institutions and political leadership by analyzing available data, including past experience as well as empirical data. They use logic, intuition, and common sense in reaching their conclusions. Political scientists of this group point out that human behavior is very complex. People sometimes act irrationally or emotionally, saying one thing but doing another. These political scientists argue that, human nature being what it is, it is extremely difficult to make many broad generalizations in political science. They argue that, unlike a natural scientist working in his laboratory, a political scientist cannot conduct controlled experiments in his study. These political scientists also argue that, in studying politics, no person can be completely objective and detached. In the social sciences, they say, some problems have no permanent solutions.

Political science provides many important insights into political behavior and government in the United States. It helps historians to understand American voting behavior, the way power is shared in American society, how political decision-making takes place in our government, the way our political parties function, and the importance of political leadership in America.

Concepts of Political Science

A concept in political science is a fundamental idea that helps to explain how people behave politically. Consider, for instance, the concept of **political behavior.** In political science, this concept centers on the behavior of important groups or power blocs. In the United States—and in every nation—certain large groups of people share common interests and values. Such groups often develop certain ways of behaving to protect their interests and values. For example, in American society and in many societies, workers, particularly industrial workers, form a loosely united class. Their common interests include higher wages and shorter working hours. If their wages or their work rules are not satisfactory, they tend to react in a given way, usually by strikes or demonstrations. Political scientists have also discovered that workers tend to have a special way of acting in the area of politics. They tend to have similar attitudes toward their union leaders, as well as toward the political leaders of their country.

Political scientists also examine the concept of **political ideology.** Political ideology refers to a common set of beliefs and values that influence how political decisions are made in a society. The dominant, or most important, groups in a society generally have a certain ideology, or set of beliefs. These beliefs affect how political decisions are made in their society and how power is distributed. In the Soviet Union, for example, the leaders and members of the Communist Party are the dominant group. Their beliefs and values have a decisive influence on who wields the power in the Soviet Union and on how political decisions are made. In the United States, the dominant groups are somewhat harder to identify. American leaders tend to have a wider range of beliefs, rather than one set ideology. Yet American leaders do tend to share certain common, basic values, such as freedom of speech, the worth of an individual, and acceptance of the rule of the majority. These common beliefs influence decision-making and political behavior in the United States.

Why do political scientists study voting patterns?

Political scientists studying the concept of political ideology try to identify the dominant groups in various societies and try to determine their beliefs and values. They try to see how these beliefs affect political decision-making.

Political scientists also devote much of their time to the study of the concept of **leadership.** In studying leadership, political scientists must take into account many subjective factors, or elements of human nature, which affect what leaders do and how they behave. President Taft, for example, believed that the President's role must be an extremely limited one. President Franklin Roosevelt, on the other hand, believed that the President's role was to use the vast powers of his office to the utmost. The subjective beliefs of these men greatly influenced the kind of leadership they gave to the country. Knowing about the beliefs and personality traits of American Presidents would obviously be of great value in examining the records of their administrations.

Political scientists also study the concept of **power structure.** This concept refers to the group of political, industrial, and social leaders in a nation who generally shape the important decisions in that nation. In spite of certain differences, these leaders share basic beliefs and values, and they help to make most of the important decisions affecting the nation. In the United States the power structure is sometimes popularly referred to as "the Establishment." The study of the power structure in American states and cities can help us understand more clearly who wields the power in the United States and who makes the decisions. However, studies made by political scientists have shown the complexity of the American power structure. Some studies suggest that the United States is ruled by a small, tightly knit group, or a power elite. Others suggest that power in American society is diffuse and balanced among many different groups. Whatever the answer, the concept of the power structure is useful in increasing our understanding of important aspects of political behavior.

Many political scientists are interested in the concept of **political socialization;** that is, the methods a society uses to transmit its political values to its children. Political scientists working in this area have found that American society—in the home and in the classroom—takes a variety of steps to pass along certain political values from one generation to the next. The findings suggest, for example, that the first political image that an American child recognizes is the figure of the President. Next children recognize Congress and voting. These studies, which are still going on, should give us a better understanding of the values and attitudes of American citizenship.

Methods of Political Science

Some political scientists emphasize the scientific aspect of political science, some give it less emphasis. Nevertheless, all political scientists, to a greater or lesser degree, are committed to a scientific method of investigation in collecting their data or information. That is, they study and observe their subject objectively, and they carefully classify and measure the data and information they collect. Of course some political scientists still use intuition, logic, and common sense to make their conclusions and even to predict political behavior. But most political scientists today search for laws, or patterns, of political behavior by using a modern scientific method. What does this mean?

Take, for example, the political scientists who study political socialization of children—that is, the ways in which a society transmits political attitudes to its children. What methods do they use to make their investigation? To collect their data, these political scientists rely on **field work** and the use of **observa-**

The Presidential seal

tions, questionnaires, and **interviews.** They go to schools and homes and observe how parents and teachers pass along certain political attitudes to children. They prepare questionnaires and conduct interviews with children, parents, and teachers. Then they collect all their data and analyze it statistically, often using computers. Finally, they form tentative conclusions. This type of study is, of course, clearly based on scientific method.

The same would be true for a study of the voting patterns of American voters. Suppose a political scientist wants to study the voting patterns of the people living in the 4th ward of St. Louis. How would he proceed? He would go to St. Louis and assemble the voting records in that ward for a number of years. He would interview and question a representative cross-section of the voters who presently live in the area. Finally he would analyze his data statistically and form his conclusions.

Generally speaking, most political scientists today rely more on field work than on scholarly research and reading in libraries. That is, they become first-hand observers of the workings of a local, state, or federal government. Instead of studying the past behavior of governments and of political leaders, they concentrate more on the present political scene. Suppose a political scientist wants to study how decisions are made at Presidential nominating conventions. He would go to the parties' conventions and carefully observe the proceedings first hand. He would interview party leaders and convention delegates. He would examine the roll call records.

Sometimes, the nature of his study will require a political scientist to rely on both field work and library research. Suppose that he wants to study the political views of military leaders. His field work would involve interviews with generals and admirals. He would question them about their educational and social backgrounds, their reading habits, their voting preferences. He would also interview and question members of their staffs and families. Finally, he would go to the library and carefully read their speeches, articles, books, and statements. Only then would he analyze his data and formulate his conclusions.

Political scientists also make use of **comparative studies.** Using this method of investigation, political scientists can compare, for example, similar governmental institutions, such as the two major American political parties. In what ways are the aims of the Democratic and Republican parties similar? In what ways are they different? Or a political scientist might compare the political institutions of two different countries. A comparative study of the British Parliament and the United States Congress is an especially interesting one because the two institutions share similar origins, purposes, and characteristics. Similarly, a comparative study of the Congress of the United States and the Supreme Soviet in the Soviet Union would reveal the many differences between two institutions supposed to serve the same political purposes.

Political scientists search for "laws" or patterns that govern some aspect of a nation's political life. But they are also vitally interested in finding the reasons that lie behind these patterns. In other words, political scientists not only want to answer the question "how," they also want to answer the question "why." In studying the voting patterns of people who have recently moved to a suburb, for example, political scientists want to find out why these people tend to vote Republican, even if they previously voted Democratic. In studying differences in political leadership, political scientists want to find out not only *how* various government leaders act but *why* they act the way they do. In so doing, political scientists hope to formulate accurate generalizations that describe and illuminate political behavior.

CASE STUDY IN POLITICAL SCIENCE

The Big City Political "Machine"

American cities have had a long tradition of "machine" politics involving both major political parties. In the Republican and Democratic parties alike, municipal politics has centered around the competing ambitions of the leaders, or "bosses," of the local party organizations, or "machines." Most big city governments in the United States, including those of Chicago, Boston, Philadelphia, Baltimore, Memphis, and New York, have at one time or another been dominated by political party "bosses" and their "machines." How can this phenomenon be explained?

On the positive side, it can be said that at the height of their power, in the late 1800's and early 1900's, the political "machines" fulfilled a real social need. They provided jobs and housing and food to needy city dwellers at a time when few American institutions—public or private—had been set up to meet the needs of the poor. But at the same time, on the negative side, the "machine" politicians did many things that we would today condemn as wrong and corrupt. They frequently stole public funds and permitted illegal activities such as gambling. They granted large and lucrative city contracts to businessmen in exchange for bribes and kickbacks. They gave government jobs to people who helped them win elections rather than to people who were qualified.

It is easy to condemn these corrupt practices, but that does not really increase our understanding of "machine" politics. Why was the political "machine" able to dominate urban politics? How did the "machine" manage to hold itself together as a political organization? Why did so many people vote for "machine" politicians? Why did the "machine" eventually lose most of its power? These are some of the questions we shall investigate as we study the rise and fall of the political "machine" as the dominant influence in the power structure of American cities in the late 1800's and early 1900's.

Why the "Machine" Dominated the Urban Power Structure

From the earliest days of settlement there was no well-defined power structure in America, as there was in Europe. In Europe the wealthy, titled aristocracy formed the established power structure. They were the ruling class who undertook the responsibility for ruling all of society. The United States had no such ruling class. By the late 1800's the United States was a rapidly growing country in which many people were making a lot of money. But unlike their European counterparts, these wealthy Americans had no long tradition of taking on the responsibilities of government.

Since the ideology of newly rich Americans did not emphasize public service, political leadership in America's growing cities was open to anyone who wanted to enter politics. In practice, this meant that men often entered city politics in the same way that Americans entered any business enterprise—to make a profit and to get rich. If more money could be made in politics than in selling shoes, then politics was the business to enter. Thus, the urban political "machine"—organized to make as large a profit out of politics as possible—was born.

How the "Machine" Held Itself Together

The political "machine" was an efficient business organization that attracted members and won their loyalty by relying primarily on the methods used by all businesses—material incentives. Individuals who worked for the "machine" were either paid cash for their work, given positions in the gov-

The political "machine" was frequently condemned for its injustices and corruption.

ernment, or favored with some other special privilege such as quiet permission to carry on an illegal practice.

Another popular method used by the "machine" was to avoid taking a stand on important and emotional issues. By the 1890's, when one of the most durable of political "machines," New York's Tammany Hall, was at the height of its power, Tammany's top political leader avoided a question concerning free silver, the most controversial issue of the day, by declaring, "I'm in favor of all kinds of money—the more the better." By remaining neutral on the issues, the "machine" avoided losing votes and at the same time focused the party worker's attention on material incentives.

The organization which often opposed political "machines" in many cities was the reform movement. As the word "movement" suggests, reformers were not as well organized as the "machines." Even more important, their basis for organizing was entirely different. Reformers relied on the support and zeal of those citizens who were so upset about the corruption in city government that they would work hard during political campaigns without pay. Rather than giving material rewards to their supporters, the reformers hoped that the psychic, or inner, satisfaction that individuals received from supporting crusading causes would be enough to encourage their active work. Consequently, reformers needed issues that aroused moral fervor. If they were to win an election, they had to have a cause that so aroused the enthusiastic support of many Americans that they would work hard to "throw the rascals" out of office.

Unfortunately the reformers' emphasis on crusading zeal sometimes was less successful than the "machine's" ways of sustaining its organization. It was easier to gain voters' support by paying them than by relying on their enthusiasm and good will. As George Washington Plunkitt, one of New York's Tammany Hall politicians, observed, the reformers were only "mornin' glories." They "looked lovely in the mornin' and withered up in a short time, while the regular machines went on flourishin' forever, like fine old oaks."

Who Supported "Machine" Candidates

Even though the "machine" politicians were guilty of much graft and corruption, they still did not have enough money and jobs to buy the vote of every citizen. How then did the "machine" get enough votes to win elections? Why did people who received no lucrative contracts or soft city jobs vote for "machine" candidates?

By and large the "machine" received the support of the immigrants who flooded into American cities during the late 1800's and early 1900's. The Irish, the first of many immigrants to arrive, rapidly secured leadership positions in the "machine." They in turn wooed the support of succeeding immigrant groups, such as Italians, Germans, Poles, Russians, Lithuanians, and Negroes migrating North from the rural South.

The immigrants supported the "machine" because it was one of the few urban institutions which gave them help in time of need. Plunkitt best explained the popularity of the "machine" among the poor as follows: "If a family is burned out I don't ask whether they are Republicans or Democrats, and I don't refer them to the Charity Organization Society, which would investigate their case in a month or two and decide they were worthy of help about the time they are dead from starvation. I just get quarters for them, buy clothes for them if their clothes were burned up, and fix them up till they get things runnin' again. . . . The consequences is that the poor look up to George W. Plunkitt as a father, come to him in trouble and don't forget him on election day."

In addition to meeting the emergency needs of the immigrant community, the "machine" attracted the support of the ethnic groups by running a "balanced ticket" for the various city offices. For example, in New York City the Tammany candidate for mayor often was Irish, while the candidates for the other two important city offices usually included an Italian and a Jew. In this way the ticket was "balanced" so that each of the major ethnic and religious groups was represented in the top positions of city government. The immigrant groups were delighted to vote for the "machine" candidates and thus register publicly their belief and pride that a member of their ethnic group was just as good as any other man in the community.

Why the "Machine" Declined in Power

Even today one should not underestimate the strength of the "machine" in the power structure of many American cities. Yet it is true that the "machine" is not as strong today as it was 50 years ago. Ever since the 1920's immigration to the United States has been restricted, and there simply are not as many new people who need the help of the "machine" in adjusting to life in a strange country. The children and grandchildren of the immigrants know of the "old country" only through stories, and they are not so likely to vote for a man simply because he is a member of their ethnic group.

As people earn more money, most people find that a few dollars is not enough to buy their vote. As more and more people obtain high school and college educations, they no longer need to depend on the local precinct workers as their main source for learning about political candidates. Radio and television provide means through which candidates can appeal to the people directly rather than through an elaborate political organization.

As city services and welfare programs improve, the individual in need can find other sources of help besides the precinct captain. Finally, the reformers' own innovations, implemented in their "mornin's" of triumph, weakened "machine" politics. The reformers set up a civil service system which eliminated patronage. They appointed professionals as leaders of the police, fire, welfare, and other city departments so that politicians could no longer influence the operations of these departments. In many cities local elections were made nonpartisan so that the party organizations would find it more difficult to influence voters.

Some of these changes have been for the better, but they have also created new problems. If the people are dependent on radio and television for information, how can they distinguish a good leader from a clever salesman? If the politicians no longer control professionals in city departments, what is to prevent the professionals from creating small bureaucratic kingdoms which neither the politician nor the citizen can hope to influence? If political parties are taken out of politics, on what basis can the voter determine the differences between the candidates? Eliminating patronage and corruption from the power structure of urban politics is certainly a good idea, but it does not solve the political problems of the cities. Sometimes, in fact, it may create new ones.

What functions did the "machine" fulfill?

■ How did political "machines" exercise leadership in large American cities? Explain.

■ Cite evidence from this case study that helps explain the rise of political "machines" and their later decline.

THOMAS JEFFERSON
1743–1826

ABRAHAM LINCOLN
1809–1865

THEODORE ROOSEVELT
1858–1919

AMERICANS TODAY

PART **4**

The Nation as a World Leader

How thirteen colonies on the fringe of a vast, untamed wilderness eventually became a nation holding a position of world leadership—such is the dramatic story of the United States. This story has unfolded in less than 200 years.

One way to visualize the swift rise of the American nation is to think of Jefferson, Lincoln, and Theodore Roosevelt. Each of these men lived through a distinct period in the rapidly developing life of the nation.

Theodore Roosevelt, the last of the three, was born before the Civil War. He lived to see the reunited country grow from 36 to 48 states; acquire Alaska, Hawaii, Puerto Rico, and other far-flung territories; fight in World War I; and develop into the leading industrial power of the world.

Part 4 of Rise of the American Nation begins with the Spanish-American War of 1898 and brings us to the present. This period of the nation's history is marked by the impressive developments that have carried the United States to a position of leadership in the world.

Millions of Americans living today hold vivid memories of the "Golden Twenties"; the Great Depression of the 1930's; the excitement, tragedy, and overwhelming sorrow of World War II; and the years since 1945, years filled with trouble and yet not without promise for the future.

In Part 4 of Rise of the American Nation we, the living, are writing our own history and adding still another chapter to the dramatic story of the nation that now carries the burden and the opportunity of world leadership.

UNIT NINE

Becoming a World Power

1898–1920

From 1823 until the 1890's, Americans devoted most of their energy to the settlement and development of the continental United States. To be sure, Americans traveled to Europe and Europeans traveled to America. The two-way flow of people and ideas across the Atlantic never ceased. And always, of course, there was vigorous trade between the two continents. But it was the conquest of the untamed West and, after 1865, the development of industry that engaged the major energy of the American people.

By the 1890's, however, a revolution was taking place in American opinion. With the American West becoming a major industrial area, an increasing number of Americans became interested in securing overseas markets where they could sell the surplus products of farm and factory. Some Americans even became interested in acquiring or controlling lands beyond their continental boundaries.

In this chapter you will see how Americans acquired a new interest in world affairs. You will see how they emerged from the Spanish-American War of 1898 in possession of the Philippine Islands and other islands in the Pacific Ocean. You will see how this growing Pacific empire created new problems for the United States, and how it forced America's leaders to develop new policies for dealing with the nations of the Far East.

THE CHAPTER IN OUTLINE

1. Reasons behind the nation's growing interest in overseas expansion.

2. Deepening American involvement overseas after the war with Spain.

3. Establishing American control over the Philippines, Hawaii, and Samoa.

4. The increasing influence of the United States in the Far East.

■ *The charge up San Juan Hill, 1898*

CHAPTER **30**

American Expansion Overseas

1898 – 1914

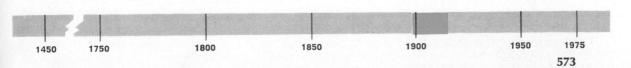

1 Reasons behind the nation's growing interest in overseas expansion

Great Britain, France, the Netherlands, Spain, Portugal—these were the old colonial powers. They had started their policies of *imperialism*—of establishing colonies and building empires—back in the 1500's and 1600's. Now, in the mid-1800's, they owned and controlled a large portion of the world. But huge areas of the earth still remained unclaimed by any colonial nation.

The race for empire. During the latter half of the 1800's, there was a mad rush to gain ownership or control of the remainder of the underdeveloped areas of the earth. Nations previously little interested in expansion joined the race—among them Belgium, Germany, Italy, Japan, and Russia. Within a few years the rival colonial powers seized control over almost all of Africa and sliced off large portions of China and other areas in the Far East. By the early 1900's nearly all of the underdeveloped regions of the world had been divided among the rival colonial empires.

Reasons for the New Imperialism. The Industrial Revolution was to a great extent responsible for the mounting interest in colonies. Factories needed raw materials in ever-growing quantities. Manufacturers, to keep their factories operating, had to find new markets for their finished products. Improvements in transportation, especially in the steamship, enabled businessmen to buy and sell in a truly worldwide market. And as trade increased and profits accumulated, businessmen and bankers began to look overseas for opportunities to invest savings. More than any other single factor, the growth of industry speeded up the race to secure colonies and to control underdeveloped lands.

It is not surprising that Great Britain, the world's leading industrial power before 1900, built the largest empire. Right behind Britain were France, Belgium, and the Netherlands. Industrialization in each of these countries was in full swing by the late 1800's.

Nor is it surprising that the countries that were late in achieving national unity or in industrializing were also late in entering the race for empire. Germany, Italy, and Japan were among these countries. As a result, when they began to look around for colonial possessions, they found most of the world divided up, and they became jealous rivals for the territory that remained.

There were still other reasons for the growth of worldwide imperialism in the late 1800's and the early 1900's. One was the invention of new instruments of warfare, notably repeating rifles and machine guns. By 1900 these new weapons were becoming standard army equipment, enabling small bands of professional soldiers to conquer and control people in underdeveloped regions who did not have similar weapons.

Public support for imperialism. Another reason for the growth of imperialism was the attitude of people in the colonial powers. No government could have built an empire without public support. There were objectors in every country, but, in general, men-in-the-street were as eager for empire as statesmen or businessmen. English factory workers, French shopkeepers, German farmers—these and other solid citizens of the colonial powers were all proud of their country's empires. Supported by their own citizens, the governments of the colonial nations were able to spend the huge sums of money needed for armies to occupy the colonial territories and for navies to guard the ever-lengthening sea lanes to and from the colonies.

End of the American frontier. Americans, with a few exceptions, had never been interested in acquiring colonies. Indeed, Americans had cast off their own colonial status in the American Revolution. Thus American sympathies were with colonial peoples, not with the colonizing powers.

America's lack of interest in acquiring colonies is, of course, easy to understand. For 300 years the undeveloped American West was, in a sense, an American "colony." Even as late as 1867, when Secretary of State Seward bought Alaska from Russia for more than $7 million, Americans referred to Alaska as "Seward's folly" and "Seward's icebox." It was not until 30 years later, in 1897, when gold was discovered in Alaska, that Americans began to realize what a great bargain they had made. But in 1867 when Alaska was purchased, it was not unreasonable for people to ask, "What does the United States want with more land?"

In 1890, however, the Census Office announced that a frontier line separating settled areas from wilderness could no longer be drawn between the Canadian and Mexican boundaries. There was still, to be sure, plenty of good land waiting to be settled. But the best land was becoming more expensive, and an important phase of American development was ending.

The expanding American business economy. During the late 1800's the United States became the world's leading exporter of agricultural prod-

■ During the Alaskan gold rush, thousands of men landed at Juneau, Alaska, and headed inland through the treacherous, snow-covered Chilkoot Pass (shown above), gateway to the gold fields.

ucts. By 1890, however, it was beginning to feel the competition of such agricultural nations as Canada and Argentina. American growers and processors of grain, livestock, and cotton, as well as the manufacturers of agricultural machinery, were eager to sell their products abroad. It was not surprising, therefore, that America's agricultural interests in general supported vigorous government efforts to open up new markets overseas.

Moreover, by 1890 the United States was rapidly becoming one of the world's leading industrial nations. American manufacturers, like manufacturers in Europe, needed a continuous flow of raw materials. They also needed markets for the products of their factories.

There was, to be sure, a big difference between American and European businessmen. Europeans, lacking sufficient raw materials and markets at home, were under considerable pressure to get firm control of new sources of raw materials and new markets. American businessmen, operating in a young and only partly developed country, were not under the same pressure. The country as a whole, and especially the great American West, still offered large supplies of raw materials and almost limitless opportunities for the sale of manufactured goods and investment of surplus money.

But some American businessmen realized that the existing situation would not last forever. For this reason, by 1890 a growing number of American businessmen as well as the nation's agricultural interests were pleased to have the United States pursue an active race for overseas economic opportunities, if not for actual colonies.

American expansionists. Until 1898, at least, American interest in colonies was stimulated not so much by businessmen as by preachers, scholars, politicians, and military leaders.

One influential advocate of American expansion was Josiah Strong, a Congregational minister and social reformer. His widely read book *Our Country,* written in 1885, argued that the American branch of the efficient and freedom-loving "Anglo-Saxon race" was destined to extend its civilizing influence in Latin America, Asia, and Africa.

An even more influential book was written by Captain Alfred Mahan in 1890 under the title *The Influence of Sea Power upon History, 1660–1783.* Mahan's book attempted to show that the world's greatest nations had risen largely because of their sea power, and that greatness depended upon sea power. Therefore, he argued, the United States must strengthen its navy and must also secure colonies overseas. Mahan claimed that colonies were needed as naval bases and as refueling stations, or "coaling stations." He also pointed out that colonies would provide raw materials and markets. Colonies would thereby strengthen the

575

industrial organization on which a modern sea power is forced to rely.

Strengthening the navy. Even before Captain Mahan's book appeared, Congress had taken steps to strengthen the navy. These steps were needed. In 1880, for example, the United States had fewer than 100 "seagoing vessels"—and many were "seagoing" in name only, with rusty boilers and planking rotted beyond repair.

Starting in 1882, however, the situation began to change when Congress authorized the construction of "two steam-cruising vessels of war." Three years later the Navy Department created the Naval War College at Newport, Rhode Island. About this time the Bethlehem Steel Corporation began to build a plant for the manufacture of "armor plate" —tough steel sheets to protect the hulls and superstructures of warships. By 1895 the "White Squadron," sometimes called the "Great White Fleet," was under construction.

Ready for a new role. In 1895 the United States had not yet really entered the race for empire. But the ground had been prepared. For various reasons, Americans were becoming increasingly interested in colonies. Some businessmen were becoming uneasy at the prospect that their European competitors might gain control of the markets of underdeveloped areas. The nation's industrial system was rapidly becoming one of the most productive in the world. And a new navy, small but modern and efficient, was ready for action. For these reasons and others, more and more Americans came to believe that the United States was destined to play a leading role in world affairs.

SECTION SURVEY

IDENTIFY: imperialism, colonial empire; Alfred Mahan, Josiah Strong.

1. The Industrial Revolution was responsible for the mounting interest in acquiring colonies by nations which had become industrialized. Explain.
2. How did the transportation and communication revolutions encourage the quest for colonies?
3. Why was the United States not interested in acquiring colonies before the late 1800's?
4. Show how each of the following affected American interest in colonies: (a) closing of the frontier, (b) industrial development, (c) growing power in world affairs.
5. Why were the industrial nations able to maintain control over the nonindustrialized areas of the world?

2 Deepening American involvement overseas after the war with Spain

The Spanish-American War of 1898 marked a turning point in American history. Before the war, which lasted only a few weeks in the spring and summer of 1898, the Midway Islands—occupied in 1867 in the name of the United States—and Alaska were the only lands that the United States owned beyond its immediate boundaries. Within a few years after the war ended, the American flag was flying over a number of islands in the Pacific Ocean, the United States was deeply involved in the Far East, and American influence was being strongly exerted in the lands bordering the Caribbean Sea.

Trouble in Cuba. Cuba and Puerto Rico, both in the Caribbean, were the last remnants of Spain's once mighty empire in the New World. Spaniards had once called Cuba "the Ever Faithful Isle." In 1868, however, when a violent revolution broke out, the Cubans proved to be something less than faithful to their Spanish rulers. It took Spain 10 years to crush this uprising, and even then Spain did so only with a promise to provide long-awaited reforms. But discontent continued to smolder.

The trouble was that most Cubans worked at starvation wages for extremely wealthy landowners. To make matters worse, the Spanish government in Madrid exploited the Cubans, antagonizing landowners as well as landless workers.

Spanish misrule plus an economic crisis finally plunged Cuba into another revolution. The United States was partly responsible for the economic crisis. In 1890, as you have seen, Congress adopted the McKinley Tariff Act. This act allowed Cuban sugar, the major crop of the island, to enter the United States free of duty. As a result, trade between the United States and Cuba prospered, reaching a total of more than $100 million a year. However, in 1894 the United States adopted the Wilson-Gorman Tariff Act, which placed a 40 percent duty on all raw sugar imported into the United States. When the 1894 tariff went into effect, sugar piled up in Cuban warehouses, plantations closed down, and thousands of Cubans lost their jobs.

Revolution in Cuba. Driven to desperation by the economic crisis and angry at Spain's failure to provide the long-promised reforms, the Cubans rose in revolution in 1895, one year after the Wilson-Gorman tariff went into effect. Bands of revolutionists roamed the countryside, killing, burning, and plundering.

The Spaniards, led by General Valeriano Weyler, nicknamed "The Butcher," retaliated with a policy of savage repression. General Weyler ordered all people living in territory controlled by the revolutionists into concentration camps, or prison camps, run by the Spaniards. Spanish soldiers then marched through the abandoned countryside, destroying buildings and putting to death all persons found in the area without permission. What the revolutionists had not destroyed, the Spaniards did. Large areas of Cuba were reduced to utter ruin. Starvation and disease plagued the land.

The revolution's effects on America. In a strictly legal sense, the revolution in Cuba was no concern of the United States. Spain was a sovereign, independent nation, free to do as it pleased with its own colonies. This was freely admitted by the American government, which officially adopted a policy of neutrality.

But the effects of the revolution could not be confined to Cuba. The revolutionists themselves did everything possible to win American sympathy and support. Despite Spanish protests, the revolutionists waged a vigorous propaganda campaign in America. They also bought American arms and ammunition which they smuggled into Cuba.

The revolution also affected some American pocketbooks. Before the uprising began, Americans had invested more than $50 million in Cuban plantations, transportation projects, and business establishments. Moreover, trade between Cuba and the United States was crippled by the revolution.

As months passed, more and more Americans expressed their sympathy for the revolutionists. They recalled their own efforts to win independence from the British during the American Revolution.

Sensation and sympathy in the press. American newspapers helped to inflame public opinion. Two New York papers—William Randolph Hearst's New York *Journal* and Joseph Pulitzer's New York *World*—were especially active in supporting the revolutionists. The owners of these papers discovered that sales skyrocketed when they published sensational stories and pictures of Spanish atrocities in Cuba.

Newspapers in other towns and cities quickly copied the financially successful methods of Hearst and Pulitzer. Before long, many Americans, feeding on the sensational stories and pictures, began to clamor for United States intervention in Cuba.

By 1898 even the more conservative newspapers, including weekly religious journals, insisted that the United States had a moral responsibility to restore order in Cuba.

McKinley's attempts to avoid war. When President William McKinley was inaugurated on March 4, 1897, he was strongly opposed to war. The United States was just emerging from the depression that had started in 1893, and the President, many of his advisers, and businessmen in general were fearful that war, or even the threat of war, would throw the country back into a depression.

For nearly a year the President managed to maintain the official policy of neutrality. But early in 1898 several events forced his hand.

On February 9, 1898, American newspapers headlined a letter written by the Spanish minister to the United States. In the letter, Señor De Lôme (LOH·may) characterized President McKinley as "weak and a bidder for the admiration of the crowd," and as a "would-be politician." The Spanish minister had written the letter to a friend in Havana. It was not intended for publication. Indeed, it had been stolen from the mails and sold to the press. But the harm was done. Unthinking Americans concluded that the uncomplimentary remark reflected the attitude of all Spaniards.

A few days later, on February 16, Americans read even more startling news in their papers. The night before, the United States battleship *Maine,* which had been sent to Cuba in January to protect American lives and property, had gone down in Havana harbor with the loss of more than 250 American lives. Captain Charles D. Sigsbee, commander of the *Maine,* stated that the disaster followed an explosion of unknown origin and urged that "public opinion should be suspended until further report." In Havana flags were flown at half-mast, theaters and places of business were closed, and expressions of sorrow and sympathy were forwarded to Washington. All of this was brushed aside by the public. People jumped to the conclusion that the Spaniards had destroyed the ship. "Remember the *Maine!*" became a national slogan.

Despite these incidents, President McKinley refused to declare war. Assistant Secretary of the Navy Theodore Roosevelt declared that the President "has no more backbone than a chocolate eclair." But McKinley still hoped for a peaceable solution.

SPANISH-AMERICAN WAR: 1
(PHILIPPINE ISLANDS)

CAPTURED
AUG. 13, 1898

BATAAN

MANILA
BAY

Manila

CORREGIDOR I.

SPANISH
FLEET

DEWEY'S FLEET

0   10
Miles

CHINA SEA

LUZON

Manila

DEWEY
from Hong Kong

SOUTH

MINDORO

P H I L I P P I N E

PACIFIC

SAMAR

PANAY

LEYTE

CEBU

NEGROS

BOHOL

PALAWAN

I S L A N D S

O C E A N

MINDANAO

BORNEO

0   200
Scale of miles

Spanish concessions. Late in March, with the President's approval, the Department of State sent an *ultimatum* ° to Spain. In the ultimatum the United States demanded (1) that Spain immediately cease all fighting in Cuba and grant an armistice to the revolutionists, and (2) that the Spanish forces in Cuba immediately abolish the concentration camps.

On April 9 the Spanish government accepted the ultimatum. The Spaniards, however, hedged on the question of Cuban independence, which in the American view could alone bring peace to the island. But the American minister in Madrid felt that, with patience, independence for Cuba could be achieved. In cabling the good news to President McKinley, he added, "I hope that nothing will now be done to humiliate Spain. . . ."

War declared. Despite the Spanish concession, on April 11, 1898, President McKinley asked

---

° *ultimatum:* in diplomatic language, a final statement of terms whose rejection may lead to the breaking off of diplomatic relations or to war.

Congress to intervene in Cuba. What was his reason for doing so?

The most likely explanation seems to be that the war spirit had proved too strong for the President to resist.

On April 19, after a week of debate, Congress by large majorities voted to use the land and naval forces of the United States to secure the full independence of Cuba. But Congress also adopted the Teller Resolution. This resolution stated that the United States claimed no "sovereignty, jurisdiction, or control" over Cuba except for *pacifying,* or bringing peace to, the island and promised that once Cuba was free the United States would "leave the government and control of the island to its people."

Victory in the Pacific. Curiously enough, fighting in the "war for Cuban liberty" started not in Cuba but in the Pacific. For weeks before Congress declared war, Theodore Roosevelt, the Assistant Secretary of the Navy, had been preparing for any developments. Roosevelt had sent orders to Commodore George Dewey, then in command of a fleet anchored at Hong Kong, to prepare his ships for action. When Dewey received word that war had been declared, he promptly headed for the Philippine Islands, the center of Spanish power in the Pacific.

On the night of April 30, 1898, Dewey's six ships slipped past the fortress of Corregidor and into the harbor of Manila, capital of the Philippines (see map, this page). At daybreak on May 1 the American warships opened fire. Their guns outranged those of the Spanish vessels, and by noon the one-sided battle was over. The Spaniards lost nearly 170 men and all their vessels. The Americans lost one man—who died of heatstroke.

Although Commodore Dewey controlled Manila harbor, he did not have enough men to land and seize the city. While he waited for a landing force to arrive from the United States, he sent arms and ammunition to a band of Filipinos led by Emilio Aguinaldo (ay·MEE·lyo ah·ge·NAHL·do). The Filipinos, eager to throw off Spanish rule and win their independence, began to organize for an attack on Manila.

Two months passed. Then, early in August, American transports arrived with a strong landing party. The position of the Spanish garrison was hopeless. Cut off by Dewey's warships from all hope of relief, surrounded on the land side by the Filipino revolutionists, and faced with an attack by an American army, Manila surrendered on August 13, 1898.

Victory in the Atlantic. Meanwhile, Spain's Atlantic fleet under Admiral Cervera (sehr·VEH·rah), on April 29 had sailed westward from the Cape Verde Islands.

News that Admiral Cervera's fleet was steaming toward America threw Americans living in coastal areas into a panic. One coastal town after another begged for naval protection.

The alarm was unwarranted. Cervera's fleet was hopelessly inadequate for the task assigned to it, and the gallant admiral sailed only with the thought of saving the honor of Spain, not with the hope of victory. Instead of attacking, the Spaniards slipped into the harbor at Santiago, Cuba, for refueling. Here they were bottled up by an American squadron commanded by Admiral William T. Sampson and Commodore W. S. Schley (see map, this page).

On Sunday morning, July 3, 1898, Cervera's fleet made a wild dash for the open sea. But the American ships were waiting, and as the Spanish fleet raced out of the harbor and steamed along the coast, it was met by murderous fire. Within four hours the battle was over. Not a single Spanish vessel escaped.

Land fighting in Cuba. In contrast to the United States Navy, which moved swiftly and efficiently, the War Department was quite unprepared. When the war began, the regular army, numbering fewer than 30,000 officers and men, including four regiments of black soldiers, was scattered in small contingents over the country.

More than 200,000 men immediately volunteered for war service, including four more units of black soldiers recruited under a special act of Congress. The volunteers also included Theodore Roosevelt, who resigned as Assistant Secretary of the Navy to become lieutenant colonel of a volunteer regiment of cavalry known as the "Rough Riders."

The first American troops to arrive in Cuba were poorly trained and equipped. Many of them carried antiquated rifles. The food was poor, and the army was without adequate hospital and sanitary facilities. Hundreds of American soldiers died needlessly from dysentery, typhoid, malaria, and yellow fever.

On June 24 the two armies clashed. Slowly, by hard fighting, the Americans under General William Shafter pushed the enemy back through the fortified village of El Caney and across San Juan Hill (see map, this page). By July 2 American forces had advanced to within a mile and a half of

Santiago. It was this fact that led Admiral Cervera to make his desperate attempt to escape with the Spanish fleet. The destruction of the Spanish navy was the final blow. The Spanish commander at Santiago surrendered his forces on July 17.

Black soldiers, who had not been allowed to mix with white troops· on the ships carrying them to Cuba, fought well in several engagements of the war. Frank Knox, later to be Secretary of the Navy, became separated from the Rough Riders at San Juan Hill and joined a troop of the all-black Tenth Cavalry. After the battle he wrote home that he had never seen "braver men anywhere," and he added, "Some of those who rushed up the hill will live in my memory forever."

Meanwhile, another American army, under General Nelson A. Miles, landed on the Spanish island of Puerto Rico, east of Cuba. The Americans encountered no opposition, and by the end of July were in control of the island.

The fruits of victory. The United States entered the war with the argument that it was fighting merely to free the oppressed Cubans. It ended the war with an empire on its hands.

American and Spanish commissioners met in Paris in October 1898 to negotiate a peace treaty. By the terms of the treaty, Spain agreed to sur-

■ Members of a black signal corps that served in the Spanish-American War are shown above. Commenting on race relations during the war, one American officer wrote, "White regiments, black regiments, regulars and Rough Riders, representing the young manhood of the North and the South, fought shoulder to shoulder, unmindful of race or color, unmindful of whether commanded by an ex-Confederate or not, and mindful only of their common duty as Americans."

render all claim to Cuba. In addition, Spain agreed to cede to the United States the following territories: (1) Puerto Rico; (2) the Pacific island of Guam (see map, pages 874–75); and (3) the Philippines—in exchange for which the United States agreed to pay Spain $20 million.

As a result of the war, the United States also acquired Wake Island in the Pacific (see map, page 874). American armed forces had landed on Wake on July 4, 1898, and raised the American flag. Congress later annexed Wake.

Until 1898, except for the two square miles of the Midway Islands, the United States owned no overseas possessions. When the Senate ratified the peace treaty, however, the United States became a colonial power.

The expansionists—followers of Alfred Mahan, Theodore Roosevelt, and others—were delighted. But many Americans were deeply troubled. Was it wise and proper for the United States to join the European powers in the race for empire? Did the United States want to assume responsibility for a colonial empire scattered over the Pacific Ocean and the Caribbean Sea?

SECTION SURVEY

IDENTIFY: ultimatum, "Rough Riders," Teller resolution; Joseph Pulitzer, William Randolph Hearst, Commodore Dewey, Emilio Aguinaldo, Admiral Cervera; 1898.

1. (a) What were the causes of the Cuban revolt against Spain? (b) Why did this revolt affect the United States?
2. To what extent did each of the following help bring about the Spanish-American War: (a) sensational press coverage, (b) the De Lôme letter, (c) destruction of the *Maine,* (d) American investments and trade with Cuba?
3. Describe briefly the highlights of the fighting in (a) the Pacific, (b) Cuba.
4. The Spanish-American War marked a turning point in American history. Explain.

3 Establishing American control over the Philippines, Hawaii, and Samoa

The Philippine Islands presented Americans with an immediate and difficult problem: Should the United States set the islands free, just as it intended to set Cuba free? Or should it now turn on the Filipinos and force them to accept American rule?

American dilemma. President McKinley was one of countless Americans who wrestled with this problem. Finally he decided to establish American rule in the Philippine Islands.

As he later explained to a group of fellow Americans, the United States could not return the Philippines to Spain, for "that would be cowardly and dishonorable." It could not give them to France, Germany, or Great Britain, for "that would be bad business and discreditable." It could not turn them over to the Filipinos, for they were "unfit for self-government."

". . . There was nothing left for us to do," McKinley concluded, "but to take them all, and to educate the Filipinos, and uplift and civilize and Christianize them. . . ."

President McKinley's motives were good, but his knowledge of the facts was incomplete. Indeed, he later confessed that when he had first heard of Dewey's victory, he had had to look for the islands on the map. As for "Christianizing" the Filipinos, they had long since been converted to Catholicism, except the Moros, a group of people who were Moslems.

Divided public opinion. Many Americans agreed with McKinley that it was America's duty to "educate" and "uplift and civilize and Christianize" the Filipinos. These Americans believed that the strong and wealthy nations shared the moral responsibility to assume what the British poet Rudyard Kipling had called "the white man's burden." Others hoped to profit economically by following the path of world empire. Still others, mostly military leaders, believed that America needed the islands as strategic bases.

But opponents of imperialism viewed the decision with serious misgivings. They argued that, in taking the Philippines, the United States was violating its own Declaration of Independence and the principle that people had the right to live under a government of their own choice. "It will be only the old tale of a free people seduced by false ambitions and running headlong after riches and luxu-

ries and military glory," warned Carl Schurz, a prominent Republican. A few opponents, including some Negro spokesmen, argued that American imperialism was based in part on the false assumption of white racial superiority, as reflected in such phrases as "white man's burden." They argued that American expansion abroad could only work to the disadvantage of black Americans seeking to improve their lives in the United States.

Conquest and early rule. The conquest of the Philippines turned out to be more difficult than the defeat of Spain. The Filipinos were no more willing to accept American rule than they had been to endure Spanish rule. For three years 70,000 American troops fought in the islands at a cost of $175 million, and with a casualty list as high as that of the Spanish-American War. By 1902, however, the American forces were victorious.

Despite this unhappy beginning the United States tried to live up to McKinley's promise "not to exploit, but to develop; to civilize, to educate, to train in the science of self-government." In the Philippine Government Act of 1902, Congress created a government for the islands under which they were to be ruled by a governor and a small legislative body—an elected assembly and an appointed upper house. The United States Congress had the power to veto all legislation. The plan did not go into effect until 1907. Meanwhile, William Howard Taft, the first governor, ruled wisely. He cooperated closely with the Filipinos, and included many Filipinos in the new government.

Filipino dissatisfaction. But many Filipinos wanted full self-government—nothing less. Their dissatisfaction became apparent in 1907 when the elected lower house met for the first time. Three quarters of the representatives were pledged to work for independence. Their hopes rose high in 1913 when Woodrow Wilson became President of the United States. Leading Democrats had opposed the conquest of the Philippines, and the Democratic Party had pledged itself to grant independence at the earliest possible date.

These hopes, however, were soon dashed. Although the Jones Act of 1916 did give the Filipinos the right to elect the members of both houses of the legislature, Congress did not grant independence. The act merely promised independence "as soon as a stable government can be established."

Independence granted. Meanwhile the islands prospered. Highways, railroads, telegraph and telephone lines were built. Education reduced illiteracy from 85 percent in 1898 to 37 percent in 1921. Disease was greatly reduced and Filipino health steadily improved. Exports and imports swelled in volume as the result of an American tariff policy which, in 1902, gave a 25 percent tariff reduction to products from the Philippines and, in 1913, removed all tariffs on many articles traded between the islands and the United States.

Most important of all, the United States eventually kept its promise to set the islands free (Chapter 38).

Early relations with Hawaii. In 1898 Hawaii (see map, page 874) also occupied American attention. United States interest in the Hawaiian Islands went back many years.

Before 1865 about the only relations that the United States had with these central Pacific islands were through traders and missionaries. But after 1865 American businessmen began to develop the resources of Hawaii—chiefly sugar cane and pine-

apples. In 1875 Hawaii signed a treaty with the United States. In return for the right to sell sugar in the United States without payment of any duty, the Hawaiians promised not to sell or lease territory to any foreign power. In 1887, when this treaty was renewed, the United States leased Pearl Harbor as a naval base.

The Hawaiians became increasingly alarmed as the wealth and power of the islands passed into foreign hands. Finally, led by Queen Liliuokalani (le-LEE·wo·kah·LAH·ne), they announced their intentions to end foreign influence.

Foreign seizure and control. American businessmen, aided by influential Hawaiians, met this challenge with prompt action. They started a revolution.

At this critical moment the American minister to Hawaii intervened. Claiming that he was acting only to protect American lives and property, he requested the aid of the marines who were con-

■ In 1898 Hawaii became a Territory of the United States; in 1959 it became the fiftieth state in the Union. This photograph of Kauai Island shows some of Hawaii's natural beauty.

veniently at hand on a nearby warship. The Hawaiian soldiers, concluding that the marines had come to help the revolutionists, refused to fight. The new government, controlled by the foreign business interests and missionaries, asked to be annexed to the United States. The American minister promptly raised the Stars and Stripes, and on February 1, 1893, marines began to patrol the islands.

Refusal to annex Hawaii. When news of these events reached the United States, furious protests poured into Congress. Many Americans did not want island territory. They were indignant at the manner in which American marines had been used. They were afraid that overseas expansion would lead to heavy military expenditures.

President Cleveland sent a commission to Hawaii to investigate. The commission ordered the American flag hauled down and heard evidence from both sides. In its report, the commission stated that the revolution had been started largely by American businessmen, aided by the American minister and the marines.

After studying the report, Cleveland concluded that the only way to make amends was to apologize to Queen Liliuokalani and to restore her to her throne. But this would have required the exercise of force against the new government. By now Congress was fed up with the whole affair, and in 1894 it adopted a resolution refusing to interfere further in Hawaii.

Annexation of Hawaii. Then came the Spanish-American War, which, as you have seen, generated a new spirit in America. The question of Hawaii once again was brought up on the floor of Congress. This time, in 1898, by an overwhelming vote, the islands were annexed to the United States and given Territorial status.

American control of Samoa. As in Hawaii, American interests in the Samoan Islands were of long standing. In 1878 the United States secured from a Samoan chief the right to use the harbor of Pago Pago (PAHN·goh PAHN·goh) on the island of Tutuila (too·too·EE·lah) as a naval base. The Samoans granted similar privileges to Germany and Great Britain.

The three countries—Great Britain, Germany, and the United States—then became involved in a scramble to control the islands. At one point, in 1889, a naval clash among the three powers was narrowly avoided, largely because a typhoon blew the rival squadrons out to sea.

Finally, in 1899, the British withdrew and the islands were divided between Germany and the

■ Queen Liliuokalani of Hawaii led her people in an unsuccessful attempt to end the influence of American businessmen and missionaries in the islands. She was forced from her throne in 1893.

United States. Germany lost control of its share of the islands when it was defeated in World War I. But Tutuila, with its excellent anchorage in the harbor of Pago Pago, remained in the hands of the United States, which developed it into a major naval base in the Pacific.

SECTION SURVEY

IDENTIFY: "white man's burden," Jones Act; William Howard Taft, Queen Liliuokalani.

1. Do you agree or disagree with the anti-imperialists who argued that, in taking the Philippines, the United States violated the Declaration of Independence? Explain.
2. How did the United States finally acquire Hawaii?
3. The intense rivalry between nations to acquire colonies was demonstrated in the scramble for the Samoan Islands. Explain.
4. Some anti-imperialists argued that American imperialist policy worked to the disadvantage of black Americans at home. (a) Why did they feel this way? (b) Do you agree or disagree with their argument? Why? (c) What was the position of black Americans at home in the 1890's? (Review pages 504–05 and 536–37.)

4 The increasing influence of the United States in the Far East

By 1900 United States territory in the Pacific included Hawaii, Midway, Guam, Wake, the Philippine Islands, and part of Samoa. With this new territory the American people assumed heavy responsibilities. These new responsibilities, plus events taking place in the Far East, led the United States in 1899–1900 to proclaim the *Open Door policy* for China. This policy formed the basis for American action in the Far East, and involved the United States in the affairs of Russia and Japan. To understand the Open Door policy, it is necessary to review American relations with China during the 1800's.

The China trade. America's interest in China began back in 1784, when the *Empress of China* sailed from New York with a cargo intended for the Chinese seaport of Canton. The venture proved profitable, and enterprising Yankees were quick to seize the new trading opportunity.

Most of the Orient trade started in Philadelphia, New York, and New England ports. After a long voyage around South America, the ships anchored in the Pacific Northwest. There they traded with the Indians, exchanging blankets, axes, guns, and other goods for furs. When they had a full cargo, the Yankee skippers then headed out across the Pacific Ocean for China (see map, page 292).

Early diplomatic relations. Despite this growing trade, the word "China" did not appear in a public or Presidential message or paper until 1831. In the 1840's, however, relations between the United States and China grew closer.

As time passed, China's rulers began to fear the influence that foreigners were exerting in their country. When China began placing restrictions on British traders, however, Great Britain waged a successful war (1839–42) and forced the Chinese to open certain "treaty ports" to British trade.

Americans demanded and secured similar privileges when the American envoy to China, Caleb Cushing, negotiated a treaty which gave the United States all trading privileges granted by China to other nations and extended to Americans the right of *extraterritoriality*. This meant that American citizens in China who were charged with violations of China's civil or criminal laws had the right to be tried in American courts in China. Other foreign nations also secured trading privileges and extraterritorial rights in China.

These concessions from China encouraged foreign businessmen to settle there. As time passed, outsiders began to exercise more and more influ-

■ A Japanese artist painted this picture of United States troops marching through Peking after the Boxer Rebellion in 1900.

ence in China. Many of China's leaders resented this, but were powerless to prevent the growing foreign influence.

Among all the imperialistic powers interested in the Far East, the United States seemed least eager to grab Chinese territory. As a result, relations between the two countries remained friendly through the 1800's.

Crisis in China.   In the 1890's, however, a major crisis developed. Japan entered the race for colonies with an attack upon China in the Sino-Japanese War of 1894–95. In this war Japan won the large island of Formosa, certain territory on the Shantung Peninsula, and control of Korea (see map, page 744).

While China was helpless as a result of the Japanese attack, Germany, Russia, Great Britain, and France rushed in to seize their share of the booty. It appeared for a time that China would soon share the fate of Africa, which had already been carved up and divided among the European imperial powers.

The crisis in China posed a problem for the United States. Americans did not want Chinese territory. On the other hand, Americans did not intend to be squeezed out of Chinese markets.

The Open Door policy.   John Hay, who became Secretary of State in 1898, had a solution for the problem. He sent a note to all the powers concerned asking them to assure the United States (1) that they would keep open all "treaty ports"; and (2) that they would guarantee to all nations engaged in trade with China equal railroad, harbor, and tariff rates. In short, Hay asked for an Open Door policy that would insure American businessmen the opportunity to compete on equal terms with other traders in China. Although the response to his note was not encouraging, Hay announced on March 20, 1900, that the Open Door policy was in effect.

The Boxer Rebellion.   Naturally enough, the Chinese deeply resented the efforts by Japan, Russia, and the European powers to control their country. On the rising tide of resentment, the Chinese launched a movement to drive all "foreign devils" from their country. The movement was led by members of a Chinese secret society whom westerners called "the Boxers." °

° *the Boxers:* the Chinese name for this society literally meant "righteous harmonious band." But westerners wrongly translated the Chinese name to "righteous harmonious *fists*" and hence called the society the "Boxers."

In the spring of 1900 the Boxers suddenly attacked. They killed about 300 foreigners in northern China. Then they surrounded the foreign settlement in Tientsin (TIN·TSIN) and the foreign legations in Peking, where men and women from many nations had gathered for protection.

The foreign powers promptly rushed troops to relieve the besieged people. The joint expeditionary force included 2,500 American troops from the Philippines as well as military units from Japan and several European nations. By August 14 the expeditionary force had relieved the foreigners in Tientsin and Peking, but not before 65 of the besieged had been killed.

The Boxer Rebellion provided the colonial powers with an excellent excuse to seize additional Chinese territory. But John Hay took a firm stand in opposition. On July 3, even while the expeditionary force was fighting its way inland to Peking, Hay announced that the United States wanted to "preserve Chinese territorial and administrative entity . . . and safeguard for the world the principle of equal and impartial trade with all parts of the Chinese Empire."

Largely because of American influence, China did not lose any territory as a result of the Boxer Rebellion. China did, however, have to pay the foreign powers an indemnity of $333 million as compensation for loss, damage, and injury. The American share of the indemnity amounted to about $24 million, half of which the United States government turned over to American citizens to compensate them for losses of personal property in China. The American government then returned the remainder of the money to China.

Grateful for this American action, the Chinese government put the money into an educational fund to send Chinese students to the United States. This fund enabled thousands of China's ablest youth to study in American colleges and universities. These students helped to build closer understanding between the two countries.

The Open Door policy in China had other far-reaching results. It immediately involved the United States in the affairs of Russia and Japan, both of whom were expanding in the Far East.

The opening of Japan.   Before 1853 the Japanese had lived in almost complete isolation from the rest of the world. Japan's rulers forbade foreigners to enter Japan; only the Dutch had won the right to carry on a limited amount of trade through one small Japanese port. In 1853, however,

Japan's isolation was abruptly shattered when Commodore Matthew C. Perry arrived in Japanese waters with a squadron of American naval vessels and demanded an audience with the Japanese rulers.

The exchange of presents that took place between the Americans and Japanese during a conference in 1854 symbolized the difference between the two countries. The United States received gifts of silk, brocades, lacquer ware, and other fine handmade articles; the Japanese received tokens of the new industrial world—a telegraph set, guns, and model railroad trains.

As a result of this conference and a later one, the United States and Japan signed the Treaty of Kanagawa. With this treaty both countries expressed a desire for peace, friendship, and developing trade. Japan also agreed to open two ports to United States trading vessels. Later, Japan opened other ports.

Japan and the race for empire. Few events in modern history have had such far-reaching effects as the opening by the United States of the doors of Japan. Two major developments followed at once. First, American and other traders started a lively commerce with Japan that grew to large proportions in the 1900's. Second, Japanese leaders were convinced that they should adopt the industrial techniques of the western nations. And once started, the process of modernization in Japan went on at an astonishingly rapid rate.

By the late 1800's Japan was a transformed country. But the "new" Japan faced new problems. Knowledge of science, medicine, and sanitation had reduced the death rate—a welcome development. But the lower death rate also meant a larger population—and this created difficulties, for Japan was a small country without enough farm land to feed all of its people adequately. The Japanese also needed raw materials for their new factories and markets for their products.

Faced with these problems, Japan started upon a program of imperialism similar to that being followed by the other industrial nations of the world. Japan needed colonies to secure food for its surplus population and to provide raw materials and markets for its growing industries. Thus Japan entered the race for empire and became one of the rivals for control of the Far East.

As you have seen, Japan started its career as an imperial power with an attack upon China in the Sino-Japanese War of 1894–95. Ten years later Japan plunged into war with Russia.

The United States in the Pacific. Although the Russo-Japanese War of 1904–05 took place on land nearly half a world away from the continental boundaries of the United States, Americans were immediately concerned. Their new commitments in the Pacific had given Americans a direct interest in the affairs of the Far East. The war between Russia and Japan, fought on Chinese soil and in Pacific waters, threatened to interfere with American trading and missionary interests in China. It also threatened to weaken, if not destroy, the Open Door policy.

Acting on his own authority, President Theodore Roosevelt warned Germany and France that, if they aided Russia, the United States would side with Japan. With Roosevelt acting as mediator, representatives from Russia and Japan met at Portsmouth, New Hampshire, during the summer of 1905 and worked out terms for settling the conflict. In 1906, for his efforts, Roosevelt received the Nobel peace prize.

The Treaty of Portsmouth transferred Russia's interests in Korea and Manchuria to Japan. The treaty also gave Japan the southern half of Sakhalin Island (see map, page 744). But the Russians refused to grant Japan's demand for a cash indemnity, and Roosevelt persuaded the Japanese, against their will, to waive this demand.

Roosevelt was delighted with the results of his efforts to end the Russo-Japanese War. The Treaty of Portsmouth left the Open Door policy intact. It maintained for a time the balance of power in the Far East. Neither Japan nor Russia nor any other colonial power had a dominant position in China. The doors of China remained open to American business and trade.

SECTION SURVEY

IDENTIFY: extraterritoriality, Boxer Rebellion, Treaty of Portsmouth, Nobel peace prize; John Hay, Commodore Perry.

1. (a) Describe the circumstances which led to the Open Door policy. (b) State the provisions of this policy.
2. Give the reasons for Chinese-American friendship during this period.
3. (a) Why did Japan become imperialistic? (b) Why were Americans concerned about Japanese imperialism?
4. Japan won the 1904–05 war against Russia. Why do you think this was significant?

TRACING THE MAIN IDEAS

During the latter half of the 1800's the major colonial powers of Europe were engaged in a race for empire. The United States, however, was not especially interested in entering the race. To be sure, in 1867–68 Secretary of State Seward persuaded Congress to annex the Midway Islands and to purchase Alaska, but Congress did so reluctantly and Americans on the whole were indifferent.

Toward the end of the 1800's American sentiment began to change. It was the Spanish-American War, however, that finally started the United States down the road of imperialism.

The Spanish-American War of 1898 was begun in protest against Spain's policy in Cuba. It ended with a treaty in which Spain agreed to give up its claim to Cuba and in which the United States gained the Philippine Islands, as well as Guam and Puerto Rico. In addition to the Philippines and Guam, the United States acquired other territories in the Pacific area. Hawaii was annexed in 1898, and a portion of Samoa was acquired in 1899. To protect its growing interests, the United States insisted upon an equal opportunity to share in the business and trade of the Far East. This policy, the Open Door policy, involved Americans in the troubled affairs of eastern Asia, and committed the nation to a role of power politics in the Pacific.

But America's interest in colonies was not confined to the Pacific area. As you will see in the next chapter, the Caribbean offered even larger and more inviting opportunities for the development of American interests.

CHAPTER SURVEY

QUESTIONS FOR DISCUSSION

1. Why did the foreign policy of the United States change from one of isolationism to one of expansionism?
2. What arguments did the expansionists use to defend their position?
3. In your opinion, does expansionism contradict the ideals of self-government expressed in the Declaration of Independence? Why or why not?
4. Do you think the American people were in agreement with the statement by John Hay that "[The Spanish-American War] has been a splendid little war; begun with the highest motives, carried on with magnificent intelligence and spirit, favored by that fortune which loves the brave"? Why or why not?
5. (a) How did the areas acquired by the United States in 1898 differ from those acquired through the Louisiana Purchase and the Mexican Cession? (b) What problems of government do you think these new areas presented? (Remember that the Northwest Ordinance of 1787 served as a plan of government for possessions in the continental United States.)
6. Recall American attitudes toward mercantilism before the American Revolution. What was our attitude toward our "mother country," Great Britain? Do you think we can generalize and say that most colonies feel this way about their mother country? Why or why not?
7. Comment: Compared to other nations possessing colonies, the United States was more successful in helping other peoples to establish self-government. Thus, Americans demonstrated their belief in the ideals of the Declaration of Independence and the Constitution.
8. Was there a contradiction in the United States' favoring the Open Door policy for China and the policy of the Monroe Doctrine for the Western Hemisphere? Explain.
9. By moving into the Pacific and the Far East, the United States embarked upon a policy that was to have lasting consequences for foreign affairs and domestic conditions. Explain.

RELATING PAST TO PRESENT

1. Until World War II, the United States had amicable relations with China. The foundation for this friendship was established during the period just studied. Explain.
2. Is the United States involved overseas today for the same reasons it was involved during the period just studied? Explain.
3. Compare the role of the press today with the "yellow press" of Hearst and Pulitzer during the Spanish-American War.

USING MAPS AND CHARTS

1. (a) Since the war against Spain was designed to free Cuba, why was Dewey's fleet ordered to the Philippine Islands? (See map, page 578.) (b) What was the significance of Dewey's victory?
2. Using the map on pages 874–75, point out the possessions that the United States acquired as a result of the Treaty of Paris of 1898.

■ *Theodore Roosevelt as "policeman of the world"*

CHAPTER **31**

American Expansion in the Caribbean

1898 – 1914

O N AUGUST 12, 1898, the Spaniards signed the armistice that brought the Spanish-American War to an end. For both the United States and Spain this was a turning point.

By the terms of the armistice, Spain agreed (1) to leave Cuba, (2) to cede Puerto Rico and Guam to the United States, and (3) to allow American troops to occupy the Philippine Islands until a formal peace treaty could be drawn up and signed.

August 12, 1898, was a sad day for the Spanish nation. The Spaniards had reason for sorrow, for the Spanish-American War did indeed strike the final blow to the once mighty Spanish empire.

For the American people, however, the Spanish-American War marked an important milestone on the path of empire and world power. After 1898, as you know, the United States rapidly became a major power in the Pacific and in the Far East. And between 1898 and 1914, as you will read in this chapter, the course of events turned the Caribbean Sea into what was sometimes called "an American lake."

THE CHAPTER IN OUTLINE

1. The start of an American empire in the Caribbean area.

2. Intervention in Latin America under a modified Monroe Doctrine.

3. The outbreak of conflict between the United States and Mexico.

| 1450 | 1750 | 1800 | 1850 | 1900 | 1950 | 1975 |

1 The start of an American empire in the Caribbean area

With the Spanish-American War in 1898, the United States began to move into the Caribbean area. Less than 20 years later the American flag was flying not only over Puerto Rico, but also over the Panama Canal Zone and the Virgin Islands; American advisers were helping to govern small countries in and around the Caribbean; and the United States had developed a revised foreign policy for the Western Hemisphere.

"Does the Constitution follow the flag?" The acquisition of overseas possessions brought the American government face to face with an important question: Were the people who lived in these areas entitled to all the rights guaranteed by the Constitution to citizens of the United States? Or, as the question was often stated, "Does the Constitution follow the flag?"

This question began to bother many Congressmen. Millions of people in the newly acquired territories had little understanding of the word "democracy." But if the Constitution did "follow the flag," these people were entitled to the rights of American citizenship. Many Congressmen refused to accept this reasoning.

The Supreme Court's answer. In the so-called Insular Cases of 1901 the Supreme Court ruled that there are two kinds of possessions—"incorporated" and "unincorporated." The "incorporated" possessions—Hawaii and Alaska—were destined for statehood, and the citizens of these possessions were therefore entitled to all the constitutional rights guaranteed to United States citizens. The "unincorporated" possessions—Puerto Rico, the Philippines, Samoa, and others—were not destined for statehood, and the people of these areas were *not,* therefore, entitled to all constitutional guarantees. The people of the "unincorporated" possessions were, however, entitled to certain fundamental rights, such as the guarantee that they would not be deprived of life, liberty, or property without due process of law.

The Insular Cases, and several similar Supreme Court decisions between 1901 and 1922, helped to develop an American colonial policy. However, it was Congress that passed the laws ruling America's growing colonial empire, subject only to certain broad limitations derived from the Constitution of the United States.

■ **Below, Theodore Roosevelt patrols Latin America. This political cartoon criticized the growing imperialism of United States foreign policy.**

A government for Puerto Rico. In 1900, with the Foraker Act, Congress provided for the government of Puerto Rico. The new government consisted of a governor and an executive council appointed by the President of the United States, and a lower house elected by the Puerto Ricans.

Discontented Puerto Ricans, however, continued to demand a larger voice in their own government. In 1917, shortly after the Filipinos won a similar victory in the Jones Act of 1916, the United States adopted a second Jones Act making Puerto Rico a United States Territory and making the Puerto Ricans American citizens. Puerto Ricans were also granted the right to elect members of both houses of their legislature. Finally, in 1950, Congress gave Puerto Ricans the power to write their own constitution. In 1952, after the constitution had been ratified by popular vote, Puerto Rico became a Commonwealth. As a Commonwealth, Puerto Rico is self-governing. It makes its own laws and controls its own finances. The United States, however, provides for the island's defense, includes Puerto Rico within its own tariff system, and places no restrictions on immigration from Puerto Rico to the United States (Chapter 44). Today Puerto Rico is, as one of its statesmen said, "associated with the American Union by bonds of affection, common citizenship, and free choice."

Strings on Cuban independence. Although Cuba was never considered an American colony, American influence over Cuban affairs remained strong after the Spanish-American War.

The Teller Resolution, which Congress adopted in 1898 when it declared war on Spain, pledged that the Cubans would be given their independence (page 578). But for three years after the war, while Congress was deciding what to do about the island, Cuba was ruled by an American army of occupation under General Leonard Wood.

In 1901 Congress finally decided to turn Cuba over to the Cuban people, subject, however, to certain conditions. These conditions, incorporated in the Army Act of 1901 as the Platt Amendment, declared: (1) The Cuban government must never enter into any foreign agreements that might endanger Cuban independence. (2) The Cuban government must never incur debts that it could not repay in a reasonable time. (3) The Cuban government must give the United States "The right to intervene for the preservation of Cuban independence, the maintenance of a government adequate for the protection of life, property, and individual liberty." (4) The Cuban government must place naval bases at the disposal of the United States. Congress also announced that the United States would not withdraw its military forces until the Platt Amendment had been written into the Cuban constitution.

This was not the "independence" that many Cubans had expected, yet they had to agree to American demands. Accordingly, they accepted the Platt Amendment, and in 1902 the American forces were withdrawn.

An American protectorate. Actually, Cuba became a "protectorate" of the United States. That is, the United States, a strong nation, attempted to protect Cuba, a weaker nation, by retaining partial control over Cuban affairs. Cubans were not happy with this relationship because of their previous experience under Spanish rule.

On three different occasions between 1906 and 1920, American troops landed in Cuba to maintain order and to protect American business and property. Moreover, American diplomatic pressure frequently forced the Cubans to accept policies formulated in the United States.

In 1934, as you will see, Congress abolished the Platt Amendment, thus ending America's role as "protector" of Cuba.

Growing interest in a canal. In the years following the Spanish-American War, the United States was being pulled along a path of empire. As the empire grew, people began to say that the United States needed two navies—one to protect its interests in the Pacific, the other to safeguard the Atlantic and the Caribbean.

But there was an alternative to a two-ocean navy. That was a canal across the narrow Isthmus of Panama separating the Atlantic and the Pacific oceans. Indeed, a French company in the 1880's had tried but had failed to build such a canal. Another possible canal route was through Nicaragua (see map, page 591). A canal in either place would enable a fleet to pass easily and quickly from one ocean to the other. It would also be of enormous commercial value to the United States, as well as to the merchant fleets of the entire world.

When the Spanish-American War began, the U.S. battleship *Oregon,* then in California waters, started a run around South America in an effort to reach the Atlantic fleet. Public imagination was stirred, and for six weeks daily reports of the ship's progress appeared in every newspaper. The *Oregon's* voyage convinced many Americans that a canal was needed and that the canal must be controlled by the United States.

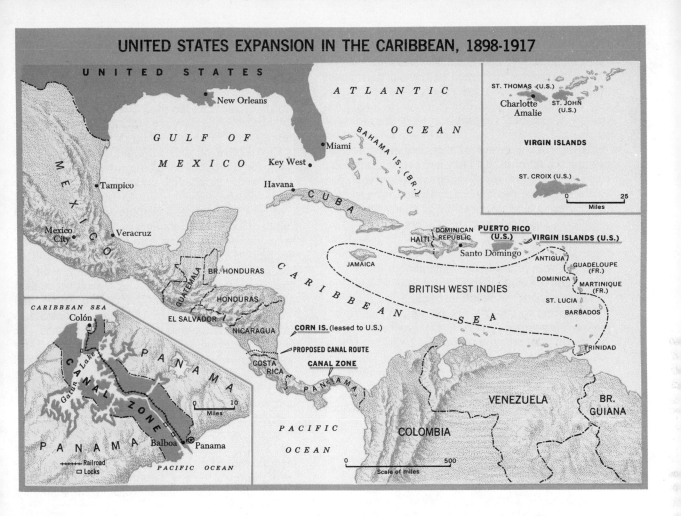

UNITED STATES EXPANSION IN THE CARIBBEAN, 1898-1917

Withdrawal of British canal rights. Talk about building a canal through the Isthmus of Panama had gone on for many years. As early as 1850 the United States and Great Britain had agreed in the Clayton-Bulwer Treaty that, if a canal were built, they would together control it and guarantee that it be unfortified and open to all nations in wartime.

By 1898, however, the United States had changed its thinking. Americans had concluded that the canal was so important to their national interests that the United States must have exclusive control over it.

Negotiations with Great Britain resulted, in 1901, in the Hay-Pauncefote Treaty. In this treaty Great Britain abandoned all rights to share in the building and management of the canal. The United States was now free to build and operate the canal. But it was understood that the canal would be open to all nations, even in time of war.

Difficulties encountered. The next step was to secure a right of way either through Nicaragua or across the Isthmus of Panama. The United States decided in favor of the Isthmus, which was then a province of Colombia, and Secretary of State John Hay immediately opened negotiations with the foreign minister of the Colombian government, Señor Herrán. Soon the Hay-Herrán Treaty was ready for ratification. In return for a 99-year lease to a six-mile strip of land across the province of Panama, the United States agreed to pay Colombia $10 million and a yearly rental of $250,000.

Matters stood at this promising point when the legislators of Colombia adjourned without taking action. They hoped to secure better terms through further negotiations. But many Americans, including President Theodore Roosevelt, were furious because Colombia's delay effectively blocked the entire canal project.

591

Revolution in Panama. Fortunately for the United States, many leaders in the province of Panama were also indignant at Colombia's delay. These leaders had dreamed of a canal that would place Panama at a crossroads of world commerce. For years the people of Panama had resented control by Colombia. Colombia's delay was the last straw.

In Panama a group of men began secretly to organize a revolution. They were encouraged by representatives of the French company that had earlier attempted to build a canal and now wanted to recover as much as possible of its investment.

One of the Panamanian leaders journeyed to Washington—secretly, of course—and asked the American government for assistance. Although open aid was refused, the Panamanian left Washington convinced that the United States would not interfere once the revolution began.

According to rumors, the revolution was to begin on November 4, 1903. On November 2 an American gunboat, the *Nashville,* arrived at Colón (see inset map, page 591). Hardly had it landed before a Colombian transport arrived with Colombian soldiers. The Colombian generals commanding the expedition immediately proceeded to the city of Panama, leaving orders for the troops to follow. Shortly after they arrived in Panama, however, the Colombian generals were seized and thrown into jail.

The seizure of the Colombian generals was a signal for the outbreak of the revolution. The city of Panama quickly fell under the control of the revolutionists.

Meanwhile, during a dispute that broke out in Colón, Colombian soldiers and naval officers threatened to kill every American in the city. At this point United States marines landed. Colombian authorities demanded to know what right the Americans had to interfere. The Americans replied that in a treaty between the United States and Colombia signed back in 1846 the United States had guaranteed the free transit of the Isthmus. The United States government also added that no Colombian troops would be permitted to land within 50 miles of Panama. By this time the United States had more than enough naval strength on hand to make its warning effective.

Right of way through Panama. Largely because of American aid, the revolution in Panama was a success. On November 4, 1903, the new government of Panama was installed in office. Acting with unusual speed, two days later, on November 6, the United States recognized Panama's independence.

Two weeks later, on November 18, Panama granted the United States the long-sought canal right of way across the Isthmus. In the Hay-Bunau-Varilla (boo·NOH vah·REE·yah) Treaty, Panama gave the United States a perpetual lease to a 10-mile strip of land between the Atlantic and the Pacific. In return, the United States agreed to pay Panama $10 million and a yearly rental of $250,000.

Did the United States help to start the revolution in Panama? President Theodore Roosevelt once boastfully remarked, "I took Panama." On other occasions he denied that the United States had in any way helped to carry out the revolution. But no matter how the revolution started, one fact is certain: It worked to the advantage of the United States, and President Theodore Roosevelt did not lose a minute in making the most of the situation to advance American interests in Central America and the Caribbean.

■ The building of the Panama Canal was an enormous undertaking, requiring the leveling of mountains and the conquest of tropical diseases. The canal was finally completed in 1914, at a cost of approximately $400 million.

Compensation for Colombia. Colombia was furious, of course, and the affair did much to stimulate the fear and distrust of the "Yankee" that was already strong in Latin America. In later years the United States tried to pacify the Colombian people. In 1921 the United States Senate ratified an agreement giving Colombia $25 million as partial compensation for the loss of the province of Panama.

Building the canal. Meanwhile, work on the canal progressed under the direct supervision of the United States Army Corps of Engineers. One of the first and most difficult tasks was to conquer malaria, yellow fever, and other tropical diseases. Until these diseases were brought under control, workmen from the United States found it almost impossible to live in the Canal Zone.

Dr. Walter Reed and his colleagues working in Cuba discovered that yellow fever was transmitted by a certain mosquito, the *Stegomyia*. Armed with this and other medical discoveries, Dr. William C. Gorgas, the surgeon in charge of the American health program in Panama, was able to turn a deadly, steaming tropical jungle into a relatively healthful region.

By 1914 the canal was completed (see inset map, page 591) at a cost of approximately $400 million. Its completion was a major triumph of engineering and a personal triumph for the engineer in charge, Colonel George W. Goethals (GOH·thalz). The first traffic moved through the canal just as World War I broke out in Europe. During both world wars, the canal added immeasurably to the naval strength of the United States, while its value as a peacetime artery of trade and commerce has been almost incalculable.

SECTION SURVEY

IDENTIFY: Insular Cases, protectorate, Hay-Pauncefote Treaty, Hay-Bunau-Varilla Treaty; Walter Reed, George Goethals.

1. How did the Supreme Court answer the question, "Does the Constitution follow the flag"?
2. What provisions did Congress make for the government of Puerto Rico?
3. Why has it been said that the Platt Amendment made Cuba an American protectorate?
4. Give the economic and military reasons for American interest in a canal through Central America.
5. American policies helped to stimulate the fear and distrust of the "Yankee" that was already strong in Latin America. Comment.

2 Intervention in Latin America under a modified Monroe Doctrine

During the early 1900's, as you have seen, the United States on a number of occasions intervened in the internal affairs of the smaller countries in the Caribbean area. On what grounds did the United States justify this interference?

Reasons for interference. Intervention was necessary, Americans argued, to maintain law and order in countries bordering on the United States. In the first place, the United States government had an obligation to protect the lives and properties of its own citizens living in other countries. Second, the United States was determined as a matter of self-interest and self-defense to prevent European countries from intervening in the political affairs of the Western Hemisphere, and there would be less temptation for such intervention if law and order prevailed. Third, the United States was concerned about the defense of the canal it was then building across the Isthmus of Panama.

Americans developed the argument of self-defense into a well-defined foreign policy. This foreign policy consisted of the Monroe Doctrine strengthened, as you will see, by Theodore Roosevelt's interpretation of the doctrine, called the Roosevelt Corollary.

The Monroe Doctrine of 1823. As you have learned (pages 259–60), the original Monroe Doctrine of 1823 warned the European powers (1) not to attempt any further colonization in the Americas, and (2) not to interfere with independent governments in the Western Hemisphere.

When this warning was first issued and for long thereafter, the United States did not have the necessary naval strength to enforce the policy. But the support of Latin Americans and the backing of the British Royal Navy gave weight to Monroe's words.

The first major test. The first major test of the Monroe Doctrine came during the 1860's when Emperor Napoleon III of France attempted to establish a French empire in Mexico.

Napoleon III's desire to seize control of Mexico had the support of many Frenchmen—of military men and others seeking adventure and of businessmen seeking trade. It began when Napoleon III, together with Great Britain and Spain, sent an expedition to Mexico, supposedly to force Mexico to repay some of its debts. After Mexico repaid its debts, Great Britain and Spain withdrew. But Napoleon III refused to pull out his troops. Instead,

■ During the Venezuelan crisis of 1902, the United States warned European nations not to violate the Monroe Doctrine. In a cartoon of that year, Uncle Sam tells Great Britain and Germany, "That's a live wire, gentlemen!"

aided by Mexicans opposed to President Benito Juárez (HWAH·res), the French troops installed Maximilian of Austria as emperor of Mexico. President Juárez fled to El Paso del Norte near the United States border.

The United States immediately protested that French occupation of Mexico was a clear violation of the Monroe Doctrine. But the United States was fighting the Civil War, and until 1865 was unable to take firm action. Then, with the war ended, the United States prepared to send an American army to the Mexican border—farther, if necessary.

But the American army was not needed. Napoleon, faced with the danger of war in Europe and convinced that he could not hold Mexico, withdrew his forces. Juárez and his followers destroyed Maximilian's army and executed Maximilian in 1867.

It was a sorry affair all around. However, by upholding the Monroe Doctrine, Americans greatly increased their standing in the eyes of the rest of the world.

A second major test. A second major test of the Monroe Doctrine came in 1895. The immediate issue was a boundary dispute between Venezuela and British Guiana (see map, page 591).

This dispute originated when Great Britain acquired British Guiana back in 1814. Despite the protests of Venezuela, Great Britain had time and again pushed the western boundary of British Guiana on to territory claimed by Venezuela. Finally, in 1882, Venezuela demanded that Great Britain submit the controversy to arbitration, meaning that the British would have to agree in advance to accept the decision of a neutral party.

The British refused to submit the boundary controversy to arbitration. In 1895 Venezuela asked the United States to intervene. President Cleveland decided to act. In an extremely strong message, Secretary of State Richard Olney warned Great Britain that the United States would not tolerate any further interference with Venezuela and demanded an immediate settlement of the problem by arbitration.

Great Britain indignantly rejected Olney's demands. In the first place, the British retorted, the Monroe Doctrine had not been violated. Second, the Monroe Doctrine was not a recognized part of international law. And third, the United States had no business interfering.

President Cleveland refused to accept this explanation. When the British refusal to arbitrate reached him, he appointed an American commission to investigate the controversy and reach a decision. This was a direct challenge to British imperial power.

Realizing that war between Great Britain and the United States was a real possibility, responsible men in both countries urged moderation. Partly because of their efforts and partly because of British difficulties in South Africa at the time, the British government suddenly reversed its position and agreed to arbitrate the boundary dispute. It even offered to help the American commission with its investigation.

Once more the Monroe Doctrine had been successfully upheld by the United States. And on this occasion the United States could claim that it had used its foreign policy to protect a weak nation against a great power. Even more important, perhaps, was the fact that the British, desiring American friendship, now in effect recognized that the United States had special interests in the Caribbean area.

A third major test. In 1902, seven years later, Venezuela again became involved in a dispute with European countries. Venezuela was unable to repay debts owed to Great Britain, Germany, and Italy. After their demands for repayment produced no results, the three countries took joint action. They withdrew their diplomatic representatives, blockaded the Venezuelan coast, and seized several small gunboats.

At this point President Theodore Roosevelt warned the European powers that any attempt to seize territory in the Western Hemisphere would violate the Monroe Doctrine. Then he urged the countries involved to submit the dispute to arbitration. They did, and the matter was settled.

The Drago Doctrine. In the case of Mexico and in both of the Venezuelan controversies, the United States had intervened in the name of the Monroe Doctrine to warn European nations to keep out of the politics of the Western Hemisphere. In all of these controversies, the United States had helped to protect its weaker neighbors.

By 1902, however, many Americans were eager to promote their own interests in Latin America. The United States had gone into the Spanish-American War in 1898 to help the oppressed Cubans. It had come out of the war in control of Cuba and owning Puerto Rico. Moreover, by the early 1900's Americans in growing numbers were investing money in Caribbean countries.

Latin-American leaders were becoming alarmed at the growing influence of the United States. In 1902 one of these leaders, Luis M. Drago, Argentine Minister of Foreign Affairs, announced a policy for Latin America that came to be known as the Drago Doctrine.

Señor Drago declared that Argentina would not admit the right of any European nation to use force to collect debts from a Latin-American nation. The Argentine Minister of Foreign Affairs stated that, when individuals or nations lent money, they did so at their own risk.

Nearly all of Latin America's leaders, as well as many United States citizens, agreed with Luis M. Drago. But in 1904, when trouble broke out in the Dominican Republic, President Roosevelt announced a policy that exempted the United States from the principle that foreign debts concerned only the debtor country and foreign investors.

The Roosevelt Corollary. The Dominican Republic (see map, page 591) owed long-overdue debts to several European countries as well as to American investors. When the European countries threatened to use armed force to collect the money, President Roosevelt at once intervened.

Roosevelt boldly announced in 1904 that, if it became necessary for any nation to interfere in the affairs of a Latin-American country, it would be the United States that interfered, not a European government. Roosevelt declared that ". . . in the Western Hemisphere the adherence of the United States to the Monroe Doctrine may force the United States, however reluctantly, in flagrant cases of . . . wrongdoing or impotence, to the exercise of an international police power."

The new policy laid down in 1904 by President Roosevelt came to be known as the Roosevelt Corollary to the Monroe Doctrine. With this policy, the United States assumed the role of "big policeman" in the Western Hemisphere. On several occasions during the next two decades, the United States used the Roosevelt Corollary to justify its intervention in the affairs of its neighbors south of the Rio Grande.

There was, of course, another side to the Roosevelt Corollary. It aimed to make conditions in the Latin-American countries such that European governments would have no excuse for intervention. In this sense, the Roosevelt Corollary helped all of the American countries. But Latin Americans could not forget that it was also a weapon that could be used against them and was thus an insult to their national pride.

The United States purchased three of the Virgin Islands from Denmark in 1917. This purchase helped to guarantee American control over the Caribbean Sea and the approaches to the Panama Canal.

A protectorate over the Dominican Republic. The United States first exercised its "international police power" by intervening in the affairs of the Dominican Republic. As part of an agreement reached with the Dominican government in 1905, President Roosevelt promised to guarantee the Republic's *territorial integrity*. That is, he promised to use American armed forces, if necessary, to prevent any European country from seizing Dominican territory. In exchange for this guarantee, the Dominican government agreed to allow an American agent to collect its customs duties, to turn over 45 percent of the duties to the Dominican government, and to use the remainder of the money to pay foreign creditors.

Although customs duties doubled under American supervision and the financial position of the Dominican Republic improved, the Dominican

people resented United States control. Finally, in 1916, during President Wilson's administration, the Dominican government announced that it intended to end the protectorate.

The United States answered this challenge by landing marines and suspending the Dominican legislature. For eight years, until 1924, the Dominican Republic was ruled by a Dominican military dictatorship under the American government. The United States withdrew its military forces in 1924, but did not end its role of "protector" until 1940.

A protectorate over Haiti. The same general methods used to secure control of the Dominican Republic were applied to the Republic of Haiti (see map, page 591).

When, in 1914, during President Wilson's administration, revolutions shook the debt-ridden Haitian republic, the United States landed marines.

The Haitians were then asked to ratify a treaty prepared by the United States Department of State. This treaty gave the United States the right to (1) supervise Haiti's finances, (2) intervene to maintain order, and (3) control the Haitian police force. After considerable American pressure, the legislature of Haiti ratified the treaty, which went into effect early in 1916.

Unfortunately, neither the treaty nor the continued presence of an American military force was sufficient to restore order completely. During the next four or five years nearly 2,000 Haitians were killed in riots and other outbreaks of violence.

Nevertheless, some improvements did come to Haiti during the years of United States control. Some Americans, however, agreed with those Haitians who argued that better sanitation, health, and education, and increased prosperity, were not worth the loss of freedom.

Despite continued resentment in Haiti and growing pressure from the American public to end military occupation of the island, the treaty permitting American control was renewed in 1926, as you will see. But in 1930 President Herbert Hoover announced that all American troops would be withdrawn when the treaty expired in 1936. Two years before that date, in 1934, President Franklin D. Roosevelt withdrew all military forces and gave the Haitian government a greater share of authority over the republic's finances.

American interference in Central America. Twice between 1900 and 1920 American military forces were used in Nicaragua and Honduras to gain a large measure of control over these republics. In addition, the United States exercised a large

596

amount of influence over the governments of Colombia, Costa Rica, and Guatemala (see map, page 591). This influence was secured by means of a policy that its critics referred to as "dollar diplomacy."

Under the so-called "dollar diplomacy," American bankers, sometimes by invitation of the Department of State, lent money to Caribbean governments. When the debtors failed to repay their debts or the interest on their loans, the United States government intervened to protect American investments. This intervention took various forms, including the landing of marines, the supervision of elections, and support to the political group that favored the United States.

Purchase of the Virgin Islands. By purchase of three of the Virgin Islands from Denmark, the United States completed its colonial holdings in the Caribbean (see map, page 591).

Back in 1868 Secretary of State Seward had tried to get Congress to buy the Virgin Islands. Congress had refused then, and refused again in 1902.

In 1917, however, with World War I raging in Europe, the United States was fearful that Germany might secure control of these strategic bases, and it renewed the offer to buy the islands. This time negotiations were completed. With the payment of $25 million to Denmark, the islands became outposts of America's Caribbean empire.

As the map on page 591 shows, the Virgin Islands lie at the eastern edge of the West Indies. United States naval bases on the islands, and on Puerto Rico, help to guarantee American control over the Caribbean Sea and the approaches to the Panama Canal.

(see map, page 591)

SECTION SURVEY

IDENTIFY: Drago Doctrine, territorial integrity, "dollar diplomacy"; Napoleon III, Benito Juárez, Richard Olney.

1. (a) How did the United States justify its intervention in Latin-American affairs? (b) Do you agree that this intervention was justified? Explain.
2. (a) What were the provisions of the original Monroe Doctrine of 1823? (b) Describe two occasions on which the Monroe Doctrine was tested and upheld.
3. (a) In what way did the Roosevelt Corollary modify the original Monroe Doctrine? (b) Cite examples of the application of the Roosevelt Corollary.
4. Latin Americans had strong reactions to events in the Caribbean resulting from United States policy. Comment.

3 The outbreak of conflict between the United States and Mexico

American investments south of the Rio Grande in time involved the United States in conflict with Mexico. By the time Woodrow Wilson became President in 1913, American citizens had invested nearly $1 billion in Mexican oil wells, mines, railroads, and ranches. Most of Mexico's trade was with the United States.

Dictatorship and revolution. Mexico was closely tied to the United States, and Mexico's President Porfirio Diaz was largely responsible for this fact. Diaz, although called "president," was actually a dictator who had ruled Mexico since 1877. During his long rule he had brought peace and order to Mexico and had helped to develop the country's resources. But, to develop Mexico's resources, he had encouraged foreign investors to finance and operate mines, factories, and other industries by offering them special privileges. Given this encouragement, foreign capital, much of it from American investors, had poured into Mexico. As a result, however, foreign investors and the privileged friends of dictator Diaz enjoyed most of the material benefits of Mexico's developing economy.

Finally, in 1910, the Mexicans staged a successful revolution. Diaz resigned and left for Europe. A sincere reformer, Francisco Madero, then became president—but only for a short time. Early in 1913 Madero was assassinated and Victoriano Huerta (WAIR·tah) seized the government.

Huerta had many enemies, including the friends of the late President Madero. The struggle between Huerta and his enemies, led by Venustiano Carranza, plunged Mexico into more bloodshed.

Wilson's policy of "watchful waiting." Americans with investments in Mexico were deeply troubled by the situation. And millions of people throughout the Americas were extremely dismayed because Huerta had risen to power as the result of a cold-blooded murder.

Under the circumstances, some Americans wanted President Wilson to send an armed force into Mexico to protect American investments and restore law and order. Wilson chose, instead, to follow a policy that he hoped would preserve the independence of the Mexican people.

Wilson outlined his policy in a speech given shortly after he had been elected. "The United States will never again seek one additional foot of territory by conquest," he declared. "We have seen material interests threaten constitutional freedom in the United States," he went on to say. "Therefore we will now know how to sympathize with those in the rest of America who have to contend with such powers, not only within their borders but from outside their borders also." He then urged the Latin-American countries to settle the Mexican problem in their own way.

Although a number of European countries promptly recognized the Huerta government, Wilson refused to do so. He pointed out that Huerta had come to power not by the will of the Mexican people, but by means of force and murder. Moreover, he was convinced that the Mexicans themselves would soon get rid of Huerta. Meanwhile, Wilson announced that the United States would follow a policy of "watchful waiting."

Wilson's refusal to intervene pleased most Latin Americans, who could hardly believe their ears. But many American businessmen with Mexican investments savagely attacked the President as they saw American lives and property destroyed in Mexico.

American intervention. As the months passed, however, even President Wilson began to lose patience. Hundreds of small revolutionary bands roamed Mexico, but they were not organized, and Huerta remained in power. More disturbing, Huerta seemed to take delight in taunting the United States. Nor did he stop with taunts. American citizens were killed in Mexico, and there were rumors that Huerta might try to confiscate, or seize, American property.

The final crisis came in April 1914 when a Mexican official arbitrarily arrested several American sailors who had landed in a zone of Tampico, Mexico, then under martial law, to buy gasoline. The sailors were soon released, but Huerta refused to apologize for the incident. To make matters worse, a German ship arrived at Veracruz with machine guns and other military supplies for Huerta. President Wilson then ordered United States marines to seize Veracruz. Emboldened by America's action, the anti-Huerta forces in Mexico began to gain strength.

The "ABC mediation." The United States was now in a position to dictate the choice of the new Mexican president. But Wilson had no such intention. Instead, he accepted an invitation from Argentina, Brazil, and Chile—sometimes called the "ABC powers"—for United States representatives to meet with Mexican leaders and those of the other nations to try to reach a solution. Huerta could not afford to ignore a similar invitation, and the conference was held at Niagara Falls, Canada. As a result of the "ABC mediation," Huerta resigned.

Venustiano Carranza then established himself in power in Mexico, and American forces were withdrawn from Veracruz. And in 1915, after

■ "Pancho" Villa, a brilliant horseman (left, foreground), was thought of by many Mexicans as a modern Robin Hood. In Mexico he is remembered in ballads and tales.

■ General John J. Pershing is shown above crossing the Santa Maria River near El Valle, Mexico, in 1916. He left Mexico the following year, having been unable to capture "Pancho" Villa.

Carranza guaranteed that Mexico would respect foreign lives and property, the United States recognized him as leader of the Mexican government.

American troops in Mexico. But trouble still continued, for the people Carranza chose to help him rule began to quarrel among themselves. One of the men who turned against Carranza was Francisco (Pancho) Villa (VEE·yah). Angry at the United States for helping Carranza and hoping at the same time to force American interference in Mexico, Villa and his followers in 1916 seized 18 Americans in northern Mexico and cold-bloodedly put them to death. Later, he crossed the border and raided Columbus, New Mexico, killing 17 Americans.

President Wilson immediately declared that he intended to send an expedition into Mexico to capture Villa, "dead or alive." Carranza agreed, although with understandable reluctance, and General John J. Pershing led an initial force of some 5,000 men across the border. But the deeper Pershing penetrated into Mexican territory, the more hostile the Mexicans became. For a time the shadow of full-scale war hung over both countries. Finally, in January 1917, American troops withdrew from Mexico, with Villa still at large.

President Wilson had tried, and tried sincerely, to respect the independence and freedom of the Mexican people. In the end, however, he had to use force to maintain law and order and protect American lives and property. In the course of these troubled years in Mexican–United States relations, Wilson learned that it was not easy for the United States to keep aloof from a nearby country where disorder threatened Americans.

SECTION SURVEY

IDENTIFY: confiscate, ABC powers; Porfirio Diaz, Victoriano Huerta, Venustiano Carranza, Pancho Villa, John Pershing.

1. Show how the economic interests of the United States and Mexico were closely interwoven.
2. (a) Describe the circumstances that led to Wilson's policy of "watchful waiting." (b) Explain this policy.
3. Why did Wilson abandon "watchful waiting"?
4. What important lesson did Americans learn from their experiences with Mexico during the years 1910–17?

TRACING THE MAIN IDEAS

The Spanish-American War of 1898 marked a turning point in America's position in the world. During the opening decade of the 1900's, the United States embarked upon a program of imperialism similar in many ways to that being followed by the major European nations, as well as by Japan.

Driven by complex forces that were reshaping the pattern of life throughout the world, the United States began at the turn of the century to extend its influence in the Pacific and the Caribbean. The Panama Canal provided a connecting link between the various parts of America's rapidly growing empire. To protect that vital artery of trade, the United States took steps to bring the Caribbean countries under its influence. Each new step the United States government took, each new commitment it assumed, led to additional steps and additional commitments.

By 1914 the United States had formulated two basic foreign policies. The Open Door policy aimed to secure equality of opportunity for Americans in the Far East. The Monroe Doctrine, now strengthened by the Roosevelt Corollary, aimed to safeguard United States interests in the Western Hemisphere.

During the opening years of the 1900's the United States became a world power. But the position of world power brought with it new problems and new responsibilities. In the next chapter you will see why and how the United States was drawn into World War I, and how the nation emerged from that conflict as a great world power.

CHAPTER SURVEY

QUESTIONS FOR DISCUSSION

1. Theodore Roosevelt once said: "I took Panama." (a) What did he mean? (b) What does this say about the power of the Presidency? (c) Why did the United States pay Colombia $25 million in 1921?
2. If, during the period just studied, the Canadian ambassador to the United States had said to the Mexican ambassador to the United States, "We have a common problem between us," what do you think he might have meant?
3. What is your opinion concerning Taft's "dollar diplomacy"? Explain.
4. (a) How would you justify Theodore Roosevelt's policies in the Caribbean? (b) How would you criticize them?
5. The Panama Canal created new commitments for the United States. Explain.
6. How has Puerto Rico benefited from its relationship with the United States?

RELATING PAST TO PRESENT

1. The United States is considering building another canal in Central America, as indicated on the map on page 591. How have political conditions in Panama encouraged this plan?
2. Compare the attitudes of two Latin-American countries toward the United States during the period just studied and in recent years.
3. Some have said that the Monroe Doctrine protected Latin America from Europe but not from the United States. Do you agree or disagree? Explain the reasons for your opinion.

USING MAPS AND CHARTS

1. Use the map on page 591 to help you explain why the Caribbean Sea was once called an "American lake."
2. What is the approximate distance from Miami, Florida, to Havana, Cuba? Why is this information of concern to us today?
3. (a) Identify the countries in Central America. (b) What are their chief products? (Consult an encyclopedia or almanac.) What might this information tell you about their standard of living?
4. On a map of the world, indicate which areas were affected by the major foreign policies and involvements of the United States by 1917.

On THE MORNING of July 28, 1914, Americans opened their newspapers with shocked surprise. In screaming headlines the New York *Tribune* reported, "AUSTRIA DECLARES WAR, RUSHES VAST ARMY INTO SERBIA; RUSSIA MASSES 80,000 MEN ON BORDER." All other American papers that day carried the same news.

In general, the reaction of the American public was one of both stunned disbelief and withdrawal. Europeans could not be so reckless. But if they were, well, then they alone must reap the consequences. Americans wanted no part of this European madness.

The summer of 1914 ushered in a new age—an age characterized by violence and revolution. Within the course of a few fateful months, the fabric of peace went up in flames, and the world was swept into what until then was the most terrible war in history.

The conflict that started in the summer of 1914 spread rapidly. Before it ended four years later, 30 nations on six continents were involved; more than 8 million fighting men had been killed; an equal number of civilians had lost their lives; and property worth countless billions of dollars had gone up in flames.

But before looking at the war itself, it is necessary to answer several important questions: Why did the news of war come as such a surprise to Americans? Why did Americans think that the war was no concern of theirs? And, finally, what at last drew the United States into the conflict?

■ *The sinking of the Lusitania, 1915*

CHAPTER **32**

America's Entry into World War I

1914 – 1920

THE CHAPTER IN OUTLINE

1. American efforts to encourage international cooperation.

2. The outbreak of World War I in Europe despite efforts toward peace.

3. The failure of American attempts to remain neutral.

4. Mobilizing American strength for the war effort.

5. The role of American troops and ideals in helping to win the war.

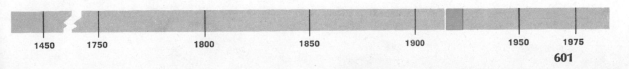

| 1450 | 1750 | 1800 | 1850 | 1900 | 1950 | 1975 |

1 American efforts to encourage international cooperation

During the late 1800's and the early 1900's, the great nations of the world had taken important steps toward international cooperation. By 1914 millions of men and women in both Europe and America were convinced that major wars were a thing of the past.

The peace movement. For nearly 100 years a movement for international peace had been steadily gaining strength (page 335). During the early 1900's antiwar societies in both Europe and America prepared numerous antiwar pamphlets. The pamphlets emphasized that war was wasteful and failed to solve the problems it was intended to solve—that even the victors paid too high a price.

Growing interdependence. It was obvious to everyone that science and technology were rapidly breaking down the barriers of space and time and bringing the peoples of the earth closer together. Railway trains rumbled across national boundaries carrying freight and passengers. Liners and freighters sailed back and forth across the oceans. The telegraph, the telephone, and underwater cables enabled men in all parts of the world to communicate almost instantaneously.

These and other technological developments greatly increased the number, variety, and importance of activities that people of different nations could and did carry on together. Businessmen bought and sold in truly worldwide markets and built industries in foreign countries. Humanitarian associations, among them the Red Cross, organized on an international basis. Professional groups—scientists, engineers, doctors, and scholars—formed international societies and pooled their knowledge for the benefit of all peoples.

International agencies. Governments as well as individual citizens were also engaged in a growing number of activities requiring international cooperation. By 1914, 30 different international agencies of government had been organized to deal with problems shared by many nations, such as transportation, communication, disease and sanitation, weights and measures, postal regulations, and maritime rules.

By bringing the nations of the world together in such cooperative efforts, all of these agencies seemed to strengthen international understanding.

The Pan-American Union. Meanwhile, the governments of the leading nations of the world had been taking direct steps to prevent war. On several occasions during the late 1800's and the early 1900's delegates from many different nations met to discuss the issues of war and peace.

The First International Conference of American States of 1889–90 was one of the early meetings. Delegates from the Latin-American countries and the United States met in Washington, D.C., where, with Secretary of State James G. Blaine serving as

■ During the early 1900's antiwar societies were formed in both Europe and America. The women shown below belonged to a "Peace Party" that urged Americans to stay out of war.

chairman, they organized the International Union of American Republics.

Secretary of State Blaine told the delegates, "We hold up this new Magna Carta, which abolishes war and substitutes arbitration between the American republics, as the first and great fruit of the International American Conference."

In 1910 the name of the International Union of American Republics was changed to the Pan-American Union, and under that name it continued to hold periodic meetings to discuss common problems. (Later, in 1948, the members of the Pan-American Union created the Organization of American States, known as the O.A.S.)

In the early 1900's United States expansion and interference in the Caribbean area aroused the antagonism of a number of Latin-American countries and thus weakened the influence of the Pan-American Union. Nevertheless, to people throughout the Americas, the Pan-American Union was the symbol of a new, more peaceful world that was coming into being.

The Hague Conferences. Millions of people in both Europe and the Americas had also taken hope from two conferences held in Europe.

The First Hague Conference, called by the tsar of Russia, met at The Hague in the Netherlands in 1899. Twenty-six nations sent delegates. The delegates strongly urged nations to try to settle disputes through mediation or arbitration. In cases involving mediation, two or more nations engaged in a dispute would ask a disinterested third party or nation to "recommend" a solution. In cases involving arbitration, two or more nations engaged in a dispute would agree in advance to accept the decision of a neutral party. To encourage nations to submit their disputes to arbitration, the First Hague Conference organized the Permanent Court of Arbitration with headquarters at The Hague. The conference also tried to lessen the horrors of warfare by outlawing certain weapons and by drawing up rules for the conduct of war.

The Second Hague Conference, called by the tsar of Russia and President Theodore Roosevelt, met at The Hague in 1907. This time 44 nations sent delegates. The conference drafted additional "rules" for the conduct of war. It also adopted the Drago Doctrine (page 595), which stated that no nation should use force to collect debts "unless the debtor country refused arbitration, or having accepted arbitration, failed to submit to the award."

The first two Hague Conferences encouraged men who were working to promote peace. Plans were under way for a third conference when war broke out in Europe.

Individual efforts to promote peace. American citizens, both in public office and private life, took an active part in the search for ways to prevent war. Edward Ginn, a well-known Boston publisher, provided a grant of money to establish the World Peace Foundation. Andrew Carnegie set up the Carnegie Endowment for International Peace; donated money to construct the building for the Permanent Court of Arbitration at The Hague; and gave a grant to help construct the Pan-American Union building in Washington, D.C.

Although President Theodore Roosevelt believed that some wars were necessary, he played a leading role in the peace movement. He was responsible, as you know, for the 1905 peace conference held at Portsmouth, New Hampshire, at which Japan and Russia reached an agreement ending the Russo-Japanese War. President Roosevelt and his successor, President Taft, also played an active part in other international negotiations.

President Wilson, who entered the White House in 1913, was an even stronger champion of international understanding. He supported his Secretary of State, William Jennings Bryan, who negotiated antiwar treaties with 21 nations in 1913 and 1914. These treaties declared that every controversy, without exception, must be submitted to a joint commission for investigation and recommendation. The nations signing these treaties promised not to go to war until the commissions had made their reports.

By 1914 men had built what seemed to be a solid and enduring structure of peace. Why, then, did war break out?

SECTION SURVEY

IDENTIFY: interdependence of men and nations, mediation, arbitration.

1. Describe the factors which led to the peace movement of the early 1900's.
2. Why did many people think that the Pan-American Union held bright promise for the future?
3. Why did the first two Hague Conferences greatly encourage men who were working to promote peace?
4. Describe briefly the efforts made by individuals to promote peace and international understanding in the years preceding World War I.

2 The outbreak of World War I in Europe despite efforts toward peace

War broke out in 1914 because the elaborate safeguards men had built to prevent war were less strong than the divisive forces pulling nations apart. Despite the many efforts made to preserve peace in the early 1900's, the European nations during these years were standing on a powder keg. When a spark was struck to the powder, all men's hopes and plans for peace exploded.

The "spark" that led to war. The spark was struck in the Balkan Peninsula of Europe (see map, this page) in the early summer of 1914 by Serbian nationalists who were pledged to free all

fellow Slavs ° living under the rule of the Austro-Hungarian empire. The Serbian nationalists assassinated the Archduke Franz Ferdinand, heir to the throne of Austria-Hungary, and his wife as they rode through the streets of Sarajevo (SAH·rah·yeh·vo), capital of the province of Bosnia. Bosnia had only recently been incorporated into the Austro-Hungarian empire.

The Serbian conspirators were caught and brought to trial. But Franz Joseph, the 83-year-old emperor of Austria-Hungary, and his advisers decided to use this opportunity to destroy Serbia's

° *Slavs:* a people widely spread over central, eastern, and southeastern Europe whose languages come from the same basic root. The Slavs under Austro-Hungarian rule were called South Slavs.

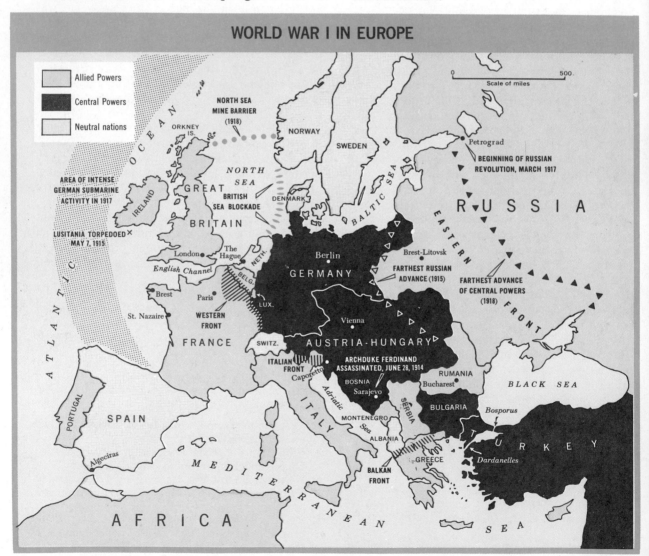

WORLD WAR I IN EUROPE

■ The spark that set off World War I was only minutes away on June 28, 1914, when Archduke Franz Ferdinand and his wife, both fated for assassination, drove away from the Senate House at Sarajevo. (They are seated in the back of the car.)

power completely. Accordingly, Austria-Hungary made certain harsh demands against Serbia, which Serbia refused to meet.

As tension mounted, European diplomats struggled to solve the differences between Austria-Hungary and Serbia. But Austria lined up the support of its main ally, Germany, and prepared for war. Austria-Hungary declared war on Serbia on July 28, 1914, and Austrian armies began to move southward across the border.

The spread of war. The action of Austria-Hungary set in motion a chain of explosive events. Russia, a Slavic country sometimes called the "Protector of the Slavs," immediately prepared to go to Serbia's aid. Germany promptly declared war on Russia on August 1. When France, an ally of Russia, refused to declare its neutrality, Germany on August 3 declared war on France. Great Britain, an ally of France, then declared war on Germany on August 4 and on Austria on August 12.

A week after Austria-Hungary's attack on Serbia, then, five major European nations were at war. Before the conflict ended, it had engulfed 30 nations on six continents. The nations siding with Austria-Hungary and Germany were known as the Central Powers. Those allying themselves with Russia, France, and Great Britain were referred to as the Allied Powers, or simply as the Allies.

Did the tragic incident at Sarajevo really start World War I? Yes and no. It was the immediate cause, the spark that touched off the explosion. But there were deep, underlying causes which help to explain why the war came and why it spread so rapidly and so widely.

Nationalism as a cause. An intense spirit of nationalism was one of the underlying sources of tension. The term *nationalism* often refers to the strong feeling people have for their own country, but it may also refer to the desire of a subjugated people to throw off foreign rule and create their

605

own nation. As you have seen, it was a desire to free certain Slavs from Austro-Hungarian rule that prompted the Serbian conspirators to assassinate the heir to the throne of Austria-Hungary. And Austria-Hungary declared war on Serbia in order to crush the rising spirit of nationalism among the Slavic people and to hold the Austro-Hungarian empire together. But the spirit of nationalism was not confined to the Balkan Peninsula. In almost every country of Europe, as well as in the colonies overseas, subjugated people longed for independence.

Imperialism as a cause. Another disruptive force was imperialism—the struggle for colonies. As you have read (pages 574–86), during the late 1800's and the early 1900's the major powers of the world were engaged in a race for empire. By 1914, so far as colonies were concerned, the nations of Europe could be grouped into two classes: the "have" nations and the "have-not."

Great Britain and France, each with huge colonial empires, were among the "have" powers. Although Russia owned no colonies, it did possess immense areas of underdeveloped land, and thus was also a "have" nation.

Germany, on the other hand, was a "have-not" nation. It did own colonies in Africa and in the Pacific, but its colonial empire was relatively small, and Germany wanted additional territory. Italy was in a similar situation—and one of the reasons that finally brought Italy into the war on the Allied side was a promise of colonies when the war ended.

International rivalries. Rivalry among nations was not, however, confined to the race for colonies. Austria-Hungary attacked Serbia partly to strengthen its hold on the Slavic peoples and to increase its influence in the Balkan Peninsula. Russia, on the other hand, came to Serbia's aid to prevent Austria-Hungary from increasing its influence.

France supported Russia not only because it was Russia's ally, but also because it wanted to recover Alsace-Lorraine, a former French area which the Germans had secured in 1871. Italy desired nearby territories within the Austro-Hungarian empire. Every Balkan country looked greedily at territory belonging to its neighbors. Russia longed for ice-free harbors in the Baltic Sea and for an outlet through the Dardanelles and the Bosporus into the Mediterranean Sea. Germany, the major Baltic Sea power, and Turkey, which controlled the Dardanelles, feared and distrusted Russia.

Search for a system of alliances. The mounting tensions with their accompanying plots and intrigues led inevitably to an armament race. Long before 1914 the relative sizes of navies and armies occupied a major part of the attention of every European government.

Besides building up their military forces, European nations tried to gain security with the *balance-of-power system*. This meant, in the simplest terms, that every nation tried to increase its own strength by securing as many allies as possible. Thus Germany, Austria-Hungary, and Italy joined in what became known as the Triple Alliance. And, to maintain a balance of power, Great Britain, France, and Russia formed what became known as the "Triple Entente" (ahn·TAHNT). Both of these rival alliances had been completed by 1907.

Austria's declaration of war on Serbia immediately set the whole system of alliances into motion. Of all the nations, only Italy failed to live up to its obligations under the treaties binding it to Austria-Hungary and Germany. Holding out to see which side would promise the most, Italy did not enter the war until 1915, and then on the Allied side.

Peace or war? During the early 1900's, as you have seen, strong forces pulled men and nations in two directions at the same time. With one hand, governments tried to strengthen the bonds between nations and build a solid structure of peace. With the other hand, governments plotted and schemed against one another and desperately planned for war or for the protection of their national interests in the event that war broke out.

SECTION SURVEY

IDENTIFY: Slavs, nationalism, imperialism, balance-of-power system, "have" and "have-not" nations, Central Powers, Allied Powers; 1914.

1. Why is the incident at Sarajevo considered the spark that set off World War I?
2. Discuss how the following factors help to explain why World War I came and why it spread so rapidly and so widely: (a) nationalism, (b) imperialism, (c) international rivalries, (d) the balance-of-power system.
3. How are the four factors listed in question 2 interrelated?
4. How do you think a nation prepares itself psychologically for war?

3 The failure of American attempts to remain neutral

America's first reaction to the outbreak of war in Europe, as you have seen, was one of shocked surprise and withdrawal. The war seemed unreal, a nightmare that would not last.

American neutrality. But the war was all too real, and on August 19, 1914, President Wilson urged the American people to be "neutral in fact as well as in name" and "impartial in thought as well as in action." Americans did not find it easy to follow President Wilson's advice. From the beginning they were torn between the desire to avoid war and sympathy for one side or the other.

Millions of recently naturalized Americans had friends and relations in Europe. Men and women of German origin—or of Austrian or Turkish origin—wanted the Central Powers to win. Those of Irish origin saw in the war a chance for Ireland to win independence from Great Britain.

On the other hand, most Americans were sympathetic to the Allied Powers. The ties of language, similar democratic governments, and deep-rooted traditions bound Americans to Great Britain. The ties with France were also strong.

After all, the French back in 1778 had come to the aid of Americans fighting for their independence. As World War I went on, this sympathy for the Allies led thousands of young Americans to enlist in the British, Canadian, and French armies. A special unit of volunteer American fliers, called the Lafayette Escadrille, was created as part of the new French flying force.

Although in 1914 American sympathies were divided, the great majority of Americans hoped for an Allied victory. On the other hand, most Americans supported the President's policy of neutrality and prayed for an early end to the war.

The German plan of attack. The Central Powers, under the leadership of the German High Command, had every intention of ending the war quickly. They intended to conquer France before the Russians could fully mobilize. With France at their mercy, they could then turn against Russia.

Long before the war the French, fearful of German attack, had built powerful fortifications along the entire Franco-German frontier. But the French had not fortified the border between France and Belgium. The French counted on an international agreement, which the Germans had signed, that in the event of war Belgium would be respected as a neutral nation.

■ Disregarding an international agreement that, in the event of war, Belgium's neutrality would be respected, German troops marched into Belgium in 1914.

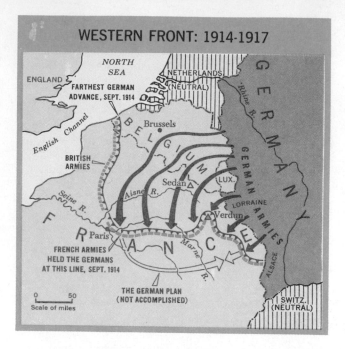

WESTERN FRONT: 1914-1917

NORTH SEA

ENGLAND

NETHERLANDS (NEUTRAL)

FARTHEST GERMAN ADVANCE, SEPT. 1914

GERMANY

English Channel

Rhine R.

BELGIUM

Brussels

BRITISH ARMIES

GERMAN ARMIES

Aisne R.

Sedan

LUX.

Seine R.

LORRAINE

Verdun

FRANCE

Paris

Marne R.

ALSACE

FRENCH ARMIES HELD THE GERMANS AT THIS LINE, SEPT. 1914

THE GERMAN PLAN (NOT ACCOMPLISHED)

0   50
Scale of miles

SWITZ. (NEUTRAL)

The German Chancellor, however, called the international agreement respecting Belgium's neutrality merely "a scrap of paper," and the German High Command launched its offensive against neutral Belgium and against Luxembourg as well, intending to reach the borders of France in six days. As shown on the map above, seven powerful German armies were to strike in a great wheeling motion at northern France.

Failure of the German plan. The German plan failed, largely because Belgium resisted. Fighting gallantly, the small Belgian army compelled the Germans to take 18 days to cross Belgium, not the six called for in the German timetable. This delay gave General Joffre, commander of the French armies, time to rush troops to the Belgian border. It also gave the British time to transport an army of about 90,000 men to northern France.

The French and the British arrived too late to save Belgium. Nor were they able to stop the Germans at the Belgian frontier. Crushed by the superior might of the Germans, the French and British retreated to the Marne River, where Joffre hastily prepared his main defense.

Fighting against seemingly hopeless odds, the French and British stopped the German offensive early in September 1914 at the Marne River in the First Battle of the Marne. The Germans then fell back to the Aisne (AYN) River, where they dug a line of trenches and checked an Allied counter-offensive.

The First Battle of the Marne was one of the most decisive battles of the war. If the Germans had won, they might have crushed all remaining French and British resistance in a few weeks.

"All quiet on the Western Front." By 1915 the war in Western Europe had reached a stalemate. Both sides were entrenched along a 600-mile line reaching from the Swiss border to the English Channel. During the next three years both the Germans and the Allies, with only a thin strip of land called "no man's land" separating their trenches, fought desperately to gain control of the Western Front. But neither side was able to break through the enemy line or to end the trench warfare. Many thousands of men died in this bloody struggle, but until the spring of 1918 neither side made any significant gains.

There were, to be sure, other fronts—and on all of them, as well in Western Europe, men were fighting and dying. The Central Powers and Russia were locked in combat along the entire Eastern Front. Turkish troops defended a precarious line that reached southward through Palestine as far as Medina, in Arabia, against the British and French and their allies. Fighting men of Austria-Hungary and Italy faced each other in the area of their common boundary north of the Adriatic Sea (see map, page 604).

British interference with American trade. The prospect of a long war was bad news indeed for Americans who hoped to remain neutral. It meant, among other things, that warfare on the high seas would be intensified as Great Britain and Germany tried to prevent supplies from the United States and other neutral countries from reaching the other side.

The British fleet, which controlled the seas, at least during the opening months of the war, blockaded the German coast (see map, page 604) and laid explosive mines in the North Sea. To the angry astonishment of Americans, the British navy also blockaded neutral countries, such as Norway, Sweden, Denmark, and the Netherlands, through which American goods flowed into Germany. American anger increased when the British began to examine American mail bound for Europe and ordered all neutral ships to stop at British ports, where their cargoes were searched.

The United States vigorously protested that Great Britain's actions were "illegal" and a flagrant violation of the "rights of neutrals" to travel the

■ During the long stalemate along the 600-mile front in Europe, British soldiers left their trenches for frequent harassing raids against the Germans.

high seas provided they were not carrying war materials.

Submarine warfare. American anger at Great Britain subsided, however, in the face of German submarine warfare.

According to international law, naval vessels of countries at war had the right to stop and search a neutral ship. If the neutral ship carried arms, munitions, and other materials useful in war, known as *contraband*, the naval vessel had the right to seize the neutral ship and take it into port as a prize of war. If it were impossible to take the neutral vessel into port, the warship was required to take passengers and crew to a safe place before sinking the prize.

Submarines, however, could not take seized vessels into port because they were not armed to defend themselves against enemy warships while on the surface. Nor could submarines take the passengers and crew of a large vessel on board. Least of all could they surface and search neutral ships, for the moment that they rose to the surface they were "sitting ducks" for even one well-aimed shot from a naval gun. By their very nature, submarines were designed to lurk in the ocean depths, to strike suddenly without warning at an enemy ship, and to get away before a counterattack.

German submarines unleashed. The German surface fleet, although powerful, was still no match for the British navy. The Germans, therefore, had concentrated on building submarines, called U-boats. Early in the war the Germans notified President Wilson that they intended to turn their submarines loose in the Atlantic. President Wilson promptly replied that the United States would hold Germany responsible for any acts that endangered American property and lives on the high seas.

Sinking of the *Lusitania*. The Germans were convinced that their submarine blockade would ruin Great Britain. They therefore ignored President Wilson's warning and ordered their U-boats to patrol the Atlantic shipping lanes. On March 28, 1915, a British steamer was torpedoed and sunk near Ireland, carrying to death more than 100 persons, including an American.

This and other incidents were the prelude to the sinking of the British liner *Lusitania* off the southern coast of Ireland on May 7, 1915, with the loss of 1,198 lives, including 128 Americans. Since the *Lusitania* was carrying war materials bound for England, the Germans held that they were not responsible.

In three vigorous messages to the German government in Berlin, the American State Department protested against the sinking of the *Lusitania* and warned that any repetition of such action would lead to serious consequences. American anger at the *Lusitania* affair was still at the boiling point when on August 19, 1915, another U-boat sank the *Arabic,* a British liner, with the loss of two American lives.

Alarmed at the furious indignation of the American people, Germany on September 1 gave a written promise that in the future "Liners will not be sunk by our submarines without warning . . . provided that the liners do not try to escape or offer resistance." Americans had to be content with this promise.

The sinking of the *Lusitania* marked a turning point in American feeling about the war. Increasing numbers of Americans began to realize that the conflict in Europe was not far off but close at hand. They began to understand that neutrality might become impossible. Nevertheless, in 1915 most Americans continued to hope that the United States could avoid war.

SECTION SURVEY

IDENTIFY: "All quiet on the Western Front," trench warfare, "no man's land," contraband, U-boats, *Lusitania.*

1. The United States, Wilson asserted, "must be neutral in fact as well as in name" and "impartial in thought as well as in action." Why did Americans find it difficult to heed President Wilson's appeal?
2. America's neutral rights were violated by Great Britain and Germany. Explain.
3. How did Americans react to submarine warfare? Why?
4. Wilson was faced with the dilemma of keeping the United States out of war while making sure that the nation's neutral rights were protected. Comment.

610

4 Mobilizing American strength for the war effort

From the summer of 1914 to the spring of 1917, the United States moved slowly toward war. As time passed, more and more Americans came to believe that neutrality was impossible.

More sinkings, more promises. In March 1916 the Germans broke their promise and attacked a French passenger vessel, the *Sussex*. Lives were lost and several Americans were injured. President Wilson promptly threatened to break off diplomatic relations with Germany unless it agreed to abandon its methods of submarine warfare.

In what became known as the *"Sussex* pledge," Germany renewed its earlier promise not to sink liners without warning and without providing for the safety of the passengers. But the Germans added an important reservation. They would keep the promise on condition that the United States would persuade the Allies to modify the food blockade of Germany, which, according to Berlin, was inflicting hunger and starvation on German women and children. The United States replied that the British blockade had nothing to do with German violation of American neutral rights on the high seas.

A rising war spirit. American opinion was divided over Wilson's efforts to enforce neutrality. Some people, including former President Theodore Roosevelt, felt that the United States was not firm enough. Others believed that the American government was unwisely going too far in its threatening demands on Berlin. Secretary of State Bryan, for example, resigned during the *Lusitania* crisis. In Bryan's opinion, the United States should forbid American citizens to travel on British and French ships. Bryan also believed that Congress should stop Americans from selling war materials to belligerents.

Preparing for war. President Wilson refused to follow the advice of Bryan and others who shared Bryan's views. Instead, Wilson helped to arouse the public to support a program for strengthening the army and the navy. The National Defense Act, passed in June 1916, increased America's regular army from 106,000 to 175,000 men and provided for officers' training camps. A three-year naval program, begun in 1916, was carried out vigorously. In 1916 the government also created the Council of National Defense and the United States Shipping Board. These agencies planned for the mobilization of the country's resources in case of war and launched a huge shipbuilding program.

The war preparations did not mean that either the administration or the American public had abandoned all hope of remaining neutral. Indeed, many Americans voted for the re-election of Wilson in November 1916 on the ground that "he kept us out of war."

But six months later, under the leadership of the President and Congress, the American people entered the conflict, millions of them with considerable enthusiasm. What happened to lead the administration to take this momentous step?

Diplomatic relations broken. On February 1, 1917, Germany renewed its unrestricted submarine warfare, thus going back on the *"Sussex* pledge." A German proposal to permit only one American passenger ship to sail to England each week added insult to injury.

The German High Command decided to renew unrestricted submarine warfare, fully aware that this decision would almost certainly bring the United States into the war. The High Command took the calculated risk that submarines could destroy Great Britain's power and will to fight before the United States could provide effective help.

Wilson met the new challenge promptly. On February 3 he broke off diplomatic relations with the German government.

Moving toward war. On February 24 British naval intelligence agents handed to the American ambassador to Great Britain a German message they had intercepted and decoded. The message had been sent from Germany by Foreign Secretary Alfred Zimmerman to the German minister in Mexico. It contained instructions about what to do in case war broke out between Germany and the United States. In this event, the German minister was to offer Mexico an alliance with Germany. With German support Mexico was to attack the United States and "reconquer the lost territory in New Mexico, Texas, and Arizona." President Wilson released the Zimmerman note to the Associated Press on March 1. Americans were shocked and angry.

On March 12 President Wilson, through the State Department, announced that all American merchant vessels operating through war zones would be armed for defense against German submarines. The public received this announcement with mixed reactions, but in general approved.

Still other and deeper forces moved American sympathies toward the Allies and toward war with Germany. For one thing, American ties with Great Britain and France were traditionally closer than those with Germany. Not least important, American shipments of munitions to the Allied Powers had risen from $6 million in 1914 to nearly $500 million in 1916, and by April 1917 American bankers had lent about $2 billion to the Allies. Naturally, these American investors wanted an Allied victory. But historians have found no evidence to indicate that economic interests influenced President Wilson's conduct in the critical weeks before the war.

The President's "War Message." As the weeks passed, President Wilson reluctantly concluded

■ The United States officially entered World War I in April 1917. Before the year was out, nearly 2 million Americans had poured into military training camps. Below, raw recruits, not yet in uniform, are shown how to salute.

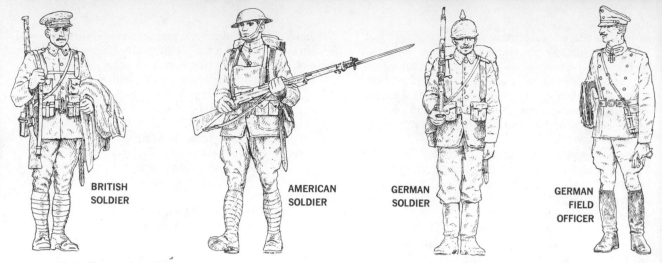

BRITISH
SOLDIER

AMERICAN
SOLDIER

GERMAN
SOLDIER

GERMAN
FIELD
OFFICER

■ Uniforms of World War I

that America's entrance into the war was inevitable. On March 20 he called an emergency cabinet meeting. He and his official advisers gravely considered the entire situation, from the long-standing grievances against Germany to the recent disturbing incidents. Supported by his entire cabinet, the President on March 21 called a special session of Congress for April 2. On April 2, 1917, a solemn and hushed group of Senators, Representatives, and a number of distinguished guests gathered to hear President Wilson present his "War Message."

The President condemned Germany's submarine

■ **Machine Gun.** By the time of World War I, this deadly 30-caliber Browning machine gun had evolved. Mounted on tripod legs (shown in part), the gun fired rapidly when the trigger was pulled and the "cartridge belt" moved automatically past the "barrel," bringing the "cartridges" one after another into position for firing. The "barrel" was cooled by water contained in the "water jacket."

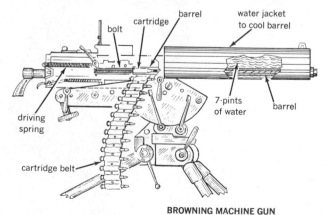

BROWNING MACHINE GUN

warfare as "the wanton and wholesale destruction of the lives of noncombatants, men, women, and children, engaged in pursuits which have always, even in the darkest periods of modern history, been deemed innocent and legitimate. Property can be paid for; the lives of peaceful and innocent people cannot be. . . . The challenge is to all mankind. . . . We will not choose the path of submission and suffer the most sacred rights of our Nation and our people to be ignored or violated," the President declared. "The wrongs against which we now array ourselves are no common wrongs; they cut to the very roots of human life."

Making the world "safe for democracy." But Wilson was too great an idealist to rest his case upon the evils of unrestricted submarine warfare alone. He also summoned the American people to rise in a crusade for a better world: "We are glad, now that we see the facts with no veil of false pretense about them, to fight thus for the ultimate peace of the world and for the liberation of its peoples, the German peoples included: for the rights of nations great and small and the privilege of men everywhere to choose their way of life and of obedience. The world must be made safe for democracy. Its peace must be planted upon the tested foundations of political liberty. We have no selfish ends to serve. We desire no conquest, no dominion. We seek no indemnities for ourselves, no material compensation for the sacrifices we shall freely make."

War declared. Congress promptly declared war. The Senate approved a war declaration on April 4, the House on April 6, 1917.

America's entry into the conflict had an immediate effect upon other neutral countries. Between

April 1917 and July 1918 a number of Latin-American states declared war. Most of the other American countries, although unwilling to enter the war, severed diplomatic relations with Germany.

Raising an army.   As soon as war was declared the United States set in motion a vast mobilization of its manpower, its industries, and its natural resources. On May 18 Congress adopted the Selective Service Act, which provided for the registration of all men between the ages of 21 and 30. The act was amended on August 31, 1918, to include all men between 18 and 45. Before the war ended, more than 24 million men were registered by their local draft boards, and 2.8 million of this group were drafted into the army. Before the war ended more than 4.7 million men served in the United States armed forces.

Even before the draft began to operate, construction had been started on training camps. During the summer and fall of 1917 nearly 2 million Americans poured into these camps to begin military training.

Negroes in uniform.   About 371,000 Negroes served in World War I, but, as in earlier wars, they often met prejudice and discrimination. Black servicemen were restricted to separate units, recreation centers, and living accommodations. Most of the 200,000 black troops sent to Europe served in noncombat battalions, though many of these men requested combat duty. All of the 10,000 Negroes who served in the navy were assigned to non-combat duties.

As the war progressed, the bravery and courage of black units under fire were plain to see. The first Allied unit to drive through to the River Rhine was the 369th, a Negro regiment attached to the Ninety-Third Division. For outstanding courage in battle, Henry Johnson and Needham Roberts of the 369th became the first black Americans to receive the *Croix de Guerre,* or "cross of war," a coveted French military honor.

Financing the war.   To secure money to finance the war, Congress decided to raise approximately two thirds by borrowing, the remaining one third by taxing current income.

The government borrowed money by selling war bonds. Through four "Liberty Loan Drives" and a "Victory Loan Drive," the government borrowed more than $21 billion. The government also raised money by boosting income-tax rates and by levying excise taxes on railroad tickets, telegraph and telephone messages, alcoholic beverages, tobacco, and certain amusements.

Mobilizing industry.   Materials were as important as manpower and money. The big problem was to stimulate production and prevent waste. To achieve this goal, Congress gave the President sweeping wartime powers. He was authorized to set prices on many commodities, including food and fuels. He was also authorized to regulate, or even to take possession of, factories, mines, meat-packing houses, food-processing plants, and all transportation and communication facilities. The President exercised these vast powers through a number of wartime agencies, or boards.

The War Industries Board, established in 1917, became the virtual dictator of manufacturing. It

■ These soldiers attending a radio class were among the 371,000 Negroes who served in World War I. As in earlier wars, black servicemen often met with prejudice and discrimination and were restricted to separate units.

developed new industries needed in the war effort. It regulated business to eliminate waste and nonessential goods. Before the war's end, the War Industries Board was regulating the production of some 30,000 commodities.

Other federal agencies also took an active part in planning the war program. The War Finance Corporation lent public funds to businesses needing aid in manufacturing war materials. The Emergency Fleet Corporation built ships faster than German submarines could destroy them. The Railroad Administration took over the operation of the railroads, reorganized the lines, and controlled rates and wages in the interest of war efficiency. The Fuel Administration stimulated a larger output of coal and oil, and encouraged economies in their use.

Mobilizing labor. The successful mobilization of industry depended, of course, upon the complete cooperation of labor. In an effort to deal with labor disputes, President Wilson in April 1918 appointed the National War Labor Board. This board was authorized to arbitrate disputes between workers and employers. In June Wilson appointed the War Labor Policies Board. This board was authorized to establish general policies affecting wages, hours, and working conditions. These measures and the cooperation of organized labor reduced labor disputes to a minimum during the war years.

Conserving food. The problem of food was equally critical. Late in 1917, in part to help conserve grain, which is used in making alcohol, Congress adopted and submitted to the states an amendment to the Constitution prohibiting the manufacture, sale, or transportation of alcoholic liquors. This Eighteenth Amendment was ratified by the necessary three fourths of the states in 1919, and went into effect on January 16, 1920.

The government also made other moves to guarantee food for the American people and their allies. Herbert Hoover, who had successfully managed food relief in war-stricken Belgium, was placed in charge of the Food Administration. Hoover brought about a vast expansion of agriculture, curtailed the hoarding and waste of food, encouraged people to plant "victory gardens," and urged them to observe "wheatless" and "meatless" days. The sale of sugar and other commodities was limited. All this took place without rationing, or actual limiting of the sale of food. Under Hoover, the Food Administration depended on publicity and persuasion to get people to cooperate in conserving food.

Mobilizing public opinion. The government also undertook to gain the cooperation of all Americans in the war effort.

The Committee on Public Information circulated millions of leaflets describing in glowing language America's official war aims and denouncing the German government. Colleges, schools, the press, churches, fraternal lodges, women's organizations, and civic groups all cooperated with the government's campaign "to sell the war to the American people." In all sorts of public gatherings, the war aims were publicized in brief speeches delivered by well-known people called "Four-Minute Men." Never before had the government tried to influence the minds of the people on so vast a scale.

■ Colleges, schools, the press, churches, fraternal lodges, women's organizations, and civic groups all cooperated with the government's campaign "to sell the war to the American people." The poster shown below illustrates some of the roles taken by women during the war.

SERVICE

FALL IN!

NATIONAL LEAGUE FoR WOMANS SERVICE

Controlling dissent. From the beginning most Americans enthusiastically supported the war. There were, however, some dissenters, who, in greater or lesser measure, were not in sympathy with the war effort.

To deal with these people, Congress in June 1917 adopted the Espionage Act. This act was aimed at treasonable and disloyal activities. In May 1918 Congress strengthened the Espionage Act by an amendment, often called the Sedition Act. This act provided penalties of up to $10,000 in fines and 20 years' imprisonment, or both, for anyone found guilty of interfering with the sale of war bonds, attempting to curtail production, or using "disloyal, profane, scurrilous, or abusive language" about the American form of government or any of its agencies.

Operating under these laws, the Department of Justice arrested at least 1,597 persons. Of these, 41 received prison sentences of from 10 to 20 years. In addition, newspapers and periodicals that criticized the government's conduct of the war were deprived of their mailing privileges.

Many loyal Americans, themselves thoroughly in sympathy with the war effort, objected to the Espionage Act and the Sedition Act. They held that the constitutional rights of citizens should not be interfered with, even in wartime.

For the most part, however, Americans did not need persuasive arguments or restrictive laws to secure their loyalty. Americans entered the war on a great wave of enthusiasm, convinced, as Wilson had put it, that this was indeed a crusade "to make the world safe for democracy."

SECTION SURVEY

IDENTIFY: *"Sussex* pledge," Zimmerman note, unrestricted submarine warfare, Selective Service Act, Espionage Act; Henry Johnson; April 1917.

1. In his War Message, President Wilson asked Congress to declare war on Germany. (a) What reasons did he give? (b) Why did he view the war as a crusade?
2. How did the United States mobilize its (a) manpower, (b) industries, (c) natural resources, (d) public opinion?
3. In the crusade "to make the world safe for democracy," black servicemen often faced discrimination. How do you explain this contradiction?
4. During wartime, the right to dissent should be curtailed by the federal government. Do you agree or disagree? Explain.

5 The role of American troops and ideals in helping to win the war

America's declaration of war came none too soon. In the spring of 1917 the Allies were facing a grim situation, and by the end of the year their position was desperate.

The military situation in 1917. By early 1917 the Allies, who had suffered enormous losses, were war-weary and discouraged. In March they were further disturbed by news that the tsar of Russia had been deposed and a new revolutionary government established.

America's entry into the conflict in April was one of the few bright spots in a year during which Allied fortunes sank lower and lower.

In the fall Germany threw a number of crack divisions into the Austrian campaign, and on October 24 a combined force of Austrians and Germans crashed through the Italian lines at Caporetto (see map, page 604). French and British troops, rushed from the Western Front, helped to stop the rout and saved Italy from collapse.

Most serious of all, however, was the news from Russia. On November 7 the Bolsheviks, a party of radical Communists, seized power. A month later the Bolsheviks signed an armistice with Germany. Almost three months later, in March 1918, they concluded the peace treaty of Brest-Litovsk (BREST lih-TOFSK). Meanwhile Rumania, unable to stand alone against the Central Powers in eastern Europe, had sued for peace and in 1918 signed a peace treaty at Bucharest.

Thus by the end of 1917 the Germans were free to concentrate most of their forces on the Western Front. General Ludendorff, commander of the German armies, prepared for an offensive intended to end the war before American troops could play an important role.

American naval forces. Meanwhile the United States Navy, which had been rapidly building its strength since 1916, went into action. Before the war ended, Admiral William S. Sims, Commander of the United States Naval Forces Operating in European Waters, had established 45 naval bases, which were located as far north as Murmansk, in Russia, and as far south as Greece.

In cooperation with the British navy, American naval forces patrolled the North Sea and effectively bottled up the German fleet. They also laid most of a 230-mile barrier of mines that stretched across the North Sea from Norway to the Orkney Islands (see map, page 604). This barrier greatly increased the hazards for German submarines seeking to reach the open waters of the Atlantic Ocean or to return to their bases in Germany.

Meanwhile other naval vessels helped to convoy merchant ships and troop transports through the submarine-infested waters of the Atlantic Ocean. The Anglo-American convoy system was so effective that 2 million men or more were transported to Europe with the loss of only a few hundred lives. It was a remarkable tribute to naval efficiency. It was also a severe blow to the German High Command.

Arrival of the A.E.F. in France. While the United States Navy was busy on the high seas, the land forces were being organized.

President Wilson appointed General John J. Pershing as Commander of the American Expeditionary Forces (the A.E.F.). A West Point graduate, Pershing had served in Cuba, in the Philippines, and in 1916 as commander of the expedition sent into Mexico to capture Pancho Villa.

Pershing landed in France early in June 1917. By the end of June the first regiments of the First Division arrived, and on July 4 several thousand "Yanks" marched through Paris amid the heartfelt cheers of the French people.

American troops arrived in ever-swelling numbers. By May 1918 they were pouring in at the rate of 10,000 a day. By the fall of 1918 more than 2 million had landed in France. To supply and maintain this huge army, the Americans built docks, 1,000 miles of railroad, and thousands of miles of telephone and telegraph lines in Europe. They landed 17,000 freight cars and more than 40,000 trucks. The Americans also built training camps, hospitals, storage houses, and ammunition dumps.

Germany's last bid for victory. On March 21, 1918, the Western Front exploded into violent action as the Germans, reinforced by seasoned troops released from the Russian front, launched a powerful campaign, or "peace offensive," to end the war. At the end of two weeks, the Germans had gained 1,500 square miles and inflicted 160,000 casualties. By the end of May they were at the River Marne, only 37 miles from Paris.

Pershing's original plans had called for a period of training behind the lines before his troops went into action. He had also insisted that American troops fight as a separate army under their own top command. But in the spring of 1918 he con-

sented to putting every available man into the lines immediately. French, British, and American troops fought under a unified Allied command directed by the French military leader, Marshal Foch (FOSH).

Stopping the German advance. Fighting desperately, French, British, Belgian, and American troops finally stopped the Germans. On May 28 the First Division of the United States Army took Cantigny (kahn·tee·NYEE). Three days later the Third Division, in a last ditch defense of Paris, only 40 miles away, helped the French hold the Germans at Château-Thierry (shah·TOH teh·REE). At Belleau (BEL·loh) Wood the Second Division, strengthened by the 4th Marine Brigade, held back the Germans in six days of fighting (see map, page 617).

Then, on July 15, the Germans threw everything they could into one final ferocious assault around Reims (REEMZ). In this action, the beginning of the Second Battle of the Marne, the Allied lines held, and on July 18 Marshal Foch ordered a counterattack spearheaded by the First and Second American Divisions and the First French Morocco Division. The Germans began to fall back. The tide at last had turned.

The Allied victory drive. The Allies now took the initiative. In July Foch launched a terrific offensive along the entire length of the line. The Germans were driven back.

Fighting as a separate American army under General Pershing's command, the American troops, 500,000 strong and supported by French troops and British planes, launched a powerful attack on the area around St. Mihiel (SAN mee·YEL) in September 1918. After three days of savage fighting, this section of the southern front was under American control.

Then, against withering artillery and machine-gun fire, the Americans drove toward Sedan, the highly fortified position that the Germans had held since 1914. For 47 days the United States troops pushed toward their objective. The fighting in this tremendous Meuse-Argonne (MYOOZ ahr·GUN) offensive involved 1.2 million combatants. The Americans alone suffered 120,000 casualties. But they pushed the German line back 30 miles and captured 28,000 prisoners and large supplies of war materials.

Important though they were, the American victories represented only part of the tremendous offensive against the crumbling German lines. Bel-

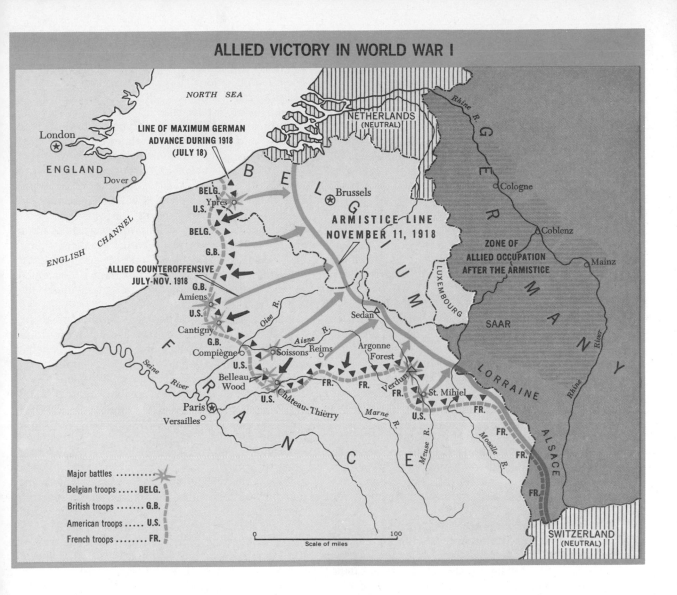

Allied Victory in World War I map showing: NORTH SEA, London, Dover, ENGLAND, ENGLISH CHANNEL, LINE OF MAXIMUM GERMAN ADVANCE DURING 1918 (JULY 18), NETHERLANDS (NEUTRAL), Rhine R., GERMANY, Cologne, Coblenz, Mainz, Brussels, BELGIUM, ARMISTICE LINE NOVEMBER 11, 1918, LUXEMBOURG, ZONE OF ALLIED OCCUPATION AFTER THE ARMISTICE, SAAR, ALLIED COUNTEROFFENSIVE JULY-NOV. 1918, BELG., Ypres, U.S., G.B., Amiens, Cantigny, Compiègne, Soissons, Sedan, Reims, Aisne R., Argonne Forest, Oise R., Belleau Wood, Château-Thierry, U.S., FR., Verdun, St. Mihiel, LORRAINE, ALSACE, Rhine River, Moselle R., Meuse R., Marne R., Seine River, FRANCE, Paris, Versailles, SWITZERLAND (NEUTRAL). Legend: Major battles, Belgian troops BELG., British troops G.B., American troops U.S., French troops FR. Scale of miles 0-100.

gians, British, and French, confident of victory, were fighting fiercely against the enemy along the entire front.

Under these hammer blows German morale began to sag, and Germany's allies lost heart. In September the Turkish armies in Palestine and Arabia suffered crushing blows, and Bulgaria surrendered unconditionally. On November 3 the crews of the German ships at Kiel, a German naval base, mutinied rather than put to sea. Army units also mutinied, and riots broke out in German cities. On November 3 Austria signed an armistice with the Italians.

Convinced at last that the war was lost, Kaiser Wilhelm II, ruler of Germany, fled to the Netherlands, leaving his country in the hands of revolutionists, who signed an armistice with the Allies on November 11, 1918.

The armistice terms. The armistice was signed in a railroad car on a siding in the forest of Compiègne (kon·PYEN·y) on the eleventh hour of the eleventh day of the eleventh month of 1918. The Germans signed grimly, for the terms of the armistice were severe.

The Germans agreed to evacuate France, Belgium, Luxembourg, and Alsace-Lorraine without delay. They agreed to surrender to the Allies an enormous amount of war materials, including most of Germany's naval vessels, and to return prisoners, money, and all valuables taken from the occupied countries. They agreed to renounce the Treaty of Brest-Litovsk with Russia and the Treaty of Bucharest with Rumania.

In addition, the Allies reserved the right to occupy all German territory west of the Rhine as well as a strip of territory about 18 miles wide that lay along the east bank of the Rhine (see map, page 617).

Wilson's Fourteen Points. An American expression of idealism, as well as American fighting strength, played a large part in breaking the Central Powers' will to fight. This important part of the story of World War I goes back to the early winter of 1917–18.

As you recall, in November 1917 the Bolsheviks seized control of Russia and shortly thereafter signed a peace treaty with Germany. At this time the Bolsheviks published a number of secret treaties that the Allies had drawn up at the beginning of the war. These secret treaties outlined in detail how the Allies planned to divide the spoils of war if they were successful in defeating the Central Powers.

President Wilson chose this opportunity to lay before the world what he firmly believed was "the only possible program for world peace." Wilson's program, which he presented to Congress on January 8, 1918, included fourteen principles, or "points."

The first group of points aimed to end the causes of modern war, as Wilson understood these causes. Specifically, he called for open, instead of secret, diplomacy; for freedom of the seas instead of their control by the strong naval powers; for removal of tariffs and other economic barriers between nations; for reduction of land armaments; and for temporary international control of colonies in place of the existing imperialism.

President Wilson also called for the liberation of peoples long held in bondage by Russia, Austria-Hungary, Germany, and Turkey. Among these peoples were the Poles, Czechs, Slovaks, and South Slavs. Wilson's proposal also included the people living in the German-held region of Alsace-Lorraine. These and other groups were to have the right of "self-determination." That is, they were to decide for themselves the country in which they wished to live.

But the "Fourteenth Point" was the heart of President Wilson's program. With this famous point Wilson urged the creation of a "general association of nations" to give "mutual guarantees of political independence and territorial integrity to great and small states alike."

Influence of Wilson's program. The Fourteen Points and statements explaining them were printed during the war in the languages of the peoples of central Europe and dropped by plane into the heart of enemy country. All this publicity encouraged the Slavic peoples within Germany and Austria-Hungary to boycott the war efforts of their masters and to speed up their own liberation. Even the German people read the Fourteen Points and found in President Wilson's program hope for a just and lasting peace rather than a continued regime of absolute rule and militarism under the Kaiser and his associates.

Moreover, as defeat pressed closer upon them, the German and Austrian peoples saw in the Fourteen Points an escape from the harsh penalties that the Allies would otherwise impose upon them. Thus, when the great German military offensives failed in the summer of 1918, and when President Wilson made it clear that he would not negotiate with any German authority that was not representative of the people, the people of Germany and Austria-Hungary took steps to overthrow their rulers.

President Wilson and millions of Americans had entered the conflict with the burning conviction that they were waging a crusade "to make the world safe for democracy." In the winter of 1918–19 many Americans believed that this goal was at last in sight.

SECTION SURVEY

IDENTIFY: Bolsheviks, "Yanks," convoy, armistice, idealism, self-determination; Admiral Sims, General Pershing, Marshal Foch; November 11, 1918.

1. What contributions did the United States Navy make to winning the war?
2. Discuss the part played by the A.E.F. in defeating the German army.
3. Who considered the armistice terms of 1918 severe? Why?
4. (a) Why were Wilson's Fourteen Points considered an expression of American idealism? (b) Why was the Fourteenth Point the heart of Wilson's program?

TRACING THE MAIN IDEAS

The outbreak of World War I in the summer of 1914 came as a blow to millions of Americans and other peoples throughout the world. During the early 1900's great strides had been made in the direction of international cooperation. Suddenly, in 1914, all men's hopes for peace were destroyed.

Despite America's desire to remain neutral, the United States was drawn closer and closer into the conflict. As the months passed, President Wilson and a growing number of Americans began to believe that the war was essentially a conflict between autocracy on the one hand and democracy on the other. On this high note of idealism, the United States entered the conflict.

Hundreds of millions of people throughout the Americas, Europe, the Middle East, and the Far East rejoiced when the armistice was signed on November 11, 1918. These people believed that they had won "the war to end war," one "to make the world safe for democracy." Many of these people looked to the United States for leadership in the difficult task of building a peaceful world.

In the winter of 1918–19 it was clear to Americans and to people in other lands that the United States had become a major world power. It was also clear that with Europe in ruins the United States had the opportunity of becoming the most influential nation on earth.

CHAPTER SURVEY

QUESTIONS FOR DISCUSSION

1. What part did American troops play in the victory of the Allies?
2. President Wilson preached a moral crusade in the fighting of World War I. Comment on how this helped win victory for the Allies.
3. What powers of the President are important in time of war?
4. (a) How do you think war advances technological development? (b) How did technological developments change the nature of war by 1914?
5. (a) Why have scientists become as important in modern warfare as politicians and soldiers? (b) Do you think scientists should make value judgments about the kinds of weapons their research will lead to? Explain.
6. The armistice that ended World War I brought with it a spirit of high idealism and hope to people throughout the world. Explain.
7. Nearly 20 million persons, both military and civilian, were killed or disabled during World War I. The material damage due to the war is estimated at 28 billion dollars. How do you think these losses affected world conditions after the war?

RELATING PAST TO PRESENT

1. Were American newspapers completely objective during World War I? Do you think they are objective in reporting current conflicts? Explain.
2. Why are civil liberties often restricted during a period of crisis? Are civil liberties in the United States being restricted today? Explain.
3. Do other nations still look to the United States for leadership in the difficult task of building a peaceful world? Explain.

USING MAPS AND CHARTS

1. Using the map on page 604, identify (a) the Allied Powers, (b) the Central Powers, and (c) the major neutral nations.
2. Using the map on page 608 and consulting the text, (a) show why the Germans violated the neutrality of Belgium, and (b) explain the reason for the failure of the Germans to conquer the French armies in 1914.
3. Referring to the map on page 617, (a) locate the positions held by American troops, (b) identify American victories, and (c) indicate the area which the Allied armies occupied after the war.

UNIT SURVEY

FOR FURTHER INQUIRY

1. Why did the Spanish-American War symbolize a change in American foreign policy?
2. Comment: In acquiring overseas possessions, the United States was acting in the tradition of "manifest destiny."
3. How did Theodore Roosevelt interpret the power of the President in regard to foreign policy? Cite your evidence in answering this question.
4. How can national ideals of neutrality and peaceful co-existence with other nations come into conflict with national self-interest? In your answer, cite examples from events described in Unit Nine.

PROJECTS AND ACTIVITIES

1. For an interesting account of the Spanish-American War, read Walter Millis' *The Martial Spirit* (Houghton Mifflin). Compare it with Frank Freidel's *The Splendid Little War* (Little, Brown).
2. For more information concerning the entrance of the United States into World War I, see Chapter 32 of Joseph E. Gould's *Challenge and Change: Guided Readings in American History* (Harcourt Brace Jovanovich).
3. If possible, interview members of your family or community for first-hand accounts of life during World War I.

USING THE SOCIAL SCIENCES

(Read pages 622–24 before you answer the following questions.)

1. What do you think determines the view taken by an individual or a nation on the question of imperialism?

2. What did Carl Schurz mean when he stated "And I warn the American people that a democracy . . . cannot long play the king over subject populations without creating in itself ways of thinking and habits of action most dangerous to its own vitality. . . ." Does this statement apply to current events? Explain.
3. In Unit 9's case study, statements reflecting belief in racial superiority and racial inferiority were made by some anti-imperialists and some pro-imperialists as well. Explain.

SUGGESTED FURTHER READING

Biography

BLUM, JOHN MORTON, *Woodrow Wilson and the Politics of Morality*, Little, Brown.

GORGAS, M. D., and B. J. HENDRICK, *William Crawford Gorgas: His Life and Work*, Doubleday.

LUTZ, ALMA, *Susan Anthony*, Harper & Row (Beacon).

MORISON, ELTING E., *Turmoil and Tradition: A Study of the Life and Times of Henry L. Stimson*, Houghton Mifflin.

RICKENBACKER, EDWARD V., *Fighting the Flying Circus*, Lippincott. About World War I pilot; autobiographical.

ROLLINS, ALFRED B., JR., *Woodrow Wilson and the New America*, Dell (paper). Original speeches, letters, official documents, journalistic commentary, and the words and writings of close friends and bitter adversaries concerning the public and private life of Woodrow Wilson.

ROOSEVELT, THEODORE, *Rough Riders*, Scribner.

WOOD, L. N., *Walter Reed: Doctor in Uniform*, Messner.

Other Nonfiction

ANGLE, PAUL, ed. *The Making of a World Power*, Fawcett (Premier Books, paper). Drawn largely from primary sources, a description of the United States at the turn of the century, and during World War I and the Depression.

BAILEY, THOMAS A., *Wilson and the Peacemakers*, Macmillan.

BALDWIN, HANSON W., *World War I*, Grove (paper). Written by a competent military analyst, it surveys many of the theaters of the war and discusses politics, economics, personalities, and the war's place in history.

BEALE, HOWARD K., *Theodore Roosevelt and the Rise of America to World Power*, Johns Hopkins Press.

BEMIS, SAMUEL FLAGG, *The Latin-American Policy of the United States: An Historical Interpretation*, Harcourt Brace Jovanovich.

BREBNER, JOHN B., *North Atlantic Triangle*, Columbia Univ. Press.

CLENDENEN, CLARENCE C., *The United States and Pancho Villa: A Study in Unconventional Diplomacy*, Cornell Univ. Press.

CONGDON, DON, ed. *Combat: World War I*, Dell. Various first-hand accounts; contains maps of the major battlegrounds.

DULLES, FOSTER RHEA, *America's Rise to World Power: 1898–1954*, Harper & Row.

FLEMING, D. F., *The United States and the League of Nations 1918–1920*, Putnam.

FREIDEL, FRANK, *The Splendid Little War*, Little, Brown. War with Spain.

GRATTAN, C. HARTLEY, *The United States and the Southwest Pacific*, Harvard Univ. Press.

GRISWOLD, A. WHITNEY, *The Far Eastern Policy of the United States*, Harcourt Brace Jovanovich.

LINK, ARTHUR, S., *Wilson: The Struggle for Neutrality, 1914–1915*, Princeton Univ. Press.

——, *Woodrow Wilson and the Progressive Era: 1910–1917*, Harper & Row (Torchbooks, paper). An evaluation of Wilson's goals and achievements.

LIPPMANN, WALTER, *United States Foreign Policy: Shield of the Republic*, Little, Brown.

MARSHALL, S. L. A., *The American Heritage History of World War I*, Dell (paper).

MAY, ERNEST R., *Imperial Democracy: The Emergence of America as a Great Power*, Harcourt Brace Jovanovich.

MECHAM, J. LLOYD, *The United States and Inter-American Security, 1889–1960*, Univ. of Texas Press.

MILLIS, WALTER, *The Martial Spirit*, Houghton Mifflin. Spanish-American War.

——, *The Road to War*, Houghton Mifflin. Why Americans entered World War I.

PRATT, JULIUS W., *America's Colonial Experiment*, Prentice-Hall (text ed.).

REYNOLDS, QUENTIN, *They Fought for the Sky*, Bantam (paper). The great pilot-heroes of World War I; illustrated with drawings of early fighting planes.

ROOSEVELT, THEODORE, *The Rough Riders*, New American Library (Signet Books, paper). The Spanish-American War.

SMITH, GENE, *When the Cheering Stopped*, Bantam (paper). The last years of Wilson's administration.

TANSILL, CHARLES C., *America Goes to War*, Little, Brown. World War I.

TUCHMAN, BARBARA W., *The Guns of August*, Dell (paper). The events leading up to World War I.

WEEMS, JOHN E., *The Fate of the Maine,* Holt, Rinehart & Winston.

WERSTEIN, IRVING, *1898: The Spanish-American War Told with Pictures*, Cooper Square Publishers (paper).

Historical Fiction

BOYD, THOMAS, *Through the Wheat*, Scribner. Novel about American soldier.

DOS PASSOS, JOHN, *Three Soldiers*, Random House (Modern Library); and others. About World War I.

HEMINGWAY, ERNEST, *A Farewell to Arms*, Scribner (text ed.). Love story and fighting on Italian front.

HETH, EDWARD H., *Told with a Drum*, Harper & Row. German-American city.

MARCH, WILLIAM, *Company K*, New American Library (Signet Books).

NASON, LEONARD H., *Chevrons*, Doubleday; Grosset & Dunlap. Soldiers in World War I.

REMARQUE, ERICH MARIA, *All Quiet on the Western Front*, Little, Brown; Fawcett (Crest Books). Novel about German soldier in World War I.

SCANLON, W. T., *God Have Mercy on Us!*, Houghton Mifflin. A story of 1918.

STALLING, LAURENCE, *Plumes*, Harcourt Brace Jovanovich; Grosset & Dunlap. A family that fights in all the American wars.

THOMASON, JOHN WILLIAMS, *Fix Bayonets!*, Scribner. Fighting in World War I.

WHARTON, JAMES B., *Squad*, Coward-McCann; Grosset & Dunlap. Group of soldiers in World War I.

HISTORY AND THE SOCIAL SCIENCES

A naval battle of the Spanish-American War

The Imperialist Debate

Americans today seldom associate empire-building, or imperialism, with their own country. Yet there was a brief period in American history when imperialism and territorial expansion by conquest (which the word implies) were the subjects of lively debate in this country.

Between 1880 and 1910 the United States did in fact become the possessor of vast territories acquired by the force of arms. Pro-imperialists maintained that it was the destiny of the United States to expand. Anti-imperialists argued that expansion by force of arms was incompatible with the basic values on which the United States was founded. Which side had the more valid argument? This is a question we shall try to investigate as we examine the imperialist debate that once raged in the United States.

America's "Manifest Destiny"

In the late 1800's the notion of "manifest destiny," a phrase coined in the 1840's during the Mexican War, enjoyed widespread popularity in the United States. Pro-imperialists argued that the United States, enjoying the best government on earth and representing the best ideals of Western civilization, had the *manifest destiny*—the clearly ordained duty—to share its blessings with other less fortunate peoples by extending to them the protection of the American flag and the benefits of American government.

The Reverend Josiah Strong, an early apostle of American imperialism, preached that Americans were the possessors of the two great needs of mankind—"pure, spiritual Christianity" and "civil liberty." "It follows then," he wrote, "that the Anglo-Saxon, as the great representative of these two great blessings . . . is divinely commissioned to be . . . his brother's keeper. It seems to me that God . . . is training the Anglo-Saxon race for an hour sure to come in the world's future."

The need for new markets for expanding American industry and for farm products was another major reason cited in favor of expansion. The pro-imperialists pointed out that the Asian and African continents were being carved up and divided among the European powers. Unless the United States stepped into this race, they argued, there would be no places left where Americans could secure raw materials for their industries or consumers for their products. Albert Beveridge, a United States Senator from Indiana, declared: "American factories are making more than the American people can use. . . . Fate has written our policy for us; the trade of the world must and shall be ours. We will establish trading posts throughout the world as distributing points for American products. We will cover the world with our merchant marine. We will build a navy to the measure of our greatness."

Beveridge's dream of a powerful American navy was given eloquent elaboration by one of America's greatest naval strategists, Captain Alfred Mahan. Mahan maintained that the United States must secure its vital interests—economic, political, and strategic—and achieve its destiny by establishing a network of far-flung markets maintained by a large merchant fleet and backed up by a navy capable of operating in the oceans and seas of the world. To achieve this objective, Mahan urged, the United States must become a first-rate naval power, acquiring overseas naval bases and building battleships and other large naval vessels. Captain Mahan recruited a powerful ally to his cause, the influential Assistant Secretary of the Navy, Theodore Roosevelt.

Caught by the fever of imperialism, the United States began flexing its new-found muscles—and seemed ready for a fight. The revolution by the people of Cuba against the corrupt and oppressive control of the Spaniards who ruled over them presented America with the opportunity it was seeking. On April 11, 1898, the United States declared war on Spain.

There were, of course, many reasons behind the outbreak of the Spanish-American War in 1898. First, many Americans had a genuine sympathy for the plight of the Cubans and were eager to expel the Spaniards from the island. Second, there was a great deal of belligerent, warlike fervor in the United States which was skillfully fanned against Spain by the press and by the spokesmen for American expansion. Third, after years of relying on the British fleet for the enforcement of the Monroe Doctrine, the United States was determined to show the world that it was a great power and that its word was supreme—at least in the Western Hemisphere. Fourth, some Americans welcomed foreign adventure as a diversion from the seemingly endless series of economic and political crises that demanded their attention at home.

The war itself was almost an anticlimax. In a matter of weeks the American forces had triumphed over those of Spain and the war was over. The end of the fighting brought new, complex problems to the United States, for with the signing of the peace treaty in October 1898 the United States found itself with an empire on its hands. The problem now was what to do with it.

Controversy over the Philippines

In the months following the war a great deal of controversy centered on the Philippines, which had been ceded to the United States by Spain. The anti-imperialists argued that the United States should set the islands free. The pro-imperialists argued that American rule must be established over the Philippines. Senate debate was prolonged and stormy.

The pro-imperialists were led by Senator Henry Cabot Lodge who argued that the annexation of the Philippines would be in the best interests of the Filipinos themselves. To abandon the islands, he declared, would be a "base betrayal of the Filipinos" because only under the protection of the American flag would they be able to enjoy the freedoms guaranteed under the Constitution and the Declaration of Independence. "The Filipinos," he added, "are not today in the least fitted for self-government."

U.S. troops in the Philippines

Lodge then went on to point out that the annexation of the Philippines, with their rich supplies of such raw materials as hemp and gold, would also be in the best interests of the United States. The islands, he argued, would soon provide an important market for American products. Manila, Lodge predicted, would become a strong American naval base to protect American interests in the Far East. Senator Lodge warned against an isolationist America. "Even now," he concluded, "we can abandon the Monroe Doctrine, we can reject the Pacific, we can shut ourselves up between our oceans, as Switzerland is enclosed among its hills, and then it would be inevitable that we should sink out from among the great powers of the world. . . ."

Senator Beveridge, also speaking for the pro-imperialists, argued in favor of the acquisition of the Philippines, stating: "God has . . . made us the master organizers of the world to establish system where chaos reigns. . . . This is the divine mission of America. . . . What shall history say of us? Shall it say that we renounced that holy trust? . . . Our fathers would not have had it so. No! They . . . unfurled no retreating flag. That flag has never paused in its onward march. Who dares halt it now—now, when history's largest events are carrying it forward?"

The anti-imperialists were led by Carl Schurz, a former cabinet member under President Hayes. Schurz, speaking against the annexation, warned that permitting racially mixed foreigners to participate in the American political process might eventually endanger the purity of America's "Anglo-Saxon population." Schurz, a former abolitionist, clearly understood the racist nature of his basic argument—concern for the "purity" of the white race.

Schurz also argued that the annexation of the Philippines might lead the United States to build up its military forces and extend its control to still other territories—with disastrous results. "I deny," he said, "that the duties we owe to the Cubans and the Puerto Ricans and Filipinos . . . absolve us of our duties to the 75 millions of our own people and to their posterity. . . . I deny that they compel us to . . . bring upon us the constant danger of war and to subject our people to the galling burden of increasing armaments."

Finally Schurz argued that aggressive expansion might have an adverse effect on America itself: "And I warn the American people that a democracy . . . cannot long play the king over subject populations without creating in itself ways of thinking and habits of action most dangerous to its own vitality. . . ."

Also speaking for the anti-imperialists was the Anti-Imperialist League, which issued the following statement in opposition to American policy in the Philippines: "We regret that it has become necessary in the land of Washington and Lincoln to reaffirm that all men, of whatsoever race or color, are entitled to life, liberty, and the pursuit of happiness. We maintain that governments derive their just powers from the consent of the governed. We insist that the subjugation of any people is 'criminal aggression' and open disloyalty to the distinctive principles of our government. . . .

"We hold, with Abraham Lincoln, that 'no man is good enough to govern another man without that man's consent. When the white man governs himself, that is self-government, but when he governs himself and also governs another man, that is more than self-government—that is despotism.' 'Our reliance is in the love of liberty which God has planted in us. Our defense is in the spirit which prizes liberty as the heritage of all men in all lands. Those who deny freedom to others deserve it not for themselves, and under a just God cannot long retain it.' "

These then were the arguments of both sides. The Philippines were annexed, but this proved to be the last territorial expansion of the United States. There were many reasons that the imperialist crusade came to a halt. The American takeover of the islands was bitterly resisted for two years by Filipino guerrillas, and the final subjugation of the islands came only at the cost of many lives and much money. It soon became the settled policy of the United States that the occupation would last only until the Filipinos were ready to govern themselves. Even in the early years of the occupation, Americans became increasingly convinced that American democratic traditions were not exportable and that the United States was not suited for the role of an imperialist ruler. The Philippines gained independence in 1946, but long before that date opposition to imperialism and support for the self-determination of nations became the accepted principles of American foreign policy.

■ In the long run, who had the more valid argument—the pro-imperialists or the anti-imperialists? Why? Did the men on either side of the debate agree in all their ideas and viewpoints? Explain.

■ Analyze the arguments of one pro-imperialist and one anti-imperialist and explain how their thinking compares with that of Americans today.

Celebrating Philippine independence, 1946

RISE OF THE AMERICAN NATION

INTRODUCTION: THE COLONIAL PERIOD	Unit One: Building the Colonies	1450–1763
PART 1: CREATING A NEW NATION	Unit Two: Winning Independence	1763–1789
	Unit Three: Building the Nation	1789–1845
PART 2: THE NATION DIVIDED	Unit Four: The Rise of Sectionalism	1820's–1860's
	Unit Five: The Nation Torn Apart	1845–1865
PART 3: THE NATION REUNITED	Unit Six: Rebuilding the Nation	1865–1900
	Unit Seven: The Rise of Industrialism	1860's–1890's
	Unit Eight: The Arrival of Reform	1897–1920
PART 4: THE NATION AS A WORLD LEADER	Unit Nine: Becoming a World Power	1898–1920
	Unit Ten: The "Golden Twenties"	1920–1932
	Unit Eleven: The New Deal and World War II	1932–1945
	Unit Twelve: The Challenges of a New Era	1945–1970's

UNIT TEN

The "Golden Twenties"

1920 – 1932

This Fabulous Century 1920–1930, by the Editors of Time–Life Books, photograph by Henry Groskinsky © 1969 Time Inc.

■ A big city movie theater in the 1920's

CHAPTER **33**

From Prosperity to Economic Collapse

1920 – 1932

ON DECEMBER 4, 1918, President Wilson and many of his official advisers left New York harbor on the army transport *George Washington* bound for Europe and the peace conference at Versailles (vair·SI) near Paris. The vessel docked at Brest, France, on December 13. While waiting for the conference to open, President Wilson visited Paris, London, Rome, and other European cities. People gave him a tumultuous welcome everywhere he went.

But Wilson's triumph was short-lived. At the peace conference all the bitterness of four long years of warfare burst into the open. Wilson did win acceptance of his proposal for a League of Nations designed to safeguard the peace. But in the process he had to compromise many of his principles.

By 1920 it was clear that a large majority of the American people had rejected Wilson's leadership. As you will see in Chapter 34, the United States refused to join the League of Nations and, in a sense, turned its back upon Europe. And, as you will see in the following pages, Americans by and large also turned their backs upon Wilson's domestic policies. In the election of 1920 they chose a Republican President to lead the nation.

During the decade of the 1920's three Republican Presidents—Warren G. Harding, Calvin Coolidge, and Herbert Hoover—presided over a country that on the whole enjoyed a period of unparalleled prosperity. But the era of the "Golden Twenties" ended with an economic collapse and the most shattering depression in American history.

THE CHAPTER IN OUTLINE

1. Loss of popularity for Woodrow Wilson and the Democratic Party.

2. Republican control of the government during the "Golden Twenties."

3. The prosperity of the 1920's shattered by the Great Depression.

| 1450 | 1750 | 1800 | 1850 | 1900 | 1950 | 1975 |

1 Loss of popularity for Woodrow Wilson and the Democratic Party

Before America's entry into the war, President Wilson had concentrated on his program of domestic reform. As you have seen, his first administration, from 1913 to 1917, reduced tariffs, strengthened the antitrust laws, and established the Federal Reserve System. In these and other ways, Wilson tried to restore competition in American business and to protect the consumer.

Even before the war, however, Wilson felt that the "New Freedom" program had largely achieved its goals. And after the war he became deeply involved in organizing world peace. As a result, he had little time left for such pressing domestic problems as a postwar business slump, a decline of farm prices, and widespread unemployment.

Losing support at home. The American people, however, were tired of international issues. They were more interested in their nation's domestic affairs than in a peace treaty or a League of Nations. The Congressional elections of 1918, held just a few days before the armistice, showed how the political winds were blowing. President Wilson appealed to the voters to return a Democratic Congress. Ignoring his appeal, they elected a Republican majority in both the House and Senate.

Wilson's illness. When Wilson returned from the Versailles Conference in the summer of 1919, he found many Senators critical of the Covenant, or constitution, of the League of Nations. But the President refused to compromise on the covenant's basic points. Instead, he tried to win the American public to his point of view.

Late in the summer of 1919, after three weeks of a grueling nationwide speaking tour, Wilson suffered a stroke which left him partially paralyzed. His condition improved somewhat, but he remained an invalid until his death in 1924.

The postwar depression. Wilson's illness came at a time when the country was suffering from a severe postwar depression. With the signing of the armistice, the government began to cancel its wartime contracts. Businessmen in wartime industries suddenly faced the problem of reconverting their plants to peacetime production. New machinery had to be installed, new customers found. During the reconversion, factories closed down or operated with greatly reduced labor forces.

Farmers also suffered during the transition from war to peace. As European farm lands returned to normal production, the American farmer's wartime markets in Europe disappeared. Farm prices, which had soared during the war, dropped as competition increased. Wheat, for example, which had sold for as high as $2.26 a bushel, dropped to less than

■ When President Wilson found many Senators critical of the Covenant of the League of Nations, he tried to win the American public to his point of view. This cartoon, referring to his nationwide speaking tour, shows him "going to talk to the boss."

$1.00 a bushel in 1922. Almost half a million American farmers lost their farms during this troubled period.

Meanwhile wage earners were also suffering. Many men who had worked in government wartime agencies lost their jobs when the war ended. Hundreds of thousands of industrial wage earners were thrown out of work when factories closed down or curtailed operations. Many of the 4.5 million returning servicemen could not find work.

As the depression deepened, as wages fell, and as more people lost their jobs, discontent swelled alarmingly. To make things worse, the high cost of living, stimulated by the war, rose even higher. In 1919 it climbed 77 percent above pre-war levels. In 1920 it rose an additional 28 percent. Under such conditions, many workers understandably resorted to strikes. During 1919 more than 4 million workers were at one time or another out on strike. Three of the strikes were especially serious.

The Boston police strike. On September 9 the Boston police force left their posts to strike for higher wages and improved conditions. The strike left Boston without police protection. When rioting and looting broke out, the state guard was called in. The policemen, realizing that the strike was lost, announced that they would return to their posts.

At this point, however, the Boston police commissioner refused to allow the strikers to return to their jobs. He announced that he intended to hire a new police force. Governor Calvin Coolidge supported the commissioner. "There is no right," Coolidge flatly stated, "to strike against the public safety by anybody, anywhere, any time." Coolidge's statement was widely applauded all over the country. It brought him to public attention and helped him to win the Vice-Presidential nomination on the 1920 Republican ticket.

The coal strike. Less than two months after this police strike, on November 1, 1919, the United Mine Workers (U.M.W.) went out on strike. Led by their newly elected, colorful, and pugnacious president, John L. Lewis, they demanded higher wages and a shorter work week. On November 9 United States Attorney General A. Mitchell Palmer secured an injunction against the union, which ordered the officers of the U.M.W. to stop all activities tending to encourage the strikers.

But the coal miners refused to return to work. Finally, on President Wilson's suggestion, the problem was submitted to a board of arbitration. The board gave the miners a 27-percent wage increase, but refused to consider a reduction in the weekly hours of work.

The steel strike. Meanwhile, discontent in the steel industry led to a strike involving more than 300,000 workers. The steelworkers had long been dissatisfied with their working conditions. In some plants they worked as long as 12 hours a day, 7 days a week. Moreover, they had not been able to form a union to bargain for them. During the summer of 1919, however, a number of A. F. of L. unions formed a committee which launched a vigorous organizing campaign in the steel towns. The strike started on September 22, 1919, after management refused to recognize the committee's right to speak for all steelworkers.

As the weeks passed, violence erupted around some of the steel mills. At Gary, Indiana, martial law was declared, and federal troops moved in to keep order. Finally, with public opinion running against the steelworkers, the strike was called off, and in January 1920 the men returned to their jobs. Three years later, however, the steel companies agreed to establish an 8-hour day.

Labor's declining strength. The postwar depression did not last long. By early 1920 American export trade was soaring as orders for goods poured in from the war-devastated countries. The value of American exports rose to three times the 1913 level.

As economic conditions improved and jobs became more plentiful, many workers lost interest in unions. Membership in the A. F. of L., which had reached a peak of more than 4 million early in 1920, began to decline.

There were, of course, other reasons for the decline of the labor movement. The failure of the steel strike and of other strikes during 1919 discouraged workers. The use of the injunction, as in the strike of the United Mine Workers, was another discouraging factor. And the Supreme Court, in a series of decisions, broadened the base for use of the injunction, restricted labor organizing activities, and ruled unconstitutional legislation intended to improve working conditions. Industrial management, moreover, launched a widely publicized campaign against "the union shop," and identified labor unions with socialism and Communism. A "Red scare" that swept the country in 1919–20 caused large numbers of citizens, including many workers, to turn against organized labor.

The "Red scare." During the postwar years, federal and state governments conducted a vigorous drive against anarchists, Communists, and

■ During the Boston police strike of 1919, a few policemen remained on duty. One is shown here talking in the street to a mounted member of the state guard.

socialists. The Espionage Act (page 615), passed in wartime to punish treasonable or disloyal activities, remained in effect after the war. Under this law, revolutionists and suspected revolutionists were arrested and fined. Some of those arrested were aliens who were deported to the countries from which they had come.

One important reason for the postwar concern with radicals was the Russian Bolshevik Revolution of 1917 (page 615). This event frightened many Americans who feared that radicals in the United States might try to follow the Bolshevik example. Rumors of revolutionary plots circulated widely from 1917 through 1920.

But there was more than rumor to arouse alarm, even though radical leaders disapproved of acts of irresponsible violence. During the spring and summer of 1919 more than 30 bombs were discovered by postal authorities in packages addressed to prominent citizens. And in New York City on September 16, 1920, a bomb exploded in crowded

Wall Street at noontime, killing 38 persons, injuring hundreds, and causing property damage that was variously estimated at from $500,000 to $2.5 million.

Meanwhile, in the fall of 1919 Attorney General Palmer had instructed his agents in the Department of Justice to arrest radical agitators throughout the country. Among those arrested were several hundred aliens who were deported.

Criticism of the "Palmer raids." A number of Americans, both Democrats and Republicans, criticized this drive against radical movements, pointing out that many of the raids were conducted without search warrants. They argued that the Attorney General sometimes ignored the constitutional rights of free citizens.

But it was not just against Attorney General Palmer that the critics directed their fire. During this postwar period about one third of the states had passed laws to punish advocates of revolutionary change. By 1920 a growing number of Americans

629

■ In the summer of 1917, 15,000 Negroes in New York City marched in a "silent parade," to the beat of muffled drums, to protest the rising racial tension and violence against Negroes.

who had no sympathy with radicals were becoming increasingly alarmed at the widespread violation of civil liberties. Many leaders of both political parties agreed with President Wilson that Americans could not solve their problems by trying to suppress unpopular political views.

Rising racial tensions. With the growth of northern industry before World War I, many black families had moved from the South to northern industrial centers, hoping to escape lives of poverty and discrimination. The war, with its heavy demand for industrial manpower, caused this migration to increase. During the war about half a million southern black wage earners found jobs in the coal mines of West Virginia and Illinois, the meat-packing plants of Chicago, the steel mills of Pittsburgh, the automobile factories of Detroit, and the industries of other large cities.

But Negroes did not find in the North the equality of opportunity they sought. Black wage earners got the hardest jobs and the lowest pay. Northern white wage earners sometimes staged protest strikes against employment of black workers, especially when industrialists used black laborers as strike breakers. Racial tensions in the North began to arise alarmingly.

Disappointed hopes. A war being fought "to make the world safe for democracy" naturally aroused the hopes of black Americans, who looked forward to new and greater freedom at home. Many decided to hasten the day by taking a stronger stand for their rights. In the summer of 1917, 15,000 Negroes in New York City marched in a "silent parade," to the beat of muffled drums, to protest the rising racial tension and violence directed against Negroes.

630

Black soldiers returning from Europe, where they had been treated as equals, especially by the French, were angry and disappointed that conditions in the United States were little changed. They were especially discouraged to find a new Ku Klux Klan operating in the North as well as in the South. The new Klan harassed Jews, Catholics, foreign-born citizens, and everyone else it chose to call dangerous and "un-American." But Negroes were the special object of Klan violence.

There were other reasons for bitterness among black Americans in the North. During the postwar business depression, competition for jobs between white and black workers became fierce, and the white workers usually got the jobs. There was also a troublesome housing shortage as a result of wartime building restrictions. And when black families tried to move into white neighborhoods, racial friction became acute.

The riots of 1919. During 1919 riots in more than 20 cities, North and South, brought death and injury to hundreds of men and women and caused the destruction of thousands of tenements in slum areas.

The riots generally began when Negroes fought against some especially discriminatory act. Frightened white citizens, convinced that black Americans were trying to threaten them and gain control, responded with violence. Police forces, ill-equipped to deal with riots, usually sided with white citizens, making black Americans take even more desperate actions.

The riots solved no problems. Nor did they spur local or national officials to try to remedy even the more obvious causes of the trouble. As a result, some black Americans decided to take more militant actions. They were now more ready to follow leaders who insisted that black citizens, no less than white, had a lawful right to defend themselves when the law failed to do so.

Despite the many proofs that the North was no utopia for Negroes, southern black families continued to migrate to northern cities. Between 1910 and 1930 the black population of the northern states more than doubled, rising from a little over 1 million to nearly 2.5 million. The racial problem in the United States was no longer largely a southern problem—it was now a national concern.

Election of 1920. In the Presidential election of 1920, the country's unsettled condition gave the Republican candidate, Senator Warren G. Harding of Ohio, a decided advantage over his Democratic opponent, Governor James M. Cox of Ohio. Many voters naturally blamed the administration in office for the troubled times. The Republican candidate's plea for a return to "normalcy" had great appeal. Many Americans were tired of Europe and its wars, tired of Wilson's attempts to "save the world for democracy." Businessmen were worried about the 1919 depression of business. Workers and farmers felt that their problems, among them unemployment and falling prices, were being neglected.

Thus, Harding won the election with approximately 16 million votes to Cox's 9 million. The electoral vote was even more sweeping, giving Harding 404 to Cox's 127. Eugene V. Debs, the Socialist candidate, who was in prison for violating the Espionage Act, received nearly 1 million votes.

The election of 1920 was the first Presidential contest in which all eligible women could vote. The long struggle for woman suffrage had been won in August 1920, when the Nineteenth Amendment went into effect.

Fading party differences. In the decade that followed their defeat in 1920, the Democrats failed, with a few exceptions, to work out a clear-cut program to challenge the Republicans. They turned away from the spirit of reform that had characterized Wilson's first administration. More and more the Democrats accepted the same conservative principles followed by the Republicans. Both parties supported high tariffs and believed that big business should be let alone. As the years passed, it became increasingly difficult to distinguish between the two parties.

SECTION SURVEY

IDENTIFY: Bolshevik Revolution, return to "normalcy," Nineteenth Amendment, the riots of 1919; John L. Lewis, Warren G. Harding.

1. World War I brought about many dislocations in American life, including a rising cost of living, increased unemployment, and declining profits for large corporations. How does this information relate to the following: (a) strikes, (b) rising racial tensions, (c) the election of 1920?

2. (a) What conditions produced the "Red scare"? (b) How was organized labor affected by the "Red scare"? Why?

3. Many Americans criticized the drive against radical movements because it involved a widespread violation of civil liberties. Comment.

4. Why were poor Americans, both black and white, particularly affected by the economic conditions of the postwar period?

2 Republican control of the government during the "Golden Twenties"

Warren G. Harding, who was inaugurated on March 4, 1921, was a genial Ohio newspaperman who had climbed to the top of the political ladder in his own state. Before becoming President he had served as United States Senator in Washington. Handsome and distinguished, with a warm, easygoing manner—much too easygoing, as it turned out—he had many friends in every walk of life.

Farm relief and financial reform. Harding did not take over an easy job when he entered the White House. Late in 1920 a second postwar depression had hit the country. Farmers, wage earners, businessmen, and the public in general were clamoring for government action and for the fulfillment of the President's promise of a return to "normalcy."

Responding to widespread demands for help, Congress adopted the Emergency Tariff on May

■ Warren G. Harding had been an Ohio newspaperman and a United States Senator before he was nominated for the Presidency by the Republican Party and elected in 1920. His warm, friendly personality was one of his greatest assets as President.

27, 1921. This measure raised rates on some farm products, but failed to raise farm prices generally.

In June Congress adopted the Budget and Accounting Act. The new measure was designed to reduce extravagance and waste in government, and to provide a more efficient method of handling government expenditures. It also created a Bureau of the Budget in the Treasury Department, with a director appointed by the President.

Up to this time Congress had made annual appropriations on a piecemeal basis, with no great concern for "balancing the budget." Under the new system, all government agencies and departments had to submit annual requests for funds to the Director of the Budget. The director then had to draw up a detailed budget, listing estimated income and expenditures for the coming *fiscal year.*° Once the budget was prepared, the President submitted it to Congress, which could, if it chose, raise or lower the estimates.

Charles G. Dawes, the first director of the budget, was an extremely capable administrator. Under his leadership and that of the Secretary of the Treasury, Andrew W. Mellon, the government began to use surplus revenues to reduce the national debt. At the end of World War I the debt totaled more than $25 billion. During the 1920's it was cut by about one third.

Some critics held that Mellon's financial measures reduced the taxes of the wealthy while checking a needed expansion of social services for the poor. But most Americans approved of the emphasis on economy in government spending, along with the reduction of the debt associated with Mellon's 12-year administration of the Treasury.

War veterans and the bonus. Meanwhile, Congress tackled the problem of the war veterans. Many war veterans, as well as many other Americans, felt that the government should provide "adjusted compensation" for ex-servicemen. These people pointed out that during the war the servicemen had received low pay while workers at home earned high wartime wages in more or less safe jobs.

In August 1921 Congress created the Veterans' Bureau. President Harding then appointed Charles R. Forbes as its first director. The Veterans' Bureau was authorized to handle veterans' claims for compensation and hospitalization, to provide med-

° *fiscal year:* the 12-month period considered as a year for general accounting and budgeting purposes. The fiscal year of the United States government begins on July 1.

ical care for sick veterans, and to administer the government program for veterans' insurance.

The Veterans' Bureau was only a partial answer to the demands of veterans. The American Legion, the Veterans of Foreign Wars, and other veterans' organizations continued to press for adjusted compensation. Congress responded in 1922 with a bonus bill. President Harding vetoed the bill because it did not include any provision for raising the money to be spent.

Finally—to glance ahead—in 1924 Congress passed another bonus bill over President Coolidge's veto. The bill provided adjusted compensation for all veterans except those with ranks above captain. The payments were not to be given in cash but in the form of a paid-up 20-year life insurance policy. Veterans who held the policy for 20 years would receive full compensation.

The Fordney-McCumber Tariff. On September 21, 1922, Harding signed the Fordney-McCumber Tariff Act into law. The new tariff wiped out the reductions made in the Underwood Tariff of 1913 (page 547) and established considerably higher rates. It continued the limited protection for farmers provided by the Emergency Tariff of 1921. It revised sharply upward the tariff rates on hundreds of manufactured products.

The Fordney-McCumber Tariff also authorized the President, under certain circumstances, to raise or lower any of the tariff rates by as much as 50 percent. As it turned out, most of the adjustments made were upward rather than downward.

Public scandals. Despite some solid accomplishments, the Harding administration left a long, sorry record of corruption. President Harding was not himself involved in the corruption. His mistake was in appointing certain undeserving men to office. Of course, his cabinet did contain such able and respected men as Charles Evans Hughes, who became Secretary of State; Andrew W. Mellon, who headed the Treasury Department; and Herbert Hoover, who served as Secretary of Commerce. But Harding's administration also contained dishonest politicians who brought disgrace upon his administration.

Self-seeking politicians from Harding's home state, known as the "Ohio Gang," succeeded in placing one of their number, Harry M. Daugherty, in the cabinet as Attorney General. An investigation later revealed that Daugherty had used his position to protect men who violated the prohibition amendment. Another Harding official, Thomas W. Miller, defrauded the government in the sale of

IT'S WASHDAY EVERY DAY IN WASHINGTON

■ This cartoon shows the Senate washing out the "dirty linen" of the Harding administration. Several prominent government officials who had been appointed to office by the President were involved in the political scandals.

alien properties—that is, foreign-owned properties seized by the American government during World War I. Charles R. Forbes, who headed the Veterans' Bureau, could not satisfactorily account for $200 million spent by his organization.

The most notorious scandal took its name from the naval oil reserve lands at Teapot Dome in Wyoming. Secretary of the Interior Albert B. Fall persuaded the Secretary of the Navy, Edwin C. Denby, to transfer the Teapot Dome reserve and another oil reserve at Elk Hills, California, to Fall's jurisdiction. In return for bribes, Fall leased the oil reserves to private oil speculators.

These scandals did not become publicly known until Coolidge took office, when Fall, Forbes, and Miller were each prosecuted and imprisoned. Some hint of what was going on reached Harding in 1923, however, and his health broke under the strain. He died suddenly in the summer of 1923.

Calvin Coolidge. On Harding's death, Calvin Coolidge, the Vice-President, became President.

■ This portrait of President Calvin Coolidge reflects the honesty and forthrightness that helped to regain for the Republican Party the public confidence that had been lost during the Harding administration.

Coolidge, a man of unquestioned honesty, had built his political career in Massachusetts, advancing from state legislator to governor.

To millions of Americans, Calvin Coolidge became a symbol of the thrifty, old-fashioned, simple, country American. In a period of extravagance and "big money," his simplicity helped to regain for the Republican Party the public confidence that had been lost as a result of the scandals of the Harding administration.

The election of 1924. Only once during the 1920's did the Republican program face any serious opposition. Curiously enough, the opposition came in part from within Republican ranks.

The revolt broke out in 1924 when the Republicans nominated the staunchly conservative Calvin Coolidge for the Presidency. Coolidge believed that government should encourage, but not regulate, business. He also disapproved of special legislation to help workers or farmers.

Resisting these conservative policies, a group of progressive Republicans broke away from the Republican Party and formed a new Progressive Party. They nominated Senator Robert M. La Follette of Wisconsin as their standard bearer. The Progressive Party received the backing of three important groups of Americans who were dissatisfied with both major parties—western farmers, organized labor, and the socialists. The Progressive Party called for government action on a number of fronts. It urged federal credit and other assistance for farmers, social legislation and additional laws to protect the rights of labor, and government ownership of railroads and water power resources.

La Follette received almost 5 million votes, the largest number any third party had ever mustered. With La Follette's death shortly after the campaign, however, the Progressive Party lost its strength and faded into insignificance.

The Democrats in 1924 nominated John W. Davis, a conservative corporation lawyer. During his campaign Davis concentrated on the scandals of the Harding era. But the Republicans met this challenge by claiming credit for the prevailing prosperity. The argument of prosperity proved effective. Despite the Progressive revolt, which split the Republicans into two factions, Coolidge won by a landslide, piling up 382 electoral votes to 136 for Davis and 13 for La Follette.

Coolidge and thrifty government. President Coolidge continued to emphasize thrift in government. In the name of economy, he vetoed a bonus bill for veterans of World War I. As you have read (page 633), Congress passed this bill over his veto. Coolidge also vetoed the McNary-Haugen Bill which was designed to stabilize farm prices by allowing the government to buy up farm surpluses and sell them abroad.

In other matters, too, Congress and the President did not see eye to eye. But the President remained popular. "Keep cool with Coolidge" was a slogan of the day. He probably could have been re-elected in 1928 had he wished. But a year before the election he announced that he did not choose to run.

The election of 1928. With Coolidge out of the Presidential race, the Republicans nominated Herbert C. Hoover of California, a successful mining engineer with a notable record as administrator of food relief in Europe during and after the war and as Secretary of Commerce after 1921.

The Democrats nominated New York's Governor Alfred E. Smith. Smith advocated a federal farm relief program and also urged stricter regulation of public utilities. These planks in the Democratic platform had strong appeal for many Americans. But Smith had political handicaps that cost him support within his own party. He was opposed to prohibition, he was a Roman Catholic, and he was connected with the Tammany political machine in New York City—all of which made him unpopular with large groups of voters, especially in the South and West.

Hoover won the election, receiving 444 electoral votes to Smith's 87. Smith lost not only his own state of New York, but also several traditionally Democratic states in the South, which for the first time since the Civil War gave their votes to a Republican.

Herbert C. Hoover. President Hoover summed up his political beliefs in the phrase "rugged individualism." His general point of view was very close to Harding's idea of "normalcy" and to Coolidge's belief that government should encourage business but not give special assistance to individuals. Hoover, however, displayed greater imagination than his Republican predecessors. He believed that "experts" in fields other than government could make important contributions to government. He also believed that the government should assume at least a moderate amount of guidance, or planning, for the social and economic development of the nation.

When Hoover took office, he looked forward to a long period of increasing prosperity. He believed that Americans now expected more than the necessities of life. "The slogan of progress," he declared, "is changing from the full dinner pail to the full garage." For about six months, booming business and heavy consumer buying seemed to bear out this prediction.

The Hawley-Smoot Tariff. In 1929, with a great many Americans enjoying unprecedented prosperity, Hoover called Congress into special session to consider farm relief and a "limited revision" of tariffs.

Instead of a "limited revision," Congress passed the Hawley-Smoot Tariff bill, providing for the

LIVING AMERICAN DOCUMENTS

Herbert Hoover's
"Rugged Individualism" Speech (1928)

During one hundred and fifty years we have built up a form of self-government and a social system which is peculiarly our own. It differs essentially from all others in the world. It is the American system. It is just as definite and positive a political and social system as has ever been developed on earth. It is founded upon a particular conception of self-government in which decentralized local responsibility is the very base. Further than this, it is founded upon the conception that only through ordered liberty, freedom, and equal opportunity to the individual will his initiative and enterprise spur on the march of progress. And in our insistence upon equality of opportunity has our system advanced beyond all the world. . . .

highest tariff in American history. President Hoover felt that some of the rates were too high. He also pondered a petition signed by 1,000 leading economists who argued that such high tariffs would raise prices, create hardships for American consumers, seriously interfere with world trade, and invite economic reprisals from other countries. But in 1930, believing that protective tariffs encouraged business prosperity, Hoover put aside his doubts and signed the bill.

The Hawley-Smoot Tariff created problems for many countries (page 648). Driven to resistance, during the next two years some 25 countries took steps to cut down their imports of American products.

The Agricultural Marketing Act. Hoover did depart from the policies of his Republican predecessors, however, in supporting the Agricultural Marketing Act. This act created a Federal Farm Board, empowered to lend up to $500 million to cooperative farm groups to help them store crops during years when a surplus of farm products brought falling prices. The theory was that the farmers could sell their stored products later when prices rose. Unfortunately, surpluses continued year after year and prices continued to fall. As a result, the Federal Farm Board used up its financial resources without bolstering farm income.

In his support of federal legislation to aid farmers, Hoover was taking a modest turn away from

■ When Herbert Hoover (center) first became President, he believed that the nation could look forward to a long period of prosperity. But the events of 1929 were to prove him wrong.

the "rugged individualism" that he favored in theory. As you will see later, the stock market crash in 1929 and the Great Depression that followed brought new and ever heavier pressures for government action to aid farmers, wage earners, businessmen, and consumers in general.

SECTION SURVEY

IDENTIFY: "Ohio Gang," Teapot Dome scandal, rugged individualism; Alfred E. Smith.

1. How did Coolidge's election to the Presidency in 1924 reflect the temper of the times?
2. Both the Fordney-McCumber Tariff of 1922 and the Hawley-Smoot Tariff of 1930 established high tariff rates. (a) How would these tariffs affect foreign countries? (b) How would they affect American industries? (c) How would they affect American farmers?
3. Despite some solid accomplishments, the Harding administration left a long, sorry record of corruption. Explain.
4. Compare the parties, candidates, issues, and results of the elections of 1924 and 1928.

3 The prosperity of the 1920's shattered by the Great Depression

Flourishing business conditions and a rising standard of living contributed to the political success of the Republican Party during the 1920's. Between 1922 and 1929 jobs were plentiful. Americans were, on the whole, better fed, clothed, and housed than ever before.

"Easy money." During the prosperity of the so-called "Golden Twenties" many Americans made and spent money with ease. Millions of workmen received relatively high wages, many businessmen earned large profits, and an ever-growing number of stockholders received substantial dividends.

As Americans bought more and more consumer goods, the retail trade recorded ever-increasing sales. Some of the profits of successful business enterprises went back into industry, to pay for expansion and new product research. Some paid for workers' recreational facilities, some for company programs providing insurance and pensions for employees. Large sums flowed into medical research, education, and the welfare of the poor.

As surplus income piled higher and higher, more and more Americans from all walks of life were tempted to invest their savings or their profits in the stock market, hoping for big returns.

The limits of prosperity. Not all Americans shared in the prosperity of the "Golden Twenties." Many workers lost their jobs when new machines were installed in factories. Some craftsmen, such as blacksmiths and harness makers, whose skills were no longer needed, found it difficult to adapt to the monotonous work on assembly lines. Furthermore, some industries—such as coal, textiles, and leather —never fully recovered from the postwar slump of the early 1920's. Finally, many farmers did not share in the prosperity that other Americans were enjoying.

The plight of the farmers. After the war, as you have seen, American farmers lost many European markets. Also, as you will see, laws passed in the early 1920's virtually ended immigration. Thus, this traditional source of new customers was now lost to the farmer. But, although markets were shrinking, farm production—with the help of new machines and new techniques—jumped more than 20 percent between 1919 and 1929.

When supply is high and demand is low, when more people want to sell goods and fewer people are able or willing to buy them, prices inevitably drop. And while farm prices were falling, the prices of the industrial goods that the farmer needed rose higher and higher. As a result, many farmers found it increasingly difficult to meet their mortgage payments or the installments on their farm machinery. Thus, during the industrial prosperity of the 1920's, many farmers were sinking deeper into debt, and many lost their farms. The plight of sharecroppers and tenants, white and black alike, was even worse than that of the small farmers.

Belief in prosperity. But few people in the 1920's paid much attention to these limitations of prosperity. Most Americans believed, with Herbert Hoover, that "we in America are nearer to the final triumph over poverty than ever before in the history of any land." Thus, the depression that started late in 1929 came as a stunning blow to most Americans.

The stock market crash. For years the prices of stocks had been moving upward. After Hoover's election in November 1928, moreover, a frenzy of speculation gripped the country. Convinced that they were entering "four more years of prosperity," investors bought feverishly. Despite repeated warnings that stock prices were much too high, Amer-

■ A photograph of New York City's Wall Street is superimposed below on the front page of a newspaper reporting the "nation-wide stampede" to unload stocks.

The New York Times.

Copyright, 1929, by The New York Times Company.

THE WEATHER
Rain today and probably tomorrow; somewhat colder tomorrow.
Temperature Yesterday—Max. 54, Min. 47.
£70 S. Weather Forecast—For South see Page 48.

NEW YORK, TUESDAY, OCTOBER 29, 1929.

TWO CENTS In Greater | THREE CENTS | FOUR CENTS Elsewhere
New York | Within 200 Miles | Except 7th and 8th Postal Zones

S SENATORS RENEW DEMAND ON HOOVER

Roosevelt's Memory Honored In Navy Day Fete on Ships

EUROPE IS DISTURBED ...CTION ...DEBT

STOCK PRICES SLUMP $14,000,000,000 IN NATION-WIDE STAMPEDE TO UNLOAD; BANKERS TO SUPPORT MARKET TODAY

Sixteen Leading Issues Down $2,893,520,108;
Tel. & Tel. and Steel Among Heaviest Losers

A shrinkage of $2,893,520,108 in the open market value of the shares of sixteen representative companies resulted from yesterday's sweeping decline on the New York Stock Exchange.

American Telephone and Telegraph was the heaviest loser, $448,905,162 having been lopped off of its total value. United States Steel common, traditional bellwether of the stock market, made its greatest nose-dive in recent years by falling from a high of 202½ to a low of 185. In a feeble last-minute rally it snapped back to 186, at which it closed, showing a net loss of 17¼ points. This represented for the 8,131,055 shares of common stock outstanding a total loss in value of $142,293,446.

In the following table are shown the day's net depreciation in the outstanding shares of the sixteen companies referred to:

Issues.	Shares Listed.	Losses in Points.	Depreciation
American Radiator	10,096,289	10%	$104,748,997
American Tel. & Tel.........	13,203,093	34	448,905,162
Commonwealth & Southern....	30,764,468	3⅛	96,138,963
Columbia Gas & Electric......	8,477,307	22	186,500,754
Consolidated Gas...........	11,451,188	20	229,023,760
DuPont E. I.................	10,322,481	18½	190,960,628
Eastman Kodak	2,229,703	41½	93,368,813
General Electric	7,231,684	47¼	342,345,480
General Motors.............	43,500,000	6½	283,675,000
International Nickel..........	13,777,696	7⅝	108,497,088
New York Central...........	4,637,088	22⅞	106,214,071
Standard Oil of New Jersey...	24,843,643	8	198,749,144
Union Carbide & Carbon			

PREMIER ISSUES HARD HIT

Unexpected Torrent o Liquidation Again Rocks Markets.

DAY'S SALES 9,212,80(

Nearly 3,000,000 Shares Ar Traded In Final Hour—The Tickers Lag 167 Minutes.

NEW RALLY SOON BROKER

Selling by Europeans and "Mot Psychology" Big Factors in Second Big Break.

icans from many walks of life invested in stocks. During most of 1929, stock prices soared to higher and higher levels.

Then the bubble burst. On October 24, 1929, a panic of selling hit the New York Stock Exchange as frantic orders to sell stock came pouring in. The causes of this panic were chiefly overproduction and overspeculation. More goods had been produced than could be profitably sold. And a great many stocks were either worthless or overinflated. That is, the business behind such stocks either existed on paper only, or their actual value was far less than the market value of the stock.

Overproduction and overspeculation had caught up with the American people. The overinflated prices of stocks tumbled downward. On October 29 prices sank to a shattering new low when over 16 million shares of stock were dumped on the market. By mid-November the average value of leading stocks had been cut in half, and stockholders had lost $30 billion. With this "crash" of the stock market, the Great Depression started.

At first business and government leaders tried to reassure the American people. "Business is fundamentally sound," announced Secretary of the Treasury Andrew Mellon. But such words, no matter how reassuring, could not stem the tide of economic disaster sweeping the country.

Spread of the Great Depression.   Before 1929 ended, banks all over the country were closing their doors. Businesses everywhere cut back production, and many concerns, finding themselves without customers, were forced out of business. Factories and mines were shut down. Empty railroad cars piled up on the sidings. By 1930 between 6 and 7 million Americans were unemployed. The result was a chain reaction. Unemployment meant fewer customers; a decrease in customers caused further cutbacks in production; these cutbacks, in turn, resulted in more unemployment. By 1932 nearly 12 million Americans were out of work.

The depression struck at all classes. Many well-to-do Americans helplessly watched their fortunes, invested in stocks or businesses, disappear. But the industrial workers and the farmers suffered most. Most wage earners had no savings to tide them over a period of unemployment. In every city thousands of unfortunate men and women stood in lines to get free meals of bread and soup. Families forced out of their homes moved to makeshift huts that they built on unused land at the edges of the cities, using scrap lumber, packing boxes, and corrugated iron.

For the farmers the depression came as a final blow. As you have seen, most farmers had never shared fully in the prosperity of the twenties. But bad as conditions were before, they became steadily worse between 1929 and 1932. Farm prices fell lower and lower. As their incomes shrank, more and more farmers lost their farms. In some midwestern states desperate farmers used force to prevent sheriffs from foreclosing mortgages on their farms.

Many thousands of men from cities and farms wandered over the land seeking jobs at any wages, hitchhiking or hiding in freight trains, and sleeping on park benches. Never had America known such widespread suffering.

What caused the depression?   There is no simple way to explain the Great Depression. Economists agree that there were many causes, but they disagree about which was most important.

President Hoover insisted that the major cause was the worldwide economic disorder that followed World War I. Many economists agreed. They pointed to the vast destruction of property during the war and the worldwide dislocation of trade during and after the war.

Other economists argued that America's high tariff policies helped to stifle world trade and hurt American business. High tariffs, they claimed, prevented other countries from selling their goods in the United States. This in turn prevented them from securing the dollars that they needed to buy American products.

Still other economists blamed the depression on the excessive borrowing of money—for stocks, for comforts purchased on the installment plan, or for the expansion of businesses. These critics also claimed that the federal government failed to control bank loans and to protect the public against the sale of stocks that had no value.

Some economists have argued that depressions are an inevitable part of the American economic system. According to this view, business expands during periods of prosperity in order to obtain the largest possible profits. But when factories produce more goods than consumers can buy, the factories have to cut down on production, at least until their surpluses are consumed. For this reason, these economists have argued, prosperity and depression are inevitable parts of the business cycle.

Finally, some economists have traced the Great Depression to uneven distribution of income. These economists have argued that, if farmers had received better prices for their products and if workers had received higher wages, the American people

■ **The depression struck at all classes. In every American city thousands of men and women stood in lines, like the one shown above, to get free meals of bread and soup.**

would have been able to buy a larger proportion of the surplus goods. Had this happened, these economists claim, the factories would have kept busy and the depression could have been avoided.

Hoover and the depression. Whatever its causes, the depression confronted the Hoover administration with two emergencies. First, there was the widespread misery of people without jobs or farms, without money to buy enough food or clothing, and increasingly without hope. Some Americans urged the federal government to extend direct relief to those in need. President Hoover, however, believed that direct aid was a responsibility of local communities. Direct federal relief, he said, would create a vast, inefficient bureaucracy and undermine the self-respect of the persons receiving it. Unfortunately, local communities did not have the resources to cope with the ever-rising tide of human misery.

To the second emergency, the collapse of business and agriculture, Hoover responded more actively. He instructed the Federal Farm Board to buy up agricultural surpluses in an effort to raise falling farm prices. With the support of Congress, he started several public works programs, among them Boulder Dam (later called Hoover Dam) on the Colorado River. These projects were intended to stimulate business and provide employment for jobless workers.

Also at Hoover's urging, Congress created the Reconstruction Finance Corporation (RFC) in February 1932. The Reconstruction Finance Corporation was authorized to lend large sums of money to banks, life insurance companies, railroads, farm mortgage associations, and other enterprises. President Hoover and his associates hoped that federal loans would strengthen these key businesses and thus provide jobs for millions of workers. The RFC advanced nearly $2 billion in loans to American business during the remaining years of the Hoover administration, but the depression grew worse.

In response to a recommendation by Hoover, Congress also passed the Home Loan Bank Act in July 1932. This act created a series of special banks designed to provide financial assistance to savings banks, building and loan associations, and insurance companies—all of which lent money on mortgages. By providing financial aid to these key mortgage institutions, Hoover hoped to reduce foreclosures on homes and farms and to stimulate construction of residential buildings.

639

■ To American farmers, the depression came as a final blow. Many lost their farms and wandered over the land as migrant workers. This moving photograph shows the troubled mother of a migrant family with her children.

In adopting these measures, the President and Congress were accepting, for the first time, the idea that the federal government must assume certain responsibilities when the nation's economy becomes disordered. Unfortunately, the measures that they adopted did not stop the downward trend.

The election campaign of 1932. Although several issues, among them prohibition, entered into the Presidential campaign of 1932, there was really only one important issue—the depression. The Republicans renominated Herbert Hoover. During the campaign Hoover continued to blame the depression on international conditions, and declared that his policies were beginning to bring recovery.

Both of these claims were vigorously rejected by the Democratic Presidential candidate, New York Governor Franklin Delano Roosevelt. Roosevelt maintained that Republican policies, not international conditions, were to blame for the depression. He argued that the federal government should help provide direct relief to the needy and direct aid to

640

farmers. He called for a broad program of public works. And he demanded that safeguards be set up to prevent wild speculation and fraudulent issues of stock. To this end he proposed laws to protect the bank depositor, the purchaser of stocks, and the home owner. Referring to unemployed workers, desperate farmers, and others, Roosevelt stated that the "forgotten man" must have a "new deal."

Roosevelt's victory. Franklin D. Roosevelt and his running mate, John Nance Garner of Texas, swept the country in the election of 1932, with Roosevelt winning 23 million popular votes to Hoover's 16 million. Roosevelt carried 42 states and piled up 472 electoral votes to Hoover's 59. Moreover, the Democrats secured decisive majorities in both houses of Congress. Not since the Civil War had the Democratic Party won such a sweeping victory.

A majority of voters throughout the 1920's had given the Republicans credit for the prosperity of those years. Now a great many Americans seemed to be saying that the Republicans should take the blame for the depression. Many who voted for the Democrats were really voting against Hoover rather than for Roosevelt. But many more saw in Roosevelt the kind of dynamic personality that they believed was needed to lead the country out of its troubles.

Roosevelt had promised the American people a "new deal." During the four months between Election Day and Inauguration Day—March 4, 1933 —workers, farmers, and even many businessmen waited impatiently and hopefully to see how the new President would carry out his pledge. You will read about the New Deal in Chapters 36 and 37.

SECTION SURVEY

IDENTIFY: depression, Great Depression, the stock market crash, "the forgotten man," RFC; Franklin D. Roosevelt; October 1929.

1. The "Golden Twenties" were golden for some, but for the majority of Americans there was little gold in them. Do you agree or disagree? Explain.
2. How do economists exp'ain the major causes of the Great Depression?
3. How did the measures taken by Hoover to combat the depression reflect his philosophy of government and its role in economic affairs?
4. According to the 1920 census, more Americans were living in cities than on farms. How does this fact relate to the hardships experienced by the "little people" with the coming of the depression?

TRACING THE MAIN IDEAS

After three years of unrest and readjustment following World War I, Americans enjoyed a decade of enormous prosperity. During the "Golden Twenties" business prospered, wages were high, and most workers were employed.

Here and there warning voices called attention to the difficulties faced by large numbers of farmers and to other weaknesses of the economic system. Most Americans, however, believed that prosperity had come to stay.

And then, toward the end of 1929, the great American industrial machine began to grind to a halt. At first people could not believe that the situation was serious. But as the months passed, it became increasingly evident that the nation was facing a major crisis.

What was wrong? Americans did not agree on all the answers to this very important question. But they did agree that something must be done to save the country from complete economic collapse.

The election campaign of 1932 was waged in this atmosphere. With the victory of Franklin D. Roosevelt and the Democratic Party, Congress began a series of experiments collectively referred to as the New Deal.

But the shock and disillusionment that swept across the United States in the early 1930's were not confined to domestic affairs. As you will see, by the time Franklin D. Roosevelt entered the White House in 1933, the structure of peace that men had been building since World War I was crumbling. At home and abroad Americans were confronted with the most serious problems they had ever faced.

CHAPTER SURVEY

QUESTIONS FOR DISCUSSION

1. Why were Americans more interested in domestic affairs than in international relations in the year 1920?
2. Was the "Red scare" the first experience of this kind in our history? Explain your answer.
3. During the Boston police strike, Governor Coolidge made the following statement: "There is no right to strike against the public safety by anybody, anywhere, any time." What did he mean? Do you agree or disagree with his viewpoint? Why?
4. When the cost of living goes up, how does it affect (a) buying power, (b) people living on fixed incomes?
5. Speaking in the 1920's, Herbert Hoover said: "We in America are nearer to the final triumph over poverty than ever before in the history of any land." (a) What facts supported his opinion? (b) Why were some Americans critical of his view?
6. How did business conditions contribute to the Republican Party's success during the 1920's?

RELATING PAST TO PRESENT

1. Compare the racial riots of 1919 with those of the 1960's with regard to where they occurred, their causes, and their results.
2. Is it fair to blame or praise a President or a political party for (a) a war, (b) a depression, (c) prosperity? Explain.
3. Compare the attitudes of the American people toward labor unions today and during the period of the 1920's.
4. Do you think the slogan "rugged individualism" still applies to our economic theories today? Explain.
5. During the depression years, black Americans were one of the groups hardest hit by unemployment. Why was this so? If the country suffered another depression, do you think the same thing would happen today? Why or why not?

USING MAPS AND CHARTS

1. Using chart 1 on page 876, (a) calculate the approximate percentage of the population included in the labor force in 1920. What is the significance of this percentage compared with the figures for the previous years? (b) In 1920, how many workers were employed in farming, in manufacturing, and in trade, services, and government? (Refer to chart 3 on page 876.) What conclusion can you draw from these figures?
2. Consulting chart 4 on page 873, answer the following: (a) Compare the rates of the Fordney-McCumber Tariff with those tariffs that preceded and followed it. (b) What does this information tell you? How well does this information reflect the times?
3. Using chart 3 on page 873, answer the following: (a) In 1920, what was the relation of our exports to our imports? (b) How does this relationship differ from that in the year 1900?

Detail from George Luks' "Armistice Night." Anonymous gift. Oil on canvas. 1918. 37 x 68¾. Collection Whitney Museum of American Art, New York.

■ *Celebrating the armistice*

CHAPTER 34

American Rejection of World Leadership

1920 – 1932

ON NOVEMBER 11, 1918, almost everyone in America took the day off from work. Factories, offices, stores, and schools closed their doors while Americans, old and young, poured into the streets of every city and town and village across the land to celebrate the armistice that brought an end to World War I. In an exultant statement to the press, President Wilson announced, "Everything for which America fought has been accomplished." So it seemed to him, and so it seemed to Americans in general on November 11, 1918.

But Wilson realized, as millions of Americans did not, that it is easier to win a victory on the battlefield than to build a lasting peace. He warned his fellow Americans of the tremendous problems that remained to be solved and challenged them to assume the responsibility of world leadership. Americans, however, were tired of wartime restrictions, and eager to return to the everyday business of living. And when, as the months passed, the European nations began to quarrel over the spoils of war, Americans became increasingly disillusioned.

President Wilson struggled hard to get his fellow Americans to support his plans for peace. But by the early 1920's the American people had repudiated Wilson, rejected the League of Nations, and, at least in the political sphere, had turned their backs upon Europe and the opportunities and risks of assuming world leadership.

THE CHAPTER IN OUTLINE

1. America's refusal to join the League of Nations.

2. America's exclusion of Europe's people and goods.

3. Moving toward better relations with Latin America.

4. Working with other nations to build peace and prevent war.

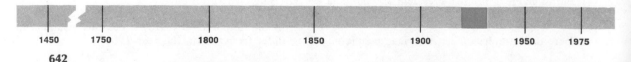

1450   1750   1800   1850   1900   1950   1975

1 America's refusal to join the League of Nations

On December 4, 1918, the army transport *George Washington* sailed out of New York harbor and steamed toward Europe. Its most distinguished passenger was President Wilson, who was bound for the peace conference at Paris.

Wilson was the first President ever to leave the Western Hemisphere during his term of office. He hoped to persuade the other representatives at the conference to adopt the Fourteen Points that he had earlier outlined as "the only possible program for world peace" (page 618).

The "Big Four."   The peace conference, which opened on January 18, 1919, had much of the tension of a melodrama. The stage, however, was the world; the principal characters were the chief officials of the four leading powers—Great Britain, France, Italy, and the United States; and the outcome of the drama would affect millions of people.

Wilson arrived at the conference after a triumphal journey through Great Britain, Italy, and France, where masses of people had turned out to greet the man who symbolized their hope for a better world. Encouraged by this reception, Wilson felt that he could use his great popularity to bring about a just peace based on his Fourteen Points. But the three other leading delegates at Paris, supported by powerful interests in their homelands, had very different aims.

David Lloyd George, the British Prime Minister, had just won a general election by using the vindictive slogans "Hang the Kaiser" and "Make Germany Pay." He had no intention of becoming unpopular with the British voters by showing generosity toward the Germans, or by giving up England's naval supremacy and accepting Wilson's idea of "freedom of the seas."

The "Tiger" of French politics, Premier Georges Clemenceau (ZHORZH klay·mahn·SOH), believed that the only way to defend France was to crush Germany. And Italy's Vittorio Orlando wanted to acquire territory that had been secretly promised to Italy when Italy joined the Allies in 1915.

The problem of secret treaties.   The united opposition of Lloyd George, Clemenceau, and Orlando was not the only problem President Wilson faced. There was also the problem of secret treaties.

As you have read (page 618), in 1917 the Russian Bolsheviks published certain secret treaties that the Allies had made before the United States entered the war. The new Communist rulers of Russia hoped to discredit the Allies by exposing these treaties as "imperialist diplomacy," and to some extent they succeeded.

Under these treaties, the Allies agreed to divide the spoils of victory. Great Britain was to take over

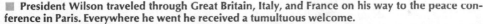

■ President Wilson traveled through Great Britain, Italy, and France on his way to the peace conference in Paris. Everywhere he went he received a tumultuous welcome.

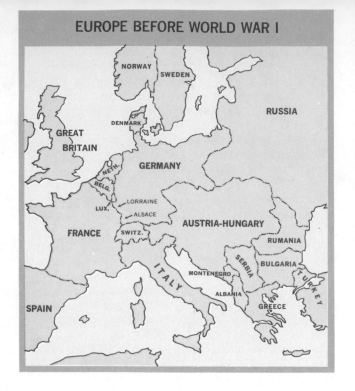

EUROPE BEFORE WORLD WAR I

Germany's colonies, except for certain territories in the Pacific Ocean which were to go to Japan. (Japan had declared war on Germany in 1914.) France, Russia, Serbia, and Italy were to enlarge their national boundaries at the expense of Germany and Austria-Hungary. And, finally, Germany was to make huge payments, called *reparations,* to the Allies to compensate for damages resulting from the war. These secret arrangements obviously contradicted several of Wilson's Fourteen Points, such as open diplomacy, national self-determination, and the end of colonialism.

Wilson's dilemma. Faced with these secret treaties and with the united opposition of Lloyd George, Clemenceau, and Orlando, Wilson could either compromise—or walk out of the Paris Peace Conference. Indeed, at one point he almost did walk out, but he realized that such a step might be taken as a confession of failure. He was also afraid that Communism might spread from Russia into central Europe if a peace treaty were delayed and conditions remained unstable. His strongest reason for staying, however, was his faith in a League of Nations. Such a League, he was convinced, would in time remedy any injustices that the peace treaty might contain.

The Treaty of Versailles. The final peace treaty, called the Treaty of Versailles, was com-

■ The "Big Four" at the Versailles peace conference of 1919 were (from left to right) David Lloyd George of Great Britain, Vittorio Orlando of Italy, Georges Clemenceau of France, and Woodrow Wilson of the United States. In an effort to satisfy some national groups they

pleted and signed late in June 1919. The treaty showed the results of bargaining between Wilson on one side and Lloyd George, Clemenceau, and Orlando on the other.

The Treaty of Versailles and related treaties made important changes in the map of the world, and especially in the map of Europe. Germany's colonies were given to the Allied victors, but under a *mandate system* which required the new owners to account for their colonial administration to the League of Nations.

Certain border areas of pre-war Germany were lopped off. One important area, Alsace-Lorraine, was assigned to France. Other areas were included in a new country, Czechoslovakia, and in a re-created Poland. To satisfy the nationalist desires of various peoples in eastern Europe, several other independent states were created, including Finland, Estonia, Latvia, Lithuania, and Yugoslavia. Certain border changes were made for Italy, Greece, Rumania, and Belgium (see maps, this page and page 645).

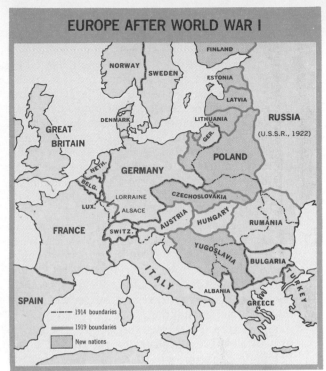

EUROPE AFTER WORLD WAR I

NORWAY SWEDEN FINLAND
ESTONIA
LATVIA
DENMARK LITHUANIA
GREAT BRITAIN RUSSIA (U.S.S.R., 1922)
GER.
POLAND
NETH. GERMANY
BELG. LORRAINE CZECHOSLOVAKIA
LUX. ALSACE AUSTRIA HUNGARY RUMANIA
FRANCE SWITZ. YUGOSLAVIA BULGARIA
ITALY TURKEY
SPAIN ALBANIA GREECE

- - - - 1914 boundaries
———— 1919 boundaries
New nations

remade the map of Europe, as shown in these pages. But in doing so, they antagonized other national groups, whose dissatisfaction later arose to be among the causes leading to World War II. Thus Wilson's ideals were shattered against the harsh realities of European affairs.

Under the Treaty of Versailles, the German government reluctantly accepted full responsibility for starting the war, and agreed to remain disarmed. Germany also agreed to pay large reparations for war damage.

Wilson failed to convince the other Allied representatives that vengeance and greed were weak foundations for a lasting peace. But he did successfully oppose some of the more unreasonable Allied demands. And he had the great personal satisfaction of seeing the Covenant of the League of Nations written into the Treaty of Versailles.

The League of Nations. The League of Nations, with headquarters at Geneva, Switzerland, provided international machinery to make war less likely. The machinery consisted of (1) a permanent Secretariat, or administrative and secretarial staff; (2) an Assembly in which each member nation had one vote; and (3) a Council, the all-important executive body. The Council had five permanent members—the five great powers of France, Great Britain, Italy, Japan, and the United States—al-

though other nations were also represented by means of rotating membership. Germany and the Soviet Union (Russia) were excluded from League membership. Closely related to the League were the Permanent Court of International Justice, the International Labor Organization, and other international agencies.

The League Covenant did not outlaw war. But each League member agreed, before going to war, to make every effort to solve its difficulties in a friendly way, and even then to wait during a "cooling off" period before striking a blow. If any member failed to do this, the other members might then decide, through the Council, to apply "economic sanctions" by refusing to trade with the offender. Moreover, the Council might go further and recommend the use of force against the "aggressor" state. To forestall efforts to change the new map of the world by force, Article Ten of the Covenant provided that each League member was to guarantee the territorial integrity and political independence of every other member.

The League Covenant also created agencies for many worthwhile causes: improving conditions of labor and health throughout the world, working for the reduction of armaments, and trying to abolish slavery and the narcotics trade. These were important steps toward international cooperation.

645

League weaknesses. The League of Nations was not, of course, a perfect organization. It had several serious weaknesses. For one thing, taking action against an aggressor was almost impossible for several reasons. First, the term "aggressor" was not clearly defined. Second, the Council could only recommend that nations take action, but could not compel them to act. Third, any Council member could block the wishes of the other members because all important Council decisions had to be unanimous. In brief, the work of the League depended upon the willingness of its members to cooperate.

Another basic weakness of the League was its guarantee of existing political boundaries. When the map of Europe was redrawn, some peoples found that they were now part of a different nation —one that they did not want to belong to. Yet these peoples had no way to secure further changes in their national boundaries.

A third weakness was the League's failure to provide adequate machinery for recommending solutions to economic problems that might lead to war. Trade rivalries and tariff barriers still existed, as did imperialism, yet the League could not do much more than study such problems. Still another weakness was exclusion of the Soviet Union and Germany from membership. And finally, the League was in no position to tackle the problem of reducing armaments.

Despite its shortcomings, however, the League of Nations was a promising beginning in the difficult task of creating a new, cooperative world order, dedicated to international peace and justice. In the 1930's about 60 nations belonged to the League, which was bringing an important new ingredient into international affairs—the organized moral judgment of a majority of the nations of the world.

Senate rejection of the League. Early in July 1919 President Wilson returned from Paris to ask the Senate to approve the Treaty of Versailles, and thus bring the United States into the League. The Senate shattered his hopes by rejecting the treaty. Senator Henry Cabot Lodge of Massachusetts, chairman of the important Committee on Foreign Relations, and other Republican Senators opposed the League.

Many Americans thought that the Treaty of Versailles was unjust, and they were unwilling to have the United States join a League which pledged its members to carry out the provisions of the treaty. Many Americans pointed with alarm to Article Ten of the League Covenant, which pledged each member to guarantee the existing political boundaries of the other members. Americans argued that such a pledge might involve the United States in war.

Wilson's refusal to compromise. Despite the opposition to the League of Nations, the Senate might have voted for it if President Wilson had been willing to accept amendments proposed by Senator Lodge and his supporters. These amendments were designed to safeguard American interests and to prevent the United States from being drawn into European conflicts. Wilson believed, however, that these amendments would so weaken the League that it would become ineffective. He refused to compromise.

To win public support, Wilson traveled across the country making speeches in defense of the League. Finally, exhausted by the long strain, in the fall of 1919 he collapsed, and for seven months lived in seclusion. His one remaining hope was that the public would support his cause by electing a Democratic President in the 1920 election. But the Republican landslide of that year and the election of President Harding (page 631) seemed to indicate that Americans preferred to forget the League and world problems in general. They paid no heed to Wilson when he warned, "Arrangements of the present peace cannot stand a generation unless they are guaranteed by the united forces of the civilized world."

The rise of Japanese, Italian, and German expansionism in the 1930's bore out Wilson's prophecy. But by that time, as you will see, the League had become too weak to prevent the outbreak of World War II.

SECTION SURVEY

IDENTIFY: "Big Four," Treaty of Versailles, reparations, mandate system, economic sanctions; Henry Cabot Lodge.

1. Compare the views of Wilson, Lloyd George, Clemenceau, and Orlando concerning the treaty of peace.
2. Give four ways in which the Treaty of Versailles changed the map of the world.
3. (a) Describe the structure of the League of Nations. (b) What machinery did the League set up for the prevention of war?
4. What were some of the major weaknesses of the League? Explain.
5. (a) List two arguments presented by Americans who rejected the League. (b) Do you think it is really possible to say what would have happened if the United States had joined the League? Explain.

2 America's exclusion of Europe's people and goods

America's refusal to join the League of Nations was based in part upon a desire to avoid becoming involved again in Europe's troubles and quarrels. But this desire led much further than the rejection of the League.

The United States also tried, with considerable success, to keep out the people and products of Europe and Asia. The immigration and tariff laws passed during this period were the most restrictive in American history.

Closing the gates. During the 1920's the United States reversed one of its oldest traditions by almost completely halting immigration. Earlier, it is true, specific laws and international agreements had excluded the Chinese, the Japanese, and most other Asians. But despite exceptions, few Americans had seriously questioned the historic role of the United States as a haven of refuge and a land of opportunity for immigrants. Indeed, during the decade before World War I, more Europeans settled in the United States than in any previous 10-year period.

Reasons for closing the gates. Why did a nation of immigrants and descendants of immigrants suddenly close its doors? One reason was the general anti-European feeling that swept over America after the war. But certain groups of Americans had special reasons of their own.

Organized labor, for example, argued that new immigrants were willing to work for lower wages than American workers and thus pulled down the standard of living. Industrialists who had formerly favored immigration as a source of plentiful, cheap, unskilled labor no longer needed masses of unskilled workers, for by 1920 the railroads had been built and the basic industries such as steel were well developed. Finally, many established Americans felt that the newer immigrants, mainly from eastern and southern Europe, did not easily become "Americanized." These Americans thought that it was harmful to the country to admit settlers whose languages and customs were so different from those of older inhabitants.

The immigration laws. Responding to these and other arguments, Congress passed three laws in the 1920's that progressively restricted immigration from Europe. The Emergency Quota Act of 1921 introduced a *quota system* which limited the number of Europeans and others who could be admitted to 3 percent of the total number of persons of their nationality residing in the United States in the year 1910. The 1921 act also set a total yearly limit of about 350,000 immigrants.

In 1924 an even more restrictive law was passed which reduced the annual quota from 3 to 2 percent, and changed the base year from 1910

■ For decades before the 1920's, most immigrants to the United States had made their first American homes in overcrowded neighborhoods such as Orchard Street (below) in New York City.

■ This cartoon comments on the new, restrictive immigration law passed by Congress in 1924. Do you think the cartoon is an accurate representation of what the law signified?

to 1890. This change in the base year discriminated against Italians, Austrians, Russians, and other eastern and southern Europeans who had immigrated to the United States mainly after 1890.

Finally, the National Origins Act of 1929 shifted the base year of immigration to 1920, but counterbalanced this more liberal provision by reducing to 150,000 the total number of immigrants to be admitted during any one year.

The new immigration policies aroused a great deal of bitterness, especially among eastern and southern Europeans. The Japanese were also aroused because the immigration act of 1924 ended the Gentlemen's Agreement of 1907, which Japan

had faithfully observed, and closed the doors completely to Japanese immigrants.

The war of tariffs. While closing its doors to immigrants, the United States was also, like other nations, raising tariff barriers to keep out foreign products. As you have seen, the Fordney-McCumber Tariff of 1922 increased import duties on hundreds of items. And in 1930 the Hawley-Smoot Tariff lifted tariff rates to the highest level in American history.

America's high tariff policy proved a cruel blow to many countries in Latin America and in Europe. When America's high tariffs deprived these countries of their best markets in the United States, their economic strength declined. Factories closed, men were thrown out of work, and the surplus of farm products mounted steadily.

Some countries struck back by raising their own tariff barriers against American goods. Thus the high tariffs that Congress hoped would aid American industry helped in the end to deprive many American businessmen and farmers of the foreign markets they badly needed. The peace treaties had barely been signed before the nations of the world were engaged in another war—a trade war fought with tariffs.

War debts and high tariffs. America's high tariff policy created still another problem. How could European countries pay their war debts to the United States if they could not sell their goods in this country?

The war had changed America's relation to Europe from debtor to creditor. Before the war American businessmen had borrowed money from Europeans to finance new industries. During the period before the United States entered the war in 1917, however, Europeans began to sell their American stocks and bonds to buy war goods. And, as the war progressed, the American government lent huge sums to the warring countries. As a result, by 1918 nearly all the European countries owed money to the United States. The total amounted to about $10 billion.

The American government reduced the interest rates on the loans and arranged for the debtor nations to repay the money over a long time period. Yet, despite the generous terms, the bankrupt European countries emerged from the war not knowing how they could repay their debts.

President Wilson reminded Congress of one possible solution to Europe's problems when he declared, "If we wish to have Europe settle her debts, we must be prepared to buy from her." But this solution became impossible when the United States adopted a high-tariff policy.

War debts and reparations. The only other solution open to the European Allies was to collect war damages, or reparations, from Germany, and to use this money to repay their war debts to the United States. In 1921 a Reparations Commission fixed the total of German reparations at $33 billion. Germany, however, was in the midst of severe economic troubles, and in no position to pay such a huge sum. In an effort to secure the money, Germany borrowed heavily from bankers in the United States and Europe.

But there was a limit to the amount that the German government could borrow, and, as the years passed, the reparations had to be reduced—once in 1924 and again in 1929. In spite of this relief, however, Germany's economic situation grew steadily worse. By 1930 it looked as though the Germans could make no further payments.

A legacy of bitterness. Faced with this situation, the debtor countries notified the United States that they could no longer meet their payments on the war debts. After all, they argued, they had contributed far more to victory in blood and sacrifice than had America and it would be only fair of the United States to cancel all war debts.

The American government, supported by most Americans, refused to admit such a claim. It insisted that the war debts to the United States and German reparations payments to the Allies were two entirely separate matters. Americans pointed out that some of the loans—perhaps as much as a third of the total amount—had, in fact, been made after the armistice. Americans also reminded the European countries that they were not too poor to spend large sums for armaments.

Then in 1931 the debtors, with the exception of Finland, refused to make even a token payment. President Hoover then declared a year's halt, or *moratorium,* on the payment of war debts and reparations. But Germany did not make any more payments, and the whole question was left unsolved.

In the end, most of the war debts and most of Germany's reparations remained unpaid. But America's unsuccessful attempt to collect the war debts increased Europe's resentment against the United States. And the European victors' attempt to collect reparations from Germany, though equally unsuccessful, created a feeling of bitterness among the German people, which, as you will see, contributed to the rise of Adolf Hitler in the early 1930's.

SECTION SURVEY

IDENTIFY: quota system, armaments, moratorium.

1. Give four reasons why the United States closed its gates to immigrants after World War I.
2. How did the emotions created by the war, the "Red scare," and a decreased need for "cheap" labor lead to demands for the restriction of immigration?
3. Who do you think would be more anti-immigrant—people living in rural areas or in urban areas? Explain.
4. (a) What reasons did the European Allies give for stopping payments on their war debts? (b) How did Americans answer these arguments?
5. In what ways did America's high-tariff policies backfire?

3 Moving toward better relations with Latin America

During the early 1900's, as you have read, Presidents Theodore Roosevelt, William Howard Taft, and Woodrow Wilson had all intervened in Latin-American affairs. They had justified their intervention on the grounds that it was necessary (1) to safeguard the Panama Canal, (2) to prevent European countries from extending their influence in the Caribbean, and (3) to protect American citizens and property in Latin America.

This Caribbean policy, as it was called, was continued by Presidents Harding and Coolidge. Critics of the policy—and there were many on both sides of the border—referred to it as "dollar diplomacy." Many Latin Americans called it "Yankee imperialism."

Investments in Latin America. During the "Golden Twenties," as you have read, many Americans had money to invest. The underdeveloped countries of Latin America offered inviting opportunities for investment, and American dollars financed the building of factories, railroads, mines, and ranches in the lands to the south. Whereas in 1913 United States investments in Latin America totaled $1.3 billion, by 1928 they totaled more than $5 billion.

American intervention. American interest in Latin America grew in proportion to the amount of American money invested there. President Coolidge frankly declared that the United States government would protect the property and lives of American citizens wherever they went.

During these years many Latin-American countries were undergoing social and economic revolutions. Frequently two groups in a country struggled to gain control, and each group claimed that it alone represented the people and the legal government. When this happened, the United States tended to recognize the group most friendly to American interests.

In some instances the United States played an active role in the struggle for power. On occasions it forbade the sale of arms to the group it disliked and armed the group it supported. Worst of all from the Latin-American point of view, the United States sometimes sent armed forces to protect American lives and property.

Relations with Nicaragua. American policy toward Nicaragua offers an example of the kind of intervention that Latin Americans fiercely resented. The United States was particularly concerned about Nicaragua because of large American investments there. Moreover, Nicaragua was close to the vital Panama Canal. Finally, there was the prospect that a new canal might eventually be built through Nicaragua itself. President Taft had sent marines into the country during an internal conflict to protect American investments and the nearby Panama Canal. President Coolidge withdrew the marines in 1925, but sent them back in 1926 when new disturbances broke out.

This policy was unpopular throughout Latin America. It was also unpopular with many Americans who claimed that the United States was really making war. President Coolidge denied this and spoke of the American occupation as a police duty. But criticism was so strong that the administration took measures to solve the problem by more peaceful means.

In 1927 President Coolidge withdrew most of the marines, leaving only enough to assure the protection of American property if violence again broke out. This helped to relieve the tension between the United States and Nicaragua. But the Nicaraguans demanded the complete withdrawal of *all* marines and the end of American interference. In 1933 President Hoover finally withdrew all United States troops.

Strained relations with Mexico. United States relations with Mexico also reflected the determination of the United States to protect American interests south of the Rio Grande. As you will recall (page 597), during Wilson's administration a sweeping social revolution in Mexico had raised new problems in the traditionally uneasy relations between the two countries. American lives and property suffered in the upheaval. But far more threatening to Americans who had invested in Mexican property was the new policy established in the Mexican constitution of 1917.

Article 27 of the Mexican constitution declared that "only Mexicans . . . have the right to acquire ownership [of, or] . . . to develop mines, waters, or mineral fuels in the Republic of Mexico. The nation may grant the same right to foreigners, provided they agree to be considered Mexicans in respect of such property, and accordingly not to involve the protection of their government in respect of the same." This article also canceled concessions made to foreigners by earlier governments. Foreign businessmen and investors were quick to protest.

During 1917 and 1918 the United States was too involved in the European war to take any action in regard to Mexico. Moreover, not all of the provisions of the constitution were at once applied. But immediately after the armistice in 1918, oil investors and other American owners of property in Mexico clamored for intervention. These businessmen were joined by many American Catholics who were greatly disturbed over anti-Catholic provisions in the Mexican constitution and the anti-clerical policies of the Mexican government. The situation grew worse when the Mexicans supported the anti-American faction in Nicaragua. By 1927 relations between the United States and Mexico were close to the breaking point.

Improved relations. In 1927, however, the United States began slowly to modify its policy. President Coolidge took the first step by sending Dwight W. Morrow, a successful banker, as ambassador to Mexico.

Instead of threatening Mexico with United States power, Morrow tried to understand the Mexican point of view. His sincerity, intelligence, and charm quickly won him many friends in Mexico. The skillful work of Morrow and other American "ambassadors of good will" repaired much of the damage done in the past. The Mexicans agreed to recognize American titles to subsoil minerals, such as petroleum, that had been in effect before the constitution of 1917.

Moving toward a new policy. The Morrow mission marked a turning point in American relations with Mexico and with other Latin-American countries. From 1927 on, both Calvin Coolidge and his successor, Herbert Hoover, went out of their way to cultivate friendlier relations with the Caribbean republics and with the South American nations. Coolidge went to Havana, Cuba, in 1928

■ Herbert Hoover toured South America in 1929, before his inauguration as President of the United States. Above, he descends from a horse-drawn carriage in Santiago, Chile.

and personally opened a Pan-American Conference. Hoover toured South America in the months before his inauguration.

Latin Americans were pleased by the friendly attention of an American President and a President-elect. Their governments encouraged American investments and gave those investments greater protection than in the past. The United States, in turn, stopped intervening by force in the internal affairs of Latin-American nations.

The Monroe Doctrine modified. But Latin Americans still resented the 1904 Roosevelt Corollary to the Monroe Doctrine. As you have read (page 595), the Roosevelt Corollary stated that the United States had the right to act as policeman of the Western Hemisphere.

In the hope of improving United States relations with Latin America still further, the Department of State declared in 1930 that the Monroe Doctrine no longer would be used to justify United States intervention in Latin-American domestic affairs. Thus, by the end of the 1920's relations with Latin America had been considerably improved.

SECTION SURVEY

IDENTIFY: "dollar diplomacy," "Yankee imperialism," police duty; Dwight W. Morrow.

1. Why did America's Caribbean policy arouse resentment in Latin America and criticism in the United States?
2. Why were American policies toward Nicaragua resented by Latin Americans?
3. What were the reasons for American hostility toward Mexico from 1917 to 1927?
4. Summarize the steps taken by the United States from 1927 to 1930 to improve its relations with Latin America.

4 Working with other nations to build peace and prevent war

While the United States was moving toward improved relations with Latin America, it also began to move toward international cooperation. In 1920, it is true, the Department of State completely ignored communications from the newly established League of Nations in Geneva. But as time passed American experts in international law, public health, and finance became important advisers in League activities. During Harding's administration the United States began to send "observers" to Geneva to take unofficial parts in League committee work dealing with epidemics, slavery, and the narcotics trade. By 1924 American delegates were attending League conferences.

The World Court. Both Harding and Coolidge recommended that the United States join the Permanent Court of International Justice, popularly known as the World Court, created in 1920 to arbitrate international disputes. But the Senate, jealous of its right to make treaties and influenced by Americans who were fearful of "entangling alliances," agreed to join only on its own terms. The nations already belonging to the World Court refused to accept the Senate's terms, and the matter was dropped.

The armaments race. The government was more successful in its efforts to stop the naval armaments race in which it was engaged with Great Britain and Japan. Relations between the United States and Japan were particularly strained after World War I. Americans resented the Japanese occupation of the Shantung Peninsula in China. This occupation, begun in 1914, violated America's Open Door policy, which was designed to keep China's territory intact and to prevent any single power from dominating China. Americans were concerned because Japan was allied with Great Britain.

As a result of the tension created by this situation, each of the three powers was rapidly building up its naval strength. Many people in all three countries were afraid that the naval arms race might lead to war.

The Washington Conference. Against this disturbing background, nine powers with interests in Asia met in the American capital on November 12, 1921. Secretary of State Charles Evans Hughes opened the Washington Naval Conference by boldly proposing a 10-year "naval holiday" during which no new warships were to be built. He suggested that the United States, Great Britain, and Japan each scrap enough of its own warships to bring the naval strength of the three great sea powers into a ratio of 5:5:3. These limitations applied only to "capital ships," that is, to battleships and heavy cruisers of 10,000 tons or more. According to this plan, Great Britain and the United States would be equal in naval strength while Japan would have three fifths as much tonnage as each of the other two countries. France and Italy, moreover, were to have fleets of equal size, with a ratio of 1.75 to the other powers.

At first, Japan refused to accept the plan. But, eager to make economies at home, the Japanese delegates finally accepted the proposal on the condition that Great Britain and the United States should not further fortify any Pacific colonies, except Hawaii. These agreements were included in what came to be called the Five-Power Treaty.

Other agreements. The Five-Power Treaty was only one of the agreements reached at the conference. Among others were the Four-Power Pact and the Nine-Power Treaty.

In the Four-Power Pact, Japan, Great Britain, France, and the United States agreed to respect one another's rights in the Pacific. They also agreed to consult with one another in the event of any act of aggression in the Pacific area.

In the Nine-Power Treaty, the nations represented at the conference guaranteed the territorial integrity of China and promised to uphold the Open Door policy by promoting trade and other relations "between China and the other powers upon the basis of equality of opportunity."

Developments in the Pacific area following the Washington Conference seemed to justify the widespread belief that a major step toward economy and peace had been taken. Japan withdrew, at least partially, from the Shantung Peninsula. Japan also withdrew troops that had occupied parts of Siberia during the Russian Revolution. At a London Naval Conference in 1930 Japan agreed to extend the naval holiday. As you will see, however, this agreement marked the high tide of Japanese cooperation with the Western powers.

The attempt to "outlaw war." In addition to favoring disarmament, the United States tried to prevent war by what has been called a policy of "wishful thinking." In 1928 Secretary of State Frank B. Kellogg joined with the French foreign minister, Aristide Briand (ah·rees·TEED bree·AHN), in asking all nations to sign a pledge outlawing war

BILLY MITCHELL

The German dreadnought *Ostfriesland* was considered unsinkable. With her triple hull, her 85 watertight compartments, and her heavy armor plating, she had survived 18 direct hits from 12- and 14-inch guns in the Battle of Jutland in 1916. Now, on Thursday, July 21, 1921, she was anchored off the Atlantic coast not far from Washington, D.C. Seized by the Allies at the end of the war, by international agreement the battleship was to be sunk, and the deadline for the sinking had been set at Sunday, July 24. The American navy was prepared to do the job. The Atlantic fleet stood ready to blast the captured vessel to pieces, and, if gunfire failed, to rip her apart with demolition charges placed inside her hull.

But a different method was to be tried first. General Billy Mitchell of the Army Air Service, a pioneer in the development of modern air power, had rashly promised to sink the unsinkable *Ostfriesland* with bombs. Many high-ranking naval officers ridiculed the idea that planes could sink a powerful battleship, but General Mitchell had won the opportunity to try.

Shortly after noon Mitchell's bombers appeared in the distance, small specks on the horizon that grew rapidly in size as they roared toward their target. Then the bombs fell. Great columns of water were hurled high into the air, and the ships of the Atlantic fleet, standing off at a safe distance, were shaken by the explosions.

Slowly the *Ostfriesland* began to sink. The observers watched in silence as her bow came up. They could see the enormous holes torn in her sides by the bombs. Her stern went under water. She rolled over completely, and within half an hour after the first bomb was dropped the supposedly unsinkable dreadnought disappeared beneath the waves.

Billy Mitchell had demonstrated that a new era in military history had begun.

"as an instrument of foreign policy." The signers were also to agree to settle all disputes by peaceful methods.

Eventually 62 nations initialed the document, but the Kellogg-Briand Pact, or the Pact of Paris as it was called, proved to be little more than a statement of good intentions. In signing, each nation added its own reservations. None was willing to outlaw war waged in self-defense. Since nearly every nation going to war justifies its action by pleading self-defense, this reservation destroyed the pact's effectiveness.

Finally, the document said nothing about enforcement. Those who signed it were not even bound to consult with one another in case some government acted aggressively. At best, the Kellogg-Briand Pact represented little more than an agreement that war was evil.

The crumbling peace structure. The opening act in the tragedy that later engulfed the entire world began in 1931, although at the time its full significance was not understood. Without warning, the Japanese army rolled across the frontiers of Manchuria (see map, page 723). China, large but helpless, could do little to defend its great northern province. Within a few months the Japanese had torn the province away from the Chinese. A Japanese program to sweep "foreign" influence out of the Far East and to build an Asia for Asians was under way.

Japan's aggression was a violation of the Covenant of the League of Nations and an outright challenge to the Open Door policy of the United States. Japan was bluntly reminded of these facts by Secretary of State Henry L. Stimson. In a formal note issued in 1932, Stimson protested Japan's flagrant violation of the Nine-Power Treaty and of the Kellogg-Briand Pact, both of which Japan had signed. President Hoover and Congress, however, were unwilling to commit the United States to the use of force, or even to economic sanctions, to enforce the Stimson declaration.

653

■ The League of Nations, shown here at its first meeting, represented a beginning in the difficult task of creating a cooperative world order.

Meanwhile, the League of Nations was summoned to consider what action, if any, should be taken. To this meeting President Hoover sent an American representative. The League sent a commission to Manchuria to investigate. But beyond a statement of its agreement with the so-called Stimson Doctrine, the League failed to act. Confident that the nations of the world would not act collectively in order to preserve peace, the Japanese withdrew from the League of Nations and prepared to invade and conquer China and Southeast Asia.

The structure of peace had begun to crumble. As you will see, Fascist Italy and, after 1933, the rising Nazi regime in Germany realized that they too could safely embark upon programs of aggression. The peace structure was not firm enough to stand a heavy blow. And the world powers, which by collective action might have bolstered the crumbling structure of peace, were unwilling and unable to act together.

SECTION SURVEY

IDENTIFY: World Court, armaments race, "naval holiday"; Charles Evan Hughes, Frank B. Kellogg, Henry L. Stimson.

1. What conditions led to the Washington Naval Conference of 1921–22?
2. (a) What were the major provisions of the Five-Power Treaty? (b) Indicate the reason for the Four-Power Pact.
3. Why was the Nine-Power Treaty significant for (a) China, (b) the United States, (c) Japan?
4. Why was the Kellogg-Briand Pact of 1928 "little more than a statement of good intentions"?
5. (a) How did the United States react to the Japanese invasion of Manchuria? (b) What was the reaction of the League of Nations? Why?

TRACING THE MAIN IDEAS

In the United States and in other countries, war-weary people hailed the armistice of November 11, 1918, as a turning point in history. Men and women everywhere were filled with faith in the future. They looked forward to a far better world than they had ever known. They were prepared to cooperate in a mighty effort "to make the world safe for democracy."

President Wilson reminded American citizens that they had a major responsibility in the building of a lasting peace. "It will now be our fortunate duty," he declared, "to assist by example, by sober friendly counsel, and by material aid in the establishment of just democracy throughout the world." But Wilson's advice went unheeded.

In the immediate postwar years the United States did help Europe by supplying food, clothing, medical supplies, and huge loans of money. And during the 1920's the United States worked closely with the League of Nations to remove sources of international friction, and also tried to establish better relations with Latin America. But when the United States refused to join the League, barred its doors to immigration, and raised tariff barriers to a new high, few friends were won for America.

By 1932 the faith and good will that had been so widespread throughout the world in 1918 were rapidly evaporating. In place of the prosperity of the 1920's, people everywhere faced a deepening economic depression. In place of faith and good will, the world was divided by intense international rivalry and growing feelings of suspicion and distrust. Japan had already begun its program of aggression, Italy was threatening its neighbors, the Nazi movement was gathering strength in Germany, and the structure of peace was breaking into fragments.

CHAPTER SURVEY

QUESTIONS FOR DISCUSSION

1. If either Senator Lodge or President Wilson had compromised, the Treaty of Versailles would have been approved by the United States Senate. Comment.
2. How was the League of Nations supposed to protect world peace?
3. What efforts toward world peace did the United States make during the 1920's?
4. The Kellogg-Briand Pact did not survive the challenges posed by the Japanese invasion of Manchuria. Comment.
5. Explain the relationship between each of the following pairs of terms: (a) reparations—moratorium, (b) capital ships—naval holiday, (c) aggression—Stimson Doctrine, and (d) colony—mandate system.
6. During the period just studied, the United States shut its doors to immigrants and to foreign goods. Did it act for the same reason in both cases?
7. The Treaty of Versailles showed the results of bargaining between Wilson on the one side and Lloyd George, Clemenceau, and Orlando on the other. Discuss.
8. The League of Nations represented the organized moral judgment of the great majority of nations. Explain.

RELATING PAST TO PRESENT

1. There has not been a global war since 1945. To what developments do you think this can be attributed?
2. Does the United States follow one or several policies in dealing with the nations of the world today? Explain.

USING MAPS AND CHARTS

1. Comparing the maps on pages 644 and 645, (a) identify the new nations that appeared in Europe after World War I. (b) Do you think their appearance could have created new problems? Explain. (c) Which nations lost territory as a result of World War I? (d) Do you think people can change their nationalities easily? Explain.
2. Using chart 2 on page 858, (a) compare the immigration to the United States in 1914 with that in 1940. (b) How do you explain this radical change? (c) What effect did it have on the composition of our population? (d) Can you think of other effects it may have had on our nation? (Consider the contributions that immigrants have made to the United States throughout its history.)

CHANGING WAYS
OF AMERICAN LIFE

CHAPTER **35**

An Accelerated Pace of Living in the "Golden Twenties"

1920 – 1932

Eᴠᴇʀʏ ᴀɢᴇ, or period of years, in history has certain characteristics that distinguish it from every other age. The decade of the 1920's was no exception. Writers, combing the records and in many cases searching their personal memories, have pinned various labels on the 1920's—among them the "Golden Twenties," the "Roaring Twenties," the "Age of Disillusionment," the "Decade of Wonderful Nonsense," the "Jazz Age," and the "Ballyhoo Years."

These labels suggest that the 1920's were characterized by widespread prosperity, by an unusual outpouring of energy, by a sharp increase in the productivity of American industry, by disillusionment with the outcome of the crusade to make the world safe for democracy, by an emphasis on materialism, and by the desire "to get rich quick" and to have a good time. All of this was true.

But people's ideas, beliefs, and everyday habits did not suddenly change as though by some stroke of magic on Armistice Day in 1918. Neither did their ideas, beliefs, and habits suddenly change when the shadow of the Great Depression fell over the land in the early 1930's.

The forces that gave new directions to American life in the 1920's were deeply rooted in American history and, for that matter, in the history of the Western world. Stimulated in part by World War I, the Industrial Revolution gathered new momentum in the 1920's. Power-driven machines, new sources of energy, more efficient factories, better methods of marketing goods—all of these helped to bring prosperity to the American people.

But the influence of industrialization reached far beyond the nation's economic life. It continued to transform everyday life in urban and rural areas alike. It gave new directions to science and education. It affected literature, art, architecture, and recreation.

THE CHAPTER IN OUTLINE

1. The increasing momentum of the Industrial Revolution.

2. New ways of living in country, town, and city.

3. New ways of living reflected in education, literature, and the arts.

4. Striking changes in the daily life of Americans.

1 The increasing momentum of the Industrial Revolution

By 1920 the power-driven machine was one of the dominant symbols of America. There were machines in factories, on farms, and in the home—and still the number and variety of machines kept multiplying. The development of the machine depended, however, upon other developments, including new sources of energy, increased production of metals, and more efficient methods of business.

New sources of energy. Energy to drive its machines—this is the first requirement of an industrial nation. And the United States had sources of energy in abundance. It had enormous deposits of coal, huge underground pockets of oil and natural gas, water-power sites, and the technological "know-how" to generate huge amounts of electric power.

By the 1920's coal, the traditional source of energy for the Industrial Revolution, was meeting stiff competition from petroleum, natural gas, and electricity. Between 1920 and 1930 the annual consumption of coal actually dropped by about 20 percent, while petroleum production more than doubled, and the production of natural gas increased 150 percent.

But the most phenomenal development was in the production and use of electricity. In 1900 this new energy source had hardly been tapped. By 1920 Americans were producing 56 billion kilowatt-hours annually; by 1930, 114 billion. In brief, the United States was using more electricity than all other countries of the world combined.

The assembly line. As energy to drive machines became increasingly abundant, businessmen and engineers tackled the problem of using it most efficiently. Older machines were improved, and new machines were developed for factory, farm, and home. But it was the organization of machines on a conveyor-belt assembly line that provided one of the striking characteristics of the American economy in the 1920's.

As you have seen, mass production was an essential element of American industry long before the 1920's. Manufacturers had been using standardized interchangeable parts ever since Eli Whitney and European inventors had developed the technique more than a century earlier (page 250). But the conveyor-belt assembly line was relatively new. First used on a large scale by Henry Ford in 1914, the assembly line was soon adopted by other industries.

Bigger and bigger industries. Mass production could be carried on only by large, highly organized industrial concerns. During the "Golden Twenties" there was plenty of surplus capital to finance industrial development. As a result older industries grew by leaps and bounds, while new industries climbed into the ranks of the giants.

Most of the growth of industry was the result of *mergers*—that is, the combining of two or more independent companies into one larger company. Between 1919 and 1929, for example, more than 1,000 mergers took place in manufacturing and mining. By 1930, only 200 corporations owned nearly half of the country's corporate wealth and one fifth of the total national wealth.

Industrial efficiency. As industries continued to grow, they also continued to become more efficient. Efficiency engineering was not, of course, a product of the 1920's. As you have read (page 556), in the early 1900's Frederick W. Taylor had pioneered in studies of machines and the workmen who operated them. During the 1920's these "time-and-motion" studies were generally undertaken before a new machine or process was installed in an industrial plant.

Businessmen also applied efficiency engineering, or "scientific management," to the problems of business planning and office bookkeeping. This new approach to industrial efficiency was called "cost accounting." Cost accountants found out the cost of every item of machinery, materials, and labor that went into the total cost of producing or selling a product. They could then show businessmen how to cut costs and thus gain greater production at lower prices.

Herbert C. Hoover, as Secretary of Commerce under Presidents Harding and Coolidge, helped to spread the idea of scientific management. He encouraged industry to use fewer and simpler standardized parts and models as a way of achieving economy and efficiency.

Hoover also tried to minimize the waste involved in competition. He urged business organizations to share information, to work out common policies, and to draw up codes of fair prices.

This government attitude naturally encouraged the growth of large-scale industry. In the 1920's the government did not make any great effort to enforce the Sherman and the Clayton Antitrust Acts. Business and government were more interested in industrial efficiency than in industrial competition.

■ By the 1920's, advertising had become an essential part of American business success. It was used to sell virtually everything, from soap flakes to limousines. This automobile ad appeared in 1926.

Advertising and marketing. Marketing techniques also became more effective during the 1920's. Manufacturers spent large sums on advertising to encourage the public to choose their products over those of their competitors. Advertising firms devoted more time to the study of public psychology to discover how to appeal to consumers most effectively. Advertising firms also urged Americans to abandon the deeply rooted American ideal of thrift. In "an age of abundance," they said, continued prosperity depended upon spending, not saving.

Mail-order houses, department stores, and chain stores continued to grow in number and size. The companies that had pioneered in new methods of marketing during the late 1800's—Montgomery Ward; Sears, Roebuck; the Great Atlantic and Pacific Tea Company; F. W. Woolworth; Marshall Field—were still among the leaders in their fields. These companies and many new ones were getting a big portion of the nation's retail business.

Two new developments, both destined to contribute to a future revolution in the packaging of goods, first emerged in the 1920's. In 1923 Clarence Birdseye developed a method of quick-freezing for preserving perishable foods. In the same year the Du Pont company bought the American patent rights to cellophane, a transparent wrapping material. By the late 1920's frozen foods were being sold in stores, and cellophane was attracting attention.

The automobile industry. Even more important to the story of America's economic expansion in the 1920's was the development of the automobile. In 1920 about 8 million passenger cars and about 1 million trucks were registered in the United States. By 1930 about 23 million passenger cars—an average of one car for every six citizens—and 3.5 million trucks were traveling the nation's roads, and the "automobile revolution" was in full swing.

This revolution had far-reaching consequences. By 1930 cars, trucks, and buses had almost completely replaced horse-drawn vehicles, and even the railroads and trolley cars were beginning to suffer from the competition of the gasoline-driven vehicles.

By the end of the 1920's the automobile industry had become the nation's biggest business, with an annual product valued at $3.5 billion in 1929. Moreover, this new industrial giant used huge quantities of steel, glass, rubber, and other materials. It created a rising demand for materials to build paved roads, garages, and service stations. It is estimated that 5 million persons, or one of every nine American workers, were employed in the automobile industry or a related business by 1930.

New industries. Garages, service stations, and trucking firms were only a few of the new industries that emerged during the 1920's. The increasing availability of electricity stimulated production of many laborsaving devices for the home—refrigerators, vacuum cleaners, toasters, electric irons, electric fans, and electric stoves.

The chemical industry, in which Germany had led the world before World War I, became in the 1920's one of America's most rapidly growing enterprises. By 1929 several American chemical companies were larger than any European competitors. In 1930 Du Pont, the giant among chemical companies, was producing 1,100 different products in 80 different factories in the United States. Among the products pouring out of the chemical plants were rayon, synthetic resins, and a growing variety of plastics.

■ The booming economy of the 1920's was characterized by an "automobile revolution," the emergence of many new industries—and increased pollution.

Problems of industrialization. Despite all its benefits, however, there was a negative side to this rapid process of industrialization. Chemicals, gasoline, and other technical innovations began to pollute America's rivers and lakes—and even the air. In the cities, traffic and air pollution became problems, while crowded housing conditions spurred the spread of slums. In the 1920's, however, few Americans paid much attention to these results of rapid changes in the economy. Most people living in the United States were content to enjoy the advantages of the quickening tempo of the machine age.

SECTION SURVEY

IDENTIFY: merger, scientific management, cost accounting, marketing techniques; Henry Ford, Clarence Birdseye.

1. The machine and the word "efficiency" characterized the America of the 1920's. Comment.
2. What was the attitude of the federal government toward big business in the 1920's? Why?
3. What is the function of advertising? Do you think the advertising industry should regulate itself? Explain.
4. What do you think is the relationship between advertising and easy credit?

2 New ways of living in country, town, and city

During the 1920's the onward march of industrialization continued to affect the lives of all Americans as the nation continued to grow in industrial power and in population.

Facts and figures. The 1920 census revealed that the population of the United States was almost 106 million. And for the first time in American history, those living in towns and cities outnumbered farm and country dwellers. The urban population then totaled 54 million, the rural population 51 million.

The onward march of urbanization and industrialization was even more apparent by the end of the decade. The census of 1930 showed that the population of the United States had climbed to nearly 123 million, an increase of 17 million. Most of the increase was in urban areas, where almost 69 million people lived by 1930. The rural population, on the other hand, totaled only about 54 million.

And even a large part of the rural population lived in small towns and villages. Between 1920 and 1930 the farm population decreased from 31.6 million to 30.4 million, as young people in growing numbers left the farms to seek new opportunities in the booming cities.

Changing ways on the farm. By the 1920's, also, the farmer's isolation and loneliness seemed to be things of the past. Paved roads covered the countryside. Telephone and electric wires stretched along roads and across fields to farmhouses. Single-wire antennas, called "aerials" in the 1920's, carried music, news, and entertainment by way of the new radio sets into living rooms. Henry Ford's "Tin Lizzies" were parked beside barns and houses.

Machines were also transforming farm life and helping to ease the farmer's burden. Where electricity was available, it was used for lighting, for pumping water, and for operating refrigerators, vacuum cleaners, sewing machines, and other laborsaving devices for the home. Milking machines could be found on many dairy farms. And trucks, tractors, and many power-driven farm implements were being used in growing numbers.

Power-driven machines enabled farmers to do much more work in much less time with much less effort. More efficient farming methods and better plants and breeds of livestock also helped to increase farm productivity.

Farm problems. But increased productivity also created problems. A surplus of farm products drove farm prices downward. To be sure, not all farmers were hit equally hard by rising surpluses and falling prices. Dairy and truck farmers profited from the shift in American eating habits away from cereals toward more milk, butter, vegetables, and fruit. Indeed, the citrus fruit industries of California, Texas, and Florida enjoyed a spectacular development as a result of the rising demand for fruit and the organization of cooperative advertising and marketing organizations. Tobacco growers also enjoyed a "sellers' market" as cigarette smoking became more popular. The large mechanized farms continued to prosper, mainly because they could afford the best equipment and could market their products most economically.

But although some farmers prospered, many suffered. Hardest hit were the owners of small farms. Many of them, handicapped by lack of money to buy expensive equipment and by limited acreage, found it increasingly difficult to make a living. At the start of the Great Depression in 1929 and 1930, it was the small farmer who first lost his home and his land.

Changing ways in town and city. Meanwhile, towns and cities were undergoing spectacular growth. Between 1920 and 1930 the rapidly growing population pushed 25 of America's older cities above the 100,000 figure; by 1930, 93 cities had populations of 100,000 or more. Some urban areas more than doubled their populations during this decade.

The very appearance of urban centers began to change. Huge new apartment houses appeared on what had been vacant lots or the sites of one-family houses. New skyscrapers pierced the sky line as builders tried to provide office space for the growing industries.

Less spectacular but no less significant was the changing appearance of shopping areas. From one end of the city to another—and it was the same in all the towns and cities—merchants remodeled older stores or built new stores to provide for the needs of the growing population.

Streets built in earlier times for horse-drawn vehicles and for a more leisurely way of life became increasingly crowded and noisy as automobiles and trucks multiplied. And during the 1920's a new method of transportation, the bus, began to compete with the older electric trolleys. Although not a single bus was registered in the United States in 1920, about 40,500 were registered by 1930.

Perhaps most spectacular of all was the development of suburban areas. Streetcar lines and paved roads pushed out from the cities into the surrounding countryside. Farms in outlying areas were divided into building lots, and row after row of houses appeared in developments with such fanciful names as "Sunset Acres," "Grand View," and "American Venice."

New opportunities for women. The changing appearance of the cities reflected larger and deeper changes in American life. One of the most striking developments was the growing freedom and opportunity for women.

For 100 years before the 1920's, women had been winning larger opportunities in political, economic, and social affairs. But their greatest gains came in the 1920's. With the adoption of the Nineteenth Amendment in 1920, women won the right to vote in national elections. This was a landmark in women's long struggle to win equality with men.

Equally important were women's gains made as a result of industrialization. The housewife's burden was eased by new laborsaving devices—washing machines and irons, new types of stoves, vacuum cleaners, and refrigerators. Ready-made garments and inexpensive sewing machines also relieved women of much of their labor. Packaged foods and canned goods helped to lighten the task of preparing meals.

Middle-class women who could afford these new services found new uses for their leisure time. Many now had more time to read books and magazines, to attend art exhibits, to hear lectures. Others now had time to work for civic improvements by promoting playgrounds, by taking part in political affairs, and by influencing public opinion through such organizations as the League of Women Voters. Still others took active parts in parent-teacher associations. Never before had so many women found time and opportunity to develop their interests and hobbies.

The rapidly multiplying machines in mills, plants, and factories created new jobs on assembly

■ Paved roads and automobiles, the radio and the telephone, all helped to ease the isolation and loneliness of the farmer's life.

lines for less privileged women. This was especially true in the textile and tobacco factories springing up in the South. Moreover, women were finding increasing opportunities to work at selling jobs and as clerks and stenographers.

Workers' gains and losses. The surge of women into offices and factories was only one phase of the revolution that was transforming the lives of wage earners. The ever more rapid development of power-driven machines continued to free workers from backbreaking toil. Increased productivity brought generally higher wages, with which workers could buy products they had never before been able to afford.

Wage earners also benefited from studies undertaken to find ways of lessening fatigue and eliminating accidents on the job. From these studies businessmen learned that workers were happier and actually produced more when their employers showed an interest in them. Profiting from this lesson, some employers introduced profit sharing and retirement plans and provided cafeterias, game rooms, and ball parks for employees.

But although employers as a whole showed increasing interest in working conditions, they opposed labor unions even more vigorously than before the war. A growing number of corporations in the 1920's organized "company unions"—that is, unions organized by the employers or their representatives, and dominated by the employers rather than the workers. Company unions, as well as the higher standard of living of the workers, contributed to the decline in strength of organized labor during the 1920's.

Limited progress for Negroes. As you have read (pages 630–31), many black families who moved into northern cities in the 1900's met with discrimination in jobs and housing, as well as in almost every aspect of their social life. But they also found new opportunities.

The number of black wage earners in American industries nearly doubled between 1910 and 1930, rising from about 600,000 to more than 1 million. During the same period, black employees in clerical occupations rose from 19,000 to nearly 41,000. Negroes employed in civil service jobs increased from about 22,000 to around 50,000, most of them as postal employees. By 1930 some 70,000 Negroes owned their own businesses.

In the late 1800's and early 1900's, opportunities for black Americans in most fields had remained quite limited. But despite this, individual Negroes had made outstanding contributions to American

life. For example, in 1893 Dr. Daniel H. Williams successfully performed the first open-heart surgical operation. And in 1909 Matthew Hensen, adventurer and explorer, together with Admiral Robert E. Peary, reached the North Pole. In artistic fields Meta Warwick Fuller, a sculptor, and Henry O. Tanner, a painter, among many others, enriched American life with work of high technical skill and great beauty. Finally, in the field of applied science, George Washington Carver's achievements were truly impressive. In the early 1900's Carver became famous for his work at Tuskegee Institute in developing hybrid crops, and in instructing southern farmers, white as well as black, how to increase their crop yields and how to put familiar agricultural products to new uses.

In the 1920's black Americans continued to make significant, though limited, gains in education. A growing number of Negroes, in the North and the South, received a high school education, and more attended colleges and universities. By 1930 about 15,000 black Americans held academic degrees. Yet black leaders, as well as white citizens who shared their concern, pointed out that in 1930 many doors of opportunity still remained closed to black Americans. They also pointed out that the postwar advances, limited though they were, showed clearly what American Negroes could accomplish when given the opportunity.

Negro rights. In the 1920's the Republican Party was trying to build strong political organizations among white Americans in the South. As a result, the Republican administration did little to meet the demands of southern Negroes for federal protection of their voting rights or for a fair share of federally appointed jobs. But in northern urban centers, black voters showed increasing strength. In 1928 a northern Negro, Oscar de Priest of Chicago, was elected to Congress where he served three terms.

And black Americans in both the North and the South were making progress in their struggle for equal justice before the law. Here the efforts of the NAACP (page 549) to bring law suits to enforce the equal rights of black Americans began to make important progress.

Black self-identification. In the 1920's black Americans began to feel a growing sense of racial identification and pride, along with increasing interest in their African backgrounds. These feelings were strongly expressed by Marcus Garvey, a black immigrant from the West Indies.

Garvey became convinced that Negroes could never win true freedom and equality in the United

■ Between 1910 and 1930, black Americans made significant, though limited, gains in education and job opportunities. This photograph of the staff of a city bank was made in 1928.

States. He popularized among black city slum dwellers a form of black nationalism which emphasized a "back to Africa" movement. He eloquently described the achievements of black Africans, and urged his listeners to return "home," where they might enjoy opportunities they could never find in white-dominated America. Although none of Garvey's half million followers actually moved to Africa, his movement gave many Negroes a new sense of racial pride.

Most black leaders of the 1920's opposed Garvey's movement as unrealistic and as escapism. They insisted that Negroes, having long been Americans, could and must win the rights and opportunities that other Americans enjoyed. But these leaders also encouraged American Negroes to interest themselves in the achievements and aspira-

tions of black people in Africa and other parts of the world. Racial solidarity, they urged, should replace the narrow outlook that separated black Americans from black people in other lands, and that also separated black Americans themselves into different economic and social groups.

The "new Negro." The rise of younger black leaders in the 1920's was stimulated by a book entitled *The New Negro* by Alain Locke, a professor at Howard University. This important book both reflected and encouraged changes taking place in black communities.

The new black leaders insisted that the "new Negro" must be proud of his heritage and his people's achievements. He must stop being apologetic and defensive toward white Americans. The "new Negro" must realize that self-assertiveness, not ac-

663

■ Among the great jazz bands of the 1920's, none was more popular than that of Duke Ellington (seated at the piano).

commodation, was the only effective way to gain equality and full implementation of America's democratic creed.

The "Harlem renaissance." Inspired by the image of the "new Negro," a cultural renaissance, or rebirth, aroused the interest of many white Americans, while strengthening the growing pride of black Americans. This cultural rebirth of the 1920's centered in New York City's black community of Harlem, and has been called the "Harlem renaissance." But its rich expressions were not confined to Harlem.

These new cultural contributions were marked by originality, freshness of style, and vigor. "Jazz" music, with its exciting and spontaneous rhythms, and "the blues," reflecting the joy, laughter, sadness, and pain of black Americans, found outstanding exponents and performers in the 1920's. Among these were W. C. Handy, Scott Joplin, Jelly Roll Morton, and Duke Ellington. Black "spirituals" became part of the repertory of Marian Anderson, who in the 1920's was just beginning her career as one of the world's greatest singers of classical as well as folk music.

The literature of the Harlem renaissance reflected the racial pride of the "new Negro." Langston Hughes, Claude McKay, and Countee Cullen wrote verse marked by haunting bitterness and defiance, but also by joy and hope. This many-sided emotional richness among black writers was exemplified in Jean Towner's *Cane*. This work portrayed black environments in the rural South, in Washington, D.C., and in New York City, starkly revealing its characters' intense emotions while also portraying their beauty and dignity.

SECTION SURVEY

IDENTIFY: urbanization, company union, *The New Negro*, "Harlem renaissance"; Marian Anderson, Matthew Hensen, George Washington Carver, Marcus Garvey.

1. What conflicts began to emerge in the 1920's between urban and rural values as they related to (a) the family, (b) politics, (c) morals, (d) recreation?
2. What are the relationships between women, freedom, and industrialization?
3. Describe the contributions made by (a) individual Negroes in the early 1920's, (b) leading figures in the "Harlem renaissance."
4. (a) What is meant by black self-identification? (b) How was it accomplished? (c) What is meant by the term "new Negro"?
5. What positions were taken by various black leaders in their effort to improve the position of black Americans?

3 New ways of living reflected in education, literature, and the arts

As the industrial society expanded, it became increasingly clear that Americans needed a far more extensive education than that which had been considered adequate in earlier times. Under the impact of the machine, the educational system continued to change.

Growth of enrollment. One important development was the increase in school enrollment. Between 1900 and 1920, for instance, the total high school enrollment rose from under 700,000 to about 2.5 million. By 1930 the enrollment had soared to about 4.8 million.

The colleges showed similar gains. Between 1900 and 1920 college enrollments jumped from about 237,000 to 597,000. During the 1920's this figure almost doubled, climbing to 1.1 million by 1930.

To meet the needs of this enormously increased student body, American states and communities had to spend huge sums for new school buildings, textbooks and equipment, and teachers' salaries. The wealth created by the growing industrialization provided taxes for education. There were, of course, many youths who still could not afford to go beyond elementary school. But after 1920 a larger proportion than ever before obtained a high school education.

Curriculum changes. The growing complexity of the industrial society with its emphasis upon highly specialized skills called for men and women trained in mathematics, engineering, science, and the skilled trades. To meet the new needs, educators began to enlarge the curriculum to include more work in vocational training, home economics, commercial courses, health, physical education, modern foreign languages, and civic education. Special trade schools, technical schools, and commercial schools were built in an effort to adapt the educational system to the machine age.

Changes in school administration. The machine age also affected the organization and administration of the schools. The development of cars and buses, for example, enabled students from widely scattered areas to attend centrally located schools. As a result, in rural regions consolidated schools of good quality replaced the scattered, one-room "little red schoolhouses." In the cities a few high schools were built for as many as 5,000 to 10,000 students. Some people worried, however, that American schools and colleges might be too much influenced by industrial techniques of organization and administration—speed-up, efficiency methods, and standardization.

Toward a more effective education. Students of education were reaching new conclusions about how people actually learn and about the purposes of education. Educators, following in the path earlier marked out by psychologists William James and G. Stanley Hall, were proving that a child's mind can be molded—within limits. Other scholars, among them John Dewey, continued to emphasize that life itself is an education, and that the way to produce effective citizens is to give boys and girls actual experience in democratic living. Still other scholars, led by psychologists like Edward L. Thorndike, worked out tests for measuring intelligence and for evaluating the educational process. Educators met frequently to lay plans for adapting schools to a changing society.

Journalism. Newspapers and magazines also reflected the influence of the machine age. By the 1920's journalism had become big business, highly organized and highly standardized. The *Reader's Digest,* started in 1922, quickly won nationwide circulation with its digests of articles from other journals. *Time* magazine, started in 1923, also won a wide circle of readers with its terse comments on current affairs.

Many of the individually owned older newspapers were being bought up by the great newspaper chains. Chain newspapers ran the same syndicated columns and editorials, the same comics, sports news, and advertisements, and subscribed to the same news services—the Associated Press, the United Press, and the International News Service. The newspapers, like the magazines, reflected the ideals, interests, and problems of industrial America.

Literature. Much of the literature of the late 1920's dealt with such ever-popular themes as love, personal conflicts, and adventure. Many authors, however, wrote about the conflicts and confusions of the machine age. In his poem *The Waste Land* T. S. Eliot pictured society in the machine age as grim, barren, standardized, commercialized, cheap, and vulgar. Carl Sandburg, who found much to admire in the new industrialized society, also showed how terrible life could be when man glorified the machine and neglected himself.

The fiction of the 1920's also reflected the influence of the machine age. *This Side of Paradise,* a popular novel by F. Scott Fitzgerald, revealed the tragic confusion of America's youth in a society all

HIGHLIGHTS OF AMERICAN
WRITING

Robert Frost (1874–1963), who described a complete poem as one "where an emotion has found its thought and the thought has found the words," won the Pulitzer prize for poetry four times. Among his most famous poems are "The Death of the Hired Man" and "Mending Wall."

Amy Lowell (1874–1925), a poet and critic, is remembered most for two romantic poems, "Patterns" and "Lilacs."

H. L. Mencken (1880–1956), an essayist and editor, wrote many witty and biting essays and compiled *The American Language*, described by one critic as "a wonderful combination of scholarship, festivity, social history, . . . political and literary feuding, industry, genuine love of country, unashamed bias, humor, commentary on the world, compendium of American manners, and anthology of Mencken prejudices."

Eugene O'Neill (1888–1953), often called America's first important dramatist, wrote several long and deeply psychological dramas; some short plays; and a comedy, *Ah, Wilderness!* He won the Pulitzer prize three times.

Edna St. Vincent Millay (1892–1950) was still a student when one of her best-known poems, "Renascence," was published. She won the Pulitzer prize for poetry with her book of sonnets entitled *The Harp-Weaver*.

Pearl Buck (1892–   ), who grew up and worked as a missionary in China, drew upon her many years there to write several novels about Chinese life. Her Pulitzer-prize-winning novel *The Good Earth* traces a Chinese family through several generations and through many troubles.

Thornton Wilder (1897–   ) is both a novelist and a playwright. His novel *The Bridge of San Luis Rey*, his well-known play *Our Town*, and his allegorical play *The Skin of Our Teeth* all won Pulitzer prizes.

Stephen Vincent Benét (1898–1943) became obsessed with the desire to write a long narrative poem using the military information which so interested him. As a result he produced *John Brown's Body*, which won him a Pultizer prize for poetry. His short story "The Devil and Daniel Webster" is a minor American classic.

---

too often characterized by fast living and hard drinking. In *Main Street, Babbitt,* and other novels, Sinclair Lewis portrayed the hypocrisy and the shallowness of men who worshiped the dollar and the material comforts of the machine age. The short stories of Sherwood Anderson poignantly reflected the loss of the old craft skills. Ernest Hemingway, one of the so-called "hard-boiled realists," told of the tragic plight of Americans who lived abroad to escape the standardized culture of machine-dominated America.

Theodore Dreiser, in the novel *An American Tragedy,* pictured youth caught in the mad drive for power and wealth, and condemned a society whose ideals and morals were materialistic and grasping. Willa Cather's *The Professor's House* dealt with the contrasting values of an older world that had time for poetry and the newer world that

was so much concerned with material possessions. In his novels, John Dos Passos wrote of the crushing effect the machine had on the individual's ideals and aspirations.

Painting and design. In painting and design Americans were more and more influenced by Europeans like Cézanne, Manet, Monet, Degas, Matisse, and Picasso. Some modernists boldly experimented with geometric designs that often resembled machines in their emphasis on hard angles, masses, and abstract form. Many American artists continued to paint the more conventional themes, but they painted them in new ways. Others tried to reveal the meaning of the machine age in their paintings of factories, warehouses, slums, railroads, and other scenes of urban life.

New art forms. The machine age also opened up entirely new forms of art. In the hands of artists,

666

the camera captured the spirit and meaning of the new age. New methods of art reproduction enabled people to own inexpensive yet excellent copies of the world's outstanding works of art. When these reproduction techniques were adopted by the mass-circulation magazines, millions of Americans were able to see the work of the world's greatest photographers, illustrators, and artists.

Aided by commercial artists and industrial designers, manufacturers began to produce telephones, furniture, fabrics, clothing, typewriters, glassware, refrigerators, stoves, automobiles, and a host of other articles that showed that machines and machine products might be beautiful in design and structure.

Architecture. Inspired by outstanding architects like Louis Sullivan and Frank Lloyd Wright (page 516), other architects began to promote the idea that a building ought to use the materials and follow the forms most suitable to the purposes for which it was to be used.

For many people the skyscraper became a symbol of the influence of the machine upon architecture. Built of steel, glass, and concrete, it towered into the sky in order to use as little expensive ground space as possible, with its upper stories set back to prevent the streets from being darkened. In its emphasis upon clear-cut vertical lines and its massing of windows, the skyscraper was an excellent example of how purpose and materials dictated design.

Music. Music, too, reflected the influence of the new industrial age. Many people believed that the syncopated jazz of the 1920's expressed the rhythms and the accelerated speed and energy of the machine.

Music also became increasingly available to all the people through the radio, the phonograph, and musical instruments manufactured at lower and lower costs. Moreover, wealth created by the new industrial age supported symphony orchestras and opera companies.

SECTION SURVEY

IDENTIFY: machine age, *An American Tragedy, Reader's Digest, Time* Magazine; Edward L. Thorndike, William James, Sinclair Lewis, F. Scott Fitzgerald.

1. How did some writers show their disillusionment with the America of the 1920's?
2. What is the responsibility of the writer—to transmit values or to convey the spirit of his times?

■ This detail from Lyonel Feininger's painting "The Church of the Minorites" shows the artist's concern with the techniques of "cubism." In their paintings, cubists attempted to show various perspectives of an object simultaneously.

3. (a) Do you think the artists of the 1920's conveyed the spirit of their times? Explain. (b) Take four artists or writers of the period and show whether they did or did not reflect the 1920's.
4. The skyscraper was a symbol of the influence of the machine upon architecture. Comment.

4 Striking changes in the daily life of Americans

With money in their pockets and more leisure time than ever before, Americans in the 1920's poured into the countryside, packed stadiums, and jammed motion picture theaters. Indeed, it was this vigorous pursuit of entertainment that led historians to refer to the 1920's as the "Jazz Age" and the "Age of Wonderful Nonsense."

The automobile. The automobile was a major source of American recreation, as entire families piled into the car for an evening's ride or a weekend trip.

Many Americans who were otherwise law-abiding citizens refused to take Prohibition seriously. Below, a couple is scrutinized before being admitted to a "speakeasy," where liquor was served illegally.

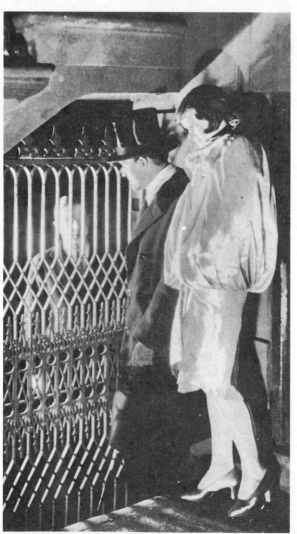

By the 1920's the automobile was no longer the exclusive possession of the well-to-do. Of 123 working-class families interviewed in a typical midwestern city in 1923, as many as 60 owned cars. The 1920's also saw the swing from the open to the closed car, with car design becoming an endless topic of conversation.

But although the automobile made travel comfortable and private, it also created new problems. Traffic accidents and deaths kept rising. Young people asserted their independence by driving off in the family car, free from parental supervision. Many Americans believed in fact that the automobile was disrupting the family and destroying the nation's moral code.

National prohibition of liquor. As you have read (page 614), the Eighteenth Amendment was ratified in January 1919. This amendment gave the federal government power to prohibit "the manufacture, sale, or transportation of intoxicating liquors within, the importation thereof into, or the exportation thereof from the United States and all territory subject to the jurisdiction thereof. . . ."

In October 1919 Congress passed the Prohibition Enforcement Act, usually called the Volstead Act, over President Wilson's veto. This act defined as "intoxicating liquor" any beverage containing more than one half of one percent of alcohol. The Volstead Act turned enforcement of the law over to the Bureau of Internal Revenue, and created the special office of Commissioner of Prohibition.

Prohibition problems. The prohibition experiment created serious problems in American life. Long coastlines in the east and west and unguarded frontiers to the north and south made it impossible to stop the flow of illegal liquor into the country.

Bootlegging became big business controlled by criminal elements in the large cities. The gangster Al Capone, who ruled Chicago's underworld, commanded a small "army" of gangsters equipped with revolvers, sawed-off shotguns, and submachine guns. Gang wars and other violence became common in many American cities during the "Roaring Twenties." Moreover, the gangs branched out to seize control of gambling establishments and dance halls. By the end of the decade, they had begun to develop the so-called "rackets." The racketeers collected "protection" money from businessmen, threatening violence if their victims failed to pay.

The people themselves were partly to blame for this widespread violation of the law. Many Americans who were otherwise law-abiding refused to take prohibition seriously. Finally, in 1933, the prohibition era ended when the necessary number of states ratified the Twenty-first Amendment. This amendment repealed the Eighteenth Amendment and returned the power to control the sale of intoxicating drinks to the states themselves.

Radio. Meanwhile, another new development —radio—was transforming the lives of millions of Americans, young and old alike.

KDKA, the first commercial broadcasting station, began to operate in Pittsburgh on November 2, 1920. Radio immediately became a craze. By 1922 sales of receiving sets and radio parts totaled more than $60 million. By 1929 sales amounted to almost $400 million, more than 600 broadcasting stations had been licensed, and one third of all American homes owned radio receivers.

Radio brought an enormous variety of information and entertainment directly into the home. The most popular programs featured "crooners," jazz musicians, comedians, sports announcers, and newscasters. But many Americans felt that radio was not fulfilling its great promise as an instrument of education and culture. They criticized the dominant role of the advertiser who paid the broadcasting companies and entertainers, and therefore often determined what programs would be presented.

Despite the trivial content of many programs, however, radio served the nation in a variety of ways. By providing common experiences for all Americans, it increased the feeling of national unity. Radio also helped to overcome the isolation of rural life. It encouraged popular interest in current events, including sports, and offered useful information on health, home economics, and farming techniques. It made serious music available to more Americans than ever before. Finally, radio provided greater safety for airplanes and ships.

Movies. The motion picture industry also enjoyed a spectacular growth during the 1920's. By the 1920's, the nickelodeons (page 555) had been replaced by huge and lavish motion picture "palaces." By the end of the decade, weekly audiences approached the 100 million mark, and the industry itself had become big business, the fourth largest in the nation.

A major step forward was made in 1927 when Warner Brothers released the first successful "talkie"—*The Jazz Singer,* featuring Al Jolson. For years the industry had been working on the problem of using sound with pictures. Within a year of the first success, the old silent films were being replaced by the even more popular sound pictures.

During the 1920's the movie industry turned out many films more polished in technique and more sophisticated in content than the pre-war films. These new films emphasized such popular themes as social advancement, the reckless enjoyment of life, and the independence of women. In the prosperous "Golden Twenties," many Americans who hoped to become rich learned from the films produced by Cecil B. de Mille and Ernst Lubitsch how the rich behaved, or were thought to behave.

Not all the films of this period, however, were concerned with such popular themes. Erich von Stroheim's *Greed* transformed a realistic novel by Frank Norris into a film which described with great power how greed for money warped the character and finally destroyed the lives of a working-class couple. Lewis Milestone's *All Quiet on the Western Front,* based on a novel about World War I by Erich Remarque, expressed very movingly the widespread antiwar feeling of the 1920's. Other films, such as Robert J. Flaherty's *Nanook of the North,* successfully captured the grandeur of nature in distant places.

Sports. During the 1920's interest in spectator sports grew markedly. Baseball remained the most popular professional game, with between 9 and 10 million people attending major league games annually. Babe Ruth, who replaced Ty Cobb as the idol of fans, in 1927 astounded the baseball world by hitting a record number of 60 home runs. College football drew some 30 million spectators in the same year. Red Grange, a halfback for the University of Illinois, became a national hero and won a movie contract. In 1927, also, ardent boxing fans spent over $2.6 million to see the famous Dempsey-Tunney match. Professional golf and tennis matches also became more popular during the 1920's.

Some critics claimed that Americans had become a nation of spectators, satisfied to watch passively while a small group of professionals played for money or glory. Others denied this, and pointed to the active participation of Americans in golf, tennis, sand-lot baseball, swimming, camping, skating, bowling, and other sports.

Feats and fads. Americans in the 1920's were unusually responsive to new fads and fashions and dramatic public events. This period has been called the "Jazz Age" with some justice, for the rhythmic music of jazz was perhaps the most consistently

George Bellows. "Dempsey and Firpo." Oil on canvas. 1924. 51 x 63¼. Collection Whitney Museum of American Art, New York.

■ Boxing was one of the most popular spectator sports of the 1920's. The artist George Bellows painted this scene of Jack Dempsey being knocked out of the ring by his opponent, Luis Firpo.

popular of the new fashions. Most of the other fads shifted rapidly from year to year: from the Chinese-originated game of mah-jongg to crossword puzzles, to vigorous dances like the Charleston, to eccentric activities like flagpole sitting and marathon dances.

But some of the nation's enthusiasm was directed to individual accomplishments. By far the most glorified hero of the 1920's was Charles A. Lindbergh, who in May 1927 made the first nonstop flight from New York to Paris in his plane, *The Spirit of St. Louis.* Another fearless voyager was Commander (later Admiral) Richard E. Byrd, who made the first flights to both the North and the South Pole. Other Americans who followed the example of Lindbergh and Byrd proved that the postwar period was an age of authentic feats as well as eccentric fads.

SECTION SURVEY

IDENTIFY: Volstead Act, KDKA, *The Spirit of St. Louis, The Jazz Singer, Nanook of the North;* Commander Byrd, Babe Ruth.

1. What do you think accounts for the fact that America became a nation of spectators in the 1920's?
2. In what ways did the radio and movies serve the American people in this period?
3. The Eighteenth Amendment provides a good example of a segment of the American public trying to legislate moral behavior for all Americans. Comment.
4. How did the prohibition era help to create a breakdown in morality and a lack of respect for the law?
5. How did the hero-worship of Charles Lindbergh fulfill a need of many Americans living in the 1920's? What did Lindbergh stand for when compared to the youth of the "Lost Generation"?

TRACING THE MAIN IDEAS

Many critics of American life during the 1920's claimed that modern technology was standardizing people's lives. They pointed out that every night people all over America turned their radios to the same programs, becoming as passive and uncreative as the machine itself. The critics also were disturbed because the machine which had given men such vast power was being used largely to make money, to provide more or less meaningless recreation, and to bring about destruction in wartime. The machine, they insisted, might ultimately spell man's ruin unless men learned to use it for beneficial human and social ends.

Other students of American civilization defended the machine. They insisted that it relieved men of backbreaking toil and that it made possible higher standards of living, more leisure, more consumer goods, more comforts, more time for educa-tion and pleasure. As evidence of the machine's contribution to better living, they pointed out, for example, that good music was available to nearly all Americans who cared to tune their radios to the proper station. Education in the machine age, also argued its defenders, did not need to lead to standardization; rather, it might use motion pictures, radio, and the growing knowledge of psychology to break away from binding traditions and to enlarge the freedom and strengthen the personality of the individual.

As the 1920's drew to a close, however, arguments about the advantages and disadvantages of modern technology were suddenly pushed into the background. As you will see in the next chapter, during the 1930's the American people struggled through the greatest economic depression in their history.

CHAPTER SURVEY

QUESTIONS FOR DISCUSSION

1. What do you think accounted for the "fads" of the 1920's?
2. What were some of the elements in American life that American writers and artists of the 1920's criticized? Do you agree with them? Why or why not?
3. Would you say that there was a "generation gap" during the 1920's? Explain.
4. How did the radio, movies, and newspapers contribute to conformity? How did they contribute to individualism?
5. Why did "practical" courses supersede classical studies in high schools and colleges by 1930?
6. What factors do you think contributed to the change in American manners and morals in the 1920's?
7. How did industrialization affect the lives of people (a) on farms and (b) in cities? Does industrialization always mean progress? Explain.
8. Why do you think Marcus Garvey's message—pride in race and economic self-sufficiency—appealed to black Americans in the 1920's?
9. Justify the use of each of the following terms to describe the tempo of the 1920's: (a) "Golden Twenties," (b) "Roaring Twenties," (c) "Age of Disillusionment." Which do you think best describes the era? Explain.

RELATING PAST TO PRESENT

1. The mass communications media depend upon the public for economic support. Keeping this in mind, do you think the media should cater to the tastes of the "average" person, or should they strive for above-average quality? Explain.
2. Should the federal government be responsible for what the mass media transmit to the American public? Explain.
3. The "Harlem Renaissance" was an expression by black Americans of their discontent as well as of their racial pride. Are black Americans today involved in a new renaissance? Explain.
4. During the 1920's, many black Americans left the South to come North. Did the northern cities turn out to be an escape to freedom or a new imprisonment? Does a similar situation exist today? Explain.

USING MAPS AND CHARTS

1. Using chart 7 on page 859, (a) make a list of the ten largest cities in 1890 and in 1930. (b) Explain the changes that you note.
2. Basing your answer on the charts on pages 866–67, indicate the change in the power output by sources between 1900 and 1920. Show how this development affected manufacturing, agriculture, and transportation.

UNIT SURVEY

FOR FURTHER INQUIRY

1. Explain the relationship between nationalism, tariff legislation, and restrictions upon immigration as it existed during the 1920's.
2. Was the United States completely isolationist in its foreign affairs during the 1920's? Explain.
3. Explain how each of the following demonstrates a rejection of Progressivism and the ideals of the New Freedom: (a) President Harding's campaign slogan of "a return to normalcy"; (b) President Coolidge's statement, "The business of America is business"; (c) President Hoover's belief in "The American system of rugged individualism."
4. In the 1920's, newspapers became big business. (a) What role did advertisers in newspapers now play? (b) How do you think that the objectivity of newspapers was affected by these developments? Explain.
5. In your opinion, what was the real reason that Prohibition failed? Explain.

PROJECTS AND ACTIVITIES

1. Compare the popular songs of the 1920's with those of today. How do they differ? How are they alike? How does music reflect the times?
2. Research the history of the Ku Klux Klan. How did the various stages of its history reflect the times?
3. Make a comparative analysis of the causes of the Great Depression by studying the following: J. K. Galbraith, *The Great Crash;* Dixon Wecter, *The Age of the Great Depression, 1929–1941;* and Herbert Hoover, *Memoirs,* Vol. 3.
4. Interview members of your family in order to obtain first-hand accounts of life during the Great Depression.

USING THE SOCIAL SCIENCES

(Read pages 674–80 before you answer the following questions.)

1. Explain the concept of cultural socialization. Does this concept support the theory of America as a "melting pot"? Explain.
2. What cultural conflicts would an immigrant encounter when settling in the United States?
3. What kinds of cultural conflict might result between immigrant parents and the children born to them in their newly adopted country?
4. What would our society gain if America had a single, uniform cultural pattern? What would it lose?

SUGGESTED FURTHER READING

Biography

BARUCH, BERNARD M., *My Own Story,* Holt, Rinehart & Winston.

COBEN, STANLEY, *A. Mitchell Palmer: Politician,* Columbia Univ. Press.

GARWOOD, DARRELL, *Artist in Iowa: The Life of Grant Wood,* Norton.

HANDLIN, OSCAR, *Al Smith and His America,* Little, Brown.

HOOVER, HERBERT, *Memoirs,* Macmillan, 3 vols.

LINDBERGH, CHARLES A., *The Spirit of St. Louis,* Scribner (paper). Woven into the hour-by-hour details of the first transatlantic flight are flashbacks that tell the story of the author's boyhood and youth.

——, *We,* Grosset & Dunlap; Putnam.

MERZ, CHARLES, *And Then Came Ford,* Doubleday.

MITANG, HERBERT, *The Man Who Rode the Tiger,* Lippincott. Story of Samuel Seabury.

MORRISON, HUGH, *Louis Sullivan, Prophet of Modern Architecture,* Norton.

NEVINS, ALLAN, *Ford,* Scribner, 2 vols.

REYNOLDS, QUENTIN, *The Wright Brothers,* Random House.

STONE, IRVING, *Clarence Darrow for the Defense,* Doubleday.

WHITE, WILLIAM ALLEN, *A Puritan in Babylon,* Macmillan. Calvin Coolidge.

WISE, W. E., *Jane Addams of Hull House,* Harcourt Brace Jovanovich.

Other Nonfiction

ALLEN, FREDERICK LEWIS, *The Big Change,* Bantam (paper). Some of the major changes that took place in art, literature, morals, sports, business, and everyday living in the United States from 1900 to 1950.

——, *Only Yesterday,* Bantam (paper). The manners, morals, and politics of the 1920's.

AMORY, CLEVELAND, *The Proper Bostonians,* Dutton (Everyman's Library).

ELLIS, ETHAN L., *Frank B. Kellogg and American Foreign Relations, 1925–1929,* Rutgers Univ. Press.

FAULKNER, HAROLD U., *From Versailles to the New Deal,* Yale Univ. Press. The times of Harding, Coolidge, Hoover.

FRANKFURTER, FELIX, *The Case of Sacco and Vanzetti,* Grosset & Dunlap (Universal Library, paper). An analysis of one of the most controversial court trials in American history.

FRAZIER, FRANKLIN E., *The Negro in the United States,* Macmillan.

GALBRAITH, J. K., *The Great Crash,* Houghton Mifflin. An economist discusses the causes of the Great Depression.

HANDLIN, OSCAR, *The Uprooted,* Grosset & Dunlap (Universal Library, paper). The story of the immigrants who came to America and what they found here.

HICKS, JOHN D., *Republican Ascendancy: 1921–1933,* Harper & Row.

HOOVER, HERBERT, *The Great Depression,* Macmillan.

JOHNSON, GERALD W., *The Lines Are Drawn,* Lippincott. Pulitzer prize cartoons.

LEIGHTON, ISABEL, ed. *The Aspirin Age,* Simon and Schuster. Light essays on the years 1914–1941.

LEUCHTENBERG, WILLIAM E., *The Perils of Prosperity, 1914–1932,* Univ. of Chicago Press.

LOCHNER, LOUIS P., *Herbert Hoover and Germany,* Macmillan.

MADISON, CHARLES A., *Leaders and Liberals in Twentieth Century America,* Ungar.

MELLQUIST, JEROME, *The Emergence of an American Art,* Scribner. Art at the turn of the century.

MITCHELL, BROADUS, *Depression Decade,* Holt, Rinehart & Winston.

MOWRY, GEORGE E., ed. *The Twenties: Ford, Flappers and Fantastics,* Prentice-Hall. Excerpts from contemporary magazine articles, newspaper stories, and personal accounts.

MURRAY, ROBERT K., *Red Scare: A Study in National Hysteria, 1919–1920,* McGraw-Hill. An analysis of the sensational propaganda and mass hysteria directed against radicalism following World War I.

NEVINS, ALLAN, *The United States in a Chaotic World,* Yale Univ. Press. International affairs 1918–1933.

SLOSSON, PRESTON W., *The Great Crusade and After, 1914–1928,* Macmillan.

SOULE, GEORGE, *Prosperity Decade,* Holt, Rinehart & Winston. From 1917 to 1929.

STEARNS, MARSHALL, *The Story of Jazz,* New American Library (Mentor Books, paper). The men who created and played this uniquely American music.

TRAVERSO, EDMUND, and VAN R. HALSEY, eds. *The 1920's: Rhetoric or Reality?,* New Dimensions in American History series, Heath (paper). Based upon source materials; includes material on the debate over the League of Nations, and on the ideals of the period.

WECTER, DIXON, *The Age of the Great Depression, 1929–1941,* Macmillan.

Historical Fiction

ADAMS, SAMUEL HOPKINS, *Revelry,* Liveright. Scandals during Harding's administration.

BACHELLER, IRVING, *Uncle Peel,* Grosset & Dunlap; Lippincott. The 1920's.

BAKER, DOROTHY, *Young Man with a Horn,* Houghton Mifflin. Jazz trumpeter who lived in the 1920's.

BARNES, MARGARET A., *Years of Grace,* Houghton Mifflin. Jazz Age in Chicago.

CATHER, WILLA, *The Professor's House,* Knopf. Conflict between culture and materialism.

DREISER, THEODORE, *An American Tragedy,* World Publishing; and others. Novel about a young weakling.

LAWRENCE, JOSEPHINE, *If I Have Four Apples,* Grosset & Dunlap. Novel about Great Depression.

LEWIS, SINCLAIR, *Arrowsmith,* Harcourt Brace Jovanovich. Novel about idealistic doctor.

——, *Babbitt,* Harcourt Brace Jovanovich. Satirical novel about businessman.

——, *Main Street,* Harcourt Brace Jovanovich. Novel about pettiness of small-town life.

MARQUAND, JOHN P., *The Late George Apley,* Little, Brown; Pocket Books. Story of a Boston aristocrat.

SINCLAIR, UPTON, *Between Two Worlds,* Viking. The decade 1919–1929.

——, *Oil!,* Laurie [London]. Oil scandal during Harding's administration.

HISTORY AND THE SOCIAL SCIENCES

ANTHROPOLOGY

Nature of Anthropology

The word "anthropology" literally means "the study of man." But man, of course, is the object of study of all the social sciences, as well as history. How then does anthropology differ from the other social sciences? Most anthropologists would answer that the central concern of anthropology is the study of human cultures.

Anthropology today has several different areas of specialization, but the two most important are *cultural anthropology* and *physical anthropology*. Physical anthropology is the study of the physical origins of man; cultural anthropology is the study of the many different patterns of culture in the modern world. While physical anthropology remains a respected and important part of the discipline, most anthropologists today consider the study of cultures—their history and their changing patterns—to be their central concern. Thus we shall limit our discussion primarily to cultural anthropology.

Some years ago, anthropologists were mainly interested in studying the cultures of primitive peoples. The titles of three major books written in the late 1920's and early 1930's by a famous American anthropologist, Margaret Mead, indicate the areas that interested an older generation of anthropologists: *Coming of Age in Samoa, Growing Up in New Guinea,* and *Sex and Temperament in Three Primitive Societies.*

But anthropology today has greatly broadened its scope. A famous anthropologist wrote, in 1949, that "Anthropology is no longer just the science of the long-ago and faraway." In the 1970's, this statement about anthropology is even more accurate.

Some anthropologists still study primitive groups. But today, the few remaining primitive societies are dying out. Even the most primitive peoples in the world's remotest regions are directly or indirectly in contact with other peoples. Many anthropologists now are studying contemporary cultures throughout the non-Western world, such as rural communities in modern India or cultural change among the peoples of east Africa. American anthropologists also have begun to examine cultural patterns among certain groups within their own society, such as rural communities in Appalachia, or cultural changes affecting Pueblo Indians in Arizona or Mexican-Americans in California or Greek-Americans in Chicago.

No matter which cultural group an anthropologist chooses to study, he shares a common goal with all other anthropologists. Anthropologists in general try to understand the relationship between man and his culture. They want especially to investigate the patterns of cultural behavior that develop as man adapts to, and changes, his environment.

In making their inquiries, anthropologists examine all aspects of a society's culture. Like sociologists, anthropologists are not searching for unique behavior or bizarre customs. Rather, they are searching for patterns of similarity or regularity that explain and describe man's cultural behavior. Patterns of behavior and thought are the subject matter of cultural anthropology.

The anthropologist operates under the assumption that all over the world different peoples, in adapting to their environment, have developed different habits and customs. Different peoples have developed different ways of building houses, of preparing food, of bringing up children, of arranging marriages, of coping with illness, of earning a living, of burying the dead. The anthropologist also examines the ideas—the different ways of thinking and

A Navajo Indian creating a sand painting

believing—developed by different peoples around the world. In some societies, for example, sick people are considered cursed, while in others they are honored as favorites of the gods. If an American bride gets married on a rainy day, she might consider the rain to be a sign of bad luck. But among many Arabs living in the arid regions of the Middle East, a rainy wedding day is considered a sign of good fortune.

Anthropologists, then, in trying to understand culture, investigate the habits and ideas shared by members of whole societies. In recent years, they have come to view culture as a total, integrated way of life, not just an accumulation of customs. And anthropologists today also believe that, to be understood properly, this total way of life must be studied on its own terms. It must not be judged by using the standards of another culture.

Peoples of different cultures sometimes find it difficult to understand one another. Most people believe that their own culture is best for them. Such pride is normal. But it can become dangerous when people think that their modes of thinking and doing things are the only ways, or the only right ways. Anthropology, in helping us to understand the cultural patterns of many different societies, helps us to see our own culture in proper perspective. An understanding of the diversity among cultures makes it more difficult for people to look upon other peoples and other cultures as inferior—just because they are different.

Culture is learned, and language is an integral part of culture.

Concepts of Anthropology

Culture is the key concept in anthropology. Culture includes all the ideas that a people believe in and all the things that they do. It includes their habits and customs, their religion and education, their arts and their government. In short, a people's culture is their entire way of life, including everything they have learned from the time they were born. Anthropologists maintain that babies are not born with a culture. Cultural behavior is not something that a child inherits biologically from his parents. Rather, cultural behavior is behavior that is learned.

Each society of men has its own distinctive culture which makes it different from any other culture. Members of each society behave differently from members of all other societies in some ways. Frenchmen greet one another by kissing on both cheeks. Americans greet by pumping right hands. Inhabitants of the Andaman Islands in the Indian Ocean weep when greeting friends whom they have not seen for some time. Notice, however, that although these people behave differently, they are all trying to solve the same problem—greeting a friend.

Anthropologists are also interested in studying the concept of **cultural socialization;** that is, how cultural patterns are transmitted from one generation to the next. They want to find out how the older generation teaches the younger generation to conform to the established patterns of cultural behavior. An American child, for example, learns the accepted patterns of cultural behaivor from his family, his teachers, his friends, his religious leaders. The group—society in general—approves if he learns his lessons well and disapproves if he does not. And every culture also has different patterns of behavior for different groups within the society. For example, in American culture as in all others, different behavior patterns are expected of the very young and the very old, of men and of women, of married people and of unmarried people. Anthropologists want to find out what these patterns of behavior are and how they are maintained and transmitted.

In studying the process of socialization, anthropologists also study deviations from the accepted modes of behavior. Members of the older generation generally frown upon or even punish lapses or deviations from the established modes. Nonetheless, such lapses do exist. Consider, for example, a society such as the United States, in which stealing is not an accepted mode of behavior. Even though American society condemns stealing, nonetheless some Americans do steal. And in tribes where young men are expected to be good fighters, some boys do not like to fight, and a few even try to avoid combat completely. Thus every culture has some patterns of behavior that are not followed by all members.

Cultural change is another important concept in anthropology. Anthropologists have found that cultures do not stay the same—even for short periods of time. Cultural change takes place all the time—even in primitive societies. In recent years, because of the transportation and communications revolution, many primitive societies have become less primitive and have accepted some modern ways of dress and sanitation. Some anthropologists say this is progress; others are not so sure.

Anthropologists have also found that cultural change does not occur evenly in any society. Change may deeply affect some members of the society, while leaving others clinging to the old ways. This situation, if acute enough, results in **social conflict**—another important concept investigated by anthropologists.

The Japanese tea-serving ceremony

Social conflict develops most often between the younger and older generations, especially in developing countries. Consider, for example, a young African who leaves his farming village to study in one of Africa's modern cities. He soon finds himself torn between two worlds. He wants his village to retain its traditional cultures, and yet he wants to help his people by introducing new scientific ways of farming that he has learned in the city. The young African must find a way to balance his new ideas with his old.

Cultural **customs, habits,** and **mores** are other important concepts investigated by anthropologists in their study of culture. Anthropologists generally use these terms interchangeably to describe a particular culture's patterns of behavior. The power of a custom is very great. The government of India today has a difficult time restraining widows from the centuries-old custom of *suttee,* which commanded them to leap to their deaths into the funeral pyres of their husbands. It is custom which dictates the elaborate rules for the tea-serving ceremony in Japan. And it is custom which forces a guest at a Bedouin feast to eat beyond his capacity for fear of giving grave offense to his Arab host. It is very difficult, if not impossible, to change these customs, whose origin is usually hidden in the distant past.

Methods of Anthropology

Anthropologists use many of the methods of inquiry developed in other social sciences, especially in sociology. But anthropologists have adopted and refined their own original method of inquiry—the **field study.**

In studying the culture of a particular group of people, the anthropologist depends mainly on empirical research; that is, his method of investigation is based on first-hand research. As a rule, he goes to live in the culture he is studying as a participant and as an observer. He lives in the group for a reasonably long period of time, making every effort not to disturb the routine of life that he is observing.

The anthropological field study has been refined in recent years, but its fundamental principles, as defined by Bronislaw Malinowski in the early 1900's, are still widely followed by anthropologists today. Malinowski, one of the founders of modern anthropology, lived for two years on the Trobriand

Islands in the South Pacific in order to study the cultural patterns of the people living on the islands. Describing his experience, he wrote, "I did my work entirely alone, living for the greater part of the time right in the villages. I therefore had constantly the daily life of the natives before my eyes, while accidental dramatic occurrences, deaths, quarrels, village brawls, public and ceremonial events could not escape my notice."

Anthropologists today, in accordance with principles established by Malinowski, believe that the observing anthropologist must be a participant—he must live in the native environment in order to gain the confidence of the people he is studying. Winning the people's confidence is essential if they are to confide in the anthropologist and tell him of their private lives, their inner thoughts, their fears, their joys. The anthropologist must blend into his environment and accept the pleasant, as well as the unpleasant, aspects of his surroundings. And he must record everything he sees and learns and experiences in a detailed diary, or log, of his observations.

To make sure that his field work is objective and useful, the anthropologist must observe a fundamental precept. He must *not* concentrate on the unique and the odd aspects of the culture he is studying and thereby neglect the ordinary and the routine aspects of the people's lives. His research must be aimed at portraying the *entire* culture, not merely fragments which intrigue him. And equally important, the investigator must take pains not to allow his own value judgments and cultural preferences to influence him in any way.

The anthropologist must record his observations in his field study log in an accurate, detailed, and thoroughly methodical manner. His field study must be exhaustive; that is, it must not record only some examples of the people's behavior, or a few selected interviews, but rather it must include as far as possible all examples within reach. Until the anthropologist has made such an exhaustive study, he cannot begin with confidence his search for patterns of regularity in the behavior of the group under study. And this search for regular patterns is his main reason for making the field study in the first place.

A village in New Guinea

However, the aim of the anthropological study—the charting of patterns of regularity in group behavior—cannot be obtained by observation alone. Observation must be supplemented by carefully conducted **interviews** with members of the group who know a great deal about the various aspects of life in their particular community and are willing to talk about them. Moreover, it is especially helpful if the anthropologist can conduct these interviews in the native language. Interviews are the best ways of learning the modes of thinking and the ways of eeling of the people under study. Anthropologists also feel that the statements elicited during interviews should be written down verbatim in order to capture, in Malinowski's memorable phrase, "the verbal contour of native thought."

Some modern anthropologists, while accepting the validity of the classical field study, have expressed doubts about the anthropologist's ability to maintain complete detachment in conducting his study. Professor H. L. Shapiro of the American Museum of Natural History wrote recently that many anthropologists who live for years with primitive peoples and study every aspect of their behavior and then write reports on their observations often forget that the people observed are individuals. He contended that "The passions that move primitive man become lost in the generalization that describes the rules under which he lives."

Thus, the anthropologist's task is a difficult one. But in his search for objective truth, the anthropologist helps to explain particular modes of behavior that throw light on human behavior in general.

CASE STUDY IN ANTHROPOLOGY

Greek-Americans

The American Melting Pot—Fact or Fantasy?

During the past 150 years a marvelously complicated myth was created by a great many people. Over and over Americans were told that the special genius of the United States stemmed from its makeup as a nation of immigrants—of people from diverse backgrounds and cultures who were slowly being molded into one great society with a common culture—American society and culture. There were two theories on how this American culture was being formed. Some people thought that the earliest settlers had established an American culture and that each immigrant group as it arrived learned the language and accepted the established customs, thus becoming assimilated into the American way of life. Other people said that all immigrant groups were making different contributions to an evolving culture and that one day a new, homogeneous American culture would be produced. But however they explained what was happening, they pictured immigrant peoples, speaking many languages, wearing exotic costumes, and practicing "Old World" customs, coming together in the great American "melting pot" and being melted down into the metal of Americans.

In some cases, of course, these people were right. Some "melting" did take place. But now when we look at the metal we see that the groups that went into the pot did not melt down completely, but kept much of their own shape. The metal which is American society and culture today is lumpy. Many groups share in a common American culture, but these groups also retain some feeling of separate identity in their own communities as Japanese-Americans, Irish-Americans, Jewish-Americans, Puerto Rican-Americans, German-Americans, black Americans, Greek-Americans, Polish-Americans, Chinese-Americans, Italian-Americans.

Why are these communities—or ethnic groups as they are called—still such important forces in the United States today? All of us can think of some reasons. (1) Identification with a small, familiar ethnic group gives people help and comfort in adjusting to modern industrial life. (2) Black Americans, Japanese-Americans, and Chinese-Americans, because they are easily identifiable by distinct racial characteristics, continue to be treated as special groups by the rest of American society. (3) Some institutions in American society—religious, political, and economic—continue to be based on ethnic identity.

In this case study we shall examine the **culture** of one ethnic group, Greek-Americans, to see how this group maintains its cultural identity—its unique patterns of cultural behavior—within the larger American community. We shall also try to discover how the process of **cultural socialization** takes place among these Greek-Americans—how their habits and ideas are maintained and transmitted from one generation to the next.

Greek-Americans—The Enduring Strength of Ethnic Identity

Many people are gathering at a large Greek-Orthodox church on the south side of Chicago. It is Greek Easter. Most who come to the service drive up in American cars. The men are discussing baseball and the cost of a color television set; a few are discussing the political crisis in Greece. The women are comparing notes on children's schools and the length of skirts. The boys and girls are discussing homework and dates. All of them—men, women, and children—are aware that on this day they are members of a special

Greek icons

group. They are Greek-Americans, and they are proud of it. This Easter is a day which is uniquely Greek-American. Christmas and the Fourth of July are holidays which they share with other Americans. Greek Easter is theirs.

The church which this group enters has a bay at the altar side facing east. Near the center the church is divided by a great grill wall, separating the altar from the nave. On the grill hang several *icons,* stylized pictures of sacred figures. Because the Greek church uses the Julian calendar, Greek Easter falls later in the year than the Easter celebrated by Protestants and Roman Catholics, who use the Gregorian calendar. Greek Easter is the climax of Holy Week, with special ceremonies both in the church and at home, leading up to the midnight service and the lighting of candles by the entire congregation. Easter Sunday dinner is an occasion for great family gatherings, featuring roast lamb, *kulurakia*—special Easter bread—and after dinner, a breaking of the dyed red eggs.

Some of the people coming to church on this Easter have not been to church since last Easter, while others come every day bringing their children to the parochial school run by the church. Not everyone in the Greek-American ethnic group participates in the special Greek Easter ceremonies, but everyone knows that Greeks do these things and feels a sense of identification with the group that observes these Easter customs. In various ways their identification as Greek-Americans is a source of support, deep and enduring, to most Americans of Greek descent.

The congregation of the church we have been describing now lives scattered throughout the south side of Chicago, but once they all lived in the neighborhood around the church. Before that the first generation of immigrants lived in the Harrison-Halstead area, the first center of the Greek community in Chicago. At that time the area was called "Greektown"—the center of the first *kinotitos* (community), the location of the major Greek coffee houses and restaurants, the sites of the first candy factories and the food dispensing businesses. It was in Greektown that the Chicago political "machine" made its appeal for Greek votes in return for political services.

Most of Greektown has now been pulled down as part of an urban renewal project, and several Greek-American communities have been established elsewhere in the city, around new churches. Most Greek-Americans in Chicago now feel their connection to their ethnic group through one of these churches or through friendships with other Greek-American families. Contacts are kept very much alive for many reasons, but most especially because older Greek-Americans want to encourage their young people to marry within the group so that the Greek traditions will be carried on. They feel that happier, more satisfactory marriages can be made within the group than outside it. The women will know Greek cooking, the men will be able to find business associates, and the children will be brought up in the church.

Nowadays some younger members of the Greek-American community do not marry within the group. Most older Greek-Americans are unhappy when this happens. It is true that some outsiders who marry into the group become communicants in the church, and learn Greek ways. However, these people can never really become Greek-Americans because the basis for being a Greek-American is thought to be "blood"—heredity. Greek-Americans think of themselves as descendants of Greek immigrants, not as a group which can be voluntarily joined. Most members of the group also feel that, to be a Greek-American, it is necessary to be of the Orthodox religion. They would be astonished, for example, to meet a Greek-American who is a Protestant or a Roman Catholic.

Many Greek-Americans can tell in detail the history of their ancestors who came to America as immigrants, mainly between 1910 and 1920. Many came fully expecting to return to Greece once they had made some money; often these were men alone. However, many did not return, and they later went back, or sent back, for wives. Some immigrants did return to fight for Greece in the Balkan Wars or in World War I. The older generation is proud that, as American citizens, many fought in the United States army during World War I and World War II. All Greek-Americans know stories of Greek immigrants successful in business, academic life, and politics—even a Vice-President of the United States. For many, the American dream came true—poor immigrants or their children made good in America, although often after long years of loneliness and struggle. However, contrary to the prediction often made, they were not entirely melted down into Americans. A sense of ethnic community continued. They became Americans, but a special kind of Americans—Greek-Americans.

Over the years Greek-Americans have had serious struggles among themselves. Often the struggles centered around political problems in Greece. Those who supported the Greek monarchy fought bitterly with those who supported the republican cause. Neither group planned to return to Greece, but wanted to raise money to support the appropriate cause.

Sometimes the struggles reflected differences about church organization. Over the years the Greek Orthodox church has had two centers: Constantinople (Istanbul) and Athens. Some churches in the United States were founded with support from the Patriarch of the Greek Orthodox church in Constantinople; others with support from the Holy Synod in Athens.

Both common customs and common history and, paradoxically, common feuds and struggles have helped to hold the Greek-American community together. Probably equally important in keeping the group identity has been the treatment of Greek-Americans by other Americans. When Greek immigrants came to Chicago and started in the restaurant business and the candy business, those already in these businesses feared their competition. When Greeks moved into the Harrison-Halsted area, their customs and language were regarded as strange. Families were laughed at, students in school were ridiculed, men in business were abused, church doctrine and ritual were considered odd. The acceptance of new immigrants into American life has often been reluctant. For Greek-Americans, the fact that their church was different from the three more common religions—Protestant, Roman Catholic, and Jewish—tended to keep them apart socially even as they became accepted economically and politically.

The two sides of the American experience are clear when we look at Greek-Americans. Part of the time the United States has been a land of economic opportunity, of tolerance of religious and ethnic differences, of hope for political and legal equality. Part of the time, however, it has been a land of intolerance and distrust among ethnic groups who fear one another while remaining ignorant of what the other groups are really like. The Greek-American community has seen and contributed to both, and the historical experience has created an ethnic group which is now strong and a real part of the American scene.

A Greek-American family

■ What unique patterns of cultural behavior are found among Greek-Americans?

■ How does the Greek-American community in Chicago illustrate "the enduring strength of ethnic identity"? Explain.

UNIT ELEVEN

The New Deal and World War II

1932–1945

Detail from Isaac Soyer's "Employment Agency." Oil on canvas. 34½ x 45. 1937. Collection Whitney Museum of American Art, New York.

■ *Out of work during the Depression*

CHAPTER **36**

Undertaking a Great Experiment

1932 – 1936

P̲RESIDENT FRANKLIN DELANO ROOSEVELT took office on March 4, 1933, in the midst of the Great Depression. He began his administration with a ringing summons to the American people to face the future with courage and faith. "The only thing we have to fear is fear itself," he confidently stated. His calm words helped to lift the nation from its despair and helped to rally the people behind the government.

The President outlined his New Deal program in a crisp, dramatic Inaugural Address. He then presented his reform proposals, with recommendations for immediate action, to a special session of Congress that he called soon after taking office.

The New Deal had in general three aims—relief, recovery, and reform. Because Americans were clamoring for action, the three aims were often mixed together as objectives of a single act of Congress. Sometimes measures adopted to realize one of the aims interfered with other measures designed to achieve the other aims.

But for purposes of analysis, it is convenient to divide the New Deal into its three essential parts: (1) measures to provide relief for the unemployed; (2) measures to speed the recovery of agriculture, industry, commerce, and labor; and (3) measures to remedy certain weaknesses in the economic system.

Such was the general nature of the Great Experiment that President Roosevelt and Congress launched in the spring of 1933.

THE CHAPTER IN OUTLINE

1. New Deal measures to provide relief and work for the unemployed.

2. Recovery measures to stimulate agriculture and help farmers.

3. Recovery measures to aid banking, building, and transportation.

4. Recovery measures to help industry and encourage labor.

5. Various reform measures carried out by the New Deal.

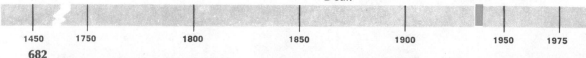

| 1450 | 1750 | 1800 | 1850 | 1900 | 1950 | 1975 |

1 New Deal measures to provide relief and work for the unemployed

The most urgent task facing Roosevelt when he took office was to provide assistance for millions of jobless, hungry Americans. By 1933 nearly 14 million people were out of work.

Direct relief. The Roosevelt administration immediately launched what seemed at the time to be a colossal program of direct relief. In two years the Federal Emergency Relief Administration (FERA), created in 1933, and other federal agencies distributed $3 billion to needy Americans. Money was distributed to the states, allowing state and local officials to use the money as they chose— for direct relief or to provide jobs. At one time nearly 8 million families were on direct relief. But few Americans liked this kind of relief. The unemployed wanted jobs, not charity. Thus plans were made to replace direct relief with a program to provide work.

Work relief. The federal government attacked the problem of providing jobs in several different ways. For instance, during 1933–34 it paid nearly $1 billion in wages to men and women drawn from the relief rolls who were given jobs on "made work" projects. Many of the "made work" projects— raking leaves and picking up litter in parks—had relatively little value. Critics of the New Deal called this kind of work "boondoggling."

President Roosevelt and other New Dealers knew that federal charity and "made work" were at best necessary evils. What Americans needed and what the New Dealers wanted to provide was socially useful work. To accomplish this purpose, a new agency, the Works Progress Administration (WPA), was created in 1935, with Harry L. Hopkins as its head. The WPA cooperated with state and local governments, which shared in both the cost and the administration of the work relief program. During 1935 and 1936 Congress voted about $6.3 billion in funds for the new agency.

The WPA program helped people in many walks of life. By 1936 more than 6,000 schoolhouses had been constructed or repaired; new sewage plants had been built in 5,000 communities; about 128,-000 miles of secondary roads had been constructed or improved; and other public improvements had been made. Unemployed actors, musicians, and writers enriched American life by providing plays, concerts, guidebooks, and other forms of recreation. At the peak of its activity, in March 1936,

■ During the Depression, most unemployed Americans wanted jobs, not charity. To meet this demand, the Roosevelt administration created such agencies as the WPA and the CCC. A group of CCC workers is shown above.

nearly 4 million Americans were working for the WPA.

Work for youth. Perhaps the greatest tragedy of the depression was its effect upon millions of young Americans. Many could not continue in school—elementary school, secondary school, or college—because they lacked food and clothing or were homeless. Those who graduated during the depression years faced unemployment. Thousands of jobless young Americans roamed the nation in search of work.

Two agencies were created to bring immediate work relief to the nation's youth. In 1933 the Civilian Conservation Corps (CCC) was organized. At times as many as 500,000 young men between 18 and 25 were enrolled in the CCC. Nearly all of them were unmarried; most came from poverty-stricken families. These youths were scattered across the land in 2,600 work camps. They received food, clothing, and shelter; they were paid wages which they were expected to share with their families; and they were offered opportunities for recreation and education.

The young people in the CCC did socially useful work. They built fire trails in the forests, cleared

683

■ Mary McLeod Bethune (left) was one of the prominent leaders who made up President Roosevelt's "black cabinet." Above, she meets with Eleanor Roosevelt and a government official.

swamps, planted trees, built small dams for flood control, cleared land for public parks, and in other ways helped to conserve the nation's natural resources.

A second New Deal work relief measure aided young people still in school. The National Youth Administration (NYA), created in 1935, distributed federal money to needy students, who were paid regular wages for tasks which the local educational authorities arranged in and around the school. During its first year the NYA gave jobs to more than 400,000 students.

The New Deal youth program saved hundreds of thousands of youths from idleness, helped them to maintain their self-respect, and enabled many to get an education. It also kept many young Americans out of the overcrowded job market in business and industry.

Negroes and the New Deal. Along with destitute white Americans, needy black Americans gained relief and employment in the Works Prog-

ress Administration, the Civilian Conservation Corps, and the National Youth Administration. But the depression hit black wage earners and farmers even harder than it did white workers. Though black Americans made up one tenth of the nation's population, by 1936 one sixth of those on relief were Negroes. Black tenant farmers and sharecroppers were especially hard hit, and they often suffered discrimination in the allocation of benefits from the New Deal agricultural agencies. Discrimination also existed in the administration of federal housing programs and, especially at local levels, in other New Deal programs.

Yet the depression and the doors opened by the New Deal stimulated Negroes to struggle with renewed determination for their legal and constitutional rights. In many northern cities black leaders organized "don't buy where you can't work" campaigns. In the Southern Tenant Farmers' Union, tenant farmers, black and white, often joined together against wealthy landlords. The National

Negro Congress, launched in 1935 with some support from white liberals and radicals, promoted the interests of black Americans within the New Deal agencies.

Finally, responding to pressures such as these and to the prodding of Eleanor Roosevelt, the President's wife, the New Deal administration appointed prominent Negroes to important federal positions. Among them were Mary McLeod Bethune, Ralph Bunche, and Robert C. Weaver. These leaders and others made up an informal group of advisers often called the "black cabinet."

Evaluating the relief program. The New Deal relief projects aroused much criticism, not only from Republicans, but also from members of the President's own party. It is true that many mistakes were made. There was incompetence. There was waste.

Some New Dealers admitted the truth of these criticisms. They explained, however, that there had been no large, successful precedents for the gigantic task they had been forced to undertake. They also pointed out that they had been handicapped by lack of adequately trained personnel to carry out some of their programs.

But, despite admitted weaknesses in the work relief program, all New Dealers claimed that it had fully justified itself. Work provided by the federal government, they insisted, had saved millions of Americans from hunger and had allowed them to retain some measure of self-respect.

SECTION SURVEY

IDENTIFY: New Deal, FERA, direct relief, CCC, work relief, WPA, "black cabinet"; Ralph Bunche, Eleanor Roosevelt, Robert Weaver.

1. (a) What immediate problems confronted Roosevelt when he took office in 1933? (b) How was he able to get Congress to pass almost all of the initial legislation he proposed?
2. How did the New Deal respect states' rights in distributing funds for relief purposes?
3. Perhaps the greatest tragedy of the depression was its effect upon millions of young Americans. Why was this so?
4. (a) What criticisms were leveled against the New Deal relief program? (b) How did the New Dealers answer these criticisms?
5. What was the experience of Negroes during the New Deal?
6. The New Deal was not radical in concept. Comment.

LIVING AMERICAN DOCUMENTS

Franklin D. Roosevelt's
First Inaugural Address (1933)

So, first of all, let me assert my firm belief that the only thing we have to fear is fear itself—nameless, unreasoning, unjustified terror which paralyzes needed efforts to convert retreat into advance. . . .

Our greatest primary task is to put people to work. This is no unsolvable problem if we face it wisely and courageously.

It can be accomplished in part by direct recruiting by the government itself, treating the task as we would treat the emergency of a war, but at the same time, through this employment, accomplishing greatly needed projects to stimulate and reorganize the use of our natural resources.

Hand in hand with this, we must frankly recognize the overbalance of population in our industrial centers and, by engaging on a national scale in a redistribution, endeavor to provide a better use of the land for those best fitted for the land. . . .

In the field of world policy I would dedicate this nation to the policy of the good neighbor—the neighbor who resolutely respects himself and, because he does so, respects the rights of others—the neighbor who respects his obligations and respects the sanctity of his agreements in and with a world of neighbors. . . .

2 Recovery measures to stimulate agriculture and help farmers

The New Deal measures to provide direct relief and work relief were intended to meet the urgent needs of millions of suffering Americans. Simultaneously, the New Deal administration launched a recovery program designed to restore the nation's economic health.

Saving the farmers' homes. When Roosevelt became President, two out of every five American farms were mortgaged. Moreover, farmers all over the country were faced with mounting debts—back taxes, interest payments, and payments on the principal of their loans. Unable to pay their debts, many farmers watched their farms pass into the hands of banks, insurance companies, and private

A dust storm in Oklahoma

THE DUST BOWL

The year 1934 brought a long-drawn-out nightmare to thousands of farmers living in western Kansas, southeastern Colorado, the Oklahoma Panhandle, northeastern New Mexico, and the semiarid plains of Texas. Relentless winds swept over drought-ridden land, burying fields, fences, and houses under thousands of tons of drifting dust. Cattle and poultry died. A young boy on his way home from school was found buried in the dust only a quarter of a mile from his home. Farmers were driven to despair. Millions of acres were abandoned by poverty-stricken families who, in desperation, piled their possessions in trucks and moved to the cities or to California.

What caused this dreadful situation? The plains had experienced drought and dust storms even when buffalo and cattle grazed on their long grasses. But as farmers moved in and plowed more than a third of the area, partly as a result of pressure to grow more wheat during World War I, they destroyed the protecting cover of grass, and the soil lay bare beneath the burning sun, defenseless against the driving wind. Only a prolonged drought was required to bring disaster. In 1934 the drought came.

After this disaster, the Soil Conservation Service encouraged farmers to use contour plowing, to plant soil-saving crops, and to set out trees in shelter-belt strips to break the force of the wind. By the late 1930's the farmers in the Dust Bowl were beginning to win their battle against drought, wind, and dust.

mortgage holders. The farmers then rented their former land as tenants or were left homeless and jobless.

To relieve this desperate situation, the federal government made available a huge sum of money to be lent to farmers at a low interest rate. Some farmers borrowed money to buy seed, fertilizer, and equipment necessary to continue operations. Others borrowed money to buy back their farms or pay their taxes.

Still others borrowed money from the government to refinance loans that they could not repay at the time. Suppose, for instance, that Mr. Grumman, a farmer, owed $5,000 that he had to repay over a 20-year period with interest at 5 percent. Because of the depression, Mr. Grumman could not meet his yearly payments on his debt. He was faced with the foreclosure of his mortgage and the loss of his farm and home. But under the new government program he could borrow $5,000 from Federal Land Banks to pay off his debt to the mortgage holder. The new debt could run for as long as 50 years, with interest at 2.25 percent.

This liberal system of federal credit enabled hundreds of thousands of farmers to protect their land and homes. The farm credit programs were administered by the Farm Credit Administration (FCA), created in 1933.

Higher incomes for farmers. In a second major attack upon the farm problem, the New Dealers tried to increase the farmers' income. The basic government formula for farm recovery was simple. The first step was to raise the prices of farm products. With more dollars in their pockets, the farmers—then about one fourth of the nation's population—would buy more manufactured goods. This new demand would help to reopen factories. These factories would hire more workers, thus reducing industrial unemployment. The industrial workers, in turn, would spend more money, which in time would help to reopen still more factories. The demand for goods of all sorts, from farm and factory, would spiral upward. The key to the situation, as the New Dealers saw it, was higher farm prices.

The government set out to increase farm prices by utilizing the principle of supply and demand. Consider the example of a grocery store which has bought more oranges than it can sell to customers. The surplus oranges are about to rot. What does the storekeeper do? He reduces the price of the oranges. Next time, of course, he will order fewer oranges, hoping that by reducing the available supply he can sell all the oranges at a good price. This is essentially the policy that the New Deal applied to farm goods in the Agricultural Adjustment Act of 1933.

Limiting farm production.   The government reduced the supply of farm products by several methods. To begin with, government agents, acting under the authority of the Agricultural Adjustment Administration (AAA), urged farmers to sign agreements not to use one quarter to one half of their land. By thus limiting the amount of farm produce, the government hoped to raise prices. But even with higher prices the farmer had less income because he had fewer products to sell. The government therefore paid each farmer a certain sum of money for each acre that he took out of production. The money for these subsidies, or "benefit payments," was secured by collecting taxes from the food processors—meat packers, canners, flour millers, and others who prepared, or "processed," farm products.

Under this program, millions of acres of farm land were taken out of production. In 1933 a million cotton planters plowed under cotton, and they did not plant about 10 million acres which would ordinarily have been under production. As a result, the 1933 cotton crop was reduced by about 4 million bales and the price of cotton almost doubled, while the planters received almost $200 million in federal subsidies. Producers of wheat, corn, hogs, rice, tobacco, dairy products, cattle, rye, barley, peanuts, flax, grain, sorghum, and sugar signed similar agreements to limit production.

Evaluating the farm program.   New Dealers were pleased with their agricultural recovery program. They pointed out that the prices of farm products had risen and farmers were earning more money. They also pointed out that with this increased purchasing power farmers were spending more money and thus helping to get industry rolling again. These favorable results, the New Dealers said, were the outcome of a sound program of federal planning.

But there was also severe criticism of the New Deal farm program. In the first place, critics pointed out, it was necessary to levy taxes on the food processors to get money for the subsidy payments. These taxes were passed along to the consumer in the form of higher prices. Thus, money was being taken from the urban consumer and given to the farmer. While farmers were getting more money, city dwellers were experiencing an actual decline in purchasing power.

In the second place, larger farmers benefited far more from the program than did small farmers. Poorer farmers felt that the benefit payments which finally filtered down to them were inadequate for their needs. In the third place, many critics considered the program bureaucratic—concentrating too much power in an unnecessary number of administrative bureaus—full of red tape, confusion, and inefficiency. Finally, millions of Americans condemned a program which deliberately produced scarcities at a time when hunger was widespread.

The program declared unconstitutional.   It was the Supreme Court, however, that brought the Agricultural Adjustment Act of 1933 to an end by declaring it unconstitutional. In a 1936 decision in the case of *United States v. Butler,* the Supreme Court stated that Congress had no constitutional right to regulate agricultural production. The Court also ruled that the power to regulate agriculture belonged to the states, and that the federal government had no authority to interfere.

As you will see in the next chapter, however, the adverse Supreme Court decision did not end New Deal efforts to help farmers.

SECTION SURVEY

IDENTIFY: AAA, subsidy, bureaucratic, *United States v. Butler.*

1. Explain the basic New Deal formula for farm recovery.
2. What measures did the New Dealers introduce to help farmers retain their homes and land?
3. Give the arguments for and against the New Deal farm recovery program.
4. Why did the Supreme Court declare the Agricultural Adjustment Act of 1933 unconstitutional?
5. Do you think the New Deal formula for farm recovery supported the principles of capitalism? Explain.

3 Recovery measures to aid banking, building, and transportation

While trying to stimulate agriculture, the New Deal was also trying to restore the health of the country's banks and currency. When Roosevelt took office on March 4, 1933, the nation was in the grip of an unprecedented financial collapse.

Bank failures.   For months crowds of panic-stricken Americans had been selling stocks and

■ Above, depositors wait anxiously at an Ohio bank during the 1933 "bank holiday." Closings prevented "runs" on sound banks, which reopened after examination by the Treasury Department.

rushing to banks to withdraw their deposits before the banks failed. By March 1933 nearly every stock exchange and many banks had closed. Many states, in a belated effort to save their financial institutions, had ordered all banks to suspend activities until further notice. Americans across the country were hiding money in mattresses, under carpets, or in any place considered safe.

With so many banks closed, the everyday business life of the nation could not be carried on. People could not pay their bills by check, and there was not enough currency in circulation to meet the needs of even a depressed economy.

The bank holiday. One of Roosevelt's first acts was to issue a proclamation effective on March 6, 1933, closing every bank in the country for an indefinite period. Congress then enacted laws forbidding any bank to reopen until it could prove its soundness and its ability to carry on business without endangering its customers' deposits. Most banks across the country were able to satisfy the financial experts in the Treasury Department and quickly reopened.

Abandoning the gold standard. Shortly after Roosevelt ordered the "bank holiday," Congress authorized the Secretary of the Treasury to call in all gold coins and gold certificates then in circulation, and provided a maximum penalty of a $10,-000 fine and 10 years in jail for anyone found guilty of hoarding gold. With this action Congress abandoned the gold standard, which in the past had

meant that all paper currency was redeemable in gold on request.

Later, in October 1933, Roosevelt undertook to stabilize the price of gold. He authorized the Reconstruction Finance Corporation (page 639) to buy and sell gold on the world market so that the United States could take "in its own hands the control of the gold value of our dollar." If the price of gold dropped, the RFC could raise it immediately merely by offering to buy gold at a higher price. If the price rose too high, the RFC could begin to sell gold at lower prices.

Still later, at the end of January 1934, President Roosevelt announced that the gold value of the dollar would be established at 59.06 cents in relation to the old "gold" dollar, whose value had been 100 cents in gold. By "devaluing" the dollar, the New Deal administration hoped to force prices upward and thus help the farmers. In this respect, however, the new measure was a disappointment.

"Pump priming." To revive the nation's economy, the New Deal followed a procedure called "pump priming." When the pump in a well does not draw water, it is sometimes necessary to "prime the pump" by pouring a little water down the well shaft. This water seals the crack around a washer in the shaft and thus helps to create a vacuum into which the well water rises so that it can be pumped up.

One of the major "pump priming" agencies was the Reconstruction Finance Corporation. By October 1936 the RFC had poured large sums of money into the nation's economy. It did this in the form of loans totaling $11 billion to railroads, banks, insurance firms, and industrial enterprises. Much of this money was quickly repaid.

But the New Deal also "primed the pump" in other ways. It undertook a huge building program. The New Dealers recognized that the building industry is one of the keys to a nation's economic health. It draws materials from many sources, and when construction work is going on, men are busy in forests, mines, and factories throughout the land. In normal times the building industry employs hundreds of thousands of workers and thus concerns all Americans.

Construction of public works. The building program of the New Deal started in June 1933, when the Public Works Administration (PWA), headed by Harold L. Ickes, Secretary of the Interior, began to contract with private firms for the construction of public works, such as bridges, government buildings, power plants, conservation projects, and dams. The federal government also encouraged states and municipalities to carry on their own building programs, offering them loans and outright gifts amounting to from 30 to 45 percent of the total cost of the projects.

By the summer of 1936 public projects completed under this program included about 70 municipal power plants; several hundred schools and hospitals; nearly 1,500 waterworks; and many federal, state, county, and municipal buildings.

Repair and building of homes. The New Dealers also sought to revive the key building industry by stimulating the building of homes. Like so many New Deal measures, this program was double-barreled. It had as a second goal the relief of home owners.

When President Roosevelt took office, an average of 1,000 American homes were being foreclosed and sold at public auction every day. In June 1933 Congress tried to end this situation by creating the Home Owners' Loan Corporation (HOLC). With money borrowed at low interest rates from this government agency, many home owners paid off their old mortgages. At the same time, they arranged with the HOLC to pay off their new mortgages over a long period with much smaller monthly payments. Between 1933 and 1936 the homes of more than 1 million American families were saved by the HOLC.

To provide further aid to the owners of homes and businesses, as well as to stimulate the building

industry, the Federal Housing Administration (FHA) was established in 1934. Acting through the FHA, the government encouraged banks to lend money to individuals for repairing and building houses and business properties by insuring the banks against losses on such loans. Yet so desperate was the financial position of most Americans that up until 1936 relatively few people were able to take advantage of the FHA loans, and little residential construction was started.

A federal housing program to provide homes for the very poor was no more successful. Although the PWA lent and gave money to some 27 cities for slum clearance and for the erection of "low cost" apartment houses, results were disappointing. For one thing, rents for the finished apartments were usually beyond the reach of poor families.

Aid to transportation. No less important than the building industry to a nation's economic life is its transportation system. The depression hit the railroads a stunning blow. Between 1929 and 1933 their income was cut in half, and almost one third of all the railway companies in the United States went bankrupt. Others were saved from complete collapse only by loans from the RFC.

To recover lost business, some western railways lowered their passenger rates from 3.2 cents to 2 cents per mile. The experiment proved so successful that the Interstate Commerce Commission ordered all lines to adopt the same rate. Government loans also enabled the railroads to install modern equipment, such as diesel engines and streamlined trains.

All of these measures helped the railways. But at the same time that the government was aiding the railroads, it was also spending huge sums of money to improve the nation's highways and waterways, thereby giving a boost to the competitors of rail traffic.

SECTION SURVEY

IDENTIFY: bank holiday, "pump priming," devaluing the dollar, RFC, PWA, FHA.

1. How did the bank holiday restore public confidence in the banks?
2. (a) "Pump priming" was basic to New Deal economic theory. Explain. (b) In what ways did the New Deal "prime the pump"?
3. What steps were taken at this time to help the transportation industry? Why?
4. Why is the building industry a key industry in the United States?

4 Recovery measures to help industry and encourage labor

All of the New Deal recovery measures were more or less indirect methods of reviving the nation's industrial machine. With the National Industrial Recovery Act, usually referred to as the NIRA, the New Deal tackled the problem head on.

The NIRA. The National Industrial Recovery Act went into effect in June 1933 as a two-year emergency measure. It was intended to revive industry by enabling American employers to cooperate in a great planned effort for the re-employment of jobless workers and the raising of wages. Cooperation was to replace competition as one of the major driving forces of American industry. Antitrust legislation, such as the Sherman and Clayton antitrust acts, was disregarded. Instead, the government officially encouraged businessmen to forego competition and form cooperative trade associations.

■ This 1934 cartoon shows Uncle Sam entangled by the multitude of government agencies created under the New Deal. How many of the agencies indicated in the cartoon can you identify?

The NIRA provided that each industry should, with the aid of the National Recovery Administration (NRA), adopt a "code of fair practices." Once these codes had been approved by the President, they became binding upon the entire industry.

Under the vigorous leadership of General Hugh S. Johnson, administrative head of the NRA, some 95 percent of American industries adopted fair practice codes within a few months. The codes differed a great deal. But, in general, they limited production and provided for the common control of prices and sales practices. Most codes also outlawed child labor and stipulated that adults should not work more than 40 hours a week and that wages should not be less than $12 to $15 a week.

Labor under the NIRA. Perhaps the most important—and certainly the most controversial—provisions in the NIRA were contained in the famous Section 7a. This section guaranteed workers the right to bargain collectively with their employers. Employers were forbidden to pressure a worker to join a particular union or to remain a nonunion worker. Employers were also forbidden to refuse work to a man simply because he belonged to a union.

Arguments for the NIRA. President Roosevelt defended the NIRA on the grounds that it allowed labor to organize in order to get a share of profits 'hrough higher wages, that it abolished child labor, and that it ended many unfair trade practices. He also argued that it was responsible for putting 4 million people to work and for raising the total annual wages of the nation by $3 billion.

Criticisms of the NIRA. The NIRA also had its critics, who became increasingly outspoken. In the first place, owners of small businesses charged that the NRA codes of fair practices had mostly been made by and for large corporations. They claimed that some codes, in assigning quotas of production, gave unfairly small quotas to smaller plants. They also insisted that the minimum-wage provisions in the codes favored the highly mechanized factories, whose owners could afford to pay higher wages.

In the second place, it was difficult to enforce the codes. When "chiselers" ignored codes they had promised to obey, honest manufacturers and dealers suffered from unfair competition. In the third place, the courts for the most part refused to enforce the "fair practices" provisions of the codes. And finally, while a major purpose of the NRA was to aid recovery by increasing the purchasing power of consumers, many manufacturers defeated this purpose by raising prices to cover the increase in wages.

The main objection of the NIRA, however, came from many businessmen who opposed it because it stimulated unionization and collective bargaining. Moreover, certain provisions in Section 7a of the act were not clear. For instance, did company unions, under the influence of managers and owners, have the right to engage in collective bargaining? Labor said that company unions could not honestly represent the workers and should be outlawed. Management disagreed.

The National Labor Board. To settle the confused points of the law, Congress established the National Labor Board (NLB), which later became the National Labor Relations Board (NLRB). The National Labor Board was given the power to conduct elections in plants and to determine which labor organization had the right to bargain for all the workers in that particular plant. It also served as a board of arbitration to settle labor disputes brought before it by labor and management.

But the NLB was unpopular with businessmen, who claimed that it usually settled disputes in favor of labor. As a result, business began to oppose the entire NRA program. When management refused to grant union demands, a wave of strikes broke out. Yet, despite these problems, the National Labor Board, before the summer of 1935, settled more than four fifths of the 3,755 disputes referred to it and averted nearly 500 strikes.

The NIRA declared unconstitutional. In May 1935, in the case of *Schechter v. United States,* the Supreme Court declared the NIRA unconstitutional. The judges ruled that Congress had delegated too much of its legislative power to the President, that the President had no power to approve or disapprove of industry codes, and that such codes were not legally binding upon industry. The Court also insisted that, in giving the federal government the right to regulate interstate commerce, the Constitution did not give the government the power to regulate every aspect of business.

The Wagner Act. One important idea in the NIRA was quickly reborn. In 1935 Congress passed the famous National Labor Relations Act, often called the Wagner Act after one of its sponsors, Senator Robert F. Wagner of New York. Workers hailed the Wagner Act as the "Magna Carta of Labor."

The Wagner Act, like the equally well-known Section 7a of the NIRA, guaranteed to labor the right to organize, to bargain collectively with employers for better wages and working conditions, and to engage in "concerted activities . . . for other mutual aid." The Wagner Act specifically condemned as unfair to labor such employer practices as discriminating against or discharging a worker for belonging to a union. It also declared that the majority of the workers in any plant or industry could select representatives for bargaining with management.

Under the Wagner Act the organization of labor proceeded rapidly. While the Wagner Act was in a sense a reform measure, it was also intended to promote industrial recovery by guaranteeing to organized labor a better chance of raising its wages and of thus increasing its purchasing power. No single measure of the New Deal aroused more controversy than the Wagner Act.

SECTION SURVEY

IDENTIFY: NIRA, Section 7a, collective bargaining, *Schechter v. United States*, NLRB; Robert F. Wagner.

1. (a) What was the intent of the NIRA? (b) How was it to be implemented?
2. (a) Give the two most effective arguments in favor of the NIRA. (b) Did these arguments meet the criticisms leveled against the NIRA? Explain.
3. Why did the Supreme Court declare the NIRA unconstitutional?
4. Workers hailed the National Labor Relations Act as the "Magna Carta of Labor." Why?

5 Various reform measures carried out by the New Deal

The New Dealers reasoned that relief and recovery measures were urgently needed in the early 1930's, but that only fundamental reforms could protect the nation against another depression. Under Roosevelt's leadership, the objectives of providing basic economic reform and security became increasingly important in 1935 and in the following years.

Protecting savings. In one of its major reform acts, the New Deal in 1933 established the Federal Deposit Insurance Corporation (FDIC), which guaranteed the savings of bank depositors. At first set at $2,500, the guarantee was raised in 1934 to $5,000. (In later years, it was raised to $10,000, then to $20,000.)

The New Deal also strengthened banks in other ways. For example, it increased the power of the Federal Reserve System by placing industrial and savings banks under its supervision. The Federal Reserve Board was given additional power to regulate credit as a check upon reckless speculation.

Another series of laws was designed to protect the public against worthless stocks. Any salesman —bank, brokerage house, or individual—who failed to give full and honest information about the true value of the stocks and bonds that he sold was subject to a severe penalty. In 1934 the Securities and Exchange Commission (SEC) was created to administer these laws and to regulate the stock exchanges.

Social security for the people. In another fundamental reform measure, the New Deal attacked the problem of individual security.

The Social Security Act of 1935 had three major goals. First, it provided unemployment insurance for individuals who lost their jobs. The money for this purpose was raised by a payroll tax on employers in businesses employing more than eight workers. The unemployment insurance fund was administered by state insurance systems, in cooperation with the federal government.

A second goal of the Social Security Act was to provide old-age pensions ranging from $10 to $85 a month for persons over 65. The money for this purpose was raised by a payroll tax on employers and a social security tax on the wages of employees.

A third goal of the Social Security Act was to help the handicapped—the blind, the deaf-mutes, the crippled, the aged, and dependent children. Federal pensions up to $20 a month were available for needy persons over 65, provided that the states appropriated an equal amount. Federal funds were also available for those states which sought to protect the welfare of the handicapped.

President Roosevelt called the Social Security Act "a cornerstone in a structure which is being built." It was admittedly only a beginning; excluded from its provisions were public employees, farm laborers, domestic servants, and employees of religious, charitable, and nonprofit educational institutions. Nevertheless, by 1937 nearly 21 million workers were entitled to unemployment benefits, and 36 million workers to old-age pensions.

Electricity for homes. Another reform movement sought to bring electricity to more Americans. Despite widespread development of electric power up to the 1930's, only one third of America's homes had electricity; in rural areas only 15 out of every 100 houses were wired.

To solve this problem, the President in 1935 created the Rural Electrification Administration

(REA). The REA had the responsibility of developing a program for generating and distributing electricity in isolated rural areas.

Regulating utility companies. In 1935 also, Congress passed the Public Utility Holding Company Act, also called the Wheeler-Rayburn Act. This measure was intended to give the federal government greater power over the nation's gas and electric industries. The act gave the Federal Power Commission authority to regulate the interstate production, transmission, and sale of electricity. It gave the Federal Trade Commission similar authority over gas. It gave the Securities and Exchange Commission authority to regulate the financial practices of public utility holding companies.

By regulating the financial operations of the public utility holding companies, the New Deal hoped to end an increasing trend toward monopoly in public utilities. The measure was designed to prevent any holding company from controlling more than a "single integrated public utility system" operating in a single area of the country. Under the law, utility companies were forbidden to engage in any business other than the production and distribution of gas or electric power. They were also forbidden to issue new stocks and bonds without first getting the approval of the Securities and Exchange Commission.

Finally, in a "death sentence" clause the Public Utility Holding Company Act gave the public utility holding companies five years to readjust their financial affairs. At the end of five years, any company that could not prove that it was actually distributing gas or electricity in a given area would be dissolved.

The TVA. With the creation of the Tennessee Valley Authority (TVA), Congress in 1933 launched the United States upon an experiment which had no parallel in American history. The scene of the experiment included parts of seven states in the region drained by the Tennessee River and its tributaries (see map, page 693).

The TVA moved into this region with a plan for the unified development of all its resources. The plan was to improve economic and social conditions for the benefit of the people who lived in the valley, as well as for the benefit of all Americans, by setting a standard of cost for producing and distributing electric power. After a decade of trial and error, New Dealers justified their enthusiasm over the TVA by pointing to several accomplishments.

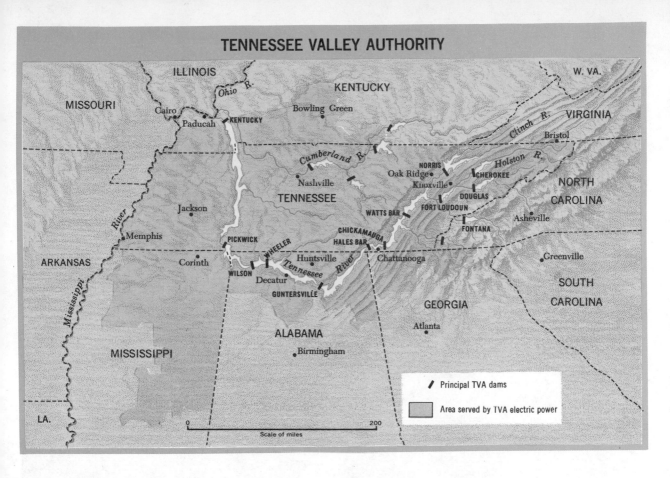

TENNESSEE VALLEY AUTHORITY

Power development. TVA enthusiasts were especially proud of the construction of 21 large dams on the Tennessee River and its major tributaries (see map, this page) and thousands of smaller dams on creeks and brooks. Power plants had been erected to convert the "white coal" of the river into vast quantities of electricity. From these federally owned power plants, high-voltage transmission lines fanned out to cover the region with a network of wires leading into farmhouses in even the most remote valleys. Whereas in 1935 only 1 in every 100 homes in Mississippi had electricity, by 1945 about 20 homes out of 100 were wired. The per capita consumption of electric power in the TVA region was 50 percent higher than the average for the entire United States. Moreover, rates for electric power had been cut by about one third.

Flood control. The TVA dams were also planned as part of a system of flood control. Into a central control room now come daily reports from all over the valley, as well as radio reports from automatic rain gauges, telling of the amount of rain-

fall and the volume of water flowing in each brook, creek, and river. By pushing buttons, sluice gates in great dams can be opened or closed, and millions of tons of water released or stored for future use.

Prevention of soil erosion. Hand in hand with flood control has gone a program to prevent soil erosion and restore the fertility of the land. Millions of trees have been planted. Their roots hold the soil in place, and their leaves pile up to absorb and hold rain and melted snow. Fertilizer produced by the electric power of TVA dams has been sold at cost to the farmers of the Tennessee Valley. Agents from the Department of Agriculture have helped the farmers by teaching them the value of fertilizers, contour plowing, crop rotation, and the planting of soil-restoring crops.

Other purposes. The TVA program includes many other features. River transportation has been improved. New roads have been built. Factories have sprung up, providing jobs for thousands of workers. Hundreds of thousands of acres of land have been converted into public parks for Ameri-

693

■ The TVA system of flood control includes many dams, some of which produce hydroelectric power. Fontana Dam, shown here, is on the Little Tennessee River in North Carolina.

cans to enjoy. Lakes have been stocked with fish for the pleasure of vacationists and the profit of commercial fishermen. Schools, libraries, and hospitals have been constructed.

Criticisms of the TVA. There is another side to the TVA story. Private power companies, representing a $12-billion industry, bitterly fought the TVA. Spokesmen for the private power interests declared that the TVA was an unwarranted intervention by the federal government in private industry. They insisted that the lower rates charged by the TVA for its electric power were not the result of more efficient production. If the TVA paid taxes as all private industries did, critics insisted, it would have to charge much more for its electricity. Advocates of the TVA believed that its rates should be used as a "yardstick" to govern the rates charged by private power producers. But the private power companies insisted that the TVA was

an unfair, "16-inch yardstick," and the cheap electricity that it generated was a gift from the taxpayers of the entire nation to the people of one region.

SECTION SURVEY

IDENTIFY: social security, public utilities, REA, TVA, soil erosion.

1. The FDIC restored full public confidence in the banks as saving institutions. Explain.
2. (a) What were the three main purposes of the Social Security Act of 1935? (b) This legislation was long overdue. Comment.
3. (a) The TVA experiment had no parallel in American history. Explain. (b) How did raising the standard of living in the TVA region benefit the rest of the nation?
4. (a) What arguments have been advanced against the TVA? (b) Do you think these arguments have validity? Explain.

TRACING THE MAIN IDEAS

When Franklin D. Roosevelt became President of the United States in 1933, the nation was in the depths of the worst depression it had ever experienced. President Roosevelt, a person of great energy and overwhelming enthusiasm, took, at least publicly, an optimistic view of the situation.

Surrounding himself with people who for the most part shared his own views about the nation's problems, Roosevelt immediately opened a three-pronged attack upon the depression. In a series of relief measures, Congress, led by the administration, tried to provide adequate food, clothing, and shelter for the millions of unemployed and needy Americans. In a second series of recovery measures, Congress attempted to revive the nation's industrial machine and put the nation's economy back on a solid foundation. In a third series of reform measures, Congress undertook to strengthen the economic system by correcting what the New Dealers believed to be basic weaknesses.

CHAPTER SURVEY

QUESTIONS FOR DISCUSSION

1. In his first Inaugural Address, Franklin D. Roosevelt said: "The only thing we have to fear is fear itself." What did he mean?
2. In an interdependent, complex, industrialized society such as ours, who do you think should be responsible for (a) the poor, (b) the unemployed, (c) the handicapped, (d) the aged? Explain what changes were made in regard to these groups under the New Deal.
3. Was the planned-scarcity aspect of the New Deal farm relief program effective? Why or why not?
4. Compare Hoover's "trickle-down" theory with Roosevelt's "pump-priming" theory. Which theory was more effective in helping to remedy the ills of the depression? Why?
5. List the social and economic reforms made under the New Deal. Next to each reform, state briefly the purpose it was meant to accomplish.
6. (a) Why was the New Deal controversial? (b) Which Americans were the strongest supporters of the New Deal? (c) Which were most opposed to it?

7. Study the pictures on pages 683, 686, 688, and 694. How do they relate to the period just studied?

RELATING PAST TO PRESENT

1. Which federal programs begun during the New Deal era are still in operation today?
2. How has history substantiated the criticisms leveled at the New Deal? How has history substantiated the praise given to the New Deal?

USING MAPS AND CHARTS

1. Answer the following questions, using the chart on page 701: (a) Explain the increase in labor-union membership between 1900 and 1920. (b) Why was there a decrease between 1920 and 1930?
2. Using chart 3 on page 876, describe and explain the shifts in major occupations that occurred between 1920 and 1940.
3. Using chart 6 on page 877, explain the drop in elementary school enrollment and the rise in high school enrollment between 1930 and 1940.

■ *Franklin Delano Roosevelt*

CHAPTER 37

The Great Experiment on Trial

1936 – 1940

By 1936 the United States was beginning to recover from the Great Depression. National income had risen sharply since 1932, having jumped from a low of less than $47 billion to almost $70 billion. Industrial production, once again on the rise, was double that of 1932. These and other figures gave convincing proof that in four years the nation had made considerable progress in its battle against the depression.

How much this progress could be attributed to the New Deal was, however, an open question. Some Americans, including large numbers of Republicans, argued that progress had been made in spite of the New Deal. Others, including many Democrats, argued that the New Deal had saved the country from complete catastrophe and had started it on the road to recovery.

But the depression was far from conquered. In 1936 as many as 3.5 million people were still working on government relief projects. Nine million men and women were still unemployed. Many factories and mines were still closed or were working at far less than full capacity. Although the country was on the road to recovery, the American people still faced many problems.

Such was the situation when in 1936 the voters entered another Presidential election year. Should Roosevelt be re-elected? Should the New Deal be continued? These were the big questions facing the voters.

As you will see, Roosevelt won by an overwhelming majority. But, as you will also see, during his second term in office he faced mounting problems. In a real sense the New Deal was on trial.

THE CHAPTER IN OUTLINE

1. Mounting opposition to New Deal policies and programs.

2. Continuing New Deal reforms despite growing criticism.

3. The end of the New Deal's "great experiment."

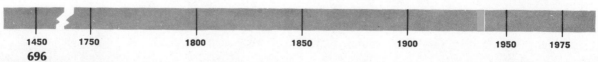

| 1450 | 1750 | 1800 | 1850 | 1900 | 1950 | 1975 |

1 Mounting opposition to New Deal policies and programs

By 1936 President Roosevelt and New Deal supporters were running into growing difficulties. But in the 1936 Presidential election campaign, they fought back vigorously and successfully.

Roosevelt's campaign promises. In June 1936 the Democrats enthusiastically renominated Roosevelt for a second term, and again chose John Nance Garner of Texas as his running mate. The Democratic platform strongly endorsed the New Deal.

During the campaign Roosevelt again showed his great skill in rallying support. He emphasized production and employment gains made during his first term. Business activity, he declared, was almost normal again, thanks to "pump priming." He promised to balance the budget, warning, however, that it was even more important "to balance the human budget." Great steps, he repeated, had been taken toward that goal. But, he added, the New Deal still had a long, hard road to follow.

Roosevelt's supporters. Lined up behind the President were not only most Democrats, but also countless rank-and-file Republicans. Most of the progressive Republican leaders who had supported him in 1932 continued to do so. Labor was overwhelmingly for the President, as were many farmers who remembered the New Deal benefits they had recently received. Many of those who had received federal relief money also supported Roosevelt. The local Democratic political "machines," some of which had used relief money to strengthen their own power, stood solidly for the re-election of the entire Democratic ticket. And finally, black voters in the North almost solidly rejected their traditional Republican affiliation and supported the party that, in some measure, had responded to their needs and grievances.

Roosevelt's critics. But the President and the New Deal also had many critics, including a number of influential Democrats who "took a walk" from the party and supported the Republican candidate. And Roosevelt's Republican critics included most big business leaders, many small businessmen who had suffered under the NRA, bankers, private power companies, newspapers, and many professional men.

Opponents of President Roosevelt sometimes likened him to a dictator, claiming that he was undermining the Constitution. They pointed out that the Supreme Court had declared unconstitutional seven out of nine important New Deal measures. They insisted that the American way of life —individualism, free enterprise, and private property—was being abandoned for socialism and regimentation. Roosevelt's critics denied that the New Deal had restored prosperity. They pointed to continued unemployment. They made much of the fact that the administration had piled up a huge national debt of over $33 billion and had failed to balance the budget.

Republican promises. The Republican leaders, however, could not win the election of 1936 merely by opposing the New Deal. They had to secure the votes of a great many people who had been helped by the New Deal. To secure these votes, they nominated friendly, thrifty Alfred M. Landon, Governor of Kansas, for President.

Governor Landon was a "liberal" Republican. Although he was in the oil business, he had the support of many farmers who trusted his judgment. Moreover, in a period when most states and the federal government had piled up huge debts, Governor Landon had balanced the Kansas budget.

■ Critics of the New Deal believed that it undermined the Constitution of the United States and the American way of life. This cartoon likens the New Deal to the Trojan horse of the ancient Greeks and implies that Roosevelt's policies would result in tyrannical government.

■ President Roosevelt, shown here during his 1936 campaign, was able to rally widespread public support despite the growing difficulties of the New Deal.

The Republican platform promised to continue agricultural benefits to farmers, to befriend labor, and to keep the controls on the stock markets and on reckless speculation. Although these were all New Deal measures, the Republicans insisted that they could carry them out more effectively and economically than the Democrats. The Republicans also promised to balance the budget and to restore to the states certain powers that the federal government had seized to carry out the New Deal program. Thus the Republicans adopted what had traditionally been the Democratic states' rights position.

Roosevelt's victory. The election campaign was filled with angry charges and countercharges. Into the campaign the Republicans poured more than $9 million—a huge sum for those years—the Democrats somewhat more than half that amount. More than 45 million Americans voted, reflecting keen popular interest.

Roosevelt and Garner swept the country with an electoral vote of 523 to 8. Roosevelt's popular vote was also impressive—27,476,673 to Landon's 16,679,583. Moreover, the Democrats won or kept

control of all but six governorships and maintained their leadership of both houses of Congress. Not since the re-election of President Monroe in 1820 had a Presidential candidate won such backing.

Roosevelt's criticism of the Court. In 1937, early in his second term, President Roosevelt opened an attack on the Supreme Court. Roosevelt was upset because the Court had set aside as unconstitutional seven important New Deal laws. He was also disturbed because the Court had declared unconstitutional a New York state measure providing minimum wages for women and children. Moreover, the federal courts had used the injunction to block federal agencies from carrying out New Deal measures.

Roosevelt declared that all too often certain Supreme Court justices thought in terms of the "horse and buggy" era. "A dead hand was being laid upon this whole program of progress," the President later declared. It was, he said, the hand of the Supreme Court.

Roosevelt and Court "reform." On February 5, 1937, President Roosevelt asked Congress for power to appoint an extra justice to the Supreme

Court for each existing justice who did not retire upon reaching age 70. At the time, six of the nine justices were 70 or older. Roosevelt's proposal, therefore, would have enabled him to appoint six new justices more favorable to the New Deal.

Changes in the Supreme Court. Although the President fought vigorously for his "reform" proposal, he lost. Congressmen in his own party refused to support him, and public opinion ran strongly against him. In general, people did not want to tamper with the delicate balance of legislative, executive, and judicial powers that the Founding Fathers had written into the Constitution.

But although Roosevelt lost the battle for Court reform, he gained most of the things he wanted. The Court began to approve important New Deal measures. The National Labor Relations Act (page 691) and the Social Security Act (page 692) were tested and found constitutional. Moreover, the Court approved an act passed by the state of Washington establishing minimum pay for women and children. This act was almost identical to the New York state law that the Court had earlier declared unconstitutional.

Had the Court suddenly realized that it might be well to approve certain popular legislation to prevent a drastic reform of the Court itself? Many Americans believed that such was the case.

Moreover, during Roosevelt's second administration a whole series of court vacancies occurred through death and retirement. By 1941 Roosevelt had been able to replace all but two of the original justices with men who appeared to be more sympathetic to New Deal legislation.

The business slump of 1937–38. Early in 1937, while the issue of the Supreme Court was being argued across the land, the nation's industrial machinery once again slowed down. By the autumn of 1937 factories were closing, and unemployment was rising.

The Democrats spoke of what was taking place as a *recession;* that is, a business slump less severe than a "depression." The Republicans, on the other hand, called it the "Roosevelt depression." Roosevelt's opponents blamed the Democrats and the New Deal for the business slump, just as the Democrats in 1931 had blamed the Republicans for the Great Depression.

Politics aside, there was fairly widespread agreement on the major cause of the slump. Instead of balancing the budget as he had promised to do back in 1932, Roosevelt had piled up the largest national debt in history. The Republicans, as you have read,

had made the most of this fact in the 1936 election campaign. But many Democrats and friends of the New Deal had also become increasingly uneasy about the mounting debt.

Mindful of the growing criticism, the New Deal administration had seized the first chance to reduce expenditures. In 1936, with business conditions steadily improving, the administration had begun to cut expenditures for relief and public works. Unfortunately, private industry was not yet strong enough to give jobs to the men and women dropped from relief projects. Once again, therefore, the nation's economic system started on a downward spiral.

New "pump priming." Fortunately, measures adopted to fight the Great Depression automatically began to act as brakes against the 1937–38 recession. More than 2 million wage earners in 25 states, protected by the Social Security Act, began to collect unemployment insurance. The new banking laws protected the savings of depositors. And many government agencies were ready to lend money to business and to construct public works, thus creating new jobs.

President Roosevelt and Congress began once again to "prime the economic pump" by increasing

■ Clifford Berryman drew this cartoon of President Roosevelt during the Supreme Court battle of 1937 and wrote under it: "Thus ended the Era of Good Feeling."

ALL I SAID WAS "GIMME SIX MORE JUSTICES!"

government lending and spending. The Reconstruction Finance Corporation again came to the rescue of business enterprises in distress. The WPA doubled the number of workers on its payroll from 1.5 million to 3 million.

By the end of 1938, the nation's economic machinery was once again picking up speed. The Democrats were quick to claim another victory for the New Deal. The Republicans, on the other hand, insisted again that recovery had come in spite of the New Deal. And many Americans, Democrats and Republicans alike, continued to express alarm at the ever-growing national debt.

SECTION SURVEY

IDENTIFY: recession; John Nance Garner, Alfred M. Landon.

1. Compare the parties, candidates, issues, and results of the election of 1936 with those of the election of 1932.
2. (a) Why did Roosevelt say that certain members of the Supreme Court thought in terms of the "horse and buggy" era? (b) How did he propose to remedy this situation? (c) How would his proposal have affected the balance of powers among the branches of the federal government?
3. Show how the measures adopted to combat the Great Depression acted as brakes against the recession of 1937–38.

2 Continuing New Deal reforms despite growing criticism

During the 1936 election campaign President Roosevelt had promised that, if re-elected, he would continue the New Deal. Neither the business recession of 1937–38 nor the mounting criticism of his policies prevented Roosevelt from continuing his program.

Growth of the A. F. of L. As you have read (page 691), the Wagner Act of 1935 guaranteed to workers the right of collective bargaining and forbade employers to discriminate against organized labor. Under the protection of this law, the A. F. of L. began to recruit and organize unskilled workers in the mass production industries—steel, automobiles, aluminum, aircraft, utilities. But the A. F. of L. drive to organize unskilled workers did not move rapidly enough to please many labor leaders.

Organization of the CIO. Growing impatience with the A. F. of L. led John L. Lewis, powerful head of the United Mine Workers, and a group of like-minded labor leaders to organize in 1935 the Committee for Industrial Organization. The CIO immediately launched a drive to organize workers in the automobile, steel, rubber, oil, radio, and other industries in industrial unions. The new industrial unions included all workers, skilled and unskilled, in an industry. The United Automobile Workers (UAW), for example, represented all workers in automotive plants. Whereas in earlier times workers in the automobile industry had negotiated contracts through many separate unions —electrical, welding, metalworking, and the like— they now negotiated as a single powerful organization.

The CIO also encouraged the inclusion of black workers in the new industrial unions. Integrated, rather than segregated, locals heralded a new day in the long-standing effort to organize white workers and black workers in a common cause.

Disturbed by the growing influence of the CIO, A. F. of L. leaders ordered it to disband. When John L. Lewis and other CIO leaders refused to obey this order, the A. F. of L. expelled them. But the CIO continued to operate, and in May 1938 it reorganized as a separate body, the Congress of Industrial Organizations (still called CIO), with John L. Lewis as its first president. By 1940, when Philip Murray succeeded Lewis as president, the CIO had a membership of 3.6 million, a figure roughly equal to that of the older A. F. of L.

The sit-down strike. Meanwhile, spirited organizational campaigns by both the A. F. of L. and the CIO resulted in a wave of strikes.

In November 1936 several hundred workers in the General Motors plants at Flint, Michigan, staged a *sit-down strike*. Instead of leaving the plant and organizing picket lines, the workers simply sat down at their machines and announced that they would not leave until management granted their demands.

The sit-down strike, which made it impossible for management to bring in strike breakers, proved extremely effective. Within a few months this relatively new labor weapon spread to many other plants, involving more than half a million workers. All of the leading automobile manufacturers except Ford now recognized the United Automobile Workers, the powerful new CIO union, as bargaining agent for the automobile industry. The United States Steel Corporation, long a foe of unions, finally accepted the CIO steelworkers' union as the bargaining agent of the steelworkers. The CIO also organized workers in many other industries and made some headway in persuading agricultural laborers to join a CIO union.

In 1939 the Supreme Court ruled that sit-down strikes were illegal. But the CIO—as well as the A.F. of L.—continued to forge ahead. In general, the Wagner Act of 1935 with its guarantee of the right to collective bargaining had given organized labor its great opportunity for growth.

Jurisdictional strikes. Much of the labor unrest during the late 1930's sprang from bitter rivalry between the A. F. of L. and the CIO. Disputes arose over which one had the "jurisdiction," or right, to enroll a particular group of workers, and sometimes these disputes led to *jurisdictional strikes*. Management thus was put in a difficult spot. If it recognized the CIO union, the A. F. of L. workers would go out on strike; if it recognized the A. F. of L. union, the CIO workers would go out on strike; and if it refused to recognize either union, it would run the risk of violating the Wagner Act!

The New Deal administration in general followed a "hands-off" policy in the conflicts between the A. F. of L. and the CIO unions, though many people felt that the National Labor Relations Board favored the CIO. The NLRB, with the support of President Roosevelt, tried with increasing success to settle disputes between the two rival labor organizations, and to prevent or mediate strikes. The great wave of strikes that reached its peak in 1937 and 1938 diminished in the following years as both labor and management reluctantly came to accept government intervention.

The Fair Labor Standards Act. Largely as a result of New Deal labor policies and laws, organized labor became a powerful force during the 1930's. But the New Deal program did not merely encourage and support organized workers; it also aimed at reforming labor conditions in the United States. To this end, President Roosevelt in 1937 proposed the Fair Labor Standards Act, sometimes called the Wages and Hours Law, which provided a minimum wage scale and a maximum work week for many workers. In the President's words, this bill would put "a floor below which wages shall not fall, and a ceiling beyond which the hours of industrial labor shall not rise."

Stubborn opposition quickly developed to the Fair Labor Standards Act. Many employers claimed that the bill encouraged unwarranted and unwise government interference and control over

■ One of the goals that the labor leader John L. Lewis worked toward was greater safety for miners. In 1957 he soberly inspected the results of an Illinois mine disaster.

LABOR UNION MEMBERSHIP

PERCENTAGE OF LABOR FORCE COMPOSED OF UNION MEMBERS	
1900	4%
1920	12%
1930	7%
1940	16%
1950	22%
1968	24%

Each symbol represents 1 million members.

industry. But the bill was pushed through Congress and went into effect in October 1938.

The Fair Labor Standards Act provided that a legal maximum work week of 44 hours in 1938 be decreased to 40 hours by 1940, with time-and-a-half pay for overtime. It also provided that minimum wages of 25 cents an hour in 1938 be increased to 40 cents an hour by 1945. It prohibited the employment of children under 16 in industries producing goods for interstate commerce. The Department of Labor was charged with enforcing the act.

Importance of the act. The Fair Labor Standards Act was important for several reasons. First, it marked a great extension of the federal government's control over industry. Second, it aimed not only to stimulate employment by providing for a shorter working day, but also to increase the purchasing power of a large part of labor. Third, the act made it unnecessary to amend the Constitution in order to prohibit child labor. Fourth, it encouraged social legislation by the states, since it removed some of the most marked differences in hours and wages between the North and the South. Fifth, it brought the benefit of federal support to the unorganized as well as to the organized workers of the nation.

Although the Fair Labor Standards Act affected only workers employed in interstate industries, by 1940 about 13 million men and women were benefiting from the law. Roosevelt hailed the new law as being, after the Social Security Act, "the most farsighted program for the benefit of workers ever adopted in this or in any other country."

Important though the Fair Labor Standards Act was, it did not insure freedom from racial discrimination in employment. In 1941, A. Philip Randolph, a powerful and militant black labor leader, threatened to march on the national capital with 10,000 Negroes to demand equal employment opportunities. Responding to this pressure, President Roosevelt in June 1941 established the Fair Employment Practices Committee (FEPC) to counteract racial discrimination in industries that were expanding through government contracts to meet the needs of World War II.

Helping the farmers. Other far-reaching New Deal measures were meant to improve the economic position of the nation's farmers. When in 1936 the Supreme Court ruled against the Agricultural Adjustment Act of 1933 (page 687), Congress promptly passed another law.

The Soil Conservation and Domestic Allotment Act of 1936 gave benefit payments to farmers who cooperated in a soil conservation program. Farmers who participated in the program leased part of their lands to the government. Under the supervision of state farm agencies, the farmers then began to restore the fertility of the leased land by practicing the best conservation measures, by using fertilizers, and by sowing soil-restoring plants, such as clover. In return, the farmers received a certain sum of money for every acre they withdrew from production.

By this means the government hoped to develop nationwide knowledge of sound conservation practices. Equally important, by limiting production the government hoped to raise the prices of farm products.

The Bankhead-Jones Act. With the Bankhead-Jones Farm Tenant Act of 1937, the New Deal undertook to help tenant farmers, sharecroppers, and migratory farm workers, who moved from place to place in search of jobs. The new law created the Farm Security Administration (FSA). The FSA was authorized to lend money at low interest rates to tenant farmers, sharecroppers, and farm laborers who wished to buy farms. Farmers who received the loans had 40 years to repay.

The Agricultural Adjustment Act of 1938. But the heart of the New Deal agricultural reform program was the second Agricultural Adjustment Act, passed in 1938. This act contained a number of important provisions:

(1) It provided benefit payments to farmers in proportion to the number of acres that they withdrew from production and planted in soil-conserving crops.

(2) The government was authorized to decide the amount of various staple crops that could be marketed each year. With the approval of two thirds of the producers of these commodities in each locality, the government then assigned a certain allotment to each farmer. If he exceeded this allotment, he had to pay a fine when he marketed such crops during a time of surplus.

(3) When harvests were large, the surpluses were stored by the government for eventual release in "lean" years. But the farmer did not lose his income from the surplus crops. The government gave him "commodity loans" on all stored crops.

The amount of these loans was fixed at slightly below *parity*—that is, below a figure based on average prices of each of the commodities for the "base" period from August 1909 to July 1914, a relatively prosperous period for farmers. When the market price of a commodity rose to the "parity" level, the farmer was to sell his stored crop and repay the loan. If the market price remained below "parity," the farmer kept the money and the government kept his crop. By this method, the government hoped to keep the price of agricultural products at a steady level, thus benefiting both farmers and consumers. It was a program of "price supports based on parity."

(4) The act also authorized the government to insure wheat crops against drought, flood, hail, and plant diseases.

Evaluating the farm program. In 1932, in the depths of the Great Depression, farm income had sunk to less than $5 billion. By 1938 it had risen to more than $8 billion. By 1940 it totaled more than $9 billion.

But critics were quick to point out that the increased income came from higher prices paid by consumers and from subsidies paid by the government—with taxpayers' money. These critics charged that "money had been taken from Peter to pay Paul."

Critics, including many farmers, also resented increasing government controls over farm production. They feared that subsidies would destroy the farmer's independence. Moreover, critics charged that the government's price support program was causing America's agricultural products to lose out in foreign markets.

Such criticisms vanished, at least temporarily, in 1941 when the United States was plunged into World War II. Then, as New Deal supporters were quick to point out, the country owed much to the farm legislation of the 1930's. This legislation had improved the economic condition of many Americans, had increased the fertility of millions of acres of land, and had enabled the United States to feed a large portion of the war-devastated world.

Shelter for low-income groups. During his second term in office, President Roosevelt also continued his attack upon the housing problem. The National Housing Act of 1937, usually called the Wagner-Steagall Act, had two aims: (1) to stimulate business by government spending for the construction of houses; and (2) to "remedy the unsafe

■ A. Philip Randolph (shown seated before the microphone) rallied black Americans to support New Deal efforts to end job discrimination in defense industries.

and unsatisfactory housing conditions and the acute shortage of decent, safe, and sanitary dwellings for families of low income in rural and urban communities."

The National Housing Act created the United States Housing Authority (USHA), which embarked on an ambitious program of housing construction. In 1941 the USHA had lent $750 million for the construction of more than 160,000 housing units.

Other New Deal reforms. In 1938 Congress passed the Food, Drug, and Cosmetic Act, which replaced the earlier Pure Food and Drug Act of 1906 (page 539). The 1938 act required adequate testing of new drugs before they were offered for sale. It also required manufacturers to list the exact ingredients of their products on their labels. In addition, the Wheeler-Lea Act, also passed in 1938, prohibited manufacturers from making false or misleading claims in their advertising.

In 1939 Congress tackled the problem of improper political practices. The Hatch Act placed restrictions upon federal officeholders below the policymaking level in the executive branch of the government. Such officeholders were prohibited (1) from taking an active part in political campaigns, (2) from soliciting or accepting political contributions from workers on relief, and (3) from using their official positions to influence the course of Presidential or Congressional elections. In 1940 the Hatch Act was amended to include state and local government employees whose pay came completely or even partially from federal funds. The 1940 amendment also limited the amount of money a political party could spend in any one year to a maximum of $3 million, and the amount any individual could contribute to $5,000 annually.

SECTION SURVEY

IDENTIFY: CIO, sit-down strike, minimum wage, migratory farm workers, parity, price supports, Hatch Act, FEPC; John L. Lewis, A. Philip Randolph, Philip Murray.

1. (a) What prompted the organization of the CIO? (b) How did it differ from the A. F. of L.?
2. How did the Fair Labor Standards Act influence labor conditions in the United States?
3. What measures were taken from 1936 to 1938 to alleviate the economic condition of farmers?
4. What steps did the New Dealers take (a) to provide homes for low-income families, (b) to aid consumers?

3 The end of the New Deal's "great experiment"

By the middle of his second term, President Roosevelt's influence was beginning to decline. In 1937, as you have seen, he had suffered a major defeat when he failed to push through Congress his bill for reorganizing the Supreme Court. In the Congressional elections of 1938, he suffered an even more serious defeat.

Roosevelt's failure to "purge" his party. As the elections approached, Roosevelt decided to "liberalize" the Democratic Party and to "purge," or rid, Congress of those conservative Democrats who had voted against his reform program. Singling out several Democrats by name, he urged voters to defeat them at the polls.

Roosevelt's campaign to liberalize the Democratic Party failed. With only one exception all of the Congressmen whom Roosevelt had opposed were re-elected. Moreover, the voters chose a great many new Democratic Congressmen who were opponents of the New Deal. To add to Roosevelt's dismay, the Republicans won additional seats in Congress. Nevertheless, the Democrats continued to hold a substantial majority in both the House and the Senate.

New Deal activities suspended. President Roosevelt, a shrewd politician, was quick to see the meaning of the 1938 elections. Realizing that public opinion was turning against him, he began to suspend earlier New Deal activities. By 1939 Congress was cutting appropriations for many New Deal agencies.

As a result of the threatening world situation (Chapter 38), the PWA and the WPA began shifting their attention from public works to projects involving national defense, such as the building of airports and military highways. Other New Deal agencies, such as the Civilian Conservation Corps and the National Youth Administration, ended operations when Congress cut off further appropriations. Although the TVA weathered attacks both in and out of Congress, the President's recommendation that similar projects be developed in six other areas of the country received little support.

The driving impulse of the New Deal had spent itself. Those who maintained that the reform objectives of the New Deal were still far from being realized faced stiffer opposition and growing public indifference. This changed attitude toward the New Deal can be explained, in part at least, by recovery from the business recession of 1937–38 and by growing concern over national defense.

Roosevelt's financial policies opposed. Much of the opposition to the New Deal came from people who believed that Roosevelt's financial policies were undermining the nation's economic system. With the return of better times, this group became larger and more outspoken.

The New Dealers used three different methods for financing their relief, recovery, and reform programs.

One method was inflation. Although Congress authorized President Roosevelt to print paper money, he never did so. He did, however, decrease the gold content of the dollar (page 688).

A second method was *deficit spending*. This meant that the government spent more than it received in taxes, leaving the budget unbalanced, or showing a deficit. In the 1930's the national debt increased from about $16 billion to more than $40 billion. Men and women in both parties were highly critical of the failure of the Roosevelt administration to balance the budget. Businessmen in particular lost confidence in an administration that piled up a larger and larger national debt.

Another method by which the New Deal had financed its operations was by raising taxes. In 1935 the administration asked Congress to increase taxes on corporations and to levy taxes on gifts and inheritances. Critics called this a "soak the rich" proposal because it put a new tax burden upon the well-to-do. Despite strong opposition, however, Congress passed the Revenue Act of 1935, often called the Wealth Tax Act. With this measure Congress increased the income tax for individuals and large corporations and levied taxes on gifts and estates. But the revenue thus obtained did not balance the budget, and the national debt continued to grow.

In the Revenue Act of 1936, Congress moved still further in the direction of taxing corporation profits. It laid a steeply graduated tax on corporation profits which were not distributed to stockholders. Business bitterly complained that the new tax would discourage business expansion and prevent the accumulation of surpluses for use in depression years.

In 1938, however, as a result of growing opposition to the New Deal, Congress began to reverse the taxation policy of earlier years. The Revenue Act of 1938 provided for a sharp reduction of corporation taxes. And in 1939 Congress abolished the tax on undistributed profits. At the same time, how-

Broadcasting "The War of the Worlds"

INVASION FROM MARS

At eight o'clock on the evening of October 30, 1938, millions of radio listeners throughout the country heard the following announcement: "The Columbia Broadcasting System and its affiliated stations present Orson Welles and the Mercury Theater of the Air in *The War of the Worlds* by H. G. Wells."

There was a brief pause, followed by a weather report. Then an announcer declared that the program would be continued from a New York hotel. A jazz band came on the air. Suddenly the music stopped. An announcer, his voice tense and anxious, broke in to declare that a professor had just observed a series of explosions on Mars. Other announcements followed in rapid order. A meteor had landed near Princeton, New Jersey. Fifteen hundred people had been killed. No, it wasn't a meteor. It was a spaceship from Mars. Martian creatures were emerging. They were armed with death rays. They had come to wage war against the people living on earth.

An untold number of listeners were seized with panic. Some fell to their knees and began to pray. Others gathered their families, rushed from their homes, and fled on foot or by car into the night.

And yet it was only a radio play. CBS stated this fact clearly four different times during the hour-long program. Numerous explanations were advanced for this outburst of mass hysteria. But one thing was clear—the extraordinary power of broadcasting.

ever, it raised the corporation income tax to a maximum of 19 percent. In addition, for the first time in history Congress required employees of cities and states to pay taxes to the federal government.

A third term for Roosevelt. Despite the fact that Roosevelt's influence was weakening, and despite the fact that the two-term tradition for Presidents was widely accepted as part of the unwritten Constitution, Roosevelt decided to run for a third term. The President did not at first announce his decision, although he hinted that the critical foreign situation might compel him to be a candidate. But behind the scenes he quietly arranged matters so that it would have been almost impossible for any Democrat to run against him without his consent.

As a result of Roosevelt's influence in his own party, the Democratic convention chose him on the first ballot at Chicago in July 1940. It also, without general enthusiasm, accepted his Secretary of Agriculture, Henry A. Wallace of Iowa, formerly a Republican, as his running mate.

■ In a political cartoon of 1938, Uncle Sam is saying to President Franklin D. Roosevelt: "But, Doctor, isn't it time she went on a diet?"

GOVERNMENT
EXPENSES

The Democratic platform promised to extend social security, to stress the low-cost housing program, and to advance government ownership of public utilities. It also promised to keep the United States out of war and to send no armies abroad unless the nation were attacked.

Wendell Willkie. The Republicans chose as their candidate Wendell L. Willkie, a New York lawyer with a long progressive record. Willkie favored many of the principles of the New Deal. But he believed that the New Deal had been administered in such a way as to endanger individualism, free enterprise, and democracy. Warmhearted, engaging, and informal, Willkie proved a strong candidate.

The Republican platform condemned the New Deal for its "shifting, contradictory, and overlapping administrations and policies." It promised to revise the tax system to stimulate private enterprise and to promote prosperity. It also promised to keep the major New Deal reforms, but to administer the laws with greater efficiency and less waste. The Republicans also demanded a constitutional amendment that would limit Presidents to a maximum of two terms. Like the Democrats, the Republicans promised to keep America out of war unless the nation were attacked.

The campaign of 1940. The ominous threat of a second World War hung over the election campaign of 1940. Indeed, in the fall of 1940, while the American people were preparing to vote, Great Britain was fighting desperately for survival.

Both Roosevelt and Willkie advocated a vigorous program of national defense. Both urged all aid to Great Britain short of war. In general, there was no important difference in their attitudes toward the terrible conflict raging abroad.

On domestic issues, however, they differed sharply, with Willkie attacking Roosevelt for irresponsibility and Roosevelt attacking Willkie for "unwitting falsifications of fact." Willkie traveled 30,000 miles through 34 states in a whirlwind campaign. Roosevelt limited himself to a few speeches.

The election returns. Roosevelt won a sweeping victory in an election in which more Americans voted than in any previous contest in American history. But the returns clearly showed that the President had lost some of his earlier popularity. Roosevelt's 60 percent popular majority in the election of 1936 was reduced to just under 55 percent in the 1940 election. In round numbers this meant that 27 million Americans voted for Roosevelt, and 22 million for Willkie. The popular vote

■ Wendell Willkie, on August 17, 1940, rode through the crowded streets of his home town, Elwood, Indiana, on the way to deliver his speech accepting the Presidential nomination of the Republican Party. Willkie was popular and drew many votes, but lost the election.

was, therefore, much closer than indicated by the electoral vote of 449 for Roosevelt and 82 for Willkie. Although the Democrats retained control of Congress, the Republicans increased their strength in both Congress and the state legislatures.

During Roosevelt's third term the New Deal domestic programs of relief, recovery, and reform received less attention as foreign problems and war itself absorbed American energies. Thus a great period of reform in American history came to an end. Whether this suspension of reform activities was the result of war, or whether the reform impulse had spent itself, remains unanswered.

SECTION SURVEY

IDENTIFY: purge, deficit spending, national debt; Henry A. Wallace, Wendell Willkie.

1. By 1938 the driving impulse of the New Deal had spent itself. Explain.
2. (a) Describe the three methods used by New Dealers to raise money. (b) Why were these methods criticized?
3. Compare the parties, candidates, issues, and results of the election of 1940 with those of the election of 1936.
4. Did the New Deal give more people an opportunity to share in the benefits of capitalism? Explain.

TRACING THE MAIN IDEAS

By 1936 the New Deal faced growing opposition, some of which came from within the Democratic Party itself. Despite this opposition President Franklin D. Roosevelt was re-elected by an even larger majority than he had won in 1932.

In his Inaugural Address the President admitted that the New Deal had not yet accomplished many of its objectives. As he said, the New Deal had not yet reached "the promised land."

The major New Deal reforms during Roosevelt's second administration were designed to improve the lot of the wage earner and the farmer and to provide better housing for middle-income and lower-income families. These and other measures were extremely popular with many Americans and extremely unpopular with many other Americans.

As the years passed, opposition to the New Deal program began to mount. Many critics felt that the government was interfering too much with the long-established rights of free enterprise and, in so doing, was threatening individualism and democracy in the United States.

By the end of 1938 the opposition had become so strong that President Roosevelt decided to postpone other far-reaching reforms that he had been considering. Indeed, during 1939, 1940, and 1941 the administration began to suspend the activities of several New Deal agencies.

Another reason for the President's decision to postpone the reform program was his growing concern over international affairs. This concern, as you will see, was well founded.

CHAPTER SURVEY

QUESTIONS FOR DISCUSSION

1. In your opinion, did the New Deal infringe upon the individual's economic rights? Explain.
2. The AAA was designed to take care of the farmer's main problem—surplus crops. Comment.
3. In what ways did President Roosevelt and the New Deal break with the past?
4. What do you think the proper role of government should be in times of national crisis?
5. (a) Why did Roosevelt try to reform the Supreme Court? (b) Give reasons for the failure of his plan. (c) What position would you have taken on the issue? Give arguments to support your opinion.
6. Summarize the various ways in which the New Deal tried to help (a) the consumer, (b) low-income families on farms and in cities, (c) young people, (d) the aged, and (e) workers.
7. Compare the (a) parties, (b) candidates, (c) issues, and (d) results in the elections of 1936 and 1940.
8. Why was the New Deal largely suspended after 1938?

RELATING PAST TO PRESENT

1. The CCC really created a new frontier. Explain. With what might the CCC be compared today in terms of a new frontier for young people?
2. Using the Great Depression as a basis for comparison, describe how you think the United States would react to a severe economic crisis if one occurred today.

USING MAPS AND CHARTS

1. Answer the following questions based on the chart on page 701. (a) Explain the increase in labor-union membership between 1930 and 1940. (b) Why is it that in 1940 only 16 percent of the labor force belonged to unions?
2. Which of the charts on pages 862–63 reflect the Agricultural Revolution? What evidence is presented here of the effect of this revolution on the life of the farmer?

In 1933, when Franklin Delano Roosevelt became President for the first time, it was clear that few Presidents had entered office under more unfavorable circumstances.

The Great Depression, the worst depression the country has ever experienced, was becoming worse week by week, not only in the United States but throughout the world.

Equally disturbing was the growth of warlike dictatorships in Asia and Europe. To American dismay, the Japanese war machine had already rolled across the borders of Manchuria and, as you have seen, seized that province from the Chinese.

But there was no way for President-elect Roosevelt or anyone else to foresee that in 1933 Hitler would win control of Germany; that by 1936 a powerful German army would move into the Rhineland in defiance of the Versailles Treaty; and that by 1940 Hitler's Nazis, Mussolini's Fascists, and the Japanese warlords would have plunged the world into the most devastating conflict in history.

During the 1930's the United States took an increasingly active interest in foreign affairs. It recognized the Soviet Union. It made provisions to grant independence to the Filipinos. It expanded the Good Neighbor policy. And, although the United States tried to remain neutral in a war-torn world, by the end of 1941 the American people found themselves playing a leading role in the struggle against the dictatorships.

■ *The attack on Pearl Harbor, December 7, 1941*

CHAPTER **38**

Moving from Isolationism into War

1932 – 1941

THE CHAPTER IN OUTLINE

1. Broadening American relations with other countries.

2. The roots of the American policy of isolationism.

3. The difficulties of isolationism in a war-threatened world.

4. America's involvement in World War II.

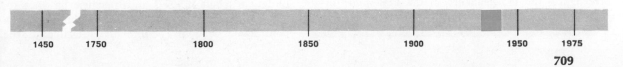

| 1450 | 1750 | 1800 | 1850 | 1900 | 1950 | 1975 |

1 Broadening American relations with other countries

American foreign policy in the 1930's was influenced by two basic considerations: (1) the Great Depression at home and abroad and (2) the rising threat of dictatorships in Europe and Asia. Both of these developments played a part in nearly every American decision made during these troubled years.

Recognition of the Soviet Union. In 1933, during the first year of the New Deal administration, the United States recognized the Soviet Union. Those favoring this move argued that it was only realistic to recognize a regime that had been in power for 16 years. They pointed out that an increased flow of trade between the two countries would be advantageous to the United States, and they reminded their fellow Americans that the two countries shared a common concern about the threat of Japanese aggression.

In reply to these arguments, the opponents of recognition pointed out that the Communists made no secret of their dream of world conquest. But this objection was met when the Soviet Union promised to stop all propaganda activities in the United States. As it turned out, this promise was not kept. Moreover, United States recognition of the Soviet Union did not result in a substantial increase in trade between the two countries.

Steps toward Philippine independence. In the Jones Act of 1916, as you have read (page 581), the United States promised to give the Filipinos their independence. During the 1920's one administration after another postponed this action, claiming that the Filipinos were not yet ready for independence. In 1933, however, late in Hoover's administration, Congress passed an independence act for the Philippines over the President's veto.

The Philippine legislature rejected this measure. Many Filipinos feared that one of the act's provisions, giving the United States the right to retain military and naval bases, would enable Americans to continue their control in the Philippines. Other Filipinos argued that once they were free, the United States would raise tariff barriers against Philippine products.

In an effort to overcome these fears, Congress in 1934 passed the Tydings-McDuffie Act. This measure was more acceptable to the Filipinos. It provided for the establishment of a Philippine Commonwealth and outlined a gradual 10-year tariff increase on Philippine goods imported into the United States. This would give the Filipinos an opportunity to adjust to an independent economy. Ten years after the establishment of a commonwealth—on July 4, 1946, as it turned out—the Philippines were to become entirely independent, except for the retention of naval bases by the United States.

The Good Neighbor policy. During the 1930's the United States also redoubled earlier efforts to improve relations with Latin America. The friendly policy started by Presidents Coolidge and Hoover (page 650) was expanded by President Roosevelt.

Self-interest as well as a genuine desire for friendship motivated the Good Neighbor policy. During the 1920's many Americans began to realize that the United States could not afford to continue antagonizing its Latin-American neighbors. When the Great Depression came in the early 1930's, this realization hardened into firm conviction. The United States needed Latin-American trade. The rise of dictatorships in both Europe and Asia further strengthened the conviction that the United States must establish friendlier relations with its Latin-American neighbors.

Carrying out the Good Neighbor policy. In 1933 President Roosevelt expressed a widely shared feeling when he declared, "In the field of foreign policy, I would dedicate this nation to the policy of the good neighbor—the neighbor who resolutely respects himself and, because he does so, respects the rights of others." Later that year, in a conference held in Montevideo, Uruguay, the

---

LIVING AMERICAN DOCUMENTS

Proclamation of Philippine
Independence (1946)

Whereas it has been the repeated declaration of the . . . government of the United States of America that full independence would be granted the Philippines as soon as the people of the Philippines were prepared to assume this obligation; and

Whereas the people of the Philippines have clearly demonstrated their capacity for self-government; . . .

Now, therefore, I, Harry S. Truman, . . . do hereby recognize the independence of the Philippines as a separate and self-governing nation. . . .

United States joined the other American countries in a pledge not to interfere in the affairs of their neighbors. "No state," the pledge declared, "has the right to intervene in the internal or external affairs of another state."

The Montevideo Pact marked a turning point in United States relations with Latin America. As President Roosevelt put it, "The definite policy of the United States from now on is one opposed to armed intervention."

Nor were these mere words. In 1934 the United States canceled the Platt Amendment (page 595), which for 33 years had given it the right to intervene in Cuban affairs. That same year the remainder of American troops were finally withdrawn from Haiti. In 1936 the United States signed a new treaty with Panama giving up its right to intervene in Panama's affairs. And gradually the United States ended its control over the customhouses of the Dominican Republic—a control exercised since 1905.

Testing the Good Neighbor policy. The Good Neighbor policy was put to a severe test in 1938 when President Lázaro Cárdenas (LAH·sah·ro KAHR·day·nahs) of Mexico confiscated the properties of all foreign oil companies. Foreign investors, including Americans, protested vigorously and demanded action from their governments. President Roosevelt refused to intervene on behalf of American investors. Instead, he urged the American oil companies to negotiate directly with the Mexican government. As a result of these negotiations, the Mexican government agreed to pay American oil claims.

International trade agreements. The United States also tried to promote an international revival of trade. The Roosevelt administration offered to negotiate with any country special trade agreements that would provide for lowering tariffs.

In the Trade Agreements Act of 1934, Congress authorized the President to raise or lower existing tariffs by as much as 50 percent without Senate approval. As a result, the Roosevelt administration could bargain, or "reciprocate," with other countries. A nation that lowered its tariffs on United States goods would, in turn, receive more favorable tariffs on the goods that it sent to the United States. By 1940 Secretary of State Cordell Hull had signed 22 reciprocal trade agreements.

Equally important was the provision of the Trade Agreements Act known as the "most-favored nation" clause. This clause offered any country the opportunity to be treated as well as the nation

LIVING AMERICAN DOCUMENTS

Abrogation of the Platt Amendment (1934)

The United States of America and the Republic of Cuba, being animated by the desire to fortify the relations of friendship between the two countries, and to modify with this purpose the relations established between them by the Treaty of Relations signed at Havana, May 22, 1903 . . . have agreed upon the following articles:

Article I. **The Treaty of Relations which was concluded between the two contracting parties on May 22, 1903, shall cease to be in force, and is abrogated, from the date on which the present treaty goes into effect.**

Article II. **All the acts effected in Cuba by the United States of America during its military occupation of the island, up to May 20, 1902, the date on which the Republic of Cuba was established, have been ratified and held as valid; and all rights legally acquired by virtue of those acts shall be maintained and protected. . . .**

seemingly "most favored" in any tariff agreement. This act therefore helped to end tariff discriminations against the United States. It also was an effective instrument for stimulating American business by improving trade relations with other nations.

New tariff agreements worked out with Canada and Great Britain under the Trade Agreements Act were especially important. They stimulated a great increase of trade between these countries and the United States, providing an economic foundation for the political cooperation that became so important in World War II.

SECTION SURVEY

IDENTIFY: dictatorship, Good Neighbor policy, Montevideo Pact, reciprocal tariff, "most-favored nation" clause; Lázaro Cárdenas, Cordell Hull.

1. What were the arguments for and against recognition of the Soviet Union in 1933?
2. What was the major provision of the Tydings-McDuffie Act?
3. What were the conditions that prompted renewal of the Good Neighbor policy?
4. Many obstacles had to be overcome before real cooperation between the United States and Latin America could be achieved. Comment.

2 The roots of the American policy of isolationism

In the early 1930's, the threat of war became increasingly ominous. In Asia and Europe the militaristic leaders of Japan, Italy, and Germany started their armies down the road of aggression.

The rise of dictatorships. As the years passed, the Roosevelt administration had to deal with a growing number of totalitarian ° rulers. Benito Mussolini, who seized power as the leader of Italian Fascism in 1922, was a swaggering, domineering ruler who dreamed of controlling the Mediterranean and the Middle East. The Japanese warlords, who seized control of Japan in the late 1920's, also had unlimited ambitions. Their seizure of Manchuria in 1931 (page 653) was only one step in a program to win control of the Far East and the Pacific. Adolf Hitler, the Austrian-born fanatic who climbed to power in Germany in 1933, was a ruthless dictator who also longed for conquest. Joseph Stalin, who in the 1920's succeeded Nikolai Lenin as the strong man of the Soviet Union, made no secret of his intention to spread Communism throughout the world.

There were other dictators, including General Francisco Franco, who came to power in Spain in 1939 after a bloody civil war. But in the 1930's the dictatorships of Japan, Italy, and Germany proved to be the most aggressive.

The totalitarian threat to democracy. Hitler, Mussolini, and the Japanese warlords openly expressed their contempt for democracy. It was, in Mussolini's words, "a rotting corpse" that must be replaced by a more "efficient" form of government and a "superior" way of life.

All of the dictatorships scorned the democratic rights of free speech and a free press. In the eyes of the totalitarian rulers, the individual existed to serve the state and had no rights except those that the state chose to give him.

All of the dictatorships glorified force. Compelling the people to work for "bullets rather than butter," they converted their industries to war production and devoted their major efforts to building powerful military machines.

Aggression and mounting tension. By the mid-1930's the dictators were ready to move. In 1935 Mussolini's blackshirted Fascists attacked the Af-rican nation of Ethiopia (see map, page 716), using bombers and poison gas against a virtually defenseless people.

Meanwhile, in 1934 and 1935 the Japanese demanded the right to build a navy equal in size to that of any other power. When the other powers refused, Japan withdrew from agreements reached at the Washington Naval Conference of 1921–22 (page 652) and in subsequent treaties, and began a rapid buildup of its naval forces.

Then, in March 1936, German troops moved into the Rhineland (see map, page 716) in clear violation of the Treaty of Versailles. In July civil war broke out in Spain. In October Germany and Italy signed a military alliance and began to call themselves the Axis ° Powers. In November 1936 Germany, Italy, and Japan announced that they were joining in an Anti-Comintern ° Pact, thus hiding their aggressive designs under the pretense of resisting Communism.

And on July 7, 1937, Japanese and Chinese troops clashed on the Chinese-Manchurian border. This border "incident" developed into a full-scale war. In time, historians referred to it as the beginning of World War II in the Far East.

Roots of American isolationism. Despite the growing threat to peace, most Americans clung to their determination to avoid becoming involved in war. They believed that the United States could and should remain isolated. Why did Americans feel this way?

In the first place, most Americans were disillusioned about the results of World War I. The war had not brought the peace, disarmament, and democracy which millions had hoped to see established across the earth. Instead, it had been followed by constant quarreling among the European powers, by tariff wars, and by failures to reduce armaments.

Most important, the war had been followed by an unwillingness or an inability to make the League of Nations an effective instrument for peace. The isolationists refused to accept the argument that the League might have been more successful had the

---

° *Axis:* a name made up by Mussolini, who said the line from Rome to Berlin formed the "axis" on which the world would turn thereafter. Eventually Japan was included among the Axis Powers. The nations who fought the Axis Powers were known as the Allies.

° *Comintern:* an international organization, dominated by the Russian Communist Party, whose aim was to spread Communism throughout the world.

° *totalitarian:* designating a dictatorship that exercises total control over a nation and suppresses individual freedom.

712

■ All of the dictatorships of the 1930's glorified force and military might. This photograph shows steel-helmeted Storm Troopers at a military review in Nuremberg, Germany.

United States joined. They argued that the League's weakness was the best possible evidence that the United States had been wise *not* to join. This widespread disillusionment became increasingly intense when the League failed to check the aggressions of Italy, Germany, and Japan in 1935–37.

American disillusionment over World War I was intensified in 1934 when the Senate Munitions Investigating Committee started to investigate war profits. Figures released by the committee suggested that many American bankers and munitions makers had reaped rich profits from World War I. Many people concluded that America's loans to the Allies had been largely responsible for drawing the United States into the conflict. This conclusion has since been rejected by most historians. In the mid-1930's, however, it fed the spirit of disillusionment.

But disillusionment about World War I was not the only basis for American isolationism. Most Americans believed that the Atlantic and Pacific oceans would protect the United States from at-

tack even if the dictators crushed all opposition in Europe and Asia. Many also argued that improved relations with Latin America gave the nation another safeguard against attack.

The isolationists were strengthened by two other groups. Many Americans believed that the government's first responsibility was to combat the Great Depression. Many others, deeply convinced pacifists, believed that all wars were unjustifiable and that the United States must avoid being drawn into another conflict. Pacifism was strong, especially among young people, in both the United States and Great Britain during the 1930's.

Isolationism in practice. In 1934 American isolationists won a victory when Congress passed the Johnson Debt Default Act. This act forbade the American government and private citizens from lending money to any country that had defaulted, or failed to repay, its war debts.

The Johnson Debt Default Act underscored Americans' annoyance at the failure of all Euro-

713

■ This poster was one of many efforts made by various groups to keep the United States out of World War II. The Japanese settled the question when they attacked Pearl Harbor on December 7, 1941.

pean nations except Finland to repay their war debts. Americans were especially annoyed because some of the defaulting nations were pouring money into armaments. Americans did not intend to provide them any more money for armaments, or to risk becoming involved in another war because of entangling investments.

Neutrality acts.   Between 1935 and 1937 the isolationists won other victories in a series of neutrality acts passed by Congress. These acts, which reflected widespread public sentiment against war, were occasioned by Mussolini's unprovoked attack upon Ethiopia, by the civil war in Spain, and by the aggressive actions of the nations of Germany and Japan.

In general, the neutrality laws (1) prohibited the shipment of munitions to "belligerents," or warring nations; (2) authorized the President to list commodities other than munitions that could be sold to belligerents only on a "cash-and-carry" basis; (3) made it unlawful for Americans to travel on the vessels of belligerent nations.

The neutrality laws were intended to keep Americans out of war and to prevent the involvement of American citizens in such disasters as the sinking of

the *Lusitania* in 1915. With these laws the United States abandoned its long-established doctrine of freedom of the seas and withdrew the traditional rights of citizens to travel where they wished.

Dissatisfaction with neutrality.   Strong though it was, isolationism by no means represented the thinking of all Americans. Many Americans were dismayed by the abandonment of individual rights that earlier generations had fought so hard to establish.

Still other Americans regretted that the neutrality laws made it difficult for the United States to help the victims of aggression. They feared that the totalitarian aggressors would become bolder if the United States refused to aid weaker nations. In their view, if the United States allowed aggressors to crush their weaker neighbors, the United States might one day find itself surrounded by powerful enemies.

Finally, many international-minded citizens argued that the United States had a moral duty to aid the victims of unprovoked aggression. This attitude cut across party lines. There were internationalists as well as isolationists in both the Democratic and the Republican parties.

Policy changes.   Between 1933 and 1937 President Roosevelt did not take a firm stand on America's responsibility in a troubled world. At times he sided with the isolationists; at other times with the internationalists.

In 1933 Roosevelt failed to support the work of the London Economic Conference, an important conference called by the League of Nations. The delegates to the conference wanted to find a way to stabilize world currencies in order to boost trade and encourage worldwide economic recovery. Shortly before the conference opened, the United States abandoned the gold standard (page 688). President Roosevelt, therefore, did not want to support the stabilization of currency by countries still on the gold standard. He ordered American delegates at the conference to limit their discussions to tariff problems. As a result, the conference failed. Also, Roosevelt no longer pressed for American entrance into the League of Nations, as he had done in the 1920's.

By 1937 Roosevelt was becoming more deeply impressed with the seriousness of the world situation and with the need for the United States to take a positive stand against aggression. In a speech on October 5, 1937, the President said: "If we are to have a world in which we can breathe freely and live in amity without fear—the peace-loving nations must make a concerted effort to uphold laws and principles on which alone peace can rest secure. . . .

"When an epidemic of physical disease starts to spread, the community approves and joins in a quarantine of the patients in order to protect the health of the community against the spread of the disease. . . ."

Continuing isolationism. In his famous "quarantine" speech Roosevelt expressed views that most Americans were not yet ready to accept. Proof of this came with the *Panay* incident." On December 12, 1937, Japanese planes bombed and strafed a United States gunboat, the *Panay,* and three American oil tankers on the Yangtze River in China (see map, page 744). Several Americans were killed, and many were wounded.

Secretary of State Hull immediately sent a sharp note to the Japanese government. He demanded full apologies, compensation, and a promise that no such incident would recur. The Japanese agreed to all of Hull's demands.

During this "incident," the American public revealed how strongly it favored keeping out of war. A public opinion poll showed that 54 percent of all Americans felt that the United States should completely withdraw from China.

By the end of 1937 the tide of aggression was rising rapidly in Asia as well as in Europe. Many Americans, including President Roosevelt, were becoming increasingly alarmed. But most Americans still clung to the belief that the United States could remain isolated.

3 The difficulties of isolationism in a war-threatened world

By 1938 the dictators were becoming more ruthless. During 1938 and 1939 headlines of new aggressions and new crises often crowded other news off the front pages of America's newspapers.

The spread of warfare. In 1938 Japanese forces were attacking along the length of the Chinese coast and pushing inland up the river valleys. Meanwhile, halfway around the world, the Spanish Civil War was bringing misery to hundreds of thousands of other people.

Spain had become an international battleground. Hitler and Mussolini were helping Franco, making the most of the opportunity to test their latest military equipment and to give picked "volunteers" actual battle experience. Soviet "volunteers" were fighting against Franco and his Nazi and Fascist allies. Among Franco's foes in the "International Brigade" were volunteers from many other countries, including the United States.

The United States reacted to this threat to world peace by joining France and Great Britain in a program of nonintervention. With President Roo-

■ British Prime Minister Neville Chamberlain (left) met with Adolf Hitler on September 23, 1938, to discuss peace. The meeting led to the ill-fated four-power peace pact that was signed a week later at Munich.

SECTION SURVEY

IDENTIFY: totalitarian, Axis Powers, isolationism, pacifists, "quarantine" speech, *"Panay"* incident"; Benito Mussolini, Adolf Hitler, Joseph Stalin, Francisco Franco.

1. Discuss the philosophy of government shared by the totalitarian dictators; for example, their ideas about the role of the individual and the role of the state.
2. List the events of 1935–37 which posed a threat to peace.
3. What were the roots of the widespread feeling of isolationism among Americans from 1920 to 1937?
4. (a) Upon what major experience in American history were the neutrality acts based? (b) Could this be called a misreading of history? Comment.
5. Roosevelt's attitude toward world affairs was changing, but the attitude of the American people was not. Comment.

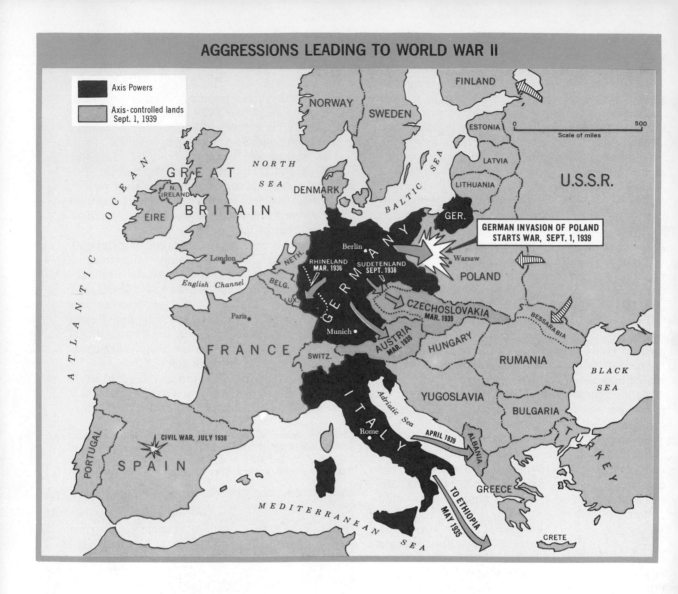

AGGRESSIONS LEADING TO WORLD WAR II

Axis Powers

Axis-controlled lands
Sept. 1, 1939

Scale of miles

GERMAN INVASION OF POLAND
STARTS WAR, SEPT. 1, 1939

RHINELAND
MAR. 1936

SUDETENLAND
SEPT. 1938

CZECHOSLOVAKIA
MAR. 1939

AUSTRIA
MAR. 1938

CIVIL WAR, JULY 1936

APRIL 1939

TO ETHIOPIA
MAY 1935

---

sevelt's approval, Congress in January 1937 barred all shipments of war materials to either side in the civil war in Spain.

New aggressions—and Munich.   Another crisis developed when, on March 11, 1938, Hitler's powerful army moved into Austria (see map, this page). Two days later Hitler announced the union of Austria and Germany.

With Austria under his control, Hitler turned greedy eyes toward western Czechoslovakia. This area, known as the Sudetenland (SOO·DAY·t'n·land), contained a large proportion of German-speaking people. Hitler demanded that Czechoslovakia turn over the Sudeten region to Germany. By the end

of the summer a major crisis was at hand, for Czechoslovakia, with one of the best trained armies in Europe and with the sympathy of other democratic nations overwhelmingly on its side, refused to bow to Hitler.

Tension was at the breaking point when British Prime Minister Neville Chamberlain, French Premier Édouard Daladier, Mussolini, and Hitler met at Munich. There on September 30, 1938, the four men signed a pact, agreeing to accept nearly all Hitler's demands. The Czechs, forsaken by their friends, turned over most of the Sudeten region to Germany. Prime Minister Chamberlain, whose intense desire for peace blinded him to Hitler's designs, returned to England confident that the Munich Agreement had ended the threat of aggression in Europe. "I believe," he said, "it is peace for our time."

Other leaders did not share Chamberlain's confidence. They believed his policy of "appeasement" would only lead Hitler to make further demands. Throughout Europe nation after nation re-armed with redoubled speed.

Growing American concern. President Roosevelt viewed the events of 1938 with deepening concern. As early as January 28, in a special message to Congress, he coupled a promise to work for peace with a warning that it was time for the United States to build up its defenses. Congress increased appropriations for the armed forces and, in May, authorized more than $1 billion for a "two-ocean navy."

Roosevelt privately referred to the aggressions of Japan, Italy, and Germany as "armed banditry," and Secretary of the Interior Harold L. Ickes called Hitler a "maniac." Officially, however, the President contented himself with personal notes to foreign rulers, including Mussolini and Hitler, urging them to settle their differences by negotiation and international cooperation. But since the United States was committed to a hands-off isolationist policy, no one paid much attention to the President's words.

Hemispheric defense. As the Sudeten crisis approached the breaking point, however, Roosevelt did make one commitment. In August 1938, in a speech in Ontario, Canada, he extended the protection of the Monroe Doctrine to Canada. He solemnly promised Canadians that "the people of the United States will not stand idly by if domination of Canadian soil is threatened by any other Empire."

Roosevelt's promise to Canada was only one of several steps the United States was taking to develop a hemispheric defense policy. Earlier, at the Buenos Aires Conference of 1936, the United States and the 20 other members of the Pan-American Union had agreed to regard a threat to any American country as a threat to the security of all American countries. The 21 members also agreed

■ Great Britain and France declared war on Germany after Hitler ordered the invasion of Poland in September 1939. Above, German soldiers fire at snipers in the Polish capital of Warsaw.

LIVING AMERICAN DOCUMENTS

Franklin D. Roosevelt's
"Four Freedoms" Speech (1941)

In the future days, which we seek to make secure, we look forward to a world founded upon four essential human freedoms.

The first is freedom of speech and expression—everywhere in the world.

The second is freedom of every person to worship God in his own way—everywhere in the world.

The third is freedom from want—which, translated into world terms, means economic understandings which will secure to every nation a healthy peacetime life for its inhabitants—everywhere in the world.

The fourth is freedom from fear—which, translated into world terms, means a worldwide reduction of armaments to such a point and in such a thorough fashion that no nation will be in a position to commit an act of physical aggression against any neighbor—anywhere in the world. . . .

to consult together if such a threat developed.

In December 1938, with the clouds of war rapidly gathering, the Pan-American Union met again in Lima, Peru. The delegates repeated their pledge of solid opposition to any threat of foreign intervention in the Western Hemisphere. But they went a step further, agreeing that at the first sign of trouble the foreign ministers of the Western Hemisphere would meet to decide what action their countries should take.

Roosevelt's promise to Canada and the Declaration of Lima provided additional assurance that the Monroe Doctrine had become a "multilateral," or many-sided, policy, rather than a "unilateral," or one-sided, policy. By 1938 it was clear, as Roosevelt said, that "national defense has now become a problem of continental defense."

New crises leading to World War II. On January 4, 1939, in his annual message to Congress, President Roosevelt warned that the world situation had become extremely grave. He urged greatly increased appropriations for the armed services. He also urged Congress to reconsider the neutrality legislation adopted during 1935–37.

The President's worst fears were soon confirmed. On March 15, 1939, Hitler's armies moved into the rest of Czechoslovakia. On April 7 Mussolini's troops invaded Albania (see map, page 716).

Awakening at long last to their common peril, Great Britain and France announced that an attack upon Poland would mean war. Great Britain and France also tried belatedly to get the Soviet Union to join them in an agreement to oppose by armed force any further aggression by either Hitler or Mussolini. It was with shock, therefore, that the democratic nations learned on August 23, 1939, that the U.S.S.R. had just signed a nonaggression pact with Germany.

Seemingly freed by the Soviet pact from the danger of a two-front war, Hitler struck swiftly. On September 1, without warning, German bombers and powerful mechanized divisions crossed the border into Poland (see map, page 716). Two days later, on September 3, 1939, Great Britain and France declared war on Germany.

While Great Britain and France were mobilizing, Soviet troops invaded Poland from the east. By the end of September all organized Polish resistance had been crushed, and Germany and the U.S.S.R. divided Poland between them. The Soviets then demanded and won the right to establish military and naval bases in Estonia, Latvia, and Lithuania (see map, page 716). And on November 30, after Finland refused to grant Soviet demands to establish military bases on Finnish soil, the U.S.S.R. attacked its small neighbor. The Soviet government claimed that its actions were necessary to protect the Russian homeland from invasion.

And thus, in 1939, World War II started and began to spread across Europe.

SECTION SURVEY

IDENTIFY: Declaration of Lima, appeasement, nonaggression pact; Neville Chamberlain; 1938, 1939.

1. At Munich, Western leaders had a choice between shame or war. They chose shame with war an inevitability. Comment.
2. Compare the American attitude toward the war in Europe in 1914–15 with that in 1939.
3. In 1938 the Latin-American nations became partners with the United States in enforcing the Monroe Doctrine. This was an effect of the Good Neighbor policy. Comment.
4. Draw a time line covering 1931 to 1939. (a) Below the line list the events abroad that led to World War II. (b) Above the line list United States actions or foreign policy decisions. (c) Some American foreign policies of the 1930's were dictated by the past. Explain, using the time line.

4 America's involvement in World War II

American sympathies in 1939 were overwhelmingly in favor of the Allies. At the same time, however, Americans were determined to stay out of war. President Roosevelt was merely voicing a widely shared feeling when, in a "fireside chat" over radio on September 3, he said, "As long as it remains in my power to prevent, there will be no blackout of peace in the United States."

Neutrality laws amended. On September 21, 1939, however, Roosevelt urged a special session of Congress to amend the Neutrality Act of 1937. "I regret that Congress passed the Act. I regret equally that I signed the Act," he declared. As Roosevelt pointed out, the existing embargo on the export of munitions actually favored Germany. If it were not for the embargo, Great Britain and France could use their control of the seas to secure from the United States the arms that they desperately needed. Hitler, on the other hand, did not need military equipment, for he had been preparing for war for years.

After a six-week debate, with many Congressmen demanding outright repeal of the neutrality laws and many others insisting on retaining them, Congress finally agreed on a compromise proposal. The new law abolished the arms embargo and allowed any country to buy weapons or munitions from the United States provided that the goods were transported to Europe on foreign ships. This law, which went into effect on November 4, 1939, greatly helped the Allied nations resisting Hitler.

Declaration of Panama. While Congress was debating the problem of neutrality, the Pan-American Union met at Panama to consider problems of hemispheric defense.

On October 3, 1939, the delegates to the Panama Conference issued a declaration warning all belligerent war vessels to stay out of a "safety zone" around the Americas roughly 300 to 1,000 miles wide. Germany, Great Britain, and France challenged this declaration on the ground that no nation or group of nations had the right to close any part of the high seas to their ships. The declaration was important, however, as an indication of genuine cooperation among the nations of the Western Hemisphere.

The fall of France. While Hitler was carrying on his *blitzkrieg,* or "lightning war," against Poland in 1939, the French rapidly mobilized. They braced themselves for an attack against the Maginot (mah-

Stukas in flight

BLITZKRIEG

With the blitzkrieg, Hitler unleashed a new type of warfare. Before the war started he had assembled a number of highly mobile, highly mechanized units, including tanks and mounted artillery. These units, known as Panzer divisions, were supported by a new type of specially designed aircraft, the Stuka, or dive bomber. Concentrating intense fire power upon a single section of the enemy line, the Panzers and Stukas drove through and fanned out in the rear. Then they raced over the countryside, overrunning command posts and supply depots and paralyzing lines of transportation and communication. When the enemy was completely disorganized, the German infantry moved in and "mopped up" all remaining resistance.

Using the blitzkrieg, Hitler was invincible in the early days of the war. But, in time, the Allies organized their own mobile units and their own clouds of fighters and bombers. Then it was a different story. They, too, could use the methods of the blitzkrieg. Sometimes, when it suited their purposes, they allowed Hitler's Panzers to pierce their own lines. Then the Allies sealed off the gap, shot down the Stukas, and moved in to destroy the Nazi tanks and armored equipment with their own mechanized units.

zhee·NOH) Line—the formidable chain of forts guarding their eastern frontier. But Hitler did not attack. People began to joke about the "phony war," which some called a *sitzkrieg,* or "sitting war."

On April 9, 1940, the joking ceased. On that date Hitler demonstrated the true meaning of "blitzkrieg." In the following weeks, his powerful armored divisions, supported by fighters and bombers, rapidly overran Denmark, Norway, the Netherlands, Belgium, Luxembourg, and northern France (see map, page 730). On May 26 the British began a heroic evacuation of their expeditionary forces from the beaches of Dunkirk, a seaport in northern France on the Strait of Dover. Although the British were forced to leave much of their equipment, they succeeded in saving most of their men. On June 10 Italy, sensing that France was doomed, declared war on France and Great Britain.

Hitler's blitzkrieg did not halt until June 22, 1940, when France signed an armistice with Germany. In London the French National Committee pledged continued resistance by the "Free French" under General Charles de Gaulle, and began to rally part of the French colonial empire against the Nazis. Meanwhile, Marshal Pétain (pay·TAN) became the leader of a German-controlled French government with headquarters at Vichy (vee·SHEE) in central France (see map, page 730).

The Battle of Britain.   With the fall of France, Great Britain stood alone and almost defenseless, for the British had left most of their war equipment on the beaches of Dunkirk.

On May 10, 1940, Winston Churchill replaced Neville Chamberlain as Prime Minister of Great Britain. With a gift for leadership given to very few men, Churchill rallied the British people, strengthening their hopes and their determination to fight. Churchill promised that the British would never surrender. If by chance Great Britain itself were to fall, he declared, "Then our Empire beyond the seas, armed and guarded by the British fleet, would carry on the struggle until, in God's good time, the New World, with all its power and might, steps forth to the rescue and liberation of the Old."

By the end of June, with France under Nazi control, Churchill was preparing his people for the coming "Battle of Britain." "Hitler knows that he will have to break us in this island or lose the war," Churchill said. "If we can stand up to him, all Europe may be free and the life of the world may move forward into broad, sunlit uplands. But if we fail, then the whole world, including the United States,

including all that we have known and cared for, will sink into the abyss of a new Dark Age. . . .

"Let us therefore brace ourselves to our duties, and so bear ourselves that, if the British Empire and its Commonwealth last for a thousand years, men will still say, 'This was their finest hour.' "

The supreme test for the British came in the late summer of 1940. In August Hitler unleashed his fighters and bombers against Great Britain in an all-out effort to sweep the Royal Navy from the English Channel and the Royal Air Force from the skies. The Royal Navy fought back furiously, and the Royal Air Force, though almost hopelessly outnumbered, flew day and night, sometimes shooting down as many as 100 Nazi bombers in a single 24-hour period. In October, advised by his military chiefs that an attempt to invade Great Britain would be suicidal, Hitler postponed his invasion plan, "Operation Sea Lion," until spring.

"Never in the field of human conflict," Churchill declared, referring to the Royal Air Force, "was so much owed by so many to so few."

American defense measures.   During the summer and fall of 1940, the United States was taking steps to strengthen its own defenses.

To check subversive activities, Congress passed the Alien Registration Act, commonly known as the Smith Act. This law strengthened legislation controlling aliens and made it illegal for any person in the United States to advocate the overthrow of the government by force or violence, or to belong to an organization that advocated the violent overthrow of the government.

In July Secretary of State Hull and the foreign ministers of the other American nations gathered in Havana, Cuba, to make plans for preventing Germany from seizing the Western Hemisphere colonies of the countries it had conquered. The Act of Havana stated that the moment the territorial integrity of any colony was in danger, the American republics, acting singly or collectively, would take control of the colony. From then until the end of the war, the colony would be governed by a group of trustees from the American republics.

Two weeks later President Roosevelt met with Prime Minister Mackenzie King of Canada. At this meeting the two leaders created a Permanent Joint Board of Defense to plan for the "defense of the north half of the Western Hemisphere."

In the meantime Congress was furiously debating the pros and cons of the first peacetime draft in American history. The Burke-Wadsworth Act was finally passed and signed by President Roosevelt on September 16, 1940. The law required all men between 21 and 35 to register for the draft, and made them liable for one year of military training.

Roosevelt's Lend-Lease proposal. By the end of 1940 American supplies were flowing to Great Britain, and America's defense program was gathering momentum. But President Roosevelt was not satisfied that the government was doing all it could "to keep war away from our country and our people."

What worried Roosevelt most was the fact that the British could not much longer afford to pay cash for the war materials they desperately needed. In his annual message to Congress, Roosevelt declared, "Our country is going to be what our people have proclaimed it to be—the arsenal of democracy." Roosevelt proposed that the United States increase greatly its production of military equipment of all kinds so that it could lend or lease to the British and to the other Allies any materials needed to carry on the fight.

Roosevelt's Lend-Lease proposal provoked a storm of controversy. Many people agreed with the President that the Lend-Lease proposal offered America's best hope of avoiding full-fledged participation in the war. Others, including the isolationists, took a directly opposite position—that Lend-Lease would surely involve America in a shooting war.

Overriding all objections, Congress passed the Lend-Lease Act in March 1941 and appropriated an initial sum of $7 billion for ships, planes, tanks, and anything else that the Allies needed. When on June 22, 1941, Hitler's armies invaded the Soviet Union despite the German-Russian nonaggression pact, the United States made Lend-Lease materials available to the U.S.S.R.

(continued on page 724)

■ Winston Churchill, shown here making his famous "V for victory" sign, became Prime Minister of Great Britain in 1940. Churchill's leadership united the British people, strengthening their hopes and their determination to fight.

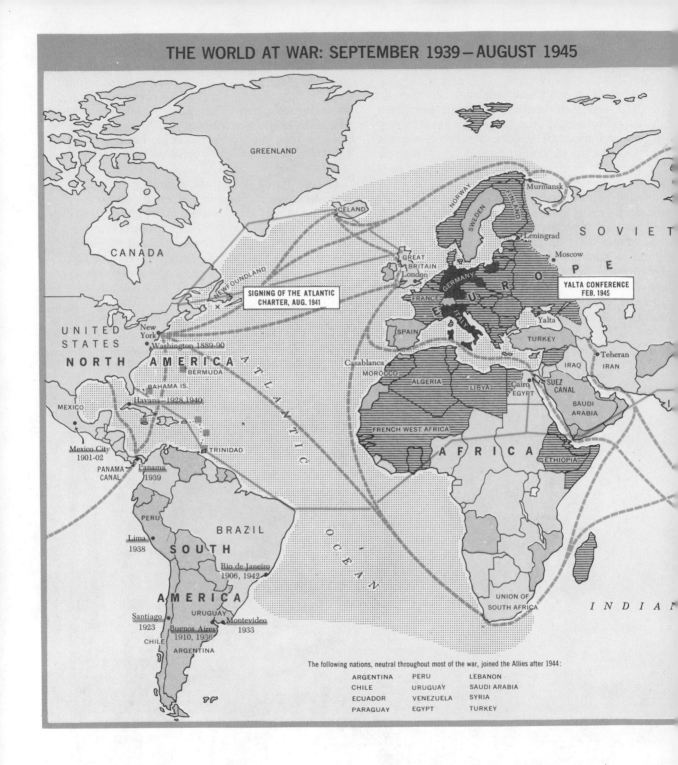

THE WORLD AT WAR: SEPTEMBER 1939 – AUGUST 1945

GREENLAND

CANADA

SOVIET

NORWAY
SWEDEN
FINLAND
Murmansk
Leningrad
Moscow

ICELAND

GREAT
BRITAIN
London

NEWFOUNDLAND

**SIGNING OF THE ATLANTIC
CHARTER, AUG. 1941**

GERMANY
FRANCE
EUROPE
ITALY

**YALTA CONFERENCE
FEB. 1945**

UNITED
STATES

New
York
Washington 1889-90

SPAIN

Yalta

TURKEY

NORTH   AMERICA

Casablanca
MOROCCO

Teheran
IRAQ
IRAN

BERMUDA

BAHAMA IS.

MEXICO

Havana—1928,1940

ALGERIA
LIBYA

Cairo
EGYPT

SUEZ
CANAL

SAUDI
ARABIA

Mexico City
1901-02

TRINIDAD

FRENCH WEST AFRICA

A F R I C A

PANAMA
CANAL

Panama
1939

ETHIOPIA

PERU

BRAZIL

ATLANTIC

SOUTH

Lima
1938

Rio de Janeiro
1906, 1942

OCEAN

AMERICA

UNION OF
SOUTH AFRICA

INDIAN

URUGUAY

Santiago
1923

Buenos Aires
1910, 1936

Montevideo
1933

CHILE

ARGENTINA

The following nations, neutral throughout most of the war, joined the Allies after 1944:

ARGENTINA	PERU	LEBANON
CHILE	URUGUAY	SAUDI ARABIA
ECUADOR	VENEZUELA	SYRIA
PARAGUAY	EGYPT	TURKEY

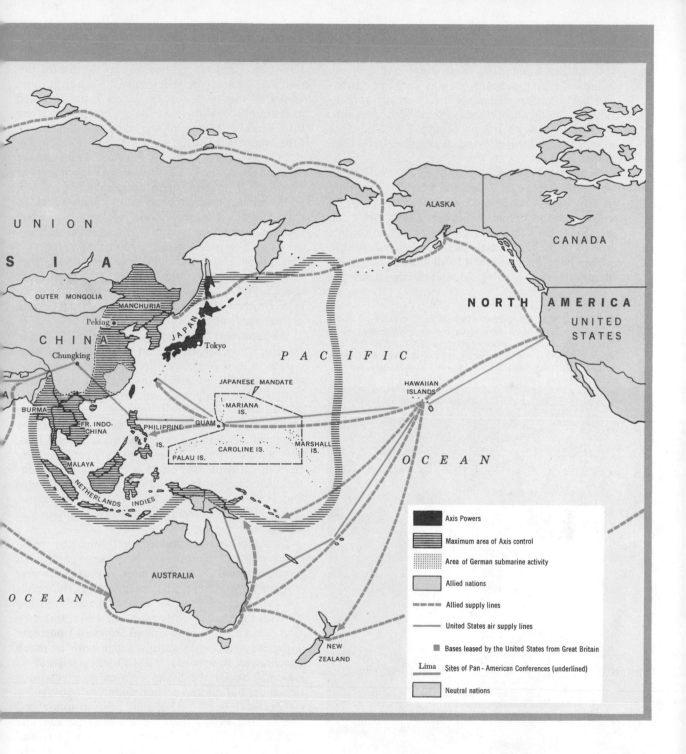

■	Axis Powers
▦	Maximum area of Axis control
▦	Area of German submarine activity
▢	Allied nations
- - -	Allied supply lines
——	United States air supply lines
■	Bases leased by the United States from Great Britain
Lima	Sites of Pan - American Conferences (underlined)
▢	Neutral nations

UNION

S I A

OUTER MONGOLIA

MANCHURIA

Peking

CHINA

JAPAN

Tokyo

Chungking

P A C I F I C

BURMA

FR. INDO-
CHINA

PHILIPPINE

IS.

GUAM

JAPANESE MANDATE

MARIANA
IS.

CAROLINE IS.

MARSHALL
IS.

PALAU IS.

MALAYA

NETHERLANDS INDIES

HAWAIIAN
ISLANDS

O C E A N

ALASKA

CANADA

NORTH AMERICA
UNITED
STATES

AUSTRALIA

OCEAN

NEW
ZEALAND

The Battle of the Atlantic. The Lend-Lease arrangement inevitably drew the United States closer to war. By the spring of 1941 German and Italian submarines were turning the North Atlantic into a graveyard of ships. In April American naval vessels began to "trail" enemy submarines, radioing their location to British warships. In July American troops occupied Iceland (see map, page 722) to prevent its occupation by Germany.

In September President Roosevelt issued "shoot on sight" orders to American warships operating in the "safety zone" established back in 1939 at the Panama Conference (page 719). American warships also began to accompany and protect, or *convoy,* merchant vessels as far as Iceland. And in November Congress voted to allow American merchant vessels to enter combat areas. Roosevelt

■ Cordell Hull, President Roosevelt's Secretary of State, is shown above with two Japanese diplomats sent on a "peace" mission to Washington in 1941. It is still not known whether or not these representatives had been informed of the planned attack on Pearl Harbor.

promptly armed the merchant vessels and provided them with navy gun crews.

The Atlantic Charter. In August 1941, while the United States was moving rapidly toward undeclared war with Germany, Roosevelt and Churchill met to discuss the larger issues involved in the conflict. At this meeting the two leaders drew up a broad statement of war aims that came to be called the Atlantic Charter.

Like Woodrow Wilson's Fourteen Points (page 618), the Atlantic Charter listed a number of "common principles" upon which men of good will could build a lasting peace and a better world. In the Atlantic Charter, Roosevelt and Churchill pledged themselves to work for a world free of aggression, a world in which every nation, large or small, would have the right to adopt its own form of government. Once the aggressors were crushed, the Charter declared, all nations must work together to free all men everywhere from the burden of fear and want.

Rising threat from Japan. While war raged in the European theater, Japan was pushing its conquests in the Far East. In July 1941 Japanese troops occupied French Indo-China (see map, page 744). Thoroughly alarmed, President Roosevelt immediately "froze" all Japanese assets in the United States. He also placed an embargo on the shipment of gasoline, machine tools, scrap iron, and steel to Japan. Japan promptly retaliated by freezing all American assets in areas under its control. As a result, trade between the United States and Japan practically ended. And then in August the United States sent a Lend-Lease mission to China.

The Japanese, convinced that American resistance was stiffening, began to make plans for an attack upon the United States. Even as its war leaders were making final preparations, however, the Japanese government sent a "peace" mission to Washington. On November 20, 1941, this mission demanded that the United States (1) unfreeze Japanese assets, (2) supply Japan with as much gasoline as it needed, and (3) cease all aid to China. The United States refused to meet these demands, but offered several counterproposals.

On December 7 the Japanese mission announced that further negotiations were useless because the United States clung to "impractical principles" and had failed "to display in the slightest degree a spirit of conciliation."

The attack on Pearl Harbor. On Sunday morning, December 7, 1941—even before Japan's reply

■ The Japanese attack on the American naval and air base at Pearl Harbor, in Hawaii, killed 2,000 Americans and wounded almost 2,000 more.

had been delivered to the American government—Japanese planes roared down without warning upon the United States fleet anchored in the huge American naval and air base at Pearl Harbor, in Hawaii (see map, page 745). Victims of this surprise attack, the Americans lost almost all of their planes and eight battleships and suffered the partial destruction of several other naval units. More than 2,000 soldiers, sailors, and civilians were killed, and almost 2,000 more were wounded. The same day the Japanese also attacked Wake, Midway, Guam, the Philippine Islands, and other American bases.

War declared. Americans were shocked and angered as the radio announced what had happened on the morning of December 7, 1941. With almost complete unanimity, the American people supported President Roosevelt the next day when he asked Congress for a declaration of war against Japan. The Senate declared war unanimously; the House, with only one dissenting vote. Great Britain and the governments-in-exile that had fled their countries when Hitler conquered them also immediately declared war against Japan. Three days later, on December 11, Germany and Italy declared that a state of war with the United States existed, whereupon Congress declared war upon those two countries.

SECTION SURVEY

IDENTIFY: blitzkrieg, Smith Act, "arsenal of democracy," Atlantic Charter, Lend-Lease; Charles de Gaulle, Marshal Pétain, Winston Churchill; December 7, 1941.

1. Without extraordinary heroism on the part of the Royal Air Force and the British people, the Battle of Britain could not have been won. Comment.
2. At certain times in a country's history, the power of a single personality becomes an extremely important force. How does this apply to (a) Churchill's role in Great Britain, (b) Hitler's role in Germany?
3. Trace the events that led to the Japanese attack on Pearl Harbor.
4. The American people were isolationist before 1939 because they believed they were safe behind a two-ocean moat. Comment.

725

TRACING THE MAIN IDEAS

The 1930's was to be a decade of crisis and tragedy. The decade started with the Great Depression, which plunged millions of people all over the world into unemployment, confusion, and unrest. Then, in the middle 1930's, the armies of Japan, Italy, and Germany started on their paths of conquest and aggression. By the end of the 1930's many of the nations of the world were involved in what was to become the most terrible conflict in human history.

The overwhelming majority of the American people were at first determined to remain aloof from the war. They supported Congress when it enacted neutrality legislation in 1935, 1936, and 1937. But as the dictators crushed their weaker neighbors, Americans began to realize that the democratic way of life and free people everywhere were in danger. More and more Americans came to feel that, by helping other nations resist aggression, the United States would strengthen democracy and protect itself.

By 1939, when World War II broke out in Europe, the United States had begun to reverse its traditional policy of isolationism. During the next two years the United States abandoned neutrality and became "the arsenal of democracy." American ships carried cargoes of war materials to Great Britain, the Soviet Union, and China. America's navy, air force, and army were strengthened with feverish speed. On December 7, 1941, the Japanese struck at Pearl Harbor. The United States was at war.

CHAPTER SURVEY

QUESTIONS FOR DISCUSSION

1. How were nationalism, imperialism, and ideologies of racial superiority related to the causes of World War II?
2. Under Franklin D. Roosevelt's Good Neighbor policy, the Monroe Doctrine was transformed into a principle supported by several nations. (a) Explain. (b) Trace the steps which led to the change.
3. How did the United States' arms embargo aid the aggressor nations?
4. (a) Munich has become synonymous with the word appeasement. Explain. (b) How did appeasement help lead to World War II?
5. Pearl Harbor solidified American public opinion and ended the great debate between the internationalists and the isolationists. Explain.
6. Why did many Americans believe in isolationism during the 1930's?

RELATING PAST TO PRESENT

1. How do you think America's international affairs today have been affected by what was learned from the events preceding World War II?
2. Why might it be necessary to recognize the existence of a new country, even if the United States does not approve of its government?

USING MAPS AND CHARTS

1. Consulting the map on page 716, answer the following: (a) Identify the Axis Powers. (b) Point out the lands seized by Nazi Germany. (c) Which of Mussolini's conquests are shown? (d) Identify the lands controlled by the Axis Powers on September 1, 1939.
2. What conclusions about the "shrinking globe" can you draw from a study of the map on pages 874–75?

WORLD WAR II had been under way a little more than two years when on December 7, 1941, Japan's savage blow at Pearl Harbor plunged America into the global conflict.

America's enemies had the great advantage of what military men call "interior lines of supply and communication." Germany, Italy, and Japan were so situated geographically that the supply lines from their farms and factories to the fighting fronts were relatively short.

The United States and its Allies, on the other hand, had to establish and protect supply lines that often stretched thousands of miles across sea and land to fighting men in far-off areas of the earth.

America's enemies had an even greater advantage. They had been preparing for war for many years. During these years they had trained huge armies; they had converted their factories to war production; and they had accumulated vast stores of rifles, machine guns, tanks, planes, and hundreds of other instruments of modern warfare.

The United States, on the other hand, had not really begun to prepare for war until the summer of 1940, and even then preparations had been limited. Indeed, it was America's lack of preparation that led Hitler, Mussolini, and the Japanese warlords to believe that they could win the war before the United States could mobilize its enormous resources and manpower.

Faced by such overwhelming odds, the American people grimly entered the conflict.

■ *The Marine Corps war memorial at Arlington, Virginia*

CHAPTER **39**

Americans in the Second World War

1941 – 1945

THE CHAPTER IN OUTLINE

1. Allied disasters on all fronts followed by Allied offensives.

2. Fighting the "battle of production" on the American home front.

3. Paving the way toward an Allied victory in Europe.

4. Allied victory in the Pacific and the end of World War II.

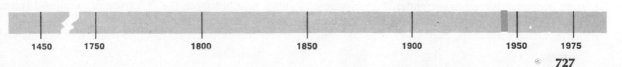

| 1450 | 1750 | 1800 | 1850 | 1900 | 1950 | 1975 |

1 Allied disasters on all fronts followed by Allied offensives

During most of 1942, as the Americans were converting to a wartime economy, the United States and its allies suffered a series of almost unrelieved disasters in every theater of the war.

Early Japanese gains. The scene at Pearl Harbor on the evening of December 7, 1941, was one of utter destruction. America's offensive power in the Pacific had been wiped out by the Japanese surprise attack. And the Japanese soon struck again in the Pacific. By the end of December Japan had seized the American islands of Guam and Wake; had captured the British colony of Hong Kong; and had launched attacks upon Thailand, British Malaya, and the American-controlled Philippines and Midway (see map, page 744).

Disaster in the Pacific. The new year brought a mounting fury of destruction, with Japanese conquests covering a widening area of the Pacific and Far East (see map, pages 744–45). On January 2, 1942, Japanese troops poured into Manila, capital of the Philippines. On January 11 the Japanese invaded Borneo and Celebes (SEL·eh·beez) in the Netherlands Indies. On February 15 the advancing tide of Japanese troops overran the British naval base at Singapore. Later in the month, in the Battle of the Java Sea, a Japanese naval force delivered a crushing blow to an Allied fleet composed of American, British, Dutch, and Australian warships.

By the end of March the Japanese had conquered most of the Netherlands Indies with its rich supplies of oil, tin, rubber, quinine, and other vital war materials. They had also seized Rangoon, Burma, and were relentlessly driving British, Indian, and Chinese troops out of Burma.

Meanwhile, in the Philippines, a small force of Americans and Filipinos under General Douglas MacArthur continued their heroic but hopeless resistance against the invading Japanese. In January 1942 Manila surrendered, and MacArthur's forces retired to the Bataan Peninsula. In March MacArthur himself was ordered to Australia to take command of the Allied forces in the South Pacific. Fighting against overwhelming odds, the hungry, sick, exhausted survivors on Bataan were captured on April 9. On May 6 the outnumbered and starving troops on the fortress of Corregidor guarding Manila Bay were forced to surrender. The Japanese also cut the Burma Road, destroying the last land route to China (see map, page 744).

Thus, by the end of May 1942, almost six months after their attack on Pearl Harbor, the Japanese had overcome all opposition and were poised to strike westward at India; southward at Australia; and eastward through Hawaii at the Pacific coast of the United States. These were dark days for Americans and their weary allies. But by the end of May, Japanese success had reached its peak.

American gains in the Pacific. Despite some opposition at home, the United States accepted the British argument that the defeat of Hitler in Europe must be the first Allied objective. But the war in the Pacific soon proved to be more than a mere holding operation.

Japan suffered its first serious reverse early in May 1942. Carrier-based planes from a British-American naval force caught a Japanese fleet moving southward in the Coral Sea, off the northeastern coast of Australia, and sank or severely damaged more than 30 Japanese warships.

Japanese forces received another setback early in June 1942 when they launched a two-pronged sea-borne attack on the Aleutian Islands and Hawaii. The ultimate Japanese objective was an invasion of the United States. American forces stopped the northern campaign, but only after Japanese troops had occupied the Aleutian islands of Attu and Kiska (see map, page 744). American naval forces blocked the southern campaign by defeating the Japanese in a major battle off the island of Midway.

There are several reasons why the United States began to stem the Japanese tide. First, early in 1942 the United States and Great Britain had pooled their resources to create a unified Pacific command. Second, the American people were beginning to win the important "battle of production" at home. The products of the nation's farms and factories were pouring into Pacific supply depots and forward bases. Finally, time had been gained by the courageous resistance of Americans and Filipinos on Bataan and Corregidor.

The turning tide in the Pacific. On August 7, 1942, the United States undertook its first major offensive action when marines stormed ashore at Guadalcanal in the Solomon Islands (see map, page 744). For four desperate months American marines and army troops clung to a toehold around Guadalcanal's airport, repelling one savage attack after another from the air, from the sea, and from the surrounding jungle.

In November the Japanese made a desperate ef-

■ This painting shows United States troops landing on the Pacific island of Bougainville in 1943. Island by island, American and British forces sought to push back the Japanese.

fort to regain their former bases in the Solomons, which they needed to carry out their planned invasion of Australia. But Admiral William F. Halsey intercepted the huge Japanese fleet, and in a furious battle, November 12–15, completely routed the Japanese. Guadalcanal was at last secure. The tide of battle in the Pacific had turned. From then on, the United States held the initiative in the Pacific.

Disaster in Europe. The situation in the Atlantic and in Europe during most of 1942 was gravely serious. German and Italian submarines in the Atlantic sank ships more rapidly than the United States and Great Britain could build new ones. Britain, now an isolated fortress in the Atlantic, could not hold out much longer unless reinforcements arrived, and unless the devastating Nazi bombings of vital British industrial areas were stopped.

On the continent of Europe, as in the Pacific, the tide of Axis conquest was rolling with terrifying speed. Yugoslavia lay beneath the Axis yoke. The Greeks had been reduced to near starvation. The Soviet Union had lost its rich grainfields in the Ukraine region, and many major Soviet industrial centers had been leveled. Part of the destruction was done by the Soviet people themselves, for, as they retreated before the Germans, they applied a "scorched earth" policy to their land, destroying everything that they could not carry with them.

Despite Soviet resistance the Nazi divisions rolled on in the summer offensive of 1942, over-running the oil fields of the Caucasus and rumbling into the outskirts of Stalingrad on the Volga River (see map, page 731). Beyond lay the Ural Mountains, where the Soviet people had moved much factory equipment that they had snatched from the path of the Germans, and where they were feverishly building new industries.

In the Mediterranean the Axis forces were triumphant everywhere. German and Italian aircraft with bases in Italy, Greece, the Greek island of Crete, and North Africa virtually forced British naval craft out of the Mediterranean, and thus denied the British the use of the Suez Canal route to the Indian Ocean. Great Britain was compelled to send its ships thousands of miles around Africa to reach Egypt, the Middle East, and India. By the autumn of 1942 the German *Afrika Korps* under General Erwin Rommel had advanced to the frontiers of Egypt, where it stood poised for a final thrust at the Suez Canal and the oil fields of the Middle East.

(continued on page 732)

WORLD WAR II AND ALLIED VICTORY IN EUROPE

ICELAND

ATLANTIC

GREAT

NORTH SEA

NORWAY

SWEDEN

FINLAND

Leningrad

EIRE

N. IRELAND

BRITAIN

DENMARK

BALTIC SEA

ESTONIA

LATVIA

LITHUANIA

GER.

SOV

1942-45

1940-44

OCEAN

London

Dunkirk

NETH.

Berlin

1945

Warsaw

1944

Kiev

English Channel

JUNE 6, 1944

BELG.

GERMANY

POLAND

U.K

NORMANDY

LUX.

1944

1945

Paris

CZECHOSLOVAKIA

FRANCE

1944

1945

Vienna

AUSTRIA

HUNGARY

1944

SWITZ.

Vichy

"VICHY FRANCE"

RUMANIA

1945

PORTUGAL

SPAIN

ITALY

ADRIATIC SEA

YUGOSLAVIA

1944

1944

Rome

BULGARIA

SARDINIA

Anzio

Cassino

Naples

Salerno

ALBANIA

GREECE

T

1944

1943

Strait of
Gibraltar

SP.
MOROCCO

1942

Algiers

1943

Bizerte

Palermo

1944

1943

Casablanca

Tunis

SICILY

1942

MOROCCO (Fr.)

ALGERIA (Fr.)

TUNISIA (Fr.)

MALTA

CRETE

1943

MEDITERRANEAN

El Alamein

1942

0   1000

Scale of miles

LIBYA

E G

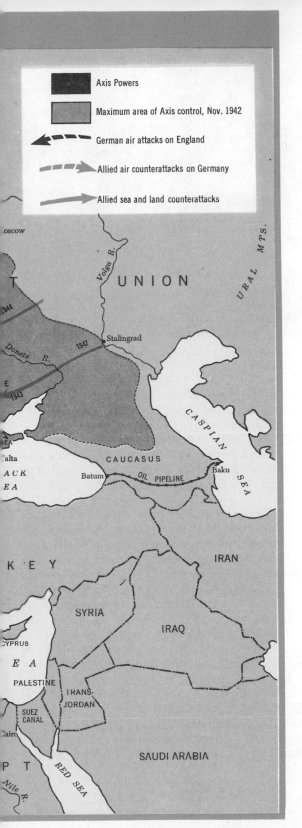

Axis Powers

Maximum area of Axis control, Nov. 1942

German air attacks on England

Allied air counterattacks on Germany

Allied sea and land counterattacks

Dark days for the Allies

1939

SEPT.–OCT.	German invasion and conquest of Poland.

1940

APR.–JUNE	German invasion of Denmark, Norway, Luxembourg, Belgium, Netherlands, France.
MAY	British evacuation from Dunkirk.
JUNE–JULY	Fall of France; establishment of Vichy government.
AUG.–OCT.	Battle of Britain (German air attacks).
OCT.	Axis aggressions in Balkans.
NOV.– FEB. 1941	British offensive in Mediterranean and North Africa.

1941

FEB.–MAY	Battle of the Atlantic begins.
MAR.–APR.	Axis counteroffensive in North Africa.
APR.–JUNE	German invasion of Greece, Yugoslavia, Crete.
JUNE	German invasion of U.S.S.R. begins.

Allied gains: the tide turns

1942

MAY–AUG.	Allied air attacks on Germany begin.
OCT.–NOV.	Allied counteroffensive in North Africa begins.
NOV.– MAR. 1943	Russian counteroffensives in U.S.S.R.; German surrender of Stalingrad (in February).

1943

MAY	Allied victory in North Africa; end of African campaign.
JULY–AUG.	Allied invasion of Sicily.
JULY– JAN. 1944	Russians drive Germans back in U.S.S.R. and enter Poland.
SEPT.	Allies begin Italian campaigns.
SEPT. 8	Italy surrenders.

1944

JUNE 6	Allied invasion along Normandy coast (Operation Overlord).
AUG.	Allied forces land in southern France.
AUG. 25	Allies liberate Paris.
SEPT.	Allies liberate Belgium, Luxembourg.
SEPT.	Battle for Germany begins.
SEPT.–DEC.	Russians conquer Yugoslavia and Hungary.
DEC.	Battle of the Bulge (last German counteroffensive).

Allied victory in Germany

1945

FEB.–APR.	Allied invasion of Germany.
MAY 7	Germany surrenders.
MAY 8	V-E Day (end of war in Europe).

■ Smiling crowds, making the "V for victory" sign, greeted the United States soldiers who entered Algeria during the campaign in North Africa.

Allied November victories. November 1942 marked a turning point of the war. In the Pacific, as you have seen, the three-day naval battle of Guadalcanal, on November 12–15, started the Allies on their long island-hopping drive toward Tokyo. In North Africa the British General Bernard L. Montgomery caught Rommel by surprise late in October at El Alamein in Egypt, and drove him back across the desert toward eventual and complete defeat.

A few days later, on November 8, a mighty invasion armada led by General Dwight D. Eisenhower landed thousands of British, Canadian, and American troops on the northern coast of Africa (see map, page 730). On November 19 the Soviet troops began an encircling movement around the German forces at Stalingrad. Within several weeks, after a heroic defense of their city, the Soviet troops forced the Germans at Stalingrad to surrender.

"This is not the end," Winston Churchill said in November 1942. "It is not even the beginning of the end. But it is, perhaps, the end of the beginning." Subsequent events justified Churchill's words. Before 1942 was over, the Allies held the initiative in Europe, as in the Pacific. From then until the war's end, they exerted steady pressure until they finally pierced the Axis defenses and plunged into the heart of the aggressor nations.

Wartime cooperation. How had the Allies been able to survive the earlier disasters? Why were they able in November 1942 to begin to seize the initiative? One answer is that the tremendous strength of America's manpower and war materials was beginning to have its effect. Another answer is that in their struggle for survival the Allies worked as a team.

On January 1, 1942, the 26 Allied nations, calling themselves the United Nations,° issued a declaration. In this joint Declaration of the United Nations, the 26 countries (1) promised full cooperation in the war effort, (2) agreed not to make a separate peace, and (3) endorsed the war aims outlined in the Atlantic Charter (page 724).

Lend-Lease. Early in 1941, as you recall, even before the United States had entered the war, Congress laid the basis for large-scale aid to the Allies with the Lend-Lease program (page 721).

After the attack on Pearl Harbor, the aid program went into high gear. The United States shipped immense quantities of war materials across the submarine-infested sea routes to its allies in the Pacific and to Great Britain, the U.S.S.R., and the British armies in Egypt and the Middle East. Be-

° The wartime Allies called themselves the "United Nations." Later, when in 1945 they formed a permanent organization, they continued the use of this same name.

fore the war ended, Lend-Lease aid reached more than $50 billion, of which 69 percent went to Great Britain, about 25 percent to the U.S.S.R., and small quantities to other Allies.

But Lend-Lease was not a one-way arrangement. During the war the United States received, in exchange, goods and services valued at nearly $8 billion, most of which came from Great Britain. For example, when the American air forces began to arrive in England, the British provided bases, housing, and equipment. The Lend-Lease program was an outstanding example of Allied wartime cooperation.

Cooperative planning. But joint planning of strategy was an even more decisive Allied effort. Shortly after the attack on Pearl Harbor, Prime Minister Churchill and a group of military, naval, and technical aides met in Washington, D.C., with General George C. Marshall, Chief of Staff of the Army, and the commanders of America's air, land, and sea forces. This meeting was the first of a series held by the Allied military leaders.

These conferences required a tremendous spirit of give and take. Final decisions were not always popular with all concerned. For example, the Soviets, hard-pressed in the summer of 1942, urged their Allies to relieve the pressure on the Soviet Union in Eastern Europe by opening a "second front" in Western Europe. Roosevelt and American military leaders finally agreed with Churchill that the Allies were not sufficiently prepared to do this and decided instead to land troops in North Africa, from where they could strike at southern Europe. Despite these and other differences among the Allies, the high degree of cooperation achieved was an indispensable factor in the final victory.

SECTION SURVEY

IDENTIFY: "scorched earth" policy, *Afrika Korps,* United Nations, "second front"; Douglas MacArthur, William Halsey, Erwin Rommel, Bernard Montgomery, Dwight D. Eisenhower.

1. December 1941 to May 1942 were dark days for Americans and their weary Allies. Explain.
2. Describe the strategy of the United States and its Allies in fighting the Axis Powers.
3. How did the Lend-Lease program help both the United States and its Allies?
4. "November 1942 marked a turning point of the war." Why?
5. Why was Allied cooperation so decisive a factor in winning the war?

2 Fighting the "battle of production" on the American home front

The Allied victories beginning in November 1942 were won on the farms and in the factories of the Allied nations, as well as on the fighting fronts. By the end of 1942 the United States in particular had made itself "the arsenal of democracy."

Hitler's errors. When he declared war upon the United States, Hitler had already made two grave mistakes. First, he had failed to conquer Great Britain, which he might have done had he launched an invasion immediately after the British armies lost most of their equipment at Dunkirk. Second, his surprise attack upon the U.S.S.R. in June 1941 and his failure to take Moscow led to the disaster of his troops at Stalingrad.

On December 11, 1941, Hitler made a third major mistake by declaring war upon the United States. He miscalculated the speed with which the American people could convert their peacetime industries to war production.

America's soaring production. One of the amazing demonstrations of America's productivity took place on the nation's farm lands. Despite the fact that 2 million agricultural workers served in the armed forces, farmers managed to raise record-breaking crops. They raised enough food to supply the American people as well as their Allies.

The output of America's mines and factories was equally impressive. For example, between July 1, 1940, and July 31, 1945, United States manufacturing plants produced 296,601 military planes, including 97,000 bombers; 86,388 tanks; 88,077 scout cars and carriers; 16,438 armored cars; 2.4 million trucks; 991,299 light vehicles, such as jeeps; 123,707 tractors; 17.4 million rifles and side arms; 2.7 million machine guns; 315,000 pieces of artillery; and 41.4 billion rounds of ammunition.

In addition, America's shipbuilders launched 71,060 naval vessels and 45 million tons of merchant ships, creating the greatest navy and merchant marine the world had ever seen. By 1943 five ocean-going vessels were being launched every 24 hours to join the growing fleet linking America's farms and factories with the far-flung battle fronts.

All in all, production during the war years was 75 percent greater than in peacetime. According to Donald M. Nelson, first chief of the War Production Board, created in January 1942, "American industry turned out more goods for war than we ever produced for our peacetime needs—yet had enough power left over to keep civilian standards of living at an astonishingly high level."

Financing the war. Where did the money come from to finance the war? A little more than one third came from taxes, which were raised to the highest level in American history. The government borrowed the remainder, chiefly by selling huge issues of bonds. Because of this borrowing, the national debt shot upward from about $49 billion in 1941 to nearly $259 billion by the spring of 1945.

The dollar cost of the war was staggering. By 1945 military expenditures totaled $400 billion— twice the sum that the federal government had spent for all of its activities, including all wars, between 1789 and 1940!

Government control of production. The task of mobilizing the nation's manpower and resources required tremendous planning. This was the job of the federal government, which created a complicated network of agencies to organize the war effort.

At the top there was a policy-making board called the Office of War Mobilization (OWM). Its job was to unify the activities of the many war agencies.

Just below the OWM was the War Production Board (WPB), which affected the daily lives of nearly every man, woman, and child in the United States. The WPB controlled the allocations of raw materials to industrial plants. It searched the country for scrap iron and canvassed the nation's kitchens for fats, tin, and aluminum. It directed the

conversion of factories from peacetime to wartime production, and also stimulated the construction of new industrial plants.

In addition, the WPB restricted the production of all consumer goods which required materials necessary to the war effort. It rationed gasoline to conserve oil and rubber. It even controlled clothing styles to save wool, cotton, rayon, and other vital materials.

Mobilizing resources. The War Manpower Commission (WMC) was another agency that closely affected the lives of many Americans. The WMC discouraged men and women from working in nonessential occupations. By 1945 it had channeled nearly 30 million wage earners, including about 2 million black workers, into war-related jobs.

The WMC also operated the Selective Service System which, by the end of the war, had drafted nearly 10 million out of the more than 15 million Americans who served in the armed forces. Included were more than 1 million black Americans, both volunteers and draftees, about half of whom served overseas. Despite black protests, official military policy, as in previous wars, required Negroes to serve in segregated units. In 1944-45, however, some white and black troops on the European front were integrated to meet an emergency situation.

In its effort to mobilize the nation's resources and to direct America's wartime activities, the federal government also created the War Shipping Administration and the Office of Defense Transportation. These agencies closely supervised the railroads, express services, and shipping, with the result that freight and troops were moved efficiently over land and sea. Another agency, the Office of War Information, bolstered the morale of the armed forces as well as of civilians by publicizing the achievements of war production. It also presented the Allied war aims by broadcasting them in dozens of languages to people all over the world.

Government control of prices. One of the ways in which the government most closely regulated the lives of civilians was through price controls. In World War I the shortage of consumer goods and the increased purchasing power of industrial and agricultural workers had driven prices skyward, bringing on inflation and causing suffering, especially among the poor. The government was determined to prevent prices from skyrocketing again. In its first step against inflation, the government raised income taxes, thus draining off dollars that would otherwise have been spent on goods in the

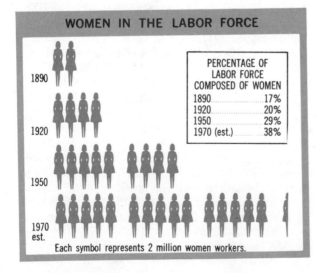

WOMEN IN THE LABOR FORCE

PERCENTAGE OF LABOR FORCE COMPOSED OF WOMEN	
1890	17%
1920	20%
1950	29%
1970 (est.)	38%

1890
1920
1950
1970 est.

Each symbol represents 2 million women workers.

stores. As a second step, the government encouraged Americans to buy war bonds, arguing that such purchases were both a patriotic duty and a sound investment. But these measures alone could not prevent inflation.

In 1942, following the example of European governments, Congress authorized the Office of Price Administration (OPA) to establish ceilings, or top limits, on prices and to set up a rationing system. The OPA issued ration books containing coupons which purchasers had to use in addition to money to buy gasoline, fuel, shoes, coffee, sugar, fats and oils, meat, butter, and canned foods. The OPA also established rent controls. By these measures it protected consumers from price increases and unfair distribution as the available supply of goods dwindled and as the housing shortage became acute.

Despite these efforts, the prices of consumer goods rose, especially food prices. By 1944 the cost of living had risen 30 percent above 1941 prewar levels. Americans resented government controls over their daily lives, and some violated the price control and rationing system by paying exorbitant prices on the "black market" to obtain more than their share of rationed products. Most Americans, however, accepted price controls and rationing as a wartime necessity.

Government control of wages. Shortly after the attack on Pearl Harbor, the leaders of organized labor promised President Roosevelt that American workers would not strike during the war. At the same time they insisted that the government, in return for the "no-strike pledge," must ensure that workers would be fairly treated. By the spring of 1942, however, the cost of living had risen, and workers were becoming restless.

In July 1942 the National War Labor Board (WLB) tried to work out a compromise. It granted a 15-percent wage increase to readjust the workers' incomes to the rise in living costs. Several months later Congress and President Roosevelt authorized the WLB to "freeze" the wages and salaries of all workers at the newly established levels.

For a time there was relatively little trouble. But as prices continued to rise, labor again became restless, and here and there strikes broke out. In such instances the government usually intervened, and for the most part settled the disputes quickly.

Government control of profits. Paralleling its efforts to control prices and wages, the government also tried to regulate profits—mainly by means of taxation. Personal income taxes were greatly increased for people in the higher income brackets.

■ After the Japanese attack on Pearl Harbor, most Japanese-Americans were forced to leave their homes and to stay in detention camps, such as the one shown here. Do you believe such government actions were justified?

But the most drastic means of controlling profits was the excess profits tax, levied in 1940, which obliged corporations to pay to the government as much as 90 percent of all excess profits.

Americans did not like government controls, but accepted them with the understanding that they would be removed when the emergency was over.

The plight of Japanese-Americans. The upheaval in everyday life resulting from these controls and from the whole vast war effort revealed the extraordinary willingness of the American people to make sacrifices for the national emergency. Despite discomforts, sacrifices, and some displays of selfishness, a remarkably high level of morale was maintained.

To be sure, Americans suffered deep anxieties and fears. But these fears did not lead to the widespread repressions of unpopular and suspected mi-

735

nority groups that occurred in World War I. The tragic exception to this overall tolerance was the forced relocation of some 100,000 Americans of Japanese birth or parentage.

After the Japanese attack on Pearl Harbor, many Americans were genuinely fearful of a Japanese attack on the United States. This fear was soon turned against the Nisei—native-born Americans whose ancestors came from Japan. As a result, most Japanese-Americans—the great majority of whom lived in California—were forced to leave their homes and were taken to detention camps in other states, where they remained as virtual prisoners until the end of the war. Most of the Nisei lost their homes and businesses. Yet there had never been any real proof that these Japanese-Americans had been disloyal. Indeed, nearly all of the Nisei remained loyal, patriotic American citizens despite their harsh, unfair treatment.

After the war, Americans regretted their unjustified actions against the Nisei. In 1945 the Nisei were permitted to leave the detention camps and settle wherever they wished. In 1948 Congress passed an act to help the Nisei recover their property losses.

Negro advances and setbacks at home. As in previous wars, black Americans contributed their full share not only to the fighting, but to efforts on the home front as well. In 1941, President Roosevelt directed that a Fair Employment Practices Committee be set up to eliminate discriminatory hiring policies in defense industries. As a result, the doors of the nation's defense industries were opened to hundreds of thousands of willing black workers.

Less was accomplished, however, in promoting equal housing opportunities for Negroes in the overcrowded cities in which defense industries were concentrated. Unfair treatment and discrimination on the part of white Americans—especially those white workers who, like many Negroes, had recently migrated from the South—led to outbursts of violence and even riots in several cities. In Detroit in 1943, federal troops restored order after a riot cost the lives of 25 black Americans and 9 white Americans.

Aware of their contributions to the war effort, many black Americans became restless. As they listened to patriotic speeches about freedom for all, they became more determined to make these ideas truly meaningful for themselves. Thus, black leaders continued the fight for equal rights at home throughout the war years.

IDENTIFY: OWM, WPB, Selective Service System, price controls, ration books, black market, Nisei.

1. Why was the United States called the "arsenal of democracy"?
2. It was necessary for the federal government to establish controls and regulations over virtually every aspect of American life during the war. Explain.
3. By 1945 military expenditures totaled $400 billion —twice the sum that the federal government had spent for all activities between 1789 and 1940. What are your reactions to this statement?
4. How did each of the following contribute to the war effort: (a) unions, (b) scientists, (c) women, (d) farmers, (e) black Americans?
5. United States action against the Nisei was justified because the constitutional rights of all citizens are suspended in wartime. Comment.

3 Paving the way toward an Allied victory in Europe

In the summer of 1942, as the tide of war was beginning to turn in favor of the Allies, President Roosevelt and Prime Minister Churchill decided to strike at what Churchill called the "soft underbelly" of the Axis.

Victory in North Africa. The opening blow, as you recall, fell late in October 1942, when the British broke through Rommel's lines at El Alamein and began to drive the Germans back into Libya. Meanwhile, on November 8, a force of 500 troop transports and 350 warships under General Eisenhower's command landed British, Canadian, and American troops on the coasts of French Morocco and Algeria. It was the greatest combination of land, sea, and air forces assembled up to that time.

The loss of French areas in North Africa was a serious blow to the Germans. Although they continued to fight with great skill, their efforts were hopeless. Allied planes and ships cut their supply lines from Italy. General Montgomery's British Eighth Army drove steadily westward, while American forces moved eastward. Outnumbered and caught between the jaws of two enemy forces in Tunisia (see map, page 730), the Germans and Italians surrendered early in May 1943.

As a result of the victory in North Africa, the Allies captured more than 250,000 Axis troops. Far more important, the Allied nations now had control of the Mediterranean. Allied warships could now operate freely, protected by planes based at airfields along the North African coast. The Allies could ship supplies to India through the Suez Canal. They could also ship supplies to the U.S.S.R. by way of Iran.

Invasion of Italy. From their newly won North African bases the Allies subjected Sicily and Italy to merciless bombing. Then, early in July 1943, British, Canadian, and American troops landed in Sicily. The Sicilians offered little resistance, and the crack German troops were greatly outnumbered by the invaders, who swiftly overran the island.

Americans and other Allied peoples were thrilled at the rapid conquest of Sicily and by other good news that came over the radio during the summer of 1943. Late in July the Italians ended Mussolini's dictatorial rule and organized a new government. Before dawn on September 3 the British Eighth Army landed on the southern coast of the Italian mainland. On September 8 the Italian government surrendered unconditionally, and the following day an Allied invasion force landed at Salerno.

Despite these great successes the campaign for Italy was one of the longest and most difficult of the war. Veteran German troops were rushed in to fill the gaps left by the Italians. Difficult mountain terrain and bad weather helped the Germans. On October 1 Naples fell to an American army under General Mark W. Clark, but for several months the Allies were unable to advance beyond Cassino (see map, page 730). In an effort to outflank the German lines, Allied troops landed on the Anzio beaches on January 22, 1944. But the Nazis fought desperately, and it was not until June 4, 1944, that the Allied armies entered Rome.

From Rome they moved northward. Progress was slow, and every inch of soil was won at great cost by fighting men of the Allied nations—Americans, British, Canadians, Indians, New Zealanders, South Africans, French, Moroccans, Algerians, Senegalese, Italians, Poles, Greeks, Arabs, Brazilians, and a Jewish brigade from Palestine. Although the Nazis were pushed steadily northward, fighting continued in Italy until the last few months of the war in Europe.

Importance of the gains in Italy. The victories of 1943–44 in Italy were immensely important. Through them the Allies strengthened their control of the Mediterranean. The loss of Italy deprived Germany of desperately needed manpower. Moreover, from Italian bases Allied airmen were able

"Kilroy" in Japan, after the war

"KILROY WAS HERE"

Of the millions of Americans in the armed forces during World War II, none was more famous than Kilroy. Not "General" Kilroy. Just plain Kilroy. Kilroy with no initials.

Kilroy was amazing. He was anywhere, everywhere, and always the first to arrive. Soldiers drove Japanese troops out of a mountainside cave, and when they cautiously entered, they saw the familiar writing on the cave wall: "Kilroy was here." The writing appeared on the Marco Polo Bridge in China, on the Tomb of the Unknown Soldier in Paris, on packing boxes and the walls of buildings on every continent.

Who was Kilroy? No one knew. Some thought that he was a sergeant, absent without leave, who wandered mysteriously over the world, writing the familiar inscription wherever he went. In 1946, a year after the war had ended, the American Transit Company staged a radio contest in an effort to identify the original Kilroy. The winner turned out to be James Kilroy, a Boston city councilor, who, during the war, had been an inspector for the Bethlehem Steel Plant in Quincy, Massachusetts. When criticized for being inattentive to his work, he began to write on packing cases "Kilroy was here" to prove that he was on the job.

Whether this was the true origin of the famous inscription cannot be certainly known. Kilroy had become a mythical figure, a modern counterpart of such legendary American heroes as Paul Bunyan and John Henry. Tall tales of Kilroy's exploits provided relief for the loneliness and boredom of GIs far from home. Kilroy also served as an inspiration to American fighting men, for he was a symbol of the unconquerable spirit that could overcome every obstacle and squarely meet every danger.

to bomb southern Germany and the German-held Balkans, including the rich oil fields in Rumania.

Finally, in their efforts to check the Allies in North Africa and Italy, the Germans had been forced to withdraw troops from the Soviet front. This had helped the Soviet Union to regain great stretches of valuable farm land in the Ukraine. Despite the Italian campaign, however, the Nazis continued to concentrate most of their military forces against the Soviet Union, and the Soviets continued to call for a "second front" in Western Europe.

Victory in the Atlantic. The victories in Italy were possible only because the Allies had won control of the Atlantic Ocean. During the early months of the war, German submarines waged a mighty battle against ships carrying supplies to Europe. On April 23, 1942, Winston Churchill reported secretly to Parliament:

"I will begin with the gravest matter; namely, the enormous losses and destruction of shipping by German U-boats off the east coast of the United States. In a period of less than sixty days, more tonnage was sunk in this one stretch than we had lost all over the world during the last five months of the Battle of the Atlantic before America entered the war. . . ."

Gradually, however, the Allies began to gain the upper hand. Radar and other devices for detecting planes and submarines were developed. New warships, including small aircraft carriers, began to slide down the ways of American and British shipyards. During 1942 the Axis sank 585 Allied and neutral vessels in the Atlantic. During 1943 the Axis sank only 110 ships. By the end of 1943 the Battle of the Atlantic was won.

Over the sea lanes great convoys carried urgently needed military supplies to the Mediterranean war fronts and to Great Britain, which by 1943 had been converted into a vast base for the invasion of Western Europe.

Victory in the air. While the Allies were winning the Battle of the Atlantic, Allied planes began their offensive against Germany and German-occupied Europe. In 1942 American airmen began taking part in Royal Air Force raids. By early 1943 the combined Anglo-American air assault had become a major and increasingly important factor in the struggle. During the last year of the war, fleets of as many as 2,000 heavy bombers were dropping tons of bombs on a single target area.

The destruction was enormous. The constant blows against German transportation centers, industrial plants, and military installations weakened German morale and power to resist. The Allied air raids brought relief to Great Britain, which had suffered tremendous damage from German air attacks. They also helped Soviet armies seeking to drive the Nazis from Soviet soil.

Liberation of Western Europe. The terrific air assault on Germany was merely part of a larger strategy—the invasion and conquest of Germany. By June 1944 General Eisenhower, who had been named Supreme Commander of the Allied invasion armies in Western Europe, was satisfied that it was time to launch the attack.

"Operation Overlord," as the invasion was called, began before dawn on the morning of June 6, 1944 (D-Day). More than 11,000 planes roared into the air. Some dropped airborne troops at key points a few miles inland from the German-occupied French coast. Others bombed roads, bridges, railway junctions, and German troop concentrations. Still others formed a mighty umbrella under which a huge invasion fleet of nearly 4,000 troop transports, landing craft, and warships moved across the English Channel to the Normandy beaches (see map, page 730).

The Germans had worked for years to make these beaches impregnable. Heavy artillery and machine guns were located in reinforced concrete pillboxes. Barbed wire and tank traps lined the shores. Other tangles of barbed wire were strung on steel and concrete piles and sunk just below the water's surface for hundreds of feet offshore.

Despite the years of preparation, the Germans were powerless to stop the invasion. Field Marshal Karl von Rundstedt later explained: "Terrific air power broke up all bridges and pinned me down completely, and the terrific power of the naval guns made it absolutely impossible for reserves to come up." The Nazis resisted fiercely, but they were outplanned, outnumbered, and outfought.

Allied tank forces ripped through the German defenses and fanned out behind the lines. Aided by the French resistance, or underground movement, they quickly overran the countryside. On August 25, 1944, Paris fell. By this time the Allies had landed more than 2 million men, nearly 500,000 more vehicles, and millions of tons of munitions and supplies.

Meanwhile, early in August, the United States Seventh Army landed on the southern coast of France and pushed rapidly up the Rhone Valley to join the Allied troops pouring in from Normandy. Within six months after D-Day, France had been liberated and the Allies had swept into the outer defenses of Germany's famous Siegfried Line (see map, this page). Here the attack at last ground to a halt, and the Allied armies paused while new ports were opened, supplies were brought up, and military units were regrouped.

The election of 1944. The preparations for the final drive into Germany did not interfere with the regular November elections in the United States. The Republican candidate for the Presidency, Thomas E. Dewey, governor of New York, had attracted national attention when, as a district attorney, he had successfully prosecuted racketeers in New York. The Republicans considered Dewey a strong candidate. But the war was going well, and the Democrats argued that it would be unwise to replace experienced leaders with new men. The argument proved convincing. Roosevelt, running for a fourth term, won with an electoral vote of 432 to Dewey's 99. The new Vice-President was Harry S. Truman of Missouri.

Germany's last counterattack. While the Allies were regrouping and the Americans were electing a President, the Germans were preparing a counterattack. On December 16 some 24 German divisions struck at a weakly held point in the Allied lines. German armored forces broke through, creating a dangerous "bulge" in the Allied lines. Christmas 1944 found the Allies fighting desperately in the Battle of the Bulge (see map, this page), trying to prevent the Germans from plunging onward to the sea. Reinforcements were rushed up. The German divisions were shattered and thrown back behind the Siegfried Line. This was the final major counterattack by the Nazis. Their defeat cost them dearly in men and equipment. Even more important, as General Eisenhower pointed out, was "the widespread disillusionment within the German army and Germany itself."

Invasion of Germany. By February 1945 Allied preparations had been completed for the invasion of Germany itself. The air forces continued to blast industrial areas, military bases, and transportation lines. Then, in March, the Allies crossed the Rhine, encircled Nazi troop concentrations, and plunged toward the heart of Germany (see map, this page).

Meanwhile, the Soviets had been driving the Germans out of the Ukraine, had conquered Nazi-held Rumania and Hungary, and were closing in upon the Nazis from the south and east. Churchill, by now greatly concerned over the Soviet Union's postwar intentions and alarmed at the deep penetration of the Soviet armies into Europe, argued that

ALLIED VICTORY IN EUROPE

the Allies should race the Soviets to Berlin and Prague. This was a vital political problem, which should have been decided by the leaders of the Allied governments including, of course, President Roosevelt. But the civilian leaders left the decision to General Eisenhower, who, as Supreme Commander, concluded that his first objective should be the total destruction of the German armies. It would be "militarily unsound," he declared, to depart from this objective for political considerations. As a result of this decision, American forces under Eisenhower's command advanced only as far as the Elbe River (see map, this page), where on April 25 they joined with the Soviet forces at Torgau.

Allied victory in Germany. Events that ended the war in Europe then followed in rapid order. On May 1 Hitler reportedly took his own life in the burning ruins of Berlin. On May 2 the Soviet troops hammered their way into the last Nazi strongholds of the city, and nearly 1 million German soldiers in Italy and Austria surrendered. Germany was in chaos. Within a week the Nazi forces in the Netherlands, Denmark, and Germany stopped fighting.

739

Early on the morning of May 8 the German High Command surrendered unconditionally. Thus, May 8, 1945 (V-E Day) marked the formal end of the war in Europe.

In Churchill's words, the victory over Germany was "the signal for the greatest outburst of joy in the history of mankind." As for himself, he wrote, his joy was tempered by "an aching heart and a mind oppressed by forebodings." He was weighed down by the awful tragedy of the war and concerned over the postwar intentions of the U.S.S.R.

Shocking revelations of Nazi horrors. The first outbursts of joy and relief at the end of the war in Europe were soon dulled by the shocking news coming out of Germany. As the Allied armies occupied the conquered country, the full extent of Nazi horrors came to light. The world now heard in detail the bloodcurdling crimes the Nazis had perpetrated in their concentration camps. In one of the most terrible displays of brutality in human history, the Nazis had created these camps, or "death factories," to destroy their "political enemies" and to exterminate the entire Jewish population.

With a horror almost beyond belief, the world learned that 6 million men, women, and children, most of them Jews, had been slaughtered after suffering unspeakable anxieties, agonies, indignities, and tortures.

Roosevelt's death. President Roosevelt did not live to see the end of the war nor to share in the world's horror over the full extent of Nazi atrocities. Worn out by his vast responsibilities, he died suddenly on April 12, 1945, in the "Little White House" at Warm Springs, Georgia. People all over the world were stunned at the news of his death. For three days American radio stations canceled programs to devote time to his memory. And Vice-President Harry S. Truman, who now became President, declared, "His fellow countrymen will sorely miss his fortitude and faith and courage in the time to come. The peoples of the earth who love the ways of freedom and hope will mourn for him."

■ In one of the most moving pictures of World War II, the famous photographer Margaret Bourke-White photographed these bewildered prisoners in the notorious Buchenwald concentration camp as horrified American troops arrived to set them free.

1. Why was it vital for the Allies to win the Battle of the Atlantic?
2. Describe the events of 1945 that led to the fall of Germany and to the end of the war in Europe.
3. What events led to a working relationship between the United States and the Soviet Union during World War II?
4. (a) What is meant by "genocide"? (b) The Nazi atrocities—their policy of genocide—were among the most brutal crimes ever committed against humanity. Comment.

4 Allied victory in the Pacific and the end of World War II

President Roosevelt died in April 1945, only a month before the Allied victory in Europe and only four months before the defeat of the Japanese brought World War II to an end.

By 1943, as you have seen, the United States and its Allies were taking the offensive in the Pacific. The overall strategy, directed by Admiral Chester W. Nimitz, called for air, land, and naval forces to strike westward at the Japanese-held islands in the Central Pacific; for a fleet under Admiral Halsey to drive the Japanese from the Solomon Islands; and for General MacArthur to advance with troops along the New Guinea coast and on to the Philippines. The ultimate objective was Japan.

Early victories. During 1943 American, Australian, and New Zealand troops pushed forward through the steaming jungles and across the vast stretches of the Central and South Pacific. The struggle was grim, for the Japanese clung to every foot of land. Few prisoners were taken.

Driving the Japanese from their threatening position before Port Moresby, which defended Australia, American and Australian troops fought their way up the New Guinea coast. Before the end of 1943 much of New Guinea had been recovered. American and New Zealand forces also won victories in the Solomons.

Meanwhile, in the Central Pacific, Admiral Nimitz' powerful fleet moved into the Gilbert Islands, and American marines seized Tarawa and Makin (see map, page 744). Far to the north Japan's troops were dislodged from the Aleutian strongholds of Attu and Kiska. The threat to Alaska was now ended.

Despite these successes, won at extreme cost in lives after ferocious fighting, the Allied gains in 1943 were limited. The major Japanese positions remained untouched.

Island hopping to the Philippines. By 1944 a growing volume of men and supplies was arriving in the Pacific, and many areas conquered by the Allies in 1943 were being converted into great staging bases from which new advances could be made. Powerful new warships and aircraft carriers, temporarily grouped into swift task forces, were sweeping through the outer screen of protecting islands to blast Japanese installations and shipping routes. Carrier planes were raining explosives on the Japanese-held islands prior to invasion.

Suddenly, on January 31, 1944, the Allies struck again, this time against the Marshall Islands (see map, page 744). Three days later they seized Kwajalein (KWOJ·ah·lin), one of the keys to Japanese control of the Marshalls. Kwajalein was the first Japanese possession occupied by the Allies. Three weeks later Eniwetok (en·ih·WEE·tok) was stormed successfully. From these two newly acquired bases, strong fleets of B-24 bombers began to blast Truk, major stronghold in the Carolines and key to Japanese control of the Southwest and Central Pacific. Meanwhile, General MacArthur, continuing his methodical advance up the New Guinea coast, seized Hollandia. By July all of New Guinea was in his hands, with only bypassed pockets of Japanese troops left to surrender or to starve.

A month earlier, in June 1944, the Pacific war had erupted with extreme violence. Task-force raids and swift strikes by carrier-based planes pinned down Japanese air and naval forces and hammered the defenses of Saipan and Guam in the Mariana Islands (see map, page 744). Then, under cover of intense air and naval bombardment, landing craft swept in upon the beaches. From fleet concentrations near the Philippines, the Japanese sent out swarms of planes, only to lose more than 400 in a few hours. The following day hundreds of American planes roared from the decks of carriers to strike a severe blow at the retreating Japanese fleet.

Though shocked and saddened by the appalling loss of life, the American people were thrilled at the victories on Guam and Saipan. They had long dreaded the thought of a slow, bloody, island-by-island advance to Japan. Now, as they saw the larger strategy unfolding, Americans realized that

741

America's tremendous sea and air power enabled it to seize key positions in the Pacific, leaving Japanese forces isolated and helpless on numerous islands far behind the line of battle.

Victory in the Philippines.   But probably the most gratifying news from the Pacific in 1944 was the reconquest of the Philippines. In October a vast naval armada moved up from the New Guinea–Solomons theater of war and in from Saipan and Guam. Under naval and air cover the converging forces poured upon the beaches of Leyte (LAY·teh) in the central Philippines (see map, page 744) and eventually captured the island. Meanwhile, in the Battle of Leyte Gulf, American naval forces struck a shattering blow at Japan's remaining sea power.

Overcoming bitter land resistance, the conquering troops then spread over the Philippines, and early in February 1945 Manila fell to the Americans. "I shall return," MacArthur had promised when, following orders, he had left Corregidor in March 1942. "I'm a little late, but we finally came," he said in Manila in 1945 as the American and Filipino flags were raised above the city.

The Yalta Conference.   Long before the Allied victories in 1945, leaders of the great powers had met at a series of conferences to develop a common strategy for defeating the Axis and to formulate plans for a lasting peace.

Early in February 1945 President Roosevelt, Prime Minister Churchill, and Premier Stalin met at Yalta in the southern part of the Soviet Union (see map, page 722) to make plans for the final stages of the war. At Yalta they made far-reaching decisions concerning the postwar world.

One group of decisions involved the creation of a new world organization. The three heads of state agreed to call a conference to meet in San Francisco on April 25, 1945, to draw up a charter for a new international organization. They also agreed on some crucial details regarding the nature of the new organization (Chapter 41).

In another group of decisions, Roosevelt, Churchill, and Stalin made plans for the occupation of postwar Germany and the treatment of Poland and the other liberated nations in Eastern and Central Europe. They agreed to divide Germany into four military zones to be occupied and controlled by the United States, Great Britain, the Soviet Union, and France, respectively. They also agreed that the "Big Three"—the United States, Great Britain, and the Soviet Union—would support free elections in Poland and throughout Europe, thereby guaranteeing the right of Europeans to choose their own governments. These and other agreements were announced to the public.

But the "Big Three" also reached several secret agreements. In one of these, Stalin promised that the Soviet Union would enter the war against Japan within three months after the war in Europe ended. In exchange for this promise, Roosevelt and Churchill, upon recommendation of top military men, agreed (1) to recognize the Mongolian People's Republic, which had once been part of China but now claimed its independence under Soviet protection; and (2) to allow the Soviet Union to have the Kurile Islands, the southern half of Sakhalin Island, an occupation zone in Korea, and certain rights in Manchuria (see map, page 744). Several of these territories and privileges had been held by Russia before it lost them to the Japanese in the Russo-Japanese War of 1904–05.

Details of the Yalta Conference did not become public until long after Roosevelt's death. Down through the years critics have severely condemned Roosevelt for what they called his "surrender" to Soviet demands. The critics charged that as a result of his "surrender," Roosevelt gave the Soviet Union control of Manchuria, paved the way for the Chinese Communists' victory over Chiang Kai-shek (CHY·AHNG KI·SHEK), the Chinese Nationalist leader, and opened the door to Communist aggression in Korea. They also held him responsible for permitting Soviet occupation of East Berlin and East Germany, and the creation of Communist governments in Eastern Europe. These governments were created without the free elections which Stalin had promised.

Roosevelt's defenders have replied to these charges by reminding the critics of the military situation at the time of the Yalta Conference. Soviet armies had already conquered most of Eastern Europe, including Poland. American troops, on the other hand, had not yet crossed the Rhine and were still fighting the Japanese in the Philippines. Moreover, Allied military leaders had warned that the invasion of Japan, scheduled for the spring of 1946, would be extremely costly, and that Americans should be prepared for as many as 1 million casualties.

Perhaps most important, Roosevelt's defenders insisted, was the fact that Stalin had given Churchill and Roosevelt reason to believe that the Soviet Union would cooperate in the construction of a new world organization designed to establish the foundations of a lasting peace. As Churchill himself later wrote, "Our hopeful assumptions were soon to be falsified. Still, they were the only ones possible at the time."

The road to victory. On February 19, 1945, a week after the Yalta Conference ended, United States marines landed on the murderous beaches of Iwo Jima (EE·woh JEE·mah). Nearly 20,000 American marines were killed or wounded in the successful effort to gain control of the airfields on this barren volcanic island, only 750 miles from Tokyo (see map, page 744).

A few weeks later the largest landing force in Pacific history began the invasion of Okinawa (oh·kih·NAH·wah), a Japanese island some 300 miles from the Japanese homeland. Japanese "suicide planes," manned by pilots who were pledged to die by diving bomb-laden planes into their targets, struck at the American fleet as it closed in on the inner defenses of Japan. Despite bitter Japanese resistance, Okinawa fell in June.

Japan's air and sea power were broken. But Japan still had many well-trained and well-equipped divisions of soldiers. It still controlled large areas of China, although badly needed American supplies were being flown across the eastern Himalayas and transported by trucks over the newly opened Stilwell Road (see map, page 744) to Chiang Kai-shek's embattled troops. But these supplies were only a fraction of what China needed, and Chinese troops were in no position to undertake a major offensive. Moreover, the inner defenses on the Japanese homeland were strong. On the other hand, Japan was blockaded, and, after the war in Europe ended in the spring of 1945, the full weight of the Allies was available for the final struggle in the Pacific.

Day by day the American task forces grew bolder, driving the remaining Japanese ships from the seas and sweeping in to shell shore installations on the Japanese mainland. Day by day huge fleets of bombers, now within easier striking distance of Japan, dropped fire bombs and high explosives in devastating raids upon transportation, industrial, and military centers of the Japanese home islands. By the early summer of 1945 the blockade and the relentless bombings were destroying Japan's power to resist. How long could Japan hold out?

The Potsdam Ultimatum. With President Roosevelt's death in April 1945, the responsibility for making decisions to bring about the defeat of Japan fell upon his successor, President Truman. In July Truman met with Stalin and Clement

■ This war painting depicts a Filipino guerrilla on the island of Luzon. He is waving an American flag to signal United States troops engaged in a pre-invasion bombardment of the island that the Japanese have fled.

Attlee, the new British Prime Minister, at Potsdam, Germany. At this meeting the leaders discussed plans for the control and occupation of Germany. They also issued an ultimatum to Japan, calling for unconditional surrender. Japan formally rejected the ultimatum on July 29.

(*continued on page 746*)

WORLD WAR II AND ALLIED VICTORY IN THE PACIFIC

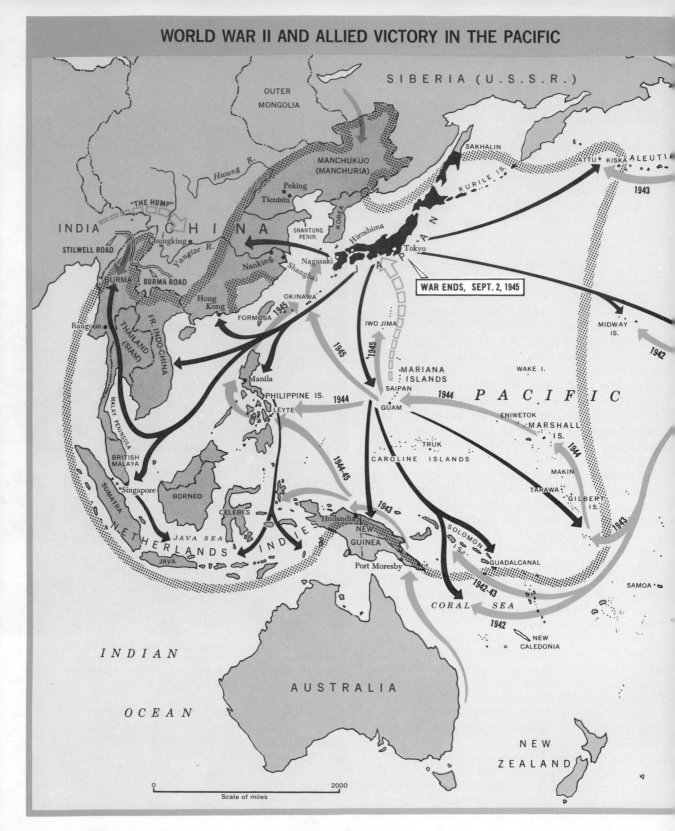

SIBERIA (U.S.S.R.)

OUTER MONGOLIA

MANCHUKUO (MANCHURIA)

SAKHALIN

KURILE IS.

ATTU · KISKA · ALEUTI

1943

"THE HUMP"

Hwang R.

Peking

Tientsin

SHANTUNG PENIN.

KOREA

INDIA CHINA

STILWELL ROAD

Chungking

Yangtze R.

Nanking

Shanghai

Nagasaki

Hiroshima

Tokyo

WAR ENDS, SEPT. 2, 1945

MIDWAY IS.

1942

BURMA BURMA ROAD

Hong Kong

OKINAWA

1945

FORMOSA

IWO JIMA

1945

1945

Rangoon

THAILAND (SIAM)

FR. INDO-CHINA

WAKE I.

PACIFIC

Manila

PHILIPPINE IS.

LEYTE

1944

MARIANA ISLANDS

SAIPAN

GUAM

1944

ENIWETOK

MARSHALL IS.

1944

MALAY PENINSULA

MAKIN

TARAWA

GILBERT IS.

1943

TRUK

CAROLINE ISLANDS

BRITISH MALAYA

Singapore

BORNEO

1944-45

CELEBES

SUMATRA

NETHERLANDS

JAVA SEA

JAVA

INDIES

Hollandia

NEW GUINEA

Port Moresby

1943

SOLOMON IS.

GUADALCANAL

1943

1942-43

INDIAN

OCEAN

AUSTRALIA

CORAL SEA

1942

NEW CALEDONIA

SAMOA

NEW ZEALAND

0   2000

Scale of miles

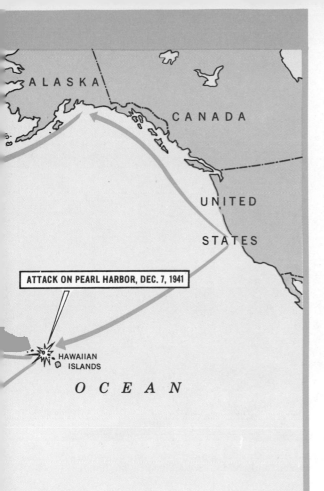

WORLD WAR II IN THE PACIFIC

Dark days for the Allies

1941

JULY	Japanese invasion of French Indo-China.
DEC. 7	Japanese attack Pearl Harbor.
DEC. 8–11	United States declares war against the Axis.
DEC.	Japanese invasion of Thailand and Br. Malaya; capture of Wake, Guam, Hong Kong; invasion of Philippines, Midway.

1942

JAN.	Fall of Manila.
JAN.–MAY	Japanese occupy Netherlands Indies and Burma.
FEB.	Singapore surrenders to Japanese.
FEB.–MAR.	Battle of the Java Sea.
APR.–MAY	Fall of Bataan and Corregidor.
MAY	Battle of the Coral Sea.
JUNE	Battle of Midway.
JUNE	Japanese occupy Attu and Kiska in Aleutians.

Allied gains: the tide turns

AUG.	U.S. marines land on Guadalcanal.
NOV.	Allied victory in naval battle of Guadalcanal.

1943

JAN.–SEPT	Allied gains in New Guinea.
MAR.–AUG.	Allies force Japanese from Aleutians.
JUNE–DEC.	Allied offensive in South Pacific: Solomon Is.
NOV.–FEB. 1944	Allied offensive in Central Pacific: Gilbert Is., Marshall Is., Kwajalein, Eniwetok.

1944

APR.–JULY	Allies seize Hollandia and regain New Guinea.
JUNE–AUG.	Allies capture Saipan and Guam in Mariana Is.
OCT.	Allied campaign to reconquer Philippines begins.

1945

FEB.	Allies liberate Manila; end of Philippines campaign.
FEB.–MAR.	U.S. marines conquer Iwo Jima.
APR.–JUNE	U.S. marines conquer Okinawa.
MAY–AUG.	Allied air offensive against Japanese home islands.

Allied victory in the Pacific

AUG. 6	Atomic bomb dropped on Hiroshima.
AUG. 9	Atomic bomb dropped on Nagasaki.
AUG. 10	Japan surrenders.
AUG. 14	V-J Day (end of war in Pacific).
SEPT. 2	Japan signs formal surrender on U.S.S. *Missouri*.

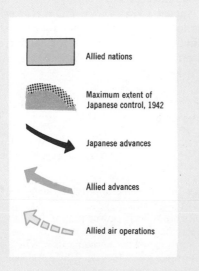

745

■ The atomic bomb dropped on the Japanese city of Hiroshima fell approximately one mile from the site of this photograph. Nearly 100,000 men, women, and children were killed by the bomb.

The end of World War II.　On August 6, 1945, at 8:15 A.M. a solitary plane flew high over the Japanese city of Hiroshima (hee·ro·SHEE·mah). No alarm was sounded. Then, suddenly, the city disintegrated in a single searing atomic blast. Nearly 100,000 of the 245,000 men, women, and children in Hiroshima were killed instantly or died soon after. A new force had been added to warfare, a force that would enormously complicate the postwar world.

In authorizing the bombing of Hiroshima, President Truman knew that he had made an extremely grave decision. He had given the order only after days of conferring with his key military and political advisers. His decision was made as a last resort to force Japan to surrender immediately, and thus to save the lives of hundreds of thousands of American fighting men. But despite the devastation of Hiroshima, the Japanese failed to surrender.

On August 8 the Soviet Union declared war on Japan. On August 9 a second atomic bomb destroyed the city of Nagasaki. On August 10 the Japanese government finally asked for peace.

On August 14, 1945 (V-J Day), President Truman announced by radio that Japan had accepted the Allied peace terms. The formal surrender was signed on September 2, 1945. World War II had come to an end.

SECTION SURVEY

IDENTIFY: Potsdam Ultimatum, V-J Day; Chester Nimitz, Harry S. Truman, Chiang Kai-shek; August 14, 1945.

1. Trace the "island-hopping" strategy of the Americans in the Pacific.
2. What role did air power play in both the European and Pacific theaters of the war?
3. (a) Summarize the agreements reached at the Yalta Conference in 1945. (b) Why are these agreements considered controversial?
4. (a) Why did the Japanese finally surrender? (b) Was the dropping of the atomic bomb necessary to end the war? Explain.

TRACING THE MAIN IDEAS

The cost of World War II in human lives, money, and property was enormous. In the United States alone the federal government spent more money than it had during its entire history from 1789 to 1940, including the cost of all earlier wars. Parts of many of the world's major cities were reduced to rubble. Billions of dollars worth of property disappeared in smoke and flames.

The loss of human life was staggering. According to General Marshall's final report, 201,367 Americans had been killed by the end of June 1945, about 600,000 had been wounded, and 57,000 were missing. Other nations lost even more heavily. It has been estimated that more than 3 million Germans, more than 3 million Russians, more than 1.5 million Japanese, and more than 375,000 British troops were killed in battle. Civilian deaths resulting from bombs, starvation, disease, and concentration camps ran into the millions. The exact number can never be known, for vast numbers of people simply disappeared from the face of the earth. Many other millions were uprooted and left homeless.

These were only some of the immediate and terrible effects of the most devastating war in history.

CHAPTER SURVEY

QUESTIONS FOR DISCUSSION

1. Despite their deeply rooted belief in individualism and free enterprise, Americans accepted many new governmental controls during World War II. Why?
2. What were the most important reasons for the Allied victory in Europe?
3. What role did science and technology play in winning the war?
4. Japanese-Americans born in the United States proved their loyalty to America with their lives by serving in the American armed forces during World War II. Not one Japanese-American was ever convicted of sabotage or of spying. Yet Japanese-Americans were interned in prison camps at the beginning of the war. Why? In your opinion, can this violation of civil liberties be justified? Explain your answer.

RELATING PAST TO PRESENT

1. If another world war were to come, there would be very few survivors. Comment.
2. Evaluate current American efforts to prevent international conflicts. Do you believe our foreign policy has overcommitted our nation? Is the United States too isolationist? Explain.

USING MAPS AND CHARTS

1. Using the map on pages 730–31, answer the following: (a) Explain the objectives of the Allied land attacks. (b) How was Allied naval strategy co-ordinated with Allied land attacks? (c) In November 1942, which countries were under Axis control?
2. Base your answers to the following on the map on page 739. (a) What was the objective of each of the four Allied drives into Germany from the west and the south? (b) Indicate the strategy of the Russian drives from the east. (c) Why was the Battle of the Bulge a critical military event?
3. Using the map on pages 744–45, answer the following questions: (a) By 1942, which countries had been conquered by Japan? Why? (b) When the Japanese attacked Pearl Harbor, how far were they from the continental United States?

UNIT SURVEY

FOR FURTHER INQUIRY

1. In your opinion, did the New Deal change the basic character of the federal government? Explain.
2. The TVA project was unique. Why? What difficulties are inherent in this approach to a regional problem? What advantages does this approach have?
3. Would either Jefferson or Hamilton have approved of the New Deal? Explain.
4. During the 1930's, some of the nations of the world resorted to dictatorship government in order to resolve problems caused by the worldwide depression. Why didn't the United States do this?
5. Has the federal government been forced to assume more power because our nation has become so complex and interdependent? Or has the federal government seized more power while ignoring other possible solutions to the problems of our society? Explain your answer.
6. What impact do you think Roosevelt's Four Freedoms had on colonial peoples around the world? What impact do you think it had upon minority groups in the United States?
7. Black Americans encountered discrimination in the armed forces and in the job market during World War II. Comment.
8. President Roosevelt "saved" capitalism. Do you agree or disagree? Explain.

PROJECTS AND ACTIVITIES

1. Review America's attempts to maintain neutrality before the War of 1812, before World War I, and before World War II. (a) What were the similarities and the differences? (b) Why did each of these attempts fail?
2. Read and report to the class on "A Latin-American View of the Monroe Doctrine" in Brown and Brown's *Impressions of America* (Harcourt Brace Jovanovich).
3. Read the biography *Roosevelt: The Lion and the Fox* by James McGregor Burns (Harcourt Brace Jovanovich) to gain an understanding of this important figure in American history.
4. Present a report to the class on the songs or the movies that were popular during World War II.
5. Follow up earlier interviews by asking members of your family or community for their first-hand accounts of life during the New Deal and World War II.

USING THE SOCIAL SCIENCES

(Read pages 750–52 before you answer the following questions.)

1. How did the depression affect the relationship between Americans and their government?
2. What adaptations had to be made by the individuals affected by the depression?
3. What economic statistics would help you to understand the nature and depth of the depression?
4. What changes took place in the concept of leadership during Franklin Roosevelt's administration?

SUGGESTED FURTHER READING
Biography

BEARD, CHARLES A., *President Roosevelt and the Coming of the War, 1941*, Yale Univ. Press.

BRADLEY, OMAR N., *A Soldier's Story*, Popular Library (paper). General Bradley describes his own wartime experiences.

BULLOCK, ALAN, *A Study in Tyranny*, Bantam (paper). A documented study of Adolf Hitler.

BURNS, J. M., *Roosevelt: The Lion and the Fox*, Harcourt Brace Jovanovich.

FAHEY, JAMES J., *Pacific War Diary, 1942–1945*, Hearst (Avon Books, paper). The diary, written in secret and against strict Navy regulations, of an American sailor who fought in every major engagement of the Pacific war.

GUTHRIE, WOODY, *Bound for Glory*, Dutton (paper). Illustrated autobiography of the famous folk singer and composer; focuses on America in the 1920's and 1930's.

JOSEPHSON, MATTHEW, *Sidney Hillman, Statesman of American Labor,* Doubleday.

POGUE, FORREST C., and HARRISON GORDON, *George C. Marshall,* Viking.

ROOSEVELT, ELEANOR, *This I Remember,* Doubleday (Dolphin Books, paper). The famous wife of Franklin D. Roosevelt describes the years of the Depression and World War II as she lived them.

SHERWOOD, ROBERT E., *Roosevelt and Hopkins: An Intimate History,* Harper & Row.

TUGWELL, REXFORD G., *The Democratic Roosevelt,* Doubleday. Treats of the early New Deal.

Other Nonfiction

AGEE, JAMES, and W. EVANS, *Let Us Now Praise Famous Men,* Intext (Ballantine Books, paper). Excellent photographs and commentary on the Great Depression.

ALLEN, FREDERICK LEWIS, *The Big Change: America Transforms Itself: 1900–1950,* Harper & Row (text ed.).

ASBELL, BERNARD, *When FDR Died,* New American Library (Mentor Books).

BAILEY, THOMAS A., *The Man in the Street,* Macmillan. Impact of American public opinion on foreign policy.

BEARD, CHARLES A., *American Foreign Policy in the Making, 1932–1940,* Yale Univ. Press.

BRICKHILL, PAUL, *The Great Escape,* Fawcett (Crest Books, paper). The true account of an escape from a German prison camp.

COMMAGER, HENRY STEELE, ed. *The Pocket History of the Second World War,* Pocket Books (paper).

EISENHOWER, DWIGHT D., *Crusade in Europe,* Doubleday.

FAIRBANK, JOHN D., *The United States and China,* Harvard Univ. Press.

FOGELMAN, EDWIN, ed. *Hiroshima: The Decision to Use the A-Bomb,* Scribner (paper). Essays examining the moral, scientific, and political implications of the decision.

FREIDEL, FRANK, ed. *The New Deal and the American People,* Prentice-Hall (Spectrum Books, paper). Documentary cross section of opinions on the New Deal.

GREW, JOSEPH CLARK, *Ten Years in Japan,* Simon and Schuster.

HERRING, HERBERT CLINTON, *Good Neighbors,* Yale Univ. Press.

HERSEY, JOHN, *Hiroshima,* Knopf; Bantam (paper). Interviews with six survivors.

JOHNSON, DONALD B., *The Republican Party and Wendell Willkie,* Univ. of Illinois Press.

JOHNSON, WALTER, *1600 Pennsylvania Avenue: Presidents and the People, 1929–1959,* Little, Brown.

JONES, CHESTER LLOYD, *The Caribbean Since 1900,* Prentice-Hall.

KENNAN, GEORGE F., *American Diplomacy, 1900–1950,* Univ. of Chicago Press.

KOGON, EUGEN, *The Theory and Practice of Hell,* Putnam (Berkley, paper). The author's six years in a Nazi concentration camp.

LANGER, WILLIAM L., and S. EVERETT GLEASON, *The Challenge to Isolation: 1937–1940,* Harper & Row.

——, *The Undeclared War: September 1940–December 1941,* Harper & Row.

Life MAGAZINE, *Picture History of World War II,* by the Editors of *Life,* Simon and Schuster.

MILLIS, WALTER, *This Is Pearl! The United States and Japan—1941,* Morrow.

NEVINS, ALLAN, *The New Deal in World Affairs,* Yale Univ. Press.

PRITCHETT, C. HERMAN, *The Roosevelt Court: A Study in Judicial Politics and Values, 1937–1947,* Farrar, Straus (Octagon Books).

PYLE, ERNIE, *Brave Men,* Popular Library (paper). Narrative account of World War II by a news correspondent who lived with the men he wrote about.

SCHLESINGER, ARTHUR M., JR., *The Age of Roosevelt,* Houghton Mifflin, 3 vols.

SCHNEIDER, FRANZ, and CHARLES GULLANS, *Last Letters from Stalingrad,* New American Library (Signet Books, paper). Contains farewell messages that were written by German soldiers and that were flown out on the last German airlift from Stalingrad.

SHANNON, DAVID, *The Great Depression,* Prentice-Hall (Spectrum Books, paper). Contains case histories, interviews, newspaper accounts, etc.

TANSILL, CHARLES C., *Back Door to War: The Roosevelt Foreign Policy, 1933–1941,* Regnery.

Historical Fiction

DOS PASSOS, JOHN, *Number One,* Houghton Mifflin. Novel treating of southern political boss.

——, *The Grand Design,* Houghton Mifflin. Treats of situation in Washington during the New Deal.

KANTOR, MAC KINLAY, *The Good Family,* Coward-McCann. Novel traces family history from 1925 to 1950.

LEWIS, SINCLAIR, *It Can't Happen Here!* Doubleday. Prediction of what would happen if the United States were ruled by dictator.

NATHAN, ROBERT, *One More Spring,* Knopf. The Great Depression affects several individuals.

SINCLAIR, UPTON, *Dragon Harvest,* Viking. Novel tracing the events from Munich to fall of France.

——, *Dragon's Teeth,* Viking. Novel discussing road to Hitlerism.

WARREN, ROBERT PENN, *All the King's Men,* Harcourt Brace Jovanovich; and others. Southern political boss.

WOUK, HERMAN, *The Caine Mutiny,* Doubleday. A navy crew mutinies against its commander.

HISTORY AND THE SOCIAL SCIENCES

Some experiences in a nation's history have a lasting influence. They not only are remembered, but their effects and even lessons are quite clear many, many years after the event. The New Deal era was surely such an experience in the history of the United States.

There is no question that the New Deal era was a traumatic experience for the American people. The trauma began with the shock and suffering of the Great Depression and continued through the revolutionary legislation of the "First Hundred Days" of Franklin Delano Roosevelt's administration. But historians of the New Deal differ in their appraisal of the period. Professor Raymond Moley, a former adviser of President Roosevelt, wrote: "As the weeks ran by in March, the city of Washington became a mecca for the old socialists, single-taxers, utility reformers, Civil Service reformers, and goo-goos of all types. . . . That a government composed of men who could agree on neither the nature of our economic disease nor the character of the treatment would be the last blow for the stricken country never occurred to them. Each wanted to put on his surgical mask and rubber gloves and go to work."

Professor Arthur Schlesinger, Jr., however, pictured the New Dealers in a different light: "The New Dealers brought with them alertness, an excitement, an appetite for power, an instinct for crisis, and a dedication for public service which became during the thirties the essence of Washington. . . . At his worst, the New Dealer became an arrant sentimentalist or a cynical operator. At his best, he was the ablest, most intelligent, and most disinterested public servant the United States ever had."

Which appraisal is the more correct? This is what we shall investigate.

Revolution Through Legislation

The Great Depression began with an almost catastrophic crash of the stock market. As stock prices tumbled downward, millions of stockholders lost large sums of money or were completely wiped out. The disaster on Wall Street was followed by a drastic downward spiral in production and in prices. Businesses went bankrupt, farmers lost their farms, unemployment rose to a frightening level, and misery and hunger abounded.

President Herbert Hoover, a firm believer in the free enterprise system and in the ability of American business to handle any situation, was reluctant to use the powers of the federal government to cope with the emergency. He was sure that once confidence was restored things would be better again. Moved by the suffering of so many citizens, however, Hoover did urge more contributions to private charities, but he adamantly opposed government relief for the poor. Only as the depression deepened did President Hoover sign a bill creating the Reconstruction Finance Corporation, which was authorized to lend money to banks, railroads, and industrial firms to prevent their going bankrupt. While this measure provided some help to these segments of the economy, it was ineffective in dealing with the situation as a whole.

At his inauguration in March 1932, President Franklin Delano Roosevelt, elected by a landslide Democratic vote, asserted that his election was a mandate for him and for the federal government to take immediate and unprecedented steps to fight the depression and to alleviate the suffering of the American people. He concluded: "The people of the United States . . . in their

Many small businesses failed during the Great Depression.

need . . . have registered a mandate that they want direct, vigorous leadership. They have asked for discipline and direction under leadership. They have made me the present instrument of their wishes. . . . May God guide me in the days to come."

If proof is needed that the American system of government can be changed by the will of the majority of the people acting through their representatives in Congress, the New Deal provides that proof. Taking advantage of a House and a Senate controlled by Democrats, President Roosevelt pressured Congress into passing a number of epoch-making laws which amounted to a "new deal," a new era, for the American people. These legislative acts, most of which were passed within the "First Hundred Days" of Roosevelt's administration, were a virtual revolution by legislation. They drastically changed the economic and social order of the United States.

During the New Deal the view of Herbert Hoover and most earlier Presidents that the federal government's power was limited and that its purpose was only to provide an honest and efficient administration was superseded by a new philosophy, affirmed by the Supreme Court, that the responsibility and duty of the federal government was to provide for the "general welfare" of the entire population. To that end, Congress, under Roosevelt's leadership and prodding, passed laws aimed at alleviating the suffering of the unemployed and at ensuring a new and better future for businessmen, workers, and farmers. President Roosevelt defined these objectives in one of his campaign speeches: "We have two problems: first to meet the immediate distress; second to build up a basis for permanent employment. As to 'immediate relief,' the first principle is that this nation, this national government, if you like, owes a positive duty that no citizen shall be permitted to starve."

Reactions to the New Deal

Since the New Deal brought such far-reaching changes to almost all aspects of American society and since it rested on a new and novel interpretation of the Constitution approved by the Supreme Court, the reaction to it ranged from enthusiastic praise to outright condemnation. To some, the New Deal was a distortion of the Constitution, a veritable orgy of waste, and an inexcusable example of federal interference with the rights of the states and of individual citizens. Opponents of the New Deal charged that the welfare measures, unemployment compensation, and other New Deal legislation threatened traditional American values of self-reliance and encouraged Americans to rely on the government to make up for their own inadequacies.

On the other hand, supporters of the New Deal maintained that the New Deal had saved the country from economic collapse and had proved that a democratic government, using peaceful, legal means, could deal successfully with even the gravest situation. They argued further that the New Deal legislation had improved the nation's economic development by creating new sources of production and by turning many millions of unemployed Americans into productive and prospering workers.

One historian, Edgar E. Robinson, saw unprecedented disaster ahead for the nation as a result of the New Deal. "Did the nation," Robinson asked, "emerge from 12 years of Roosevelt leadership economically sound? A national debt approaching $300 billion dollars must raise a serious question. . . . Huge government expenditures had saved millions of people and had won a war, but at a cost of grave concern to all citizens. Could this road lead eventually to anything but national bankruptcy?"

But Professor Richard Hofstadter, in his Pulitzer-prize winning book *The*

According to this cartoonist, why did the Republicans oppose the New Deal?

President Franklin D. Roosevelt

Age of Reform, wrote that the New Deal had saved America from disaster. Hofstadter argued that when Roosevelt took office "the entire working apparatus of American economic life had gone to smash." As a result of New Deal reforms, he stated, the federal government "was fated henceforth to take responsibility on a large scale for social security, unemployment insurance, wages and hours, and housing." To Hofstadter, the New Deal represented a creative response to the urgent problems of widespread unemployment and the growing lack of confidence in the ability of the American political and economic system to cope with emergency situations.

The Legacy of the New Deal Today

In assessing the New Deal from a 40-year perspective, it is important to recognize that the New Deal had its failures and negative results. The New Dealers, for example, did engage in excessive spending and did manage to pile up a huge national debt. But it is also important to acknowledge that many New Deal measures and laws remained on the statute books long after the New Deal era was past. In fact, most welfare reforms initiated under the New Deal have ceased to be a partisan issue in American politics. The example of the Social Security Act makes this clear.

Dwight D. Eisenhower, who became the first Republican President to lead the country after the Presidency of Franklin Roosevelt, did not demand the repeal of the Social Security Act. On the contrary, under the Eisenhower administration social security payments were increased as was the minimum wage rate. And it is significant also that among the first acts of Congress signed by the Republican President Richard M. Nixon was a law increasing social security payments by 15 percent and providing greatly increased benefits for retired miners.

The most significant legacy of the New Deal is the firm consensus today of most political leaders and of the great majority of Americans that in case of a threatened economic recession or depression it is the duty of the federal government to take all measures necessary to restore prosperity to the country. This idea was not shared by many Americans before the Great Depression. In fact, before that time most Americans believed that in a free, capitalistic society the government must stand aloof from the economic process.

As late as 1892, for example, President Grover Cleveland vetoed a bill which provided a modest sum to help Texas farmers whose crops were destroyed by a prolonged drought. In his veto message Cleveland stated that while his personal sympathy was with the farmers it was not the government's responsibility to help individuals in financial distress.

The depression and the New Deal changed this philosophy quite radically. It is now generally assumed that the federal government has a responsibility for citizens who suffer from a natural disaster such as a flood or a tornado and for those who are unemployed, disabled, or aged. The Great Depression and the New Deal seem to have convinced the American people that free competition and free enterprise alone are not enough to assure a fair measure of economic security to all segments of the population. For good or for bad, this is the legacy of the New Deal.

■ Do you agree with the conclusions of historians like Moley and Robinson or do you agree with those of Schlesinger and Hofstadter? Why?

■ Why is the New Deal a good example of continuity in American history? Discuss some of its lasting influences in American life.

RISE OF THE AMERICAN NATION

UNIT TWELVE

The Challenges of a New Era

1945 – 1970's

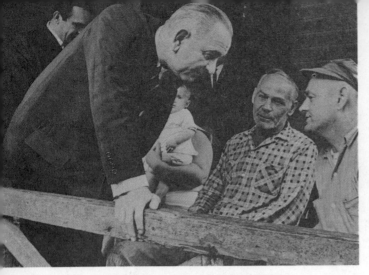

■ *President Johnson in Appalachia, 1964*

CHAPTER **40**

Problems on the Domestic Front

1945 – 1970's

P RESIDENT ROOSEVELT did not live to see the victorious conclusion of World War II or the organization of the United Nations. Worn out by more than 12 years of constant pressure as President, he died suddenly on April 12, 1945.

With Roosevelt's death the burden of present and future problems fell upon his successor, President Harry S. Truman. The new leader was almost 61 years old, lean, gray-haired, plain and folksy, with a winning grin and a liking for mixing with ordinary people.

Born and raised on a farm in Missouri, Truman had served overseas in World War I. After a successful career in local politics, he had been elected to the United States Senate. In the Senate he had supported the New Deal program, and had come to public attention during the early years of World War II when he served as chairman of a key Senate committee—the Special Committee to Investigate the National Defense Program. In 1945, after only a few months in the Vice-Presidency, he was suddenly elevated to the highest office in the land.

At the simple oath-taking ceremony in which he assumed the Presidency, Truman spoke humbly. He promised that he would carry on Roosevelt's policies, both domestic and foreign. Led by a new President, the United States prepared to enter the postwar world.

THE CHAPTER IN OUTLINE

1. Truman's efforts to solve postwar problems through a "Fair Deal."

2. Eisenhower's role in developing "Modern Republicanism."

3. Kennedy's challenge to the nation to advance to a "New Frontier."

4. Johnson's invitation to Americans to build the "Great Society."

5. Nixon's plans "to bring America together."

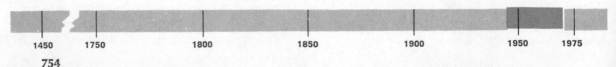

| 1450 | 1750 | 1800 | 1850 | 1900 | 1950 | 1975 |

1 Truman's efforts to solve postwar problems through a "Fair Deal"

With the defeat of Japan in August 1945, Americans were eager to return to the ways of peace. They wanted their sons and daughters, brothers and sisters, husbands and friends home again— and servicemen and women were just as eager to return.

Demobilization. American military leaders, faced with the problem of stationing occupation troops in Germany, Italy, and Japan, warned that hasty demobilization would be dangerous. Their warnings went unheeded. Reluctantly, the military authorities gave in to public pressure. Within two years the air force had been reduced from 85,000 to 9,000 planes, the navy had withdrawn hundreds of ships from active service, and the army had reduced its forces from 89 to 12 divisions.

Aid to veterans. After World War II the government did far more to help veterans adjust to civilian life than had ever been done before. Government help came through the Servicemen's Readjustment Act of 1944. This "GI ° Bill of Rights," as it was called, provided for (1) government loans to help ex-servicemen set themselves up in business or on farms, (2) government loans to buy homes, (3) pensions and hospital care, and (4) educational opportunities. Under the GI Bill, hundreds of thousands of veterans received money for tuition, books, and part of their living expenses while they attended school or college.

The Employment Act of 1946. The government also assumed responsibility for maintaining a high level of employment. Although the Employment Act of 1946 fell short of the guarantee of "full employment," it did commit the federal government to maintain a vigorous economy and high employment through a policy of federal spending and investment.

Reconversion of industry. While veterans were returning to civilian life, industry was rapidly shifting from wartime to peacetime production. Thus there was no serious unemployment during the postwar years. On the contrary, from 1945 to 1948 the number of employed workers rose from about 54 million to more than 61 million. Instead of a feared postwar depression, Americans enjoyed a high degree of prosperity.

° **GI:** a nickname describing enlisted men. The initials stand for "Government Issue."

Postwar inflation. But prosperity brought problems, including the danger of runaway inflation. For more than a year after the war ended, President Truman continued the wartime price controls (page 734). But the demand for ending these controls grew increasingly insistent.

Not until November 1946 did President Truman yield to the pressure. In the Congressional elections of that year, the Republicans won control of both houses of Congress. Four days later the President issued an Executive Order ending all controls on prices and wages. He did, however, continue controls on rent.

Prices immediately started to rise. High wartime wages, plus savings accumulated during the war years, had created an enormous reservoir of purchasing power. With money to spend and a mounting demand for goods of all kinds, Americans engaged in a buying splurge. It was a "seller's market," and prices soared higher and higher.

Shortage of housing. Although rent controls kept rents from climbing to disastrous levels, they did not ease the postwar housing shortage. Relatively few houses had been built during the depression years, and almost none during the war years. Meanwhile the population had been growing— from nearly 123 million in 1930 to more than 140 million by 1945. After the war the housing situation became increasingly desperate as millions of veterans returned to civilian life.

During 1945 and 1946 President Truman led a drive to provide federal subsidies for the construction of new housing. But his efforts failed because of widespread opposition to any proposal that would increase the already swollen national debt. By 1947, however, the private building industry was rolling into high gear, and the housing situation, though still serious, began to improve.

Labor unrest. Rising prices inevitably led to demands for higher wages. In many cases industry met the demands—but promptly raised prices to recover the increased costs of production. The rise in prices, in turn, spurred labor to demand higher wage boosts. Thus inflation continued its upward spiral, with workers blaming industry, industry blaming workers, and consumers caught in the middle.

Labor unrest led to strikes. Two of the most serious involved the railroads and the coal-mining industry. President Truman, who was generally sympathetic to organized labor, finally ended the railroad strike by threatening to declare a national emergency and draft the strikers into the army.

■ After World War II, the government did far more to help veterans adjust to civilian life than had ever been done before. Above, homecoming Pacific veterans come down the gangplank at San Francisco.

The federal government also ended the United Mine Workers' coal strike by seizing the mines and issuing an injunction that forced the miners to return to work.

The Taft-Hartley Act of 1947. The postwar labor unrest and strikes led to public demand for stronger federal controls over organized labor. When the Republicans won control of Congress in 1946, they attributed their victory in part to the rising demand for new labor legislation. In June 1947, after bitter debate, Congress passed the Labor Management Relations Act, better known as the Taft-Hartley Act, over President Truman's veto.

In general, the new law aimed to reduce the power that organized labor had won under the New Deal. The Taft-Hartley Act prohibited unions from making contributions to political campaigns. It permitted management to seek injunctions in times of strikes, and to sue union officials for violations of contracts or for engaging in strikes arising from jurisdictional disputes with rival unions. The law forbade "closed shop" agreements. It also gave the President power to secure a court injunction calling for an 80-day "cooling-off" period when a strike threatened to affect national health and safety. Moreover, the law required employers and union leaders to sign non-Communist oaths.

The Taft-Hartley Act proved to be a highly controversial measure. Supporters of the law argued that it restored equality of bargaining power between employers and workers. They insisted that it merely corrected the unfair advantages granted to organized labor in the Wagner Act of 1935 (page 691). But organized labor protested that the new law deprived workers of many benefits won over a long period.

Gains for organized labor. During the postwar years, however, organized labor did make notable gains. Workers in general won substantial wage increases. More significant in the long run were certain techniques adopted by management and labor to protect workers against inflation and ill health, and to offer them greater security for their old age.

An industry-wide trend was stimulated in 1948 with a contract signed by the United Automobile Workers and the General Motors Corporation. This contract included three noteworthy provisions. (1) It contained a two-way *escalator clause*, which provided that wages should be adjusted upward or downward every three months to keep pace with the rise or fall in the cost of living. (2) The contract contained an *annual improvement provision*, which provided automatic wage increases of from 2 to 2.5 percent to compensate workers for increased production resulting from improvements in machines and processes. (3) The contract contained several *welfare provisions*, including retirement pensions and health insurance.

The UAW-GM contract of 1948 was only one of many similar contracts negotiated by labor and management in the postwar years. Even more important than the contracts was the fact that both labor and management were increasingly seeking agreements that would provide fair returns to both workers and owners.

Candidates in the 1948 election. By 1948 the nation was enjoying a high degree of prosperity.

756

With this in their favor, the Democrats met to choose their Presidential candidate.

The delegates to the Democratic convention nominated President Truman on the first ballot and chose Senator Alben W. Barkley of Kentucky as his running mate. Then, largely at the insistence of President Truman and Mayor Hubert H. Humphrey, Jr., of Minneapolis, the delegates wrote a strong civil rights plank into the platform. This plank urged Congress to support the President in guaranteeing (1) the right of every adult to vote and participate in politics; (2) the right of everyone to an equal opportunity to work at a job of his own choosing; (3) the right of everyone to have personal security; and (4) the right of equal treatment in the armed services. The Democratic platform also called for repeal of the Taft-Hartley Act and for federal legislation in support of housing, education, farm income, and broader social security benefits.

The Democratic platform split the party. Southern delegates vigorously objected to the civil rights plank. A number of southern Democrats, calling themselves "Dixiecrats," formed a separate States' Rights Party and nominated Governor J. Strom Thurmond of South Carolina for President.

Former Vice-President Henry A. Wallace also left the Democrats to head a new Progressive Party. The Progressive Party tried to win the support of labor and of liberal Democrats by adopting planks that promised to renew and to extend many New Deal measures.

The Republicans were jubilant. Having won control of Congress in 1946, and with the Democrats split into three segments, the Republicans were confident of winning the election. After again nominating Governor Thomas E. Dewey of New York as their candidate, they adopted a platform praising free enterprise and calling for minimum government control over business. The Republican platform also promised to protect "both workers and employers against coercion and exploitation," and urged that the states be given greater responsibility for housing, public health, and social security.

Truman's victory. The public opinion polls indicated and most newspapers and many Americans assumed that Dewey would win. But President Truman confidently carried on a vigorous campaign. He asked a special session of the Republican-dominated Congress to live up to its 1946 campaign promises and do something to halt rising prices and to meet the housing crisis. When Congress adjourned without acting on these issues,

President Truman toured the country denouncing the legislators for failing to meet their responsibilities.

The election result was a stunning surprise victory for President Truman. Truman polled 49.4 percent of the popular vote; Dewey, 45 percent; the other candidates divided the remaining 5.6 percent. In the Electoral College, Truman won 303 votes, Dewey 189, and Thurmond 39. Wallace failed to win a single electoral vote. The Democrats regained control of Congress and won many state and city elections.

The "Fair Deal." Heartened by his victory, President Truman decided to launch a broad program of reform. In his State of the Union Message in January 1949, he urged Congress to adopt a "Fair Deal" program and extend some of the New Deal reforms.

Politically wise observers doubted whether the President could win support for his program from the various wings of his own party. This skepticism proved to be well founded. Time after time during Truman's second term, many southern and some northern Democrats joined the Republicans to block Fair Deal measures.

President Truman did, however, have some success with his Fair Deal program. Between 1949 and 1952 Congress (1) extended social security benefits to include 10 million more persons; (2) raised the minimum wage for workers in interstate industries under the Fair Labor Standards Act (page 701) from 40 to 75 cents an hour; (3) authorized the federal government to undertake a program of slum clearance and to build 810,000 low-income housing units over a six-year period; (4) continued rent controls to March 31, 1951; (5) adopted a new Agricultural Act in 1949 that established farm price supports at 90 percent of parity through 1950, and thereafter on a sliding scale of 75 to 90 percent; (6) brought more employees of the Internal Revenue Service under civil service; and (7) expanded the activities of the Reclamation Bureau in the development of flood control, hydroelectric plants, and irrigation projects.

Other laws under Truman. During Truman's two terms Congress adopted other important measures.

The Atomic Energy Act, signed by the President on August 1, 1946, gave the government a monopoly on the production of all fissionable materials—that is, elements such as uranium which can be split to produce atomic energy. The act placed the control of research and production under a five-man civilian Atomic Energy Commission (AEC).

The National Security Act of 1947 centralized the responsibility for military research and planning. It created a new cabinet department—the Department of Defense—headed by a civilian Secretary of Defense. The act provided the new Secretary with three assistants—the Secretaries of the Army, Navy, and Air Force, who were not to be cabinet members.

The Presidential Succession Act of 1947 changed the line of succession to the Presidency in case both the President and Vice-President died in office. Under the new law, succession passed first to the Speaker of the House, then to the President *pro tempore* of the Senate—both elected officers— and finally to the Secretary of State and the other appointed cabinet officers, in the order in which their offices had been created.

In 1947 Congress also proposed the Twenty-second Amendment (page 200), which became part of the Constitution in 1951. This amendment limited a President's tenure to two terms in office. The two-term limitation did not apply to President Truman who was in office at the time.

In an effort to bring greater efficiency into the vast, sprawling structure of government, President Truman asked former President Herbert Hoover to head a commission to study the problem of governmental reorganization. In the Reorganization Act of 1949 Congress wrote many of the commission's recommendations into law.

Concern over internal security. A stepped-up drive against subversive elements in government began in 1947 when President Truman called for an investigation by the Federal Bureau of Investigation (FBI) and the Civil Service Commission into the loyalty of all federal employees. By the end of 1951 more than 3 million employees had been investigated and cleared, 2,000 had resigned, and 212 had been dismissed as "security risks."

Meanwhile, in 1948 the FBI and the Department of Justice launched an intensive investigation into Communist activity in the United States. Before the year ended 11 Communist leaders had been indicted under the Smith Act of 1940 (page 720), tried, and sentenced to prison for conspiracy to advocate the violent overthrow of the government.

Finally, Congress passed the Internal Security Act of 1950, popularly known as the McCarran Act. This law required all Communist organizations in the United States to file their membership lists with the Attorney General and to give him a statement of their financial operations.

In its deepening concern over internal security, Congress was reacting not only to the possibility of Communist subversion at home but also to the increasingly serious international situation (Chapter 41). Both of these issues played major roles in the Presidential election of 1952. As a result of this election, Dwight D. Eisenhower became President of the United States.

SECTION SURVEY

IDENTIFY: GI Bill, demobilization, "Dixiecrats," Twenty-second Amendment; Strom Thurmond, Hubert H. Humphrey.

1. (a) What problems confronted the American government after World War II? Why? (b) How did the government meet these problems?
2. (a) Why was the Taft-Hartley Act passed? (b) Has history supported labor's arguments against this act? Explain.
3. Give the parties, candidates, issues, and results of the election of 1948.
4. Describe some important achievements of Truman's Fair Deal program.
5. Why was there a deepening concern over internal security at this time?
6. (a) What were the provisions of the civil rights plank of 1948? (b) Why did these provisions arouse controversy?

2 Eisenhower's role in developing "Modern Republicanism"

In the 1952 campaign the Republicans adopted the slogan "It's time for a change." But they did not agree among themselves as to what this change should be. Like the Democrats, they were split into a conservative and a liberal wing.

The election of 1952. Confident of a Republican victory, each wing of the Republican Party fought to control the nominating convention. The conservatives failed to gain the nomination for Senator Robert A. Taft of Ohio. The liberals won, nominating General Dwight D. Eisenhower for the Presidency and Richard M. Nixon of California for the Vice-Presidency.

The Democrats also entered their 1952 nominating convention as a divided party. In general, conservative Democrats had little liking for the New Deal and the Fair Deal. Moreover, southern

Democrats opposed their party's stand on civil rights. Faced with this split, the Democrats finally chose Governor Adlai E. Stevenson of Illinois as their Presidential choice, and Senator John Sparkman of Alabama as his running mate.

Both parties waged hard-fought campaigns. The Republicans charged the Democrats with "political corruption" and promised to "clean up the mess in Washington." The Republicans condemned their opponents for steadily enlarging the powers of the federal government over the states. They also declared that the Democrats had been "soft" on Communism, both at home and abroad. According to some Republicans, the government was "honeycombed" with Communists and Communist sympathizers. Further, Eisenhower charged the Truman administration with "bungling" in the Korean War (Chapter 41).

Stevenson was an effective campaigner. He eloquently defended Truman's foreign and domestic policies. And he insisted that there was no easy road to the "peace, prosperity, and progress" that the Republicans were promising the voters.

On November 4, 1952, voters in record numbers cast their ballots. Eisenhower won 57 percent of the popular vote—33.8 million to Stevenson's 27.3 million. Eisenhower's majority in the electoral count was overwhelming, 442 to 89. But the Republicans managed to control Congress by only bare majorities in both houses.

Control of Congress won by the Democrats. The Republicans held their slender majority in Congress for only two years. In the 1954 Congressional elections the Democrats won control of the legislative branch by majorities of 27 seats in the House and 2 in the Senate.

During the summer of 1956 the Republicans enthusiastically renominated Eisenhower and Nixon for President and Vice-President. The Democrats renominated Adlai Stevenson, choosing Senator Estes Kefauver of Tennessee as his running mate.

In the campaign the Republicans reminded voters that the nation was enjoying the highest standard of living in its history. The Democrats blamed the Republicans for the rising cost of living and for falling farm prices. They also charged that the Republicans had failed to develop an effective foreign policy.

Eisenhower's popularity returned him to the White House with a vote of more than 35 million to Stevenson's nearly 26 million. The electoral count was 457 to 73. But the voters returned a substantial Democratic majority to Congress.

■ Shown here campaigning in the East, the Republican candidate Dwight D. Eisenhower won the Presidency in 1952 and again in 1956. In both campaigns, he defeated the Democratic candidate, Adlai E. Stevenson.

In the 1958 Congressional elections the Democrats won by a landslide, piling up large majorities in both houses. Thus, from 1954 to 1960 the government operated with a Republican President and a Congress controlled by Democrats.

Encouraging private business. The Eisenhower administration generally tried to reduce government interference in the affairs of the states and of private business. For many years there had been controversy over whether the federal government or the states owned oil fields lying off the coasts of Florida, Louisiana, Texas, and California. With the approval of the Eisenhower administration, Congress settled this offshore oil controversy with the Submerged Lands Act of 1953, giving control of the underwater oil deposits to the states.

The Tennessee Valley Authority again became an issue in 1954. The administration opposed a TVA proposal to build steam plants to generate needed electricity for the Atomic Energy Commission and awarded the contract instead to the Dixon-Yates group of private utility companies. But the

Dixon-Yates contract aroused a storm of controversy over the issue of special favors to private interests, and it was canceled.

The Eisenhower administration made other determined efforts to encourage private enterprise. (1) Former President Hoover agreed to head a new commission to recommend ways of securing greater efficiency in government and ending government competition with private business. (2) In 1954 Congress amended the Atomic Energy Act, giving private industry a larger opportunity to develop atomic energy for peaceful purposes. (3) The federal government reduced or completely ended its participation in business activities, including the manufacture of synthetic rubber, the operation of railroads, ships, and hotels, and the production of motion pictures.

Balancing the budget. Once in office, Eisenhower made government economy and a balanced budget "the first order of business." Appropriations for defense and foreign aid were reduced despite arguments from some Democrats that the administration was weakening national security. In 1956 for the first time in eight years the government ended its fiscal year with a surplus.

"Modern Republicanism." The Eisenhower administration did not try to repeal the basic social and economic legislation of the New Deal and Fair Deal eras. President Eisenhower personally favored a "middle-of-the-road" policy. This included a moderate extension of some New Deal and Fair Deal programs—an expansion of social security and of federal support for education, housing, slum clearance, and public health activities. This policy —together with support for the United Nations, military aid for American allies, and economic and military help for underdeveloped countries—came to be called "Modern Republicanism."

Social legislation. Shortly after taking office in 1953 President Eisenhower signed a joint resolution of Congress, transforming the Federal Security Agency into the Department of Health, Education, and Welfare and making the Secretary of the new department a member of the cabinet. In January 1954, in his State of the Union Message, he urged Congress to expand the social security program and to consider ways of providing additional federal aid for health, housing, and education.

Congress responded by extending social security to an additional 10.5 million persons and by increasing benefits. By 1955 about 90 percent of the nation's workers were covered by social security.

Congress also set aside additional money for hospital construction and for medical research. And in 1955 it authorized $500 million for slum clearance and urban redevelopment.

But Congress refused to appropriate money to build schools and raise teachers' salaries. Many members of both political parties feared that federal support of education might lead to federal control. In 1958, however, after the Russians had successfully launched several earth satellites, Congress adopted legislation providing loans for able students, principally students of science.

Gains for organized labor. During the Eisenhower administration Congress raised the hourly minimum wage under the Fair Labor Standards Act from 75 cents to $1.00. In June 1955 the Ford Motor Company and the General Motors Corporation signed contracts (renewed in 1958) with the United Automobile Workers which provided, among other things, that the companies would pay unemployment benefits.

During the 1950's many unions set up welfare funds to take care of unemployed, disabled, and retired workers. In December 1955 the A. F. of L. and the CIO voted to combine. The new organization, called the AFL-CIO, with George Meany as president and Walter Reuther as vice-president, had about 15 million members.

The Labor Act of 1959. There were also problems for organized labor. In 1957–58 a Congressional committee revealed corrupt leadership in certain unions, notably in the powerful Teamsters Union. Several union officials were brought into court and given jail sentences. The AFL-CIO leaders insisted that the corrupt practices were limited to only a small segment of organized labor. They took steps, however, to put their house in order.

In the meantime, Congress adopted the Labor-Management Reporting and Disclosure Act of 1959. This law contained several important provisions: (1) It prohibited Communists or persons convicted of felonies within the five previous years from serving as union officials or employees. (2) It prohibited secondary boycotts and the picketing of parties other than those directly involved in a strike. (3) It required labor unions to file annual financial reports with the Secretary of the Treasury. (4) It required employers to report loans or payments made to labor unions. (5) It required national labor organizations to hold elections at least every five years. (6) It provided a "bill of rights" guaranteeing union members the right to attend meetings, nominate candidates for political office, and vote in elections using secret ballots.

The new labor legislation went into effect in September 1959. Meanwhile President Eisenhower and Congress had been facing another difficult problem of labor-management relations.

The steel strike of 1959.   In 1959 the contract between the steel industry and the United Steel Workers of America came up for renegotiation. The workers asked for a wage increase and other benefits, claiming that the steel industry could afford to meet these requests without raising steel prices. The industry refused to discuss a wage increase unless the union agreed to eliminate "featherbedding," or the assignment of more men to a piece of work than management felt were needed.

On July 15 the union called a strike involving 500,000 steel workers and plants that produced 85 percent of the nation's steel. Negotiations dragged on. Finally President Eisenhower, using powers granted him in the Taft-Hartley Act, asked for an 80-day anti-strike injunction. On November 7 the injunction went into effect and the workers returned to their jobs.

The injunction did not, however, settle any of the issues. Not until January 4, 1960, did the union and the industry reach an agreement. The new agreement provided for step-by-step wage increases over 30 months. A committee was formed to study the dispute over work rules.

The farm problem.   With the exception of large commercial producers, farmers in the 1950's did not share as fully as other Americans in the "Eisenhower prosperity." Between 1952 and 1956 farm income dropped 26 percent.

There were a number of reasons for this situation, including the loss of foreign markets and growing competition from farmers in other countries. Basically, however, the problem was an old one—overproduction in relation to national demand. Since the early 1930's farm workers' productivity had almost doubled, largely because of advances in technology.

From 1942 to 1954 the government tried to guarantee farmers a *fixed* price support of 90 percent of parity. When prices dropped below this 90 percent level, the government bought surplus crops at the fixed price.

Under this policy, storage facilities were bursting. Storage charges alone were costing the government nearly $1 million a day. But surplus continued to pile up, and prices continued to fall.

Secretary of Agriculture Ezra Taft Benson per-

suaded the Eisenhower administration to abandon fixed price supports and adopt a flexible scale of 82.5 to 90 percent. This, he maintained, would discourage farmers from growing crops that were glutting the market.

Despite opposition the Eisenhower administration backed Benson's program of flexible price supports. In 1956, however, the government made a major change in the farm program. Money from a "soil bank" was to be paid to farmers who withdrew land from commercial production and planted it in trees or, wherever possible, built dams and created reservoirs. By the end of 1958 the "soil bank" had paid $1.6 billion to farmers for withdrawing land previously used for growing wheat, corn, cotton, tobacco, and rice.

Internal security.   The Eisenhower administration also inherited the problem of protecting the country against subversion without denying Americans their constitutional rights of freedom to criticize and to associate with whomever they wished. Congressional committees were sometimes accused of handling individuals suspected of subversion without proper regard for fair judicial practices. The most controversial of these was a subcommittee headed by Senator Joseph McCarthy of Wisconsin.

During the first two years of the Eisenhower administration, Senator McCarthy carried on intensive investigations of possible Communist influences in the government. He brought charges against leading Americans no longer in government service, against the State Department, and against the army. Many Americans applauded McCarthy, but others criticized what they called his recklessness and his disregard for constitutional rights. In 1954 McCarthy's influence declined, partly as a result of a Senate resolution censuring him for some of his actions.

During this troubled period Congress adopted the Immunity Act of 1954. This act provided that witnesses could be compelled to testify before courts, grand juries, and Congressional committees on matters involving national security. But the act also provided that the witnesses would be granted immunity from prosecution for any criminal activities they might confess. The Supreme Court upheld the constitutionality of this law.

Continuing prosperity.   Although Americans in 1960 still faced stubborn domestic and foreign problems, an impressive majority continued to enjoy a rising standard of living. To be sure, economic progress in the 1950's had been slowed twice by recessions—the first in 1953–54, the second in 1957–58. In the 1957–58 recession, the more severe of the two, unemployment climbed to more than 5.5 million, the stock market slumped, and many Americans feared another serious depression. But by 1959 unemployed workers were returning to their jobs, the stock market had reached record high levels, business was improving, and a spirit of optimism prevailed.

The "Eisenhower prosperity" was tempered, however, by the continuing struggle with Communism, by growing tensions abroad, and by unresolved problems at home, including the fact that many Americans, white as well as black, did not share in the widespread "good times." As a result, the election campaign of 1960 was one of the hardest fought in the nation's history.

SECTION SURVEY

IDENTIFY: AFL-CIO, immunity from prosecution, soil bank; Adlai E. Stevenson, Joseph McCarthy, George Meany, Walter Reuther.

1. Compare the elections of 1952 and 1956 with respect to parties, candidates, issues, and results.
2. From 1954 to 1960 the government operated with a Republican President and a Congress controlled by Democrats. (a) What does this tell you about the state of national politics at this time? (b) What difficulties would this situation present in the functioning of government?
3. In what ways did the Eisenhower administration encourage private enterprise?
4. What is meant by "modern Republicanism"?
5. (a) Describe the tensions between internal security and constitutional rights that arose during this period. (b) How did fear contribute to these tensions?

3 Kennedy's challenge to the nation to advance to a "New Frontier"

Which of the nation's leaders was best qualified to guide the United States through its problems at home and abroad? This was the question confronting Americans in the summer and fall of 1960.

The 1960 election. Both the Republicans and the Democrats nominated relatively young, energetic candidates for the Presidency. The Republican nominee, Richard M. Nixon of California, was 47. He had served in both houses of Congress and since 1953 had been Vice-President under Eisenhower. The Democratic nominee, John F.

Kennedy of Massachusetts, was 43. He, too, had served in both houses of Congress.

The Vice-Presidential candidates also had distinguished records. Henry Cabot Lodge, Jr., a former Senator from Massachusetts, was serving as Ambassador to the United Nations when chosen as Nixon's running mate. Lyndon B. Johnson of Texas, who shared the Democratic ticket with Kennedy, had served in Congress since 1937—for 11 years in the House, and then, since 1948, in the Senate, where since 1954 he had served as his party's leader.

During the campaign the Presidential candidates faced each other in a series of television debates. The central issue was the condition of the nation. Kennedy charged that, as a result of the Eisenhower administration's failure to deal adequately with urgent issues, the United States was losing prestige and influence to the Communists throughout the world. He called for "a supreme national effort" to reverse what he believed to be a downward trend in the nation's fortunes, and promised if elected "to get America moving again." What the nation needed, he said, was to advance to a "New Frontier."

Nixon insisted that the United States was stronger than it had ever been. "Communist prestige in the world is at an all-time low and American prestige is at an all-time high," he declared. Nixon charged Kennedy with advocating "wild experimentation" and "reckless" policies. He promised if elected to continue Eisenhower's programs and to build a more secure nation on their foundations.

The voters, disturbed by the gravity of the charges and countercharges, turned out in record numbers. Kennedy won 303 electoral votes to Nixon's 219. But out of more than 68 million popular votes cast, Kennedy squeezed through by a margin of only about 118,000 votes.

The new administration. The incoming President attracted a great deal of attention. Kennedy, at 43, was the youngest man ever elected to the Presidency. Moreover, he was the first Roman Catholic to win the highest office in the land.

John F. Kennedy was acutely aware of the problems confronting his administration. Barely half of the voters had showed a willingness to follow the new administration toward a "New Frontier." Moreover, although the Democrats controlled Congress, conservative Democrats, mostly from the South, had in the past voted with conservative Republicans to defeat measures similar to those Kennedy now wanted.

■ President John F. Kennedy, shown here with his wife Jacqueline, inspired Americans of all ages to take a greater interest in government affairs.

Mindful also of the gravity of the problems facing the nation at home and abroad, Kennedy tried to secure the ablest men and women he could get for his administrative staff. Among his advisers were prominent business leaders and Republicans.

Economic problems. With his staff organized, the President prepared to attack the related problems of unemployment and economic growth. The immediate problem was unemployment. In January 1961 more than 5 million Americans, or nearly 8 percent of the total labor force, were unemployed. In certain depressed areas, such as the coal fields of West Virginia, the percentage of unemployment was far higher. The unemployment rate among black Americans was double the rate for the nation as a whole. Among teenagers it was even higher— nearly three times the national average.

The problem of unemployment had its roots deep in the nation's rapidly changing economic life, as you will see (Chapter 43). Some economists contended that the American economy was not growing as rapidly as it could and should grow. Industries were not modernizing older plants and building new ones as rapidly as they had done in the past.

Coupled with the sluggish economic growth rate was the problem of automation, or the use of machines to do work formerly done by men and women. Moreover, the increasingly complex American economy called for new skills on the part of workers, with the result that there was less opportunity for the untrained and the poorly educated.

Measures to stimulate the economy. In line with administration proposals, Congress took steps to increase spending power and retrain workers. Amendments to the Social Security Act increased

763

LIVING AMERICAN DOCUMENTS

John F. Kennedy's
Inaugural Address (1961)

We dare not forget today that we are the heirs of that first revolution. Let the word go forth from this time and place, to friend and foe alike, that the torch has been passed to a new generation of Americans— born in this century, tempered by war, disciplined by a hard and bitter peace, proud of our ancient heritage—and unwilling to witness or permit the slow undoing of those human rights to which this nation has always been committed, and to which we are committed today at home and around the world.

Let every nation know, whether it wishes us well or ill, that we shall pay any price, bear any burden, meet any hardship, support any friend, oppose any foe to assure the survival and the success of liberty. . . .

the minimum monthly benefits for retired workers. Minimum wages under the Fair Labor Standards Act were raised to $1.25 an hour, and 4 million more workers were included under such wage-hour protection. With the Area Redevelopment Act of 1961 Congress authorized the federal government to make loans and grants to stimulate business and retrain workers in depressed areas. In 1962 Congress set aside $900 million for building public works in areas where unemployment exceeded 6 percent of the labor force. In 1962 the Manpower Development and Training Act provided for a three-year manpower retraining program.

Even with these and other measures, unemployment remained a major problem. Faced with this discouraging situation, President Kennedy proposed a substantial reduction of individual and corporate income taxes. The proposed reduction would leave consumers with more money to spend and companies with more money to invest in modernizing and enlarging their plants. These results, the administration hoped, would stimulate production and provide more jobs. But Congress failed to act on this proposal in 1963.

Housing and urban renewal. Another effort to strengthen the nation's economic and social fabric was the Housing Act of 1961. This act added $4.9 billion more in funds for the government's housing program. By means of long-term loans at low interest rates, the Housing Act tried to stimulate the construction of moderate-income housing. It included additional funds to provide hospitals and housing for the elderly. The largest single authorization was for urban renewal, including the planning and improvement of mass transportation facilities. Congress also appropriated nearly $1.5 billion to aid in the construction of buildings for medical and dental schools, and to assist colleges in building classrooms, libraries, and laboratories.

The money appropriated for housing opened up jobs for workers in the building trades. It also stimulated employment in mining, lumbering, and the manufacturing industries that supplied construction materials. At the same time, it provided better buildings and housing for some Americans.

The Trade Expansion Act. In 1962 Congress took a major step to stimulate America's foreign trade, a step prompted in part by the creation of the Common Market in Western Europe.

The Common Market, created in 1957, was a large trading area composed of six European nations—France, West Germany, Italy, Belgium, the Netherlands, and Luxembourg. To improve trade among themselves, the Common Market nations had gradually lowered the tariffs that had been crippling their trade relations. By 1962 the Common Market nations were enjoying increasing prosperity. Recognizing that the Common Market could greatly affect the United States, Congress passed the Trade Expansion Act of 1962.

This act—perhaps the most important measure adopted during the Kennedy administration— placed large powers in the hands of the President. Over a five-year period he could cut tariff rates 50 percent below the 1962 level, or raise them 50 percent above the 1934 level. He could also remove *all* tariffs on products for which the United States and the Common Market countries together accounted for 80 percent of all world trade.

The act contained an "escape clause" that allowed the President to retain or reimpose tariffs to protect industries which were seriously hurt by tariff reduction. Industries exposed to damaging foreign competition could also apply for technical assistance and for loans to finance a shift into other manufacturing. Workers in these industries could apply for retraining or relocation allowances.

The continuing farm problem. The Trade Expansion Act was designed, among other things, to help American farmers dispose of their surplus commodities. In 1962 Congress passed still another in the long series of laws that tried to deal with this problem. The new act provided for payments to farmers who agreed to turn farm land into forest, wildlife, or recreation areas. It authorized loans to state and local agencies to carry out conservation programs. It tightened controls over the production of crops used mainly to feed livestock, and placed new limitations on wheat production.

The wheat limitation program, like earlier government programs to support prices and limit the output of crops, required farmers' approval. In a nationwide referendum held in May 1963, however, a majority of farmers rejected the program.

The rejection of its wheat limitation program was a severe blow to the Kennedy administration's agricultural plans. The blow was softened somewhat when the Soviet Union, suffering from widespread crop shortages, offered to buy $250 million worth of wheat in 1963. After extended debate, Congress approved the sale.

Despite the possibility of selling grain to Communist countries, the basic farm problem remained unchanged. At the end of 1963 the nation's farmers continued to struggle with surplus products and declining incomes.

Changes in suffrage. During the Kennedy administration several major changes took place in voting rights. The Twenty-third Amendment to the Constitution, adopted in 1961, enabled residents of the District of Columbia to vote in Presidential elections. The Twenty-fourth Amendment, adopted in 1964, forbade the poll tax as a requirement for voting in federal elections.

While voting barriers were being lifted for some citizens, others fought for fairer representation in their state and local legislatures. In a number of states there had been no *redistricting,* or changes in representation, for many years. During that time some communities had grown into big population centers, while others with a similar number of legislators had not grown or had grown only slightly.

Between 1962 and 1964 the Supreme Court handed down several history-making decisions relating to representation in state legislatures and in the House of Representatives. The most far-reaching in its effects was the Court's "one person, one vote" ruling. According to this decision, election districts for state legislatures as well as for the House of Representatives must be as nearly equal in population as practicable. In other words, according to the Court, "one man's vote is to be worth as much as another man's vote" in an election for Congressman and state legislator. The Supreme Court thus set in motion a political revolution intended to give approximately equal value

to every citizen's vote and so provide genuinely representative government at both state and federal levels.

The Supreme Court rulings aroused a storm of controversy. Many citizens, including influential Congressmen, criticized the Court for interfering "unduly" in matters that, in their judgment, belonged to the states. Others praised the Court for forcing the states to take what they considered long-overdue action.

Unfinished business. By November 1963, John F. Kennedy had served nearly three years as President. He had become increasingly popular and influential, both at home and abroad. But despite his popularity, and despite Democratic control of both the House and the Senate, several major "New Frontier" projects were stalled in Congress.

As you will see (Chapter 44), Congress had not acted on the civil rights bill President Kennedy had recommended. And, despite an increasingly serious crisis in education, Congress would not adopt an administration proposal to grant extensive federal aid to education. The administration also had failed to get Congress to reduce taxes or to adopt a bill adding medical care for the aged to the social security program.

Thus matters stood when, on November 22, 1963, President Kennedy was assassinated.

The assassination of John F. Kennedy. At 12:30 noon on Friday, November 22, 1963, while riding in a motorcade through Dallas, Texas, President Kennedy was struck by two bullets·from the rifle of an assassin. He died within minutes without regaining consciousness.

As soon as Vice-President Johnson, who was also in the motorcade, learned that the President had died, he drove under close guard to Love Field and boarded the Presidential plane. There, in the cabin of the plane at 2:38 P.M., Lyndon B. Johnson was sworn in as the thirty-sixth President of the United States.

The tragic weekend. Americans reacted to the tragic news with shocked disbelief, then with deeply felt anger and grief. For three days, while the body of John F. Kennedy lay in state in the rotunda of the Capitol, radio and television stations suspended regular programing, and all but the most essential businesses closed their doors. Messages of sorrow and sympathy poured in from all over the world. The leaders of many nations flew to Washington to pay their respects to the late President.

In the meantime, within an hour and a half of the fatal shooting the Dallas police had seized a suspect, Lee Harvey Oswald. They charged him with the murder of a Dallas policeman as well as the assassination of the President. Oswald was placed under heavy guard in a Dallas jail. Two days later, while being transferred to another jail, he was shot and killed in full view of millions of Americans who watched the scene on their television screens. His murderer, Jack Ruby, the operator of a Dallas night club, pushed through a group of police officers to shoot Oswald at arm's-length range.

Americans were deeply troubled by this new act of brutality. With Oswald gone, grave questions remained unanswered: Was Lee Harvey Oswald the assassin? If so, had he acted alone, or did he have accomplices? Was he the trigger man in a conspiracy to assassinate President Kennedy? Was Jack Ruby part of that conspiracy, and did he kill Oswald to keep him from talking?

The Warren Commission Report. To answer these questions and to put an end to wild rumors and speculation, President Johnson promptly appointed a seven-man commission to investigate the case. The commission was headed by Earl Warren, Chief Justice of the Supreme Court.

In its unanimous report released 10 months later, on September 27, 1964, the seven-man Warren Commission, after carefully examining all available evidence and the testimony of 532 witnesses, concluded that: (1) Lee Harvey Oswald had assassinated President Kennedy. (2) He had acted alone. (3) Jack Ruby had also acted alone. (4) There was no evidence of a conspiracy. ". . . if there is any such evidence," the report said, "it has been beyond the reach of all the investigative agencies and resources of the U.S."

SECTION SURVEY

IDENTIFY: New Frontier, depressed areas, Common Market; Lee Harvey Oswald, Jack Ruby, Earl Warren.

1. Give the parties, candidates, issues, and results of the election of 1960.
2. (a) Describe measures taken by the Kennedy administration to stimulate the economy. (b) Why were these measures less than fully successful?
3. Discuss the significance for democratic government of the (a) Twenty-third Amendment, (b) Twenty-fourth Amendment, (c) "one person, one vote" ruling.
4. Was President Kennedy able to bring the nation to a New Frontier before his assassination? Explain.

4 Johnson's invitation to Americans to build the "Great Society"

In the midst of the tragic events of the weekend of November 22–25, 1963, Americans could take pride in the fact that even the assassination of a President did not break down the orderly procedure of government. Five days after the assassination, Lyndon B. Johnson, in his first Presidential address to Congress, dedicated himself to the "ideas and the ideals" which John F. Kennedy had "so nobly represented."

President Johnson meant what he said. In his State of the Union Message to Congress in January 1964, he assigned top priority to three items—a civil rights law, a tax cut, and an "unconditional war on poverty." Speaking quietly but firmly, he declared: "All this and more can and must be done." Then, appealing to economy-minded Congressmen, he added, "And it can be done without any increase in spending."

An impressive Congressional record. Congress responded to President Johnson's leadership. Before adjourning in October 1964, the legislators chalked up one of the most impressive legislative records in the nation's history. Most far-reaching was the Civil Rights Act of 1964 (Chapter 44). But there were other important measures.

The Revenue Act of 1964 provided for an $11.5 billion reduction in personal and corporate income taxes. By leaving more money in the hands of consumers and business managers, the new law greatly stimulated the economy. President Johnson called it "the single most important step that we have taken to strengthen our economy since World War II."

The Economic Opportunity Act of 1964 marked another important attempt to "break the cycle of poverty." It created an Office of Economic Opportunity (OEO) and authorized an initial expenditure of $1 billion to finance the war against poverty. The new agency was directed to work with state and local governments in developing larger opportunities for employment and in expanding training programs, especially among young people.

Congress also acted favorably on several other administration measures. These included (1) authorization of $375 million to help cities improve urban and commuter transit facilities; (2) establishment of a wilderness system to preserve federally owned wild areas; (3) pay increases for all federal officials and employees, including Congressmen. But two measures strongly supported by the administration, the Medicare and Appalachia bills, were still before the legislature when they adjourned to join the 1964 election campaign.

The Medicare bill proposed by the administration would provide medical care for the aged as part of the social security program; the Appalachia bill was designed to tackle the problem of economically distressed communities in Appalachia, a large area, mostly mountainous, including parts of Pennsylvania, Maryland, West Virginia, Ohio, Kentucky, Virginia, Tennessee, North Carolina, South Carolina, Georgia, and Alabama. Johnson's program also included slum clearance, housing, and VISTA, a domestic version of the Peace Corps.

The election campaign of 1964.   The Republicans, meeting in the Cow Palace near San Francisco in July of 1964, nominated Senator Barry M. Goldwater of Arizona for the Presidency. Following Goldwater's wishes, they chose Representative William E. Miller of New York as his running mate. Goldwater, an ardent conservative, had been serving in the United States Senate since 1953; Miller, in the House of Representatives since 1951.

The Democrats, meeting in Atlantic City in August, nominated President Lyndon B. Johnson by acclamation. He, too, indicated his choice for Vice-President—Senator Hubert H. Humphrey of Minnesota, a Senator since 1949.

The Presidential race was bitterly contested. From the beginning both parties were divided. Many moderate Republicans, unable to accept Goldwater's position on several critical issues, refused to endorse his candidacy. The Republicans also lost the support of most black voters. Negroes deeply resented the fact that Goldwater had been one of only six Republican Senators who voted against the Civil Rights Act in the belief that certain of its provisions were unconstitutional.

But the Democrats also had to contend with the loss of large numbers of normally Democratic voters. Many white southern Democrats felt that President Johnson, a Texan, had betrayed them by leading the battle for the Civil Rights Act. They threw their support to Goldwater because of his vote against the act and because of his strong support of states' rights.

Johnson's sweeping victory.   At the peak of the campaign two far-reaching events swept the election news from the headlines. In mid-October the Soviet Union released the startling announcement that Premier Nikita Khrushchev had been deposed and replaced by Leonid I. Brezhnev as First

■ Eugene J. McCarthy (right) sought the Democratic nomination for President in the election campaign of 1968. He was aided in his campaign by thousands of young volunteers from all over the nation.

Secretary of the Communist Party and Aleksei N. Kosygin as Premier. And, while the world was still trying to evaluate the upheaval in the U.S.S.R., Communist China exploded an atomic "device" and thus took a significant step toward becoming the world's fifth nuclear power.

On November 3 a record-breaking number of almost 70 million voters decisively elected President Johnson by an overwhelming electoral vote of 486 to 52. The popular vote, 42 million to 26 million, also gave Johnson a very large plurality. The Democrats also won substantial victories in state and local elections and in Congress.

Starting toward the "Great Society."   Encouraged by his sweeping victory, President Johnson challenged Americans to join him in building the "Great Society." He emphasized that Americans could help build a new world, not just a new nation.

"We are in the midst of the greatest upward surge of economic well-being in the history of any nation," the President declared. "But we are only at the beginning of the road to the Great Society." Ahead, he said, lay three major tasks: "To keep our economy growing. To open for all Americans the opportunities now enjoyed by most Americans. To improve the quality of life for all."

President Johnson then outlined the proposals he intended to put before Congress. High on his list of domestic priorities were voting rights, education, and medical care.

"Great Society" legislation. By the time Congress adjourned in the fall of 1965, it had adopted laws dealing with all of the President's major recommendations. In one of the most far-reaching laws, the legislators came to grips with education (Chapter 44). In another far-reaching measure, Congress established Medicare, a program of health insurance for citizens over 65.

The Medicare law contained two major sections: (1) Basic health coverage, providing up to 90 days of hospital care for each illness. The patient would pay the first $40 of the hospital bill, and an additional $10 for each day he remained after 60 days. The remainder of the bill would be paid by social security. The basic-coverage section also included nursing-home care and home nursing, with the patient paying a small part of the cost himself. (2) Voluntary supplementary coverage, which enabled individuals covered by social security to buy inexpensive health insurance to take care of doctors' bills and the cost of other health services.

Following another of President Johnson's recommendations, Congress provided for the gradual reduction, over a four-year period, of federal excise taxes on automobiles, television sets, and other consumer items. The $4.6 billion cut in excise taxes was designed to encourage consumers to buy more goods. This in turn would stimulate production and, by creating more jobs, reduce unemployment.

In a redoubled effort to raise the standard of living of the nation's underprivileged citizens, the legislators adopted several measures:

Congress increased to $1.5 billion the appropriation under which the Office of Economic Opportunity was carrying on the anti-poverty program.

Congress authorized $1 billion to develop the economy of the 11-state Appalachia region. This money was to be spent for highways, flood control, the development of new industries, and for other measures to create new and better employment opportunities for the 15 million people in that depressed area. Congress also authorized $3.3 billion to revive the economies of other depressed areas throughout the nation.

Congress authorized $7.5 billion to improve the nation's housing. The housing act included the following provisions: (1) It increased allocations for slum clearance and urban renewal. (2) It provided additional funds for building public housing projects. (3) It allocated money for urban planning, the beautification of cities, and the development of parks and other recreational areas. (4) It authorized the federal government to pay part of the rent of low-income families so that needy families would not pay more than roughly 25 percent of their total income for rent. (5) It authorized federal grants for the restoration of run-down properties.

These and other laws added up to an impressive body of legislation. By the end of 1965 the President's Great Society program was making encouraging progress.

Loss of momentum. As it turned out, however, 1965 marked the peak in Johnson's program and in his popularity. By 1966 the war in Vietnam (Chapter 42) was absorbing more and more of the nation's resources and the administration's time and energy. And as the war intensified and the Great Society program slowed down, criticism of the President became increasingly widespread.

Eugene McCarthy's challenge. It was Eugene J. McCarthy, Democratic Senator from Minnesota, who first revealed the extent of the dissatisfaction. In November 1967 Senator McCarthy made the surprising announcement that he intended to campaign for the Presidency. His basic purpose, he said, was to challenge President Johnson and to give the voters an alternative to the administration's Vietnam policy.

At first few political observers took McCarthy's campaign seriously. But as the weeks passed, McCarthy made surprising gains. In the nation's first 1968 Presidential primary, held in New Hampshire in March, he won a resounding victory.

One of the outstanding developments of the McCarthy campaign was the response of the nation's youth. Thousands of young volunteers from all over the country poured into New Hampshire to work within the established political system for a candidate who had inspired them with new hope.

Political developments. The New Hampshire primary triggered a series of political developments. The first development came within a few days after McCarthy's outstanding victory, when Senator Robert F. Kennedy of New York announced that he, too, would seek the Democratic nomination for President. Senator Kennedy was an outspoken critic of President Johnson's Vietnam policy.

A second political development, one that came as a stunning surprise to the nation, was President Johnson's declaration that he would not run for re-election. "I shall not seek, and I will not accept, the nomination of my party for another term as your President," he declared at the end of a nationally televised program on March 31.

As Johnson later explained, by removing himself from the political arena he hoped to be in a much stronger position to work for a peaceful settlement of the war in Vietnam and to unite his own divided country. Even some of President Johnson's most inflexible political enemies praised his decision as an act of statesmanship.

President Johnson's withdrawal opened the door to the candidacy of Vice-President Hubert Humphrey, who soon joined McCarthy and Kennedy in the race for the Democratic nomination.

The assassination of Robert F. Kennedy. Early in April the nation mourned a fallen civil rights leader, Martin Luther King, Jr. (Chapter 44). In June the nation again went into mourning, this time for one of the leading Presidential aspirants, Robert F. Kennedy.

Senator Kennedy was cut down by an assassin's bullet only a few minutes after he learned that he had won a close victory over Senator McCarthy in the California primary. He was leaving a victory celebration in a Los Angeles hotel when the assassin fired the fatal shot.

The assassination of President John F. Kennedy, of Martin Luther King, Jr., and now of Robert F. Kennedy caused many people at home and abroad to wonder if violence was becoming characteristic of American society. In a televised speech, President Johnson rejected the suggestion that the American people as a whole were guilty of the murder. "Two hundred million Americans did not strike down Robert Kennedy," the President said. Then solemnly, he pleaded: "Let us, for God's sake, resolve to live under the law! Let us put an end to violence and to the preaching of violence."

The President's words did not, however, dispel a widespread feeling of discontent among many Americans. What, people asked, was happening to the nation? There was no easy answer. But President Johnson did appoint a commission to study the question of violence; the television networks removed several of their most violent programs from the air; and Congress finally enacted a gun-control law, despite strong opposition by forces opposed to such legislation.

■ This photograph was taken minutes before Robert F. Kennedy's assassination. He is making a victory sign to some of his campaign workers in a Los Angeles hotel. His wife stands at his right.

Gun-control legislation. The gun-control legislation made it illegal for a person to buy a handgun in a state other than his own. It also prohibited mentally incompetent persons, convicted felons, and military veterans who had received less-than-honorable discharges from owning any kind of firearms. But it did nothing to control the sale of rifles and shotguns, causing President Johnson to call it a "halfway measure."

Fallen hopes for the "Great Society." When Lyndon Johnson assumed the Presidency, he had dedicated himself to building the "Great Society" —one free from poverty, discrimination, and injustice. Working with a responsive Congress, during his first two years in office he had made substantial progress toward that goal. Then, as the Vietnam war began to absorb more and more of the administration's attention, domestic programs had inevitably suffered. The dream of a "Great Society" became marred by war abroad and unrest and violence at home.

1. Under President Johnson, Congress chalked up one of the most impressive legislative records in the nation's history. Explain.
2. With reference to the election of 1964, discuss (a) candidates and parties, (b) results for the political parties and the nation.
3. How did the Great Society follow the New Deal and Fair Deal philosophies of reform?
4. Eugene McCarthy triggered a series of political developments. (a) What were they? (b) How did they relate to Vietnam?
5. (a) How did Americans respond to the assassinations of the 1960's? (b) Has violence become characteristic of American society? Explain.

5 Nixon's plans "to bring America together"

It was a restless, disturbed nation that in August 1968 watched the Presidential nominating conventions on television. The two major political parties, reflecting the nation's uneasiness and uncertainty, met to choose their candidates.

Choosing candidates. The Republicans, meeting first, gathered at Miami Beach in Florida. Richard M. Nixon, who represented the middle ground as well as the old-line "establishment" of the Republican Party, won the Presidential nomination easily on the first ballot. He chose Spiro T. Agnew, Governor of Maryland, as his running mate. The general mood of the Republican convention was optimistic and placid. This placid mood was disturbed when a riot broke out in a ghetto area of Miami. Although quickly suppressed, the riot resulted in six deaths.

The Democratic convention, held later in Chicago, proved to be one of the most tumultuous in American history. To many millions watching on television, the convention hall appeared to be a disorderly arena in which the McCarthy and Kennedy forces were contending bitterly against the old-line Democrats represented by Humphrey. As with the Republicans in Miami, victory went to the old-line establishment. Hubert H. Humphrey, winning on the first ballot, chose Senator Edmund S. Muskie of Maine as the Vice-Presidential candidate.

The bitterness of the proceedings in the convention hall itself was reflected in the streets of the city. Indeed, Chicago seemed to be a battleground. Thousands of young people had gathered in the city to demonstrate against the Vietnam conflict and in favor of their candidate. Claiming that the demonstrations had gotten out of hand, the Chicago police moved in on the demonstrators. The violent confrontations that followed, resulting in numerous injuries but no deaths, were again witnessed by millions of television viewers.

The candidates and the issues. During the campaign neither Nixon nor Humphrey aroused marked enthusiasm among voters. Large numbers of Americans remained uncertain as to how to vote. The emergence of a third-party candidate, George C. Wallace of Alabama, founder of the American Independent Party, further complicated the situation.

The three principal issues of the campaign were violence and disorder, Vietnam, and racial strife. Public opinion polls showed that seven out of every ten Americans were convinced that "law and order had broken down in the country." Two out of every three felt that the war in Vietnam was being badly managed. The overwhelming majority of white citizens believed that the Negro revolt was going "too fast," while an equally large majority of black citizens were convinced that the movement to improve conditions was "not going fast enough."

George C. Wallace. From the beginning third-party candidate Wallace concentrated on the issue of law and order. He promised to "make the cities safe" by strengthening the police forces and by using federal troops if necessary.

On the closely related issues of poverty and racial unrest, Wallace expressed opposition to existing welfare programs, the busing of school children, and the federal enforcement of integration. He pledged, if elected, to repeal the open housing legislation, to give the police greater power to deal with demonstrations and civil disorders, and to "restore" to the states and local communities control over welfare programs and the schools.

As to Vietnam, he promised to end the war by negotiation, if possible, but if this failed, to secure military victory by means of "conventional weapons." Wallace emphasized "conventional weapons" because his Vice-Presidential running mate, General Curtis LeMay, had startled the public by saying that the nuclear bomb was "just another weapon."

Richard M. Nixon. Throughout the campaign Nixon stressed the need for new leadership. He maintained that the Democrats had brought the nation close to disaster, and that it was "time for a change." Like Wallace, he promised to restore law and order, but he added the word "justice" to his pledge. As part of his formula for combating crime and violence, he called for higher police salaries, a "major overhaul" of the prison system, and an improvement in rehabilitation programs.

Turning to the problem of poverty and the crisis of the urban ghettos, Nixon insisted that the Democratic programs involving massive federal spending had failed. He promised to review the entire welfare program and to turn over to private enterprise the primary responsibility for retraining unemployed workers and rebuilding the cities. "One of the first requirements," he said, "is the development of black-owned and black-run businesses." He proposed to finance the attack on the urban crisis more by tax incentives to private enterprise than by federal appropriations.

On the issue of Vietnam, Nixon assured the nation that he would "bring an honorable end to the war," explaining that he did not wish to interfere with the delicate peace talks going on in Paris.

Nixon was more specific, however, in his comments on military policy and national defense. Pointing to what he called a "security gap," he advocated a buildup of American nuclear capability to insure that the United States held clear "superiority" over all potential enemies. His recommendations included the development of an anti-ballistic missile system (ABM). This missile system was, he admitted, enormously expensive, but, in his view, "a necessary investment in peace."

In early 1968 the United States and the Soviet Union had agreed upon the details of a treaty limiting the further spread of nuclear weapons. President Johnson called this nonproliferation treaty "the most important international agreement in the field of disarmament since the nuclear age began." At that time Nixon had endorsed the treaty. But in the summer of 1968, when the Soviet Union sent troops into Czechoslovakia to suppress the growing spirit of liberalism in that country, Nixon qualified his earlier endorsement. He maintained that if the United States were to ratify the treaty at that time, the world might assume that the United States accepted the aggressive Soviet action.

Hubert H. Humphrey. During most of the campaign Humphrey found himself in a difficult situation. His party was badly divided. Millions of people associated the violence in Chicago with the Democrats. And, perhaps most serious of all, Humphrey was obliged to defend the unpopular administration he was serving as Vice-President; at the same time, as a Presidential candidate, he had to convince the voters that he was not committed to these policies and would provide more effective leadership.

Humphrey was convinced that force, no matter how strongly applied, would not end the unrest and violence afflicting the nation. "We can only cut crime," he declared, "by getting at its causes: slums, unemployment, run-down schools and houses. This is where crime begins and that is where it must end." Although he advocated "vigorous federal support of state and local law enforcement," he cautioned that the attack against crime "must not jeopardize hard-won liberties of our citizens."

To meet the problems of poverty and urban decay, Humphrey called for "a Marshall Plan for the cities based upon self-help, local initiative, coordinated planning, and private capital." He advocated job training by private enterprise with government support wherever necessary.

It was the issue of Vietnam that caused Humphrey the most difficulty. At the start of his campaign he continued a steadfast defense of the unpopular administration policy. Had the election been held any time during that period, Humphrey would probably have suffered a crushing defeat. But when, at the end of September, he abandoned his earlier position and advocated a halt to the bombing of North Vietnam, his prospects began to improve. They improved still further when, less than a week before election day, President Johnson announced that he had ordered a halt to all bombing north of the DMZ (Demilitarized Zone), offering hope for an earlier end to the conflict. Public opinion polls taken the weekend before the election indicated that it was a neck-and-neck race.

The election. The election was indeed a close one. Out of over 71 million popular votes cast, Nixon's margin of victory over Humphrey was only 260,000 votes. The electoral vote of 302 for Nixon, 191 for Humphrey, and 45 for Wallace did not, however, reflect this closeness.

Keenly aware of the narrow margin of his victory, President-elect Nixon pledged that the "great objective" of his administration would be to unite the country. "We want to bridge the generation gap," he declared in his victory speech. "We want to bridge the gap between the races. We want to bring America together. And I am convinced that this task is one that we can undertake and one in which we will be successful."

771

■ President Richard M. Nixon frequently spoke to the American people on television and radio to ask their support for his foreign and domestic policies. Above, he discusses a new tax bill.

The "style" of the Nixon administration. In his news conferences and television broadcasts President Nixon tried to give the impression of moderation, realism, and responsibility to the public interest even when taking an unpopular position on any given issue. In contrast, Vice President Spiro T. Agnew's rhetoric reflected a "hard line" when, for example, he denounced the major television networks for alleged "liberal" bias in news coverage, when he referred to peace demonstrators and campus radicals as "effete" and "impudent snobs," and when he charged that the President's Congressional opponents kowtowed to pressures from civil rights and labor lobbyists. Other members of the administration seemed, in their public announcements, to be trying to satisfy varied views. Thus the influential Attorney General, John Mitchell, ignored exponents of civil liberties and due process in urging Congress to curb traditional rights of the accused as a means of checking and controlling crime. On the other hand, Secretary of Health, Education, and Welfare Robert Finch seemed to speak for the less "hard line" positions of the administration in holding that education, including desegregation, health, and welfare should not be curtailed by any re-ordering of priorities. Finch's actions, however, failed to satisfy exponents of

federal support for health and welfare. Without complete success, Secretary of the Interior Walter Hickel tried to erase the impression that he favored private interests by speaking out in favor of anti-pollution measures. Hickel also surprised many of his critics by urging the administration to be sensitive to the claims and interests of restless youth. Despite these and other efforts, the Nixon administration made no marked gains in counteracting the dissatisfaction of the exponents of federal support for education, welfare, civil rights, and a speedier de-escalation of the war in Southeast Asia.

Difficulties with Congress. The Nixon administration, handicapped by not having a sympathetic majority in Congress, ran into trouble in its efforts to implement its policies. In some cases the result was inaction; in others, compromise. Thus the extension of the Voting Rights Act of 1965 did not include some of the restrictions the administration favored. In the effort to place on the Supreme Court a justice committed to the Nixon view of a strict interpretation of the Constitution, the President found himself unable to secure the needed majority vote in the Senate to confirm his nomination, first, of Judge Clement Haynsworth, Jr., and second, of Judge Harrold Carswell. Judge Haynsworth was rejected on the ground that he was committed to an anti-labor position by reason of personal investments in corporations; Judge Carswell on the grounds that he was a "racist" and mediocre in his judicial ability. Nixon's third nominee, Judge Harry Blackmun, however, met no opposition and easily won Senate confirmation.

In the matter of appropriations, the differences between the administration and Congress also led to compromises or stalemates. The President insisted on paring down federal expenditures, contending that the nation had overspent itself and that many programs were unwise and poorly administered. Critics of the administration in Congress insisted, on the other hand, that cuts in military expenditures were inadequate and must remain so as long as the war in Southeast Asia continued. At the same time, the critics charged that the cuts in spending for social welfare, education, and other domestic programs were not justified.

The problem of inflation. Among the serious challenges confronting President Nixon when he entered the White House was the growing pressure of inflation. The President refused to adopt the wage and price controls some economists insisted were necessary. The administration did, however, take several steps to bring inflation under control.

The Nixon administration continued through 1969 the 10 percent increase in the federal income tax that had been introduced in 1968. And it did succeed in squeezing several billion dollars out of what it considered the swollen national budget, although much of the saving came at the expense of pressing domestic programs. Moreover, as a further measure the Federal Reserve Board increased interest rates to their highest level in many years. This "tight money" policy made borrowing expensive and thereby reduced the amount of money and credit available to the American people.

By the end of 1969 the administration was hopeful that these measures were beginning to reduce the inflationary pressures on the economy. During the opening months of 1970, however, prices continued to rise at a disturbing rate. Compounding the problem, by summer corporate profits were 10 percent lower than in 1969, factories were operating at only 80 percent of capacity, and unemployment had risen to more than 5 percent of the working force—the highest level since 1965. Senator Mike Mansfield, Democratic majority leader in the Senate, voiced a concern widely shared throughout the nation when he warned that the economy was approaching "a crisis stage" and called for a "short-term freeze" on wages, profits, and prices.

Reforming the welfare program. For a year and a half after Nixon became President, the problems of inflation and the war in Vietnam (Chapter 42) commanded the major share of the President's attention. Preoccupation with these two issues distracted the administration and Congress from other urgent problems facing the nation. In August 1969, however, President Nixon made a bold proposal for a fundamental reform of the public welfare system. The program Nixon outlined was so sweeping in implications that it left conservatives in his own party bewildered. A spokesman for the administration called the proposal "the single most important piece of social legislation to be sent to the Congress in a generation."

The Family Assistance Program, as it was called, included three major proposals: (1) a guaranteed annual payment of $1,600 for every family of four in the nation; (2) a job-training program that would place major responsibility for planning and administration upon local communities; and (3) a requirement that able-bodied recipients (except mothers of preschool children) must accept "suitable" jobs or, if these were not available, must enter the job-training program.

Pros and cons of the Nixon proposal. Critics of the existing welfare system had often pointed out that it actually discouraged recipients from working. Any money a person on welfare managed to earn was deducted from his or her welfare payments. The Family Assistance Program, on the other hand, contained a provision that allowed recipients to earn a specified amount of money before any deductions were made from the $1,600 guaranteed annual income. It therefore provided an incentive for recipients to seek work and, hopefully, to become entirely self-supporting. This feature of the proposal was widely applauded.

There were, however, major criticisms. Some critics maintained that the proposed annual payment of $1,600 was grossly inadequate, and argued instead for a minimum guarantee of at least $3,200. Critics also opposed the work requirement. "It's open to too much abuse," one critic warned. Opponents of the proposal also objected to the fact that it was limited to families with children.

For months Congress and the public discussed the pros and cons of the Nixon Family Assistance Program. A Gallup poll taken in the spring of 1970 indicated that a large majority of the American people favored the general principle of the proposal. It remained for Congress to write the necessary legislation.

The nation's welfare program inherited by the Nixon administration had been born back in the 1930's in the days of the "New Deal." It had been extended and modified during Truman's "Fair Deal," Eisenhower's "Modern Republicanism," Kennedy's "New Frontier," and Johnson's "Great Society." Now President Nixon proposed to modify sharply the direction of the traditional program and to redirect its purpose.

SECTION SURVEY

IDENTIFY: "law and order," Family Assistance Program; Spiro T. Agnew, Edmund S. Muskie.

1. With reference to the election of 1968, discuss (a) the candidates, issues, nominating conventions, (b) the results for the political parties.
2. (a) What were the basic issues of the 1968 campaign? (b) How did each of the candidates resolve these issues? (c) How did the majority of American people seem to feel about these issues?
3. What did George Wallace and his platform as well as his showing in the election reflect?
4. Evaluate the pros and cons of Nixon's Family Assistance Program.

TRACING THE MAIN IDEAS

"I feel as though the moon and all the stars and all the planets have fallen on me," Harry S. Truman said to reporters when on April 12, 1945, he learned that President Franklin D. Roosevelt had died. In the following decades four other Presidents —Eisenhower, Kennedy, Johnson, and Nixon— each in his own way revealed his awareness of the awesome responsibilities he carried as Chief Executive of the United States and leader of the free world.

In 1945 the immediate problem facing the nation was that of converting from a wartime to a peacetime economy. Americans met this problem squarely, made the necessary postwar adjustments, and entered a period of rising prosperity that continued into the 1970's. Over the years many of the nation's domestic programs evolved during President Roosevelt's "New Deal" were expanded—in the "Fair Deal" by Truman, "Modern Republicanism" by Eisenhower, the "New Frontier" by Kennedy, the "Great Society" by Johnson, and the new social legislation outlined by Nixon.

But prosperity and legislation designed to advance the general welfare were only part of a larger story. Both on the domestic front and on the international stage, Americans were confronted with the challenge of unsolved problems of the utmost complexity. Indeed, in an increasingly interdependent world, domestic affairs and foreign policies could no longer be considered separately, for the strength and well-being of the American people depended more and more upon the strength and well-being of others. America's allies and friends depended upon the United States for military aid and economic and technical assistance. The anti-Communist world and the uncommitted nations expected the American people to exercise moral leadership befitting their enormous military and economic power. In the next chapter you will learn how the United States met this difficult challenge.

CHAPTER SURVEY

QUESTIONS FOR DISCUSSION

1. The Eisenhower administration did not attempt to undo the social and economic changes that came about during the New Deal and Fair Deal eras. Do you agree or disagree? Explain.
2. What in your opinion were President Kennedy's most important contributions to our national life? Explain.
3. Compare the Johnson and Nixon administrations with regard to their (a) policy in Southeast Asia, (b) social welfare programs.
4. Does a President have the responsibility to lead or follow the majority view? Explain.
5. Compare the demobilization and reconversion problems at the end of World Wars I and II. Explain which of these postwar periods provided the more difficult task.
6. Why did the Taft-Hartley Act of 1947 and the Labor-Management Reporting and Disclosure Act of 1959 prove to be highly controversial?
7. Both the Truman and Eisenhower administrations were confronted with the problem of protecting the country against subversion without, at the same time, denying Americans their constitutional rights to freedom of criticism and association. Did they succeed in this objective? Support your opinion.

8. The election of 1960 has been described as one of the most important in American history. Discuss.

RELATING PAST TO PRESENT

1. Give evidence to show that during recent years the federal government has tried to balance the powers of labor and management by means of various laws.
2. President Nixon's Family Assistance Program includes a provision for a guaranteed minimum annual income. In your opinion, is this provision a wholly new idea in social legislation or is it related to programs begun during the New Deal era? Explain your answer.

USING MAPS AND CHARTS

1. Basing your answer on the Chronology of Events, pages 888–90, answer the following: Compare the records of Truman, Eisenhower, Kennedy, Johnson, and Nixon with reference to domestic affairs, and indicate which one, in your opinion, has the most impressive achievements.
2. Using the maps on pages 852–53, 864–65, and 870–71, locate Appalachia and discuss the reasons for the depressed economic conditions in that area.

THE END OF the war in 1945 brought nothing comparable to the delirious celebrations that had followed Allied victory in World War I. There was rejoicing, to be sure, in all the victorious countries, but the joy and gaiety were restrained, for the dominant feeling was one of immense relief.

The mood of the American people was summarized by the reporter who wrote that in his city "everybody talked of the 'end of the war,' not of 'victory.'"

It was all so different from 1918. In 1918 Americans had been content to let the world take care of itself. In 1945 they felt they knew better. Senator Arthur H. Vandenberg of Michigan, who through the 1930's had been one of the leading isolationists in Congress, spoke for millions of Americans when in London in 1944 during a German rocket attack he turned to a friend. "How can there be immunity or isolation," he asked, "when man can devise weapons like that?"

Later, in the Senate, Senator Vandenberg renounced his isolationism and came out in favor of American cooperation in the building of a new world order. "I want a new dignity and a new authority for international law," he announced; "I think American self-interest requires it."

In 1945 the American people were rapidly becoming aware that, like it or not, the United States was destined to play a new role on the world stage. But not even the most farsighted among them could foresee the heavy burden of responsibility they would have to carry in the troubled years ahead.

THE CHAPTER IN OUTLINE

1. The role of the United States in organizing the United Nations.

2. "Cold War" between the United States and the U.S.S.R. in Europe.

3. "Hot War" in Asia as a result of Communist aggression.

4. Continuing American efforts to meet the Communist challenge.

5. The development of American policies to deal with world crises.

■ The formal ceremonies of the Japanese surrender, 1945

CHAPTER 41

The Challenges of World Leadership

1945 – 1960

1450   1750   1800   1850   1900   1950   1975

1 The role of the United States in organizing the United Nations

Even before World War II ended, many world statesmen were soberly considering ways to build an enduring peace. American statesmen were among the leaders in this effort.

Roots of the United Nations. As early as January 1, 1942, the Allies—or United Nations, as they called themselves—promised to fight as a team for the defeat of Italy, Germany, and Japan (page 732). Many Allied leaders—among them Roosevelt, Churchill, and Stalin—agreed that it would be wise to convert the wartime alliance into a permanent organization for peace.

Many Americans shared this point of view. Members of both political parties pledged their support to an international organization of nations. Democrats and Republicans alike agreed to abandon isolationism and to cooperate in a bipartisan, or nonpolitical, program of international cooperation.

Conference at Dumbarton Oaks. Encouraged by enthusiastic American support, delegates from the United States, Great Britain, the U.S.S.R., and China met in 1944 at Dumbarton Oaks, an estate in Washington, D.C., to prepare a plan for a postwar United Nations organization. On most questions of procedure the delegates quickly reached agreement. Some problems, however, were more difficult to solve.

What, for instance, should they do about the demand of Soviet Ambassador Andrei Gromyko (gro·MEE·ko) that the U.S.S.R. be represented in the United Nations not by one delegation but by 16—one for each of the 16 Soviet Republics? And what should they do about the thorny problem of the voting procedure in the Security Council, the body in which the great powers would hold permanent seats and which was to be mainly charged with keeping peace in the world?

Agreements at Yalta. Meeting at Yalta early in February 1945 (page 742), Roosevelt, Churchill, and Stalin reached agreements on several of the issues that had deadlocked the Dumbarton Oaks Conference. They agreed that two of the Soviet Union's 16 republics would be admitted to the United Nations under the fiction that they were independent nations. The leaders also worked out a compromise proposal on voting procedure in the Security Council and agreed to support this proposal when the United Nations Charter, or constitution, was drafted. Finally, they agreed to call a United Nations Conference in San Francisco on April 25, 1945, to draw up the Charter of a permanent organization.

The San Francisco Conference. Delegates from 50 nations, representing three fourths of the peoples of the earth, took part in the San Francisco Conference. Despite differences in language, dress, religious ideas, and modes of living, the delegates were all working for one objective—the formation of a world peace organization.

At first the delegates disagreed sharply on certain issues. However, the controversies were quickly settled by compromise, and in the surprisingly short time of eight weeks the Dumbarton Oaks and the Yalta proposals had been reshaped into the United Nations Charter.

The United States Senate voted to join the new world organization, and on August 9, 1945—three days after the bombing of Hiroshima—President

■ The General Assembly of the United Nations serves as the "town meeting" of the world. In the photograph below, President Nixon is addressing the General Assembly on the Vietnam conflict.

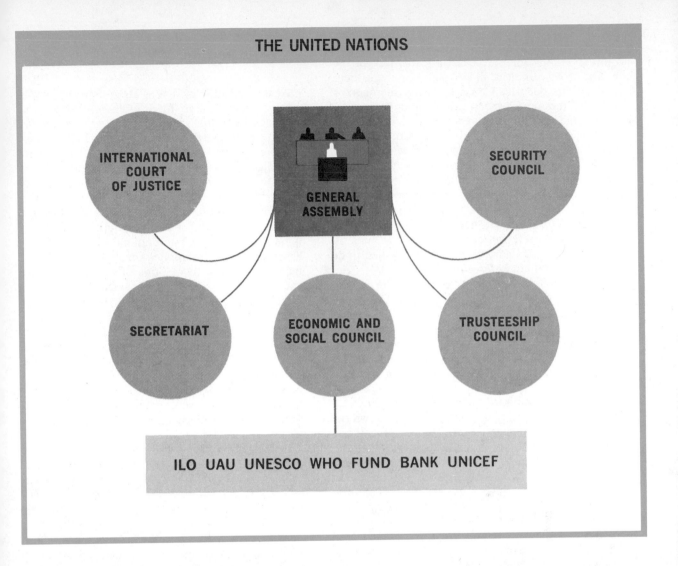

THE UNITED NATIONS

INTERNATIONAL COURT OF JUSTICE

GENERAL ASSEMBLY

SECURITY COUNCIL

SECRETARIAT

ECONOMIC AND SOCIAL COUNCIL

TRUSTEESHIP COUNCIL

ILO UAU UNESCO WHO FUND BANK UNICEF

Truman signed the Charter. On October 24—now celebrated as United Nations Day—the United Nations (UN) came into existence, its charter having been ratified by the required number of countries.

Purposes and organization. The purposes of the UN are clearly stated in the Preamble to the Charter: "We the peoples of the United Nations, determined to save succeeding generations from the scourge of war . . . to promote social progress and better standards of life in larger freedom . . . have resolved to combine our efforts to accomplish these aims. . . ."

In general, the UN seeks to maintain peace, to provide security, to promote justice, to increase the general welfare, and to establish human rights. Six major organs and many related agencies were created by the UN in order to carry on its work.

(1) The Security Council was to be the police authority of the world, charged with preventing war. It was to consist of 11 members.° Five of these, the so-called "Big Five" powers—the United States, China, France, the Soviet Union, and Great Britain—were to hold permanent seats. The six nonpermanent members were to be elected for two-year terms. The Security Council was to meet in continuous session, and to be ready to go into action at a moment's notice. It was to have at its command an international military force to check aggression. But on matters of peace and security any one of the five permanent members could prevent all action by a single negative vote, or veto.

(2) The General Assembly was to be the "town

° It later was increased to 15 members—the five permanent members, plus ten nonpermanent members.

meeting" of the world, in which all UN members were to be equally represented. It was to make recommendations for the peaceful settlement of disputes. It was to elect all the nonpermanent members of the Security Council, certain members of the Trusteeship Council, and all members of the Economic and Social Council.

(3) The Economic and Social Council, composed of 18 members (now 27), was to study world economic, social, cultural, and health problems, and to make recommendations to the General Assembly or to individual member countries.

(4) The International Court of Justice, modeled after the World Court (page 652), was to decide legal disputes referred to it by disputing nations. It was to give advisory opinions when asked to do so, but it could not enforce its decisions.

(5) The Secretariat was to handle the administrative work of the UN.

(6) The Trusteeship Council was to look after the welfare of peoples living in colonial areas.

Early years of the UN. Early critics of the UN insisted that it was doomed to fail because the member nations had not given up any of their national sovereignty. Other people, however, shared the opinion expressed by President Truman in 1945. "This Charter," he stated, "points down the only road to enduring peace. There is no other."

As crises broke out in many parts of the world, Truman's statement took on new meaning. By 1948 the world situation had become so tense that Trygve Lie (TRIG·vuh LEE), the first Secretary-General of the UN, issued a pointed warning. "The trouble," he declared, "lies in the intense conflict over the settlement of the last war between East and West, and, especially, between the two most powerful single nations in the world today—the United States and the Soviet Union."

SECTION SURVEY

IDENTIFY: Dumbarton Oaks Conference, San Francisco Conference, "Big Five"; Andrei Gromyko, Trygve Lie.

1. (a) What major problems had to be solved before a United Nations organization could be created? (b) Which of these conflicts were settled at the Yalta Conference?
2. Describe the purposes of the United Nations.
3. Indicate the chief functions of the Security Council and the General Assembly.
4. "The United Nations is not a world government." Explain.

778

2 "Cold War" between the United States and the U.S.S.R. in Europe

At the end of World War II, millions of people suffered from lack of food, clothing, shelter, and medical attention. The United States responded generously to the desperate need for help.

America's new role in the world. During and immediately after the war, the United States played an active role in creating three important UN agencies: (1) the United Nations Relief and Rehabilitation Administration (UNRRA), (2) the International Bank for Reconstruction and Development, and (3) the International Monetary Fund. These UN agencies supplied food, clothing, shelter, and medical care to millions of needy persons in war-damaged nations and provided money to rebuild ruined industries. A large part of the money for these activities came from the United States.

After the war ended, American dollars and supplies flowed directly to the war-devastated areas. Major contributions came from private American organizations—churches, schools, fraternal societies, and civic associations. An even larger contribution came from the United States government —in the form of supplies, equipment, loans, and the assistance of specialists and experts.

In their foreign aid programs Americans were motivated by generosity, self-interest, and considerations of military strategy. Many Americans believed that it was their duty to share their products and technical skills with others less fortunate. An increasing number began to feel that America's high standard of living could be maintained only if other nations were also in a position to buy and to sell. And many Americans, including leaders of both major political parties, had learned from World War II the value of controlling strategic areas of the earth as military bases and as sources of vital raw materials.

Expanding Soviet influence. America's new role of world leadership brought it into conflict with the Soviet Union, which also emerged from the war as a major power. The postwar policies of the Soviet Union represented, at least in part, a continuation of the expansionist ambitions of tsarist Russia. But now the U.S.S.R. regarded itself as the leader of a Communist revolution destined to replace the "capitalist" and "imperialist" world— a world in which the United States was the principal power.

Thus, even before the war ended, the Soviets

began to move aggressively against their weaker neighbors, whom they regarded as "ripe" for a Communist revolution. Moscow-trained Communists were at work in nearly every country. Their aim was to hasten the revolutions which, from the Communist point of view, were the only means of freeing the "workers of the world" from "capitalist and imperialist domination."

In 1940 Latvia, Lithuania, and Estonia—countries to which the Russians had some historical claims—were incorporated into the Soviet Union. As a consequence of World War II, the U.S.S.R. also acquired large parts of Poland and Rumania. Through Communist governments which they helped to set up, the Soviets by 1948 had secured control of the "free" governments of Poland, Rumania, Hungary, Czechoslovakia, and the eastern part of Germany (see map, page 790). Moreover, Soviet influence reached beyond Eastern Europe into the Mediterranean. Moscow-trained Communists were especially active in Greece and Italy.

The U.S.S.R. was deeply entrenched in the Far East, as well as in Europe. As a result of the Yalta agreements (page 790) and because of Russia's last-minute entry into the war against Japan, the Soviet Union secured control of large areas that had been Chinese and Japanese territory.

Mounting tension. The Communist leaders defended their actions on the ground of self-defense. They pointed out that during the Bolshevik Revolution the Allies, including the United States, had sent troops into northern Russia and Russian Siberia. They feared, they said, that the United States would lead the "capitalist nations" in a new attack against the U.S.S.R. They claimed that, to defend themselves against such an attack, they were required to maintain powerful military forces and to control bordering countries from which an attack could be launched.

The United States, on the other hand, objected bitterly to the Soviet Union's domination of its weaker neighbors. The United States, which had demobilized most of its own troops, resented the Soviet policy of maintaining huge military forces. Moreover, Americans loathed the ruthless methods used by the Communists to crush all opposition. Most Americans regarded the Soviet Union as the world's newest aggressor. Americans were convinced that Communism was the mortal enemy of democracy and human rights.

As friction increased, the Soviet press and radio, rigidly controlled by the government, became increasingly anti-American. The Soviet government

■ At the end of World War II, millions of people suffered from lack of food, clothing, shelter, and medical attention. Above, a Belgian mother and her three children walk through their home town after the Germans had bombed it.

779

refused to join the United Nations Educational, Scientific, and Cultural Organization (UNESCO), which had been established to promote understanding among the peoples of the world. It permitted very few Americans to visit the U.S.S.R. or its "satellite" nations—those nations dominated by the U.S.S.R. As time passed many Americans began to wonder why the Soviets were hiding their activities behind an "iron curtain."

Deadlock over atomic energy. Inability to reach agreement on international control of the atomic bomb greatly added to the mounting tension. Early in 1946, acting on American initiative, the UN created an Atomic Energy Commission. On June 14, 1946, at the Commission's first meeting, the United States representative, Bernard M. Baruch (buh·ROOK), presented America's proposal for international control. "Let us not deceive ourselves," Baruch said, "We must elect world peace or world destruction. . . ."

Baruch proposed that complete control of atomic energy be turned over to an international agency responsible to the UN. This agency would have full authority to enter any country to inspect atomic energy installations. The United States—at that time the only nation that had atomic bombs—was ready, Baruch announced, to give up its secrets to the new world authority. But, he warned, the United States would not reveal any secrets until the UN provided for "immediate, swift, and sure punishment for those who violate the agreements that are reached by the nations." Baruch insisted that each of the "Big Five" on the Security Council give up its right to the veto on all matters involving atomic energy.

When the United States proposal reached the Security Council, the Soviet Union killed it by a veto.

The Soviet Union then advanced a counterproposal. It opposed any system of international inspection and control. Instead, it insisted that the United States destroy its atomic bombs, that the UN declare atomic warfare illegal, and that all nations promise not to manufacture atomic bombs. But the Soviet Union flatly refused to abandon the veto right in the Security Council. This meant that if any nation, including the U.S.S.R., violated its promise not to make atomic bombs, the Soviet Union or any permanent Security Council member could block all UN action by a single veto.

As months passed and the UN failed to find an acceptable compromise, more people began to ~~~ree with an American official who declared,

"Apparently the rulers of the Soviet Union do not desire—perhaps do not dare—to raise the iron curtain at this time."

The Truman Doctrine. Faced with the menace of Communist aggression, the United States began to formulate a policy of "containment." This policy aimed to "contain," or restrict, Soviet expansion and to check the spread of Communism. The new policy was first applied to Greece and Turkey.

In 1947 Greek Communists, supported by the Soviets, were about to seize control of the Greek government. At the same time the Soviet Union was trying to force Turkey to give up control of the Dardanelles, the strait between European and Asiatic Turkey. Soviet control of Greece and of the Dardanelles would enable the U.S.S.R. to dominate the northeastern Mediterranean and the Suez Canal.

This situation prompted President Truman on March 12, 1947, to announce the "Truman Doctrine." This doctrine stated that the United States must "help free people to maintain their free institutions and their national integrity." He then asked Congress for authority to help the Greeks and Turks to strengthen their armed forces and to check the spread of Communism. Congress responded with an initial appropriation of $400 million.

The Marshall Plan. Aid to Greece and Turkey, however, was not enough to prevent the spread of Communism. All of war-torn Europe was in economic difficulty, and Communists were winning converts among hungry, disillusioned people.

Early in June 1947 Secretary of State George C. Marshall suggested a solution to Europe's economic problems. The "Marshall Plan," as his program came to be called, proposed to help European countries in self-efforts to get their farms, factories, and transportation systems operating efficiently again. The United States would provide money, supplies, and machinery to any nation, including the Soviet Union and its satellites, that agreed to cooperate in the program.

The Marshall Plan provoked heated Congressional debate. Those who favored the proposal insisted that the best way to block Communism and strengthen America's own economic system was to restore Europe's economic health. Opponents declared that the United States could not afford to "carry Europe on its back." In the spring of 1948, however, Congress overcame opposition and approved the Marshall Plan, officially known as the European Recovery Program.

Despite the opposition of the Soviet Union and

its satellites, all of whom denounced the plan as "Yankee imperialism," the Marshall Plan was an outstanding success. Slowly but steadily Europe began to recover from the war.

The Berlin airlift. Meanwhile tension mounted in Germany. In 1945 the great powers had agreed to a joint occupation of Germany. Great Britain, France, and the United States occupied western and southern Germany, and the Soviet Union occupied eastern Germany. Berlin, within the Soviet-controlled zone, was also divided into four sections, each controlled by one of the four powers.

On June 24, 1948, the Soviets suddenly blocked all roads, canals, and railways connecting Berlin and the Western Zone of Germany. By this move they apparently hoped to force the three Western powers out of Berlin.

The British-American answer to the Soviet challenge was the Berlin airlift. Starting in the summer of 1948 and continuing for nearly a year, British and American planes transported more than 2 million tons of food and supplies, including coal, to Berlin. This crisis in East-West relations was finally resolved in 1949 with the aid of the UN.

North Atlantic Treaty Organization. The Soviet blockade of Berlin and Communist efforts to wreck the Marshall Plan aroused growing alarm in Western Europe. In April 1949 nine Western European nations,° determined to meet the Soviet threat, joined the United States, Canada, and Iceland in an alliance known as the North Atlantic Treaty Organization (NATO).

In the Atlantic Pact—the treaty proposing such an alliance—each member nation agreed that "... an armed attack against one or more of them in Europe or North America shall be considered an attack against them all. . . ." They also agreed to resist such an attack with armed force, if necessary.

Since the Atlantic Pact was a treaty, it had to be approved by the United States Senate. The chief issue of Senate debate was whether or not the Atlantic Pact would compel the United States to go to war to assist another country without an act of Congress. This, as you recall, was the main issue that had kept the United States out of the League of Nations in 1919. However, in July 1949 the Senate did ratify the agreement. Eventually General Eisenhower was appointed Supreme Commander of the NATO forces.

Thus, by the end of 1949 an American policy of "containment" had begun to take shape, at least in regard to Europe. NATO strengthened the military defenses of Western Europe. The Marshall Plan strengthened its economic structure, thus eliminating much of the discontent that had so often led people into Communism.

Meanwhile, however, trouble was brewing in the Middle East and in Asia.

° Great Britain, France, Belgium, the Netherlands, Luxembourg, Italy, Denmark, Norway, and Portugal. West Germany, Turkey, and Greece joined later (see map, pages 790-91).

LIVING AMERICAN DOCUMENTS

Marshall Plan (1947)

It is logical that the United States should do whatever it is able to do to assist in the return of normal economic health in the world, without which there can be no political stability and no assured peace.

Our policy is directed not against any country or doctrine but against hunger, poverty, desperation, and chaos. Its purpose should be the revival of a working economy in the world so as to permit the emergence of political and social conditions in which free institutions can exist. . . .

Any government that is willing to assist in the task of recovery will find full cooperation, I am sure, on the part of the United States government. Any government which maneuvers to block the recovery of other countries cannot expect help from us. Furthermore, governments, political parties, or groups which seek to perpetuate human misery in order to profit therefrom, politically or otherwise, will encounter the opposition of the United States. . . .

SECTION SURVEY

IDENTIFY: UNESCO, satellite nations, iron curtain, containment; Bernard Baruch, George C. Marshall.

1. Explain America's new role in the postwar world in regard to (a) foreign aid, (b) the Soviet Union.
2. (a) Why did the Soviet Union expand its influence during the postwar period? (b) How did the Soviets justify their actions?
3. (a) Compare the Soviet and the American plans for control of atomic energy. (b) Why did the plans end in deadlock?
4. How did each of the following help to "contain" Communism: (a) Truman Doctrine, (b) Marshall Plan, (c) Berlin airlift, (d) NATO?

781

3 "Hot War" in Asia as a result of Communist aggression

Postwar troubles were not confined to Europe. During President Truman's administration they seriously threatened peace in the Middle East and Asia.

Tensions in the Middle East.   Iran soon became a trouble spot. During World War II both American and Soviet troops were stationed in Iran. After the war the United States pulled out its troops, but the Soviets, eager to control the oil-rich land adjoining their borders, did not. Tension mounted. Finally, after the UN intervened in 1946, the Soviets withdrew their military forces.

Meanwhile shadows were gathering over Palestine on the eastern Mediterranean. Since the end of World War I Great Britain had ruled Palestine under a mandate from the League of Nations. On May 14, 1948, when Great Britain voluntarily gave up this mandate, the Jews in Palestine proclaimed the independence of the new state of Israel. This action plunged Israel into war with the neighboring

■ A UN mission under the leadership of an American, Dr. Ralph J. Bunche, arranged an armistice ending the Palestinian War. Below, Dr. Bunche (right) receives the Nobel peace prize for his efforts.

Arab countries of Egypt, Transjordan (later renamed Jordan), Lebanon, Syria, Iraq, and Saudi Arabia. The UN at once took steps to end the fighting. Finally a UN mission under the leadership of an American, Dr. Ralph J. Bunche, managed to get both sides to agree to an armistice. As a result of his energetic services Dr. Bunche received the Nobel peace prize.

Communist victory in China.   While an uneasy peace was being restored in the Middle East, Chinese Communists, backed by their Soviet allies, were rapidly winning control of China. The struggle for control of China began long before World War II.

In 1927, four years before the Japanese moved into Manchuria (page 791), Chiang Kai-shek, leader of the Chinese Nationalist forces, opened war on the Chinese Communists. For a time China was torn by civil conflict. But after Japan attacked China, both of the opposing Chinese factions fought against Japanese troops. During World War II the United States encouraged such cooperation. Chinese troops, for the most part poorly armed, heroically resisted the invading armies of Japan. In 1945, in recognition of its valiant efforts, China was admitted to the United Nations as one of the "Big Five."

But China's troubles were not over. With the end of World War II the struggle between Chiang's Nationalist forces and the Chinese Communists for control of China once again erupted in armed conflict. The Soviet Union supported and supplied the Chinese Communists, led by Mao Tse-tung (MAU DZUH-DOONG). The United States provided military and other assistance to Chiang's Nationalist movement. American military authorities differed on what would best serve United States interests. General Albert C. Wedemeyer felt that American military support was both belated and insufficient. General George C. Marshall, on the other hand, believed that Chiang's regime could not be sufficiently strengthened to warrant further American support in his struggle against the Communists. The Truman administration followed Marshall's advice and withdrew military support.

By 1949 the Communists had conquered most of China. Completely defeated on the mainland, Chiang and his Nationalist government, together with a small army, retreated to the island of Formosa, or Taiwan (see map, page 791).

The United States continued to recognize the Nationalists as the legal government of China, and the Nationalists continued to represent China in the

UN Security Council.° Nevertheless, the Communist victory was a major triumph for the U.S.S.R. and a disaster for the United States and its allies.

The division of Korea. Meanwhile, trouble was brewing in Korea. Between 1910 and 1945 the Koreans had been ruled by Japan. During the closing days of World War II, however, Soviet and American troops swept the Japanese out of Korea. After the war General Douglas MacArthur was appointed Supreme Commander of the Allied Powers, and placed in charge of the occupation forces in Japan.° His responsibilities also included the southern portion of Korea.

At the end of the war, a line drawn across the Korean peninsula at the 38th parallel (see map, this page) separated American occupation forces in the south from Soviet occupation forces in the north. Americans and most other peoples considered this to be a temporary arrangement.

But despite UN efforts to unite the country, Korea remained divided, and Soviet and American troops were not withdrawn. Then in 1948 North Korea and South Korea set up separate governments, both claiming authority to rule the entire country. The North Korean government, controlled by Communists and supported by the Soviets, called itself the "People's Republic." The South Korean government, of which Syngman Rhee (SING·man REE) had been chosen president in an election sponsored by the UN, called itself the "Republic of Korea" (ROK). The United States and 30 UN members (but not the Soviet Union) recognized the Republic of Korea as the lawful government.

Finally the United States and the Soviet Union withdrew their troops. Each left behind the Korean army that it had helped to train—two armies now facing each other across the 38th parallel. Now and then the North Koreans sent raiding parties across the border into South Korea.

The Korean challenge. On June 25, 1950, the North Korean army suddenly launched a full-scale invasion of South Korea. In an emergency session the UN Security Council adopted a resolution branding the invasion as an "armed attack" and ordering an immediate cease-fire. The Soviet delegate, Jacob A. Malik, did not attend this meeting. Six months earlier the Soviet Union, angered by

° The People's Republic of China replaced Nationalist China on the Security Council in 1972.

° During the occupation period relations between Japan and the Western powers were restored to a friendly basis. In 1951 Japan received independence in a treaty signed at San Francisco.

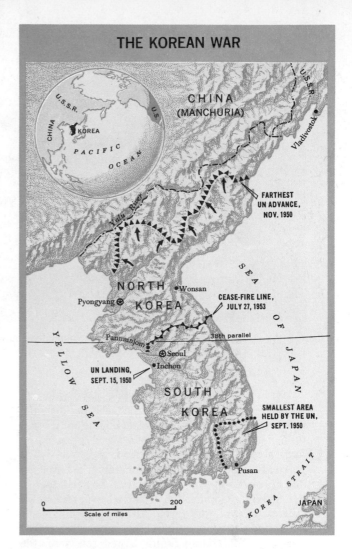

THE KOREAN WAR

FARTHEST UN ADVANCE, NOV. 1950

CEASE-FIRE LINE, JULY 27, 1953

UN LANDING, SEPT. 15, 1950

SMALLEST AREA HELD BY THE UN, SEPT. 1950

CHINA (MANCHURIA)

U.S.S.R.

Vladivostok

Yalu River

NORTH KOREA

Wonsan

Pyongyang

Panmunjom

38th parallel

Seoul

Inchon

SOUTH KOREA

Pusan

YELLOW SEA

SEA OF JAPAN

KOREA STRAIT

JAPAN

PACIFIC OCEAN

U.S.S.R.

CHINA

KOREA

U.S.

0   200
Scale of miles

the Security Council's refusal to admit a delegate from Communist China, had recalled Malik to the Soviet Union. Not even the Korean crisis could make the Soviets change their minds. Had Malik been present, he could have used his veto power to block all UN action. His absence enabled the UN to act vigorously.

Answering the challenge. Meanwhile President Truman was busy conferring with the heads of the State and Defense Departments. On Tuesday, June 27, 1950, the big news broke: The President had pledged American arms to Korea's defense. That same evening the Security Council adopted a second resolution in which it used the term "aggressor" to describe North Korea and called upon UN members to furnish all possible assistance to the South Koreans.

■ General Douglas MacArthur commanded South Korean and UN troops during the Korean War. He is shown above (seated next to the driver of the jeep) inspecting UN positions along the front line.

By Friday, June 30, 1950, six days after the North Koreans had crossed the 38th parallel, the UN was firmly committed to action. For the first time in history the members of a world organization had dared to challenge aggression.

The Korean War. Unfortunately, the UN itself had no troops to throw into action. Soviet vetoes in the Security Council had blocked every effort to create a UN military force. Although 19 UN members finally contributed assistance, the major burden of defending South Korea fell upon the United States.

In response to the UN's call, President Truman ordered the United States Seventh Fleet to prevent any attack upon Formosa and to blockade the Korean coast. Truman also ordered United States air and ground forces into Korea.

For a time it looked as though the North Koreans would overrun all of Korea. The South Koreans were hopelessly outnumbered. Neither they nor the first American troops rushed to the scene had the equipment to stand up against the heavily armored, Soviet-made tanks of the North Korean army. By early August the South Korean and UN troops under General MacArthur were desperately defending a small area around Pusan in southeast Korea (see map, page 783).

Then the tide suddenly turned. On September 15, 1950, General MacArthur staged an amphibious attack against Inchon and then swept eastward, recapturing Seoul (SOHL), the capital of South Korea. At the same time a strongly reinforced UN army, now well equipped and powerfully supported from the air, launched a counteroffensive from southeastern Korea. The North Korean forces, caught in a huge trap, began to break up. Thousands surrendered. The rest fled northward across the 38th parallel, with MacArthur's troops in hot pursuit. By November advance units of the UN forces were at the Yalu River, the boundary between North Korea and Communist China. MacArthur was convinced the war would end soon.

Then suddenly the tide turned again. Late in November hundreds of thousands of Chinese Communist "volunteers" swarmed across the Yalu River to reinforce the North Korean troops. In a conference at Wake Island on October 15, General MacArthur had assured President Truman that the Chinese Communists would not enter the war, and that if they did, the UN forces could handle them. But now UN troops, their lines extended, were outnumbered in many cases by hundreds to one. Finally, after weeks of the most desperate fighting, MacArthur's forces managed to stabilize their defense line near the 38th parallel.

The "Great Debate." The entry of Chinese Communist troops—"volunteers" or otherwise—completely changed the nature of the war. The UN now faced a problem of the utmost gravity. Should it heed MacArthur's request and allow him to blockade the China coast, bomb the Chinese mainland, and help Chiang Kai-shek's Nationalist forces launch an invasion of China?

MacArthur's proposal provoked heated debate. MacArthur's supporters argued that quick, decisive action would bring a speedy end to the Korean conflict. Those who disagreed argued that an attack upon Communist China might bring the U.S.S.R. openly to the aid of its Communist ally and thus start another world war.

MacArthur's opponents also pointed to another danger. If the United States committed its military forces to a major war in Asia, the Soviet Union would be free to do as it pleased in Europe. As summed up by General Omar Bradley, Chairman of the Joint Chiefs of Staff, an attack upon Communist China "would involve us in the wrong war, at the wrong place, at the wrong time, and with the wrong enemy."

Stalemate in Korea. By January 1951 President Truman had reached his decision. He ordered General MacArthur to establish the strongest possible defense line near the 38th parallel, but forbade a blockade of the China coast, the bombing of China, and the use of Chiang's troops to invade China. The war in Korea was to remain strictly a "police action" intended only to protect South Korea.

In 1951, therefore, the Korean War reached a stalemate. The North Koreans and the Chinese Communist "volunteers" from time to time hurled themselves against the UN defenses, only to be killed by the thousands. UN planes continued to bomb and strafe North Korean lines of communication as far as the Yalu River. And UN troops, mostly Americans, continued to fight—and to die —in a war for which there seemed to be no solution.

Meanwhile General MacArthur, refusing to accept Truman's decision as final, tried to carry his case over the President's head to prominent Congressmen. In April 1951 President Truman relieved MacArthur of his command. "I could do nothing else and still be President," Truman explained. General Matthew B. Ridgeway replaced MacArthur as Commander of the UN forces.

American policy and "Point Four." During 1951 and 1952, while the UN worked for peace in Korea, the United States continued the rapid buildup of its land, sea, and air forces. The military buildup, however, was only part of America's response to the challenge of Communism. Through economic aid and technical assistance, the United States assumed a major responsibility for helping less fortunate areas of the world to raise their standards of living. The Marshall Plan was intended primarily for Europe. A new plan, the "Point Four" program, was aimed at underdeveloped areas anywhere in the world.

President Truman first announced the Point Four program in January 1949. "The United States," he said, "is embarking on a bold new program for making the benefits of our scientific advances and industrial progress available for the improvement and growth of underdeveloped areas." To be sure, private business as well as the government had been assisting underdeveloped countries for many years. The "bold new" part of the program consisted of bringing the many scattered activities into a carefully planned, coordinated program. As the President warned, the United States would have to carry the major financial burden of the Point Four program. But, he promised, much of the work would be conducted by and through the UN.

The Point Four program got off to a slow start. But the Korean War convinced even the most hesitant Americans that the world was facing a grave crisis. By 1952 most Americans were persuaded that United States policy should include provision for foreign aid and the strengthening of military defenses throughout the free world. However, the question of how much aid and to whom it should be granted remained a subject for debate, for the so-called "free world" included uncommitted nations and dictatorships as well as democracies.

SECTION SURVEY

IDENTIFY: Chinese Nationalists, 38th parallel, police action; Ralph Bunche, Mao Tse-tung, Syngman Rhee, Douglas MacArthur.

1. Describe the postwar events that created tension in (a) the Middle East, (b) the Far East.
2. (a) How did the United States answer the challenge of the Korean situation? (b) Did the President take upon himself powers not stated in the Constitution? Explain.
3. What issues provoked the "Great Debate" during the Korean War?
4. What made the Point Four program unique?

4 Continuing American efforts to meet the Communist challenge

In 1953 when President Eisenhower took office, he and his Secretary of State, John Foster Dulles, continued the bipartisanship in foreign affairs that had been followed by the Democrats since America's entry into World War II.

Ending the Korean War. During the 1952 election campaign Eisenhower had promised to do everything within his power to end the Korean War. In December 1952 he visited the battle area for talks with political and military leaders. Peace talks were being carried on at this time in Panmunjom (PAN·MUHN·JUM) in Korea (see map, page 783). These talks had dragged on and on.

On March 5, 1953, only a few weeks after Eisenhower took office, Joseph Stalin died. The new leaders of the Soviet Union seemed to be more conciliatory, and the North Korean Communists were now willing to negotiate. Finally, on July 27, 1953, representatives of North Korea and the UN signed an armistice agreement. This agreement recognized the division of Korea into two countries—North Korea (Communist) and the Republic of South Korea.

In a formal treaty the United States promised to defend South Korea against attack. The United States also undertook to help the South Koreans improve their economic and social conditions.

Crisis in Indo-China. Only a few months after the Korean armistice, world peace was threatened by another crisis in the Far East. Ever since the end of World War II, Indo-China, a French colony, had been torn by armed conflict. The Vietminh (VYET·meen), a Communist group, had been fighting to win control of the entire country from the French and their loyal, anti-Communist Vietnamese allies. When it became clear that Communist China was actively aiding the Vietminh, the United States began to send military equipment to the Vietnamese and French armies.

Early in 1954 the Vietminh, supported by the Chinese, launched a powerful drive against the French and their Vietnamese supporters. On May 7, 1954, the key French fortress of Dienbienphu (dyen·byen·FOO) (see map, page 801) fell to the Communists.

In July a meeting was held in Geneva, Switzerland, to discuss Indo-China's fate. Representatives from France, Indo-China, Communist China, the Soviet Union, and Great Britain agreed to divide Indo-China into three nations—Laos, Cambodia, and Vietnam. The area of Vietnam north of the 17th parallel became the Communist state of Vietminh, later North Vietnam; the portion of Vietnam south of that line became South Vietnam (see map, page 801).

Organization of SEATO. With an uneasy peace established in Southeast Asia, the Southeast Asia Treaty Organization (SEATO) came into being on September 8, 1954, at a conference in Manila. Among the nations that were members of SEATO were the United States, Great Britain, France, Australia, New Zealand, Pakistan, Thailand, and the Philippines.

SEATO was much weaker than its European counterpart, NATO. For one thing, such important Asian countries as India, Burma, Ceylon, and Indonesia refused to join. Moreover, unlike NATO, SEATO did not provide for an armed force to resist aggression. The members of SEATO agreed, however, to consider an attack upon any of their number as a threat to the peace and safety of all the others. They also pledged to resist attacks on Laos, Cambodia, and South Vietnam.

Strengthening Western Europe. The United States also continued its efforts to strengthen Western Europe. In October 1954 the United States and its European allies agreed to give the Federal Republic of West Germany full sovereign powers. They also agreed to admit West Germany to NATO, and to allow the new state to build an army of 500,000 men to serve under the NATO command. The United States, Great Britain, and France also agreed to regard an attack upon West Germany as an attack upon themselves.

The inclusion of West Germany greatly increased NATO's military potential. American supplies, equipment, and armed forces, however, continued to provide an essential part of NATO's power.

Atomic and hydrogen weapons. By 1954 both the United States and the Soviet Union possessed hydrogen bombs. In the face of this fearsome development, the United States made vigorous efforts to work out an agreement with the Soviet Union to end the arms race. But the Soviets refused to accept international inspection within their own borders. Without such inspection, the United States refused to consider any agreement to destroy stockpiles of existing weapons or to stop the manufacture of nuclear weapons.

The "open skies" proposal. In 1955, however, President Eisenhower advanced a bold proposal for ending the armaments race. At a Big Four "summit conference" in Geneva in June, Eisenhower proposed that the Soviet Union and the United States exchange blueprints of their military establishments and permit mutual aerial, or "open skies," observation of military installations. Eisenhower also declared that Americans were ready to make concessions to enable the two great powers to live in peace.

The Geneva Conference, however, produced no tangible results. The four powers were unable to reach an agreement.

Hopes for a change. On February 25, 1956, startling news came out of the Soviet Union. Communist Party leader Nikita Khrushchev publicly attacked his predecessor, Stalin, calling him a cruel tyrant.

What was behind this attack? Was Khrushchev about to adopt a friendlier attitude toward the "free world"? Was he about to loosen the U.S.S.R.'s tight grip over its satellites in Eastern Europe? Hope began to stir, and in the satellite countries people began to demand a greater degree of freedom from Soviet control.

Revolt in Poland. In October 1956 the leaders of the Communist Party in Poland elected an ardent Polish nationalist, Wladyslaw Gomulka (VLAH-dee-slaf go-MUL-ka), as first secretary of their party. Although a devoted Communist, Gomulka promised the Poles freedom of speech, press, and religion. Encouraged by Gomulka's stand, Poles staged anti-Soviet demonstrations in the streets. On several occasions, they exchanged shots with Soviet troops.

The Polish revolt attracted world attention. What would Khrushchev do? Instead of crushing the revolt, Khrushchev granted concessions. He withdrew some Soviet troops from Poland and granted some of the freedom the Poles demanded. But the Poles won a limited victory. Final power still rested in Khrushchev's hands.

The Hungarian tragedy. Inspired by the example of the Poles, the Hungarians also rebelled against the Soviets. On October 23, 1956, students and workers rioted in the streets of Budapest (see map, page 790).

The next morning Soviet tanks, artillery, and armored cars supported by jet planes moved into Budapest. Violent fighting broke out as the heroic Hungarian "freedom fighters" resisted with improvised weapons. The rebellion spread as entire units of the Hungarian army joined the "freedom fighters."

LIVING AMERICAN DOCUMENTS

Dwight D. Eisenhower's
Disarmament Proposals (1955)

I should address myself for a moment principally to the delegates from the Soviet Union, because our two great countries admittedly possess new and terrible weapons in quantities which do give rise in other parts of the world, or reciprocally, to the fear and danger of surprise attack.

I propose, therefore, that we take a practical step, that we begin an arrangement very quickly; as between ourselves—immediately. These steps would include:

To give each other a complete blueprint of our military establishments . . .

Next, to provide within our countries facilities for aerial photography to the other country. . . .

For four days the fighting continued. Then, on October 28, the U.S.S.R. agreed to pull its troops out of Budapest. Two days later Imre Nagy (IM-reh NAHZH), who was now premier, promised the Hungarians free elections and an early end to the one-party dictatorship. At the same time, the Soviet Union declared that it was willing to consider withdrawing all its troops from Hungary, Poland, and Rumania.

But even while the Hungarians were celebrating, the Soviet army was preparing another assault. On November 4 Soviet forces launched a massive attack upon Budapest. "All Budapest is under fire," the Budapest radio reported. "The Russian gangsters have betrayed us."

In the meantime Premier Nagy had asked the UN for help. The General Assembly adopted a resolution condemning the Soviet action and demanding the immediate withdrawal of all Soviet troops from Hungary. But the U.S.S.R. paid no attention to this resolution. And when the UN asked for permission to send observers to Budapest, the Soviet Union refused.

Within a few days the Hungarian fight for freedom came to a tragic end. With all organized resistance ruthlessly crushed, a new Hungarian government, a puppet of the U.S.S.R., began to round up the rebels and imprison them or deport them to the Soviet Union. Refugees by the thousands fled across the frontier into Austria, seeking freedom in exile.

1. Show how each of the following revealed the continuing challenge of Communism: (a) the Korean armistice, (b) the crisis in Indo-China, (c) the formation of SEATO.
2. Explain the reason for Eisenhower's bold proposal at the 1955 Geneva Conference.
3. Why did the revolt in Poland attract worldwide attention?
4. (a) What was the outcome of the Hungarian revolution? (b) Why did the United States respond differently to the crisis in Hungary than it had responded to the earlier crisis in Korea?

5 The development of American policies to deal with world crises

In the same week that the gallant Hungarians rebelled, another crisis developed over the Suez Canal. For a few tense days the world hovered on the brink of another war.

Egypt and the Suez Canal. The Suez Canal, connecting the Mediterranean with the Red Sea, ran entirely through Egyptian territory. Owned and operated by an international company, the Canal was open on equal terms to ships of all nations. By arrangement with Egypt, British troops were stationed in the Canal Zone to safeguard the Canal and to protect British interests.

After World War II the Egyptians became increasingly dissatisfied with British military occupation of the Canal Zone. Finally, in 1954 the British government agreed to withdraw its forces. In June 1956 the last British troops did withdraw from the Canal Zone.

In the meantime, in 1954, Colonel Gamal Abdel Nasser led a successful revolution, overthrew the king of Egypt, and became President of the Republic of Egypt. Nasser was determined to improve and modernize the country and extend Egyptian influence throughout the Middle East. One of his major plans involved the building of a great irrigation dam and electric generating plant at Aswan on the Nile River. When the Soviet Union indicated an interest in financing the dam, the United States offered Egypt a $56 million loan for the Aswan project. But when it became clear that the U.S.S.R. could not at the time afford to finance the project, Secretary of State Dulles withdrew the United States of-

fer.° Great Britain and the World Bank immediately withdrew similar offers. Nasser, furious at this blow to his plans, announced that Egypt was going to seize the Canal and operate it as a national enterprise. The Western powers tried in vain to persuade Nasser to agree to international control by the 18 nations that regularly used the Canal.

The Suez Crisis. Such was the tense situation when, on October 29, 1956, the Israeli army moved rapidly westward through the Sinai Peninsula toward the Suez Canal. The Israeli government announced that its troops had invaded Egyptian territory to forestall a carefully planned attack upon Israel by Egypt.

On October 30 the British and French issued a 12-hour ultimatum. They demanded that Egypt and Israel cease fighting and allow French and British troops temporarily to occupy key points in the Canal Zone. When Egypt refused, the British and French bombed Egyptian airfields and moved troops into the northern part of the Canal Zone.

Then, denouncing Israel, France, and Great Britain as aggressors, the Soviet Union threatened to intervene with force if the three nations did not immediately withdraw.

The United States now found itself in an embarrassing position. Great Britain and France, its allies in NATO, had ignored the UN, and had created a situation that could easily lead to a general war. Moreover, the United States was unwilling to permit the Soviet Union to claim that it was the only champion of Egypt and other small nations against "Western imperialism." Reluctantly, the United States delegates to the UN voted in favor of a General Assembly resolution calling for an immediate cease-fire and the withdrawal of British, French, and Israeli troops. Great Britain, France, and Israel accepted these terms.

The Eisenhower Doctrine. As an immediate result of the Suez crisis, the United States adopted what came to be known as the Eisenhower Doctrine. Early in January 1957 President Eisenhower asked Congress (1) to authorize him to use military force if this were requested by any Middle Eastern nation to check Communist aggression and (2) to set aside $200 million to help those Middle Eastern countries that desired such aid from the United States. Congress granted both requests. The United States thus indicated its intention of check-

---

° In 1959 the Soviet Union agreed to provide finances and engineers to build the dam. Construction began in 1960 and was completed in 1969.

■ One of the major plans of Gamal Abdel Nasser, President of the Republic of Egypt, involved the building of a great irrigation dam at Aswan on the Nile River. The temples of Abu Simbel, one of which is shown above, were threatened by the project and had to be moved to a new site.

ing Communist influence in the Middle East by "filling the vacuum" left by the decline of British and French influence.

The Eisenhower Doctrine was soon tested. Early in 1958 Egypt and Syria joined together to form the United Arab Republic (U.A.R.). The U.A.R., supported by Communists throughout the Arab world, was strongly anti-Western. Egypt's Nasser, President of the U.A.R., urged the other Arab nations to join the U.A.R.

During the next few months the Arab world was torn by intrigue. Rebellion broke out against the pro-Western government of Lebanon. In Iraq a group of army officers killed the pro-Western leaders and seized control of the Iraqi government. The new government had the support of the Soviet Union and the U.A.R. The neighboring states of Lebanon and Jordan, now convinced that their pro-Western governments would soon be overthrown too, appealed to the United States and Great Britain for help. President Eisenhower immediately sent American marines to Lebanon, and Great Britain flew 2,000 crack paratroopers into Jordan.

For several weeks American and British forces remained poised for any emergency. Late in September, after the Secretary-General of the UN re-

ported that the situation in Lebanon was improving, Great Britain and the United States withdrew their troops.

The race into space. The crisis in the Middle East was not the major development of 1957–58. The most startling news, which broke on October 4, 1957, was compressed into a single word: *Sputnik*. The Russians had succeeded in hurling an artificial satellite into orbit around the earth.

The American public, long convinced that the United States had no superior in science and technology, was stunned. Recognizing the Soviet achievement, President Eisenhower assured the American people that the United States was pursuing its own rocket and missile program, which would soon show concrete results. On January 31, 1958, the United States launched a small satellite, Explorer I, into orbit, and the space race was under way.

Rockets powerful enough to carry satellites into space could also be used to hurl atomic and hydrogen bombs into an enemy country. By 1960 both the Soviet Union and the United States were building stockpiles of Intercontinental Ballistic Missiles (ICBM's) equipped with nuclear warheads. Push-

(*continued on page 792*)

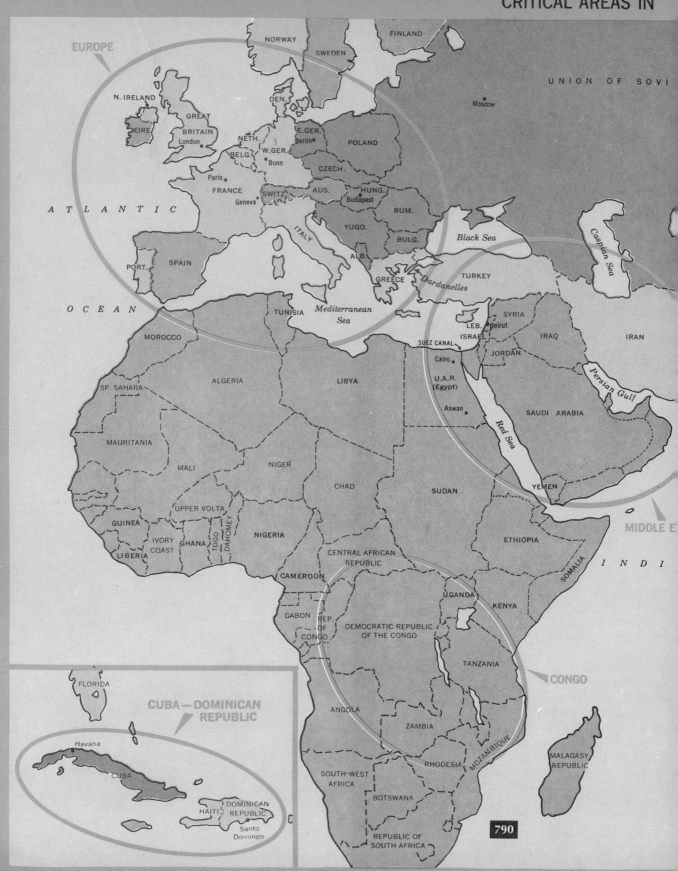

EUROPE

NORWAY

SWEDEN

FINLAND

UNION OF SOVI

Moscow

N. IRELAND

DEN.

EIRE

GREAT
BRITAIN

London

NETH.

E. GER.

Berlin

POLAND

BELG.

W. GER.

Bonn

CZECH.

Paris

FRANCE

SWITZ.

AUS.

HUNG.

Budapest

RUM.

Geneva

YUGO.

BULG.

Black Sea

Caspian Sea

A T L A N T I C

ITALY

ALB.

GREECE

Dardanelles

TURKEY

O C E A N

SPAIN

PORT.

Mediterranean
Sea

TUNISIA

SYRIA

LEB.

Beirut

CYPRUS

IRAQ

IRAN

MOROCCO

SUEZ CANAL

ISRAEL

JORDAN

Cairo

U.A.R.
(Egypt)

Persian Gulf

ALGERIA

LIBYA

SP. SAHARA

Aswan

SAUDI ARABIA

Red Sea

MAURITANIA

MALI

NIGER

CHAD

SUDAN

YEMEN

MIDDLE E

GUINEA

UPPER VOLTA

NIGERIA

ETHIOPIA

I N D I

IVORY
COAST

GHANA

TOGO

DAHOMEY

CENTRAL AFRICAN
REPUBLIC

SOMALIA

LIBERIA

CAMEROON

UGANDA

KENYA

GABON

REP.
OF
CONGO

DEMOCRATIC REPUBLIC
OF THE CONGO

CONGO

ANGOLA

TANZANIA

FLORIDA

CUBA — DOMINICAN
REPUBLIC

ZAMBIA

MALAGASY
REPUBLIC

Havana

CUBA

RHODESIA

MOZAMBIQUE

SOUTH-WEST
AFRICA

HAITI

DOMINICAN
REPUBLIC

Santo
Domingo

BOTSWANA

REPUBLIC OF
SOUTH AFRICA

790

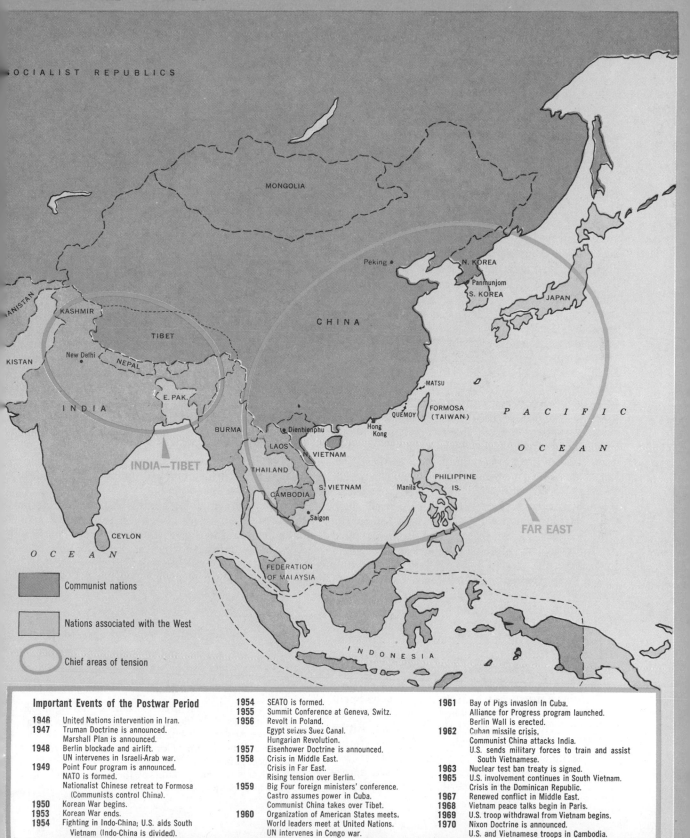

THE WORLD AFTER 1945

SOCIALIST REPUBLICS

MONGOLIA

Peking •

N. KOREA
Panmunjom
S. KOREA
JAPAN

CHINA

KASHMIR

TIBET

New Delhi •

NEPAL

E. PAK.

INDIA

BURMA

MATSU

FORMOSA
(TAIWAN)

QUEMOY

Hong Kong

Dienbienphu

LAOS

N. VIETNAM

THAILAND

CAMBODIA

S. VIETNAM

Saigon

Manila

PHILIPPINE
IS.

PACIFIC

OCEAN

INDIA—TIBET

FAR EAST

CEYLON

OCEAN

FEDERATION
OF MALAYSIA

INDONESIA

Communist nations

Nations associated with the West

Chief areas of tension

Important Events of the Postwar Period

1946	United Nations intervention in Iran.
1947	Truman Doctrine is announced.
	Marshall Plan is announced.
1948	Berlin blockade and airlift.
	UN intervenes in Israeli-Arab war.
1949	Point Four program is announced.
	NATO is formed.
	Nationalist Chinese retreat to Formosa
	(Communists control China).
1950	Korean War begins.
1953	Korean War ends.
1954	Fighting in Indo-China; U.S. aids South
	Vietnam (Indo-China is divided).

1954	SEATO is formed.
1955	Summit Conference at Geneva, Switz.
1956	Revolt in Poland.
	Egypt seizes Suez Canal.
	Hungarian Revolution.
1957	Eisenhower Doctrine is announced.
1958	Crisis in Middle East.
	Crisis in Far East.
	Rising tension over Berlin.
1959	Big Four foreign ministers' conference.
	Castro assumes power in Cuba.
	Communist China takes over Tibet.
1960	Organization of American States meets.
	World leaders meet at United Nations.
	UN intervenes in Congo war.

1961	Bay of Pigs invasion in Cuba.
	Alliance for Progress program launched.
	Berlin Wall is erected.
1962	Cuban missile crisis.
	Communist China attacks India.
	U.S. sends military forces to train and assist
	South Vietnamese.
1963	Nuclear test ban treaty is signed.
1965	U.S. involvement continues in South Vietnam.
	Crisis in the Dominican Republic.
1967	Renewed conflict in Middle East.
1968	Vietnam peace talks begin in Paris.
1969	U.S. troop withdrawal from Vietnam begins.
1970	Nixon Doctrine is announced.
	U.S. and Vietnamese troops in Cambodia.

button war that could destroy millions of lives in a single instant had become a dreadful possibility.

Another crisis in the Far East. In the summer of 1958 a new crisis developed in the Far East. Communist China began to bombard the Nationalist-held islands of Quemoy and Matsu, west of Formosa and only a few miles off Communist China's coast, as though in preparation for an invasion.

Secretary of State Dulles answered this threat with a declaration that the United States would take "timely and effective" action to repel any invasion of Quemoy and Matsu and to defend Formosa. The Soviet Union immediately declared that it considered Communist China's claims to the islands "lawful and just."

By October the crisis passed, but the major issue remained unsettled. Communist China's Foreign Minister made this clear when, on November 1, he declared: "The Americans must pull away their hand from the Taiwan Strait. . . . We are determined to liberate Formosa and the offshore islands. . . ."

Rising tensions over Berlin. The Far East crisis was hardly past when, on November 27, the Soviet premier issued an ultimatum on Berlin. Khrushchev gave the Western powers six months to agree to withdraw from Berlin and make it a free, demilitarized city. If by May 27, 1959, the Western powers had not agreed, the Soviet Union would turn over to Communist East Germany complete control of all lines of communication to West Berlin. If the Western powers then tried to gain access to West Berlin without the permission of the East German government, the Soviet Union would help the East Germans to meet force with force. The United States, Great Britain, and France replied by firmly repeating their determination to remain in West Berlin.

The temporary easing of tension. During 1959, however, the situation began to improve. Instead of insisting that the Western powers get out of Berlin by May 27, the Soviet Union met with the Western leaders in a Big Four foreign ministers' conference. Although the conference failed to reach any important agreements, it did open the door to further negotiations.

Premier Khrushchev himself seemed to be opening the door a bit wider when, in September, he visited the United States. At the end of his visit he and Eisenhower issued a joint declaration, stating that the most serious issue facing the world was general disarmament. They also expressed agreement that the problem of Berlin and "all outstanding international questions should be settled, not by the application of force, but by peaceful means through negotiation."

Encouraged by Khrushchev's apparent willingness to negotiate, the Western powers agreed to meet with the Soviet Premier at a Summit Conference.

Summit Conference plans abandoned. The Summit Conference was never held. Early in May 1960, shortly before it was scheduled to open in Paris, Premier Khrushchev charged the United States with "aggression." He announced that, on May 1, the Soviets had shot down a high-flying United States plane over the heart of the Soviet Union.

American officials at first insisted that the U-2, as the plane was called, was engaged in weather research and had strayed off its course. Later the United States admitted that the U-2 had been engaged in aerial reconnaissance.

Premier Khrushchev was furious. He refused to take part in the Summit Conference unless Eisenhower (1) agreed to stop all such future flights; (2) apologized for past acts of "aggression"; and (3) promised to punish those responsible for the flights.

Hoping against hope that the conference could still be held, President Eisenhower announced that the U-2 flights had been stopped and would not be resumed. He refused, however, to apologize. Khrushchev, refusing to accept anything less than an apology, left for home. All plans for the conference had to be abandoned.

During the remaining months of his second term President Eisenhower continued to seek ways of reducing world tensions. His efforts were fruitless. Khrushchev refused to budge. As an Indian delegate to the UN expressed it, Eisenhower opened the door and Khrushchev slammed it shut.

SECTION SURVEY

IDENTIFY: Sputnik, U-2, Aswan Dam, ICBM; Gamal Nasser.

1. (a) What were the causes and results of the Suez crisis? (b) Explain the position taken by the United States.
2. Many international crises occurred during 1958. Explain this statement by referring to events in (a) Europe, (b) the Middle East, (c) the Far East.
3. Why did the Summit Conference of May 1960 fail to materialize?
4. What was the importance of the Eisenhower Doctrine as a move in the Cold War?

TRACING THE MAIN IDEAS

World War II transformed America's relations with the rest of the world. Any lingering hopes that the United States could return to a position of isolationism vanished in the smoke and flames of the conflict. As the world's richest and most powerful nation, the United States felt that it had no choice but to accept the responsibilities of world leadership. During the postwar years these responsibilities proved far heavier than even the keenest observer could have foreseen as the war ended in 1945.

The immediate postwar problem was the worldwide challenge of Communism. During the Truman administration the United States developed a foreign policy which sought to "contain" the Soviet Union and to check the spread of Communism. Through military aid to friendly as well as "uncommitted" nations, and through collective defense arrangements, notably NATO, the United States undertook to build a shield of military might around the "free world."

Meanwhile the United States sought to remove the threat of war and to strengthen the foundations of peace. Under Democratic and Republican Presidents alike, the United States continued to support the UN, to work for disarmament, and to aid many other countries overseas. Through the Marshall Plan and other programs of economic and technical assistance, the United States brought new hope, first to the war-ravaged countries of Europe, later to the emerging, underdeveloped nations of the world.

Through the decade of the 1950's both Democratic and Republican administrations followed these two basic policies—one which sought to maintain the military defenses of the uncommitted and the anti-Communist nations, the other to strengthen their economic foundations. By means of these policies the United States succeeded in emerging safely from one world crisis after another. In 1960, however, it was evident that even greater trials faced the nation in the years ahead.

CHAPTER SURVEY

QUESTIONS FOR DISCUSSION

1. Was the Korean War a victory for the United States and the United Nations? Why or why not?
2. How successful was the Marshall Plan? What was its basic philosophy? Explain.
3. How effective were the steps taken by the United States between the years 1945–60 in meeting the challenge of Communism?
4. "The United Nations will not be able to prevent a third world war." Do you agree or disagree? Explain.
5. Compare SEATO and NATO in (a) member nations, (b) aims, and (c) effectiveness.
6. The Eisenhower Doctrine was actually an extension of the old containment policy first developed during the Truman administration. Discuss.
7. The launching of Sputnik I led to much self-examination and self-criticism on the part of Americans. (a) Explain. (b) Indicate specific results.
8. (a) In your opinion, what have been the outstanding contributions of the United Nations to world peace during the period since it was founded? (b) In your opinion, what have been its failures?

RELATING PAST TO PRESENT

1. What do you think would be gained if the United Nations were given additional powers in order to protect world peace? What might be lost?
2. Compare the twentieth-century "race into space" with the fifteenth-century search for an all-water route to Asia. What are some similarities? What are some dissimilarities?

USING MAPS AND CHARTS

1. Using the map on pages 790–91, locate Lebanon, U.A.R., Iraq, Quemoy, Matsu, and Formosa.
2. Using the map on page 783, answer these questions: (a) Why was United Nations morale in the Korean War at its lowest ebb in the early part of September 1950? (b) Which event in that same month bolstered United Nations morale? Why? (c) Locate the line of farthest United Nations advance. (d) Compare the cease-fire line of July 1953 with the 38th parallel. (e) What is the distance from the 38th parallel to the Yalu River? to the Soviet Union?

■ *American soldiers in Vietnam*

CHAPTER 42

Re-examining the Nation's Role in World Affairs

1960 – 1970's

WORLD TENSIONS were close to the snapping point when in January 1961 President Eisenhower turned over the office of Chief Executive to his successor, John F. Kennedy. During the election campaign Kennedy had predicted that the 1960's would be one of the most critical periods in the nation's history—perhaps the most critical. As the years passed, first under the leadership of President Kennedy, then under Presidents Johnson and Nixon, this prediction proved to be well founded.

By the closing years of the decade older unresolved problems had reached the crisis point and newer problems clamored for attention. Compounding the challenges confronting the American people was the fact that many of the most urgent problems were worldwide in nature— pollution of the environment, nuclear disarmament, food for the rapidly growing population— and could be solved only through international cooperation.

Of first concern, because it affected all other problems, was America's military involvement in Vietnam. The Southeast Asian conflict, costly in lives and resources, deeply troubled large numbers of Americans.

In one sense, Vietnam was part of a larger issue confronting Americans. The larger issue could be reduced to a clear and direct question: Was the United States overcommitted? In other words, had the United States assumed more responsibilities around the world than it could meet, even with all its wealth and power?

These were among the issues troubling Americans as the decade of the 1960's drew to a close and, under the leadership of President Nixon, Americans entered the 1970's.

THE CHAPTER IN OUTLINE

1. American assumption of global responsibilities.

2. Increasing American involvement in the conflict in Vietnam.

3. Re-evaluating the nation's responsibilities as a world leader.

| 1450 | 1750 | 1800 | 1850 | 1900 | 1950 | 1975 |

1 American assumption of global responsibilities

During the 1960's the deadly possibility of nuclear war and the challenge of Communist aggression continued to haunt Americans. Even as the nation grappled with these problems, however, other far-reaching developments thrust increasingly heavy demands upon the American people and their leaders.

The world in swift transition. One of the major developments was the growing competition American business faced from Japan, the Soviet Union, and the Common Market countries of Western Europe (page 764). These nations, with modern industrial plants built largely in recent years and operating with the newest, most efficient equipment, had become serious competitors with the United States for world markets.

Another revolutionary development was the entry of new nations into the world community. Between 1945 and 1969 UN membership grew from 51 to 126. The greatest part of the growth in membership occurred during the 1960's. Most of the new nations, whose population included more than 1 billion people, had emerged from former colonies in the underdeveloped areas of Asia and Africa. President Kennedy was speaking of these people when he declared in his Inaugural Address: "To those peoples in the huts and villages of half the globe struggling to break the bonds of mass misery, we pledge our best efforts to help them help themselves, for whatever period is required— not because the Communists may be doing it, not because we seek their votes, but because it is right. If a free society cannot help the many who are poor, it cannot save the few who are rich."

Changing relationships of nations. Still another far-reaching development was the shifting balance of world power. Since the end of World War II the Communists led by the Soviet Union had been aligned on one side, with the United States and its allies aligned on the other. During the 1960's this alignment began to crumble.

The newly independent nations of Asia and Africa were reluctant to tie themselves to either the Soviet Union or the United States. Led by India, these "uncommitted" nations exerted an increasingly influential voice in world affairs.

Meanwhile the solid front of Communism was breaking up as Communist China challenged the Soviet Union's leadership of world Communism.

By the mid-1960's the split between the two most powerful Communist countries was nearly complete.

The solid front of the anti-Communist alignment was also being strained. In 1964 President Charles de Gaulle of France began to challenge America's leadership role. De Gaulle looked at the rising industrial strength of Europe, the growing influence of the "uncommitted" nations, and the breakup of the once solid Communist front, and decided that it was time for a realignment of power. He hoped to establish France at the head of a "third force," a group of nations with power and influence equal to those of the United States and the Soviet Union.

By the 1960's all of the powerful nations— both of the Communist and the non-Communist world—were competing for both the markets and the political support of the underdeveloped nations. Thus many of the world crises facing the Kennedy administration grew out of the problems of Africa, Asia, and Latin America.

Trouble in Africa. President Kennedy had to deal with the problems of America's relations to the new emerging African nations. The most serious crisis developed in the Democratic Republic of the Congo.°

The Congo, a former Belgian colony, became independent in June 1960. Even before the independence celebrations ended, many rival groups—among them pro-Communist and pro-Western factions—began to battle for control of the government. The situation became desperate when Congolese troops mutinied against their Belgian officers and the Congo was swept by atrocities. Terrified Europeans fled the country, and Belgian paratroopers, defying the wishes of the Congo government, occupied key cities. The problem was compounded when the mineral-rich Katanga province seceded from the newly formed nation.

In the midst of this chaos, the Congo government appealed to the UN. The UN responded by sending a security force, composed largely of troops from African and Asian nations, to police the troubled country.

Although the UN force managed to prevent a full-scale civil war, it was not at first able to end the bloodshed. A new crisis developed in February

---

° Not to be confused with the nearby Republic of Congo, the new nation formed from the southern part of French Equatorial Africa.

795

■ In his Inaugural Address, President Kennedy pledged that the United States would aid the underdeveloped nations of the world "not because we seek their votes, but because it is right."

1961 when Patrice Lumumba, leader of the pro-Communist faction, was assassinated. Soviet Premier Khrushchev demanded withdrawal of all UN troops and threatened to intervene. President Kennedy replied with a warning that the United States would defend the UN operation "by opposing any attempt by any government to interfere unilaterally in the Congo."

With firm American backing, the UN continued its difficult peacemaking operation in the Congo and by 1965 the fighting ended and Katanga province rejoined the nation. By the late 1960's, most scars of the civil war seemed healed and the Congo was one of the most prosperous of the African nations.

The Arab-Israeli conflict. As you have read, the Middle East had long been an area of international tension (pages 782 and 788–89). After the Suez crisis, the bitter quarrel and occasional raids between Israel and the Arab nations continued.

In 1967, Israelis believed that the Arab nations were massing large military forces to destroy Israel. In June 1967, powerful Israeli forces struck at Egypt, Jordan, and Syria, defeating them in a war lasting only six days. After the war, Israel remained in control of large areas of land that had belonged to the nations of Egypt, Jordan, and Syria.

The Arab nations were bitter at their defeat and now more determined than ever to destroy Israel. They began sending trained guerrilla fighters into Israel. The Israelis continued to strike back.

For many years, the Soviet Union sent aid of various kinds, including military aid, to the Arab nations but not to Israel. The United States tried to help the Arab nations overcome their poverty, and it gave military aid to help those nations resist Communism. It also gave military aid to Israel.

In the years after the June 1967 war, the Middle East remained a danger spot in the world. The Arab nations and Israel were constantly raiding or attacking each other's border areas. The United States and the Soviet Union continued to provide military aid and tried to strengthen their influence in the Middle East. Finally in 1970 the United States was able to secure a truce in the border raids and the fighting, though a peaceful settlement of the 1967 war still seemed only a distant prospect.

Cuba, a Communist beachhead. The Kennedy administration also inherited the extremely serious problem of Cuba. For many years the Cubans had suffered under the repressive rule of dictator Fulgencio Batista (ful·JEN·cee·oh bah·TEES·tah). During the late 1950's a band of Cubans led by Fidel Castro opened war on the Batista regime. Castro's forces, armed in large part with American weapons, operated out of the remote mountainous regions of eastern Cuba. Early in 1959, supported by the Cuban people, they overthrew Batista's government. The United States welcomed Castro's rise to power as a victory for democracy.

American sympathy rapidly evaporated, however, when Castro began to act like another power-crazed dictator. He failed to hold the elections he had promised. He put to death hundreds of his political enemies and jailed thousands unsympathetic to his regime. He expropriated foreign-owned property. In addition, Castro began to lash out at the "Yankees" and to turn to the Communist powers for support. Castro accepted a Soviet offer of military aid if the United States interfered in Cuba.

At first the United States adopted a policy of patient waiting. During the summer of 1960, however, American policy hardened. The United States (1) placed a temporary embargo on the purchase of Cuban sugar; (2) announced a sweeping program of economic aid to Latin America; and (3) urged the Organization of American States (O.A.S.), formerly the Pan-American Union, to condemn Cuba's actions.

Late in August the 21 members of the O.A.S. met in San José, Costa Rica. The conference adopted a resolution condemning Communist interference in the Western Hemisphere and urging the American countries to negotiate their differences through the O.A.S.

The Bay of Pigs. When Kennedy took office in January 1961 he inherited a plan developed during the Eisenhower administration to overthrow the Castro government. During 1960 a force of anti-Castro Cubans had been trained at bases in Central America with the active support of the United States Central Intelligence Agency (CIA). The plan called for an invasion of Cuba, during which the Cuban underground would rise and join the invasion forces and overthrow the Castro government. President Kennedy, after long discussions with his close advisers, decided to allow the plan to be carried out.

On April 17, 1961, the invasion force landed on the beaches of the Bahía de Cochinos, or the Bay of Pigs. The landing ended in tragedy for the anti-Castro "Freedom Fighters," most of whom were killed or captured. In reply to a storm of criticism, President Kennedy admitted that the invasion attempt had been a mistake, for which he personally assumed full responsibility.

Following the Bay of Pigs invasion attempt, the Soviet Union stepped up its shipments of military equipment to Cuba. In December 1961 Castro declared publicly, "I am a Marxist-Leninist and will be one until the day I die." A month later the O.A.S. voted to exclude Cuba from that organization. The United States had already cut off its trade with Cuba, but failed to persuade the O.A.S. to take similar action.

A world crisis. The crisis that brought the world to the brink of a nuclear holocaust came in the fall of 1962. In mid-October American intelligence sources confirmed reports that the Soviet Union was equipping Cuba with long-range jet bombers and offensive missiles capable of delivering nuclear bombs throughout the Caribbean, much of Central and South America, and most of the eastern United States. On October 22, with the evidence before him, President Kennedy ordered the United States Navy to establish a blockade—or "quarantine"—against any further shipment of "offensive" weapons to Cuba. He also demanded that the Soviet Union immediately dismantle the missile bases and withdraw Soviet missiles and bombers from Cuba.

The world waited tensely for Khrushchev's reaction. Confronted with the choice between nuclear war or meeting Kennedy's demands, Khrushchev backed down. During the next few weeks the Soviets began to dismantle the missile bases and remove the missiles and bombers. Nonetheless, the Communists had succeeded in establishing a beachhead only 90 miles from America's shores.

The Alliance for Progress. One of the Western Hemisphere's answers to the Communist challenge was an ambitious program called the Alliance for Progress, outlined by President Kennedy in March 1961. The charter launching the program was signed by the United States and 19 Latin-American countries (all but Cuba) five months later.

The Alliance members agreed to undertake a 10-year program to improve social and economic conditions in Latin America. Finances for the program were to come from private and government sources in Latin America and the United States, as well as from Japan, Western Europe, and international agencies such as the World Bank. To be eligible for aid, each country had to develop a program of land and tax reform to improve social conditions and living standards.

The Alliance for Progress got off to a slow start, partly because many of the large property owners in Latin America were reluctant to initiate reforms. Nevertheless, during the first four years the United States contributed $4.5 billion to the program, the Latin-American countries $22 billion. Some progress was made, but the results were disappointing. Much of the money was used to help the business elite and the military establishments of Latin America rather than the masses of poor people. Congress, increasingly impatient, began to reduce the budgets for the Alliance, slashing them in 1969 to an all-time low of $336 million.

In the spring of 1969 Sol M. Linowitz, retiring from his post as United States Ambassador to the O.A.S., summed up his concern for deteriorating relations between Latin America and the United States. "Latin America," he said, "is a microcosm of all the problems of the have-not world: high mortality rates, widespread disease, underdeveloped industry and agriculture, low life expectancy, high birth rates, insufficient housing, lack of schools. . . . If we cannot intelligently, wisely, maturely deal with these problems in our own hemisphere, we are not going to succeed anywhere else."

The Dominican crisis.   One of the most serious crises in United States relations with Latin America developed in the spring of 1965 when revolution plunged the Dominican Republic into chaos.

From 1930 until 1961 the Dominican Republic (see map, page 591) was ruled by an iron-handed dictator, General Trujillo (troo-HE-yoh). Then Trujillo was assassinated, and in 1963 the country held its first free elections for government leaders in 38 years. The new government was only seven months old when it was driven out by an army-backed committee known as the *junta.* But the junta was unable to win the support of the common people, and in the spring of 1965 a violent uprising broke out. Santo Domingo, the capital, was torn by savage fighting between a hastily organized rebel force and the armed forces of the junta government.

Calling the situation "grave," President Johnson promptly ordered 400 marines into the capital to protect the lives of Americans there. This was the first time since 1926 that the marines had been ordered into a Latin-American country. Many Latin-American leaders admitted that the action was necessary. At the same time they expressed fear that the use of marines might mark the start of a new United States policy toward Latin America.

Latin-American fear of United States intervention increased, when, within two weeks, more than 22,000 American troops had landed in Santo Domingo, with another 10,000 standing by in navy vessels offshore. These troops drove a neutral zone between the rebel and junta forces and secured a cease-fire.

President Johnson justified the large-scale intervention on the ground that it was necessary to (1) end the blood bath, (2) prevent a possible Communist takeover, and (3) enable the people to hold free elections. He made it clear, however, that the American forces would be withdrawn as soon as the O.A.S. assumed responsibility for maintaining order.

Meeting in emergency sessions, representatives of the O.A.S. accepted the responsibility. By mid-summer a small contingent of troops from four Latin-American nations had joined the American forces in Santo Domingo, and some of the United States troops had been withdrawn. Meanwhile an O.A.S. commission urged the rebel and junta leaders to accept a provisional, or temporary, government that would rule the country until free elections could be held. In late August both sides accepted a provisional president who governed the country until free elections were held in June 1966.

Continuing conflict in Southeast Asia.   Crises continued to develop in Asia, as well as in Latin America and Africa, during the 1960's. The major crisis areas were the new countries of Southeast Asia—Laos, Cambodia, and North and South Vietnam (page 786).

The tiny kingdom of Laos was divided into three political factions—pro-Western, Communist, and neutral. In an effort to secure a strong pro-Western government, the United States poured millions of dollars into Laos. When these efforts failed, the Kennedy administration reversed its policy. In July 1962, after lengthy negotiations with the Laotian factions and the Communist powers, a truly neutral government was established in Laos.

The United States also gave considerable military and economic aid to Cambodia in an effort to secure a pro-Western government. As in Laos, however, the policy failed. In the autumn of 1963, apparently yielding to strong pressures from the Communists, the Cambodian government asked the United States to withdraw its military and technical personnel.

American efforts to prevent a Communist takeover in the new Southeast Asian countries were put to their severest test in South Vietnam. As you will read (pages 800–04), in its efforts to support the South Vietnamese government, the United States moved step by step into what turned out to be the longest and the most unpopular war in American history.

Communist China. Meanwhile the shadow of aggression by Communist China continued to darken all of Southeast Asia.

In 1959 the Chinese Communists took over Tibet, and in 1962, following a border dispute, they launched a large-scale attack on India. In response to appeals from the Indian government, the United States and Great Britain began to airlift military supplies to the hard-pressed Indian troops. Then, as suddenly as the Communist Chinese had attacked, they announced a cease-fire and called for negotiations. But India, shocked by what it considered unprovoked aggression, began to build up its defenses to prepare for any future trouble.

The Sino-Soviet break. Communist China's attack on India was embarrassing to the Soviet Union, which had long maintained friendly relations with India. Western observers believed that Communist China had launched its offensive without consulting the Soviets.

But there was clearer evidence that the Chinese and Soviet Communists were drawing apart. During the early 1960's the Soviets began pulling their military and technical advisers out of Communist China. And by 1964 the leaders of the Soviet Union and Communist China were openly attacking each other's policies. Khrushchev insisted that "peaceful co-existence" was possible, and that in any event nuclear war was unthinkable. Communist China, on the other hand, flatly declared that there could be no peace with "the capitalistic warmongers," and accused the Soviet Union of abandoning the cause of world Communism.

The smoldering issue of Berlin. The break in the solid front of Communism provided one reason for Khrushchev's failure to press his threats against West Berlin (page 781). In 1961, Khrushchev had renewed his threat to conclude a separate peace treaty with East Germany. He warned that the treaty would end the Western nations' rights of free access to West Berlin. President Kennedy in turn warned that the United States would not abandon the people of West Berlin.

In August 1961 the East German government began to erect a wall along the line between East and West Berlin. The Berlin wall cut off the escape of East Germans into West Germany and became a grim symbol of the conflicts between the Communist and anti-Communist nations. President Kennedy repeated that the Western powers would not be forced out by Soviet threats. Khrushchev abandoned his 1961 treaty deadline, only to renew it for 1962. Although by the end of 1963 the Soviet leader had not carried out his threats, the Berlin issue remained unresolved.

The nuclear test ban and disarmament. In August 1961 Premier Khrushchev also announced that the Soviet Union intended to resume nuclear testing. The announcement shocked people everywhere, for in 1958 the nuclear powers—the United States, Great Britain, and the Soviet Union—had reached a "gentlemen's agreement" to suspend all testing for three years. The three-year period had not yet expired. President Kennedy reacted promptly, warning that if the Soviets carried out their plans, the United States would be compelled in the interest of its own defense to resume nuclear testing.

Disregarding this warning and earnest pleas from nations throughout the world, the U.S.S.R. began a series of nuclear tests in the fall of 1961. The following spring, after the Soviet Union had turned down repeated pleas for a fully effective test ban, the United States began its own tests.

Despite the breakdown of the "gentlemen's agreement," the United States continued to press for a nuclear test ban and a general arms reduction. The Soviet Union finally agreed to return to the conference table. During 1962, however, negotiations continued to be deadlocked on the old question of international inspection.

The first break in the long deadlock came in 1963. In June Moscow and Washington agreed on a "hot line" to provide direct teletype communications between the two capitals to help prevent nuclear war by accident. The line installed by September was hailed by both sides as a major breakthrough.

Meanwhile progress was also made on the nuclear test ban. On July 25, 1963, American, British, and Soviet representatives reached an agreement to ban nuclear tests in the atmosphere, under water, and in space. The treaty was formally signed on August 5. The United States Senate, after some debate, ratified the agreement, and it was declared in effect on October 10, 1963.

Continuity and change in foreign policy. To meet the nation's responsibilities in a rapidly changing world, the Kennedy-Johnson administration generally followed the basic foreign policy developed under Truman and Eisenhower. It continued to resist Communist aggression, to strengthen the nation's military defenses, to maintain America's missile lead, and to catch up with the Soviet Union in the space race. The administration also continued to support the UN and to make determined efforts to reduce international tensions.

But there were new phases as well as continuity in foreign policy during the early 1960's. The Trade Expansion Act of 1962 (page 764) was designed to increase the flow of world trade as well as to meet the growing competition of the Common Market countries of Western Europe. The Kennedy-Johnson administration also sponsored programs to strengthen international cultural relations by sending outstanding American musicians, theater groups, writers, and artists to visit friendly, neutral, and Communist countries. By far the most imaginative innovation, however, was the Peace Corps.

The Peace Corps. President Kennedy himself created the Peace Corps by executive order in March 1961 on a "temporary pilot basis." The following September Congress authorized the establishment of a permanent organization. That same month the first volunteers, most of them young Americans, arrived in the African nation of Ghana to serve as teachers.

From the beginning the Peace Corps was a notable success. By 1970 about 10,000 Americans, mostly young men and women, were serving overseas in 59 different countries. The Peace Corps, with its emphasis on youth and its dedication to the service of humanity, embodied John F. Kennedy's loftiest ideals. It symbolized America's determination to assume the moral as well as economic and military leadership of the non-Communist world.

SECTION SURVEY

IDENTIFY: Congo crisis, Sino-Soviet break, Berlin Wall, CIA, hot line, O.A.S., Peace Corps; Fidel Castro, General Trujillo.

1. (a) Describe developments taking place in the world that placed heavy demands upon the United States in the 1960's. (b) Why did the United States feel an obligation to respond to these demands?
2. The Cuban missile crisis brought the world to the brink of a nuclear holocaust in 1962. Explain.
3. Review United States relations with Latin America in (a) the Alliance for Progress, (b) the Dominican crisis.
4. In the 1960's Communist China and Southeast Asia again became major American concerns. Why?
5. The nuclear test ban and disarmament were issues that reflected the "balance of power" concept between the major powers. Comment.

2 Increasing American involvement in the conflict in Vietnam

In January 1965, when Lyndon B. Johnson started his first full term as President, he dedicated his administration primarily to the solution of crucial domestic problems—racial tensions, poverty, injustice. By the end of 1965, however, it was evident that the United States was waging two major wars—the war against prejudice and poverty and injustice at home and the conflict in Vietnam abroad.

America's limited involvement. American involvement in Vietnam grew out of United States efforts to prevent the Communists from taking over the new Southeast Asian countries (page 801). During the late 1950's and early 1960's, guerrillas, known as the Vietcong and supported from Communist North Vietnam, ranged over the entire countryside, sometimes striking on the very outskirts of the capital of Saigon (see map, page 801). By the spring of 1961 the struggle was going badly for the anti-Communist government of President Ngo Dinh Diem (NOH DIN ZIM), whose repressive policies had antagonized many of his own people, especially the Buddhists, who represented a large majority of the population.

To strengthen South Vietnam, the Kennedy administration in 1962 sent some 8,000 troops to train the South Vietnamese armies, to transport the South Vietnamese forces from one danger point to another, and to serve as military advisers. American efforts were frustrated, however, by the refusal of many South Vietnamese to support Ngo Dinh Diem's unpopular government. Finally Diem was assassinated and his government overthrown in the autumn of 1963. Efforts to establish a stable civilian government failed, however, and for most of the next two years military leaders ruled the country.

Although by the end of 1964 the number of American advisers and technicians had risen to some 23,000, they were not authorized to engage in combat. As late as October of 1964 President Johnson had stated that his administration had no intention of committing American troops to a war in Asia. "We are not," he declared, "about to send American boys nine or ten thousand miles away from home to do what Asian boys ought to be doing for themselves."

A turning point. Only two months earlier, however, the United States had taken a major step toward deeper involvement. In spite of some uncertainty as to what exactly had happened, the

President announced on August 4, 1964, that two American destroyers had been attacked in the Gulf of Tonkin by North Vietnamese patrol torpedo boats and that he had immediately ordered retaliatory attacks against the enemy boats and coastal military installations.

Three days later Congress adopted what became known as the Gulf of Tonkin Resolution. This resolution gave the President power to "take all necessary measures to repel any armed attack against the forces of the United States and to prevent further aggression." Three years later, as you will see, the resolution became the subject of bitter debate.

Persuasion and force. By early 1965 the Johnson administration was convinced that the South Vietnamese armies, although outnumbering the Vietcong by about six to one, were in danger of being defeated. To prevent this from happening, on February 28 President Johnson ordered United States planes to begin the bombing of selected targets in North Vietnam. The air strikes were intended to slow down North Vietnamese infiltration into South Vietnam and to force the North Vietnamese government in the capital at Hanoi to negotiate a settlement. In March, as a further demonstration of America's determination to support South Vietnam, the President for the first time committed American troops to active combat.

But President Johnson added persuasion to force in his effort to bring Hanoi to the conference table. In April he declared that the United States was prepared to offer $1 billion of economic aid to Southeast Asia, including North Vietnam, as soon as the fighting ended and the Southeast Asian countries established peaceful relations. Several weeks later, in May, the President ordered a halt to all air attacks.

None of these actions produced the hoped-for results. Hanoi continued to insist that negotiations would not be considered until the bombing had been ended unconditionally and all American troops had been withdrawn from Vietnam. Washington responded by resuming the air strikes and by increasing American troop strength. By the end of 1965, nearly 125,000 American servicemen had been committed to the war effort.

Late in December President Johnson made another major effort to reach a peaceful settlement. All bombing was suspended from December 24 to January 31. During this period the State Department carried on what it called an "unprecedented" diplomatic effort, involving consultations with 115 governments, in the hope that their concern would

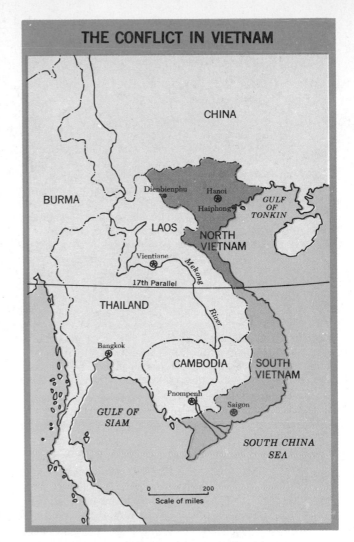

THE CONFLICT IN VIETNAM

CHINA

BURMA

Dienbienphu Hanoi
Haiphong GULF OF TONKIN

LAOS NORTH VIETNAM

Vientiane

17th Parallel

THAILAND

Bangkok

Mekong River

CAMBODIA SOUTH VIETNAM

Pnompenh

Saigon

GULF OF SIAM

SOUTH CHINA SEA

0   200
Scale of miles

persuade Hanoi to negotiate. The effort failed.

Escalation of the war. Frustrated by the failure of its "peace offensive," the United States began to increase its military pressure on North Vietnam. Critics charged that President Johnson had begun to rely on force rather than diplomacy to bring Hanoi to the conference table.

The bombing was steadily intensified. By 1968 the United States had dropped an enormous tonnage of bombs on North Vietnam—a total greater than all the bombs dropped in all the theaters of war in World War II.

By September 1968 the war was costing Americans more than $25 billion a year. Some 540,000 American fighting men were in Vietnam, and American casualties totaled more than 27,000 service-

LIVING AMERICAN DOCUMENTS

The Gulf of

Tonkin Resolution (1964)

Whereas naval units of the Communist regime in Vietnam, in violation of the principles of the Charter of the United Nations and of international law, have deliberately and repeatedly attacked United States naval vessels lawfully present in international waters, and have thereby created a serious threat to international peace; and

Whereas these attacks are part of a deliberate and systematic campaign of aggression that the Communist regime in North Vietnam has been waging against its neighbors and the nations joined with them in the collective defense of their freedom; ... Now therefore, be it

Resolved by the Senate and House of Representatives of the United States of America in Congress assembled, That the Congress approves and supports the determination of the President, as Commander in Chief, to take all necessary measures to repel any armed attack against the forces of the United States and to prevent further aggression.

---

men killed and an additional 92,000 seriously wounded.

Dislocation of Vietnamese life.   The war had a shattering impact on the Vietnamese, North and South alike. Although the air strikes in North Vietnam were aimed at storage depots, roads, bridges, and infiltration routes, bombs are not pinpoint weapons, and North Vietnamese villagers were often the victims.

The people of South Vietnam, however—men, women, and children—bore the heaviest burden. By 1968 more than 1.6 million troops ° were engaged in a country about the size of the state of Washington. Moreover, there were no "front lines," for this was guerrilla warfare. Every village was a potential battleground.

The Vietcong, well organized and strengthened in some areas by North Vietnamese army regulars, avoided large-scale frontal engagements. Instead they employed terrorism—bombs planted in a marketplace or in a busy city and the torture or assas-

° On the allied side almost 750,000 South Vietnamese, 540,000 Americans, about 45,000 South Koreans, and about 15,000 Australians, New Zealanders, Thais, and Filipinos. For the enemy, an estimated 300,000, including the Vietcong and North Vietnamese regulars.

sination of unfriendly village leaders. The Vietcong relied largely on hit-and-run tactics, striking suddenly and then disappearing into the forest or jungle. Only when they were reasonably certain of military superiority did the Vietcong strike directly.

The Americans in turn relied heavily upon air power. They poured bombs and napalm, rockets and machinegun fire, upon supply routes, on suspected jungle hideouts, and on villages controlled by or suspected of harboring guerrillas. Ground troops—South Vietnamese and Americans—carried out "search-and-destroy" operations. In areas they could not hold and defend they moved the people to refugee centers and burned the villages.

This kind of warfare inevitably produced widespread devastation and human misery. By the end of 1967 civilian casualties, the victims of Vietcong terror or allied counterattack, totaled about 100,000 to 150,000 a year. By 1968 at least 2 million of the 16 million people of South Vietnam had become refugees. These people were crowded into the cities, housed in refugee camps, or relocated in "secure" villages free from Vietcong control.

The NLF.   The Vietcong were the fighting arm of a political organization known as the National Liberation Front (NLF). The NLF was organized in 1960 for the purpose of overthrowing the South Vietnamese government and seizing control of the country. It operated as a "shadow" organization, with its own members paralleling legal South Vietnamese officials at every government level.

From its national headquarters (assumed to be mobile but possibly located in the jungle close to the Cambodian border), the NLF directed its "officials" in the cities, towns, and hamlets of South Vietnam. Through this "shadow" government it levied taxes, "enlisted" men and women for its fighting forces, and organized terrorism and guerrilla warfare. The NLF included many Communists who, it is assumed, took their orders from Hanoi and probably dominated the organization. As the war intensified, the fighting arm of the NLF was strengthened by troops from the well-trained and well-equipped armies of North Vietnam.

The "other" war.   The Saigon government (supported by the United States) was, in fact, engaged in two major contests—one military, the other political. To win the military effort, it had to root out the NLF "shadow" government and protect South Vietnam's cities and hamlets from terrorism and guerrilla warfare. To win the political contest, the Saigon government had to convince the Vietnamese people that it genuinely cared about their welfare and could guarantee them a better way of life than that promised by the Communists.

From the start the United States stimulated Saigon's social and economic efforts with economic aid and technical assistance. As time passed the United States redoubled its support, sending teachers, social workers, agricultural specialists, and other experts to Vietnam. At the same time it urged the Saigon government to move more rapidly toward the reform of its undemocratic character and the elimination of existing graft and corruption.

The balance sheet in the "other" war. A South Vietnamese election in the autumn of 1967 was somewhat encouraging. Since President Diem's assassination in 1963 the country had been ruled by military leaders. The election was the first step toward the return of an elected government and the drafting of a constitution. Defying the Vietcong, who tried everything including violence to sabotage the elections, an estimated 51 percent of the eligible voters went to the polls. General Nguyen Van Thieu (NWIN VAN TYOO) became President, Air Marshal Nguyen Cao Ky (NWIN KOW KEY) Vice-President. Although military leaders were still in control, they promised to step up reforms.

Further encouragement came at the end of 1967 with a report by the civilian head of America's social and economic program in South Vietnam. According to his report, two thirds of the hamlets (about 8,650 out of 12,650) were "totally" or "reasonably" secure and free from Vietcong control. However, many Americans in Vietnam did not share the report's optimism. Other studies revealed that many South Vietnamese did not believe that the Saigon government was really interested in their welfare or that it could protect them from the Vietcong even if it wanted to.

The Tet offensive. Events in early 1968 demonstrated that Vietnamese doubts and fears were justified. Early in February the Vietcong and North Vietnamese army regulars opened the powerful Tet offensive—so-called because it was carried out during the Tet, or lunar New Year holidays. In a coordinated campaign they attacked the supposedly "secure" cities of South Vietnam, seizing partial control of or terrorizing 26 provincial capitals.

The South Vietnamese and American troops soon regained control of the capitals. But the price of "victory" came high, for in the course of battle large sections of several cities were blasted into rubble. Equally serious, the Vietcong recovered control of large areas of the countryside left defenseless when South Vietnamese and American

■ American servicemen are shown above carrying one of their wounded to a helicopter.

troops were withdrawn to defend the cities.

The Tet offensive dealt a staggering blow to an earlier prediction by General William Westmoreland, commander of America's military forces in South Vietnam, that the enemy was being defeated. It also demonstrated that the "other war"—the effort of the Saigon government to win the allegiance of the Vietnamese people—was still far from won.

The start of the Paris peace talks. At the end of March, with the Tet offensive still a raw memory, President Johnson declared that the United States intended to limit its bombing of North Vietnam. Starting immediately, he said, the air strikes would be confined to invasion routes and to the area immediately north of the Demilitarized Zone (DMZ) —a supposedly "neutral" strip of land separating North and South Vietnam.

Hanoi responded with the long-awaited offer to begin peace talks. After weeks of discussion the United States and North Vietnam finally agreed to hold the talks in Paris, where they began in May 1968. Meanwhile the fighting continued, and by midsummer 540,000 American troops were serving in Vietnam.

By 1969 the Vietnam conflict had become the second longest war in American history and the third largest in terms of lives and money expended. Only the Revolutionary War had lasted longer, and only World War I and World War II had consumed more American money, resources, and lives. Equally disturbing, the conflict had divided the nation more sharply than it had been divided since the Civil War.

SECTION SURVEY

IDENTIFY: Vietcong, Gulf of Tonkin Resolution, guerrilla warfare, NLF, DMZ; President Diem, President Thieu, General Westmoreland.

1. By 1965 the United States was waging two major wars. How were they interrelated?
2. Trace the evolution of American involvement in South Vietnam starting in 1962.
3. What position did the United States take in Vietnam by 1965?
4. (a) Describe the impact of the war on North and South Vietnam. (b) Describe the impact of the war on the United States and the rest of the world.

3 Re-evaluating the nation's responsibilities as a world leader

By 1968 many Americans were becoming concerned over President Johnson's conduct of foreign affairs. The immediate issue was, of course, Vietnam. But beyond that conflict was the larger problem of America's role as a world leader.

Was the United States trying to police the world? If so, did it have the wealth and the power to carry out this policy successfully? And did it have the duty or even the right to assume such an awesome responsibility? By 1968 these questions were troubling Americans all over the country.

The specter of Communist China. In the official view of the Johnson administration, perhaps the major threat to world peace was Communist China. In 1964 Chinese scientists tested their first atomic bomb. By 1968 they had also tested a hydrogen bomb and were working on the development of missiles that would make China a nuclear power in the 1970's.

Since 1949, when they won control of the country, the Chinese Communists had followed a policy of bitter hostility to "the U.S. imperialists" and their "lackeys" in the capitalistic world. Led by Mao Tse-tung, they had developed a theory of world revolution.

At the heart of Mao's theory was the idea of "people's wars," or "wars of liberation." Revolutions would be started in one after another of the underdeveloped countries by dedicated native Communists trained in guerrilla warfare. The guerrillas would avoid frontal assaults unless they had

clear superiority over their enemy. They would live off the countryside, using rural villages as their bases. When the enemy was worn down by an endless series of minor engagements, the guerrillas, supported by well-trained troops from the regular armies of a friendly Communist state, would attack and conquer the cities. By means of such revolutions, or "people's wars," the Communists would in time win control of the underdeveloped nations of Asia, Africa, and Latin America. They would then be able to move against the industrialized nations, already weakened by the endless "wars of liberation," and the Communist dream of worldwide Communism would be fulfilled.

America's Asian policy. The immediate objective of America's Asian policy, developed during the 1950's, was to counter the challenge of Communist China. This challenge was to be met by (1) "containing" Communist China within its existing borders, (2) providing military support to nations threatened by "wars of liberation," and (3) providing economic aid that would, as Secretary of State Dean Rusk later explained, "assist the countries of Asia in building broadly based governments . . . which can better withstand Communist pressure."

In support of this policy, the United States went to the aid of South Korea when it was invaded in 1950 by the Communist forces of North Korea (page 783). It maintained the powerful Seventh Fleet in Asian waters, as well as troops and air bases in South Korea, Taiwan (Nationalist China), and Thailand. It provided military and economic aid to the Philippines, Nationalist China, Laos, South Vietnam, and (until 1963) Cambodia. And in a continuing effort to isolate Communist China, the United States consistently voted against admitting that nation to the UN.

Meanwhile, as an essential part of its Asian policy, the United States continued to recognize Nationalist China on the island of Formosa, or Taiwan, as the only legal government for the whole of China.

Defense of America's role in Vietnam. In the view of the Johnson administration, American troops were fighting in Vietnam for the same reason they had fought in South Korea and that the Seventh Fleet had been standing guard off Formosa; namely, to prevent the spread of Communism and the possibility of a third world war. In the case of Vietnam, however, a new element had been introduced. As the administration saw it, Vietnam was merely a prelude to other "wars of liberation" —first in the neighboring states of Southeast Asia but eventually in the other underdeveloped nations of the world. In brief, Vietnam was a testing ground for Mao Tse-tung's theory of "people's wars."

Given this analysis, the Johnson administration logically concluded that the way to meet the threat was to demonstrate that aggression could not succeed. President Johnson clearly outlined this position in 1966. "Our purpose in Vietnam," he declared, "is to prevent the success of aggression. It is not conquest; it is not empire; it is not foreign bases; it is not domination. It is, simply put, just to prevent the forceful conquest of South Vietnam by North Vietnam."

Those Americans who shared this view predicted that North Vietnam would quickly back down when confronted by America's military might. When Hanoi failed to respond in this way, the United States increased its military pressure. But Hanoi countered each new step by a buildup of its own forces, and the conflict steadily intensified.

Criticisms of the Vietnam policy.   Critics of the Johnson administration's Vietnam policy grew more numerous and more vocal as the war increased in intensity. Those who urged the government to work harder to secure a negotiated settlement were labeled "doves." Those who urged the administration to increase the military pressure on Hanoi were labeled "hawks." There were wide differences of opinion within each of the groups.

Extremists among the hawks wanted President Johnson to bomb and mine Haiphong harbor and, if necessary, to invade North Vietnam. The administration resisted this course on the ground that it might precipitate World War III by drawing Communist China and the Soviet Union openly into the conflict.

Extremists among the doves wanted President Johnson to end the fighting by withdrawing all American troops from Vietnam as quickly as possible. The administration also dismissed this proposal, arguing that the withdrawal of American troops would (1) repudiate pledges made to South Vietnam, (2) leave millions of South Vietnamese at the mercy of their enemies, (3) open the door to a Communist takeover of all of Southeast Asia, and (4) strengthen the Communist threat to India and the island nations of the Far East.

Most opposition to the administration's policy fell between these two extremes. However, growing numbers of citizens felt that the commitment of American troops to a land war in Asia had been a grave mistake. They rejected the administration's

© 1966 Chicago Sun-Times, reproduced by courtesy of WIL-JO Associates, Inc. and Bill Mauldin.

■ Extreme positions taken by both doves and hawks on the issue of Vietnam were satirized in this political cartoon entitled "The Strategists."

contention that the principal enemy was the Communist government of North Vietnam. On the contrary, they argued, the war was largely a civil conflict in which the Vietcong were trying to overthrow what they considered the corrupt and unrepresentative government of South Vietnam. Moreover, they added, the United States was destroying South Vietnam in the process of "saving it from Communists." They urged the President to end the bombing of North Vietnam, to redouble his efforts to get peace talks started, and to include the National Liberation Front in the negotiations.

The issue of Presidential authority.   In March of 1968, with criticism of administration policies mounting, the Senate Foreign Relations Committee held a televised hearing to review the conduct of the war. As the hearing progressed, Chairman J. William Fulbright and other committee members expressed concern not only over American involvement in Vietnam but also over the issue of Presidential authority.

When Secretary of State Rusk appeared before the committee, Senator Fulbright asked him if President Johnson intended to escalate the war by sending more troops to Vietnam. Rusk responded that this was a matter for the President to decide. Rusk reminded the committee that in the Gulf of Tonkin Resolution of 1964 Congress had authorized President Johnson "to take all necessary measures to repel any armed attack against the forces of the United States and to prevent further aggression." Senator Fulbright replied that when he voted for the resolution, he had not intended to give the President a "blank check" to commit American troops to a land war in Asia.

At the heart of this issue was a fundamental question of constitutional powers. The Constitution designates the President as commander in chief of the nation's armed forces and gives him extensive powers over the conduct of foreign affairs. But the Constitution reserves to Congress the power "to declare war." In the case of Vietnam, however, the United States was engaged in an undeclared war over which Congress had little control.

To be sure, Congress, through its control of the purse strings and its right to reject treaties, has a check on Presidential powers. But as a practical matter, once large numbers of American troops are committed to an area, a refusal by Congress to provide them with adequate supplies and equipment would seem to be unthinkable.

Most Americans agreed that there were times when the President had to make far-reaching decisions without waiting for Congress to act. But did this mean that in matters of war and peace the role of Congress was no longer relevant? No one, it seemed, had a conclusive answer.

Was the United States overcommitted? Beyond the issue of Presidential authority was the larger issue of American foreign policy in general. Since World War II American commitments to prevent the spread of Communism had grown steadily. By 1969 the United States was providing military or economic assistance, or both, to more than 70 nations. It had formal commitments to defend 42 nations against any form of aggression, Communist or otherwise. It was prepared to wage major wars on two different fronts simultaneously, as well as to fight "brushfire" conflicts anywhere in the world.

In support of these formidable worldwide commitments, the Defense Department had 3.5 million men under arms—1.5 million overseas—and an additional 1.2 million civilian employees. As of January 1968 annual appropriations for military activities totaled $87.6 billion, or $439 for every man, woman, and child in the United States.

Increasing criticism. During the late 1960's Congress began to question what critics called the "swollen" defense budgets. By 1969 defense budgets were being subjected to searching examinations.

No one questioned the need to maintain the nation's military defenses. What the critics *did* question was what they believed was the alarming imbalance between the huge sums devoted to military projects and the relatively meager amounts devoted to the nation's domestic problems and the desperate needs of the underdeveloped nations.

In 1968, for example, in contrast to the approximately $88 billion appropriated for military and defense activities, Congress voted only $24 billion, or $118 per capita, for the nation's human needs—welfare, housing, health, and education. And Congress voted only $2.7 billion, or $13 per capita, for aid to the underdeveloped world.

Nor was the imbalance simply a matter of money. As critics pointed out, the many highly skilled men and women working on defense projects were not available to tackle the urgent human problems at home or abroad. The "brain drain" into war industries was robbing the nation's economy of precious and desperately needed human resources.

By the late 1960's the cost and magnitude of America's global commitments had become matters of widespread concern. It was evident, for example, that the enormous military expenditures were helping to fuel the growing inflation in the economy. As the value of the dollar declined (or, to state it differently, as prices rose), American products began to lose their competitive advantage in foreign markets. And as the inflationary pressures increased, foreign governments and private investors abroad, fearing that the dollar would lose its value, began to withdraw gold from the United States Treasury. The flow of gold out of the country weakened the dollar even further.

The Johnson administration took steps, including a 10 percent increase in the income tax, to combat inflation and to stabilize the value of the dollar. But critics continued to insist that until the government ended the Vietnam war and re-evaluated its total foreign policy the nation would remain in deep trouble.

Cautious moves made by Nixon. Such was the situation in January 1969 when President Richard M. Nixon took office. The war in Vietnam, as you have read (page 800), and the increasingly serious problem of inflation occupied Nixon's main attention during his first year in office.

During the election campaign Nixon had declared that if elected he would "bring an honorable end to the war." For several months after his election, however, no apparent plan emerged, and critics of the war became increasingly impatient.

In the spring and summer of 1969, however, the administration took several encouraging steps. In June President Nixon announced that he was withdrawing troops from Vietnam and that before the end of 1969 he planned to bring 60,000 men home. Two months later Secretary of Defense Melvin Laird declared that he was replacing the old "search-and-destroy" policy with a policy of "protective reaction." Under the new policy American troops would engage the enemy only when attacked or threatened by attack. The Nixon administration hoped that the new tactics would reduce American casualties and thus quiet some of the opposition to the war.

The administration's hope was only partially realized. The casualty rate dropped to the lowest in three years, and remained low as the level of fighting was reduced. But the opposition, led by those who now demanded the "immediate withdrawal" of all American troops, continued as vigorously as ever. Indeed, charging that President Nixon really had no plan for ending American involvement, opponents organized a series of nationwide demonstrations, the first held on October 15, 1969. On Moratorium Day, as it was called, several million Americans, mostly young people, gathered in public places across the country to register by their presence their demand for peace. "It was," *Life* Magazine reported, "a display without historical parallel, the largest expression of public dissent ever seen in this country."

Nixon's plan for Vietnam. Three weeks after the nationwide demonstration President Nixon appeared on national television to outline his proposal for ending the war. He also appealed to "the silent majority" of Americans to give him time to carry out his "plan for peace." "We intend," Nixon said, "to persist in our search for a just peace through negotiated settlement, if possible, or through continued Vietnamization if necessary—a plan in which we will withdraw all our forces from Vietnam

on a schedule . . . as the South Vietnamese become strong enough to defend their own freedom."

Shortly before Christmas President Nixon again appeared on national television to give what he called "a progress report." There were, he said, no further developments in the peace talks. However, recent developments in South Vietnam had made him "cautiously optimistic" over the ability of the South Vietnamese to defend themselves in the not-too-distant future. Nixon then announced his intention of withdrawing another 50,000 troops by April 15, 1970.

Public reaction. Americans who believed that the only way to end United States involvement in the war was to withdraw all troops at the earliest possible date were disappointed. But public opinion polls taken after the address indicated that the majority of Americans supported the President's plan.

The Nixon administration's "protective-reaction" policy and the gradual withdrawal of American troops reversed the earlier "search-and-destroy" policy and the increasing escalation of the war. Nixon was fully aware that the success of the new policy depended upon the reaction of Hanoi and the South Vietnamese. If the North Vietnamese and the Vietcong increased their pressure, the withdrawal of American troops would have to be slowed down or even stopped entirely. The same situation would prevail if the South Vietnamese proved unable to defend themselves. Only one thing was certain. The great majority of Americans wanted to end the nation's military involvement in Vietnam, one way or another, as soon as possible.

The Cambodian venture. The millions of Americans who shared this desire were heartened by President Nixon's promise in April 1970 to withdraw an additional 150,000 troops during the next twelve months. But ten days later the President startled the public with the announcement that South Vietnamese and American troops were crossing the border into Cambodia. Their objective, he said, was to destroy the string of North Vietnamese and Vietcong ammunition depots and camps along the eastern border of Cambodia. As soon as the sanctuaries from which the enemy had been launching their attacks against South Vietnam had been wiped out, the troops would be withdrawn. Nixon promised that all American forces would be out of Cambodia by the end of June.

President Nixon kept his promise. In the meantime, however, the Cambodian venture had shocked many Americans and triggered widespread anti-war demonstrations. It also strengthened the general conviction that the time had come for a complete re-evaluation of the nation's foreign policy, a re-evaluation that was already under way.

An outline for a new foreign policy. Early in 1970 President Nixon, in a special message to Congress, had outlined a new foreign policy. His title for the 40,000-word message was "United States Foreign Policy for the 1970's: A New Strategy for Peace."

The President began by reviewing conditions in the years following World War II. The war had left much of the world in ruins. New nations, created out of the former colonial empires, were struggling to secure their independence and build stable political and economic institutions. And the Communists, united under the leadership of the Soviet Union, had as their goal the overthrow of existing governments and the establishment of Communism across the earth.

Through the Marshall Plan and other foreign-aid programs the United States had helped its friends and allies to rebuild their war-torn countries. At the same time it had countered the Communist threat with a policy of containment. America's leaders had offered military and economic assistance to any nation anywhere that was threatened by a Communist takeover. To carry out this policy the United States had built a military establishment that was capable of fighting "two and one-half wars" simultaneously—a major war in Europe, a major war in Asia, and a smaller war in Latin America or Africa.

By 1970, however, conditions had changed dramatically. "We deal now," the President said, "with a world of stronger allies, a community of independent developing nations, and a Communist world still hostile but now divided." As he put it, "international Communism has been shattered. . . . The Marxist dream of international Communism has disintegrated."

In view of the changes abroad and the growing pressure of domestic problems, the time had come for the United States to begin a "limited withdrawal" from its worldwide commitments. The time had come for other nations, large and small, to assume a greater responsibility for building a prosperous and peaceful world. The time had come in America's relations with other countries, including the Soviet Union and Communist China, to emphasize "negotiation" rather than confrontation, "partnership" rather than domination.

The "central thesis" of the "Nixon Doctrine," the President declared, "is that the United States will participate in the defense and development of allies and friends, but that America cannot—and will not—conceive *all* the plans, design *all* the programs, execute *all* the decisions, and undertake *all* the defense of the free nations of the world. We will help where it makes a real difference and is considered in our interest."

Evaluating the Nixon Doctrine. Nixon's promise to scale down America's overseas commitments and reduce the size of its military forces won widespread approval. At the same time critics were quick to charge that the President's message "was long on rhetoric, short on specific proposals."

The phrase "peace through partnership" had a happy ring. But what would the United States do, critics asked, if the partners failed to cooperate? Why, they wanted to know, did the President pay only passing attention to the United Nations, the *only* existing global partnership for peace? And why did he make no mention of "world law"? In the critics' view, the basic flaw in Nixon's "foreign policy for the 1970's" was that it depended for success upon the exercise of self-restraint by all the nations of the world—and this was indeed a shaky foundation upon which to build a structure of lasting peace.

On one essential, however, there was general agreement. The Nixon Doctrine marked a major turning point in American history. In the words of one observer, the new approach to international relations was "as significant as the nation's emergence from isolation a generation ago."

SECTION SURVEY

IDENTIFY: hawks, doves, "people's wars," moratorium, "silent majority," Vietnamization, Nixon Doctrine; Dean Rusk, Melvin Laird.

1. Explain Mao Tse-tung's theory of world revolution.
2. Describe the provisions and purposes of America's Asian policy.
3. (a) Describe the arguments supporting America's role in Vietnam. (b) Describe the criticisms.
4. What constitutional questions were involved in President Johnson's Vietnam policy?
5. (a) Is the United States overextended in its foreign policy commitments? (b) Why does the question of priorities enter into a discussion of American commitments?

TRACING THE MAIN IDEAS

For more than a decade after World War II world power was divided between two giants—the United States and the Soviet Union. The United States was the acknowledged leader of the so-called "free world," the Soviet Union of the Communist nations.

By the 1960's, however, power was being dispersed. The solid front of Communism was breaking up as Communist China challenged Soviet leadership and the Communist nations of Eastern Europe began to demand a larger measure of independence. America's influence was also weakening as Japan and the Common Market countries of Western Europe became more and more prosperous and began to compete seriously for world markets. Moreover, the new nations that had emerged out of the former colonial empires were becoming increasingly restless.

Faced with these changes, each of the giant powers played the dangerous game of fishing in troubled waters in an effort to bring the underdeveloped nations into its own camp. As a consequence the United States became involved in one crisis after another in Asia, Africa, and Latin America. The most serious crisis developed in 1962 when the Soviet Union's attempt to equip Cuba with offensive missiles brought the world to the brink of nuclear war. Confronted by the determined opposition of the United States, the Soviets backed down and war was avoided.

By the mid-1960's America's policy of resisting the spread of Communism anywhere in the world had drawn the nation into a full-scale conflict in Southeast Asia. Fearful of a Communist takeover of South Vietnam, America's leaders provided massive air, naval, and ground support for the South Vietnamese. Before the end of the decade the conflict had become the third largest in the nation's history. Only World War I and World War II had been more costly in money, resources, and lives.

Widespread dissatisfaction with America's involvement in Vietnam led President Johnson to withdraw from the 1968 Presidential race and resulted in the election of a Republican President, Richard M. Nixon. It also led to a searching re-evaluation of the nation's entire foreign policy. By the early 1970's this re-evaluation was well under way.

CHAPTER SURVEY

QUESTIONS FOR DISCUSSION

1. Give your own evaluation of the Nixon Doctrine.
2. What are the implications of the Sino-Soviet split for United States foreign policy?
3. Should the United States permit Communist China to become a member of the United Nations? Why or why not?
4. Japan and the Common Market countries of Western Europe are becoming increasingly prosperous. How do you think such prosperity affects the relationship of the United States with these countries?
5. Why has the United States committed itself to opposing Communist expansion in Southeast Asia? Describe the steps taken by the Kennedy, Johnson, and Nixon administrations with regard to the conflict in Vietnam.
6. Some American critics of the government's Vietnam policy have declared that the United States could win the war but would destroy Vietnam in the process. What is meant by this statement?

7. Is the United States following the policy of the "Good Neighbor" with regard to Latin America today? Give facts to support your opinion.

RELATING PAST TO PRESENT

1. What was the attitude of the American public toward United States involvement in World War I? in World War II? in the Vietnam War? Explain the reasons for each of these attitudes.
2. Does the Nixon Doctrine constitute a return to isolationism? Why or why not?

USING MAPS AND CHARTS

1. Using the map on page 801, identify the four nations created out of what was formerly French Indo-China.
2. Refer to the map on page 801 to locate the Gulf of Tonkin. What connection does it have with American involvement in Vietnam?

CHANGING WAYS
OF AMERICAN LIFE

CHAPTER 43

America's Entry into a New Era

1945 – 1970's

THE WORD IS *change*. No single word better characterizes the years since 1945. Nor has anything been more striking than the *speed* with which every aspect of life has been transformed in the United States and throughout the world.

To be sure, change has been a central characteristic of American life from the day the first European settlers landed on the shores of the New World. Through the course of three and one-half centuries Americans have subdued a continent and converted the wilderness into the world's most prosperous and dynamic nation.

But the new and startling fact in the postwar years has been the *rapid acceleration* of change. Not since life first appeared on earth has so much change been compressed into such a brief span of time. One observer, writing in the early 1960's, declared that these changes were "so wide-sweeping that they are taking us from one epoch of human history into another." In his judgment, the world of the future will be as different from the world of today as our world is different from that of the Stone Age hunters who in the dawn of human history roamed the forests and grasslands in search of food.

During the opening years of the 1940's, however, not even the most far-sighted American could foresee the amazing developments that would in the years immediately ahead influence and alter older ways of living in the United States and increasingly throughout the world. In 1945 the opportunities and challenges of a new age had not yet been revealed. But by the late 1960's and early 1970's Americans in all walks of life were keenly aware of both opportunity and challenge as they looked at the rapidly changing scene and peered anxiously into the future.

THE CHAPTER IN OUTLINE

1. The increasing momentum of the scientific revolution.

2. Building an economy of abundance in the nation.

3. The effects of growth and change on the quality of American life.

1 The increasing momentum of the scientific revolution

The scientific revolution that has transformed—and continues to transform—almost every aspect of life had its roots in and was nourished by highly organized research and development. Even as recently as the 1930's the major advances in science in both Europe and America had been made by individual scientists working alone or with a few colleagues in the laboratories of universities or private industry. During the years following World War II, however, scientific research and development became increasingly a systematically organized team effort in which the federal government played an important role.

One of the most eminent twentieth-century scholars, Alfred North Whitehead, observed that when men began to organize research they invented "the art of inventing." This "invention," he concluded, was one of mankind's greatest achievements. The first dramatic demonstration of what scientists and engineers could accomplish by such large-scale cooperation occurred during World War II.

Harnessing the energy of the stars. On Wednesday, December 2, 1942, with the temperature down to 10 degrees, Chicago pedestrians hurried about their business, eager to get out of the cold. Fortunately for their peace of mind, the people of Chicago were unaware of what was going on in a laboratory under the stands of the Stagg Athletic Field at the University of Chicago. In the laboratory, which only a few weeks earlier had been a squash court, a group of scientists led by Enrico Fermi, an Italian émigré, were about to conduct the most fateful experiment ever undertaken by man.

The scientists, after months of feverish research, were about to discover whether an atomic reaction could be started and, if started, whether it could be controlled and stopped before it got out of hand. If the reaction proved uncontrollable, the most fearful "explosion" ever produced by man might devastate a vast area of Chicago and wipe out untold thousands of lives.

Only the pressure of a national emergency justified the risk. German scientists were trying to develop an atomic bomb. Confronted with this terrifying challenge, President Roosevelt had ordered a select group of the nation's leading scientists and engineers to spare no cost in the effort to beat the Germans to this awesome discovery.

The all-out effort conducted in the utmost secrecy was officially launched on December 6, 1941, under the innocent-sounding code name "Manhattan Project." Only a handful of the nation's top leaders knew that the project's goal was an atomic bomb.

Writing years later, one of these leaders, Arthur Holly Compton, described the suspenseful moment when Dr. Fermi gave the order to begin the test. "The counters registering the rays from the pile began to click faster and faster until the sound became a rattle. . . . Finally after many minutes the meters showed a reading that meant the radiation reaching the balcony was beginning to be dangerous. 'Throw in the safety rods,' came Fermi's order. They went in with a clatter. . . . The rattle of the counters died down to an occasional click. I imagine that I can still hear the sigh of relief. . . .

"Atomic Power! It had been produced, kept under control, and stopped. . . ."

The experiment was a success. For the first time in human history men had grasped, if only for a fleeting moment, the most elemental force in nature—the energy that keeps the stars blazing in the skies.

Organizing human intelligence. But it was a long step from a laboratory experiment to the production of an atomic bomb, and an even longer step to the development of atomic energy for peacetime uses. For three years, in an all-out effort to develop the bomb, thousands of the nation's leading scientists, engineers, and construction workers devoted their time and talents to the Manhattan Project. Never before had so much money ($2 billion), so much intelligence, and so much effort been channeled into a single undertaking. The atomic bombs that largely obliterated Hiroshima and Nagasaki in August 1945 provided evidence, terrible though it was in this case, of the effectiveness of organized cooperative research.

The growth of organized research. Mindful of the results achieved by the Manhattan Project and other wartime ventures, such as the development of radar, in the postwar years both government and private industry devoted more and more money to scientific research and development. Whereas in 1930 only $166 million was spent for this purpose, by 1953 the total had risen to $5 billion and by 1969 to $25 billion, almost two thirds of which came from the federal government. Although the federal government is the major investor in scientific research and development, most of the work is carried on in the laboratories of private industry,

■ Above, a mushroom cloud rises from the Nevada desert following the test detonation of an atomic bomb. Are nuclear weapons still being tested above ground?

universities, and independent research institutes.

As a result of highly organized scientific activities, new knowledge began to accumulate at such a staggering rate that men began to speak of the "knowledge explosion." The amount of information available to the human race was doubling every 10 years. The new methods of discovery and invention were self-generating. Each advance, each gain in knowledge, opened up new horizons for science. As you will see, new industries were created and thousands of new products became available. And most important, man was making fantastic progress in understanding the basic forces of nature.

But as you will also see, each fresh discovery also created new problems. With the invention of the "art of inventing," men built change into society, and the world could never be the same again.

International aspects of the revolution. As the years passed, international scientific activity came to be carried on by well-organized teams of scien-

tists from many lands. The period from July 1, 1957, to December 31, 1958, was proclaimed the International Geophysical Year. During this period scientists of 66 nations worked together in a worldwide study of gravity, geomagnetism, meteorology, oceanography, solar activity, cosmic rays, and other fundamental subjects.

In 1959 the United States and 11 other nations, including the Soviet Union, signed a treaty agreeing (1) to exercise no territorial claim over the vast, ice-covered continent of Antarctica and (2) to set it aside as a scientific preserve open to the scientists of all nations.

Early in 1967 a somewhat similar treaty in regard to outer space was signed by 62 countries. The treaty (1) prohibits the orbiting of nuclear weapons and (2) prohibits any nation from claiming sovereignty over the moon or any planet. President Johnson called the treaty "the first, firm step toward keeping outer space free forever from the implements of war." But efforts during the 1960's to work out collaborative arrangements for space exploration with the Soviet Union were unsuccessful.

Computers and the scientific revolution. The electronic computer was one of the most significant postwar products of the scientific revolution. Computers perform mathematical calculations and store and analyze vast amounts of information about literally any subject.

The first modern computers were developed shortly after World War II. By 1956 fewer than 1,000 were being used. By 1968 more than 15,000 were installed in laboratories, business offices, and government agencies, and predictions were that the number would double in the 1970's.

In a fraction of a second computers can perform calculations that even the most efficient individual could not complete in a lifetime. Computers available by the mid-1960's could perform in *one second* 357,000 additions or subtractions or 178,500 multiplications or 102,000 divisions. They were being used in laboratories to provide lightning solutions to complex technical problems that could not be solved in any other way. They were being used by businesses and banks for accounting, bookkeeping, and billing. They were being used by government to check tax returns and record data on births, marriages, public health, car registrations, and criminal records. They were being used in industry to forecast economic trends and control assembly lines in automated factories. And by the late 1960's computers were being developed that could automatically translate languages.

In brief, machines were doing much of certain kinds of mental work once performed by men and women. In fact, any data that could be measured or counted could be handled more efficiently by computers than by human beings.

Automation: promise or threat? Other equipment performed still other operations far more swiftly and efficiently than individuals could hope to do. For example, the Bell Telephone Company reported that if it had not installed automatic switchboards, all the women in the nation between ages 18 and 30 would have been required to handle the 90 billion telephone calls made in the United States in 1962.

The more complex machines used in many industries performed an entire sequence of operations and adjusted themselves to correct their own errors. By the 1960's "pushbutton factories" could turn raw materials into finished products with only a handful of technicians to plan and control the manufacturing process.

Observers in the United States and other lands watched the rapid increase in automation—the use of machines to do the work formerly done by men and women—with mixed feelings. Some hailed it as a triumph of human ingenuity which would lead to ever higher standards of living. Others shared the deep concern of Walter Reuther, president of the United Automobile Workers. After touring an efficient, automated automobile plant in which machines had reduced the number of workers from 800 to 15, Reuther asked pointedly, "Are these machines going to buy cars?" Organized labor leaders were not opposed to automation as such but, rather, to what they called "irresponsibly introduced" machines that could "result in unprecedented unemployment and an economic depression which may threaten the very foundation of our free society."

■ **By the 1960's "pushbutton factories" could turn raw materials into finished products with only a handful of technicians to plan and control the manufacturing process. A modern aluminum rolling mill is shown in the photograph below.**

Built-in change. History provides an almost endless list of examples that demonstrate the revolutionary impact of technological change. The invention of the chariot and its use in warfare terrified foot soldiers and transformed the nature of war in ancient times as much as the tank did in World War I. The development of the compass, the sternpost rudder, and three-masted ships resulted in the shift of economic and political power from the Mediterranean to the Atlantic and led to the discovery of the New World.

But the new element of change in the postwar world was the speed with which new inventions and new techniques were introduced into society. Nothing like it had ever happened before. As a consequence of this postwar revolution in science and technology, change has become the most striking characteristic of life in America and increasingly throughout the world. And as Americans entered the 1970's the revolution was continuing to gain momentum.

SECTION SURVEY

IDENTIFY: "the art of inventing," Manhattan Project, "knowledge explosion," International Geophysical Year, automation; Enrico Fermi.

1. Large-scale cooperation by scientists and engineers occurred during World War II. Why?
2. What new pressures does the "knowledge explosion" place on the people and schools of the United States?
3. The slogan of International Business Machines (IBM) is "Men Think—Machines Work." Relate this slogan to computers and automation.
4. Technological change has a revolutionary impact upon a society and the world. Explain.
5. (a) Automation can have a dehumanizing effect on society. Comment. (b) Where does the responsibility for how automation is utilized rest? Why?

2 Building an economy of abundance in the nation

The most obvious impact of the postwar revolution in science and technology was upon the nation's economic life. After World War II ended, the United States entered a period of unprecedented prosperity built on what economists called "an economy of abundance." This term described an economic system with the capacity to produce more goods than the people able to buy them could consume.

Growing productivity. In *USA in New Dimensions,* a study based on the nation's economy at the mid-century mark, a group of distinguished economists concluded that "America today has the strongest, most productive economic system in human history. . . . The United States, with little more than 6 percent of the world's population and less than 7 percent of its land area, now produces and consumes well over one third of the world's goods and services, and turns out nearly one half of the world's factory-produced goods."

Even more significant than the high level of prosperity at mid-century were the predictions of future growth based on past trends. During the 75 years preceding World War II the United States doubled its output of goods about once every 24 years. During the postwar period the rate of growth climbed sharply, indicating that the United States would double its output every 18 years.

The roots of prosperity. There were many reasons for America's remarkable economic growth. Among them were an abundance of natural resources, an excellent transportation system, an abundance of skilled workers, steadily improving labor-management relations, highly organized and efficiently managed industries, efficient methods of distribution, and an economic system that placed a premium on both individual initiative and teamwork.

But above all it was the astonishing advances in science and technology during and after World War II that sent the economy spiraling upward. "It has become apparent," the head of General Motors research laboratories said, "that the growth of a country's economy is increasingly linked with, not its natural resources, but the use it makes of its technological resources." The United States was the foremost nation in learning this lesson and in applying it to the development of its economy.

New and expanding industries. As the scientific revolution gathered momentum, new industries joined older ones in providing the products, services, and opportunities available to more and more Americans.

The aircraft industry, still in its infancy in the 1920's, grew in the postwar years to a multi-billion-dollar enterprise. The commercial airlines directly employed thousands of men and women. Many other thousands were employed in the plants producing aircraft for the airlines, private individuals, business firms, and the armed services.

The electronics industry, also an infant in the early 1920's, boomed during World War II with the production of radio, radar, and other equipment for the military forces. During the postwar years it gained still greater momentum with the production of television sets, electronic computers, transistor radios, and an incredible variety of complex instruments for the control and guidance of rockets and missiles.

In the late 1950's, when Soviet and American space exploration began in earnest, the aircraft and electronics industries joined hundreds of other enterprises in an entirely new undertaking—the space program. By the early 1960's some 9,000 American firms were actively participating in research and development of space-related items. By 1964 more than 30,000 scientists and other specialists were working for the National Aeronautics and Space Administration (NASA). Estimates of the total number of Americans engaged in some phase of the space program ranged from 3 to 5 million. Moreover, by 1964 the space research program had created some 3,200 different products, many of which had become part of the nation's everyday life.

Another completely new industry, atomic energy, also expanded greatly during the postwar years. By the early 1960's nearly 140,000 scientists, engineers, and other workers were engaged in atomic energy activities. Although military developments continued to dominate the effort, peacetime applications of atomic energy were growing more numerous. For example, the first commercial atomic-powered plant for generating electricity began operations near Pittsburgh in 1957. By the early 1970's more than 90 generating plants were operating throughout the country.

Meanwhile the older established industries were modernizing their plants and expanding their operations by mergers and by the continuing development of new products. Among the postwar industrial giants were the steel, automobile, petroleum, chemical, pharmaceutical supplies, and business machine industries, and the giant of all giants, the American Telephone and Telegraph Company, the largest corporation in the world. As incomes rose and as more people had more leisure time, companies manufacturing sports equipment also moved into the big business category.

The revolution in transportation. The nation's swift advance into an "economy of abundance" would not have been possible without revolutionary developments in transportation.

In 1945 the commercial airlines were still operating out of small airports and carrying only about 3

■ In the late 1950's, the aircraft and electronics industries joined hundreds of other enterprises in an entirely new undertaking—the space program. Above, Apollo 11 lifts off from the Kennedy Space Center.

million passengers annually, mainly in two-engine, propeller-driven planes capable of carrying only 20 to 40 passengers. By the 1960's they were operating out of huge, overcrowded airports and carrying more than 60 million passengers annually as well as ever-growing amounts of freight. And by 1970 planes with a carrying capacity of 360 passengers and 20 tons of freight were in operation.

Speed as well as size and versatility became a major factor in aircraft design during the postwar years. By the late 1950's 10-miles-a-minute jet aircraft were in operation on the commercial airlines. By the late 1960's designers were developing supersonic planes that would fly at more than 2,000 miles an hour, or about three times the speed of sound. Engineers planning airports and developing meth-

■ During the past few decades, the revolutionary growth of commercial air transportation has often resulted in overcrowded airports and plane traffic jams.

ods for regulating traffic in the increasingly crowded skyways often found their plans out of date before they left the drawing boards.

During the postwar years traffic problems on the nation's streets and highways also became an engineer's nightmare. Between 1945 and 1970 the number of automobiles, buses, and trucks more than tripled, increasing from 31 million to more than 100 million. The Federal Aid Highway Act, adopted by Congress in 1956, provided for the construction of 42,500 new miles of superhighways by 1972. Almost as soon as the act was passed traffic experts began to talk of the need to expand it. By the early 1970's federal, state, and local governments were pouring billions of dollars annually into the construction of new roads, highways, and city parking facilities. But with an addition of more than 2 million new motor vehicles each year, the problem was far from solution. Indeed, figures compiled by traffic engineers indicated that the automobile manufacturers were making cars and trucks faster than the nation was building roads and parking facilities to handle them.

The railroads, once the nation's main carriers of passengers and freight, did not share in the postwar transportation boom. Faced with mounting taxes, rising costs of labor and equipment, and falling incomes, by the 1960's many railroads were either bankrupt or on the verge of bankruptcy.

Although the rail carriers still carried nearly one half of the nation's freight, they were facing stiffer and stiffer competition from the trucking industry. Moreover, they had lost most of their passenger business to automobiles, buses, and aircraft. To be sure, the daily commuter trains carrying workers to and from their city jobs were still crowded. But with a few exceptions the commuter railroads were operating at a loss. Railroad managers contended that if commuter services were to continue, federal, state, and local governments would have to lower railroad taxes and bear a share of the cost of operating the trains. By the late 1960's, with the situation becoming critical, states and cities—particularly in the Northeast—were seeking new ways to improve commuter service. And in an effort to restore efficient passenger service between large cities, the federal government was subsidizing the development of high-speed trains capable of traveling at almost 150 miles an hour.

The changing scene. By the 1960's the revolution transforming older ways of living was in full swing. There was every reason to believe that the American scene would continue to change with steadily increasing speed. What these changes would be no one, of course, could foresee.

Who in 1945, for example, could have predicted the developments of the next 10, 20, or 25 years? In 1945 the corner store was still a familiar sight in every American town; by the 1960's giant shopping centers were within easy driving distance of most housewives. Between 1945 and the early 1970's an almost limitless variety of new products and services became available to many Americans. Medical scientists and the pharmaceutical industry produced penicillin and other antibiotics, anti-polio vaccine, and thousands of other new medical products. Manufacturers of household equipment produced, among other things, portable air-conditioners, washing machines, power-driven lawnmowers, dishwashers, and garbage disposal units. Housewives could purchase frozen food, dehydrated food, and pre-cooked food.

Prosperity and problems. But the postwar prosperity was only one side of the story. As you will see (Chapter 44), a disturbingly large number of Americans, including an alarmingly high percentage of Negroes, did not share in the general prosperity. And as you will also see, the changes transforming the nation's economic and social life and the face of the land itself created new problems for individuals and for society as a whole. As older problems became more acute and new problems clamored for attention, tensions mounted and observers of the American scene began to refer to the postwar years as "the age of anxiety."

SECTION SURVEY

IDENTIFY: "economy of abundance," "the age of anxiety."

1. Explain the reasons for America's remarkable economic growth after World War II.
2. What businesses, industries, and occupations can you list that were nonexistent before World War II?
3. Revolutionary developments in transportation took place in the postwar years. Comment on the benefits as well as the problems that flowed from these developments.
4. (a) What is progress? (b) What standards did you use to arrive at your definition?

3 The effects of growth and change on the quality of American life

The revolution in science and technology had an explosive effect not only on the nation's economy but on every aspect of American life. Each major development triggered a series of chain reactions. Equipped with new power, new techniques, and new machines, men refashioned the very face of the land itself. Life in the countryside and the city alike was transformed.

The rapid growth of population. One of the most far-reaching postwar developments was the world's rapid population growth. By the late 1960's the population of the earth was increasing at the rate of close to 70 million each year.

The upward population surge had not been foreseen. On the contrary, during the 1930's students of population trends, or *demographers,* had predicted that the United States population would shortly reach a peak and level off. By the early 1940's, however, they were swallowing their words. In 1940 the nation's population was 131 million. By the early 1970's it had grown to more than 210 million and was increasing upward each year by nearly 3.5 million—a yearly growth rate greater than the country's total population on the eve of the American Revolution.

To be sure, since 1957 the *rate of growth* had been declining. But even so the estimates of future growth were sobering. An American population of 335 million was forecast for the year 2000, and some demographers predicted 500 million by the year 2015.

The basic explanation for the upward surge of population in the United States and throughout the world was to be found in the remarkable advances made by medical science. Using the new "wonder drugs," as well as new methods and improved instruments for diagnosis and treatment, physicians were able to reduce the death rate, especially among children, and to prolong life.

Other developments in the United States also contributed to the rapid population growth. Prosperity enabled young people to marry earlier and to raise larger families. And large numbers of immigrants—some 2 million during the 1950's and even more during the 1960's—helped to swell the total.

The redistribution of people. An equally far-reaching development in postwar America was the growing mobility of a people that had always been

■ By the mid-1960's almost 85 percent of the total increase in the nation's population was taking place in urban areas. It was predicted that by the mid-1970's three fourths of all Americans would be living in metropolitan areas.

unusually mobile. Americans became increasingly able and willing to move from place to place. In earlier times when life was simpler large numbers of Americans had lived their lives in the area in which they were born, but by the 1960's one out of every five Americans was changing his place of residence each year.

These population shifts affected different states and different sections of the country in different ways. The western states grew at twice the rate of the nation as a whole, and in 1963 California, fastest growing of all, passed New York to become the nation's most populous state. Meanwhile the Northeast and the South were losing ground in relation to the rest of the nation.

Among the flowing tides of people three were especially significant: (1) the continuing exodus from the farms; (2) the rapidly increasing movement of middle-class families out of the central cities into the suburbs; and (3) the swelling migration of black Americans out of the South into other sections of the country.

The exodus from the farms. Among the dramatic developments of the new age was the sharp decline in farm population. Between 1940 and

1970 the number of people living on farms dropped from more than 30 million to fewer than 10 million. In some years more than 1 million men and women left the farms to seek better opportunities in the nation's growing urban areas. In 1940, 23 percent of all Americans lived on farms; by 1970 fewer than 6 percent remained.

Despite a rapidly shrinking farm population America was producing more food and other farm products than ever before. In 1940, for example, each farm worker produced enough food for 10 people; by 1970 each worker was producing enough food for more than 40 people.

The remarkable rise in American farm productivity sprang from the rapid increase of efficient, large-scale corporation farms and even more from the spectacular developments in agricultural science and technology. Better strains of plants, improved breeds of livestock, increasing attention to soil conservation and the enrichment of farm lands —all these combined to raise the average yield per acre of some standard farm crops by as much as 50 percent. Electricity, gasoline, and new farm machines also played major roles in boosting production.

There was cruel irony in the fact that every increase in productivity only added to the problem of farm surpluses. Some observers hoped that when the number of farmers decreased enough and the nation's population grew large enough the problem of agricultural surpluses would solve itself. Other observers maintained that there could be no such thing as a surplus. How, they asked, could one speak of too much food in a world in which two thirds of the people went hungry? And how could one speak of surplus food in a nation in which one fifth of the citizens—between 30 and 40 million men, women, and children—suffered from poverty and undernourishment?

Still other observers expressed another reason for concern over the rapid decline of the farm population. They argued that something important was vanishing from American life. From the beginning of American history, they pointed out, the small, independent farmer operating a family-size farm had added strength and vitality to democracy and free enterprise.

From a rural to an urban nation. The decline of the farm population was accompanied by a sharp increase in the urban population. This trend toward urbanization was worldwide. In the United States, however, cities expanded at what seemed to be an explosive rate.

By the mid-1960's almost 85 percent of the total increase in the nation's population was taking place in urban areas. Students of urban affairs predicted that by the mid-1970's three fourths of all Americans would be living in metropolitan areas. These areas included the central or *core* cities and the surrounding suburbs.

Two great migrations of people—one out of the central cities, the other into them—were producing revolutionary changes in American life.

The growth of suburban America. The migration out of the cities was led by young married couples seeking better living conditions for raising their families. This movement strengthened the trend toward a more widespread ownership of homes.

All over the nation people who could afford to do so were moving out of the older cities into the suburbs. The countryside around the cities was being leveled by bulldozers—at a rate, according to one estimate, of some five square miles every day—and huge suburban housing developments were springing up almost overnight. Department stores and banks were opening branches in the new suburban shopping areas, many industries were follow-

ing the people out of the central cities, and the expanding metropolitan areas were being tied together by a complex network of highways and superhighways.

These changes were impressive. They were transforming the face of the land itself. They were also creating problems.

As the suburbs spread in an unplanned sprawl over the countryside, the housing developments, shopping centers, highways, and roads ate up irreplaceable farm lands at an alarming rate. As you will see (Chapter 44), one consequence of the lack of planning was a deterioration of the total environment and therefore of the quality of life itself. Meanwhile the citizens of the new suburban communities were confronted with the immediate problems of creating almost from scratch new schools, police departments, fire departments, water and sewage systems, churches, libraries, hospitals, parks, and scores of other public services.

The growth of supercities. As the suburbs expanded, the metropolitan areas began to grow together to form supercities. This phenomenon, like the explosive growth of population, was worldwide.

In the United States by the 1970's three great supercities had begun to take shape. One extended along the Atlantic seaboard from Portland, Maine, to Richmond, Virginia. A second stretched along the shores of the Great Lakes from Chicago, Illinois, to Pittsburgh, Pennsylvania. A third reached down the California coast from San Francisco to San Diego. Each of these three great concentrations of buildings and people was sometimes called a "megalopolis" from the Greek words *megalo* meaning "very large" and *polis* meaning "city."

In both physical appearance and character the "very large cities" represented something totally new in human experience. Throughout history the city had been a compactly organized unit of activity. The new supercities were entirely different. They were neither urban nor suburban; they were a mixture of both. The megalopolis was an almost continuous system of interwoven urban and suburban areas covering thousands of square miles.

Unfortunately, political developments had failed to keep pace with these enormous concentrations of people and activities. For example, some 1,400 different governments operated in the metropolitan area of New York. Thus it was often difficult if not impossible to come to grips with problems common to the entire area—traffic congestion; health and sanitation; pollution of water, land, and air. No single one of the 1,400 different political units

■ In many large American cities, slum areas became a major problem. City governments increasingly found it difficult to help provide adequate housing for low-income citizens.

city after city across the land blocks of gleaming new office buildings and expensive apartment houses towered as visible symbols of the nation's growing affluence and vitality. Moreover, in most cities rows of low-income apartments were replacing the rundown tenements of an earlier age.

Equally visible, however, were signs of decay. Traffic clogged the streets and highways leading into the central cities—streets and highways built in an earlier age for horses and wagons and carriages, not for swarms of automobiles, buses, and trucks. Neglected areas deteriorated into slums when property owners, discouraged by the flight of the middle class from the city, refused to spend money for repairs and improvements. Faced with the decline of property values, city governments found it difficult to collect the amount of tax money they needed to provide essential public services.

As you will see, the problems confronting the cities were compounded by the revolutionary changes taking place in the composition of the urban population. The middle-class families leaving the cities were being replaced mainly by men, women, and children, black and white alike, from rural areas of the country, particularly from the South.

As early as 1961 James B. Conant, noted scientist and educator and former president of Harvard University, had issued a report titled *Slums and Suburbs* that attracted nationwide attention. The report pointed out the alarming contrast between the poverty of life in the decaying cores of the cities and the growing affluence of the suburbs. "We are allowing social dynamite to accumulate in our large cities," Dr. Conant warned. As you will read in the next chapter, this dynamite finally exploded.

could deal with the problems; the solutions required a complex cooperative effort, and this was not easy to secure.

It appeared increasingly evident to some observers that the overlapping and competing governments in the metropolitan areas would have to be replaced by a single government with overall jurisdiction. But political traditions and long-established institutions are hard to change, and only limited progress had been made by the early 1970's.

The changing faces of the central city. Meanwhile the original cities—now called the central or core cities—were also experiencing far-reaching changes—and some critical problems.

On the positive side, the hearts of the cities, the business areas, were being completely rebuilt. In

SECTION SURVEY

IDENTIFY: demographer, population shift, megalopolis, central or core city, suburb, *Slums and Suburbs*.

1. (a) What has contributed to the growth of population in the United States and the world? (b) What are some of the consequences of the population explosion?
2. (a) What have been the effects upon the United States of the growing mobility of its people? (b) Give the three basic sources of migration in the United States today.
3. (a) How did science and technology affect agriculture? (b) With what results?
4. The United States has become an urban nation. Explain.
5. The quality of life in the United States has become a major concern of many Americans. Why?

TRACING THE MAIN IDEAS

During the years following World War II the United States and the world entered a new epoch in human history. Americans led the way. They moved into the new age through the gateway opened by revolutionary developments in science and technology.

Among the most far-reaching of all the developments of the postwar years was the discovery of the effectiveness of organized research. In earlier times, even as recently as the 1930's, most research had been carried on by individuals working alone or with a few colleagues. In the postwar world research became a highly organized team effort. Scientists and engineers by the hundreds of thousands systematically undertook to unravel further secrets of nature and to develop more efficient instruments and machines and techniques.

One of the immediate consequences of the scientific revolution was a dramatic increase in the wealth and power of the United States. Americans became the first people in history to build an economy capable of producing more goods—food, clothing, housing—than the people as a whole needed. The fact that millions of Americans did not share in the prosperity, and the fact that the vast power acquired by the nation did not bring it the security it longed to have, became increasingly disturbing problems to the citizens of the United States as the years passed.

Another dramatic change in America in the postwar years was the rapid, even startling, increase in population. As the population grew and moved back and forth across the land in great human tides, the very face of America was transformed. But with change following change in ever more rapid succession, older problems became increasingly acute and newly created problems clamored for attention.

CHAPTER SURVEY

QUESTIONS FOR DISCUSSION

1. An experiment performed in Chicago in the year 1942 marked a turning point in the history of the United States and of the world. Explain.
2. The twentieth-century scholar Alfred North Whitehead observed that when men began to organize research, they invented "the art of inventing." Explain what he meant.
3. What are some of the benefits that have resulted from America's economic growth after World War II? What are some of the problems that have resulted?
4. In your opinion, what may be the long-range effects of the world's population explosion? Explain.

RELATING PAST TO PRESENT

1. "With the invention of the 'art of inventing,' men built change into society." Explain this statement, referring to inventions which are currently bringing about changes in our society.
2. The Founding Fathers created a Constitution that can adapt to a changing society. Defend or refute this statement, using evidence from current events to support your argument.

USING MAPS AND CHARTS

1. Using charts 1, 2, 3, 4, 6, 7, and 8 on pages 858–59, discuss the population explosion with regard to (a) rate of population growth in the past 30 years, (b) causes of the population explosion, and (c) effects of the rural-urban population shift on American life.
2. Referring to the charts on pages 868–69, discuss the revolutionary changes in transportation and communication that have taken place in the United States during recent decades.

CHANGING WAYS
OF AMERICAN LIFE

CHAPTER 44

Problems as Well as Promise for a New Generation of Americans

1945 – 1970's

B<small>Y THE</small> 1970's the United States had become a nation of ever sharper contrasts and contradictions.

On the one hand the American people could point with pride to a continuing succession of world-shaking technological triumphs. Their nation had been the first to unlock the secret of the atom and harness the awesome energy of the stars. It had been the first to develop an economic system capable of producing more goods—food, clothing, housing, even luxuries—than the people as a whole could consume. In the momentous effort to conquer space the United States had been the first to take the giant step of landing astronauts on the moon. These and other striking achievements flowed from highly organized research and development.

On the other hand Americans were acutely aware of an accumulation of unsolved problems—alarming racial tensions, the widespread poverty of an estimated one fifth of the nation, the worsening urban crisis, the rapidly widening gap between the rich industrialized nations and the ever-deepening poverty of the rest of the world, and the deteriorating quality of the environment.

These problems were especially alarming because by the 1970's the United States and the other technologically advanced nations had the capability—or could acquire the capability—of doing just about anything men wanted to do. Stated concisely, through science and technology men had acquired God-like powers.

Would Americans use the God-like powers they possessed to tackle and solve the enormous problems confronting them and a troubled world? This was the crucial challenge facing the nation as it moved into the decade of the 1970's.

THE CHAPTER IN OUTLINE

1. The black revolution's challenge to the "American dream."

2. The crises confronting Americans in the early 1970's.

3. A re-examination of a troubled nation's goals and priorities.

4. America's entry into the decisive decade of the 1970's.

1 The black revolution's challenge to the "American dream"

No group was more keenly aware of the discrepancy between America's technological achievements and its limited progress toward solving urgent social problems than the nation's 22 million black Americans. By the 1960's and early 1970's Negroes, frustrated with what they considered much too slow progress toward the goal of full equality of opportunity, were becoming increasingly insistent upon "freedom now."

The roots of the problem. The struggle that had reached crisis proportions by the late 1960's had its roots deep in the past. More than a century earlier, in 1863, President Lincoln had signed the Emancipation Proclamation, and by 1870 the Thirteenth, Fourteenth, and Fifteenth Amendments had been added to the Constitution. These three amendments freed the Negroes from slavery, gave them full citizenship, and guaranteed them and all other Americans "the equal protection of the laws," including the specific assurance that the right to vote would not be denied because of "race, color, or previous condition of servitude."

For a number of years after the adoption of these amendments many black southerners voted and held public offices in local and state governments. A number were elected to and served in Congress. After a few years, however, one after another of the southern states adopted laws establishing a new pattern of race relations. By the 1890's, as a result of both law and custom, the Negroes' right to vote had been limited. Black southerners were segregated from white southerners in railroad stations, on trains and streetcars, in public parks and buildings, in schools, churches, and hospitals, and in prisons and cemeteries.

Most northerners raised no protest against these laws. On the contrary, Negroes in the North faced increasing discrimination. Then, in 1896, the Supreme Court ruled that laws establishing segregation did not violate the Fourteenth Amendment. In the case of *Plessy v. Ferguson* the Court declared that "separate but equal" facilities met the requirement that all citizens were entitled to "the equal protection of the laws."

Black Americans thus entered the 1900's handicapped by problems they had not anticipated during the first hopeful years of freedom. Yet despite these handicaps they made impressive advances. As you have read (pages 662–64), Negroes won increasing success in every field of activity—science, medicine, the professions, business, music and art, entertainment and sports. By the end of World War II they had made marked—although still drastically limited—progress toward fuller political, legal, and social rights.

Legal action. During the postwar years the movement to end discrimination in government, business, education, and sports began to accelerate. President Truman took steps to insure equal opportunities for black Americans, and a number of barriers began to break down.

■ The "March on Washington" took place in 1963, on the hundredth anniversary of the Emancipation Proclamation. Some 200,000 Americans, black and white, marched in support of equal rights.

Acting on the recommendations of a Presidential Committee on Civil Rights set up in 1946, President Truman urged Congress to adopt legislation strengthening civil rights laws and enforcement machinery. When Congress failed to act, Truman used his executive powers to order an end to segregation in the armed forces and in the government.

Under President Eisenhower progress in civil rights continued. The most important development of the Eisenhower years was a Supreme Court decision of 1954. In *Brown v. Board of Education of Topeka* the Court reversed the 58-year-old *Plessy v. Ferguson* ruling that "separate but equal" facilities for Negroes were constitutional. The Court unanimously ruled that state or local laws requiring black citizens to send their children to separate schools violated the Fourteenth Amendment.

Several months after the momentous 1954 decision the Supreme Court placed on local school authorities the responsibility for working out plans for gradually desegregating public school systems. The Supreme Court also instructed federal district courts to require local school authorities to "make a prompt and reasonable start toward full compliance" and to move "with all deliberate speed."

Encouraged by the Supreme Court ruling, civil rights supporters redoubled their efforts to break down discrimination. As one of their major tactics they undertook to secure the passage of effective legislation. Congress responded with the adoption of five civil rights acts—those of 1957, 1960, 1964, 1965, and 1968.

These five measures were designed to speed up desegregation and to secure for black Americans the voting and other rights guaranteed them in the Constitution but often denied them in practice. This legislation achieved some of its objectives. By the mid-1960's race barriers had been largely broken down in hotels and restaurants, in buses and trains and airlines, and in other public facilities. Impressive gains had also been made in voter registration. Whereas in 1965 only 6 percent of the Negroes in Mississippi were registered to vote, by 1967 more than one third had been registered. The gains in school desegregation were less impressive. Although token desegregation was a fact throughout the South, by 1967 only 16 percent of black southerners enrolled as students were attending integrated schools. Each year, however, the pace quickened. And in the fall of 1969 the Supreme Court gave new impetus to the process with its toughest order to date. Completely reversing its earlier ruling

that desegregation be carried on "with all deliberate speed," the Court ordered an end to all dual school systems "at once." During the opening years of the Nixon administration, however, the Department of Justice showed less inclination to force southern school districts to desegregate.

Direct action.   Meanwhile the civil rights movement was employing another tactic, that of direct action, to speed integration and eliminate discrimination. By means of bus strikes, sit-ins, "Freedom Rides" through the South, and a 1963 "March on Washington," civil rights workers dramatized their determination to make court decisions and legislation effective. Students, both black and white, including many from northern colleges and universities, took a leading part in these peaceful demonstrations.

The tactic of direct action had two immediate results. It antagonized many white citizens in the North as well as in the South, helping to create what became known as "white backlash." But at the same time it drew into the movement many working-class Negroes who had not been involved when the emphasis had been mainly upon legislative action.

Growing frustration and shifting emphasis. During the early 1960's the outlook among Negroes was on the whole hopeful. New legislation, favorable court decisions, and the growing support of many white citizens were encouraging. Moreover, large-scale involvement in demonstrations and other forms of direct action, especially by young people, had given black Americans a deeper sense of self-respect and a growing confidence in the achievement of their goals.

By the mid-1960's, however, rising frustration was replacing earlier optimism. Essential though civil rights were, they did not provide jobs for the unemployed. They did not provide adequate housing in either the nation's rural areas or the overcrowded city slums. They did not provide the training or education needed to give underprivileged men and women the opportunity to raise their standard of living and build a better way of life. More and more it was becoming evident that integrated schools were not necessarily better schools in terms of the quality of education they provided.

Thus by the mid-1960's the goals of the movement shifted from civil rights to economic and social issues—jobs, housing, de facto segregation,°

° *de facto segregation:* segregation that exists not by law, but because of neighborhood residence patterns.

■ Dr. Martin Luther King, Jr., the most influential of all black leaders and staunch advocate of nonviolence, is shown above speaking in support of civil rights.

and discrimination by businesses and by organized labor in hiring practices. But with the war in Vietnam absorbing more and more of the nation's resources, Negroes felt that their problems were being neglected, and the goal of equal opportunity seemed as remote as ever. The growing strength of the "white backlash" and the failure of Congress in 1966 to adopt an open housing law ° provided additional fuel for the resulting bitterness, frustration, and despair.

Violence in the ghetto. The depth of black frustration was starkly revealed in riots that broke out in the community of Watts in Los Angeles, California, in the summer of 1965. The National Guard was called in to restore order, but before the rioting was brought under control 4,000 persons were arrested, hundreds were injured, 34 were killed, and

---

° *open housing law:* a law forbidding discrimination in the sale or rental of houses and apartments.

the damage from burning and looting totaled more than $35 million.

The extent and fury of the violence shocked the nation. It was especially alarming to those Americans, black and white alike, who had believed that the civil rights movement was making progress and that race relations were improving. Any lingering optimism in that regard was swept away during the next two years when rioting broke out in cities across the nation. Among the hardest hit were Detroit, Cleveland, Newark, and the nation's capital, Washington, D.C.

Many Americans, black as well as white, blamed the violence on a group of new militant black leaders. Although there was some truth in this explanation, it was by no means the whole truth. The rate of unemployment among black workers the country over was double that of white workers, and among black teenagers in the ghettos the discrepancy was much greater. Even these figures tell only part of

Malcolm X (above) was one of the first radical black leaders to attract national attention. Early in his career he advocated a policy of complete segregation of the races, but later abandoned this extreme viewpoint. Another of the new black leaders, Stokely Carmichael (below), was active in militant civil rights organizations.

the story, for Negroes in general worked at the lowest paying jobs. Figures released by the Social Security Administration revealed that in 1966 about 11.9 percent of the nation's white citizens had incomes below the poverty level, as against about 40.6 percent of nonwhite citizens. As the riots demonstrated, poverty from which there seems to be no escape is a fertile breeding ground for violence.

New leaders and "black power." Malcolm X was one of the first of the new radical black leaders to attract national attention. At first Malcolm X had a large following as one of the influential members of the Black Muslim organization. After he was suspended as a Muslim minister and broke with Elijah Muhammad, the Black Muslims' leader, he formed his own organization. In the early days of his brief but controversial career Malcolm X preached that all white men were devils and that the two races could live only completely separated from each other. Before his death, however, he abandoned this rigid racist position. "The sickness and madness of those days," he said to a friend, "I'm glad to be free of them." He was assassinated in 1965 by black radicals he had antagonized.

By the mid-1960's revolutionary black nationalism was making rapid strides. It embraced a variety of programs and organizations. Its leaders included Floyd McKissick and Stokely Carmichael, who had been active in militant civil rights organizations. It also included the founders of the Black Panther Party—Huey P. Newton, Bobby Seale, and Eldridge Cleaver. These men and others who shared their views tapped the desperation and despair in the ghettos. Scorning integration and, in some instances, any cooperation with white "liberals," they advocated complete racial separation. In their own organizations, black people must, they declared, achieve immediately their right to self-determination and full equality. Revolutionary black nationalism asserted the inevitability of direct confrontation with the white "power structure," including if necessary the use of force to protect black Americans against the aggressive "racism" of the white "establishment." "Black power," they maintained, was the only solution to black problems.

Many older black leaders, including Roy Wilkins of the NAACP and Martin Luther King, Jr., of the Southern Christian Leadership Conference, rejected this appeal to black racism and the use of force. Dr. King, most influential of all black leaders and an unbending advocate of nonviolence, declared: "In advocating violence, it [the black power movement] is imitating the worst, the most brutal, and the most uncivilized value of American life." Those who reject integration and call for separation of the races, he added, do a cruel disservice to Negroes. In his words, "There is no salvation in isolation."

When extremists first used the term 'black power," most citizens, black and white alike, were deeply alarmed, taking it to be an appeal to violence. Before long, however, different groups defined the phrase in their own way, and "black power" became a widely used rallying cry, even among black conservatives.

In economics "black power" meant the growth of independent black businesses. In education it meant local community control of ghetto schools. In politics it meant the growth of political power by either the formation of a black political party or the control of ghetto politics through bloc voting. And socially it meant self-reliance, self-respect, and racial pride. Phrases like "Black is beautiful" and terms such as "Afro-Americans" and "blacks" as well as "black power" came to be widely used in the Negro community.

Signs of progress. By the mid-1960's the black power movement was making gains. Politically these were revealed in the election of Negroes to public office—for example, Edward W. Brooke of Massachusetts to the United States Senate; Carl B. Stokes and R. G. Hatcher as mayors of Cleveland, Ohio, and Gary, Indiana, respectively; Julian Bond to the Georgia legislature.

Growing black influence was also apparent in other fields. In communities throughout the country black citizens were organizing to exercise greater control over schools in their own neighborhoods. They appeared with growing frequency in ads and on national television and radio programs.

And in the spring of 1968 Congress adopted a new civil rights act. The new act extended federal protection to civil rights workers and included the long-sought open-housing measure. The open-housing provision barred discrimination in the sale or rental of all housing with the exception of owner-occupied homes sold directly by the owner. The new law marked a significant legal victory in the battle against discrimination. Whether it would be effective in practice remained to be seen.

The Kerner Commission Report. The Spring of 1968 also brought to the American public the most comprehensive report on the race problem ever released by the federal government. In the summer of 1967 President Johnson had appointed

LIVING AMERICAN DOCUMENTS

Martin Luther King, Jr.'s,
"I Have a Dream" Speech (1963)

I say to you today, my friends, that in spite of the difficulties and frustrations of the moment I still have a dream. It is a dream deeply rooted in the American dream.

I have a dream that one day this nation will rise up and live out the true meaning of its creed: "We hold these truths to be self-evident; that all men are created equal."

I have a dream that one day on the red hills of Georgia the sons of former slaves and the sons of former slaveowners will be able to sit down together at the table of brotherhood. . . .

I have a dream that my four little children will one day live in a nation where they will not be judged by the color of their skin but by the content of their character.

I have a dream today. . . .

a National Advisory Commission on Civil Disorders to study the causes of ghetto rioting and disorder. The "basic conclusion" of the commission's report, issued in March 1968, was immensely disturbing.

"Our Nation is moving toward two societies, one black, one white—separate and unequal," the Commission warned. "Discrimination and segregation have long permeated much of American life; they now threaten the future of every American. . . . What white Americans have never fully understood—but what the Negro can never forget—is that white society is deeply implicated in the ghetto. White institutions created it, white institutions maintain it, and white society condones it."

The 425-page report contained detailed analyses of the race issue and comprehensive recommendations involving employment, housing, education, and welfare. If the programs recommended by the commission were to be carried out, the cost over the next decade would total scores of billions of dollars. The alternative, the commission concluded, was continued disorder and "the destruction of basic democratic values."

The assassination of Martin Luther King, Jr. The assassination of Martin Luther King, Jr., Nobel peace prize recipient and most respected of black leaders, fell with stunning force on all Americans, white and black alike. Dr. King was in Memphis, Tennessee, leading a nonviolent demonstration, when on April 4 he was cut down by an assassin's bullets.

"It is no longer a question of violence or nonviolence," Dr. King said in the last speech he made before his death. "It is nonviolence or nonexistence."

In that last speech he indicated that he had a premonition of death. "I've been to the mountain top . . ." he said, "And I've looked over, and I've seen the promised land. . . . I may not get there with you, but I want you to know tonight that we as a people will get to the promised land. . . ."

Dr. King's death served as a grim reminder of the importance of the Kerner Commission's warnings. While the nation mourned the loss of a leader who had devoted his life to a nonviolent solution of the race issue, riots broke out in various cities across the country. Chicago and Washington were worst hit.

The balance sheet. An economist, testifying before the Kerner Commission, struck a balance sheet. "No one can deny that all Negroes have benefited from civil rights laws and desegregation in public life in one way or another," he said. "The fact is, however, that the masses of Negroes have not experienced tangible benefits in a significant way. This is so in education and housing. It is critically so in the area of jobs and economic security. Expectations of Negro masses for equal job opportunity programs have fallen far short of fulfillment."

The economist went on to sum up his findings for the Commission: "Negroes have made gains. . . . There have been important gains. But . . . the masses of Negroes have been virtually untouched by these gains."

Martin Luther King, Jr., had dreamed of a nation in which men and women of every race and creed would be united in freedom and justice. Whether this dream would be realized remained an open question as Americans moved into the 1970's. The answer, as the Kerner Commission pointed out, was to be found in the minds and hearts of the American people. In the commission's words, the solution "will require a commitment to national action—compassionate, massive, and sustained, backed by the resources of the most powerful and the richest nation on this earth. From every American it will require new attitudes, new understanding, and, above all, new will."

828

IDENTIFY: *Brown v. Board of Education of Topeka,* de facto segregation, "white backlash," Kerner Commission Report; Malcolm X, Stokely Carmichael, Martin Luther King., Jr.

1. Summarize steps taken by the President, Congress, and the Supreme Court since 1954 in the field of civil rights.
2. Why by the mid-1960's did the black movement shift its emphasis from civil rights to economic and social issues?
3. What are some possible definitions of "black power"?
4. (a) What is the relationship between poverty and violence? (b) What does Negro rioting in the cities tell us?
5. "Our Nation is moving toward two societies, one black, one white—separate and unequal." (a) What are the implications of this warning? (b) What is required of Americans as individuals and as a nation to prevent this prediction from coming true?

2 The crises confronting Americans in the early 1970's

Closely related to the racial strife disrupting the nation were two other unresolved problems—widespread poverty and the crisis of America's cities. These problems were especially alarming because they had been permitted to develop in the world's richest nation, a nation with the resources of money, technology, and talent needed to try to solve the problems if it chose to do so.

Growing affluence. One of the encouraging developments in postwar America was the continuing growth in the productivity of the economic system. By 1970, for example, the Gross National Product—the total of all goods and services produced—approached the $1 trillion figure. Compared to 1960, this represented a gain of about 100 percent. For Americans as a whole it meant a continuing rise in the standard of living. As you have read, however, by 1970 inflation had become a serious threat to the nation's economic health.

The changing role of women. Another remarkable postwar development was the increasingly important role women were playing in the nation's work life. The contrast with earlier years was striking. Whereas in 1900 men made up most of the work force, by the early 1970's more than 40 percent of all gainfully employed workers were women.

A large percentage of the female workers were married. Steadily growing numbers of women were entering the professions of medicine, law, education, religion, science, and engineering. More and more were occupying positions of leadership in business and government formerly held only by men.

But it was also true that women continued to face discrimination. Many employers did not accept the principle that women were entitled to the same pay and the same opportunities that men enjoyed. Determined to overcome this handicap, militant organizations of women, "the new feminists," demanded full equality of rights and opportunities in every sphere of American life.

Although the entry of women into the work force had been gaining momentum since 1900, two major developments greatly speeded the process. First, the demand for manpower during World War II broke down many deeply rooted prejudices and gave women a chance to show that they could do as well as men in many different jobs. Second, and far more significant, the rapidly expanding economy created thousands of new jobs, nearly all of which demanded skilled brainpower rather than muscle.

Growth of the middle class. As one result of the changes occurring in the economy, America became increasingly a middle-class society. By the 1970's blue-collar workers, who in 1945 had held the majority of jobs, were outnumbered almost two to one by other workers. The great gains in employment were in the service industries and in work requiring professional and technical skills—teaching, science, engineering, medicine, nursing. Between 1960 and 1968 college enrollments doubled, and by 1970 an estimated 7 million students and 500,-000 teachers were working in the colleges and universities.

It was encouraging, too, that black citizens as well as white citizens were sharing in the nation's growing affluence. According to the Kerner Commission's Report, "the proportion of Negroes employed in high-skill, high-status, and well-paying jobs rose faster than comparable proportions among whites from 1960 to 1966." And this trend continued as the 1970's began.

Unhappily, there was another America, the America of the nation's poor—rural and urban, black and white. One fifth of the nation's men, women, and children remained outside the circle of prosperity.

The nation's poor. According to the Social Security Administration, in 1967 nearly 26 million Americans were living on incomes below what was considered the poverty line—$3,335 annual income for a nonfarm family of four. Another 15 million men, women, and children were living just above this poverty line. The total of 40 million represented one out of every five Americans. Moreover, 4 million homes had no running water or plumbing. New low- and moderate-income housing was not being built fast enough to replace rundown, wornout buildings, let alone to meet the needs of the rapidly growing population—over 2.5 million more people every year.

Poverty was a rural as well as an urban problem. In a report released late in 1967 a Presidential commission declared that for 14 million Americans "poverty is so widespread and so acute as to be a national disgrace, and its consequences have swept into our cities, violently."

Although two thirds of America's poor were white, the nonwhite population bore the heaviest burden of poverty. About 12 percent of the white population was below the poverty line, in contrast to some 40 percent of the nonwhite population.

In both rural and urban areas, poverty was most prevalent among certain groups—men and women over 65, unskilled workers, and migratory laborers. Hardest hit of all were several of the nation's minority groups. In addition to black Americans and American Indians, these minorities included men, women, and children of Spanish-speaking backgrounds—the descendants of the original Spanish settlers in the Southwest, Mexican-Americans, and Puerto Ricans.

The Spanish-speaking minority. The poverty and discrimination Negroes and Indians commonly experienced was shared by the great majority of the Spanish-speaking population that numbered, by the 1960's, somewhere between 3 and 5 million. Although the different groups of Spanish-speaking people differed from one another in important ways, all possessed certain characteristics that set them apart from the mainstream of American life. Their way of life was rural in background, simple in its technology, resistant to social change, strong in its sense of group identification, and proud of its Spanish and Catholic heritage.

The "Hispanos." The descendants of the original Spanish settlers in the Southwest continued to live, in general, a rural or village life. For their livelihood they mainly depended upon the raising of cattle and sheep. These "Hispanos" or "Latinos" were proud of their past and devoted to their way of life. At the same time they deeply resented their

■ In 1966 Cesar Chavez (in the plaid shirt) led Mexican-American farm workers on a march to dramatize their demand for better working conditions.

poverty and the widespread discrimination against them. They attributed their unhappy condition to the sharp practices of the "Anglos," especially in regard to water and mineral rights and the titles to ranch lands.

By the 1960's the members of this old and proud minority, numbering a few hundred thousand at the most, were actively resisting "Anglo exploitation" and discrimination. They were demanding full equality of opportunity as American citizens.

Mexican-Americans. Even more unfortunate were the Mexican-Americans. Before World War I many Mexicans had entered the United States to work on railroads and ranches in the Southwest and as unskilled laborers in the border cities. They lived in segregated shantytowns. English-speaking Americans regarded these immigrant workers as aliens and often treated them unfairly.

During and after World War I hundreds of thousands of Mexicans poured across the border to seek jobs in the United States. Most of them became migrant workers in the cotton and sugar-beet fields and in the rapidly developing commercial fruit and vegetable orchards and farms of California. Some,

called "braceros," came under contract. Others, called "wetbacks," entered the country illegally by swimming or wading across the Rio Grande. Many returned home after the crops had been harvested but recrossed the border again the next season. Many others became permanent residents of Los Angeles, El Paso, Dallas, Denver, and other cities. As migrant workers in the fields and as laborers in the cities, the Mexican-Americans played an essential role in the economic life of the Southwest.

By mid-century the cities along the southwestern border included large numbers of Mexican-Americans. Largely unskilled and uneducated, handicapped by not knowing English, discriminated against in wages and housing, most were forced to live in slums. By the 1960's, however, many of the sons and daughters of the earlier immigrants were enrolled in the high schools, and to a lesser extent in the colleges, of California and other southwestern states. More and more of these young people were demanding an end to the discrimination their parents had endured.

Most Mexican-Americans who did not settle in the cities continued to work as migratory farm workers. Efforts by labor unions in the 1930's and 1940's to organize them were largely unsuccessful. In the 1960's, however, the workers, led by Cesar Chavez and other new leaders, began to make real if still limited progress toward their goal of fair wages and decent living and working conditions.

The Puerto Ricans. Puerto Ricans made up the third Spanish-speaking minority group. As you have read (page 590), Puerto Rico had been an American territory since 1898, and the inhabitants of the Caribbean island were legally entitled to the rights and privileges of American citizenship. Even before the worldwide depression of the 1930's brought severe hardships to the already poor and overcrowded island, many Puerto Ricans had migrated to New York in search of jobs. During and after the depression they came in ever-swelling numbers.

Puerto Ricans who moved to New York were badly handicapped. Most came from rural villages. They lacked the skills necessary for life in a highly complex and competitive urban environment. They had at best a limited command of English. And perhaps most serious, they were victims of prejudice and discrimination.

Because of these handicaps most of the newcomers were able to get only unskilled jobs that paid the lowest of wages. They were crowded into wretched tenements in Spanish Harlem and other segregated areas in metropolitan New York and, increasingly, in other major cities, where their lives were marked by poverty and hardship. Many returned to Puerto Rico.

The lot of young Puerto Ricans was especially difficult. In school they were handicapped by unfamiliarity with English and embittered by the antagonism they often met from other children.

In some ways the experiences of the approximately 1 million Puerto Ricans in the United States resembled those of earlier immigrants. Many managed to move up the economic ladder and to find places in small businesses, semi-skilled trades, the professions, and the arts. When their voting power became obvious in the large cities, Puerto Ricans became a "force" as well as a "problem." Nevertheless the deprivations and discrimination most Puerto Ricans experienced stood in marked contrast to the widespread affluence of most American groups.

The war on poverty. "Poverty in the midst of plenty is a paradox that must not go unchallenged," President Kennedy had declared in 1963. And President Johnson, sharing this conviction,

launched an "unconditional war on poverty" (page 766). In 1964, responding to the administration's urging, Congress created the Office of Economic Opportunity. Under the OEO a number of programs were started—a Head Start education program for preschool children; a Neighborhood Youth Corps for unemployed teenagers; a Job Corps for youngsters who had dropped out of school; an Upward Bound program to help boys and girls go to college; and the VISTA program (a domestic version of the Peace Corps) in which volunteers worked with and among the nation's poor.

In 1965 Congress continued the war on poverty with several important measures aimed at improving conditions in job training, health, education, and housing. It expanded the 1964 Economic Opportunity Act. It adopted a Medicare bill providing for hospital care and other medical services for persons over 65. It enacted into law two major education bills, one providing federal aid for elementary and secondary education, and the other for higher education. It created a new federal department, the Department of Housing and Urban Development. To head the new department President Johnson appointed Robert C. Weaver, the first Negro to serve in the cabinet.

The plight of the cities. By 1966 the Vietnam conflict was intensifying (page 801), and as a consequence the anti-poverty drive began to lose momentum. Meanwhile, however, the rioting and disorder in the nation's cities were sobering warnings that the urban crisis could not be ignored.

Congress responded with two measures. It created another cabinet-level agency, the Department of Transportation. The new department was charged with coordinating the activities of some 34 federal agencies dealing with air, rail, and road travel and transportation.

Congress also set up a $1.3 billion Model Cities program. Under this program a selected group of about 75 cities were to develop "model" plans for rebuilding decaying slum areas. The plans were to provide for the coordination of all federal programs —job training, health, education, housing, and welfare. All planning was to be done in cooperation with the citizens in the communities to be rebuilt.

Mounting tensions. Encouraging though it was, the Model Cities program offered no immediate relief for the nation's cities. Moreover, after 1966 the anti-poverty program began to lag as the government became more involved in Vietnam.

The resulting frustration and despair were reflected in unprecedented outbreaks of violence dur-

PUERTO RICO'S PEACEFUL REVOLUTION

Puerto Rico is sometimes called "the showcase of Latin America." This beautiful but overcrowded Caribbean island, the home of some 2.5 million people, richly deserves its showcase reputation.

In 1945 the Puerto Ricans launched a program to eliminate poverty and unemployment and to raise the prevailing low standard of living. This program, known as "Operation Bootstrap," was well under way when, in 1952, Puerto Rico became a self-governing commonwealth associated with the United States (page 590). Today, with a stable democratic government and a flourishing economy, Puerto Ricans enjoy a per capita income higher than that of any other Latin-American country with the single exception of oil-rich Venezuela.

The peaceful revolution through which the Puerto Ricans secured self-government and better living standards was carried out under the remarkable leadership of Luis Muñoz-Marín (LWEES MOON·yos-mah·REEN). With United States help, the Puerto Ricans have instituted land reforms and eliminated the worst slums. They have built roads, factories, modern tourist hotels, housing projects, and schools. One way the United States has helped Puerto Ricans in their efforts to raise living standards is through free trade. There are no tariff barriers between the United States and Puerto Rico.

It is significant that Puerto Ricans have transformed their island without sacrificing their own cultural traditions. Puerto Rico's victory over poverty, although by no means complete, represents one of the most dramatic chapters in recent history.

ing the first nine months of 1967. These outbreaks of violence caused property damage amounting to hundreds of millions of dollars and resulted in hundreds of injuries and scores of deaths.

The Poor People's Campaign. By 1968 the tensions in rural as well as urban America were acute. The Poor People's Campaign, organized in the spring, was designed to dramatize the plight of the poor and to compel government action.

In May the vanguard of the "army of the poor," led by Dr. Ralph D. Abernathy, reached the nation's capital. In the heart of the city, along the length of the Lincoln Memorial's reflecting pool, they began to build Resurrection City—a makeshift cluster of plywood huts to shelter the thousands who were to join in the nonviolent demonstration.

The campaign drew men and women from every corner of the nation. There were whites and blacks, Indians, Mexican-Americans, Puerto Ricans, migrant workers, the poor from the ghettos and from the rural areas of the land. The culminating event was Solidarity Day, so named to remind America that the poor of every race and creed were determined to unite to win freedom from the burden of poverty. Dr. Abernathy voiced the pleas of millions when he said: "Let no child go hungry. . . . Let no man be without a job. . . . Let no citizen be denied an adequate income."

The demonstration ended on June 16. For six weeks it had focused the nation's eyes on the shame of widespread poverty in a prosperous land. Whether it had accomplished any further purpose only the future would reveal.

The urban crisis. It was in the great urban centers that the nation's domestic problems were focused. The problems were staggering—poverty; racial strife; the breakdown of a sense of community; the alarming problem of drug addiction; soaring crime rates; inadequate health, educational, and recreational facilities; traffic congestion; the physical decay of the central cities; the pollution of water and air; and the increasingly rapid division of the city population into a minority of the well-to-do and the majority of the poor.

As you have read (page 820), two great streams of migration were transforming the nation's urban areas. Middle-class families, mostly white, were moving out of the cities into the suburbs. Underprivileged Americans, white as well as black, were moving from rural areas into the cities.

The migration from the country to the city was largely the result of technological change. Farm workers, displaced by machines, moved to the city in search of work. In earlier times they would have found jobs. But work for unskilled, inadequately educated men and women was becoming increasingly scarce in a technological society. Compounding the problem was the fact that the service industries which still required a substantial number of unskilled or semi-skilled workers were following the middle class into the suburbs.

Hardest hit of all were black Americans. For Negroes as a whole, the unemployment rate in 1967 was double that of whites, and for black teenagers it was 26.5 percent compared to 10.6 percent for white teenagers. These were national averages. In the city slums unemployment rates were much higher.

By the late 1960's the conditions in America's large cities had become desperate. The core areas of the cities had decayed so badly that they needed to be entirely rebuilt. This would take years and billions upon billions of dollars. Meanwhile the underprivileged in the slums, white and black alike, needed more and better public services—health, education, sanitation, recreation, police and fire protection. Jobs and retraining for jobs had to be provided.

But the cities did not have the finances to do the work that had to be done. The people most able to pay the necessary taxes were abandoning the cities; those least able to pay and most in need of the services were becoming more numerous. Between 1950 and 1966 municipal revenues increased by only 29.8 percent, while expenditures increased by 43.7 percent.

By the late 1960's the urban crisis was in fact a national crisis. Only a massive and coordinated effort by the federal government and the cities—by the nation as a whole—could prevent a disaster.

SECTION SURVEY

IDENTIFY: migrant workers, Hispanos, braceros, "wetbacks," OEO, VISTA; Cesar Chavez, Robert Weaver, Dr. Ralph Abernathy.

1. Who comprise the poor in America? Why?
2. Trace the measures adopted by the Johnson administration to fight the war on poverty.
3. What was the significance of the "Poor People's March" on Washington?
4. The urban crisis is a national crisis. Explain.
5. For many Americans "poverty is so widespread and so acute as to be a national disgrace, and its consequences have swept into our cities violently." Comment.

3 A re-examination of a troubled nation's goals and priorities

In 1492 it took more than six weeks for the news of Columbus' great discovery to reach the privileged classes in Europe. In 1969 an estimated 600 million people around the globe watched on television and uncounted millions more listened on radio as the first Earthmen, America's astronauts, set foot on the moon. The striking contrast between these two world-shaking events provided graphic evidence of mankind's progress toward the conquest of time and space.

Just as millions of men and women followed the trail Columbus had blazed to the New World, so other Earthmen would explore the lunar surface and, in the fullness of time, land on other planets. But no event could ever match in sheer dramatic excitement mankind's first triumphant expedition into outer space.

Behind the successful flight of Apollo 11 was a vast cooperative effort extending over eight years and involving the energy and talents of an estimated half million men and women and an expenditure of more than $30 billion—15 times the amount of money invested in the development of the first atomic bomb. The Apollo 11 flight was without question the most magnificent technological achievement up to that moment in human history.

But in the midst of rejoicing over the grandeur of man's conquest of space, many Americans were troubled. Why had the nation that had landed men on the moon not made greater progress toward solving the urgent problems confronting it on earth?

The question in regard to national purposes was not a new one. Americans had been asking it with growing concern for more than a decade. By the 1970's, however, it had become crucially important.

From self-confidence to self-appraisal. Americans in 1945 entered the postwar years with confidence. The United States had emerged from the war as the richest, most powerful nation on earth. The future seemed full of promise.

During the next few years this unqualified optimism melted away. To be sure, the nation's booming economy continued to bring prosperity and the assurance of still more material comforts in the years ahead. But this bright picture was blurred by dark shadows. The threat of nuclear war was a haunting reality. Communism, with its continuing efforts to win over the two thirds of the world's people living on the ragged edge of hunger

■ In 1969 an estimated 600 million people around the globe watched on television and uncounted millions more listened on radio as the first Earthmen, America's astronauts, set foot on the moon.

and need, remained a challenge. The swift advance of the scientific revolution was multiplying problems even as it created greater wealth and larger opportunities.

Faced with revolution throughout the world and increasingly difficult problems at home, Americans experienced a growing sense of doubt and uncertainty. In the midst of prosperity they were anxious and troubled. As the years passed they began to ask what had become of the peaceful and orderly world that in 1945 had seemed such a promising possibility.

What had gone wrong? Had Americans, as individuals and as a nation, failed to make the most of their opportunities? If so, where had they failed? What needed to be done? Troubled by questions like these, Americans entered the 1960's, as one historian put it, "in a mood of anxious self-appraisal."

Ideals versus practices. In 1959, hoping to clarify the goals toward which America might strive, President Eisenhower appointed a group of distinguished citizens to study the problem. In the

fall of 1960 the Commission published its report, *Goals for Americans.*

"The paramount goal of the United States was set long ago," the report began. "It is to guard the right of the individual, to ensure his development, and to enlarge his opportunity. It is set forth in the Declaration of Independence. . . .

"The way to preserve freedom is to live it. Our enduring aim is to build a nation and help build a world in which every human being shall be free to develop his capacities to the fullest. We must rededicate ourselves to this principle and thereby strengthen its appeal to a world in political, social, economic, and technological revolution."

The Commission's report outlined objectives for every major activity of American life. Throughout the report the Commission held before readers the "mighty vision" of a nation whose fundamental concern was for the development of every individual's spiritual and intellectual capacities.

These were noble words. They expressed a noble ideal—the ideal often called the "American Dream." As the years passed, however, it became increasingly evident to many Americans, particularly young Americans, that in far too many ways the nation was failing to live up to this ideal.

Youth's questioning of older values. One of the most striking phenomenons of the 1960's was the rapidly widening gap between the generations. By the early 1970's many young people were questioning and some were rejecting the values and practices of the older generation.

In their attitudes and behavior young Americans had gone through several distinct phases during the postwar years. Those growing up in the 1950's were characterized as "the uncommitted generation." With the exception of an extremely few "hipsters" and "beatniks," young people in the 1950's seemed to be conformists. On the whole, their goals in life were the security of a steady job, a home in the suburbs, and a safe, comfortable life. For the most part they avoided political activity.

In the early 1960's, however, a spirit of idealism seemed to be replacing the earlier widespread apathy. Inspired by a relatively young President, John F. Kennedy, the young began to commit themselves to causes. Some joined the Peace Corps. Others became active in the civil rights movement. Many began to work within the framework of the major political parties. The college campuses stirred with new political and intellectual activity.

By 1964, however, some of the idealism was draining away. After President Kennedy's assassination a wave of unrest and protest swept through the ranks of the nation's young people. The growing unrest was not confined to the United States.

In the United States it was relatively easy to identify some of the reasons for the unrest. No one pretended these were all of the reasons. Unemployment, especially among high-school dropouts and teenagers in the ghettos, was an obvious source of discontent. College students were becoming increasingly restless as enrollments soared and the overcrowded universities tended to become vast impersonal educational factories. Many young people were deeply disturbed over America's involvement in Vietnam, which they considered immoral and futile. They were concerned, too, over continuing poverty and prejudice and discrimination in a nation that professed democratic principles.

These alienated young people reacted in two different ways. One relatively small group, the "hippies," rejecting the adult world and all it represented, refused to make any commitments or assume any responsibilities. Another small group turned to active rebellion, their goal the overthrow of "the establishment" and the creation of what they considered a better form of society.

Many Americans hoped that the new generation could be encouraged to work for social and political change within the democratic system; one means to this end was the Voting Rights Act of 1970, which gave eighteen-year-olds the right to vote in federal elections. In 1971 the 26th Amendment extended this right to state and local elections. It was often observed that the alienated remained only a small minority of the new generation. Even so, no thoughtful observer dismissed the group as inconsequential. Their protest, whether in the form of passive withdrawal or active rebellion, served as a disturbing reminder of America's unfinished business.

Private or public priorities? Many Americans —and not merely the alienated younger generation—shared a basic question involving the economy itself: Was the nation making the best use of its enormously productive economic system? Or, stated more simply, were Americans spending their money and using their resources, human and material, in ways most beneficial to them and to the nation as a whole?

On one side of the debate were those citizens, young and old alike, who argued that too much of America's income and wealth was being used to satisfy private needs—the latest model automobiles, labor-saving devices and gadgets for the home, and other consumer goods of all kinds. As a result, this group argued, Americans were failing to devote enough of their income to public services—schools, hospitals, the war on poverty, urban renewal, parks and recreational facilities, the renewal of the environment. Those who argued this way reminded their fellow citizens that the economy was already producing more goods than the people with money could consume. Despite this fact, however, the nation was devoting a smaller proportion of its total income to public services than it had in 1939.

In a widely read book, *The Affluent Society,* economist J. K. Galbraith reminded Americans that in their pursuit of material things they were neglecting many essentials of the good life. In a scathing word portrayal he described an American family on its way to a vacation in the country. He pictured them driving their new luxury model car through city streets littered with rubbish and congested with traffic into a countryside defaced by billboards. "They picnic," he wrote, "on exquisitely packaged food from a portable icebox by a polluted stream and go on to spend the night at a park which is a menace to public health and morals. Just before dozing off on an air mattress, beneath a nylon tent, amid the stench of decaying refuse, they may reflect on the curious unevenness of their blessings. Is this," Galbraith asked, "indeed the American genius?"

Many Americans took sharp issue with economist Galbraith and those who supported his views. The critics did not deny the need for greater attention to public services. They were concerned, however, with the danger of a welfare state in which the government would drain off a larger and larger proportion of the national income in taxes and thus decide for the people how they should spend their money. Were this to happen, the critics warned, the government would discourage individual initiative and stifle the creativity that had produced the most productive economic system in history. Such a policy would, they claimed, kill the goose that had been laying the golden eggs of prosperity.

Foreign aid: How much and what kind? Coupled with the question of how best to strengthen freedom, equality of opportunity, and prosperity at home was the equally urgent question of America's role in a changing world.

One dramatic measure of the change could be seen in the United Nations. When the UN charter was signed in June 1945 the organization included 50 members, only two of which were from black Africa, only three from Asia. By 1970 more than

■ By the 1970's, many young Americans were questioning the values and practices of the older generation. Their protests served as a disturbing reminder of America's unfinished business.

half of the 126 members were African or Asian; almost three fourths of them were economically underdeveloped countries.

The delegates from the underdeveloped nations represented the poor people of the world, and the poor were becoming increasingly impatient with their lot. As historian Arnold Toynbee put it, "In the most remote villages of the world, hundreds of millions of people have at long last sensed the possibility of a better life." The black militancy in the United States and the rising voices of America's poor, white and black, were only the domestic manifestations of a worldwide revolution. Moreover, the gap between the rich, industrialized countries and the poor, underdeveloped nations was becoming steadily wider and deeper.

By the 1960's it was becoming increasingly evident to America's leaders that the war against poverty and injustice must be waged on a world scale. Self-interest, as well as America's cherished belief in the dignity of life and the "unalienable right" of every individual to equality of opportunity, left the nation no choice but to accept the challenge. Americans were beginning to understand that the United States could maintain its military defenses against the Communist powers and still lose the war for freedom and democracy by failing to support the underdeveloped nations in their struggle for a better life.

Few thoughtful Americans opposed foreign aid as such. There was, however, much disagreement about how much of the nation's resources should be devoted to this effort. And there were equally vigorous disagreements as to where foreign aid should go and how it could be used most effectively.

America's foreign-aid program was reduced as a result of these differences of opinion. The $1.75 billion Congress appropriated for foreign aid in

836

1969 was the lowest in the program's 21-year history. Critics were quick to contrast America's meager effort to relieve worldwide poverty and suffering with the nearly $80 billion the Department of Defense spent in the same year. Critics were also quick to remind their fellow Americans that 11 nations ranked ahead of the United States in the percentage of Gross National Product devoted to helping underdeveloped nations. In the words of one Congressman, the United States had set for itself "priorities of power, not priorities of need." To the critics at least, the evidence seemed to indicate that the American nation was failing to make an adequate response to the challenge of a restless world.

SECTION SURVEY

IDENTIFY: generation gap, apathy, commitment, alienation, *The Affluent Society,* "priorities of power, not priorities of need."

1. Why had the nation that had landed men on the moon not made greater progress toward solving the urgent problems confronting it on earth?
2. What accounted for the "mood of anxious self-appraisal" on the part of many Americans in the 1960's?
3. (a) Do you think that Presidents Jefferson, Jackson, Lincoln, or Theodore Roosevelt needed a committee to clarify the nation's goals? Explain. (b) How is the appointment of such a committee by President Eisenhower itself a reflection of America's problems?
4. Why have some alienated youths turned their backs on the values of the older generation?
5. Suppose you think: "The world is a global village." What would this mean for Americans?

4 America's entry into the decisive decade of the 1970's

By the late 1960's many Americans shared with thoughtful men and women throughout the world the conviction that they were about to enter the most decisive decade in human history. Speaking in the spring of 1969, the Secretary-General of the United Nations, U Thant, expressed this widely held concern.

The need for cooperative action. "Members of the UN," the Secretary-General warned, "have perhaps 10 years left in which to subordinate their ancient quarrels and launch a global partnership to curb the arms race, to improve the human environment, to defuse the population explosion, and to supply the required momentum to world development efforts."

The problems U Thant mentioned, as well as others, including racial tensions, were worldwide. As such, they could be solved only by the cooperative efforts of all nations. But the major responsibility, and therefore the obligation of leadership, rested upon the rich, industrialized countries. The obvious first step was for each nation to put its own house in order.

The deteriorating environment. High on the list of worldwide problems was the deteriorating quality of the natural environment. "History tells us," Secretary of the Interior Stewart Udall wrote in 1963, "that earlier civilizations declined because they did not learn to live in harmony with the land. Our successes in space and our triumphs of technology hold a hidden danger," he warned. "As modern man increasingly arrogates to himself dominion over the physical environment, there is the risk that his false pride will cause him to take the resources of the earth for granted—and to lose all reverence for the land.

"America today stands poised on a pinnacle of wealth and power, yet we live in a land of vanishing beauty, of increasing ugliness, of shrinking open space, and of an overall environment that is diminished daily by pollution and noise and blight."

During the next few years growing numbers of ecologists,° biologists, and other scientists concerned with the life processes expressed deepening alarm over man's reckless misuse of his environment. They warned that it was suicidal for men to continue to abuse the land, water, and air upon which all life depends. They pointed out that during the past century more than 200 species of mammals, birds, and fish had vanished from the earth, and that 1,000 more—including man himself—were now endangered.

The worst offenders were the prosperous, productive, industrial nations like the United States. In 1969, for example, Americans were throwing away an estimated 400,000 tons of trash every day. The disposal of junk had become a major problem for every city and town. Each year Americans discarded 48 billion rustproof cans, 26 billion indestructible bottles, 9 million cars and trucks and

---

° *ecologist:* a scientist concerned with the relationships between the environment and living organisms—plants, animals, and man.

buses, 4 million tons of plastic products, and millions of pounds of paper. Trash and garbage littered the countryside and piled up in ugly, mountainous heaps on city dumps.

Less visible but even more serious was the problem of pollution. The air of all the major industrial cities was dangerously contaminated with smoke and noxious fumes from automobile exhausts, industrial plants, and the chimneys of homes, apartments, and office buildings. Lakes and rivers had become "open sewers," heavily polluted with human and industrial wastes. One river that flowed through a midwestern city was so heavily coated with oil and grease that it was declared a "fire hazard"! Pesticides, insecticides, and herbicides used in agriculture, forestry, and on suburban lawns to control "harmful" insects and weeds also killed birds and other wild creatures. The residue of these poisonous chemicals washed into the streams and rivers and flowed to the sea, destroying fish and other marine life in the process.

Moreover, new hazards were developing. Oil companies, already drawing oil from wells in coastal waters, were beginning to drill in the frozen wastes of the Arctic. And scientists and engineers were developing the technology to mine the beds of the oceans. By the 1970's men and machines were exploiting even the most remote and forbidding regions of the earth.

It was becoming glaringly evident that the "triumphs of technology" did indeed "hold a hidden danger." With their new powers men were disrupting the delicate balances of nature. The fact that many species had already been wiped out was a danger signal that the human species could not afford to ignore.

Population and resources. The problems posed by technology were compounded by an exploding population. As rapidly multiplying numbers of people placed heavier and heavier demands upon the earth's limited resources, the question of human survival became increasingly grave. How many people *could* the earth support? That question was beginning to haunt many world leaders.

During the late 1950's President Eisenhower had declared that the related problems of population growth and family planning were not proper government concerns. But a decade later, in 1969, President Richard M. Nixon sent a special message to Congress urging larger federal support for birth-control programs in the United States and overseas. It was generally agreed throughout the world that population growth must be checked and brought

under control. The only question was how this should be accomplished.

Demographers reported that in 1965 the world's population totaled about 3 billion. By 1980 it was expected to total 4 billion, and by the year 2000 to pass 6 billion.

Meanwhile, to support these growing numbers of people, the industrialized world of power-driven machines was devouring increasingly enormous quantities of natural resources. For example, it was estimated that "the total amounts of water, copper, and iron needed just to sustain the present United States population for the remaining years of their lives is larger than the total used by *all* men, women, and children who previously lived on the earth." Similar exhausting demands were being made on other vital resources. By the 1960's the United States had become more and more dependent upon imports of essential raw materials from other lands to feed its hungry machines and maintain its standard of living.

The slow awakening. As early as the 1890's the federal government had begun to reveal concern about the conservation of irreplenishable resources. As you have read (page 540), the early conservation movement, important though it was, had limited goals. The early conservationists were mainly concerned with regulating the use of particular resources—wildlife, forests, minerals, and soil. By mid-century, however, more people were beginning to understand that the planet itself—including *all* its resources and *all* forms of life—was in danger as a result of human recklessness.

Major credit for first arousing widespread public concern probably belongs more to Rachel Carson than to any other single individual. In her best-selling book *Silent Spring,* published in 1962, she warned that "along with the possibility of the extinction of mankind by nuclear war, the central problem of our age has . . . become the contamination of man's total environment."

Starting with the Kennedy and Johnson administrations, federal and state governments stepped up their conservation efforts with legislation designed to slow down and reverse the process of deterioration. By 1970 an impressive body of federal and state laws was in effect. The legislation included measures (1) to regulate the use of pesticides, insecticides, and other dangerous poisons; (2) to protect species of wildlife threatened with extinction; (3) to require automobile manufacturers to clean up the exhausts of the cars, trucks, and buses they sold; (4) to require factories, office buildings, apartment houses, and home-owners to meet certain minimum anti-air pollution standards; (5) to halt pollution of the land and water and clean up the rivers and lakes; (6) to restore the natural beauty of the countryside by screening and in other ways controlling unsightly junkyards and dumps; and (7) to create new national and state parks, and to preserve certain areas as untouched wilderness for future generations.

These measures, though impressive when viewed as a whole, represented only the first steps toward the solution of what Rachel Carson had called "the central problem of our age." A much greater effort would have to be made at every level of government—local, state, national, and international. By 1970 there was wide agreement throughout the United States and the world that the survival of man depended upon his ability to control and upgrade the quality of his total environment.

Religion's response to changing times. Religion, like all other aspects of life, was affected by the revolutions transforming the world. One of the notable developments in the United States was the growth of church membership.

Between 1940 and 1961 membership increased at twice the rate of the population, rising from about 64 million in 1940 to more than 116 million, or 64 percent of the population, by 1961. The sharp upward trend slowed during the 1960's. Church membership continued to increase, however, reaching 126 million by 1968.

Perhaps more significant than growth in membership was the changing attitude toward the church's role in the new age. Many clergymen from practically every denomination began to take a more active part in social and economic affairs. They became involved in civil rights movements, in efforts to combat poverty, in opposition to the war in Vietnam, and in efforts to halt the armaments race.

A controversial issue. During the 1960's a controversial religious question developed as a result of several Supreme Court decisions. In *Engel v. Vitale,* decided in 1962, the Court declared unconstitutional a regulation by a board of education that a prayer be recited in the public schools in New York state. A year later, in *Abington School District v. Schempp* and in *Murray v. Baltimore School Board,* the Supreme Court ruled unconstitutional a state law and a board of education regulation requiring recitation of the Lord's Prayer and Bible readings in public schools. In all of these decisions the Court held that laws or regulations

■ The air of all the major American industrial cities was dangerously contaminated with smoke and pollutants from automobile exhausts, industrial plants, and the chimneys of apartment houses and office buildings.

requiring religious practices in public schools violated the constitutional provision in the First Amendment that prohibited "an establishment of religion."

The "prayer cases" aroused a storm of controversy. Some citizens praised the Court for strengthening the principle of separation between church and state. Others branded the Court's actions as "anti-religious."

World religious response. One of the far-reaching developments in religion was the meeting of the Ecumenical (or worldwide) Council convened in Rome in the fall of 1962 by Pope John XXIII. It included Roman Catholic leaders from all over the world as well as delegate-observers from most major Protestant denominations. The Council sought, among other objectives, to increase understanding among Christians of all denominations and to unite Christians and those of other faiths in an effort to strengthen the forces of justice, morality, and peace throughout the world.

In the spring of 1963 Pope John addressed a special message, *Pacem in Terris* ("Peace on Earth"), to "all men of good will." Speaking in the name of humanity, he analyzed the central problems confronting mankind and called upon men to cast out their crippling prejudices and turn from folly toward the light of reason and truth and "the universal good." The message was proclaimed throughout the world.

Another widely discussed encyclical, this one issued in 1968 by John XXIII's successor, dealt with the problems of world poverty, the explosive growth of population, and the related issue of birth control. In the encyclical *Humanae Vitae* ("Of Human Life"), Pope Paul VI firmly restated the Roman Catholic Church's traditional condemnation of artifical birth control. The encyclical provoked a storm of criticism from within the Roman Catholic Church as well as from world leaders of every faith. In the critics' view, the papal statement failed to deal realistically with the growing threat of an exploding population.

Mounting unrest in education. The revolutionary developments reshaping the world created both problems and opportunities for the nation's educational institutions as well as its political and religious institutions.

One of the more obvious problems was overcrowding. The rapidly multiplying population placed increasingly heavy burdens on the entire educational system. For example, between 1940 and 1970 the number of students enrolled in the nation's schools and institutions of higher education more than doubled, rising from 30 million to more than 70 million. Even more dramatic was the increase in college and university enrollments, which rose 45 percent in the five-year period from 1963 to 1968. By 1968 at least one third of all young people between 18 and 21 were attending institutions of higher education.

As the shortage of buildings, equipment, and teachers became more acute, college students became increasingly restless. In the late 1960's demonstrations and even riots occurred on campuses across the nation. To be sure, the students were demonstrating against the war in Vietnam, racial injustice, and widespread poverty. But they were also complaining that the colleges and universities had become huge, impersonal "educational factories" and that the education provided had little relevance to the contemporary world. By the early 1970's the unrest had begun to spread to the nation's high schools.

Defense-orientation of higher education. One of the developments in education that troubled many university students was the growing emphasis on science and technology. This emphasis had received new impetus in 1957 when the Soviet Union launched its first Sputnik. This demonstration of advanced Soviet military science shocked Americans who had come to believe that their own country was the undisputed leader in science and technology.

A concerned Congress reacted in 1958 with the National Defense Education Act. The act was designed to strengthen the teaching of science, mathematics, engineering, and modern foreign languages. It provided funds for laboratory and other equipment and for loans to college students.

Criticism that the act neglected the humanities and the social sciences prompted Congress to revise it in 1964. The revised measure increased the money available for student loans. It also provided funds for the purchase of equipment in the teaching of English, history, geography, and civics as well as science, mathematics, and modern foreign languages.

Even more disturbing to many students was the growing involvement of the universities in war-oriented activities. Students charged that the universities were no longer "free" but were becoming "servants of the government."

By the late 1960's the universities as a whole depended upon the federal government for more than two thirds of their research funds. Several of the leading universities actually depended upon federal research grants for more than half of their total budgets. Especially disturbing to many students was the fact that a large percentage of federal research money was allocated to military and defense-related research. In contrast, less than one half of 1 percent of the billions the federal government was spending on research was devoted to efforts to improve the quality of education.

Growing federal support of education. The growth of federal financial support for education was a significant development of the 1960's.

In both 1961 and 1962 Congress refused, after heated debate, to adopt administration-sponsored bills that included the authorization of funds to help build classrooms and raise teachers' salaries. One group of opponents feared that federal aid would lead to federal control. Another group refused to vote for bills that did not include assistance for church-affiliated schools and other independent schools. Still another group raised an equally controversial issue by insisting that federal aid should go only to schools that had complied with federal law in regard to desegregation.

In 1963, however, the tide began to turn when Congress voted $231 million for construction of buildings for medical and dental schools. It also voted $1.2 billion to assist colleges in building classrooms, libraries, and laboratories. And, as you have just read, in 1964 it greatly expanded the National Defense Education Act.

By far the most significant development was the $1.3 billion Education Act of 1965. The act provided $1 billion in federal aid to the nation's public elementary and secondary schools. The money was to go to school districts in direct proportion to the number of children in those districts who came from families whose annual incomes were less than $2,000 a year. "I deeply believe," President Johnson declared, "that no law I have signed, or will ever sign, means more to the nation."

The Education Act of 1965 provided a pattern for continuing financial assistance to the nation's public elementary and secondary schools. Congress, now committed to the principle of federal support for every level and type of education, began to loosen the purse strings still further. Whereas in 1964 federal aid for all types of education totaled $2.4 billion, by 1969 the figure had risen to $7.8 billion.

It was evident, however, that unless much greater federal support was provided the nation's educational institutions could not meet their responsibilities. Growing enrollments, soaring costs of buildings, equipment, and salaries, and the problem of upgrading the quality of education for every American youth were thrusting heavier and heavier burdens upon America's schools and colleges.

Questions of quality. The educational crisis confronting Americans as they entered the 1970's could not be solved without money. But money alone was not enough. Questions involving the quality of education had to be answered.

In brief, what kind of education should the schools provide to equip students for life in a rapidly changing world? How could the schools best prepare young people to grasp the opportunities and to meet the challenges of the modern world?

■ Student demonstrations in the late 1960's and early 1970's were directed not only against the war in Vietnam, racial injustice, and widespread poverty, but also against the quality of education in the colleges.

The evidence was overwhelming that poorly educated, poorly trained men and women had little hope of earning an adequate living in an increasingly complex society. Far more serious from society's point of view was the fact that inadequately educated citizens could not help to solve the increasingly critical problems facing the nation and the world.

Extensive efforts to improve the quality of education began in the late 1950's with improvements in the teaching of mathematics, physics, chemistry, biology, and other natural sciences. By the mid-1960's these efforts had broadened to include the humanities and the social sciences. Aided by grants of money from the federal government and from private foundations, projects designed to improve the curriculum and methods of learning were being developed and tried out in research centers and in hundreds of schools throughout the country. In general the new programs undertook to discourage older methods in which students learned by memorizing data from a lecture or from a textbook. Instead the new projects emphasized an approach in which students assumed major responsibility for

841

■ By the 1970's Americans increasingly looked toward education to solve the problems that faced the nation and the world. Above, children work on a community art project.

solving problems by gathering and analyzing data and arriving at their own conclusions.

Another major development was the effort to improve the quality of education for disadvantaged boys and girls. The Head Start program (page 831) sponsored by the federal government brought preschool children together in an effort to provide them with learning experiences they could not enjoy in culturally deprived homes. "Store-front academies" operating in abandoned buildings in the ghettos and supported by industry and other private organizations gave older "dropouts" the opportunity to resume their education.

These and other developments, including the use of computers and other types of educational technology in the classrooms, represented a determined effort to improve the quality of American education. Years before historian H. G. Wells had warned that "human history becomes more and more a race between education and catastrophe." By the 1970's America's leaders and growing numbers of Amer-

ica's citizens were acutely aware that, to win the race, education must become the nation's first priority.

SECTION SURVEY

IDENTIFY: ecology, *Silent Spring, Pacem in Terris;* Stewart Udall, Rachel Carson.

1. Why is there a need for cooperative action on the part of the nations of the world in dealing with ecological problems?
2. The triumphs of technology hold a hidden danger. Comment.
3. Why are population levels closely interrelated to most other ecological problems?
4. What changes in religion took place during the 1960's? Why?
5. Discuss the steps which must be taken to improve the quality of American education.
6. Discuss the steps which must be taken to improve the quality of American life.
7. In what ways do the 1970's represent a decisive decade?

TRACING THE MAIN IDEAS

As Americans entered the 1970's they were becoming more and more aware of the fact that the desperate need of their time was for intellectual competence and moral responsibility. Only by creative thinking and bold action of the highest order could Americans solve the compelling problems confronting them—racial tensions, widespread poverty in the midst of plenty, the crisis facing the cities, unrest throughout the world, and the increasingly grave challenge of a deteriorating environment. Americans increasingly felt the need for renewed dedication to man's age-old quest for dignity and self-respect and the spiritual values that give life meaning. It was hoped that in this way Americans could nourish and strengthen the free way of life that had sustained them throughout their history.

Urgent though the problems were, the American people had good reason to move into the future with confidence. Beginning on that day when a small handful of men had landed at Jamestown, Americans had repeatedly demonstrated an amazing ability to adjust to changing ways and changing times. They had made the transition from small villages and towns to huge metropolitan centers; from the simple tools of self-sufficient farming to the infinitely more complex technology of an industrial society; from relative isolation to a role of world leadership.

Now, as the United States moved through the most decisive decade of its history, the nation's material, intellectual, and spiritual resources were being tested to the utmost. It remained for the American people to prove that they could meet the challenge successfully.

CHAPTER SURVEY

QUESTIONS FOR DISCUSSION

1. President Nixon, in talking about pollution in the United States, has said "it is literally now or never." What do you think he meant?
2. It has been suggested that America's victories in World War II and its success in sending the first men to the moon could not have been possible without sustained national interest. Is this same interest necessary in dealing with the problems of poverty and pollution in the United States? Do you think Americans will solve these problems? Explain your answers.
3. Have black Americans gained more for the cause of civil rights through the use of militant or non-militant tactics? (Define the term militancy before attempting to answer this question; also provide evidence to support your answer.)
4. The United States will celebrate its two-hundredth anniversary in the decade of the 1970's. What do you think Americans should be celebrating on this anniversary?
5. Why has Puerto Rico been called "the showcase of Latin America"?
6. Compare the problems faced by two of the minority groups discussed in this chapter. How are the problems similar? How are they dissimilar?
7. A nation moves forward in history only if it can respond successfully to the challenges which confront it. Select the four most important challenges confronting our country during the past two decades, and indicate how the American people are meeting these conditions.
8. Explain the differences between the Civil Rights Acts of 1957, 1960, and 1964.

RELATING PAST TO PRESENT

1. In your opinion, are our current national goals different from those outlined in the Declaration of Independence? Explain your answer.
2. "Human history becomes more and more a race between education and catastrophe." How does this statement apply to our world today?

USING MAPS AND CHARTS

1. Make a time line showing the important events of the civil rights movement between 1945 and the present.
2. Consult the Chronology of Events on pages 889–90 and select what you consider to be the 5 most important occurrences in American history during the past 10 years. Explain the reasons for your selections.

UNIT SURVEY

FOR FURTHER INQUIRY

1. What in your opinion is the single most crucial challenge faced by the United States today? Explain.
2. What do you believe is the wisest policy for the United States to follow in Southeast Asia? Explain.
3. Because the American society is growing and changing so rapidly, far-reaching changes will have to be made in American government as well. Do you agree or disagree with this statement? Explain.

PROJECTS AND ACTIVITIES

1. Draw a time line of the Vietnam War, including the major diplomatic and military events of the conflict.
2. Prepare a report for class presentation on anti-pollution efforts in your city or state.
3. Draw a political cartoon to illustrate your views on the issue of student dissent.
4. Collect newspaper clippings dealing with the struggles of various minority groups to attain their civil rights. What similarities do you find among these news stories? What dissimilarities do you find?

USING THE SOCIAL SCIENCES

(Read pages 846–48 before you answer the following questions.)

1. During the Cuban missile crisis, what do you think President Kennedy's main concern was? How did he view his own role in the crisis?
2. What did this incident reveal about the nature of decision-making during a national crisis?
3. Is the 1961 Bay of Pigs invasion of Cuba related to the Cuban missile crisis? Explain.
4. If you had been President during the Cuban missile crisis, would you have behaved as President Kennedy did? Explain.

SUGGESTED FURTHER READING

Biography

BEAL, JOHN R., *John Foster Dulles: A Biography,* Harper & Row.

BROWN, CLAUDE, *Manchild in the Promised Land,* New American Library (Signet Books, paper). Story of a Harlem youth who fought his way out of the New York ghetto.

DAVIS, KENNETH S., *A Prophet in His Own Country,* Doubleday. About Adlai Stevenson.

EISENHOWER, DWIGHT D., *The White House Years: Mandate for Change, 1953–56,* Doubleday.

GRIFFIN, JOHN HOWARD, *Black Like Me,* New American Library (Signet Books, paper). A white professor dyes his skin and enters the South as a Negro.

SIDEY, HUGH, *John F. Kennedy: A Reporter's Inside Story,* Atheneum.

TRUMAN, HARRY S., *Year of Decisions,* Doubleday. Volume I of *Memoirs,* covering his first year in office.

WHITE, WILLIAM S., *The Professional: Lyndon B. Johnson,* Houghton Mifflin.

X, MALCOLM, *The Autobiography of Malcolm X,* Grove (paper). The life of the Negro leader and his relationship to Black Nationalism.

Other Nonfiction

BERGMAN, PETER M., and MORT N. BERGMAN, eds. *The Chronological History of the Negro in America,* Harper & Row.

BLAUSTEIN, ALBERT P., and ROBERT L. ZANGRANDO, eds. *Civil Rights and the American Negro,* Simon and Schuster (Washington Square Press). Three centuries of laws, court decisions, executive orders, editorials, and speeches.

CARSON, RACHEL, *Silent Spring,* Fawcett (paper). One

of the first books to warn about the threat of pollution to our natural environment.

DEAN, VERA MICHELES, *The United States and Russia,* Harvard Univ. Press.

EHRLICH, PAUL R., *Population Bomb,* Intext (Ballantine Books, paper). The author contends that overpopulation will be the root cause of major world problems unless it is brought under control.

GOLDMAN, ERIC, *The Crucial Decade,* Knopf. America 1945–1955.

HANDLIN, OSCAR, *Fire Ball in the Night,* Atlantic–Little, Brown. The racial crisis.

HARRINGTON, MICHAEL, *The Other America,* Penguin. The twenty percent of America's population that lives below the minimum standard of economic well-being.

HIGGINS, MARGUERITE, *War in Korea,* Doubleday.

HOOVER, J. EDGAR, *Masters of Deceit,* Holt, Rinehart & Winston. Communism in the United States.

JOSEPHY, ALVIN M., JR., *The Indian Heritage of America,* Bantam (paper). A complete history of the Indians of North, South, and Central America.

KENNAN, GEORGE F., *Democracy and the Student Left,* Bantam (paper). Analyzes the nature and causes of student discontent: their opposition to the war in Vietnam; their concern for minority groups; their suspicion of the Establishment.

——, *Realities of American Foreign Policy,* Princeton Univ. Press.

KING, MARTIN LUTHER, JR., *Stride Toward Freedom,* Harper & Row. Discusses the Montgomery bus boycott and the theory of nonviolence; it won Dr. King the Nobel peace prize.

——, *Why We Can't Wait,* New American Library (Signet Books, paper). The civil rights crusade of the early 1960's, described by its leader.

KISSINGER, HENRY A., *Nuclear Weapons and Foreign Policy,* Harper & Row (text ed.).

LILIENTHAL, DAVID E., *Change, Hope and the Bomb,* Princeton Univ. Press.

LIPPMANN, WALTER, *The Communist World and Ours,* Little, Brown.

LUBELL, SAMUEL, *The Future of American Politics,* Harper & Row; Doubleday (Anchor Books).

MAILER, NORMAN, *The Armies of the Night,* New American Library (Signet Books, paper). The October 1967 march to the Pentagon by war protesters; the author took part in the march and was arrested for his actions.

MORGENTHAU, HANS J., *The Purpose of American Politics,* Random House.

POTTER, DAVID, *People of Plenty,* Univ. of Chicago Press. Economic abundance and the American character.

SHANNON, DAVID, *The Decline of American Communism,* Harcourt Brace Jovanovich.

SILBERMAN, CHARLES E., *Crisis in Black and White,* Random House (Vintage Books, paper). Analyzes race relations in the United States.

UDALL, STUART L., *Quiet Crisis,* Hearst (Avon Books, paper). Emphasizes the necessity of protecting our environment and natural resources.

Historical Fiction

DOS PASSOS, JOHN, *Midcentury,* Houghton Mifflin. Mingling of fiction, history, and biography.

HERSEY, JOHN, *A Bell for Adano,* Knopf. United States military government in Italy.

MASTERS, DEXTER, *The Accident,* Knopf. Scientist is killed by radiation.

MICHENER, JAMES, *The Bridges at Toko-ri,* Random House. Korean War.

HISTORY AND THE SOCIAL SCIENCES

CASE STUDY IN HISTORY

The Cuban Missile Crisis

On Tuesday morning, October 16, 1962, the Central Intelligence Agency [CIA] informed President John F. Kennedy that photographs taken by American U-2 reconnaissance planes showed conclusively that the Soviet Union was building missile sites in Cuba and was supplying the Cubans with ballistic missiles and jet bombers capable of carrying nuclear weapons. The Cuban missile crisis had begun.

The crisis, although it lasted only 13 days, was one of the most dangerous periods in our nation's history. This direct confrontation between the United States and the Soviet Union gives us an excellent opportunity to investigate the decision-making process at work at the highest levels of American government. Who are the leaders who in times of crisis make the decisions that affect the lives of every American? How do these leaders arrive at their decisions? With these questions in mind, we can proceed to an in-depth study of the Cuban missile crisis of 1962.

High-Level Conferences to Deal with a National Emergency

At 11:45 A.M. on October 16, President Kennedy invited a number of high-level government officials, the Joint Chiefs of Staff, and a number of distinguished private citizens to attend a White House meeting. At the meeting CIA experts presented photographs showing missile bases under construction in Cuba. The areas photographed were clearly being prepared for surface-to-surface offensive ballistic missiles armed with atomic warheads capable of striking at any point in the United States. Other photographs showed that about 30 missiles were already installed. It was estimated that, within a matter of minutes, these missiles could kill 80 million Americans.

It was clear that immediate action was imperative. President Kennedy, whose awesome and personal responsibility it was as President to protect and defend the security of the United States, asked his civilian and military advisers to make recommendations. The Joint Chiefs of Staff favored a massive air strike which would completely wipe out the missile sites. Secretary of Defense Robert McNamara and the President's brother, Attorney General Robert Kennedy, favored a naval quarantine, or blockade, of Cuba which would prevent the Soviets from bringing more missiles and site equipment into Cuba. The Joint Chiefs of Staff argued that a blockade would not destroy the bases and missiles already on the island and that the Soviets would extract a high price in Berlin or elsewhere for the missiles' removal.

General Curtis Le May, the Air Force Chief of Staff, urged the President to take swift and drastic military action. The air force, he argued, was ready to destroy the Soviet missile menace in Cuba and to provide effective air cover for the island's invasion. General Le May assured the President that the Soviets would not retaliate. President Kennedy expressed his doubts, stating "They, no more than we, can let these things go by without doing something. They can't, after all their statements, permit us to take out their missiles, kill a lot of Russians, and do nothing. If they don't take action in Cuba, they certainly will in Berlin."

Former Secretary of State Dean Acheson argued that it was the President's clear responsibility to order an air attack and invasion of Cuba. The missiles had to be destroyed, Acheson said, if the free world were to continue to rely on the United States to protect its freedom.

LAUNCH STANDS

A U-2 photograph of a Cuban missile site

Robert Kennedy stated that a blockade was preferable to a direct attack because a blockade would give the Soviets a chance to retreat. An air attack, on the other hand, would kill thousands of Cuban civilians and hundreds of Soviet advisers, and might force the Soviets to retaliate either in Cuba or in Western Europe—or start an atomic holocaust by a direct attack on the United States.

The debate among the advisers highlighted the complexity of the decision demanded of the President, but slowly, the proposal for a naval and air blockade of Cuba gained the support of a majority of the advisers. A special committee appointed by the President announced that it had agreed on a blockade. After questioning the committee members at length, the President ordered them to continue their deliberations. Robert Kennedy, a committee member, later commented on the strain: "Each one of us was being asked to make a recommendation which would affect the future of all mankind, a recommendation which, if wrong and if accepted, could mean the destruction of the human race. That kind of pressure does strange things to a human being, even to brilliant, self-confident, mature, experienced men. For some it brings out characteristics and strengths that perhaps even they never knew they had, and for others the pressure is too overwhelming."

After considering the alternatives, the committee decided to present to the President all the arguments for and against an air strike and a blockade. The President listened, but he did not tell the committee what his decision would be. The President made sure, however, that Congressional leaders of both major parties were kept informed of the developments.

Finally, all the recommendations were in. Now the final decision—and the final responsibility—rested with the President. President Kennedy decided in favor of a blockade. He told his advisers that two arguments had influenced his decision. One was a statement from the commander in chief of the Strategic Air Command that even a major surprise air attack might not destroy all the missiles. The other was his conviction that a direct attack would severely damage or even destroy the moral position of the United States throughout the world.

Having made up his mind, the President decided that it was his duty to go on television and give the American people a complete history of the crisis. Before his speech, the President informed a bipartisan group of Congressional leaders of his decision and invited their comments. Some influential Senators, convinced that Congress and the country wanted stronger action, urged the President to launch a direct attack. The President explained that in his view the blockade was advisable as an initial step because it could lead to a resolution of the crisis while an air attack might bring catastrophic results.

On Monday, October 22, President Kennedy spoke to the American people. He spoke soberly and candidly. He emphasized that the Soviet Union must withdraw the missiles or the United States would destroy them on the ground. The blockade, he said, was an initial step; the United States was prepared to take far more drastic action. He expressed the hope that the Soviets would consider the consequences and avoid a confrontation.

President Kennedy sent a letter to Premier Nikita Khrushchev of the Soviet Union, informing him of the blockade and urging him not to attempt to break it by force—a step which the United States would counter by force. Kennedy concluded by saying, "I am concerned that we both show prudence and do nothing to allow events to make the situation more difficult to control than it is."

President John F. Kennedy

847

Days of Anxiety and Confrontation

Missiles aboard a Soviet ship carrying them toward Cuba

The blockade went into effect on Wednesday, October 24. United States naval vessels received orders to disable any foreign vessel attempting to run the blockade, but to spare the lives of seamen as far as possible.

Reports received in the White House and published in the press announced that many Soviet vessels were sailing directly toward Cuba. Robert Kennedy later wrote that, when the President received these reports, his "face seemed drawn, his eyes pained, almost gray." Then more encouraging reports came in from the director of the CIA. Twenty Soviet ships approaching the blockade barrier had stopped dead in the water and some had even turned around. The Soviets apparently had decided not to run the blockade.

However, aerial photographs showed that work on the missile sites in Cuba was proceeding rapidly. Moreover, toward the end of the week Khrushchev accused the United States of trying to destroy the Castro regime and warned the United States navy not to interfere with Soviet ships. Disappointed with this response, President Kennedy determined to show Khrushchev that he would not retreat until the missiles were withdrawn. He ordered American naval vessels to board and search a Panamanian-owned ship bound for Cuba under a Soviet charter. The ship was searched but was allowed to proceed to Cuba when no military goods were found on board.

The President once again appealed to Khrushchev to remove the missiles. At the same time, however, he gave orders to the Joint Chiefs of Staff to prepare for an invasion of Cuba and a massive air strike on the missile sites using conventional weapons. The people of the United States and of the world waited for the next Soviet move. Finally Khrushchev replied in a vague way that, if the United States would promise not to invade or blockade Cuba, the missiles would be removed. He warned that interference with Soviet ships would mean nuclear confrontation. Privately, however, the Soviets stated more clearly that in return for an American pledge guaranteeing Cuba's sovereignty under Castro, the Soviet Union would remove the missiles.

But another letter from Khrushchev demanded that subsequently the United States also withdraw its missiles from Turkey. President Kennedy had decided some time before to remove the missiles from Turkey, but he refused to do so under the threat of "nuclear blackmail." The situation worsened when a Soviet missile launched from a Cuban site destroyed a U-2 observation plane and killed an American pilot. The demands for an invasion of Cuba grew more insistent, but the President decided for one more try at diplomacy. He wrote again to Khrushchev and, ignoring the demand for the withdrawal of American missiles from Turkey, demanded the immediate withdrawal of Soviet missiles from Cuba. In return the President agreed: (1) to remove promptly the quarantine measures in effect against Cuba and (2) to give assurances that Cuba would not be invaded.

At 10:00 A.M. on Sunday, October 28, Kennedy received another message from Khrushchev. The Soviet Union agreed to withdraw the missiles in return for a guarantee that the United States would not invade Cuba. President Kennedy agreed. The 13-day ordeal in decision-making had come to an end.

■ How does the government's decision-making process work? What role does the President play? What is his advisers' role? What beliefs basic to American democracy affect the way in which decisions are made?
■ At all times during the crisis President Kennedy tried not to disgrace or humiliate Premier Khrushchev. Was this a wise policy? Why or why not?

HISTORICAL ATLAS
OF THE
UNITED STATES

A century has passed since Jules Verne drew from his fertile imagination a fantastic story of man's first flight to the moon. What was then pure science fiction became exciting fact in July of 1969 as millions of people throughout the world watched spellbound on their television sets as two American astronauts landed on the moon and explored its surface. For many people this remarkable feat was proof, indeed, that they were living in the Space Age. Only the infinite reaches of outer space still remained unconquered by man.

It may well be that the exploration of outer space will be, as some have predicted, "the greatest adventure man has ever dared to take." But we do violence to the record when we ignore other great adventures, one of which was the discovery, exploration, and settlement of what is now the United States.

The first small band of Englishmen who landed at Jamestown in the winter of 1607 knew less about the North American continent than we know today about the moon and the more distant planets. They stood, a mere handful of men, on the fringe of a vast, unexplored wilderness that reached, as we now know, from sea to sea. They were the first of many thousands of pioneers who through the next three centuries moved steadily westward to win one of the richest and most varied lands on earth.

The elevation profile below gives a generalized view of the country that the pioneers crossed. It does not show Daniel Boone's first group of settlers struggling over the Wilderness Road on their way to "the dark and bloody ground" west of the Appalachian Mountains. It does not show the covered wagons of the Mormons crawling across the apparently endless plains toward their final destination on the shores of the Great Salt Lake. It does not show the Donner Party caught in a blizzard in the high Sierras when within a few days' journey of their goal, the sun-drenched valleys of California. To the uninformed reader, the elevation profile means little. But to those who know something of the geography of the United States and the great drama of American history, the profile is rich in meaning.

850

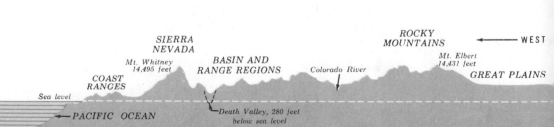

Turning the page, we come to a map which gives another generalized view of the country. The map shows the great sweep of the land mass that is the United States and the variety of its natural features. The men and women who explored this continent would have given a great deal for such a map.

Like the elevation profile, the map gives only part of the total picture. It gives an over-all view of the stage on which the great adventure which is American history has been carried on, and is being carried on today. The stage embraces half a continent; there is room on it for coastal plains, masses of mountain ranges, the broad expanse of high plateaus, a mighty network of rivers and lakes, and the immense sweep of the central lowlands and the Great Plains.

But the map shows us only the stage. It is a stage bare of both scenery and actors. There is no hint of the dark and brooding forest that once covered so much of the continent, no hint of the immense grasslands or the fertile valleys, no hint of the buried mineral wealth that has provided the raw material for the most productive industrial economy the world has ever known.

It takes many maps and many different charts to reveal even partially what the American people have built on this part of the North American continent that they claim as their own. In this Atlas, the seven double-page maps and the 44 charts, tables, and graphic summaries of significant developments give a much larger concept of the variety of the natural and human resources that help to explain the rise of the American nation.

Using the pages that follow, you can review, by way of charts, maps, and text, some major strands of American history and speculate on where these continuing strands may lead in the future. No one can tell you exactly what the challenges and opportunities of the future will be, either for you personally, or for the nation as a whole. But using the background of American history, you can speculate on certain *areas* of opportunity and challenge that seem sure to arise.

See map, pages 852–53 ⟶

EAST ⟶

CENTRAL   LOWLAND

PRAIRIES   OZARK MTS.   ⌐Mississippi River

APPALACHIAN
HIGHLANDS

Mt. Mitchell
6,684 feet

COASTAL
PLAIN

Sea level

ATLANTIC OCEAN ⟶

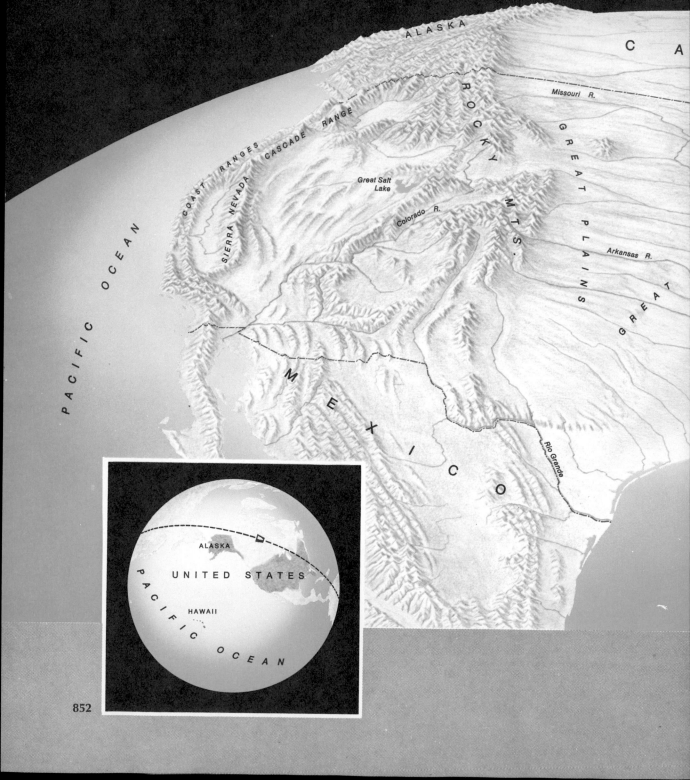

ALASKA

CA

ROCKY

Missouri R.

GREAT PLAINS

GREAT

COAST RANGES

CASCADE RANGE

SIERRA NEVADA

Great Salt
Lake

Colorado R.

M T S.

Arkansas R.

PACIFIC OCEAN

M E X I C O

Rio Grande

ALASKA

UNITED STATES

PACIFIC OCEAN

HAWAII

NADA

HUDSON BAY

Mississippi R.

CENTRAL

GREAT LAKES

Missouri R.

LOWLAND

Ohio R.

Mississippi R.

APPALACHIAN MOUNTAINS

PIEDMONT

COASTAL

PLAINS

ATLANTIC OCEAN

GULF OF

MEXICO

☐ This view of the United States—from about 2,000 miles out in space—shows rivers and mountain ranges more clearly than they would actually appear from far out in space. Unlike an astronaut's view, which is usually hidden in part by clouds, this space view enables you to examine the various natural features of the United States. The inset map at the left traces an imaginary path of a space capsule circling the earth.

853

TERRITORIAL GROWTH OF THE UNITED STATES

Within the overlapping life spans of three of its Presidents—Jefferson, Lincoln, and "Teddy" Roosevelt—the United States grew from a relatively narrow strip along the Atlantic seaboard to a nation embracing half a continent. And by 1959, the United States included Alaska to the north and the faraway islands of Hawaii. Data of this story appear here and on pages 856–57.

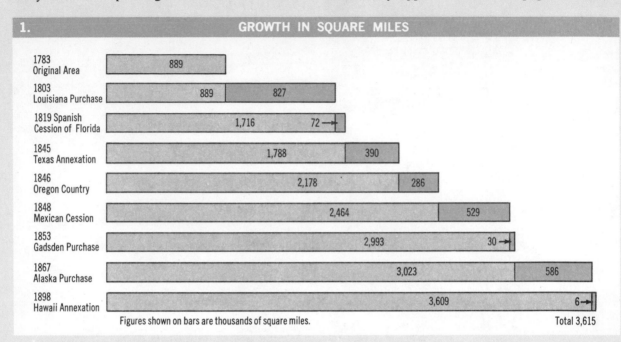

1. GROWTH IN SQUARE MILES

1783 Original Area	889
1803 Louisiana Purchase	889 — 827
1819 Spanish Cession of Florida	1,716 — 72 →
1845 Texas Annexation	1,788 — 390
1846 Oregon Country	2,178 — 286
1848 Mexican Cession	2,464 — 529
1853 Gadsden Purchase	2,993 — 30 →
1867 Alaska Purchase	3,023 — 586
1898 Hawaii Annexation	3,609 — 6 →

Figures shown on bars are thousands of square miles.   Total 3,615

2. TERRITORIAL ACQUISITIONS

Name	Date	How Acquired	Area (sq. mi.)	Percent of Present Area	Present States
Original Area	1783	Won from Great Britain; established by Treaty of Paris	888,685	24%	Original 13 states, plus Illinois, Indiana, Kentucky, Maine, Michigan, Ohio, Tennessee, Vermont, West Virginia, Wisconsin, and part of Alabama, Minnesota, Mississippi
Louisiana Purchase	1803	Purchased from France	827,192	23%	Arkansas, Iowa, Missouri, Nebraska, North Dakota, South Dakota, and part of Colorado, Kansas, Louisiana, Minnesota, Montana, Oklahoma, Wyoming
Florida	1819	Treaty with Spain	72,003	2%	Florida, and part of Alabama, Louisiana, Mississippi
Texas	1845	Annexed	390,144	11%	Texas, and part of Colorado, Kansas, New Mexico, Oklahoma, Wyoming
Oregon Country	1846	Treaty with Great Britain	285,580	8%	Idaho, Oregon, Washington, and part of Montana, Wyoming
Mexican Cession	1848	Treaty with Mexico	529,017	15%	California, Nevada, Utah, and part of Arizona, Colorado, New Mexico, Wyoming
Gadsden Purchase	1853	Purchased from Mexico	29,640	1%	Part of Arizona, New Mexico
Alaska	1867	Purchased from Russia	586,412	16%	Alaska
Hawaii	1898	Annexed	6,450	Less than 1/10th %	Hawaii

Total Present Area 3,615,123

It was not just a nation that grew from "sea to shining sea"; it was a federal union. Each new state has been admitted by act of Congress as a full and equal partner in the Union. The achievement recorded on the map on pages 856–57 and in the table below is a tribute to the men who drafted a Constitution that provided for the orderly admission of new states.

3. STAGES IN THE GROWTH OF THE FEDERAL UNION

Original 13 states
1791-1844
1845-1863
1864- present

4. DATE OF ENTRY, AREA, AND CAPITAL OF STATES

Order of Entry	State	Date of Entry	Area (in sq. mi.)	Capital	Order of Entry	State	Date of Entry	Area (in sq. mi.)	Capital
1	Delaware	1787	2,057	Dover	27	Florida	1845	58,560	Tallahassee
2	Pennsylvania	1787	45,333	Harrisburg	28	Texas	1845	267,339	Austin
3	New Jersey	1787	7,836	Trenton	29	Iowa	1846	56,290	Des Moines
4	Georgia	1788	58,876	Atlanta	30	Wisconsin	1848	56,154	Madison
5	Connecticut	1788	5,009	Hartford	31	California	1850	158,693	Sacramento
6	Massachusetts	1788	8,257	Boston	32	Minnesota	1858	84,068	St. Paul
7	Maryland	1788	10,577	Annapolis	33	Oregon	1859	96,981	Salem
8	South Carolina	1788	31,055	Columbia	34	Kansas	1861	82,264	Topeka
9	New Hampshire	1788	9,304	Concord	35	West Virginia	1863	24,181	Charleston
10	Virginia	1788	40,817	Richmond	36	Nevada	1864	110,540	Carson City
11	New York	1788	49,576	Albany	37	Nebraska	1867	77,227	Lincoln
12	North Carolina	1789	52,586	Raleigh	38	Colorado	1876	104,247	Denver
13	Rhode Island	1790	1,214	Providence	39	North Dakota	1889	70,665	Bismarck
14	Vermont	1791	9,609	Montpelier	40	South Dakota	1889	77,047	Pierre
15	Kentucky	1792	40,395	Frankfort	41	Montana	1889	147,138	Helena
16	Tennessee	1796	42,244	Nashville	42	Washington	1889	68,192	Olympia
17	Ohio	1803	41,222	Columbus	43	Idaho	1890	83,557	Boise
18	Louisiana	1812	48,523	Baton Rouge	44	Wyoming	1890	97,914	Cheyenne
19	Indiana	1816	36,291	Indianapolis	45	Utah	1896	84,916	Salt Lake City
20	Mississippi	1817	47,716	Jackson	46	Oklahoma	1907	69,919	Oklahoma City
21	Illinois	1818	56,400	Springfield	47	New Mexico	1912	121,666	Santa Fe
22	Alabama	1819	51,609	Montgomery	48	Arizona	1912	113,909	Phoenix
23	Maine	1820	33,215	Augusta	49	Alaska	1959	586,412	Juneau
24	Missouri	1821	69,686	Jefferson City	50	Hawaii	1959	6,450	Honolulu
25	Arkansas	1836	53,104	Little Rock		District of Columbia (1791)		67	
26	Michigan	1837	58,216	Lansing					

See map, pages 856-57 ——————►

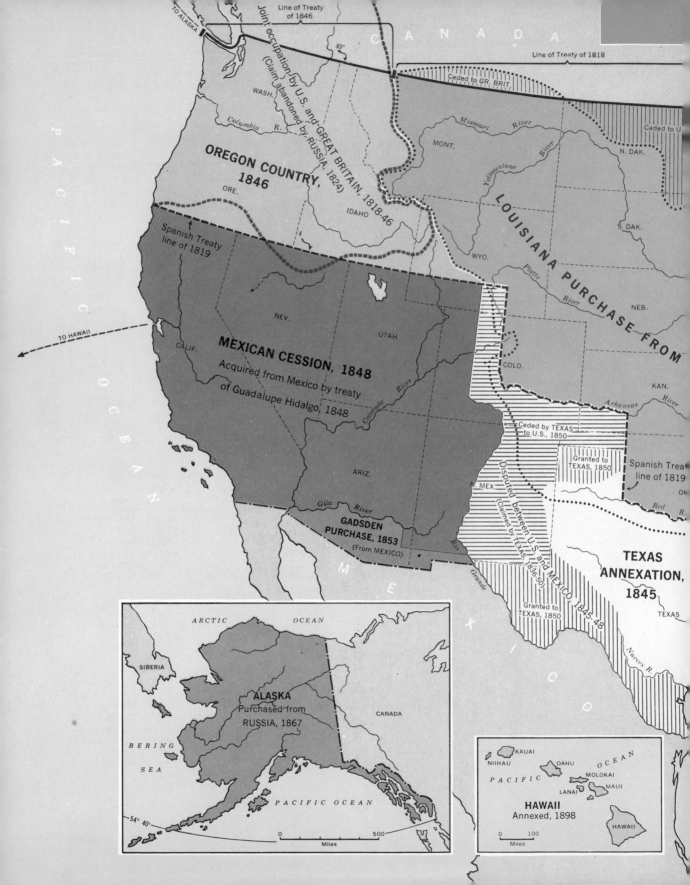

TO ALASKA

Line of Treaty of 1846

CANADA

49°

Line of Treaty of 1818

Joint occupation by U.S. and GREAT BRITAIN, 1818-46
(Claim abandoned by RUSSIA, 1824)

Ceded to GR. BRIT.

Ceded to U

OREGON COUNTRY, 1846

WASH.

Columbia R.

ORE.

IDAHO

MONT.

Missouri River

Yellowstone River

N. DAK.

S. DAK.

WYO.

NEB.

LOUISIANA PURCHASE FROM

Spanish Treaty line of 1819

TO HAWAII

CALIF.

NEV.

UTAH

Colorado River

ARIZ.

Gila River

Platte River

COLO.

KAN.

Arkansas River

Ceded by TEXAS to U.S., 1850

Granted to TEXAS, 1850

Spanish Trea line of 1819

Ok

Red R.

MEXICAN CESSION, 1848

Acquired from Mexico by treaty
of Guadalupe Hidalgo, 1848

GADSDEN PURCHASE, 1853
(From MEXICO)

Rio Grande

N. MEX.

Disputed between U.S. and MEXICO, 1845-48
(Claimed by TEXAS, 1836-50)

Granted to TEXAS, 1850

TEXAS ANNEXATION, 1845

TEXAS

Nueces R.

P A C I F I C   O C E A N

M E X I C O

ARCTIC OCEAN

SIBERIA

ALASKA
Purchased from
RUSSIA, 1867

CANADA

BERING SEA

PACIFIC OCEAN

54° 40'

0   500
Miles

KAUAI

NIIHAU

OAHU

PACIFIC OCEAN

MOLOKAI

LANAI

MAUI

HAWAII
Annexed, 1898

HAWAII

0   100
Miles

TERRITORIAL GROWTH OF THE UNITED STATES

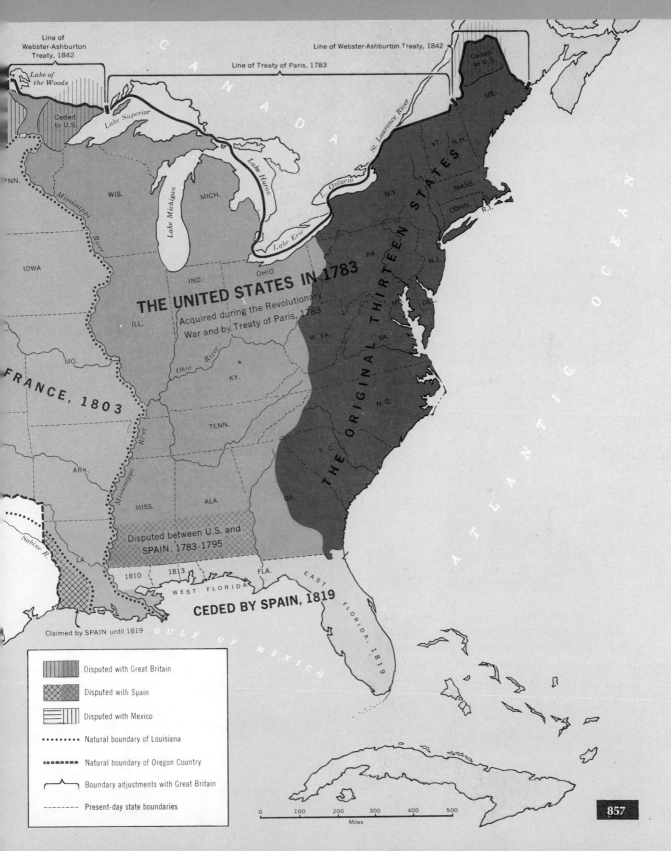

Line of
Webster-Ashburton
Treaty, 1842

Line of Webster-Ashburton Treaty, 1842

Line of Treaty of Paris, 1783

Ceded
to U.S.

*Lake of
the Woods*

CANADA

Ceded
to U.S.

ME.

Lake Superior

Lake Huron

St. Lawrence River

VT. N.H.

MINN.

WIS.

Lake Michigan

MICH.

L. Ontario

NY.

MASS.

Mississippi River

IOWA

Lake Erie

PA.

CONN.

R.I.

IND.

OHIO

THE UNITED STATES IN 1783
Acquired during the Revolutionary
War and by Treaty of Paris, 1783

N.J.

ILL.

DE.

MO.

MD.

FRANCE, 1803

Ohio River

KY.

W. VA.

VA.

THE ORIGINAL THIRTEEN STATES

Mississippi River

TENN.

N.C.

ARK.

S.C.

MISS.

ALA.

GA.

Disputed between U.S. and
SPAIN, 1783-1795

Sabine R.

LA.

1810   1813   FLA.

EAST
FLORIDA

WEST FLORIDA

CEDED BY SPAIN, 1819

FLORIDA, 1819

Claimed by SPAIN until 1819

GULF OF MEXICO

ATLANTIC OCEAN

Legend

▥	Disputed with Great Britain
▦	Disputed with Spain
▤	Disputed with Mexico
••••••	Natural boundary of Louisiana
▬ ▬ ▬	Natural boundary of Oregon Country
⌐‾⌐	Boundary adjustments with Great Britain
- - - -	Present-day state boundaries

0   100   200   300   400   500
Miles

POPULATION GROWTH OF THE UNITED STATES

People! They came from many lands to work in the growing cities and to build a new way of life in the rapidly expanding nation. Whereas in 1790 there were only about 4 million people, by 1970 there were more than 200 million. In earlier times, immigration accounted for much of the increase; today, a sharp rise in life expectancy helps to swell the nation's population.

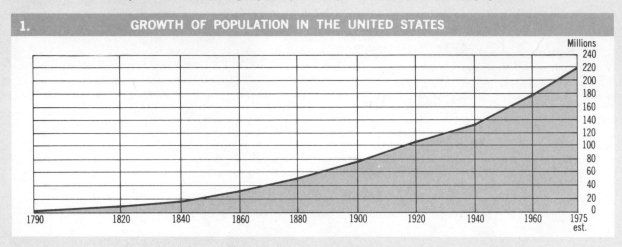

1. GROWTH OF POPULATION IN THE UNITED STATES

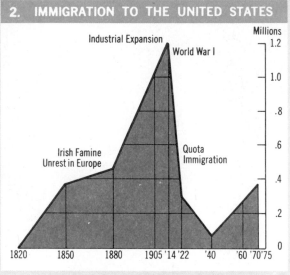

2. IMMIGRATION TO THE UNITED STATES

3. BIRTH RATE

4. DEATH RATE

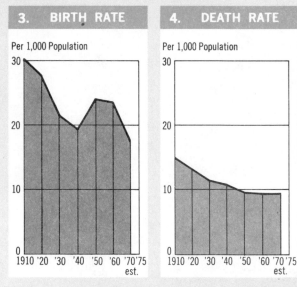

5. FOREIGN-BORN RESIDENTS

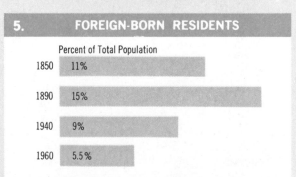

Percent of Total Population

1850 — 11%
1890 — 15%
1940 — 9%
1960 — 5.5%

6. AVERAGE LIFE EXPECTANCY AT BIRTH

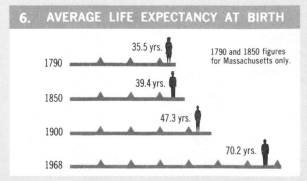

1790 — 35.5 yrs.
1850 — 39.4 yrs.
1900 — 47.3 yrs.
1968 — 70.2 yrs.

1790 and 1850 figures for Massachusetts only.

	State	Population at First Census After Entry	State Population 1970	Representatives in Congress	Largest City in 1970 (prel.)	City Population 1890	City Population 1930	City Population 1970 (prel.)
1	Delaware	59,000	548,104	1	Wilmington	61,431	106,597	80,386
2	Pennsylvania	434,000	11,793,909	25	Philadelphia	1,046,964	1,950,961	1,926,529
3	New Jersey	184,000	7,168,164	15	Newark	181,830	442,337	378,222
4	Georgia	83,000	4,589,575	10	Atlanta	65,533	270,366	487,553
5	Connecticut	238,000	3,032,217	6	Hartford	53,230	164,072	155,868
6	Massachusetts	379,000	5,689,170	12	Boston	448,477	781,188	628,215
7	Maryland	320,000	3,922,399	8	Baltimore	434,439	804,874	895,222
8	South Carolina	249,000	2,590,516	6	Columbia	15,353	51,581	111,706
9	New Hampshire	142,000	737,681	2	Manchester	44,126	76,834	87,754
10	Virginia	692,000	4,648,494	10	Norfolk	34,871	129,710	268,331
11	New York	340,000	18,190,740	39	New York	2,507,414	6,930,446	7,771,730
12	North Carolina	394,000	5,082,059	11	Charlotte	11,557	82,675	239,056
13	Rhode Island	69,000	949,723	2	Providence	132,146	252,981	176,920
14	Vermont	154,000	444,732	1	Burlington	14,500	24,789	38,633
15	Kentucky	221,000	3,219,311	7	Louisville	161,129	307,745	356,982
16	Tennessee	106,000	3,924,164	8	Memphis	64,495	253,143	620,873
17	Ohio	231,000	10,652,017	23	Cleveland	261,353	900,429	738,956
18	Louisiana	153,000	3,643,180	8	New Orleans	242,039	458,762	585,787
19	Indiana	147,000	5,193,669	11	Indianapolis	105,436	364,161	742,613
20	Mississippi	75,000	2,216,912	5	Jackson	5,920	48,282	150,332
21	Illinois	55,000	11,113,976	24	Chicago	1,099,850	3,376,438	3,325,263
22	Alabama	128,000	3,444,165	7	Birmingham	26,178	259,678	297,364
23	Maine	298,000	993,663	2	Portland	36,425	70,810	65,116
24	Missouri	140,000	4,677,399	10	St. Louis	451,770	821,960	607,718
25	Arkansas	98,000	1,923,295	4	Little Rock	25,874	81,679	128,880
26	Michigan	212,000	8,875,083	19	Detroit	205,876	1,568,662	1,492,914
27	Florida	87,000	6,789,443	15	Jacksonville	17,201	129,549	513,439
28	Texas	213,000	11,196,730	24	Houston	27,557	292,352	1,213,064
29	Iowa	192,000	2,825,041	6	Des Moines	50,093	142,559	198,427
30	Wisconsin	305,000	4,417,933	9	Milwaukee	204,468	578,249	709,537
31	California	93,000	19,953,134	43	Los Angeles	50,395	1,238,048	2,782,400
32	Minnesota	172,000	3,805,069	8	Minneapolis	164,738	464,356	431,977
33	Oregon	52,000	2,091,385	4	Portland	46,385	301,815	375,161
34	Kansas	364,000	2,249,071	5	Wichita	23,853	111,110	274,448
35	West Virginia	442,000	1,744,237	4	Huntington	10,108	75,572	72,970
36	Nevada	42,000	488,738	1	Las Vegas	0	5,165	124,161
37	Nebraska	123,000	1,483,791	3	Omaha	148,514	214,006	327,789
38	Colorado	194,000	2,207,259	5	Denver	106,713	287,861	512,691
39	North Dakota	191,000	617,761	1	Fargo	5,664	28,619	53,365
40	South Dakota	349,000	666,257	2	Sioux Falls	7,205	33,362	72,488
41	Montana	143,000	694,409	2	Billings	836	16,380	60,549
42	Washington	357,000	3,409,169	7	Seattle	42,837	365,583	524,263
43	Idaho	89,000	713,008	2	Boise City	2,311	21,544	73,330
44	Wyoming	63,000	332,416	1	Cheyenne	11,690	17,361	40,020
45	Utah	277,000	1,059,273	2	Salt Lake City	44,843	140,267	176,793
46	Oklahoma	1,657,000	2,559,253	6	Oklahoma City	4,151	185,389	363,225
47	New Mexico	360,000	1,016,000	2	Albuquerque	3,785	26,570	242,411
48	Arizona	334,000	1,772,482	4	Phoenix	3,152	48,118	580,275
49	Alaska	229,000	302,173	1	Anchorage	0	2,500	48,029
50	Hawaii	642,000	769,913	2	Honolulu	22,907	138,445	319,784
	District of Columbia	8,000 (1800)	756,510	—	Washington	188,932	486,869	756,510

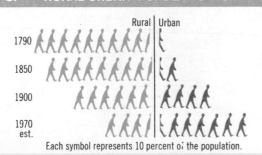

	Rural	Urban
1790		
1850		
1900		
1970 est.		

Each symbol represents 10 percent of the population.

The maps on pages 860–61 give a graphic summary of the Westward Movement. In 1790, all but a few hardy pioneers lived in the 13 original states along the Atlantic seaboard. Then, as the nation grew, people poured westward. In 1970, the most heavily populated state was California.

Equally striking has been the shift of population from rural to urban areas. In 1790 more than 90 percent of Americans lived in rural areas; by 1970 only about one third.

See maps, pages 860-61 ⟶

POPULATION GROWTH

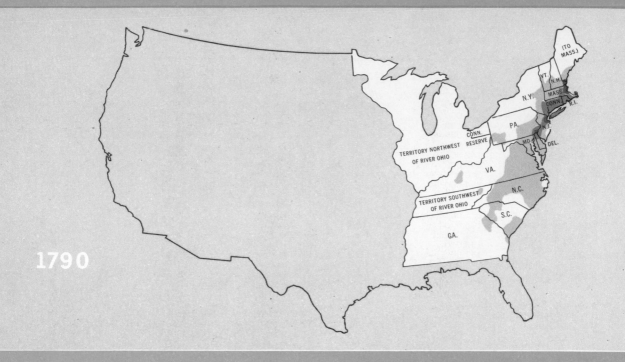

1790

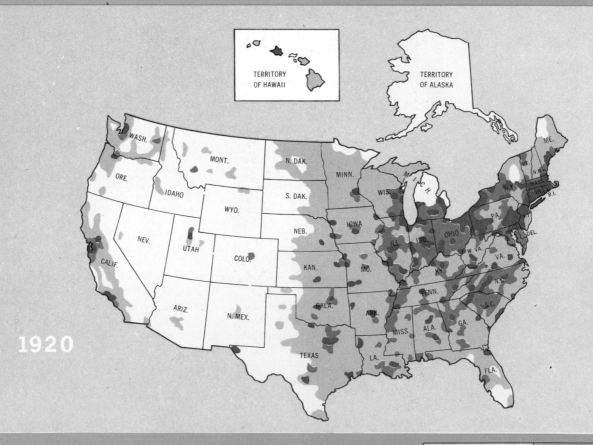

1920

PERSONS PER SQUARE MILE | Fewer than 5 | 5 to 45

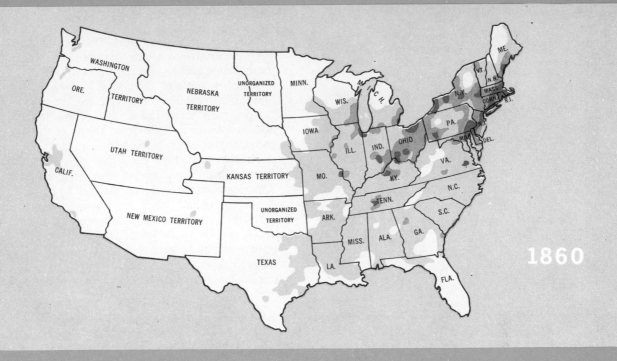

1860

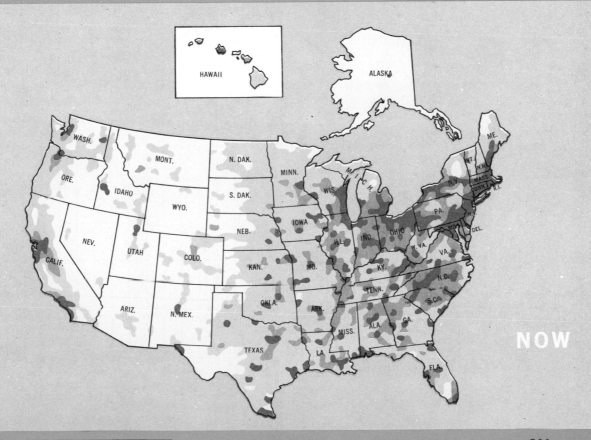

NOW

46 to 90	More than 90

1. THE FARM POPULATION

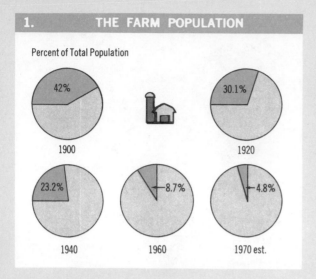

Percent of Total Population

42% — 1900
30.1% — 1920
23.2% — 1940
8.7% — 1960
4.8% — 1970 est.

The conquest of hunger! This is the dramatic story summarized in bare outline in the charts on these pages and on the map on pages 864–65.

Through most of their long history, men have lived in the shadow of starvation. When, for any reason, their crops failed, famine swept the land and people died. Today, two thirds of the world's people have barely enough to eat.

Famine has never been part of the American story. From the days of the first settlements, America's fertile soil has yielded food in abundance. In recent times, even though the number of farmers has declined, and even though fewer acres are being harvested, productivity of each American farm acre has risen greatly. Today, through modern methods, fewer farmers are producing more food on less land than ever before.

2. PEOPLE FED BY ONE FARM WORKER

1900 — 6.9 People
1950 — 15.5 People
1969 est. — 45.3 People

3. TRACTORS REPLACE HORSES AND MULES

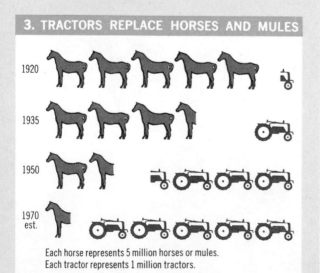

1920
1935
1950
1970 est.

Each horse represents 5 million horses or mules.
Each tractor represents 1 million tractors.

4. FARM PRODUCTION — ACRES HARVESTED

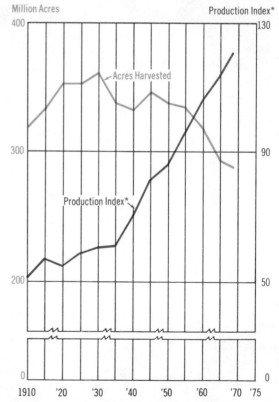

Million Acres

Production Index*

400 — 130
300 — 90
200 — 50
0 — 0

Acres Harvested

Production Index*

1910 '20 '30 '40 '50 '60 '70 '75

* The production index is a standard of measurement which indicates the increase or decrease of total farm production. Farm production for 1957-59 = 100.

5. NUMBER OF FARMS

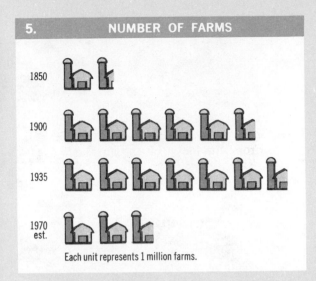

1850

1900

1935

1970 est.

Each unit represents 1 million farms.

6. AVERAGE SIZE OF FARMS

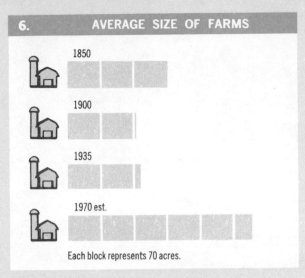

1850

1900

1935

1970 est.

Each block represents 70 acres.

7. USE OF FERTILIZER

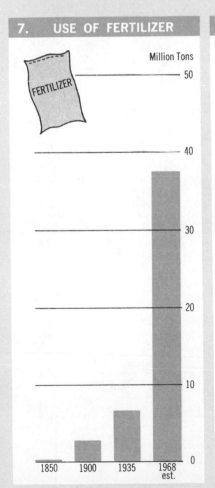

Million Tons

50

40

30

20

10

0

1850 1900 1935 1968 est.

8. FARM MACHINERY

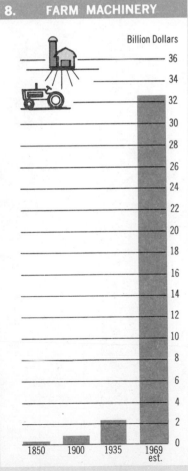

Billion Dollars

36
34
32
30
28
26
24
22
20
18
16
14
12
10
8
6
4
2
0

1850 1900 1935 1969 est.

9. AGRICULTURAL EXPORTS

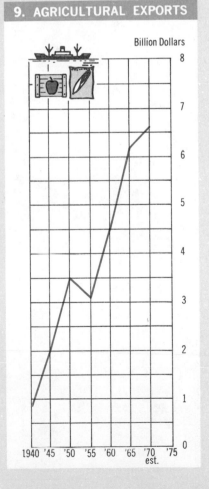

Billion Dollars

8

7

6

5

4

3

2

1

0

1940 '45 '50 '55 '60 '65 '70 '75 est.

See map, pages 864-65 ⟶

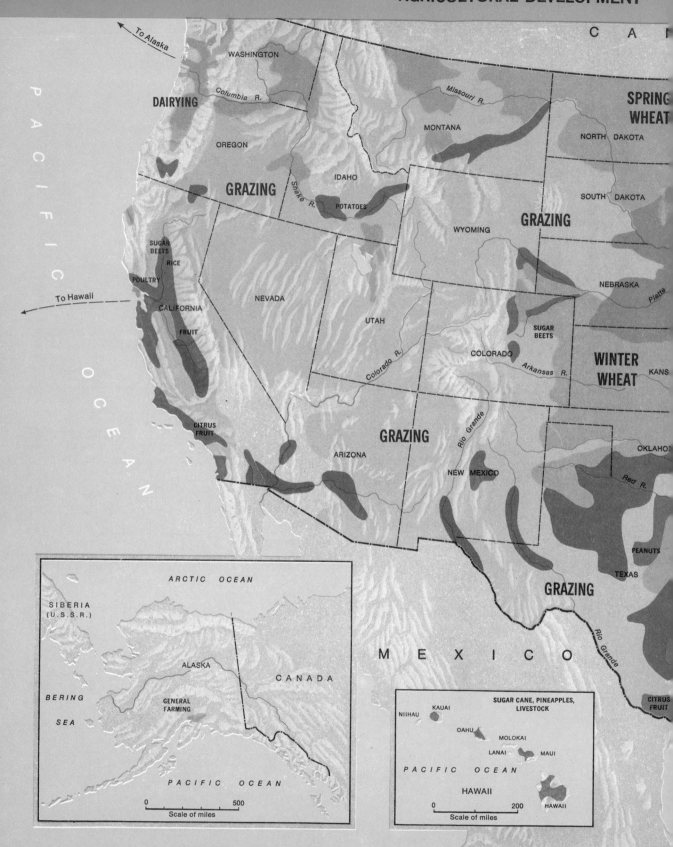

To Alaska

WASHINGTON

DAIRYING

Columbia R.

OREGON

Missouri R.

MONTANA

SPRING
WHEAT

NORTH DAKOTA

PACIFIC

GRAZING

Snake R.

IDAHO

POTATOES

SOUTH DAKOTA

WYOMING

GRAZING

SUGAR
BEETS

RICE

NEVADA

UTAH

NEBRASKA

Platte

To Hawaii

POULTRY

CALIFORNIA

FRUIT

COLORADO

SUGAR
BEETS

Colorado R.

Arkansas R.

WINTER
WHEAT

KANS.

O
C
E
A
N

CITRUS
FRUIT

GRAZING

ARIZONA

Rio Grande

NEW MEXICO

OKLAHO.

Red R.

PEANUTS

TEXAS

GRAZING

MEXICO

Rio Grande

CITRUS
FRUIT

ARCTIC OCEAN

SIBERIA
(U.S.S.R.)

ALASKA

CANADA

BERING
SEA

GENERAL
FARMING

PACIFIC OCEAN

0   500
Scale of miles

SUGAR CANE, PINEAPPLES,
LIVESTOCK

NIIHAU

KAUAI

OAHU

MOLOKAI

LANAI

MAUI

PACIFIC OCEAN

HAWAII

0   200
Scale of miles

HAWAII

C A N

C

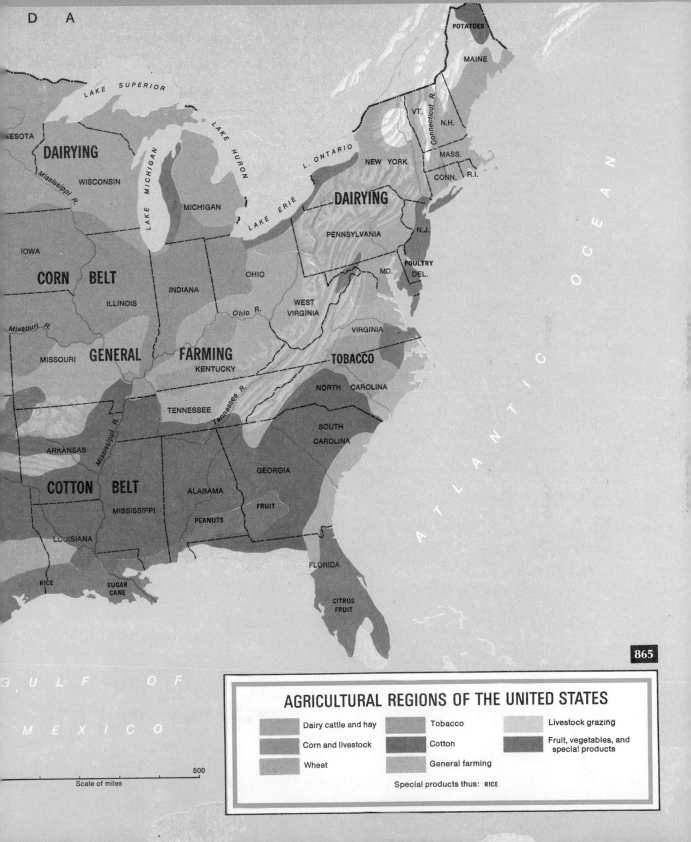

D A

POTATOES

MAINE

LAKE SUPERIOR

VT.

N.H.

NESOTA

DAIRYING

L. ONTARIO

MASS.

LAKE HURON

WISCONSIN

CONN. R.I.

NEW YORK

LAKE MICHIGAN

Connecticut R.

Mississippi R.

MICHIGAN

LAKE ERIE

DAIRYING

N.J.

IOWA

PENNSYLVANIA

OHIO

POULTRY

CORN BELT

INDIANA

MD. DEL.

ILLINOIS

Ohio R.

WEST VIRGINIA

Missouri R.

VIRGINIA

GENERAL FARMING

MISSOURI

KENTUCKY

TOBACCO

NORTH CAROLINA

TENNESSEE

Tennessee R.

SOUTH CAROLINA

ARKANSAS

Mississippi R.

GEORGIA

COTTON BELT

ALABAMA

FRUIT

MISSISSIPPI

PEANUTS

LOUISIANA

FLORIDA

RICE

SUGAR CANE

CITRUS FRUIT

ATLANTIC OCEAN

GULF OF

MEXICO

865

AGRICULTURAL REGIONS OF THE UNITED STATES

Dairy cattle and hay	Tobacco	Livestock grazing
Corn and livestock	Cotton	Fruit, vegetables, and special products
Wheat	General farming	

Special products thus: RICE

500

Scale of miles

Industry and agriculture have advanced side by side to produce today in the United States the highest standard of living that man has ever known. Behind the amazing advance of American industry stand the scientists and engineers who invented new machines and new products, discovered new sources of power, and learned to tap the wealth of natural resources buried in the earth (see map, pages 870–71).

But scientists and engineers are only one part of the story. Marching by their side have been the businessmen—the owners and managers of the nation's industries—who have contributed their ingenuity and their organizing ability to the creation of America's great industrial economy.

And beside the owners and managers have marched the armies of workers, men and women whose energy, skill, and creative efforts have opened up mines, built factories, dug canals, laid railroad tracks, strung telegraph and telephone wires, and supplied the manpower to produce and distribute the almost endless variety of products that keep pouring out in ever-mounting volume. An important part of this remarkable industrial development has been the use of power from coal, oil, gas, water, and nuclear energy.

1. MAJOR ADVANCES OF

	The Colonists Had
POWER	Human Muscles Animal Muscles Wind and Water Power
PHYSICAL MATERIALS	Copper and Bronze Iron Wood and Clay Plant and Animal Fibers
MANUFACTURING	Hand Forges and Tools Man-powered Spinning Wheels and Looms
AGRICULTURE	Wooden Plow Spade Ax and Other Hand Tools
TRANSPORTATION	Horses Animal-drawn Vehicles Sailing Vessels
COMMUNICATION	Hand Printing Presses Local Newspapers

2. OUTPUT PER WORKER

National Income per Man-Hour

1850	50¢
1900	50¢ 50¢
1950	50¢ 50¢ 50¢ 50¢ 50¢
1960	50¢ 50¢ 50¢ 50¢ 50¢ 50¢ 50¢
1975 est.	50¢ 50¢ 50¢ 50¢ 50¢ 50¢ 50¢ 50¢ 50¢ 50¢

Each unit represents 50 cents in 1960 prices.

3. WORKERS IN MANUFACTURING

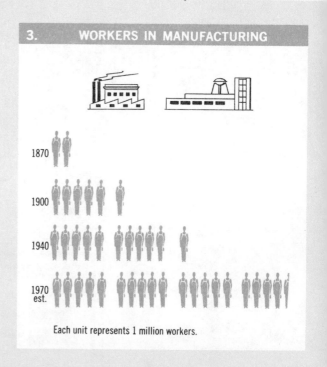

1870	♀♀
1900	♀♀♀♀♀
1940	♀♀♀♀♀♀♀♀
1970 est.	♀♀♀♀♀♀♀♀♀♀♀♀♀♀♀♀♀♀

Each unit represents 1 million workers.

AMERICAN INDUSTRY: COLONIAL PERIOD TO THE PRESENT

1783–1850	1850–1900	1900–1920	1920–Present
Steam Power	Hydraulic-turbine Engines Internal-combustion Engines Steam Turbines Dynamos, Electric Motors		Nuclear Energy Solar Energy
Large-scale Production of Iron	Large-scale Production of Steel Development of Combustion Fuels: Coal, Oil, Gas Development of Light Metals and Alloys	Large-scale Production of Light Metals and Alloys Development of Plastics and Synthetics	Large-scale Production of Plastics and Synthetics Development of Nuclear Fuels
Water- and Steam-powered Factories Interchangeable Parts	Mass Production with Centralized Assembly of Interchangeable Parts	Conveyer-belt Assembly Line	Automation Computers
New Iron and Steel Tools Early Agricultural Machines: Cotton Gin, Reaper, Harvester	Steam Power	Genetics and Soil Science Gasoline and Electric Power	Large-scale Mechanized Farming
Development of Steamships Development of Railroads Development of Canals	Large-scale Transport by Steamship and Rail Early Development of Internal Combustion Engines	Automobiles, Trucks, Buses Development of Propeller-driven Aircraft	Development of Jet Propulsion Rocket Flights Manned Flights to Moon
Large-scale Printing Presses Telegraph Development of Magazine and Book Printing	Transoceanic Cable Telephone Wireless Telegraphy Phonograph	Motion Pictures Radio Transcontinental Telephone	Television; Transistors; Communication Satellites; Lasers; Magnetic Tape; Video Cartridges

4. SHIFT IN POWER SOURCES

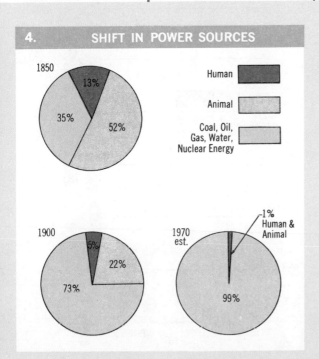

1850
13%
35%
52%

Human

Animal

Coal, Oil,
Gas, Water,
Nuclear Energy

1900
5%
22%
73%

1970
est.
1% Human & Animal
99%

5. RESEARCH AND DEVELOPMENT

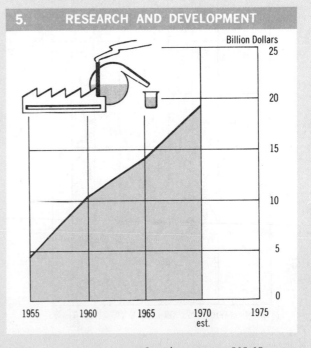

Billion Dollars
25
20
15
10
5
0

1955 1960 1965 1970 est. 1975

See charts, pages 868-69
and map, pages 870-71

During the early 1800's, when a great wave of pioneers was rolling westward, many Americans feared that the far reaches of the country would eventually break away from the Union. The distances seemed too great, the means of communication too slow and uncertain. These early fears proved groundless. The charts on these pages and the map on pages 870–71 reveal the developments and the resources that conquered time and space and made the Union possible.

Settlers carried west by the spreading network of railroads turned virgin lands into rich farms,

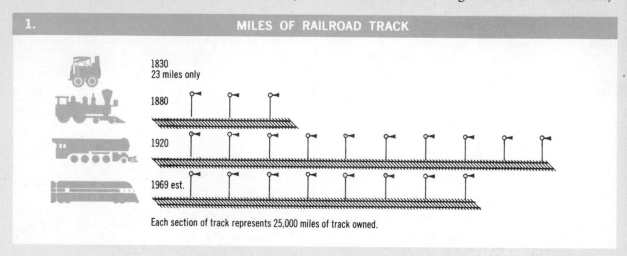

1. MILES OF RAILROAD TRACK

1830
23 miles only

1880

1920

1969 est.

Each section of track represents 25,000 miles of track owned.

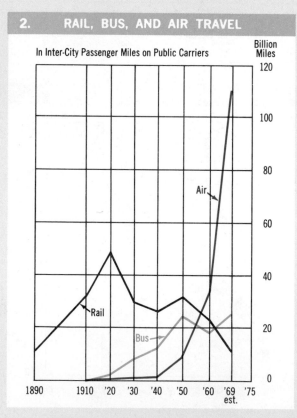

2. RAIL, BUS, AND AIR TRAVEL

In Inter-City Passenger Miles on Public Carriers

Billion Miles

Air

Rail

Bus

1890   1910   '20   '30   '40   '50   '60   '69 est.   '75

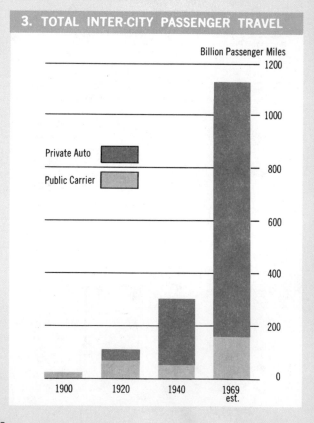

3. TOTAL INTER-CITY PASSENGER TRAVEL

Billion Passenger Miles

Private Auto

Public Carrier

1900   1920   1940   1969 est.

built cities in what had once been wilderness, and took long-buried mineral wealth from the earth for the benefit of all the people. Improved highways and mass production of automobiles, buses, and trucks put the nation on wheels. The telephone, radio, and television gave the people eyes and ears that could see and hear across the continent—and beyond. These inventions, along with the airplane, made the whole world neighbors. And this is only the beginning, for men have already begun to conquer the vast distances of outer space.

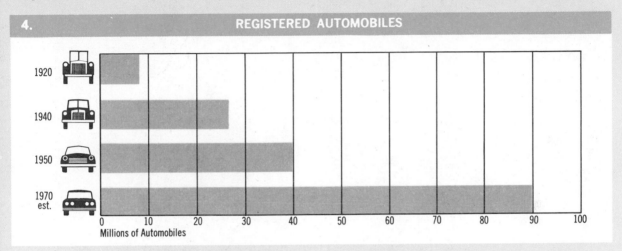

4. REGISTERED AUTOMOBILES

1920
1940
1950
1970 est.

0   10   20   30   40   50   60   70   80   90   100
Millions of Automobiles

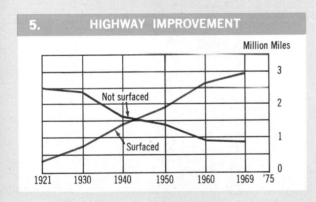

5. HIGHWAY IMPROVEMENT

Million Miles

Not surfaced

Surfaced

1921   1930   1940   1950   1960   1969 '75

3
2
1
0

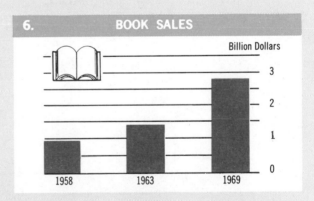

6. BOOK SALES

Billion Dollars

3
2
1
0

1958   1963   1969

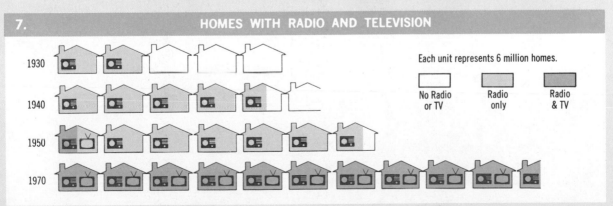

7. HOMES WITH RADIO AND TELEVISION

1930
1940
1950
1970

Each unit represents 6 million homes.

No Radio or TV   Radio only   Radio & TV

INDUSTRIAL RESOURCES

C A

To Alaska

CHIEF
JOSEPH
ROCKY
REACH   GRAND
COULEE   HUNGRY HORSE
WASH.   NOXON
PRIEST   RAPIDS
RAPIDS
THE DALLES   McNARY
BONNEVILLE
Columbia R.

MONT.   Missouri R.   GARRISON
N. DAK.

HELLS
CANYON

ORE.   YELLOWTAIL

IDAHO   S. DAK.
Snake R.   OAHE
                                                              BIG BEND
SHASTA   WYO.   FORT RANDALL

FOLSOM   NEBR.
                                                                   Platte R.

CALIF.   NEV.   UTAH
                                              COLO.   KANS
                                          Arkansas R.

HOOVER   GLEN
                CANYON

                ARIZ.   N. MEX.

                                                              TEXAS

Colorado R.

M E X I C O
                                                              Rio Grande

ARCTIC   OCEAN

SIBERIA
(U.S.S.R.)

                              CANADA

Yukon R.
ALASKA

BERING

SEA

PACIFIC   OCEAN

0   500

Scale of miles

0   500

Scale of miles

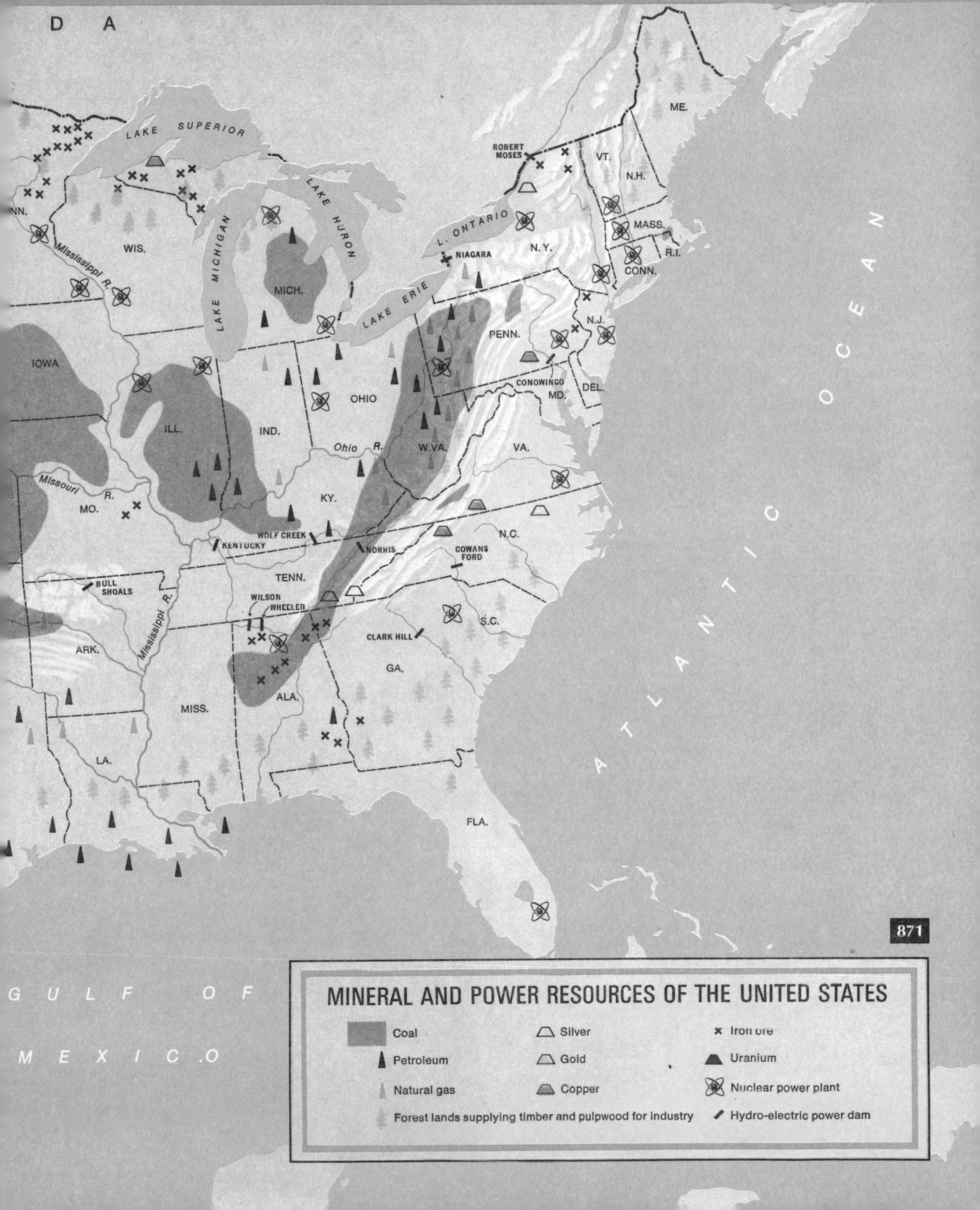

D A

ME.

LAKE SUPERIOR

ROBERT
MOSES

VT.

N.H.

NN.

Mississippi R.

WIS.

MICH.

LAKE MICHIGAN

LAKE HURON

LAKE ERIE

L. ONTARIO

NIAGARA

N.Y.

MASS.

R.I.

CONN.

IOWA

OHIO

PENN.

N.J.

CONOWINGO

MD.

DEL.

ILL.

IND.

Ohio R.

W.VA.

VA.

Missouri R.

MO.

KY.

WOLF CREEK

KENTUCKY

NORRIS

N.C.

COWANS
FORD

Mississippi R.

BULL
SHOALS

TENN.

WILSON
WHEELER

S.C.

ARK.

CLARK HILL

MISS.

ALA.

GA.

LA.

FLA.

ATLANTIC OCEAN

GULF OF

MEXICO

MINERAL AND POWER RESOURCES OF THE UNITED STATES

▮ Coal	△ Silver	✗ Iron ore
▮ Petroleum	△ Gold	▲ Uranium
▮ Natural gas	▰ Copper	⊛ Nuclear power plant
▲ Forest lands supplying timber and pulpwood for industry		╱ Hydro-electric power dam

In the early 1800's, when the nation was young, the bulk of its exports consisted of raw materials—such as lumber and cotton—and foodstuffs (chart 2, right). Such products continued to form most of America's exports until well into the twentieth century. By that time, the American economic system had become so productive that the total export of American manufactured goods considerably exceeded that of raw materials and foodstuffs.

America's industries and its complex transportation and communication system—the arteries of the economy—developed behind a high wall of protective tariffs (chart 4, right).

During the 1800's, Americans neither bought a great deal from other countries nor sold much to them (chart 3, right). They were pouring their money into capital goods. These were the formative years when the pioneers were moving westward across the continent, and the industrial economy was developing from an infant into a

giant. In the 1800's Americans needed for their own use most of what they could produce. They needed steel for railroads, for bridges across rivers and canyons, for the framework of factory and office buildings, for machines in factories and on farms. They needed copper for telegraph and telephone wires and for power lines to carry electricity. They needed tools, utensils, and household equipment to furnish the homes of a population that was growing at an extremely rapid rate.

By the early 1900's, however, America's giant industrial economy was rolling in high gear. Americans were producing more than enough for their own needs and were creating surpluses of both foodstuffs and manufactured goods for export to other countries of the world (charts 2 and 3, right). But trade has always been and must always be a two-way street (chart 5, right). Today Americans are carrying on an ever-swelling volume of world trade.

1. UNITED STATES' SHARE OF THE WORLD'S WEALTH

Each symbol represents 10 percent of world total. Percentages shown are for 1969.

PRINCIPAL U.S. EXPORTS

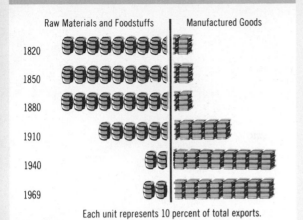

Raw Materials and Foodstuffs   Manufactured Goods

1820

1850

1880

1910

1940

1969

Each unit represents 10 percent of total exports.

3.

U.S. EXPORTS AND IMPORTS

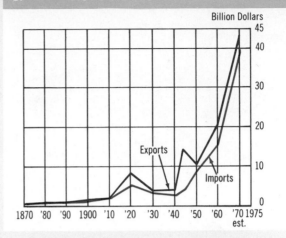

Billion Dollars

Exports

Imports

1870 '80 '90 1900 '10 '20 '30 '40 '50 '60 '70 1975
est.

4.

THE RISE AND FALL OF U.S. TARIFFS

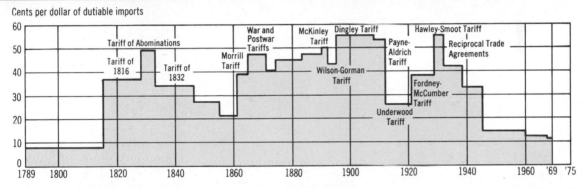

Cents per dollar of dutiable imports

Tariff of Abominations

Tariff of 1816

Tariff of 1832

Morrill Tariff

War and Postwar Tariffs

McKinley Tariff

Dingley Tariff

Wilson-Gorman Tariff

Payne-Aldrich Tariff

Hawley-Smoot Tariff

Reciprocal Trade Agreements

Fordney-McCumber Tariff

Underwood Tariff

1789 1800 1820 1840 1860 1880 1900 1920 1940 1960 '69 '75

5.

DIRECTION AND VOLUME OF U.S. WORLD TRADE

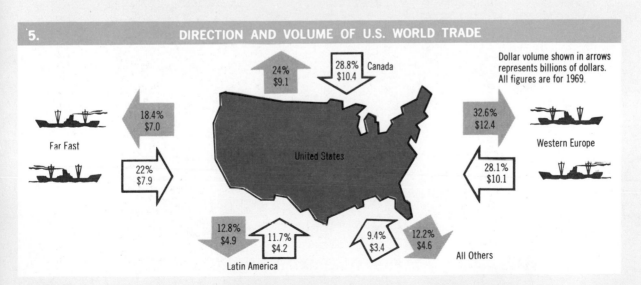

Dollar volume shown in arrows represents billions of dollars. All figures are for 1969.

24%
$9.1

28.8% Canada
$10.4

18.4%
$7.0

Far East

32.6%
$12.4

Western Europe

22%
$7.9

28.1%
$10.1

United States

12.8%
$4.9

11.7%
$4.2

9.4%
$3.4

12.2%
$4.6

Latin America

All Others

873

See map, pages 874-75 ⟶

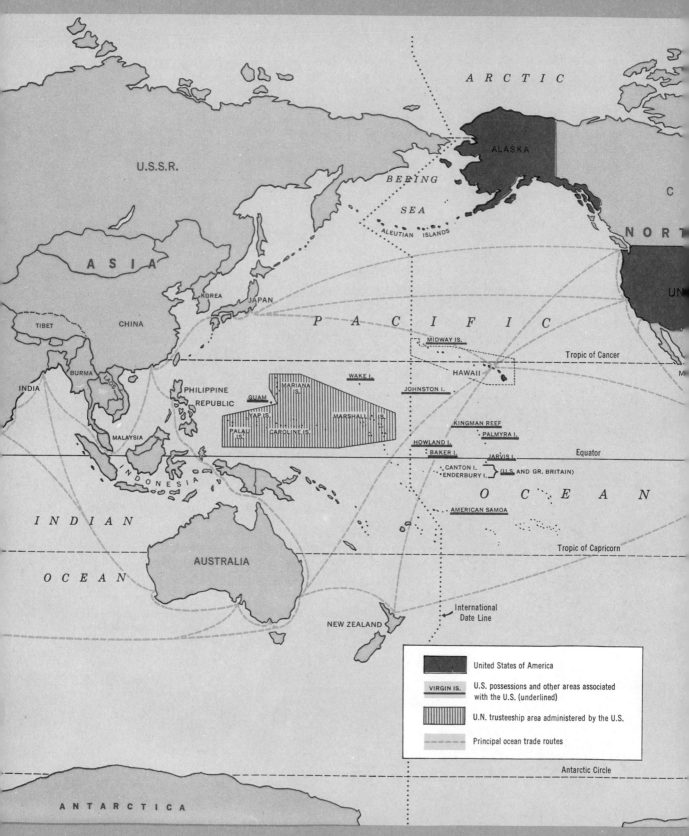

ARCTIC

ALASKA

U.S.S.R.

BERING

SEA

ALEUTIAN ISLANDS

C

NORT

ASIA

KOREA

JAPAN

PACIFIC

TIBET

CHINA

BURMA

INDIA

LAOS

PHILIPPINE
REPUBLIC

GUAM

MARIANA
IS.

YAP IS.

PALAU
IS.

CAROLINE IS.

MARSHALL IS.

WAKE I.

MALAYSIA

INDONESIA

MIDWAY IS.

HAWAII

JOHNSTON I.

KINGMAN REEF

PALMYRA I.

HOWLAND I.
BAKER I.

JARVIS I.

CANTON I.
ENDERBURY I.

(U.S. AND GR. BRITAIN)

AMERICAN SAMOA

OCEAN

UN

M

Tropic of Cancer

Equator

INDIAN

OCEAN

AUSTRALIA

Tropic of Capricorn

NEW ZEALAND

International
Date Line

Antarctic Circle

ANTARCTICA

United States of America	
VIRGIN IS.	U.S. possessions and other areas associated with the U.S. (underlined)
	U.N. trusteeship area administered by the U.S.
	Principal ocean trade routes

GREENLAND

OCEAN

Arctic Circle

ICELAND

NORWAY

SWEDEN

FINLAND

ASIA

U.S.S.R.

GREAT
BRITAIN

EIRE

GER.

POLAND

EUROPE

AMERICA

FRANCE

TES

ITALY

TURKEY

PORTUGAL

SPAIN

AFGHANISTAN

TUNISIA

ISRAEL

IRAQ

IRAN

MOROCCO

PAKISTAN

ALGERIA

LIBYA

U.A.R.
(EGYPT)

SAUDI
ARABIA

ATLANTIC

INDIA

CUBA

PUERTO RICO

MAURITANIA

MALI

NIGER

CHAD

SUDAN

CANAL ZONE

VIRGIN IS.

AFRICA

RAL

VENEZUELA

NIGERIA

ETHIOPIA

SOMALIA

MERICA

COLOMBIA

LIBERIA

GHANA

KENYA

INDIAN

ECUADOR

DEMOCRATIC
REPUBLIC
OF CONGO

PERU

SOUTH

OCEAN

TANZANIA

BRAZIL

OCEAN

AMERICA

ANGOLA

BOLIVIA

MALAGASY

PARAGUAY

S.W. AFRICA

CHILE

URUGUAY

REPUBLIC OF
SOUTH AFRICA

ARGENTINA

ANTARCTICA

1. LABOR FORCE AND POPULATION

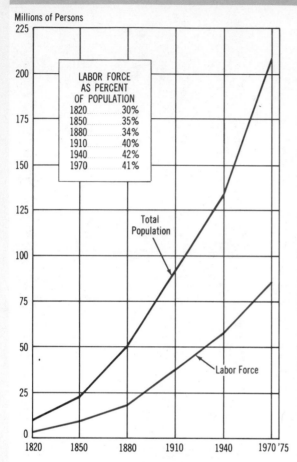

Millions of Persons

LABOR FORCE
AS PERCENT
OF POPULATION
1820	30%
1850	35%
1880	34%
1910	40%
1940	42%
1970	41%

Total Population

Labor Force

2. DISTRIBUTION OF INCOME

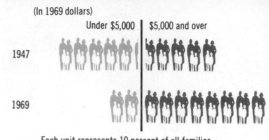

(In 1969 dollars)

Under $5,000 $5,000 and over

1947

1969

Each unit represents 10 percent of all families.

3. SHIFTS IN MAJOR OCCUPATIONS

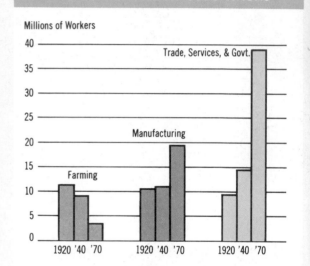

Millions of Workers

Trade, Services, & Govt.

Manufacturing

Farming

1920 '40 '70   1920 '40 '70   1920 '40 '70

When, in May 1790, Rhode Island ratified the Constitution and entered the Union as the thirteenth state, the total population of the United States was only about 4 million. More than nine out of every ten Americans lived on farms or in small villages. Most Europeans who gave the United States even a second thought looked down on the infant republic with mingled scorn and amusement and predicted that it would last only a few years. Although President Washington was more optimistic, he reminded his fellow citizens that the new nation was an "experiment" entrusted to the hands of the American people.

The experiment succeeded beyond even the most daring dreams of the Founding Fathers. By the opening years of the twentieth century,

the United States had become a world power. By mid-twentieth century it had become the leader of the non-Communist world.

Measured by material things—by the things men can see and touch—the United States of the 1970's bears little resemblance to the infant republic of 1790. As you have seen throughout this book, the country has grown and changed through the years. Today, science and technology are transforming the face of the nation—and for that matter, the whole world—with bewildering speed.

As the charts on these pages remind you, however, it is not just the material aspects of life that are being transformed in this swiftly moving age. One of the most striking aspects of American life today is the amazing variety of occupa-

AVERAGE WORKWEEK

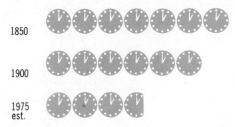

1850

1900

1975 est.

Each symbol represents 10 hours worked per week.

5.   CHURCH MEMBERSHIP

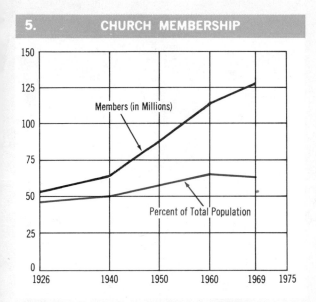

Members (in Millions)

Percent of Total Population

150
125
100
75
50
25
0

1926   1940   1950   1960   1969   1975

6.   SCHOOL AND COLLEGE ENROLLMENT

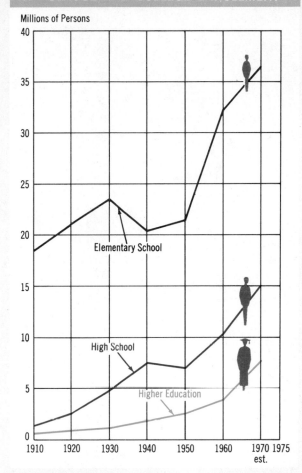

Millions of Persons

40

35

30

25

20

Elementary School

15

High School

10

Higher Education

5

0

1910   1920   1930   1940   1950   1960   1970 1975
est.

tions open to the rapidly growing army of workers. Whereas in 1790 more than 90 percent of all Americans worked on the land, by the 1970's a young person had the opportunity to choose from many thousands of types of jobs.

Equally striking is the steadily rising standard of living and the growing amount of leisure time enjoyed by the American people. What are Americans doing with their leisure?

More and more Americans are joining the church of their choice. Many of the country's leaders believe that above all Americans need rededication to the values that have from the beginning sustained the growing nation through its trials and triumphs.

Enrollments in schools and colleges are rising rapidly. "If a nation expects to be ignorant and

free," Thomas Jefferson warned, "it expects what never was and never will be." The American people as a whole have come to share this faith in education.

Despite a growing concern for matters of the spirit, Americans are still confronted with disturbing questions. Are the American people developing the attitudes, understanding, and skills they need to meet the formidable challenges of a fast-changing world? Are they developing the minds and strengthening their understanding the moral principles upon which the nation founded?

These are extremely important questions important, perhaps, as any questions the American people can ask themselves as the the future.

See map, pages 8

STATES AND CITIES OF THE UNITED STATES

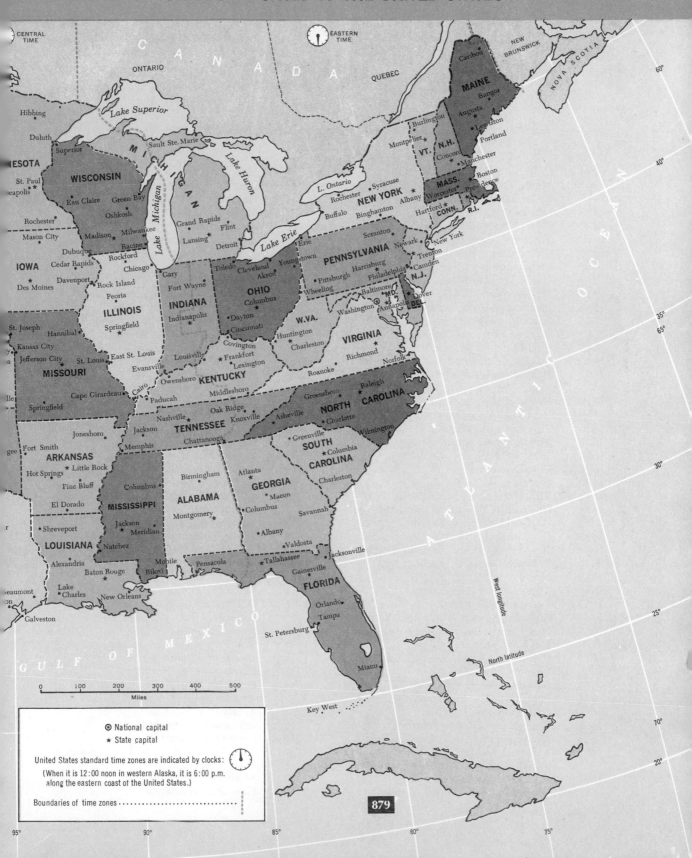

CENTRAL TIME

EASTERN TIME

C A N A D A

ONTARIO

QUEBEC

NEW BRUNSWICK

NOVA SCOTIA

Lake Superior

Hibbing

Duluth

Superior

Sault Ste. Marie

MAINE

Caribou

Bangor

Augusta ★

Lewiston

Portland

MINNESOTA

St. Paul ★

Minneapolis ★

WISCONSIN

M I C H I G A N

Lake Huron

Burlington

Montpelier ★

VT.

N.H.

Concord ★

Manchester

Rochester

Mason City

Eau Claire

Green Bay

Oshkosh

Madison ★

Milwaukee

Racine

Grand Rapids

Lansing

Flint

L. Ontario

Rochester

Syracuse

NEW YORK

Albany ★

MASS.

Worcester

Boston

Providence ★

R.I.

IOWA

Des Moines ★

Dubuque

Cedar Rapids

Davenport

Rockford

Chicago

Gary

Fort Wayne

Toledo

Detroit

Lake Michigan

Lake Erie

Buffalo

Binghamton

Erie

Hartford ★

CONN.

Scranton

Newark

New York

Rock Island

Peoria

ILLINOIS

Springfield ★

INDIANA

Indianapolis ★

OHIO

Columbus ★

Cleveland

Akron

Youngstown

PENNSYLVANIA

Pittsburgh

Harrisburg ★

Philadelphia

Trenton ★

Camden

N.J.

St. Joseph

Hannibal

Kansas City

Jefferson City ★

St. Louis ★

East St. Louis

Evansville

Dayton

Cincinnati

Wheeling

W.VA.

Huntington

Charleston ★

Washington

Annapolis ★

MD.

Baltimore

Dover ★

DEL.

Louisville

Covington

Frankfort ★

Lexington

VIRGINIA

Richmond ★

Norfolk

MISSOURI

Cape Girardeau

Cairo

Paducah

Owensboro

KENTUCKY

Middlesboro

Roanoke

Springfield

Jonesboro

Nashville ★

Oak Ridge

Knoxville

Asheville

Greensboro

Raleigh ★

NORTH CAROLINA

Wilmington

Fort Smith

Hot Springs

Little Rock ★

ARKANSAS

Memphis

Jackson

TENNESSEE

Chattanooga

Charlotte

Greenville

SOUTH CAROLINA

Columbia ★

Pine Bluff

El Dorado

Birmingham

Atlanta ★

Columbus

GEORGIA

Macon

Charleston

Columbus

MISSISSIPPI

Jackson ★

Meridian

ALABAMA

Montgomery ★

Albany

Savannah

Shreveport

LOUISIANA

Natchez

Alexandria

Beaumont

Houston

Galveston

Lake Charles

New Orleans

Baton Rouge ★

Mobile

Biloxi

Pensacola

Valdosta

Jacksonville

Tallahassee ★

Gainesville

FLORIDA

Orlando

Tampa

St. Petersburg

Miami

Key West

G U L F   O F   M E X I C O

A T L A N T I C   O C E A N

West longitude

North latitude

60°

40°

35°

30°

25°

65°

70°

20°

95°

90°

85°

80°

75°

0   100   200   300   400   500

Miles

⊕ National capital

★ State capital

United States standard time zones are indicated by clocks:
(When it is 12:00 noon in western Alaska, it is 6:00 p.m.
along the eastern coast of the United States.)

Boundaries of time zones ·················

879

CHRONOLOGY OF EVENTS IN AMERICAN HISTORY

(The state given after each President's name was the state of residence at time of election.)

1096	Crusades to Holy Land start.
1271–95	Marco Polo's travels in Far East.
1492	**Columbus discovers America.**
1494	Line of demarcation.
1497–98	John Cabot's explorations.
1498	Vasco da Gama reaches India.
1500	Cabral claims Brazil.
1513	Balboa discovers Pacific Ocean.
1519	Cortés lands in Mexico.
1519–22	Magellan's men circle earth.
1531–35	Pizarro conquers Incas.
1534	Cartier makes first voyage.
1539–42	De Soto explores Southeast.
1588	English defeat Spanish Armada.
1603	Champlain makes first voyage.
1607	**Jamestown is founded.**
1609	Hudson explores Hudson River.
1619	**House of Burgesses meets.**
1619	First Negroes arrive in Virginia.
1620	Pilgrims reach Cape Cod.
1620	**Mayflower Compact.**
1624	Virginia becomes royal colony.
1630	Massachusetts Bay Colony founded.
1632	Maryland is chartered.
1636	Roger Williams founds Providence.
1636	Hartford (Connecticut) settled.
1636	Harvard University founded.
1639	Fundamenal Orders of Connecticut.
1643	New England Confederation formed.
1647	**Massachusetts passes school law.**
1649	Maryland Toleration Act.
1651–63	Principal Navigation Acts.
1663	Carolina is chartered.
1664	English take over Dutch colonies.
1664	New Netherland becomes New Jersey and New York.
1673	Exploration by Marquette, Joilet.
1675–76	Bacon's Rebellion.
1679	New Hampshire is chartered.
1681	Pennsylvania is chartered.
1681–82	Exploration by La Salle.
1682	Delaware granted to Penn.
1686	Dominion of New England created.
1689–1748	France and Great Britain intermittently at war.
1693	College of William and Mary founded.
1699	Woolens Act.

1701	Yale University founded.
1732	Georgia is chartered.
1732	Hat Act.
1733	Molasses Act.
1735	**Zenger trial.**
1740	University of Pennsylvania founded.
1746	Princeton University founded.
1750	Iron Act.
1754	French and Indian War starts.
1754	Albany Plan of Union proposed.
1754	Columbia University founded.
1755	Braddock defeated disastrously.
1756	Pitt heads British government.
1759	British capture Quebec.
1763	**Treaty of Paris.**
1763	Proclamation of 1763.
1764	Sugar Act, Currency Act.
1764	Brown University founded.
1765	Stamp Act.
1765	Stamp Act Congress meets.
1766	Stamp Act repealed.
1766	Rutgers University founded.
1767	Townshend Acts.
1769	Dartmouth College founded.
1770	Boston Massacre.
1772	Committees of Correspondence.
1773	Boston Tea Party.
1774	**First Continental Congress.**
1775	Fighting at Lexington, Concord.
1775	Second Continental Congress.
1775	Battle of Bunker Hill.
1776	Paine's *Common Sense* appears.
1776	**Declaration of Independence.**
1776	American victory at Trenton.
1777–78	Howe occupies Philadelphia.
1777	Burgoyne surrenders at Saratoga.
1778	Treaty of alliance with France.
1778–79	Clark takes the Northwest.
1781	Cornwallis surrenders.
1781	Articles of Confederation go into effect.
1783	**Treaty of Paris; United States independence recognized.**
1785	Land Ordinance.
1786	Virginia Statute for Religious Freedom.
1786–87	Shays' Rebellion.
1787	Northwest Ordinance.
1787	**Constitution drafted.**

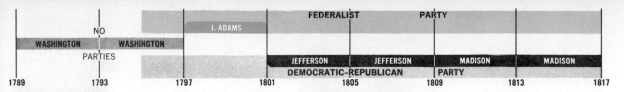

NO PARTIES

WASHINGTON   WASHINGTON

J. ADAMS

FEDERALIST   PARTY

JEFFERSON   JEFFERSON   MADISON   MADISON

DEMOCRATIC-REPUBLICAN   PARTY

1789   1793   1797   1801   1805   1809   1813   1817

1
George Washington
1732–1799; Virginia
In office: 1789–1797

1789	Congress creates Departments of State, Treasury, and War.
1789	United States courts are organized.
1789	French Revolution begins.
1789	Slater brings knowledge of power-driven machines to U.S.
1790	Assumption Bill provides for federal payment of states' war debts.
1790	Patent and copyright law.
1791	Bill of Rights ratified.
1791	Vermont enters Union.
1791	Bank of United States chartered.
1791	Lancaster Turnpike is begun.
1792	Kentucky enters Union.
1792	Gray discovers Columbia River.
1793	Genêt visit.
1793	Proclamation of Neutrality.
1793	Eli Whitney invents cotton gin.
1794	"Whisky Rebellion" is crushed in Pennsylvania.
1794	Battle of Fallen Timbers.
1794	Jay Treaty.
1795	Pinckney Treaty.
1796	Tennessee enters Union.

2
John Adams
1735–1826; Massachusetts
Federalist
In office: 1797–1801

1797	XYZ Affair angers Americans.
1798	Navy Department is created.
1798	Eleventh Amendment ratified.
1798	Alien and Sedition Acts.
1798–99	Kentucky and Virginia Resolutions.
1800	Interchangeable parts demonstrated.
1801	Marshall becomes Chief Justice.

3
Thomas Jefferson
1743–1826; Virginia
Democratic-Republican
In office: 1801–1809

1803	Ohio enters Union.
1803	*Marbury v. Madison.*
1803	Louisiana Purchase adds immense area to United States.
1804	Twelfth Amendment ratified.
1804–06	Lewis and Clark expedition.
1805–07	Pike explores western regions.
1805	War with Barbary pirates ends.
1807	Embargo Act.
1807	Steamboat *Clermont* demonstrated.
1808	Astor builds fort and trading post in Oregon country.
1809	Non-Intercourse Act.

4
James Madison
1751–1836; Virginia
Democratic-Republican
In office: 1809–1817

1811	Indian fight at Tippecanoe.
1811	National Road is begun.
1811	Fulton builds steamboat *New Orleans.*
1812	Louisiana enters Union.
1812–14	War of 1812 is fought between United States and Great Britain.
1813	Waltham experiment begins—attempt to help factory workers.
1814	Hartford Convention meets; restates Kentucky and Virginia Resolutions.
1814	Treaty of Ghent restores peace.
1815	Battle of New Orleans.
1816	Second Bank of United States chartered.
1816	Protective tariff adopted.
1816	Indiana enters Union.

BUSINESS ACTIVITY CHART

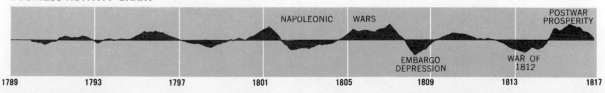

NAPOLEONIC WARS

POSTWAR PROSPERITY

EMBARGO DEPRESSION

WAR OF 1812

1789   1793   1797   1801   1805   1809   1813   1817

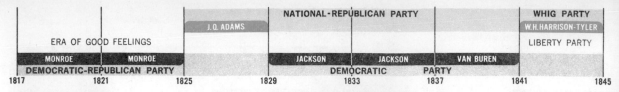

| | | | NATIONAL-REPUBLICAN PARTY | | | WHIG PARTY |
| ERA OF GOOD FEELINGS | | | J.Q. ADAMS | | | W.H.HARRISON-TYLER / LIBERTY PARTY |

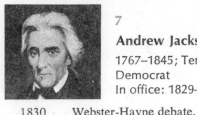

MONROE | MONROE | | | JACKSON | JACKSON | VAN BUREN
DEMOCRATIC-REPUBLICAN PARTY | | | DEMOCRATIC PARTY

1817   1821   1825   1829   1833   1837   1841   1845

5
James Monroe

1758–1831; Virginia
Democratic-Republican
In office: 1817–1825

1817–25	"Era of Good Feelings."
1817	Mississippi enters Union.
1818	Rush-Bagot Agreement approved.
1818	Illinois enters Union.
1818	Treaty settles Canadian boundary.
1818	Philadelphia-Pittsburgh Turnpike is completed.
1819	*McCulloch v. Maryland.*
1819	*Dartmouth College v. Woodward.*
1819	Financial panic.
1819	Alabama enters Union.
1819	Tallmadge Amendment introduced.
1819	Treaty gives Florida to U.S.
1820	Missouri Compromise.
1820	Maine enters Union.
1821	Missouri enters Union.
1821	Austin starts colony in Texas.
1821	First public high school opens.
1822	U.S. recognizes revolutionary governments of Latin America.
1823	Monroe Doctrine proclaimed.
1824	*Gibbons v. Ogden.*
1825	Utopian community started by Robert Owen at New Harmony.

6
John Quincy Adams

1767–1848; Massachusetts
National-Republican
In office: 1825–1829

1825	Erie Canal opens.
1828	"Tariff of Abominations."
1828	"South Carolina Exposition and Protest."
1828	Work begun on Baltimore and Ohio Railroad.
1828	Webster publishes his dictionary.

7
Andrew Jackson

1767–1845; Tennessee
Democrat
In office: 1829–1837

1830	Webster-Hayne debate.
1831	First nominating conventions.
1831	Slave uprising in Virginia.
1831	First issue of the *Liberator*.
1832	Tariff of 1832.
1832	Ordinance of Nullification.
1832	Telegraph is developed.
1832	Jackson vetoes renewal of charter for Bank of United States.
1833	Jackson withdraws deposits from Bank of United States.
1833	Compromise tariff act.
1834	National Trades Union formed.
1836	Texas declares its independence.
1836	Arkansas enters Union.
1836	Jackson issues "Specie Circular."
1837	Michigan enters Union.

8
Martin Van Buren

1782–1862; New York
Democrat
In office: 1837–1841

1837	Panic; economic depression begins.
1837	Horace Mann starts school reform.
1838	Oberlin admits women.
1841	Jacksonian era ends.

9
William Henry Harrison

1773–1841; Ohio
Whig
In office: March 4–April 4, 1841

1841	Harrison dies.

BUSINESS ACTIVITY CHART

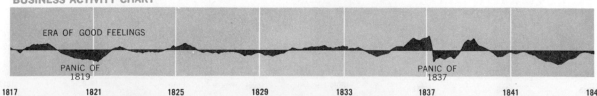

ERA OF GOOD FEELINGS

PANIC OF 1819

PANIC OF 1837

1817   1821   1825   1829   1833   1837   1841   1845

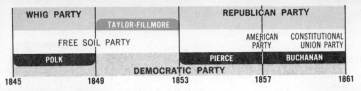

WHIG PARTY			REPUBLICAN PARTY		
	TAYLOR-FILLMORE				
FREE SOIL PARTY				AMERICAN PARTY	CONSTITUTIONAL UNION PARTY
POLK			PIERCE	BUCHANAN	
		DEMOCRATIC PARTY			

1845	1849	1853	1857	1861

10

John Tyler

1790–1862; Virginia
Whig
In office: 1841–1845

1842	Massachusetts recognizes legal right of labor unions to exist.
1842	Webster-Ashburton Treaty.
1844	Vulcanizing process patented.
1844	Telegraph put into operation.
1845	Florida enters Union.

11

James K. Polk

1795–1849; Tennessee
Democrat
In office: 1845–1849

1845	Texas enters Union.
1846	Irish Potato Famine.
1846	Treaty settles Oregon boundary.
1846	Sewing machine is patented.
1846	Iowa enters Union.
1846	Congress declares war on Mexico.
1846	Wilmot Proviso is presented.
1846	Ether used as anesthetic.
1847	Mormons settle at Great Salt Lake.
1848	Treaty ends Mexican War; gives U.S. Mexican Cession.
1848	Polk tries to buy Cuba.
1848	Women's rights convention.
1848	Wisconsin enters Union.

12

Zachary Taylor

1784–1850; Louisiana
Whig
In office: 1849–1850

1849	Gold rush to California.
1850	Taylor dies.

13

Millard Fillmore

1800–1874; New York
Whig
In office: 1850–1853

1850	Compromise of 1850.
1850	California admitted to Union.
1851–56	Kelly, Bessemer develop processes for making steel cheaply.
1852	*Uncle Tom's Cabin* is published.

14

Franklin Pierce

1804–1869; New Hampshire
Democrat
In office: 1853–1857

1853	Gadsden Purchase approved.
1853	Perry arrives in Japan.
1854	Kansas-Nebraska Act.
1854	Republican Party is formed.
1855	*Leaves of Grass* is published.
1856	Violence breaks out in Kansas.

15

James Buchanan

1791–1868; Pennsylvania
Democrat
In office: 1857–1861

1857	Dred Scott decision.
1858	Lincoln-Douglas debates.
1858	Minnesota enters Union.
1859	John Brown raids Harpers Ferry.
1859	Drake drills first oil well.
1859	Oregon enters Union.
1860	South Carolina secedes.
1861	Kansas enters Union.
1861	Confederacy is formed.
1861	Morrill Tariff Act.

MEXICAN WAR — CALIFORNIA GOLD RUSH

1845	1849	1853	1857	1861

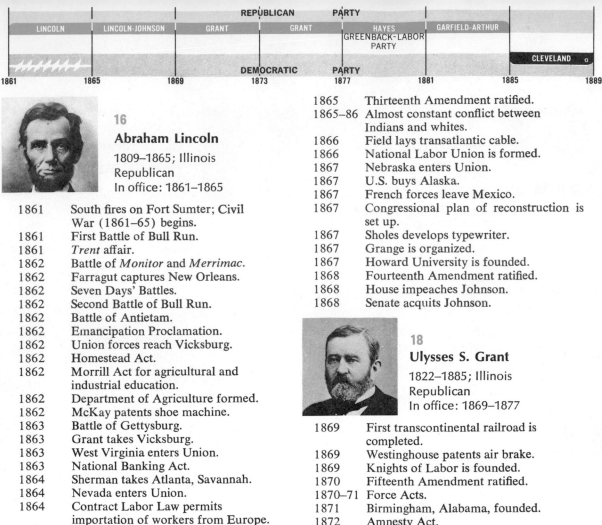

REPUBLICAN   PARTY

| LINCOLN | LINCOLN-JOHNSON | GRANT | GRANT | HAYES | GARFIELD-ARTHUR | |

GREENBACK-LABOR
PARTY

CLEVELAND

DEMOCRATIC   PARTY

1861   1865   1869   1873   1877   1881   1885   1889

16
Abraham Lincoln

1809–1865; Illinois
Republican
In office: 1861–1865

1861	South fires on Fort Sumter; Civil War (1861–65) begins.
1861	First Battle of Bull Run.
1861	*Trent* affair.
1862	Battle of *Monitor* and *Merrimac*.
1862	Farragut captures New Orleans.
1862	Seven Days' Battles.
1862	Second Battle of Bull Run.
1862	Battle of Antietam.
1862	Emancipation Proclamation.
1862	Union forces reach Vicksburg.
1862	Homestead Act.
1862	Morrill Act for agricultural and industrial education.
1862	Department of Agriculture formed.
1862	McKay patents shoe machine.
1863	Battle of Gettysburg.
1863	Grant takes Vicksburg.
1863	West Virginia enters Union.
1863	National Banking Act.
1864	Sherman takes Atlanta, Savannah.
1864	Nevada enters Union.
1864	Contract Labor Law permits importation of workers from Europe.
1864	Railroad sleeping car developed.
1865	Freedmen's Bureau is created.
1865	Lee withdraws from Richmond.
1865	Lee surrenders to Grant.
1865	Lincoln is assassinated.

17
Andrew Johnson

1808–1875; Tennessee
Republican
In office: 1865–1869

1865	Johnson recognizes four reconstructed governments.

1865	Thirteenth Amendment ratified.
1865–86	Almost constant conflict between Indians and whites.
1866	Field lays transatlantic cable.
1866	National Labor Union is formed.
1867	Nebraska enters Union.
1867	U.S. buys Alaska.
1867	French forces leave Mexico.
1867	Congressional plan of reconstruction is set up.
1867	Sholes develops typewriter.
1867	Grange is organized.
1867	Howard University is founded.
1868	Fourteenth Amendment ratified.
1868	House impeaches Johnson.
1868	Senate acquits Johnson.

18
Ulysses S. Grant

1822–1885; Illinois
Republican
In office: 1869–1877

1869	First transcontinental railroad is completed.
1869	Westinghouse patents air brake.
1869	Knights of Labor is founded.
1870	Fifteenth Amendment ratified.
1870–71	Force Acts.
1871	Birmingham, Alabama, founded.
1872	Amnesty Act.
1872	"*Alabama* Claims" are settled.
1872	Crédit Mobilier scandal.
1873	Silver dollars dropped from list of standard coins.
1873	Nationwide economic depression.
1874	Glidden patents barbed wire.
1874	Chautauqua movement is started.
1875	Resumption Act.
1876	Colorado enters Union.
1876	Centennial Exhibition.
1876	Patent on telephone applied for.
1876	National League (of baseball teams) is organized.
1876	Presidential election disputed.
1876–77	"Granger cases" decided.

BUSINESS ACTIVITY CHART

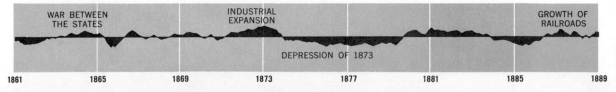

WAR BETWEEN
THE STATES

INDUSTRIAL
EXPANSION

GROWTH OF
RAILROADS

DEPRESSION OF 1873

1861   1865   1869   1873   1877   1881   1885   1889

REPUBLICAN PARTY
POPULIST PARTY
B.HARRISON
CLEVELAND
DEMOCRATIC PARTY
1889   1893   1897

19

Rutherford B. Hayes

1822–1893; Ohio
Republican
In office: 1877–1881

1877	Troops withdrawn from South.
1877	Series of railroad strikes.
1878	Bland-Allison Act.
1879	U.S. Geological Survey organized.
1880–90	Immigration swells.

20

James A. Garfield

1831–1881; Ohio
Republican
In office: March 4–
September 19, 1881

1881	Garfield is assassinated.

21

Chester A. Arthur

1830–1886; New York
Republican
In office: 1881–1885

1882	First large central electric-power plant in U.S.
1882	Chinese Exclusion Act.
1882	Standard Oil Trust organized.
1883	Civil Service Commission set up.

22

Grover Cleveland

1837–1908; New York
Democrat
In office: 1885–1889

1885	Severe drought in "Cattle Kingdom."
1885	Linotype is invented.

PANIC OF
1893

1889   1893   1897

1886	Presidential Succession Act.
1886	Knights of Labor number 700,000.
1886	A. F. of L. is organized.
1886	Haymarket Riot.
1886	Supreme Court qualifies 1876–77 decisions in "Granger cases."
1887	Electoral Count Act.
1887	Interstate Commerce Act.
1887	Hatch Act.
1887	Division of Forestry created.
1887	Dawes Act.

23

Benjamin Harrison

1833–1901; Indiana
Republican
In office: 1889–1893

1889	Washington, Montana, North Dakota, South Dakota enter Union.
1889	Hull House is opened to public.
1889–90	Pan-American Conference.
1890	Wyoming, Idaho enter Union.
1890	McKinley Tariff.
1890	Sherman Antitrust Act.
1890	Sherman Silver Purchase Act.
1890	End of frontier.
1891	Populist Party is organized.
1891	Congress authorizes President to withdraw timberlands from sale.
1892	Homestead steel strike.

24

Grover Cleveland

1837–1908; New York
Democrat
In office: 1893–1897

1893	Silver Purchase Act is repealed.
1893	Business slump; lasts until 1896.
1893	World's Fair held in Chicago.
1894	Wilson-Gorman Tariff.
1894	Pullman strike.
1895	First large plant for producing electricity from water power.
1895	Banks lend gold to government.
1895	Cubans revolt against Spain.
1895	Venezuelan boundary dispute.
1895	Armat invents movie projector.
1896	Bryan is free silver candidate.
1896	Utah enters Union.
1896	Gold discovered in Klondike.

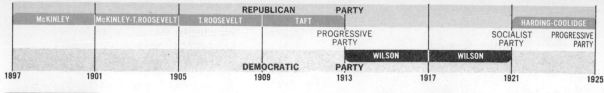

REPUBLICAN PARTY			
McKINLEY	McKINLEY-T.ROOSEVELT	T.ROOSEVELT	TAFT

PROGRESSIVE PARTY

HARDING-COOLIDGE

SOCIALIST PARTY

PROGRESSIVE PARTY

WILSON   WILSON

DEMOCRATIC PARTY

1897   1901   1905   1909   1913   1917   1921   1925

25
William McKinley
1843–1901; Ohio
Republican
In office: 1897–1901

1897	Dingley Tariff.
1898	Spanish-American War.
1898	Treaty of Paris gives U.S. Puerto Rico, Guam, Philippines.
1898	U.S. annexes Hawaiian Islands.
1898	South Dakota adopts initiative and referendum.
1899	U.S. controls American Samoa.
1899	First Hague Conference.
1899–1900	Open Door policy proclaimed.
1900	Boxer Rebellion.
1900	Galveston, Texas, adopts commission government.
1901	Platt Amendment.
1901	Insular Cases are decided.
1901	McKinley is assassinated.

26
Theodore Roosevelt
1858–1919; New York
Republican
In office: 1901–1909

1901	Hay-Pauncefote Treaty.
1901	United States Steel is formed.
1901–02	Pan-American Conference.
1902	Newlands Reclamation Act.
1902	Coal strike in Pennsylvania.
1902	*The History of the Standard Oil Company* is published.
1902	Drago Doctrine is announced.
1902	American forces withdrawn from Cuba.
1903	Department of Commerce and Labor is created.
1903	Elkins Act.
1903	Wisconsin adopts direct primary.
1903	Radio message is sent from U.S. to England.

1903	First powered flight.
1903	Canal Zone is acquired by U.S.
1904	Northern Securities Company ruling.
1904	Roosevelt Corollary to Monroe Doctrine is announced.
1905	Treaty of Portsmouth.
1905	*Lochner v. New York.*
1905	I.W.W. is formed.
1906	Pure Food and Drug Act.
1906	Meat Inspection Act.
1906	Hepburn Act.
1906	Burke Act modifies provisions of Dawes Act.
1906	Upton Sinclair's *The Jungle* is published.
1906	Three-element vacuum tube invented.
1906	Pan-American Conference.
1907	Oklahoma enters Union.
1907	Financial panic and depression.
1907	"Gentlemen's Agreement" with Japan.
1907	Second Hague Conference.
1908	State ten-hour-day law is upheld.
1908	White House Conservation Conference.
1908	Supreme Court rules against union in Danbury Hatters' case.

27
William H. Taft
1857–1930; Ohio
Republican
In office: 1909–1913

1909	Payne-Aldrich Tariff.
1910	Mann-Elkins Act.
1910	Postal savings system started.
1910	Pan-American Conference.
1910–11	Speaker of the House loses power.
1911	"Rule of reason" is adopted.
1911	Roosevelt, Shoshone dams opened.
1911	Transcontinental plane flight.
1912	New Mexico, Arizona enter Union.
1912	Progressive Party is formed.
1912	First state minimum-wage law.
1913	Sixteenth Amendment ratified.

BUSINESS ACTIVITY CHART

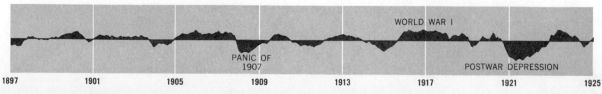

WORLD WAR I

PANIC OF 1907

POSTWAR DEPRESSION

1897   1901   1905   1909   1913   1917   1921   1925

REPUBLICAN PARTY

| COOLIDGE | HOOVER |

DEMOCRATIC PARTY

1925   1929   1933

28
Woodrow Wilson
1856–1924; New Jersey
Democrat
In office: 1913–1921

1913	Seventeenth Amendment ratified.
1913	Underwood Tariff.
1913	Federal Reserve Act.
1914	World War I starts.
1914	Panama Canal opened to traffic.
1914	Ford's conveyor-belt assembly.
1914	FTC is created.
1914	Clayton Antitrust Act.
1914	Smith-Lever Act.
1915	New York and San Francisco are linked by telephone.
1916	Jones Act.
1916	*"Sussex* pledge."
1917	Russian Revolution.
1917	U.S. enters World War I.
1917	Smith-Hughes Act.
1917	Government takes over railroads.
1917	U.S. buys Virgin Islands.
1918	Fighting at Château-Thierry.
1918	Fighting at St. Mihiel.
1918	Meuse-Argonne offensive.
1918	World War I ends.
1918	Wilson presents Fourteen Points.
1919	Eighteenth Amendment ratified.
1919	"Palmer raids."
1919	Treaty of Versailles (includes provision for League of Nations).
1920	Nineteenth Amendment ratified.
1920	World Court is created.
1920	KDKA begins operation.

29
Warren G. Harding
1865–1923; Ohio
Republican
In office: 1921–1923

| 1921 | Bureau of the Budget is created. |
| 1921 | Veterans' Bureau is created. |

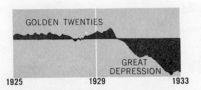

GOLDEN TWENTIES

GREAT
DEPRESSION

1925   1929   1933

1921–22	Washington Naval Conference.
1921–29	Laws restricting immigration are enacted.
1922	Mussolini seizes power in Italy.
1922	Fordney-McCumber Tariff.
1923	Harding dies suddenly.

30
Calvin Coolidge
1872–1933; Massachusetts
Republican
In office: 1923–1929

1923	Du Pont buys cellophane rights.
1923	Quick-frozen foods developed.
1923	Pan-American Conference.
1924	Teapot Dome scandal, involving oil-reserve lands.
1924	Veterans' bonus bill passed.
1924	All Indians given citizenship.
1924	New Progressive Party formed.
1927	McNary-Haugen Bill vetoed.
1927	First talking movie.
1927	Lindbergh flies Atlantic.
1927	International Health Service reports that hookworm has almost disappeared from U.S.
1928	Kellogg-Briand Pact attempts to outlaw war.
1928	Pan-American Conference.

31
Herbert Hoover
1874–1964; California
Republican
In office: 1929–1933

1929	Agricultural Marketing Act.
1929	Stock market crash; beginning of Great Depression.
1930	Public-works programs started; Boulder (later Hoover) Dam began.
1930	London Naval Conference.
1930	Hawley-Smoot Tariff.
1931	Moratorium declared on war debts owed to U.S. by European nations.
1931	Japan invades Manchuria.
1932	RFC is created.
1932	Home Loan Bank Act.
1932	Stimson Doctrine is announced.
1932–33	Federal Reserve powers enlarged.
1933	Hitler comes to power in Germany.
1933	Twentieth Amendment ratified.

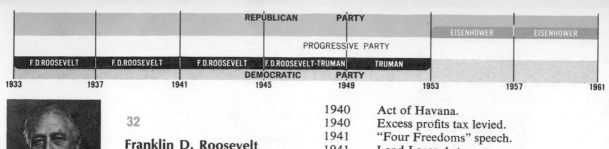

| | REPUBLICAN PARTY | | | | EISENHOWER | EISENHOWER |

PROGRESSIVE PARTY

| F.D.ROOSEVELT | F.D.ROOSEVELT | F.D.ROOSEVELT | F.D.ROOSEVELT-TRUMAN | TRUMAN | | |

DEMOCRATIC PARTY

1933   1937   1941   1945   1949   1953   1957   1961

32

Franklin D. Roosevelt

1882–1945; New York
Democrat
In office: 1933–1945

1933	CCC is created.
1933	Agricultural Adjustment Act.
1933	FCA is created.
1933	Roosevelt declares bank holiday.
1933	Congress abandons gold standard.
1933	NIRA goes into effect.
1933	NLB (later NLRB) is created.
1933	FDIC is established.
1933	TVA is created.
1933	U.S. recognizes Soviet Union.
1933	Good Neighbor policy announced.
1933	Twenty-first Amendment ratified.
1934	Roosevelt "devalues" dollar.
1934	SEC is created.
1934	Trade Agreements Act.
1934	Drought creates Dust Bowl.
1934	Platt Amendment canceled.
1935	WPA is created.
1935	Buses, trucks placed under ICC.
1935	NIRA declared unconstitutional.
1935	National Labor Relations Act.
1935	Social Security Act.
1935–37	Neutrality Acts.
1936	AAA ruled unconstitutional.
1936	Pan-American Conference.
1937	Plan to reorganize Supreme Court.
1937	*Panay* incident.
1937–38	Business slump.
1938	CIO separates from A. F. of L.
1938	Fair Labor Standards Act.
1938	New Agricultural Adjustment Act.
1938	Food, Drug, and Cosmetic Act.
1938	Munich Agreement.
1938	Declaration of Lima.
1939	Germany invades Poland; World War II begins.
1939	Neutrality Act of 1937 amended.
1940	Alien Registration Act.
1940	France signs armistice.

1940	Act of Havana.
1940	Excess profits tax levied.
1941	"Four Freedoms" speech.
1941	Lend-Lease Act.
1941	Hitler attacks U.S.S.R.
1941	Atlantic Charter states war aims.
1941	Japanese attack Pearl Harbor; U.S. enters World War II.
1942	Corregidor surrenders to Japanese.
1942	Marines invade Guadalcanal.
1942	Allied invasion of North Africa.
1942	Pan-American Conference.
1942	OPA is established.
1943	Allied invasion of Italy.
1943	Cairo and Teheran Conferences.
1944	Allies attack Marshall Islands.
1944	Invasion of Marianas.
1944	Allies invade Western Europe.
1944	France is liberated.
1944	Dumbarton Oaks Conference.
1945	Yalta Conference.
1945	Roosevelt dies suddenly.

33

Harry S. Truman

1884–1972; Missouri
Democrat
In office: 1945–1953

1945	San Francisco Conference.
1945	War ends in Europe.
1945	Atomic bombs dropped on Hiroshima and Nagasaki.
1945	Truman signs UN Charter.
1945	World War II ends.
1946	Coal strike by U.M.W.
1946	Philippines become independent.
1946	End to wage and price controls.
1947	Truman Doctrine is announced.
1947	Marshall Plan is proposed.
1947	Taft-Hartley Act.
1947	Presidential Succession Act.
1948	Religious exercises in schools ruled unconstitutional.

BUSINESS ACTIVITY CHART

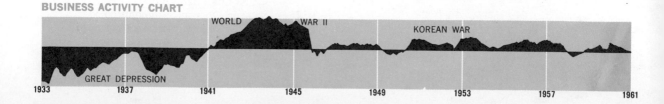

WORLD WAR II   KOREAN WAR

GREAT DEPRESSION

1933   1937   1941   1945   1949   1953   1957   1961

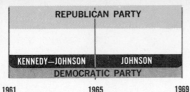

KENNEDY—JOHNSON | JOHNSON
DEMOCRATIC PARTY

1961   1965   1969

1948	UAW—GM contract with "escalator."
1948–49	Berlin airlift.
1949	Point Four program is announced.
1949	NATO is formed.
1949	Communists control China.
1949	Agricultural Act.
1950	Internal Security Act.
1950	Korean War starts.
1951	Twenty-second Amendment ratified.
1952	U.S. tests hydrogen bomb.

34

Dwight D. Eisenhower

1890–1969; New York, Penna.
Republican
In office: 1953–1961

1953	Department of Health, Education, and Welfare is set up.
1953	States get title to offshore oil.
1953	Korean armistice signed.
1953	Stalin dies.
1954	Supreme Court rules segregated public schools unconstitutional.
1954	Indo-China is divided.
1954	SEATO is formed.
1954	West Germany is admitted to NATO.
1954	Both U.S. and U.S.S.R. have H-bombs.
1955	Congress authorizes $500 million for urban redevelopment.
1955	UAW contracts move toward guaranteed annual wage.
1955	Summit conference.
1956	Revolts in Poland and Hungary.
1956	Suez crisis.
1957	Eisenhower Doctrine announced.
1957	Civil Rights Commission created.
1957	*Sputnik* in orbit.
1958	First U.S. satellite in orbit.
1958	Marines land in Lebanon.
1958	Matsu and Quemoy are shelled.
1958	Congress admits Alaska to the Union.
1958–59	Berlin crisis.
1959	St. Lawrence Seaway is opened.

VIETNAM WAR

1961   1965

1959	Labor-Management Reporting and Disclosure Act.
1959	Congress admits Hawaii to the Union.
1959	Foreign ministers' conference.
1960	Summit Conference called off.
1960	O.A.S. meeting.
1960	World leaders gather at UN.

35

John F. Kennedy

1917–1963; Massachusetts
Democrat
In office: 1961–1963

1961	Peace Corps created.
1961	Alliance for Progress started.
1961	First Soviet cosmonaut orbits earth.
1961	Invasion of Cuba fails.
1961	Area Redevelopment Act.
1961	Housing Act.
1961	Berlin wall built.
1962	First American astronaut orbits earth.
1962	U.S. troops sent to South Vietnam.
1962	Manpower Development and Training Act.
1962	Trade Expansion Act.
1962	Cuban missile crisis.
1963	Nuclear test-ban treaty.
1963	Kennedy is assassinated.

36

Lyndon B. Johnson

1908–1973; Texas
Democrat
In office: 1963—1969

1964	Revenue Act lowers income taxes.
1964	Economic Opportunity Act.
1964	Civil Rights Act.
1964	Twenty-fourth Amendment ratified.
1964	Political redistricting begins.
1964	Report of Warren Commission released.
1964	Khrushchev deposed.
1965	Voting Rights Act.
1965	Medicare established.
1965	Crisis in Dominican Republic.
1965	Escalation in South Vietnam.
1965	Elementary and Secondary Education Act.

1969

1965	Department of Housing and Urban Development created.
1966	Department of Transportation created.
1967	Racial disturbances break out in several large cities.
1967	Twenty-fifth Amendment ratified.
1968	Vietcong and North Vietnamese carry out Tet offensive.
1968	Martin Luther King, Jr., is assassinated.
1968	Robert F. Kennedy is assassinated.
1968	Vietnam peace talks begin in Paris.

37

Richard M. Nixon

1913–   ; New York
Republican
In office: 1969–

1969	American troop withdrawals from Vietnam begin.
1969	American astronauts land on the moon.
1969	President Nixon proposes the Family Assistance Program.
1970	U.S. and South Vietnamese troops enter Cambodia; Americans withdraw after two months; American troop withdrawals from Vietnam continue.
1970	Voting Rights Act enables 18-year-olds to vote in federal elections.
1971	In his State of the Union message, President Nixon proposes a shift in power from federal to state and local governments.

Data up to January 1970 courtesy of Cleveland Trust Co.

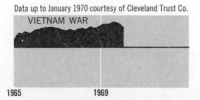

VIETNAM WAR

1965   1969

INDEX

Italicized page numbers preceded by *c*, *m*, or *p* refer to a chart (*c*), map (*m*), or picture (*p*) on the page.

Boldface page numbers are pages on which a definition or explanation is given.

For list of Maps and Charts, see page xiii.

For list of Special Features, see page xv.

For list of Living American Documents, see page xv.

Civil rights (cont.)
Magna Carta, 19, 106, *p 106*; reconstruction governments, 416; "Red scare," 629–30; relativeness of, 167; slaves, 15, 65, 66; Supreme Court decisions, 168; women, 167, 333–34; World War I, 615. *See also* Bill of Rights; specific subjects.
Civil Rights Acts: (1865), 410–11; (1875), 422; (1964), 766, 767; (1957, 1960, 1964, 1965, and 1968), 824
Civil Service, 430, 662, 757; merit system, **430**–33; reform, 430–33, 434, 544, 750; spoils system, **268,** 281, **430,** 435
Civil Service Commission, 758
Civil War: abolition movement, 383, 385; advantages of North v. South, 374–75; agriculture, 374, 388, 390–91; aims, 374–75, 383; campaigns and strategies, 375, 376, *m 377,* 378–80, *m 378, m 379, m 380;* devastation of, 408, *p 409;* end, 382, *p 387,* 403, 404; finances, 197, 374, 387, 389–90, 411, 413; foreign relations, 376, 379, 391–92; industry, 374, *p 375,* 387–88; naval war, 376, *m 737,* 378, *m 379,* 385, 392, *p 392;* outbreak, *m 369,* 370; pensions, 434–36; "rebellion of individuals" v. "state suicide," 410; secession, 369, *m 365;* transportation, 388, 391; uniforms, *p 373. See also* Confederate States of America; Reconstruction.
Clark, George Rogers, 133, *m 133*
Clark, Jonas, 509
Clark, Mark W., 737
Clark, M. B., 476
Clark, William, *m 232,* 233–34, *p 233*
Clay, Henry, 240, 251, *p 251,* 356; Adams election, 265, 280; American system, 252, 265; Bank supporter, 270, 272; Compromise of 1850, 359–61, *p 360, m 363;* "Great Compromiser," 265, 269–70, 274, 359–60; Missouri Compromise, 355, *m 356;* Secretary of State, 265; tariffs, 356; War Hawk, 240
Clayton Antitrust Act, 548, 549, 560, 657
Clayton-Bulwer Treaty, 591
Cleaver, Eldridge, 826
Clemenceau, Georges, 643, 644
Clemens, Samuel L., 514, 515
Cleveland, Grover, 433, 492, 583; conservation, 434, 540; depression, 436–37; farm subsidies, 752; reform, 433, 434; silver issue, 493–94; strikes, 505–06; tariff policy, 436; Venezuela boundary dispute, 594–95
Cleveland, Ohio, *m 290, m 879;* immigration, 298; race relations, 825, 827
Clinton, DeWitt, 241
Clinton, George, 221, 235, 238
Clinton, Sir Henry, 119–20, 130–31, 133
Clipper ships, *p 291,* 293
Closed shop, 503
Clothing: colonial, *p 54,* 55,

p 56, 60, *p 60,* 62, *p 62;* farm, 480, 481; industry, 294–95, 304, 390
Coal, 374, 539, 657; strike, 536, 628, 756
Cobb, Ty, 669
Coins, 104
"Cold War," 778–81
Collective bargaining, 294, 691
Colleges, 308–09; agricultural, 419; black Americans, 338, 662; coeducation, 333; colonial, 71, 77, *p 78;* curriculum, 77, 512–13; defense-orientation, 840; enrollment, 665, *c 877;* land grant, 391, 512, 549, 558; public, 338; Spanish America, 14; women, 333, 509, *p 510;* "Wisconsin Idea," 531
Collier, John, 68
Colombia, *m 591,* 597; compensation for Panama, 593; independence, *m 259;* canal negotiations, 591; Panama revolt, 592
Colon, Panama, 592, *m 591*
Colonies, 11. *See also* Colonies, American; names of colonies and of owning countries.
Colonies, American, *m 31, m 47,* 99; agriculture, 20, 21, 27, 32–33, *p 30,* 36–38, *p 39,* 54, 59–62; "breadbasket," 35; charter rights, 18–19; colonizing companies, 18–21, 26, 28; communities, 32–33; defense, 33, 34, 45, 47, 83, 102; defense costs, 102, 104, 105, 108; education, 71, 77–80, *p 80,* 336; failures, 18; French and, 40, 43–47, 74, 117, 119, 121; French Canadians and, 119; government, 20–21, 26–32, 34–35, 37, 81–85, 96–98, 104, 107, 108, 110; independence, 101, 121–23; Indians and, 20, 21, 27–29, *p 30,* 33, 35, *p 36,* 43, 44–45, 68–71, 102; industries and occupations, 20, 21, 29, 35–36, 37, 48–50, *p 49,* 104, *p 105 (see also* Agriculture*)*; labor, 20, 21, *p 21,* 25, 28, 54, 56–58, *p 56,* 65 (see *also* Slaves and slavery); land claims, 44, 102, *m 103,* 104, 112; land settlement policy, 145; "melting pots," 36, 57–58; mercantile laws, 48–50; money, 104–05; Netherlands and, 33–34, 119; philosophy, 61–62, 63–64; population, 19–20, 29, 32, 33, 36–37, 54, 56, 64, 99; proprietary colonies, **35,** 81, 84; radical and conservative attitudes, **117;** religion in, 28–30, 34, 36, 37, 65, 74–76, 96–98; resistance to British laws, 104–13, *p 107, p 113;* Revolutionary War, 115, 116–38; royal, **21,** 32, 34, 37, 81, 84–85; salutary neglect of, **50;** self-sufficiency, 61–62, 63–64; slavery and slave trade, 14–15, 21, 32, 35, 37–38, *p 38,* 50, *p 50, m 51,* 56, 64–67, *p 66, p 67,* 121; social divisions, 56; Spain and, 37, 47, 74, 117, 119, 121; taxation, 35, 49, 74, 76, 102, 104–13; tensions between Britain and, 48–50, 102–13; trade, 20, 36, 33–34, 35, 48–50, 54, 56, 102, 104–06, 107, 110, 111; way of life, 38, 53–71 (see *also* spe-

cific aspects). *See also* names.
Colorado, 321, *m 878;* admitted, 451; agriculture, 446, 686; mining, 451, 488; Territory, *m 369,* 451; women's suffrage, 533, 553
Colorado River, 12, *m 13, m 232,* 639
Colored Alliance, 489
Columbia River, *m 232,* 234, 317, 318, *m 319*
Columbus, N.M., 599
Columbus, Christopher, 5, 7–10, *m 7, m 9,* 11
Columbus, Ohio, 286, *m 287, m 879*
Comanches, 318, 321
Commerce and Labor, Department of, 538
Commerce. *See* Trade and commerce; subjects.
Commerce Compromise, 159, 210
Commercial Revolution, 6
Commission government, 533–34
Committees of Correspondence, 110–11
Common law, 473
Common Market, 764, 795, 800
Common Sense (Paine), 120–21
Commonwealth v. Hunt, 297
Communications, 467, 555, *c 868–69;* internationalism and, 602; regulation, 539, 544. *See also* Transportation; subjects.
Communism: Anti-Comintern Pact, 712; "cold war," 778–81; containment efforts, 780–81, 782–85, 788–89, 798–800, 804–05, 808; election issue, 762; internal security, 758, 761; labor movement, 506, 628–29, 756, 760; McCarthyism, 761; "peaceful co-existence," 799; "Red scare," 628–30; spread of, 644, 710, 712, 742, 778–81, 795, 797; world alignment, 795. *See also* Communist China; Soviet Union; other countries.
Communist China, 742, 782–83; atomic explosion, 767; Indo-China crisis, 786; Korean War, 784–85; Quemoy and Formosa crises, 792; Soviet break, 799; Soviet Union and, 795; Tibet and India, 799; world communism and "people's wars," 804, 805
Comparative studies, 567
Competition, 93–94
Compromise of 1850, 359–61, *p 360,* 362, *m 363,* 365
Compton, Arthur Holly, 811
Computers, 813
Comstock Lode, 451, *m 445*
Conant, James B., 820
Concentration camps, 740, *p 740*
Concord, Mass., 115, 116, *m 116, p 117,* 135
Confederate army, 374, *p 375,* 386, 388, 400. *See also* Confederate States of America; names, battles.
Confederate States of America, *m 369,* 373–74; advantages, 374; agriculture, 388; aims, 374; armed forces, 374, *p 375,* 386, 388, 392, *p 392;* blockade of, 376, *m 377,* 387; campaigns and strategy, 375, *m 377;* con-

scription, 386; Constitution, 369; dissensions, 386–87; finance, 197, 387, 405, 411; foreign relations, 376, 379, 391–92; formation, 369; industry, 387–88; naval war, 376, *m 377,* 392, *p 392;* states' rights theory, 369, 386–87. *See also* Civil War; Reconstruction; state names.
Confederation, 34, 144. *See also* Articles of Confederation; Congress of the Confederation.
Confiscation Act, 398
Conflict concept, 93–94
Congo, Democratic Republic of, *m 790–91,* 795–96
Congregational Church, 74, 143
Congress of the Confederation, 144, 156; Constitutional Convention, 155; economic conditions and, 152–53; financial problems, 146, 150–51; military weakness, 152, 153; Northwest Territory and, 145–48; powers of, 148–52, 153, 162; trade regulation, 150–51, 155; treaty enforcement, 151; voting in, 148–50
Congress for Industrial Organizations (CIO), 700, 701, 760
Congress, United States, 157–58, 171–82; blocs, **355;** caucuses, **222,** 280; checks and balances of and by, 164–65; corruption and scandals, 428; Executive Department guidance, 215; first, 161, 214–16; judiciary and, 165, 168, 228; "lame duck," 198–99; law passing method, 176, *c 177;* lobbies and, 436–37; number of members, 173; powers delegated to, 159, **163,** 164, 168, 171, 178–79; President and, 164–65, 176, 282; public opinion and, 165, 282; readmission of South, 407, 409, 412; representation in, 159, 173, 196; sessions, 174, 175, 198–99; slavery and, 159, 179; Territories, 187–88. *See also* Congress of the Confederation; House of Representatives; Senate; specific names and subjects.
Conkling, Roscoe, 432
Connecticut, 160, *m 287, p 289, m 290,* 449, 536, *m 879;* colonial, 30, *m 31,* 74, 81, *p 82, m 103,* 112; Constitution, 141; government, 30, 81; land claims, *m 103,* 112; religion in, 142, 143; settlement, 30, *p 82*
Connecticut Compromise, 157–58
Connecticut River and Valley, *m 31,* 33, 34
Conquistadores, 12
Conscription, 386; Act, 388
Conservation, 531; Cleveland, 434, 540; Eisenhower, 761; environment deterioration, 837–39; Johnson, L. B., 766, 838–39; Kennedy, 765, 838; McKinley, 540; New Deal, 693–94, 702; Roosevelt, Theodore, 539–41, *p 540,* 545; "soil banks," 761; Taft, 544–45; Truman, 757; TVA, 693–94
Constitutional Convention, 155, *p 161, p 162;* case study in

New England (Colonial) (cont.) 34; development of, 32–33; education, 78–79, p 80, 336; government, 83; immigration to, 32; land settlement policy, 145; life in, 56, 59–62; mercantile laws, 50; religious tolerance in, 30, 74–75, 76; settlement, 23, 26–33; slavery in, 65; trade, 50, m 51. See also New England; place names.

New England Confederation, 34

New France, m 31, 40, 74; French and Indian War, 44–47, m 45, m 47; fur trade, 42–43, 68; settlements, 41, p 41

New Freedom, 543, 547–50, 627

New Frontier, 282, 762–65, 773, 774

New Guinea, 741–42, m 744

New Hampshire, 160, m 290, 768, m 879; colonial, 30–32, m 31, 71, 74, m 103; Constitution, 141; Dartmouth College case, 256–57; Indian education, 71; religion in, 142, 143

New Harmony, Ind., 336

New Haven, Conn., 30, m 31, 34

New Jersey, 160, m 287, m 290, 546, m 879; colonial, m 31, 34, 35, 59–62, 65, m 103; Revolutionary War, 127–28, m 127, m 128, p 129, 132, m 134, 135; rural colonial life in, 59–62; settlement, 34; slavery, 65

New Jersey Plan, 157

New Mexico, 14, 321, 599, 686, m 878; admitted, 451; Mexican War, 325–26, m 326, 327; slavery, 359; Territory, m 319, m 363, m 369, 446; Texas boundary, 358–59

"New Nationalism," 292, 535, 546

New Netherland, m 31, 33, 65

New Orleans, La., 41, m 42, 47, m 47, m 137, m 149, p 153, m 290, 302, m 443, m 879; Civil War, 376, m 377, 378, m 379, m 381; closed to Americans, 152; immigration, 298, 304; Louisiana Purchase and, 231; right of deposit, 219; riots, 411; slave auctions, 306; War of 1812, 243, m 244–45

New South, 418–23

New Sweden, m 31, 33

New World, m 3. See also names of countries; subjects.

New York (Colony), m 31, 35, m 103; French and Indian War, 44–46, m 45; government, 34–35, 83, 108; press freedom, 80; religion, 34, 74; resistance to British laws, 107, 108, 112; slavery, 65, 66. See also New York City; New York State.

New York City, m 31, p 162, 468, 555, 670; colonial, 35, p 48, p 49, 59, 107, 112; draft riots, 388; Harlem, 664, 831; immigration, 298, p 299, p 647; labor riots, 297; "machine" politics and corruption, 429–30, p 429, 568–70,

635; national capital, 161, 212–15; public schools, 337; race relations, 630, p 630, 831; resistance to British laws, 107, 112; Revolutionary War, 127, 128, m 127, m 128, 132, 133, m 134; settlement, 33, 65; skyscrapers, 516, p 516; Tammany Hall, 427, 429, 430, 569–70, 635; transportation, 467, p 553; transportation to and from, 254, 286, m 287, 289, m 290, m 319, 475; Wall Street explosion, 529. See also New York (Colony); New York State.

New York State, m 879; corruption, 429; Erie Canal, 286, m 287; land claims, m 149; labor, 559, 698, 699; population, 808; progressive movement, 536; ratification of Constitution, 160–61; Revolutionary War, 127–30, m 127, m 130, 132–33, m 134; roads, 251, m 287; school prayers, 839; War of 1812, 242, p 242, 243, m 244–45. See also New York (Colony); New York City.

New York Stock Exchange, p 48, 436, p 437, 638

New Zealand, m 723, 737, 741, 786

Newfoundland, m 9, m 13, 14, 18, 36, 55; fishing rights, 137, m 137

Newlands Reclamation Act, 541

Newport, R.I., 576

Newspapers and periodicals, 467, 513–14, 665; abolitionist, 339, 340, 343, 350–51, p 357; colonial, 59, 73, 80; freedom of press, 80, 167, 191; mass circulation, 513–14; "muckrakers," 531–32, p 532; reporting services, 514, 665

Newton, Huey P., 826

Nez Percé Indians, 439

Niagara Falls, 468, 598

Niagara Movement, 423

Nicaragua, 590, m 591, 596, 650

Nile River, m 713, 788, p 789

Nimitz, Chester W., 741

Nine-Power Treaty, 652, 653

Nineteenth Amendment, 167, 198, 631, 661

Ninth Amendment, 163, 193

Nixon, Richard M., p 772, p 776, 794; Cambodia, 807–08; defeat by Kennedy, 762; Doctrine, 807; economy, 772; election as President, 770–71; Indian policy, 444; inflation problem, 772–73; national unity, 282, 771; population control, 838; race relations, 771, 824; social legislation, 752; 773; "style," 772; Supreme Court appointments, 772; Vice-President, 758, 759; Vietnam War, 771, 773, 807

Nobel peace prize, 510, 782

Nonimportation agreements, 107

Non-Intercourse Act, 238–39

Normandy, m 730, m 731, 738

Norris, Frank, 532, 669

Norris, George W., 545

Norsemen, m 9, 10, p 10

North (Union side in Civil War), m 369, 373–75; agriculture, 374, 390–91; aims, 374–75, 383; armed forces,

372, p 375, 376, 384–86, p 384, p 385, 388–89, p 389, 398–400; blockade by, 375, 376, m 377, 387; border states, 373; bounty system, 388–89; campaigns and strategy, 375–82, m 377, m 379, m 381, m 382; draft, 388; finances, 374, 389–90; industry, 374, p 375; opposition to war, 392–93; transportation, 374, 391

North Africa: Barbary pirates, 235, m 235, p 236; World War II, m 730–31

North America, m 3, m 8–9; in 1763, m 47; in 1783, m 137. See also names of countries, subjects.

North Atlantic Treaty Organization (NATO), 781, 786, 788, 793

North Carolina, m 149, m 290, p 694, 767, m 879; agriculture, 38, 54, 302, m 302; Civil War, 373, m 377, 381, m 382, 387; colonial, 18, m 31, 36, 38, 54, 67, m 103; population, 54; ratification of Constitution, 161; Revolutionary War, 119–20, 132, m 133; settlement, 36; slavery, 65; state university, 338

North Carolina, University of, 338

North Dakota, 451, 490, m 878

North Korea, m 783, m 791; People's Republic, 783; war, m 783, 783–84, 786, 804

North, Lord Frederick, 109

North Pole, 662, 670

North Sea, m 604, 608, 615, 729, m 730–31

North Vietnam, m 791, m 801; bombing of, 771, 786, 798, 800, 801, m 801, 803. See also Vietnam War.

Northern (Northwestern) Farmers' Alliance, 489

Northern Pacific R.R., 440, m 445

Northern Securities Co., 537, 538

Northwest Ordinance, 147–48, 169, 214

Northwest Territory, p 140, m 149, p 151; British in, 151–52, 219; government, 147, 214; land hunger, 239; Revolutionary War, 133, m 133; slavery, 355

Norway, m 9, 448, m 604, 608, 615, 720, 781; NATO, 781; World War II, m 730–31

Nova Scotia, 14

Nuclear: test ban, 799; weapons, see Weapons. See also Atomic bomb.

Nueces River, 324, m 326

Nullification: Calhoun and South Carolina, 273–74; Kentucky and Virginia Resolutions, 226; Ordinance of, 273

Oberlin, 333, 338

Observation, as technique, 566

Office of Economic Opportunity (OEO), 766, 768, 831

Office of Price Administration (OPA), 735

Office of War Information (OWI), 734

Office of War Mobilization (OWM), 734

Officeholding: black Americans, 415–16; colonial, 29, 65; ex-Confederate disability, 196–97; Reconstruction, 414–17; religious tests for, 189; spoils system, 268, 281, 430, 435. See also Civil service.

Oglethorpe, James, 37

Ohio, m 149, 767, 827, m 879; admission, 253; immigration, 298

"Ohio Gang," 633

Ohio River and Valley, 44, m 45, 46, 133, m 133, 152, 287, m 287, 288

Oil, p 468; discovery, 468; power source, 468, 657; production, 555, 657

Okinawa, 743, m 744–45

Oklahoma, 443, 686, m 878–79; admitted, 451; District and "Sooners," 450–51

"Old Guard," 432, 435

Olney, Richard, 594

Omaha, Neb., 391, 428, 440, 447, m 445, 491, m 879

Oneida Community, 336

O'Neill, Eugene, 666

Open Door policy, 584, 585, 652, 653

"Open skies" proposal, 786–87

Operation Bootstrap, 832

Operation Overlord, 738

Operation Sea Lion, 720

Optic, Oliver (W. T. Adams), 514

Orders in Council, 237, 239

Oregon, m 369, 374, m 878; Civil War, 373; Hayes election, 431; labor, 559; Territory, m 319, 320, m 363. See also Oregon Country.

Oregon Country, m 232, 258, 259, 357, 439, m 856–57; claim conflicts, 259, 317–20; exploration, 317–18; missionaries, 318; slavery, 318. See also Oregon.

Oregon Trail, 318, m 319, p 320

Organization of American States (O.A.S.), 603, 797–98

Orkney Islands, m 604, 615–16

Orlando, Vittorio, 643, 644, p 644

Osage Indians, 443

Osgood, Samuel, 214

Ostend Manifesto, 362

Oswald, Lee Harvey, 766

Otis, James, 108, 110

Ottawa Indians, 102

Owen, Robert, 336

Pacific Northwest, 317; trade, 291–92, m 292–93. See also Far West; state names.

Pacific Ocean, m 8–9, 11

Page, Thomas Nelson, 515

Pago Pago, 583

Paine, Thomas, 120–21, 123, 186

Painting, 517, 662, 666

Pakenham, General, 243

Pakistan, 786, m 791

Palestine, 608, 617, m 730–31, 737, 782

Palmer, A. Mitchell, 628, 629

"Palmer raids," 629

Palo Alto, Battle of, 326, m 326

Panama, m 9, 11, m 13, m 17; health program, 593; independence, 592; nonintervention treaty, 711; revolution, 592; route to California, m 319, 330. See also Panama

Princeton, N.J., 128, *m 128*, *p 129*
Princeton University, 309, 518, 546
Printing, 467; colonial, 14, 80
Prison reform, 335
Privateers, 136–37
Proclamation Line (1763), *m 103*, 146
Production, factors of, **523**
Profiteering, **134**
Progressive movement, 530, 550; aims, 531; government reforms, 532–34; leadership, 531, 535; "muckrakers," 531–32; powers of Speaker of House, 545–46; race relations, 536–37; regulatory laws, 537–39; "square deal," 535–37; tariff policy, 544
Progressive Party, 494, 546, 634; new, 757
Prohibition, 635, 667, 668–69; amendments, 198, 199; colonial, 37; temperance movement, 335
Promontory, Utah, 440, *m 445*
Prophet, the, 240
Prosser, Gabriel, 313
Protective tariff, **216**. See also Tariffs.
Protestants, 24–25; immigrants, 35, 37. See also Religion; names of denominations.
Providence, R.I., 30, *m 31*, 294
Provincetown, Mass., 27
Prussia, 131, 137, 252
Public health, 59; pure food and drug laws, 539, 704; Medicare, 767, 768, 831
Public Health Service, 443
Public Information, Committee on, 614
Public schools, 78–79, *c 145*, 146, 336–38, *p 337*. See also Education.
Public Utility Holding Company Act, 692
Public Works Administration (PWA), 689, 704
Publicity Act, 544
Pueblo Indians, 674
Puerto Rican-Americans, 678, 829, 831
Puerto Rico, *m 137*, *m 225*, 257, *m 259*, *m 591*, 576; Commonwealth, 590; economic development, 832; immigration, 831; naval base, 597; Spanish-American War, 571, 579, 580, 588, 595; Territory, 590
Pulaski, Casimir, 131
Pulitzer, Joseph, 513, 577
Pullman, George M., 466
Pullman Palace Car Co., 505
"Pump priming," 688–89, 699–700
Pure Food and Drug Act, 539, 704
Puritan Revolution, **25**
Puritans, 25, 28–29, 65, 70, 74, 77; education, 78–79; sociological case study of, 96–98
Purvis, Robert, 342–43
Pusan, S. Korea, *m 783*, 784

Quadruple Alliance, 258, 259
Quakers, 35, 71, 75, 78; slavery opposed by, 65, 67, 143, 399; persecution of, 98
Quartering Acts: (1765), 105, 110; (1774), 112
Quebec, Can., 14, 41, *m 42*, 43;

Act, *m 103*, 112, 146; Battle of, *p 40*, 46–47
Quemoy, *m 791*, 792
Questionnaires, as technique, **567**
Quincy, Josiah, Jr., 109
Quota system, **647**

Radical Republicans, 398; decline, 412–13; governments in South, 414–17; Johnson impeachment, 412–13; Reconstruction, *see* Reconstruction.
Radio, 555, 669, 705, *c 869*; "Mars" broadcast, 705
Railroad Administration, 614
Railroads, 289, *p 289*, *m 290*, 362, 420, *m 445*; agriculture, 361, 484–85, 486–87; buffalo destruction and, 440–41; Civil War, 374, 375, 391; cattle industry and, 444–45, *m 445*, 447; city growth and, 465–66; consolidation, 475; decline, 816; equipment, 289, 465–66, 475; labor, *p 499*, 500, 560; land grants, 448, 466; mileage, 289, 302, 361, 465, 553, *c 869*; New Deal, 689; passenger services, 816–17; pools, 486–87; rebates, 487; regulation, 434, 486–87, 537, 538; scandals, 428; settlement and, 448, *p 450*; strikes, 502, 505–06, 755; subsidies, 391, 448, 466; transcontinental, 391, 428, 440, 466
Raleigh, Sir Walter, *m 17*, 18
Ramsay, David, 140
Randall, James G., 350
Randolph, A. Philip, 702, *p 703*
Randolph, Edmund, 157, 214
Randolph, John, 241
Rate of growth concept, **817**
Ratification, **144**; Articles of Confederation, 144; Constitution, 160–61, 190
Rationing, 734, 735
Real wages, **498**
Rebates, **487**
Recall, **533**
Recession, 699, 762
Reclamation Bureau, 757
Reconstruction, **403**, 404–17; amnesty, 416–17; black codes, 409; end of, 417, 432; Freedmen's Bureau, 414; governments in South, 414–17; Johnson's plan, 407, 409–11, 416; Lincoln's plan, 400, 404–07, 409–11; military districts, 411; "rebellion of individuals" and "state suicide," 410; secret societies, 416–17; suffrage question, 405, 411–12, 416; Wade-Davis Bill, 405–06
Reconstruction Finance Corp. (RFC), 639, 688, 689, 700, 750
Recreation, 467, 487, 517, 555, 668–70; colonial, 54–55, 56, 60–61, *p 61*, 62; rural, 517, 518; urban, 517–18
Red Cross, 602
"Red scare," 628–30
Red Sea, 788, *m 791*
Redistricting, **765**
Reed, Doctor Walter, 593
Referendum, **533**
Reform movements: Indian policies, 442–44; political, 430–37, 486–94, 531–50, 634, 704; social, 332–46, 510, 511. *See also* specific subjects.
Reformation, 24–25, 78

Region, as concept, **457**
Regional approach concept, **458**
Reims, Fr., 616, *m 617*
Religion: Afro-American churches, 75, *p 76*; border conflicts, 74; Canada, 112; church membership, 839, *c 877*; Constitutional provisions, 189, 191; ecumenicalism, 840; education, 75, 77, 336, 338; election issue, 433, 635; emigration motive, 24–25, 26, 28, 36, 37, 327–28; European influence, 74, 261; freedom of, 142, 167, 191; freedom of in colonies, 30, 34, 36, 74–75; Great Britain, 24–25, *p 25*, 26, 28, 35; of immigrants, 35, 37, 298; officeholding qualification, 189; intolerance, 29, 98, 298, 327, 631; Puritan social control and, 56, 96–98; racial attitudes, 65, 75–76; school prayers, 839; separation of church and state, 29, 77, 96, 98, 142; slavery attitudes, 15, 67, 75, 351, 352; Spanish colonies, 11, 14, 15, 68, 321, 328; social involvement, 839, 840; state churches, **74**, 76, 142, 143; suffrage qualifications, 29, 65, 82, 97, 143; taxation to support, 74, 143, 147, 339; tolerance in colonies, 35, 36, 37, 74–76, 98. *See also* denominations.
Remarque, Erich, 669
Renaissance, 5
Rent controls, 735, 755, 757
Reorganization Act (1949), 758
Reparations, **644**, 649; Commission, 649
Republican Party: (1865–97), 426, 435–36, 544; beginning of, 364–65, *p 365*; elephant symbol, 429; "Modern Republicanism," 760; Radical Reconstruction, 416–17; similarity to Democrats, 631; splits (1872), 430–31, (1876), 431–32, (1884), 433, (1912), 546, (1924), 634, (1952), 758. *See also* Republican Party (Jeffersonian); Elections, presidential; names, subjects.
Republican Party (Jeffersonian), 221, 225–26, 230–31, 241; American System, 251–52; decline of, 265. *See also* Republican Party.
Resaca de la Palma, Battle of, 326, *m 326*
Research, growth of, 811–12
Resumption Act, 488
Resurrection City, 832
Reuther, Walter, 760
Revels, Hiram, 415
Revenue, **104**; bills, 176; tariff, **216** (*see also* Tariffs). *See also* Taxation.
Revenue Acts: (1936), 705; (1938), 705; (1939), 705; (1964), 766
Revere, Paul, 116, *m 116*, *p 150*
Revolutionary War, 55, 115–38, *m 118*, 574, 803; American problems, 135; armed forces, *see* Continental Army, Militia, Patriots; blockade, 136–37, 151; British problems, 135–37; casualties, *p 121*; declaration of, 123, 126; Declaration of

Independence, 55, 121, 122–26; end of, 135; finances and debts, 135, 146, 215, 235; foreign aid, 119, 130–31, *p 132*, 133–34, *m 133*, 215; Hessians, 127–28, 129, 136; Lexington and Concord, 115, 116, 135; naval war, 133–34, 135, 136–37; New England, 115–19, *m 116*, *p 117*, *m 118*, *m 119*, 128, 129, *m 130*; New York and New Jersey, 127–30, *m 127*, *m 128*, *p 129*, *m 130*, 132, 133, *m 134*, 135; Northwest, 133, *m 133*; peace treaty, 134, 137–38; Pennsylvania, 127, *m 127*, 130, 131, *p 132*, *m 134*, 135; South, *m 118*, 119–20, 132–34, *m 133*, *m 134*, 135; tensions leading up to, 102–13; uniforms, 131; weapons, 63, *p 63*, *p 131*
Rhee, Syngman, 783
Rhineland, 709, 712, *m 716*
Rhine River, *m 617*, 618, 739, 742
Rhode Island, *m 287*, *m 290*, 576, *m 879*; constitution, 141; ratification of Constitution, 161. *See also* Rhode Island (Colony).
Rhode Island (Colony), *m 31*, *m 103*; Gaspee affair, 110; government, 30, 81, 110; religious freedom, 30, 74–75; settlement, 29–30
Rhone Valley, 738
Rice, 37, 38, 54, 65, 302, *m 302*, 310, 312, 419
Richardson, Henry Hobson, 516
Richardson, William A., 428
Richelieu River, 41, 128–29, *m 130*
Richmond, Va., *m 287*, *m 290*, 302, 420, 819, *m 879*; Civil War, 375, *m 377*, 378–79, *m 379*, 381–82, *m 382*, *p 390*, 408, *p 409*
Ridgeway, Matthew B., 785
Right of deposit, **219**
Rio Grande, *m 13*, *m 232*, *m 319*, 650, 830; boundary, 322, *m 322*, 324–25, *m 326*
Roads, 256, *p 256*, *m 287*; automobiles and, 554–55; federal, 254, 286; first important, 253; mileage, 286, 333, 816, *c 869*; national growth and, 253–54, 286; private companies, 253–54; toll, 254
Roanoke, *m 17*, 18, *m 20*, *m 31*
"Roaring Twenties," 668
Roberts, Needham, 613
Robinson, Edgar E., 751
Rochester, N.Y., 256, *m 287*, *m 879*
Rockefeller, John D., 476, 509
Rocky Mountain Fur Co., 317–18
Rocky Mountains, 41, *m 232*, 245; routes, 318, *m 319*
Rodgers, Moses, 330
Role and role conflict concepts, **94**
Rolfe, John, 20
Rölvaag, O. E., 450
Roman Catholicism, 74, 112; colonial, 35, 36, 75; election issue, 433; immigrants, 298; missionaries, 11, 14, 15, 68, 318, 321, 328; Protestant conflict, 24–25, 74; slaveholding, 15; Spanish America, 15, 74

Transportation (*cont.*)
Civil War, 374, 375, 388, 391; colonial, 56; costs, 286; desegregation, 394; federal aid, 764, 766, 831; industry and, 252, 253, 285–91, *m 287*, 493, 602; mass, 764, 766; national growth and, 253–54, 285, 440, 448, 465–67; New Deal, 689; revolutions, 553–55, 815–17; segregation, 422; trade and improvements in, 291–93; urban, *p 553*, 658, 661, 764, 766; water (*see also* Canals), 158, *p 220*, 253, *m 281*; World War II, 734. *See also* Roads; specific forms.

Transportation, Department of, 831

Travis, William B., 322

Treason, **166**, 186–87

Treasury, Department of, 214, 632, 688, 806; scandal, 428

Treaty of: (1778), 131, 224; (1818), *m 858*; (1819–Adams Onis), 258, 317, *m 856*; (1846), 245, 319, *m 319*, *m 856*

Trent Affair, 392

Trenton, N.J., 127–28, *m 128*, *m 879*

Triple Alliance, 606

Triple Entente, 606

Tripoli, 235, *m 235*, *p 236*

Trolleys, 660–61

Troy, N.Y., 286, *m 287*, 333

Trujillo, Rafael, 798

Truk, 741, *m 744*

Truman Doctrine, 780

Truman, Harry S., 754, 782; atom bombing, 746; Communist containment, 780, 793, 799–80; Congress as issue, 282; election as President, 757; Fair Deal, 757, 773; government reorganization, 758; housing, 755; internal security, 758; Korean War, 759, 783–85; labor relations, 755–56; MacArthur dismissal, 785; Potsdam Ultimatum, 743; price controls, 755; race relations, 823–24; Roosevelt death, 740; Senator, 754; UN, 777, 778; Vice-President, 739, 753; World War II, 743, 746

Trumbull, John, 262

Trustees of Dartmouth College v. Woodward, 256–57

Trusts, 436, **472**–73; antitrust laws, 473–74, 537–38, 544, 548–49

Truth, Sojourner, *p 393*, 394

Tubman, Harriet, 343, 352

Tucker, George, 309–10

Tunis, *p 30–31*, 235, *m 235*

Tunisia, *m 730–31*, 736

Tunney, Gene, 669

Turkey, *m 644*, *m 645*; NATO, 781; Truman Doctrine, 780; U.S. missiles in, 848; World War I, *m 604*, 606, 608, 617, 618; World War II, *m 730–31*

Turner, Nat, 313, *p 314*, 343

Tuskegee Institute, 422, 662

Twain, Mark (Samuel L. Clemens), 451, 514, 515

Tweed Ring, 429–30, 431

Tweed, William M., 429, 430

Twelfth Amendment, 194, 227, 265

Twentieth Amendment, 198–99

Twenty-fifth Amendment, 201

Twenty-first Amendment, 199, 669

Twenty-fourth Amendment, 200, 765

Twenty-second Amendment, 200, 758

Twenty-third Amendment, 200, 765

Two-party system, 221–22

Tydings-McDuffie Act, 710

Tyler, John, 276

U-boats, 609–10. *See also* Submarine warfare.

Udall, Stewart, 837

Ukraine, 729, *m 730–31*, 738, 739

Ultimatum, **578**

Uncle Tom's Cabin (Stowe), 334, 343, 361

Underground railroad, 342–43, *p 343*, 352

Underwood Tariff Act, 547, 550, 633

Unemployment: (1893), 436; (1961), 764, 765; black Americans, 763, 833; business cycle, 498; "full employment," 755; Great Britain, 25; Great Depression, 638, *p 639*, 640, *p 640*, 683; New Deal programs and, 683–84, 700; Panic of 1837, 275, *p 275*, 297; post-World War I, 628; recessions, 762; technological, 497, 833. *See also* Employment; Labor.

Union army, 372, *p 375*, 376, 384–86, *p 384*, *p 385*, 388–89, *p 389*, 434–36. *See also* Civil War; specific battles.

Union Pacific R.R., 391, 428, 440, 445

United Arab Republic (U.A.R.), 789

United Automobile Workers (UAW), 700, 756, 760, 812

United Mine Workers (U.M.W.), 504, 536, 628, 700, 756

United Nations, 760, 781, 800, 837; Allied Powers, 732, 776; Arab-Israeli crises, 782; atomic energy control, 780; Charter, 776, 777; Conference, 776; Congo crisis, 795–96; Day, 777; early years, 778; Educational, Scientific, and Cultural Organization (UNESCO), 780; formation, 776–78; Korean War, 783–85, 786; Lebanon crisis, 789; membership, 795, 835–36; Nixon Doctrine and, 808; organization and agencies, 777–78; Relief and Rehabilitation Administration (UNRRA), 778; Suez Crisis, 788; Trusteeship Council, 778

United Press (UP), 514, 665

United States Housing Authority, 704

United States Shipping Board, 610

United States Steel Corp., 476, 700–01

United States v. Butler, 687

United Steel Workers of America, 761

Universities. *See* Colleges.

Upper California, 324–27, *p 325*, *m 326*, 328

Upward Bound program, 831

Urban League, 423

Uruguay, *m 259*, 710

U.S.S.R. *See* Soviet Union.

U.S. v. E. C. Knight Co., 473

Utah, 321, 452, 533, 553, *m 878*; admitted, 328, 451; labor, 559; Mormons, *p 255*, *m 319*, 327–28; slavery, 359; Territory, *m 363*, *m 369*, 451

Utica, N.Y., 286, *m 287*

Utopian communities, 336

U-2 incident, 792

Vallandigham, Clement L., 393

Valley Forge, Pa., 130, *m 130*, 131, *p 132*, 135

Van Buren, Martin, 272, 274–76, 295; slavery issue, 356, 358

Van Hise, Charles, 531

Vandalia, Ill., 254, 286, *m 287*

Vandenberg, Arthur H., 775

Vanderbilt, Cornelius, 475, 509

Vaqueros, **444**

Vassar, Matthew, 509

Venezuela, 594–95, *m 591*, 832; independence, *m 259*

Veracruz, Mex., 326, *m 326*, 598

Vergennes, Count, 101, 138

Vermont, *m 149*, 253, 262, *m 290*, *m 879*

Versailles, Fr., *m 617*; Conference, 626–27

Versailles, Treaty of, 282, 644, 645, 646, 709, 712

Verrazano, Giovanni da, *m 13*, 14, 41

Vesey, Denmark, 313

Vespucci, Amerigo, *m 9*, 11

Veterans' Bureau, 632, 633

Veterans of Foreign Wars, 633

Veto power, **164**, 165, 176

Vice-President: election, 160, 182–83, 194, 210, 222–23, 227; first, 161; impeachment provisions, 174, 184; nomination, 222, 268; Senate president, 174; succession of, 199, 201, 434, 758; succession to Presidency, 183, 199, 201; term, 182, 198–99

Viceroy, **16**

Vichy, France, 720, *m 730–31*

Vicksburg, Miss., *m 377*, 378, 380, *m 381*, 400

Victory Loan, 613

Vietcong, 800–05. *See also* Vietnam War.

Vietnam War, 773, 794, *p 794*, 799, *m 801*, *p 803*, 831; bombing of North Vietnam, 771, 801, 803; Cambodia and, 807–08; cost, 801, 803; criticism of role in, 805–07, 831, 835; defense of role in, 804–05; economic aid, 801, 803; election issue, 768, 770, 771; escalation, 801; Gulf of Tonkin resolution, 801, 802, 806; guerrilla warfare and terrorism, 802; limited involvement, 800; peace efforts, 801, 803; Tet offensive, 803; troops, 801–02, 803, 807; Vietnamization and withdrawal of troops, 807

Vigilantes, **451**

Villa, Francisco (Pancho), *p 598*, 599, *p 599*, 616

Vincennes, Ind., 133, *m 133*

Virgin Islands, *m 591*, 596, 597

Virginia, *m 287*, *m 290*, 419, 767, *m 879*; Civil War, 373, 376, *m 377*, 378–79, *m 378*, *m 379*, 381–82, *m 382*, *p 390*, 408, *p 409*; government, 309; Harpers Ferry raid, 366–67;

land claims, 133, *m 149*; ratification of Constitution, 160–61; readmission, 412, 414; Reconstruction, 407; religious freedom, 142; slave revolts, 313, *p 314*; slavery, 383; Revolutionary War, 133–34, *m 134*, 135; states' rights theory, 226. *See also* Virginia (Colony).

Virginia (Colony), *m 17*, 18, *m 20*, 26, *m 31*, 34, 36, 37, 38, 80, 145; agriculture, 38, 54; Bacon's Rebellion, 82–83, *p 83*; French and Indian War, 44, 45; government, 20–21, 81, 82–83, *p 85*, 309; Indian education, 71; land claims, 44, *m 103*, 112; population, 54; resistance to British laws, 108–09; settlement, 18–21; slavery, 65–66, *p 66*. *See also* Virginia; place names.

Virginia Convention, 119

Virginia Plan, 157

Virginia Resolutions, 226, 242

Virginia, University of, *308*, 546

VISTA, 767, 831

Volga River, 729, *m 731*

Volstead Act, 668

Volta, Alessandro, 468

Von Rundstedt, Karl, 738

Von Steuben, Baron, 131, *p 132*, 133

Voting: ballot reforms, 532–33. *See also* Disenfranchisement; Suffrage.

Voting Rights Acts: (1965), 772; (1970), 835

Wabash River, 240, *m 244*

Wade-Davis Bill, 405–06

Wadsworth, James, 400

Wages and Hours Law, 701

Wagner, Robert F., 691

Wagner Act, 691, 700, 701, 756

Wagner-Steagall Act, 703

Wake Island, 580, 584, 725, 727, *m 744–45*, 784

Walker, David, 340

Wall Street, 491

Wallace, George C., 770, 771

Wallace, Henry A., 706, 757

Wallace, Lew, 515

Walpole, Robert, 50

Waltham, Mass., 285, 294

Wanamaker, John C., 470

War: antiwar movements, 335, 602–03, *p 602*, 652–53; declaration power, 176, 178–79; Department of, 214, 429, 544, 579

War Between the States. *See* Civil War.

War Finance Corporation, 614

War Hawks, 240

War Industries Board, 613, 614

War Labor Policies Board, 614

War Manpower Commission (WMC), 734

War of 1812, 291; aftermath, 243–45, 335; campaigns, *p 242*, 243, *m 244–45*; causes, 237–40; letters of marque and reprisal, **179**; opposition to, 241–42; peace treaty, 243

War Production Board, 733, 734

War Shipping Administration, 734

Ward, Aaron Montgomery, 470

Waring, E. J., 422

Warner, Charles Dudley, 514

ACKNOWLEDGMENTS

All drawings by Samuel H. Bryant, except those on pp. 65 and 68, which are by William Sauts Bock. Illustration of American Eagle weathervane by Harry Rosenbaum. Maps by Harold K. Faye, except those on pp. 304 and 801, which are by Harbrace.

KEY Bettmann, The Bettmann Archive; BB, Brown Brothers; C, Culver Pictures, Inc.; HSP, The Historical Society of Pennsylvania; LOC, Library of Congress; MCNY, Museum of the City of New York; MMA, The Metropolitan Museum of Art; NYHS, New-York Historical Society; NYPL, New York Public Library; UPI, United Press International, Inc.; WW, Wide World Photos, Inc.

PART TITLE PHOTOGRAPHS: p. 1, Washington and Lee University; pp. 99, 283, Bettmann; p. 401, White House Historical Society; p. 571, repetition from pp. 99, 283, 401, plus Jim Theologos.

TEXT PHOTOGRAPHS: p. 3, from *The Discovery of the World* by Albert Bettex, photo courtesy of Zentralbibliothek, Zurich; p. 4, courtesy of the Mariners Museum, Newport News, Va.; p. 5, The Pierpont Morgan Library; p. 6, Trustees of the British Museum; p. 7, attributed to Ridolfo Ghirlandajo, Museo Navale, Genoa-Pegli; p. 10, Kunstindustrimusset, Oslo; p. 12, Hans Erni, courtesy of Rathbone Books, London; p. 15, from *The Discovery of the World* by Albert Bettex, photo courtesy of Zentralbibliothek, Zurich; p. 16, Howard Pyle Collection, Delaware Art Museum, Wilmington, Delaware; p. 19, C; p. 21, BB; p. 23, John Hancock Mutual Life Insurance Co.; pp. 24, 25, Trustees of the British Museum; p. 27, Pilgrim Society, Plymouth, Mass., courtesy of American Heritage; p. 28, New England Mutual Life Insurance Co.; p. 30, NYHS; p. 32, Massachusetts Historical Society; p. 34, MCNY; p. 38, Charleston Library Society; p. 40, Royal Ontario Museum, Toronto, Canada; p. 43, The Continental Insurance Co.; p. 46, State Historical Society of Wisconsin; pp. 48, 49, NYHS; p. 50, NYPL Picture Collection; p. 55, Detail, MMA, gift of Mrs. A. Wordsworth Thompson, 1899; p. 57, HSP; p. 66, NYPL Arents Collection; p. 67, LOC; p. 69, painting by A. A. Jansson, Courtesy of The American Museum of Natural History; p. 70, Pitman Studios, Cambridge, Mass., photo courtesy of American Heritage; p. 74, NYHS; p. 76, from *A Pictorial History of the Negro in America,* by Langston Hughes and Milton Meltzer; p. 78, LOC; p. 79, Boston Atheneum; p. 80, NYPL; p. 82, NYPL, Astor, Lenox and Tilden Foundations; p. 83, Brown County Library, Green Bay, Wis.; p. 85, Bettmann: p. 89, New Hampshire Historical Society; p. 91, BB; p. 92, John Vachon, *Look* Magazine; p. 94, U.S. Army; p. 96, Bettmann; p. 97, American Antiquarian Society; p. 98, Bettmann; p. 101, NYPL Prints Division; p. 105, HSP; p. 106, NYPL Picture Collection; p. 107, LOC; p. 109, C; pp. 110, 113, Bettmann; p. 115, Collection of Gilbert Darlington, N.Y.; p. 117, Collection of Walter Perry III, courtesy of American Heritage; pp. 121, 122, LOC; p. 129, HSP; p. 132, A. Devaney, Inc., N.Y.; p. 134, Detail, Yale University Art Gallery; p. 136, BB; p. 138, NYPL Picture Collection; p. 140, Burton Historical Collection of the Detroit Public Library; pp. 141, 143, BB; p. 146, Washington University Gallery of Art, St. Louis; p. 147, NYPL Prints Division; p. 150, Bettmann; p. 151, LOC; p. 155, detail from "Washington Addressing the Constitutional Convention," by J. B. Stearns, Virginia Museum of Fine Arts, gift of Colonel and Mrs. Edgar W. Garbisch; p. 156, Bettmann; p. 157, BB; p. 158, American Philosophical Society, Philadelphia; p. 161, HSP; p. 162, C; p. 163, BB; p. 165, LOC; p. 166, NYHS; p. 169, C; p. 204, Bettmann; p. 206, Imperial War Museum; p. 207, BB; pp. 208, 209, 210, Bettmann; p. 212, detail from "Lady Washington's Reception," by Daniel Huntington, in the Brooklyn Museum Collection; p. 213, NYHS, p. 214, Bettmann; p. 217, detail, MMA, Joseph Pulitzer Bequest, 1942; p. 220, Herbert and Claiborne Pell Collection; p. 222, NYHS; p. 224, C; p. 227, BB; p. 230, Mr. Warren Sturgis, NYC., courtesy of American Heritage; p. 233, Oregon State Highway Travel Division; pp. 234, 236, NYHS; p. 238, courtesy Musée du Louvre, photo by Editorial Photocolor Archives; p. 241, BB; p. 242, from *A Pictorial History of the Negro in America,* by Langston Hughes and Milton Meltzer; p. 247, Smithsonian Institution; p. 249, Detail, Yale University Art Gallery, Mable Brady Garvan Collection; p. 251, Harbrace Archives; p. 252, The Granger Collection; p. 255, DeVenney-Wood, *Life* Magazine © Time Inc.; p. 256, from the collection of the Maryland Historical Society; p. 258, BB; p. 261, HSP; p. 262, NYPL, Schomburg Collection; p. 264, Museum of Art, Rhode Island School of Design; p. 266, LOC; p. 273, BB; pp. 275, 276, NYHS; p. 280, The Boatman's National Bank of St. Louis, Neil Sauer photo; p. 282, LOC; p. 288, MCNY, The Harry T. Peters Collection; p. 291, Calendars of Distinction, Ltd., London. Copyright; courtesy of American Heritage; p. 295, detail, Yale University Art Gallery; p. 296, BB; p. 299, MCNY; p. 303, courtesy Musée de Pau, photo by Giraudon; pp. 305, 306, top and bottom, photos by Lisa Little, in the Collection of the Museum of Primitive Art, N.Y.; p. 307, NYHS Landauer Collection; p. 309, Collection of the J. B. Speed Art Museum, Louisville, Kentucky; p. 310, NYHS; p. 313, MCNY, The Harry T. Peters Collection; p. 314, The Granger Collection; p. 320, The Butler Art Institute; p. 323, Mrs. J. Bill Arthur and Mrs. Al Warner, San Antonio, Texas; p. 325, M. H. De Young Memorial Museum; p. 329, courtesy of the Suffolk Museum and Carriage House at Stony Brook, L.I., Melville Collection; p. 330, History Division, Los Angeles County Museum of Natural History; p. 334, C; p. 335, BB; p. 337, Detail, Yale University Art Gallery, The Mable Brady Garvan Collection; p. 338, from Robert S. Fletcher, *A History of Oberlin College* (1943), photograph in the collection of Mrs. Florence P. Clark, Washington, D.C.; p. 341, Bettmann; p. 342, photo from *Narrative of Frederick Douglass,* as seen in *A Pictorial History of the Negro in America,* by Langston Hughes and Milton Meltzer; p. 343, Ohio State Archaeological and Historical Society; p. 345, courtesy of Kenneth M. Newman, The Old Print Shop, N.Y.C.; p. 346, Bettmann; p. 350, MMA, Gift of Mr. & Mrs. Carl Stoeckel, 1897; p. 351, Sophia Smith Collection, Smith College Library; p. 352, LOC; p. 354, Office of the Secretary of State, Topeka, Kansas; p. 357, BB; p. 359, Southwest Museum, Collection of Dr. Carl Dentzel; p. 360, Bettmann; p. 364, BB; p. 365, Bettmann; p. 367, courtesy of the Illinois State Historical Library; p. 370, The Museum of the Confederacy; p. 372, Detail, Courtesy of the Cooper-Hewitt Museum of Decorative Arts and Design, Smithsonian Institution; p. 375, The Putnam County Historical Society; p. 384, LOC, photo by William M. Smith; p. 385, LOC; p. 387, West Point Museum, collection of Alexander McCook Craighald; p. 389, LOC; p. 390, Valentine Museum, Richmond, Va.; p. 393, NYHS; p. 394, C; p. 398, LOC; p. 399, Bettmann; p. 400, Frederick Lewis Photo; p. 405, LOC; p. 406, NYPL, from *Harper's Weekly,* 1865; p. 409, LOC; p. 412, NYPL, from *Harper's Weekly,* April 4, 1868; p. 413, The National Archives; p. 417, NYPL, Astor, Lenox and Tilden Foundations; p. 419, The Granger Collection; p. 421, C; p. 423, The Association for the Study of Negro Life and History, Washington, D.C., as seen in *International Library of Negro Life and History, Vol. 7;* p. 425, NYHS; p. 427, LOC; p. 429, NYPL, Astor, Lenox and Tilden Foundations; p. 433, NYPL, *Frank Leslie's Illustrated Newspaper,* Aug. 20, 1881; p. 437, NYPL, from *Harper's Weekly,* Aug. 12, 1893; p. 441, Taft Museum, Cincinnati, Ohio; p. 447, U.S. Dept. of Agriculture; p. 449, Nebraska State Historical Society; p. 450, Bettmann; p. 452, Gene Autry; p. 456, Jerome Tucker; p. 458, Monkmeyer Press Photo; p. 459, Harbrace; p. 460, Thomas Gilcrease Institute, Tulsa, Oklahoma; p. 462, California State Library; p. 465, NYPL, *Harper's Weekly,* Oct. 29, 1892; p. 468, NYPL, *The Century Magazine,* Vol. xxvi–31; p. 470, F. W. Woolworth Co.; p. 472, C; p. 474, LOC; p. 475, © ARNOLD NEWMAN; p. 477, Weir: "Forging the Shaft: a Welding Heat," MMA, gift of Lyman G. Bloomingdale, 1901; p. 481, Homer: "Snap the Whip," MMA, gift of Christian A. Zabriskie, 1950; p. 485, N.Y. State Historical Association; p. 497, BB; p. 499, Thomas Gilcrease Institute, Tulsa, Oklahoma; pp. 501, 503, Bettmann; p. 504, UPI, photo courtesy Johnson Publishing Co., Chicago; p. 510, BB; p. 512, MCNY, The J. Clarence Davies Collection; p. 514, C; p. 516, MCNY; p. 518, *Harper's Weekly,* 1879; p. 522, William Finch, Editorial Photocolor Archives; p. 523, Monkmeyer Press Photo; p. 525, Harbrace; p. 527, LOC; p. 528, Nebraska State Historical Society; p. 530, courtesy of Kennedy Galleries, Inc.; p. 532, C; p. 534, Bettmann; p. 536, Detail, George Eastman House Collection, photo by Lewis W. Hine; p. 537, both left and right, Association for the Study of Negro Life and History, Washington, D.C.; p. 538, LOC; p. 540, Theodore Roosevelt Collection, Harvard College Library; p. 541, James E. Wilkie, Jr.; p. 543, Bettmann; p. 545, BB; p. 548, Detail, Los Angeles County Museum of Art; p. 550, James Vanderzee Institute; p. 553, MCNY; p. 554, Bettmann; p. 557, LOC; p. 560, Detail, George Eastman House Collection; p. 564, UPI; p. 565, Burt Glinn, Magnum; pp. 566, 568, Bettmann; p. 570, BB; p. 573, Charles Johnson Post Collection; p. 575, LOC; p. 580, U.S. Signal Corps Photo No. 111–RB–2839 in the National Archives; p. 582, Photo Researchers; p. 583, C; p. 584, LOC; p. 588, C; p. 589, BB; p. 592, Historical Pictures Service–Chicago; p. 594, NYPL, New York *Herald,* Dec. 16, 1902; p. 596, Alpha Photo Association; p. 598, BB; p. 599, Bettmann; p. 601, Mansell Collection; p. 602, Photoworld, Inc.; p. 605, UPI; p. 607, BB; p. 609, Imperial War Museum, London; p. 611, C; p. 613, BB; p. 614, Collection of Huntington Hartford; p. 622, Cowlitz County Historical Museum; p. 623, C; p. 624, UPI; p. 626, Henry Groskinsky, *Life* Magazine © Time Inc.; p. 627, Chicago *News;* p. 629, BB; p. 630, NAACP Photo; p. 632, UPI; p. 633, BB; p. 634, NYHS; pp. 636, 637, BB; p. 639, Bettmann; p. 640, LOC; p. 643, National Archives; pp. 644–45, Radio Times Hulton Picture; p. 647, Detail, Lewis W. Hine, George Eastman House Collection; p. 648, *The Columbus Dispatch,* Historical Pictures Service-Chicago; p. 651, UPI; p. 653, WW; p. 654, BB; p. 658, Harbrace, NYPL; p. 659, Memorial Art Gallery of the University of Rochester; p. 661, BB; p. 663, NYPL Schomburg Collection; p. 664, Stanley Dance; p. 667, Walker Art Center, Minneapolis, Minn.; p. 668, C; p. 674, Monkmeyer Press Photo; p. 675, Thomas Benner, Shostal Associates; pp. 676, 677, Monkmeyer Press Photo; p. 678, Editorial Photocolor Archives; p. 680, Jim Theologos; p. 683, C; p. 684, UPI; pp. 686, 688, 690, BB; p. 694, Tennessee Valley Authority; p. 696, George Skadding; pp. 697, 698, BB; p. 699, LOC; pp. 701, 703, WW; pp. 705, 706, BB; pp. 707, 709, 713, WW; p. 714, C; pp. 715, 717, 719, WW; p. 721, Bettmann; p. 724, WW; p. 725, U.S. Navy Photo No. 80–6–32414 in the National Archives; p. 727, Charles Phelps Cushing, photo by Alice C. Cushing; p. 729, U.S. Navy Photo; p. 732, WW; p. 735, BB; p. 737, Richard C. Ferguson, Acme Photo; p. 740, Margaret Bourke-White, *Life* Magazine, 1945 © Time, Inc.; p. 743, U.S. Navy Photo; p. 746, BB; p. 750, LOC; p. 751, BB; p. 752, George Skadding; p. 754, WW; pp. 756, 759, UPI; p. 763, Black Star; p. 767, UPI; p. 769, WW; p. 772, UPI; p. 775, Office of the Secretary of Defense, U.S. Army Photo; p. 776, UPI; p. 779, Acme Photo; pp. 782, 784, 789, UPI; p. 794, Philip Jones Griffiths, Magnum; pp. 796, 803, UPI; p. 812, USAF Photo; p. 813, Aluminum Company of America; p. 815, NASA Photo; p. 816, Burt Glinn, Magnum; p. 818, Design Photographers International; p. 820, Bruce Davidson, Magnum; p. 823, Fred Ward, Black Star; p. 825, WW; p. 826, top, Burt Shavitz, PIX; bottom, Camera Press, PIX; p. 830, George Ballis, Black Star; p. 832, LOC; p. 834, WW; p. 836, Nacio Jan Brown, BBM, Berkeley, Calif., p. 839, John Launois, Black Star; p. 841, Dan McCoy, Black Star; p. 842, Katrina Thomas; p. 846, UPI; p. 847, Fred Ward, Black Star; p. 848, UPI.

CHRONOLOGY PHOTOGRAPHS: All from the Library of Congress except the following: p. 881, 1, Detail, MMA, G. Stuart; p. 882, 5, MMA, bequest of Seth Low; p. 883, 12, Charles Phelps Cushing; p. 884, 16, Bettmann; p. 887, 29, Ewing Galloway; 31, Fabian Bachrach; p. 888, 32, Franklin D. Roosevelt Library, Hyde Park, N.Y.; 33, Charles Phelps Cushing; p. 889, 34, Chase News Photo; 35, Henry Grossman; 36, Fabian Bachrach; p. 890, 37, Official White House Photograph.

9
0
1
2
3
4
N 5